The Handbook of Language and Gender

EDITED BY

Janet Holmes and Miriam Meyerhoff

Blackwell
Publishing

© 2003, 2005 by Blackwell Publishing Ltd

BLACKWELL PUBLISHING
350 Main Street, Malden, MA 02148-5020, USA
9600 Garsington Road, Oxford OX4 2DQ, UK
550 Swanston Street, Carlton, Victoria 3053, Australia

First published 2003 by Blackwell Publishing Ltd
First published in paperback 2005

1   2006

Library of Congress Cataloging-in-Publication Data

The handbook of language and gender/edited by Janet Holmes and
Miriam Meyerhoff.
      p. cm. – (Blackwell handbooks in linguistics; 13)
   Includes bibliographical references and index.
   ISBN 0-631-22502-1 (alk. paper)—ISBN 0-631-22503-X (alk. paper : pbk)
   1. Language and sex. I. Holmes, Janet, 1947– II. Meyerhoff,
Miriam. III. Series.
P120.S48 H36 2003
306.44–dc21

               2002006515

ISBN-13: 978-0-631-22502-7 (alk. paper)—ISBN-13: 978-0-631-22503-4 (alk. paper : pbk)

A catalogue record for this title is available from the British Library.

Set in 10/12pt Palatino
by Graphicraft Ltd, Hong Kong

For further information on
Blackwell Publishing, visit our website:
www.blackwellpublishing.com

THE HANDBOOK OF LANGUAGE AND GENDER

Blackwell Handbooks in Linguistics

This outstanding multi-volume series covers all the major subdisciplines within linguistics today and, when complete, will offer a comprehensive survey of linguistics as a whole.

Already published:

The Handbook of Child Language
Edited by Paul Fletcher and Brian MacWhinney

The Handbook of Phonological Theory
Edited by John A. Goldsmith

The Handbook of Contemporary Semantic Theory
Edited by Shalom Lappin

The Handbook of Sociolinguistics
Edited by Florian Coulmas

The Handbook of Phonetic Sciences
Edited by William J. Hardcastle and John Laver

The Handbook of Morphology
Edited by Andrew Spencer and Arnold Zwicky

The Handbook of Japanese Linguistics
Edited by Natsuko Tsujimura

The Handbook of Linguistics
Edited by Mark Aronoff and Janie Rees-Miller

The Handbook of Contemporary Syntactic Theory
Edited by Mark Baltin and Chris Collins

The Handbook of Discourse Analysis
Edited by Deborah Schiffrin, Deborah Tannen, and Heidi E. Hamilton

The Handbook of Language Variation and Change
Edited by J. K. Chambers, Peter Trudgill, and Natalie Schilling-Estes

The Handbook of Historical Linguistics
Edited by Brian D. Joseph and Richard D. Janda

The Handbook of Language and Gender
Edited by Janet Holmes and Miriam Meyerhoff

The Handbook of Second Language Acquisition
Edited by Catherine J. Doughty and Michael H. Long

The Handbook of Bilingualism
Edited by Tej K. Bhatia and William C. Ritchie

The Handbook of Pragmatics
Edited by Laurence R. Horn and Gregory Ward

The Handbook of Applied Linguistics
Edited by Alan Davies and Catherine Elder

The Handbook of Speech Perception
Edited by David B. Pisoni and Robert E. Remez

For Sam

Contents

Notes on Contributors   x

Acknowledgments   xvi

Different Voices, Different Views: An Introduction to
Current Research in Language and Gender
Janet Holmes and Miriam Meyerhoff   1

**Part I   History and Theoretical Background to the Study
           of Language and Gender**   19

  1 Theorizing Gender in Sociolinguistics and Linguistic
     Anthropology   21
     Bonnie McElhinny

  2 Theories of Discourse as Theories of Gender:
     Discourse Analysis in Language and Gender Studies   43
     Mary Bucholtz

  3 "What's in a Name?" Social Labeling and Gender Practices   69
     Sally McConnell-Ginet

  4 Variation in Language and Gender   98
     Suzanne Romaine

  5 Language and Desire   119
     Don Kulick

  6 "One Man in Two is a Woman": Linguistic Approaches
     to Gender in Literary Texts   142
     Anna Livia

Part II Negotiating Relations   159

7 Language, Gender, and Politics: Putting "Women" and
   "Power" in the Same Sentence   161
   Robin Lakoff

8 Gender and Family Interaction   179
   Deborah Tannen

9 Gender and Power in On-line Communication   202
   Susan C. Herring

10 The Relevance of Ethnicity, Class, and Gender in Children's
    Peer Negotiations   229
    Marjorie Harness Goodwin

11 The Power of Gender Ideologies in Discourse   252
    Susan U. Philips

Part III Authenticity and Place   277

12 Crossing Genders, Mixing Languages: The Linguistic
    Construction of Transgenderism in Tonga   279
    Niko Besnier

13 Claiming a Place: Gender, Knowledge, and Authority
    as Emergent Properties   302
    Miriam Meyerhoff

14 Constructing and Managing Male Exclusivity in
    Talk-in-interaction   327
    Jack Sidnell

15 Exceptional Speakers: Contested and Problematized
    Gender Identities   353
    Kira Hall

16 Language and Gender in Adolescence   381
    Penelope Eckert

17 Language and Gendered Modernity   401
    William L. Leap

18 A Marked Man: The Contexts of Gender and Ethnicity   423
    Sara Trechter

Part IV Stereotypes and Norms   445

19 Gender and Language Ideologies   447
    Deborah Cameron

20 Gender Stereotypes: Reproduction and Challenge   468
    Mary Talbot

21 Gender and Identity: Representation and Social Action 487
Ann Weatherall and Cindy Gallois

22 Prestige, Cultural Models, and Other Ways of Talking About
Underlying Norms and Gender 509
Scott Fabius Kiesling

23 Communicating Gendered Professional Identity: Competence,
Cooperation, and Conflict in the Workplace 528
Caja Thimm, Sabine C. Koch, and Sabine Schey

24 Linguistic Sexism and Feminist Linguistic Activism 550
Anne Pauwels

Part V   Institutional Discourse 571

25 "Feminine" Workplaces: Stereotype and Reality 573
Janet Holmes and Maria Stubbe

26 Creating Gendered Demeanors of Authority at Work and
at Home 600
Shari Kendall

27 Schooled Language: Language and Gender in Educational
Settings 624
Joan Swann

28 Coercing Gender: Language in Sexual Assault Adjudication
Processes 645
Susan Ehrlich

29 Multiple Identities: The Roles of Female Parliamentarians
in the EU Parliament 671
Ruth Wodak

Epilogue: Reflections on Language and Gender Research 699
Alice F. Freed

Index 722

Notes on Contributors

Niko Besnier is Professor of Anthropology at Victoria University of Wellington, New Zealand. He has published on a variety of topics in social anthropology and linguistic anthropology, based on extensive field research in two areas of Polynesia, Tuvalu and Tonga. His current research focus is the range of transnational experience among Tongans in Tonga and Tongans in migrant communities around the Pacific. He is also developing a research programme that will focus on contemporary urban Japanese society.

Mary Bucholtz is Assistant Professor of Linguistics at the University of California, Santa Barbara. She has co-edited several books on language and gender, including *Gender Articulated: Language and the Socially Constructed Self* (with Kira Hall; Routledge, 1995) and *Reinventing Identities: The Gendered Self in Discourse* (with Anita C. Liang and Laurel A. Sutton; Oxford University Press, 1999). Her research focuses on the relationship of language, power, and social identity, especially race and gender. She is currently at work on a book entitled *Signifying Nothing: Language, Youth, and Whiteness.*

Deborah Cameron is Professor of Languages at the Institute of Education, London. She has written and edited numerous contributions to language and gender studies, including *Feminism and Linguistic Theory* (Macmillan, 1992), *The Feminist Critique of Language* (Routledge, 1998), and *Women in Their Speech Communities* (with Jennifer Coates; Longman, 1988).

Penelope Eckert is Professor of Linguistics, Professor by courtesy of Cultural and Social Anthropology, and Director of the Program in Feminist Studies at Stanford University, California. She has published work in pure ethnography as well as ethnographically based sociolinguistics. Her most recent books are *Linguistic Variation as Social Practice* (Blackwell, 2000) and *Style and Sociolinguistic Variation* (Cambridge University Press, 2001).

Susan Ehrlich is Professor in the Department of Languages, Literatures, and Linguistics at York University, Toronto, Canada. She has published in the areas of language and gender, discourse analysis, linguistic approaches to literature, and second language acquisition in journals such as *Text, The Journal of Pragmatics, Discourse & Society,* and *Language in Society.* Her most recent book is *Representing Rape: Language and Sexual Consent* (Routledge, 2001).

Alice F. Freed is Professor of Linguistics and a member of the Women's Studies faculty at Montclair State University, New Jersey. Her research interests include discourse analysis and sociolinguistics with a focus on issues of gender. She is the author of *The Semantics of English Aspectual Complementation* (Reidel, 1979), co-editor (with Victoria Bergvall and Janet Bing) of *Rethinking Language and Gender Research: Theory and Practice* (Longman, 1996), and author of various articles that have appeared in *Language in Society, The Journal of Pragmatics,* and others.

Cindy Gallois is Professor of Psychology at the University of Queensland, Australia. Her research centers on intergroup communication and accommodation in organizational, health, and cross-cultural contexts; she has published over 100 books and papers on these topics. She is a past president of the International Communication Association and a Fellow of the Academy of the Social Sciences in Australia.

Marjorie Harness Goodwin is Professor of Linguistic Anthropology at the University of California, Los Angeles. Her work investigates how talk is used to build social organization within face-to-face interaction, with particular emphasis on the social worlds of young girls. Her monograph *He-Said-She-Said: Talk as Social Organization among Black Children* (Indiana University Press, 1990) is a study of the gendered language practices of African American children.

Kira Hall received her PhD in Linguistics from the University of California, Berkeley in 1995 and is currently Assistant Professor of Anthropology and Linguistics at the University of Colorado at Boulder. Specializing in the area of language, gender, and sexuality, her major publications include *Gender Articulated: Language and the Socially Constructed Self* (with Mary Bucholtz; Routledge, 1995) and *Queerly Phrased: Language, Gender, and Sexuality* (with Anna Livia; Oxford University Press, 1997). She is currently writing a book on the language and cultural practices of Hindi-speaking *hijras* (eunuchs) in northern India.

Susan Herring received her PhD from the University of California, Berkeley in 1991, and is currently Associate Professor of Information Science at Indiana University. Her recent work has focused on the linguistic and social aspects of communication mediated by new technologies (the Internet, the World Wide Web), especially gender patterns in these media. She has edited two books on computer-mediated communication and is author of 20 articles on the subject.

Janet Holmes holds a personal Chair in Linguistics at Victoria University of Wellington, New Zealand, where she teaches sociolinguistics. She is Director of the Wellington Corpus of Spoken New Zealand English and of a project on Language in the Workplace. Her publications include *An Introduction to Sociolinguistics* (2nd edition, Longman, 2001), *Women, Men and Politeness* (Longman, 1995), and an edited book, *Gendered Speech in Social Context* (Victoria University Press, 2000). She is a Fellow of the Royal Society of New Zealand.

Shari Kendall is Research Associate in the Department of Linguistics at Georgetown University, Washington, DC. She is Co-Principal Investigator with Deborah Tannen of the Sociolinguistics Work-Family Project. Her work investigates the discursive creation of identities in work and family discourse. She is co-author (with Deborah Tannen) of "Language and Gender" in *The Handbook of Discourse Analysis* (Academic Press, 1985) and "Gender and Language in the Workplace" in *Gender and Discourse* (Sage, 1997), and (with Keller Magenau) of " 'He's calling her Da Da!': A Sociolinguistic Analysis of the 'Lesbianism as Disease' Metaphor in Child Custody Cases" in the *Journal of the Association for Research on Mothering*.

Scott F. Kiesling is Assistant Professor of Linguistics at the University of Pittsburgh, Pennsylvania. His dissertation work (1996) focused on language, power, and masculinity. He is currently working on language variation and change in Australian English, with a focus on ethnicity and gender.

Sabine C. Koch is a Social Psychologist and Communication Researcher. She studied psychology at the University of Heidelberg, Germany and Madrid, Spain, and dance/movement therapy at Hahnemann University in Philadelphia, USA. Presently she is working on her PhD in a national research project at the University of Heidelberg, conducting verbal and nonverbal analyses of gendered communication in work teams.

Don Kulick is Professor of Anthropology at New York University. His most recent publications on topics of sexuality and gender include "Gay and Lesbian Language" (*Annual Review of Anthropology*, 2000), "Transgender and Language" (*GLQ*, 1999) and the book *Travesti* (University of Chicago Press, 1998).

Robin Tolmach Lakoff has been a Professor of Linguistics at the University of California, Berkeley, since 1972. Among her books are: *Language and Woman's Place* (Harper & Row, 1975); *Talking Power* (Basic Books, 1990), and *The Language War* (University of California Press, 2000).

William L. Leap is Professor of Anthropology at American University, Washington, DC, where he teaches courses in language and culture studies, lesbian/gay studies, cultural geography, and the anthropology of education. He is the author of *Word's Out: Gay Men's English* (University of Minnesota,

1996), editor of *Public Sex/Gay Space,* and co-editor (with Ellen Lewin) of *Out in the Field* (University of Illinois, 1996) and *Out in Theory* (University of Illinois, 2002). He co-ordinates the annual Lavender Languages and Linguistics Conference and works through other channels to support the visibility of lgbtq (lesbian, gay, bisexual, transgender, and queer) scholarship (and of lgbtq scholars!) in anthropology and linguistics.

Anna Livia is a visiting Assistant Professor in the French department at the University of California, Berkeley. Her book on the uses of linguistic gender, *Pronoun Envy,* was published in 2000 by Oxford University Press. With Kira Hall, she is editor of *Queerly Phrased* (Oxford University Press, 1997), the first anthology to examine the interconnection of language, gender, and sexuality from a linguistic perspective. She is currently doing research on the collocation of gender and class.

Sally McConnell-Ginet is Professor of Linguistics at Cornell University, New York, and active in Women's Studies (recently rechristened Feminist, Gender, and Sexuality Studies). She began publishing on language and gender topics in 1975 and has been collaborating in this area with Penelope Eckert of Stanford University since the early 1990s. She also teaches and does research in formal semantics and pragmatics.

Bonnie McElhinny is Assistant Professor of Anthropology at the University of Toronto, Canada. Her research focuses on language, gender, and political economy. Her publications appear in *Gender and Discourse* (Ruth Wodak, ed.; Sage, 1997); *Sociolinguistics and Language Teaching* (Sandra McKay and Nancy Hornberger, eds; Cambridge University Press, 1996), *Dislocating Masculinity* (A. Cornwall and N. Lindisfarne, eds; Routledge, 1994); *Gender Articulated* (Kira Hall and Mary Bucholtz, eds; Routledge, 1995), and various journals. She is currently completing a book manuscript entitled *Policing Language and Gender.*

Miriam Meyerhoff is Lecturer in Theoretical and Applied Linguistics at the University of Edinburgh, Scotland. Her research on language and gender focuses on the covert and overt linguistic expressions of ideologies about gender and about the social order. She also studies syntactic change and grammaticalization.

Anne Pauwels is Executive Dean of the Faculty of Arts and Professor of Linguistics at the University of Western Australia, Perth. Her research in the area of gender focuses on the linguistic representation of the sexes, feminist language planning and change, as well as gender and bilingualism/language contact. *Women Changing Language* (Longman, 1998) is her most recent book on gender and language.

Susan U. Philips is Professor of Anthropology at the University of Arizona. She received her PhD in Anthropology from the University of Pennsylvania. Her current research focuses on diversity in gender ideology in Tongan discourse. Her most recent book, *Ideology in the Language of Judges* (Oxford University Press, 1998) addresses the discourse organization of ideological diversity in American judges' courtroom language use.

Suzanne Romaine has been Merton Professor of English Language in the University of Oxford since 1984. Her recent publications are *Communicating Gender* (Erlbaum, 1999), *Language in Society: An Introduction to Sociolinguistics* (Oxford University Press, 2000, 2nd edn.), and (jointly with Daniel Nettle) *Vanishing Voices: The Extinction of the World's Languages* (Oxford University Press, 2000).

Sabine Schey completed a Master's (Magister) degree in linguistics at the University of Heidelberg, under the supervision of Caja Thimm. While at the University of Heidelberg she also worked on the WorkComm research project (communication of gender at the workplace). In this project, she was responsible for interviews and content analysis of interview data. She is now working in the private sector doing market research.

Jack Sidnell gained his PhD in Anthropology from the University of Toronto, Canada. Currently he is an Assistant Professor in the Department of Anthropology, Northwestern University and a Visiting Assistant Professor in the Department of Anthropology, University of Toronto. His research interests include talk and social organization, conversation analysis, language contact, pidgins and creoles, and language variation and change. Current work in progress includes a book about talk, knowledge, and everyday life in a Guyanese village.

Maria Stubbe is a Research Fellow in the School of Linguistics and Applied Language Studies at Victoria University of Wellington, New Zealand. She has worked on the Wellington Language in the Workplace Project since it began in 1996. Her research currently focuses on the analysis of spoken discourse in workplace communication, with a particular focus on problematic discourse and on how gender and ethnicity relate to organizational culture and communicative practices.

Joan Swann is a senior lecturer in the Centre for Language and Communications, Faculty of Education and Language Studies at the Open University, England. Much of her research on language and gender has been carried out in educational contexts, and she is particularly interested in the relationship between research on language and gender and educational policy and practice. Recent publications include *Introducing Sociolinguistics* (Edinburgh University Press, 2001; co-authored with Rajend Mesthrie, Andrea Deumert, and William Leap).

Mary M. Talbot is Reader in Language and Culture at the University of Sunderland, England. Her recent publications include *Fictions at Work: Language and Social Practice in Fiction* (Longman, 1995), *Studies in Valency 1* (edited with Lene Schøsler; Odense University Press, 1995), *Language and Gender: An*

Introduction (Polity, 1998), and *All the World and Her Husband: Women in 20th Century Consumer Culture* (edited with Maggie Andrews; Cassell, 2000). She has also contributed to numerous journals and edited collections on aspects of power, gender, and language in social life.

Deborah Tannen is University Professor and Professor of Linguistics at Georgetown University, Washington, DC. Her books include *Talking Voices: Repetition, Dialogue, and Imagery in Conversational Discourse* (Cambridge University Press, 1989); *Conversational Style: Analyzing Talk Among Friends* (Ablex, 1984); *Gender and Discourse* (Oxford University Press, 1994); *The Argument Culture* (Random House, 1997); *Talking from 9 to 5* (Avon, 1994); *You Just Don't Understand* (Morrow, 1990); and, most recently, *I Only Say This Because I Love You*. Though she is best known for her writing on communication between women and men, her research interests have also included spoken and written language, cross-cultural communication, modern Greek discourse, and the relationship between conversational and literary discourse.

Caja Thimm is University Professor for Communication and Media Studies at the University of Bonn, Germany. She has studied political science, communication studies, and linguistics at the universities of Heidelberg, San Francisco, and Berkeley, and published books on gendered language and dominance, and on intergenerational interaction. Her more recent work focuses on business communication online/offline and electronic democracy.

Sara Trechter is an Associate Professor of Linguistics in the English Department at California State University, Chico. Her work in language, gender, and ethnicity focuses on the use of gender deictics in Siouan languages and the Lakhota discourse construction of Whiteness.

Ann Weatherall is Senior Lecturer in Psychology at Victoria University of Wellington, New Zealand. Her interest in the field of gender, language, power, and discourse was inspired by a public lecture in 1987 by Dale Spender. Her recently completed book, *Shifting Perspectives on Gender, Language and Discourse* (Routledge) summarizes 15 years of research and thinking in this field.

Ruth Wodak is Professor of Applied Linguistics and Discourse Analysis at the University of Vienna, Austria, and Director of the Research Center on Discourse, Politics, and Identity at the Austrian Academy of Sciences. She has held visiting professorships in Stanford, Uppsala, Minnesota, and Georgetown, Washington DC. She is co-editor of *Discourse & Society* and *Language and Politics*. Her research domains are identity, gender, political rhetoric, racism, anti-Semitism, and institutional discourse. Her most recent books include *Gender and Discourse* (Sage, 1997), *The Discursive Construction of Identity* (Edinburgh University Press, 1999), *Racism at the Top* (Drava, 2000), and *Discourse and Discrimination* (Routledge, 2001). In 1996 she was awarded the Wittgenstein Prize for Elite Researchers.

Acknowledgments

We would like to express our appreciation to the contributors to this volume who responded pleasantly and in some cases even speedily to our requests for drafts, revisions, and final versions of their papers. We would also like to express appreciation to the helpful and supportive volume editors with whom we worked, Tami Kaplan and Sarah Coleman. We owe a large debt to Martin Paviour-Smith who was a meticulous copy-editor and general assistant in getting the book ready for press; to Margaret Aherne, our patient and thorough copy-editor; to Tina Chiles and Marie Lorimer for proofreading; and to Vivien Trott who carefully checked that references were in order. Finally we express our gratitude to Tony, Rob, David, Andrew, and Sam who provided wonderful support, or in some cases diversions, to keep us sane during the long and demanding process of interacting with so many different personalities in putting together such a large collection of excellent papers.

Different Voices, Different Views: An Introduction to Current Research in Language and Gender

JANET HOLMES AND MIRIAM MEYERHOFF

1 Introduction

The purpose of *The Handbook of Language and Gender* is to provide an authoritative, comprehensive, and original collection of articles representing the richness and diversity of contemporary research in the area. Currently, language and gender is a particularly vibrant area of research and theory development within the larger study of language and society, and the contributions in this volume focus especially on more recent trends and developments. The volume comprises specially commissioned articles in five distinguishable but closely related areas, identified because of their importance in current language and gender research, and encompassing the breadth of interdisciplinary interests of researchers and students in this dynamic area.

This collection of articles will prove a valuable resource to students of linguistics, and especially to those interested in sociolinguistics and discourse studies from undergraduate level upwards. A quick glance at the contents will indicate, however, that the collection should also have much wider appeal; it is truly interdisciplinary, drawing on work from many different academic areas. There are articles which will be of interest to anthropologists and those interested in cultural studies, to sociologists and social psychologists, and to those concerned with organizational communication. There are articles which have obvious relevance to feminists, and to those working in gender studies, as well as to professional women, and those engaged in business and management. Moreover, because of the more practical orientation of some of the articles, especially in the final two sections, the collection will also be of interest to applied linguists, to those working in education and language policy, to professionals engaged in the areas of Human Relations and Human Resources, and, we predict, to the educated reader.

Many collections of readings on language and gender are compilations of papers already written and published. Some consist of articles which are best described as "classic" (e.g. Tannen 1993; Cameron 1998; Coates 1998; Cheshire and Trudgill 1998). Many are constructed around a specific theme, such as power (Hall, Bucholtz, and Moonwomon 1992), gender identity (e.g. Hall and Bucholtz 1995; Bucholtz, Liang, and Sutton 1999), masculinity (Johnson and Meinhof 1997), communication (Wertheim, Bailey, and Corston-Oliver 1998), belief systems (Warner et al. 1996), bilingualism (e.g. Burton, Dyson, and Ardener 1994), second language education (Sunderland 1994), or sexist language (Hellinger and Bussmann 2001). Others focus more on a specific theoretical approach, such as social constructionism (e.g. Bergvall, Bing, and Freed 1996; Bucholtz, Liang, Sutton, and Hines 1994), communities of practice (e.g. Holmes 1999), or interactional sociolinguistics (e.g. Tannen 1994). Still others take a predominantly descriptive approach, covering a wide range of contrasting languages and cultures (e.g. Kotthoff and Wodak 1997; Hellinger and Bussmann 2001).

By contrast, and as a useful complement to these varied emphases, the papers in this Handbook provide an indication of the range of issues currently under debate in the area, and outline the topical concerns of those working at the forefront of research in language and gender. The main themes are indicated by the five broad section headings, and a diversity of methodologies is represented (discussed further below). A wide range of languages are invoked in the different papers, in some cases as a core component of particular case studies, in others as brief but specific examples to illustrate a more general point. So, while most papers use English for exemplification, readers will also find references to languages as varied as Tongan, Tagalog, French, Bislama, Guyanese Creole, Gaelic, Dutch, German, Afrikaans, and Lakhota. Most authors provide an indication of where their own areas of research strength and interest fit into the wider field, and they also indicate how their own positions can be distinguished from those of others. Hence, readers are typically provided both with an authoritative overview of a theme or issue, and a thought-provoking specific illustration of current research in a particular area.

2   Overview of the Contents of the Handbook

The Handbook has five sections: Part I is made up of chapters that review aspects of the history of the study of language and gender, and provide theoretical background to this study. The chapters in Part II deal to some extent with negotiations of relations and the role gender and language play in such negotiations. In Part III, the chapters are concerned with issues of authenticity (e.g. who gets to define what it means to be a "real" woman or a "real" man or a "real" Lakhota), and the task individuals face of finding a "place" for themselves in the complex social worlds they populate. A strong theme here is the processes by which identities emerge, or are effaced and disappear. In Part IV, the chapters deal with the importance, functionality, and invidiousness of stereotypes and norms. Finally, Part V reviews issues relating to language and gender in institutional discourse. Hence, the Handbook has an overall progression leading from highly theoretical chapters, to those which discuss very practical applications of language and gender research in various specific locales.

Within each section, too, the chapters are ordered in a manner that we hope will aid readers' appreciation of the themes of that section and allow them to select the chapters we think may be of most direct use to them, depending on their personal goals and interests. The first and last chapters bracket each section: in general, the first chapter is one that provides a particularly accessible lead-in to the issues, and the last is generally one which to a greater or lesser extent rounds off the section, and often provides a link to the next section. In other words, there is at least one chapter in each section (the lead-in) which we feel is a particularly approachable communication of the theme(s) of that section, and it is intended that this will provide a useful balance to chapters that are more demanding.

There are implications of this organization for the use of the Handbook. For example, readers using the Handbook as a text or supplement to texts in the classroom should find the most accessible papers can be read even by those without a lot of background in the field of language and gender research, while also providing a helpful basis for regrounding more advanced readers. In addition, readers who come from outside the academy with, for example, practical and applied interests in language and gender should find that the initial chapter in each section will provide them with a good overview of significant themes in research on language and gender, and give some idea of ways to communicate the relevance of these themes to a general audience.

As is traditional in introducing such a collection, we next provide a brief synopsis of each chapter. We hope that these will help readers of the Handbook locate the chapters that are most likely to fulfill their immediate goals, and also to plan further explorations to satisfy their future goals.

Bonnie McElhinny's chapter opens the volume with a survey of the study of language and gender within the traditions and methods of linguistic anthropology. Her analysis of the way the concept of "gender" is treated in different approaches introduces an issue which recurs throughout the collection, and she highlights, in particular, the problematic consequences of assuming that gender is adequately analyzed as a simple dichotomy. Mary Bucholtz provides a different historical and theoretical perspective, looking at how gender has been a part of the analysis of discourse over time. Bucholtz traces the emergence of feminist theories of gender in discourse analysis and directs our attention to more recent moves to incorporate historicity into analyses of interaction and social identities. Sally McConnell-Ginet considers how naming and reference

work within different communities of practice. As well as referential information, labels may convey information about gender depending on how they are
used within different communities of practice. Because practice-based models
are adopted by many of the researchers in subsequent sections, readers may
find this chapter very helpful. Suzanne Romaine discusses work that has been
undertaken within the variationist, or quantitative, sociolinguistic paradigms,
and which makes reference to the significance of gender at the macro-level of
analysis. She reviews the descriptive generalizations (which have sometimes
been treated as predictive) ensuing from this research, and critiques its methods
and the assumptions underlying such analyses. Don Kulick provides a psychoanalytic perspective on the study of language and gender. Assuming that
gender identities are at least partly the consequence of psychological drives to
express desire and social constraints on the expression of desire, he asks whether
we can identify linguistic routines or patterns that reveal underlying (and paradoxically, often unspoken) motivations and constraints. Finally in this section,
Anna Livia presents a thought-provoking discussion of the way gender may
be relevant to the analysis of texts, reviewing evidence that conventions of
masculine and feminine style exist, and examining the ways in which the
conventions of the linguistic system facilitate the creation of alternative,
oppositional, or conventional identities. She also examines the role of the
translator and the metaphors used for the process of translation, along with
their implications in analyzing gender in texts.

In Part II ("Negotiating Relations"), Robin Lakoff explores the complex
relationship between women and power through a discourse analysis of written texts taken from three major American institutions: academia (Schegloff's
arguments about the appropriate way of treating gender in Conversation Analysis), the arts (including the distribution of talk in the controversial Mamet
play *Oleanna*), and politics proper (the way the print media sexualize, objectify,
and ridicule women in politics). She exposes the disruption of conventional
discourse patterns which is being caused by women's entrance into domains
traditionally regarded as exclusively male. Deborah Tannen's chapter presents data from intra-family communication which suggests that participants
are attending to strategies which will build solidarity between them as well as
strategies that bolster, or undermine, a power differential between the inter-
actants. She locates her analysis of interactions in the tradition of foundational
work by Elinor Ochs on family communication and Brown and Gilman on
politeness. Susan Herring reviews issues relating to gender in mediated communication, especially on the Internet. She shows that (despite utopian hopes
for equality in this medium) issues of power relations resurface, reproducing the
gender norms of society at large. At the same time she also shows how women
have made places for themselves in the virtual world, and she concludes by
considering directions in which the medium and women's participation in it
might go in the future. Marjorie Goodwin's chapter provides a valuable review
of current debates in language and gender research which focus on children's
negotiation. She examines ethnographic studies of the interactive practices

used by children of different social class, age, and ethnic groups to construct gendered social relationships in and across girls' and boys' play groups. She focuses especially on the sequencing strategies employed in children's disputes, and on the strategies of exclusion used by girls in particular. Closing Part II, Susan Philips presents a very approachable exploration of the relationship between gender ideologies and power in anthropology. Combining a helpful historical overview of how anthropologists have understood gender ideologies with an examination of the most salient gender roles in Tonga, she gives the reader a clear model both of how gender ideologies can be studied and also how their routinized nature can be analyzed in terms of dominant and subordinate ideologies.

Part III ("Authenticity and Place") examines gender identity in the widest range of linguistic situations. Niko Besnier's chapter discusses aspects of how Tongan *fakaleitī* (i.e., roughly, a transgendered individual in Tonga) employ linguistic and non-linguistic strategies to establish a social place for themselves within the larger Tongan ideological system of who or what defines the constitutive properties of "real" women and "real" Tongans. Besnier shows how *fakaleitīs'* code-switching between Tongan and English (which has significance as a global language) functions to contest normative Tongan ideals about such categories. Miriam Meyerhoff's discussion of gender and language in Vanuatu similarly finds close and very overt associations between having a claim to a specific place and authority to speak or to control the flow of information. She argues that some linguistic strategies often employed by women are a means of responding to, working with, and challenging their exclusion from authority by the general ideology that men, and only men, really have a claim to "place." She also looks at continuities between historical patterns of gendered interaction and the synchronic patterns of gendered speech discussed earlier. Jack Sidnell examines what is required in the way of linguistic and other social performance for a rumshop in Guyana to be constituted as a "male-only" environment. He examines contextualization cues serving to include men, exclude women, and to weave "male" histories into the rumshop domain. Kira Hall considers the way gender identities have been problematized in research on language and gender. She argues that we can only fully understand the significance of recent theoretical shifts in the study of language and gender if we also understand the non-peripheral nature of gender identities traditionally treated as exceptional or deviant. Penelope Eckert's chapter builds on her research on the interplay of gender and more locally defined identities among adolescents and pre-adolescents. She makes the case that adolescence is a particularly significant period (especially in the USA) for the creation and contestation of social categories, and this is reflected in the enormous stylistic creativity of adolescents. The kinds of linguistic styling they undertake, she argues, reverberates through the speech community far beyond adolescent communities of practice.

William Leap's chapter tackles the question of what gender identities are in the global world of late modernity. He discusses a lonely hearts ad, a poem, and a narrative to illustrate how very local meanings of language choice and specific lexical items serve to place their users in the matrix of a more global homosexual community. He argues that such possibilities are derived from the social flux and movement associated with late modernity. The section concludes with Sara Trechter's chapter which, like others in this section, explores the discursive dimension of the emergence and negotiation of social identities. Trechter, however, articulates a more fundamental problem. She argues that language and gender research should begin to engage with the processes by which identities are effaced or disappear (rather than emerge) through both local and meta-discursive (e.g. academic) practices.

Part IV ("Stereotypes and Norms") begins with a chapter by Deborah Cameron which explores the issue of the ideological work done by representations of language, and especially the role that language plays in maintaining gender distinctions and naturalizing gender hierarchies. To illustrate, she traces recent changes in communication ideologies, with which representations of gendered language are strongly linked. Mary Talbot's chapter also examines how gender stereotypes support gender ideologies. She characterizes stereotypes, including stereotypes of "women's language," as powerful hegemonic constructs or ideo-logical prescriptions for behavior, noting that traditional sexist stereotypes are so resilient that they may be repeatedly contested without undermining their commonsensical status. She provides further evidence to support Cameron's observation that men's communication deficits have recently become a focus of concern, and notes that gender stereotypes are increasingly being contested in some contexts. Ann Weatherall and Cindy Gallois contrast social cognitive approaches (and especially communication accommodation theory) to the study of language and gender with the methods of discursive psychology. Starting from stereotypes, the social cognitive approach in social psychology proceeds to analyze gender on the assumption that the differentiation of categories is conceptually prior to language. By contrast, discursive psychology treats social categories as salient in interaction only when and as they are activated in talk. Scott Kiesling makes the point in his chapter that it is possible to relate indi-vidual stances, such as competence and electability in a fraternity meeting, to underlying, widely held norms. He also discusses the relevance of prestige norms to the analysis of language and gender. He dissects the oft-made dis-tinction between overt and covert prestige, raising some questions about the validity of the latter in particular. Approaching language and gender research from a communications framework, Caja Thimm, Sabine Koch, and Sabine Schey examine the influence of interpersonal relations and communication styles at work on women's professional development. Their research analyzes responses to interview questions as evidence of gender stereotypes and gendered expect-ations in workplace interaction, as well as differences in the kinds of com-municative strategies used by women and men in workplace role-plays. Anne Pauwels' chapter continues her extensive work documenting sexist language usages and attempts at language reform. She explores the specifically feminist concerns which may motivate some of the strategies employed in response to sexist usages, as well as responses to such strategies.

Part V ("Institutional Discourse") opens with Janet Holmes and Maria Stubbe's chapter, which explores the notion of the gendered workplace. They first describe a number of broad patterns identified in three different aspects of workplace interaction, namely the distribution of talk and humor in meetings, and of small talk at work more generally. They then adopt a community of practice framework to examine in more detail the discursive practices of two women managers in a stereotypically "feminine" and a stereotypically "masculine" workplace respectively, demonstrating the value of combining different theoretical and methodological approaches for illuminating the complexity of gendered discourse. Shari Kendall's chapter in this section provides a detailed case-study of the way one particular woman, pseudonymed "Elaine," gives directives, comparing the strategies Elaine uses in the linguistic creation of authority first as a parent with her ten-year-old daughter at home, and then as a manager with her two female subordinates at work. The analysis indicates that while Elaine uses face-saving strategies in both domains, the frequency and form of these strategies differ in significant ways in different contexts, reflecting the fact that she constructs different authoritative demeanors when speaking as a mother and as a manager. In another institutional domain, Joan Swann examines three shifts in research orientation that are relevant to research in education, and considers their implications for educational policy and practice. The first is well documented in this collection – the shift from essentialist and dichotomous conceptions of gender to a differentiated, contextualized, and performative model which questions generalized claims about gender, and about educational inequality. The second is a shift from responsive attitudes to feminist educational research in the 1980s to a much "colder" current climate in which feminist interests have been marginalized. The third shift involves contexts of communication, and especially the differential impact of computer-mediated communication on the educational opportunities of boys and girls, with its potential to return researchers to traditional polarized notions of gender difference and disadvantage.

Susan Ehrlich's chapter is also concerned with the linguistic representation and (re)production of gender ideologies in institutional discourse. She demonstrates how dominant ideologies of sexual violence against women are reproduced, sustained, and (potentially) contested through coercive interactional devices in sexual assault adjudication processes. These strategies result in what she calls "coerced identities"; they render invisible or efface the complainants' attempts to represent themselves as conscious agents, and rather "produce" them as subjects who had not acted strategically. Ruth Wodak's chapter is concerned with the fragmented and multiple identities of elite women, specifically female members of the European Union (EU) Parliament, a complex public domain which she characterizes as determined by intercultural, ideological, ethnic, national, and gender conflicts. She provides statistical data as background, and then draws on excerpts from interviews with female EU parliamentarians to demonstrate how women establish themselves in this complex setting, and what strategies they employ to present and promote themselves, and to guarantee that they are taken seriously.

Finally, the volume concludes with an Epilogue by Alice Freed. Freed asks why stereotypes about language and gender remain relatively unchanged after several decades of empirical research on language and gender. Why has it been so difficult for language and gender researchers to show the public that there is a lot more to language than the usual stereotypes? Rather than summarize the contents of the other chapters in the Handbook (as this Introduction does), Freed's Epilogue positions them in relation to directions of the field of research, thus tying the contributions of Parts I–III more closely to the discussions of stereotypes and applied language and gender research in Parts IV and V.

3   Themes and Issues in the Handbook

As is often the case, there are a number of possible ways in which the contents of the Handbook might have been arranged. The five sections just outlined reflect one way in which the articles can be grouped, but there are other axes which cross-cut the divisions of the five major sections.

One issue which serves to unify and draw together most, if not all, of the contributors is a fundamental concern with the question of how best to represent and even talk about gender and language. The field has moved well beyond descriptions of (perceived or actual) differences between men's and women's speech, or finger-pointing that maps power hierarchies with gender hierarchies.[1] The writers in this Handbook (like those writing for many of the other texts mentioned at the beginning of this Introduction) are trying to understand and represent the interaction between language and gender in much more subtle and nuanced ways. The very notion of gender as a category is a topic which is problematized at the outset, and many of the chapters in the Handbook explicitly distance themselves from essentialist analyses of gender which treat it as a deterministic quality. These researchers try to avoid assuming that there is a natural basis for separating the social world into two and only two sexes or genders, that is, they resist assuming that this difference is part of the essence of every human being. Furthermore, they try to avoid the assumption that categorizing any given individual as "female" or "male" necessarily determines or predicts characteristics of their speech and verbal interactions. This concern has been central to the discussion of gender since the late 1980s and early 1990s. (The concern has also been articulated with respect to other social categories widely used in social dialectology, such as social class, age, and ethnicity.)

This approach has typically also been marked by a methodological shift. Analyses of gender and language that are influenced by the move away from essentialized notions of gender tend to start with people's participation in their immediate and most salient social groups. To the extent that they then work outwards in the social sphere, they attempt to relate generalizations about larger trends in society to specific evidence of how gender is understood, contested, and absorbed as a category for social membership in the very "local" domains from which the analysis started. Most of the chapters in this Handbook do try to make such connections between the local and the supra-local; many of the contributors see their research and their field of interest as being inescapably involved in social action and social change. But one criticism of the move toward highly context-dependent analyses of gender is that it may focus too heavily on the descriptive particulars of any given example. It is sometimes claimed that this is at the expense of advancing more general understandings of the relationships between social categories and language behavior (Philips provides a clear discussion of the advantages to be gained from highlighting both the variability and the similarity of gender ideologies cross-culturally). A loss of generalization need not necessarily be the case, as Eckert (2000) shows in her textured analysis of linguistic and social variation during the transition years of adolescence in a Detroit high school. It is worth bearing in mind, though, that the work of Eckert (2000), Holmes (1997), and Herring (this volume) indicates that there are costs associated with attempting to blend quantitative and qualitative research; the most successful and informative examples of this integration are the result of many years of data collection and/or analysis.

Many of the researchers represented in this volume argue, then, that eschewing essentialized notions of gender provides a way for more voices to be heard; a gendered dimension to interactions *emerges* rather than being assumed at the outset. This, they suggest, provides a more comprehensive theoretical representation of gender in society, and it may even be a more accurate description of how gender and language interact. However, another theme that emerges from the chapters in the Handbook is the sense that this approach may ignore facts about gender and language which have been repeatedly pointed out in the language and gender literature over the decades, and which, as socially responsible academics, we cannot and do not want to ignore. No matter what we say about the inadequacy or invidiousness of essentialized, dichotomous conceptions of gender, and no matter how justifiable such comments may be, in everyday life it really is often the case that gender is "essential." We can argue about whether people ought to see male and female as a natural and essential distinction, and we can point to evidence showing that all social categories leak. However, that has not changed the fact that gender as a social category *matters*. There is extensive evidence to suggest that gender is a crucial component of people's social world; many people really do find it vital to be able to pigeonhole others into the normative, binary set of female–male, and they find linguistic or social behaviors which threaten the apparent stability of this "essential" distinction extremely disturbing. Thus, they censure women (overtly or indirectly) for behavior that is typically associated with males, they beat up transvestites, they pathologize or murder homosexuals.

Two issues arise from this: the relevance of our research outside the small circle of academics and theoreticians, and the use that people outside our in-group may make of the research conducted within these frameworks. Deborah

Cameron has been a consistent and articulate voice on both these issues (e.g. Cameron et al. 1992; Cameron 1995, 2000). She has long been concerned with making sure that linguistic research is responsive and directed by the needs and interests of the communities of speakers studied and does not simply feed academic appetites. She has also explored the appropriation of linguistic research, examining the way sometimes complex findings in the literature end up being stripped down in the mainstream press to fit societal preconceptions and stereotypes about issues such as gender. Alice Freed (among others) has also pointed out that there is a sense in which anyone engaged in research on language and gender must take responsibility for feeding the popular obsession with identifying and reifying sex-based differences in language, or any other form of behavior (a theme she expands on in this volume; see also Stokoe and Smitherson 2001). So there is a real tension here which all researchers in language and gender have to deal with. If we truly believed a radical version of the anti-essentialism that has recently become an axiom of the field, then we would put away our pens, our tape-recorders, and our notebooks, and the field of language and gender research would disappear. There would be no meaning to a handbook of language and gender because gender would have become such an idiosyncratic quality that it would be non-existent as a category across individuals.

This tension makes itself felt in this Handbook in a number of ways. One is the debate over the "proper" use of gender as a category in the analysis of discourse. Several contributors to the volume (Bucholtz, Lakoff, Sidnell, Weatherall and Gallois) bring up a recent debate over how overtly speakers must mark their orientation to, and the conversational salience of, gender in order for it to be analyzed as a social category being attended to in talk. In some ways, Schegloff's argument that analysts have to find something very "local" in the conversation before invoking gender as a salient category is an extremely pure application of the anti-essentialist posture adopted by many of the researchers who have rejected his argument as being too limited. We see this Handbook as being an excellent site for bringing such ironies and paradoxes within the field of study into fresh perspective, and providing the wherewithal for cordial and constructive continued discussion of how we are to resolve, or simply live with, them.

4   Theory and Methodologies

Finally, it is useful to draw attention to the range of theoretical frameworks and the many different methodologies included in this collection. A number of chapters examine the relationship between an individual's gender and specific features of their language: that is, the focus in these chapters is on characteristics of speech and writing which correlate with membership of gender as one particular social category. Analysts who adopt this approach treat gender as an identifiable social variable for the purposes of their analyses, a position justified by the fact that most people intuitively agree on what gender categories mean, and share a common conception of gender. Thus, the focus of such researchers is on the insights to be gained by identifying patterns in speech and writing which, to a greater or lesser extent, correlate with gender-based social categories. Much (though not all) variationist research adopts this approach, as Romaine's overview of the social dialect literature in the area of language and gender clearly indicates. Thimm, Koch, and Schey also use this approach in their examination of the influence of a speaker's gender on their choice of particular pragmatic particles and technical terms in interviews and role-plays, as does Herring's analysis of linguistic evidence of gender identity in computer-based on-line communication. A social cognitive perspective, described in Weatherall and Gallois' article, similarly involves "an assumption that gender identity develops as a relatively stable, pre-discursive trait, which resides in individuals and which is more or less salient, depending on its relevance to a particular social context. . . . cognition is conceptually prior to its expression in language and communication" (p. 488).

On the other hand, many of the analyses in the collection are conceptualized within a broadly social constructionist framework. As indicated in the previous section, analysts adopting this approach tend to question the notion of gender as a social category, and they often treat the social as well as the linguistic dimensions of their analyses as equally deserving of attention. So, these researchers conceive of social identity, and more particularly gender identity, as a social construct rather than a "given" social category to which people are assigned. Gender is treated as the accomplishment and product of social interaction. The focus is on the way individuals "do" or "perform" their gender identity in interaction with others, and there is an emphasis on dynamic aspects of interaction. Gender emerges over time in interaction with others. Language is a resource which can be drawn on creatively to perform different aspects of one's social identity at different points in an interaction. Speakers sensitively respond to the ongoing process of interaction, including changes of attitude and mood, and their linguistic choices may emphasize different aspects of their social identity and indicate a different orientation to their audience from moment to moment. So, not only do people speak differently in different social contexts, as sociolinguistic analyses of different styles have demonstrated (e.g. see Romaine's chapter), but, more radically, talk itself actively creates different styles and constructs different social contexts and social identities as it proceeds. The community of practice model which is outlined in McConnell-Ginet's chapter, and further invoked in Eckert's analysis of adolescent interaction, is firmly grounded within a social constructionist framework. Similarly, the discursive psychology perspective outlined by Weatherall and Gallois considers gender to be the accomplishment and product of social interaction. These chapters indicate the potential of this approach for illuminating the more dynamic aspects of interaction, and for identifying sites of potential social change. They also draw attention to the strategies by which social change is typically resisted or facilitated, demonstrating "people's active engagement in the reproduction of or resistance to gender arrangements in their communities" (Eckert and McConnell-Ginet 1992: 466). Moreover, as McElhinny points out, this approach more comfortably accommodates the analysis of communities, cultures, and linguistic behaviors that do not fit the standard gender dichotomy, and facilitates research which challenges the "dominant ideologies [which] help to perpetuate inequities in Western contexts" (p. 36).

Within this broad conceptual framework, however, there is room for a range of contrasting emphases and methodologies. One of the more popular methodologies in this collection is the ethnographically grounded and postmodern analyses illustrated in the detailed case-studies of talk in interaction provided by Leap and Kulick, for example, and illustrated in relation to written discourse by Livia. These post-structural analyses are very clearly at home under a social constructionist umbrella. Besnier, Meyerhoff, and Philips equally exemplify their arguments by drawing on their detailed ethnographic research in specific, and non-Western, speech communities.

It is also worth noting, as Bucholtz points out, that many researchers fruitfully combine aspects of different methodologies to answer the questions that arise in the course of their research. Meyerhoff, for example, demonstrates, in her discussion of *sore* in Bislama, that variationist approaches are not inconsistent with detailed ethnographic sociolinguistic description, and a social constructionist focus on the emergent nature of gender. Sidnell's detailed analysis of male talk in a Guyanese rumshop illustrates how a classic conversation analysis (CA) approach to the text is illuminated by ethnographic detail about the community in which it is located. CA is based fundamentally on a model of communication as joint activity (Sacks 1984), and Sidnell illustrates this while specifically exploring how gender is oriented to in the sample of talk-in-interaction which he examines. Drawing on her extensive ethnographic research, Goodwin also uses CA to examine turn types, and the function of features of sequential organization in the management of children's disputes. Weatherall and Gallois indicate the value of CA-based analyses in discursive psychology, while Holmes and Stubbe's chapter also illustrates the value of combining different methodologies. They explore the relationship between the quantitative patterns identified using a predominantly variationist approach, and the insights revealed by more detailed qualitative discourse analysis of interactions involving particular women in their workplaces, conceptualized as contrasting communities of practice.

Sociolinguists and discourse analysts who work within a social constructionist framework typically engage in qualitative analysis of discourse, paying careful attention to the context of interaction, as illustrated by many of the chapters in this collection: for example Leap, Ehrlich, Kendall, and Tannen. Following Goffman (1974), Tannen and Kendall, for example, use a "framing" approach, relating the linguistic forms and meanings of utterances to the speaker's frame of the activity, for example as a socialization exercise, or as a learning experience. In the context of language and gender research, a framing approach conceptualizes the creation of gendered identities as one component of the creation of social identities more generally. As Kendall (p. 604) notes, following Ochs (1992):

> Women and men do not generally choose linguistic options for the purpose of creating masculine or feminine identities; instead, they draw upon gendered linguistic strategies to perform pragmatic and interactional functions of language and, thus, constitute roles in a gendered way. It is the manner in which people constitute their identities when acting within a social role that is linked with gender – that is, being a "good mother," being a "good manager."

Detailed discourse analysis of relevant social interactions clearly provides the crucial basis for frame analysis, as for other kinds of qualitative analysis. However, the analyses which underpin at least some of the research described by Kiesling, Meyerhoff, Eckert, Wodak, Pauwels, and Holmes and Stubbe make it clear that there is also a place for quantitatively oriented studies, at least as a background for understanding the social significance of particular linguistic choices at specific points in an interaction.

Another very distinctive theoretical approach, perhaps best exemplified by Wodak's analysis of the language of women politicians in the European Parliament, is Critical Discourse Analysis (CDA). CDA aims to reveal connections between language, power, and ideology, describing the way power and dominance are produced and reproduced in social practice through discourse structures in interaction. As with social constructionism, CDA accommodates a variety of methodologies. Some researchers, such as Wodak, Cameron, and Talbot, focus mainly on macro-level discourse strategies, examining distinctive rhetorical patterns, for instance, while others adopt a detailed CA or an interactionally oriented approach. Still others, such as Ehrlich, take a more grammatical approach, exploring relevant details of syntactic and semantic organization, while Pauwels' analysis of sexist usages examines the grammatical and lexical components of several different linguistic systems as a whole.

Another approach to the analysis of gender in discourse is a more cognitive approach, typically exemplified in the work of social psychologists such as Weatherall and Gallois, but in this collection, also evident in many discussions of the relevance of stereotypes in the analysis of gendered interaction: e.g. Thimm et al., Talbot, Pauwels, and Livia (Philips too attends to the routine and repeated as well as the fluid and creative). As Livia comments, stereotypes and norms have an important backgrounding function in that "the traditional gender norms are often used as a foil against which more experimental positions are understood" (p. 149). Finally, Weatherall and Gallois also provide a useful overview of recent gender-oriented research within Communication Accommodation Theory, a framework which emphasizes the centrality of social identity and the relevance of the addressee in accounting for language variation in intergroup interactions.

This collection illustrates, then, that a wide range of theoretical approaches and methodologies are currently in use by researchers in the area of language and gender. Moreover, it is evident that it is often impossible to categorize individual chapters as exemplars of one rather than another approach. Many researchers clearly find it productive to combine different approaches and integrate various methodologies in their attempts to throw light on the questions which intrigue them.

5   Conclusion

Putting together this collection has been a stimulating and challenging experience. In concluding, we draw attention to two important issues which have crystallized in the process of editing the volume. The first relates to potential applications of language and gender research, the second to productive future directions for theoretical paradigms in the area.

A number of chapters in the Handbook point to very pragmatic lessons which can be learnt from language and gender research, and provide an opening for our academic work to participate in and contribute to social activism. For instance, what we can draw from Cameron's, Talbot's, and Holmes and Stubbe's work is a clearer sense of the way findings in social science research are often manipulated to match existing preconceptions about the natural relationship between gender and power in the workforce, in advertising, and in employment and education policies. There seems little point to our academic interests if they do not at some stage articulate with real-world concerns and enable us or our readers to identify, for example, certain employment practices as unfair and ill-informed, based more on stereotypes and prejudice than they are on people's actual behavior in the real world. At some point, our research has to be able to travel out of the academy in order to draw attention to and challenge unquestioned practices that reify certain behaviors as being morally, or aesthetically, better than others. Most, if not all, the contributors to this volume would share an appreciation of being able to highlight and resist practices that (1) reserve the expression of authority for a subset of speakers in possession of certain (arbitrary) properties, and (2) withhold the allocation of authority from others. Philips' contribution to this volume makes a particularly strong argument for the political and social relevance of research on gender ideologies. As responsible researchers in the area of language and gender, then, we should never cease to engage actively with and challenge assumptions about gender norms, and loudly draw attention to the way power, privilege, and social authority interact with and are naturalized as properties of independent social categories.

However, as Herring points out, such stances of committed engagement may themselves distance us from younger women, or from more widespread contemporary attitudes which valorize diversity and individual expression.

Yet, somehow researchers on language and gender have to deal with these sorts of applied paradoxes too, since our work is increasingly evaluated on its relevance to and connection with issues that are topical in the community that funds us either directly (assigning tax dollars to higher education) or indirectly (through funding agencies).

This leads to our second point, namely, our awareness of the tensions, the contradictions, and the sites of potential paradigm conflict among the diverse materials and analyses collected together in this Handbook. Our own strongly held position amid these different perspectives and potential conflicts is one which welcomes the fruitful interaction generated by the expression of different points of view, and encourages the exploration of areas of difference and disagreement. We believe that valuable progress can result when researchers hold different theoretical positions or adopt different methodologies, provided they are willing to engage in discussion and debate.

Reflecting on the progress indicated by the research represented in this collection, it seems that language and gender research is at a stage when it can accommodate, and even begin to integrate, a range of different approaches to understanding how and to what extent gender is relevant (or not) in negotiating interaction and constructing complex sociocultural identities. While social constructionist approaches predominate, it is clear that the contribution and important influence of gender stereotypes, gender-based cognitive categories, and sociocultural conceptions of differently gendered roles must be factored into our research. The crucial point, in our view, is to avoid adopting narrow paradigms which are potentially damaging to the spirit of enquiry, and to resist pressures toward the development of a restrictive and limiting orthodoxy in the kinds of theoretical frameworks and research methodologies which are judged acceptable.

Like other contributors to this collection, we have consistently argued for, and indeed, adopted approaches which attempt to integrate quantitative and qualitative methods of analysis, using the patterns identified by the quantitative analysis as essential background to assist in the detailed qualitative interpretation of the discourse. Macro-level quantitative research identifies the gendered norms on which speakers are drawing, the ground against which individual choices must be interpreted. Research is inevitably an additive and an iterative process.

It may be useful if those working in language and gender research resolved to avoid using terms such as "essentialist" to dismiss research which focuses on the big picture, research which attempts to identify regularities and make generalizations about global patterns observable in the relationship between language and gender – that is, research which aims to uncover some of the patterns regulating "the gender order" (as it is referred to in Eckert and McConnell-Ginet, forthcoming). All research is an attempt to get a best fit between intuitive conceptions and insights about the specific details of an interaction, and a satisfactory and illuminating theoretical account of the interaction. Yet we are all aware of the fact that research is unavoidably messy and fuzzy-edged. We will make greater progress if we seek to accommodate insights from a variety of sources, rather than dismissing, in a blinkered and unreflecting manner, results from currently unfashionable paradigms.

In conclusion, we consider that this collection provides an inspiring kaleidoscope of theoretical models and concepts, methodological approaches and strategic pathways for feminist social action for researchers in the field of language and gender. It certainly provides a wide range of addressees for people to engage with in furthering their own research, a great variety of people to talk to about the research issues that are besetting them, and a remarkably varied set of starting points for those just beginning research in this area.

NOTE

1   Though sadly that does not mean that such simplistic representations of the field and of the findings of language and gender research do not continue to work their way into texts, from introductions to sociolinguistics and advanced surveys of the field through to popular texts written for non-academic audiences.

REFERENCES

Bergvall, Victoria L., Bing, Janet M., and Freed, Alice F. (eds) 1996: *Rethinking Language and Gender Research: Theory and Practice.* New York: Longman.

Bucholtz, Mary, Liang, Anita C., Sutton, Laurel A., and Hines, Caitlin (eds) 1994: *Cultural Performances: Proceedings of the Third Berkeley Women and Language Conference, April 1994.* Berkeley, CA: Berkeley Woman and Language Group, University of California.

Bucholtz, Mary, Liang, Anita C., and Sutton, Laurel A. (eds) 1999: *Reinventing Identities: The Gendered Self in Discourse.* New York: Oxford University Press.

Burton, Pauline, Dyson, Ketaki Kushari, and Ardener, Shirley (eds) 1994: *Bilingual Women: Anthropological Approaches to Second-Language Use.* Oxford: Berg.

Cameron, Deborah 1995: *Verbal Hygiene.* London: Routledge.

Cameron, Deborah (ed.) 1998: *The Feminist Critique of Language.* London and New York: Routledge.

Cameron, Deborah 2000: *Good to Talk? Living and Working in a Communication Culture.* London: Sage.

Cameron, Deborah, Frazer, Elizabeth, Harvey, Penelope, Rampton, Ben, and Richardson, Kay (eds) 1992: *Researching Language: Issues of Power and Method.* London: Routledge.

Cheshire, Jenny and Trudgill, Peter (eds) 1998: *The Sociolinguistics Reader,* vol. 2: *Gender and Discourse.* London: Arnold.

Coates, Jennifer (ed.) 1998: *Language and Gender: A Reader.* Oxford: Blackwell.

Eckert, Penelope 2000: *Linguistic Variation as Social Practice.* Oxford: Blackwell.

Eckert, Penelope and McConnell-Ginet, Sally 1992: Think practically and look locally: Language and gender as community-based practice. *Annual Review of Anthropology* 21: 461–90.

Eckert, Penelope and McConnell-Ginet, Sally (forthcoming): *Language and Gender Practice.* Cambridge: Cambridge University Press.

Goffman, Erving 1974: *Frame Analysis.* Harmondsworth: Penguin.

Hall, Kira and Bucholtz, Mary (eds) 1995: *Gender Articulated: Language and the Socially Constructed Self.* London: Routledge.

Hall, Kira, Bucholtz, Mary, and Moonwomon, Birch (eds) 1992: *Locating Power: Proceedings of the Second Berkeley Women and Language Conference,* April 4 and 5, 1992, vol. 1. Berkeley, CA: Berkeley Women and Language Group, University of California.

Hellinger, Marlis and Bussmann, Hadumod (eds) 2001: *Gender Across Languages: The Linguistic Representation of Women and Men.* Amsterdam: John Benjamins.

Holmes, Janet 1997: Women, language and identity. *Journal of Sociolinguistics* 1(2): 195–223.

Holmes, Janet (ed.) 1999: *Communities of Practice in Language and Gender Research. Language in Society,* Special Issue, 28(2): 171–320.

Johnson, Sally and Meinhof, Ulrike Hanna (eds) 1997: *Language and Masculinity.* Oxford: Blackwell.

Kotthoff, Helga and Wodak, Ruth (eds) 1997: *Communicating Gender in Context.* Amsterdam and Philadelphia: John Benjamins.

Ochs, Elinor 1992: Indexing gender. In Alessandro Duranti and Charles

Goodwin (eds) *Rethinking Context: Language as an Interactive Phenomenon.* Cambridge: Cambridge University Press, pp. 335–58.

Sacks, Harvey 1984: Notes on methodology. In J. Maxwell Atkinson and John Heritage (eds) *Structures of Social Action: Studies in Conversation Analysis.* Cambridge: Cambridge University Press, pp. 21–7.

Stokoe, Elizabeth H. and Smitherson, Janet 2001: Making gender relevant: conversation analysis and gender categories in interaction. *Discourse and Society* 12(2): 217–45.

Sunderland, Jane (ed.) 1994: *Exploring Gender: Questions for English Language Education.* London: Prentice-Hall.

Tannen, Deborah (ed.) 1993: *Gender and Conversational Interaction.* Oxford: Oxford University Press.

Tannen, Deborah (ed.) 1994: *Gender and Discourse.* Oxford: Oxford University Press.

Warner, Natasha, Ahlers, Jocelyn, Bilmes, Leela, Oliver, Monica, Wertheim, Suzanne, and Chen, Melinda (eds) 1996: *Gender and Belief Systems: Proceedings of the Fourth Berkeley Women and Language Conference,* April 19–21, 1996. Berkeley, CA: Berkeley Women and Language Group, University of California.

Wertheim, Suzanne, Bailey, Ashlee C., and Corston-Oliver, Monica (eds) 1998: *Engendering Communication: Proceedings of the Fifth Berkeley Women and Language Conference,* April 24–26, 1998. Berkeley, CA: Berkeley Women and Language Group, University of California.

Part I
History and Theoretical Background to the Study of Language and Gender

1 Theorizing Gender in Sociolinguistics and Linguistic Anthropology

BONNIE MCELHINNY

1 Introduction

Increasingly, feminist scholars in linguistics and in other fields have realized that we must ask how empirical gaps come to be created. Feminist scholars have discovered "that many gaps were there for a reason, i.e. that existing paradigms systematically ignore or erase the significance of women's experiences and the organization of gender" (Thorne and Stacey 1993: 168). The task of feminist scholarship thus goes beyond simply adding discussions of women and women's experiences into our disciplines, to encompass the broader task of interrogating and transforming existing conceptual schemes. In history, for instance, feminist and other radical scholars have challenged the assumption that history is primarily about politics, public policy, and famous individuals. The inclusion of women has led to a rethinking of the notion of historical periodization itself, since historical turning points are not necessarily the same for women as for men (Kelly-Gadol 1977). In literature, feminist scholars have extended their project from the critique of texts by male authors and the recovery of texts written by female authors to asking questions about how literary periods and notions of dominant aesthetic modes are established, and thus how certain writers, texts, and genres become valued as central or canonical (see e.g. Feldman and Kelley 1995). Feminist anthropologists have also asked questions about how the canon of anthropological thought gets constructed (Behar and Gordan 1995).

Feminist sociolinguists and linguistic anthropologists are also increasingly asking questions about fundamental analytic concepts that must be revalued when women and gender are taken seriously. The definition of hypercorrection (Cameron and Coates 1988), standard and vernacular language (Morgan 1994), definitions of speech community (Eckert and McConnell-Ginet 1992; Holmes 1999), and even theories about the way language constructs social identity (Ochs 1992) have all been examined by feminist sociolinguists. It is not only, however, analytic concepts which are distinctively sociolinguistic that require feminist re-examination. We also need to consider how certain basic categories of analysis found in other disciplines are implemented in our own. I argue here that the fundamental feminist category of "gender," as implemented in sociolinguistics, has often included certain political and social assumptions which prematurely narrow our area of inquiry.

Early sociolinguistic studies of gender often assumed that gender should be studied where it was most salient, and that gender was most salient "in cross-sex interaction between potentially sexually accessible interlocutors, or same-sex interaction in gender-specific tasks" (Brown and Levinson 1983: 53). At its best, work based on this assumption led to a series of insightful studies of the linguistic styles of men and women in romantic heterosexual relationships or in experimental settings designed to simulate such relationships (e.g. Fishman 1983; Gleason 1987; Tannen 1990; West and Zimmerman 1983). There are, however, at least four significant, and increasingly controversial, theoretical assumptions about gender embedded in this recommendation: (1) gender is closely wedded to sex, and the study of gender is closely wedded to the study of heterosexuality; (2) gender is an attribute; (3) the study of gender is the study of individuals; and (4) gender is best studied where most salient. In this chapter I explore each of these in turn. In this discussion, as elsewhere, theories about gender always have more than theoretical significance; they always suggest the cause of inequities and thus indicate where society should direct its resources to redress inequity (see Jaggar 1983). Deciding amongst different theories of gender is thus no mere theoretical exercise; it is directly linked to deciding upon political strategies for feminist activism.

1.1   *The relationship of gender to sex and sexuality*

The distinction between sex and gender has been one of the foundations of Western feminist thought. The following pairs of definitions are typical.

> [Sex and gender] serve a useful analytic purpose in contrasting a set of biological facts with a set of cultural facts. Were I to be scrupulous in my use of terms, I would use the term "sex" only when I was speaking of biological differences between males and females and use "gender" whenever I was referring to the social, cultural, psychological constructs that are imposed upon these biological differences. . . . [G]ender designates a set of categories to which we can give the same label crosslinguistically or crossculturally because they have some connection to sex differences. These categories are however conventional or arbitrary insofar as they are not reducible to or directly derivative of natural, biological facts; they vary from one language to another, one culture to another, in the way in which they order experience and action.   (Shapiro (1981), cited in Yanagisako and Collier 1990: 139)

The distinction between sex and gender attempts to counter views which attribute differences and inequalities between women and men to sex or biology, as in opinions like the following:

> In all primate societies the division of labor by gender creates a highly stable social system, the dominant males controlling territorial boundaries and maintaining order among lesser males by containing and preventing their aggression, the females tending the young and forming alliances with other females. Human primates follow this same pattern so remarkably that it is not difficult to argue for biological bases for the type of social order that channels aggression to guard the territory which in turn maintains an equable environment for the young.   (McGuinness and Pribam, cited in Sperling 1991: 208)

In this sociobiological view there is no gender, for there are no cultural determinants of human life. All is "sex." This view of sex as naturally dictating behavior and roles supports a functionalist model of human social organization. Feminists who make a distinction between sex and gender do not necessarily abandon the idea that there are some biological differences between women and men, but most attempt to sharply circumscribe that which can be attributed to such differences. Often implicit in such distinctions is the idea that what is socially constructed (gender) can be more easily transformed than what is biological (sex).

An increasing number of feminists argue that sex/gender models like Shapiro's are problematic, both in their conception of gender and in their assumptions about sex (see also Cameron 1997b). To say that "gender" refers "to the social, cultural, psychological constructs that are imposed upon these biological differences" implies that there are TWO genders, based upon two sexes. Linda Nicholson (1994) calls this the "coat-rack" model of sex and gender. This dichotomous picture of gender is problematic because it overstates similarity within each of the categories so designated, and understates similarities across these categories. Further, underlying the assumption that the sex–gender distinction is dualistic is an assumption that these differences are necessary for procreative sexuality, which is understood as heterosexuality (see e.g. Kapchan 1996: 19). The methodological recommendation to study gender "in cross-sex interaction between potentially sexually accessible interlocutors" illustrates how the idea of just two genders can be conflated with a presumption of heterosexuality. Historically and cross-culturally sexual attachment has not always been ideologically organized in terms of a dichotomy, but in Western capitalist countries at present "objects of desire are generally defined by the dichotomy and opposition of feminine and masculine; and sexual practice is mainly organized in couple relationships" (Connell 1987: 113).[1] Assumptions about heterosexuality as normative thus directly inform notions of sex and gender, while normative notions of sex and gender inform those about heterosexuality. To focus only on studying gender, then, in heterosexual interactions may be quite misleading: gender differences may be *exaggerated* in such interactions.

Feminist scholars have taken two different paths to redressing problems with the sex/gender distinction. One path, often followed by physical anthropologists and biologists, is to offer a more nuanced picture of the biological, and how it interacts with the social (Sperling 1991; Worthman 1995). This approach challenges the notion of biology as more fixed and less amenable to change than culture is. For instance, Worthman (1995) considers the ways that gender as a principle for social organization affects biological development in terms of risk factors for breast cancer. Much recent work in sociolinguistics adopts a second approach, one which in effect subsumes what was traditionally placed under the domain of sex into the domain of gender. Scholars with this view look at the social construction of "sex." In addition to recognizing cultural differences in understanding the body (Nicholson 1994), proponents of this view may argue that we need to look at how certain definitions of sex/gender become hegemonic and are contested within a given society. Philosopher Judith Butler argues that:

> Gender ought not to be conceived merely as the cultural inscription of meaning on a pregiven sex. . . . gender must also designate the very apparatus of production whereby the sexes themselves are established. As a result, gender is not to culture as sex is to nature; gender is also the discursive/cultural means by which "sexed nature" or "a natural sex" is produced and established as "prediscursive" prior to culture, a politically neutral surface on which culture acts.   (1990: 7)

Instead of asking "what are the gender differences?", this approach (an approach which has been called *post-structuralist* or *deconstructive* feminist) leads one to ask "what difference does gender make?" and "how did gender come to make a difference?" To argue that differences found in people's behavior, including their speech behavior, can simply be explained by invoking gender is to fail to question how gender is constructed. Instead, one needs to ask how and why gender differences are being constructed in that way, or what notion of gender is being normalized in such behavior. This approach, then, proposes to investigate how categories such as "woman" are created and which political interests the creation and perpetuation of certain identities and distinctions serves. Where people's behavior does not conform to dominant norms of masculinity or femininity, it is rendered unintelligible or incoherent: certain people or certain behaviors may not be recognized as legitimately human. Because they deviate from normative conceptions of how sex, gender, and sexuality should be aligned they are subject to repercussions and sanctions which vary according to local context. Some are economic, with people being confined to certain kinds of work and expelled from others. In the USA, women working as police officers often find themselves addressed as "sir" and occasionally find that others assume they are lesbians, regardless of any other information about sexual identity, simply because of the work that they do. Other sanctions are physical interventions, in the form of violence ("gay-bashing") or medical procedures (in North America, intersexed infants are operated on in order to be easily categorizable as male or female). Yet other sanctions are emotional: witness the expulsion from biological families of many Indian *hijras*, Nigerian *'yan daudu* (both discussed below), and American gays and lesbians. That the boundaries of what is seen as appropriate gendered behavior are policed and sanctioned is seen as evidence that certain definitions of gender are used to maintain a certain social order. (Below I suggest that the detailed specification of what "social order" means remains one of the tasks that scholarship in language and gender has yet to adequately address.)

Challenges to norms of sex and gender can cast a particularly illuminating light on the construction of sex and gender because they make visible norms and counternorms of gender. Indeed, the study of such challenges has become one methodological corollary of a post-structuralist theoretical approach. Although one argument against a deconstructive feminist approach has been that it focuses on marginal cases of gender construction, cases of deviance, in ways that do not explain gender construction in the majority of people's lives, this argument fails to recognize the principal point being made by this approach, a point that is more familiar perhaps in the study of other marginalized groups. From the perspective of Marxism, the notions of elite groups about why and how social stratification and conflict comes about are suspect because they are more likely to reify the status quo than to question it. For instance, a bourgeois perspective might see each worker as a free agent, constrained only by free will in how s/he contracts out labor power, while workers see domination, exploitation, and the accumulation of wealth among a few.[2] Similarly, gender "outliers" bear the costs of hegemonic views about gender in ways that may cause them to question why such views are so powerful and so widely held.

In linguistics and elsewhere, a post-structuralist approach has led to a recent series of studies which focus on various kinds of sex/gender "transgression," in part for what they help reveal about dominant norms of sex/gender/sexual identity. For instance, Hall's work with Indian *hijras* (ritual specialists, mostly men, who describe themselves as hermaphrodites but have often undergone a castration operation) highlights the process of socialization into gender: femaleness and femininity must be learned by *hijra*, much like others acquire a second language. Hall's work also interrogates the assumption that highly visible and culturally central gender ambiguity suggests higher cultural tolerance for gender variation, pointing out the range of exclusion and abuse experienced by *hijra* in India (Hall 1997; Hall and O'Donovan 1996). By looking at the ways that *'yan daudu* (Nigerian men who talk like women, and often have men as sexual partners) transgress norms of gender and sexuality, Gaudio (1996, 1997) suggests how, even in a patriarchal Islamic society that in principle accords all men potential access to masculine power, this access is not equally distributed, nor unconditional. Cameron's (1997a) study of college men watching a basketball game, and gossiping about other men whom they label "gay," shows how some men continually construct themselves as heterosexual by denigrating other men, labeling them as "gay" in the absence of any information or even any indicators about their sexuality because their clothes or behavior or speech are perceived as "insufficiently masculine." Kulick's work on Brazilian *travestis* addresses the question of what it is about the hegemonic definitions of sexuality and gender in Brazil that make it logical and meaningful for males who desire other males to radically modify their bodies (1998: 225). See also Besnier (1993, this volume) for work on gender liminality in Polynesia.

Studying discourse from or about sexual minorities is not, however, the only strategy for highlighting how gender is learned and performed. Indeed, to study gender in this way may suggest or assume that there is a closer relationship between sexuality and gender than between either of these and any other aspect of social identity, a question which itself deserves empirical investigation (Sedgwick 1990). It may also suggest that the construction of hegemonic gender norms is most closely linked to procreational needs (Hawkesworth 1997). The ways in which gender is imbricated in other axes of identity, the ways in which certain notions of gender can reinforce or challenge certain notions about class and ethnicity, is part of what we must begin to investigate more closely. Barrett's (1994) study of the linguistic strategies used by African American drag queens shows how they appropriate stereotypes of White women's speech in order to parody and critique certain White stereotypes about Black men (including the myth of the Black male rapist). Inoue's (forthcoming) genealogical approach to Japanese women's language (JWL) highlights the co-construction of gender, class, and national identity. Although some linguists have described JWL as a speech variety spoken by all Japanese women, traceable back to feudal Japan, Inoue shows how JWL was actively constructed during the late nineteenth century as part of the construction and consolidation of a modern nation-state meant to withstand the Western colonial inroads visible elsewhere in Asia. Similarly, Siegal's (1994) study of White women in Japan who resist using certain Japanese linguistic strategies deemed appropriate for women because they perceive them as overly hesitant or humble suggests both how certain kinds of Japanese femininity are constructed with language use and what gendered norms prevail for these White Westerners. Finally, my work on women working in a traditionally masculine, working-class workplace highlights some prevailing notions of what it means to be a woman, what it means to be a man, and what it means to be a police officer, as it examines how those notions are critiqued and changed by female police officers (McElhinny 1994, 1995, 1996). By looking at men and women's crossover into spheres and spaces often predominantly associated with the other, we begin to get a sense of how the boundaries between those spheres are actively maintained, how gender is policed, how people resist these boundaries, and perhaps what transformation requires.

It is worth considering why post-structuralist models of gender have been so readily embraced by sociolinguists and linguistic anthropologists working on gender. Our very subject matter – language – may lend itself to an ability to focus on gender and the social construction of "sex." People's ability to adapt language readily and rapidly from situation to situation, addressee to addressee, may accord people an unusual degree of agency and flexibility in their construction of themselves in a way that other forms of cultural and actual capital can and do not (e.g. body hexus, occupational opportunities). The fruitfulness of this approach for sociolinguistic inquiry should not too quickly lead us into endorsing this approach as "the" appropriate model for understanding gender/sex systems, without carefully attending to the ways different cultural and economic contexts may lead to other ways of understanding sex, gender, and sexuality. The question of how to think of gender as something which is structure and practice, institutional and individual, is one I develop in the next two sections.

2   Gender as Activity and Relation

To suggest that gender is something one continually does is to challenge the idea that gender is something one has. A variety of metaphors have arisen to capture this idea: gender as activity, gender as performance, gender as accomplishment. As a group they can be understood as embodying a practice-based approach to gender, and as such they participate in a wider move within linguistic and sociocultural anthropology since the mid-1970s to use practice-based models (Abu-Lughod 1991; Hanks 1990; Ochs 1996; Ortner 1984, 1996). Practice theory reacts against structural-determinist social theories (e.g. British-American structural-functionalism, determinist strands of Marxism and French structuralism) that did not incorporate a sufficient sense of how human actions make structure. Although Ortner (1996) argues that key practice theorists (she lists Pierre Bourdieu, Anthony Giddens, Marshall Sahlins, and Michel de Certeau) often make little attempt to engage with work by feminist, subaltern, post-colonial, and minority scholars, and vice versa, her argument ignores feminist linguistic anthropological work, perhaps in part because it works outside the intellectual genealogy she establishes here (see McElhinny 1998). A number of recent works in feminist linguistic anthropology *do* draw on practice theory, but they have been often as influenced by the work of Soviet psychology (especially Vygotsky and his students) as by the theorists she names. Before exploring these works, it is, however, useful to consider the roots of the notion of gender as an attribute, and the problems with that notion that a practice-based approach tries to address.

Judith Butler argues that:

> [H]umanist conceptions of the subject tend to assume a substantive person who is the bearer of various essential and nonessential attributes. A humanist feminist position might understand gender as an attribute of a person who is characterized essentially as a pregendered substance or "core" called the person, denoting a universal capacity for reason, moral deliberation or language. (1990: 10)

She goes on to contrast this view with those historical and anthropological approaches that understand gender as a relation among socially constituted subjects in specifiable contexts. The model of personhood described by Butler has been called abstract individualism, defined as an approach to understanding the relationship of people to society which "considers individual human beings as social atoms, abstracted from their social contexts, and disregards the role of social relationships and human community in constituting the very identity and nature of individual human beings" (Weiss 1995: 163). Although Butler does not make this point, others have pointed out that abstract individualism is a part of the liberal political philosophy which arose alongside and helps undergird capitalist social relations in Western nation-states. Liberal philosophy argued for the inherent equality of men (I use the masculine noun advisedly), based on each man's inherent rationality. Each was supposed to be able to identify his own interests, and to be enabled to pursue them. Ensuring the conditions for each man's autonomy and fulfillment has been linked to preserving the right to private property (Jaggar 1983: 34). The focus on rationality as the essence of human nature has, as has been frequently remarked, led to an ahistoricism and universalism in liberal theory: "[liberalism] does not place any philosophical importance on such 'accidental' differences between human individuals as the historical period in which they live, their rank or class position, their race or their sex" (Jaggar 1983: 32).

Contrasting conceptions of gender in commodity- and in gift-based societies helps make clear how and why gender comes to be seen as possessed by individuals in capitalist societies, as Strathern has pointed out. Commodity and gift each refer to ways to organize social relations. In commodity societies, a relationship is established between the objects exchanged, while in gift exchange a relation is established between the exchanging subjects. In a commodity-oriented economy, people experience a desire to appropriate goods; in a gift-oriented economy, people desire to expand social relations. In a commodity society, "both the capabilities available to the person and the resources available to society are construed as 'things' having a prior natural or utilitarian value in themselves" (Strathern 1988: 135). People who are understood as owning their own labor also "own their minds . . . and their minds turn the proprietor of his or her own actions also into the author of them" (1988: 135). It is an idiosyncratic feature of a Western bourgeois way of understanding property that suggests that singular items are attached to singular owners, with the fact of possession constructing the possessor as a unitary social entity. Individuals, in this view, are understood as a source of action, an embodiment of sentiment and emotion, and an author of ideas.[3]

Often enough, anthropologists working from within a Western tradition have continued to use a commodity logic to understand gender. They have, that is, continued to be fascinated by the attributes of things, and to locate possession, ownership, control, in a one-to-one relation between discrete attributes and the unitary individual. In Melanesia, however, metaphors of interaction are more useful than metaphors of possession for understanding gender: selves are understood as registers of their encounters with one another, microcosms of interaction. People are understood as dependent upon others for knowledge of their internal selves, rather than as authors of accounts of them.

Now, ways of conceiving gender as something other than a possession or attribute are not only found in non-Western cultural systems. They also are part of a challenge to hegemonic world-views in North America and Western Europe. Significantly, one of the best-developed scholarly accounts in the sociolinguistic tradition of gender as an activity draws on a Marxist psychological tradition: Soviet activity theory. The roots of activity theory are in the work of Vygotsky, with its emphasis on the social origins of consciousness (drawing upon Marx's Sixth Thesis on Feuerbach). The concept of activity was further developed by Leontyev, who elaborated upon Marx's First Thesis on Feuerbach. In *He-Said-She-Said*, Marjorie Harness Goodwin (1990) draws on the Vygotskyan tradition to argue that activities, rather than cultures, groups, individuals, or gender, should be the basic unit of analysis for the study of interactive phenomena.[4]

Goodwin examines the different social structures created by African American boys and girls in a range of speech activities (directives, argument, gossip/ dispute, instigating, and stories) and in a range of play activities (playing house, making slingshots, making glass rings, arguments). In some activities she finds girls and boys building systematically different social organizations and gender identities through their use of talk, and in others she finds them building similar structures.[5] A focus on activities suggests that individuals have access to *different* activities, and thus to *different* cultures and different social identities, including a range of different genders. We discover that

> stereotypes about women's speech . . . fall apart when talk in a range of activities is examined; in order to construct social personae appropriate to the events of the moment, the same individuals [will] articulate talk and gender differently as they move from one activity to another.   (Goodwin 1990: 9)

Crucial to note here is that it is not just talk which varies across context, a point long familiar in sociolinguistics. Gender identity also varies across context. Language and gender co-vary. The particular contribution a focus on activities makes to linguistic research on gender, then, is that it changes the research question from what the differences are between men's and women's speech (an approach which serves to perpetuate and exaggerate the dichotomous gender categories, and to undergird the idea of gender as a possession) to when, whether, and how men and women's speech are done in similar and different ways.

In theoretically related work, Penelope Eckert and Sally McConnell-Ginet have argued that studying how gender is constructed in communities of practice challenges existing approaches to the study of gender in sociolinguistics. A *community of practice* "is an aggregate of people who come together around mutual engagement in an endeavour. Ways of doing things, ways of talking, beliefs, values, power relations – in short practices – emerge in the course of this mutual endeavour" (1992: 464).[6] A community of practice identifies a somewhat larger analytic domain than does *activity*. Communities of practice articulate between macro-sociological structures such as class and everyday interactional practices by considering the groups in which individuals participate and how these shape their interactions. The groups in which they participate are in turn determined and constituted by their place within larger social structures. The notion of community of practice thus serves as a mediating region between local and global analysis (Bucholtz 1993). Studying communities of practice also allows us to investigate how gender interacts with other aspects of identity because "people's access and exposure to, need for, and interest in different communities of practice are related to such things as their class, age, and ethnicity as well as to their sex" (Eckert and McConnell-Ginet 1992: 472). In addition to investigating which communities speakers belong to, one can investigate how people manage memberships in different communities or different (perhaps hierarchical) positionalities within communities of practice, and how communities of practice are linked with other communities of practice. Sociolinguists still, however, need to explore the ways in which recent critiques of practice theory may or may not apply to our use of the concept of community of practice. Ortner (1996) points out that the practice-based approach moves beyond a view of social behavior as ordered by rules and norms, but that it also grants actors a great deal of agency, thus perhaps reproducing the hegemonic model of personhood (abstract individualism) of Western commodity-based societies. A deeper-seated critique of practice theory has arisen from the work of some Marxist scholars (see e.g. Smith 1999) who see the invocation of practice theory too often as the end of analysis rather than the beginning of a careful historical and cultural enquiry.

To focus on activities and practices does not lead us in precisely the same direction. Practice, in particular, allows one to retain some sense of the sedimentation of practice that occurs in certain institutional or cultural contexts. Still, the projects are similar in this sense: Eckert and McConnell-Ginet and Goodwin are each trying to find a way to critique essentializing analytic categories. This may not require us to abandon such notions as "gender," as Goodwin recommends. "Gender" retains significance for people living their lives, not just people analyzing how people live their lives. This, too, is part of what we must capture in our analysis, without *assuming* the significance of gender. Ortner's comments on the need to retain some notion of culture could equally well apply to gender:

> Yet for all the problems with the use of the culture concept – the tendency to use it in such a way as to efface internal politics/difference, and to make others radically other – it does more violence to deny its presence and force in the social process than to keep it in the picture. For "culture" in the borderlands is both the grounds of negotiation and its object: it sets the terms of the encounters, but it is also what is at stake.   (1996: 182)

The study of gender in workplaces also suggests some need to modify the strong claim that "the relevant unit for the analysis of cultural phenomena, including gender, is thus not the group as a whole, or the individual, but rather situated activities" (Goodwin 1990: 9). Gender is used as a way of allocating access to different forms of work and other resources. To focus on gender in activities alone may be to focus on the gender of individuals, but to lose sight of the gender of institutions. In this, activity theory may be said to betray its psychological origins. Many activity theorists, drawing on Marxist social theory, have remained cognizant of the importance of situating activities within larger social systems (cf. Leontyev 1981: 47). Nevertheless, in Soviet psychology, and in American practices influenced by it, the move beyond small-group interactions to the analysis of "the *system* of social relations," the study of "collectivities, institutions and historical processes" (Connell 1987: 139) is endlessly deferred. I believe, however, that the use of activities as a unit of analysis can be readily reconciled with a systemic focus, if it is adopted as a methodological tool rather than a theoretical approach.

A careful focus on activity becomes a rigorous tool for ethnographic analysis, asking either that one demonstrate that activities are understood as the "same" by participants, or that one find principled ways to explain differences. Different individuals may agree that they are participating in the same social activity (e.g. working as police officers), and even agree on the goals of that activity (e.g. preventing and punishing crime), but believe that there are different ways of achieving those same goals (for instance, writing an excellent report or stopping suspicious people on the street). The choice of an appropriate activity, then, for comparing the verbal strategies of men and women is crucial, and even after that choice is made, it must be demonstrated (rather than assumed) that the activity is the same for all participants, that they all interpret the goals of that activity in the same way, and that they believe the same interactional strategies are required for effecting those goals.

The study of work activities also highlights some problems with a notion related to "activity" and "practice" which currently enjoys significant popularity in gender theory, that of *performativity* (see Butler 1990; Case 1990; Parker and Sedgwick 1995). A focus on the construction of gender in activities seems to accord speakers a great deal of agency in their language choice, and in their construction of social identity. And yet, gender is perhaps only so malleable in a limited range of activities, including play activities, movies, masquerades. To focus only on the situations where gender is malleable diverts focus from continuing patterns of exclusion, subordination, normalization, and discrimination (see my discussion of when gender is relevant, below, as well as Cameron 1997b). Critiques such as this have led Butler to develop a revised notion of performativity, going under the name *citationality* (1993), that in its very name seems to focus less on agency and more on institutional constraints. Livia and Hall (1997) make a strong case that Butler's use of speech act theory attends closely to institutional constraints, while Butler herself has repeatedly argued against an approach to agency that does not take political conditions underlying its possibility into account (Butler 1992). However, this later version of her work may have swung too far in the opposite direction, with too great a focus on construction in ways which make agency invisible. In addition, "institutional constraints," as described by Butler, remain abstract rather than historically or socially precise.

3   The Gender of Institutions

The third problem with a focus on studying gender in heterosexual dyads is that it suggests that "gendered talk is mainly a personal characteristic or limited to the institution of the family" (Gal 1991: 185). This is then accompanied by a preference for studying gender in "informal conversations, often in one-to-one or small-group relationships in the family or neighborhood" (Gal 1991: 185). A focus on interactions between romantic partners in sociolinguistics draws attention away from the importance of studying the ways that "gender is a structural principle [organizing] other social institutions: workplaces, schools, courts, political assemblies and the state" and the patterns they display in "the recruitment, allocation, treatment, and mobility of men as opposed to women" (Gal 1991: 185). Because certain linguistic strategies are indirectly and indexically linked with certain groups, institutions need only be organized to define, demonstrate, and enforce the legitimacy and authority of linguistic strategies associated with one gender while denying the power of others to exclude one group without needing to make that exclusion explicit. In the case of policing, the downplaying of the importance of talk for effectively doing the job, and the overplaying of the importance of physical strength, can be seen as one strategy for excluding women from the job.[7]

Gender differences are created, for instance, in the division of labor into paid and unpaid work, in the sexual segregation of workplaces and the creation of "men's" and "women's" work, in differences in wages, and in discrimination in job training and promotion (see Connell 1987: 96). Gender differences are created in bureaucratic interactions in legal, medical, psychiatric, and welfare settings (McElhinny 1997). Gender thus should be understood as a principle for allocating access to resources, and a defense for systematic inequalities. It is, like class and racialized ethnicity, an axis for the organization of inequality, though the way each of these axes work may have their own distinctive features (Scott 1986: 1054, 1069). Though an institutional definition of gender has been influential in history (Scott 1986), sociology (Connell 1987: 139), and sociocultural anthropology (Ortner 1996; Silverblatt 1991), its implications have yet to be fully explored in sociolinguistics and linguistic anthropology (though see Gal 1997; Inoue 2000; Kuipers 1998; McElhinny 1994, 1995, forthcoming; Philips 2000), as well as recent work on gender and language ideology (Philips, this volume).

To assume that gender is attached only to individuals is to adopt uncritically the hegemonic ideology of gender in the USA. Perhaps the most elegant exposition of this is in Ortner (1991), where she points out that one analytic puzzle for anthropologists studying the USA is how to talk about class when Americans rarely use this analytic category themselves.[8] She argues class must be understood in terms of its displacement onto other categories: because hegemonic American culture takes both the ideology of social mobility and the ideology of individualism seriously, explanations for non-mobility not only focus on the failure of individuals (because they are said to be inherently lazy or stupid or whatever), but shift the domain of discourse to arenas that are taken to be "locked into" individuals – gender, race, ethnic origin, and so forth (1991: 171). Such an account becomes a serious critique of definitions of gender that uncritically adopt this hegemonic American notion of gender as attached to individuals in ways that fail to allow the theorizing of gender as a structural principle or the interaction of gender with systems of inequity.

4 When Gender is Relevant

Finally, we arrive at a question about the theorizing of gender that strikes at the heart of feminist analytic practice: is gender always salient and relevant? When she began her study of elementary school children, sociologist Barrie Thorne found that she was drawn to the moments when gender divisions were highlighted. These gender-marked moments seemed, she wrote, "to express core truths: that boys and girls are separate and fundamentally different as individuals and as groups. They help[ed] sustain a sense of dualism in the face of enormous variation and complex circumstances" (1990: 107). But the "truth," she argues, turned out to be much more complex: we need, she maintains, to understand when gender is largely irrelevant, and when it seems central, when gender is marked and when it is unmarked, for it is only in "developing a sense of the whole and attending to the waning as well as the waxing of gender salience [that] we can specify not only the social relations that uphold but also those that undermine the construction of gender as binary opposition" (1990: 108). If part of the strategy, then, for studying gender is not assuming that gender is always relevant, do we need some method for determining and demonstrating when and how gender is relevant?

The question of relevance has been extensively discussed within conversational analysis. One of the implications of the recommendation that we study when gender is relevant and when it is not, is that even though a woman may be speaking, that does not mean that she is always speaking "as a woman." To determine which aspects of an identity or a setting are relevant a conversational analyst must demonstrate that they are relevant to participants, something which is taken to be evident in their behavior since they must display to one another what they take their relevant identities to be as the basis for their ongoing interaction (Schegloff 1987, 1992). The principle of relevance means that "CA transcripts of talk pay little attention to social relations and to what other approaches call 'social context,' e.g. social identities of participants, setting, personal attributes, and so on. By intentionally ignoring what are often assumed to be static features of a social world . . . CA reflects . . . the ethnomethodological avoidance of premature generalizations and idealizations" (Schiffrin 1994: 235).

An example of work which arrives at such premature generalizations, in Schegloff's view, is a well-known series of studies of interruptions, by Candace West and Don Zimmerman, which argues that men interrupt women more frequently than women interrupt men (West and Zimmerman 1983; Zimmerman and West 1975). The problem with such work, argues Schegloff, is that it is not at all clear that the characterizations which the investigator makes are those which are grounded in the participants' own orientations in the interaction (1987: 215). So far, this argument resonates with some of the most careful and sensitive critiques of studies of interruption (cf. especially Tannen 1989, 1990) which argue that studies focusing solely on gender fail to take into account ethnicity, personality, ongoing relationships, and other aspects of identity which might be relevant. However, this is not the way Schegloff's argument proceeds. The problem, he argues, is that gender (and class and ethnicity) are not "analytically linked to specific conversational mechanisms by which the outcomes might be produced" (1987: 215). They are not, he argues, linked to conversation in any specific way:

> the resolution of an overlap is, in the first instance, not determined or effectuated by the attributes of the parties; otherwise the outcome of an interruption would be entirely determined at its beginning. . . . It may well be that women are interrupted more than they interrupt, but the introduction of such an "external" attribute early in the research process or the account can deflect attention from how the outcome of the conversational course of action is determined *in its course, in real time.*   (emphasis in original – 1987: 216)

The principle of demonstrating relevance leads Schegloff to believe that analysts can often only responsibly talk about people's identities in terms of the roles they play in conversation:

> [A]lthough it may be problematic to warrant "in a hospital" as a formulation of context, or "doctor/patient" as an identification of the participants, it may be relatively straightforward to warrant "two-party conversation" or "on the telephone" as contexts and "caller/called" as identifications of the participants. Because they are procedurally related to the doing of the talk, evidence of orientation to them ordinarily is readily available.   (1987: 219–20)

Talking about identity in this way leads one, as Schegloff freely acknowledges (1987: 228–9), to grant priority to a "unitarian" approach to social theory rather than an approach that focuses on variations in social identity. Although Schegloff quite reasonably asks why the differences linked to class, ethnicity, gender, and institution should be perceived as more interesting than what is similar, his recommendation does not seem to accord much space for determining whether a focus on difference or similarity is more important in a given context. Schegloff's argument thus challenges the idea that gender is always relevant with an approach that suggests analysts should ask when gender is relevant; but he ultimately seems to suggest that gender is never relevant. This approach simply returns us to abstract individualism. It is perhaps noteworthy that Marjorie Harness Goodwin, a feminist practitioner of conversational analysis, does not use this rigorous criterion for gender relevance.

Feminist scholars in all disciplines have rightly been suspicious of theories which seem to focus on abstract individuals and which leave little space for the study of gender and other aspects of social identity. Although invoking similarities between men and women may be warranted by, and politically effective in, some situations (see McElhinny 1996; Scott 1990), in many others such invocations have led to the application of unacknowledged masculine norms to women in ways that have led their behavior to be judged as inferior. The solution to this problem may be not to focus on *when* gender is relevant but *how* it is relevant, a question which has been recently addressed by Ochs (1992). Ochs critiques earlier feminist work on language (e.g. Lakoff 1975) which assumes that there is a straightforward mapping of language onto gender (or that, in more technical terms, language is a referential index of gender). Such referential models have been shown to be the dominant ideology of language in many Western capitalist countries (e.g. Silverstein 1979). Schegloff also adopts a referential model of language and social identity, though instead of using that model (as Lakoff 1975 does) to specify the features of "women's" language, he denies that there is any such possibility. Ochs argues that in any given community there is only a small set of linguistic forms that referentially, or directly and exclusively, index gender. Examples in English include third-person pronouns – *he, she, him, her* – and some address forms like *Mr, Mrs*, and *Ms*. Instead gender and other aspects of social identity are much more frequently non-referentially, or indirectly, indexed with language. Non-referential indices are non-exclusive (that is, a given form is not used only by a single group, such as women) and constitutive (that is, the relationship between a linguistic form and a social identity is not direct but mediated). With this view the relationship of language and social identity moves from a model which suggests that *A means B* to one in which *A can mean B, which can mean C*. It moves, for example, from a claim that the use of tag questions means that you are a female speaker, to a claim that the use of a tag question is sometimes a way of softening a harsh utterance, or indicating tentativeness, or eliciting contributions from a silent or isolated person. One or other of these strategies may be more often adopted by women because of cultural and ideological expectations about femininity, *or* a given hearer may be more likely to assume that a woman speaker is using one of these strategies because of cultural and ideological expectations about femininity.

This indexical model of the relationship between linguistic forms and the construction of social identity thus accounts for different interpretations that different hearers may assign to a single speaker's utterance: someone with an ideology about women that suggests that they are hesitant and tentative may interpret a tag question in one way, while another hearer interprets the same tag question as that speaker's attempt to mitigate an otherwise harsh statement. Crucially, the assignment of situational meaning is interactionally governed: "Interlocutors may use these structures to index a particular identity, affect, or other situational meaning; however, others co-present may not necessarily assign the same meaning" (Ochs 1996: 413). Indeed, speakers and hearers may exploit this ambiguity. The range of meanings that a form potentially indexes is larger than those it actually indexes in any given instance of use. This structurally limited indeterminacy means language can be used to build different social orders: either simultaneously, or sequentially. Thus, "members of societies are agents of culture rather than merely bearers of a culture that has been handed down to them and encoded in grammatical form. The constitutive perspective on indexicality incorporates the post-structural view that the relation between person and society is dynamic and mediated by language" (1996: 416). Clearly part of what we must ask when asking if gender is relevant is "to whom? for what?"

Duranti argues that ultimately the question of relevance is one which requires ethnographic investigation (1997: 271–5), but even this may not suffice if one is not also cautious in one's definition of culture and ethnography.[9] What is taken for granted about reality and what is questioned may not be a function of the culture taken as a whole, since members of a culture do not accept the same parts of the world as granted, in part because people's horizons of relevance are shaped by the tasks in which they are engaged, and in part because knowledge of the world is shaped and regulated by power (Blommaert 1999; Smith 1999).

5   Conclusion

This chapter has suggested that certain theoretical assumptions about gender have led to a focus on certain kinds of studies in sociolinguistics (especially studies of heterosexual dyads), to the neglect of others. Indeed, "theoretical assumptions" is perhaps too general a description. Instead, it is possible to speak of these presuppositions as ideologies linked to some dominant ways of conceptualizing gender in Western capitalist contexts. If studies of gender proceed without assuming a close association between gender, sex, and (hetero)sexuality, if gender is understood as an activity rather than a relation, if we consider gender as an institutionalized principle for allocating access to resources, and if we carefully explore when, and how, and why, and to whom gender is relevant, then it becomes possible to study gender and language in communities, contexts, cultures, and times where alternative assumptions prevail, and to challenge these dominant ideologies where they help to perpetuate inequities in Western contexts.

NOTES

1 Thorne (1990) points out that the assumption that gender is best studied when maximally contrastive has led to opposed assumptions about how gender should be studied amongst children and adults.

2 For descriptions of feminist standpoint theory see Harding (1991), Collins (1990), and Jaggar (1983).

3 For further ethnographic critiques of this focus on individual "ownership" of utterances see Duranti (1992), Morgan (1991), and Rosaldo (1982).

4 Goodwin's recommendation that we focus on activities has parallels in the recommendations of cultural anthropologist Lila Abu-Lughod (1991).

5 Edelsky's (1981) work on the construction of conversational floors in mixed-gender committee meetings at a university supports a similar conclusion.

6 See Holmes and Meyerhoff (1999) and Bucholtz (1999) for discussions of how "community of practice" differs from traditional sociolinguistic definitions of speech community. Other papers in Holmes (1999) explore the potential and limits of the concept.

7 Bergvall (1999) also calls for more attention to larger-scale formations that sustain and regulate gender, though in ways different from those described here.

8 Di Leonardo (1998) rightly critiques Ortner (1991) for claiming that research on social class is a marginal anthropological concern. Nonetheless, Ortner's consideration of complex interactions of systems of inequity asks us to do research in ways that not only consider gender, ethnicity, class, age, etc., but also the relative local prominence of these, and the ways inequities in one can be obscured by ideologies which foreground another (see also Ortner 1996; Ortner and Whitehead 1981).

9 See Cameron (1997b) for a recommendation similar to Duranti's.

REFERENCES

Abu-Lughod, Lila 1991: Writing against culture. In Richard Fox (ed.) *Recapturing Anthropology: Working in the Present*. Santa Fe, NM: School of American Research Press, pp. 137–62.

Barrett, Rusty 1994: "She is *not* white woman": Appropriation of white women's language by African American drag queens. In Mary Bucholtz, Anita C. Liang, Laurel A. Sutton, and Caitlin Hines (eds) *Cultural Performances: Proceedings of the Third Berkeley Women and Language Conference*. Berkeley, CA: Berkeley Women and Language Group, University of California, pp. 1–14.

Behar, Ruth and Gordan, Deborah (eds) 1995: *Women Writing Culture*. Berkeley, CA: University of California Press.

Bergvall, Victoria 1999: Toward a comprehensive theory of language and gender. *Language in Society* 28(2): 273–93.

Besnier, Niko 1993: Polynesian gender liminality through time and space.

In Gilbert Herdt (ed.) *Third Sex, Third Gender: Beyond Sexual Dimorphism in Culture and History*. New York: Zone Books, pp. 285–328.

Blommaert, Jan 1999: Context is/as critique. Paper presented at the Annual Meetings of the American Anthropological Association, Chicago, November 1999.

Brown, Penelope and Levinson, Stephen 1983: *Politeness: Some Universals in Language Usage*. Cambridge: Cambridge University Press.

Bucholtz, Mary 1993: Theory and practice in African-American women's speech. Paper presented at the Language–Gender Interface, Linguistic Institute, Columbus, Ohio.

Bucholtz, Mary 1999: Why be normal? Language and identity practices in a community of nerd girls. *Language in Society* 28(2): 203–24.

Butler, Judith 1990: *Gender Trouble: Feminism and the Subversion of Identity*. New York: Routledge.

Butler, Judith 1992: Contingent foundations: Feminism and the question of "postmodernism". In Judith Butler and Joan Scott (eds) *Feminists Theorize the Political*. New York: Routledge, pp. 3–21.

Butler, Judith 1993: *Bodies That Matter*. New York: Routledge.

Cameron, Deborah 1997a: Performing gender identity: Young men's talk and the construction of heterosexual masculinity. In Sally Johnson and Ulrike Hanna Meinhof (eds) *Language and Masculinity*. Oxford: Blackwell, pp. 47–64.

Cameron, Deborah 1997b: Theoretical debates in feminist linguistics: Questions of sex and gender. In Ruth Wodak (ed.) *Gender and Discourse*. London: Sage, pp. 21–36.

Cameron, Deborah and Coates, Jennifer 1988: Some problems in the sociolinguistic explanation of sex differences. In Deborah Cameron

and Jennifer Coates (eds) *Women in Their Speech Communities*. London: Longman, pp. 13–26.

Case, Sue-Ellen (ed.) 1990: *Performing Feminisms: Feminist Critical Theory and Theatre*. Baltimore: Johns Hopkins University Press.

Collins, Patricia Hill 1990: *Black Feminist Thought*. New York: Routledge.

Connell, Robert W. 1987: *Gender and Power: Society, the Person and Sexual Politics*. Stanford, CA: Stanford University Press.

Di Leonardo, Micaela 1998: *Exotics at Home: Anthropologies, Others, American Modernity*. Chicago: University of Chicago Press.

Duranti, Alessandro 1992: Intentions, self and responsibility: An essay in Samoan ethnopragmatics. In Jane Hill and Judith Irvine (eds) *Responsibility and Evidence in Oral Discourse*. Cambridge: Cambridge University Press, pp. 24–47.

Duranti, Alessandro 1997: *Linguistic Anthropology*. Cambridge: Cambridge University Press.

Eckert, Penelope and McConnell-Ginet, Sally 1992: Think practically and look locally: Language and gender as community-based practice. *Annual Review of Anthropology* 21: 461–90.

Edelsky, Carole 1981: Who's got the floor? *Language in Society* 10: 383–421.

Feldman, P. and Kelley, T. (eds) 1995: *Romantic Women Writers: Voices/ Countervoices*. Hanover, NH: University Press of New England.

Fishman, Pamela 1983: Interaction: The work women do. In Barrie Thorne, Cheris Kramarae and Nancy Henley (eds) *Language, Gender and Society*. Cambridge, MA: Newbury House, pp. 89–101.

Gal, Susan 1991: Between speech and silence: The problematics of research on language and gender. In Micaela di Leonardo (ed.) *Gender at the*

Crossroads of Knowledge: Feminist Anthropology in the Postmodern Era. Berkeley, CA: University of California Press, pp. 175–203.

Gal, Susan 1997: Gender in the post-socialist transition: The abortion debate in Hungary. In Roger Lancaster and Micaela di Leonardo (eds) *The Gender/Sexuality Reader.* New York: Routledge, pp. 122–33.

Gaudio, Rudolf P. 1996: Men Who Talk Like Women: Language, Gender and Sexuality in Hausa Muslim Society. PhD dissertation, Stanford University, Department of Linguistics.

Gaudio, Rudolf P. 1997: Not talking straight in Hausa. In Anna Livia and Kira Hall (eds) *Queerly Phrased: Language, Gender, and Sexuality.* New York: Oxford University Press, pp. 416–29.

Gleason, Jean Berko 1987: Sex differences in parent–child interaction. In Susan Philips, Susan Steele, and Christine Tanz (eds) *Language, Gender and Sex in Comparative Perspective.* Cambridge: Cambridge University Press, pp. 189–99.

Goodwin, Marjorie Harness 1990: *He-Said-She-Said: Talk as Social Organization among Black Children.* Bloomington: Indiana University Press.

Hall, Kira 1997: "Go suck your husband's sugarcane": Hijras and the use of sexual insult. In Anna Livia and Kira Hall (eds) *Queerly Phrased: Language, Gender and Sexuality.* New York: Oxford University Press, pp. 430–60.

Hall, Kira and O'Donovan, Veronica 1996: Shifting gender positions among Hindi-speaking Hijras. In Victoria Bergvall, Janet Bing, and Alice Freed (eds) *Rethinking Language and Gender Research: Theory and Practice.* London: Longman, pp. 228–66.

Hanks, William 1990: *Referential Practices: Language and Lived Space among the Maya.* Chicago: Chicago University Press.

Harding, Sandra 1991: *Whose Science? Whose Knowledge?* Ithaca, NY: Cornell University Press.

Hawkesworth, Mary 1997: Confounding gender. *Signs* 22(1): 649–86.

Holmes, Janet (ed.) 1999: *Communities of Practice in Language and Gender Research.* Special Issue of *Language in Society,* 28(2): 171–320.

Holmes, Janet and Meyerhoff, Miriam 1999: The Community of Practice: Theories and methodologies in language and gender research. *Language in Society* 28(2): 173–84.

Inoue, Miyako forthcoming: Gender, language and modernity: Toward an effective history of "Japanese women's language." *American Ethnologist.*

Jaggar, Alison 1983: *Feminist Politics and Human Nature.* Totowa, NJ: Rowman and Allanheld.

Kapchan, Deborah 1996: *Gender on the Market: Moroccan Women and the Revoicing of Tradition.* Philadelphia: University of Pennsylvania Press.

Kelly-Gadol, Joan 1977: Did women have a renaissance? In R. Bridenthal and C. Koonz (eds) *Becoming Visible: Women in European History.* Boston: Houghton-Mifflin, pp. 139–63.

Kuipers, Joel 1998: "Towering in rage and cowering in fear": Emotion, self and verbal expression in Sumba. In Joel Kuipers (ed.) *Language, Identity and Marginality in Indonesia: The Changing Nature of Ritual Speech on the Island of Sumba.* Cambridge: Cambridge University Press, pp. 42–66.

Kulick, Don 1998: *Travesti: Sex, Gender and Culture among Brazilian Transgendered Prostitutes.* Chicago: University of Chicago Press.

Lakoff, Robin 1975: *Language and Woman's Place*. New York: Harper and Row.

Leontyev, Aleksei N. 1981: *Problems of the Development of the Mind*. Moscow: Progress Publishers.

Livia, Anna and Hall, Kira 1997: "It's a girl!" Bringing performativity back to linguistics. In Anna Livia and Kira Hall (eds) *Queerly Phrased: Language, Gender, and Sexuality*. New York: Oxford University Press, pp. 1–18.

McElhinny, Bonnie 1994: An economy of affect: Objectivity, masculinity and the gendering of police work. In Andrea Cornwall and Nancy Lindisfarne (eds) *Dislocating Masculinity: Comparative Ethnographies*. London: Routledge, pp. 159–71.

McElhinny, Bonnie 1995: Challenging hegemonic masculinities: Female and male police officers handling domestic violence. In Kira Hall and Mary Bucholtz (eds) *Gender Articulated: Language and the Socially Constructed Self*. New York: Routledge, pp. 217–43.

McElhinny, Bonnie 1996: Strategic essentialism in sociolinguistic studies of gender. In Natasha Warner, Jocelyn Ahlers, Leela Bilmes, Monica Oliver, Suzanne Wertheim, and Melinda Chen (eds) *Gender and Belief Systems: Proceedings of the Fourth Berkeley Conference on Women and Language*. Berkeley, CA: Berkeley Women and Language Group, University of California, pp. 469–80.

McElhinny, Bonnie 1997: Ideologies of public and private language in sociolinguistics. In Ruth Wodak (ed.) *Gender and Discourse*. London: Sage, pp. 106–39.

McElhinny, Bonnie 1998: Genealogies of gender theory: Practice theory and feminism in sociocultural and linguistic anthropology. *Social Analysis* 42(3): 164–89.

McElhinny, Bonnie forthcoming: *Policing Language and Gender*.

Morgan, Marcyliena 1991: Indirectness and interpretation in African-American women's discourse. *Pragmatics* 1(4): 421–51.

Morgan, Marcyliena 1994: No woman, no cry: The linguistic representation of African American women. In Mary Bucholtz, Anita C. Liang, Laurel Sutton, and Caitlin Hines (eds) *Cultural Performances: Proceedings of the Third Berkeley Women and Language Conference*. Berkeley, CA: Berkeley Women and Language Group, University of California, pp. 525–41.

Nicholson, Linda 1994: Interpreting gender. *Signs* 20(1): 79–105.

Ochs, Elinor 1992: Indexing gender. In Alessandro Duranti and Charles Goodwin (eds) *Rethinking Context: Language as an Interactive Phenomenon*. Cambridge: Cambridge University Press, pp. 335–58.

Ochs, Elinor 1996: Linguistic resources for socializing humanity. In John J. Gumperz and Stephen Levinson (eds) *Rethinking Linguistic Relativity*. Cambridge: Cambridge University Press, pp. 407–37.

Ortner, Sherry 1984: Theory in anthropology since the Sixties. *Comparative Studies in Society and History* 26(1): 126–66.

Ortner, Sherry 1991: Reading America: Preliminary notes on class and culture. In Richard Fox (ed.) *Recapturing Anthropology: Working in the Present*. Santa Fe, NM: School of American Research Press, pp. 163–90.

Ortner, Sherry 1996: *Making Gender: The Politics and Erotics of Gender*. Boston: Beacon Press.

Ortner, Sherry and Whitehead, Harriet 1981: Introduction: Accounting for sexual meanings. In Sherry Ortner and Harriet Whitehead (eds) *Sexual Meanings: The Cultural Construction of Gender and Sexuality.* Cambridge: Cambridge University Press, pp. 1–27.

Parker, Andrew and Sedgwick, Eve Kosofsky (eds) 1995: *Performativity and Performance.* New York: Routledge.

Philips, Susan 2000: Constructing a Tongan nation-state through language ideology in the courtroom. In Paul Kroskrity (ed.) *Regimes of Language: Ideologies, Polities and Identities.* Santa Fe, NM: School of American Research Press, pp. 229–58.

Rosaldo, Michelle 1982: The things we do with words: Ilongot speech acts and speech act theory in philosophy. *Language in Society* 11: 203–37.

Schegloff, Emanuel 1987: Between micro and macro: Contexts and other connections. In J. Alexander, B. Giesen, R. Munch, and N. Smelser (eds) *The Micro-Macro Link.* Berkeley, CA: University of California Press, pp. 207–36.

Schegloff, Emanuel 1992: In another context. In Alessandro Duranti and Charles Goodwin (eds) *Rethinking Context: Language as an Interactive Phenomenon.* Cambridge: Cambridge University Press, pp. 191–228.

Schiffrin, Deborah 1994: *Approaches to Discourse Analysis.* Cambridge: Cambridge University Press.

Scott, Joan 1986: Gender: A useful category of historical analysis. *American Historical Review* 91(5): 1053–75.

Scott, Joan 1990: Deconstructing equality-vs-difference; or, the uses of post-structuralist theory for feminism. In Marianne Hirsch and Evelyn Fox Keller (eds) *Conflicts in Feminism.* New York: Routledge, pp. 134–48.

Sedgwick, Eve Kosofsky 1990: *Epistemology of the Closet.* Berkeley, CA: University of California Press.

Shapiro, Judith 1981: Anthropology and the study of gender. *Soundings: An Interdisciplinary Journal* 64: 446–65.

Siegal, Meryl 1994: Second-language learning, identity and resistance: White women studying Japanese in Japan. In Mary Bucholtz, Anita C. Liang, Laurel Sutton, and Caitlin Hines (eds) *Cultural Performances: Proceedings of the Third Berkeley Women and Language Conference.* Berkeley, CA: Berkeley Women and Language Group, University of California, pp. 642–50.

Silverblatt, Irene 1991: "Interpreting women in states": New feminist ethnohistories. In Micaela di Leonardo (ed.) *Gender at the Crossroads of Knowledge: Feminist Anthropology in the Postmodern Era.* Berkeley, CA: University of California Press, pp. 140–74.

Silverstein, Michael 1979: Language structure and linguistic ideology. In Paul R. Clyne, William F. Hanks and Carol L. Hofbauer (eds) *The Elements: A Parasession on Linguistic Units and Levels.* Chicago: Chicago Linguistic Society, pp. 193–247.

Smith, Gavin 1999: *Confronting the Present: Towards a Politically Engaged Anthropology.* Oxford: Berg.

Sperling, Susan 1991: Baboons with briefcases vs. Langurs in lipstick: Feminism and functionalism in primate studies. In Micaela di Leonardo (ed.) *Gender at the Crossroads of Knowledge: Feminist Anthropology in the Postmodern Era.* Berkeley, CA: University of California Press, pp. 204–34.

Strathern, Marilyn 1988: *The Gender of the Gift.* Berkeley, CA: University of California Press.

Tannen, Deborah 1989: Interpreting interruption in conversation. In

Caroline Wiltshire, Randolph Graczyk, and Bradley Music (eds) *CLS 25: Papers from the 25th Annual Regional Meeting of the Chicago Linguistic Society (Part 2: Parasession on Language in Context)*. Chicago: Chicago Linguistic Society, pp. 266–87.

Tannen, Deborah 1990: *You Just Don't Understand: Women and Men in Conversation*. New York: William Morrow.

Thorne, Barrie 1990: Children and gender: Constructions of difference. In Deborah Rhode (ed.) *Theoretical Perspectives on Sexual Difference*. New Haven, CT: Yale University Press, pp. 100–13.

Thorne, Barrie and Stacey, Judith 1993: The missing feminist revolution in sociology. In Linda Kauffman (ed.) *American Feminist Thought at Century's End*. Cambridge, MA: Blackwell, pp. 167–88.

Weiss, Penny 1995: Feminism and communitarianism: Comparing critiques of liberalism. In Penny Weiss and Marilyn Friedman (eds) *Feminism and Community*. Philadelphia: Temple University Press, pp. 161–86.

West, Candace and Zimmerman, Don 1983: Small insults: A study of interruptions in cross-sex conversations between unacquainted persons. In Barrie Thorne, Cheris Kramarae, and Nancy Henley (eds) *Language, Gender and Society*. Cambridge, MA: Newbury House, pp. 102–17.

Worthman, Carol 1995: Hormones, sex and gender. *Annual Review of Anthropology* 24: 593–616.

Yanagisako, Sylvia and Collier, Jane F. 1990: The mode of reproduction in anthropology. In Deborah Rhode (ed.) *Theoretical Perspectives on Sexual Difference*. New Haven, CT: Yale University Press, pp. 131–44.

Zimmerman, Don and West, Candace 1975: Sex roles, interruptions, and silences in conversation. In Barrie Thorne and Nancy Henley (eds) *Language and Sex: Difference and Dominance*. Rowley, MA: Newbury House, pp. 105–29.

2 Theories of Discourse as Theories of Gender: Discourse Analysis in Language and Gender Studies

MARY BUCHOLTZ

1 Introduction

The study of language and gender has increasingly become the study of discourse and gender. While phonological, lexical, and other kinds of linguistic analysis continue to be influential, the interdisciplinary investigation of discourse-level phenomena, always a robust area of language and gender scholarship, has become the central approach of the field. It is some indication of the impact of discourse analysis that no fewer than four books treating the topic of language and gender share the title *Gender and Discourse* (Cheshire and Trudgill 1998; Tannen 1994a; Todd and Fisher 1988; Wodak 1997a). In addition, hundreds of books, articles, and dissertations in numerous disciplines examine the intersection between discourse and gender from a variety of analytic perspectives. This proliferation of research presents problems for any attempt at a comprehensive overview, for although many of these studies are explicitly framed as drawing on the insights of discourse analysis, their approaches are so different that it is impossible to offer a unified treatment of discourse analysis as a tool for the study of language and gender. Hence there is no well-defined approach to discourse that can be labeled "feminist discourse analysis"; indeed, not all approaches to gender and discourse are feminist in their orientation, nor is there a single form of feminism to which all feminist scholars subscribe.

The goal of this chapter is instead to provide a sketch of some of the various forms that discourse analysis can take and how they have been put to use in the investigation of gender. I focus in particular on qualitative approaches to discourse analysis, although there have been many studies of gender in discourse that use quantitative methods, some of which draw upon the frameworks outlined here. The approaches to discourse analysis considered in this chapter stem from four different but often interconnected research traditions: an anthropological tradition that focuses on cultural practices; a sociological tradition that emphasizes social action; a critical tradition that concentrates on texts; and a more recent anthropological tradition that considers the historical trajectories of discourse. After first examining the linguistic and non-linguistic definitions of discourse that inform scholarship on gender, the chapter traces the history and development of each approach and highlights debates and faultlines between competing frameworks. And because the application of any discourse-analytic framework to questions of gender brings along a set of theoretical assumptions about the interrelationship of discourse, identity, and power, this chapter also considers the ways in which particular theories of discourse imply particular theories of gender. Finally, it is important to note before proceeding that in many instances it is difficult to pinpoint the precise framework within which a given study was carried out, for most studies of language and gender do not rely on a single approach to discourse. The studies described here were selected not for their adherence to a particular framework, but for their ability to illustrate details of specific kinds of discourse analysis as applied to gender.

2   Defining Discourse

The term *discourse* is itself subject to dispute, with different scholarly traditions offering different definitions of the term, some of which venture far beyond language-centered approaches. Within linguistics, the predominant definition of *discourse* is a formal one, deriving from the organization of the discipline into levels of linguistic units, such as phonology, morphology, and syntax. According to the formal definition, just as morphology is the level of language in which sounds are combined into words, and syntax is the level in which words are combined into sentences, so discourse is the linguistic level in which sentences are combined into larger units. An alternative definition focuses not on linguistic form but on function. Discourse, in this view, is language in context: that is, language as it is put to use in social situations, not the more idealized and abstracted linguistic forms that are the central concern of much linguistic theory. Given its attention to the broader context of language use, the study of language and gender has overwhelmingly relied on the second definition of discourse. In practice, however, both definitions are often compatible, for much of the situated language that discourse analysts study is larger than a single sentence, and even the formal analysis of discourse may require an appeal to the context in which it occurs.

   If formal linguistic definitions of discourse are too narrow for the needs of language and gender research, then some non-linguistic definitions emerging from post-structuralist theory have been too diffuse. Michel Foucault's (1972) view of discourses as historically contingent cultural systems of knowledge, belief, and power does not require close attention to the details of linguistic form. Discourse analysis within a Foucauldian framework tends to consider instead how language invokes the knowledge systems of particular institutions, such as medical or penal discourse. This post-structuralist definition of discourse is inadequate for many discourse analysts, although some believe that Foucauldian "discourses" (culturally and historically specific ways of organizing knowledge) can and should be incorporated into the analysis of linguistic "discourse" (contextually specific ways of using language). Such an integrated approach may increase the relevance of linguistic discourse analysis for the study of gender in other disciplines. Indeed, the main influence of discourse analysis on non-linguistic feminist scholarship has come from Foucault and related perspectives rather than from the linguistic side of discourse analysis, which often involves a degree of technical detail that can be daunting to those untrained in the field.

Despite the range of scholarly practices that fall under the rubric of discourse analysis, it is possible to identify areas of convergence. Neither a single theory nor a single method, discourse analysis is a collection of perspectives on situated language use that involve a general shared theoretical orientation and a broadly similar methodological approach. Although the forms that discourse analysis takes vary widely, those that emphasize discourse as a social, cultural, or political phenomenon have in common a theory of discourse not merely as the reflection of society, culture, and power but as their constantly replenished source. In other words, for most discourse analysts the social world is produced and reproduced in great part through discourse. The method that emerges from this theoretical stance is one of close analysis of discursive detail in relation to its context. Where discourse analysts often differ is in such questions as the limits of context (how much background knowledge is necessary and admissible in order to understand a particular discursive form?), the place of agency (are speakers entirely in control of discourse? Are they merely a discursive effect?), and the role of the analyst (is the researcher's role to discover the participants' own perspectives, or to offer an interpretation that may shed new light on the discourse?). In answering such questions, discourse analysts working within different frameworks are influenced by their own disciplinary traditions as well as the distinctive theoretical developments of their chosen discursive paradigm. Consequently, in addition to broad areas of agreement, practitioners of different kinds of discourse analysis have found ample room for mutual critique and debate. The differences between approaches are especially evident when examining how various strands of discourse analysis interact with the field of language and gender studies, which has its own tradition of controversy and scholarly disagreement (see e.g. Bucholtz 1999a, forthcoming). In every case, however, the use of discourse-analytic tools has helped to clarify and expand our knowledge of how gender and language mutually shape and inform each other.

3   Discourse as Culture

Within linguistic anthropology, gender has been a frequent site of discursive investigation, and gender-based research helped to establish the utility of discourse-centered approaches to anthropology. These approaches have provided an alternative to much previous linguistic work within anthropology, which emphasized the description of linguistic systems through elicitation of decontextualized words and sentences from native speakers. By contrast with this tradition of data elicitation, the anthropologically oriented forms of discourse analysis that developed in the 1960s and 1970s emphasized the value of "naturally occurring" (that is, unelicited) data, often involving multiple participants and varied kinds of language use. These new methods of data collection also opened up new directions for the anthropological study of gender.

The two frameworks considered here, the ethnography of communication and interactional sociolinguistics, offer compatible and complementary perspectives on the relationship between language and culture. Both take from their roots in anthropology a concerted focus on cultural specificity and variability. And both view culture and discourse as intimately interconnected. Within language and gender scholarship, these approaches have therefore provided the impetus for research that expands the field's early focus on the European American middle class to include a broad range of languages and cultures. Yet each approach has made very different kinds of contributions to language and gender research, based on the different ways in which it has used the concept of culture to frame the study of gender.

3.1   *Ethnography of communication*

The ethnography of communication (earlier termed the ethnography of speaking) was established by Dell Hymes (1962, 1974) as a way of bringing language use more centrally into the anthropological enterprise. The framework seeks to apply ethnographic methods to the study of language use: that is, it aims to understand discourse from the perspective of members of the culture being studied, and not primarily or pre-emptively from the perspective of the anthropologist. To this end, ethnographers of communication often focus on "ways of speaking" – discourse genres through which competent cultural members display their cultural knowledge – by considering speakers' own systems of discursive classification rather than importing their own academically based analytic categories. They also examine, from native speakers' point of view, how specific kinds of language use (speech events) are put to use in particular contexts (speech situations). In keeping with its anthropological origins, research in the ethnography of communication framework has concentrated primarily on language use beyond that of White middle-class speakers in industrialized societies. Perhaps for the same reason, the emphasis is on spoken language, as indicated by much of the terminology of the approach.

One of the most influential examples of this paradigm is Elinor (Ochs) Keenan's ([1974] 1989) account of gender differences in a Malagasy-speaking community in Madagascar. Keenan observes that among the Malagasy villagers she studied, women were associated with a direct speech style and men with an indirect style. Keenan does not explicitly contrast this pattern with the scholarly and popular view, common at the time she did her research, of Western women's speech as indirect and men's as direct (e.g. Lakoff 1975), but many other scholars called attention to the implications of these findings for language and gender research. However, Keenan's analysis does not stop with the identification of gender differences. She goes on to point out that each mode of discourse provides a distinct form of power. Malagasy women's direct style of discourse allows them to engage in politically and economically powerful activities, such as confrontation, bargaining, and gossip, that men participate in less often or not at all. But this is not a simple distribution of discursive labor; as Keenan shows, Malagasy language ideologies privilege indirect language as skilled and artful, the style most suited for public oratory, while devaluing direct language as unsophisticated and as indicative of Malagasy cultural decline.

The finding that women's ways of speaking are less valued than men's is echoed in other studies in the ethnography of communication paradigm. In addition, many studies support Keenan's observation that men's discourse genres tend to be more public and women's tend to be more domestic. Both these general patterns, however, are challenged by the work of Joel Sherzer (1987), who notes that among the Kuna, an indigenous group in Panama, women's discursive forms are sometimes different from men's, sometimes the same; sometimes superior or equal, sometimes inferior; sometimes public, sometimes private.

Where many ethnographies of communication address gender primarily from the standpoint of differences between women and men, another approach focuses on discourse genres used by women and girls without extensive comparison to men's and boys' discursive practices. Much of this work focuses on African American women's discourse, redressing the overwhelming scholarly emphasis on male discourse forms among African Americans. Claudia Mitchell-Kernan (1971), for example, elaborates the concept of signifying, which was initially described as a publicly performed game of ritual insults between boys (e.g. Abrahams 1962). Mitchell-Kernan reports on the practice of conversational signifying, a discourse genre involving indirect critique at which adult female speakers are especially adept. More recently, language and gender scholars have extended Mitchell-Kernan's research by documenting other discourse genres through which African American women and girls accomplish social, cultural, and political work, such as he-said-she-said, or accusing another party of gossiping (Goodwin 1980); instigating, or initiating a conflict between two other parties through storytelling (Goodwin 1990); reading dialect, or juxtaposing African American Vernacular English and Standard English to critique an addressee (Morgan 1999); and others. Although this work may discuss similarities and differences between female and male speakers, comparison is not the main point. Rather, the purpose is to examine women's and girls' discursive competence on its own terms.

In both its comparative and non-comparative modes, the ethnography of communication as an approach to gender highlights speaker competence, local understandings of cultural practice, and cross-cultural variation. It therefore contributes to the feminist project of calling attention to women's abilities and agency, while reminding scholars that gendered language use is not everywhere the same. But because within this framework speakers are preeminently viewed as cultural actors, especially in earlier research individual language practices are often taken as representative of cultural patterns of gendered discourse. Generalizations may be made not about how "women" speak, but about how women of a particular culture speak; variation between women within a given cultural context is rarely discussed. In addition, the ethnography of communication has historically had a tendency to focus on more public, ritualized, and performance-oriented speech events – precisely those types of discourse that in most cultures have fewer female participants. Women's ways of speaking may therefore be considered, by native speakers and the analyst alike, as less culturally significant than those available to men. Hence the shift in emphasis from public and ritual speech events to conversational and everyday interaction, as evidenced particularly in the non-comparative study of discourse genres, also enables a more complete assessment of women's uses of discourse.

The ethnography of communication has been largely devoted to the description and analysis of relatively discrete and culturally salient discourse forms: speech acts, events, and genres that are recognized and often labeled by members of the culture. Yet much of social life takes place in ordinary conversation, and many cultures do not necessarily name or consciously recognize discourse practices that take place in the sphere of the everyday. The ethnography of communication also focuses mainly on discourse internal to a single culture rather than on how the same discursive form may be understood by members of different cultural backgrounds. A complementary approach to discourse within anthropology, interactional sociolinguistics, takes interaction and cultural contact as central to the cultural investigation of language use. This approach results in a very different view of gender and discourse.

3.2   *Interactional sociolinguistics*

Growing out of John Gumperz's work on language contact and code-switching in India and Norway, interactional sociolinguistics has been since its beginning a model of language in use that emphasizes the effects of cultural and linguistic contact. Ethnographies of communication are frequently carried out in small, non-Western, non-industrialized societies, or in culturally distinctive smaller groupings within Western societies. By contrast, interactional sociolinguistics primarily examines language use in heterogeneous, multicultural societies that are often highly industrialized, concentrating especially on how language is used across linguistic and cultural groups within a single society. As developed in the work of John Gumperz and his associates (e.g. Gumperz 1982a, 1982b), the approach emphasizes how implied meanings can be derived from details of interaction that signal the appropriate cultural frame of reference for inter-pretation. These contextualization cues are culturally specific, and hence may give rise to miscommunication when used between speakers with different cultural systems of conversational inference. The main arena for the investiga-tion of such communicative breakdowns is in inter-ethnic interaction of various kinds, usually between members of the dominant social group who often occupy more powerful roles in the interaction (such as employer, lawyer, teacher, or interviewer) and members of subordinated ethnic groups who often have less powerful positions (such as employee, witness, student, or interviewee).

Gender-based research within interactional sociolinguistics developed from this concern with cross-cultural differences in communicative norms. In fact, the scholar who is most closely associated with this approach, Deborah Tannen, has explicitly linked her study of gender to her work on ethnic differences in communication. Tannen's research on inter-ethnic communication – which con-trasts the conversational styles of Greeks, Greek Americans, Jewish Americans, and Americans of other backgrounds – demonstrates that interlocutors with different cultural backgrounds can misinterpret one another's conversational styles as personality traits such as pushiness or inconsistency (e.g. Tannen 1981, 1982). In developing her approach to gender and discourse, Tannen combined insights from this ethnically based research with the work of Daniel Maltz and Ruth Borker (1982), who argue that even within a single culture gender is best understood in cultural terms, with distinctive female and male discursive practices emerging from gender-segregated play patterns in child-hood. Tannen elaborates this line of reasoning in both popular and scholarly works on cross-gender interaction in intimate relationships and in the work-place (e.g. Tannen 1990, 1994a, 1994b, 1999), in which she analyzes how the conversational style associated with each gender can lead to miscommun-ication and difficulties in accomplishing one's goals.

Although this approach to gender and discourse has been widely criticized by other language and gender scholars (e.g. Davis 1996; Freed 1992; Troemel-Ploetz 1991), both for emphasizing gender difference over male dominance as the crucial factor in female–male communication and for downplaying the heterogeneity of women's (and men's) discursive practices, the contributions of the perspective should also be acknowledged. Like the ethnography of communication, interactional sociolinguistics highlights women's competence as users of discourse who have mastered the interactional rules appropriate to their gender. In fact, unlike the ethnography of communication, which may include native speakers' or the analyst's evaluations of female versus male discourse forms, interactional sociolinguists resolutely resist favoring one style over another. And, in contrast to some other feminist perspectives, interactional-sociolinguistic work on gender may challenge the view of women as victims.

Radical feminists, for example, analyze marriage as a patriarchal institution in which women have little agency or autonomy, a perspective that has the unfortunate effect of representing heterosexual women as colluding in their own oppression by entering willingly into a relationship of unequal power. Interactional sociolinguists complicate the radical-feminist position by pointing out that male communicative strategies in intimate relationships may not always be intended to dominate or silence women. Yet there are limits to the power that interactional sociolinguistics cedes to women (and men): in this framework, speakers are understood as largely constrained by the gender-based cultural system they learned as children, which they may transcend only through conscious awareness and effort.

Finally, although both interactional sociolinguistics and the ethnography of communication would certainly view culture and discourse as mutually constitutive, the two approaches focus on different aspects of this relationship. Within the ethnography of communication, the analytic emphasis is on discourse as the substance of culture, the means by which shared cultural practice and identity are forged and displayed. Within interactional sociolinguistics, on the other hand, researchers highlight the ways in which culture underlies discourse, shaping how language is used and what it can mean. For scholars of language and gender, this difference in emphasis has led to markedly different theories of gender. Ethnographers of communication concentrate on how women, as discourse producers, are makers of culture. The focus on women as cultural agents also calls attention to the diversity of women's discursive practices in different cultures. Interactional sociolinguists, by contrast, emphasize not how women's discourse produces culture but how it is produced by culture. And in equating gender with culture, interactional sociolinguists view the primary point of comparison as between women and men. While the interactional sociolinguistic framework allows for differences in discourse style between women of different cultures, there is a tendency in much of the research in the field to downplay intragender variation and to highlight intergender variation in discourse patterns. Despite such significant differences in their views of gender and of discourse, these anthropological approaches have in common an analytic focus on cultural variability that sets them apart from many other forms of discourse analysis.

4   Discourse as Society

In these anthropological versions of discourse analysis, discourse is understood in terms of culture, especially in terms of cultural variation and specificity. In sociological and social-psychological paradigms, discourse is instead linked to society, especially in terms of how discourse structures society. The central principles that inform this perspective derive from ethnomethodology, a theory developed by sociologist Harold Garfinkel (1967) which views the social world as organized through everyday interaction. Garfinkel consequently advocated applying close analytic attention to the ordinary activities from which social order emerges. Gender played an important role in the development of ethnomethodological ideas, in part due to Garfinkel's study of Agnes, a bio-logical male who identified as female. Agnes's successful display of herself as a woman was accomplished through the management of routine activities related to gender. The insight that social identities such as gender are achieve-ments or accomplishments, that gender is something that people "do" rather than simply have (Kessler and McKenna 1978; West and Zimmerman 1987), is one that has had a powerful impact on language and gender research, as well as on gender studies more generally.

As an outgrowth of ethnomethodology, conversation analysis has applied these ideas to the organization of talk. Recently, conversation analysis has in turn been put to use in the fields of social psychology and discursive psychol-ogy. Gender has figured centrally as an issue in all of these frameworks, but despite shared techniques of discourse analysis, feminist and non-feminist approaches to conversation analysis have often been in conflict concerning the appropriate method of studying gender in interaction.

5 Conversation Analysis

Conversation analysis has in common with interactional sociolinguistics a commitment to analyzing the details of interaction. But where interactional sociolinguistics takes as its main task the description of how culturally based interactional systems are signaled and put to use, the primary undertaking of conversation analysis is to examine the sequential unfolding of conversation moment by moment, turn by turn, to show how interactional structure con-structs social organization. Some of the earliest and most influential studies of language and gender come from a conversation-analytic/ethnomethodological framework (Fishman 1983; Zimmerman and West 1975; West 1979; West and Zimmerman 1983). Such research demonstrated that gender-based power differences are an emergent property of interaction: men's one-up discursive position *vis-à-vis* women, as indicated through their greater propensity for interruption and their lesser engagement in interactional maintenance work, does not merely reflect but actually produces male power as an effect of discourse.

These explicitly feminist studies contrast with the approach to conversation analysis articulated by Emanuel Schegloff, a co-founder and in many ways the standard-bearer of the framework, who in a series of programmatic state-ments, critiques, debates, and challenges has sought to preserve conversation analysis against the encroachment of "self-indulgent" (that is, politically motivated) modes of analysis (Schegloff 1999). Gender is pivotal to this con-troversy, for Schegloff (1997), in an article that launched a flurry of rebuttals and counter-rebuttals, uses gender to illustrate his position that social categories cannot be assumed to be analytically relevant without demonstrable evidence from within the interaction. Arguing against the theories and methods of critical discourse analysis, an explicitly political approach (see below), Schegloff twice analyzes the same data transcript, a telephone conversation between a divorced couple about their son: first according to a feminist model, and second according to a strict version of conversation analysis. By looking closely at the sequential organization of the conversation, Schegloff builds his argument that what some feminist analysts might interpret as male power enacted through interruptions of the female speaker is instead an outcome of interactional issues, such as the negotiation of turn-taking, responses, agreements, and assessments. Schegloff does not rule out the possibility of a gender-based analysis of these or other interactional data that meet his standards for conversation analysis – indeed, he provides a second example in which he performs such an analysis – but he insists that feminist analyses of conversation must be based on the clearly evident interactional salience of gender rather than on analysts' own theoretical and political concerns.

Schegloff's critique of linguistic research on social identities is a useful addition to a discussion that is by no means new; a number of language and gender scholars have raised similar issues regarding the dangers of assuming a priori that gender is always operative in discourse, and in predictable ways (see e.g. Eckert and McConnell-Ginet 1992). But Schegloff's proposed solution, as a number of critics have noted, limits admissible context so severely that only the most blatant aspects of gendered discursive practice, such as the overt topicalizing of gender in conversation, are likely candidates for Schegloffian analysis. And while political critique is possible in principle, in practice the analyst rarely moves to the critical level. Finally, Schegloff's article has also come in for some textual critique of its own, due to the covert gender politics that his rhetoric reveals (Billig 1999a, 1999b; Lakoff, this volume).

Some researchers of gender have succeeded in expanding the range of issues that are authorized by Schegloff's version of conversation analysis by using the fine-grained analytic methods associated with this framework in conjunction with the rich contextual grounding of ethnography. This multiple-method approach was pioneered by Marjorie Harness Goodwin (e.g. 1980, 1990, 1999; see also Mendoza-Denton, 1999).

5.1   Discursive psychology and feminist conversation analysis

In England, a new research tradition has developed using the combined tools of conversation analysis, feminism, and social psychology. This approach to discourse includes several strands, which differ theoretically and methodologically in spite of their broadly similar feminist project. (See Weatherall and Gallois, this volume, for a fuller discussion of the distinctions between these subfields in their approach to gender and discourse.) Many of these scholars have been influenced by and have contributed to the development of discursive psychology, a branch of psychology that uses discourse analysis rather than controlled experimentation as its primary method (Edwards and Potter 1992).

Elizabeth Stokoe (2000) follows Schegloff's line of argument to make a case for a feminist conversation analysis founded on participants' own interactional orientations to gender; in her examples such an orientation is indicated through the discursive use of gendered nouns and pronouns. Stokoe leaves open the question that she raises in her conclusion: must analysis be restricted to such explicit signaling of gender? Other feminist scholars within psychology find the two perspectives largely incompatible for precisely this reason. Ann Weatherall (2000) rejects the conversation-analytic premise that analysis of gender is admissible only when speakers overtly demonstrate an orientation to it, maintaining *contra* Schegloff that gender is omni-relevant in interaction. Margaret Wetherell (1998) aims to balance these two views of what counts as appropriate context. Responding to Schegloff's (1997) critique of critical discourse analysis, Wetherell argues that a complete analysis of discourse data requires both the technical analysis that conversation analysis provides and a critical (in her example, post-structuralist) analysis of the ideologies that make discourse socially interpretable. She demonstrates this approach in an analysis of a discussion of sexual exploits among a group of young men, noting that a strictly sequential account would miss the ways that cultural ideologies of heterosexual masculinity lend meaning to the speakers' interactional moves.

While such debates have centered on the applicability of conversation-analytic theory to language and gender research, other scholars within feminist psychology have focused instead on how the findings of conversation analysis can be applied to issues of gender. Celia Kitzinger and Hannah Frith (2000), for example, utilize the conversation-analytic concept of dispreferred response to point out the problems with campaigns to stop date rape. (Susan Ehrlich's chapter in this volume offers a complementary approach to the issue of date rape.) The authors note that when such campaigns instruct young women to "just say no" to unwanted sex forcefully and without explanation, they ask women to violate the interactional norm that a negative response to a request or suggestion (or demand) is dispreferred and thus must be mitigated through additional interactional work such as hedging or justifying. In addition, several scholars have offered recommendations for improving the compatibility of feminism and conversation analysis (e.g. Kitzinger 2000; Speer 1999). The range of feminist uses and critiques of conversation analysis makes clear that the question of the proper bounds of a conversation-analytic approach to gender is still far from settled. Nevertheless, practitioners of conversation analysis in all its forms share a view of gender as a phenomenon whose meaning and relevance must be analytically grounded in (though not, for some feminist scholars, necessarily restricted to) participants' own understandings of the interaction and not smuggled into the analysis via the researcher's assumptions and commitments.

This approach is consistent with both the ethnography of communication and interactional sociolinguistics in its insight that participants in conversation are highly skilled users of a complex set of flexible rules for conducting interaction, a point which for language and gender researchers underscores women's discursive agency and ability. Another commonality is the conversationanalytic principle of privileging the viewpoint of cultural members over that of the analyst. But the restriction of context to the immediate interaction, as advocated by Schegloff, contrasts with the broader cultural questions asked by these anthropological forms of discourse analysis. Where interactional sociolinguistics frequently uses playback interviews as a way of ascertaining participants' views of their interaction, and the ethnography of communication may examine the same speaker or speech event over time, the strictest form of conversation analysis does not admit any historical dimension to its analysis. Nor does it often stray far from the study of unelicited conversation, which, as its name suggests, is the foundation of conversation analysis.

Feminist conversation-analytic research takes a broader view, including research interviews among its data and incorporating historical patterns of gender and sexism into its analysis. But while historical context supplies crucial background for feminist conversation analysis, it does not take center stage. The fine-grained view of gender in interaction that conversation analysis yields therefore contrasts with approaches where the relationship of discourse to larger historical forces often drives the analysis. A clear connection between discourse and history may of course be difficult to locate when the discourse under investigation is casual conversation; it is often much easier to identify the broader context of language use in more formal, institutional, and codified forms of discourse, especially writing. Hence for a fuller picture of the discourse genres that may provide insights into the study of gender, it is necessary to consider those strands of discourse analysis that attend primarily to the discursive structures and functions of written texts.

6   Discourse as Text

Just as contemporary linguistics has tended to focus on spoken rather than written language, all of the preceding approaches to discourse analysis limit their investigations almost exclusively to oral discourse, and especially to dialogic interaction. Under the general rubric of text linguistics, other discourse-analytic frameworks – stylistics and critical discourse analysis – instead make written texts central to scholarly inquiry. The shift in emphasis from spoken to written language has important consequences for the theorizing and analysis of gender in discourse.

While both stylistics and critical discourse analysis are critical approaches to discourse, what is meant by *critical* in each case is quite different. Stylistics began as a linguistic approach to literary criticism, where *critical* originally referred to a scholar's evaluative role in assessing the effectiveness of a text as art. The use of *critical* within critical discourse analysis is instead borrowed from the language of Marxism, especially critical theory, which emerged from the Frankfurt school of literary and cultural criticism. In this context, *critical* signifies a leftist (usually socialist) political stance on the part of the analyst; the goal of such research is to comment on society in order to change it. These two kinds of inquiry can be integrated, but in practice either the aesthetic or the political perspective tends to predominate.

Because stylistics has historically been concerned with the analysis of an author's style (the distinctive ways that she or he uses language to achieve aesthetic effects), traditional stylistics has often been criticized for restricting its analytic gaze to the text alone, a methodological principle it shares with conversation analysis. More recently, however, some stylisticians have taken up the frameworks of critical linguistics and critical discourse analysis as productive approaches for the analysis of written discourse. This move has broadened the contextual field of stylistic inquiry by making connections between texts and the ideologies that produce and are produced by them. At the same time, the expansion of literary criticism into cultural criticism has enlarged the range of texts that are available for literary (and hence stylistic) analysis, especially texts from popular or mass culture such as genre fiction, films and television shows, music lyrics, advertisements, and newspaper and magazine articles.

With respect to gender, stylistics and critical discourse analysis have considerable overlap, and it is not always easy to separate the two approaches. Their differences are largely a matter of data selection: feminist stylistics continues to examine literary discourse alongside popular texts, while feminist critical discourse analysis studies both spoken and written data in a number of institutional contexts such as the media, government, medicine, and education. Both investigate the way that ideologies (or discourses, in the Foucauldian sense) of gender are circulated and reworked in a range of cultural texts, and both seek to call attention to the linguistic strategies whereby texts locate readers within these discourses.

6.1 Stylistics

Within language and gender research, stylistics has been informed by feminist literary criticism as well as by feminist linguistics (see Livia, this volume). But although some approaches have an explicitly liberatory aim, not all linguistic studies of gender in literature have as a primary goal the active fostering of critical awareness in readers. As a result of their political purpose, liberatory forms of stylistics tend to focus primarily on texts that promote dominant cultural ideologies, which are revealed and challenged in the course of the analysis. By contrast, recent research by Anna Livia (2000, this volume) on linguistic gender in literature demonstrates how authors may subvert or flout prevailing ideologies of social gender through their strategic use of gender-marked linguistic resources such as pronouns, nouns, and modifiers. Livia considers how linguistic gender in English and in French, in which gender marking is much more prevalent, is used in texts ranging from feminist science fiction to transsexual autobiography to undermine the notion of an absolute and binary division between genders on social or biological grounds. This research complements liberatory stylistics in documenting the possibilities as well as the constraints of gender positionings in written texts.

The most fully articulated theory of stylistics as a critical and liberatory feminist project has been carried out by Sara Mills (1992, 1995, 1998). Under the label of feminist stylistics or (post-) feminist text analysis, Mills's form of stylistics greatly expands the contextual parameters of traditional stylistic analysis to include, in addition to the text and its author, its history, its relationship to other texts, and its relationship to readers. Her central concern is with the ways in which a text signals through its language how it is to be read. This "dominant reading" draws on ideologies of gender, often in ways that assign a gender position to the reader as well. Feminist text analysis therefore involves an explication not only of how gender is represented within the text but also of how the text draws the reader into its ideological framework, and of how, through raised awareness, the reader can resist these representations and positionings. Mills (1992, 1995) exposes the underlying assumptions about gender in advertising discourse directed at women, such as "Removes all unsightly, embarrassing facial and body hair" or "Styled to make you look slimmer," as well as in literature from popular romance to poetry and literary prose. A recurring theme in these earlier analyses is that in mainstream texts women are positioned – both as textual figures and as readers – as objects of heterosexual desire and violence whose agency is limited to a replication of this arrangement of power. Mills offers alternative, resistant readings of such texts as a way of destabilizing normative discourses of gender. In her more recent work, Mills (1998) draws on contemporary feminist theory and language and gender scholarship to argue for the possibility of multiple and contradictory interpretations of texts. Continuing her earlier focus on advertisements, she suggests that the widespread influence of feminism has made sexism less overt but no less present in mainstream discourses of gender and heterosexuality.

The emancipatory orientation of stylistic research like Mills's has moved the field much closer to critical discourse analysis, and in fact the work of many authors contributes to both frameworks (e.g. Talbot 1995a; Thornborrow 1997). Yet the analysis of literary discourse remains a distinct tradition, which with respect to gender engages with specifically literary questions such as the possibility of a gendered writing style. The concept of authorial style is of less interest to critical discourse analysts, who often deal with texts for mass distribution that are not the product of a single identifiable author. Texts are therefore examined for what they reveal not about the author's gender but about the author's assumptions about gender – or, more accurately, about the representation of gender that the text offers up.

6.2   Critical discourse analysis

In its current form, critical discourse analysis has been shaped by several different scholars, most prominently Norman Fairclough (1989; Fairclough and Chouliaraki 1999), Teun van Dijk (1993a, 1993b), and Ruth Wodak (1989, 1999, this volume). Blending Marxist and post-structuralist theories of language, critical discourse analysis is an approach to language as a primary force for the production and reproduction of ideology – of belief systems that come to be accepted as "common sense." The beliefs that are put forth in the texts of greatest interest to critical discourse analysts are those that encourage the acceptance of unequal arrangements of power as natural and inevitable, perhaps even as right and good. In this way discourse has not merely a symbolic but also a material effect on the lives of human beings (cf. Cameron, this volume).

Institutions are of special concern to critical discourse analysts both because of their disproportionate power to produce and circulate discourse and because they promote dominant interests over those of politically marginalized groups such as racial and ethnic minorities, the lower classes, children, and women. Some of the clearest examples of this discursive control can be found in the media, which have been a primary target of critical discourse-analytic research.

Whereas stylistics, almost by definition, restricts itself to written – or at least to scripted – discourse, critical discourse analysis may be carried out on either written or oral data. But while some feminist research aligned with critical discourse analysis features data from spoken interaction (e.g. Coates 1997; Wodak 1997b), the dominant strain of critical discourse-analytic work on gender concentrates on written discourse. One of the most productive scholars working within this tradition is Mary Talbot, who takes her data primarily from the popular print media and fiction. A central argument in much of Talbot's work is that such texts seem to promise readers one thing but instead provide something else: a lipstick article in a magazine for teenage girls is a call to consumption under the guise of a friendly chat (Talbot 1995b); a report on sexual harassment in a British tabloid reinforces normative gender positions even as it seems to align itself with the female victim (Talbot 1997); an advice column uses a liberal discourse of sexual tolerance to cast homosexuality as a phase on the way to heterosexuality (Gough and Talbot 1996); a British Telecom advertisement appears to assume a pro-feminist stance while representing women and women's language negatively (Talbot 2000; see Cameron, this volume, for a fuller discussion of this advertisement). Identifying such reversals between what a text does and what it purports to do is at the heart of critical discourse analysis.

The use of mainly written data in feminist forms of text linguistics, and especially the concerted attention given to written discourse genres in which issues of gender and power are prominent features, encourages a different kind of analysis than is seen in other discourse-analytic studies. Both feminist stylistics and feminist critical discourse analysis put gender ideologies at the forefront of analysis. Where conversation analysis insists that power must be discovered in interaction and cannot be the point from which analysis proceeds, critical text analysis maintains that power permeates every aspect of society and hence is operative in all discourse. These scholars' refusal to shy away from politicized analysis provides a valuable model of engaged scholarship for researchers working within other approaches to discourse and gender.

In calling attention to the ideologies of gender embedded in the most pervasive forms of discourse in contemporary society, however, critical text linguistics presents women primarily as the consumers and the subjects of discourse rather than its producers. Agency in this approach is based primarily in the capacity of the consumer of the text to identify and reject these dominant discourses as a result of critical discourse analysis. And because critical discourse analysis does not usually investigate readers' relationships to such texts, it is not clear whether the potential effects of the discourse that the analyst identifies are in fact the effects experienced by the text's consumers.

Critical text linguistics is an important contributor to language and gender studies in its close attention to the discursive reproduction of power via the "top-down" processes whereby ideologies become established through discourse. But it does not give equal attention to the "bottom-up" strategies of those who may contest or subvert these ideologies through creative appropriation or production of new discourses (see e.g. Bucholtz 1996, 1999b). Thus neither discourse nor ideology is ever finished, in the sense that both can repeatedly enter new configurations that may constitute gender in ways unanticipated by analysts. Stylistics and critical discourse analysis, as primarily textual approaches to discourse, rarely indicate how texts circulate or how audiences interpret and use them; however, two new strains of discursive inquiry within linguistic anthropology examine the relationship between discourse and ideology from a more dynamic perspective. These approaches focus on specific discursive processes: ideologies and histories of discourse.

7   Discourse as History

Critical discourse analysis, with its foundations in Marxist thought, takes a special interest in history, at least in its theoretical outlines (Fairclough 1992). Other approaches to discourse analysis which have recently developed within linguistic anthropology also emphasize historical context, but in a more focused way. In one body of work, scholars follow the paths of ideology – the historically permeable systems of knowledge and power that Foucault termed *discourses*. The other scholarly trend considers instead discourse in the linguistic sense of the word, tracking its movement through time and space. This historicizing of discourse and discourses brings a much-needed temporal depth to the study of language and gender.

7.1 Language ideologies

The historical embeddedness of discourse is found in recent analyses within anthropology which focus not on discourse itself but on metadiscourse: discourse about discourse. Several recent essays and collections have laid out, from an anthropological viewpoint, a variety of issues involving language ideologies (Kroskrity 2000; Schieffelin et al. 1998; Woolard and Schieffelin 1994), developing issues first raised by Michael Silverstein's (1979) formulation of the concept. The study of language ideologies is both like and unlike critical discourse analysis. The similarity lies in the primacy given to ideology in both approaches, but the frameworks differ in their theoretical influences, their methods, and their scope. Critical discourse analysis uses language as a means of understanding ideology, and hence social and political relations, while the study of language ideologies turns this relationship in on itself by asking how ideologies that are *about* language, and not merely expressed in language, may themselves carry ideas about the social distribution of power (Cameron, this volume). Theoretically, research on language ideologies is less bound to the influence of Marxist perspectives; methodologically, it is both more linguistic (in focusing on socially and politically interested representations of language itself) and more anthropological (in concentrating on a broad range of specific cultural and geographic contexts from which language ideologies emerge). Relatedly and perhaps most importantly, it is less inclined to assume a privileged analytic perspective with respect to its data: whereas critical discourse analysis centers its discovery procedures on the analyst's interpretations of discourse (which are in turn thought to be the same as those of a reader, though made more explicit), anthropological research on language ideologies is more likely to appeal to the evidence of how ideologies are taken up, interrupted, or rerouted by those who participate in metadiscourse in various ways.

Among the work that informs and expands this young tradition of scholarship is Michael Silverstein's (1985) discussion of the language ideologies that feminist linguists challenge as well as those they hold; and Deborah Cameron's (1995) work on linguistic prescriptivism, or "verbal hygiene," as a language ideology with profoundly gendered effects. Much of the work on language ideologies and gender, however, centers on issues of emotion as indexed in discourse. Don Kulick's (1998) account of ideologies of language, gender, and emotion in a Papua New Guinean village recalls Elinor Ochs's (Keenan [1974] 1989) work in Madagascar in its delineation of an ideology that associates angry discourse with women and conciliatory discourse with men (see also Kulick, this volume). But where in Madagascar women's discursive practices came to be ideologically associated with modernity and cultural decline, in Papua New Guinea it is the men's discursive forms that are tied to modernity and "civilization" and usher in a shift away from the local language. Similarly, Charles Briggs (1998) contrasts two gendered discourses among the Warao, an indigenous group in Venezuela: the ritual wailing of women and the curing songs of men. But where Kulick focuses primarily on such points of gendered contrast, Briggs uses the language ideologies he outlines to make sense of gossip as a site of political struggle in which ideologies of gender are cross-cut by faultlines based on age, tradition, and political power. He shows how gendered ideologies of language allow powerful Warao men to counteract women's gossip against them by representing it as a marginal discourse form. By demonstrating that the associations between specific language ideologies and particular discursive practices are emergent and negotiated outcomes of interaction, Briggs opens the door to a far greater degree of social and political agency than critical discourse analysis – or, indeed, than much comparative language and gender research – allows. In contrast to the assumptions of critical discourse analysis, Briggs challenges any approach to language ideologies that places the researcher in a position of analytic authority *vis-à-vis* the community under study.

A historical approach to language ideology is also taken by Miyako Inoue (forthcoming) in her study of the emergence of "Japanese women's language" in the late nineteenth and early twentieth centuries. Here again modernity is a crucial element of ideologies of language and gender: Inoue demonstrates that a distinct system of gender-marking in Japanese arose in the first instance through the representation of women's speech in the modern Japanese novel, using schoolgirls' speech as a model. She argues that in thus constituting "Japanese women's language" modern novelists also created "the Japanese woman." Such appeals to historical as well as linguistic detail point the way to a more historically nuanced analysis of ideology than is available in other frameworks.

Research on language ideology attests to the inextricability of gender from other historically situated social and political processes. Although critical discourse analysis shares with language-ideology scholarship a commitment to recognizing ideologies and demonstrating their historical contingency, its preference for close textual analysis over historical and cultural depth has limited the extent to which it has been able to unsettle rather than reify existing relations of power. By bringing discursive practices and language ideologies together and by locating both within the mesh of culture and history, anthropological researchers of language ideologies are able to provide a more nuanced picture of female agency in the face of potent cultural ideologies of gender. In this body of scholarship, ideologies interact in complex ways: beliefs about gender are also beliefs about language, and conversely. Moreover, ideology is never total or foreclosed to other, countervailing ideologies.

The language-ideology framework therefore provides a richer theorizing of ideology than critical discourse analysis provides, one in which the analysis of discourse foregrounds the fact that discursive practices are not determined by ideology and hence are always available for negotiation and change. Linguistic anthropology has also recently been the source of another historical perspective on discourse, one closely allied with the language-ideology research; indeed, a number of the same scholars have made use of both perspectives in their work. Although it has not yet been fully tapped for its potential as a model for language and gender research, this form of discourse analysis may prove extremely useful in opening up new lines of inquiry through its investigation of the trajectory not of discourses, or ideologies, as in critical discourse analysis and research on language ideologies, but of discourse itself.

7.2 *Natural histories of discourse*

The study of how discourse becomes text – how it becomes bounded, defined, and movable from one context into another – has been termed recontextualization (Bauman and Briggs 1990) or natural histories of discourse (Silverstein and Urban 1996), the latter something of a misnomer insofar as there is nothing "natural" about how discourse enters into new text formations. If some approaches to discourse analysis emphasize oral discourse, and others focus on written texts, then natural histories of discourse call attention instead to the interplay between the oral and the written and between earlier and later versions of the "same" oral or written discourse: in short, to intertextuality. (Some work within critical discourse analysis also takes an interest in intertextuality, but this is an outcome of analysis, not its starting point.) Both conversation analysis and text linguistics take as given the notion of an unproblematically bounded text, whether spoken or written; investigations of natural histories of discourse instead take the formation of a "text" as an autonomous object (entextualization) and its mobility across contexts (recontextualization) as the central questions. The natural history of discourse is the path that discourse takes on its way to becoming text, the transformations it undergoes, as well as the changes wrought when a text is transplanted into a new discursive situation. This approach encompasses a wide range of phenomena in which intertextual relations are highlighted, including quotation, translation, literacy practices, and the performance of scripted texts, as well as the transcription practices of discourse analysts themselves. This research is closely related to work on language ideologies in that the possibilities for entextualization are often ideologically constrained, and ideologies can often be tracked through ensuing processes of discursive recontextualization. In both bodies of work gender emerges from the interaction of ideologies and discursive practices. Yet natural histories of discourse offer a different vantage point on this process from that taken by language-ideology scholarship by emphasizing the circulation not of ideologies but of discourse across contexts.

In Charles Briggs's research (1992) on women's discourse genres among the Warao, for example, he argues that ritual weeping, as a discourse form reserved for women, provides the opportunity for women to transgress social norms in order to critique the behavior of powerful men. Warao women extract (and invent) textual material from men's discourse and recontextualize it. As Briggs points out, such critiques may have consequences beyond the discourse itself, including limiting the authority of male community leaders.

Another approach to natural histories of discourse can be seen in Vincent Crapanzano's (1996) study of the nineteenth-century autobiographical narrative of Herculine Barbin, whom French medical and legal authorities reclassified from female to male. Crapanzano considers how the narrative conventions of autobiography limit the ability of Barbin to produce a continuous identity throughout the text: both Barbin's narrative and her/his identity are fragmented; it is only their conjunction in a single text that gives them both unity. While Crapanzano does not frame his work in relation to its implications for the investigation of gender, it may recall the work of Livia (2000, this volume) described above in showing the limits on the exploitation of textual conventions by an author writing outside the traditional binary gender system.

Theories of gender within natural histories of discourse favor a perspective in which gender, like the discourse through which it is produced as a socially meaningful category, is inherently unstable and manipulable. Gender identities and power relations cannot be determined from a reading of social structures alone, or from an ahistorical investigation of a given bit of discourse, for every text has a history of previous contexts in which those identities and relations may have operated very differently, and may continue to carry a trace of their prior effects. Yet given the name under which some research on such matters is carried out, it may be necessary to expand the scope for agency within this approach. If the history of discourse is construed as natural, then discourses may be understood as circulating independently of purposeful human action, a post-structuralist notion that many feminists and gender critics have faulted (e.g. Livia and Hall 1997). Fortunately, most work within this paradigm has not succumbed to the temptation of literalizing the idea of naturalness in the analysis of discourse.

Although natural histories of discourse and language-ideology research offer new ways of looking at discourse, they do not diverge dramatically from the ethnography of communication and interactional sociolinguistics, whose theoretical and methodological foundations they generally share. As already noted, the earlier approaches accommodate ideologies of language use, and both use the concept of context or even, as in the case of interactional sociolinguistics, of contextualization. And like these frameworks, newer historicized anthropological perspectives on discourse understand gender as an inherently cultural notion.

Language and gender research on discourse trajectories has barely begun, and if researchers take up the approach they will no doubt continue to develop it in fruitful new directions. Future work on language and gender from this perspective might document how processes of entextualization yield gendered results (a task begun with Inoue's work on Japanese women's language) or how gendered structures may be challenged by mobilizing texts into new contexts (as in Briggs's research). Because histories of discourse and of discourses are also potentially histories of gender, even scholars drawing on other traditions of discourse analysis would be well advised to make greater use of historical and contextual processes in analyzing how gender is produced in discourse.

8 Conclusion

The importance of discourse analysis in language and gender scholarship shows no signs of abating, and the forms of discourse analysis surveyed in this chapter do not exhaust the frameworks available for the analysis of discourse as a social phenomenon. All the research discussed in these pages can be connected to additional approaches to discourse analysis, including some that have not been sketched here, or that have yet to be formulated as distinctive frameworks. Moreover, some of the work discussed in this chapter does not address itself to an audience of language and gender scholars, yet all of it is useful for the linguistic study of social gender. The classification of discourse-analytic models offered here is therefore not intended as an absolute categorization, but rather a tentative and suggestive taxonomy that allows similarities and differences among approaches to come into relief, in particular with regard to the theories of gender that they employ and imply.

For language and gender research, the most prominent issues in discourse analysis are the nature of context, the role of agency versus dominant forms of power, and the analytic stance of the researcher. The problem of context is one that has become central to theoretical discussions of discourse analysis. Some approaches, such as conversation analysis, seek to limit context to what can be recovered from the discourse itself, while others, such as the ethnography of communication, consider a much wider range of contextual factors to be potentially relevant to analysis; others still, especially the natural histories of discourse, problematize the very notion of context by focusing on how contexts bring texts into being and give them (provisional) meaning. For language and gender scholars, this question is vital to an understanding of the nature of gender itself: is gender, as many feminist conversation analysts would have it, an achievement of discourse, or is it an ideological system with broad contextual parameters, as suggested in different ways by critical textual analysts and by those who study language ideologies? Likewise, the question of agency remains a point of divergence across approaches. In interactional sociolinguistics, individual agency is limited by cultural constraints, and it is almost invisible in some textual analysis; but agency is more fully realized in other anthropological models. With respect to analytic perspective, both conversation analysts and linguistic anthropologists advocate that researchers analyze discourse from the viewpoint of its participants, although more socially engaged approaches such as interactional sociolinguistics also endorse the analyst's role in revealing to participants other possible interpretations. The liberatory goal of critical textual analysis, meanwhile, considers it the researcher's political responsibility to make explicit how power relations may have been missed or mistaken by a text's audience. Natural histories of discourse instead invite greater reflexive awareness on the part of the analyst, suggesting that she attend to her own practices of text-making and how they circumscribe available interpretations. Such tensions are not easily resolved (cf. Bucholtz 2001). For the study of gender, these differences have meant that discourse analysis offers multiple and conflicting theories of the relationship of gender, discourse, and the researcher herself.

Few scholars, however, take a rigid or absolutist position on the appropriate methods for the analysis of gender in discourse. Researchers tend to draw on multiple approaches as needed to answer the questions that arise in the course of research. But there is a general tendency for certain types of discourse analysis to converge on certain types of data, a tendency that is both reasonable and limiting. Certainly, each form of discourse analysis has been developed to address specific issues, and hence in some ways it is best suited for those tasks and ill adapted for others. Yet there is always room for scholars to adapt and even appropriate what they need from diverse perspectives. Innovation requires that scholars of language and gender push their theories both of discourse and of gender as hard as they can; it is always worth bringing new models to bear on one's data, as well as interrogating familiar frameworks with novel research questions. By using the insights of other modes of discourse analysis, advocates of particular approaches can improve upon them and apply them to new situations. Drawing on various approaches allows the researcher to highlight issues of agency, power, interaction, and history at different moments in the analysis. The approaches to discourse analysis surveyed in this chapter are separated by real and sizeable differences in their understanding of the nature of language, the nature of gender, and their intersection. But a great deal of room remains for intellectual cross-fertilization. Such an undertaking requires discussion, and perhaps collaboration, across the dividing lines of different analytic traditions. An ongoing dialogue among discourse analysts of all stripes will ensure the continuing viability of discourse analysis as a flexible and incisive tool for the study of gender.

REFERENCES

Abrahams, Roger D. 1962: Playing the dozens. *Journal of American Folklore* 75: 209–20.

Bauman, Richard and Briggs, Charles L. 1990: Poetics and performance as critical perspectives on language and social life. *Annual Review of Anthropology* 19: 59–88.

Billig, Michael 1999a: Whose terms? Whose ordinariness? Rhetoric and ideology in Conversation Analysis. *Discourse & Society* 10(4): 543–58.

Billig, Michael 1999b: Conversation Analysis and the claims of naivety. *Discourse & Society* 10(4): 572–6.

Briggs, Charles L. 1992: "Since I am a woman, I will chastise my relatives": Gender, reported speech, and the (re)production of social relations in Warao ritual wailing. *American Ethnologist* 19(2): 337–61.

Briggs, Charles L. 1998: "You're a liar – you're just like a woman!": Constructing dominant ideologies of language in Warao men's gossip. In Bambi B. Schieffelin, Kathryn A. Woolard, and Paul V. Kroskrity (eds) *Language Ideologies: Practice and Theory*. New York: Oxford University Press, pp. 229–55.

Bucholtz, Mary 1996: Black feminist theory and African American women's linguistic practice. In Victoria L. Bergvall, Janet M. Bing, and Alice F. Freed (eds) *Rethinking Language and Gender Research: Theory and Practice*. London: Longman, pp. 267–90.

Bucholtz, Mary 1999a: Bad examples: Transgression and progress in language and gender studies. In Mary Bucholtz, Anita C. Liang, and Laurel A. Sutton (eds) *Reinventing Identities: The Gendered Self in Discourse*. New York: Oxford University Press, pp. 3–24.

Bucholtz, Mary 1999b: Purchasing power: The gender and class imaginary on the shopping channel. In Mary Bucholtz, Anita C. Liang, and Laurel A. Sutton (eds) *Reinventing Identities: The Gendered Self in Discourse*. New York: Oxford University Press, pp. 348–68.

Bucholtz, Mary 2001: Reflexivity and critique in discourse analysis. *Critique of Anthropology* 21(1): 157–75.

Bucholtz, Mary (forthcoming): Language, gender, and sexuality. In Edward Finegan and John Rickford (eds) *Language in the USA*, 2nd edn. Cambridge: Cambridge University Press.

Cameron, Deborah 1995: *Verbal Hygiene*. London: Routledge.

Cheshire, Jenny and Trudgill, Peter (eds) 1998: *The Sociolinguistics Reader*, vol. 2: *Gender and Discourse*. London: Arnold.

Coates, Jennifer 1997: Competing discourses of femininity. In Helga Kotthoff and Ruth Wodak (eds) *Communicating Gender in Context*. Amsterdam: John Benjamins, pp. 285–314.

Crapanzano, Vincent 1996: "Self"-centering narratives. In Michael Silverstein and Greg Urban (eds) *Natural Histories of Discourse*. Chicago: University of Chicago Press, pp. 106–27.

Davis, Hayley 1996: Review article: Theorizing women's and men's language. *Language and Communication* 16(1): 71–9.

Eckert, Penelope, and McConnell-Ginet, Sally 1992: Think practically and look locally: Language and gender as community-based practice. *Annual Review of Anthropology* 21: 461–90.

Edwards, Derek, and Potter, Jonathon 1992: *Discursive Psychology*. London: Sage.

Fairclough, Norman 1989: *Language and Power*. London: Longman.

Fairclough, Norman 1992: *Discourse and Social Change*. Cambridge: Polity Press.

Fairclough, Norman, and Chouliaraki, Lilie 1999: *Discourse in Late Modernity: Rethinking Critical Discourse Analysis*. Edinburgh: Edinburgh University Press.

Fishman, Pamela 1983: Interaction: The work women do. In Barrie Thorne, Cheris Kramarae, and Nancy Henley (eds) *Language, Gender, and Society*. Cambridge, MA: Newbury House, pp. 89–101.

Foucault, Michel 1972: *The Archaeology of Knowledge*. New York: Pantheon.

Freed, Alice 1992: We understand perfectly: A critique of Tannen's view of cross-sex communication. In Kira Hall, Mary Bucholtz, and Birch Moonwomon (eds) *Locating Power: Proceedings of the Second Berkeley Women and Language Conference*, vol. 2. Berkeley, CA: Berkeley Women and Language Group, University of California, pp. 144–52.

Garfinkel, Harold 1967: *Studies in Ethnomethodology*. Cambridge: Polity Press.

Goodwin, Marjorie Harness 1980: "He-said-she-said": Formal cultural procedures for the construction of a gossip dispute activity. *American Ethnologist* 7: 674–95.

Goodwin, Marjorie Harness 1990: *He-Said-She-Said: Talk as Social Organization among Black Children.* Bloomington: Indiana University Press.

Goodwin, Marjorie Harness 1999: Constructing opposition within girls' games. In Mary Bucholtz, Anita C. Liang, and Laurel A. Sutton (eds) *Reinventing Identities: The Gendered Self in Discourse.* New York: Oxford University Press, pp. 388–409.

Gough, Val and Talbot, Mary 1996: "Guilt over games boys play": Coherence as a focus for examining the constitution of heterosexual subjectivity on a problem page. In Carmen Rosa Caldas-Coulthard and Malcolm Coulthard (eds) *Texts and Practices: Readings in Critical Discourse Analysis.* London: Routledge, pp. 215–30.

Gumperz, John J. 1982a: *Discourse Strategies.* Cambridge: Cambridge University Press.

Gumperz, John J. (ed.) 1982b: *Language and Social Identity.* Cambridge: Cambridge University Press.

Hymes, Dell 1962: The ethnography of speaking. In *Anthropology and Human Behavior.* Washington, DC: Anthropological Society of Washington, pp. 13–53.

Hymes, Dell 1974: *Foundations in Sociolinguistics: An Ethnographic Approach.* Philadelphia: University of Pennsylvania Press.

Inoue, Miyako (forthcoming): Gender, language, and modernity: Toward an effective history of "Japanese women's language." *American Ethnologist.*

Keenan, Elinor (Ochs) [1974] 1989: Norm-makers, norm-breakers: Uses of speech by men and women in a Malagasy community. In Richard Bauman and Joel Sherzer (eds) *Explorations in the Ethnography of Speaking,* 2nd edn. Cambridge: Cambridge University Press, pp. 125–43.

Kessler, Suzanne J. and McKenna, Wendy 1978: *Gender: An Ethnomethodological Approach.* New York: Wiley.

Kitzinger, Celia 2000: Doing feminist conversation analysis. *Feminism and Psychology* 10(2): 163–93.

Kitzinger, Celia and Frith, Hannah 2000: Just say no? The use of conversation analysis in developing a feminist perspective on sexual refusal. *Discourse and Society* 10(3): 293–316.

Kroskrity, Paul V. (ed.) 2000: *Regimes of Language: Ideologies, Polities, and Identities.* Santa Fe, NM: School of American Research Press.

Kulick, Don 1998: Anger, gender, language shift, and the politics of revelation in a Papua New Guinean village. In Bambi B. Schieffelin, Kathryn A. Woolard, and Paul V. Kroskrity (eds) *Language Ideologies: Practice and Theory.* New York: Oxford University Press, pp. 87–102.

Lakoff, Robin 1975: *Language and Woman's Place.* New York: Harper and Row.

Livia, Anna 2000: *Pronoun Envy: Literary Uses of Linguistic Gender.* Oxford: Oxford University Press.

Livia, Anna and Hall, Kira 1997: "It's a girl!": Bringing performativity back to linguistics. In Anna Livia and Kira Hall (eds) *Queerly Phrased: Language, Gender, and Sexuality.* New York: Oxford University Press, pp. 3–18.

Maltz, Daniel N. and Borker, Ruth A. 1982: A cultural approach to male–female miscommunication. In John J. Gumperz (ed.) *Language and Social Identity.* Cambridge: Cambridge University Press, pp. 196–216.

Mendoza-Denton, Norma 1999: Turn-initial *no*: Collaborative

opposition among Latina
adolescents. In Mary Bucholtz, Anita
C. Liang, and Laurel A. Sutton (eds)
*Reinventing Identities: The Gendered
Self in Discourse*. New York: Oxford
University Press, pp. 273–92.

Mills, Sara 1992: Knowing your place:
A Marxist feminist stylistic analysis.
In Michael Toolan (ed.) *Language,
Text and Context: Essays in Stylistics*.
London: Routledge, pp. 182–205.

Mills, Sara 1995: *Feminist Stylistics*.
London: Routledge.

Mills, Sara 1998: Post-feminist text
analysis. *Language and Literature*
7(3): 235–53.

Mitchell-Kernan, Claudia 1971: *Language
Behavior in a Black Urban Community*.
Berkeley, CA: Language Behavior
Research Laboratory.

Morgan, Marcyliena 1999: No woman
no cry: Claiming African American
women's place. In Mary Bucholtz,
Anita C. Liang, and Laurel A.
Sutton (eds) *Reinventing Identities:
The Gendered Self in Discourse*.
New York: Oxford University
Press, pp. 27–45.

Schegloff, Emanuel A. 1997: Whose text?
Whose context? *Discourse & Society*
8(2): 165–87.

Schegloff, Emanuel A. 1999: Naivete vs.
sophistication or discipline vs.
self-indulgence: A rejoinder to
Billig. *Discourse & Society* 10(4):
577–82.

Schieffelin, Bambi B., Woolard, Kathryn
A., and Kroskrity, Paul V. (eds)
1998: *Language Ideologies: Practice
and Theory*. New York: Oxford
University Press.

Sherzer, Joel 1987: A diversity of voices:
Men's and women's speech in
ethnographic perspective. In
Susan U. Philips, Susan Steele,
and Christine Tanz (eds) *Language,
Gender and Sex in Comparative
Perspective*. Cambridge: Cambridge
University Press, pp. 95–120.

Silverstein, Michael 1979: Language
structure and linguistic ideology.
In Paul R. Clyne, William F. Hanks,
and Carol L. Hofbauer (eds) *The
Elements: A Parasession on Linguistic
Units and Levels*. Chicago: Chicago
Linguistic Society, pp. 193–247.

Silverstein, Michael 1985: Language
and the culture of gender: At the
intersection of structure, usage,
and ideology. In Elizabeth Mertz
and Richard J. Parmentier (eds)
*Semiotic Mediation: Sociocultural
and Psychological Perspectives*.
Orlando, FL: Academic Press,
pp. 219–59.

Silverstein, Michael and Urban, Greg
(eds) 1996: *Natural Histories of
Discourse*. Chicago: University
of Chicago Press.

Speer, Susan A. 1999: Feminism and
conversation analysis: An
oxymoron? *Feminism and Psychology*
9(4): 471–8.

Stokoe, Elizabeth H. 2000: Toward a
conversation analytic approach to
gender and discourse. *Feminism
and Psychology* 10(4): 552–63.

Talbot, Mary 1995a: *Fictions at Work:
Language and Social Practice in
Fiction*. London: Longman.

Talbot, Mary 1995b: A synthetic
sisterhood: False friends in a
teenage magazine. In Kira Hall
and Mary Bucholtz (eds) *Gender
Articulated: Language and the
Socially Constructed Self*. New York:
Routledge, pp. 143–65.

Talbot, Mary M. 1997: "Randy fish boss
branded a stinker": Coherence and
the construction of masculinities in
a British tabloid newspaper. In Sally
Johnson and Ulrike Hanna Meinhof
(eds) *Language and Masculinity*.
Oxford: Blackwell, pp. 173–87.

Talbot, Mary M. 2000: "It's good to
talk?" The undermining of feminism
in a British Telecom advertisement.
Journal of Sociolinguistics 4(1): 108–19.

Tannen, Deborah 1981: New York Jewish conversational style. *International Journal of the Sociology of Language* 30: 133–9.

Tannen, Deborah 1982: Ethnic style in male–female conversation. In John J. Gumperz (ed.) *Language and Social Identity*. Cambridge: Cambridge University Press, pp. 217–31.

Tannen, Deborah 1990: *You Just Don't Understand: Women and Men in Conversation*. New York: William Morrow.

Tannen, Deborah 1994a: *Gender and Discourse*. New York: Oxford University Press.

Tannen, Deborah 1994b: *Talking from 9 to 5*. New York: William Morrow.

Tannen, Deborah 1999: The display of (gendered) identities in talk at work. In Mary Bucholtz, Anita C. Liang, and Laurel A. Sutton (eds) *Reinventing Identities: The Gendered Self in Discourse*. New York: Oxford University Press, pp. 221–40.

Thornborrow, Joanna 1997: Playing power: Gendered discourses in a computer games magazine. *Language and Literature* 6(1): 43–55.

Todd, Alexandra Dundas and Fisher, Sue (eds) 1988: *Gender and Discourse: The Power of Talk*. Norwood, NJ: Ablex.

Troemel-Ploetz, Senta 1991: Review article: Selling the apolitical. *Discourse and Society* 2(4): 489–502.

van Dijk, Teun A. 1993a: *Elite Discourse and Racism*. Newbury Park, CA: Sage.

van Dijk, Teun A. 1993b: Principles of critical discourse analysis. *Discourse and Society* 4(2): 249–83.

Weatherall, Ann 2000: Gender relevance in talk-in-interaction and discourse. *Discourse & Society* 11(2): 286–8.

West, Candace 1979: Against our will: Male interruptions of females in cross-sex conversation. *Annals of the New York Academy of Sciences* 327: 81–100.

West, Candace and Zimmerman, Don H. 1983: Small insults: A study of interruptions in cross-sex conversations between unacquainted persons. In Barrie Thorne, Cheris Kramarae, and Nancy Henley (eds) *Language, Gender, and Society*. Cambridge, MA: Newbury House, pp. 102–17.

West, Candace and Zimmerman, Don H. 1987: Doing gender. *Gender and Society* 1(2): 125–51.

Wetherell, Margaret 1998: Positioning and interpretative repertoires: Conversation analysis and post-structuralism in dialogue. *Discourse & Society* 9(3): 387–412.

Wodak, Ruth (ed.) 1989: *Language, Power, and Ideology: Studies in Political Discourse*. Amsterdam: John Benjamins.

Wodak, Ruth (ed.) 1997a: *Gender and Discourse*. London: Sage.

Wodak, Ruth 1997b: "I know, we won't revolutionize the world with it, but . . .": Styles of female leadership in institutions. In Helga Kotthoff and Ruth Wodak (eds) *Communicating Gender in Context*. Amsterdam: John Benjamins, pp. 335–70.

Wodak, Ruth 1999: Critical discourse analysis at the end of the 20th century. *Research on Language and Social Interaction* 32(1–2): 185–93.

Woolard, Kathryn A. and Schieffelin, Bambi B. 1994: Language ideology. *Annual Review of Anthropology* 23: 55–82.

Zimmerman, Don H. and West, Candace 1975: Sex roles, interruptions, and silences in conversation. In Barrie Thorne and Nancy Henley (eds) *Language and Sex: Difference and Dominance*. Rowley, MA: Newbury House, pp. 105–29.

3 "What's in a Name?" Social Labeling and Gender Practices

SALLY MCCONNELL-GINET

1 Categorizing Labels

What do we call one another? How do we identify ourselves? When and how do we label ourselves and others? What is the significance of rejecting labels for ourselves or others? Of adopting new labels? Social labeling practices offer a window on the construction of gendered identities and social relations in social practice.

To get the flavor of some ways that labeling can enter into gender practice, consider the English nominal labels italicized in (1), which are being used to describe or to evaluate, to sort people into *kinds*. These predicative labels characterize and *categorize* people.

(1) a. He's *a real dork*.
     b. She's *a total airhead*.
     c. I'm not *a feminist*, but . . .
     d. You are a *fierce faggot*, and I love you.
     e. We're not just *soccer moms*.
     f. What *a slut* (s/he is)!
     g. You're *a dear*.
     h. That blood is the sign that you're now *a woman*.

(1a) and (1b) are both negative characterizations, but they are gendered and they are different: (1a) alleges male social incompetence, (1b) attributes female brainlessness. (See James 1996 for these and other different semantic categories predominating in insulting labels applied to males and females in her study with Toronto students.) In (1c), the *but* signals that the speaker's rejection of the label is probably linked to acceptance of a negative evaluation that others have placed on those who openly identify with change-oriented gender agendas, often by misrepresenting their actions and attitudes (e.g. presenting feminists as humorless and unattractive man-haters). Another speaker might embrace the alternative label *womanist* as a way of criticizing self-described feminists who have ignored issues of race and class, effectively equating "women" with "well-to-do White women." (This particular example is discussed at some length in Eckert and McConnell-Ginet, forthcoming, ch. 7.) In (1d), "faggot," a label that is standardly only applied derogatorily to others by those not so labeled, is being proudly and defiantly reappropriated and joined to a modifier ("fierce") that completely subverts the weak, wishy-washy image so often associated with the nominal label. The speaker, an "out" gay man interviewed by one of my students, directly challenges the homophobic attitudes and assumptions that give the label its more usual negative value. A group's appropriation of labels that have been derogatorily applied by outsiders is often a powerful strategy: the word *queer* has been (almost) rehabilitated through this process and can now be used without suggesting prejudice against sexual minorities within certain groups (e.g. academic-based communities of practice) even by those who don't apply the label to themselves. (See McConnell-Ginet 2002 for further discussion.) And in (1e), there is an implicit criticism of the gendered political assumptions that are carried by the label, a media invention that marries gender and class privilege. (1f) attributes sexual promiscuity to the person so labeled, and, although it is sometimes applied to males these days, it overwhelmingly evokes a female image (see James 1996). Used jokingly, it may mock sexual double standards; in another context, it may reinforce them. The speaker in (1g) is gently stroking the addressee with kind words; to offer this particular form of appreciation is generally to "do" a certain kind of femininity. And in (1h), the addressee is pushed along a trajectory of gender identity, and a strong link is forged between her menarche and her new status as "woman."

As *feminist* in (1c) illustrates, labels often identify social, political, and attitudinal groupings into which people quite self-consciously do or do not enter. Others may, of course, monitor their suitability by refusing to accord them a claimed label: *Well, she's no feminist* can serve in a group defining itself as feminist to criticize the intellectual or political credentials of the person in question, and perhaps to exclude her from membership in the group. Of course, uttering that same sentence in some other group might function as a prelude to welcoming in a new member. In May 2001, the potential potency of embracing or rejecting certain labels was brought home dramatically in US news by the defection of Vermont Senator James Jeffords from the Republican Party. "I have changed my party label," he noted, "but I have not changed my beliefs" (*New York Times*, May 25, 2001: A20). Jeffords' rejection of the label *Republican*, while it may not have been associated with any change in his beliefs and values, nonetheless set into motion a quite significant chain of events with enormous political repercussions. And as news analysts pointed out, all that was required by the laws of Vermont and the rules of the US Senate for Jeffords to cease being a Republican was for him to reject the label, to say "I am no longer a Republican."

It was reportedly very wrenching for Jeffords to change his party label: being a Republican was not only an important part of how he thought of himself but of his friendships and alliances. It would be even harder for the addressee in (1h) to change or reject the gender label being attached to her. Yet, as we will see, labeling (including relabeling and label rejection) is deeply implicated not only in ascribing gender but in giving content to and helping shape gender identities and in challenging gender dichotomies.

2 Social Practice: Local Communities of Practice and Global Connections

Although I have offered a sketch of what is probably going on when each of the sentences in (1) is uttered, precisely what each labeling does will depend on how the utterance fits into the other aspects of ongoing social practice. As Penelope Eckert and I have argued in our joint work on language and gender (Eckert and McConnell-Ginet 1992a, 1992b, 1995, 1999, forthcoming), social identities, including gendered identities, arise primarily from articulating memberships in different communities of practice. A community of practice (CofP) is a group of people brought together by some mutual endeavor, some common enterprise in which they are engaged and to which they bring a shared repertoire of resources, including linguistic resources, and for which they are mutually accountable. Jean Lave and Etienne Wenger (1991) introduced the notion in their work on learning as an ongoing and thoroughly social process, and Wenger (1998) further develops the analytic framework.

Gender is a global social category that cuts across communities of practice, but much of the real substance of gendered experience arises as people participate in the endeavors of the local communities of practice to which they belong and as they move between such communities. The special June 1999 issue of *Language in Society*, edited by Janet Holmes and Miriam Meyerhoff, contains a number of interesting discussions and applications of the idea to language and gender research, and the editors' contribution (Holmes and Meyerhoff 1999) discusses its theoretical and methodological implications for language and gender research. Meyerhoff (2001) details the implications of the CofP framework more generally for the study of language variation and change, comparing the CofP to related constructs and frameworks: the speech community, social networks, and intergroup theory. As Meyerhoff makes clear, much sociolinguistic work that has not used the terminology "community of practice" has nonetheless drawn on similar ideas in attempting to gain insight into the connection between individual speech and broader general social and linguistic patterns. Penelope Eckert (2000) has developed a sustained argument for viewing linguistic variation as social practice, drawing on her extensive sociolinguistic investigations in a Detroit area high school.

Communities of practice are not free-floating but are linked to one another and to various institutions. They draw on resources with a more general history – languages as well as various kinds of technologies and artefacts. Their members align themselves not only with one another but with others whom they imagine have shared values and interests. It is not only those we directly encounter who have significant impact on our sense of possibilities for social practice and identity. Benedict Anderson (1983) introduced the notion of an "imagined community" to talk about national identity, and Andrew Wong and Qing Zhang (2000) talk about sexual minorities developing a sense of themselves as members of an imagined community in which they align themselves with others and thereby affirm and shape their sexual identities. Media, including books as well as newer communicative technologies, feed the imagination and offer glimpses of social practices that may be possible alternatives to those found in one's local communities of practice. Religious, political, and educational institutions also offer more global perspectives and resources, although they often have their main impact on individuals through their participation in connected local communities of practice (particular church groups, political action groups, classroom-based teams).

3   "Empty" Labels: Reference and Address

The idea that there might be nothing (or very little) in a name arises most naturally when labels are not used predicatively to characterize, as in (1) above, but are used to refer to or address someone. In (2) and (3), the italicized labels are being used to refer and to address respectively:

(2)   a.   *That bastard* didn't even say hello!
     b.   When are *you guys* going to supper?
     c.   Have *you* seen *my sister*?
     d.   *Jill* said *she'd* talked with *the professors in the department*.
     e.   It's *the welfare queens* who undermine the system.
     f.   *I'd* like *you* to meet *my partner, Chris*.

(3)   a.   Hey, *lady* – watch where you're going!
     b.   Why're you in such a rush, *stuck-up bitch*?
     c.   Go, *girl*!
     d.   How're you doing, *tiger*?
     e.   Frankly, *my dear*, I don't give a damn.
     f.   I'll try, *mom*, to make you proud of me.
     g.   Be good, *Joanie*.
     h.   Wait for me, *you guys*.

Referring is basic to conveying information: we refer to the people we talk about (and also, of course, to other things we talk about). Referring expressions play grammatical roles such as *subject* or *object*. Typically, they identify the participants in the eventuality designated by the verb: they are what linguists call *arguments* of the verb (or sometimes of another expression, for example a preposition). Addressing, on the other hand, exists only because of the social nature of linguistic interaction. Address forms tag an utterance with some label for the addressee, the target to whom an utterance is directed. Unlike referring expressions (and the predicative use of labels we saw in (1)), they are not grammatically related to other expressions in the utterance; in English, they are often set off intonationally much as other "parenthetical" expressions. The expression *you guys* is used to refer in (2b), to address in (3h).

The idea that names don't (or shouldn't) matter – "a rose by any other name would smell as sweet" – is linked to the idea that labeling for referential or address purposes does not characterize an individual or group but simply identifies them: points to the proper entity about whom something is said in the referring case, or indicates to whom an utterance is directed in the addressing case. Indeed, the standard analysis of what referring proper names and pronouns contribute in the way of informational content to sentences like those in (2) fits with this view of things. If my sister is named Alison (and I assume that you know that) then I could ask *Have you seen Alison?* and achieve much the same effect as if (2c) is uttered. Of course, (2c) does attribute the property of being my sister to the individual about whose whereabouts I'm inquiring. If you have some other way to identify the individual in question (perhaps you've recently seen the two of us together and note that I'm carrying and looking at the hat she was then wearing), my utterance might indeed inform you that the individual in question is my sister though that might not have been my intent (I might have been assuming that you already knew she was my sister).

In general, when a referring expression uses a nominal that can be used to characterize or categorize, the speaker is assuming that the referent is indeed categorized by that nominal. But the content of the nominal label – its potential characterizing value – is very often just a way to get attention focused on the particular individual, and other ways might in many cases do equally well. (Not in all cases, however: a matter to which we will return below.) Address forms too can include contentful nominals, and that content is often presupposed applicable to the addressee.

Of course, proper names and pronouns do not standardly have content in the same way as ordinary common nouns do. Their relative semantic emptiness precludes their occurring as predicate expressions like those in (1): rather than characterizing, they indicate a person or group. English does, of course, sometimes allow what look like characterizing uses of names and pronouns. In the case of proper names, an ordinary "common" noun – a category label – can be derived from a proper name, where the content of the noun usually derives from some specially notable characteristics of some particular person bearing that name, as in the first three examples in (4). (The person may be a fictional character as in (4c), where the expression *Lolita* serves to cast young girls as seductive and thus responsible for men's sexual interest in them.) Sometimes, though, a proper name is used just to help personify a typical member of some group or a person with some particular personal qualities; in these cases, the capital letter associated with proper names often disappears, as in the last five examples (but the original gendering of the names contributes to their significance):

(4)   a.   Kim's *no Mother Teresa.*
      b.   Lee's *a regular Einstein.*
      c.   Some of those fourth-graders are already *little Lolitas.*
      d.   She's *your typical sorority sue.* [1980s slang at University of North Carolina: Eble 1996]
      e.   He's *a nervous nellie.*
      f.   She's just *a sheila I met in Sydney.* [Australian English]
      g.   He's just *a guy I know.*
      h.   The legislators quickest to criminalize prostitutes are often *johns* themselves.

Notice also that some proper names are formally equivalent to labels that do have descriptive content: *Faith, Hope, Rose, Pearl, Iris,* and *Joy* are examples of English names (not coincidentally, all female names) that evoke content. A given girl named *Rose* is not, of course, literally a flower, but her name may suggest the beauty of those fragrant blossoms. I don't mean to suggest that men's given names are immune from content associations; the widely increased prevalence of *dick* as a vulgar term for "penis" and also as an insult has virtually killed off *Dick* as a shortened form of *Richard* among Americans under the age of 40. Here, of course, the content is seen as far more problematic than that associated with the female names mentioned above. Overall, content-bearing names are no longer the norm in English, but they certainly are in many other cultures. Even non-contentful names often link a child to a family history, to someone else who bore the same name in the family or in the family's cultural heritage. Whether that person must be of the same sex as that to which the child is assigned varies. Some languages have devices that can feminize an originally masculine name (e.g. we find English *Georgina, Paulette,* and *Roberta* alongside *George, Paul,* and *Robert*), and there are languages where there are masculine/feminine pairs of names (e.g. Italian *Mario* and *Maria*), neither of which is derivationally more basic. (There may be cases of masculinizing processes, but I have not uncovered them.) In some cultural traditions, given names are generally contentful, and those naming a child try to pick something auspicious.

How names work varies significantly in different cultural settings. Catholic children, for example, acquire a confirmation name, generally with some special significance. Felly Nkweto Simmonds (1995) discusses this and other features of the place of her own different names in her life history. The custom (and one-time legal requirement) in many Western societies of a woman's adopting her husband's surname has meant that women were more likely than men to face name changes during their lives, at least "official" name changes. Many men leave behind childhood diminutive forms of their given names (*Bobby* becomes *Bob*, *Willie* becomes *Will* or *William*), but many also acquire new nick-names on sports teams or in fraternities or the military, new names that some-times persist over the rest of the life-course. And some men are changing their surnames upon marriage nowadays, hyphenating names or choosing with their partner a name that ties into the heritage of both (e.g. my local paper reported on a couple, one named *Hill* and one with an Italian surname and heritage, who chose *Collina*, "hill" in Italian, as their common new surname).

Some cultures institutionalize an array of different personal names, others do not use family names as most Europeans understand them, and still others tie names very tightly to life-stages. Among the Tamang in Nepal, people of both sexes bear a variety of different names during their lives. Babies are given a name selected by a religious expert to contain appropriate sounds, but those names are seldom used and are generally known only to close family. Young children are typically given rather derogatory labels ("little pock-marked one"), designed to deflect unwanted attention from evil spirits. And adolescents take for themselves joyful sounding names ("Bright Flower") that they use during courtship song festivals and similar occasions in the period between childhood and (relatively late) marriage. Adults, on the other hand, are often labeled in terms of their parental roles ("Maya's mother" or "father of Mohan") or other kinship relations ("grandfather" or "youngest daughter-in-law"), seldom being addressed or referred to by what Westerners would count as a name (though close friends from youth may continue to use the courtship-period names, at least in some contexts). (See March, forthcoming, for discussion of Tamang naming.)

Labels for people that identify them only through their relation to someone else – teknonyms – do occur in some English-speaking communities (I was addressed as *Alan's mom* or *Lisa's mother* on many occasions when my children were young), but they are pervasive in some cultures. During some historical periods, Chinese women in certain regions often received nothing but such relational forms, moving from designations such as *second daughter* and *oldest sister* to *Lee's wife* and the like; men, in contrast, were far more often named as individuals (Naran Bilik, personal communication, May 2001; see Blum 1997 for a very useful discussion of naming and other features of address and reference practices among speakers of Chinese). Bernsten (1994) discusses Shona address practices, which construct adult women mainly via their relationships to others. After marriage (when a woman moves to her husband's locale) but before having children, a young woman is generally not called (at least pub-licly) by her principal childhood name but *amain'ini* (lit. "little mother"), the term for a young aunt, or, to show respect and recognition of her ancestral ties to another place, by the totem name associated with her natal family or clan. But once she has children the principal form of address to a woman is *amai* ("mother") + the name of her eldest child. Or at least such teknonymy was the predominant pattern before European colonizers and missionaries came and began to promote Western-style naming practices.

Labeling practices that de-emphasize women's status as very particular individuals can be found closer to home. For example, in American and British history, tombstones have often named male children (*James, Richard, Kenneth, and Thomas*) but not female (*and three daughters*). And *Mrs. John Doe* names a station, whoever the occupant may be, whereas *Mr. John Doe* picks out an individual. This point was brought home to me early in my married life when I came across a box of stationery made for my husband's first wife, bearing what I had until then thought of as "my" new name. (Stannard 1977 remains a fascinating account of "Mrs. Man"; the epigraph she chooses from a letter Henry James wrote to a friend in 1884 is eloquent: "we talk of you and Mrs you.")

The many ways in which proper names may enter into gender practice is itself the topic for a book. The two critical points for present purposes are that (1) although proper names are not fundamentally characterizing, they nonetheless have considerable significance beyond their picking out particular individuals, and (2) the significance of proper names lies in how they are bestowed and deployed in particular cultures and communities of practice.

There are also occasional characterizing uses of forms identical to pronouns. These are analogous to the occasional transformation of a proper name into a characterizing expression that we saw in (4):

(5)   a.   Max thinks he's a real *he*-man.
      b.   Bernadette's a *she*-wolf.
      c.   I really hope their baby is a *she*.
      d.   This *me*-generation has forgotten what it means to care about others.

In (5a–c), *he* and *she* draw on the background gender assumptions they carry in their ordinary referring uses. But they are otherwise lacking in content.

Neither proper names nor pronouns are what people generally have in mind when they speak of *name-calling*. Name-calling is like address in being specifically targeted, but unlike address in that the label itself constitutes a full utterance whose explicit function is to characterize (more particularly, to evaluate) its target. Popular usage speaks of name-calling only when the content of the label applied is overtly disparaging, but I include approving labels in this category as well. In (6) there are some examples. The first two might be hurled at a target by someone intending to hurt, the third is more likely to be used jokingly, whereas the last three might well function as expressions of affection or thanks or appreciative positive evaluation. (Interestingly, it seems significantly harder to omit the pronominal *you* with the positive than with the negative.)

(6)   a.   (You) *jerk.*   cf. What *a jerk* (you are)!
      b.   *Fatso.*
      c.   (You) *klutz.*
      d.   You *sweetheart.*   cf. You are such a *sweetheart!*
      e.   You *angel.*
      f.   You *genius.*

Name-calling is directed toward a particular target and ascribes the content of the nominal to that target. What characterizing content amounts to in these cases is evaluation, which can be either (overtly) negative or positive. The strongly evaluative element is why (in English) name-calling is much like uttering a special *wh*-exclamative form – "what a(n)——(you are)" – or an exclamatory declarative – "you are such a(n)——," where the blank is filled in with some noun phrase. It is the negative cases, of course, that invoke the old playground mantra "sticks and stones may break my bones but words will never hurt me," chanted by the target of some name in a desperate attempt to prevent further assault by denying its (obvious) power. We can think of name-calling as an utterance of a characterizing expression directed at an addressee, where the whole point of such an utterance is to paste the evaluative label on the addressee.

Address forms are often used in calls (where the address form may constitute the whole utterance) or greetings or on other occasions to get the attention of the person or persons to whom an utterance is directed: such uses have been called *summons*. By analogy with the lines on an envelope that direct the message inside to a particular location, the term *address* suggests the primacy of this attention-getting or "finding" function of address forms, even though some analysts (see, for example, Schegloff 1972) want to reserve the term for non-summoning uses. In general, address forms can be parenthetically interjected at almost any point in an ongoing exchange although they are particularly common in greetings or other openings. Many address forms can also be used to refer, and I will sometimes mention differences between address and referring uses of a particular form. And second-person reference, though grammatically distinct from address, raises many of the same social issues. Ide (1990) uses "terms of address" to include both address forms and second-person reference.

4 Address Options: Beyond Power and Solidarity

Address forms are always grammatically optional, but they are often socially required and they are always socially loaded. There are many different ways that analysts have divided the field, but the following two displays give some order to the range of available options in English. Display (7) gives a typology for forms that are individualized in the sense that speaker and addressee consider them names or nicknames that have been specifically attached to this particular addressee. Of course, any given individual may get very different forms from different addressers, and some addressers may use multiple forms. Imagine these preceded by *hey* or *hi* or *hello* or a similar greeting (*yo* is increasingly common among younger Americans):

(7)   Surname plus social title: *Mr./Ms./Miss/Mrs. Robinson*
Surname plus professional title: *Dr./Prof./Judge/Sen./Capt. Robinson*
Surname only: *Robinson*
Title or kinterm plus given name: *Ms. Blanche/Auntie Blanche/Granny Rose/
Papa John*
Bare kinterm: *mother/mom/mommy/mama, dad/daddy/papa/pop(s)/father, sis(ter),
bro(ther), son, daughter, aunt(ie), uncle, grandma, grandpa*
Given name: *Christine/Christopher*
Standard short form of name: *Chris*
Special "nicknames": *Crisco* (for *Chris*), *Teddy Bear/Ace/Batgirl*

In general, the choices at the top are used reciprocally between those socially quite separated or non-reciprocally up a hierarchy, whereas the choices at the bottom are used reciprocally between people who are close to one another or non-reciprocally down a hierarchy. But the rankings of the choices may be shifted or other individualized options may be developed in particular communities of practice. Indeed, members of a particular CofP may develop their own practices that do not readily slot into this model. I will discuss some examples of other options and alternative interpretations below. English-speaking children are often instructed as to how they should address (and also refer to) various people. (Blum 1997 observes that address and reference norms are explicitly conveyed for adults as well in many Chinese communities of practice.)

The group of address options given in (8) is more general. Again, it may help to think of them as following some greeting:

(8)   Bare title: *coach, professor, doc(tor), judge, councilor, teach(er)*
Respect terms: *sir, ma'am, miss*
Stranger generic names: *Mac, Bud, Buster, Toots*
General: *man, you (guys), girl(friend), dude, lady, ladies, gentlemen, folks, babe, sexy;*
(esp. for children) *tiger, chief, princess, beautiful*
Epithets/insults: *bitch, ho, slut, prick, bastard, slimeball, nerd, dyke, faggot*
Endearments (sometimes preceded by *my*): *honey, dear, sweetie, love, darling,
baby, cutie*

Although bare kinterms appear in display (7), the category of forms used for addressing particular others (those in the designated relation to the speaker) can also be used more generally, and could have been included in display (8). In the southern United States in the mid-twentieth century (and even more recently), it was very common for White people to use *auntie* or *uncle* to (condescendingly) address Black people whom they did not know. The form *Pops* has been hurled by young toughs at old men whom they are hassling, but the form is now dying out. There are other cultural settings where kinterms equivalent to *aunt* and *uncle* are used to address elderly strangers as respectful forms. And *brother* and *sister* are sometimes used positively among African Americans, often to emphasize shared histories, and in church service contexts among some other groups of Americans. The moral: the significance of particular forms of address lies in the history of patterns of usage within and across particular communities of practice and in the connection between addressing and other aspects of social practice that build social relations and mark them with respect and affection or with contempt, condescension, or dislike.

In neither list is it sufficient to think of a cline from more to less respectful or less to more intimate. This is not to deny that respect and power, on the one hand, and intimacy and solidarity, on the other, are indeed crucial components of interactional meaning. This point was made by Roger Brown and Albert Gilman (1960), in an account of address and addressee reference in European languages with a familiar and a more formal second-person pronoun. Their classic paper, "Pronouns of Power and Solidarity," focused on what they called the T/V distinction of second-person pronouns found in many Indo-European languages, though absent for centuries now from English. The "T" form (as in French *tu* or German *du*), which is grammatically singular, is generally described as the more familiar. The "V" form (as in French *vous* or German *Sie*), grammatically plural (and historically semantically plural as well), is described as the more formal. Canonically, the V form is used reciprocally between distant (non-solidary) peers and upwards in a (power-laden) hierarchical relation, whereas the T form is used reciprocally between close peers and downwards in a hierarchical relation. Is the V respectful or deferential? Is the T friendly or condescending? This particular polysemy, produced by the interactional tension and connection between power and solidarity, is pervasive, as Deborah Tannen (1994, this volume) has argued.

In the T/V languages, it is not just the pronominal forms themselves that carry the power/solidarity values, but also verb forms. The verbal form of an imperative, for example, agrees in number with the unexpressed second-person pronominal subject, and thus obligatorily indicates a T (*Sors!* "leave") versus V (*Sortez!*) choice even if there is no overt form referring to the addressee. In contrast, English has only one form for imperatives and even if one has to refer explicitly to the addressee, the second-person pronoun *you* does not make social distinctions. Offering a historical as well as synchronic account, Brown and Gilman observed a progression in the European T/V languages toward increased reliance on the solidarity semantic – increased use of the T form. That progression has certainly continued in the decades since their paper was published, but the distinctions have not vanished, and there are almost certainly still possibilities in some communities of practice using T/V languages for subtle interactions with gender practice in choice of second-person pronouns and verbal form of second-person utterances. Even for the binary T/V split, matters are more complex than the simple split into the power and the solidarity semantic might indicate, especially if our interest is in gender and sexuality.

Historically, in many contexts where heterosexuality was presumed, it was important to preserve pronominal markings of "distance" – i.e. non-intimacy – between women and men during the years when they were presumed to be potential sexual partners. For example, children who used mutual T in their prepubescent years might switch as they matured. Paul Friedrich (1972) offered the Russian example "Petya's grown-up now. He says *vy* to the girls." And a man and a woman whose family relations forbade their intimacy – standardly presumed to be at least potentially sexual – were especially careful to stick with mutual V: for example, within families Brown and Gilman report mutual V most common between a married woman and her husband's brother. Because it was women who were expected to police and control intimacy, it was they who were normatively expected to "give permission" for a move from mutual V-address to mutual T-address. Given the general principle that Brown and Gilman enunciate, that the more powerful member of a dyad is the one able to initiate a move from either mutual V or asymmetric address to mutual T, it is surprising that they do not comment at all on their claim that in cross-sex dyads, it is women who decide whether mutual T is to be permitted. This is, of course, an instance of women's "power" to dispense or withhold sexual favors, a "power" often more symbolic than real. Increased egalitarian ideologies with their emphasis on mutual T-relations have undoubtedly eroded these distinctions, but there are still certainly some gender components of T/V usage. Brown and Gilman do note, however, another instance where the gender and the sexual order introduce some disturbances in their account of the general functioning of the T/V distinction. There is, they say, one particularly "chilling example" that runs counter to their general principle that mutual T, once established, is never withdrawn. German men visiting prostitutes engage in mutual T-address until the "business" is completed, when they revert to mutual V. Here too, practices may well have changed in the decades since their research, but notice that what address did in such cases was to construct the commercial relationship between customer and sex worker as one of temporary intimacy.

What is important to note is that there are many different "flavors" of power – of status differentials – and of solidarity – of connections between peers. These flavors are the product of the character of social practice in different communities of practice. They are often linked to gender or to race or ethnicity or class, but they ultimately derive from social practice. As a consequence, address forms from one individual to another often vary significantly, depending on such factors as the CofP in which the two are encountering one another and the nature of the particular interaction in which they are engaged.

To appreciate the different flavors of power and solidarity, consider a few cases of English address that do not really fit on the lists in (7) and (8). For example, there are people who receive a shortened form of their given name from most acquaintances but the full form, generally considered more distant, from a spouse or some other intimate. Presumably, the full form can construct intimacy precisely because most mere acquaintances do not use it. It marks the specialness of the couple's own intimate CofP. Or, consider Leeds-Hurwitz's (1980) report of a woman promoted in a company and creating address distinctions that subtly constructed her new position of ascendancy over former colleagues and (near) equality with former superiors. For her former colleagues, she developed multiple names (signaling more "familiarity"), whereas they continued simply to use her given name. Her former (male) superiors continued to use her given name, but she dropped the title plus surname forms she had once used to them. She moved to the unusual combination of given name plus surname, perhaps avoiding given name alone either because she had not been explicitly invited to use it, the norm in such changes, or because she found it difficult to break the old taboo. This woman drew on familiar resources but put them together in somewhat novel patterns to help sustain the social challenges of her new form of participation in the workplace CofP.

There are also a number of "off-the-list" ways to combine intimacy with deference to age. In some communities of practice in the southeastern USA, for example, it is still relatively common for young people to use a social title plus given name for an older woman (*Miz Anne*), a form that combines the "respect" of the title with the closeness and familiarity implied by the given name. Although the same formula can be used to address an older man, it is somewhat more common to get social title plus some shortened form of the surname. For example, my father, Charles McConnell, was called *Mr. Mac* by college-age friends when he was in his forties and living in North Carolina. This pattern of title plus shortened surname is much less restricted regionally and is frequently used by children to their teachers of both sexes; the initial of the surname is a frequent "shortening": *Ms. G* (or *Miss G* or *Mrs. G*) or *Mr. G*. Similarly, in some communities of practice, children use *Aunt* or *Uncle* plus first name not only for kin but also for close family friends of their parents' generation or older. A young friend of mine, who's been taught to use respectful titles to adults, recently sent me an e-mail that began "Dear Dr. Sally."

Even when we stay "on the list," it is obvious that many address forms are canonically gendered but that matters are seldom so simple as restricting application or use of a form to a single sex. In English, first names are often (though not always) gendered, social titles and kinterms are gendered, and there is considerable gendered differentiation in the use of other forms. Here we will focus on cases that seem to indicate something about ongoing changes in the gender order.

Bare surname, for example, is still far more common among men and boys than among women and girls, but there are changes afoot. (The still prevalent expectation that women will change surnames when they marry probably helps sustain the sense that surnames are more firmly attached to men than to women. But that expectation is certainly weakening, as more women retain birth names or join with partners willing to effect a common change to a new name for the new family unit.) Surnames are not part of address within the nuclear family (not these days, when women no longer use title plus surnames in addressing their husbands as was the custom in some English-speaking circles in the nineteenth century), and the surname is associated with the move from the nuclear family to other communities of practice and with leaving babyhood behind. It is often used reciprocally as a form of address (and of reference) in communities of practice where relationships focus on camaraderie and collective performance under pressure rather than emotional intimacy. (Non-reciprocal bare surname use is also associated with such communities of practice when they are hierarchically organized. In the military, for example, the higher-ranking individual may use surname to those below and receive title plus surname. Hicks Kennard (2001) offers examples from women in the US Marine Corps.) Reciprocal bare surname address is certainly increasingly used among women; what is noteworthy is that such usage is especially common in communities of practice such as sports teams (or the military) where the relationships called for are those for which such address is especially apt, where there is a friendship of equals and "sentimentality" is excluded. That this pattern of address is increasing among women, for whom its main provenance in earlier generations seems to have been nursing units, testifies to the increase in women's participation in communities of practice of the sort that promote mutual dependence and teamwork but eschew anything that might suggest vulnerability.

Of course, bare surname address and reference are not completely confined to arenas such as playing fields and hospital floors. A friend of mine refers to her now dead husband this way, and apparently that was how she and almost everyone other than his family of origin addressed and referred to him most frequently. Such cases, however, are exceptional; a young woman whose relationship with a young man moves from simple comradeship to heterosexual romance often finds herself also moving away from initial bare surname address to given name and/or special names and endearments. Bare surname, then, is not simply gendered; the gender differentiation in its use follows from its relation to kinds of social practice and social relations, and changes in the gender patterns of its use are part and parcel of changes in the content of gender practice.

The jocular use of epithets in address – "It's great to see you, you old sonofabitch!" – is in some ways similar to the use of bare surname, especially when the usage is reciprocal. It is, however, more age-sensitive, with peak use among young men, and more situationally restricted, being paradigmatically associated with male locker-room or fraternity registers and at least normatively censored in mixed-sex and general public settings (like swearing in general). Like bare surnames (and swearing), however, jocular epithets are becoming more and more commonly used by young women to their close friends and siblings (see, for example, Hinton 1992).

Less jocular (and non-reciprocal) usage of the epithets that are standardly thought of as applied to females is associated with such contexts as male construction workers yelling at female strangers walking by (on street calls generally, see Gardner 1981; Kissling 1991; Kissling and Kramarae 1991). The only instances reported by Leanne Hinton's students surveyed in 1991 of a man's calling a woman *bitch* were from strangers (see also (3b), an example reported to me by a young woman I know) – i.e. the addresser and addressee are not within a common community of practice. Address from strangers to women often also uses "complimenting" general terms referring to appearance, such as *beautiful* or *sexy*. Just as "insults" are often really positive marks of intimacy, such "compliments" are often really negative marks of objectification and condescension. Sometimes hostile "feminine" as well as specifically homophobic epithets are used in name-calling as well as in reference by men to harass other men. (See Cameron 1997 for use of epithets with homophobic content in reference to absent men to enforce heterosexual gender conformity.)

Epithets, often quite overtly sexual and classified as obscene, are frequently used for reference in certain communities of practice by men talking among themselves about women. On many all-male sports teams, for example, such references to women are extremely common and may serve both to display a kind of superiority to women and to effect "bonding" via shared "othering" and denigration of women. In some such communities of practice, the men using these terms routinely for reference to women would never think of using them in address or in reference in the mixed-sex communities of practice to which they belong. But men are not the only insulters. Abusive referential terms are sometimes used in communities of practice by women talking about other women who are not there to defend themselves. In the woman–woman uses, however, the forms tend to be personally directed, whereas in a number of all-male groups the forms are used to refer to virtually any woman (at least, any female age-mate). Of course, women do sometimes "bond" by speaking negatively of men; a brilliant cartoon in a recent *New Yorker* magazine shows some women gathered around a water cooler, with one saying: "I'd love to join you in saying nasty things about men but I used to be one."

The reports I have gotten of this kind of anti-male "bonding" phenomenon among women speak primarily of labelings that characterize men in general or particular men, many of these characterizations being focused on the men's (alleged) sexual mistreatment of women or their general inconsiderateness. These contrasts point to the somewhat different place of cross-sex hostility in the social practices of all-female and of all-male communities of practice. The negative labeling of women that some groups of men are using to bond tends to be backgrounded, a matter of the default forms of reference some of them use for female individuals of whom they are implicitly dismissive. For women, the negative labeling tends to be more explicitly descriptive or evaluative: they are characterizing the men in a disapproving way, taking men as their topic rather than relegating cross-sex derogation to the background. (These comments are based on reports from my own and others' students as well as on other kinds of informal observations. Systematic study of actual usage in this arena is not easy to undertake, given the relatively "private" nature of such exchanges.)

In the past several decades there have been a number of studies of abusive terms referring to or used to address women (Schultz 1975 and Penelope [Stanley] 1977 are classic references; Sutton 1995 is a more recent study), many of which note the predominance of words that have sexual allusions. Some studies also look at abusive terms designating men (e.g. Baker 1975; Risch

1987; James 1996). Interestingly, some terms (e.g. *bitch, slut, bastard*) are becoming less strongly gendered in two ways: they can now apply to both sexes, and women use them far more than they once did, both seriously and in joking contexts among themselves. In spite of this, James (1996) still found strong gendered stereotypes for referents and for users of most such epithets, which suggests they still convey gendered meanings, though perhaps more complex and somewhat different ones than they once did. According to Sutton (1995), a significant number of young women report using *ho* affirmatively to one another (a smaller number have also reclaimed *bitch*) – and in jocular contexts, also forms like *slut* and *dork*. These reports fit with the accounts my own students offer of the evolving scene. Most studies have relied on self-reports of usage and interpretation. Just how well such accounts reflect the range of actual practices remains unclear.

Nicknaming can be important in certain communities of practice. Many all-male sports teams or living units such as fraternities bestow special nicknames on new members, names that are virtually always used in the CofP and are often used in encounters between members in other contexts. Some all-female and some mixed communities of practice have such naming practices as well. Some evidence suggests, however, both that the practices are more common in all-male groups and that group-bestowed nicknames are much more frequently used among male teammates or fraternity members than they are in the parallel female or mixed communities of practice. Nicknames are often based on a person's "real" name (like *Crisco* for *Chris* in display (7)) but can come from other sources, often with a special meaning for a particular CofP.

The general terms in display (8) are often used reciprocally among intimates as well as with strangers. They are much more common from and to men but are beginning to be used among women; *dude*, for example, is by no means any longer confined to male addressees or male addressers, and even *man* is now occasionally addressed to young women (see Hinton 1992). Such forms, most of which began with males as their only referents, seem now to signal casual good will. In the plural *you guys* is now widely used for group address and second-person reference, no matter what the composition of the group. My mother (in her late eighties) and I (in my sixties) were recently so addressed by a young male server in a restaurant. (The singular *guy* is still pretty strongly male-gendered.) The formality of *ladies* and the frequent condescension of age-inappropriate *girls* help explain why *guys* has become so popular even for female-only referents.

But women are beginning to turn not only to originally male forms for such casual but friendly, though impersonal, address. For example, in some communities of practice, especially those whose members are mainly African American, *girl* can readily be used to adult female addressees by both other women and men to express a supportive and friendly connection. This use is spreading, probably because of its occurrence in such contexts as US advertisements featuring women basketball stars and popular music lyrics. The form *girlfriend* as a term of address is even more restricted to communities of practice in which African Americans predominate. Among women, it can express affection and ongoing co-membership in some emotionally important community of practice. So used, the form is warm but casual. Importantly, the affection being expressed is that of a non-sexual friendship, which depends on the general referential properties of *girlfriend* in American English. Unlike *boyfriend*, which must mean a male romantic interest (and can be so used by both straight women and gay men), *girlfriend* in reference or description can mean either romantic/sexual object (this use is common to straight men and lesbians) or important close friend. This latter use is only open to women – a man who speaks of *my girlfriend* thereby indicates a romantic interest, perhaps because of heterosexual assumptions that relations of men and women are always erotically charged. Although many European American women do use *girlfriend* to refer to their close women friends, they seldom draw on it as an address form. There are attested uses of *girlfriend* by a White lesbian to address her lover, but this use is not the same as the asexual friendship use among African American women. Will this friendship use of *girlfriend* in address spread to other American women, as so many other social and linguistic practices originating in African American communities have? (Note, for example, the appropriation of *yo* and *dude*.) We may eventually see such a spread, but at the moment, the address signals not only warm woman-to-woman friendship but also underscores shared racial heritage. African American men also sometimes use the bare term *girlfriend* in addressing women who may be relative strangers to express good will and to underscore shared heritage; of course, its particular significance depends very much on other features of the setting in which the exchange occurs. It is not surprising, however, that African American men do not use *boyfriend* as a casually friendly form of address to one another; its erotic charge in male–male referential usage spills over to address.

Forms like *honey* and *dear*, classified as endearments in (8), have been widely discussed. Just as epithets do not always insult, so endearments do not always express affection. They can do so, of course, when used in a CofP between intimates, but they can also condescend or be otherwise problematic (see, for example, Wolfson and Manes 1980), especially from a man to a woman he does not know well (or perhaps not at all). Most of them are widely used from adults (especially women) to children, even children they don't know. And older women sometimes use them to much younger men who are strangers to them, in what is often described as a "maternal" way. But their condescension potential, especially in address from men to women, has been widely noted and thus many men now avoid them outside of genuinely intimate contexts. (Except to very young boys, American men very seldom use them to other males.) There are, however, still English-using communities of practice in Britain where some of these endearments apparently function in much the same way as general terms like *guys* or *dude* or *folks*. They can come from strangers of either sex to addressees of either sex with no suggestion of anything other than light-hearted friendliness (and the absence of "stuffiness" or undue reserve).

The respect terms *sir* and *ma'am* show considerable local variation in their use. In the American southeast, they are frequently used by children to parents, a very intimate relation. As respect forms, the terms are not equivalent; not only does *ma'am* compete with *miss*, but neither of these feminine variants has the same authoritative impact that *sir* carries (and *ma'am* is far more restricted than *sir* regionally). The need to mark deference to authority held by females has led to some interesting usages, with women police officers (McElhinny 1995), for example, occasionally receiving the normally masculine *sir*, presumably because the femaleness of the more standard *ma'am* tends to limit its ability to confer real authority on the addressee.

Of course, a taxonomy of the kind given for English, already strained as we have seen in organizing English speakers' address practices, will be even less adequate for other languages. For example, Japanese has the respectful affix *-san*, which can be added to various terms of address (e.g. names, kinterms). It also seems more common in Japan than in English-speaking countries for adults in a family to call each other by the terms designating their parental roles (though one certainly can find in the USA many couples who call each other "mom" and "dad" or something equivalent). In addition, Japanese has a number of second-person pronouns, a couple of which (*anata* and *anta*) are used by both women and men, and several that are rather brusque or "rough" in flavor and used primarily by men. Among married couples, wives are apparently more respectful to husbands than vice versa. Women seem to be avoiding very informal forms such as a plain first name and, as they do generally, the second-person pronouns *kimi* and *omae*. A wife's first name + *san* to her husband may be matched by his plain first name or even nickname to her, and use of forms like *kimi* and *omae*, which he would be unlikely to use to a peer. Both often use parental terms (*otosan* "father" and *okasan* "mother" are most common, but *papa* and *mama* are also used). (Ogawa and Shibamoto Smith 1997 discuss these purported patterns, drawing on Lee 1976, a study based on self-reports by Japanese couples living in the USA, and Kanemura 1993, a survey of Japanese women students reporting on their parents' practices.) Do such gender asymmetries persist among younger married couples in Japan? How do different address choices function in constructing different kinds of marital relationships? Such questions have not yet been addressed, at least not in English-language reports. What Ogawa and Shibamoto Smith demonstrate is that the patterns can be called on outside heterosexual marriage. They examined address (and also first- and third-person references) used in a documentary film by two gay men in a committed relationship, finding that in many ways the two men labeled themselves and the other in much the same ways as do the canonical husband and wife.

Families, including non-traditional families, are of course very important kinds of communities of practice. For many children, they are initially the only community of practice in which the child participates. Hinton (1992) asked entering college students at the University of California, Berkeley, to report on their address to parents and to siblings. The informal but not especially inti-mate *mom* and *dad* were the overwhelming favorites for addressing parents reported by both sexes (83 per cent of women and 89 per cent of men reported *mom*, 79 per cent of women and 90 per cent of men reported *dad*), but the women used both more diminutives (*mommy, daddy*) and more of the formal terms (*mother* and *father*, with *father* a vanishingly small usage from both sexes as an address form but *mother* used by about 14 per cent of the women as compared to only 4 per cent of the men). Both sexes were somewhat more likely to report use of a diminutive form to the opposite-sex parent, but the striking contrast was sex of user. Of the women, 33 per cent and 45 per cent reported using *mommy* and *daddy* respectively, whereas only 16 per cent and 12 per cent of the men admitted to these uses (they were, of course, reporting their current patterns, not recalling earlier uses). Many of the students re-ported multiple usages; it could be illuminating to see under what conditions a particular form was chosen. There is also an "other" category, but it is not broken down by sex of speaker or by type of form (first name? endearment?). Hinton did not ask about address from parents, but there certainly are conse-quences for learning gender practice in a household where a male child is addressed as *son* or *big guy* and his sister is called *honey* or *beautiful*. Given name or a shortened form thereof is the most common form of address to children from adults, including their parents, but other options exist and can enter into social practice within the family in many interesting ways: for example, the full name is sometimes used for "disciplining" a child who is not doing what the parent wants.

As children move beyond their natal families into other communities of practice, they encounter new address options, but they may also bring with them expectations and interpretations built on their own family's practices. A child who uses *mom* or *mommy* may be shocked by a playmate's use of first name, apparently assuming a kind of egalitarian relation, or of *mother*, appar-ently rather "stiff" or formal. Boys especially may get mocked for *mommy* or *daddy*, learning that *mom* and *dad* are considered more adult and appropriately masculine choices. There can be problems articulating address choices with other family members in a community of practice other than the family itself. A sibling may (unwittingly or deliberately) reveal a family pet name that a kid has left at home as too "childish" for school contexts. And one of my students reported that her mother and father work in the same office, where he uses endearments to her whereas she uses his first name only as the fitting choice for the workplace (and finds his endearments somewhat annoying – not sur-prisingly he is above her in the office hierarchy).

Because address forms are optional and generally admit some variation from a particular addresser to a particular addressee, their occurrence is always potentially significant. Address and addressee-reference options not only very frequently signal gendered identities and relations of interlocutors, but they often do considerable work in giving content to gender performance.

5 "Enough About You, Let's Talk About Me": Self-reference and Gender

In English there are no distinctions of gender or other social relations conveyed by the first person (*I*, *me*, *my*), but this is not always the case. Japanese, for example, provides examples of first- and second-person pronouns that are differently used by women and men and are interpreted as gendered. As Ogawa and Smith (1997) observe, Japanese speakers using first-person pronouns have a number of options, only some of which are gender-neutral. The forms *watakushi* and *watashi* are used by both sexes but the abbreviated *atakushi* and *atashi* are interpreted as feminine, whereas the abbreviated *washi*, now relatively seldom used (and mainly from older men), is interpreted as masculine (and overbearing). The forms *boku* and *ore* are listed as used by male speakers, and *atai* as a "lower-class, vulgar" women's form of self-reference. The form *jibun*, often translated as English *self* and used as a reflexive, is also sometimes used for self-reference by men and is, according to Ogawa and Smith, associated with military and other strongly hierarchical workplaces. Once again, it is apparent that the real significance of these varied forms of self-reference emerges only from their use in particular communities of practice and their association with particular kinds of social practice. And once again, there is evidence that gender norms are being challenged and changed in various ways. For example, *boku* is increasingly used for self-reference by adolescent girls, who are rejecting certain features of traditional normative girlhood, including even competing with boys in school. Reynolds (1990) reports that *boku* has spread to college-age girls and even to adult women in certain contexts. Interestingly, the speakers themselves seem quite aware that their *boku* usage is associated with certain kinds of social practice. Citing Jugaku (1979), she reports: "Girls who were interviewed in a TV program explain that they cannot compete with boys in classes, in games or in fights with *watashi*" (Reynolds 1990: 140).

As Ide (1990) observes, however, the fact that Japanese often dispenses with pronominal forms altogether (it is what syntacticians call a "pro-drop" language) means that interactions conducted in Japanese often proceed with rather fewer explicit labelings of people than would be found in comparable interactions conducted in English. In addition to imperatives, casual questions in English can omit a second-person subject (*Going to lunch soon?*) and "postcard register" allows missing first-person pronouns (*Having a wonderful time!*), which are sometimes also omitted by some speakers in casual speech (*I've* encountered this in phone conversations with certain people). Third-person references are omitted only in severely limited contexts such as answers to questions in which the third-person reference has been explicitly given, a fact about English that is of some importance in considering gendering of person references, discussed briefly in the following section. Languages with no gender distinction in the first-person pronoun but with grammatical gender agreement patterns may produce the effect of gendered self-reference through gender concord: French speakers who want to utter the equivalent of the English *I am happy* must say either *je suis heureuse* (feminine) or *je suis heureux* (masculine), thus making it as hard (or perhaps even harder) to speak gender-neutrally of the self in French as it is to speak gender-neutrally of another in English.

Even when pronouns are not themselves gendered, the question of who is "included" with the speaker by a first-person plural reference can have gender implications. Languages that grammatically mark the distinction between first person inclusive and exclusive interpretations allow for tracking of affiliations. Meyerhoff (1996) discusses Bislama, a language spoken on the Melanesian islands of Vanuatu, and argues that the choice of the inclusive *yumi* rather than the exclusive form at least sometimes is made to emphasize shared gender identity. Pronominal choice also maps boundary-drawing between Melanesian and non-Melanesian and among various family groups within the Melanesian communities.

It is possible to talk about me and you without using explicitly first- or second-person forms. Although third-person expressions generally are used to refer to people (or things) distinct from the speaker or addressee of the utterance, they can sometimes be used for speaker reference, as in (9), or addressee reference, as in (10):

(9) a. *Mommy* wants you to go to sleep now. [uttered by mother to child]
     b. Remember that *Mrs. Robinson* wants you all to send *her* postcards this summer. [uttered by teacher to kindergarten students]

(10) a. Does *my little darling* want some more spinach? [caretaker to child]
      b. *Joanie* had better be a good girl at school. [caretaker to child]
      c. *His royal highness* will have to make *his* own coffee today. [disgruntled wife to husband]

In most Anglophone communities, such uses occur mainly from adults (especially parents or other primary caretakers and teachers) to children, although they can also occur in jocular contexts between adults (as suggested by (10c)). Since the parent–child model is often called on for romance by English speakers, such usages are also sometimes encountered in the very specialized communities of practice constituted by an intimate couple (straight or gay). They are not unrelated to the playful use of alter personalities in love relations discussed in Langford (1997), who comments "on the secrecy and 'childishness' which characterizes these private cultures of love . . . and their relations to 'adult' love and the 'public' world of 'adulthood'." In Japanese, however, the use of third-person forms for self- or addressee-reference is apparently much less marked (see discussion below). English speakers too can use third-person forms for self- and addressee-reference without the "childish" flavor of the above examples. For example, Hicks Kennard (2001) reports female marine recruits being constrained to use third person for both self- and addressee-reference when speaking to their drill instructor, along with the respectful *ma'am* as an address form. In sharp contrast, the senior drill instructor uses the canonical pronominal forms for first- and second-person reference and a (non-reciprocal) surname as an address form:

(11) R: Recruit Moore [self] requests to know if she [self] can speak with Senior Drill Instructor Staff Sergeant Mason [addressee ref] when she [addressee ref] has time, ma'am [address form]
      SDI: What if I tell you I'm gonna go home, Moore?

In this case, the practice seems to be functioning to depersonalize and subjugate the recruit, to wash her of her own sense of agency.

6 Gendering

Even where the nominal content might seem purely descriptive, there can be much riding on whether or not a particular gendered label is attached to a particular individual. Thirty or more years ago linguists discussed the possibility of understanding a sentence like (12a) as equivalent to either (12b) or (12c); in that era, few people entertained (12c) as a serious possibility:

(12) a. My cousin is no longer a boy.
      b. My cousin is now a man [having become an adult].
      c. My cousin is now a girl [having changed sexes].

Although the possibility of sex changes is far more salient now than it was then, most people still fail to entertain (12c) as a possible interpretation of (12a). Judith Butler points out that the gendering process often starts with a doctor's uttering a sentence like (13a), a process that "shifts the infant from an 'it' to a 'she' or a 'he'" (Butler 1993: 7). Either (13a) or (13b) is expected as an answer from new parents to that common question, (13c):

(13) a. It's a girl.
      b. It's a boy.
      c. What is it?

The expected answers to (13c) strongly suggest that a baby's gender label is taken to be of primary importance in characterizing it: answers like those in (14) are virtually unthinkable in most social contexts:

(14) a. It's a baby who scored 10 on the Apgar test.
      b. It's my child.
      c. It's a two-month old.

In English and in many other languages, the first labels applied to a child attribute gender to it. Thus begins the ongoing process of "girling" (or "boying"), with relatively little space for creating just "kids." There is some resistance, however. A recent birth announcement card has "It's a" and a picture of a baby on the front with a marker covering its genitals; inside the card continues with "baby."

English, of course, enforces a gender distinction in third-person singular pronouns. One thing this means is that use of a singular personal pronoun carries a presumption of sex attribution. I say to a colleague: "One of my students missed the final because of a sick kid and no babysitter available." The colleague responds: "Well, did you tell her that is not acceptable?" My colleague is assuming that the student is female. If I ascribe maleness to the student and want to make that clear I might say "It's a he, actually," perhaps implying a rebuke to my colleague for the apparent assumption that anyone responsible for childcare is female. On the other hand, if there is no conflict between my colleague's presumption of sex and my assessment of the situation, I may well fail to point out that there was a presumptive leap made and thus may contribute in some measure to sustaining the gendered division of labor that supports that leap.

It is actually very difficult in English and other languages with gendered third-person pronouns to talk about a third person without ascribing sex to them – and virtually impossible to do so over an extended period. This is why Sarah Caudwell's wonderful mystery series featuring Professor Hilary Tamar, to whom sex cannot be attributed, had to be written with Hilary as a first-person narrator. (See Livia 2001 for discussion of this and many other interesting literary cases where gender attribution is an issue.) Many proper names and nominals ascribe sex, but it is the pronouns that really cause trouble because continued repetition of a name such as *Hilary* or a full nominal such as *my professor* generally seems odd. Linguists have suggested that such repetition often suggests a second individual, which is one reason why people standardly use pronouns for at least most later references. There is some use of *they* as a singular pronoun; it is quite common in generic or similar contexts, as in (15a, b), and is increasing its use in reference to specific individuals, as in (15c, d):

(15) a. If anyone calls, tell *them* I'll be back by noon and get *their* name.
      b. Every kid who turned in *their* paper on time got a gold star.
      c. Someone with a funny accent called, but *they* didn't leave *their* name.
      d. A friend of Kim's got *their* parents to buy *them* a Miata.

It is still unlikely to be used for a specific individual in many circumstances: if, for example, both interlocutors are likely to have attributed (the same) sex to that individual.

The choice of referring expressions plays an important role in gender construction. For example, kinterms in English (and many other languages) are mostly very gendered. *Wife* and *husband* are much more often used in the course of everyday practice than *spouse, brother* and *sister* are far ahead of *sib(ling)*. The gender-neutral *kid, child,* and *baby* are pretty common and can be used with a possessive to refer to someone's offspring (*Lee's kid* or *my baby*), but *daughter* and *son* are probably more common, especially since they can be freely used for adults, unlike the colloquial gender-neutral forms, which tend to suggest youth. *Mother/mom* and *father/dad* are much more common for singular reference than *parent,* and *aunt, uncle, niece,* and *nephew* have no gender-neutral alternatives; *cousin* names the only kin relation for which English offers only a gender-neutral form. There are, of course, languages that have much more richly elaborated kinship terminology. Distinctions of relative age may be marked in sibling terminology, and there may be different expressions for mother's sister and father's sister or mother's brother and father's brother. And, as is well known, it is the social relations and not the strictly biological that count most in some languages: an expression more or less equivalent to English *aunt,* for example, might designate not only sisters of one's parents but other women tied to the family in some way and construed as having somewhat similar kinds of rights and responsibilities for one. Even in English the social relations typically prevail in families in which children are adopted or in which children come from different marriages. (We noted above some uses of kinterms in English address.)

There are not many systematic studies of how often references to people are gendered and what difference this makes, but there is some relevant research. Barrie Thorne (1993) observed that "boys and girls" was far and away the most common general group form of address in the two elementary schools where she conducted ethnographic research, and that many of the teachers made heavy use of the gendered labels. She also cites research by Spencer Cahill (1987) that suggests that the gendered terms are used by school staff in opposition to the gender-neutral (and disapproving) *baby*: "you're a big girl/boy now, not a baby." Thus Cahill argues that children learn to claim the gendered identities as part of claiming their new relative maturity. Thorne herself observed that "[b]y fourth grade the terms 'big girl' and 'big boy' have largely disappeared, but teachers continue to equate mature behavior with grown-up gendered identities by using more formal and ironic terms of address, like 'ladies and gentlemen'" (Thorne 1993: 35). Of course, the sex-neutral *kid* is fairly common and may in some communities of practice outpace *girl* and *boy* for referring to children or young adults. For adults, however, *woman* and *man* are much more commonplace than *person* (which, unlike *kid,* is not only gender-neutral but also age-neutral) for referring to particular individuals.

In the 1970s there was considerable discussion of the use of *girl* for mature females and the condescension it frequently conveyed (as in *I'll have my girl call your girl*). There are many common practices that conspire to link femaleness with childishness (e.g. Goffmann 1976 argued that the male–female relation was modeled on the parent–child in media depictions), and it is probably no accident that the word *girl* once simply meant "child." Nonetheless the use of the label *girl* to refer to adult females (and, as we saw above, to address them) is by no means always inappropriately juvenilizing. In some communities of practice, *gal*, originating from a variant pronunciation of *girl*, is being used to try to provide a female equivalent of *guy*, a form appropriate for casual conversation that can happily apply to a teenager but can equally well be used to refer to a middle-aged or older man. Says science writer Natalie Angier, obviously not wanting to choose between the more serious-sounding *woman* and the sometimes too youthful *girl*, "I write with the assumption that my average reader is a gal, a word, by the way that I use liberally throughout the book [on women's biology], because I like it and because I keep thinking, against all evidence, that it is on the verge of coming back into style" (Angier 1999: xv). In spite of Angier's hopefulness, *gal* still tends to be regionally and stylistically restricted, and some readers (including me!) found her liberal use of it rather jarring. Of course the fact that the plural *guys* may be widely used for female referents and addressees complicates the picture. Even in the plural *guys* is restricted: someone who asks *how many guys were there?* is not inquiring about the number of people in general but about the number of men.

The bottom line is that it is still somewhat easier to be relatively age-neutral and informal when speaking of or to males than when speaking of or to females. Will *guys* become more completely sex-indefinite, and bring counting and singular uses under a sex-indefinite umbrella? Or will some label like *gal* widen its range?

The issue of sex attribution that pronominal choice forces in English can become particularly charged when there are challenges to conventional binary gender dichotomies. Transgendered and transsexual people generally want to be referred to by the pronoun consistent with the identity which they currently claim. Those resisting moves from initial gender attributions (former friends or colleagues, unsympathetic family members) may do so by persisting in the pronominal choice consistent with the early attribution. Stories that others tell of such lives must make choices: to use the pronoun consistent with the person's publicly claimed identity at a particular time may well lead to use of different pronouns at different stages, thus visibly/audibly fracturing personal identity. When the identity an individual claims is not the identity others are willing to recognize, pronouns are one turf on which such conflicts get played out. Even those who simply resist gender conformity in their dress or behavior may find others commenting critically on that resistance by derisively using *it* in reference to them. Of course, people who are resisting gender norms can themselves use pronouns creatively as part of constructing alternative identities. Some years ago, Esther Newton (1972) noted that male drag queens often spoke of one another using *she* and *her*, the pronoun fitting the performed identity. Like the Hindi-speaking *hijras* studied by Kira Hall and Veronica O'Donovan

(1996), they could also insult one another by using male forms of address and reference.

Hindi is a language with grammatical gender, which offers further gendering possibilities that go beyond the pronominal and nominal labels on which this paper has focused. Livia (1997) offers a compelling account of the importance of grammatical gender as a resource for transsexuals who face a dilemma in articulating new identities within the communities of practice to which they belong (or aspire to belong). Drawing on several autobiographies of French-speaking male to female transsexuals, Livia notes that each of the authors, although maintaining lifelong femaleness, "alternates between masculine and feminine gender concord with regard to herself, indicating that the situation was in fact far more complex" (Livia 1997: 352). In the original French edition of Herculine Barbin's (1978) memoir, grammatical concord in the first person is predominantly feminine in the earlier sections and progressively becomes more masculine over the course of the "discovery" of Herculine's "true" identity.

7 Conclusion

Labeling enters into gender construction within and across communities of practice in a host of different and complex ways, and no single paper (or even book) could possibly really cover this topic. I have tried, however, to point to some of the possibilities that should be kept in mind in investigating the linguistic texture of gender construction by specific individuals or in particular communities of practice or institutions. As we have seen, the particularities of the linguistic resources and practices readily available to speakers are critical for how labeling connects to gender. At the same time, the function of particular labels depends on how they are deployed in social practice generally and their connection to gender practice in particular.

Of course, speakers do many creative things. The following exchange comes from an interview conducted by an undergraduate student of mine with a gay male friend of his in the spring of 2001 (used with permission of both parties):

Interviewer: Do you realize that you call me and other gay friends *girl* a lot?
Interviewee: Yes, but it is special for a few of you guys. And it's spelled differently.
Interviewer: Yeah?
Interviewee: With a "U." G-U-R-L. [clapping hands happily]
Interviewer: Awesome.
Interviewee: And whatever, because it doesn't mean you are like a female. It's for someone who is a fierce faggot.
Interviewer: "Fierce faggot?" [Laughing hysterically]
Interviewee: Hell yeah. You know what I mean. A fierce faggot. Someone who is that fabulous and fucking knows it.

REFERENCES

Anderson, Benedict 1983: *Imagined Communities: Reflections on the Origin and Spread of Nationalism*. New York and London: Verso.

Angier, Natalie 1999: *Woman: An Intimate Geography*. Boston and New York: Houghton Mifflin.

Baker, Robert 1975: "Pricks" and "chicks": A plea for "persons". In Robert Baker and Frederick Elliston, *Philosophy and Sex*. New York: Prometheus Books, pp. 45–64.

Barbin, Herculine 1978: *Herculine Barbin, dite Alexina B., presente par Michel Foucault*. Paris: Gallimard.

Bernsten, Jan 1994: What's her name? Forms of address in Shona. Paper read at Cultural Performances: Third Berkeley Women and Language Conference, at Berkeley, California.

Blum, Susan D. 1997: Naming practices and the power of words in China. *Language in Society* 26(3): 357–80.

Brown, Roger and Gilman, Albert 1960: Pronouns of power and solidarity. In Thomas A. Sebeok (ed.) *Style in Language*. Cambridge, MA: MIT Press, pp. 253–76.

Butler, Judith 1993: *Bodies That Matter*. New York: Routledge.

Cahill, Spencer E. 1987: Language practices and self-definition: the case of gender identity acquisition. *Sociological Quarterly* 27: 295–311.

Cameron, Deborah 1997: Performing gender identity: Young men's talk and the construction of heterosexual masculinity. In Sally Johnson and Ulrike Hanna Meinhof (eds) *Language and Masculinity*. Oxford: Blackwell, pp. 47–64.

Eble, Connie 1996: *Slang and Sociability: In-group Language among College Students*. Chapel Hill and London: University of North Carolina Press.

Eckert, Penelope 2000. *Linguistic Variation as Social Practice: The Linguistic Construction of Social Meaning in Belten High*. Oxford: Blackwell.

Eckert, Penelope and McConnell-Ginet, Sally 1992a: Communities of practice: Where language, gender and power all live. In Kira Hall, Mary Bucholtz, and Birch Moonwomon (eds) *Locating Power: Proceedings of the Second Berkeley Women and Language Conference*. Berkeley, CA: Berkeley Women and Language Group, University of California, pp. 89–99.

Eckert, Penelope and McConnell-Ginet, Sally 1992b: Think practically and look locally: Language and gender as community-based practice. *Annual Review of Anthropology* 21: 461–90.

Eckert, Penelope and McConnell-Ginet, Sally 1995: Constructing meaning, constructing selves: Snapshots of language, gender and class from Belten High. In Kira Hall and Mary Bucholtz (eds) *Gender Articulated: Language and the Socially Constructed Self*. New York: Routledge, pp. 469–507.

Eckert, Penelope and McConnell-Ginet, Sally 1999: New generalizations and explanations in language and gender research. *Language in Society* 28(2): 185–201.

Eckert, Penelope and McConnell-Ginet, Sally (forthcoming): *Language and Gender: The Social Construction of Meaning*. Cambridge: Cambridge University Press.

Friedrich, Paul 1972: Social context and semantic feature: The Russian pronominal usage. In John J. Gumperz and Dell Hymes (eds) *Directions in Sociolinguistics*. Oxford: Blackwell, pp. 270–300.

Gardner, Carol Brooks 1981: Passing by: Street remarks, address rights, and the urban female. *Sociological Inquiry* 50: 328–56.

Goffman, Erving 1976: Gender advertisements. *Studies in the Anthropology of Visual Communication* 3(2): 69–154.

Hall, Kira and O'Donovan, Veronica 1996: Shifting gender positions among Hindi-speaking Hijras. In Victoria Bergvall, Janet M. Bing, and Alice F. Freed (eds) *Rethinking Language and Gender Research: Theory and Practice*. London and New York: Longman, pp. 228–66.

Hicks Kennard, Catherine 2001: Female drill instructors and the negotiation of power through pronouns. Paper given at the Annual Meetings of the Linguistic Society of America, Washington DC, January 2001.

Hinton, Leanne 1992: Sex difference in address terminology in the 1990s. Paper read at Locating Power: Second Berkeley Women and Language Conference, at Berkeley, California.

Holmes, Janet and Meyerhoff, Miriam 1999: The community of practice: Theories and methodologies in language and gender research. *Language in Society* 28(2): 173–84.

Ide, Sachiko 1990: Person references of Japanese and American children. In Sachiko Ide and Naomi H. McGloin (eds) *Aspects of Japanese Women's Language*. Tokyo: Kurosio Publishers, pp. 43–62.

James, Deborah 1996: Derogatory terms for women and men: A new look. Paper read at Gender and Belief Systems: Fourth Berkeley Women and Language Conference, at Berkeley, California.

Jugaku, A. 1979: *Nihongo to Onna [Japanese and Women]*. Tokyo: Iwanamisyoten.

Kanemura, Hasumi 1993: Ninsho Daimeishi Kosho.5-gatsu Rinji Zokango: Sehai no Joseigo Nihon no joseigo. *Nihongogaku* 12: 109–19.

Kissling, Elizabeth Arveda 1991: Street harassment: The language of sexual terrorism. *Discourse and Society* 2(4): 451–60.

Kissling, Elizabeth Arveda and Kramarae, Cheris 1991: "Stranger compliments": The interpretation of street remarks. *Women's Studies in Communication* (Spring): 77–95.

Langford, Wendy 1997: "Bunnikins, I love you snugly in your warren": Voices from subterranean cultures of love. In Keith Harvey and Celia Shalom (eds) *Language and Desire: Encoding Sex, Romance and Intimacy*. London and New York: Routledge, pp. 170–85.

Lave, Jean and Wenger, Etienne 1991: *Situated Learning: Legitimate Peripheral Participation*. Cambridge: Cambridge University Press.

Lee, Motoko Y. 1976: The married woman's status and role as reflected in Japanese: An exploratory sociolinguistic study. *Signs: Journal of Women in Culture and Society* 1(1): 991–9.

Leeds-Hurwitz, Wendy 1980: *The Use and Analysis of Uncommon Forms of Address: A Business Example*. (Working Papers in Sociolinguistics, vol. 80.) Austin, TX: Southwest Educational Development Laboratory.

Livia, Anna 1997: Disloyal to masculine identity: Linguistic gender and liminal identity in French. In Anna Livia and Kira Hall (eds) *Queerly Phrased: Language, Gender, and Sexuality*. New York and Oxford: Oxford University Press, pp. 349–68.

Livia, Anna 2001: *Pronoun Envy: Literary Uses of Linguistic Gender*. Oxford and New York: Oxford University Press.

March, Kathryn (forthcoming): *Words and Words of Tamang Women in Highland Nepal*. Ithaca, NY: Cornell University Press.

McConnell-Ginet, Sally 2002: "Queering" semantics: Definitional struggles. In

Kathryn Campbell-Kibler, Robert Podesva, Sarah Roberts, and Andrew Wong (eds) *Language and Sexuality*. Palo Alto, CA: CSLI, pp. 137–60.

McElhinny, Bonnie S. 1995: Challenging hegemonic masculinities: Female and male police officers handling domestic violence. In Kira Hall and Mary Bucholtz (eds) *Gender Articulated: Language and the Socially Constructed Self*. New York and London: Routledge, pp. 217–43.

Meyerhoff, Miriam 1996: My place or yours: Constructing intergroup boundaries in Bislama. Paper read at Gender and Belief Systems: Fourth Berkeley Women and Language Conference, at Berkeley, California.

Meyerhoff, Miriam 2001: Communities of practice. In J. K. Chambers, Peter Trudgill, and Natalie Schilling-Estes (eds) *Handbook of Language Variation and Change*. Oxford: Blackwell, pp. 526–48.

Newton, Esther 1972: *Mother Camp: Female Impersonators in America*. Englewood Cliffs, NJ: Prentice-Hall.

Ogawa, Naoko and Shibamoto Smith, Janet 1997: The gendering of the gay male sex class in Japan: A case study based on "Rasen no Sobyo". In Anna Livia and Kira Hall (eds) *Queerly Phrased: Language, Gender, and Sexuality*. New York and Oxford: Oxford University Press, pp. 402–15.

Reynolds, Katsue Akiba 1990: Female speakers of Japanese in transition. In Sachiko Ide and Naomi H. McGloin (eds) *Aspects of Japanese Women's Language*. Tokyo: Kurosio Publishers, pp. 129–46.

Risch, Barbara 1987: Women's derogatory terms for men: that's right, "dirty" words. *Language in Society* 16: 353–8.

Schegloff, Emanuel 1972: Sequencing in conversational openings. In John J. Gumperz and Dell Hymes (eds) *Directions in Sociolinguistics*. Oxford: Blackwell, pp. 346–80.

Schultz, Muriel R. 1975: The semantic derogation of women. In Barrie Thorne and Nancy Henley (eds) *Language and Sex: Difference and Dominance*. Rowley, MA: Newbury House, pp. 64–75.

Simmonds, Felly Nkweto 1995: Naming and identity. In Delia Jarrett-Macauley (ed.) *Reconstructing Womanhood, Reconstructing Feminism*. London: Routledge, pp. 109–15.

Stanley, Julia Penelope 1977: Paradigmatic woman: The prostitute. In David L. Shores and Caitlin P. Hines (eds) *Papers in Language Variation*. Montgomery: University of Alabama Press, pp. 303–21.

Stannard, Una 1977: *Mrs Man*. San Francisco: Germainbooks.

Sutton, Laurel A. 1995: Bitches and skankly hobags: The place of some women in contemporary slang. In Kira Hall and Mary Bucholtz (eds) *Gender Articulated: Language and the Socially Constructed Self*. New York and London: Routledge, pp. 279–96.

Tannen, Deborah 1994: The relativity of linguistic strategies. In Deborah Tannen (ed.) *Discourse and Gender*. Oxford: Oxford University Press, pp. 19–52.

Thorne, Barrie 1993: *Gender Play*. New Brunswick, NJ: Rutgers University Press.

Wenger, Etienne 1998: *Communities of Practice*. Cambridge: Cambridge University Press.

Wolfson, Nessa and Manes, Joan 1980: Don't "dear" me! In Sally McConnell-Ginet, Ruth A. Borker and Nelly Furman (eds) *Women and Language in Literature and Society*. New York: Praeger, pp. 79–92.

Wong, Andrew and Qing Zhang 2000: *Tongzhi men zhan qi lai!*: The linguistic construction of the *tongzhi* community. *Journal of Linguistic Anthropology* 10(2): 248–78.

4 Variation in Language and Gender

SUZANNE ROMAINE

1 Introduction

This chapter addresses some of the main research methods, trends, and findings concerning variation in language and gender. Most of the studies examined here have employed what can be referred to as quantitative variationist methodology (sometimes also called the quantitative paradigm or variation theory) to reveal and analyze sociolinguistic patterns, that is, correlations between variable features of the kind usually examined in sociolinguistic studies of urban speech communities (e.g. postvocalic /r/ in New York City, glottalization in Glasgow, initial /h/ in Norwich, etc.), and external social factors such as social class, age, sex, network, and style (see Labov 1972a).

When such large-scale systematic research into sociolinguistic variation began in the 1960s, its main focus was to illuminate the relationship between language and social structure more generally, rather than the relationship between language and gender specifically. However, the category of sex (understood simply as a binary division between males and females) was often included as a major social variable and instances of gender variation (or sex differentiation, as it was generally called) were noted in relation to other sociolinguistic patterns, particularly, social class and stylistic differentiation.

Because the way in which research questions are formed has a bearing on the findings, some of the basic methodological assumptions and the historical context in which the variationist approach emerged are discussed briefly in section 2. The general findings are the focus of section 3, with special reference to connections between sex differentiation, social class stratification, and style shifting. Section 4 discusses some of the explanations for sociolinguistic patterns involving sex differentiation. The final section examines some of these explanations in the context of some of the problematic methodological assumptions made in variation studies which may be responsible for the limited explanatory power of some of the findings.

2   Research Methods

Variationist methodology came into prominence in the late 1960s not to address the issue of language and gender, but primarily to fill perceived gaps in traditional studies of variability which for the most part were concerned with regional variation. Dialectologists in the nineteenth and early twentieth centuries concentrated their efforts on documenting the rural dialects which they believed would soon disappear. A primary concern was to map the geographical distribution of forms between one region and another. These forms were most often different words for the same thing, such as *dragon fly* versus *darning needle*, although phonological and grammatical features were also included. The results often took many years to appear in print and were most often displayed in linguistic atlases of maps showing the geographical boundaries between users of different forms (see e.g. Kurath 1949).

Many dialectologists based their surveys almost entirely on the speech of men, on the assumption that men better preserved the "real" and "purest" forms of the regional dialects they were interested in collecting. Dialect geographers usually chose one older man as representative of a particular area, a man whose social characteristics have been summed up in the acronym NORM, i.e. non-mobile, older, rural, male (see Chambers and Trudgill 1980). The extent to which social variables could be or were built into mapping was thus limited. In addition, most of the linguistic items whose geographical distribution was mapped were associated with men's rather than women's lifestyles and roles, for example terms for farming implements.

By contrast, sociolinguists turned their attention to the language of cities, where an increasing proportion of the world's population lives in modern times. Labov's (1966) sociolinguistic study of the speech of New York (and subsequent ones modeled after it) abandoned the idea that any one person could be representative of a complex urban area; it relied on speech samples collected from a random sample of 103 men and women representative of different social class backgrounds, ethnicities, and age groups. The method used in New York City to study the linguistic features was to select easily quantifiable items, especially phonological variables such as postvocalic /r/ in words such as *cart*, *barn*, etc., which was either present or absent. Most of the variables studied in detail have tended to be phonological, and to a lesser extent grammatical, although in principle any instance of variation amenable to quantitative study can be analyzed in similar fashion (see, however, Romaine 1984a, for discussion of some of the problems posed by syntactic variation). By counting variants of different kinds in tape-recorded interviews and comparing their incidence across different groups of speakers, the replication of a number of sociolinguistic patterns across many communities permits some generalizations about the relationship between linguistic variables and society.

Analysis of certain key variable speech forms showed that when variation in the speech of and between individuals was viewed against the background of the community as a whole, it was not random, but rather conditioned by social factors such as social class, age, sex, and style in predictable ways. Thus, while idiolects (or the speech of individuals) considered in isolation might seem randomly variable, the speech community as a whole behaved regularly. Using these methods, one could predict, for example, that a person of a particular social class, age, sex, etc. would pronounce postvocalic /r/ a certain percentage of the time in certain situations.

3 Findings: Examination of Some Sociolinguistic Patterns of Social Class, Style, and Sex Differentiation

Of the principal social dimensions sociolinguists have been concerned with (i.e. social class, age, sex, style, and network) social class has probably been the most researched. Moreover, social class differentiation is often assumed to be fundamental and other patterns of variation, such as stylistic and gender variation, are regarded as derivative of it. Many sociolinguistic studies have started by grouping individuals into social classes on the basis of factors such as education, occupation, income, and so on, and then looked to see how certain linguistic features were used by each group.

Through the introduction of these new quantitative methods for investigating social dialects by correlating sociolinguistic variables with social factors, sociolinguists have been able to build up a comprehensive picture of social dialect differentiation in the United States and Britain in particular, as well as in other places, where these studies have since been replicated. The view of language which emerges from the sociolinguistic study of urban dialects is that of a structured but variable system, whose use is conditioned by both internal and external factors. A major finding of urban sociolinguistic work is that differences among social dialects are quantitative and not qualitative. Thus, variants are not usually associated exclusively with one group or another; all speakers tend to make use of the same linguistic features to a greater or lesser degree.

3.1 *Language, social class, style, and sex*

Some of the same linguistic features figure in patterns of both regional and social dialect differentiation, with working-class varieties being more localized, and they also display correlations with other social factors. The intersection of social and stylistic continua is one of the most important findings of quantitative sociolinguistics: namely, if a feature occurs more frequently in working-class speech, then it will occur more frequently in the informal speech of all speakers.

Table 4.1 Social class, style, and sex differentiation in (ing) in Norwich (percentage of non-standard forms used) (from Trudgill 1974: 94, table 7.2)

	Word-list	Reading	Formal speech	Casual speech
Middle-middle				
m	0	0	4	31
f	0	0	0	0
Lower-middle				
m	0	20	27	17
f	0	0	3	67
Upper-working				
m	0	18	81	95
f	11	13	68	77
Middle-working				
m	24	43	91	97
f	20	46	81	88
Lower-working				
m	66	100	100	100
f	17	54	97	100

There are also strong correlations between patterns of social stratification and gender, with a number of now classic findings emerging repeatedly. One of these sociolinguistic patterns is that women, regardless of other social characteristics such as class, age, etc., tended to use more standard forms than men.

Table 4.1 shows the results of Trudgill's (1974) study in Norwich of the variable (ing), that is, alternation between alveolar /n/ and a velar nasal /ng/ in words with -*ing* endings such as *reading, singing*, in relation to the variables of social class, style, and sex. The scores represent the percentage of non-standard forms used by men and women in each social group in four contextual styles: when reading a word-list, reading a short text, in formal speech, and in casual speech.

Generally speaking, the use of non-standard forms increases the less formal the style and the lower one's social status, with men's scores higher than women's. This variable is often referred to popularly as "dropping one's g's." It is a well-known marker of social status over most of the English-speaking world, found in varieties of American English too. Although each class has different average scores in each style, generally speaking all groups style-shift in the same direction in their more formal speech style, that is, in the direction of the standard language. This similar behavior can be taken as an indication of membership in a speech community sharing norms for social evaluation of the relative prestige of variables. All groups recognize the overt greater prestige of standard speech and shift toward it in more formal styles.

Summing up these sociolinguistic patterns involving social class, gender, and style, sociolinguists would reply to the question of who is likely to speak most non-standardly in a community: working-class men speaking in casual conversation. Conversely, middle-class women speaking in more formal conversation are closest to the standard. In table 4.1, for instance, we can see that middle-middle-class women never use the non-standard form, while lower-working-class men use it almost all of the time. Note, however, that the differences between men and women are not equal throughout the social hierarchy. For this variable they are greatest in the lower middle and upper working class. Such patterns reveal basic linguistic faultlines in a community, and are indicative of the uneven spread of the standard and its associated prescriptive ideology in a speech community.

Similar results have been found in other places, such as Sweden and the Netherlands. In fact, Nordberg (1971) proposed that this pattern of sex differentiation is so ubiquitous in Western societies today that it could almost serve as a criterion for determining which speech forms are stigmatized and which carry prestige in a community. Similarly, Trudgill (1983: 162) emphasized the same point when he claimed that the association between women and standard speech was "the single most consistent finding to have emerged from social dialect studies over the past twenty years."

Women also tend to hypercorrect more than men, especially in the lower middle class. "Hypercorrection" refers to a deviation in the expected pattern of stylistic stratification of the kind shown in table 4.1 for (ing) in Norwich, for example. Here all speakers, regardless of social class, tend to shift more toward the standard forms in their more formal speaking styles. In some cases, however, where hypercorrection occurs, as with postvocalic /r/ in New York City, the lower middle class shows the most radical style shifting, exceeding even the highest-status group in their use of the standard forms in the most formal style. The behavior of the lower middle class is governed by their recognition of an exterior standard of correctness and their insecurity about their own speech. They see the use of postvocalic /r/ as a prestige marker of the highest social group. In their attempt to adopt the norm of this group, they manifest their aspirations of upward social mobility, but they overshoot the mark. The clearest cases of hypercorrection occur when a feature is undergoing change in response to social pressure from above, that is, a prestige norm used by the upper class. In New York City the new /r/-pronouncing norm is being imported into previously non-rhotic areas of the eastern United States. Hypercorrection by the lower middle class accelerates the introduction of this new norm. The variable (ing), on the other hand, has been a stable marker of social and stylistic variation for a very long time and does not appear to be involved in change, and hence does not display hypercorrection.

3.2   *Sociolinguistic patterns and language change*

Because variability is a prerequisite for change, synchronic variation may represent a stage in long-term change. Armed with the knowledge of how variability is embedded in a social and linguistic context in speech communities today, sociolinguists have tried to revitalize the study of historical change by incorporating within it an understanding of these sociolinguistic patterns (see Weinreich, Labov, and Herzog 1968). By examining the way in which variation is embedded into the social structure of a community, we can chart the spread of innovations just as dialect geographers mapped variation and change through geographical space.

Sociolinguists have distinguished between "change from above" and "change from below" to refer to the differing points of departure for the diffusion of linguistic innovations through the social hierarchy. Change from above is conscious change originating in more formal styles and in the upper end of the social hierarchy; change from below is below the level of conscious awareness, originating in the lower end of the social hierarchy. Gender is critical here too. Women, particularly in the lower middle class, lead in the introduction of new standard forms of many of the phonological variables studied in the United States, the UK, and other industrialized societies such as Sweden, while men tend to lead in instances of change from below (see Labov 1990). Moreover, there is evidence from studies of language shift in bilingual communities for women being in the vanguard of change to a more prestigious language. In the case of Oberwart, Austria, for instance, it was women who were ahead of men, in shifting from Hungarian to German (Gal 1979).

4   Explanations for the Connection Between Women and Standard Speech

Although many reasons have been put forward to try to explain these results, they have never been satisfactorily accounted for. After all, it is in some respects paradoxical that women should tend to use the more prestigious variants when most societies accord higher status and power to men. Moreover, as has often been the case with other patterns of gender differentiation, it is women's behavior that has been problematized and seen to be deviant and thus in need of explanation. We could just as easily ask instead why men tend to use the standard less often than women of the same status. Indeed, Labov (1966: 249–63) commented on a striking case where an upper-middle-class male, Nathan B., used a high level of non-standard variants for certain variables comparable to lower-middle- or working-class speakers. After receiving his PhD in political science, Nathan B. was being considered for a university teaching appointment, but was denied it when he refused to take corrective courses to improve his speech.

4.1   *Language, sex, and gender*

One explanation that can be dismissed relatively easily is Chambers' (1995: 132–3) view that women's greater verbal abilities are responsible for the differences.

For Chambers then, the differences are sex-based or biological rather than culturally derived or gender-based. Although there was little recognition or critical discussion of the notion of gender as a social and cultural construct in most of the early sociolinguistic literature (see McElhinny, this volume), socio-linguists often invoked explanations based on women's supposed greater status-consciousness, greater awareness of the social significance of variants, and concern for politeness. When asked to say which forms they used themselves, Norwich women, for instance, tended to "over-report" their usage and claimed that they used more standard forms than they actually did. Men, however, were likely to under-report their use of standard forms. This led Trudgill (1972) to argue that for men, speaking non-standardly has "covert" prestige, while the "overt" prestige associated with speaking the standard variety is more important to women (see James 1996; Kiesling, this volume).

Thus, women may be using linguistic means as a way to achieve status denied to them through other outlets. Since women have long been denied equality with men as far as educational and employment opportunities are concerned, these are not reliable indicators of a woman's status or the status she aspires to. Although the marketplace establishes the value of men in economic terms, the only kind of capital a woman can accumulate is symbolic. She can be a "good" housewife, a "good" mother, a "good" wife, and so on, with respect to the community's norms and stereotypes for appropriate female behavior.

In this sense, the use of the standard might be seen as yet another reflection of women's powerlessness in the public sphere. This interpretation accorded well with one of the assumptions made by early gender scholars such as Lakoff (1975), who saw women's language as the "language of powerlessness," a reflection of their subordinate place in relation to men. The importance of power rather than gender *per se* emerged in O'Barr and Atkins's (1980) finding that some of the features thought to be part of "women's language" were also used by males when in a subordinate position (see Lakoff, this volume, for discussion of women and power).

Further examination of the historical context provides ample support for the association between perceived femininity and the use of standard English. In the Victorian era "speaking properly" became associated with being female, and with being a lady, in particular (see Mugglestone 1995). That is why Sweet (1890), for instance, considered it far worse for a woman to drop initial /h/ in words such as *house* or *heart*.

Because a woman aspirant to the status of lady could not attain it independently, but only through marriage, it was incumbent on her to behave and speak like a lady. George Bernard Shaw's *Pygmalion* (1916) and the popular musical made from it, *My Fair Lady*, illustrate the power of accent in social transformation. Cockney flower seller Eliza Doolittle is trained by a phonetics professor, Henry Higgins (based on Henry Sweet), to speak like a "lady." As long as she pronounces her vowels and consonants correctly, Doolittle does not betray her working-class East London origins and is indeed received in the best of society.

Doolittle's transformation is enabled partly through changes brought about by the Industrial Revolution in nineteenth-century Britain which opened up new avenues for the accumulation of wealth, prestige, and power other than those based on hereditary landed titles. Thanks to the Universal Education Act of 1872, there were greater educational opportunities for a wider portion of the social spectrum. This facilitated the spread of what Wyld (1920) called the "newfangled English," that is, the newly codified standard. Yet it was not the highest-ranking social groups of the day but instead the nouveau riche or bourgeoisie who eagerly sought the refinements the grammarians had to offer, as signs of their emergent status as educated persons. Good grammar and the right accent became social capital in an age in which the definitions of "gentleman" and "lady" were no longer based entirely on hereditary titles and land. Anyone with money, ambition, and the right connections or education could aspire to be a gentleman or a lady – even Eliza Doolittle.

The changing times brought about a semantic shift in the meanings of the terms *gentleman* and *lady*. Titles once associated with the aristocracy became terms of social approval and moral approbation. In a letter to his sister Hannah in 1833, historian Thomas Macaulay wrote that "the curse of England is the obstinate determination of the middle classes to make their sons what they call gentlemen" (cited in Trevelyan 1878: 338). Likewise, Sarah Ellis (1839: 107), a contemporary of Macaulay, commented on the metamorphosis in the meaning of the social label *lady* brought about by modern schools:

> Amongst the changes introduced by modern taste, it is not the least striking, that all daughters of tradespeople, when sent to school, are no longer girls, but young ladies. The linen-draper whose worthy consort occupies her daily post behind the counter, receives her child from Mrs. Montagu's establishment – a young lady. At the same elegant and expensive seminary, music and Italian are taught to Hannah Smith, whose father deals in Yarmouth herrings; and there is the butcher's daughter, too, perhaps the most ladylike of them all.

It is striking that the daughters of the butcher, the herring seller, and other categories of tradespeople mentioned would all belong to the upper working class and lower middle class, precisely those levels within the social hierarchy where modern sociolinguistics finds the greatest differentiation in male and female speech (see Romaine 1996).

4.2   Sex-based versus class-based differentiation

Despite this historical support for the view that speaking properly became social capital, we may question how relevant it is for women today, given women's great strides in achieving educational and economic parity with men, partly as a result of the modern women's movement. If women are using the standard to achieve status denied to them through conventional outlets, we

Table 4.2   Gender differentiation in six morphological variables in 1967 and 1996 (percentage of standard forms; from Nordberg and Sundgren 1999: 7, table 3)

	1967		1996		Extent of gap	
	Male	Female	Male	Female	1967	1996
Neuter sg. def. art	52	60	52	68	8	16
Neuter pl. def. art.	30	47	54	69	17	15
Past part. V,						
classes 1 and 4	21	30	20	30	9	10
Past part. V, class 2	88	88	88	98	0	10
Preterite, V, class 1	16	15	12	17	−1	5
Blev/vart	26	58	28	66	32	38

might expect that this need should diminish once women have more access to high-status and high-paying jobs, for example. Furthermore, if a related assumption made by sociolinguists is also true, namely, that social structure is reflected in patterns of linguistic variation, we might expect more recent sociolinguistic studies to reveal less gender variation in some of the classic linguistic variables examined in early studies of the 1960s and 1970s.

However, Nordberg and Sundgren's (1998, 1999) comparison of sociolinguistic surveys done in Eskilstuna, a medium-sized town in central Sweden 110 kilometers west of Stockholm, in 1967 and a generation later in 1996 reveals that gender differentiation in most of the variables has been maintained, or even increased rather than decreased. Table 4.2 shows gender differentiation for six morphological variables in 1967 and 1996. For each variable, with only very minor exceptions, the women use the standard forms more frequently than men, in both 1967 and 1996. The final column shows the extent of the gap measured in terms of percentage points between the men's and women's scores at the two time periods.

The first variable is the neuter singular definite article ending in -*t* in standard Swedish, as in *huset* "the house," and without it, in non-standard usage. Although male usage has remained at the same level over time, the women have moved closer to the standard. The second variable is the neuter plural definite article, which in standard Swedish is expressed by the suffix -*en* as in *husen* "the houses"; the local dialect variant is -*ena/-a*, as in *husena* or *barna* "the children." Both men and women have shifted more toward the standard in 1996, but the gap between the sexes remains roughly the same. The third variable is the past participle forms of verbs in conjugation classes 1 and 4, whose standard forms end in -*t* in standard Swedish, e.g. *dansat* "danced," *sjungit* "sung." There has been virtually no change in this variable over time. It shows roughly the same amount of sex differentiation in both time periods. The fourth variable is the past participle of verbs in conjugation class 2. Here too there is an increase over time in the gap between men and women, with women, but not men, moving toward the standard. In fact, there was no gender differentiation in 1967, with both men and women conforming very closely to the standard norm. In 1996, however, the women have shifted almost completely to the standard.

The fifth variable, preterite forms for verbs in conjugation class 1, also shows almost no gender differentiation in 1967, but women have shifted in the direction of the standard in 1996, and men have increased their use of the non-standard forms. In the case of the sixth variable, the use of the non-standard preterite forms for the highly frequent verbs *vara* "to be" and *bli* "to become," men have hardly changed their usage between the two time periods, while women have moved closer to the standard, resulting in an increase in the gap between male and female scores.

The results are striking, all the more so for their occurrence in Sweden, a country renowned for gender equality. In Sweden as well as in other Nordic countries the position of women is more nearly equal to that of men than in most other parts of the world, thanks to legislation comparable to the proposed but eventually doomed US Equal Rights Amendment.

Another surprising finding in Nordberg and Sundgren's results is the decrease in social class differentiation between 1967 and 1996. At first glance, this too flies in the face of global trends showing an increase in the gap between rich and poor, both between developed and developing nations as well as within nations. Economists such as Sen (1999) report stark contrasts between income per person (and related measures of well-being such as life expectancy, rate of infant mortality, etc.) in developed countries, most of them in the temperate zone of the Northern hemisphere, and developing countries in the tropics and semi-tropics, particularly in South Asia and sub-Saharan Africa. The richest 20 per cent of the world's people have 150 times the income of the poorest 20 per cent.

Even within developed countries such as the USA, there are similarly extreme contrasts, despite the fact that at the turn of the twenty-first century the country had enjoyed eighteen years of almost uninterrupted growth and the longest-running economic expansion in history (Economic Policy Institute 2000). Although the gap between the poor and the middle class is shrinking, the gap between the poor and everyone else is increasing. Incomes have gone up each year since 1995 without narrowing the inequality gap: the poorest fifth of the population saw a fall of 8.9 per cent in after-tax income from 1979 to 1999, but the richest 1 per cent realized a gain of 93.4 per cent.

Eskilstuna too has undergone a number of social transformations since the late 1960s. In 1967 it was primarily a prospering industrial town engaged in steel manufacturing, with a growing population and a low rate of unemployment. Since the beginning of the 1970s, however, the population has been stagnating or diminishing, with an over-representation of older age groups. As in many other countries, the transition from an industrial to a post-industrial economy has occasioned a number of economic crises such as factory closings and high unemployment, as well as witnessing an increase in the number of immigrants from abroad. The 1996 population in Eskilstuna, in comparison both to Sweden as a whole as well as to towns of a similar size, has lower levels of education, as well as lower levels of income, along with higher social benefits per person.

These socio-economic developments make somewhat contradictory predictions about the influence of social factors on language use, based on the kinds of assumptions sociolinguists have made about the relationship between language and social structure. We might expect, for example, that the global change from an economy based on manufacturing to one based on information management and services would lead to an increase in the use of the standard. Indeed, Nordberg and Sundgren found evidence of greater use of the standard overall.

Global trends, however, tell us little about individuals and how they have behaved. A rising tide of global capital does not lift all boats. Socially mobile persons ought to increase their use of the standard more than others. For the neuter singular definite article, for instance, the highest social group (group I) did not change its usage from 1967 to 1996, while the speakers in the other social groups now use a higher number of standard forms. The other variables concerning verb forms, however, showed little or no movement toward the standard over time for this group. The biggest change occurred in the neuter plural definite article: in 1967 there was an average of 38 per cent standard forms, which increased to 61 per cent in 1996.

As part of the 1996 survey Nordberg and Sundgren (1998) also interviewed thirteen of the Eskilstuna residents who participated in the 1967 study. This enabled them to look more closely at the individual dimension of change toward the standard. For the neuter singular definite article, for example, they found that all speakers used on average more standard forms in 1996 (52 per cent) than in 1967 (42 per cent). Although members of all social groups as a whole moved toward the standard, this movement was rather small in the highest and lowest groups (I and III), and not all speakers within these groups used more standard variants. The two speakers in group II, however, more than doubled their use of standard forms, from 24 per cent in 1967 to 54 per cent in 1996. Moreover, the four speakers who belonged to the youngest age group in 1967 (16–30 years) doubled their use of the standard form from 28 per cent in 1967 to 57 per cent in 1996. Thus, change in real time toward the standard has occurred both cross-generationally and within individuals.

Both social class and gender differentiation in Eskilstuna were more pronounced, however, in the case of the definite plural of neuter nouns. The two speakers in social group II behaved in a hypercorrect fashion in that they used more standard forms than the highest social group both in 1967 (50 per cent, versus 33 per cent for group I) and in 1996 (72 per cent standard forms for group II versus 51 per cent for group III). Socially mobile speakers and women generally have changed more toward the standard (Nordberg and Sundgren 1998: 18–19). The change toward the standard since the early 1970s has been much faster for the plural than singular forms of definite neuter nouns. Overall, however, the pattern of change for all the Swedish variables followed the generally established pattern for change from above, although each was in a different phase of change toward the standard.

5   Criticisms and Limitations of Variation Studies

Over the past few decades sociolinguistic studies have been heavily criticized for their simplistic operationalization of social variables such as social class and sex. The standard sociolinguistic account of the relationship between language and society often seems to suggest, even if only implicitly, that language reflects already existing social identities rather than constructs them. This approach has limited explanatory power since it starts with the categories of male and female and social class as fixed and stable givens rather than as varying constructs themselves in need of explanation.

5.1   The roles of men and women and the functions of prestige varieties

The part played by women or men *per se* in linguistic innovation as well as their relation to the standard seems, however, to depend very much on their roles and the symbolic functions of prestige varieties in the community concerned. Just as scholars may have erred in assuming sex-based differences to be derived from social class differences, some may have misinterpreted gender differences as sex differences. A critical variable is whether women have access to education, or other institutions and contexts, where standard or prestigious forms of speech can be acquired and used.

   In many contemporary non-Western cultures women are further away from the prestige norms of society. This is true, for example, in parts of the Middle East and Africa today, just as it was also true historically in Britain, where even high-ranking women did not often have as much education as men and were therefore further away from the norms of the written language. In a study I carried out of letters written by men and women to Mary Queen of Scots in sixteenth-century Scotland, I found a higher incidence among women of non-standard features of the kind which in other texts were associated with persons of low social status (Romaine 1982).

   Nordberg and Sundgren (1998: 17) also found some interesting patterns of sex differentiation in relation to age in Eskilstuna. When they looked at the youngest age group in 1996, they found that the men used slightly more standard forms than the women, and many more than men in other age groups. In 1967, it was the oldest men in social groups II and III who used more standard forms than women. While they comment that the more recent pattern is difficult to explain, they see the earlier pattern as a reflection of the fact that the oldest women in 1967 were less active outside the home, and thus retained more local features in their speech.

Nichols's (1983) study of the Gullah Creole spoken in parts of the southeastern United States also revealed that older women were the heaviest users of Gullah because they worked in domestic and agricultural positions. Older men worked mostly in construction. Younger people of both sexes had more access to white-collar jobs and service positions which brought them into contact with standard English. Younger women were ahead of the younger men in their adoption of a more standard form of English.

A more sophisticated understanding of the different functions standard speech plays for men and women in different contexts has likewise illuminated our understanding of language change, as well as the connections between race, class, and sex in the distribution of linguistic variables. Milroy, Milroy, and Hartley (1994) have found, for example, that glottalization, a long stigmatized feature of urban varieties of British English with origins in working-class London speech, is on the increase in middle-class speech in Cardiff. They believe that the greater presence of glottal stops in female speech has led to a reversal of the stigma attached to it. Similarly, Holmes's (1995a) study of New Zealand English reveals that young working-class speakers are leading the introduction of glottalized variants of word-final /t/, e.g. *pat*. They use more of these variants than do middle-class speakers, but young women in both the working and middle classes are ahead of men. Here we have a case where a once vernacular feature has changed its status, first by losing stigma, then gaining prestige as a feature of the new variety. Milroy et al. (1994) suggest that it is the fact that women adopt a variant which gives it prestige rather than the fact that females favor prestige forms. In other words, women create prestige norms rather than follow them. Thus, they are norm-makers, whatever social connotations the forms may originally have had.

Others have proposed that it may not be so much the supposed prestige connotations of the standard that attracts women, but the stigma of non-standard speech that women are avoiding. Although this explanation would not account for why women would adopt a highly stigmatized feature such as glottalization, when we look at cases where women have led in shifts to more prestigious languages, we can see how those aspiring to be ladies had to escape both literally and figuratively from their status as rural peasants by leaving the land and their language behind. Modern European languages such as Norwegian, French, and English became symbols of modernity, in particular of the newly emergent European nation-states, at the same time as they were associated with urbanity, finery, and higher social status (see Romaine 1998).

In a study where listeners were asked to identify the sex of children from tape-recordings of their speech, Edwards (1979) found that boys who were misidentified as girls tended to be middle-class, whereas girls who sounded like boys tended to be working-class. Gordon (1994) showed how the clothes and accent associated with working-class females elicited stereotypical judgments about their morality. One ten-year-old girl in Edinburgh told me, in answer to the question of why her mother did not like her to speak "rough," that is, to use local Scots vernacular outside the home (Romaine 1984b): "Well, if I speak rough, she doesn't like it when other people are in because they think that we're rough tatties in the stair." I found clear sex differentiation in the use of certain variables in children as young as six years in this community.

The standard may also function differently for men and women. In some communities women use standard speech to gain respect and exert influence on others. Larson's (1982) study of two villages in Norway revealed that while women's speech was on the whole more standard than that of men, women produced more features of standard speech when they were trying to get someone to do something or to persuade someone to believe something. Men rarely used speech in this way.

This suggests that linguistic choices need to be seen in the light of multiple roles available to women and men and in terms of the communicative functions expressed by certain forms used in particular contexts by specific speakers (see the chapters by Kendall, Thimm, and Wodak, this volume). Naive counting of variants reveals only a superficial understanding of the relationship between language and gender. A case in point is the use of tag questions, the subject of numerous studies sparked by Lakoff's (1975) belief that women used more of them than men. Because many researchers simply counted the number of tag questions used by men and women without paying attention to either the function or the context in which they were used, the results were inconclusive on the issue of whether tags showed gender-differentiated usage (see, however, Holmes 1986). The same linguistic features can, when used by different persons in different contexts and cultures, often mean very different things. On closer examination, there are few, if any, context-independent gender differences in language.

Another methodological bias may derive from the fact that most of the early sociolinguistic studies were carried out by men and many of the questions asked of both men and women reflected a masculine bias. For example, in the New York City study, Labov (1966) asked both men and women to read a passage ending with a very unflattering comparison between dogs and a boy's first girlfriend: "I suppose it's the same thing with most of us: your first dog is like your first girl. She's more trouble than she's worth, but you can't seem to forget her." In other parts of the interview men and women were asked about their words for different things. Women were asked about childhood games, while men, among other things, were asked about terms for girls and even on occasion, terms for female sex organs. Naturally, researchers have since questioned the nature of the relationship established between male sociolinguists and the women they interviewed. It is not likely that a discussion of hopscotch would establish the same kind of rapport between the male interviewer and a female interviewee as talk about obscene language would between two men. Holmes's (1995b) research on the amount of talk in single-sex and mixed-sex interviews has suggested that at least in more formal interaction, members of each sex speak least in situations they find most uncomfortable.

5.2 *Men and women in relation to social class*

The Eskilstuna study demonstrates that language is not simply a passive reflector of society, it also creates it. There is a constant interaction between society and language. To expect that language will come to reflect whatever changes take place in society oversimplifies the complexity of the interface between language and society. (Note that a similar simplification is behind one common argument against linguistic reform. We should leave language alone because once more women become doctors, business managers, etc., linguistic discrimination will disappear as language comes to reflect the improved status of women.) In this scenario society has to change first, and that is what triggers language change.

In trying to account for the increase in sex differentiation and decrease in social class stratification in Eskilstuna, it would also be a mistake to concentrate only on women and their changing relation to the standard and the socio-economic structure, while assuming that the relationship of men to the socio-economic structure has remained the same. Masculinity is no less a historically and socially constructed script than femininity. As post-industrial economies have shifted from being societies organized around industry to ones organized around electronic technology, they have been characterized by increasing rates of female employment and male unemployment. Although most western European countries have experienced far higher rates of unemployment than the USA, even with the lowest unemployment figures accompanying unprecedented prosperity for some in the new US economy, millions of men were left behind as old-economy industries such as shipbuilding and aerospace engineering "downsized." Massive corporate restructurings led to the lay-off of millions of white- and blue-collar workers. The deindustrialization and re-structuring of the final decades of the twentieth century affected huge sectors of industrial America, including not only the defense industry, but also steel and auto plants in the mid-West, and eliminated millions of workers in corporate giants such as IBM, AT & T, and General Motors. Between 1995 and 1997, for instance, about eight million people were laid off (Faludi 1999: 52, 60, 153).

Loss of income caused by unemployment has serious and far-reaching effects, including loss of self-esteem, disruption of family life leading to social exclusion, as well as accentuation of racial tensions and gender asymmetries. If sociolinguists are right that male identity is vested more in occupation, once status and income in the marketplace lose their capacity to define traditional masculinity, we might expect men to compensate linguistically for the loss of authority derived from the family breadwinner role. Masculinity in the old economy organized around industry was defined more generally in terms of providing for a family, and specifically, with the production of manufactured goods such as airplanes, ships, and automobiles. Interestingly, Faludi (1999) characterizes the economic shift from industry to service as one leading from "heavy-lifting" masculine labor to "feminine" aid and assistance. She stresses also (1999: 298) that participation in the Second World War and the Vietnam War were defining events of different kinds of masculinity for their respective male generations. Those who fought in the Second World War had a common mission with a clearly identifiable enemy as well as endorsement by society at large. While Second World War veterans returned home victorious, those who went to Vietnam not only did not enjoy broad support at home, but were also tainted by the stigma of defeat. Those who avoided serving in Vietnam, either legally or illegally, were branded with the stigma of not having done their duty.

Class-based approaches to variation have often taken for granted that individuals can be grouped into social classes based on the prestige and status associated with occupation, income, and so on, on the assumption that those in the same group will behave similarly. The case of Nathan B. noted above, however, shows the need for a closer look at individuals, as do the results of Nordberg and Sundgren's (1998) research in Eskilstuna. Members of the same sex or social class can have quite different outlooks and orientations toward language and different degrees of integration into the local setting. The concept of "social network," adopted from anthropology into sociolinguistics, takes into account different socializing habits of individuals and their degree of involvement in the local community.

Milroy (1980) applied network analysis to the study of three working-class communities in Belfast, Northern Ireland. She examined the different types of networks within which individuals socialized and correlated network strength with linguistic variables. She devised a measure of network strength which took into account the density and multiplexity of different network types. For example, a dense network is one in which the people whom a given speaker knows and interacts with also know each other. A multiplex network is one in which the individuals who interact are tied to one another in other ways. Thus, if two men in a network interact both as workmates at the same factory and as cousins, there is more than one basis to their relationship with one another.

The results in table 4.3 show how two working-class women, Hannah and Paula, who live in the same type of housing in the same area of Belfast and have similar employment, nevertheless behave quite differently from one another linguistically. Hannah is much more standard in her speech than Paula. Scores for only two of the eight variables of the study are given here: (th) refers to the absence of intervocalic *th* in words such as *mother*, and (e) refers to the frequency of a low vowel in words such as *peck*, which then merges with *pack*. Higher scores indicate a more localized or non-standard usage.

The explanation of the difference lies in their differing socialization patterns. Paula, whose speech is more non-standard, is a member of a local bingo-playing group and has extensive kin ties in the area. Hannah has no kin in the area and does not associate with local people. In fact, she stays at home a lot watching TV. In general, those with high network scores indicating the strength of association with the local community used more local, non-standard forms

Table 4.3 Two Belfast women compared (percentage of non-standard usage) (from Milroy 1980)

	(th)	**(e)**
Hannah	0	66.7
Paula	58.34	100

of speech. Those whose networks were more open and less locally constrained used more standard speech. Networks in which individuals interact locally within a well-defined territory and whose members are linked to each other in several capacities, for example as kin, neighbor, workmate, and so on, act as a powerful influence on the maintenance of local norms. If these networks are disrupted, then people will be more open to the influence of standard speech. Speakers use their local accents as a means of affirming identity and loyalty to local groups.

Some patterns of social class stratification are actually better accounted for as gender differences. In the Belfast study there was in fact one group of working-class women, who had tighter and denser networks than all the other men and who also used more non-standard forms than men. Thus, gender differentiation may be prior to class difference, with some variants being primarily gender- rather than class-marked.

There is, however, a broad link between network and social class to the extent that middle-class speakers tend to have looser networks than the working class. Nevertheless, dense networks may also be found at the upper levels of society, as in Britain, where the so-called "old boy network," whose members have usually been educated at English public schools (i.e. private schools) and at Oxford or Cambridge University, gives rise to an equally distinctive speech variety, RP (received pronunciation). More men than women had dense networks in Belfast, which suggests an explanation for some of the patterns of sex differentiation other sociolinguists have found. The network approach has also been applied in non-Western settings such as Africa and Brazil. Bortoni-Ricardo (1985) used it in Brazil, for example, to study the extent to which rural migrants to urban areas assimilated to urban standard speech norms. Change has been slower for migrant women, who have fewer social contacts than men.

The notion of network is thus more useful than that of social class and it applies equally well to multilingual and monolingual settings. At a more general level, we can say that the same kinds of processes must operate on speakers of different cultures. Dense networks can be found at any level of society, whether it is among working-class speakers in Belfast, upper-class British RP speakers, or teenagers in Harlem (see Labov 1972b), to produce a focused set of linguistic norms. Speakers whose norms are more diffuse participate in networks whose members are geographically and socially more mobile, for example women in Oberwart and Belfast. In the village of Oberwart, where young women with social aspirations have been fueling a shift away from Hungarian toward German, the fewer peasant contacts a person has, the greater the likelihood that German will be used (Gal 1979).

In non-Western cultures, however, the relationship between gender, modernity, and mobility may be such that women's departures from traditional community norms are devalued and stigmatized. Keenan (1974) reported such a case in Madagascar, where it is women who are norm-breakers (see the papers by Besnier, and Leap, this volume).

The relationship between female speech and social dialects also needs critical re-examination from a new non-class-based standpoint because men's and women's relations to the class structure are unequal. Despite the gains made in the women's movement, women are still concentrated in specific occupations, particularly in poorly paid white-collar work, and of course housework, generally unpaid and unrecognized as related to the prevailing economic structure.

It is only within the last few decades since the modern feminist movement that government departments and academic disciplines such as sociology have come to see women's relationship to social classes as a political issue and a technical problem for official statistics. Censuses and other surveys rely on a patriarchal concept of social class, where the family is the basic unit of analysis, the man is regarded as the head of a household, and his occupation determines the family's social class. Women disappear in the analysis since their own achievements are not taken into account and their status is defined by their husband's job.

According to the 1971 British census, however, more than half of all couples had discrepant social classes. The concept of the traditional nuclear family of man, woman, and children is also outdated. Studies in both the UK and the USA have shown that even by the late 1960s the majority of families in both countries were not of this type, and over the past few years government inquiries have been mounted expressing concern that the break-up of this family structure has serious consequences for society.

In a large-scale survey of around 200 married couples from the upper working and lower middle class in the Netherlands, most of the women in the sample were actually better educated than their husbands (Brouwer and Van Hout 1992). Nevertheless, more of these Dutch women who worked were in lower-status part-time jobs. Since level of education correlates well with degree of use of standard language, if there were similar discrepancies in the other surveys I mentioned, then this could easily account for the finding that women are closer to the standard than men.

Another factor seldom considered is the effect of children, with respect to both employment patterns as well as language use in families. The Dutch study found that when a couple had children, both parents used more standard language. One of the reasons why women may adopt a more prestigious variety of language is to increase their children's social and educational prospects. Similar findings have emerged from studies of language shift, such as Bull's (1991) in northern Norway, where Sami-speaking women tried to raise their children in Norwegian to enhance their children's success in school at a time when all education was in Norwegian. Interactions between gender, age, and taking care of children require more detailed study. Older women with no responsibilities for children may also not be concerned with using prestige varieties.

6   Conclusion

Eckert (1989: 245) reminds us that "the correlations of sex with linguistic variables are only a reflection of the effects on linguistic behavior of gender – the complex social construction of sex – and it is in this construction that one must seek explanations for such correlations." Faced with seemingly contradictory findings and much *ad hoc* speculation about the relation of women to prestige varieties and the role of women in language change, investigators have moved on from simplistic correlations between language use and sex to focus on the symbolic and ideological dimensions of language. While most of this traditional sociolinguistic literature has expressed the symbolic value of dominant languages and prestige varieties in terms of their supposed economic value in a linguistic marketplace, more recent work has paid attention to ideologies of femininity and masculinity (see Romaine 1998). The way in which gender gets mapped onto language choice is not straightforward but mediated through other identities and ideologies. This is simply to admit that as variables both gender and language comprise rather complex social practices and performances.

REFERENCES

Bortoni-Ricardo, Stella M. 1985: *The Urbanisation of Rural Dialect Speakers: A Sociolinguistic Study in Brazil.* Cambridge: Cambridge University Press.

Brouwer, Dédé and Van Hout, Roeland 1992: Gender-related variation in Amsterdam vernacular. *International Journal of the Sociology of Language* 94: 99–122.

Bull, Tove 1991: Women and men speaking: The roles played by women and men in the process of language shift. *Working Papers on Language, Gender and Sexism* 1: 11–24.

Chambers, J. K. 1995: *Sociolinguistic Theory.* Oxford: Blackwell.

Chambers, J. K. and Trudgill, Peter 1980: *Dialectology.* Cambridge: Cambridge University Press.

Eckert, Penelope 1989: The whole woman: Sex and gender differences in variation. *Language Variation and Change* 1: 245–67.

Economic Policy Institute 2000: *The State of Working America 2000–2001.* Washington, DC: Economic Policy Institute.

Edwards, John 1979: Social class differences and the identification of sex in children's speech. *Journal of Child Language* 6: 121–7.

Ellis, Sarah S. 1839: *The Women of England, Their Social Duties, and Domestic Habits*, 3rd edn. London.

Faludi, Susan 1999: *Stiffed: The Betrayal of the American Man*. New York: William Morrow.

Gal, Susan 1979: *Language Shift: Social Determinants of Linguistic Change in Bilingual Austria*. New York: Academic Press.

Gordon, Elizabeth 1994: Sex, speech and stereotypes: Why women's speech is closer to the standard than men's. In Mary Bucholtz, Anita C. Liang, Laurel A. Sutton, and Caitlin Hines (eds) *Cultural Performances: Proceedings of the Third Berkeley Women and Language Conference*. Berkeley, CA: Berkeley Women and Language Group, University of California, pp. 242–50.

Holmes, Janet 1986: Functions of YOU KNOW in women's and men's speech. *Language in Society* 15: 1–22.

Holmes, Janet 1995a: Glottal stops in New Zealand English: An analysis of variants of word final /t/. *Linguistics* 33: 433–63.

Holmes, Janet 1995b: *Women, Men and Politeness*. London: Longman.

James, Deborah 1996: Women, men and prestige speech forms: A critical review. In Victoria L. Bergvall, Janet M. Bing, and Alice F. Freed (eds) *Rethinking Language and Gender Research: Theory and Practice*. Harlow: Longman, pp. 98–126.

Keenan, Elinor 1974: Norm-makers, norm-breakers: Uses of speech by men and women in a Malagasy community. In Richard Bauman and Joel Sherzer (eds) *Explorations in the Ethnography of Speaking*. Cambridge: Cambridge University Press, pp. 125–43.

Kurath, Hans 1949: *Word Geography of the Eastern United States*. Ann Arbor: University of Michigan Press.

Labov, William 1966: *The Social Stratification of English in New York City*. Washington, DC: Center for Applied Linguistics.

Labov, William 1972a: *Sociolinguistic Patterns*. Philadelphia: University of Pennsylvania Press.

Labov, William 1972b: The linguistic consequences of being a lame. In *Language in the Inner City*. Philadelphia:University of Pennsylvania Press, pp. 255–97.

Labov, William 1990: The intersection of sex and social class in the course of linguistic change. *Language Variation and Change* 2: 205–54.

Lakoff, Robin 1975: *Language and Woman's Place*. New York: Harper and Row.

Larson, Karen 1982: Role playing and the real thing: Socialization and standard speech in Norway. *Journal of Anthropological Research* 38: 401–10.

Milroy, James, Milroy, Lesley, and Hartley, Sue 1994: Local and supralocal change in British English: The case of glottalization. *English World-Wide* 15: 1–34.

Milroy, Lesley 1980: *Language and Social Networks*. Oxford: Blackwell.

Mugglestone, Lynda 1995: *"Talking Proper": The Rise of Accent as a Social Symbol*. Oxford: Oxford University Press.

Nichols, Patricia 1983: Linguistic options and choices for Black women in the rural south. In Barrie Thorne, Cheris Kramarae, and Nancy Henley (eds) *Language, Gender and Society*. Rowley, MA: Newbury House, pp. 54–68.

Nordberg, Bengt 1971: En undersökning av språket i Eskilstuna. *Språkvård* 3: 7–15.

Nordberg, Bengt and Sundgren, Eva 1998: *On Observing Language Change: A Swedish Case Study*. FUMS Rapport nr. 190. Institutionen för nordiska språk vid Uppsala Universitet.

Nordberg, Bengt and Sundgren, Eva 1999: *Från lokalspråk till standard i en mellansvensk stad: individuell eller generationell förändring?* FUMS Rapport. Institutionen för nordiska språk vid Uppsala Universitet.

O'Barr, William M. and Atkins, Bowman K. 1980: "Women's language" or "powerless language"? In Sally McConnell-Ginet, Ruth Borker, and Nelly Furman (eds) *Women and Language in Literature and Society*. New York: Praeger, pp. 93–109.

Romaine, Suzanne 1982: *Socio-historical Linguistics: Its Status and Methodology*. Cambridge: Cambridge University Press.

Romaine, Suzanne 1984a: On the problem of syntactic variation and pragmatic meaning in sociolinguistic theory. *Folia Linguistica* 18: 409–39.

Romaine, Suzanne 1984b: *The Language of Children and Adolescents. The Acquisition of Communicative Competence*. Oxford: Blackwell.

Romaine, Suzanne 1996: Why women are supposed to talk like ladies: The glamour of grammar. In Natasha Warner, Jocelyn Ahlers, Leela Bilmes, Monica Oliver, Suzanne Wertheim, and Melinda Chen (eds) *Gender and Belief Systems*. Berkeley, CA: Berkeley Women and Language Group, University of California, pp. 633–45.

Romaine, Suzanne 1998: Women, land and language: Shifting metaphors and shifting languages. In Suzanne Wertheim, Ashlee C. Bailey, and Monica Corston-Oliver (eds) *Engendering Communication: Proceedings of the Fifth Berkeley Women and Language Conference*. Berkeley, CA: Berkeley Women and Language Group, University of California, pp. 473–86.

Sen, Amartya 1999: *Development as Freedom*. New York: Alfred A. Knopf.

Shaw, George Bernard 1916: *Pygmalion*. New York: Brentano.

Sweet, Henry 1890: *A Primer of Spoken English*. Oxford: Clarendon Press.

Trevelyan, George O. 1878: *The Life and Letters of Lord Macaulay by His Nephew George Otto Trevelyan*. 2 vols. London: Longman, Green and Co.

Trudgill, Peter 1972: Sex, covert prestige and linguistic change in the urban British English of Norwich. *Language in Society* 1: 179–95.

Trudgill, Peter 1974: *The Social Differentiation of English in Norwich*. Cambridge: Cambridge University Press.

Trudgill, Peter 1983: *On Dialect*. Oxford: Blackwell.

Weinreich, Uriel, Labov, William, and Herzog, Marvin 1968: Empirical foundations for a theory of language change. In Winifred P. Lehmann and Yakov Malkiel (eds) *Directions in Historical Linguistics*. Austin: University of Texas Press, pp. 95–189.

Wyld, H. C. 1920: *A History of Modern Colloquial English*, 3rd edn. Oxford: Blackwell.

5 Language and Desire

DON KULICK

1 Introduction

Exploring the relationship between language and desire is a way of breaking past the problems that inhere in studies that investigate language and sexuality, and of opening up a new field of enquiry that links together research on language and gender, affect, repression, and erotics. Past studies of language and sexuality have overwhelmingly focused on the linguistic behavior of gay men and (to a lesser extent) lesbians. Those studies treat sexuality only in terms of sexual identity, and they focus on the ways in which speakers reveal or conceal that identity in their talk. While these are valid and important topics of investigation, the stress on identity has allowed researchers to overlook what from any perspective must be central dimensions of "sexuality," namely phenomena such as fantasy, repression, the unconscious, and desire.

Furthermore, investigative emphasis on consciously assumed or consciously concealed identities has also blocked enquiry into one of the central insights of performativity theory; namely, that who we are and what we say is in many ways dependent on who we must not be and what must remain unsaid, or unsayable. But how might students of language approach the unsaid, the unsayable? Linguistic theories are of little help, because even though the unconscious is the very resource of all linguistic analysis (deep structures, preference hierarchies), this unconscious tends to be seen entirely in terms of cognition. It is more of a "non-conscious" than an unconscious. The foundational psychoanalytic concepts of desire, or repression – the "pushing away" of thoughts from conscious awareness – have not been theorized within linguistics. Even research that explicitly takes its cue from Freud (such as the work by Victoria Fromkin and others on parapraxes, or slips of the tongue: e.g. Fromkin 1973, 1980) looks only at what language reveals about underlying grammatical knowledge, and brackets out all concern with the psychoanalytic unconscious.

Recently, work in narrative analysis, literary theory, and discursive psychology has moved in directions that suggest ways we might begin exploring how desire is expressed, negotiated, and socialized in language, and how repressions are achieved interactionally. This chapter is concerned with highlighting that work. I will first of all summarize previous work on language and sexuality in order to chart the way in which a focus on desire will differ from a focus on sexuality. Then, I will review a number of theoretical perspectives on how desire can be conceptualized. Finally, I will summarize some of the research now appearing that provides us with tools and concepts that we may use to analyze desire in language.

2   Language and Sexuality

The relationship between language and different kinds of desire is a frequent topic in texts directed at psychoanalytic practitioners, even though therapists "tend to look *through* language rather than *at* its forms" (Capps and Ochs 1995: 186, emphasis in original). Language and desire has also occasionally been analyzed in literary criticism and philosophical texts (e.g. Barthes 1978; Kristeva 1980). However, research based on empirical material – material that examines how desire is actually conveyed through language in social life – is rare. The closest type of study that investigates desire in language is work that examines how sexuality is signaled through words, innuendo, or particular linguistic registers. This kind of research has been conducted since the 1940s in a number of disciplinary fields, such as philology, linguistics, women's studies, anthropology, and speech communication. Most of the early work on this topic is not well known, largely because there isn't very much of it, and what was written often appeared in obscure or esoteric publications (for example, one early study of sexual graffiti in men's toilets was printed privately in Paris in a limited edition of seventy-five copies, and had the cover embossed with the austere command that circulation of the book must be "restricted to students of linguistics, folk-lore, abnormal psychology and allied branches of social science" (Read 1977 [1935])).

Early research on language and sexuality concerned itself almost exclusively with lexical items. There were several reasons for this, but a main one was the assumption that the specialized vocabulary of a group reveals something about "the sociocultural qualities about that group" (Sonenschein 1969: 281). This assumption is a reasonable one, but the interest in looking at language to try to understand the sociocultural qualities of a group established a pattern which persists to this day of seeing sexuality exclusively in terms of "sexual identity" which was shared with other members of the same group. Furthermore, because the only people deemed to have a "sexual identity" were deviants and perverts, it was their linguistic behavior that was examined.

Yet another effect of the focus on lexicon was to largely restrict research to the language practices of homosexual men, who were held to have an extensive in-group "lingo" that could be documented. Lesbians, it was often asserted, had no equivalent slang vocabulary. One early researcher (Legman 1941: 1156) offered two explanations for this. The first concerned "[t]he tradition of gentlemanly restraint among lesbians [that] stifles the flamboyance and conversational cynicism in sexual matters that slang coinage requires." The second explanation for this lesbian lack was that "Lesbian attachments are sufficiently feminine to be more often emotional than simply sexual" – hence an extensive sexual vocabulary would be superfluous.[1] In other words, lesbians were at once both too (gentle)manly and too womanly to talk about sex.

The early focus on gay in-group vocabulary continues today, as is evidenced by the continual appearance of such novelty books as *When Drag is not a Car Race: An Irreverent Dictionary of over 400 Gay and Lesbian Words and Phrases* (Fessler and Rauch 1997), and by articles in scholarly and popular publications that trace the etymologies and political resonances of such terms as "gay," "queer," "dyke," and "closet" (e.g. Boswell 1993; Brownworth 1994; Butters 1998; Cawqua 1982; Diallo and Krumholtz 1994; Dynes 1985; Grahn 1984; Johansson 1981; Lee 1981; Riordon 1978; Roberts 1979a, 1979b; Shapiro, F. 1988; Shapiro, M. 1990; Spears 1985; Stone 1981). By the 1980s, however, research on lexicon had been supplemented by work that examined other dimensions of language, such as pronoun usage, camp sensibility, and coming out narratives. And since then, work on gay and lesbian language has mushroomed, producing studies on everything from intonational patterns to the semiotic means by which gay men create private spaces in ostensibly public domains.

Because I have recently reviewed this research in detail (Kulick 2000), I will limit my comments here to summarizing what I have identified as the most serious problems in this work on gay and lesbian language. There are three.

The first concerns the fact that even though this research ostensibly is concerned with understanding the relationship between sexual orientation and language, *it has no theory of sexuality.* That is to say, it has no real understanding of what sexuality is, how it is acquired, and what the relationship is between what Butler would call its "literal performance" and the unconscious foreclosures and prohibitions that structure and limit that performance. Instead, as I mentioned above, from its very inception as a topic of research, the linguistic and social science literature has conceptualized sexuality exclusively in terms of identity categories. The dimensions of sexuality that define it in disciplines such as psychoanalysis – dimensions like fantasy, pleasure, repression, fear, and desire – all of these are nowhere considered. This means that research has not in fact focused on how language conveys sexuality. It has focused, instead, on how language conveys identity.

This has had consequences for the kind of language behavior that has been studied, which is the second problem. Because the concern has been to show how people with particular identities signal those identities to others, the only people whose language behavior has been examined are people who are assumed to have those identities, that is, men and women who openly identify as homosexual, or who researchers for some reason suspect are homosexual.

The assumption has been that if there is a gay or lesbian language, then that language must somehow be grounded in gay and lesbian identities, and instantiated in the speech of gays and lesbians. That non-homosexuals (imposters, actors, "fag hags," hip or unwary heterosexuals) can and do use language that signals queerness has largely been ignored, and on the few occasions when it has been considered, such usage has been dismissed by researchers as "inauthentic" (Leap 1995, 1996). The lack of attention to the inherent appropriability of language has meant that research has conflated the symbolic position of queerness with the concrete social practices of men and women who self-define as gay and lesbian. While the two can overlap, they are not exactly the same thing. They are, on the contrary, importantly different.

The third problem follows from this. Because attention has focused solely on whether or not gay-identified people reveal or conceal their sexual orientation, what has been foregrounded in the study of language and sexuality is speaker intention. So the criterion for deciding whether something constitutes gay or lesbian language is to find out whether the speaker intended for his or her language to be understood in this way. This idea has been a structuring principle of all work on gay and lesbian language, but it has only been made explicit in some of the most recent work on queer language. Livia and Hall, for example, assert that "[a]n utterance becomes typically lesbian or gay only if the hearer/reader understands that it was the speaker's intent that it should be taken up that way. Queerspeak should thus be considered an essentially intentional phenomenon . . ." (1997: 14; see also Livia 2001: 200–2; Leap 1996: 21–3).

What is theoretically untenable about the idea that "queerspeak should . . . be considered an essentially intentional phenomenon" is that *no* language can be considered an essentially intentional phenomenon. Meaning is always structured by more than will or intent – this was one of Freud's most fundamental insights, and was expressed in his articulation of the unconscious as that structure or dynamic which thwarts and subverts any attempt to fully know what we mean. That meaning must always exceed intent is also the principal point of Derrida's criticism of Austin's concept of the performative (Derrida 1995a). Derrida argues that performatives work not because they depend on the intention of the speaker, but because they embody conventional forms of language that are already in existence before the speaker utters them. Performatives work, and language generally works, because it is quotable. This is the meaning of Derrida's famous example of the signature, with which he concluded "Signature Event Context" (Derrida 1995b). In order for a mark to count as a signature, he observed, it has to be repeatable; it has to enter into a structure of what he calls *iterability*, which means both "to repeat" and "to change." Signatures are particularly good examples of iterability, because even though one repeats them every time one signs one's name, no two signatures are ever exactly the same. The main point, however, is that in order to signify, in order to be authentic, one's mark *has* to be repeatable – if I sign my name "XCFRD" one time and "W4H7V" the next time, and "LQYGMP" the next time, and so on, it won't mean anything; it will not be recognized as a signature, as a meaningful mark. To be so recognized, the mark has to be repeated.

However, if something is repeatable, this means that it simultaneously becomes available for failure: if I am drunk, my signature may not be recognized, it will fail and my check will not be cashed. If something is repeatable, it also becomes available for misuse and forgery. This availability for quotation without my permission, untethered to any intention I may have, is what Derrida means when he says that failure and fraud are not parasitical to language – they are not exceptions or distortions, as Austin (1977: 22) maintains. On the contrary, quotability is the very foundational condition that allows language to exist and work at all. The fact that all signs are quotable (and hence, available for misrepresentation) means that signification cannot be located in the intention of speakers, but, rather in the economy of difference that characterizes language itself. In this sense, failure and misuse are not accidental – they are structural: a signature succeeds not in spite of the possibility of forgery, but because of it. Derrida's point, one that Butler relies on extensively in her own work (see especially Butler 1997), is that a speaker's intention is never enough to anchor meaning, to exhaustively determine context. Language constantly evokes other meanings that both exceed, contradict, and disrupt the language user's intentions. What all this means is that any attempt to define a queer linguistics through appeals to intentionality is hopelessly flawed from the start because it is dependent on precisely the fallacy of intention that Derrida definitively dispensed with years ago.

Because of these three fundamental problems with the kind of research that until now has investigated the relationship between language and sexuality, I have proposed that scholars interested in exploring this relationship will need to reorient and develop new perspectives and methods (Kulick 2000: 272–7). My suggestion is that continuing to phrase those explorations in terms of language and sexuality might be counterproductive, especially since "sexuality" can easily segue into "sexual categories," which can lead us right back to "sexual identity." To forestall and avoid that slippage, it might be helpful to declare a moratorium on "sexuality" for a while, and to phrase enquiry, instead, in terms of "language and desire."

There are three immediate advantages to be gained by beginning to think about desire, rather than sexuality. First, a shift from "sexuality" to "desire" would compel research to decisively shift the ground of inquiry from identity categories to culturally grounded semiotic practices. The desire for recognition, for intimacy, for erotic fulfillment – none of this, in itself, is specific to any particular kind of person. What is specific to different kinds of people are the precise things they desire and the manner in which particular desires are signaled in culturally codified ways. For example, the sexual desire of a man for a woman is conveyed through a range of semiotic codes that may or may not be conscious, but that are recognizable as conveying desire because they are iterable signs that continually get recirculated in social life. The iterability of codes is what allows us to recognize desire *as* desire. This means that all the codes are resources available for anyone – be they straight, gay, bisexual, shoe fetishists, or anything else – to use. It also means that desire cannot best be thought of in terms of individual intentionality. Because it relies on structures of iterability for its expression, desire is available for appropriation and forgery; as we know from cases where men invoke the desire of the Other to claim – ingenuously or not – that they thought the woman they raped desired them; or that they thought the man they killed was coming on to them. Researchers interested in language and desire need to be able to explain this too – they need to explain not only intentional desire, but forged desire.

Second, a focus on desire rather than sexuality would move enquiry to engage with theoretical debates about what desire is, how it is structured, and how it is communicated. One of the many problems with the concept of sexuality, especially when it is linked to identity, is that it tends to be conceptualized as intransitive (one *has* a sexuality, *is* a sexuality); hence research comes to concentrate on how subjects reveal or conceal their sexuality (and hence, once again, the centrality of intentional subjects in this literature). An advantage with the concept of desire is that it is definitionally transitive – one can certainly be said to "have" desire, but that desire is always for something, directed toward something. This means that research is impelled to problematize both the subject and the object of desire, and investigate how those relationships are materialized through language. Because desire, in any theoretical framework, both encompasses and exceeds sexuality, research will, furthermore, be directed toward investigating the ways in which different kinds of desires, for different things, become bound up with or detached from erotic desire.

Third, a focus on desire rather than sexuality would allow analysis expanded scope to explore the role that fantasy, repression, and unconscious motivations play in linguistic interactions – that is to say, it would direct us to look at how language is precisely *not* an essentially intentional phenomenon. It would encourage scholars to develop theories and techniques for analyzing not only what is said, but also how that saying is in many senses dependent on what remains unsaid, or unsayable.

3 What is Desire?

Before we can begin an investigation of language and desire, however, definitional issues will have to be considered. What is desire? In most discussions, that question will be answered with reference to psychoanalysis, since psychoanalysis posits desire as the force that both enables and limits human subjectivity and action.

The distinguishing feature of desire in much psychoanalysis is that it is always, definitionally, bound up with sexuality. Sexual desire is a constitutive dimension of human existence. For Freud, "the germs of the sexual impulses are already present in the new-born child" (Freud 1975: 42). Ontogenetic development consists of learning to restrict those impulses in particular ways, managing them (or not) in relation to socially sanctioned objects and relationships. This learning occurs largely beyond conscious reflection, and is the outcome of specific prohibitions and repressions which children internalize and come to embody.

Although Freud was more inclined to speak of "sexual impulses" or "libido" than "desire" (note, though, that "libido" is a Latin word meaning "wish" or "desire"), he would undoubtedly have agreed with Lacan's Spinozan epigraph that "desire is the essence of man" (Lacan 1998: 275). Freud would probably not have agreed, however, with the specific attributions that Lacan attaches to desire. In Lacan's work, desire here has a very particular meaning. Unlike libido, which for Freud was a kind of energy or force that continually sought its own satisfaction, desire, for Lacan, is associated with absence, loss, and lack.

A starting point in Lacanian psychoanalysis is the assumption that infants come into the world with no sense of division or separation from anything. Because they sense no separation, and because their physical needs are met by others, infants do not perceive themselves to lack anything; instead, they imagine themselves to be complete and whole. This imagined wholeness is the source of the term *Imaginary*, which is one of the three registers of subjectivity identified by Lacan. Lacan argues that this psychic state must be superseded (by the *Symbolic*, which means language and culture), because to remain in it or to return to it for any length of time would be the equivalent of psychosis.

Exit from the Imaginary occurs as infants develop and come to perceive the difference between themselves and their caregiver(s). Lacan believes that this awareness is registered as traumatic, because at this point, the infant realizes that caregivers are not just *there*. Nourishment, protection, and love are not simply or always just given, or given satisfyingly; instead, they are given (always temporarily) as a result of particular signifying acts, like crying, squirming, or vocalizing. Sensing this, infants begin to signify. That is, they begin to formulate their needs as what Lacan calls "demands." In other words, whereas previously, bodily movements and vocalizations had no purpose or goal, they now come to be directed at prompting or controlling (m)others.

Once needs are formulated as demands, they are lost to us, because needs exist in a different order (Lacan's *Real*, which is his name for that which remains beyond or outside signification). In a similar way that Kant argued that language both gives us our world of experience, and also keeps us from perceiving the world in an unmediated form, Lacan asserts that signification can substitute for needs, but it cannot fulfill them. This gap between the need and its expression – between a hope and its fulfillment – is where Lacan locates the origins and workings of desire.

The idea that desire arises when an infant registers loss of (imagined) wholeness means that the real object of desire (to regain that original plenitude) will forever remain out of reach. But because we do not know that this is what we want (in an important sense, we *cannot* know this, since this dynamic is what structures the unconscious), we displace this desire onto other things, and we desire those things, hoping – always in vain – that they will satisfy our needs. As Elizabeth Grosz has summarized so clearly (1990: 61), the displacement of desire onto other things means that the demands through which desire is symbolized actually has not one, but two objects: one spoken (the object demanded), and one unspoken (the maintenance of a relationship to the other to whom the demand is addressed). So the thing demanded is a rationalization for maintaining a certain relation to the other: the demand for food is also a demand for recognition, for the other's desire. The catch is that even if this recognition is granted, we can't assume that it will always be granted ("Will you still love me tomorrow . . ."); hence, we repeat the demand, endlessly.

The relationship of all this to sexuality lies in psychoanalysis's linkage between sexual difference and desire. There is a purposeful conflation in Lacan's writing between sexuality and sex; that is, between erotics and being a man or a woman. (In English, the terms "masculine" and "feminine" express a similar conflation, since those terms denote both "ways of being" and "sexual positions".) Lacan's interest is to explain how infants, who are born unaware of sex and sexuality, come to assume particular positions in language and culture, which is where sex and sexuality are produced and sustained. Because becoming a man or a woman occurs largely through the adoption or refusal of particular sexual roles in relation to one's parents (roles that supposedly get worked out in the course of the Oedipal process), sexuality is the primary channel through which we arrive at our identities as sexed beings. In other words, gender is achieved through sexuality. Furthermore, the fact that our demands are always in some sense a demand for the desire of an other means that our sense of who we are is continually formed through libidinal relations.

This relationship between sexuality and sex is central to Butler's claims about the workings and power of what she has termed the heterosexual matrix. Her argument is that men and women are produced as such through the refusals we are required by culture to make in relation to our parents. Culture, Butler says, has come to be constituted in such a way that what she calls heterosexual cathexis (that is, a person culturally-designated-as-a-boy's desire for his mother, or a person culturally-designated-as-a-girl's desire for her father) is displaced, so that a boy's mother is forbidden to him, but women in general are not – in the case of girls, something similar happens: her father is forbidden to her, but men in general are not. In other words, the object of the desire is tabooed, but the modality of desire is not – indeed, that modality of desire is culturally incited, encouraged, and even demanded. Not so with homosexual cathexis (a person culturally-designated-as-a-boy's desire for his father, or a person culturally-designated-as-a-girl's desire for her mother). Not only is the object of that desire forbidden; in this case, the modality of desire itself is tabooed.

These prohibitions produce homosexual cathexis as something that *cannot be*. And since its very existence is not recognized, the loss we experience (of the father for the boy and of the mother for the girl) cannot be acknowledged. Drawing on Freud's writings on the psychic structure of melancholia (Freud 1957, 1960), Butler argues that when the loss of a loved one cannot be acknowledged, the desire that was directed at that loved one cannot be transferred to other objects. In effect, desire gets stuck, it stays put, it bogs down, it cannot move on. Instead, it moves *in*. It becomes incorporated into the psyche in such a way that we *become* what we cannot acknowledge losing. Hence persons culturally-designated-as-boys come to inhabit the position of that which they cannot acknowledge losing (i.e. males), and persons culturally-designated-as-girls become females, for the same reason. Once again, gender is accomplished through the achievement of particular desires.

Unlike Lacan, who equivocates on whether the psychic structures he describes are universal or culturally and historically specific, Butler is at pains to stress that the melancholic structures she postulates are the effects of particular cultural conventions. However, because she does not historicize her explanation, pinpointing when the conventions that form its backdrop are supposed to have arisen and entrenched themselves in people's psychic lives, and also because the only material she analyzes to make her points about melancholy is drawn from contemporary Western societies, it is hard to see what Butler sees as actually (rather than just theoretically) variable. Gender is a fact of social life everywhere, not just in the contemporary West. Do Butler's arguments about gender identity and melancholia apply in Andean villages, Papua New Guinean rainforests, or the Mongolian steppe? This isn't clear. And since Butler does not indicate where she sees the limits of her approach to the assumption of gendered identities, it is difficult to resist the conclusion that her model, despite her assertions to the contrary, is universalistic in scope.[2]

However one wishes to read Butler here, the point is that this explanation of why certain human beings come to be men and certain others come to be women lies at the heart of performativity theory. Note, therefore, that performativity theory, as Butler has elaborated it, is inseparable from psychoanalytic assumptions about the relationship between desire, sexuality, and sex.[3] Interestingly, this fundamental reliance on psychoanalysis is downplayed or ignored in many summaries of Butler's work (e.g. Jagose 1996; Hall 1999), and my own suspicion is that many readers of *Gender Trouble* simply skip chapter 2, which is where she develops her claim that "gender identity is a melancholic structure" (1990: 68). But performativity theory without psychoanalysis is not performativity theory, at least not in Butler's version. If you remove the psychoanalysis, what remains is simply a kind of performance theory *à la* Goffman – the kind of theory that inattentive readers mistakenly accused Butler of promoting in *Gender Trouble* (e.g. Jeffreys 1994; Weston 1993).

A dramatic contrast to psychoanalytic theories of desire is found in the work of Gilles Deleuze and Félix Guattari. Deleuze and Guattari take great pleasure in criticizing and mocking psychoanalysis (chapter 2 of *A Thousand Plateaus*, about Freud's patient the Wolf-Man, reads like a stand-up comedy routine, with psychoanalysis as the butt of all the jokes). They insist psychoanalysis has fundamentally misconstrued the nature of desire because it sees desire as always linked to sexuality. This is to misrepresent it: "Sleeping is a desire," Deleuze observes; "Walking is a desire. Listening to music, or making music, or writing, are desires. A spring, a winter, are desires. Old age is also a desire. Even death" (Deleuze and Parnet 1987: 95). None of these desires are necessarily linked to sexuality, even though sexuality may well be one dimension (one "flux") that, together with other fluxes, creates desire. That psychoanalysis distills sexuality out of every desire is symptomatic of its relentless reductionism: "For [Freud] there will always be a reduction to the One: . . . it all leads back to daddy" (Deleuze and Guattari 1996: 31, 35). Lacan's insistence that desire is related to absence and lack is also a reflex of the same reductionist impulse, and it is unable to conceptualize how voids are "fully" part of desire, not evidence of a lack (Deleuze and Parnet 1987: 90). Deleuze exemplifies this with courtly love:

> it is well known that courtly love implies tests which postpone pleasure, or at least postpone the ending of coitus. This is certainly not a method of deprivation. It is the constitution of a field of immanence, where desire constructs its own plane and lacks nothing.   (Deleuze and Parnet 1987: 101)

In contrast to psychoanalysts like Freud and Lacan (and Butler), who understand desire in terms of developmental history, Deleuze and Guattari see it in terms of geography. That is to say, they see their tasks as analysts as mapping the ways desire is made possible and charting the ways it moves, acts, and forms connections. They have no need to theorize the ontogenetic origins of desire, since desire is an immanent feature of all relations. For linguists and anthropologists, an advantage with this conceptualization of desire, regardless of whether or not one elects to adopt Deleuze and Guattari's entire analytical edifice, is that it foregrounds desire as continually being dis/re/assembled. Thus, attention can focus on whether and how different kinds of relations emit desire, fabricate it, and/or block it, exhaust it.

Deleuze and Guattari's rejection of psychoanalysis as the final arbiter of desire is not without problems – Butler, for example, has commented that a reason she has not engaged with their work in her writing is that "they don't take prohibition seriously and I do" (Butler 1999: 296). The idea that desire is immanent in all relations may also strike some as an example of metaphysics at its most fanciful. Be that as it may, the French philosophers' critical stance toward psychoanalysis does resonate with the reactions of many students who become interested in performativity theory. A great difficulty with the conceptualization of desire that animates performativity theory is the fact that it is grounded in a priori psychoanalytic assertions about its genesis and nature. The quasi-universalistic assumptions which underlie those assertions are difficult to reconcile with the kind of empirical material analyzed by linguists and anthropologists. When I teach performativity theory, for example, students are generally excited by everything *except* the assumptions that underlie the nature of the subject. While the ideas intrigue them, the majority simply do not find it helpful to assume that desire = lack, or that subjectivity is constituted through processes of melancholic foreclosure and incorporation. For students and scholars interested in the analysis of embedded practices, such as talk, appeals to highly abstract psychoanalytic theories of subjectivity and action do not free up thought; instead, they seem to constrict it. Of course, this does not mean that the theories themselves are without relevance, value, or explanatory power. But it does mean that investigations of the relationship between language and desire seem not to be most productively approached by beginning with abstract psychoanalytic theories and using them as a frame within which one collects and analyzes data.

Deleuze and Guattari's framework is not abstract psychoanalysis. In this context, though, it is hardly much improvement, since its formidable philosophical erudition, deliberately contorted presentational style, and highly idiosyncratic lexicon (hecceities, rhizomes, machines, bodies without organs . . .) make it just as daunting as even Lacan's writing (although, again, it does display a sense of humor that is substantially more satisfying than Lacan's smug double-entendres). Despite these difficulties, Deleuze and Guattari do direct attention to desire without requiring that we derive all its formations from a particular source or a specific constellation of psycho-social relations (". . . it all leads back to daddy").

This interest in mapping desire as a geographer would map a landscape links Deleuze and Guattari to Foucault. Perhaps the most productive way of thinking about desire would be to see it in more or less the same terms that Foucault conceptualized power. Although he highlighted power in all his work, Foucault was explicit about not wanting to erect a coherent theory of power. "If one tries to erect a theory of power," he argued,

> one will always be obliged to view it as emerging at a given place and time and hence to deduce it, to reconstruct its genesis. But if power is in reality an open, more or less coordinated (in the event, no doubt, ill-coordinated) cluster of relations, then the only problem is to provide oneself with a grid of analysis which makes possible an analytic of relations of power.   (Foucault 1980: 199)

Following Foucault's lead, it should be possible to study desire without having to decide in advance what it is and why it emerges; that is, without having to become a psychoanalyst. Instead of a theory of desire, the point would be to develop a means of delineating, examining, and elucidating those domains and those relations that are created through desire, not forgetting for a second to highlight the ways in which those domains and relations will always be bound up with power.

4   Investigating Desire in Language

So the question arises: if we see desire as iterable practices that can be mapped, how do we do the mapping? What kind of empirical material can we look at, and what do we look for?

At present, there are at least four kinds of work being done that address these questions, even if the researchers doing the work may not exactly see themselves as investigating language and desire. The four kinds of research I have in mind are:

- studies that examine how repressions are accomplished in everyday interactions;
- studies that document how desires are socialized;
- studies that demonstrate how silences and disavowals structure interaction;
- studies that analyze how intimacy is achieved.

The first kind of research on that list is best represented by the branch of scholarship called "discursive psychology." In discursive psychology, ethno-methodology and Conversation Analysis are crucial theoretical and methodo-logical tools (for a detailed discussion of this, see the exchange between Billig and Schegloff in *Discourse & Society*: Billig and Schegloff 1999). In an overview article, Billig (1997: 139–40) explains that discursive psychology "argues that phenomena, which traditional psychological theories have treated as 'inner processes', are, in fact, constituted through social, discursive activity. Accord-ingly, discursive psychologists argue that psychology should be based on the study of this outward activity rather than upon hypothetical, and essentially unobservable, inner states." A concrete example of this is developed extensively in Billig's more recent monograph which reconsiders the Freudian concept of repression in terms of language (Billig 1999). Billig agrees with Freud that repression is a fundamental dimension of human existence. But he disagrees with the idea that the roots of repression lie in biologically inborn urges, as Freud thought. Instead, repression is demanded by language: "in conversing, we also create silences," says Billig (1999: 261). Thus, in learning to speak, chil-dren also learn what must remain unspoken and unspeakable. This means two things: first, that repression is not beyond or outside language, but is, instead, the constitutive resource of language; and second, that repression is an inter-actional achievement.

Billig's approach to Freudian repression is readily recognizable to anyone familiar with Foucault's arguments that silences "are an integral part of the strategies that underlie and permeate discourses" (1981: 27), Derrida's asser-tions that "silence plays the irreducible role of that which bears and haunts language, outside and *against* which alone language can emerge" (Derrida 1978: 54, emphasis in original), and Butler's continual insistence that the sub-ject emerges through the repeated enactment of repudiations and foreclosures

– foreclosures that are generated through language. Billig's contribution to this discussion is to focus attention on the mundane ways in which these kinds of foreclosures are accomplished in everyday conversation, through avoidances, topic changes, and direct commands. For example, in discussing the socialization of polite behavior, Billig remarks that "each time adults tell a child how to speak politely, they are indicating how to speak rudely. 'You must say *please*' . . . 'Don't say *that* word'. All such commands tell the child what rudeness is, pointing to the forbidden phrases. . . . [I]n teaching politeness, [adults provide] a model of rudeness" (1999: 94, 95; emphasis in original).

Billig's attention to socializing contexts leads us to the second kind of study that investigates desire, namely, research on language socialization that documents how particular fears and desires are conveyed and acquired through recurring linguistic routines. An early article that examined this is Clancy's investigation of how Japanese children acquire what she calls communicative style; that is, "the way language is used and understood in a particular culture" (Clancy 1986: 213). Clancy was interested to see how children are socialized to command the strategies of indirection and intuitive understanding that characterize Japanese communicative style. In working with two-year-old children and their mothers, she discovered that these skills were acquired through early socialization routines in which mothers, among other practices, (a) juxtaposed indirect expressions (e.g. "It's already good") with direct ones ("No!"), thus conveying the idea that various forms of expression could be functionally equivalent; (b) attributed speech to others who had not actually spoken, thereby indicating to children how they should read non-verbal behavior; (c) appealed to the imagined reactions of *hito*, "other people," who are supposedly always watching and evaluating the child's behavior; and (d) used strongly affect-laden adjectives such as "scary" or "frightening" to describe a child's (mis)behavior, making it clear that such behavior is socially unacceptable and shameful. These kinds of communicative interactions sensitized children to subtle interactional expectations which in adult interactions are not expressed explicitly. They also encouraged children to acquire the specific anxieties and fears (such as the disapproval of *hito*) that undergird Japanese communicative style.

The socialization of fear is also described by Capps and Ochs (1995), in their study of an agoraphobic woman in Los Angeles. A central attribute of agoraphobia is a sense of having no control over one's feelings and actions (hence one gets gripped by paralyzing anxiety attacks). Capps and Ochs hypothesize that this sense of being unable to control one's feelings is, at least in part, socialized, and they examine how this might occur by analyzing interactions between Meg, the agoraphobic woman, and Beth, her eleven-year-old daughter, when Beth talks about how she managed to handle some threatening situation. Whenever this happens, Meg will often reframe her daughter's story in ways that undermine Beth's control as protagonist. She does this by portraying people as fundamentally and frighteningly unpredictable, no matter what Beth may think; by casting doubt on the credibility of her daughter's memory of events; by minimizing the threatening dimension of the daughter's narrative, thereby implying that Beth has not truly surmounted danger; and by reframing situations in which Beth asserts herself as situations in which the daughter has done something embarrassing.

Although the studies by Clancy and Capps and Ochs discuss fear and not desire, it is important to remember that from another perspective, *fears are desires* – the desire to avoid shame, embarrassment, danger, punishment, etc. Another study co-authored by Ochs (Ochs et al. 1996) specifically discusses desire. In this case, though, the desire is not sexual, but gustatory. Here, the research team investigated how children come to develop taste. One of their main findings was that children's likes and dislikes of different kinds of food are actively socialized at the dinner table.

In a comparison of dinnertime interactions between American and Italian middle-class families, Ochs and her collaborators found that dinners at the American tables were consistently marked by oppositional stances in relation to food, with children complaining that they did not want to eat the food they were served, and parents insisting that they must. One of the reasons why these dinnertime interactions were so oppositional is that they were framed that way by parents. American parents often assumed that children would not like the same kinds of foods that they enjoyed. This could be signaled through the preparation of different dishes, some for children and others for the adults, or by remarks that invited children to align in opposition to adults. For example, when one parent presents a novel food item at the dinner table, the other might remark "I don't know if the kids'll really like it, but I'll give them." In addition, the tendency in American homes was to "frame dessert as what their children *want* to eat, and vegetables, meat, etc., as what their children *have* to eat" (1996: 22, emphasis in original), thereby creating a situation in which certain foods were portrayed as tasty and desirable, and others as mere nutrition, or even punishment ("Eat that celery or you'll get no dessert").

Italian families, in contrast, highlighted food as pleasure. Parents did not invite their children to adopt oppositional stances (by creating distinctions between themselves and "the kids" in relation to food), they foregrounded the positive dimensions of the social relations that were materialized through food ("Hey look at this guys! Tonight Mamma delights us. Spaghetti with clams"), and they did not portray dessert as a reward to be gained only after one has first performed a laborious and unpleasant duty. The results of these kinds of differences in socializing contexts is that children acquire (rather than simply "discover") different kinds of relationships to food, different kinds of tastes, and different kinds of desires.

Studies of language socialization like those by Clancy and Ochs and her collaborators do not discuss repression or mention Freud or Lacan. Never mind: this kind of work is an important and guiding example of how linguists can link with the project of discursive psychology to demonstrate how "phenomena, which traditional psychological theories have treated as 'inner processes' [such as taste, intuition, shame, or anxiety] are, in fact, constituted through social, discursive activity" (Billig 1997: 139).

The third kind of research on my list examines the disavowals, silences, and repressions that take place in discourse in order for certain subjective positions to emerge. In other words, it is work that explores how the unsaid or the unsayable structures what is said. One of the most powerful examples of this is Toni Morrison's essay on the role that what she calls "Africanism" ("the denotative and connotative blackness that African peoples have come to signify"; Morrison 1993: 6) has played in the constitution of American literature. Morrison's point is that in this literature, Black people are often either silent, invisible, or absent. But though they might be speechless or not present, they nevertheless assert a structuring power on the coherence of American literature and the forms it has taken. Their symbolization as enslaved, unsettling, dark, childlike, savage, and raw provided American authors with a backdrop against which they could reflect upon themselves and their place in the world. "Africanism," writes Morrison,

> is the vehicle by which the American self knows itself as not enslaved, but free; not repulsive, but desirable; not helpless, but licensed and powerful; not history-less, but historical; not damned, but innocent; not a blind accident of evolution, but a progressive fulfillment of destiny.   (Morrison 1993: 52)

Morrison's project is to understand how Africanist characters act as surrogates and enablers, and to see how imaginative encounters with them enable White writers to think about themselves (1993: 51). Butler employs a similar analytic strategy in her essay on Nella Larsen's novel *Passing* (Butler 1993b). Butler's reading of *Passing* highlights how certain identifications, relational configurations, and desires exist in the novel only because the characters refuse to acknowledge certain other identifications, relational configurations, and desires. But a refusal to acknowledge something is already a form of acknowledgment; it is like ignorance: ignorance is not so much something we have failed to learn as it is something we have learned not to know. Hence, the disavowal of certain desires and relationships both sustains them and structures the desires and relationships that we do explicitly recognize and embrace.

But Morrison is a writer, Butler is a philosopher, and the material they analyze to make their points are literary texts. How can their insights about absences and repudiations be brought to bear on linguistic data?

One illuminating instance of this is Cameron's (1997) analysis of how heterosexuality is performed. The data for this study is a conversation between five White male American college students sitting at home watching a basketball game. This conversation was recorded by one of the participants, who used it in a class Cameron taught to discuss sports talk. Upon examining the tape, however, Cameron noticed something else: apart from talk about the basketball game, the single most prominent theme in the conversation was gossip about men whom the speakers identify as "gay." Cameron concludes that this kind of gossip is a performative enactment of heterosexuality, one structured by the presence of a danger that cannot be acknowledged: namely, the possibility of homosexual desire within the speakers' own homosocial group. In order to defuse this threat and constitute a solidly heterosexual in-group, the speakers localize homosexual desire outside the group, in the bodies of absent others, who become invoked as contrasts.

What is most ironic about this enactment of heterosexuality is that in order to convey to one another that the males under discussion really are "gay," the students engage in detailed descriptions of those other males' clothing and bodily appearance, commenting extensively, for example, on the fact that one supposedly gay classmate wore "French cut spandex" shorts to class in order to display his legs, despite the fact that it was winter. Discussing this aspect of the students' talk, Cameron observes that the five young men

> are caught up in a contradiction: their criticism of the "gays" centres on [the "gays'"] unmanly interest in displaying their bodies . . . But in order to pursue this line of criticism, the conversationalists themselves must show an acute awareness of such "unmanly" concerns as styles and materials ("French cut spandex" . . .), what kind of clothes go together, and which men have "good legs". They are impelled, paradoxically, to talk about men's bodies as a way of demonstrating their own total lack of sexual interest in those bodies.   (1997: 54)

In other words, the students' desire in this homosocial context to distance themselves from the specter of homosexual desire leads them to structure their talk in such a way that it is not only similar to stereotypical "women's language" (besides topics, Cameron also analyzes how the speakers engage in a variety of "cooperative" discourse moves usually associated with women) – in its fine-tuned attention to the bodies and sexualities of other men, the talk is also not unlike stereotypical Gayspeak. Imagine telling them that.

The final kind of literature that I think provides linguists with models for how it is possible to examine the relationship between language and desire is work being done on the achievement of intimacy. Intimacy is a constellation of practices that both expresses and is expressive of desire. But like all desire, intimate desires are publicly mediated and run through specific circuits of power. As Berlant and Warner (1998) have recently argued, the state plays a crucial role in the constitution of intimacy by exercising its power to legitimize some types of intimacy and delegitimize others. Together with other institutions (e.g. the church, the family) and ideological formations (e.g. ideas about what "proper"or "real" men and women should and should not do in their intimate lives), intimacies are good examples of how desires may feel private, but are, inexorably and unavoidably, shaped through public structures and in public interactions. One of the ways in which public mediation shapes desire is through processes of prohibition. These processes, which are meant to discourage particular desires, in fact often incite and sustain them. As Freud and many others before him recognized,[4] the act of prohibition is a crucial instigator of desire. Prohibition is always libidinally invested: it fixes desire on the prohibited object and raises the desire for transgression.

One consistent finding of linguists who have studied intimacy is that it is often achieved, at least in part, through the transgression of taboos. An example of this is Langford's (1997) examination of Valentine's Day personal messages in the British *Guardian* newspaper. The messages that Langford analyzes are ones in which the authors of the personal ads adopt the name and the voice of a cuddly animal for themselves and their partner, for example "Flopsy Bunny I love you, Fierce Bad Rabbit," or "Fluffy likes squeezing a pink thing at bed time! Oink says Porker." A number of taboos are transgressed in these messages, most obviously the prohibition on adults publicly behaving like infants, and by extension also the prohibition on children behaving in an overtly licentious manner. Langford draws on psychoanalytic theory to argue that the develop- ment of these alternate animal personalities may be related to the desire to create an attachment to an object which is reliable and unchanging, and which stands outside the emotional traumas of everyday adult life. (There seems also to be a particularly British preoccupation at work here, uncommented on by Langford, that appears amenable to a more thoroughgoing anthropological analysis.) Whether or not one agrees with Langford's interpretation of this phenomenon, her analysis does point the way to how psychoanalytic frame- works might be helpful in thinking about why and how desire comes to be expressed in specific sociocultural settings.

Another example of the relationship between intimacy and prohibition is Channell's (1997) use of Conversation Analysis to track how intimacy is accomplished in the infamous "Tampax" telephone conversation that alleg- edly took place between the Prince of Wales and his companion Camilla Parker-Bowles. A central argument in Channell's analysis is that intimacy is accomplished through the transgression of taboos that operate in public and non-intimate discourse; hence the Prince's notorious remark about wanting to be in Camilla's knickers so badly that he'll probably end up being reincarnated as a tampon.

That the hapless Prince's quip that he might return to us as a menstrual sponge raises vaguely pornographic images is predictable, given that porno- graphy is a discourse of intimacy and desire (it is of course a discourse of many other things as well, like all desire). One of the ways pornography conveys intimacy and incites desire is by doing what the Prince of Wales does in his conversation with Camilla, namely, invoking and transgressing public taboos and prohibitions. This dimension of pornographic language is highlighted in Heywood's (1997) study of narratives published in the gay magazine *Straight To Hell*. Those narratives, which claim to be first-person accounts of real-life sexual experiences, give shape to desire by channeling it through the trans- gression of multiple boundaries. In the stories, straight men have sex with homosexuals, that sex often takes place in liminal public settings such as in the street *outside* a gay bar, and the sexual acts described flout social norms that separate the acceptable from the unspeakable ("I Slept With My Nose Up His Ass"). Heywood discusses how the *frissons* generated by these kinds of transgressions are comprehensible in a culture that fetishizes heterosexual masculinity, elevates it to the status of hyper-desirable, and figures it as something fundamentally *other* than homosexuality. In this context, narratives of a homosexual man's sexual conquest of a supposedly straight man lubricate multiple lines of fantasy.

The social embedding and linguistic coding of fantasy is also discussed by Hall (1995), in her study of telephone sex-line workers who were employed in companies that advertise to a heterosexual male market. Hall observed that workers who earned the most money (by keeping their pay-by-minute callers on the line the longest) were speakers whose language best invoked the stereotypical image of the submissive and sexually accommodating woman. Hence, the most successful "fantasy makers," as some of the workers called themselves, were the ones who could verbally invoke a conservative frame that many callers recognized and could participate in. But as in the other cases of intimacy that I have discussed, the talk on the phone lines was also transgressive of public speech. This transgression partly concerned content, where overtly sexual acts were verbalized. However, it was also transgressive in terms of delivery. One woman explained that "to be a really good fantasy maker, you've got to have big tits in your voice" (Hall 1995: 199). The phantasmatic tits were voiced through "words that are very feminine," like "peach," and by talk about feminine bodies and articles of clothing. Other fantasy makers told Hall that they relied on high pitch, whispering, and "a loping tone of voice" to project sex through the phone lines.

Like the other research I have discussed, Hall's work is important because it directs us to examine the precise linguistic resources that people use to animate desire. But it does so without reducing desire to identity. Indeed, work like Hall's directs our attention in completely the opposite direction, since the desire emitted through the language of the sex-line workers has nothing to do with their identities – a fantasy maker may be an utterly riveting "bimbo, nymphomaniac, mistress, slave, transvestite, lesbian, foreigner [!], or virgin" (from a sex-line training manual quoted by Hall 1995: 190–1) on the phone, but it is not how she identifies herself in her day-to-day life. This disaggregation of desire from identity alerts us to the ways in which desire relies on structures of iterability for its expression – and, hence, is always available for appropriation and forgery. Hall mentions a number of forgeries that occur at the sex line, some of them about race ("European American women are more successful at performing a Black identity than African American women are": p. 201). But one particularly striking forgery involves gender. One of the sex-line workers interviewed by Hall was Andy, a 33-year-old Mexican American bisexual who earned his living on the sex lines posing as a heterosexual woman.

Paraphrasing Barthes, who was writing about love, we could say that to write about desire is "to confront the *muck* of language: that region of hysteria where language is *too much* and *too little*, excessive ... and impoverished" (Barthes 1978: 99, emphasis in original). The theoretical project I have outlined here is, to be sure, a bit mucky. But no matter: what dimension of language and life isn't? The goal of this essay has been to motivate a shift from looking at language and sexuality to interrogating and mapping language and desire. This is already being done, as I noted in my summaries of current work. But my argument is that the insights being generated by that work have not been related to a meta-theoretical discourse that encourages us to see the work as contributing to a common intellectual project. The research I have discussed shares a number of theoretical concerns that could be sharpened and developed by being made explicit and linked. And they are linked: work on the ways in which repressions and silences are constituted through language, on how those silences play a structuring role in the way in which interactions are organized, and on how specific linguistic conventions are used to structure, convey, and socialize desire – all of this contributes to an understanding of the relationship between desire and language. Recognizing this would open up new lines of enquiry, it would establish new theoretical and methodological linkages, and it would allow new connections to be made across disciplines. Those connections promise to strengthen cooperation between linguists, anthropologists, and psychologists, and they promise to enrich the study of language in exciting and highly desirable ways.

NOTES

1   Lesbian feminist scholars Penelope and Wolfe (1979: 11–12) suggest other reasons for the absence of an elaborate lesbian in-group vocabulary. They argue that such an absence is predictable, given that, in their opinion, the vocabulary of male homosexuals (and of males in general) is misogynist. "How would a group of women gain a satisfactorily expressive terminology if the only available terms were derogatory toward women?" they ask. In addition, they note that lesbians "have been socially and historically invisible . . . and isolated from each other as a consequence, and have never had a cohesive community in which a Lesbian aesthetic could have developed."

2   To my knowledge, this issue is addressed directly only once in Butler's oeuvre, when she justifies why she feels she can use terms like "heterosexuality" when discussing the work of classical authors like Aristotle and Plato. Her use of the term, she writes,

> is not meant to suggest that a single heterosexualizing imperative persists in [widely varied] historical contexts, but only that the instability by the effort to fix the site of the sexed body challenges the boundaries of discursive intelligibility in each of these contexts . . . [T]he point is to show that the uncontested status of "sex" within the heterosexual dyad secures the workings of certain symbolic orders, and that its contestation calls into question where and how the limits of symbolic intelligibility are set. (1993a: 16)

Note the slippage between the disavowal that there is "a single heterosexualizing imperative" across history and cultures, and the later invocation of "the heterosexual dyad" (singular). This is the kind of hedging that opens Butler's work to the charge that she is in fact making universalistic claims, despite her assertions to the contrary.

3 Note also that this explanation of the assumption of sexed identities is not an argument about language. Hence, the frequent accusation that Butler's theorizing is "linguisticism," at least in this, central, instance, is not sustainable.

4 See Freud (1989). In his discussion of the relationship of transgression to the Law, Žižek (1999: 148) cites Paul's Epistle to the Romans, chapter 7, verse 7, as an early argument that there can be no sin prior to or independent of the Law:

> . . . if it had not been for the law, I would not have known sin, I would not have known what it is to covet if the law had not said, "You shall not covet". But sin, seizing an opportunity in the commandment, produces in me all kinds of covetousness. Apart from the law sin lies dead.

REFERENCES

Austin, J. L. 1997: *How to Do Things with Words*, 2nd edn. Cambridge, MA: Harvard University Press.

Barthes, Roland 1978: *A Lover's Discourse*. New York: Farrar, Straus & Giroux.

Berlant, Lauren and Warner, Michael 1998: Sex in public. *Critical Inquiry* 24(2): 547–66.

Billig, Michael 1997: The dialogic unconscious: Psychoanalysis, discursive psychology and the nature of repression. *British Journal of Social Psychology* 36: 139–59.

Billig, Michael 1999: *Freudian Repression: Conversation Creating the Unconscious*. Cambridge: Cambridge University Press.

Billig, Michael and Schegloff, Emanuel A. 1999: Critical discourse analysis and Conversation Analysis: An exchange between Michael Billig and Emanuel A. Schegloff. *Discourse & Society* 10(4): 543–82.

Boswell, John 1993: On the use of the term "homo" as a derogatory epithet. In Marc Wolinsky and Kenneth Sherrill (eds) *Gays and the Military: Joseph Steffan versus the United States*. Princeton: Princeton University Press, pp. 49–55.

Brownworth, Victoria A. 1994: The name game: Or why I'm a lezzie-queer. *Deneuve*, July/August: 12.

Butler, Judith 1990: *Gender Trouble: Feminism and the Subversion of Identity*. New York and London: Routledge.

Butler, Judith 1993a: *Bodies That Matter: On the Discursive Limits of "Sex."* New York and London: Routledge.

Butler, Judith 1993b: Queering, passing: Nella Larsen's psychoanalytic challenge. In Judith Butler (ed.) *Bodies That Matter: On the Discursive Limits of "Sex."* New York and London: Routledge, pp. 167–85.

Butler, Judith 1997: *Excitable Speech: A Politics of the Performative*. New York and London: Routledge.

Butler, Judith 1999: Never mind the bollocks: An interview by Kate More. In Kate More and Stephen Whittle (eds) *Reclaiming Genders: Transsexual Grammars at the Fin de Siècle*. London and New York: Cassell, pp. 285–302.

Butters, Ronald R. 1998: Cary Grant and the emergence of gay "homosexual." *Dictionaries* 19: 188–204.

Cameron, Deborah 1997: Performing gender identity: Young men's talk and the construction of heterosexual masculinity. In Sally Johnson and Ulrike Hanna Meinhof (eds) *Language and Masculinity*. Oxford: Blackwell, pp. 47–64.

Capps, Lisa and Ochs, Elinor 1995: *Constructing Panic: The Discourse of Agoraphobia*. Cambridge, MA: Harvard University Press.

Cawqua, Urson 1982: Two etymons and a query: Gay-fairies-camping. *Maledicta* VI: 224–30.

Channell, Joanna 1997: "I just called to say I love you": Love and desire on the telephone. In Keith Harvey and Celia Shalom (eds) *Language and Desire: Encoding Sex, Romance and Intimacy*. London and New York: Routledge, pp. 143–69.

Clancy, Patricia M. 1986: The acquisition of communicative style in Japanese. In Bambi B. Schieffelin and Elinor Ochs (eds) *Language Socialization across Cultures*. Cambridge: Cambridge University Press, pp. 213–50.

Deleuze, Gilles and Guattari, Félix 1996: *A Thousand Plateaus: Capitalism and Schizophrenia*. London: The Athlone Press.

Deleuze, Gilles and Parnet, Claire 1987: *Dialogues*. New York: Columbia University Press.

Derrida, Jacques 1978: Cogito and the history of madness. In Jacques Derrida (ed.) *Writing and Difference*. London: Routledge, pp. 31–63.

Derrida, Jacques (ed.) 1995a: *Limited Inc*. Evanston, IL: Northwestern University Press.

Derrida, Jacques 1995b: Signature Event Context. In Jacques Derrida (ed.) *Limited Inc*. Evanston, IL: Northwestern University Press, pp. 1–23.

Diallo, Kevin and Krumholtz, Jack 1994: *The Unofficial Gay Manual: Living the Lifestyle, Or At Least Appearing To*. New York: Main Street.

Dynes, Wayne R. 1985: *Homolexis: A Historical and Cultural Lexicon of Homosexuality. Gai Saber Monograph No. 4*. New York: Gay Academic Union.

Fessler, Jeff and Rauch, Karen 1997: *When Drag is not a Car Race: An Irreverent Dictionary of over 400 Gay and Lesbian Words and Phrases*. New York: Fireside.

Foucault, Michel 1980: *Power/Knowledge: Selected Interviews and Other Writings, 1972–1977*, edited by Colin Gordon. New York: Pantheon Books.

Foucault, Michel 1981: *The History of Sexuality, Volume 1*. London: Pelican Books.

Freud, Sigmund 1957: Mourning and melancholia. In *Standard Edition of the Complete Psychological Works of Sigmund Freud* (24 vols), edited by James Strachey. London: Hogarth Press, vol. 14, pp. 239–58.

Freud, Sigmund 1960: *The Ego and the Id*. New York: W. W. Norton.

Freud, Sigmund 1975: *Three Essays on the Theory of Sexuality*. New York: Basic Books.

Freud, Sigmund 1989: *Totem and Taboo*. New York: W. W. Norton.

Fromkin, Victoria A. (ed.) 1973: *Speech Errors as Linguistic Evidence*. The Hague: Mouton.

Fromkin, Victoria A. (ed.) 1980: *Errors in Linguistic Performance: Slips of the Tongue, Ear, Pen, and Hand*. New York and London: Academic Press.

Grahn, Judy 1984: *Another Mother Tongue: Gay Words, Gay Worlds.* Boston: Beacon.

Grosz, Elizabeth 1990: *Jacques Lacan: A Feminist Introduction.* London: Routledge.

Hall, Kira 1995: Lip service on the fantasy lines. In Kira Hall and Mary Bucholtz (eds) *Gender Articulated: Language and the Socially Constructed Self.* New York and London: Routledge, pp. 183–216.

Hall, Kira 1999: Performativity. *Journal of Linguistic Anthropology* 9(1–2): 184–7.

Harvey, Keith and Shalom, Celia 1997: Introduction. In Keith Harvey and Celia Shalom (eds) *Language and Desire: Encoding Sex, Romance and Intimacy.* London and New York: Routledge, pp. 1–17.

Heywood, John 1997: "The object of desire is the object of contempt": Representations of masculinity in *Straight To Hell* magazine. In Sally Johnson and Ulrike Hanna Meinhof (eds), *Language and Masculinity.* Oxford: Blackwell, pp. 188–207.

Jagose, Annamarie 1996: *Queer Theory.* Melbourne: Melbourne University Press.

Jeffreys, Sheila 1994: The queer disappearance of lesbians: Sexuality in the academy. *Women's Studies International Forum* 17(5): 459–72.

Johansson, Warren 1981: The etymology of the word "faggot." *Gay Books Bulletin* 6: 16–18, 33.

Kristeva, Julia 1980: *Desire in Language: A Semiotic Approach to Literature and Art.* Oxford: Blackwell.

Kulick, Don 2000: Gay and lesbian language. *Annual Review of Anthropology* 29: 243–85.

Lacan, Jacques 1998: *The Four Fundamental Concepts of Psychoanalysis.* New York: Norton.

Langford, Wendy 1997: "Bunnikins, I love you snugly in your warren": Voices from subterranean cultures of love. In Keith Harvey and Celia Shalom (eds) *Language and Desire: Encoding Sex, Romance and Intimacy.* London and New York: Routledge, pp. 170–85.

Leap, William 1995: Introduction. In William Leap (ed.) *Beyond the Lavender Lexicon: Authenticity, Imagination and Appropriation in Lesbian and Gay Languages.* Buffalo, NY: Gordon and Breach, pp. vii–xix.

Leap, William 1996: *Word's Out: Gay Men's English.* Minneapolis and London: University of Minnesota Press.

Lee, John Allan 1981: Don't use that word! Gay, meaning homosexual. In Liora Salter (ed.) *Communication Studies in Canada.* Toronto: Butterworths, pp. 3–19.

Legman, G. 1941: The language of homosexuality: An American glossary. In George W. Henry (ed.) *Sex Variants: A Study of Homosexual Patterns,* vol. 2. New York and London: Paul B. Hoeber Inc., pp. 1149–79.

Livia, Anna 2001: *Pronoun Envy: Literary Uses of Linguistic Gender.* Oxford: Oxford University Press.

Livia, Anna and Hall, Kira 1997: "It's a girl!": Bringing performativity back to linguistics. In Anna Livia and Kira Hall (eds) *Queerly Phrased: Language, Gender, and Sexuality.* New York: Oxford University Press, pp. 3–18.

Morrison, Toni 1993: *Playing in the Dark: Whiteness and the Literary Imagination.* New York: Vintage Books.

Ochs, Elinor, Pontecorvo, Clotilde, and Fasulo, Alessandra 1996: Socializing taste. *Ethnos* 61(1–2): 5–42.

Penelope (Stanley), Julia and Wolfe, Susan J. 1979: Sexist slang and the gay community: Are you one, too? *Michigan Occasional Paper No.*

XIV. Ann Arbor: University of Michigan.

Read, Allen Walker 1977: *Classic American Graffiti: Lexical Evidence from Folk Epigraphy in Western North America*. Waukesha, WI: Maledicta Press.

Riordon, Michael 1978: A queer by any other name would smell as sweet. In Karla Jay and Allen Young (eds) *Lavender Culture*. New York: Jove Publications, pp. 308–12.

Roberts, J. R. 1979a: Notes on the etymology and usage of "dyke." *Sinister Wisdom* 11: 61–3.

Roberts, J. R. 1979b: In America they call us dykes: Notes on the etymology and usage of "dyke." *Sinister Wisdom* 9: 3–11.

Shapiro, Fred R. 1988: Earlier citations for terms characterizing homosexuals. *American Speech* 63(3): 283–5.

Shapiro, Michael 1990: Gays and lesbians. *American Speech* 65(3): 191–212.

Sonenschein, David 1969: The homosexual's language. *The Journal of Sex Research* 5(4): 281–91.

Spears, Richard A. 1985: On the etymology of "dike." *American Speech* 60(4): 318–27.

Stone, Charles 1981: The semantics of gay. *The Advocate* 325: 20–2.

Weston, Kath 1993: "Do clothes make the woman?" Gender, performance theory and lesbian eroticism. *Genders* 17: 1–21.

Žižek, Slavoj 1999: *The Ticklish Subject: The Absent Center of Political Ontology*. London and New York: Verso.

6 "One Man in Two is a Woman": Linguistic Approaches to Gender in Literary Texts

ANNA LIVIA

1 Introduction

The question of gender in literary texts has been approached by linguists in two different ways. The first involves a comparison of the fiction created by male and female authors and is typified by the search for "the female sentence" or a specifically female style of writing. The second involves a study of the uses to which the linguistic gender system of different languages has been put in literary works. In the former, gender is seen as a cultural property of the author, in the latter, a morphological property of the text. A third perspective on language and gender in literary texts is provided by translators and translation theorists. Translation theorists typically view a text as expressive of a particular time and place as well as being expressed in a particular language. The differences between source and target language may be accompanied by differences in culture and period, thus translators often work with both morphological gender and cultural gender. In this chapter, I will discuss men's and women's style in literature as well as literary uses of linguistic gender. I will also survey material on translation theory and what it offers to students of gender.

2 Male and Female Literary Styles

The most prominent modern thinker to discuss the differences between male and female literary styles is Virginia Woolf, writing at the beginning of the twentieth century. In a review of Dorothy Richardson's novel *Revolving Lights* (1923), she describes the female sentence as "of a more elastic fibre than the old, capable of stretching to the extreme, of suspending the frailest particles, of enveloping the vaguest shapes" (Woolf 1990b: 72). Assuming the traditional literary sentence to be masculine, she argues that it simply does not fit women, who need something less pompous and more elastic which they can bend in different ways to suit their purpose. However, descriptions such as "more elastic," "too loose, too heavy, too pompous" are annoyingly vague and impossible to quantify.

Woolf comes closest to giving a more specific evaluation of the female sentence in a review of Dorothy Richardson's *The Tunnel* (1919). Here she quotes a passage of interior monologue as triumphantly escaping "the him and her" and embedding the reader in the consciousness of the character: "It is like dropping everything and walking backward to something you know is there. However far you go out, you come back. I am back now" (Woolf 1990b: 71). The exact relationship between the pronouns "you" and "I" in this passage is unclear. They seem to refer to the same person, the self, but also to include the reader. Because we do not know who "I" is, we have no referent for the temporal or spatial indicators "now" or "come back" either. This slipperiness of the referent seems to be what Woolf means by "elasticity."

It is significant that Woolf chose the writings of Dorothy Richardson to illustrate the female sentence, and specifically, a passage of interior monologue. Interior monologue has the property of breaking down the boundaries between character and narrator, so that the angle of focalization (who sees the action) coincides with the narration of that action (who tells about the action). More traditional methods of storytelling present a narrator, who recounts, but is separate from the character whose point of view is related. It was one of the projects of modernism (and both Richardson and Woolf are considered modernist) to render the depths of modern experience in an appropriate form, which meant breaking away from what they considered a smug, self-satisfied Edwardian frame of social realism and an omniscient narrator. Although we cannot speak of a "modernist sentence" as such, nevertheless, the other authors usually included in the modernist canon such as T. S. Eliot, James Joyce, D. H. Lawrence, Ezra Pound, as well as Woolf and Richardson, have all experimented with sentence fragments, elimination of predicates, meandering syntax with many clauses in apposition. These are the very elements which tend also to typify interior monologue.

We would do best, therefore, to take Woolf's description of the female sentence as a literary rather than a linguistic commentary. As the stuffy Edwardian era gave way to greater freedom for women, especially in the inter-war period, so women novelists felt freer to express themselves in new ways. The literary movement of modernism coincided with (and was also itself a product of) the new social developments consequent upon the horror and paradoxical liberty of the post-First World War period. Woolf's unremitting self-consciousness is shared by her contemporaries. Indeed her precursor, Henry James, writes of his own awareness of a fragmented consciousness in a discussion of his novel *Portrait of a Lady* (quoted in Millett 1951: v): " 'Place the centre of the subject in the woman's own consciousness,' I said to myself, 'and you get as interesting and as beautiful a difficulty as you could wish'." The challenge of this "beautiful difficulty" may be taken up by men or women authors.

Although Woolf's discussion of feminine style is impressionistic and essentialist, modern theorists have looked at more subtle differences in men's and women's writing. Sara Mills examines features such as descriptions of characters and self-descriptions in personal ads. In an analysis of a romance novel by best-selling author Barbara Taylor Bradford, Mills demonstrates that the actions performed by the female character are of a different quality from those performed by the male (1995: 147–9). Parts of the woman's body move without her volition and she is represented as the passive recipient of the male's actions. The male acts while the female feels.

That male and female characters in fiction receive very different treatment is not particularly controversial, but the claim that women's writing differs in some essential way from that of men is more tendentious. Quoting Woolf's categorization of the female sentence as loose and accretive, Mills proceeds to look at some concrete examples to see what proof there may be of these differences. She concludes that the concept of a female-authored sentence stems from overgeneralization on the part of the literary critic rather than from any inherent quality in the writing, but she demonstrates that a female (or male) affiliation may be a motivating factor in certain texts (1995: 47–8). Comparing descriptions of a landscape taken from two well-known novels, Anita Brookner's *Hotel du Lac* and Malcolm Lowry's *Under the Volcano*, she shows that the first is conventionally feminine while the second is conventionally masculine (1995: 58–60). The features which mark the first as feminine include: abundant use of epistemic modality ("it was supposed," "it could be seen"); grammatically complex, meandering sentences with many clauses in apposition; and an impressionistic, subjective vocabulary such as "stiffish," "skimming," and "area of grey." In contrast, the second landscape is masculine in style, featuring the absence of an obvious authorial voice; an impersonal, objective tone; the description of amenities rather than people: "Overlooking one of these valleys, which is dominated by two volcanoes, lies, six thousand feet above sea-level, the town of Quauhnahuac" (1995: 60).

Female affiliation, or a distinctly feminist style, is a third possibility, in which the tone may be ironic or detached; female characters are presented as assertive and self-confident, and the reader is addressed directly and drawn into the text to share the narrator's point of view. Mills quotes a passage from Ellen Galford's *Moll Cutpurse* to illustrate her point: "She had a voice like a bellowing ox and a laugh like a love-sick lion" (1995: 60–1). This heroine is clearly very different from the passive female, mere object of the male's attention. The oxymoronic (apparently contradictory) quality of the comparison between Moll and a "love-sick lion" demonstrates the playful, almost parodic nature of the description. A lion is usually a symbol of masculine strength, but this lion is in love and therefore emotional. Moll thus combines a traditionally masculine quality (strength) with a traditionally feminine quality (deep feeling).

For contemporary critics, it is possible to identify certain features such as complex sentences with many subordinate clauses and a vocabulary that is vague and impressionistic as typifying the "female sentence," but there is no essential link between the fact of being a woman and this type of writing. It is a style which may be deliberately chosen by either sex. Indeed, if one considers Marcel Proust's sometimes page-length sentences, and his deliberations about the exact quality of colors and smells, one is obliged to classify his style as distinctly feminine:

> *Jamais je ne m'étais avisé qu'elle pouvait avoir une figure rouge, une cravate mauve comme Mme Sazerat, et l'ovale de ses joues me fit tellement souvenir de personnes que j'avais vues à la maison que le soupçon m'effleura, pour se dissiper aussitôt, que cette dame, en son principe générateur, en toutes ses molécules n'était peut-être pas sub-stantiellement la duchesse de Guermantes, mais que son corps, ignorant du nom qu'on lui appliquait, appartenait à un certain type féminin qui comprenait aussi des femmes de médecins et de commerçants.*

> (I had never imagined that she could have a red face, a mauve scarf like Madame Sazerat, and her oval cheeks reminded me so much of people I had seen at home that I had the fleeting suspicion, a suspicion which evaporated immediately afterwards, that this lady, in her generative principle, in each one of her molecules was perhaps not in substance the Duchess of Guermantes but that her body, ignorant of the name she had been given, belonged to a certain feminine type which also included the wives of doctors and tradespeople.)   (Proust 1954: 209–10)

Proust's sentence in the above extract is indisputably long, complex and meandering, convoluted and concerned with female apparel and appearance – all traits which have been classified "feminine."

It is equally possible for a woman author to deliberately flout this convention and write in a recognizably feminist style, or indeed a traditionally masculine one. The writer James Tiptree Junior was declared by the science fiction author Robert Silverberg to be a man in the introduction to one of her short story collections:

> For me there is something ineluctably masculine about Tiptree's writing. I don't think that a woman could have written the short stories of Hemingway, just as I don't think a man could have written the novels of Jane Austen, and in this way I think that Tiptree is male.   (Silverberg 1975: xii)

Tiptree was invited to participate in a symposium organized by the science fiction magazine *Khatru*, the ensuing discussion being published in issues 3 and 4, but "his" style was felt to be so rebarbative that "he" was asked to withdraw (Lefanu 1988: 105–6). At this point "he" revealed that "he" was none other than Alice Sheldon, a renowned, and definitely female, author. The ensuing discussion of each participant's perceptions and misconceptions turned out to be the most fruitful part of the forum.

Novels may be identified as the work of a woman purely because of their content. The British feminist publishing company Virago was about to publish a novel by a young Indian woman, when they learned that the book had in fact been written by a middle-aged English vicar. Upon hearing this, Virago stopped publication. As a company that was set up specifically to publish books by women, they were angry at being hoodwinked into accepting a manuscript written by a man. Critics of Virago's actions argued that it was the submissive, downtrodden status of the heroine which had at first convinced the editors that the novel was written by an Indian woman. This, they said, was a form of racism as the editors assumed that a victim status was typical of Asian women. Dinty Moore, a male author, was assumed to be female when he published a short story in an anthology of reminiscences of a Catholic girls' school. This also caused hot debate, though the anthology was not withdrawn (Rubin 1975).

In a study on the micro-level of text-making (looking at the immediate linguistic environment rather than the whole novel), Susan Ehrlich (1990) has analyzed the use of reported speech and thought in canonical texts, particularly the novels of Virginia Woolf. She compares Woolf's style with that of Henry James and Ernest Hemingway with regard to the types of cohesive devices each uses (1990: 101–3). James depends heavily on what is known as grammatical cohesion, or anaphora. This means he introduces a character, and as soon as the reader has had the chance to form a mental image of this character, he replaces the character's name with a pronoun (this is, of course, a very traditional strategy). Hemingway relies instead on lexical cohesion, or a simple repetition of the character's name. Woolf, in contrast, uses a much greater variety of cohesive devices including grammatical and lexical cohesion as well as semantic connectors, temporal linking, and progressive aspect. A semantic connector tells the reader explicitly to connect two pieces of information in a particular way: *at the same time; in this way; in addition.* Temporal linking gives two clauses the same time reference and is a feature that often involves hypothetical clauses which have no time reference of their own: *Edith would be sure to know; I would have arrived before the others.* Progressive aspect also links two propositions where one clause provides an anchor for the other.

The advantage of research like Ehrlich's is that it provides a concrete set of criteria by which to distinguish different literary styles. We cannot assume that all women will write like Woolf and all men like James or Hemingway, but if we know that a researcher has based his or her claims entirely on a study of canonical texts by male authors, we can predict that certain types of data will be missing.

Studies of gender in literary texts have not been confined to stylistic analysis but also include investigations into the representation of men and women and what these literary models can tell us about conversational expectations in the real world. In an insightful analysis of the preferred conversational strategies of a husband and wife at loggerheads with each other, Robin Lakoff and Deborah

Tannen (1994) propose a new methodology for interpreting communication between the sexes. They analyze the contrasting conversational strategies of Johan and Marianne in Ingmar Bergman's film, *Scenes from a Marriage*.

In this study, they introduce the concepts of pragmatic identity, pragmatic synonymy, and pragmatic homonymy, which, as they demonstrate, replicate the semantic relations of synonymy (having the same meaning but a different form), homonymy (having the same form but a different meaning), and identity (having the same form and the same meaning) (1994: 148–9). The analysis shows that the two partners often use similar strategies to very different ends and, an even more significant finding, that they also achieve the same end (avoiding conflict) by very different strategies: excessive verbiage on Marianne's part and pompous pontification on Johan's. Marianne prattles: "Here already! You weren't coming until tomorrow. What a lovely surprise. Are you hungry? And me with my hair in curlers" (1994: 152); Johann drones: "I'd been out all day at the institute with the zombie from the ministry. You wonder sometimes who those idiots are who sit on the state moneybags" (1994: 154–5). Marianne's contribution is characterized by short sentences, abrupt changes of topic, and a homely, domestic tone. Johan's style is more cohesive and elaborate; it concerns the world of work and is distanced from the current situation. Although their styles are very different, they share the same goal: each is trying to avoid a confrontation about their deteriorating marriage.

Justifying their choice of the constructed, non-spontaneous dialogue of a film script, Lakoff and Tannen explain that "artificial dialog may represent an internalized model . . . for the production of conversation – a competence model that speakers have access to" (1994: 137). They later define this type of competence as "the knowledge a speaker has at his/her disposal to determine what s/he is reasonably expected to contribute, in terms of the implicitly internalized assumptions made in her/his speech community" (1994: 139). Although this type of analysis has not been widely imitated, it demonstrates the utility of looking at constructed dialogue precisely because such pre-planned scripts allow us to see what pragmatic roles have been internalized and what expectations speakers have of patterns of speech appropriate for each sex.

In the French tradition, the *écriture féminine* school, made famous by such writers as Hélène Cixous, Chantal Chawaf, and Annie Leclerc in the 1970s, defines women's writing as corporeal, tied to the workings of the body, and at the same time multivalent and polysemic, defying syntactic norms. Chawaf challenges the reader with the rhetorical question *"l'aboutissement de l'écriture n'est-il pas de prononcer le corps?"* (1976: 18) ("is not the aim of writing to articulate the body?"), while Cixous exhorts, *"Ecris! L'Écriture est pour toi, tu es pour toi, ton corps est toi, prends-le. [. . .] Les femmes sont corps. Plus corps donc plus écriture"* (Cixous and Clément 1975: 40, 48) ("Write! Writing is for you, you are for you, your body is yours, take it. [. . .] Women are bodies. More body so more writing"). The assertion that women are bodies is a little puzzling. Are women, according to Cixous, more corporeal than men? How can writing be corporeal except in a pen and ink sense?

Écriture féminine came out of the women's liberation movement as a response to the complaint that men's writing was increasingly abstract and distanced from material concerns. Where the prevailing ideology, which dominates most text forms from highbrow novels to the language of advertising, tended to see the female body as dirty, messy, shameful, and generally problematic, *écriture féminine* set out to celebrate this body in all its wet, bloody, sticky functions and by-products from menarche to pregnancy and childbirth to menopause. Where the subliminal message of mainstream, misogynist discourse was that women were mired in their own physicality and therefore constitutionally unable to produce great works of fiction, *écriture féminine* saw men as cut off from their own bodies, decentered and more interested in the play of signifiers than in their real-world referents.

When we encounter sentences like the following from Cixous's *La Jeune née* (*The Newly Born Woman*), "*Alors elle, immobile et apparemment passive, livrée aux regards, qu'elle appelle, qu'elle prend*" ("Then she, immobile and apparently passive, prey to glances, that she calls, that she takes") (Cixous and Clément 1975: 237), which has no main verb and two subordinate clauses, we may feel lost, confused, or simply impatient. In order to appreciate the innovatory quality of this style, which provides no object for usually transitive verbs (who does she call? what does she take?), we need to feel the weight of the well-formed French sentence and the desire of the feminist writer to wriggle out from under it at all costs. For the French, their language is "la langue de Molière" (the language of Molière), while English is "la langue de Shakespeare" (the language of Shakespeare). The apex of literary achievement was apparently achieved many centuries ago, and perfected by male writers. *Écriture féminine* is a reaction to this assumption of perfection and its attribution to men.

3   Literary Uses of Linguistic Gender

In my own work on the literary uses of linguistic gender, I have examined the role of gender concord in the creation of particular stylistic effects such as focalization (or point of view), empathy, and textual cohesion (what makes everything fit together) (Livia 2000). Insofar as gender concord may be considered a choice in a given language, and not a morphological or syntactic necessity, it can be used as a stylistic device to express some aspect of character or personality. While Judith Butler's research on the performativity of gender emphasizes the iterative and citational aspects of speech, greatly reducing the role of speaker agency, my own work on the gender performances of characters such as drag queens, transsexuals, and hermaphrodites, and those whose gender is never given, demonstrates that observing (or ignoring) the requirements of gender concord allows authors to express a wide range of positions.

In her pioneering work *Gender Trouble*, Judith Butler argues that speakers, or in her words "culturally intelligible subjects," are the results, rather than the creators, "of a rule-bound discourse that inserts itself into the pervasive and mundane signifying acts of linguistic life" (1990: 145). Although her prose is a little dense, what this means in simple terms is that she sees individual speakers as being formed by the discourse they use. This discourse is "performative" because it is by uttering (or performing) it that speakers, obligatorily, gender themselves. They are compelled by the syntactic structure and vocabulary available to position themselves only in certain restricted ways with regard to gender, that is, the traditional roles of "men" and "women." They are not free to take up any gender stance they like, for this would not be "culturally intelligible." Although she does suggest three linguistic strategies by which a speaker can undermine the system (parody, subversion, and fragmentation), on the whole Butler sees agency as severely curtailed, limited merely to "variations on repetition." For her, it is the gender norms themselves which provide the lynchpins keeping "man" and "woman" in their place. She argues that "the loss of gender norms would have the effect of proliferating gender configurations, destabilizing substantive identity, depriving the naturalizing narratives of compulsory heterosexuality of their cultural protagonists" (1990: 146). Once these stabilizing norms have been lost, other possibilities become available, moving beyond the heteronormative lynchpins "man" and "woman."

This view of gender as performative has become a key tenet of queer theory, which investigates and analyzes "the naturalizing narratives of compulsory heterosexuality" and the various sexually liminal figures who do not fit into this traditional framework. Arguing against the linguistic determinism of Butler's stance, I refute the claim that gender, and particularly linguistic gender, is rigidly confining and explore the different messages it can convey. My research on a corpus of literary texts in both English and French, presented in *Pronoun Envy* (2000), shows that the realm of what is "culturally intelligible" is much wider and more diverse than queer theorists have supposed and that the traditional gender norms are often used as a foil against which more experimental positions are understood.

Anne Garréta, writing in French, and Maureen Duffy, Sarah Caudwell, and Jeanette Winterson, writing in English, have each created characters without gender in at least one of their works. Nowhere in these novels is there any grammatical clue as to whether the main protagonists are male or female. In French this is a particularly difficult feat, for gender is usually conveyed not only by the third-person pronouns *il/elle, ils/elles* (like the English *he/she* and unlike English *they*) but also in adjectives and past participles. Thus in a sentence of five words like *la vieille femme est assise* ("the old woman sat down"), the gender of the person sitting is conveyed four times: in the definite determiner *la*, in the form of the adjective *vieille*, in the lexical item *femme*, and in the form of the adjective *assise*. In English, the difficulty is decreased by the fact that morphological (or linguistic) gender is limited to the distinction between *he/she, his/her, his/hers*.

Garréta's novel *Sphinx* features both a genderless narrator and his or her genderless beloved. The novel is written in the first-person singular *je* ("I"), which is gender-neutral. Thus when the narrator describes his or her own actions, the author can avoid giving gender information by using only gender-neutral adjectives and tenses, like the *passé simple* rather than the *passé composé*. However, gender-neutral adjectives and expressions tend to be less frequently used than those which agree with the gender of the noun. The use of the *passé simple* rather than the more common *passé composé* also introduces a literary, almost anachronistic element to the text. Since the novel recounts how a White Parisian theology student becomes a disc jockey in a seedy bar and falls in love with a Black American disco dancer, the use of markedly literary tenses and descriptive expressions seems somewhat out of place. It is as though the theology student never really left the seminary.

When the narrator describes the actions and attributes of the beloved, the situation becomes even more complex and the language somewhat convo-luted, for here the use of pronouns must be avoided as well. The beloved can never simply be referred to as *il* (he) or *elle* (she) and various techniques are introduced to avoid this. Often the proper name, A***, is repeated. This repeti-tion makes it appear that a new character is being introduced, so that A*** (already confined to an initial and a string of asterisks) never becomes a familiar figure, but always seems a little strange and distant.

Another technique used by the author to avoid conveying A***'s gender is to describe A***'s body parts rather than the person himself/herself. Instead of the more straightforward *"Elle avait les hanches musculeuses, les cheveux rasés et le visage ainsi rendu à sa pure nudité"* ("she had muscular hips, a shaven head and her face was thus returned to its pure, bare state"), for example, the author is obliged to avoid mention of gender by describing A***'s body in the following, far more distanced and depersonalized way: *"Le modelé musculeux de ses hanches . . . ses cheveux rasés . . . le visage ainsi rendu à sa pure nudité"* ("the muscular moulding of her/his hips . . . her/his shaven hair . . . the face thus restored to its naked purity") (1986: 27). Because A*** is systematically referred to by a proper name, or in terms of parts of the body rather than the whole, this character seems fragmented and static.

Clearly, a text which avoids gender agreement produces a very different effect from one which follows a more orthodox pattern of reference. But it is perfectly possible to create a whole novel on this basis, as Garréta's achieve-ment has shown. One could argue that the style of *Sphinx*, whether or not it was initially imposed by the decision to avoid gender, suits the plot of the novel admirably. Given the different worlds the narrator and the beloved inhabited prior to their meeting, and the enormous social distance between them, one a White Parisian intellectual, the other a Black dancer from Harlem, the presentation of A*** as strange, constantly unfamiliar, and composed of a series of bodily fragments, creates an exoticism which well suits the story of infatuation, incomprehension, and loss.

Maureen Duffy's novel *Love Child* tells the story of the adolescent Kit and his/her murderous jealousy for Ajax, his/her father's secretary whom he/she believes to be his/her mother's lover. (In the third person, gender-neutral pronominal reference can become extremely clumsy.) While the mother and father are clearly gendered, Duffy gives no clue as to Kit or Ajax's gender. The effect of this is rather different for each character since Kit, as first-person narrator, can use the pronoun "I," while Ajax is never referred to by pronoun. In this *Love Child* resembles *Sphinx*. A character referred to without pronouns is simultaneously less empathic and less of a coherent whole. Empathy for a character may be gauged by the types of reference used for that character. Repetition of the proper name and the use of different lexical items such as "my father's secretary," "my mother's lover" create the least empathy, while pronouns and ellipsis create the most. Use of pronouns and ellipsis presuppose that the reader is already familiar with the referent and can readily access it, given minimal or zero prompts. In a similar pattern, the linguistic device which creates the strongest cohesive link is ellipsis followed by pronominalization. If the proper name is simply repeated, there is no necessary link forged between each of its appearances. In contrast, in the following sentence: "Ajax spieled, pattered, manipulated unseen puppets, drew scenes and characters" (1994: 50), in order to understand that Ajax is the subject not only of "spieled," but also of "pattered," "manipulated," and "drew," the reader must connect the four verbs, and this connection creates a strongly cohesive text.

While Kit comes across as a lonely, angry, jealous teenager who causes the death of his/her mother's lover, Ajax (like A***) seems not quite real, a mere collection of qualities and attributes, not someone who acts on his/her own behalf. We never find out if Kit is an adolescent girl witnessing a lesbian affair; a boy jealous of his mother's male suitor; a boy watching his mother flirt with another woman; or a girl who is aware of her mother's heterosexual conquests. Each interpretation gives very different readings to the text. Nevertheless, Kit is a character for whom the reader can feel some emotional connection while Ajax is not. It is the presence or absence of pronouns which creates this contrast, not information about gender, since neither character is gendered.

Jeanette Winterson's *Written on the Body* and Sarah Caudwell's mysteries revolve around a genderless narrator, but all third-person characters are assigned traditional gender markers; these novels do not, therefore, offer the same degree of complexity as Duffy's or Garréta's.

Science fiction authors, like Ursula Le Guin and Marge Piercy, have used the possibilities offered by new worlds and new biologies to invent imaginary communities whose gender positions are very different from those of twentieth-century Earth. In *The Left Hand of Darkness*, Le Guin introduces the ambisexual Gethenians whose gender status changes at different phases of their life-cycle. During most of the year their bodies are asexual, but when they enter their mating phase (called *kemmer*) they develop either male or female reproductive organs. They never know in advance which organs will develop and their gender may change from one period of *kemmer* to another. For her part, Piercy has experimented with utopian worlds in which gender is so insignificant that it is no longer encoded in the grammar. In the futuristic community of Mattapoisett, described in *Woman on the Edge of Time*, people are anatomically male or female, but this distinction is almost entirely irrelevant in determining their social roles. To demonstrate the effect this egalitarianism has on the language they speak, Piercy has invented the pronouns *person* and *per* in place of *he/she* and *his/her/hers*. These neologisms are used to describe the futuristic characters, in contrast with the twentieth-century characters.

Monique Wittig, writing in French, has experimented with a different aspect of the linguistic gender system in each one of her works. In her first novel, *l'Opoponax* (1966), she uses *on* as the voice of the narrator, recounting the daily lives and relationships among a group of young schoolchildren in a small village in eastern France. Traditional literary texts in French are narrated either in the first-person *je* or in the third-person *il* or *elle*. *On* is grammatically a third-person singular pronoun which, unlike *il/elle*, is not marked for gender. Furthermore, it may be used with the meaning of *I, we* (inclusive, i.e. *I* and *you*, or exclusive, i.e. *I* and a third party); "you" (singular or plural); "he" or "she" or "they" (masculine or feminine). This means that *on* is both remarkably flexible to manipulate and remarkably slippery in meaning. Wittig chose it because it did not encode gender information, but its effect is to neutralize other oppositions as well.

On refers most often to the narrator, a little girl called Catherine Legrand, but it is not always clear from the immediate context when it refers exclusively to Catherine, when it also refers to the other children who are all participating in the same actions and share the narrator's thoughts and feelings, and when it includes not only other children but adults as well. In one particularly memorable scene, a new child arrives at school and is instantly separated from the other children, sitting on a bench by herself. Subsequently, in a sequence of increasing violence, she is searched for lice, then beaten on the head by hand and then with rulers. Who performs each of these acts? It must be the teacher who seats the girl apart from the others, but does she also participate in, or even instigate, searching for lice? Wittig states that she uses *on* to "universalize" a very specific and somewhat unusual point of view: that of a group of young children. In fact *on* does far more than this. Because of its many possible meanings, it forces the reader to pay close attention not only to assumptions about gender, but also to assumptions about age appropriateness and common sense.

In *Les Guérillères* (1969), Wittig uses the feminine plural *elles* to tell the story of a group of women warriors who live a separatist lifestyle away from men. This feminine plural is less common than the feminine singular *elle*, the masculine plural *ils*, and the masculine singular *il*, for the following grammatical reasons. *Il* can refer either to an animate entity such as a person (*Eric arrive, il aime le chocolat*, "Eric is coming, **he** likes chocolate"); to an inanimate object (*le clou m'a griffe, il m'a fait de la peine*, "the nail scratched me, **it** hurt me"); or to an abstract idea (*le théorème est trop abstrait, il est mal expliqué*, "the theorem is too abstract, **it** is ill-explained"). *Il* is also used as a "dummy morpheme" or verb marker in meteorological and modal expressions such as *il faut venir* ("**it** is necessary to come," i.e. you must come); *il pleut* ("**it** is raining"). *Elle*, in contrast, refers to a person, inanimate object, or abstract idea, but is never used in modal or meteorological expressions. The plural *ils* refers to people, inanimate objects, abstract ideas, or a combination of these, as does *elles*. However, *ils* is also used for a combination of grammatically masculine and feminine items, while *elles* is restricted to feminine items only.

As well as these grammatical reasons for the more limited use of *elles*, the French psychoanalyst Luce Irigaray (1987: 81–123) has found that people talk more rarely about groups of women than about men, mixed groups, or singular subjects. When asked to finish sample sentences, her respondents were far more likely to speak of singular, masculine referents than of anyone else. Although *il/elle* and *ils/elles* appear to have contrasting but equal functions in the pronominal system, their frequency of use is actually steeply graded from *il* to *ils* to *elle* to *elles*. A novel in which the least favored pronoun among the third-person set, *elles*, is used as the main reference point of narration is a radical innovation.

For the narrator of *Le Corps lesbien* ("The Lesbian Body," 1973), Wittig has invented the pronoun *j/e*, a divided *I* who describes and interacts with another woman. This "barred" spelling is repeated throughout the first-person possessive paradigm: *me* is spelled *m/e*, *ma: m/a, mon: m/on*, and *moi: m/oi*. Although, as we have seen, *je* is non-gendered, it is clear in *The Lesbian Body* that the narrator is a woman since there are frequent, lyrical descriptions of specifically female body parts such as clitoris, labia, vagina.

As for exactly what this divided *j/e* represents, Wittig herself has provided two, rather different explanations. In the "Author's Note" to the English translation of 1975, Wittig states that *je*, as a feminine subject, is obliged to force her way into language since what is human is, grammatically, masculine, as *elle* and *elles* are subsumed under *il* and *ils*. The female writer must use a language which is structured to erase her (as *elle* is erased in *il*). Wittig explains that the bar through the *j/e* is intended as a visual reminder of women's alienation from (by and within) language. Ten years later, however, Wittig claims: "the bar in the *j/e* of the Lesbian Body is a sign of excess. A sign that helps to imagine an excess of *I*, an *I* exalted." This new explanation suggests that, far from signaling the difficulty for women of taking up the subject position in a linguistic structure in which the masculine is both the unmarked and the universal term, the bar through the *j/e* has the positive value of an exuberance so powerful it is "like a lava flow that nothing can stop" (ibid.). Within ten years, *j/e* has evolved from a mark of alienation to a mark of exuberance.

Members of liminal communities, such as hermaphrodites, transsexuals, drag queens and drag kings, who do not fit easily into the existing bipartite gender positions, often use the linguistic gender system to rather different effect from its traditional function. Drag queens (gay men who wear stereotypically feminine clothing and use hyper-feminine mannerisms) and drag kings (lesbians who wear stereotypically masculine clothing and use hyper-masculine mannerisms) often cross-express, using the pronouns which traditionally refer to the opposite sex. Thus a drag queen might refer to another drag queen as *her* and speak about getting her periods, engaging in a catfight, or putting on her make-up. A drag king might speak about *his* butch brothers, getting an erection, or going home to *his* wife.

In a study I carried out on the use of linguistic gender by male to female transsexuals writing in French, I found that although all the authors stated that they had always felt they were women, in fact they alternated between masculine and feminine grammatical agreement throughout their autobiographies (Livia 2000: 168–76). Masculine agreement could indicate variously a sense of belonging with other males, the gender other people ascribed to them, or a feeling of power and superiority. Feminine agreement indicated the gender they felt most comfortable in, isolation and alienation, or a triumphant affirmation. There was no simple, one-to-one alignment of masculine pronouns with the rejected gender and feminine pronouns with the desired gender.

When we turn to the descriptions of hermaphrodites in literary texts, we find that the situation is even more complex. Possessing the sexual organs of both sexes, hermaphrodites tend to vary in self-presentation far more than the transsexuals I studied. Feelings of solidarity, isolation, alienation, success, failure, are all encoded in switches from one gender to another. Indeed, the switch may be made from one sentence to another with no attempt to naturalize it, or it may be presented as a positive sign of the fluidity of gender.

4   Gender and Translation

Where the two types of analysis come together (discussion of writing styles, and discussion of uses of linguistic gender) is in investigations of gender and translation, a field in which both morphological gender and cultural gender are highly relevant. Translators work both as interpreters of the original text and, often, as guides to the culture which produced the text. If the social expectations of gender in the target culture are very different from those of the source culture, they need to deal with this anomaly. Similarly, if the languages encode gender in very different ways, they need to devise a system to encompass the differences. In their dual role as linguistic interpreters and cultural guides, translators must decide what to naturalize, what to explain, and what to exoticize.

Studying the role gender plays in translation, Sherry Simon observes that since as early as the seventeenth century translations themselves have been seen as *belles infidèles* (beautiful but unfaithful) because, like women, they can be either beautiful or faithful, but not both (1996: 10–11). Many of the metaphors for the act or process of translation are highly sexed, and indeed, heterosexed. One dominant model views translation as a power struggle between author and translator (both male) over the text (female). In this model, the translator must wrest the text away from the original author, like a son growing up to rival his father. George Steiner, himself a prominent translator, describes the translator as penetrating and capturing the text in a manner very similar to erotic possession (1975). Lori Chamberlain, another translation theorist, quotes Thomas Drant, the sixteenth-century translator of Horace, who claims: "[I have] done as the people of God were commanded to do with their captive women: I have shaved off his hair and pared off his nails" (1992: 61–2). For Drant, the original text must be utterly enslaved and deprived of its foreignness, or, in his own words, "Englished." In another model, the original author becomes the translator's mistress whose hidden charms must be revealed and whose blemishes must be improved. In yet another view, the translator is a submissive, subjugated, female, alienated, absorbed, ravished, and dispossessed, entirely taken over by the author (Chamberlain 1992: 57–66). Although the imagined relationships that prevail among author, text, and translator vary widely, at the core is the sense that translation is a sexual act.

Given this intense gendering of the process itself, it is hardly surprising that when it comes to linguistic gender in the original text, the problems posed are complex and sometimes unanswerable. The novels and poetry of French Canadian feminist writers such as Nicole Brossard and Louky Bersianik are characterized by rich alliteration, plays on words, and the creation of portmanteau words. The title of Brossard's novel *L'Amèr*, for example, is a portmanteau word containing three others: *la mer* ("the sea"), *la mère* ("the mother"), and *amère* ("bitter"). *Amer* is the masculine form of the adjective, while *amère* with a grave accent and a terminal *-e* is the feminine form. In itself *amèr* is a neologism invented by Brossard. Since the English words *sea*, *mother*, and *bitter* do not contain the same phonemes as the French words, the neatness of the alliteration is necessarily lost. The gender play is also lost in English since the adjective *bitter* has only one form. Brossard's translator, Barbara Godard, decided to use a very elaborate graphic representation for the translated title, composed of three distinct phrases: The Sea Our Mother, Sea (S)mothers, and (S)our Mothers, all twined around a large *S*. The English title can therefore read either *These Our Mothers* or *These Sour Mothers* (Simon 1996: 14). This is an elegant rendition of the original French, but it does not address the practical problem of how librarians and book catalogues are to refer to the novel.

In my own translation of Lucie Delarue-Mardrus' *l'Ange et les Pervers* ("The Angel and the Perverts," Livia 1995), I had to tackle the question of how to refer to the central character who is a hermaphrodite. Here both linguistic and cultural gender are at issue. Delarue-Mardrus describes Mario (or Marion, in her female persona), the main protagonist, as alternately masculine and feminine. The changes in gender concord in the original French are intended to produce a sense of shock, requiring the reader to work out how the grammatical system relates to Mario/n's personality and mental state. The first chapter introduces us to the young boy and his childhood in a glacial château in Normandy. Here masculine pronouns and concord are used: *Il avait toujours été seul au monde* ("he had always been alone in the world"; Delarue-Mardrus 1930: 19). The second chapter begins in the bedroom of a rich society woman in an upper-middle-class suburb of Paris. In this section, Marion is described in the feminine: *Elle n'aime rien ni personne* ("She loves nothing and no-one";

Delarue-Mardrus 1930: 21). There is no obvious connection between the *il* of the first chapter and the *elle* of the second. Furthermore, both place and social setting have changed, from Normandy to Paris, and from an old, lonely castle to a gossipy boudoir. By witholding any explicit link, Delarue-Mardrus forces readers to make the connection themselves between Mario(n)'s male and female personae. In this way, they are also implicated in his/her change of gender.

Occasionally, Delarue-Mardrus shocks the reader by referring to Mario/n in the masculine and then immediately afterwards in the feminine, without providing any intervening material or a change of context to make this seem more natural. The River Seine provides a geographical divide between Mario's bachelor garret and Marion's more luxurious rooms. In one scene we watch as Mario/n crosses the river and moves from one personality to the other: *La voilà chez elle. Le voilà chez lui* ("She was home. He was home"; Delarue-Mardrus 1930: 38). For a translator the lack of gender concord in English poses a problem. While the pronouns *la* and *le* may easily and effectively be translated as "she" and "he," their grammatical connection to the expressions *chez elle* ("at her house") and *chez lui* ("at his house") are harder to convey. "There she was at her house" and "there he was at his house" are more faithful translations than "she was home," "he was home," and they retain the naturalizing effect of grammatical necessity. They sound rather stilted in English, however.

In the memoirs of a nineteenth-century hermaphrodite, Herculine Barbin, recently rediscovered and annotated by Michel Foucault (1980), the narrator's unusual gender status is conveyed to the reader on the first page. Barbin begins her self-description in the masculine: *soucieux et rêveur* ("anxious and dreamy"), but ends in the feminine: *j'étais froide timide* ("I was cold, shy"; Barbin 1978: 9). By this movement from masculine concord in the adjective *soucieux* to feminine concord in the adjective *froide* in the next sentence, Barbin gets immediately to the crux of the matter. In contrast, in the English translation it is not until page 58 that reference is made to the grammatical ambiguity of Herculine's identity: "She took pleasure in using masculine qualifiers for me, qualifiers which would later suit my official status." The expression "using masculine qualifiers" is strangely formal, even learned, and stands out in this plaintive, simply stated autobiography.

5   Implications

We have seen that although many prominent writers have set out to discover the differences between men's and women's sentences, following in the footsteps of Virginia Woolf at the beginning of the twentieth century, no convincing linguistic evidence has yet been provided to indicate the stylistic characteristics of each. Instead, we have found that there are conventions of masculine and feminine style which any sophisticated writer, whether male or female, can follow.

When we turned to look at linguistic gender, we saw that far from being a tyrannical system which forces speakers to follow a rigid dualistic structure, it actually provides means by which speakers may create alternative, oppositional, or conventional identities. In the realm of science fiction, authors have created neologistic, non-gendered pronouns to speak of egalitarian utopias, supplementing the existing system, which is retained for more traditional worlds. Authors have experimented with non-gendered protagonists in both the first and the third person. Although these literary experiments have an effect on our reading of the novel, it is the lack of pronominal reference, not the lack of gender markers *per se*, which causes disturbance.

Finally, in our discussion of the role of the translator and the metaphors used for the process of translation, we observed that while many different metaphors exist for the act itself, the dominant metaphors place the translator in a sexual role in relation to the text and the author. Frequently, when translating from a language in which there are many linguistic gender markers into a language which has fewer, either gender information is lost, or it is overstated, overtly asserted where in the original it is more subtly presupposed.

This research on linguistic approaches to gender in literature demonstrates the utility for students of gender in society at large to investigate the uses to which gender may be put in the unspontaneous, carefully planned discourse of fiction. It reveals not what native speakers naturally do, but what they are able to understand and the inventions and models that influence their understanding.

REFERENCES

Barbin, Herculine 1978: Mes souvenirs. In Michel Foucault (ed.) *Herculine Barbin dite Alexina B*. Paris: Gallimard, pp. 9–128.

Brossard, Nicole 1977: *L'Amèr ou le chaptire effrité*. Montreal: l'Hexagone. Translated as *These Our Mothers Or: The Disintegrating Chapter* (1983) by Barbara Godard. Toronto: Coach House Quebec Translations.

Butler, Judith 1990: *Gender Trouble*. New York: Routledge.

Chamberlain, Lori 1992: Gender and the metaphorics of translation. In L. Venuti (ed.) *Rethinking Translation: Discourse, Subjectivity, Ideology*. London and New York: Routledge, pp. 57–74.

Chawaf, Chantal 1976: La chair linguistique. *Nouvelles Littéraires* (26 May): 18.

Cixous, Hélène and Clément, Catherine 1975: *La Jeune née*. Paris: Union générale d'éditions. (Translated as Cixous, Hélène and Clément, Catherine 1986: *The Newly Born Woman*. Manchester: Manchester University Press.)

Delarue-Mardrus, Lucie 1930: *L'Ange et les Pervers*. Paris: Ferenczi.

Duffy, Maureen 1994: *Love Child*. London: Virago.

Ehrlich, Susan 1990: *Point of View: A Linguistic Analysis of Literary Style*. London: Routledge.

Foucault, Michel 1980: *Herculine Barbin*. Translated by Richard MacDougall. New York: Random House.

Garréta, Anne 1986: *Sphinx*. Paris: Grasset.

Irigaray, Luce 1987: L'Ordre sexuel du discours. In *Languages: Le sexe linguistique*, vol. 85 (March): 81–123.

Lakoff, Robin and Tannen, Deborah 1994: Conversational strategy and metastrategy in a pragmatic theory: The example of *Scenes from a Marriage*. In Deborah Tannen (ed.) *Gender and Discourse*. New York: Oxford University Press, pp. 137–73.

Lefanu, Sarah 1988: *In the Chinks of the World Machine: Feminism and Science Fiction*. London: Women's Press.

Le Guin, Ursula 1973: *The Left Hand of Darkness*. St Albans: Granada.

Livia, Anna 1995: Introduction: Lucie Delarue-Mardrus and the phrenetic harlequinade. In Lucie Delarue-Mardrus (ed.) *The Angel and the Perverts*, translated by Anna Livia. New York: New York University Press, pp. 1–60.

Livia, Anna 2000: *Pronoun Envy: Literary Uses of Linguistic Gender*. New York: Oxford University Press.

Millett, Fred 1951: Introduction to *The Portrait of a Lady* by Henry James. New York: Random House, pp. v–xxxv.

Mills, Sara 1995: *Feminist Stylistics*. London: Routledge.

Piercy, Marge 1976: *Woman on the Edge of Time*. New York: Ballantine Books.

Proust, Marcel 1954: *Du côté de Chez Swann*. Paris: Gallimard.

Richardson, Dorothy 1919: *The Tunnel*. London: Duckworth.

Richardson, Dorothy 1923: *Revolving Lights*. London: Duckworth.

Rubin, Gayle 1975: The traffic in women: Notes on the "political economy" of sex. In Rayna Reiter (ed.) *Toward an Anthropology of Women*. New York: Monthly Review Press, pp. 157–210.

Silverberg, Robert 1975: Introduction to James Tiptree, *Warm Worlds and Otherwise*. New York: Ballantine.

Simon, Sherry 1996: *Gender in Translation*. New York: Routledge.

Steiner, George 1975: *After Babel*. London: Oxford University Press.

Winterson, Jeanette 1993: *Written on the Body*. London: Jonathan Cape.

Wittig, Monique 1966: *The Opoponax*. Translated by Helen Weaver. London: Peter Owen. (Originally published as Wittig, Monique 1964: *L'Opoponax*. Paris: Editions de Minuit.)

Wittig, Monique 1969: *Les Guérillères*. Paris: Editions de Minuit. (Translated as Wittig, Monique 1971: *Les Guérillères*. Translated by David Le Vay. New York: Avon.)

Wittig, Monique 1973: *Le Corps lesbien*. Paris: Editions de Minuit.

Wittig, Monique 1975: *The Lesbian Body*. Translated by David Le Vay. New York: Avon.

Woolf, Virginia 1990a: Women and fiction. In Deborah Cameron (ed.) *The Feminist Critique of Language: A Reader*. London: Routledge, pp. 33–40.

Woolf, Virginia 1990b: Dorothy Richardson and the women's sentence. In Deborah Cameron (ed.) *The Feminist Critique of Language: A Reader*. London: Routledge, pp. 70–4.

Part II
Negotiating Relations

7 Language, Gender, and Politics: Putting "Women" and "Power" in the Same Sentence

ROBIN LAKOFF

1 Introduction: Power Games

In writing a paper under the title above, an author must confront the ancient platitude that men are more comfortable with power than are women; that it is right and natural for men to seek and hold power; that for a woman to do so is strange, marking her as un-feminine and dangerous. This belief allows a culture to exclude women from full participation in any of its politics, not only in the most typical and specific sense of that word, "the art or science of government or governing"; but also in the more general sense I am assuming here, "the ways in which power is allocated and that allocation justified, among the members of a society." In its latter definition, *politics* extends beyond government to other public (and private) institutions.

There has been a fair amount of writing exploring the links among language, gender, and power: for instance the contributors to Thorne and Henley (1975), who see the triangulation through the prism of "dominance" theory; and, from the other, or "difference" perspective, Maltz and Borker (1982) and Tannen (1990). But there is much less on the role of gender in politics, from a linguistic perspective. For an example of the way gender has affected the linguistic possibilities of men versus women in a particular case, see Mendoza-Denton's (1995) discussion of the Anita Hill–Clarence Thomas hearings (a very public and political sexual harassment case).

In their writings about the connection between gender and power, several usually insightful commentators have made surprising statements. Conley, O'Barr, and Lind (1979) and Brown and Levinson (1986) argue that an observed discrepancy between male and female behavior is due not to gender but to "power" – as though one were independent of the other. Perhaps these statements must be interpreted as evidence that the collocation "women and power" still has the capacity to confuse us all.

Language reflects and contributes to the survival of the stereotype. To cite just a few examples, there are lexical differences in the way we talk about men with power, versus women with power. For example, we use different words to describe similar or identical behavior by men and by women. English (like other languages) has many words describing women who are interested in power, presupposing the inappropriateness of that attitude. *Shrew* and *bitch* are among the more polite. There are no equivalents for men. There are words presupposing negative connotations for men who do not dominate "their" women, *henpecked* and *pussywhipped* among them. There is no female equivalent.

Many proverbs and folktales function as instruction manuals for the young (and the not so young), warning women of the perils of assertiveness but encouraging it in men. In the fairy tale "Seven at a Blow," the brave little tailor, having killed seven flies with one swat, embroiders himself a belt to that effect and wears it out into the world. He gets into trouble but eventually triumphs. The lesson: verbal assertion brings a man success. On the other hand, in the story "The Seven Swans," a girl's seven brothers are changed into swans. She can transform them back into men only by sitting in a tree for seven years sewing them shirts out of daisies. If she utters one word during this period, she will fail. She succeeds, despite terrible obstacles. The moral: silence and obedience are the path to success for a woman.

Furthermore, we have different expectations about the way men and women should (or do) conduct themselves linguistically. Men are expected to be direct, women indirect. While that distinction in itself does not necessarily create a disadvantage to women, it is the basis of a familiar double-bind. If a woman is indirect (i.e. a proper woman), she is variously *manipulative* or *fuzzy-minded*. If she is direct she is apt to be called a *shrew* or a *bitch*. Denying expressive power to women is a political act.

The organization of conversation reflects the power discrepancy between men and women, especially when we compare the empirical findings about the distribution of turns between males and females with the traditional stereotypes about who does more talking than whom. Floor-holding and topic control are associated with power in the conversational dyad. The traditional assumption is that women do most of the talking, usually about nothing. Yet Spender (1980) found that typically men hold the floor 80 per cent of the time. Further, even more surprisingly, when male active participation dips below about 70 per cent both men and women assess the result as "women dominating the conversation." Other research shows that men generate most of the successful topics in mixed-group conversation: women's attempts are ignored by both men and other women in the group (Leet-Pellegrini 1980). Fishman (1978) suggests that, in intimate relationships, women do the conversational "shitwork": getting even minimal responses from men. Earlier research (e.g. Zimmerman and West 1975) suggested that one way in which men maintain their conversational dominance is by violative interruption of women. More recently these findings have been called into question (James and Clarke 1993), although the problems identified concern methodology and interpretation, rather than the existence of the phenomenon itself.

While both women and men are subject to constraint in the emotions that they may express, the constraint on both seems designed to intensify the pre-existing power imbalance between the sexes. Until very recently, men were not supposed to cry or express sadness; women were not permitted to express anger, including the use of swear words. But the expression of sorrow is an expression of powerlessness and helplessness; anger, of potency. So although these rules may seem to equalize the sexes, in fact they intensify male power and female powerlessness. When women do express anger, its power is denied ("You're cute when you're mad").

As women (and others formerly excluded, such as children) have asserted their right to use "bad" language, there has been increasing concern on the part of both right and left about the "coarsening" or growing "incivility" of the public discourse. While these words refer to different kinds of behavior, one very common use is to critique the increasing prevalence of formerly forbidden words. And while some objects of this critique are adult White males, I strongly suspect that one motivating force behind the complaints of "coarsening" is that the privilege of swearing – of expressing anger in undis-guised form – has been extended to women, and with it the right to powerful speech more generally.

This chapter illustrates the complex relationship between *women* and *power* by examining examples from three major American institutions: academia, the arts, and politics proper. In academia, publication is the analog of election in governmental politics, the determinant of success. Who, or what, decides what is publishable, what is a fit topic of discourse? Who, or what, defines and delimits academic fields?

Usually these questions are fought out clandestinely, beneath the conscious-ness of the fighters. Seldom does the battle break into publication. So such a case forms a particularly delectable object of study. And when gender and its appropriate analysis form both text and subtext of the dispute, the case becomes especially relevant. In a series of papers (1997, 1998) published in *Discourse & Society*, Emanuel Schegloff argued against the use of all but a very restricted set of conversational transcripts in doing gender-based analyses (i.e. using the data of conversation analysis (CA) to investigate power relations between females and males in conversation). Arguably, if any living person has a right to delimit the research options of CA, that person is Emanuel Schegloff; but that is a big "if." Schegloff's arguments were quickly, and vigorously, contested by Margaret Wetherell (1998) and Ann Weatherall (2000). I will examine the debate as it stood at the time of writing (December 2000).

The arts are often seen as, ideally, apolitical in aim and function. But art can be used for political persuasion. The line between art and propaganda can be fuzzy; yet much of the world's great literature, from the *Aeneid* to *Richard III* to *Nineteen Eighty-Four*, has an avowed political aim.

David Mamet's *Oleanna* is distinctly political, its politics the politics of gender. *Oleanna* opened in the spring of 1992, about seven months after the Anita Hill–Clarence Thomas contretemps and a bit less than a year after the premiere of the movie *Thelma and Louise*. Deborah Tannen's *You Just Don't Understand* (1990) was still at the top of the best-seller lists. *Oleanna* is easily viewed as a response to these perceived threats to the gender of the play's creator. Not only was the play a smash hit on at least two continents; it became the basis of a veritable cottage industry of analyses, ripostes, defenses, and apocalyptic warnings (see, for instance Rich 1992; Lahr 1992; Holmberg 1992; Mufson 1993; Showalter 1992; Silverthorne 1993; and the exchange among several prominent discussants in the *New York Times*, November 15, 1992).

My third subject is politics proper: the treatment of women as voters and as people in the public eye, in particular the campaign and election of Hillary Rodham Clinton as Senator for New York. For eight years Clinton had functioned as a standard-bearer in the gender wars, a woman cast in a traditional role trying to redefine it and herself, and thereby womanhood. The peculiarly visceral hatred of both Clintons that culminated in the presidential impeachment hearings of 1998 can be explained at least partially by the fact that, singly and as a pair, they confused gender roles (cf. Lakoff 2000). So, too, in a very real way, Hillary Clinton's fight for a US Senate seat could be seen as a referendum on new gender options. Her opponent was a non-entity; the brunt of his campaign turned on his identification as the Anti-Hillary. Gender was very much a part of the discourse, especially the unspoken part, in this campaign. Both before and during her Senate campaign, Clinton was described as "scary." What was "scary" about her?

Women play other roles in contemporary American political discourse. There are the famous "soccer moms." There is what Maureen Dowd of the *New York Times* (e.g. 1996) has derisively called the "feminization" or "pinking" of politics: concern with "compassion" and other "soft" issues. Why do commentators treat women voters and "their" issues as marked (and, therefore, often risible)? When women hold power, their treatment is equally curious, often including a peculiar attention to their sexuality (or seeming lack of it), their private lives, and their external appearance (Salter 2000).

The three cases have much in common. All are struggles over control of meaning, or interpretive rights. In the first case, the struggle centers on the definition or framing of an academic field: who decides what is appropriate subject matter, or correct methodology? In the second, one aspect of the controversy over *Oleanna* concerns who decides what it is about: is it an anti-feminist screed, or a bold attack on "political correctness"? What control does the writer of a work of art, or the creator of an academic discipline, have over the use or interpretation of that field or work? In the political arena, who decides how we, the electorate, are to perceive candidates – and other members of the electorate? What criteria are relevant?

Because the ability to make meaning is politically (in all senses) crucial, each of these cases passes what I have called the Undue Attention Test (Lakoff 2000):

each of the cases I examine below has attracted more than its normal share of commentary. Therefore the examination of the meta-texts – scholarly and popular media representations of the events described – becomes indispensable.

2   A Note on Method

How can language be gathered and analyzed to show how we create ourselves as members of a society? We can use conversation as a means of understanding the construction of individual identity and small-group cohesion. But how do we study the processes of larger-group identity and opinion formation?

These questions have been explored in other fields – political science, sociology, mass communication – using their methods (surveys, polls, focus groups), with results that are often salient. But the methods and theories of linguistics add valuable new data and a different dimension. Linguists can bring to the discussion the close and detailed analysis of language itself. What do specific choices – of topics, words, presuppositions, and other implicit devices – lead us all to believe? How do the media use language to create cohesive public meaning?

I restrict my examination in this chapter to the print media because of its accessibility. Television (and radio) may reach a wider audience and have a more pervasive influence on their beliefs, but print journalism is an equally valid focus for media analysis.

3   Schegloff: Academic Politics isn't Just Academic

By "academic politics," we normally refer to power struggles in university governance: the games we (or rather, anonymous colleagues) play on university committees or in department meetings. But similar games can be played for higher stakes within disciplines in the competition for status and definitional rights within disciplines. It is in this sense that Emanuel Schegloff's paper "Whose Text? Whose Context?" (1997) is a highly political document; and it is no surprise that it has given rise to at least two responses, the first of which has, in turn, received a response from Schegloff (1998).

As the doyen of conversation analysis, Schegloff takes issue with one way in which conversational strategies (interruption and topic control) have been used to demonstrate inequalities among participants in conversations. Schegloff's detailed and serious critique of such analyses merits close inspection. He has two major complaints.

First, these critiques start from a macro-analysis of political inequality, and only sometimes, if at all, move down to the micro-level of close observation and analysis of actual conversational behavior. Schegloff argues that the reverse should be the case: start from the micro and work up to the macro, justifying the latter, if it is invoked at all, via the former. He attacks a discipline he labels as "critical discourse analysis" for not doing as he posits. He seems to assume that all CA done from a political (e.g. feminist) perspective is a form of "critical discourse analysis" – a field he does not define in any detail.

This criticism seems related to a larger complaint often leveled by conservative critics against "engaged" analysis in any academic discipline: that it necessarily loses the "objectivity" that otherwise is the norm in academic research, and that this loss is altogether negative. The assumption is that Schegloffian CA is neutral, objective, and apolitical; and that that is the only kind that is academically worthy.

These arguments have been so pervasive for so long that they achieve an implicit rightness, or at least an implicit unmarkedness and unquestionability. But on closer inspection, they turn out to be questionable, sometimes even dubious, once we identify and discard our "normal" presuppositions.

As both Wetherell (1998) and Weatherall (2000) note, Schegloff's assumption that one must do *either* close micro-analysis *or* broader political analysis is flawed. A complete analysis requires both, and each level will inform and deepen the other. There is no reason (other than proprietary pride) to insist on purity without proof that the mixing of levels necessarily vitiates the analysis. Schegloff has not shown this; he gives no real examples of the disfavored approach, and certainly no evidence that it causes problems.

Second, Schegloff argues that an analysis must represent its subjects' own conscious rationalizations of their behavior – or at least that the analyst's explanation must involve an understanding that is accessible to the subject. So, if (let's say) a male subject's interruption of a female is not explicitly *intended* (and admitted to) as a sexist move, it cannot be *interpreted* that way by the analyst. Only, says Schegloff, if a conversation explicitly mentions gender issues can it be used as grist for a gender-based interpretation. This of course radically cuts down the amount of conversational and other behavioral data available to feminist (or other politically based) analysis.

These may seem reasonable caveats, needed to keep academic discourse from becoming dangerously engaged and subjective. But examine them a little more closely.

Schegloff offers a sample conversational text (1997: 172–3) that, he claims, might be misinterpreted if analyzed from a political stance. The subjects are an estranged couple, "Tony" and "Marsha," discussing their son "Joey." Joey's car has been vandalized while he was at Marsha's house, and therefore he had to fly rather than drive to Tony's. Immediately following the text are two paragraphs glossing it, which I reproduce below in full.

> Tony has called to find out when Joey left, presumably so as to know when to expect him. It turns out that there is trouble: Joey's car has been vandalized, and this has happened, as they say, on Marsha's watch (as she puts it at line 18,

"Right out in front of *my* house"). [Italics EAS] What is worse, nobody has bothered to inform Tony. In the segment of this conversation before us, two issues appear to be of concern: Joey and his itinerary, and the car and *its* [italics EAS] itinerary. When Tony raises the latter issue (at lines 19–20: "an eez not g'nna [. . .] bring it ba̲ck?"), Marsha gives it short shrift – providing the minimal answer (line 21: "No") and rushing ahead into a continuation of the telling she has been engaged in (the "so" marks the remainder of the turn, which could have stood as an account of the "no", as disjunctive with it, and conjunctive with her earlier talk). When that telling is brought to an analyzable conclusion (lines 29–33), Tony returns to the issue that he had raised before – the fate of the car (line 35). This is the segment on which we focus.

As it might be formulated both vernacularly and for the purposes of critically oriented analysis, we have here an interaction across gender lines, in which the asymmetries of status and power along gender lines in this society are played out in the interactional arena of interruption and overlapping talk, and this exchange needs to be understood in those terms. In this interactional contest, it may be noted, Marsha is twice "beaten down" in a metaphoric sense but nonetheless a real one, being twice induced to terminate the talk which she is in the process of producing (at line 37, "His friend"; and again at line 38, "his friend Stee-"), thereby indexing the power processes at work here. On the other hand, in the third interruption in this little episode (at lines 41–2), although Marsha does not this time yield to Tony's interruptive talk, neither does Tony yield to Marsha's. He starts while Marsha is talking, and brings his exclamation of commiseration to completion in spite of Marsha's ongoing, continuing talk. One could almost imagine that we capture in this vignette some of the elements which may account for these people no longer living together.

In what is intended as a scholarly, objective text, there are a surprising number of lexical and syntactic choices that create tendentious readings. Tony's motives are pure and uncomplicated: he calls "presumably so as to know when to expect [Joey]." "It turns out" is from Tony's perspective: Marsha knew of the situation before the initiation of the phone call. So readers are already deictically situated with Tony. Schegloff notes that "nobody has bothered to inform Tony." This sounds like grousing on Tony's (or the writer's) part: "Nobody has" really means "Marsha hasn't," and "bothered to" has a sarcastic edge: she could have and she should have. Marsha gives the beef "short shrift" – an expression implying that longer shrift would have been appropriate. I suggest that, while the analysis Schegloff argues against would be *overtly* political, his is *covertly* so – and therefore more compromised in terms of objectivity.

In the second paragraph, the politicization turns syntactic. Schegloff entertains the possibility that issues of gender and power might be producing some of the conversational strategies in the text. He refers to the conversation as an "interactional contest," suggesting that a bilateral power struggle is an integral part of any full explanation (at least that is my interpretation of his discussion), which would make sense except that he has already disqualified this mode of approach as either "vernacular" or "critically oriented analysis," that is, not scholarly CA. He notes in the paragraph immediately following that this kind of analysis is "problematic on many counts," precisely because its terms are not those that the participants themselves overtly recognize. This constitutes a bit of polemical sleight-of-hand; on the one hand (now you see it) an attractive bit of "critical discourse analysis" and on the other (now you don't) a disavowal of it. Returning to the *explication de texte*, in the second paragraph Schegloff, in discussing Tony's behavior toward Marsha, says that she is "twice 'beaten down' in a metaphoric sense," "being twice induced to terminate the talk." We note the use of two agentless passive constructions in quick order. (This paragraph is laden with such constructions, above and beyond even the academic norm: I count five in the first two sentences. Agentless passives often function as a way of avoiding responsibility and creating emotional distance between speaker and subject, or hearer.) To the same end, Schegloff imputes "metaphoric" status to "beaten down."

Later in the paragraph Schegloff argues that interruption is not being used by Tony in the interests of disempowerment – that is, Schegloff offers this sequence as a counterexample to feminist analyses of interruption. But one non-conforming case hardly constitutes a counterexample to the theory, and in fact the example he chooses would surely not be identified by most contemporary conversation analysts as a violative interruption, but rather as cooperative overlap:

41   Marsha: 'hhh <u>O</u>h it's disgusti[ng ez a <u>m</u>atter a'f]a:ct.
42   Tony: [<u>P</u> <u>o</u> or Joey,]

(The identification of this distinction, by Tannen (1981) and others, is one of the reasons why James and Clarke (1993) have cast doubt on earlier analyses of interruption as diagnostic of male control of conversation.)

In these paragraphs Schegloff uses syntactically, lexically, interpretively, and punctuationally marked choices to avoid political involvement – a choice that is political in itself. I have used Schegloff's preferred microanalytic strategy to demonstrate that his treatment is not as "neutral" as he believes. If Schegloff's arguments seem neutral, it is because they depend upon presupposed beliefs supporting traditional assignments of status, authority, and power. But claims that the discourse Schegloff analyzes is apolitical, or that we can understand why the participants made the choices they made without resorting to a gendered explanation, conveniently ignore the fact that everything we do has some political basis, and that we have to account for why it seems normal (to Schegloff, anyway) for Marsha to be beaten down, metaphorically or otherwise, and for Tony to demand full shrift but not for Marsha to, by seeing that gender and power make meaning in conversation.

Let us turn to Schegloff's second point, that analyses can only be based on concepts or constructs of which participants are in some sense aware. I'm not sure how seriously he means this: consider how many categories of CA are not normally accessible to subjects. Who is aware that a TRP (transition relevance place, or place in a conversation where a new speaker may take the floor) is approaching as they speak? Who realizes that they are producing a dispreferred second or a presequence? Non-professional subjects are much more likely nowadays to be aware, if subliminally, of gender as informing their utterances than of their choice of CA gambits.

Schegloff's example of a putatively valid case is also questionable as a proffered basis for "feminist" analysis. In it two male and two female participants are at dinner. One of the males asks for the butter. A female asks if she can have some too, to which the male says "No," and then, "Ladies last." Schegloff considers this a case where gender is "relevant," because male power is explicitly invoked. But the last remark is intended as a joke – a kind of ironic put-down of male power assumptions. Rather than demonstrating the kinds of behavior that are the subjects of feminist critique, this male speaker seems to be taking, albeit indirectly, a feminist stance. The issue then is one of control. Those who have most to lose from "politicized" analysis use the vested authority they implicitly possess to attempt to invalidate any critique. By asserting, or rather presupposing, his right to define the terms and limits of his academic field, Schegloff (nor is he alone in this) is also attempting to maintain traditional power relations between the sexes and avoid overt examination of motives. The presupposition of neutrality for non-overtly political analysis is false: the denial of power games where they occur is itself a form of manipulative control.

4   *Oleanna*: Much Ado About Something

A few months after its premiere in Cambridge, Massachusetts, *Oleanna* was brought to New York, and thereafter to many other cities. Over the next few years it was a genuine phenomenon: a work of high culture that *everyone* knew about, talked about, fought over.

Yet rereading it, I wonder whether, if it were to be performed today for the first time, anyone would pay attention. Both its topic and its reception seem very much of a time that, happily or not, has passed. So perhaps we can look at *Oleanna* now with the dispassion that comes of distance, and of once-incendiary issues more or less defused.

Oleanna was written largely in the months directly following the Anita Hill–Clarence Thomas hearings, and while the battle over "political correctness" was at its zenith in the United States. The play addresses both of these issues so directly and polemically that we may wonder whether it really constitutes literature, or – given the many deficiencies of character, plot, and construction that critics pointed to from the outset – a piece of political agitprop couched as melodrama.

Oleanna is about the intersection of gender and politics at two levels. The play itself is a discourse on power games between a male and a female; on the man's part, these games are more or less covert and essentially (in the playwright's view) benign; on the woman's, overt, shocking, and evil. At the second level the audience is invited – indeed, compelled – to weigh in, to decide not only which of the play's two characters is "right" and "good," but what the playwright intended, and whether his intentions were artistic and valid, or political and reprehensible. From opening night, opinions split drastically among both critics and audience members. The latter regularly left the theater in heated debate. Theaters presenting the play often scheduled post-performance sessions in which audiences were invited to listen to, and participate in, discussions with cast, director, and sometimes members of the larger cultural and intellectual community. These were remarkably well-attended and confrontational.

In the play, John is a professor at a prestigious research university. He is up for tenure, which at the outset he seems pretty sure of getting. He is about to buy a house; he has a wife and child. Carol is an undergraduate student in his class, from a lower social class, who has come to the university expecting it to enable her to move upward. But she has encountered trouble in the class, and goes to John's office to get some help understanding what he's been talking about.

In the first act, John does most of the talking, and Carol's contributions are mostly fragmentary and interrogative. John genuinely seems to mean well: he *wants* to help Carol, seeing in her a kindred spirit who like him comes from the working class. He wants to teach, to explain, to clarify. But he cannot get beyond his academic vocabulary and style of self-presentation: often pompous, heavily figurative, indirect. Carol's problem is that this is precisely her problem: she has not been entrusted with the decoder that would enable her to make sense of this "discourse," much less the encoder that would let her speak this way herself. While John bubbles with ideas that Carol should "get," he is of no help in enabling her to penetrate what the university, and John as its immediate representative, are really up to, what the game is and how it is played and won – which is what Carol needs to know, although of course she cannot articulate that even to herself.

Carol wants interpretations, but John won't, and probably can't, supply them: as a now middle-class White male, he is too much a part of the institution to penetrate its mysteries. John makes a few statements about how he "likes" Carol, suggests that if she will come to his office again he'll give her an A, and tells her what she's about: she's angry, she's like him, etc. Toward the end of the colloquy he embraces her – platonically, of course. None of this is what Carol bargained for, and at the end of Act I she leaves, still bewildered – in fact, doubly bewildered now.

In Act I John is the one with the power: to give Carol the passing grade she needs, and to induct her into the mysteries of the university and the middle class. Commentators have generally seen these powers, and the way John uses them, as legitimate and unremarkable – when they notice them at all, and often they do not: they are normal. Therefore, when Carol returns later, accusing John of bad faith and bad behavior, many commentators are frankly uncomprehending: how did the little ninny get these ideas put in her head? As

her detractors said of Anita Hill, she must have been put up to it by someone
. . . someone smarter . . . someone with an *agenda*, which John and people like
him certainly do not possess. They just *are*.

The most important scene in the play, to my mind, is not shown: how Carol
moves from the inarticulate and uncomprehending child of Act I to the articulate and politically astute woman of the remainder of the play. By Act II it is
Carol who is making the long, uninterrupted speeches and John who is questioning and expostulating in fragments. Some commentators see this as a flaw
of character development: how does Carol achieve this command of language?
(It is less often asked how John loses it.) The assumption of many analysts is
that she is spouting the dialogue given her by the feminist "group" we never
see, rather than that such notions might have been inchoate in her. While it is
true that Carol, like virtually all Mamet's women, is a paper cutout (and John
is not much more), if we see the ability to speak as a sign of potency, then once
Carol has been provided with explanations and with a way to get power,
articulateness might follow automatically. Similarly, deprived of his unquestioned power, John might lose his ability to speak.

By Act III it is Carol who is interpreting John, instructing him, telling him
what he means and what he should or shouldn't do – just as he was doing to
her in Act I. (Many commentators who don't notice John's behavior are upset
by Carol's.) Finally, unable to take the reversal of fortune, he beats her up,
onstage and brutally. Audiences, at least their male members, frequently
applauded at this point, some yelling, "Serves the bitch right!"

The politics of interpretation operate in a couple of ways: between John and
Carol, between the institutions they represent (the university and feminism);
and between the factions in the audience and the reviewers and commentators, who see John's interpretations as justifiable and unremarkable, Carol's as
out-of-line and deserving of punishment. The university is a proper institution
whose members properly derive from their positions interpretive powers –
over things and over subordinate people. Feminism is an improper institution,
almost oxymoronic, since institutions by their existence offer power to their
members, and members of feminist groups have no right to power. Just as
Anita Hill was castigated for demanding, very publicly, the right to give the
name to the behavior in which her boss had indulged – "sexual harassment,"
not "just kidding around" – with all that that entailed, so Carol deserves
punishment because her speech – both its content and her very articulateness
– is out of line, inappropriate for one like her.

Audiences responded as they did because, at that moment, the issues the
play explored were seething in the real world: not just Thomas–Hill, but the
movie *Thelma and Louise*, and the continuing battle over "political correctness."
Mamet, criticized for the implausibility of his characters and plot, responded
that the play was, after all, a fiction that should not be taken as realistic. But it
was understood as literal commentary on a current hot-button issue. The play
had its strong effect because audiences believed that the horrors that Carol
visited on John could really happen at a major American university: a few

harridans making enough noise could ruin the career of an innocent, deserving man. Those who have spent any time in such institutions know that this is as mythic as the minotaur: vague, unwitnessed allegations based not on actual conduct but on interpretations of ambiguous conduct do not causes of action make. Remarkably, in all the writing about the play, this fact is barely mentioned at all.

So not only is the action of the play itself implausible in several ways, but the response of professional commentators is equally so. They let Mamet get away with murder, and his protagonist with mayhem.

Most needful of interpretation is the anger that seethed all around *Oleanna*: in the play, about the play, about the "realities" represented in the play. *Oleanna* offered a comforting oversimplification at a time when life seemed extremely complicated with its new roles and new rules. We can't beat up our friends, bosses, or spouses (mostly); we can't put the genie back in the pre-feminist bottle. But we can cheer when John beats Carol.

5   Real Politics, Realpolitik: Women as Political Animals

Finally we turn to more typical "politics": how women are talked about, by the pundits and politicians, as voters; how women in prominent positions are discussed; and finally, a striking case in point, the media discussion of Hillary Rodham Clinton, former first lady of the United States and then senator from New York.

One might hope that, eighty years after achieving suffrage, women voters would have become unremarkable and unmarked. But the pundits' obsession with women voters has only grown stronger in recent years. On the one hand, this is encouraging: those who matter are finally realizing that women do have power and cannot be ignored. But the way in which women apparently must be noticed is often distressing.

Once a group has been identified as having power and needs, intelligent politicians might be expected to address themselves to those needs. Occasionally this happens for women. The Democrats regularly pay obeisance to "a woman's right to choose" (then avoid the topic when campaigning). Education, especially at the primary and secondary levels, has traditionally been considered a "women's issue" in United States politics. Recently, though, male candidates for high office have begun to identify themselves as prioritizing education. Both candidates in 2000 wanted to be "the education president." More often, appealing to the women is done by outright, and insulting, pandering: Al Gore's decision to dress in earth tones; George W. Bush's banter; the long kiss between Gore and his wife before his acceptance speech at the Democratic convention, riposted by George W. Bush's peck on Oprah Winfrey's cheek. On that show Bush, asked by Oprah for his "favorite sandwich," replied, "peanut butter and jelly on white bread." Think about it: this is the favorite sandwich only of the preschool set. Bush's people have decided that infantilization is what women want.

Other groups are stereotyped and appealed to as blocs. But women alone are appealed to as children and airheads, interested not in issues but in clothes, sex, and childish things.

New York Times Op-Ed commentator Maureen Dowd wrote several columns during the campaign (e.g. Dowd 2000a, 2000b, 2000c) about the pandering to women by both sides and politicians' judgments about what women want. There has been much discussion of the "soccer mom," the suburban mother, recently updated as the "cell-phone mom," and her electoral preferences (but nothing about the "baseball dad").

In *Newsweek* (Estrich 2000), Susan Estrich, an adviser to Democratic politicians, discusses her difficulties getting the Gore team to understand what at least one woman wanted: the presence of women (plural) at "the table," where campaign decisions were discussed. A member of the team finally got back to Estrich with the news that, among many men, there was one woman – so she should be satisfied.

Then it should be unsurprising that the public perception of powerful women is ambivalent. Powerful women are variously sexualized, objectified, or ridiculed. An item in the *San Francisco Chronicle* (Garchik 2000) would be amusing if we didn't consider the consequences. Garchik reports on South Korean Foreign Minister Lee Jung Bin's response to US Secretary of State Madeleine Albright after her visit. "Albright and I are of the same age," says Lee. "So we are both feeling intimate with each other. . . . [Upon hugging her, I found she was] really buxom . . ."

A prominent woman who, by behavior or appearance, does not function as a male sex fantasy is apt to be recast as a lesbian, as was the case with Attorney General Janet Reno as well as Hillary Rodham Clinton herself. Political males are sometimes seen as sex objects, but we should not be misled by the apparent parallels: sexual conquest enhances a man's power, but weakens a woman's (compare the connotations of *stud* and *slut*).

Even more than sexualization, objectification via elaborate discussion of appearance, usually negative, is disempowering. It is true that men in the public eye can be criticized for their looks (Al Gore's incipient bald spot; Bill Clinton's paunch; George W. Bush's "smirk"). But these barbs are both less frequent and less prominent directed at men than at women. Further, comments about looks are much more dangerous to a woman's already fragile grasp of power than to a man's: they reduce a woman to her traditional role of *object*, one who is seen rather than one who sees and acts. Because this is a conventional view of women, but not of men, comments about looks work much more effectively to disempower women than men, and are more hurtful to women, who have always been encouraged to view looks as a primary attribute – as men usually have not. Being the passive object of the gaze is presupposed for women, never for heterosexual men.

During the prolonged electoral debacle of November and December, 2000, Florida Secretary of State Katherine Harris got her fifteen minutes of fame. A great deal of the discussion centered around her looks, dress, and make-up, with New York/Washington media sophisticates sneering at the taste of Florida hicks. After a few days the media turned on themselves (Salter 2000; Scott 2000; Talbot 2000): was it *right* to spend so much energy on a woman's looks? It was as if the pundits were discovering the phenomenon for the first time, and had not seen the same sort of discussions about (to name a few) Sandra Day O'Connor, Dianne Feinstein, Hillary Rodham Clinton, Janet Reno, Monica Lewinsky, or Linda Tripp. But at least the discussion entered the public discourse.

Public women are much more subject to erosion of the wall between their public and private personae than are men, with anything unconventional about their private lives leaching into judgments of their public performance. Thus Hillary Clinton, both as first lady and as senatorial candidate, got relentless criticism largely from women about her failure to end her marriage after the Monica Lewinsky imbroglio. Not only did women respond with this critique to questions about how effective she might be as a senator; although the innocent party in the affair, it was her reactions and her private decisions that were faulted by other women.

During Clinton's first ladyship she received an extraordinary amount of media attention, immensely varied, from effusively positive to virulently negative, as was true of no modern first lady other than Eleanor Roosevelt, who was damned and praised on similar grounds.

In deciding to run for the Senate from one of America's biggest and most culturally important states, Clinton created some of her own current problems. The first ladyship, while having no official duties, functions as a symbol of ideal contemporary American womanhood (cf. Lakoff 2000). The traditional first lady mostly stays out of the limelight except for photo opportunities and virtuous deeds. She stands beside her husband and defends him when necessary, but does not speak for herself. Clinton violated these rules when she agreed to chair the health care program early in her husband's first term. Yet her approval ratings, at least for the first several months, were very high. Only after the plan failed was she castigated as "ambitious," a charge that dogs her to this day.

It is odd to find "ambition" used as a criticism of prominent women. Americans generally see "ambition" positively, as embodying the American virtues of get-up-and-go, self-esteem, and independence. A (male) politician who appears to have insufficient ambition is dismissed as lacking "fire in the belly": the expectation is that he will not be successful. Yet a woman who seeks or holds high office is called "ambitious," intended as a disqualification for the position. Early in the Clinton presidency Michael Deaver, Ronald Reagan's former press secretary, is quoted as saying of Clinton: "This is not some kind of a woman behind the scenes who's pulling the strings. This woman's out front pulling the strings" (Pollitt 1993). Since Deaver's boss's wife, Nancy

Reagan, had received some criticism for being the power behind the throne, it is clear that Deaver does not mean what he says as a compliment.

Consider an extraordinary statement by Senate Majority Leader Trent Lott, after Clinton's election to the Senate: "When this Hillary gets to the Senate, if she does – maybe lightning will strike and she won't – she will be one of 100, and we won't let her forget it" (Rosenberg 2000). Leaving aside the violation of ordinarily expected collegial courtesy, the statement boils over with resentments: *this Hillary*, the emotional deictic *this* signifying emotional connection with its subject via contempt (Lakoff 1974); the first-name reference, unilateral intimacy (such as is permitted traditionally to men for women, but not vice versa – a reminder that, in Trent Lott's Senate, the Old World Order is still in effect). I pass over the death-wish as beyond comment. And by *we* does Lott mean, "the other 99 Senators"? "all the male Senators"? In any case it is deliberately exclusive and meant to hurt: "you don't belong here, woman!"

At least as upsetting is the treatment of Clinton by women, echoed by the pundits, during her Senate campaign. Newspaper and television reports kept alluding to women's suspicions of her: "She has so much baggage," a woman voter is quoted as saying (Harden 2000). "She must have known what people would be talking about. Yet she still ran. I think she thinks a lot of herself."

The last sentence seems discordant: I would have expected instead, "She really has guts." But in this case, Clinton's guts metamorphose into nerve, reminiscent of what Oprah Winfrey has referred to as women's tendency to say of other women in positions of prominence, "Who does she think she is?"

Clinton is often referred to in these reports as "deceptive." The exact nature of the deception is seldom made explicit. Mrs. Patricia Hooks (an Alabama woman at a fund-raiser for Rick Lazio, Clinton's opponent) is quoted (Harden 2000) as saying that she had "seen through" Mrs. Clinton the first time she saw her on the television show "60 Minutes" in 1992. Clinton is, she says, "a woman who wants power, who wants control, who wants to be on the national stage." What deception has Mrs. Hooks "seen through"?

Clinton's private life is also grounds for disqualification. In the same article a professional woman, a pediatrician, is quoted as saying: "I want to like her, but I can't. I lost respect for her when she stood by him during Monica." Yet her ratings were at an all-time high during the impeachment period. And although the papers continually reported on Clinton-hating women, in the end she won election by a huge 12-point majority: women voted for her after all. The quotations might mean that women were struggling with their own personal questions, doubts, and uncertainties, using Clinton as a test case: could I, should I, do this? In the end, many must have recognized that *she* was *us*.

It is tempting to suggest that we all are using Clinton as litmus paper, Rorschach (as she has suggested), or stalking horse: a referendum on *our* marriages at the millennium, whether we're right to stay in them or leave them, who we are besides (or instead of) helpmates.

Finally, Clinton is best understood as the confluence of a set of paradoxes which women are not yet able to unravel. Many claim to hate her, but in the end show up on her side (if sometimes with misgivings); they fear her ambition, but give her high ratings when she is at her most powerful. They criticize her for standing by her man, but also give her her highest ratings when she does. Male politicians seldom have to make these delicate and dangerous choices.

6   Conclusions

A great many, perhaps most, human activities have a significant political component – that is, in some way involve the allotment of power and influence among participants. In some, the politics are interpersonal: for example, we can understand many of the structures and rules of the conversational dyad as arising out of competition for a valuable resource, floor time. In others, political concerns are institutionally organized, intra- and extra-organization. Thus within the university, intra-institutional politics is involved in tenure decisions, graduate admissions policies, and resource allocation among departments (to cite a few examples). Extra-institutional politics is manifested currently (in public universities in America) in negotiations for funding with state legislatures, and in the development and growth of public relations offices in universities to enhance the prestige of those institutions in the public eye (again, just a couple of examples).

Traditionally, discussions of "politics" have focused on the public, institutional understanding of that word and of course in particular on the workings of governments. In these frames political discourse has often been identified as a male domain, with women excluded or at best relegated to the role of interloper. One thing I have tried to do here is extend the definition of "political discourse," in terms of where it occurs, who does it, and for what purpose it is done.

In this chapter I have examined three institutions in which traditional male-only "politics as usual" are being supplanted by the entrance of women into the discourse, causing novel and in some cases rather strange reorganizations of discourse possibilities: the worlds of academia, the arts, and government. In each of these, the new roles of women are perceived by some traditional members of the institution as a threat, and the conventional language practices of the institution are channeled into new forms, or new functions, in an attempt to dispel that threat or render it innocuous. The ability to perceive what is happening in each case that I describe as a power struggle – between the proponents of the status quo, and the harbingers of the new – is often affected by the unmarkedness of male-only language forms in the institutional discourse, making it easier to view female moves toward full participation as incompetent, inappropriate, or unintelligible – and therefore worthy only of ridicule, punishment, or inattention. But the increasing numbers of women achieving speaking power in these and other public institutions are likely to render those responses non-functional before very long. In many institutions the new situation has caused confusion and dissension: how do the unspoken (and spoken) rules and assumptions of the institution bend to effect necessary change? Since institutions survive by adherence to tradition, any change is often grudging.

But as the examples above attest – change is coming. None of the cases I have examined would have been perceptible – or even imaginable – thirty years earlier. The way we talk about the relation between women and power is a language of new, tentative, but very real possibilities.

REFERENCES

Brown, Penelope and Levinson, Stephen C. 1986: *Politeness: Some Universals in Language Usage.* Cambridge: Cambridge University Press.

Conley, John, O'Barr, William M., and Lind, E. Allen 1979: The power of language: Presentational style in the courtroom. *Duke Law Journal* 1978: 1375–99.

Dowd, Maureen 1996: Liberties: Pink think. *New York Times*, September 15, 1996: 17.

Dowd, Maureen 2000a: Liberties: Rescue me, please. *New York Times*, June 7, 2000: 13.

Dowd, Maureen 2000b: Liberties: No dark victories. *New York Times*, June 18, 2000: 15.

Dowd, Maureen 2000c: Liberties: Cuddle us, or else! *New York Times*, September 21, 2000: 13.

Estrich, Susan 2000: Al Gore's woman problem. *Newsweek*, October 3, 2000: 30–1.

Fishman, Pamela 1978: Interaction: The work women do. *Social Problems* 25(4): 397–406.

Garchik, Leah 2000: Madame Secretary's Korean admirer. *San Francisco Chronicle*, November 8, 2000: D8.

Harden, Blaine 2000: Fame a two-edged sword for the candidate Clinton. Disapproval ratings: A special report. *New York Times*, September 27, 2000: 1, 22.

Holmberg, Arthur 1992: The language of misunderstanding. *American Theatre*, October 1992: 94–5.

James, Deborah and Clarke, Sandra 1993: Women, men, and interruptions. In D. Tannen (ed.) *Gender and Conversational Interaction*. New York: Oxford University Press, pp. 231–80.

Lahr, John 1992: Dogma days. *The New Yorker*, November 16, 1992: 121–5.

Lakoff, Robin 1974: Remarks on *this* and *that*. In Michael LaGaly, Robert Fox, and Anthony Bruck (eds) *Papers from the Tenth Regional Meeting of the Chicago Linguistic Society*. Chicago: Chicago Linguistic Society, pp. 345–56.

Lakoff, Robin Tolmach 2000: *The Language War*. Los Angeles and Berkeley: University of California Press.

Leet-Pellegrini, Helena M. 1980: Conversational dominance as a function of gender and expertise. In Howard Giles, W. P. Robinson, and

Phillip M. Smith (eds) *Language: Social Psychological Perspectives.* Oxford: Pergamon, pp. 97–104.

Maltz, Daniel N. and Borker, Ruth A. 1982: A cultural approach to male–female miscommunication. In John J. Gumperz (ed.) *Language and Social Identity.* Cambridge: Cambridge University Press, pp. 196–216.

Mamet, David 1992: *Oleanna.* New York: Vintage.

Mendoza-Denton, Norma 1995: Pregnant pauses: Silence and authority in the Anita Hill–Clarence Thomas Hearings. In Kira Hall and Mary Bucholtz (eds) *Gender Articulated: Language and the Socially Constructed Self.* New York: Routledge, pp. 51–66.

Mufson, Daniel 1993: Sexual perversity in viragos. *Theater* 24(1): 111–13.

Pollitt, Katha 1993: The male media's Hillary problem. *The Nation* 256(19) (May 17, 1993): 657–60.

Rich, Frank 1992: Mamet's new play detonates the fury of sexual harassment. *New York Times,* October 26, 1992: C1, C12.

Rosenberg, Deborah 2000: Hillary goes up the hill. *Newsweek,* November 20, 2000: 26–7.

Salter, Stephanie 2000: Looking at the guys in sexist, demeaning ways. *San Francisco Chronicle,* November 30, 2000: A31.

Schegloff, Emanuel 1997: Whose text? Whose context? *Discourse & Society* 8(2): 165–87.

Schegloff, Emanuel 1998: Reply to Wetherell. *Discourse & Society* 9(3): 413–16.

Scott, Janny 2000: When first impressions count: Florida face-off. *New York Times,* December 3, 2000: 3.

Showalter, Elaine 1992: Acts of violence. *Times Literary Supplement,* November 6, 1992: 16–17.

Silverthorne, Jeanne 1993: PC Playhouse. *Artforum* 31(7): 10–11.

Spender, Dale 1980: *Man Made Language.* London: Routledge and Kegan Paul.

Talbot, Margaret 2000: Mascaragate. *New York Times Magazine,* December 10, 2000: 47.

Tannen, Deborah 1981: New York Jewish conversational style. *International Journal of the Sociology of Language* 30: 133–9.

Tannen, Deborah 1990: *You Just Don't Understand.* New York: William Morrow.

Thorne, Barrie and Henley, Nancy (eds) 1975: *Language and Sex: Difference and Dominance.* Rowley, MA: Newbury House.

Weatherall, Ann 2000: Gender relevance in talk-in-interaction and discourse. *Discourse & Society* 11(2): 286–8.

Wetherell, Margaret 1998: Positioning and interpretative repertoires: Conversation analysis and post-structuralism in dialogue. *Discourse & Society* 9(3): 387–412.

Zimmerman, Don and West, Candace 1975: Sex roles, interruptions, and silences in conversation. In Barrie Thorne and Nancy Henley (eds) *Language and Sex: Difference and Dominance.* Rowley, MA: Newbury House, pp. 105–29.

8 Gender and Family Interaction

DEBORAH TANNEN

1 Introduction

In the quarter century since Lakoff's (1975) and Key's (1975) pioneering studies, there has been a mountain of research on gender and discourse – research well documented in the present volume. In recent years, discourse analysts have also undertaken studies of language in the context of family interaction. For the most part, however, the twain haven't met: few scholars writing in the area of language and gender have focused their analyses on family interaction, and few researchers concerned with family discourse have focused their analysis on gender and language. This is a gap this chapter addresses.

Drawing examples from an ongoing research project in which dual-career couples with children living at home recorded all their interaction for a week, as well as videotaped excerpts of naturally occurring family interaction that appeared on public television documentaries, I examine (1) how gender-related patterns of interaction influence and illuminate family interaction, and (2) what light this insight sheds on our ideology of language in the family as well as on theoretical approaches to discourse. In particular, I question the prevailing inclination to approach family interaction as exclusively, or primarily, a struggle for power. I will argue – and, I hope, demonstrate – that power is inseparable from connection. Therefore, in exploring how family interaction is mediated by gender-related patterns of discourse, I will also suggest that gender identity is negotiated along the dual, paradoxically related dimensions of power and connection.

2   Power and Connection in the Family: Prior Research

Researchers routinely interpret family interaction through the template of an ideology of the family as the locus of a struggle for power. In my view, this ideology needs to be reframed. Power is inextricably intertwined with connection. Discourse in the family can be seen as a struggle for power, yes, but it is also – and equally – a struggle for connection. Indeed, the family is a prime example – perhaps *the* prime example – of the nexus of needs for both power and connection in human relationships. Thus, a study of gender and family interaction becomes a means not only to understand more deeply gender and language but also to reveal, contest, and reframe the ideology of the family and of power in discourse.

Among recent research on discourse in family interaction, three book-length studies stand out. The earliest, Richard Watts' *Power in Family Discourse* (1991), is unique in analyzing conversations among adult siblings and their spouses rather than the nuclear family of parents and young children living in a single household. For Watts, as his title suggests, power is the force defining familial relations.

Published a year later, Herve Varenne's *Ambiguous Harmony* (1992) examines a conversation that took place on a single evening in the living room of a blended family: mother, father, and two children – a teenage son from the mother's previous marriage and a younger child born to this couple. Varenne, too, sees power as a central force. He writes: "The power we are interested in here is the power of the catalyst who, with a minimal amount of its own energy, gets other entities to spend large amounts of their own" (p. 76).

Shoshana Blum-Kulka's *Dinner Talk* (1997) is unique in comparing family dinner conversations in three cultural contexts: Americans of East European Jewish background; Israelis of East European Jewish background; and Israeli families in which the parents were born and raised in the United States. Although Blum-Kulka does not directly address the relationship between power and connection, she discusses the parents' dual and sometimes conflicting needs both to socialize their children in the sense of teaching them what they need to know, and at the same time to socialize with them in the sense of enjoying their company. This perspective indirectly addresses the interrelationship of power and connection in the family.

Psychologists Millar, Rogers, and Bavelas (1984) write of "control maneuvers" and note that in family therapy, "Conflict takes place within the power dimension of relationships." I do not question or deny this assumption, but I would complexify it. I have emphasized, in a number of essays (especially Tannen 1994), the ambiguity and polysemy of power and solidarity, which are in paradoxical and mutually constitutive relationship to each other. Thus family interaction (including conflict) also takes place within the intimacy dimension,

power	solidarity
hierarchy	equality
distance	closeness

Figure 8.1   Unidimensional view of power and connection

and we can also speak of "connection maneuvers." My goal in this chapter is to explicate how what researchers (and participants) would typically regard as control (or power) maneuvers can also be seen as connection maneuvers, in part because connection and control are bought with the same linguistic currency.

3   The Power/Connection Grid

Elsewhere (Tannen 1994), I explore and argue for the ambiguity and polysemy of power and solidarity – or, in different terms, of status and connection. Here I briefly recap the analysis developed in that essay.

In conventional wisdom, as well as in research tracing back to Brown and Gilman's (1960) classic study of power and solidarity, Americans have had a tendency to conceptualize the relationship between hierarchy (or power) and connection (or solidarity) as unidimensional and mutually exclusive (see figure 8.1). Family relationships are at the heart of this conception. For example, Americans frequently use the terms "sisters" and "brothers" to indicate "close and equal." So if someone says "We are like sisters" or "He is like a brother to me," the implication is, "We are as close as siblings, and there are no status games, no one-upping between us." In contrast, hierarchical relationships are assumed to preclude closeness. Thus, in work and military contexts, most Americans regard it as self-evident that friendships across levels of rank are problematic and to be discouraged, if not explicitly prohibited.

I suggest that in reality the relationship between power (or hierarchy) and solidarity (or connection) is not a single dimension but a multidimensional grid (see figure 8.2). This grid represents the dimensions of power and of connection as two intersecting axes. One axis (I represent it as a vertical one) stretches between hierarchy and equality, while the other (which I represent as a horizontal axis) stretches between closeness and distance.

Americans tend to conceptualize interpersonal relationships along an axis that runs from the upper right to the lower left: from hierarchical and distant to equal and close. Thus we would put business relations in the upper right quadrant (hierarchical and distant) and relationships between siblings and close friends in the lower left quadrant (egalitarian and close) (see figure 8.3).

In contrast, members of many other cultures, such as Japanese, Chinese, and Javanese, are inclined to conceptualize relationships along an axis that runs from the upper left to the lower right: from hierarchical and close to equal and

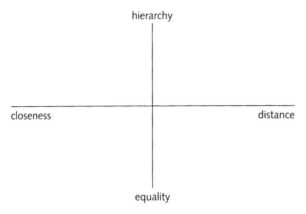

Figure 8.2   The power/connection grid

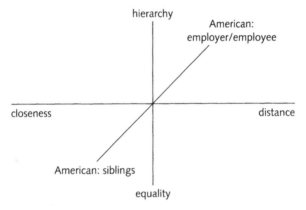

Figure 8.3   American view of the power/connection grid

distant. In this conception, the archetypal hierarchical relationship is the parent–child constellation: extremely hierarchical but also extremely close. By the same token, sibling relationships are seen as inherently hierarchical. Indeed, in Chinese (and in many other non-Western languages, such as Sinhala), siblings are addressed not by name but by designations identifying relative rank, such as "Third Eldest Brother," "Fifth Younger Sister," and so on (see figure 8.4).

It is also instructive to note that Americans are inclined to see power as inherent in an individual. Thus, Watts defines power as "the ability of an individual to achieve her/his desired goals" (1991: 145). Yet this, too, reflects peculiarly Western ideology. Wetzel (1988) points out that in Japanese cultural conceptions, power is understood to result from an individual's place in a network of alliances. Even in the most apparently hierarchical situation, such as a workplace, an individual's ability to achieve her/his goals is dependent on connections to others: the proverbial friends in high places. In other words, power is composed in part of connection, and connection entails a kind of power.

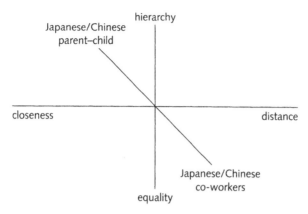

Figure 8.4   Japanese/Chinese view of power and connection

4   Mother: A Paradigm Case of the Ambiguity and Polysemy of Power and Connection

The family is a key locus for understanding the complex and inextricable relationship between power (negotiations along the hierarchy–equality axis) and connection (negotiations along the closeness–distance axis). And nowhere does this relationship become clearer than in the role of a key family member, mother. For example, Hildred Geertz (1989 [1961]: 20) writes that there are, in Javanese, "two major levels of language, respect and familiarity." (I would point out that, in light of the grid presented above, these are two different dimensions: respect is situated on the hierarchy–equality axis, whereas familiarity is a function of the closeness–distance axis.) Geertz observes that children use the familiar register when speaking with their parents and siblings until about age ten or twelve, when they gradually shift to respect in adulthood. However, she adds, "Most people continue to speak to the mother in the same way as they did as children; a few shift to respect in adulthood" (p. 22). This leaves open the question whether mothers are addressed in this way because they receive less respect than fathers, or because their children feel closer to them. I suspect it is both at once, and that trying to pick them apart may be futile.

Although the linguistic encoding of respect and familiar registers is a linguistic phenomenon not found in English, nonetheless there are phenomena in English that parallel those described by Geertz. Ervin-Tripp, O'Connor, and Rosenberg (1984) looked at the forms of "control acts" in families in order to gauge power in that context. They found that "effective power and esteem were related to age" (p. 134). Again, however, "the mothers in our sample were an important exception to the pattern . . ." (p. 135). "In their role as caregivers," the authors note, mothers "received nondeferent orders, suggesting that the children expected compliance and believed their desires to be justification enough." As with Javanese, one could ask whether children use more bald imperatives when speaking to their mothers because they have less respect for them, or because they feel closer to them, or both.

5   Power Lines – or Connection Lines – in Telling Your Day

A great deal of the research done on family discourse has focused on talk produced in the context of dinner-table conversation. The dinner table is a favorite site, no doubt, both because dinner is a prime time that family members typically come together and exchange talk, and also because it is a bounded event for which speakers gather around a table and which is therefore relatively easy to tape-record. Both Blum-Kulka and Elinor Ochs and her students (for example, Ochs and Taylor 1992) identify a ritual that typifies American dinner-table conversation in many families: a ritual that Blum-Kulka dubs "Telling Your Day." When the family includes a mother and father (as the families recorded in both these studies did), mothers typically encourage children to tell their fathers about events experienced during the day.

Ochs and Taylor give the examples of a mother who urges, "Tell Dad what you thought about gymnastics and what you did," and another who prompts, "Chuck did you tell Daddy what happened at karate when you came in your new uniform? What did Daisy do for you?" (p. 310). Ochs and Taylor note that in a majority of the instances recorded in this study, fathers responded to the resultant stories by passing judgment, assessing the rightness of their children's actions and feelings, and thereby setting up a constellation the researchers call "father knows best."

In the families Ochs and her students observed, mothers usually knew what the children had to say. This was true not only of mothers who had been at home with the children during the day but also of mothers who worked full-time, because generally they had arrived home from work earlier than the father, and they had asked the children about their day during the time they had with them before Daddy came home. At the dinner table, Daddy could have asked "How was your day?" just as Mother did before dinner. But in these families, he usually didn't.

Ochs and Taylor identify the roles in these narrative exchanges as "problematizer" and "problematizee." The "problematizer" reacts to a family member's account of an experience in a way that is critical of how the speaker handled the situation. For example, when an eight-year-old child, Josh, who has been doing homework, announced, "I'm done," his father asked in a "disbelieving tone," "Already Josh? Read me what you wrote." Thus the father questioned whether Josh really was finished or not (p. 313). In Ochs and Taylor's terms, he "problematized" Josh's announcement "I'm done."

The family power structure, Ochs and Taylor observe, is established in these storytelling dynamics. Just as Mother typically prompted a child to tell Daddy what happened, older siblings were much more likely to urge younger ones to tell about something that happened than the other way around. In this sense, older siblings were treating their younger siblings more or less the way parents treat children – something that, I would note, younger siblings often perceive and resent, especially if the older brother or sister is not all that much older.

Ochs and Taylor found that children were most often problematizees – the ones whose behavior was judged by others. Rarely were they problematizers – the ones who questioned others' behavior as problematic. This puts children firmly at the bottom of the hierarchy. Fathers were the most frequent problematizers and rarely were problematizees: rarely was their behavior held up to the scrutiny and judgment of others. This puts them firmly at the top of the hierarchy. In keeping with the findings of Ervin-Tripp, O'Connor, and Rosenberg, mothers were not up there, as parents, along with fathers. Mothers found themselves in the position of problematizee (the one whose behavior was held up for judgment) as often as they were problematizer (the one who was judging others). Thus fathers were in the position of judging their wives' actions in addition to their children's, but mothers judged only their children's behavior, not their husbands'. In other words, the storytelling dynamic placed mothers in the middle of the family hierarchy – over the children, but under the father.

The authors also observe that mothers often problematized their own actions. For example, a woman named Marie owns and runs a day care center. At dinner, she tells of a client who was taking her child out of the center, and paid her last bill. The client handed over more money than was needed to cover the time her child had spent in day care, so Marie returned the excess. But she later wondered whether she had made a mistake. After all, her policy required clients to give two weeks' notice before withdrawing a child, and this mother had not given notice. So perhaps the client had intended the overpayment to cover those two weeks, and Marie should have kept it, enforcing her policy. The father made clear that he endorsed this view: "When I say something I stick to it unless she brings it up. . . . I do not change it" (p. 312). Marie was the "problematizee" because her action was called into question. She had "problematized" herself by raising the issue of whether she had handled the situation in the best way; her husband then further problematized her by letting her know that he thought she had not. Ochs and Taylor found that this pattern was common: if mothers questioned their own actions, fathers often "dumped on" them by reinforcing the conclusion that the mothers had not acted properly. In contrast, the authors found that in the rare instances when fathers problematized themselves, mothers did not further problematize them.

In this revealing study, Ochs and Taylor identify a crucial dynamic in middle-class American families by which the family is a power structure with the father at the top. They further show that mothers play a crucial role in setting up this dynamic: "Father as problematizer," they argue, is "facilitated . . . by the active role of mothers who sometimes (perhaps inadvertently) set fathers up as potential problematizers – by introducing the stories and reports of children and mothers in the first place and orienting them towards fathers as primary recipients" (p. 329).

For me, the most important word in this excerpt is "inadvertently." I would argue that the father-knows-best dynamic results from gender differences in assumptions about the place of talk in a relationship, and that it reflects the inextricable relationship between power and connection. When a mother asks her children what they did during the day, she is creating closeness by exchanging details of daily life, a verbal ritual frequently observed to characterize women's friendships (see, for example, Tannen 1990; Coates 1996). In other words, it is a connection maneuver. If the father does not ask on his own, "How was your day?" it does not mean that he is not interested in his family, or does not feel – or wish to be – close to them. It just means that he does not assume that closeness is created by the verbal ritual of telling the details of one's day, and he probably does not regard closeness as the most important barometer of his relationship with his children.

When Mother prods a child, "Tell Daddy what you did in karate today," she is, it is true, initiating a dynamic by which the father will assess the child's actions and thus be installed as the family judge. But I would bet that her goal was to *involve* the father in the family, bring him into the circle of intimacy she feels is established by such talk. From this point of view, the father-knows-best dynamic is as much a misfire as is the common source of frustration between women and men that I have described elsewhere (Tannen 1990): for example, a woman tells a man about a frustrating experience she had that day, performing a ritual common among women friends that Gail Jefferson (1988) dubs "troubles talk." Since troubles talk is not a ritual common among men friends, he thinks he is being asked to solve the problem, which he proceeds to do – to her frustration. She protests, which frustrates him. Similarly, the mother who prods her children to tell their father what they did that day, or who talks about her own day, is trying to create connection. But the father, not recognizing the ritual nature of her comment, thinks he is being asked to judge.

In this view, it is not the mothers' initiation of the "Telling Your Day" routine in itself that sets fathers up as family judge. Instead, the "father knows best" dynamic is created by the interaction of gender-related patterns. Fathers take the role of judge of actions recounted in stories because they figure that's why they are being told the stories. Fathers are less likely to talk about their own work problems because they don't want advice about how to solve problems there, so they see no reason to talk about them. Many men feel that re-hashing what upset them at work forces them to re-live it and get upset all over again, when they'd rather put it out of their minds and enjoy the oasis of home. They may also resist telling about problems precisely to avoid being placed in the one-down position of receiving advice or of being told that they did not handle the situation in the best way. On the few occasions that Ochs and Taylor found fathers "problematizing" themselves, it is no surprise that mothers did not further dump on them – not necessarily because mothers felt they had no right to judge, but more likely because they took these revelations in the spirit of troubles talk rather than as invitations to pass judgment. These clashing rituals result in mothers finding themselves one-down in the family hierarchy without knowing how they got there.

I have discussed this example from Ochs and Taylor at length to demonstrate how gender-related patterns of discourse can explain a phenomenon observed in family interaction in prior research, and how what has been accurately identified as a matter of negotiating power is also simultaneously and inextricably a matter of negotiating connection. This analysis supports my contentions that (1) power and connection are inextricably intertwined; (2) the relationship between power and connection is fundamental to an understanding of gender and language; and (3) the relationship between gender and language is fundamental to an understanding of family interaction.

6 Self-Revelation: A Gender-Specific Conversational Ritual

The "How was your day?" ritual, for many women, is just one way that connection is created and maintained through talk. Another way is exchanging information about personal relationships and emotions. Here, too, conversations that take place in families reflect the divergent expectations of family members of different genders.

For example, one way that many women create and maintain closeness is by keeping tabs on each other's lives, including (perhaps especially) romantic relationships. When male and female family members interact, gender differences in expectations regarding the use of talk to create closeness can lead to unbalanced interchanges. The following example, which illustrates just such a conversation, comes from the research project in which both members of dual-career couples carried tape-recorders with them for at least a week, recording all the conversations they felt comfortable recording. (The digital recorders ran for four hours per tape.)

In this example, one of the project participants recorded a conversation with her unmarried brother. The sister (a woman in her thirties) is asking her brother (who is a few years younger) about his girlfriend, whom I'll call Kerry. Clearly the sister is looking for a kind of interchange that her brother is not providing:

Sister:	So how's things with Kerry?
Brother:	Cool.
Sister:	Cool. Does that mean very good?
Brother:	Yeah.
Sister:	True love?
Brother:	Pretty much.
Sister:	PRETTY much? When you say PRETTY much, what do you mean?
Brother:	I mean it's all good.

The conversation takes on an almost comic character, as the sister becomes more and more probing in reaction to her brother's minimal responses. Evident in the example is a process I call, adapting a term that Gregory Bateson (1972) applied to larger cultural processes, complementary schismogenesis. By this process, each person's verbal behavior drives the other to more and more exaggerated forms of an opposing behavior. In this example, the sister asks repeated and increasingly probing questions *because* her brother's responses are minimal, and his responses may well become more guarded *because* her questions become increasingly insistent. Indeed, she starts to sound a bit like an inquisitor.

Moreover, this conversation between sister and brother sounds rather like a mother talking to a teenage child. It is strikingly similar to the conversation represented in the next example, which took place between a mother and her twelve-year-old daughter. This conversational excerpt was identified and analyzed by Alla Yeliseyeva in connection with a seminar I taught on family interaction. The excerpt comes from a documentary made by filmmaker Jennifer Fox entitled "An American Love Story." The documentary aired in five two-hour segments on the USA's Public Broadcasting System in September 1999. In preparing the documentary, Fox followed the family of Karen Wilson, Bill Sims, and their two daughters, in Queens, New York, over two years beginning in 1992. In this episode, the younger daughter, Chaney, was anticipating her first "date" – a daytime walk – with a boy, despite her parents' misgivings. But the boy (who is thirteen) failed to appear on the appointed day. After the entire family spent several hours waiting for him, Chaney got a telephone call explaining that his grandmother had refused permission for him to go. Karen tries to discuss this development with Chaney, who responds minimally:

Karen: That's too bad. Aren't you mad?
Chaney: No.
Karen: I mean just in general.
Chaney: What do you mean?
Karen: Not at him, just in general.
Chaney: No, not that much.
Karen: Disappointed?
Chaney: No, not that much.
Karen: Relieved?
Chaney: No. [*laughs*]
Karen: What- [*also laughing*]
                Give us a feeling here, Chaney!

Through her questions and comments, Karen is showing her daughter the kind of conversation she expects to have – a conversation about how Chaney felt about what happened to her. I doubt that Chaney is unable to hold such conversations; I would bet she has them frequently with her best friend, Nelly. But, like many teenagers, she seems reluctant to divulge her feelings to her mother.

On a later day, the boy shows up unexpectedly, and Chaney goes out for a walk with him. When she returns, a similar conversation ensues, with different content. The trouble starts immediately, as Chaney heads for her room:

Karen: Come sit and tell us all about it.
Chaney: I have to call Nelly.
Karen: Come, tell us all about it first.
             I am your first priority here.

Chaney complies by sitting down, but she volunteers nothing. She offers only cryptic and minimally informative answers to her mother's questions. Through-out the conversation, Chaney laughs or chuckles.

Karen: Did he hold your hand?
Chaney: Yeah. [*laughs*]
Karen: How did that feel?
Chaney: His hands were cold.
Karen: Did you kiss?
Chaney: Yeah.
Karen: Where?
Chaney: Where do you think? [*chuckling*]
Karen: On your lip?
Chaney: Just a short one.
Karen: [*Whispering*] Oh my god!
             [*normal voice*] Where. At our door?
Chaney: Yeah.
Karen: What did you think?
Chaney: Nothing.
Karen: Did you have any feelings about it?
Chaney: Yeah.
Karen: A good one or a bad one, or a stupid one?
Chaney: Good.
Karen: Wh- When are you going to see him?
Chaney: Mmm, probably in June.
Karen: Mm, that's nice and safe.
Chaney: [*laughing and trying to get up*] Bye!
Karen: So are you happy to see him?
Chaney: Yeah.
Karen: Is he the same you thought he would be?
Chaney: He's just the same.

At this point, Chaney rises and retreats to her room. To learn how she really felt about her date, we would have to listen in on her conversation with Nelly. And that must be a source of frustration to Karen as it would be to most mothers of teenagers. Although Chaney answered her mother's questions, the interchange feels more like an interrogation than a conversation.

Why is the mother in this example and the sister in the earlier one so intent on getting a family member to divulge feelings? I have argued elsewhere

(Tannen 1990), drawing on a large body of language and gender research, that women and girls typically define their relationships with friends along the connection axis: best friends tell each other "everything." This includes not only large and small life events but also how they feel about those events. Family relationships are defined and evaluated the same way. A good family relationship is a "close" one, and that means a relationship in which one tells the other what is happening in one's life, and how one *feels* about it. When children are small, the confidences go one way: mothers want to know what their children are experiencing and feeling, though they typically do not confide their own feelings to their small children. When daughters become adults, however, as Henwood (1993) found, both daughters and mothers typically evaluate their relationship in terms of how "close" they are – and this is gauged by relative mutual revelation about feelings (as well as by discussion of the small details of daily life).

7   Gender Differences Between Parents

The significance of these gender patterns in definitions of closeness, and the significance of closeness in women's (but not men's) evaluations of family relationships, emerges in the discourse videotaped in another public television documentary, "An American Family," which aired in twelve weekly hour-long segments in 1973. For this series, filmmakers Alan and Susan Raymond filmed the family of William and Pat Loud and their five children in Santa Barbara, California, for seven months. My student Maureen Taylor examined conversations between the parents regarding their children, and in particular their teenage daughter Delilah.

Pat Loud had taken Delilah on a trip to New Mexico. Delilah came home early – and Pat, on her own return, tries to get her husband to tell her what Delilah said when she arrived home. A recurrent theme in Pat's discourse is her assumption that her daughter should confide in her. Furthermore, Pat's distress that Delilah left New Mexico without confiding her reasons for leaving to her mother is associated with Pat's general distress at seeing her children leave home.

Maureen Taylor, in a seminar paper, pointed out that Pat and Bill have very different reactions to their teenage children growing up and growing away. In talking to Pat, Bill explains that he is not concerned because he believes the separation is inevitable: "You've got to learn, Patty," he says, "that they're going to leave you." To back this up, he suggests that she think back to her own youth:

Bill: with your own father, with your own mother.
        You leave them when you're fifteen,
        and you don't come back until you're thirty, no-

In Bill's view, their children "leaving" (at this point, emotionally: all but one are still living at home) is healthy because it signals their developing independence. But Pat does not see emotional distance as a benefit:

Pat: The thing- No.
 The only thing I see from that
 is that somewhere along the line,
 she um she's afraid of me,
 or she's uh . . . something.

I would argue that the reason it is so easy for Bill to be philosophical about his teenage children's distancing, and so hard for Pat, is that being "close" to her children is crucial to Pat but not to Bill. Furthermore, for her, but not for him, being close means confiding experiences and feelings.

For Pat, seeing that her daughter is more likely to confide in her father than in her is an added blow, because she must watch someone else getting what she wants but cannot have. Bill tries to minimize the significance of this disparity with an explanation that is not complimentary to himself:

Bill: No, she's not afraid of you at all.
 She just knows that I'm weaker-
 that I'm weaker than you, that's all.

Pat does not accept this explanation and is not comforted by it:

Pat: She isn't saying these things to you
 because she thinks you're weaker.
 She is saying those things to you
 because she feels closer to you,
 which is a very healthy thing.
 I- I understand that.
 But the only thing I feel is that
 I- I want her to be able to say those things to me,
 because it's very important for her
 to have an older woman, like her mother,
 that she can say something to.
 And she doesn't tell me anything.

Pat's and Bill's differing views are foregrounded in these comments. For Pat, the most important thing is being close, and closeness is created by self-revealing talk. Pat's complaint that Delilah "doesn't tell me anything" is not only common among mothers (and not fathers) of teenage daughters, but it is also the complaint typically heard from women in heterosexual relationships about their partners.

Bill's response ignores those dynamics, probably because he is unaware of them. For him, the focus is not connection but independence. His reassurance is almost poetic with its soothing rhythms and mesmerizing repetitions. To capture this effect in print, Taylor, following Tannen (1989), laid out Bill's comments not only in lines representing breath groups but also in verses, as if it were a poem:

Bill: You want to feel blessed
        that they want to get out
        and go do their own thing.

        And you want to feel blessed
        that people aren't hanging on your neck
        for the rest of your life.

        And you want to feel blessed
        you've got a girl like that
        who doesn't want to sit around the room,
        and she wants to do,
        and she knows wh- how the hell she's going to do it.
        Don't worry about it, Patty.
        You've got your own life –
        and she'll be back again in about ten years.

But Pat is not reassured. She tries to explain her concern from the point of view of her daughter's needs rather than her own:

Pat: No- no- That isn't it.
       That isn't what bothers me.
       What bothers me is that
       I don't think that I'd be able to help her,
       or give her any assistance,
       except loaning my clothes to her,
       which, honey, is no assistance.

Bill returns to his point of view, that it is natural and fine for children to distance themselves from parents at this age:

Bill: If you haven't helped her out by now,
        the show is over.
        The blue moon went up and the sun subsided.

Pat's response comes right back to where she started: that her relationship with her daughter is defined by how close they are, and that Delilah's failure to confide in her mother is evidence of a failure of closeness:

Pat: But that's why I am so appalled and amazed is- because I always thought
       that we were extremely close
       and that she could tell me uh
       almost anything she wants to say to me.

When Pat complains again that Delilah confides more in Bill than in her, he reminds her that the reverse is true for their sons, and that this doesn't bother him at all:

Bill: Did you hear Lance tell me anything?
No!
Do I worry about that?
I just could care less.
I really could. I could care less.

Kevin?
My boy, talk to me?
Grant?
Never speaks, never says his little word.
Never, no!

Bill goes on to announce that he has decided to stop worrying. But from his point of view, that means giving up worrying not about his children's talk (whether or not they confide in him) but about their actions – whether or not they go to work and earn money:

Bill: I'm going to worry about a lot less
than I have before.
Pat: About what.
Bill: About a lot less of- of anything
that I've been worried about.

Once again, I will reproduce Taylor's presentation of Bill's comments in both lines and verses in order to capture in print the rhythmic effect of the spoken word:

Bill: Kevin doesn't want to pour the cement?
Forget it.
You don't have to pour the cement.
I don't have to support him.
He'd better start supporting himself.

She wants to dance?
She'd better get out there
and earn a couple of bucks,
and do her own dancing.

Michelle doesn't want to go play with the girls?
I'm not going to worry about it.
She can sit in her room
for the rest of her whole living days
as far as I'm concerned.

I'm not going to worry about it.
Life's too short to worry about all that jazz. That's what I've learned about this
vacation.

The conversation ends with a symphonic coda that pretty much sums up the
way mother and father are responding to their children's growing up and
leaving home:

Pat: I hate to see them go like that.
      I just hate it.
      I hate it.
Bill: I love it.

Taylor points out that the contrast between Pat's sense of desolation and Bill's
sense of liberation at their daughter's – and all their children's – growing up
reflects the gender-specific roles they took in the family. Since Pat had devoted
her married life to caring for her children, she experiences their departures as
abandonment. As she tells her brother and sister-in-law, "All my kids are
leaving me. And what have I got left? I haven't got anything left. And that
scares the hell out of me."

In contrast, Taylor points out, Bill has spent his life traveling: first in the navy
and then in connection with his business. This reinforces the interpretation he
gives to his children's growing up: although Pat sees them as leaving her, he
sees them gaining freedom and independence for themselves. Furthermore, I
would point out, Bill's description of what *he* won't worry about makes it clear
that the burden of family for him has been a financial one: the responsibility
for supporting everyone. His children's growing up liberates him from that
burden.

Thus Bill's and Pat's different reactions can be explained not only by the
different roles they took in their family but also by differences in what women
and men tend to focus on in relationships in general and family relationships
in particular. The example of Bill and Pat Loud, then, demonstrates that family
relationships are a complex intertwining of connection and power, that responses to and interpretations of these forces pattern by gender, and that an
understanding of these patterns is necessary to understand what goes on in
family interaction.

8   Balancing Power and Connection in a Family Argument

In this final section, I examine several examples from the family discourse
recorded by one of the couples who participated in the research project I
described above by recording their own conversations. (This is a different

family from the one in which the sister/brother conversation occurred.) In each of the following examples, the mother and father use complex verbal strategies to balance the needs to negotiate both power and connection as they go about the tasks required to maintain the daily life of their young family. In addition, as we will see, their discourse strategies simultaneously create gender-related parental identities.

The couple, pseudonymously called Molly and Ben, have a two-year-old daughter, Katie. Both Molly and Ben work outside the home: Ben full-time and Molly at a reduced schedule of thirty hours per week. Each regularly takes off one day a week to spend with Katie, who consequently attends day care only three days a week. At one point in the taping, Molly and Ben, both at home, become embroiled in an argument about making popcorn. Molly is in the kitchen by herself and Ben is taking care of Katie in another room when he calls out:

Ben: Molly! Mol! Let's switch.
       You take care of her.
       I'll do whatever you're doing.

Molly responds, from the kitchen, "I'm making popcorn." And then she adds, "You always burn it."

Clearly what is at stake, and what ensues, can be understood as a series of control maneuvers. Ben wants to switch roles with Molly, so that she will take over child care and he will take over popcorn preparation. Molly resists this switch. In a direct confrontation over power, Molly might simply refuse: "No, I don't want to switch." Instead, by saying "You always burn it," she resists relinquishing her task by appealing to the good of the family rather than her own preference. Insofar as she resists doing what Ben wants her to do, her statement is a control maneuver. But to the extent that she appeals to the family good rather than her own preference, it is a connection maneuver. At the same time, however, by impugning Ben's popcorn-making ability, she is putting him down. That, too, can be seen as a control maneuver.

Because Molly has based her resistance on her husband's putative deficiency, he responds on this level:

Ben: No I don't!
       I never burn it.
       I make it perfect.

Although they continue to exchange attacks, self-defense, and counterattacks focused on popcorn-making skills, Ben and Molly execute the switch: Ben takes over in the kitchen, and Molly takes charge of Katie. But she continues to try to engineer her return to the kitchen. In this endeavor, she addresses the two-year-old:

Molly: You wanna help Mommy make popcorn?
Katie: Okay.
Molly: Let's not let Daddy do it.
Katie: Okay.
Molly: Okay, come on.

Here, again, Molly's utterances are a blend of power and connection. To the extent that she is trying to get her way – take back control of the popcorn preparation – Molly is engaged in control maneuvers. But by proposing that Katie "help Mommy make popcorn," Molly is proposing to satisfy both herself and her husband: she would thereby return to the kitchen, yes, but she would also fulfill Ben's request, "You take care of her." Moreover, by involving Katie in the plan, Molly is involving the child in the interaction. Furthermore, her linguistic choices ("Let's not let Daddy do it") align herself with her daughter: "Let's" merges mother and daughter; "not let" includes the child in the mother's perspective as someone who has authority over Ben's actions, and "Daddy" includes the mother in the child's point of view. All these are connection maneuvers, though they create connection to Katie rather than Ben.

From the kitchen, Ben overhears this conversation and resists in turn. While Molly continues to urge their daughter to accompany her, Ben follows a strategy of "the best defense is a good offense":

Ben: I know how to make popcorn!
Molly: Let's hurry up so Daddy doesn't . . .
Ben: I can make popcorn better than you can!

The argument between Molly and Ben continues, as Ben retains the role of chef and maintains that his performance in this role is successful, while Molly becomes increasingly apprehensive of impending failure:

Molly: Just heat it! Heat it!
         No, I don't want you . . .
Ben: It's going, it's going. Hear it?
Molly: It's too slow.
         It's all soaking in.
         You hear that little . . .
Ben: It's not soaking in, it's fine.
Molly: It's just a few kernels.
Ben: All the popcorn is being popped!

Soon Molly tries another strategy to regain control of the kitchen, or to salvage the popcorn operation, or both:

Molly: You gotta take the trash outside.
Ben: I can't, I'm doing the popcorn.

Molly: I'll DO it, I'll watch it.
         You take the trash out
         and come back in a few minutes and –

Again, Molly proposes to reclaim the popcorn preparation, but she phrases her proposal in a way that seems to benefit him rather than her: she'll help Ben do his job of taking out the trash. This reframes the meaning of her taking over popcorn-making as temporarily spelling Ben while he fulfills another obligation.

In the end, Ben kept control of the popcorn – and he burned it. This result lends weight to Molly's reluctance to accede to his request to do it. What is interesting for my purposes here, however, is how Molly's attempts to prevent this outcome were a blend of control and connection maneuvers.

Another aspect of this example that intrigues me is Molly's use of Katie as addressee in her negotiation with Ben over popcorn-making. When Molly said "Let's not let Daddy do it," she communicated her wishes to her husband by addressing their child. Talking through the child is a strategy this mother uses frequently. By involving a third party, her attempt to get her way (a control maneuver) becomes less directly confrontational (the power play is mitigated) and also entails aligning herself with Katie (a connection maneuver).

In the next example, Molly is at home with Katie when she hears Ben's car approaching the house. She prepares Katie for her father's arrival in a way that seems designed to inspire excitement and anticipation, encouraging involvement between the child and her father in much the same way that mothers do when they encourage children to tell their fathers about their day:

Molly: Daddy's home.
Katie: Da da.
Molly: Daddy's gonna be home in a minute.
Katie: Da da pop.
         Da da pop.
         Da da pop.
Molly: You gonna give Da da a pop?
Katie: Yes.
         Shoes. Shoes. ahh.
Molly: You gonna tell Daddy to take his shoes off?

In this interchange, Molly is negotiating connection by orienting Katie toward integrating the father into the family circle. Katie's minimal utterances, "Da da pop" and "Shoes," could be interpreted in many different ways. The expansions Molly supplies ("You gonna give Da da a [fruit] pop?" and "You gonna tell Daddy to take his shoes off?") frame Katie's words as plans to involve her father in interaction. This too negotiates connection.

When Ben enters the house, however, he is tired, hungry, and out of sorts. As he sits at the table trying to eat something, Katie tries to climb on him, and he has a momentary eruption of irritation:

Ben: No! I'm eating! [*very irritated*]
         Daddy eats. [*conciliatory*]
Katie: [*cries*]
Molly: O::h. [*sympathetic tone*]
Ben: Da da eats. [*more conciliatory*]
Katie: [*cries louder*]
Ben: Wanna come up?

In a sense, Ben's first three statements are control maneuvers: he wants to prevent Katie from doing what she wants to do – climb into his lap. But the progression of modifications to his linguistic strategies evince a subtle negotiation of closeness. When Katie begins to wail, Ben retreats from his refusal to let her climb on his lap and ends up inviting her to do so ("Wanna come up?"). In building up to that invitation, he repeats the reason for his initial resistance three times: that he is eating. But each time he repeats this proposition, the way he words it and the tone in which he speaks bring him closer to his daughter.

The first iteration, "I'm eating!" is spoken in a very irritated tone and is preceded by the harsh injunction "No!" Furthermore, in using the first-person pronoun "I," Ben describes what he is doing from his own point of view. This contrasts with the perspective of his next iteration, "Daddy eats." Not only is this statement spoken in a more conciliatory tone, as if trying to make amends for the harshness of his previous burst of annoyance, but he also shifts to Katie's perspective when he says "Daddy eats," since "Daddy" identifies him from his daughter's point of view, not his own. The third repetition, "Da da eats," moves even closer to the child's perspective, since "Da da" is what she calls him. So these linguistic forms bring the father closer to the child's point of view, even as he is softening in his resistance to her attempt to climb on him, and moving toward offering her what she wanted in the first place (but no longer wants now that he has made her cry). Ben's responses to Katie, then, in these few brief lines, are a subtle negotiation of power and connection.

At this point, Molly joins the interaction in a way that blends power and connection in particularly complex and intriguing ways. She explains to Ben why Katie is crying, indirectly chastising him for causing this reaction. At the same time, she explains Katie's own feelings to her and suggests how she might, when she learns to talk, use words rather than tears to express those feelings and get her way. Because Molly does all this by talking through Katie, she is connecting the three of them as a family unit:

Molly: She got her feelings hurt.

            . . .

         I think she just wanted
         some Daddy's attention.
         You were missing Daddy today, weren't you?
         You were missing Daddy, weren't you?
         Can you say,
         "I was just missing you Daddy,
         that was all?"

Katie: [*cries*] Nnno.
Molly: And I don't really feel too good.
Katie: [*cries*] No.
Molly: No, she doesn't feel too good either.

Just as Ben moved progressively closer to Katie's point of view as he repeated his explanation that he was eating, in this example Molly's repeated explanations of why Katie is crying have the same progression. In the first line ("She got her feelings hurt"), Molly speaks of Katie in the third person, addressing Ben, so mother and daughter are linguistically distinct. She next addresses Katie directly ("You were missing Daddy, weren't you?"), bringing her into alignment with the child. She then models for Katie what the child might say to articulate her own feelings ("Can you say, 'I was just missing you, Daddy, that was all?'"). By animating Katie's feelings from the child's point of view ("And I don't really feel too good"), Molly linguistically merges with Katie. Finally, she mitigates her alignment with Katie and re-orients to Ben by addressing him and referring to Katie rather than animating her ("No, she doesn't feel too good either").

Molly's explanation of why Katie is crying ("She got her feelings hurt") is an indirect criticism because it implies that Ben should not hurt his daughter's feelings. After a short amount of intervening talk, she makes this injunction more explicit:

Molly: Why are you so edgy?
Ben: Cause I haven't eaten yet.
Molly: Why didn't you get a *snack*
         on the way home or something?
         Save your family a little stress.
Katie: Mm mm
Molly: Yeah give us a break, Daddy.
         We just miss you.
         We try to get your attention
         and then you come home
         and you go ROW ROW ROW ROW.
Katie: Row Row!

This last example is especially fascinating as an instance of what I call ventriloquizing – communicating to a second party by animating the voice of a third. Whereas Ben speaks only for himself ("I haven't eaten yet"), Molly speaks for (and as) Katie when she says "We just miss you. We try to get your attention . . ." Then, still speaking as Katie, she mimics how Ben comes across from Katie's point of view: "you go ROW ROW ROW ROW." In this utterance, Molly is animating Katie animating Ben. So the linguistic strategy by which Molly tells Ben that he should alter his behavior (a control maneuver) also linguistically merges the three of them (a connection maneuver).

9   Gender and Family Interaction: Coda

In all these examples, I have tried to show that whereas family interaction is, as researchers have been inclined to assume, an ongoing power struggle, it is also simultaneously an ongoing struggle for connection. Furthermore, family interaction is a continuing negotiation of gender identities and roles. In analyses of the interactions tape-recorded by this family, as well as others in the study, Shari Kendall has shown that whereas both mother and father espouse an ideology of equal co-parenting and wage-earning, in their ways of speaking, the mothers position themselves as primary childcare providers and their husbands as breadwinners (see Kendall, this volume). Alexandra Johnston, the research team member who spent time with Molly and Ben and transcribed their conversations, observed that one way Molly positions herself as primary caretaker is by frequently correcting Ben's parenting. In contrast, Ben rarely corrects Molly's parenting. This, indeed, is what Molly is doing in the last example when she tries to reframe Ben's interpretation of why Katie is being a pest, and to suggest how he might "save [his] family a little stress" by getting a snack on the way home.

In this way, the final example, like all those preceding it, illustrates that we need to understand family interaction – like all human interaction – not only as negotiations for power but also as negotiations for connection. Linguistic strategies that can be identified as control maneuvers must also be examined as connection maneuvers. Power and connection are the dimensions along which human relationships are negotiated, and they are also the dimensions along which gender identity is negotiated. So an appreciation of the interplay of power and connection, as well as an appreciation of the ways power and connection underlie gender identity and gender performance, are necessary to understand family interaction.

ACKNOWLEDGMENTS

The project by which four families tape-recorded their own conversations for a week each was supported by a grant from the Alfred P. Sloan Foundation to me and to Shari Kendall. I am grateful to the Foundation and to project officer Kathleen Christensen. I would also like to thank project members Alexandra Johnston and Cynthia Gordon, the research team members who worked with the families whose talk I have cited here, and who transcribed and identified the examples that I cite. The power/connection grid was first presented in Tannen (1994) and is reproduced here with permission from Oxford University Press. Some of the analyses of family interaction that I present here are also presented in Tannen (2001) and are reproduced here with permission from Random House.

REFERENCES

Bateson, Gregory 1972: A theory of play and fantasy. In *Steps to an Ecology of Mind*. New York: Ballantine, pp. 177–93.

Blum-Kulka, Shoshana 1997: *Dinner Talk: Cultural Patterns of Sociability and Socialization in Family Discourse*. Mahwah, NJ: Lawrence Erlbaum.

Brown, Roger and Gilman, Albert 1960: The pronouns of power and solidarity. In Thomas Sebeok (ed.) *Style in Language*. Cambridge, MA: MIT Press, pp. 253–76.

Coates, Jennifer 1996: *Women Talk*. Oxford: Blackwell.

Ervin-Tripp, Susan, O'Connor, Mary Catherine, and Rosenberg, Jarrett 1984: Language and power in the family. In Cheris Kramarae, Muriel Schultz, and William M. O'Barr (eds) *Language and Power*. New York: Sage, pp. 116–35.

Geertz, Hildred [1961] 1989: *The Javanese Family: A Study of Kinship and Socialization*. Prospect Heights, IL: Waveland Press.

Henwood, Karen L. 1993: Women and later life: The discursive construction of identities within family relationships. *Journal of Aging Studies* 7(3): 303–19.

Jefferson, Gail 1988. On the sequential organization of troubles-talk in ordinary conversation. *Social Problems* 35(4): 418–41.

Key, Mary Ritchie 1975: *Male/Female Language: With a Comprehensive Bibliography*. Metuchen, NJ: The Scarecrow Press.

Lakoff, Robin 1975: *Language and Woman's Place*. New York: Harper and Row.

Millar, Frank E., Rogers, L. Edna, and Bavelas, Janet Beavin 1984: Identifying patterns of verbal conflict in interpersonal dynamics. *The Western Journal of Speech Communication* 48: 231–46.

Ochs, Elinor and Taylor, Carolyn 1992: Family narrative as political activity. *Discourse & Society* 3(3): 301–40.

Tannen, Deborah 1989: *Talking Voices: Repetition, Dialogue, and Imagery in Conversational Discourse*. Cambridge: Cambridge University Press.

Tannen, Deborah 1990: *You Just Don't Understand: Women and Men in Conversation*. New York: William Morrow.

Tannen, Deborah 1994: The relativity of linguistic strategies: Rethinking power and solidarity in gender and dominance. In *Gender and Discourse*. Oxford and New York: Oxford University Press, pp. 19–52.

Tannen, Deborah 2001: *I Only Say This Because I Love You*. New York: Random House.

Varenne, Herve 1992: *Ambiguous Harmony: Family Talk in America*. Norwood, NJ: Ablex.

Watts, Richard J. 1991: *Power in Family Discourse*. Berlin: Mouton de Gruyter.

Wetzel, Patricia J. 1988: Are "powerless" communication strategies the Japanese norm? *Language in Society* 17: 555–64.

9 Gender and Power in On-line Communication

SUSAN C. HERRING

1 Introduction

New communication technologies are often invested with users' hopes for change in the social order.[1] Thus the Internet is said to be inherently democratic, leveling traditional distinctions of social status, and creating opportunities for less powerful individuals and groups to participate on a par with members of more powerful groups. Specifically, the Internet has been claimed to lead to greater gender equality, with women, as the socially, politically, and economically less powerful gender, especially likely to reap its benefits. The claims include the following:

1   Text-based computer-mediated communication, with its lack of physical and auditory cues, makes the gender of on-line communicators irrelevant or invisible, allowing women and men to participate equally, in contrast with traditional patterns of male dominance observed in face-to-face conversations (Danet 1998; Graddol and Swann 1989).
2   As a network connecting geographically dispersed users, the Internet empowers women and members of other traditionally subordinate groups to find community and organize politically in pursuit of their own interests (Balka 1993).
3   The World Wide Web allows women to self-publish and engage in profitable entrepreneurial activity on a par with men (Rickert and Sacharow 2000).

Of course, men, too, stand to benefit from anonymous communication, common-interest group formation, and the commercial potential of the Web. The difference is that for women, the Internet purportedly removes barriers to participation in domains where barriers do not exist – or at least, do not exist to the same extent – for men.

Some twenty years after the introduction of the Internet, we may ask whether these potentials have been, or are in the process of being, realized. Extrapolating from the properties of a technology to its social effects – a paradigm known as "technological determinism" (Markus 1994) – tends to overlook the fact that the development and uses of any technology are themselves embedded in a social context, and are shaped by that context (Kling et al. 2001). Does the Internet alter deeply rooted cultural patterns of gender inequality, or do those patterns carry over into on-line communication? Is Internet technology inherently gender-neutral, or does the fact that it was created by men result in an in-built structural bias that perpetuates male advantage? At the same time, the Internet is undeniably transforming social behavior as more and more people go on-line. In the early 1990s, estimates placed the number of female Internet users at 5 per cent (Sproull 1992, cited in Ebben and Kramarae 1993); females now make up slightly more than half of all Web users (Rickert and Sacharow 2000). What are the effects of millions of girls and women entering what was, until very recently, a predominantly male domain?

This chapter surveys research on gender and the Internet published or presented between 1989, when gender issues first began to be raised in print, and the time of writing (2002). It brings together research findings and speculations that bear on the claims listed above, and interprets the available evidence in relation to the larger question of whether – and if so, how – gender and power relations are affected in and through Internet communication. The body of evidence taken as a whole runs counter to the claim that gender is invisible or irrelevant on the Internet, or that the Internet equalizes gender-based power and status differentials. At the same time, limited trends toward female empowerment are identified, alongside disadvantages of Internet communication that affect both women and men.

This chapter is organized into five sections. The immediately following section considers gender in relation to issues of Internet *access*, for both users and creators of on-line resources. Basic access is a prerequisite to on-line participation, and those who create resources enjoy greater power to promote their agendas. Evidence is then evaluated that bears on claims of gender anonymity in interactive *computer-mediated communication* (CMC) on the Internet. This section is divided into two parts, the first focusing on asynchronous, and the second, on synchronous, CMC. The fourth section addresses gender on the *World Wide Web*, from the phenomenon of personal home pages, to entrepreneurial uses, and mass uses of the medium. The final section identifies possible future scenarios, based on current and emergent trends, in an attempt to answer the question: if the Internet is not yet a level playing field for women and men, is it more (or less) likely to become one in the future?

2   Access

In the early days of the Arpanet – the predecessor of the Internet[2] – on-line access was restricted to the US defense department personnel and computer scientists (almost entirely male) who designed and developed computer networking. The Internet, so called since around 1983, expanded geographically in the 1980s to include more universities, especially faculty and students in computing-related departments (mostly male). The trend by the late 1980s of increased diffusion to academicians in other disciplines and employees in a growing number of workplaces became a full-fledged sweep toward popular access in the 1990s, with the rise of Internet Service Providers (ISPs) that enabled people to connect from their homes. The percentage of female users increased along with this expansion, as did public knowledge about the Internet and ease of access to it.

Nonetheless, access remained a stumbling block for gender equity throughout much of the 1990s. Women were initially more reticent about using computers, less willing to invest time and effort in learning to use the Internet, and less likely to be employed in workplaces with Internet access (Balka 1993). When they did log on, they were more likely than men to be alienated by the sometimes contentious culture they encountered on-line (Herring 1992, 1993). However, there is evidence that all this is changing. The increasing popularization and commercialism of the Internet since the advent of the World Wide Web has brought with it ubiquity, easy-to-use graphical interfaces, and mainstream content (e.g. news, online shopping), making the Internet a "safer," more familiar-seeming place. Moreover, a new generation of young people has been raised using, and feeling comfortable with, the Internet. Given that slightly more than 50 per cent of Web users in the USA are now female, according to one study (Rickert and Sacharow 2000), it would appear that the Internet is at present no more difficult for those females to use, nor more intimidating, than it is for males.[3]

However, while the gender digital divide is being bridged in terms of who logs on to the Internet, at least in the USA, women and men still do not have equal access to the creation and control of what takes place on the Internet. Roles that require technical expertise, such as network administrator, are disproportionately filled by men, consistent with the traditional association of technology with masculinity (Wajcman 1991). Setting up one's own bulletin board system (BBS), listserver, or Web site requires not only technical skills, but an investment in equipment, Internet connectivity, and time and effort for ongoing maintenance, which taken together, presupposes a high level of motivation and interest in the technical aspects of computer networking. Women, given their lower numbers in fields such as computer science,[4] are less likely to have the necessary background and motivation to do this. As a consequence, most computer networks are set up and run by men, especially in the early days of new technologies such as the Web, when the norms for use of the technology emerge. The claim that everyone has equal access to the Internet tends to overlook the fact that all access is not equivalent – viewing a Web site or posting to a discussion group does not give an individual the same degree of power as creating and administering the Web site or as the server that hosts the discussion group. The latter remains the preserve of a technologically skilled – and mostly male – elite.

At the same time, ordinary users are empowered to create Internet content to a greater extent than in mass media such as television and radio. Not only can users participate in on-line discussion, almost anyone can create and moderate a discussion forum, or create their own Web pages. Females as well as males avail themselves of these opportunities, which require some initiation and maintenance effort, but which are mostly supported technically by others (e.g. network administrators). Moreover, since site administrators often exercise minimal control over the content available on their site, discussion group leaders and Web page creators enjoy considerable freedom to create Internet content, although that content is subject to filtering and blocking by Internet access portals. Some long-running and popular Internet sites, such as the Women's Studies List (WMST-L; Korenman and Wyatt 1996) and the Women.com Web site (Brown 2000), were developed and are run by women; in these sites, content is generated by the female owners and users, not by the technical support staff. Thus, although technological control of the Internet remains predominantly in the hands of men, women have ready access to computer-mediated communication and the Web, including the possibility of creating content therein.

3   Computer-mediated Communication

Computer-mediated communication (CMC) comprises a variety of interactive socio-technical modes including e-mail, discussion lists and newsgroups, chat, MUDs (Multi-User Dimensions) and MOOs (MUDs, Object Oriented), ICQ (I Seek You), and IM (Instant Messaging). Of these, e-mail and discussion groups have been in existence since the early 1970s; chat, social MUDs and MOOs date to the late 1980s; and ICQ and IMs were introduced in the mid-1990s.[5] All these CMC modes are textual, involving typed words that are read on computer screens.

"On the Internet, nobody knows you're a dog." A cartoon bearing this caption was published in *The New Yorker* in July of 1993, but the notion that Internet communication was anonymous had already appeared in scholarly research in the 1980s. Because you cannot see or hear your interlocutors in text-only CMC, the argument goes, you have no way of knowing who – or what – they are. A version of this claim was first advanced with reference to gender by Graddol and Swann (1989), who noted that participation by men and women tended to be equalized in an anonymous computer conferencing system used in the British Open University. They explicitly contrasted their observations on computer conferencing with the traditional pattern of male domination of mixed-sex face-to-face discourse. For the most part, however, early CMC research did not discuss gender, nor control for it in experimental studies.[6]

As more women began to venture on-line in the early 1990s, studies of gender and CMC started appearing with greater frequency. In contrast to the optimism of the 1980s, the findings of these studies tended to problematize claims of gender-free equality in cyberspace. In an important early article documenting the results of an academic listserv group's self-directed experiment with anonymity, Selfe and Meyer (1991) found that males and participants in the group who enjoyed high status off-line dominated the interaction, both under normal conditions and under conditions of anonymity. However, some individual women reported feeling freer to participate when their messages were anonymous.

Soon after, researchers began reporting the use of more aggressive tactics by men in on-line discussions, some of it explicitly targeted at female participants (Herring 1992, 1993; Herring, Johnson, and DiBenedetto 1992; Kramarae and Taylor 1993; Ebben 1994; McCormick and McCormick 1992; Sutton 1994). Using electronically distributed questionnaires, Herring (1993) found that women were more likely than men to react aversively to aggression in on-line interaction, including falling silent and dropping out of listserv groups. Around the same time, reports began to surface in the popular press of women on the Internet being the targets of male intimidation, harassment, and sexual deception (Brail 1994, 1996; Dibbell 1993; Van Gelder 1990). These findings raise an apparent paradox: how can gender disparity persist in an anonymous medium which allegedly renders gender invisible?

3.1   Asynchronous CMC

The first part of the solution to the paradox has to do with the meaning of the term "anonymity." Whereas asynchronous CMC on the Internet – the object of most of the early descriptions – offers the theoretical possibility of anonymity, in practice true anonymity was somewhat difficult to achieve in the early days of the Internet, requiring the use of an anonymizing service or the ability to forge e-mail addresses.[7] Both of these practices required knowledge not readily available to all Internet users.[8] More importantly, it seems that users are not necessarily interested in exploiting the potential for anonymous interaction – the use of one's real name lends accountability and a seriousness of purpose to one's words that anonymous messages lack. Most participants in computer-mediated discussion groups in the 1980s and 1990s interacted in their real-life identities (Collins-Jarvis 1997; Herring 1992), without attempting to disguise their gender.

Still, text-only CMC is less revealing of personal information than face-to-face communication, and some user names are neutral as to gender. Female users can choose to present themselves so as to minimize discrimination and harassment by adopting a gender-neutral name (Bruckman 1993). After all, in cyberspace others only know what you choose to present about yourself, the popular view goes. Here the second part of the solution to the paradox comes in: gender is often visible on the Internet on the basis of features of a participant's discourse style – features which the individual may not be consciously aware of or able to change easily. That is, users "give off" information about their gender unconsciously in interaction (cf. Goffman 1959), and this information does not depend in any crucial way on visual or auditory channels of communication; text alone is sufficient.

The linguistic features that signal gender in computer-mediated interaction are similar to those that have been previously described for face-to-face interaction, and include verbosity, assertiveness, use of profanity, politeness (and rudeness), typed representations of smiling and laughter, and degree of interactive engagement (cf. Coates 1993). There is an overall tendency for some of these behaviors to correlate more with female CMC users, and for others to correlate more with males. This does not mean that each and every female and male manifests the behaviors; exceptions to the tendencies can readily be found.[9] It does mean, however, that gender predicts certain on-line behaviors with greater than chance frequency when considered over aggregate populations of users, controlling for variables such as age, topic, and the synchronicity of the medium.

In asynchronous CMC of the type that takes place in discussion lists and newsgroups on the Internet and Usenet, males are more likely to post longer messages, begin and close discussions in mixed-sex groups, assert opinions strongly as "facts," use crude language (including insults and profanity), and in general, manifest an adversarial orientation toward their interlocutors (Herring 1992, 1993, 1996a, 1996b, forthcoming; Kramarae and Taylor 1993; Savicki et al. 1996; Sutton 1994). In contrast, females tend to post relatively short messages, and are more likely to qualify and justify their assertions, apologize, express support of others, and in general, manifest an "aligned" orientation toward their interlocutors (Hall 1996; Herring 1993, 1994, 1996a, 1996b; Savicki et al. 1996). Males sometimes adopt an adversarial style even in cooperative exchanges, and females often appear to be aligned even when they disagree with one another, suggesting that these behaviors are conventionalized, rather than inherent character traits based on biological sex. Moreover, there is evidence that the minority gender in an on-line forum tends to modify its communicative behavior in the direction of the majority gender: women tend to be more aggressive in male-dominated groups than among other women, and men tend to be less aggressive in female-dominated groups than in groups controlled by men[10] (Baym 1996; Herring 1996b). This observation suggests that the more numerous a gender group is on-line, the greater the influence it will have on shared discursive norms.

Politeness is one common means through which gender is cued in asynchronous CMC. Women are more likely to thank, appreciate, and apologize, and to be upset by violations of politeness; they more often challenge offenders who violate on-line rules of conduct (Smith et al. 1997), and predominantly female groups may have more, and more strictly enforced, posting rules designed to ensure the maintenance of a civil environment (Hall 1996; Herring 1996a). In contrast, men generally appear to be less concerned with politeness; they issue bald face-threatening acts such as unmitigated criticisms and insults, violate on-line rules of conduct, tolerate or even enjoy "flaming," and tend to be more concerned about threats to freedom of expression than with attending to others' social "face" (Herring 1994, 1996a, 1999). These patterns have been noted even in gay and lesbian discussion groups (Hall 1996), and among women who have succeeded in traditionally male-dominated professions such as computer science (Herring and Lombard 1995). "Inappropriately" appreciative or contentious messages can "give away" individuals in Internet discussion groups attempting to pass as the opposite gender, evidence that stereotypes about on-line gender styles based on these patterns have emerged (Herring 1996a).

Examples of a male-style message (making use of sarcasm and insults) and a female-style message (expressing appreciation, support, and a qualified assertion) are given in examples (1) and (2).[11] Females are much less likely than males to produce messages like (1), and males are much less likely than females to produce messages like (2).

(1)   *A male posting to a discussion group (responding to a male message)*

>yes, they did . . . This is why we must be allowed to remain armed . . .
>who is going to help us if our government becomes a tyranny?
>no one will.

oh yes we *must* remain armed. anyone see day one last night abt charlestown where everyone/s so scared of informing on murderers the cops have given up ? where the reply to any offense is a public killing ? knowing you/re not gonna be caught cause everyone/s to afraid to be a witness ?

yeah, right, twerp.

>   – [Ron] "the Wise" –

what a joke.

(2)   *A female posting to a discussion group (responding to a female message)*

>Aileen,
>
>I just wanted to let you know that I have really enjoyed all your
>posts about Women's herstory. They have been extremely
>informative and I've learned alot about the women's movement.
>Thank you!
>
> – Erika

DITTO!!!! They are wonderful!

Did anyone else catch the first part of a Century of Women? I really enjoyed it. Of course, I didn't agree with everything they said . . . but it was really informative.

Roberta~~~~~~~~~~~~~~~~~~~~~~~~~~

Gender differences in on-line communication tend to disfavor women. In mixed-sex public discussion groups, females post fewer messages, and are less likely to persist in posting when their messages receive no response (Broadhurst 1993; Herring forthcoming). Even when they persist, they receive fewer responses from others (both females and males), and do not control the topic or the terms of the discussion except in groups where women make up a clear majority of participants (Herring 1993, forthcoming; Herring, Johnson, and DiBenedetto 1992, 1995; Hert 1997). The lesser influence exercised by women in mixed-sex groups accounts in part[12] for why women-centered and women-only on-line groups are common (Balka 1993; Camp 1996), whereas explicitly designated men-only groups are rare.[13]

Moreover, an inherent tension exists between the conventionally masculine value on agonism and the conventionally feminine value on social harmony. The contentiousness of male messages tends to discourage women from participating, while women's concern with politeness tends to be perceived as a "waste of bandwidth" by men (Herring 1996a), or worse yet, as censorship (Grossman 1997; cf. Herring 1999). This tension does not inherently favor one gender over the other – each value system potentially constrains the other. In Internet discussion groups, however, where civil libertarian values have traditionally constituted the dominant ideological context, and where few structures are in place to sanction anti-social behavior, aggression tends to prevail over less aggressive behaviors. In a number of documented cases, repeated aggression from disruptive males has forced women-centered on-line forums to disband, move elsewhere, and/or reconfigure themselves with strict rules and regulations regarding acceptable participant conduct (Collins-Jarvis 1997; Ebben 1994; Reid 1994).

Some evidence suggests that women participate more actively and enjoy greater influence in environments where the norms of interaction are controlled by an individual or individuals entrusted with maintaining order and focus in the group. Thus women-centered groups whose moderators place restrictions on the number or nature of messages that can be posted, particularly when contentious (challenging, insulting, etc.) messages are discouraged, tend to flourish, with large, active memberships and widespread participation (Camp 1996; Korenman and Wyatt 1996). Female students also participate more – sometimes more than male students – in on-line classrooms in which the teacher controls the interaction, even when the teacher is male (Herring and Nix 1997; Herring 1999). While this result may appear initially puzzling – how can women be "freer" to participate when they are "controlled" by a group leader? – it makes sense if the leader's role is seen as one of ensuring a civil environment, free from threats of disruption and harassment. The need for such insurance points to the fundamental failure of a "self-regulating" democracy on the Internet to produce equitable participation: when left to its own devices, libertarianism favors the most aggressive individuals, who tend to be male. Consistent with this imbalance, male respondents to an Internet-wide survey cited "censorship" as the greatest threat to the Internet, whereas females cited "privacy" as their greatest concern (GVU 1997).[14]

3.2   Synchronous CMC

The studies cited above reveal some of the mechanisms by which gender disparity operates in asynchronous computer-mediated communication, despite the potential of the medium to neutralize gender differences. Some writers remain optimistic, however, as regards synchronous ("real-time") chat modes such as Internet Relay Chat (IRC) and MUDs and MOOs. Pointing out that many of the asynchronous studies focus on professional (e.g. academic) users, Grossman (1997) speculates that the real-world power hierarchies in such groups carry over into the virtual domain. Power dynamics of this sort, including gender hierarchy, should be irrelevant in casual chat in which users have no real-world connections. Danet (1998) is similarly optimistic, although for different reasons. Chatters are more anonymous than participants in asynchronous discussion groups, in that recreational chat environments encourage users to take on pseudonyms. For Danet, these pseudonyms function as masks which invite experimentation with gender identities in playful, "carnivalesque" ways, liberating users from restrictive gender binaries.

The available research suggests that in the gender realm as in other domains, synchronous CMC both differs from and resembles asynchronous CMC. Some of the research initially appears to bear out predictions of greater gender equality. Males and females tend to participate more equally in chat environments, in terms of both number of messages and average message length (Herring 1999). On average, response rates to males and females are also more balanced; if anything, females tend to receive more responses to their messages than males (Bruckman 1993; Herring and Nix 1997). In apparent support of Danet's claim, the literature also contains anecdotal reports of play with gender identity, including gender-switching sustained over periods of weeks or months (Bruckman 1993; McRae 1996).

These observations notwithstanding, gender is far from invisible or irrelevant in recreational chat. IRC users frequently ask other participants about their biological sex, along with their age and location (abbreviated "asl"). Moreover, they display their gender through their message content, use of third-person pronouns to describe their actions, and nickname choice (Herring 1998).[15] Less conscious differences in discourse style are also evident. In a study of the use of "action verbs" in a social MUD, Cherny (1994) found that female-presenting characters used mostly neutral and affectionate verbs (such as "hugs" and "whuggles"), while male characters used more violent verbs (such as "kills"), especially in actions directed toward other males. Similarly, Herring (1998) found that females on IRC typed three times as many representations of smiling and laughter as did males, while the gender ratio was reversed for aggressive and insulting speech acts. Males also produced overwhelmingly more profanity and sexual references. These findings parallel the finding that women and men in asynchronous discussions tend to use different discourse styles – aligned and supportive, as compared to oppositional and adversarial (Herring 1996a,

1996b). Rodino (1997) concludes a case study of an IRC interaction by noting that "despite multiple and conflicting gender performances [by one participant], the binary gender system is alive and well in IRC."

Examples of a female-style IRC exchange (including expressions of support, appreciation, smiling/laughter, and affectionate actions) and a male-style IRC exchange (making use of profanity, insults, sexual references, and violent actions) are given in examples (3) and (4) (from Herring 1998).[16] Not all female and male chat participants use these styles, but when they are used, they tend overwhelmingly to be produced by one, and not the other, gender.

(3)   *A chat exchange between females*

    * <u>KikiDoe</u> *huggers* beff to her death hahaah
    <<u>Beth</u>_ > :)
    <<u>Beth</u>_ > you guys are so great! *happy sobs*
    <<u>KikiDoe</u>> beth dats cause we have you

(4)   *A chat exchange among males*

    <wuzzy> any ladies wanna chat??
    <[Snoopy]> fonz: she nice
    <LiQuIdHeL> FUKCK YOU
    <[Snoopy]> fuck you little boy
    <LiQuIdHeL> NO FUCK YOU
    <mature> snoopy u r ?????????????????????
    <[Snoopy]> its past your bedtime
    <[Snoopy]> are you talking?
    * LiQuIdHeL kicks [Snoopy] in the nuts causing them to dangle out your nose like fuzzy dice on a rear view mirror . . . ;) have a nice day

Nor is the apparent equality of participation what it seems on the surface. Little variation is possible in message length in most chat modes, given constraints on buffer size and typing time in real-time interaction. Most synchronous chat messages are short, between four and twelve words in length, with the variation conditioned by the number of interlocutors (dyads tend to type longer messages than groups; see e.g. Cherny 1999) more than by participant gender. As regards frequency of posting, public chat rooms are typically frequented by more males than females (by some estimates, three males to every female), but those females who do participate receive a disproportionate amount of attention, much of it sexual in nature (Bruckman 1993; Herring 1998, 1999; Rodino 1997). The most common "gender-switching" patterns reflect this dynamic: females tend to assume gender-neutral pseudonyms in order to avoid sexual attention, while males assume female-sounding names in order to attract it (Bruckman 1993; Herring 1998).

As in asynchronous CMC, instances of aggression against women are also found, and these, too, tend to be of a sexual nature. Dibbell (1993) describes a textually enacted "rape" on a social MOO, and Reid (1994) reports an incident on a support MUD for sexual abuse survivors in which a male-presenting character named "Daddy" shouted graphic enactments of sexual abuse to all present on the MUD. Such occurrences expose the dark side of recreational CMC, in which anonymity not only fosters playful disinhibition (Danet et al. 1997), but reduces social accountability, making it easier for users to engage in hostile, aggressive acts. A number of harassment incidents target women who have gender-neutral pseudonyms (Herring 1999), suggesting that chatters, like e-mailers, give off gender cues through their interactional style, and thus that pseudonyms alone may be insufficient to mask on-line gender.

What, then, of the cases of successful on-line gender-bending that some authors point to in support of the claim that CMC deconstructs gender? Empirical observation of large populations of synchronous CMC users suggests that such cases are actually rather infrequent. Based on several years of observation, LambdaMOO founder and chief wizard Pavel Curtis (1992) concluded that sustained gender-switching is rare in LambdaMOO: because of the effort involved in trying to be something one is not, most participants interact as themselves, regardless of the name or character description they choose. In support of this, Herring (1998) found that 89 per cent of all gendered behavior in six IRC channels indexed maleness and femaleness in traditional, even stereotyped ways; instances of gender-switching constituted less than half of the remaining 11 per cent. In theory, it is possible that gender-switching takes place more often, but is so successful that it goes undetected. In practice, however, IRC users give off gender cues frequently (an average of once every three to four lines of text in the Herring (1998) study), such that the longer someone participates, the more likely it is that they will reveal their actual gender. Thus gender differences – and gender asymmetry – persist, despite the greater anonymity and relative absence of externally imposed power hierarchies in synchronous CMC.

4 The World Wide Web

The World Wide Web, introduced in the USA in 1991, began attracting widespread attention in 1993 with the launching of the Mosaic graphical browser. Currently, Web browsing is the "killer ap" (application) of the Internet (Pastore 2000), rivaling even e-mail in popularity, and its rate of use continues to grow. The Web, more than any other Internet application, was responsible for bringing women on-line in large numbers in the mid-1990s. Indeed, in their August 2000 report that women make up 50.4 per cent of Web users, Media Metrix calls it the "Women's Web" (Rickert and Sacharow 2000). Two properties of the Web set it apart from text-based CMC: first, it is multi-modal, linking text, graphics, video, and audio; second, it is primarily a one-way broadcast (mass) medium, in which "pages" created by an author are read and navigated by readers. How is gender represented, graphically and symbolically, on the Web, and to what extent are women involved in creating and administering Web content?

4.1 Graphical representation

Multimedia are celebrated for their potential to create rich "virtual realities" which mirror off-line physical reality (Lombard and Ditton 1997). At a basic level, the graphical capabilities of the Web allow photographs to be displayed on Web pages, and both males and females make use of this capability. "Anonymity" is not a particular virtue on the Web, although one is free to select any image to represent oneself, since the actual physical appearance of the creator of the pages remains hidden, as in text-based CMC. Researchers have observed that young women's self-representations in personal homepages are often sexualized, involving provocative clothing and/or postures (Blair and Takayoshi 1999). Similarly, on the amihot.com site, where women and men post photographs of themselves to be rated and commented on by others, female images are more sexually provocative, and more likely to attract comments about physical appearance, than are male images, which are more likely to be humorous or deliberately offensive in their presentation (Bella 2001). In both of the above cases, photographs of the actual individuals seem mostly to be involved, although graphical avatars in chat environments display similar tendencies when users represent themselves with photographs of famous people or cartoon images (Kolko 1999; Scheidt 2001).

Researchers are divided as to whether self-representation on the Web along stereotypical gender lines is harmful. Blair and Takayoshi (1999) critique the practice on the grounds that it perpetuates the cultural myth of woman as sex object. They point out that even when the women themselves consider displaying their images on-line as an act of self-empowerment, the reception and use of those images can objectify them. For example, the jennicam.com site, on which a young woman broadcasts a continuous live video feed of the interior of her apartment, is especially popular among men, a number of whom consider Jenni their "virtual girl friend," although she has no reciprocal knowledge of them (O'Sullivan 1999; Snyder 2000). Another well-known site, "Babes on the Web," created in the mid-1990s by a man named Robert Toups, linked to (and rated in offensively sexist terms) photographs on women's homepages without their permission (Kibby 1997; Spertus 1996). In the former case, Jenni is fetishized even though her site is not primarily sexual in content; in the latter case, serious, professional photographs of academic women were "co-opted" as part of Toups's site. Thus the problem of objectification of images of females on the Web exists independently of the "provocativeness" of the images, recalling the wider phenomenon of objectification of females off-line.

These representations become additionally problematic when they are viewed and assessed in relation to the prevalence of pornography on the Web. Internet pornography, featuring mostly images of naked or partly naked female bodies, is readily accessible for free, including hardcore types that are illegal in the United States (King 1999; Mehta and Plaza 1997). Pornography typically represents women in sexually submissive positions, in degrading circumstances, or as promiscuously wanton; it is produced primarily by men for men, constructing women's bodies as objects for male use (Fedler 1996; see also discussion in Di Filippo 2000). By the mid-1990s, a search for the word "woman" on the Internet turned up numerous porn sites, and terms like "babe" generated almost exclusively pornographic hits. The "Babes on the Web" site and the jennicam site, with its occasional female nudity, are readily subject to interpretation by their (mostly male) viewers in terms of the culture and values of on-line pornography.

However, not all writers about the Internet are troubled by sites that represent women in sexualized terms. Kibby (1997) argues that women who create their own homepages and Web sites exercise control over the representation of their bodies and personae on-line, and need not be affected by responses such as Toups's (see also Cheung 2000). "Pro-sex" feminists (Bright 1997) champion the right of women to consume and produce pornography, and see in the Internet an opportunity for them to express themselves sexually as a path to self-knowledge and empowerment (Clements 2001), as well as for financial gain (Glidewell 2000).

Finally, not all representations of women on the Web are stereotypically gendered. Kibby (1997) and Blair and Takayoshi (1999) point to Web sites created by women for women, many by Generation X-ers (young twenty-somethings), which subvert traditional representations of gender, for example, by representing women as strong and active in non-traditional domains, and by ironically adopting "retro" images (for example, of 1950s housewives) to represent them[17] (Brown 2000; Vollmer 2001). The content of such sites has been described as "edgy" and intelligent (Brown 2000), constituting a subversive discourse that co-exists alongside traditional gender discourses.[18]

4.2   *Commercialization*

The greatest single change affecting the Internet in recent years has been the commercialization of the World Wide Web. Accelerated by the termination of US federal funding for the Internet backbone in 1995 (McChesney 2000), commercialization has opened the door to mass media infiltration of the Internet, as well as creating opportunities for individual entrepreneurs to start their own on-line businesses. These developments are claimed to benefit women, who are the primary consumers in first-world economies, but who have traditionally been excluded from control and ownership in the commercial realm.

The Web can be considered a mass medium. It reaches a wide audience (Morris and Ogan 1996), and content created by individuals or organizations is broadcast to viewers, although the viewers are less passive consumers of the content than with traditional mass media such as television (O'Sullivan 1999).[19] The Web is also, increasingly, a channel of diffusion for traditional print and broadcast media. The AOL–Time Warner merger, announced publicly in January 2001, consolidated a large Internet service provider with a media conglomerate that broadcasts television news, publishes magazines and books, and owns a record label. Corporate mass media interests, on the Internet and off, are controlled almost exclusively by men.

At the same time, profit can be generated through allowing advertising banners to be placed on individual Web sites. This gives rise to a type of grassroots on-line publishing that extends beyond the personal homepage into the commercial domain. A number of women-oriented Web sites in this category, such as Cybergrrl and women.com, are analogous to general interest magazines, and originally employed a number of veterans of the alternative "zine" movement (Brown 2000). However, although started by women to provide intelligent and politicized content, many such sites now offer increasingly mainstream fare. Thus women.com, begun in 1993 as Women's Wire, an on-line discussion forum for early adopter women, has merged with the Hearst women's magazine empire; its content now includes on-line versions of mainstream women's magazines such as *Redbook, Cosmopolitan*, and *Good Housekeeping*. The most popular women's site, iVillage, was founded by a woman but has since been taken over by a man; it offers "baby clothing and pregnancy calendars, fad diets and personal shoppers" (Brown 2000), framing women as individuals whose careers are secondary, and who have a constant need to improve themselves and please others (Sarkio 2001). Brown attributes the trend toward mainstream content to commercialization, specifically, to the need for Web site producers to compete in a mass medium in which the greatest profit is achieved by catering to the lowest common denominator.

Culturally stereotyped gender roles and interests are also reflected in Web usage patterns. According to the Media Metrix report (Rickert and Sacharow 2000), women are the majority visitors to toy retailer sites, women's portals such as iVillage.com and women.com, greeting card sites, retail savings sites, and health sites. Men, in contrast, are the majority on sites containing technical content, financial information, sports, and news (CyberAtlas 2000).[20] The response of the business community to such findings is to target on-line advertising along gender lines (CyberAtlas 2000), thereby further reifying gender stereotypes. Thus while the Web may make women's (and men's) lives more convenient, it does not appear to be leveling gender asymmetries.

At the same time, if commercialization profits individual women, they can become empowered, through wealth, to make more far-reaching changes. Carlassare (2000) asserts that "women entrepreneurs are key players in the Net economy," as founders and CEOs of portal and community ventures, Web-based services ventures, e-commerce ventures, and e-business applications. Among the trends cited by Carlassare as responsible for the growing number of women entrepreneurs are an increasing recognition of the purchasing power of women on-line (in the case of businesses targeted at women), the availability of abundant capital resources, a growing number of female venture capitalists, and a shortage of people working in the technology sector. That female venture capitalists are more likely to fund female-founded businesses, which in turn are more likely to cater to women's interests, points to the importance of a critical mass of women on-line. It further suggests that the more individual women are successful, the more likely the interests of other women are to be served, through their support.

Still, the number of women-founded businesses on-line remains low compared to the number of male-founded businesses. Moreover, companies with female CEOs received only 6 per cent of all venture capital in 1999, a disproportionately low percentage (Carlassare 2000). Finally, both women- and men-owned Web companies suffered in the early 2000s because of an overall decline in technology markets. If the rise of female entrepreneurs on the Web has been predicated in part on the availability of abundant venture capital, women-owned companies are likely to suffer first, and more acutely, as a consequence of economic downturns.

Pornography sites are a special case of entrepreneurial activity in which the female entrepreneurs are often sex workers or former sex workers (Glidewell 2000; Marsh 2000). As in other domains, women's entry into the creation and marketing of on-line pornography has the potential to change the nature of the product itself, tailoring it for female consumers (Royalle 2001). On-line porn, like the porn industry in general, is highly profitable, and thus far has been largely unaffected by the profit losses that have beset other "dot coms" (Cronin and Davenport 2001; Lane 2000). Nonetheless, the big profits in on-line pornography go not to individual distributors (and even less to individual producers), but rather to a small number of people (male) who control the major distribution channels, consistent with the gendered hierarchy of power that characterizes the pornography industry more generally.

4.3   *Community and political organization*

One of the earliest gender-related claims regarding the Internet was that it would enable women to organize politically, in order better to serve their common interests (Smith and Balka 1988). To what extent has this come about? In the 1980s and early 1990s, on-line discussion forums (such as the Women's Studies List and Women's Wire) were places where women could find community and share experiences and resources, and women-focused groups proliferated (including some with a women-only membership policy, such as the Systers mailing list; see Camp 1996). Some feminist groups also used the Internet to organize for the purpose of undertaking political action, although such uses were less common (Balka 1993). The advent of the Web allowed for easier and better resource sharing: files could be accessed by clicking, rather than by downloading attachments or using a file transfer protocol, and graphics and sound, rather than just text, could be shared. A number of non-profit organizations, from the Feminist Majority Foundation to the United Nations, have made use of the Web to make information available to women on topics ranging from elections to aging to lesbian diversity to on-line harassment.

However, posting resources on a Web site is not the same as organizing politically. Brown (2000) laments the failure of the Web to fulfill the earlier dream of an on-line "feminist revolution," suggesting that this may have been a minority dream in the first place.[21] The typical female Internet user changed through the 1990s and beyond, from the educated academic woman influenced by the feminism of the 1970s and 1980s, to the middle-class post-feminist twenty-something; the political goals of the former are not necessarily shared by the latter (Wakeford 1997). This generational and demographic shift is also reflected in a discursive shift, away from grassroots politics and sisterhood, to individual self-realization, in Western discourses about feminism on-line. Thus the grrl.com site has a "fame" page listing all media citations of the founder, as an example of a "grrl" (i.e. a young woman who identifies with some sort of feminist or radical or progressive politics) who has fulfilled her personal goal – in this case, of becoming famous. And a US stripper's Web site defines stripping as a feminist act, on the grounds that it is a form of self-expression and a path to self-awareness (Clements 2001).

This trend away from social action to individual fulfillment is consistent with a larger trend on the Internet whereby communitarian discourses and discourses about participatory democracy are receding in importance as commercialism comes increasingly to the fore. Both trends are part of a larger cultural shift in the Western world in the direction of individual fulfillment, triggered by economic prosperity – much of it produced in the information technology sector itself – in the 1990s. In periods of economic expansion, plentiful resources allow all to benefit, and reduce social unrest. Social activism, in contrast, flourishes in periods of economic contraction, when biases in the distribution of resources are more apparent. The Arpanet/Internet was developed in a climate of economic inflation and high unemployment in the USA of the 1960s and 1970s. This was also, not coincidentally, a time of high social (including feminist) ideals, ideals which carried over into the conceptualization of the Internet by its early users as communal and democratic.

5 Discussion

Having presented evidence regarding gender in relation to on-line access, CMC, and the World Wide Web, we return now to consider to what extent the evidence supports the claim that the Internet fosters gender equality. The answer depends in part, of course, on how one defines "equality." On the one hand, as a dynamic, rapidly expanding technology, the Internet has created abundant opportunities for new forms of communication and commerce, from which both men and women have benefited. Women, as well as men, participate in computer-mediated communication, start discussion groups, create Web pages, and engage in entrepreneurial activity on-line. Moreover, unlike in the early days, there are as many women on-line as men.

However, to conclude from this that the Internet has lived up to its potential to create gender equality would be analogous to claiming that women and men are equal off-line because both use telephones, moderate meetings, write books, or start their own small businesses, and because they are roughly equally represented in the population of college-educated adults. While some people would indeed take this as evidence of gender equality, others would point out that men are better represented in high-status activities, encounter fewer obstacles en route to them, and receive better pay for them than do women. In other words, the fact that women are represented in those activities, while important, is not the same as doing them, and being rewarded for doing them, on a par with men. Moreover, it does not take into account that the people who own the telephone companies, run the educational institutions, publish the books, and control the financial resources (to say nothing of leading governments, the military, and religions) – in other words, the people who exercise power at the highest levels – are overwhelmingly men. To what extent, if at all, is the situation different on the Internet?

In many respects, the Internet reproduces the larger societal gender status quo. Top-level control of Internet resources, infrastructure, and content is exercised mostly by men. The largest single activity on the Internet – the distribution of pornography – is not only largely controlled by men, but casts women as sexual objects for men's use. The sexualization of women carries over into ostensibly neutral domains, such as recreational chat and personal homepages. In serious contexts, such as academic discussion groups, women participate and are responded to less than men. Moreover, it appears to be necessary for women to form their own groups to address their interests, suggesting that the default activities on the Internet address the interests of men. This evidence points to the persistence of gender disparity in on-line contexts, according to the same hierarchy that privileges males over females off-line.

Another sense in which the Internet was predicted to lead to gender equality is by rendering gender differences invisible or irrelevant. This is clearly not the case; traditional gender differences carry over into CMC, in discourse style and patterns of disparity and harassment, and on the Web, in images, content, and patterns of use. At the same time, women themselves choose to reveal their gender when they could remain anonymous, and produce gendered images (including pornography), just as women choose to frequent commercial Web sites that offer mainstream, gender stereotyped content. This leads to an apparent paradox: if traditional gender arrangements are disadvantageous to women, why do women, when adopting a new technology, actively maintain them?

Several possible explanations can be advanced to explain this paradox. The younger, less highly educated women who use the Internet today (in contrast to the more highly educated early adopters) may fail to perceive gender disparity in on-line social and commercial arrangements. The arrangements – especially inasmuch as they mirror off-line arrangements – may appear familiar, appropriate, and natural. Moreover, given the richness of opportunities the

Internet currently provides, they may not feel themselves externally constrained from doing whatever they wish on-line; that is, they may not perceive the existence of material and ideological biases.

Other women may be aware of gender asymmetries on-line and wish to change them, but find it difficult to do so. They may be unwilling or unable to forsake their own traditional gender socialization in order to "break the mold." They may feel that local resistance is futile, given the control exercised by patriarchy over the culture as a whole, of which the Internet is a product. Historical precedence and the commercialization of the Web both contribute to the appearance of inevitability of male control of the Internet. The designers and earliest users of the Internet were White, middle-class males whose norms and values (such as libertarianism) shaped its early culture (Herring 1999). The recent permeation of the Web by commerce and the mass media reinforces the traditional gender status quo and backs it with powerful financial interests (Brown 2000). Some women may comply with the status quo in their Internet use out of a sense of lack of choice.

Yet a third possible explanation holds that women (and men) maintain traditional gender arrangements out of rational self-interest, because such arrangements are perceived to be advantageous. This is the usual explanation advanced for men's resistance to social change (that is, the status quo meets their interests), but it can be extended to women on-line as well. Positive motivations for signaling (and even exaggerating) gender difference include gender pride, the social approval accorded to individuals for behaving in gender-appropriate ways, and the pleasure that can be derived from flirting, which often invokes binary gender stereotypes, in the relative safety of on-line environments. Negative rational motivations include the desire to avoid the unease one might feel in a truly gender-free environment in which one could not rely on familiar social skills and categorizations (O'Brien 1999).

It is likely that the ultimate explanation for women's complicity in reproducing traditional gender arrangements on-line involves some combination of the above factors. For the purposes of the present chapter, we may conclude that the idealistic notions that the Internet would create a gender-blind environment and would level gender-based power asymmetries receive little support from the evidence about gender and the Internet since the early 1980s. As a booming technology, the Internet provides opportunities for both male and female users, but does not appear to alter societal gender stereotypes, nor has it (yet) redistributed power at a fundamental level equally into the hands of women and men.

6 Future Projections

Framing our assessment in terms of starry-eyed ideals may not reveal the entire picture, however. The reality may fall short of the projections because the projections were unrealistic in the first place, for example, because they were based on the problematic assumption of technological determinism. Computer networks do not guarantee gender-free, equal-opportunity interaction, any more than any previous communication technology has had that effect. But the interplay of a popular technology such as the Internet with social and cultural forces over time may yet lead to change, just as technologies such as the typewriter and the telephone have altered patterns of sociability and business practice, and affected women's lives, in particular, in significant ways (Davies 1988; Martin 1991). What might the long-term effects of the Internet look like, if we could project into the future?

One possible future outcome is that as more and more women go on-line globally, a critical mass will be achieved, such that the Internet truly becomes a balanced, neutral environment. An optimistic scenario for feminists predicts that an increasing number of women would then be in control of Web content and distribution, and that more women would become computer network designers and administrators, giving them real power – both numerical and technical – to shape the nature and uses of the Internet. If this trend were to continue, the Internet could become a true "women's Web" with women constituting the majority of its users and administrators. The likelihood of this coming about depends crucially on a critical mass of women entering information technology professions. Currently, the numbers of women in IT, as well as in computer science, are declining (Catalyst 2000); this trend would need to be reversed.

A "women's Web" would not necessarily result in empowerment, however, if the Internet were then to become associated with femininity, and decline in overall status as a result. The process of "feminization" has affected professions such as those of teacher and secretary, both of which were originally restricted to men, and originally carried higher status and higher pay. It has also characterized the evolution of technologies such as the typewriter and the telephone, which were used by businessmen before they came to be associated with low-paid female labor (typists and telephone operators) (Davies 1988; Martin 1991). The Internet, like these earlier technologies, can be considered inherently well-suited to female use, because it is clean, safe, and can be used indoors. Moreover, a primary use of the Internet – interpersonal communication – is one at which women have traditionally been considered more skilled than men. As the definition of computing has evolved from number-crunching to communication, some have seen an unprecedented opening for women to embrace computer technology, symbolically as well as practically (Kramer and Lehman 1990). Feminization of the Internet – a process arguably already underway as regards e-mail use (Cohen 2001) – could erode this symbolic gain by devaluing any behavior associated preferentially with women. Carried to an extreme, the process of feminization could lead eventually to the Internet no longer being defined as a technology, as has occurred in the past with the typewriter and with domestic technologies such as sewing and washing machines (Wajcman 1991).

The final alternative is that the status quo could be maintained, with women (and some men) primarily restricted to the role of low-level users of the technology, and underlying technological and ideological control of the medium remaining in the hands of men. This scenario is not the worst outcome that could be imagined. First, the current status quo represents a gain over the recent past, in which the Internet was limited to a predominantly male elite; it has now caught up with the larger society in which it is embedded. Moreover, while the mass medium nature of the Internet makes it a powerful vehicle for the dissemination and reification of gender stereotypes (as is also true for television), its ability to be used as a medium of interpersonal communication (like the telephone) potentially empowers its users to network for non-traditional, even subversive, ends. One can imagine a future in which the Internet boom has leveled off, and in which resources become more limited – circumstances under which disempowered groups are more likely to challenge the status quo. Should the circumstances propitious for a feminist revolution arise, the Internet may yet enable a fundamentally different kind of grassroots organization than has historically been possible.

NOTES

1   Radio . . . the telephone . . . cable television . . .

2   For a history of the development of the Arpanet and the Internet, see Hafner and Lyon (1996).

3   Women's access to the Internet is considerably more limited in Islamic and developing nations, although change in the direction of greater access is taking place there as well (Harcourt 1999; Wheeler 2001).

4   Recent estimates place the number of female CS professionals at around 35 per cent, mostly clustered in lower-level positions. Moreover, the number of female college students majoring in CS has declined, rather than increased, during the growth in popularity of the Internet in the 1980s and 1990s (Klawe and Leveson 1995).

5   For a description and overview of the development of different modes of CMC, see Herring (2002).

6   E.g. Kiesler et al. (1984), who concluded on the basis of experimental studies that people are more likely to "flame" and otherwise be disinhibited in CMC than in face-to-face communication. However, subsequent Internet research (e.g. Herring 1994) identified gender differences in flaming.

7   During the "anonymity" experiment in the Selfe and Meyer study, the listowner arranged to have identifying information stripped from message headers prior to distribution of messages to the list.

8   Contemporary asynchronous discussion forums hosted by Web sites make it easier for users to be anonymous, by requiring only that they type in something that satisfies the format of an e-mail address as an identifier for purposes of registering to use the site. Since the e-mail addresses are often not

verified by the site, many users simply make them up.

9   For example, Bucholtz (forthcoming) finds differences from the generalizations presented here among female and male hackers on a Web-based discussion forum for computer specialists.

10   An exception is men who infiltrate female-centered groups for the purpose of disrupting the discourse of the group (see, e.g., Collins-Jarvis 1997; Ebben 1994).

11   The male message is from POLITICS-L; the female message is from WOMEN-L; both are by-subscription discussion lists. These examples are discussed in more detail in Herring (1996a).

12   The other part of the explanation involves freedom from harassment; see discussion below.

13   Many groups are implicitly men-centered, but they are not usually designated as such with the modifier "men" in the group's name in the way that women-centered groups have "women" as part of their names (e.g. Women's Wire, the Women's Studies list, the Society for Women in Philosophy list).

14   I interpret the women's response to reflect a concern for their personal safety, e.g. from predatory male behaviors, rather than a concern for encryption or hacking issues, the other sense in which "privacy" on the Internet could be interpreted (but cf. Gilboa 1996). Respondents were given a limited list of "concerns" to choose from in the questionnaire; this list did not include "safety" or "harassment." For further discussion of the gendered dimensions of libertarian ideology on the Internet, see Ess (1996) and Herring (1999).

15   As Danet (1998) notes, many nicknames in IRC are unrevealing as to gender, but some index gender: lisa1, CoverGirl, shyboy, GTBastard, etc. (Herring 1998).

16   The female example is from the channel #love; the male example is from the channel #teensex. Both channels are on the EFNet, a large and popular IRC network.

17   See, for example, the PlanetGrrl Web site, at http://www.planet.grrl.com/.

18   However, criticism has been directed at such sites as well, primarily for containing a considerable residue of traditional content (dating and beauty tips; horoscopes, etc.), and for their tendency to become increasingly "mainstream" over time (Brown 2000); see also below.

19   For example, viewers of Web sites can navigate through the site, choosing what to view, and in some cases, providing input to the site itself.

20   However, the most popular sites visited by both women and men are familiar portals, search engines, and general interest retail sites such as amazon.com, rather than sites offering gender-specific content (Rickert and Sacharow 2000).

21   This perspective should be balanced against the considerable evidence of women's groups outside of North America using the Internet to mobilize support for women's political causes, sometimes on an international scale (Harcourt 2000).

REFERENCES

Balka, Ellen 1993: Women's access to on-line discussions about feminism. *Electronic Journal of Communication* 3(1). http://www.cios.org/www/ejc/v3n193.htm

Baym, Nancy 1996: Agreements and disagreements in a computer-mediated discussion. *Research on Language and Social Interaction* 29(4): 315–45.

Bella, Thomas 2001: www.amihot.com: A CMC system for online flirting. Unpublished MS, Indiana University Purdue University Indianapolis.

Blair, Kristine and Takayoshi, Pamela 1999: Mapping the terrain of feminist cyberscapes. In Kristine Blair and Pamela Takayoshi (eds) *Feminist Cyberscapes: Mapping Gendered Academic Spaces*. Stamford, CT: Ablex, pp. 1–18.

Brail, Stephanie 1994: Take back the net! *On the Issues* (Winter): 40–2.

Brail, Stephanie 1996: The price of admission: Harassment and free speech in the wild, wild west. In Lynn Cherny and Elizabeth R. Weise (eds) *Wired_Women*. Seattle: Seal Press, pp. 141–57.

Bright, Susie 1997: *Susie Bright's Sexual State of the Union*. New York: Simon and Schuster.

Broadhurst, Judith 1993: Lurkers and flamers. *Online Access* 8(3): 48–51.

Brown, Janelle 2000: What happened to the Women's Web? *Salon*, August 25. http://www.salon.com/tech/feature/2000/08/25/womens_web.html

Bruckman, Amy S. 1993: Gender swapping on the Internet. In *Proceedings of INET '93*. Reston, VA: The Internet Society. (Available via anonymous ftp from http://www.inform.umd.edu/EdRes/Topic/WomensStudies/Computing/ Articles+ResearchPapers/gender-swapping)

Bucholtz, Mary (forthcoming): Geek feminism. In Sarah Benor, Mary Rose, Devyani Sharma, Julie Sweetland, and Qing Zhang (eds) *Gendered Practices in Language*. Stanford, CA: Center for the Study of Language and Information.

Camp, L. Jean 1996: We are geeks, and we are not guys: The systers mailing list. In Lynn Cherny and Elizabeth R. Weise (eds) *Wired_Women*. Seattle: Seal Press, pp. 114–25.

Carlassare, Elizabeth 2000: Introduction. In *Dotcom Divas*. http://dotcomdivas.net/intro.html

Catalyst 2000: Women in Information Technology. http://www.catalystwomen.org/press/infobriefs/infombatech.html

Cherny, Lynn 1994: Gender differences in text-based virtual reality. In Mary Bucholtz, Anita C. Liang, Laurel A. Sutton and Caitlin Hines (eds) *Cultural Performances: Proceedings of the Third Berkeley Women and Language Conference*. Berkeley, CA: Berkeley Women and Language Group, University of California, pp. 102–15.

Cherny, Lynn 1999: *Conversation and Community: Chat in a Virtual World*. Stanford, CA: Center for the Study of Language and Information.

Cheung, Charles 2000: A home on the Web: Presentations of self on personal homepages. In David Gauntlett (ed.) *Web.Studies: Rewiring Media Studies for the Digital Age*. London: Arnold, pp. 43–51.

Clements, Alysabeth 2001: Alysabeth's feminist stripper site. http://www.geocities.com/alysabethc/strippers.html

Coates, Jennifer 1993: *Women, Men and Language*, 2nd edn. London: Longman.

Cohen, Joyce 2001: He-mails, she-mails: Where sender meets gender. *New York Times*, May 17, D1 and D9.

Collins-Jarvis, Lori 1997: Discriminatory Messages and Gendered Power Relations in on-line Discussion Groups. Paper presented at the 1997 Annual Meeting of the National Communication Association, Chicago.

Cronin, Blaise and Davenport, Elisabeth 2001: E-rogenous zones: Positioning pornography in the digital economy. *The Information Society* 17(1): 33–48.

Curtis, Pavel 1992: Mudding: Social phenomena in text-based virtual realities. In Douglas Schuler (ed.) *Proceedings of DIAC92*. Palo Alto, CA: Computer Professionals for Social Responsibility. (Available by anonymous ftp from parcftp.xerox.com in pub/MOO/papers/DIAC92.)

CyberAtlas 2000: Women surpass men as US Web users. http://cyberatlas.internet.com/big_picture/demographics/article/0,,5901_434551,00.html

Danet, Brenda 1998: Text as mask: Gender and identity on the Internet. In Steve Jones (ed.) *Cybersociety 2.0*. Thousand Oaks, CA: Sage, pp. 129–58.

Danet, Brenda, Ruedenberg-Wright, Lucia, and Rosenbaum-Tamari, Yehudit 1997: Hmmm . . . where's that smoke coming from? Writing, play and performance on Internet Relay Chat. In Sheizaf Rafaeli, Fay Sudweeks, and Margaret McLaughlin (eds) *Network and Netplay: Virtual Groups on the Internet*. Cambridge, MA: AAAI/MIT Press, pp. 41–76.

Davies, Margery W. 1988: Women clerical workers and the typewriter: The writing machine. In Cheris Kramarae (ed.) *Technology and Women's Voices: Keeping in Touch*. New York: Routledge, pp. 29–40.

Dibbell, Julian 1993: A rape in cyberspace, or how an evil clown, a Haitian trickster spirit, two wizards, and a cast of dozens turned a database into a society. *Village Voice*, December 21: 36–42.

Di Filippo, JoAnn 2000: Pornography on the Web. In David Gauntlett (ed.) *Web.Studies: Rewiring Media Studies for the Digital Age*. London: Arnold, pp. 122–9.

Ebben, Maureen 1994: Women on the Net: An Exploratory Study of Gender Dynamics on the soc.women Computer Network. Unpublished doctoral dissertation, University of Illinois at Urbana-Champaign.

Ebben, Maureen and Kramarae, Cheris 1993: Women and information technologies: Creating a cyberspace of our own. In H. Jeanie Taylor, Cheris Kramarae, and Maureen Ebben (eds) *Women, Information Technology, and Scholarship*. Urbana, IL: Center for Advanced Study, pp. 15–27.

Ess, Charles 1996: Beyond false dilemmas: Men and women on the net – a plea for democracy and understanding. *Computer-Mediated Communication Magazine* 3(1), Special Issue on Philosophical Approaches to Pornography, Free Speech, and CMC, edited by Charles Ess. January 1996. http://www.december.com/cmc/mag/1996/jan/ess.html

Fedler, Joanne 1996: A feminist critique of pornography. In Jane Duncan (ed.) *Between Speech and Silence*, ch. 2. South Africa: Freedom Expression Institute and the Institute for Democracy in South Africa. http://fxi.org.za/books/chap2.htm

Gilboa, Netta "grayarea" 1996: Elites, lamers, narcs and whores: Exploring the computer underground. In Lynn Cherny and Elizabeth R. Weise (eds) *Wired_Women*. Seattle: Seal Press, pp. 98–113.

Glidewell, Robert 2000: Business lessons from online porn. *Upside Today*, February 21. http:// www.upside.com/texis/mvm/ story?id=38adbbff0

Goffman, Erving 1959: *Presentation of Self in Everyday Life*. Garden City, NY: Anchor.

Graddol, David and Swann, Joan 1989: *Gender Voices*. Oxford: Blackwell.

Grossman, Wendy M. 1997: *Net.wars*. New York: New York University Press. http:// www.nyupress.nyu.edu/ netwars.html

GVU: Graphic, Visualization, and Usability Center's 7th WWW User Survey 1997: Georgia Technological University. http:// www.cc.gatech.edu/gvu/ user_surveys/

Hafner, Katie and Lyon, Matthew 1996: *Where Wizards Stay Up Late: The Origins of the Internet*. New York: Simon and Schuster.

Hall, Kira 1996: Cyberfeminism. In S. Herring (ed.) *Computer-Mediated Communication: Linguistic, Social and Cross-cultural Perspectives*. Amsterdam: John Benjamins, pp. 147–70.

Harcourt, Wendy (ed.) 1999: *women@internet: Creating New Cultures in Cyberspace*. London: Zed Books.

Harcourt, Wendy 2000: World wide women and the web. In David Gauntlett (ed.) *Web.Studies: Rewiring Media Studies for the Digital Age*. London: Arnold, pp. 150–8.

Herring, Susan C. 1992: *Gender and Participation in Computer-mediated Linguistic Discourse*. Washington,

DC: ERIC Clearinghouse on Languages and Linguistics, Document no. ED345552.

Herring, Susan C. 1993: Gender and democracy in computer-mediated communication. *Electronic Journal of Communication* 3(2). http:// www.cios.org/www/ejc/ v3n293.htm. (Reprinted in Rob Kling (ed.) 1996: *Computerization and Controversy*, 2nd edn. New York: Academic Press, pp. 476–89.)

Herring, Susan C. 1994: Politeness in computer culture: Why women thank and men flame. In Mary Bucholtz, Anita C. Liang, Laurel A. Sutton, and Caitlin Hines (eds) *Cultural Performances: Proceedings of the Third Berkeley Women and Language Conference*. Berkeley, CA: Berkeley Women and Language Group, University of California, pp. 278–94.

Herring, Susan C. 1996a: Posting in a different voice: Gender and ethics in computer-mediated communication. In Charles Ess (ed.) *Philosophical Perspectives on Computer-Mediated Communication*. Albany: State University of New York Press, pp. 115–45.

Herring, Susan C. 1996b: Two variants of an electronic message schema. In S. Herring (ed.) *Computer-Mediated Communication: Linguistic, Social and Cross-cultural Perspectives*. Amsterdam: John Benjamins, pp. 81–106.

Herring, Susan C. 1998: Virtual gender performances. Talk presented at Texas A&M University, September 25.

Herring, Susan C. 1999: The rhetorical dynamics of gender harassment online. *The Information Society* 15(3): 151–67. Special Issue on *The Rhetorics of Gender in Computer-Mediated Communication*, edited by Laura J. Gurak.

Herring, Susan C. 2002: Computer-mediated communication and the Internet. In Blaise Cronin (ed.) *Annual Review of Information Science and Technology* 36. Medford, NJ: Information Today Inc./American Society for Information Science and Technology, pp. 109–68.

Herring, Susan C. (forthcoming): Who's got the floor in computer-mediated conversations? Edelsky's gender patterns revisited. In Susan Herring (ed.) *Computer-mediated Conversation.* Cresskill, NJ: Hampton Press.

Herring, Susan, Johnson, Deborah, and DiBenedetto, Tamra 1992: Participation in electronic discourse in a "feminist" field. In Kira Hall, Mary Bucholtz, and Birch Moonwomon (eds) *Locating Power: Proceedings of the Second Berkeley Women and Language Conference.* Berkeley, CA: Berkeley Women and Language Group, University of California, pp. 250–62.

Herring, Susan, Johnson, Deborah, and DiBenedetto, Tamra 1995: "This discussion is going too far!" Male resistance to female participation on the Internet. In Kira Hall and Mary Bucholtz (eds) *Gender Articulated: Language and the Socially Constructed Self.* New York: Routledge, pp. 67–96.

Herring, Susan and Lombard, Robin 1995: Negotiating gendered faces: Requests and disagreements among computer professionals on the Internet. Paper presented at GURT pre-session on Computer-Mediated Discourse Analysis, Georgetown University, Washington DC, March 8.

Herring, Susan and Nix, Carole 1997: Is "Serious Chat" an Oxymoron? Academic vs. Social Uses of Internet Relay Chat. Paper presented at the American Association of Applied Linguistics, Orlando, Florida, March 11.

Hert, Philippe 1997: Social dynamics of an on-line scholarly debate. *The Information Society* 13: 329–60.

Kibby, Marge 1997: Babes on the Web: Sex, identity and the home page. http://www.newcastle.edu.au/department/so/babes.htm

Kiesler, Sara, Siegel, Jane, and McGuire, Timothy W. 1984: Social-psychological aspects of computer-mediated communication. *American Psychologist* 39: 1123–34.

King, Storm 1999: Internet gambling and pornography: Illustrative examples of the psychological consequences of communication anarchy. *CyberPsychology and Behavior* 2(3): 175–93.

Klawe, M. and Nancy Leveson 1995: Women in computing: Where are we now? *Communications of the ACM* 38(1): 29–35.

Kling, Rob, McKim, Geoff, Fortuna, Joanna, and King, Adam 2001: *A Bit More to IT: Scientific Communication Forums as Socio-technical Interaction Networks.* Center for Social Informatics Working Papers. Bloomington, IN: Center for Social Informatics. http://www.slis.indiana.edu/csi/wp01–02.html

Kolko, Beth 1999: Representing bodies in virtual space: The rhetoric of avatar design. *The Information Society* 15: 177–86.

Korenman, Joan and Wyatt, Nancy 1996: Group dynamics in an e-mail forum. In Susan Herring (ed.) *Computer-Mediated Communication: Linguistic, Social and Cross-cultural Perspectives.* Amsterdam: John Benjamins, pp. 225–42.

Kramarae, Cheris and Taylor, H. Jeanie 1993: Women and men on electronic networks: A conversation or a monologue? In H. Jeanie Taylor, Cheris Kramarae, and Maureen Ebben (eds) *Women, Information*

Technology, and Scholarship. Urbana, IL: Center for Advanced Study, pp. 52–61.

Kramer, Pamela and Lehman, S. 1990: Mismeasuring women: A critique on research on computer avoidance. *Signs* 16(1): 158–72.

Lane, Frederick S. 2000: *Obscene Profits: Entrepreneurs of Pornography in the Cyber Age*. Bloomington, IN: 1stBooks Library.

Lombard, M. and Ditton, Teresa 1997: At the heart of it all: The concept of presence. *Journal of Computer-Mediated Communication* 3(2). http://www.ascusc.org/jcmc/vol3/issue2/lombard.html

Markus, M. Lynne 1994: Finding a happy medium: Explaining the negative effects of electronic communication on social life at work. *ACM Transactions on Information Systems* 12(2): 119–49.

Marsh, Taylor 2000: *My Year in Smut: The Internet Escapades inside Danni's Hard Drive*. Bloomington, IN: 1stBooks Library.

Martin, Michèle 1991: The making of the perfect operator. In *'Hello, Central?': Gender, Technology and the Re-formation of Telephone Systems*. Montreal: McGill-Queen's University Press, pp. 50–81.

McChesney, Robert 2000: So much for the magic of the technology and the free market. In Andrew Herman and Thomas Swiss (eds) *The World Wide Web and Contemporary Culture Theory*. London: Routledge, pp. 5–36.

McCormick, Naomi B. and McCormick, John W. 1992: Computer friends and foes: Content of undergraduates' electronic mail. *Computers in Human Behavior* 8: 379–405.

McRae, Shannon 1996: Coming apart at the seams: Sex, text and the virtual body. In Lynn Cherny and Elizabeth R. Weise (eds) *Wired_Women*. Seattle: Seal Press, pp. 242–63.

Mehta, Michael and Plaza, Dwaine E. 1997: Pornography in cyberspace: An exploration of what's in USENET. In Sara Kiesler (ed.) *Culture of the Internet*. Mahwah, NJ: Lawrence Erlbaum, pp. 53–67.

Morris, Merrill and Ogan, Christine 1996: The Internet as mass medium. *Journal of Communication* 46(1), Winter: 39–50.

O'Brien, Jodi 1999: Writing in the body: Gender (re)production in online interaction. In Marc A. Smith and Peter Kollock (eds) *Communities in Cyberspace*. London: Routledge, pp. 76–104.

O'Sullivan, Patrick B. 1999: "Personal broadcasting": Theoretical implications of the Web. http://www.ilstu.edu/~posull/PersBroad.htm

Pastore, Michael 2000: Women use Web to change social landscape. *CyberAtlas*, May 12. http://cyberatlas.internet.com/big_picture/demographics.html

Reid, Elizabeth M. 1994: Cultural Formations in Text-Based Virtual Realities. Master's thesis, University of Melbourne, Australia. http://www.ee.mu.oz.au/papers/emr/index.html

Rich, Frank 2001: Naked capitalists: There's no business like porn business. *New York Times*, May 20.

Rickert, Anne and Sacharow, Anya 2000: *It's a Woman's World Wide Web*. Media Metrix and Jupiter Communications. http://www.mediametrix.com/data/MMXI-JUP-WWWW.pdf

Rodino, Michelle 1997: Breaking out of binaries: Reconceptualizing gender and its relationship to language in computer-mediated communication. *Journal of Computer-Mediated Communication* 3(3). http://www.ascusc.org/jcmc/vol3/issue3/rodino.html

Royalle, Candida 2001: Candida Royalle's Femme. http://db.phenet.com/catalog/femme/home.html

Sarkio, Helena K. 2001: American Women in Cyberspace: A Case Study. Paper delivered at the Association for Education in Journalism and Mass Communication Southeast Colloquium, Columbia, South Carolina, March 10, 2001.

Savicki, Victor, Lingenfelter, Dawn, and Kelley, Merle 1996: Gender language style and group composition in Internet discussion groups. *Journal of Computer-Mediated Communication* 2(3). http://www.ascusc.org/jcmc/vol2/issue3/savicki.html

Scheidt, Lois A. 2001: Avatars and Nicknames in Adolescent Chat Spaces. Unpublished MS, Indiana University, Bloomington.

Selfe, Cynthia L. and Meyer, Paul R. 1991: Testing claims for on-line conferences. *Written Communication* 8(2): 163–92.

Smith, Christine B., McLaughlin, Margaret L., and Osborne, Kerry K. 1997: Conduct controls on Usenet. *Journal of Computer-Mediated Communication* 2(4). http://www.ascusc.org/jcmc/vol2/issue4/smith.html

Smith, Judy and Balka, Ellen 1988: Chatting on a feminist network. In Cheris Kramarae (ed.) *Technology and Women's Voices*. New York: Routledge and Kegan Paul, pp. 82–97.

Snyder, Donald 2000: Webcam women: Life on your screen. In David Gauntlett (ed.) *Web.Studies: Rewiring Media Studies for the Digital Age*. London: Arnold, pp. 68–73.

Spertus, Ellen 1996: Social and technical means for fighting online harassment. http://www.ai.mit.edu/people/ellens/Gender/gk

Sproull, Lee 1992: Women and the Networked Organization. Presentation to Women, Information Technology and Scholarship Colloquium, February 12, 1992, Center for Advanced Study, University of Illinois.

Sutton, Laurel 1994: Using Usenet: Gender, power, and silence in electronic discourse. In *Proceedings of the 20th Annual Meeting of the Berkeley Linguistics Society*, pp. 506–20. Berkeley, CA: Berkeley Linguistics Society.

Van Gelder, Lindsey 1990: The strange case of the electronic lover. In Gary Gumpert and Sandra L. Fish (eds) *Talking to Strangers: Mediated Therapeutic Communication*. Norwood, NJ: Ablex, pp. 128–42.

Vollmer, Ashley 2001: A Web of One's Own: The Online Presence of Female Gen Xers. Unpublished MS, Indiana University, Bloomington.

Wajcman, Judith 1991: *Feminism Confronts Technology*. University Park: Pennsylvania State University Press.

Wakeford, Nina 1997: Networking women and grrrls with information/communication technology: Surfing tales of the world wide web. In Jennifer Terry and Melodie Calvert (eds) *Processed Lives: Gender and Technology in Everyday Life*. London: Routledge, pp. 51–66.

Wheeler, Deborah 2001: Women, Islam, and the Internet: Findings in Kuwait. In Charles Ess (ed.) *Culture, Technology, Communication: Towards an Intercultural Global Village*. Albany: State University of New York Press, pp. 158–82.

10 The Relevance of Ethnicity, Class, and Gender in Children's Peer Negotiations

MARJORIE HARNESS GOODWIN

While considerable attention has been paid to children's skills in cognitive domains such as math and literacy in classroom settings, far less is known about children's informal social learning across peer-controlled settings. In the midst of interaction with their peers children develop their notions about ethnicity, social class, and gender-appropriate behavior, as well as their understandings of a moral self, while they play or work together and sanction those who violate group norms. This chapter reviews work on peer negotiation during children's spontaneous play which is concerned with issues of language and gender.

1 Differentiating Everyday Conflict from Aggression

Developmental psychologist Shantz (1983: 501) has argued that "the way to reveal explicit and tacit social knowledge and reasoning is to observe social interaction, that is, the child not as knower *about* the social world but as an actor *in* it." This demands the use of naturally occurring data, as neither experimental paradigms nor interview data provide adequate analogues of actual social interactions. While we know something about the features and functions of children's disputes in naturalistic (Maynard 1985a, 1985b; Corsaro and Rizzo 1990; Boggs 1978; Genishi and di Paolo 1982), as well as laboratory settings (Brenneis and Lein 1977; Eisenberg and Garvey 1981), we actually know very little about how conflicts contribute to the development of more enduring social relationships among children (see Rizzo 1992: 94).

While much attention has been paid in linguistic anthropology to studies of politeness phenomena (Brown and Levinson 1978), far less is known about the structure of disagreement or oppositional sequences. This may be because conflict is negatively valued and it is often viewed by feminist researchers as alternative to the cooperative interaction which is argued to typify female interaction. Social conflicts (Maynard 1985b; Rizzo 1992: 93) or adversative episodes (Eisenberg and Garvey 1981) are sequences in which one person opposes another's actions or statements (see Grimshaw 1990). Conflict sequences are important to investigate in that, as developmental psychologists have argued, conflict constitutes "an essential impetus to change, adaptation, and development" (Shantz 1987: 284). Routinely, conflict is equated with aggression (Shantz 1987: 284), defined as "acts done with the intention to harm another person, oneself, or an object" (Bjorkqvist and Niemela 1992: 4).

Early psychological studies on sex differences by Maccoby and Jacklin (1974) maintained that aggression was one of the clearest ways in which males and females were differentiated. More recent studies have been careful to specify alternative forms that aggressive behavior takes, and such sweeping generalizations are now less common. Bjorkqvist, Osterman, and Kaukiainen (1992), for example, distinguish three forms of aggressive behavior: direct physical, direct verbal, and indirect aggression. Indirect aggression is defined as "a kind of social manipulation: the aggressor manipulates others to attack the victim, or, by other means, makes use of the social structure in order to harm the target person, without being personally involved in attack" (ibid.: 52). Bjorkqvist et al. (1992: 55) in their study of Finnish children find that while boys are more physically aggressive than girls, boys and girls differ little in the use of verbal aggression. Lagerspetz, Bjorkqvist, and Peltonen (1988) were among the first to suggest that harm delivered circuitously, rather than in a face-to-face encounter, occurs more among girls than boys.

This chapter reviews current debates in language and gender research which focus on children's negotiation. I first examine the notion of "Separate Worlds" of males and females, an idea which has dominated much of the popular literature on gender differences in language. I critique the ideas of (1) the universality of gender segregation, and (2) essentialized views of male and female language practices which neglect considerations of context, ethnicity, or social class. A second section examines ethnographically based studies of the interactive practices which children of different social class and age groups use to construct gendered social relationships in and across girls' and boys' groups. Special attention is given to the nature of disputes, the forms of accounts, and the forms of speech actions used to construct difference and relative rank. A third section examines studies which focus on how the presentation of self, expressed through forms of character contests, is related to notions of identity within diverse ethnic groups. This section examines particular types of sequencing strategies which are employed in disputes and demonstrates how the inclusion of texts of actual sequences of interaction afford the possibility of cross-cultural comparison. A final section looks at political processes and forms of exclusion in girls' groups, noting that forms of ostracism are central to girls' social organization.

2 The Separate Worlds Hypothesis and Its Challengers

The dichotomous views of male and female personality Maccoby put forward in the 1970s were revitalized in anthropologists Maltz and Borker's (1982) Separate Worlds Hypothesis (see Kyratzis 2001a). Maltz and Borker proposed that the gender segregation that girls and boys experience results not only in differing activities which are the focus of their worlds, but also alternative ways of speaking. Girls' collaborative talk contrasts with boys' competitive talk. Maltz and Borker's hypothesis was based on selective readings of fieldwork, including my own work on African American children's interactive patterns (Goodwin 1980) and Harding's (1975) studies of gender role segregation in the Near East and Mediterranean. Henley's (1995: 361) observation that "much writing on the topic of language and gender is founded on the assumptions of White/Anglo (upper) middle-class experience" is relevant when considering the paradigm which generated research on language and gender for more than two decades.

The Separate Worlds Hypothesis, buttressed by work by Gilligan (1982) and Lever (1978), has subsequently been reified by psychologists. Leaper (1994: 68) in a review article on gender segregation has proposed that "to the extent that girls and boys emphasize different patterns of social interaction and activities in their respective peer groups, different norms for social behavior may be expected to emerge." Leaper maintains that girls' sex-typed activities help to foster nurturance and affection, as well as forms of "social sensitivity," whereas boys' physically aggressive forms of play emphasize overt competition and dominance. This argument draws on cross-cultural work by psychological anthropologists Whiting and Edwards (1988: 81), who posited that "the emergence of same-sex preferences in childhood is a cross cultural universal and robust phenomenon" and resonates with the work of Maccoby (1990, 1998) who has consistently argued that "segregated play groups constitute powerful socialization environments in which children acquire distinctive interaction skills that are adapted to same-sex partners" (Maccoby 1990: 516).

2.1 Challenging notions of gender segregation

Ethnographically based research on language in interaction has recently challenged the Separate Worlds Hypothesis with respect to (1) the universality of gender segregation, and (2) polarizations of gendered norms of social interaction and communication. Specifically, a number of researchers have analyzed how considerations of ethnicity, social class, and context are critical in the examination of gendered talk-in-interaction among children.

Forms of gender segregation affecting norms of interaction have been described for preschool children in Japan (Nakamura 2001), Norway (Berentzen

1984), Australia (Danby and Baker 1998), and the USA (Best 1983; Kyratzis and Guo 1996; Sheldon 1993). However, Thorne (1993), Goodwin (1990), Cook-Gumperz and Szymanski (2001), and Streeck (1986) caution that boys and girls are not always segregated. In a study of interaction on playgrounds in the American Midwest and California among largely White working-class schools fourth and fifth graders, Thorne (1993) found that boys and girls established "with-then-apart" social arrangements. Gender boundaries could become heightened during team handball when boys made the game competitive, through slamming the ball hard; however, at other points (for example while eating) boundaries between the gender groups were not salient.

Goodwin (1990) found that working-class African American girls ages four to thirteen in a Philadelphia neighborhood would exclude boys during more serious "he-said-she-said" disputes, when girls were ostracizing members of their group. Generally, however, girls and boys were frequently in each other's co-presence and engaged in playful cross-sex verbal disputes. Joking and teasing between girls and boys was also common among the working-class White Midwestern middle school adolescents Eder (1990, 1993, 1995) studied. Schofield (1982) and Corsaro (1997) argue that African American girls are generally more assertive and independent in their relations with one another and with boys than are upper-middle-class White girls. Gender segregation in White middle-class groups (Schofield 1981, 1982; Best 1983) prevents the development of friendships where playful conflictual types of exchanges might occur, perhaps due to "boys' and girls' notions of each other as possible romantic and sexual partners" (Schofield 1981: 72). Corsaro (1997: 150) also found age to be an important variable when considering gender segregation. More gender segregation occurs among older children (five- to six-year-olds) than among children three to five years of age. In general, White upper-middle-class children in America experience more gender segregation than African American or Italian children, regardless of age.

2.2   Challenges addressing issues of context, ethnicity, and social class

The universality of the Separate Worlds Hypothesis has been challenged by numerous studies which consider the variability of language practices across contexts. My own studies of African American working-class children (Goodwin 1990), bilingual Spanish/English speakers (Goodwin 1998), and children of diverse ethnicities at a progressive school (Goodwin 2001) refute the notion that females are non-competitive, or passive by comparison with boys (Adler, Kless, and Adler 1992: 170). Within their same-sex groups African American girls orchestrate task activities such as making rings, using directives (actions which get another to do something) which are mitigated. However, when they care for younger children, are reprimanding those who commit infractions, or play the role of mother during games of "house," girls demonstrate the ability to use bald imperatives which are equally as aggravated in form as those the boys use during task activities. In cross-sex disputes, as well, girls use bald on-record counter forms which are similar to those of males; girls are quite skilled in ritual insult and can outmaneuver boys in extended disputes.

Goodwin's (2001) study of girls' and boys' uses of directives during the game of jump-rope at a progressive elementary school attended by children of mixed ethnicities and social classes shows that the grammatical form of directives varies with levels of expertise in the activity of jumping rather than gender. This contrasts with research which has found the form of directives to be closely correlated to gender (Sachs 1987). When boys at the progressive school were unfamiliar with jump-rope, they were excluded from the game, and girls issued aggravated directives (Labov and Fanshel 1977: 84) to them; when, a month later, with practice boys became accomplished jumpers, they made use of the same imperative forms the girls used. Streeck (1986), studying ethnically mixed working-class elementary school children in the classroom, found that while boys competed with girls and worked to exclude girls during work tasks, within non-task-specific settings, such forms of competition did not occur.

Kyratzis and Guo (1996, 2001) studied cross-cultural differences in language behavior of preschoolers in Mainland China and the USA. They found that during same-sex interaction in the USA boys are more assertive than girls; the reverse is true in China. Context is important in examining who is more assertive in cross-sex conflict: while Chinese girls dominate contexts dealing with courtship, boys are dominant in contexts where work is the theme. While American girls used mitigated strategies in opposing others, both American boys and Chinese girls used bald (unmitigated) forms. Both American and Chinese girls used direct as well as third-party censures of co-present girls, rhetorical mocking questions, aggravated commands, threats, and physical force. Guo (2000) found that five-year-old Mandarin-speaking girls in a university-affiliated preschool in Beijing order boys around when issues of social status or morality are at stake, though not with respect to exchanges involving technical, problem-solving issues. In this domain boys become aggressive and controlling with playmates. Both the studies of Guo (2000) and Streeck (1986) have important implications for the organization of small groups in classrooms, as they demonstrate that within task-specific settings boys may dominate and not allow girls full participation in the activity.

Children make use of a repertoire of voices. Nakamura (2001) shows that while Japanese girls use language to create and maintain positions of closeness and equality, they can also use language to make assertive moves – negotiating roles, establishing the physical setting, and defining appropriate role behavior. Nakamura's depiction of male and female roles in a Japanese preschool has several parallels with Farris's (1991, 2000) descriptions of language use among Taiwanese preschoolers. Farris argues that boys "create a childish masculine ethos that centers on action, competition, and aggression, and that is organized and expressed discursively through loud, terse, direct forms of speech" (1991:

204). By way of contrast, Taiwanese girls attempt to maintain an ethos of "quasi-familial social relations . . . organized and expressed discursively through coy, affected, and indirect forms of speech." In comparison with Japanese female preschoolers, however, Taiwanese girls can be quite assertive; they talk pejoratively about other people in the third person *in the presence of the target*, making use of a particular style *(sajiao)*, which involves gross body movements, pouting, ambiguous lexical items, and expressive particles (ibid.: 208). Such forms might be considered instances of overt verbal aggression.

The notion of "quasi-familial social relations" discussed by Farris (1991) for Taiwanese children has parallels with the structuring of social roles among peers in a California third grade bilingual classroom described by Cook-Gumperz and Szymanski (2001). An organization of groups in terms of families was initiated by the teacher, and children themselves oriented toward ideas of quasi-family. Girls took the lead in orchestrating group activities, such as coordinating the activity of correcting answers for the group, or playing the role of "big sisters." They acted as "cultural brokers" (Vasquez, Pease-Alvarez, and Shannon 1994) who were responsible for "organizing and translating the needs and requirements of family to and from the outside world" (Cook-Gumperz and Szymanski 2001: 127). Children moved fluidly in and out of familial-based and gender-based groups; their social organization resembled the pattern of "with-then-apart" described by Thorne (1986) rather than the gender-segregated groups described by the Separate Worlds Hypothesis.

3   Constructing Gender Identity Within Boys' and Girls' Groups

Despite the fact that simple polarized depictions of gender groups cannot be established, there are differences in the criteria each gender uses for making distinctions among group members as well as procedures for achieving social organization. Close analysis of the interactive linguistic processes through which masculinity is displayed and constructed is afforded by several studies of young children. In a classic study of gender differences in the construction of social order, social anthropologist Sigurd Berentzen (1984: 17) analyzes how Norwegian preschool boys ages five to seven were constantly involved in direct comparison of one another's performances, particularly with regard to objects. Boys established their rank order through competitions such as running or wrestling; girls attached meaning to their social relationships and each other and the alliances they can enter into. While among the boys self-congratulation was common, it was sanctioned in girls' groups. A girl who was thought to "act so smart all the time" by bragging about the praise she had received from a teacher was eventually ostracized. Girls' "cultural premises and criteria of rank lead to their constantly denying each other's rank" (ibid.: 108). Patterns of fluid rather than fixed hierarchically ranked social groups were also found by Corsaro (1994) for both girls *as well as* boys in American and Italian preschools, where attempts at leadership were continually challenged and overturned. Girls in particular resisted being in the position of putting oneself above another (Corsaro 1994: 18–20).

Berentzen's observations resonate with a number of other studies. Danby (1998) and Danby and Baker (1998, 2000) examined the procedures Australian inner-city boys aged three to five used to build their social organization in the context of playing with blocks in a preschool classroom. Australian boys assert their masculinity through threats of inflicting personal injury ("smashing" down the block construction and "bashing" one of the boys) and introducing themes of terror and violence: for example, a robot shark crocodile monster who will attack and eat one of the boys, or a big dinosaur who will spit and kill someone. Because Danby and Baker provide close transcriptions of naturally occurring talk, comparisons with group processes in other studies are possible. During the boys' play coalitions of two against one are created; through subtle shifts in reference, using the third-person pronoun, boys can position themselves as talking negatively about a third party in his presence. Such negotiations within shifting coalitions are not unlike those described by Goodwin (1990) and Berentzen (1984) for girls' groups.

Best (1983), a reading teacher turned ethnographer, discusses how White upper-middle-class elementary school boys (6–8 years of age) in a school in the Central Atlantic region of the United States negotiate rank with respect to perceived toughness, often through bragging. Studying children over a four-year period, Best (1983: 4) found that a "second curriculum" of the school taught young girls to be helpful and nurturant and young boys to distance themselves from girls and look down on them; an ethos of machismo prohibited any recognition of or friendship with girls. By the third grade boys created a clique where they shared secrets and used nicknames, while excluding boys who they considered "sissies."

Sheldon (1997: 232), studying socially advantaged children in a Midwestern US preschool, located patterns of verbal and physical assertiveness in boys' social organization, finding that "insistence and brute force can be acceptable strategies for trying to get what one wants" (see also Davies 1989; Dyson 1994). Boys make use of refusals, physical intimidation (chasing, blocking), threats, and physical force, and actively attempt to escalate and extend conflict, without employing strategies that might jointly negotiate a resolution. Consistent with Berentzen's observations, boys were concerned with control of various objects (fighting for who got to push buttons or talk on the telephone). By way of contrast, girls used a feminine conflict style, "double-voice discourse," which overlays mitigation, effectively softening the force of dispute utterances (Sheldon 1996: 58). Sheldon describes the resources used to navigate disputes as both cooperative as well as competitive. The girls she studied "possess verbal negotiation skills that enable them to confront without being very confrontational; to clarify without backing down; and to use mitigators, indirectness, and even subterfuge to soften the blow while promoting their own wishes" (Sheldon 1996: 61).

Studies of accounts and countermoves during play reveal various degrees of mitigation across groups. Within the pretend play of educationally and socially advantaged White middle-class preschool children both Sheldon (1996) and Barnes and Vangelisti (1995) found interesting uses of framing during disputes. Rather than using the boys' strategy of physical force, highly aggravated talk, or insistence, girls would negotiate or verbally persuade the other for what she wanted. Four-year-old girls displayed an appreciation for the other's needs while trying to get what they wanted from their co-participants (Sheldon 1997). In a conflict exchange during pretend play, girls will often animate a voice other than their own to distance themselves from the direct and confrontational position they are taking up with respect to a present participant. For example, in the midst of a dispute in which a girl is being ostracized, she might protest how others are treating her by animating a toy person in a falsetto voice, saying "Okay, I won't be your brother any *more!*" (Sheldon 1996: 66). Sheldon argues that the "double-voice" dispute strategy of the girls is oppositional rather than passive and contradicts cultural stereotypes of girls.

Sheldon (1996) argues that the forms of justifications she locates in girls' conflict talk have close parallels with the accounts used by White middle-class California preschool girls described by Kyratzis (1992: 327). Kyratzis states that the accounts in girls' disputes "justify the fit of their control move [e.g., directives, plans] to the overall theme or topic . . . in terms of a group goal" (ibid.). Multi-layered accounts also occur in older girls' groups. Hughes, in her research among fourth and fifth grade middle- and upper-middle-class girls playing foursquare in a suburban Philadelphia Quaker school (Hughes 1988, 1991, 1993, 1995), studied the accounts that girls used during the game. When a girl got a friend out she would accompany the move with utterances such as "Sally, I'll get you in!" Though the structure of the game is perceived as competition between individual players, girls cooperate within an implicit informal team structure of friends. As Hughes (1993: 142) argues: "Girls use the rhetoric of 'niceness' and 'friends' to construct and manage competition within a complex group structure, not to avoid it."

Themes of verbal and physical aggression in boys' interaction and indirect aggression among girls are also discussed in the work of Amy Kyratzis on preschoolers' negotiation. Kyratzis (2001b) studied the "emotion talk" of a friendship group of middle-class boys in a university-based preschool where two thirds of the children were Anglo-American and one third were of diverse cultural backgrounds (including Mexican American, African American, and Asian American). Kyratzis found that boys made use of physical acts of aggression ("kick him in the butt"; "smash this girl!") and verbal aggression (put-downs and insults) while assuming an aggressive stance. Kyratzis demonstrates how alignment toward particular gendered notions about the display of emotions (particularly fear) and behavior is not static but rather can change over time, depending on context and social network.

Kyratzis and Ervin-Tripp (1999) analyzed interaction during shared fantasy among four- through seven-year-old best friend dyads in predominantly middle-class preschool classrooms of a university-based children's center; the children were 67 per cent Caucasian and 33 per cent Asian, Latino, Middle Eastern, and African American. They found that younger children, especially four-year-old boys, spend their time disputing how to maintain a joint fantasy, arguing over goods and space; girls attend to sustaining the pretend play through the developing of play employment (designing planning in the voice of directors or scriptwriters in a sequence of dramatic actions) and enactment. The preferred activity settings of boys and girls (arguing versus story retelling) makes a difference for the development of the narrative devices of global marking and ideational marking (Kyratzis and Ervin-Tripp 1999: 1322–4); girls develop these markings first because of their greater involvement in sustaining narrative-potential activities. Kyratzis (1999), in another study of creating shared fantasy with the same group of children, found that girls make more extensive use of the medium of storytelling than boys for crafting notions of possible selves. Girls make use of stories to position themselves within a form of social hierarchy (delineating who is inside and outside the group), and to explore notions of ethnic identity. The characters the girls enacted suggested their value of qualities of lovingness, graciousness, and attractiveness. Important figures for the boys to enact were Power Rangers and Smashers; the themes they developed were the powerful smasher and his weak victims.

In my own studies within an African American working-class community I found that boys, ages four to fourteen, like those described by Berentzen (1984), were concerned with comparing themselves in the endless cycle of games, verbal dueling, and narrative and activities they participated in. Conflict was enjoyed and cooperatively sustained over extended rounds of arguments and insults, without summoning adult intervention. The comparisons resulted in a fluid rather than fixed social ranking. Both boys and girls used direct or bald on-record ways of disputing in cross-sex interaction.

From fourth to seventh grade the proportion of boys involved in physical aggression with others increases to two thirds of the conflicts (Cairns and Cairns 1994: 57). Sociologists Adler and Adler (1998), studying peer groups of predominantly White, middle-class US preadolescent children ages eight to twelve (over a seven-year period), report that among boys "displaying traits such as toughness, troublemaking, domination, coolness, and interpersonal bragging and sparring skills" were important for popularity (ibid.: 55). Eder (1995), in her study of 12- to 14-year-old middle- to lower-class Euro-American children from both rural and urban backgrounds in a middle school on the outskirts of a medium-sized Midwestern community, found that boys fought both on and off the playing field to establish relative rank; physical aggression was considered the appropriate way to deal with interpersonal conflicts. Boys conveyed the importance of being tough through joint storytelling and ritual insults. Insulting or humiliating others was an acceptable means of gaining or demonstrating higher status. Weakness or interest in associating with girls was emphasized through calling someone a "squirt" or "wimp" or using terms associated with femininity or homosexuality such as "pussy," "girl," "fag," and "queer." In his study of preadolescents in Little League baseball teams Fine (1987: 79) finds that appropriate "moral themes" for behaving properly include displaying appropriate emotions, being tough or fearful when necessary, controlling one's aggression and fears, being a good sport, publicly showing a desire to win, and not betraying the bond of age-mates. Eckert's (1987, 2000) study of "the social order of Belten High" in suburban Detroit found that masculinity, toughness, and power were important for the distinct social groups of "jocks" and "burnouts" alike.

4 Gender and Ethnicity in Children's Disputes

Early work on the pragmatics of politeness examined how adult speakers display deference to their interlocutors (Goffman 1967; Brown and Levinson 1978) and work to minimize disagreement in conversation (Pomerantz 1984; Sacks 1987). However, as argued by Atkinson and Drew (1979), Goodwin (1983), Bilmes (1988), and Kotthoff (1993), within the context of argumentation the preferred next action is disagreement.

Aggravated disagreement is an activity that children work to achieve (Goodwin 1983: 675; Evaldsson and Corsaro 1998). Children engage in "character contests" (Goffman 1967: 237–8) to construct their social identities, form friendships, and reconfigure the social order of the peer group. Conflict and cooperation often exist within the same activities (Goodwin 1990: 84). The African American children I studied in Philadelphia were constantly engaging in playful disputes (Goodwin 1985, 1990). Corsaro (1997), studying "oppositional talk" of a group of Midwestern African American working-class children, found playful and teasing confrontational talk similarly used "to construct social identities, cultivate friendships, and both maintain and transform the social order of their peer group" (Corsaro 1997: 146). In studies of dispute across three groups (Italians, working-class African Americans, and White middle- and upper-class groups) Corsaro (1997) found disputes more serious and emotionally intense for Whites than they were for children of other ethnic groups or social classes. For Italian and African American children oppositional talk provides a way of displaying character (see also Morgan 1999: 37) and affirming affiliation to the norms of peer culture. *Discussione* or highly stylized and dramatic public debate (Corsaro 1997: 160) constitutes an important form of verbal interaction in both Italian adult and peer culture. *Discussione* is valued because it provides a way for children to debate things that matter to them "and in the process to develop a shared sense of control over their social world" (Corsaro 1997: 145). *Discussione* can even take over teacher-directed activities while children sustain talk about a topic of their own choosing.

While ritual insult is generally associated with African American males (Kochman 1972; Labov 1972) both Eder (1990), studying White girls, and Goodwin (1990), studying African American girls, have found that working-class girls participate in ritual insult, and develop competitive and self-defense skills. Eder (1990) reports that among working- and lower-class girls ritual insult is used as a form of "wit assessment device" (Goffman 1971: 179). According to Eder (1990: 82), "insulting skills would not only allow these females to assert and defend their rights, but might also contribute to an impression of greater intelligence and wit, since quick and clever responses are often viewed as an indicator of general cleverness and intelligence." When girls enjoyed humorous teasing bouts with boys they mocked the traditional gender role stereotypes of middle-class White girls who are routinely "educated in romance" (Holland and Eisenhart 1990). Eder suggests that ritual insult may be more likely to occur among groups of girls where "toughness" is valued.

In cross-sex disputes as well as during same-sex pretend play African American girls make use of direct assertive argumentative forms, in extended sequences of negotiation with clear displays of status differences. For example, the preadolescent girls I studied playing mothers monitor the actions of participants with utterances such as "Brenda play right. That's why nobody want you for a child!" (Goodwin 1990: 131).

Within cross-sex interaction, playful exchanges such as the following are common (transcription conventions are given at the end of the chapter):

(1) *Billy has been teasing Martha about her hair.*

Billy:	Heh heh!
Martha:	I don't know what you *laugh*in at.
Billy:	I know what I'm laughin at.
	Your *head*.
Martha:	I know I'm laughin at *your* head too.
Billy:	You know you ain't laughin
	cuz you ain't laughin.
Martha:	Ha ha ((*mirthless laughter*))
Billy:	Ha ha. I got more hair than *you*.
Martha:	You do not. Why you gotta laugh.
	You *know* you ain't got more hair than me.

Through forms of tying techniques (Sacks 1992) or format tying (Goodwin 1990: 177) children use phonological, syntactic, and semantic surface structure features of prior turns at talk to produce next turns. They explore in an almost musical way the structuring of utterances they are producing in oppositional discourse. Corsaro and Maynard (1996) found forms of format tying in the disputes of children in a *scuola materna* (Italian preschool) in Bologna, Italy, as well as in three American Midwestern children's groups: (1) predominantly White middle- and upper-middle-class children in a private developmental learning center; (2) African American children of working-class background in a Head Start Center (a pre-school aimed at preparing children for school); and (3) a first grade class of White middle-class children. Corsaro and Maynard (1996: 164) argue that debates constructed through format tying among Italian children are conducted for "a clear enjoyment of their display of knowledge about the world" while for Head Start children the purpose seemed to be winning, displaying self, building solidarity, and testing emerging friendships. Disputes among the White groups contrast with the highly stylized debates of the Italian and Head Start children in that they are often "more predictable, linear and based on a simple inversion format" (ibid.: 168) (denial–assertion opposition) and, "rather than displaying a variety of related threats or rivalries, the tying technique is monotopical" (ibid.: 171).

My studies of bilingual Spanish/English-speaking working-class elementary school girls (primarily second generation Central Americans and Mexican Americans) show that children intermix playfulness and conflict during games with ease (Goodwin 1998). Within the game of hopscotch, calling fouls and providing counters to such calls are expected next moves. In contrast to adult polite talk in which disagreement is dispreferred, often delayed and minimized through various features of turn design (Sacks 1987; Pomerantz 1984), in adversarial talk (Atkinson and Drew 1979) during children's games, "out" calls occur without doubt or delay (see also Goodwin 1985; Evaldsson and Corsaro 1998).

By way of example, in the following sequence, after Gloria makes a problematic move Carla immediately produces a strong expression of opposition, what Goffman (1978) has called a "response cry," "EY::!" which is immediately followed by a negative person descriptor "CHIRIONA" and then an explanation for why the move is illegal. By using the negative person descriptor *chiriona* meaning "cheater" a judge argues not simply that an infraction has occurred, but that the person who committed the foul is accountable in a very strong way for its occurrence. Following the opposition preface a referee further elaborates a reason for the "out" call.

(2)	Gloria:	*((jumps from square 3 to 2 changing feet))*	**Problematic Move**
	Carla:	!EY::! !CHIRIONA!	**Response Cry +**
		!MIRA!	**Negative Person Descriptor**
		Hey! Cheater! Look!	
		TE VENISTES DE AQUÍ	**Explanation**
		ASÍ!	
		You came from here like this.	
		((demonstrating how Gloria jumped	
		changing feet))	

Characteristic features of opposition turns in hopscotch include prefaces (response cries or polarity markers), which can be produced with dramatic pitch leaps, a negative person descriptor, and explanations stating the violation, often accompanied by embodied demonstrations. Children's disputes call for an intonation which makes opposition salient; pitch contours on negatives frequently accentuate rather than mitigate opposition (Goodwin, in press). While Carla's normal voice range is around 300–350 Hz, her pitch leaps to 621 Hz over the syllable /o/ of *chiriona*. In addition "EY::!" is produced with a dramatic bitonal contour and extended vowel duration.

While the forms of opposition turns are similar across a range of groups I have studied (second generation Central American and Mexican bilingual Spanish/English speakers in Los Angeles; an ESL (English as second language) class in Columbia, South Carolina, which includes newly arrived immigrant children from Saudi Arabia, Vietnam, China, Mexico, Puerto Rico, Korea, and Azerbaijan; fifth grade African American children of migrant farmworkers in rural South Carolina; working-class African American children ages four to thirteen in a Philadelphia neighborhood; and a peer group that includes mixed social classes and ethnicities in a progressive Southern California elementary school), the forms of affective stances (Goodwin 1998, 2000b), intonation contours, as well as terms of address, differ across children's groups. Working-class African American girls used terms such as "honey" and "punk" in oppositional same-sex talk; boys used terms such as "stupid," "dummy," "sucker," "big lips," "knucklehead," and "boy" in their same-sex oppositional talk. During the games of the ESL class I videotaped in Columbia, South Carolina, address terms depicting the recipient in a negative way were not used. In the same class, however, terms such as *tramposa* 'cheater', *embustera* 'liar', *chapusera* 'big cheater', *huevona* 'stinker', and *cabrona* 'bitch', were used with frequency in the "out" calls of fifth grade immigrant Puerto Rican and Mexican girls playing hopscotch together.

In contrast to studies of Latina women which accentuate forms of passivity or an ethos of collectivity (Greenfield and Cocking 1994), I found bilingual Spanish/English speakers in three separate groups involved in vivid assertive talk. Farr's (2000) studies of immigrant women from Michoacan, Mexico, in Chicago also document an assertive style of talking in which females make use of bald, on-record directives that, rather than humbling the speaker, support a stance of independence and toughness. Other sociolinguistic research on Latina women (Galindo 1992, 1994; Galindo and Gonzales Velásquez 1992; Mendoza-Denton 1994, 1996) has challenged stereotypic formulations of Latina women's speech as non-competitive.

By making language choices alternative to those of the Latina girls it is possible to construct actors, events, and social organization in a very different way (Goodwin 1998). White, middle-class Southern girls counter problematic moves in hopscotch with utterances such as "I think that's sort of on the line though" or "Uh – your foot's in the wrong spot" or "You – accidentally jumped on that. But that's okay." Rather than highlighting opposition these girls mitigate their foul calls through hedges such as "I think," "accidentally," and "sort of," and display uncertainty about the accuracy of the call. Absent from the way these girls play the game is any articulation of strong stances or accountability for one's actions.

5   Political Processes and Forms of Exclusion in Girls' Groups

Longitudinal studies by psychologists Cairns and Cairns (1994) studying fourth through tenth grade girls find that ostracism resulting from girls' disputes increases with age; from the fourth to the tenth grade the percentage of female/female conflicts involving themes of alienation, ostracism, or character defamation rose from 14 to 56 per cent (Cairns and Cairns 1994: 57). Exclusion has been documented in White middle-class elementary and middle school children's groups (Best 1983; Eder and Hallinan 1978; Adler and Adler 1998). With the exception of work by Eder and Sanford (1986), Goodwin (1982, 1990, 2000a), and Shuman (1986, 1992), little has been done to document the forms of language through which girls actually practice exclusion. Close examination of the language used in girls' disputes within narrative (Kyratzis 2000) and pretend play (Sheldon 1996) reveals that girls as young as four practice forms of exclusion.

African American girls are skillful at orchestrating confrontations between other girls through forms of storytelling they called "instigating" (Goodwin 1982, 1990). Instigating occurs when someone is accused of having talked about another girl in her absence, considered a "capital offense" in African American culture (Morgan 1999: 34). The forms of social manipulation which occur in instigating could be considered a form of "indirect aggression" (Bjorkqvist, Osterman, and Kaukiainen 1992: 53). Instigating entails telling pejorative stories about an absent party with the intent of inciting a present listener, portrayed as someone offended by the absent party, to confront the offending absent party. New alignments of the social order result from instigating – sanctioning the behavior of one of the peer group members, without the instigator herself being a participant in the eventual confrontation. Accusations are always framed as reports learned about through a third absent party, as in "Terry said that you said that I wasn't gonna go around Poplar no more!" The framing of the accusation in this way leaves open the possibility of a denial or a countermove, arguing that the intermediate party was making something up with the intent to start a fight.

While the confrontations I observed among preadolescent girls were conducted through assertive verbal actions – accusations, counter-accusations, and denials – Morgan (1999: 35) stresses that instigating among older African American girls can lead to physical confrontations. Shuman (1992: 149) investigated similar speech events among African American, White (Polish American and Irish American), and Puerto Rican working-class girls in middle school in inner-city Philadelphia; she found, however, that talking about fights provided a way of avoiding fighting: "the 'fight' consisted entirely of words, reports of what people said to one another, and reported speech consisted primarily of a description of offenses, accusations, and threats" (ibid.: 151).

Ethnographic fieldwork permits analysis of the continuum from conflict to aggression in children's verbal interaction. I conducted fieldwork at a Southern California elementary school among a group of girls of various ethnicities who regularly ate lunch and played together, and observed the clique over a three-year period as they passed from fourth to sixth grade. Forms of exclusion were quite evident in the clique with respect to their interactions with a "tagalong" – a person defined in terms of her efforts to affiliate to a particular group without being accepted by the group. Across a range of different speech activities, including storytelling in which the target is described in a derogatory manner, ritual and personal insult, and bald imperatives during recess play (Goodwin 2000a), girls sanction the behavior of the tagalong girl through actions which are totally at odds with the model of cooperative female interaction described in the Separate Worlds Hypothesis.

6 Conclusion

Some models of female interaction, based on White middle-class models, have proposed that "male speakers are socialized into a competitive style of discourse, while women are socialized into a more cooperative style of speech" (Coates 1994: 72). Barnes and Vangelisti (1995: 354) argue that the mitigation in female talk expresses female concerns for "affiliation, reciprocity, and efforts to protect others' face." Such pronouncements about differences in male and female fundamental nature gained sway in the early 1980s with the Separate Worlds Hypothesis, built on static models of child socialization propagated by the culture and personality school in anthropology. All too frequently psychological models, positing traits internal to the individual, have colored research on gender differences in language. When instead we take the lead of sociologists studying children and begin by examining actual social processes, including clique formation (Adler and Adler 1996), we find that conflict is as omnipresent in the interaction of females as in that of males. Forms of social exclusion are endemic to girls' groups (Goodwin 2000a). Extended arguments constructed through turns that highlight rather than mitigate disagreement in Latina (Goodwin 1998, 2000b, in press), African American (Goodwin 1990; Morgan 1999), and lower- and working-class White girls' groups (Eder 1995), as well as groups of mixed ethnicity (Goodwin 2001), call into question the notion that girls are fundamentally interested in cooperative, face-saving interaction.

What is needed to provide a more accurate picture of male and female interaction patterns? We first need to look beyond middle-class White groups and study the diverse social and ethnic groups which compose our society. Second, as we saw in the discussion of disputes constructed through format tying in the section "Gender and Ethnicity in Children's Disputes," making available transcripts of naturally occurring behavior in disputes rather than accounts of disputes, or descriptions of interactional norms, will render possible comparisons across groups differing in terms of ethnicity, gender, and social class. When transcripts are provided we can compare types of turn shapes (the use of response cries, polarity markers, and negative person descriptors) as well as principles of sequential organization, such as format tying, which organize disputes. Examining variation in the forms of person descriptors as well as accounts accompanying opposition turns will allow us to discern differences in the ways categorizations of person are performed and reasons are articulated by girls and boys and members of different ethnic groups and social classes. Finally, we need more ethnographically grounded accounts of children's interaction so that we can merge accounts of moment-to-moment interaction with analysis of social structure (Thorne 2001). Longitudinal studies will allow us to see how gendered forms of interaction vary with context and may change over time.

TRANSCRIPTION CONVENTIONS

Data are transcribed according to a modified version of the system developed by Jefferson and described in Sacks, Schegloff, and Jefferson (1974: 731–3).

Bold italics indicate some form of emphasis.

Lengthening: Colons (::) indicate that the sound immediately preceding has been noticeably lengthened.

Intonation: Punctuation symbols are used to mark intonation changes rather than as grammatical symbols. A period indicates a falling contour. A question mark indicates a rising contour. A comma indicates a falling–rising contour.

Capitals (CAPS) indicate increased volume.

Comments: Double parentheses (( )) enclose material that is not part of the talk being transcribed, frequently indicating gesture or body position.

Italics are used to distinguish comments in parentheses about non-vocal aspects of the interaction.

REFERENCES

Adler, Patricia and Adler, Peter 1996: Preadolescent clique stratification and the hierarchy of identity. *Sociological Inquiry* 66(2): 111–42.

Adler, Patricia A. and Adler, Peter 1998: *Peer Power: Preadolescent Culture and Identity*. New Brunswick, NJ: Rutgers University Press.

Adler, Patricia A., Kless, Steven J., and Adler, Peter 1992: Socialization to gender roles: Popularity among elementary school boys and girls. *Sociology of Education* 65(3): 169–87.

Atkinson, J. Maxwell and Drew, Paul 1979: *Order in Court: The Organisation of Verbal Interaction in Judicial Settings*. London: Macmillan.

Barnes, Melanie K. and Vangelisti, Anita L. 1995: Speaking in a double-voice: Role-making as influence in preschoolers' fantasy play situations. *Research on Language and Social Interaction* 28(4): 351–89.

Berentzen, Sigurd 1984: *Children Constructing Their Social World: An Analysis of Gender Contrast in Children's Interaction in a Nursery School*. Bergen, Norway: Bergen Occasional Papers in Social Anthropology, No. 36, Department of Social Anthropology, University of Bergen.

Best, Raphaela 1983: *We've All Got Scars*. Bloomington: Indiana University Press.

Bilmes, Jack 1988: The concept of preference in conversation analysis. *Language in Society* 17: 161–81.

Bjorkqvist, Kaj and Niemela, Prikko 1992: New trends in the study of female aggression. In Kaj Bjorkqvist and Prikko Niemala (eds) *Of Mice and Women: Aspects of Female Aggression*. San Diego, CA: Academic Press, pp. 1–15.

Bjorkqvist, Kaj, Osterman, Karin, and Kaukiainen, Ari 1992: The development of direct and indirect aggressive strategies in males and females. In Kaj Bjorkqvist and Prikko Niemela (eds) *Of Mice and Women: Aspects of Female Aggression*. San Diego, CA: Academic Press, pp. 51–64.

Boggs, Stephen T. 1978: The development of verbal disputing in part-Hawaiian children. *Language in Society* 7: 325–44.

Brenneis, Donald and Lein, Laura 1977: "You Fruithead": A sociolinguistic approach to children's disputes. In Susan Ervin-Tripp and Claudia Mitchell-Kernan (eds) *Child Discourse*. New York: Academic Press, pp. 49–66.

Brown, Penelope and Levinson, Stephen C. 1978: Universals of language usage: Politeness phenomena. In Esther N. Goody (ed.) *Questions and Politeness Strategies in Social Interaction*. Cambridge: Cambridge University Press, pp. 56–310.

Cairns, Robert B. and Cairns, Beverly D. 1994: *Lifelines and Risks: Pathways of Youth in Our Time*. New York: Cambridge University Press.

Coates, Jennifer 1994: The language of the professions: Discourse and career. In Julia Evetts (ed.) *Women and Career: Themes and Issues in Advanced Industrial Societies*. London: Longman, pp. 72–86.

Cook-Gumperz, Jenny and Szymanski, Margaret 2001: Classroom "families": Cooperating or competing – girls' and boys' interactional styles in a bilingual classroom. *Research on Language and Social Interaction* 34(1): 107–30.

Corsaro, William A. 1994: Discussion, debate, and friendship processes: Peer dispute in U.S. and Italian nursery schools. *Sociology of Education* 67: 1–26.

Corsaro, William A. 1997: *The Sociology of Childhood*. Thousand Oaks, CA: Pine Forge Press.

Corsaro, William A. and Maynard, Douglas W. 1996: Format tying in discussion and argument among Italian and American children. In Dan Isaac Slobin, Julie Gerhardt, Amy Kyratzis, and Jiansheng Guo (eds) *Social Interaction, Social Context, and Language*. Mahwah, NJ: Lawrence Erlbaum Associates, pp. 157–74.

Corsaro, William A. and Rizzo, Thomas 1990: Disputes and conflict resolution among nursery school children in the U.S. and Italy. In Allen Grimshaw (ed.) *Conflict Talk: Sociolinguistic Investigations of Arguments in Conversations*. Cambridge: Cambridge University Press, pp. 21–66.

Danby, Susan 1998: The serious and playful work of gender: Talk and social order in a preschool classroom. In Nicola Yelland (ed.) *Gender in Early Childhood*. London: Routledge, pp. 175–205.

Danby, Susan, and Baker, Carolyn 1998: How to be masculine in the block area. *Childhood* 5(2): 151–75.

Danby, Susan, and Baker, Carolyn 2000: Unraveling the fabric of social order in block area. In S. Hester and D. Francis (eds) *Local Educational Order: Ethnomethodological Studies of Knowledge in Action*. Amsterdam: John Benjamins, pp. 91–140.

Davies, Bronwyn 1989: *Frogs and Snails and Feminist Tales*. Boston: Routledge and Kegan Paul.

Dyson, Anne H. 1994: The Ninjas, the X-men, and the ladies: Playing with power and identity in an urban primary school. *Teachers College Record* 96: 219–39.

Eckert, Penelope 1987: *Jocks and Burnouts: Social Categories in a US High School*. New York: Teachers University Press.

Eckert, Penelope 2000: *Linguistic Variation as Social Practice*. Oxford: Blackwell.

Eder, Donna 1990: Serious and playful disputes: Variation in conflict talk among female adolescents. In Allen D. Grimshaw (ed.) *Conflict Talk: Sociolinguistic Investigations of Arguments in Conversations*. Cambridge: Cambridge University Press, pp. 67–84.

Eder, Donna 1993: "Go get ya a French!": Romantic and sexual teasing among adolescent girls. In Deborah Tannen (ed.) *Gender and Conversational Interaction*. Oxford: Oxford University Press, pp. 32–62.

Eder, Donna 1995: *School Talk: Gender and Adolescent Culture*. New Brunswick, NJ: Rutgers University Press.

Eder, Donna and Hallinan, Maureen T. 1978: Sex differences in children's friendships. *American Sociological Review* 43: 237–50.

Eder, Donna and Sanford, Stephanie 1986: The development and maintenance of interactional norms among early adolescents. In Patricia A. Adler and Peter Adler (eds) *Sociological Studies of Child Development*, vol. 1. Greenwich, CT: JAI Press, pp. 283–300.

Eisenberg, Ann R. and Garvey, Catherine 1981: Children's use of verbal strategies in resolving conflicts. *Discourse Processes* 4: 149–70.

Evaldsson, Ann-Carita and Corsaro, William A. 1998: Play and games in the peer cultures of preschool and preadolescent children: An interpretative approach. *Childhood* 5(4): 377–402.

Farr, Marcia 2000: "¡A mi no me manda nadie!": Individualism and identity in Mexican Ranchero speech. *Pragmatics* 10(1): 61–86.

Farris, Catherine 1991: The gender of child discourse: Same-sex peer socialization through language use in a Taiwanese preschool. *Journal of Linguistic Anthropology* 1: 198–224.

Farris, Catherine E. P. 2000: Cross-sex peer conflict and the discursive production of gender in a Chinese preschool in Taiwan. *Journal of Pragmatics* 32: 539–68.

Fine, Gary Alan 1987: *With the Boys: Little League Baseball and Preadolescent Culture*. Chicago: Chicago University Press.

Galindo, D. Letticia 1992: Dispelling the male-only myth: Chicanas and Calo. *Bilingual Review* 17(1): 3–35.

Galindo, D. Letticia 1994: Capturing Chicana voices: An interdisciplinary approach. In Mary Bucholtz, Anita C. Liang, Laurel A. Sutton, and Caitlin Hines (eds) *Cultural Performances: Proceedings of the Third Berkeley Women and Language Conference*. Berkeley, CA: Berkeley Women and Language Group, University of California, pp. 220–31.

Galindo, D. Letticia and Gonzales
    Velásquez, María Dolores 1992:
    A sociolinguistic description of
    linguistic self-expression, innovation,
    and power among Chicanas in
    Texas and New Mexico. In Kira
    Hall, Mary Bucholtz, and Birch
    Moonwomon (eds) *Locating Power:
    Proceedings of the Second Berkeley
    Women and Language Conference*,
    vol. 1. Berkeley, CA: Berkeley
    Women and Language Group,
    University of California,
    pp. 162–70.
Genishi, Celia and di Paolo, Marianna
    1982: Learning through argument
    in a preschool. In Louise Cherry
    Wilkinson (ed.) *Communicating in
    the Classroom*. New York: Academic
    Press, pp. 49–68.
Gilligan, Carol 1982: *In a Different Voice:
    Psychological Theory and Women's
    Development*. Cambridge, MA:
    Harvard University Press.
Goffman, Erving 1967: *Interaction Ritual:
    Essays in Face to Face Behavior*.
    Garden City, NY: Doubleday.
Goffman, Erving 1971: *Relations in
    Public: Microstudies of the Public
    Order*. New York: Harper and Row.
Goffman, Erving 1978: Response cries.
    Language 54: 787–815.
Goodwin, Marjorie Harness 1980:
    Directive/response speech
    sequences in girls' and boys' task
    activities. In Sally McConnell-Ginet,
    Ruth Borker, and Nelly Furman
    (eds) *Women and Language in
    Literature and Society*. New York:
    Praeger, pp. 157–73.
Goodwin, Marjorie Harness 1982:
    "Instigating": Storytelling as a
    social process. *American Ethnologist*
    9: 799–819.
Goodwin, Marjorie Harness 1983:
    Aggravated correction and
    disagreement in children's
    conversations. *Journal of
    Pragmatics* 7: 657–77.

Goodwin, Marjorie Harness 1985:
    The serious side of jump rope:
    Conversational practices and social
    organization in the frame of play.
    Journal of American Folklore 98:
    315–30.
Goodwin, Marjorie Harness 1990:
    *He-Said-She-Said: Talk as Social
    Organization among Black Children*.
    Bloomington: Indiana University
    Press.
Goodwin, Marjorie Harness 1998: Games
    of stance: Conflict and footing in
    hopscotch. In Susan Hoyle and
    Carolyn Temple Adger (eds) *Kids'
    Talk: Strategic Language Use in Later
    Childhood*. New York: Oxford
    University Press, pp. 23–46.
Goodwin, Marjorie Harness 2000a:
    Constituting the Moral Order in
    Girls' Social Organization: Language
    Practices in the Construction of
    Social Exclusion. Paper presented at
    International Gender and Language
    Association meeting, Stanford,
    California, May 5, 2000. (To
    appear in *Human Development*.)
Goodwin, Marjorie Harness 2000b:
    Morality and accountability in girls'
    play. *Texas Linguistic Forum* 43
    (Proceedings of the Seventh
    Annual Symposium about
    Language and Society, Austin):
    77–86.
Goodwin, Marjorie Harness 2001:
    Organizing participation in
    cross-sex jump rope: Situating
    gender differences within
    longitudinal studies of activities.
    *Research on Language and Social
    Interaction*, Special Issue: *Gender
    Construction in Children's Interactions:
    A Cultural Perspective*, 4(1): 75–106.
Goodwin, Marjorie Harness (in press):
    Multi-modality in girls' game
    disputes. *Journal of Pragmatics*.
Greenfield, Patricia Marks and Cocking,
    Rodney R. 1994: *Cross-Cultural Roots
    of Minority Child Development*.

Hillsdale, NJ: Lawrence Erlbaum Associates.

Grimshaw, Allen D. 1990: Introduction. In Allen D. Grimshaw (ed.) *Conflict Talk: Sociolinguistic Investigations of Arguments in Conversations.* Cambridge: Cambridge University Press, pp. 1–20.

Guo, Jiansheng 2000: When Do Chinese Girls Order Boys Around? Culture and Context in Gender Differences in Communicative Strategies by 5-year-old Mandarin-speaking Children. Paper presented at International Gender and Language Association, Stanford, California.

Harding, Susan 1975: Women and words in a Spanish village. In Rayna Reiter (ed.) *Towards an Anthropology of Women.* New York: Monthly Review Press, pp. 283–308.

Henley, Nancy M. 1995: Ethnicity and gender issues in language. In Hope Landrine (ed.) *Bringing Cultural Diversity to Feminist Psychology: Theory, Research, and Practice.* Washington, DC: American Psychological Association, pp. 361–96.

Holland, Dorothy C. and Eisenhart, Margaret A. 1990: *Educated in Romance: Women, Achievement, and College Culture.* Chicago: University of Chicago Press.

Hughes, Linda A. 1988: "But that's not really mean": Competing in a cooperative mode. *Sex Roles* 19: 669–87.

Hughes, Linda A. 1991: A conceptual framework for the study of children's gaming. *Play and Culture* 4: 284–301.

Hughes, Linda A. 1993: "You have to do it with style": Girls' games and girls' gaming. In Susan T. Hollis, Linda Pershing, and M. Jane Young (eds) *Feminist Theory and the Study of Folklore.* Urbana: University of Illinois Press, pp. 130–48.

Hughes, Linda A. 1995: Children's games and gaming. In Brian Sutton-Smith, Jay Mechling, and Thomas Johnson (eds) *A Handbook of Children's Folklore.* Washington, DC: Smithsonian Institution Press, pp. 93–119.

Kochman, Thomas 1972: Toward an ethnography of Black American speech behavior. In Thomas Kochman (ed.) *Rappin' and Stylin' Out: Communication in Urban Black America.* Chicago: University of Illinois Press, pp. 241–64.

Kotthoff, Helga 1993: Disagreement and concession in disputes: On the context sensitivity of preference structures. *Language in Society* 22: 193–216.

Kyratzis, Amy 1992: Gender differences in children's persuasive justifications during pretend play. In Kira Hall, Mary Bucholtz, and Birch Moonwomon (eds) *Locating Power: Proceedings of the Second Berkeley Women and Language Conference.* Berkeley, CA: Berkeley Women and Language Group, University of California, pp. 326–37.

Kyratzis, Amy 1999: Narrative identity: Preschoolers' self-construction through narrative in same-sex friendship group dramatic play. *Narrative Inquiry* 9(2): 427–55.

Kyratzis, Amy 2000: Tactical uses of narratives. *Discourse Processes* 29(3): 269–99.

Kyratzis, Amy 2001a: Children's gender indexing in language: From the separate worlds hypothesis to considerations of culture, context, and power. *Research on Language and Social Interaction*, Special Issue: *Gender Construction in Children's Interactions: A Cultural Perspective*, 4(1): 1–13.

Kyratzis, Amy 2001b: Constituting the emotions: A longitudinal study of emotion talk in a preschool

friendship group of boys. In Bettina
Baron and Helga Kotthoff (eds)
*Gender in Interaction: Perspectives
on Femininity and Masculinity in
Ethnography and Discourse.*
Amsterdam: John Benjamins,
pp. 51–74.

Kyratzis, Amy and Ervin-Tripp, Susan
1999: The development of discourse
markers in peer interaction. *Journal
of Pragmatics* 31: 1321–38.

Kyratzis, Amy and Guo, Jiansheng
1996: "Separate worlds for girls and
boys?" Views from U.S. and Chinese
mixed-sex friendship groups. In
Dan Slobin, Julie Gerhardt, Amy
Kyratzis, and Jiansheng Guo (eds)
*Social Interaction, Social Context, and
Language.* Mahwah, NJ: Lawrence
Erlbaum, pp. 555–78.

Kyratzis, Amy and Guo, Jiansheng 2001:
Preschool girls' and boys' verbal
conflict strategies in the U.S. and
China: Cross-cultural and contextual
considerations. *Research on Language
and Social Interaction,* Special Issue:
*Gender Construction in Children's
Interactions: A Cultural Perspective,*
4(1): 45–74.

Labov, William 1972: Rules for ritual
insults. In *Language in the Inner
City: Studies in the Black English
Vernacular.* Philadelphia: University
of Pennsylvania Press, pp. 297–353.

Labov, William and Fanshel, David 1977:
*Therapeutic Discourse: Psychotherapy
as Conversation.* New York:
Academic Press.

Lagerspetz, Kirsti M. J., Bjorkqvist, Kaj,
and Peltonen, Tarja 1988: Is indirect
aggression typical of females?
Gender differences in aggressiveness
in 11- to 12-year-old children.
Aggressive Behavior 14: 403–14.

Leaper, Campbell 1994: Exploring the
consequences of gender segregation
on social relationships. *New
Directions for Child Development*
65 (Fall): 67–86.

Lever, Janet Rae 1978: Sex differences in
the complexity of children's play
and games. *American Sociological
Review* 43: 471–83.

Maccoby, Eleanor E. 1990: Gender and
relationships: A developmental
account. *American Psychologist*
45(4): 513–20.

Maccoby, Eleanor E. 1998: *The Two Sexes:
Growing Up Apart, Coming Together.*
Cambridge, MA: Harvard University
Press.

Maccoby, Eleanor Emmons and Jacklin,
Carol Nagy 1974: *The Psychology of
Sex Differences.* Stanford, CA:
Stanford University Press.

Maltz, Daniel N. and Borker, Ruth A.
1982: A cultural approach to male–
female miscommunication. In John J.
Gumperz (ed.) *Language and Social
Identity.* Cambridge: Cambridge
University Press, pp. 196–216.

Maynard, Douglas W. 1985a: How
children start arguments.
Language in Society 14: 1–29.

Maynard, Douglas W. 1985b: On the
functions of social conflict among
children. *American Sociological
Review* 50: 207–23.

Mendoza-Denton, Norma 1994:
Language attitudes and gang
affiliation among California Latina
girls. In Mary Bucholtz, Anita C.
Liang, Laurel A. Sutton, and Caitlin
Hines (eds) *Cultural Performances:
Proceedings of the Third Berkeley
Women and Language Conference.*
Berkeley, CA: Berkeley Women
and Language Group, University
of California, pp. 478–86.

Mendoza-Denton, Norma 1996: "Muy
Macha": Gender and ideology in
gang-girls' discourse about makeup.
Ethnos 6(91–2): 47–63.

Morgan, Marcyliena 1999: No woman no
cry: Claiming African American
women's place. In Mary Bucholtz,
Anita C. Liang, and Laurel A.
Sutton (eds) *Reinventing Identities:*

The Gendered Self in Discourse. New York: Oxford University Press, pp. 27–45.

Nakamura, Keiko 2001: Gender and language use in Japanese preschool children. *Research on Language and Social Interaction* 34(1): 15–44.

Pomerantz, Anita 1984: Agreeing and disagreeing with assessments: Some features of preferred/dispreferred turn shapes. In J. Maxwell Atkinson and John Heritage (eds) *Structures of Social Action: Studies in Conversation Analysis.* Cambridge: Cambridge University Press, pp. 57–101.

Rizzo, Thomas A. 1992: The role of conflict in children's friendship development. *New Directions for Child Development* 58 (Winter): 93–111.

Sachs, Jacqueline 1987: Preschool boys' and girls' language use in pretend play. In Susan Philips, Susan Steele, and Christine Tanz (eds) *Language, Gender and Sex in Comparative Perspective.* Cambridge: Cambridge University Press, pp. 178–88.

Sacks, Harvey 1987: On the preferences for agreement and contiguity in sequences in conversation. In Graham Button and John R. E. Lee (eds) *Talk and Social Organisation.* Clevedon, England: Multilingual Matters, pp. 54–69.

Sacks, Harvey 1992: *Lectures on Conversation,* vol. 1. Edited by Gail Jefferson, with an Introduction by Emanuel A. Schegloff. Oxford: Blackwell.

Sacks, Harvey, Schegloff, Emanuel A., and Jefferson, Gail 1974: A simplest systematics for the organization of turn-taking for conversation. *Language* 50: 696–735.

Schofield, Janet Ward 1981: Complementary and conflicting identities: Images and interaction in an interracial school. In Steven R. Asher and John M. Gottman (eds)

The Development of Children's Friendships. Cambridge: Cambridge University Press, pp. 53–90.

Schofield, Janet 1982: *Black and White in School: Trust, Tension, or Tolerance?* New York: Praeger.

Shantz, Carolyn Uhlinger 1983: Social cognition. In John H. Flavell and Ellen M. Markman (eds) *Handbook of Child Psychology* (4th edn), vol. 3: *Cognitive Development.* New York: John Wiley & Sons, 495–555.

Shantz, Carolyn Uhlinger 1987: Conflicts between children. *Child Development* 58: 283–305.

Sheldon, Amy 1993: Pickle fights: Gendered talk in preschool disputes. In Deborah Tannen (ed.) *Gender and Conversational Interaction.* Oxford: Oxford University Press, pp. 83–109.

Sheldon, Amy 1996: "You can be the baby brother, but you aren't born yet": Preschool girls' negotiation for power and access in pretend play. *Research on Language and Social Interaction* 29(1): 57–80.

Sheldon, Amy 1997: Talking power: Girls, gender enculturation and discourse. In Ruth Wodak (ed.) *Gender and Discourse.* London: Sage, pp. 225–44.

Shuman, Amy 1986: *Storytelling Rights: The Uses of Oral and Written Texts by Urban Adolescents.* Cambridge: Cambridge University Press.

Shuman, Amy 1992: "Get outa my face": Entitlement and authoritative discourse. In Jane H. Hill and Judith T. Irvine (eds) *Responsibility and Evidence in Oral Discourse.* Cambridge: Cambridge University Press, pp. 135–60.

Streeck, Jürgen 1986: Towards reciprocity: Politics, rank and gender in the interaction of a group of schoolchildren. In Jenny Cook-Gumperz, William A. Corsaro, and Jürgen Streeck (eds) *Children's Worlds and Children's Language.*

Berlin: Mouton de Gruyter,
pp. 295–326.

Thorne, Barrie 1986: Girls and boys
together . . . but mostly apart:
Gender arrangements in elementary
school. In William W. Hartup and
Zick Rubin (eds) *Relationships and
Development*. Hillsdale, NJ: Lawrence
Erlbaum, pp. 167–84.

Thorne, Barrie 1993: *Gender Play*. New
Brunswick, NJ: Rutgers University
Press.

Thorne, Barrie 2001: Gender and
interaction: Widening the conceptual
scope. In Bettina Baron and Helga
Kotthoff (eds) *Gender in Interaction:*

*Perspectives on Femininity and
Masculinity in Ethnography and
Discourse*. Amsterdam: John
Benjamins, pp. 3–18.

Vasquez, Olga, Pease-Alvarez, Lucinda,
and Shannon, Sheila M. 1994:
*Pushing Boundaries: Language and
Culture in a Mexicano Community*.
New York: Cambridge University
Press.

Whiting, Beatrice Blyth and Edwards,
Carolyn Pope 1988: *Children of
Different Worlds: The Formation of
Social Behavior*. Cambridge, MA:
Harvard University Press.

11 The Power of Gender Ideologies in Discourse

SUSAN U. PHILIPS

1 Introduction

Shortly after I began my second period of fieldwork in Tonga in 1987, my Tongan research assistant, Amalia, a young woman from the village where I was living, invited me to a memorial gathering for her grandmother. "A memorial gathering?" Siale, the head of my own Tongan household, was puzzled. He had never heard of such a thing. Perhaps it was a new Mormon invention, certainly not something the Free Wesleyan Church ever sponsored. Siale's assumption that Mormonism had something to do with this mysterious event spoke volumes about the salience of Christian religious identities in Tonga. I knew huge resources were being poured into the event in terms of money for food and labor for the food preparation. I wondered, was it ego-centric for me to fear that my own pumping of cash into the local economy through my assistant's wages, in a context in which cash was not easy to come by, was altering cultural practices? When I got to the home where the event was being held, I was hooked up with a friend of the family who I was told would translate for me during the speeches. I needed more people to work for me and I knew that this woman's skills at translation of Tongan texts were being put on display. And translate she did, almost word for word as one person after another got up and tremulously remembered the woman being honored by this event.

The testimony with the greatest impact on me was that of the deceased woman's husband. He tearfully recalled how much love she showed for her family. She cooked for them, she washed clothes for them by hand, since they had no washing machine, and she always made sure none of her children left the house for school unless they were wearing immaculately clean clothing, freshly ironed without a wrinkle. I was startled by this testimony. It sounded as if the man's marriage came right out of a 1950s American family television program, like *Father Knows Best*. What did it mean? Was this a recent Mormon importation? Had Tongan marriage pervasively been influenced by Western imagery? Or was I attributing too much power to European colonialism and failing to recognize the local Tongan elements in what was being expressed?

When I got home that night, following the feast that concluded the event, Siale asked me how things had gone, what the memorial had been about. "Oh, they talked about what they remembered about her – people like her husband, her children, and friends of the family." He seemed slightly offended. "We remember things about the people we loved too," he said, "but we don't have to talk about it in public." I knew the "we" had to do with Mormons versus Free Wesleyans. But I was also aware that he had lost his own wife of forty years only a short time before, too, like the husband of the woman remembered at the memorial. So I was not surprised when he then went on to say, "When my wife was alive, she always made sure that any of us who left the house had on clean ironed clothes with no holes." He laughed, but he misted over a little as he laughed. I felt a little misty myself that this "Old Testament kind of a guy," as one American described him, or any man for that matter, should still have tender feelings for a wife after so many years together.

At the same time, inside I registered a small astonishment. Siale had talked about his wife in exactly the same terms as the man remembering his wife in the memorial event! And it was not because I had told him the specifics of what had been said at the memorial, because I had been careful not to – I had felt a little guarded in giving an account of my evening's experience because I did not know the possible consequences of anything I might report, and I was being deliberately vague; indeed, I did not know Siale well at that time. Regardless of where these ideas had come from (how Tongan, how European), I felt I was witnessing a conventionalized Tongan representation of the wifely role that had earlier appeared in a formal public event, but that was now appearing in an everyday private conversation.

In truth, the American feminist in me was mildly appalled. Was *this* what a woman was valued for? Ironing? I could hardly think of an activity I valued less myself. I had certainly systematically organized my life to avoid ironing as much as possible. I remembered my own aunt ironing all her sheets – what a waste of time! And wasn't this valuing of women as housewives precisely what presented a trap for them in American society? In order to be regarded, and to be seen as showing their regard for others, they were expected to choose mind-numbing, repetitive tasks over other more open-ended, creative, and interesting ways of showing that same regard. And here it seemed that young Tongan women like my research assistant were being exposed to the same kind of gender ideology in discourse.

Clearly I had brought feminist concerns about the nature and impact of gender ideologies into the field with me, but this was just the beginning of my effort to take what I learned about gender ideologies in Tonga and relate that knowledge to broader issues in feminist anthropology.

My purpose in this chapter is to show how an interest in the power of gender ideologies in discourse developed in linguistic anthropology, and to locate what I went on to learn about gender ideologies in Tonga within that tradition. I first take up how gender ideologies emerged as a factor in men's domination of women in the political theory of the women's movement of the late 1960s and early 1970s. Then I discuss how feminist anthropologists took up the topic in cross-cultural research. This work emphasized men's control over the public sphere and women's exclusion from the public sphere as an exercise of power that was bolstered and justified by negative gender ideologies about women. Cultural and linguistic anthropologists documented women's resistance to this domination in specific ideologically laden genres of discourse. Awareness of such opposition in turn encouraged more general documentation of diversity in gender ideologies and of the way these were ordered into relations of domination and subordination. The final major section of the chapter focuses on the need to re-locate relations of ideological domination and subordination not just in discourse, but in the institutional contexts in which discourse occurs. Such a situating is desirable in part because of the *practical* need to better understand which ideologies are more powerful and why, so that we can enhance their positive effects for women and ameliorate their negative effects.

2   The Political Roots of the Interest in Gender Ideology

The Women's Liberation Movement of the late 1960s and 1970s, which started in the United States and then spread to Europe and other parts of the world, was an important stimulus for cross-cultural research on gender ideologies, and the politics of the movement significantly influenced this research as it emerged in the early 1970s. The most general political position of the Women's Liberation Movement that shaped the study of gender ideologies was the view that women are not equal to men in American society. They do not have the same control over their own lives and the lives of others that men have. They are dominated by men in their family life, in the workplace, and in other social domains as well, particularly religion and politics.

This domination, it was argued, is bolstered by patriarchal gender ideologies that provided justification for men's domination of women. The term "patriarchal" was used to refer to ideologies that either assumed or asserted that men should dominate women, have authority over them, and tell them what to do. The use of the term "ideology" in this context had Marxist connotations. It suggested that the dominant view was one that served male interest in keeping women subordinated, without women necessarily recognizing that this was the case. Here women were seen as dominated by men in the way Marx had argued the working class was ideologically dominated by the bourgeoisie in nineteenth-century Europe. And, just as Marx had argued that an ideological critique of bourgeois ideology was needed to help the working class recognize that the present order was not necessarily in their interest and that they should resist it, so too feminists argued for the need for ideological critique of patriarchal ideology. In replacing class with gender, feminists deeply undermined the privileging of class as the primary relation of domination and subordination of interest to the social sciences, and made power central to the study of women and gender.

The American patriarchal ideology that received the greatest attention in the women's movement was the view that women are biologically inferior to men – less intelligent, physically weaker, less aggressive, and more emotional – in ways ultimately explained by differences in their biological make-up. But this was and is not the only patriarchal gender ideology in the United States or elsewhere. Biological differences between women and men are not always involved. Nor is women's inferiority always asserted. Neither is necessary for a patriarchal gender ideology. What is necessary is that there be a cultural understanding that men should have power and authority over women that women should not have over themselves or men. And some would argue that the more implicit and taken for granted this assumption is, the more powerful it is.

The role of language in expressing gender ideologies and in maintaining ideological domination over women was also articulated in the Women's Liberation Movement from its inception, and awareness of that role rapidly moved from women's consciousness-raising groups into the university along with the interest in gender ideology. While Lakoff's (1973) analysis of the ways in which particular semantic and morphological processes conveyed negative attitudes toward women marked the beginning of a tradition of analysis of such processes in linguistics, a separate tradition focusing on gender ideology in discourse emerged in anthropology, our concern here.

3   Gender Ideology in Anthropology

Anthropology's response to these ideas emerged in the early 1970s at a time when ideas were passing rapidly across the boundary between grassroots political activity and the university. The testimony to this rapid boundary crossing is the number of papers in which similar ideas about the sources of men's greater power emerged in the anthropological literature. I will focus on five such papers here that can be viewed as both pivotal and representative of these ideas.

Central here is Sherry Ortner's (1974) paper, "Is Female to Male as Nature Is to Culture?" In this very Lévi-Straussian structuralist analysis, Ortner argued that in all cultures women are seen as closer to nature than men by virtue of their involvement in the biological reproduction of the species, while men are seen as closer to culture. Culture, in turn, is more highly valued by humans in their efforts to distinguish themselves from the rest of the animal world. This provides a basis for the assertion of male superiority over women. Ortner's view was quickly taken up, empirically examined in a range of cultures, and found to have a basis in many societies (e.g. Ortner and Whitehead 1981; MacCormack and Strathern 1980). But it was also quickly criticized by others, most obviously on the grounds that not all gender ideologies are of this sort. Even within American society, while men may have controlled the arts and sciences historically, and in this sense are more associated with what is thought of as high culture, they are also symbolically associated with an animal-like aggressiveness, as in such familiar male images as the Big Bad Wolf and the Wolf Man.

The influence of Ortner's article was bolstered by the even more influential Introduction to the volume it was published in, by Michelle Rosaldo (1974), who incorporated Ortner's views into her own. Rosaldo argued that cross-culturally, and apparently in all times and social orders, both women and men have authority in the domestic sphere, but overwhelmingly men have authority in the public sphere. Like Ortner, Rosaldo saw this asymmetry as based in women's reproductive roles, which kept their activities tied to the domestic sphere. And she argued that this arrangement was also bolstered by the kind of gender ideology Ortner described, which associated women with nature and men with culture, an association that gave men superiority over women and justified their control over the public sphere.

Almost simultaneously, in a paper entitled "Men and Women in the South of France: Public and Private Domains," Rayna Reiter (1975) similarly argued that men have power by virtue of participation in the public domain that women lack in being limited to the private sphere. On the one hand, Reiter carefully documented what she meant by this in the context of a French Alps village, describing in detail the social geographies that segregated the sexes. The public sphere meant public institutions such as government and church, as well as the world of cafés where men socialized. And she also noted exceptions to her own generalizations. For example, it was predominantly women who went to church, even though men controlled the church, and women went to shops during hours when men were scarcely seen in public. On another level, Reiter limited her generalizations about the greater power of men by virtue of their control of the public sphere to societies in which state formation had taken place. She argued that the tendency in kin-based societies for men to be more involved in politics was greatly elaborated and institutionalized through state formation. She really did not give attention to gender ideology as such.

In an article in the same volume, Susan Harding (1975) reinforced Reiter's message by discussing the consequences of a sharp division of labor between men and women that placed women in private and men in public for their talk and their exercise of power in a Spanish village. Like Rosaldo and Ortner, she saw the division of labor as fundamentally determined by women being involved in reproduction, and like Reiter, she saw men's power as far greater than women's by virtue of their activity in the public sphere.

Close to this same time, in a paper many see as the beginning of the contemporary study of gender and language in linguistic anthropology, Elinor (Ochs)

Keenan (1974) similarly focused on the ways that women's language use was different from men's in a paper entitled "Norm-makers, Norm-breakers: Uses of Speech by Men and Women in a Malagasy Community." Like Ortner and Rosaldo, Keenan/Ochs had gender ideology squarely in the center of her argument. She talked about how the ideal norm for socially appropriate speech among the Malagasy was one of indirectness. Men were seen as approximating that norm, while women were seen as woefully direct in their speech. For this reason, men controlled *kabary*, the ritual speech appropriate to inter-village events such as funerals. Women did not have access to *kabary*, but rather were limited to the everyday speech of *resa* appropriate to talk within the village, which men of course also controlled. Once again gender ideology, in this case gender ideology about language use, was given a central place in justifying an allocation of roles that looked familiar, such as the greater power of men by virtue of their control of public talk. This is true even though Keenan/Ochs did not frame her ethnographic example in terms of a public–private dichotomy.

The group whose views on public and private I have been discussing really meant rather different things by the distinction. Rosaldo wasn't that specific about what she meant, but the others were ethnographically concrete. Reiter's concept of the public–private distinction was similar to that of sociologists working in Western European societies; in this concept, there were links between local manifestations of public institutions such as churches and schools and their larger institutions which transcended the local scene. Like Reiter, other anthropologists generally made a distinction between kin-based and state-based societies. But in the 1970s and even 1980s, many of us treated non-European societies as if nothing in the way of social organization existed above the village level. This entailed a setting aside of histories of colonialism and nationalism and their penetration to the village level that is no longer accepted in anthropology. At the village level, any social gathering that involved people of the village coming together could qualify as a public gathering – a rather different idea from what Reiter had in mind.

This male–female public–private dichotomy which gave power to men, bolstered by gender ideology that found women lacking in whatever was required for public participation, has been very important in feminist theory in the social sciences. Yet as soon as the idea was put forth, it was attacked. Among the key critiques launched against this view were the following: first, it is simply not true that women are not in the public sphere. They work outside the home in many societies, and in the ways public and private spheres were defined, this would put them in the public sphere. In the early twentieth century in the United States, middle-class women played a major role in social reform – in the temperance movement, in the development of child labor laws, and in the emergence of state-sponsored social welfare programs. Second, there is no basis for claiming any universality for the public–private dichotomy. It is a Western concept, indeed a particularly American concept which has been reified in law in the establishment of the limits of state penetration into the privacy of the home. Third, it is too simple to say that the power in the public sphere is greater and of a different order than that in the private or domestic sphere. Power, influence, and ideas move across the boundaries between private and public, as does the influence of women.

These critiques of the public–private distinction have had consequences for the later treatment of gender ideologies. Some, though not all (e.g. McElhinny 1997) feminist scholars dealing with Western societies regrettably drifted away from the use of this very important distinction. But many linguistic and cultural anthropologists continued to use a predominantly village-level concept of public and private in talking about gender ideology and language use (e.g. Brown 1979; Lederman 1980; Philips, Steele, and Tanz 1987). And for good reason. It simply was and still is true that men dominate public talk, and not just in village-level politics, and not just in non-Western societies. Even if this talk has been influenced backstage by women, whatever is accomplished by its production, in activities conceptualized as public ideologically, men are talking and women aren't. It is true that the particular idea of public versus private which is most salient in the United States is not universal. Indeed no *particular* idea of this distinction is. But it is still the case that in all societies there is some conceptual differentiation of social domains that is closely related to the public–private distinction.

Accordingly, it is not surprising that the distinction as applied to the local level persisted in the linguistic anthropological research looking at the relationship between gender ideology and gendered patterns of language use. In the 1980s, the distinction figured in some interesting claims about common cross-cultural patterns in gendered organization of language use. Sherzer (1987) suggested a number of cross-cultural similarities in the relations among gender, patterns of language use, and language ideology. The strongest or most unqualified pattern he described was one in which gender ideologies and gendered speaking patterns were closely related: "First, differences in men's and women's speech are probably universal. Second, these differences are evaluated by members of the society as symbolic reflections of what men and women are like . . . [S]pecific, recognized features distinguishing men's and women's speech are interpreted and reacted to by members of a society as valued or disvalued, positive or negative, according to the norms, values and power relationships of the society, in particular of course those concerning men and women" (Sherzer 1987: 116–19). Note that this is a quite different position from Ortner's, in that it allows for significant variation cross-culturally in both gender ideologies and the status of women.

Even so, for the cultural group that Sherzer was working with, the Kuna Indians of Panama, he still noted, "There is no question that men's ritual, formal, and public speech is more diversified and complex than women's and that men have more access to and control of political authority through such speaking practices" (Sherzer 1987: 110). Among the Kuna, Sherzer pointed out that women's most public contributions to the life of language were lullabies and tuneful weeping, a type of lament, one genre near the beginning and one near the end of the life-cycle. He suggested that these were genres in which women were commonly involved cross-culturally, and argued that this was due to women's intimate connection to the reproductive process. He also noted that lament sometimes entailed protest, a point to which we will return.

Note the strong tendency for gender differences in language use to be conceptualized in terms of speech events and genres, a tendency characteristic of much of the cross-cultural linguistic anthropological literature on gender, language, and power, from Keenan/Ochs' aforementioned paper up to the present (Kulick 1998). There were also other uncanny claims about widespread cross-cultural gender-and-genre patterns in the anthropological literature of this period. These included women's widespread involvement in religious spirit possession even where they were excluded from other religious roles (Charles Ferguson, personal communication), and a common ideological view of women as more emotional than men that warranted their exclusion from performance in events calling for lack of emotional intensity (Irvine 1982). Using a distinction between modern and traditional societies of which anthropologists have recently been quite critical, Sherzer (1987) suggested that gender in modern societies that are less gender-segregated is expressed through stylistic differences, while gender in traditional societies is constituted more through gendered verbal speaking roles and discourse genres.

As the linguistic anthropologists became caught up in efforts to identify broad cross-cultural patterns of gendered language use in the 1980s, mainstream feminist scholarship in the United States in the social sciences and humanities had already developed a critique of universalist claims of the sort I have been describing. Such work was said to essentialize women, by which it was meant that women were not only being written about as if they were everywhere the same, but also in a way that implied that this was their natural condition and could not be changed. Universalizing was also labeled as racist and classist, as coming out of a very middle-class women's movement that had failed to either embrace women of other backgrounds or address their concerns. These criticisms led to studies in which women were carefully and explicitly conceptualized as intersections of gender, race, ethnicity, class, and sexual orientation, some of which I will discuss in the following section. In this process, so-called third world women were often grouped with and conceptualized as analogous to women of ethnic minority background in the United States.

In the discussion so far, I have tried to carefully represent the seminal and foundational works that gave a place to the role of gender ideologies and language use in the effort to characterize and understand the power of men over women. To me these papers come across as a constant tracking back and forth between ethnographic particularities and general theoretical frameworks rather than as an unexceptioned universalizing (see also Holmes 1993 on gender and language universals). To my mind there was a careless and in some ways deliberate misunderstanding and misrepresentation of what the first generation of feminist cultural and linguistic anthropologists were doing. They were trying to demonstrate how very general and cross-cultural the problem of male power over women was and is. They also aimed to invoke a commonality among women that women from different cultural backgrounds on local levels understand and draw on when they meet one another and attempt to establish rapport with one another. While a great deal was gained by the new feminist conceptualizing of women as intersections of various aspects of social identity, a great deal was lost too. The rhetorical force of the focus on the universal key problem of a very broad male power over women, rather than the particularities of problems such as domestic violence and rape, was obscured, and really has not regained center stage in feminist writing since.

4   Diversity in Gender Ideology

Generally speaking, the early work on gender ideologies was written as if there were only one gender ideology for each society. This was a problem, because the actual existence of multiple gender ideologies in all societies made it easy to counter claims of any one such position. Moreover, while there was some documentation of the content of gender ideologies, particularly in the empirical examination of Ortner's claim that nature is to culture as woman is to man, neither the substance of gender ideologies, nor the linguistic expression of gender ideologies in discourse was given much attention by linguistic anthropologists (though see Sherzer 1987).

In this section, we see how work on gender ideologies took up the issue of ideological diversity. As earlier, the concept of speech genre continues to be of importance. Now more pointedly in some of this work, we begin to see that the actual content of gender ideologies is different in different discourse genres within a single society. Here I should emphasize that the human capacity for discourse structure, that is, the human ability to both produce and recognize *units* of discourse, is a key source of the differentiation of ideas one from another in human communication. In this context, speech genres can be thought of as *containers* of gender ideology. Speech genres are named forms of talk with recognizable routinized sequential structures of content–form relations, sometimes referred to as scripts. Laments and lullabies are examples. Speech genres are experienced and represented as bounded, as having recognizable beginnings and ends, and as continuous within those boundaries. It is this boundedness that gives them a container-like quality, so that it becomes possible to speak of one speech genre or one instance of a speech genre as entailing a gender ideology that another speech genre or instance of a speech genre does not.

In the discussion to follow I will talk about two general ideas concerning gender and ideological diversity and their variants. The first idea is that women and men have different ideologies, or different ways of looking at the world generally. The second idea is that within a given society, there is diversity in gender ideologies, a diversity that need not be conceptualized as organized along gender lines, but may be so conceptualized. While the first idea is not so central to the theme for this chapter on gender ideologies, it arguably created the climate in which the second idea could flower.

4.1 The idea that women and men have different ideologies

The idea that women and men think differently is certainly not new, and wasn't new to the women's movement of the late 1960s and 1970s. But central to the women's movement was the idea that women's views are not heard and therefore cannot have an influence. Women are silenced. In the first section, we saw how feminists of the 1970s focused on the idea that women are silenced in the public sphere. But in a broader context, that idea can be seen as a special case of the more general idea that women are silenced generally and regardless of whether one thinks about the social organization of domains for speaking at all. Ardener (1978) is credited with bringing this idea into anthropology.

Now why did feminists think this silencing mattered? It mattered for the simple injustice of it from within a broadly liberal political perspective that values people being able to have their say. It also mattered because of a disvaluing of women's words that could be harmful to their sense of self-worth. But whether implicitly or explicitly, it also mattered that women were shut down because what women had to contribute to social or cultural discourse in their point of view was different from that of men. Men would not say the things that women wanted to have said. This was one reason why anthropologists were thought to be missing a great deal of the culture of a group of people if they were talking only to men and not to women (e.g. Keesing 1985). Women's words stood for women's consciousness, and men's words for men's consciousness. Whether women are literally silenced or not, with an ideological valuing of men's words over women's, men are able to make others accept and enact their representation of the world and women are for all practical purposes silenced (Gal 1991; see also Lakoff 1995).

It is important to note that the point of this line of thinking is *not* that particular specific ideas of women are not having their just due. Rather, the point is that women have a different perspective, and *whatever* that view is, its impact is not felt in society in the way men's view is. Now there are some scholars who have also tried to characterize the specifics of how women's culture or women's world-view is different from men's, or to otherwise describe what they bring to experience that is different from what men bring. Probably the best-known example of this is Carol Gilligan's work (1982), in which she described her understanding of how women's moral perspective is different from men's. But I think it has always been easier to put forth the general idea of a difference in perspective than to characterize that perspective, without falling into unsatisfactory statements that are easily criticized as overgeneralizations, or as essentializations, as, for example, in the views that women are more nurturing and more concerned about interpersonal relationships than men.

Some scholars have offered explanations for differences in perspective between women and men. The most common explanations refer to the gender-segregated nature of early childhood (Maltz and Borker 1982; Tannen 1998) and to gender segregation in adult life (Reiter 1975; Harding 1975). However, male domination in itself is seen as a causal factor in interpretive differences too, so that the things women think about and the way they think about them are affected by their subordinated position (Gal 1991).

Scholars who posited general ideological differences between women and men, and men as ideologically dominant, have increasingly also documented women's ideological resistance against male ideological domination. The idea of women's ideological resistance has been present from early on in feminist academic writing (e.g. Reiter 1975). This should not be surprising, given the fundamental concern in the women's movement with the need for women to resist patriarchal ideological domination in a manner analogous to the Marxist concept of a need for the working class to resist ruling class ideological as well as material domination. If anything, it is surprising that this idea only really began to take hold in the late 1980s.

Analytical reliance on some notion of speech genre has been important in discussion of resistance. The most developed work on women's resistance that uses a concept of speech genre is Lila Abu-Lughod's (1986) *Veiled Sentiments*. In this book, Abu-Lughod focuses on a genre of poetry performed by Bedouin women in private contexts. In this genre, feelings of strong emotion and suffering are expressed that run counter to dominant public Bedouin values of honor, autonomy, and emotional restraint. When the words of songs can be connected to a woman's individual circumstances, they can be understood as her protest, however veiled, against those circumstances.

Other documented forms of women's protest encoded in recognizable bounded genres have this similar quality of intense emotion in the context of personal suffering. Both Feld (1982) and Briggs (1992) have documented situations in which women have used their own public laments in the context of funeral mourning for the dead as opportunities for political critique of activities going on in their communities. Following Sherzer (1987), who noted the frequent involvement of women in lament, as discussed earlier, Briggs makes it clear that Warao women regularly use one of their few rare opportunities for performance in the public sphere to raise their voices in opposition to dominant community practices or policies. Hirsch similarly characterizes women's rare opportunity to "tell their story" in Muslim courts in Southern Africa (1998) as an opportunity to raise their voices against men. But whereas the other work mentioned here suggests that the opportunity for protest comes through some specific genre associated with oppositional meanings, Hirsch focuses on a situation where women and men both get to tell their stories in public, but they do so in different ways. This is in a cultural system where women would almost never otherwise have a speaking role in a public forum. Coplan (1987) similarly finds Lesotho women workers' resistance songs to be of a different order from men's.

The logic of recognizing gender-based ideological differences has also given rise to discussion of ideological contrasts *among* women, as well as between women and men. In other words, women who are positioned differently within a society also interpret the world differently, although not necessarily in opposition to one another. One study in which bounded instances of a genre are used to tease out such differences is Shula Marks' (1988) *Not Either an Experimental Doll*. Here Marks uses letters written by three different women in early twentieth-century South Africa. These letters, particularly those by and concerning the fate of a young Black African girl, reveal gendered power dynamics of this racially segregated society that were very specific to their time. Other studies that deal specifically with different women's gender ideologies, as opposed to general ideological or interpretive differences, will be discussed in the next section.

An important development in the study of gender and ideological diversity, then, was diversity conceptualized primarily in terms of a dualistic gender system of males and females. In this development, it did not matter so much *how* they thought differently, but rather that in the context of male ideological domination, women were argued to have resisted that domination in specific genres of language use. Ultimately, then, we have a picture of ideological diversity that is organized into oppositional relations, yet seemingly in an undeniably static arrangement. Thus while one might expect that the idea of resistance could be inspiring, and its availability a comfort in the face of a vision of ideological domination, this was in some respects cold comfort indeed because the kinds of resistance described did not lead to any transformation of women's situations.

4.2   The idea of intra-societal diversity in gender ideology

As interest in ideological diversity within societies emerged in the 1980s, a second important theme in addition to that just discussed was the idea that there is more than one gender ideology within a given society. The earliest expressions of this idea typically did not ground or locate the diversity in gender ideologies within society: in other words, specific ideologies were not attributed to particular social domains or social categories (e.g. Bloch 1987; Sanday 1990). And when the view that some gender ideologies are dominant over others was expressed, the dominant and the subordinate were likewise not necessarily conceptualized as socially contextualized, or were only partially conceptualized in this way (e.g. Schlegel 1990; Fineman 1988; Kennedy and Davis 1993).

Indeed, it is common I think, both in American society and in other societies, to experience gender ideologies, and other kinds of ideologies as well, as

floating free. However, sometimes we *can* locate them socially, and the literature on gender ideologies does also abound with examples of ideologies that
belong to or are about people in specifiable social categories. It is in this work
that we again find genres of discourse in which specific gender ideologies can
be located. And here, in addition to socially occurring genres, by which I mean
those that would be performed whether or not a researcher was present, I will
also include analysis based on interviews. Interviews are arguably socially
occurring too, but they do raise questions about where the ideas expressed in
them exist outside the interviews.

There is less work delineating how men's gender ideologies differ from
those of women than one might expect, possibly because gender ideologies are
thought to be widely shared within societies. However, Emily Martin's (1987)
book *The Woman in the Body* is a major work that has located gender ideologies
in specific forms of discourse which Martin ties in part to gender differences,
but her story is more complex than that. She describes how medical books that
represent women's reproductive processes treat the body metaphorically as if
it were a machine, and she does view such a representation as male and
patriarchal. Then in interviews with American women from both middle- and
working-class backgrounds, she shows how middle-class women embrace this
same medical textual rhetoric, but women from working-class backgrounds,
both Black and White, do not. There is definitely the sense in this that the
medical images have become dominant, while the other representations are
subordinated and resistant.

A second very useful and insightful example of differences between men's
and women's gender ideologies comes from Holly Mathews' (1992) work on
different tellings of the popular Mexican folktale "La Llorona," which glosses
as "weeping woman." La Llorona is a ghost often seen along riverbanks who
is thought to try to lure men to their death by drowning in rivers. Mathews
shows how men and women in a Mexican village tell the story behind this
ghostly figure differently. In the men's version, La Llorona violated marital
expectations. She neglected her children, gossiped, and was out on the street.
Her husband turned her out of the house, so she committed suicide. In the
women's version of La Llorona the man violated the expectations of marriage.
He was unfaithful, he stayed away from home, and spent all their money.
In her distress over her inability to feed her children, La Llorona committed suicide. Here we begin to see where there is commonality culturally and
where there is difference in male and female ideas about gender roles. In this
example, it is not even clear that men and women have different ideas about
what men and women should do in a marriage, although clearly each is elab-
orating the other's role ideologically. But clearly women hold men responsible for marital failures, while men hold women responsible. However, while
Mathews does not discuss which view is dominant, other work on La Llorona
stories does. Limon (1986) suggests that the male view is the dominant view, so
that women's marital failings are more imprinted on the public consciousness
than those of men.

In Mathews' work, the stories were elicited in interview sessions, but the method is quite like that of Hirsch (1998), discussed in the last section, who compared men's and women's stories about marital conflict in a Muslim court. Both Mathews and Hirsch tape-recorded men and women producing exactly the same genre, and then identified the ways in which the male perspective is different from the female's. Hirsch too found women dwelling on men's failings while men dwelt on women's, but again the difference was that men's voices tended to dominate the public consciousness, and women's voices were rarely heard in public in the way that they were in court.

Mathews also makes the important point that a great deal of gender ideology is organized in terms of gender dyads, a point to which I will return.

The climate of the 1980s, and to some extent the 1990s, was influenced, as I noted earlier, by the critique of feminist writing that it was "essentializing" women, treating them as if they were in all times and places the same. This led to a good deal of writing that compared women in different social positions within a given society, usually American society, and this trend has included documentation of variation in women's gender ideologies in comparable forms of discourse.

Luker (1984) and others have carried out careful comparisons, based on tape-recorded interview data, of the differences between pro-abortion and anti-abortion women in the United States in their views on the proper roles for women in general and women as mothers in particular. Yanagisako (1987) has compared parallel interviews with first- and second-generation Japanese women in their views on women's roles. Both Silberstein (1988) and Kennedy and Davis (1993) have looked at the gender ideologies of women in different generations, extrapolating changes in gender ideologies through time from comparable data, also based on interviews.

Finally, there are also many fine individual works on diverse gender ideologies tied to variation in gender identities and produced in highly specific ethnographic and/or historical circumstances and forms of talk. For example, Lubiano (1992) describes the gender ideology of the Black woman on welfare that she feels underlay the treatment of Anita Hill in the Thomas–Hill hearings, where Hill had accused Clarence Thomas, a candidate for the Supreme Court, of sexual harassment, and was treated very badly for having done so. In another more recent and extended example, Lata Mani (1998) has examined specifically positioned variation in gender ideologies constituted in colonial-era written discourse genres on whether or not to ban widow-burning in India. Other fine examples include Krause (1999), Kray (1990), and Besnier (1997).

Discourse analysis has made important contributions to work of these kinds on ideological diversity. Specific discourse genres were shown to be associated with specific ideological positions, displaying the way in which discourse genres can function to create boundaries and framings for interpretive perspectives. Methodologically, the focus on speech as data in the analysis of multiple gender ideologies grounded claims about gender ideologies empirically that otherwise would not have had an empirical grounding. This body of work, however, still leaves us with some important theoretical gaps in our efforts to understand social configurations of gender ideology in discourse and to intervene in some of those configurations where they contribute to the subordination of women. While we have done reasonably well in connecting ideological stances with particular gendered social identities, our sense of other ways in which culture and social structure contribute to the social ordering of dominant and subordinate gender ideologies is relatively underdeveloped. The lack of development of the early ideas about the power of the ideologies in the public sphere as opposed to the private sphere has created a situation where theoretically we do not have a well-developed sense of institutional complexes, and of how these potentiate and constrain gender ideologies in discourse. Happily there are notable exceptions to this generalization (e.g. Hirsch 1998; McElhinny 1997).

There has also been a loss of a broader practical political perspective. While feminist concerns with women's subordination are typically still present in all of the works that have been discussed, they are often implicit, rather than explicit. And while inspiring, visions of resistance against domination that have been documented seem to be meant more to raise the idea of resistance than anything else, because the examples of resistance are often themselves pre-political, individual, or routinized in a way that does not appear to be transformative. Then too, the meanings of the terms "domination," "subordination," and "resistance" have not been closely interrogated or theoretically examined.

5   Institutional Contexts for Gender Ideologies in Discourse

We see, then, that the content of gender ideologies is different in different discourse genres within a given society. And different gender ideologies are perpetuated by women and men, and by women in different social positions and with different gender identities. There is a relationship between genre and social identity in that control of genres and their associated ideologies is gender-organized. Male power and authority are such that men achieve ideological domination over women through this gendered organization of ideology, which women resist through their production in and of specific genres of language use.

With the multiplicity of gender ideologies and their discourse manifestations, then, come ideological conflict, opposition, and struggle.

What is most apparently lacking in this way of thinking about gender ideology in discourse is some broader concept of social organization within which gender identity systems can be located and grounded. Anthropological research on gender ideology did begin with a concept of social organization within which gendered relations of power were embedded. I refer here to the ideas that societies are organized into public and private domains and that the ideological support for male control of the public domain sustains men's power over women. But as I noted earlier, the conceptual vision of society as ordered into public and private domains was severely criticized by feminists in a way that seems to have led to the fading rather than the transformation of this broad vision of societal organization.

In recent years an important domain distinction that has emerged in the language and gender literature is that between home and work (e.g. Tannen 1994; Holmes and Stubbe, this volume; Kendall, this volume). This is quite fitting, because as at least middle-class American women experience the social world, the home–work distinction is probably the most salient domain distinction, as at least middle-class women struggle in their own minds with how to have both in their lives in satisfactory ways. In actuality, research in this area has focused more on work situations than on a home–work contrast. And an important theme of the writing on women in the workplace has been how much both women and men vary in their deployment of interactional strategies that feminists have long argued were gendered in power-laden ways. Gender ideologies have not been in the foreground in this work as such until recently.

However, there are recent promising developments on gender ideologies in relation to interactional strategies in workplaces. Holmes and Stubbe (this volume) discuss the concept of "masculine" and "feminine" workplaces, as this is experienced in New Zealand. McElhinny (1995) analyzes the ways policewomen developing identities as police officers must address the hypermasculinity of police departments in their work. Both of their approaches resonate with the relatively recent emergence in the social sciences and humanities of the idea that we can speak of the "gendering" of massively complex sociocultural processes such as the military (Enloe 1989), the state (Philips 1994a), the nation (Delaney 1995), and international relations (Peterson 1992). "Gendering" is to my mind a concept similar to gender ideology, but it has stronger connotations of an implicitness and diffuseness of widely shared meaning than the concept of gender ideology.

Another promising approach that grounds diversity in practice and diversity in ideology in some concept of social organization is the recent feminist linguistic interest in communities of practice (Eckert and McConnell-Ginet 1992; Eckert, this volume; McConnell-Ginet, this volume). These are groups that engage in interaction and share interpretive orientations. Examples of communities of practice include unions, bowling teams, tennis clubs, secretarial pools, and aerobics classes. Communities of practice have relations with each other, and institutional links. People who are positioned differently in the broader sociocultural systems within which interactions occur will participate in different communities of practice. People of different genders, ages, and class positions will predictably participate in different communities of practice. One can expect to find gender ideologies that are specific to specific communities of practice and that are manifest in their discourse practices.

But I still do think that we need to work with a concept of institutions in the sociological and anthropological sense, so that one can speak of gender ideologies in religion, education, law, and family, and in their prototypical public scenes of the church, school, court, and household.

Institutions are by definition linked, interdependent, and creating of some whole. Contexts of interaction participate in broader ideological and behavioral systems that we call institutions. Thinking in terms of institutions allows us to ask the following useful questions: How are gender ideologies in different institutional settings similar and different? How are these gender ideologies shaped by their institutional contexts? Are some institutional complexes more ideologically powerful, influential, and/or hegemonic in shaping gender ideologies than others? From a Gramscian (1971) perspective, one would argue that state institutions (e.g. law, education) are the most powerful and are hegemonic and dominant in ideological struggles with civil institutions such as churches and political parties. At the same time, a Gramscian vision of state–civil articulation would also recognize that state institutions derive their hegemony in part from their ideological articulation with popular cultural ideologies in civil society.

Thinking about contemporary nations (and the whole world is organized into nations) as ideologically organized in terms of a state–civil articulation has some advantages over earlier ways of conceptualizing the contextualization of gender ideologies. It sidesteps the private–public dichotomy, without precluding the recognition of a range of kinds of public spheres (Hansen 1993). It recognizes the interconnectedness and interpenetration of different institutional contexts, allowing for the flow, or replication, of ideological representations across domain boundaries (McElhinny 1997). And a Gramscian approach still allows for recognition of such lower-level organizations as villages as social units within which ideologies flow. It is just that now the village is understood to be articulated ideologically with much more encompassing structures that may or may not be penetrating into its heart, depending on the actual situation that we are considering.

In this final discussion to follow I will try to show how the accumulated traditions for the study of gender ideologies in discourse have contributed to my thinking about gender ideologies in Tonga, taking into consideration the issues I have just raised.

In Tonga, which is a small country in the South Pacific, with one of the largest Polynesian populations, the most salient gender ideologies are encoded in three rather general gender dyads: the sister–brother relationship, the husband–wife relationship, and the sweetheart–sweetheart relationship. Mathews (1992) has argued that gender dyads are an important form of cultural model for the transmission of cultural gender systems. In saying that these three dyads and not others are key, I am saying that other kinds of dyads which might be more familiar to Americans, such as the mother–son or the father–daughter dyad, are much less often talked about and depicted, if at all. Meanwhile, the sister–brother relationship, which Americans do not elaborate, as "in story and song," is talked about and depicted all the time. Furthermore, as we will see, these dyads are depicted differently in Tongan than in American culture. This does not mean that *individual* figures are not also represented as models for women, as the Virgin is in Mexico. For example, Queen Sālote, who ruled Tonga for over forty years in the twentieth century, is a revered figure. But the dyads are more pervasive.

For each of these three dyadic representations, the concept of dominance has relevance in more than one sense. The sister–brother relationship should be considered the culturally dominant image of gender relationships in Tonga. Verbal representations of this relationship abound, and they are often highly stereotyped, but also specialized and differentiated. They are also prominent in the public sphere (Philips 1994a, 2000). This relationship is one in which the sister is represented as dominant, in the sense that her brother should subordinate himself to her, particularly through semiotic expressions of respect, but also through submission to her will, particularly the will of the oldest sister. The obligation of the brother to so submit is highlighted in images of this relationship. The brother goes to the sister to give her the privilege of naming his children. A sister goes to the US mainland to find her brother with whom the family has lost contact, and draw him back into the fold.

The husband–wife relationship, in contrast, is much less often depicted and talked about. It is a more private relationship. When it is talked about, the emphasis is not so much on the dyad itself, that is, on marriage, and the relationship between husband and wife, as it is in the United States. Instead the emphasis is on the role of the woman in relationship to her husband and children. The role of the wife is to take care of the family as a whole, much as this is said of husbands in American culture. Recall the Tongan wife being remembered fondly for her ironing in the example of gender ideology at the beginning of this chapter. A woman's ironing in that example is a conventionalized sign of the way she takes care of her whole family. The idea that she should take care of them is more important, enduring, and pervasive than any particular sign of that care. It is also the wife's job to facilitate the relationship between children and their father, to make sure they get along. In loving and ideal depictions that focus on the wife, she is neither exhorted to obey her husband, nor praised for doing so, in the way that brothers are exhorted to subordinate themselves to their sisters. However, the wife's normative subordination to her husband is understood to be part of the relationship in some sense. Her ordering of him around is depicted in humorous representations of marriage, and his beating of her can be justified on the basis of her failing to do what he thinks she should do (Kavapalu 1993; Philips 1994b).

Representations of the sweetheart–sweetheart relationship, like those of the other two dyads, also involve images of domination and subordination, but here who is dominated and who is dominating seems to flip-flop. Love poetry and love songs typically are written and sung from the perspective of a lover bereft of his or her loved one. The loss of the loved one can be due to a physical separation, an infidelity, a social gulf between the two, or other factors, but in any case it yields a rhetoric of what is essentially suffering in the voice of the lover. Love songs are canonically written for and to women by men, but there are examples of high-status women who compose songs known to be to and about men. The songs themselves are composed in such an allusive way that many, if not most, can be "heard" to be from the point of view of either a man or a woman, and they are sung by both women and men. This gender dyad is the one of the three that is most stereotypically represented in public discourse. It is dominant in the sense that it is the dyad evoked in the most pervasively performed and heard genre in the country, love songs.

Each dyad is very widespread in its representations. Each is portable, in that it can be produced and talked about in a wide range of circumstances. Each can appear or be talked about in formal, routinized, institutionalized contexts, both Western and Tongan in origin. Each can also appear in everyday forms of talk. Each appears in structured, bounded discourse genres and in less predictable conversation. At the same time, each dyad can be said to have a distinct configuration ecologically, that is, to occur in particular social environments, domains, or institutional complexes that remain predictable, in spite of the pop-up-anywhere potential of representations of all three dyads.

Sister–brother representations are part of official nation-state governmental representations. The king's daughter and *her* daughter are the most ritually prominent women in the country because she is ritually superior to her brothers, one of whom will some day be king. The fact that one of the brothers will be ruler and not the sister shows the real limits of sisterly power at this level of political organization, yet the sister's authority cannot be dismissed. If she had no brothers, she could be queen, as in the case of the earlier-mentioned Queen Sālote. The sisterly role is also celebrated in official histories of the country that explain how the high status of the sister has contributed to political configurations of the past. The sister–brother relationship is held up as the model for cross-gendered relationships in court cases involving women taking men to court (Philips 2000). In one of the best-known traditional stories a brother kills his sister over his jealousy of her preferred treatment in the family, but her supernatural powers enable her to be brought back to life (Fānua n.d.). In everyday life, the treatment of sisters to brothers and brothers to sisters is constantly an issue.

As I have already noted, the husband–wife relationship is much less publicly visible in gender dyad representations than the other two. But it too appears in a range of kinds of contexts and genres. In Queen Sālote College, the best-known private girls' high school in the country, a play written and directed by its former principal, Manu Faupula (Faupula 1972) and performed by generations of girls in the twentieth century, instructed them in the proper role of the wife in caring for husband and children. In court cases, the husband's right to beat his wife is affirmed, though only just (Philips 1994b). In a Tongatapu Hihifo District World Food Day song competition, presided over by a noble of the area, the song that won the competition and was later played on the radio depicted a husband and wife. The husband would not go out to cultivate food for the family, and his wife repeatedly exhorted him to get food for them, a depiction people found hilarious because of its violation of norms for appropriate husband and wife behavior. Schools, courts, World Food Day, the radio – these are all state-directed and state-sponsored organizational contexts in which gender representations are fostered. In a more traditional setting, speeches that are part of the kava ceremony (a ritual involving passing a drinking vessel of kava around the group) at a traditional Tongan wedding invoke gendered stereotypes of proper husbandly and wifely qualities. In every-day life at home, a husband's sisters regularly impose on his new wife their expectations of her wifely role (Bernstein 1969).

The sweetheart relationship, as represented in love songs, is within hearing day and night because of the prevalence of love songs as a musical form. They are heard on the radio all day long. They are sung in men's evening social gatherings throughout the country. They are also sung by women in work parties where bark cloth and mats are produced. Comment on the content of the songs in conversation that follows the singing is often also about the sweet-heart relationship. Anywhere where brothers and sisters are not co-present, humorous joking and teasing about romantic relationships is widespread in all adult age groups. In court, there are also silences about the sweetheart relationship. Physical and verbal aggression against women resulting in men being taken to court also occurs in the sweetheart relationship. But here the nature of the relationship will not be explicitly oriented to as an aspect of the case in the way it would be if the man and woman were husband and wife, if it is acknowledged at all. This is apparently because sexual relations between unmarried people that cannot be acknowledged in public are often thought to be involved in such cases. A young woman who has sexual relations before marriage is vulnerable to mistreatment and is unprotected in a way women in other social categories are not (Philips 2000).

These three dyadic gender ideologies are in a complementary relationship to one another. They define each other. One can't really fully comprehend any one of the dyads alone – we see the physical vulnerability of the wife and the sweetheart in a different light when we know how protected the sister is.

These gender ideologies are shared by women and men and are not overtly opposed, even though the wife and the sweetheart may appear in humorous clowning commentaries that acknowledge that ideal relationships are not always the practice. However, clearly women are best off in the sister–brother relationship, when we consider whether women's subordination is counten-anced in Tongan gender ideologies.

For all three dyads, there are Gramscian state–civil institutional ideological connections. In other words, for all three, state-funded institutions promulgate the gender ideologies in a way that penetrates people's lives on a day-to-day basis across institutional boundaries, resonating with views of the same kind that people already have. But it is the sister–brother dyad that has received greatest state sponsorship, elaboration, and proliferation. It is accordingly appropriate to speak of Tongan brother–sister gender ideology as hegemonic for Tonga.

In a context where there are multiple gender ideologies, one strategy that is available for transforming women's situation, regardless of what other strategies may be used, is to enhance, elaborate, and build on the gender ideologies that are most enabling of women. This is what happens in Tonga. There the high status of the sister has in a sense been used by women to enhance the status of the role of wife. In this regard Queen Sālote, the revered former Queen of Tonga, has been an important example for other Tongan women. As Ellem (1999) has insightfully documented, Queen Sālote interpreted her relationship to her husband, the Prince Consort, as one of brother and sister, as a way of creating a model of her partnership with him for ruling the country that would be familiar and acceptable to her subjects. In a similar way Faupula (1972), in her dramaturgical representation of the ideal woman, for the edification of the girls of Queen Sālote College, blends the roles of wife and sister, and shades them one into the other, allowing the image of the sister to dominate the image of the wife. In this way, with a little help from specific state-linked institutional contexts, the sister in a woman empowers her as a wife, and there are many powerful Tongan women in partnership-like relations with their husbands.

6 Implications

Gender ideologies play a powerful role in shaping women's lives. They are used to interpret and motivate behavior and are enacted in socially meaningful behavior. But there is no such thing as a clear one-to-one relation between one gender ideology and one society. Instead there are multiple gender ideologies in all societies. Their nature is and should be of intrinsic interest to social scientists because of the fundamental importance of gender in human life. But beyond that it is of concern to feminists to identify patriarchal gender ideologies in order to ameliorate them and enhance the development of gender ideologies that offer and encourage positive experiences for women. We need ways of thinking about gender ideologies that will enable us to do that.

When we see gender ideology manifest in a bounded speech genre or form of talk, such as story and song, we should think of it not as some representation of a whole. Rather we should think of it as a piece of a larger puzzle, where we need to understand not only the piece, but the entire picture of the larger puzzle. The production of gender ideology in discourse is located in sociocultural systems and is socially organized through those systems. People and the genres they produce are organized into relations of domination and subordination that determine which gender ideologies are powerful and where ideological conflict and struggle are. Ideologies in institutions through which the state articulates with the population it governs are particularly powerful.

There are important roles for discourse analysis of gender ideology in both the general study of gender ideology and in political critique with policy implications. Discourse analysis allows for empirical documentation of the production of gender ideologies, and can reveal in detail how these ideologies are grounded and ordered in discourse.

REFERENCES

Abu-Lughod, Lila 1986: *Veiled Sentiments.* Berkeley: University of California Press.

Ardener, Shirley 1978: Introduction. In *Perceiving Women*, edited by Shirley Ardener. London: Malaby, pp. vii–xxiii.

Bernstein, Louise 1969: Ko e lau pē (It's just talk): Ambiguity and Informal Social Control in a Tongan Village. PhD dissertation, University of California, Berkeley.

Besnier, Niko 1997: Sluts and Superwomen: The politics of gender liminality in urban Tonga. *Ethnos* 62(1–2): 5–31.

Bloch, Maurice 1987: Descent and sources of contradiction in representations of women and kinship. In Jane Collier and Sylvia Yanagisako (eds) *Gender and Kinship: Essays Toward a Unified Analysis.* Stanford, CA: Stanford University Press, pp. 324–37.

Briggs, Charles 1992: "Since I am a woman, I will chastise my relatives": Gender, reported speech, and the (re)production of social relations in Warao ritual wailing. *American Ethnologist* 19(2): 337–61.

Brown, Penny 1979: Language, Interaction and Sex Roles in a Mayan Community: A Study of Politeness and the Position of Women. PhD dissertation, University of California, Berkeley.

Coplan, David B. 1987: Eloquent knowledge: Lesotho migrants' songs and the anthropology of experience. *American Ethnologist* 14(3): 413–33.

Delaney, Carol 1995: Father state, Motherland, and the birth of modern Turkey. In *Naturalizing Power: Essays in Feminist Cultural Analysis.* New York: Routledge, pp. 177–99.

Eckert, Penelope and McConnell-Ginet, Sally 1992: Think practically and look locally: Language and gender as community-based practice. In Bernard J. Siegel, Alan R. Beals, and Stephen A. Tyler (eds) *Annual Review of Anthropology*, vol. 21. Palo Alto: Annual Reviews Inc., pp. 461–90.

Ellem, Elizabeth Wood 1999: *Queen Sālote of Tonga: The Story of an Era, 1900–1965.* Auckland: Auckland University Press.

Enloe, Cynthia 1989: *Bananas, Beaches & Bases: Making Feminist Sense of International Politics.* Berkeley, CA: University of California Press.

Fānua, Tupou Posesi (n.d.): Kuku mo Kuku/The Jealous Brother. *Pō Fananga: Folk Tales of Tonga.* Nuku'alofa, Tonga: Taulua Press, pp. 35–9.

Faupula, Manu 1972: *Mafoa E Ata (Dawn of the Light).* Mimeograph copy. Nuku'alofa, Tonga: Queen Sālote College.

Feld, Steve 1982: *Sound and Sentiment: Birds, Weeping, Poetics and Song in Kaluli Expression.* Philadelphia: University of Pennsylvania Press.

Fineman, Martha 1988: Dominant discourse, professional language, and legal change in child custody decisionmaking. *Harvard Law Review* 101: 727–74.

Gal, Susan 1991: Between speech and silence: The problematics of research on language and gender. In Micaela di Leonardo (ed.) *Gender at the Crossroads of Knowledge: Feminist Anthropology in the Postmodern Era.* Berkeley, CA: University of California Press, pp. 175–203.

Gilligan, Carol 1982: *In a Different Voice.* Cambridge, MA: Harvard University Press.

Gramsci, Antonio 1971: *Selections from the Prison Notebooks*. New York: International.

Hansen, Miriam 1993: Foreword. In Oskar Negt and Alexander Kluge (eds) *The Public Sphere and Experience: Towards an Analysis of the Bourgeois and Proletarian Public Sphere*. Minneapolis: University of Minnesota Press, pp. ix–xli.

Harding, Susan 1975: Women and words in a Spanish village. In Rayna R. Reiter (ed.) *Toward an Anthropology of Women*. New York: Monthly Review Press, pp. 283–308.

Hirsch, Susan F. 1998: *Pronouncing and Persevering: Gender and the Discourses of Disputing in an African Islamic Court*. Chicago: University of Chicago Press.

Holmes, Janet 1993: Women's talk: The question of sociolinguistic universals. *Australian Journal of Communication* 20(3): 125–49.

Irvine, Judith 1982: Language and affect: Some cross-cultural issues. In Heidi Byrnes (ed.) *Contemporary Perceptions of Language: Interdisciplinary Dimensions, GURT 1982*. Washington, DC: Georgetown University Press, pp. 31–47.

Kavapalu, Helen Morton 1993: Dealing with the dark side in the ethnography of childhood: Child punishment in Tonga. *Oceania* 63(4): 313–29.

Keenan, Elinor (Ochs) 1974: Norm-makers, norm-breakers: Uses of speech by men and women in a Malagasy community. In Richard Bauman and Joel Sherzer (eds) *Explorations in the Ethnography of Speaking*. Cambridge: Cambridge University Press, pp. 125–43.

Keesing, Roger 1985: Kwaio women speak: The micropolitics of autobiography in a Solomon Island society. *American Anthropologist* 87(1): 27–39.

Kennedy, Elizabeth and Davis, Madeleine 1993: *Boots of Leather, Slippers of Gold: The Story of a Lesbian Community*. New York: Routledge.

Krause, Elizabeth 1999: Natalism and Nationalism: The Political Economy of Love, Labor, and Low Fertility in Central Italy. PhD dissertation, University of Arizona.

Kray, Susan 1990: Never cry bull moose: Of mooses and men, the case of the scheming gene. *Women and Language* 13(1): 31–7.

Kulick, Don 1998: Anger, gender, language shift and the politics of revelation in a Papua New Guinean village. In Bambi B. Schieffelin, Kathryn A. Woolard, and Paul V. Kroskrity (eds) *Language Ideologies: Practice and Theory*. New York: Oxford University Press, pp. 87–102.

Lakoff, Robin 1973: Language and women's place. *Language in Society* 2: 45–80.

Lakoff, Robin 1995: Cries and whispers: The shattering of the silence. In Kira Hall and Mary Bucholtz (eds) *Gender Articulated: Language and the Socially Constructed Self*. New York: Routledge, pp. 25–50.

Lederman, Rena 1980: Who speaks here: Formality and the politics of gender in Mendi, Highland Papua New Guinea. *Journal of the Polynesian Society* 89: 479–98.

Limon, José 1986: La Llorona, the third legend of Greater Mexico: Cultural symbols, women and the political unconscious. *Renato Rosaldo Lecture Series Monograph* 2: 59–93.

Lubiano, Wahneema 1992: Black ladies, welfare queens, and state minstrels: Ideological war by narrative means. In Toni Morrison (ed.) *Race-ing Justice, En-gendering Power: Essays on Anita Hill, Clarence Thomas, and the Construction of Social Reality*. New York: Pantheon Books, pp. 323–63.

Luker, Kristin 1984: World view of the activists. In *Abortion and the Politics of Motherhood*, ch. 7. Berkeley, CA: University of California Press, pp. 158–91.

MacCormack, Carol and Strathern, Marilyn (eds) 1980: *Nature, Culture and Gender*. Cambridge: Cambridge University Press.

Maltz, Daniel N. and Borker, Ruth A. 1982: A cultural approach to male–female miscommunication. In John J. Gumperz (ed.) *Language and Social Identity*. Cambridge: Cambridge University Press, pp. 196–216.

Mani, Lata 1998: *Contentious Traditions: The Debate on Sati in Colonial India*. Berkeley, CA: University of California Press.

Marks, Shula 1988: *Not Either an Experimental Doll*. Bloomington: Indiana University Press.

Martin, Emily 1987: *The Woman in the Body: A Cultural Analysis of Reproduction*. Boston: Beacon Press.

Mathews, Holly 1992: The directive force of morality tales in a Mexican community. In Roy D'Andrade and Claudia Strauss (eds) *Human Motives and Cultural Models*. Cambridge: Cambridge University Press, pp. 127–61.

McElhinny, Bonnie 1995: Challenging hegemonic masculinities: Female and male police officers handling domestic violence. In Kira Hall and Mary Bucholtz (eds) *Gender Articulated: Language and the Socially Constructed Self*. New York: Routledge, pp. 217–44.

McElhinny, Bonnie 1997: Ideologies of public and private language in sociolinguistics. In Ruth Wodak (ed.) *Gender and Discourse*. London: Sage, pp. 106–39.

Ortner, Sherry 1974: Is female to male as nature is to culture? In Michelle Rosaldo and Louise Lamphere (eds) *Woman, Culture and Society*. Stanford,

CA: Stanford University Press, pp. 67–88.

Ortner, Sherry and Whitehead, Harriet (eds) 1981: *Sexual Meanings: The Cultural Construction of Gender and Sexuality*. Cambridge: Cambridge University Press.

Peterson, V. Spike 1992: *Gendered States: Feminist (Re)visions of International Relations Theory*. Boulder, CO: Lynne Rienner Publishers.

Philips, Susan U. 1994a: Local legal hegemony in the Tongan magistrate's court: How sisters fare better than wives. In Susan Hirsch and Mindy Lazarus-Black (eds) *Contested States*. London: Routledge, pp. 59–88.

Philips, Susan U. 1994b: Dominant and subordinate gender ideologies in Tongan courtroom discourse. In Mary Bucholtz, Anita C. Liang, Laurel A. Sutton and Caitlin Hines (eds) *Cultural Performances: Proceedings of the Third Berkeley Women and Language Conference*. Berkeley, CA: Berkeley Women and Language Group, University of California, pp. 593–604.

Philips, Susan U. 2000: Constructing a Tongan nation-state through language ideology in the courtroom. In Paul Kroskrity (ed.) *Regimes of Language*. Santa Fe, NM: School of American Research, pp. 229–57.

Philips, Susan U., Steele, Susan, and Tanz, Christine (eds) 1987: *Language, Gender and Sex in Comparative Perspective*. Cambridge: Cambridge University Press.

Reiter, Rayna R. 1975: Men and women in the south of France: Public and private domains. In Rayna R. Reiter (ed.) *Toward an Anthropology of Women*. New York: Monthly Review Press, pp. 252–82.

Rosaldo, Michelle 1974: Woman, culture and society: A theoretical overview. In Michelle Rosaldo and Louise

Lamphere (eds) *Woman, Culture and Society*. Stanford, CA: Stanford University Press, pp. 17–42.

Sanday, Peggy Reeves 1990: Introduction. In Peggy Reeves Sanday and Ruth Gallagher Goodenough (eds) *Beyond the Second Sex: New Directions in the Anthropology of Gender*. Philadelphia: University of Pennsylvania Press, pp. 1–19.

Schlegel, Alice 1990: Gender meanings: General and Specific. In Peggy Reeves Sanday and Ruth Gallagher Goodenough (eds) *Beyond the Second Sex: New Directions in the Anthropology of Gender*. Philadelphia: University of Pennsylvania Press, pp. 21–42.

Sherzer, Joel 1987: A diversity of voices: Men's and women's speech in ethnographic perspective. In Susan U. Philips, Susan Steele, and Christine Tanz (eds) *Language, Gender, and Sex in Comparative Perspective*. Cambridge: Cambridge University Press, pp. 95–120.

Silberstein, Sandra 1988: Ideology as process: Gender ideology in courtship narratives. In Alexandra Todd and Sue Fisher (eds) *Gender and Discourse: The Power of Talk*. Norwood, NJ: Ablex, pp. 125–49.

Tannen, Deborah 1994: *Talking 9 to 5: How Women's and Men's Conversational Styles Affect Who Gets Ahead, Who Gets Credit, and What Gets Done at Work*. New York: William Morrow.

Tannen, Deborah 1998: *The Argument Culture: Stopping America's War of Words*. New York: Ballantine Books.

Yanagisako, Sylvia 1987: Mixed metaphors: Native and anthropological models of gender and kinship domain. In Jane Collier and Sylvia Yanagisako (eds) *Gender and Kinship: Essays Toward a Unified Analysis*. Stanford, CA: Stanford University Press, pp. 86–118.

Part III
Authenticity and Place

12 Crossing Genders, Mixing Languages: The Linguistic Construction of Transgenderism in Tonga

NIKO BESNIER

1 Introduction

This chapter takes as point of departure three seemingly unrelated developments in social and cultural anthropology. The first concerns recent rethinking
of anthropological approaches to gender as a social and cultural category.
Heralded by feminist anthropologists in the last decades of the twentieth century, this shift is spurred on by the insistence that gender (and, by implication,
all other social categories) is always embedded in a complex maze of other
social divisions that criss-cross all social groups: social class, race and ethnicity,
religious identity, age, sexuality, citizenship in its various manifestations,
position in structures of production and consumption, and so on. On both
large-scale dimensions and in microscopic fashion, all aspects of social identity
and dimensions of social difference can potentially inform or even determine
the meaning of gender, dislocating sameness where it is least expected, and
potentially establishing connections between surprisingly distinct categories,
persons, and entities. A corollary to the recognition of the inherently embedded
nature of gender is the assertion that "all forms of patterned inequality merit
analysis" (di Leonardo 1991: 31), and that such analysis is the *sine qua non* of
an anthropological coming-to-terms with the meaning of gender.

The second development I am concerned with arose with the increasing
malaise among anthropologists, also characteristic of the 1980s and 1990s, with
the tacit equation of culture with place, and the continued assumption that
social groups could simply be defined in terms of geographic co-presence.
Appadurai (1996), among others, demonstrates that locality is a problematic
category for an ever-increasing number of people, for various possible reasons: place (of origin, affective ties, residence, etc.) may not be a singular, well-
defined entity, as is often the case of the migrant. Place of origin may be a site

of violence and horror, which is best erased from memories and daily lives, as in the case of refugees from civil wars and genocidal situations (e.g. Daniel 1996; Malkki 1995). Alternatively, place can have shifting, context-bound characteristics that vary with persons and contexts (Gupta and Ferguson 1997; Lovell 1998). Consequently, as Marcus (1995) argues, the age-old pattern of anthropological fieldwork that objectified "the Other" in distant lands is giving way to a more dynamic, "multi-sited" pattern of research, in which the ethnography "follows" persons, objects, or metaphors as they travel across geographies and histories.

The third anthropological preoccupation I invoke is the effort to come to grips with the various forms and meanings of modernity. Modernity, the condition of experience associated with capitalism, industrialism, consumption, and other characteristics of life in "the West," has long occupied a privileged if backstaged place in anthropology and the social sciences. At its inception, anthropology was defined as the study of what modernity was not; even recently, much work in anthropology continued to tacitly assume an unproblematic contrast between modernity and traditionalism (Spencer 1996: 378–9). However, recent thinking has unsettled the facile dichotomy between tradition and modernity, demonstrating, for instance, that the two categories are mutually constitutive, and that forms of tradition and forms of modernity are commensurable in many contexts. Furthermore, neither tradition nor modernity is a unitary condition: there many forms of modernity (as illustrated by the "alternative modernity" of Japan, for example) and, as Comaroff and Comaroff point out, "[n]or should this surprise us. With hindsight, it is clear that the cultures of industrial capitalism have never existed in the singular, either in Europe or in the myriad transformations across the surface of the earth" (1993: xi).

In this chapter, I explore how these various strands of thinking can be tied together, and inform concerns of language and gender. I explore the role of language use in constructing gender in the context of an investigation of how other social and cultural categories define gender. For example, men and women in many societies have different interests (in the various senses of the term) in "tradition" and "modernity," in the maintenance of the status quo or the emergence of new social arrangements, and language behavior and ideologies are often constitutive of these differing investments. In this project, I take gender not as a given, but as potentially emerging out of conflict and negotiation between members of a society, conflict and negotiation in which language plays an important role.

The empirical basis of my discussion is an ethnographic examination of the lives of transgendered males in Tongan society. Like all larger societies of the Polynesian region (Besnier 1994), Tongan society counts in its ranks a substantial number of men who "act like women," a category that Tongans refer to variously as *fakaleitī*, *leitī*, or *fakafefine*. The first term is the most commonly heard at this moment in history; it is a lexical compound made up of the ubiquitous polysemic prefix *faka-*, which in this context means "in the manner of"; *leitī* is borrowed from the English word "lady," which is only used to refer to transgendered persons (i.e. never to female "ladies"). Transgendered Tongans prefer the unprefixed version of the term to refer to themselves, arguing somewhat tongue-in-cheek that they are not *like* ladies but they *are* ladies (I explore additional reasons for the preference of the shorter word in Besnier 1997: 19–20). The last term, *fakafefine*, literally "in the manner of a woman," is slightly old-fashioned, but it is readily understood because its meaning is transparent from the sum of its parts.

In the discussion that follows, I first introduce Tongan society as a diaspora scattered widely in the Pacific Rim, whose center of gravity is an independent nation-state coterminous with a group of islands in the Southwestern Pacific, the Kingdom of Tonga. I briefly describe the sociocultural meaning of the two principal languages spoken by members of this diaspora, Tongan and English, a meaning which is undergoing rapid change as expatriate Tongans in New Zealand, Australia, and the United States increase in number and prominence. I then turn to the position of *fakaleitī* in Tongan society, which I show to be varied and full of inherent contradictions. I demonstrate that English has become a trademark of *fakaleitī* identity in the islands, as it encodes a cosmopolitanism and modernity which many *leitī* find useful to foreground in their daily lives. However, this trademark has a price, in that many *leitī* are not fluent in English and most do not have access to the material means of backing claims of cosmopolitanism with tangible tokens of it. In addition, mainstream society can utilize the claims associated with the use of English to dislocate *leitī* from the local context and further marginalize them.

2 Tongan Society as a Diaspora

The fieldwork on which this chapter is based was conducted principally in the capital of Tonga, Nuku'alofa. However, the Tongan diaspora figures prominently in all aspects of the economic, social, and cultural life of the island society, and its importance continues to increase, despite efforts from some quarters to contain and minimize it. As a nation-state and an island-based society, Tonga therefore cannot be considered independently of overseas Tongan communities. Altogether, about 150,000 persons claim Tongan descent, of whom about 97,500 reside in the archipelago, a loose clustering of 150 islands, 36 of which are permanently inhabited. Overseas Tongans live principally in Auckland, Sydney, the San Francisco Bay Area, urban Southern California, and Salt Lake City, but there are small groups of Tongans or single individuals just about everywhere in the world. The size, diversity, and importance of the diaspora is particularly striking in light of the fact that significant emigration only began in the 1970s.

Tongans are Polynesians, and their society has been one of the most strati-
fied and politically centralized of the region since its early-nineteenth-century
unification under the rule of a sacralized king. A British protectorate between
1900 and 1970, Tonga is today an independent state. State and society are both
founded on a marriage between selected aspects of a purported tradition and
selected aspects of a version of modernity (Philips 2000: 235–6). For example,
the State is "the only remaining Polynesian kingdom" and an upholder of
Christianity, features that Tongans consider to be illustrative of timeless tradition, while also emphasizing the fact that Tonga is an economically forward-
looking entity, a symbol of modernity. However, different elements of society
and the State may differ on key points as to which aspects of tradition and
which aspects of modernity should be made relevant to Tonga: for example,
parliamentary representation and the scope of the nobility's political power
are topics of acrid debate, particularly since the emergence of a Tongan Pro-
Democracy Movement in the 1980s (Campbell 1992: 218–22). Those in power
view dissenting voices as signs of an undesirable modernity, often associating
them with the diaspora.

Despite rapid increases in the Tongan populations of cities such as Auckland,
the most important urban centre for Tongan society continues to be Nuku'alofa,
the capital of the nation-state, inhabited by about 25,000 people, many of
whom have moved there from rural areas of the country in the last few decades.
Nuku'alofa is the prime destination of overseas Tongans' visits to the island
kingdom, in part because its international airport is the most important point
of entry into the country from Hawaii, New Zealand, Australia, and Fiji. It is
the venue of most national celebrations, including ceremonies relating to king-
ship, government, and nationhood (e.g. coronations, important funerals, and
yearly festivals of culture). Nuku'alofa is the focal point of both the rest of the
nation and the diasporic dispersion. It serves as the point of convergence for
most of the intensive flows of goods, money, and people that keep the diaspora
together.

In the context of the rapidly increasing transnationalism of their society,
many Tongans see the maintenance of a quality of "Tonganness," as well as
the very definition of this quality, as areas of concern (Morton 1996; Small 1997).
Tongans refer to this quality as *anga faka-Tonga*, "behavior in the fashion of
Tonga," or, when speaking English, "the Tongan way," echoing comparable
phrases used in neighboring societies. The quality is concretized most forcefully in high culture, including the performing arts, the manufacture and
exchange of *koloa* "valuables" (tapa-cloth and mats), ceremonies affirming
hierarchy and kinship, and of course language. However, Tongans often invoke
anga faka-Tonga when referring to culture in the broader anthropological sense,
particularly when the context calls for a contrast between locality and extra-
locality. For example, overseas Tongans and locally based but cosmopolitan
Tongans lay claims on "Tonganness" that other Tongans sometimes challenge
(Morton 1998). "Tonganness" is deeply tied to place, but in potentially conflicting ways.

3   Tongan and English

The tensions associated with the definition and maintenance of local identity and related dynamics are perhaps most clearly enacted in the competition between the two principal languages utilized in Tongan society, Tongan and English. Just about everyone in Tonga knows at least rudiments of English, which is a prominent language in schooling and even, in the case of a few schools, the only language of instruction. However, Tongans vary widely in terms of their fluency in English and the degree to which they feel comfortable speaking and writing English. Both fluency and readiness to speak English (which are not necessarily coterminous, as I will illustrate presently) depend on an aggregate of factors closely linked to the structuring of social inequality in Tonga. First, English is a prestige language, as elsewhere in the Pacific where it is the main post-colonial cosmopolitan language: linked to a colonial past, it dominates contexts of employment, education, modernity, transnationalism, contacts with the external world, and new forms of socio-economic hegemony such as entrepreneurship. Elite Tongans of either rank or wealth are more likely than non-elite Tongans to have resided in English-speaking countries under favorable circumstances (pursuing their education or visiting, for example), and therefore generally have had more opportunities to become fluent speakers of English. They are also intimate with the privilege and cosmopolitanism that English indexes.

In contrast, most non-privileged Tongans are often reluctant to speak English, ostensibly, according to explanations offered, because they fear making linguistic errors. In practice, their reluctance is not so much a matter of defective grammatical competence, but of not having the social self-assurance to assert oneself credibly as a privileged, modern, and cosmopolitan person without fearing shame (*mā*) and exposing oneself to ridicule.[1] While many non-elite Tongans have resided overseas, they have invariably been employed in menial job contexts, in which communication with native speakers of English is confined to job-related topics (e.g. understanding directives). In Tongan communities in cities such as Auckland and the San Francisco Bay Area, the life of many less-than-privileged first-generation migrant Tongans continues to be predominantly Tongan-centered and Tongan-speaking. As is the case of many migrant communities, it is only the overseas-born generation that acquires fluency in the dominant language.

The association of English with privilege is not unmitigated, for at least two reasons. First, most Tongans exhibit a high degree of allegiance to their own language. It is not uncommon to hear Tongan being used as an everyday tool of resistance to the hegemony of English. For example, it is used widely in the workplace, however steeped this workplace may be in the English language and associated symbols. In Nuku'alofa streets, youngsters do not fail to crack loud jokes in Tongan at the expense of any foreigner (*Pālangi*) they pass, whom they assume not to understand the language. But the prestige of Tongan is also asserted in contexts where English is not a competing code, as in oratory, ceremonialism, and song-and-dance concerts, and thus it is not solely associated with resistance.[2]

Second, there are contexts in which people use English widely without access to the material resources to "justify" their code choice, and without any obvious fear of shame either. One example is the very popular Nuku'alofa flea market, where English is a common medium among sellers and often also customers. What is interesting, though, is that the flea market is also one of the most visible local sites of modernity and transnationalism, for several reasons. Most simplistically, the goods sold (principally second-hand clothing) are from over-seas, and thus the market is a place where people go to buy the product of transnational links. In addition, socially marginal groups and "local Others," that is, persons who are already marginalized because of their non-mainstream religious affiliation or lifestyle (e.g. Mormons, Charismatic Christians, entre-preneurs), are over-represented among the sellers. Furthermore, the act of selling, particularly second-hand objects, flies in the face of the "traditional" order: in the "Tongan way," selling used items makes others suspect that the sellers are so poor that they are forced to sell their possessions, a state of substantial *mā* "shame." However, sellers whom I interviewed described with pride how they had overcome the strictures of traditionalism and become modern persons, a process that some attributed to their religious affiliations.[3] The prominence of English and the modernity that suffuse the flea market are thus not coincidental, and they indicate that Tongan and English are embroiled in potentially complex structures of competing prestige, along with the categories with which each language is associated, a theme which will figure prominently in the analysis that follows.

4 *Leitī* in Tongan Society

It is impossible to come up with a precise definition of who a *fakaleitī* is in Tongan society, for the same reasons that defining "man" or "woman" in any social context is neither feasible not fruitful. As for all social categories, one cannot isolate a set of necessary and sufficient conditions to determine who is a *fakaleitī* and who is not. Nevertheless, stereotypes abound, as they do wherever a marginalized minority is concerned in all social groupings. One can therefore utilize these stereotypes to provide a working definition of the category, bearing in mind at all times that they are stereotypes, and hence that they are prone to distortions, underlain with covert moral judgments, and subject to socio-political manipulation.

Mainstream Tongans stereotypically associate a *fakaleitī*'s presentation of self with a "feminine" comportment (e.g. emotional way of talking, an anim-ated face, "swishy" walk). In domestic or rural settings, *leitī* do "women's" work (e.g. laundry washing, cooking, flower gardening, child-minding, caring for elderly parents) and don't do or don't like to do physically demanding work associated with men (e.g. subsistence gardening, wood chopping, construction). In urban contexts, they hold occupations that have feminine associations (e.g. seamstress, hairdresser, cook, "house-girl"), because they either cater to women or are commonly performed by women. *Fakaleitī* are commonly characterized as wearing women's clothes and make-up, although in practice most *leitī* wear either men's or gender-neutral clothes. Their leisures and interests are concerned with beauty, creativity, and femininity (e.g. talking and doing fashion, hairstyles, and decor). They play netball and definitely not rugby (but many, like men and in contrast to women, do get drunk, and often). Finally, "because" they are like women, as the local logic goes, *fakaleitī* have sexual relations with "straight" men, that is, with men who are not identified as *fakaleitī*. Most "straight" men engage them in frequent banter over their "true" gender identity and the possibility of sexual relations, often portraying *fakaleitī* as the sexual aggressor, a strategy designed in part to emphasize the out-of-control nature of *fakaleitī*'s sexuality (a theme familiar to many sexually defined minorities around the world), and in part to invalidate their claim that they are "real women," since sexual aggression is a male trait.

What these stereotypes do not capture is that *leitī* identity is highly variable, considerably more complex, and criss-crossed by dynamics that reach far beyond the confines of narrow characterizations of gender and sexuality. An important theme that will not often arise under elicitation is the notable way in which *leitī* orient their lives toward aspects of modernity to an extent and in ways that other Tongans do not. While mainstream Tongans tacitly recognize, in their rapports with and attitudes toward *leitī*, that this orientation is part and parcel of who they are, they do not explicitly point to it as a characteristic marker of the identity. I will argue here that it is as central to understanding the meaning of the category as its gendering.

5   *Leitī* and English

It is here that language and language use begin to offer a particularly rich *entrée* into the intricacies of the problem. First of all, verbal behavior is one of the most consciously foregrounded features of *leitī* identity, yet also one of the vaguest. When asked, "How do you know when someone is a *fakaleitī*?," mainstream and *leitī* Tongans often reply, *'Oku te 'ilo'i 'i he le'o* "You know by the voice," where *le'o* "voice" also means, more generally, "way of speaking, speech mannerism." When pressed further, informants typically suggest that *leitī* speak with a high-pitched voice and at a fast tempo, and engage in dramatic emotional displays. However, attempts to determine this distinctiveness more precisely run into the same conceptual and analytic difficulties as characterizations of the linguistic characteristics of gender or sexual minorities elsewhere in the world (cf. Hall and O'Donovan 1996; Gaudio 1997; Ogawa and Smith 1997; and many others).

What is particularly striking but often left unmentioned by informants is the salience of English in *leitī*'s linguistic repertoire. The most immediate piece of evidence of this salience is the name of the category itself: a borrowing from English used exclusively to refer to transgendered males, the word "*fakaleitī*" in and of itself indexes the English language, its contexts of use, and its symbolic associations with modernity and cosmopolitanism, an indexicality that probably operates largely at a subconscious level.[4] This indexicality may be further reinforced by two factors: the original meaning and connotation of the English word "lady" (evoking sophistication, class, good breeding); and *leitī*'s own preference for the unsuffixed version of the term, which "denativizes" the term even further by stripping it of the Polynesian morpheme *faka-*. (Going one step further, *leitī* sometimes pronounce the term as if it were an English word, voicing the dental stop, diphthongizing the vowel cluster, and shifting the stress from the word-final long vowel onto the diphthong.)

The orientation to English that is part and parcel of *leitī* identity goes further. No matter how fluent or elementary their English proficiency may be, *leitī* pepper their conversations with one another and others with English. *Leitī*'s code-switching can occur in any context, and can target a wide variety of linguistic units, from single words to large discourse chunks. The most frequent examples in my corpus, not surprisingly, are to be found in face-to-face interviews with me, since *leitī* see me primarily as a speaker of English, even though my Tongan is perfectly adequate, and perhaps more importantly as someone with whom they wish to establish a rapport for which the appropriate language is English. The following excerpt from a typical one-to-one interview illustrates the ubiquitous nature of borrowings and code-switched strings[5] (I = interviewee, N = Niko [myself]):

I: Ka koe'uhí, 'e ki'i- te nau *feel secure.*
N: Hm.
I: Pea mo e anga ko e fie nofo faka-Tongá, *you know, how our culture,* 'oku- 'oku *tight up* pē 'a e *respect*
N: Hm.
I: ki he mātu'a mo e *sisters* mo e *brothers* mo e me'a.
N: Hm.
I: Ka ko e taimi ko ē 'oku nau- nau māvahe ai ko ē 'o nofo faka'apitanga, pehē
N: 'Io.
I: 'a e *camp.*
N: Hm.
I: Ko e fo'i- fai tahataha pē 'oku tu'u 'i he 'ulu, *that's all.*
N: Hm.
I: *They don't really care,* pe ma'u ha me'akai pe 'ikai.
N: Hm.
(Transcript 1993: 3, p. 6)

Translation

I: *And because, just- they will* feel secure.

N: *Hm.*

I: *And they have a desire to live in the Tongan way,* you know, how our culture, *the* respect *is quite* tight up

N: *Hm.*

I: *for the parents and the* sisters *and the* brothers *and so on.*

N: *Hm.*

I: *But when they move out and start living together as roommates in a house, it [becomes] like*

N: *Yes.*

I: *a camp* [i.e. an encampment, where norms of respectability are ignored].

N: *Hm.*

I: *Every- each does whatever goes through his head,* that's all [i.e. and nothing more].

N: *Hm.*

I: They don't really care *whether they even get food or not.*

N: *Hm.*

This excerpt, taken from an interview with a *leitī* who is relatively fluent in English, presents several interesting features. First, many words and phrases that the interviewee utters in English could equally have been uttered in Tongan, and in a couple of instances the Tongan equivalent may have been more felicitous. Second, some of the terms that my interviewee utters in English in fact refer to concepts that are highly specific to Tongan society and culture. Such is the case of "respect," a word that in Tongan English has the locally specific meaning of "avoidance behavior between cross-sex siblings and some inter-generational relations," which is much more succinctly denoted in Tongan by the widely used term *faka'apa'apa*. Such is also the case of the English kinship terms "brothers" and "sisters," which do not do a good job of capturing the kinship categories relevant to "respect," best understood in terms of cross-siblings (*tuonga'ane* "[woman's] brother", *tuofefine* "[man's] sister").

What is particularly interesting is that even *leitī* who do not have grammatical fluency in standard English nevertheless engage in code-switching with a frequency and poise that would rarely be witnessed among mainstream Tongans of comparable linguistic abilities. The following is an excerpt from an interview with a *leitī* who is much less fluent in English than the interviewee in the prior excerpt, despite years spent working in Australia. Nevertheless, English words and sentences abound in the interview:

I: Ne- 'Aositelelia, sai 'aupito 'a 'Aositelelia ia ki ke kau leitī. He ko e- *mostly* ko e sio ki he- ki he-, *have you heard about the Mardi Gras,*

N: 'Io, 'io.

I: 'Oku topu 'a 'Aositelelia hē,

N: Hm.

I: ( ) he nofo pehē.

N: Hm.

I: Ē? *Lesbian.*

N: Hm.
I: *And also the- ladies and the gay.*
N: Hm.
I: *( ) understand?*
N: Na'á ke fa'a kau ki ai?
I: *I only joins but I-* na'e kai- na'e 'ikai ke u 'alu au ki he ngaahi fale pehē.
N: 'Io.
I: *I just went inside and watch them,*
N: Hm, hm.
I: Ē? *But I never do this one.*
(Transcript 2000: 2, p. 6)

Translation
I: *It was- Australia, Australia is very good to its transgendered people. Because it's-* mostly
     if you look at the- at the- have you heard about the Mardi Gras,
N: Yes, yes.
I: *Australia is top* [topu, a recent borrowing from English] *on that front,*
N: *Hm.*
I: *( ) living like that.*
N: *Hm.*
I: *Right?* Lesbian.
N: *Hm.*
I: And also the- ladies and the gay.
N: *Hm.*
I: ( ) understand?
N: *Did you often partake in it?*
I: I only joins but I- *I didn't- I didn't go to that kind of houses* [presumably, gay bars].
N: *Yes.*
I: I just went inside and watch them,
N: *Hm, hm.*
I: *Hm?* But I never do this one.

In short, grammatical competence, concerns for efficiency of expression or the untranslatability of certain terms, and the fear of shaming are of little relevance to my interviewees' code choices. Rather, what is foregrounded in their code choices in interviews with me, as well as in face-to-face interaction with everyone else, is the indexical meaning of English and possibly the indexical meaning of the very act of code-switching (cf. Stroud 1992).

6   The Public Construction of *Leitī* Identity

With Kulick (1999: 615), I consider an analysis based on talk produced in the context of ethnographic interviews both limited and limiting (although not completely devoid of value, as long as the ethnographer places his or her own position under ethnographic scrutiny). What is of interest in the Tongan material is that the patterns of code choice I elicited during ethnographic interviews with my informants echo strikingly patterns of language use in other contexts, and thus are representative of patterns of wide social scope.[6]

Take, for example, public talk in the context of the annual beauty pageants that *leitī* have staged, with increasing aplomb since the early 1990s, in some of the most prominent venues in the country. These events are particularly interesting because, for many Tongans, they represent a context in which *fakaleitī* identity is most clearly elaborated. *Leitī* themselves and their non-*leitī* champions (principally members of a cadre of influential professional women *d'un certain âge*) see the pageant as a prime opportunity to present themselves in the best light and to seek control of their public image, and thus as a subtle but efficacious context for political affirmation. The Miss Galaxy beauty pageant is the most salient of these events, although it is only one of several comparable events held throughout the year. Like other important events in Tonga, the pageant has a high-ranking or otherwise prominent patron, who in recent years has been recruited from within the ranks of the royal family. Half of the jury of six or seven is composed of non-transgendered Tongan dignitaries (e.g. high-ranking army officers, intellectuals, and the winner of the mainstream Miss Heilala pageant for "real" women, which precedes the transgendered pageant), while the other half are "distinguished" Expatriates (i.e. temporary foreign residents of Tonga, such as businessmen, spouses of diplomats, and the occasional visiting anthropologist).

Sponsored by various businesses and organizations (e.g. hotels, hairdressing salons, rugby teams), contestants appear on stage in various costumes, ranging a gamut familiar from South Pacific pageants in general, which includes evening dress, *pule taha* "island wear" (ankle-length skirt and matching short-sleeved top, worn with a tasseled fiber belt), and "their own creations" (see Photograph 1). Each appearance is ostensibly designed to allow contestants to present themselves as attractive and feminine persons, following familiar patterns of beauty pageants around the world. The core of the pageant consists of several judged events, including an individual talent display, a brief interview (of the what-would-you-do-to-save-the-world? type), and catwalk parades. Interspersed are entertainment routines, which may include a hula performance by the emcee, a rock-and-roll standard sung by a local talent, a dance routine performed by all contestants to a popular Tahitian or disco tune, and a short classical and torch-song concert by non-transgendered performers.

What I designate "extra-locality" pervades the entire atmosphere of the Miss Galaxy pageant. It is a feature of the pageant that organizers and contestants take great pains to elaborate, and that the audience expects of the show, although these expectations are always mitigated by the view that this extra-locality is fraudulent.

The most immediate and spectacular manifestation of extra-locality is the very name of the event. Both funny and poignant, "Miss Galaxy" lays a claim on as ambitiously cosmopolitan an image as can be imagined, and plays on hyperbole in the same fashion as some of the camp aspects of the pageant (e.g. the more extravagant costumes and performances), creating humor while attempting to

Photograph 1   The contestants at the end of the pageant posing around the newly elected Miss Galaxy 1997, the incumbent, and the emcee.

retain control of this humor. But extra-locality also saturates other aspects of the pageant. For example, one of the events requires contestants to appear in "national" costume as representative of foreign "countries" (e.g. Miss Rarotonga, Miss Switzerland, Miss South America). Similarly, at the organizing stage, candidates provide their age, vital statistics, occupation, and personal aspirations, which one of the organizers enters on bio-data sheets.[7] Clearly, what participants in the pageant aim for in this emulation of international pageant practices is the appearance of a glamor whose reference reaches beyond the confines of the local context. The extent to which participants are aware of the inspiration for these practices depends on their relative worldliness. While some *leitī* involved in the programming of the show have had the opportunity to watch televised international pageants, others must rely on second-hand reports of such events, what they can infer about them from watching the mainstream Miss Heilala pageant, and their imagination.

In addition to bearing the names of the countries they represent, Miss Galaxy contestants go by female-sounding stage names of their own choosing, and which they often use in everyday contexts. These stage names are often coinages that bear linguistic similarity to the person's original Tongan name (e.g. "Suzie" from Sosefo), and are either English names (e.g. Priscilla Pressland) or exotic-sounding names with no connotation other than their generic foreignness (e.g. Aisa De Lorenzo, Aodushi Kiroshoto), but never Tongan names. The extra-local flavor also pervades the stage decorations (in 1997, flower arrangements and rather unfortunate bouquets of phallic-shaped multi-colored balloons), the background music (for the opening, a medley of triumph-alist classical themes such as the William Tell Overture), and the singing and dancing. When events are explicitly designed to add local color (e.g. a *tau'olunga* performance, a popular Tongan tune sung by one of the organizers), they are bracketed entertainment routines designed to fill the time while contestants are getting changed back-stage, and often look like strained token gestures. When a contestant does decide to perform a Tongan dance for a judged event, it is generally a spoof.

Perhaps the most powerful index of extra-locality is language use. Throughout the pageant, the dominant language is English. When contestants first present themselves, for instance, they do so in English:[8]

Aisa: ((*walks up to the mike*)) Good evening ladies and gentlemen. My name is Aisa De Lorenzo, I'm eighteen years of age, and I represent, ((*pauses, raises arms triumphantly*)) BLUE PACIFIC TAXIS! ((*walks down catwalk*))
(1997: Sony: 2 1:07:36–1:08:20)

Each contestant will have memorized and rehearsed her lines prior to the pageant, and will take utmost care to pronounce them correctly and loudly. This does not prevent occasional slip-ups, which the audience will immedi-ately ridicule boisterously. The important point is that, for most contestants, speaking English before a large and distinguished audience of elite Tongans (many of whom are bilingual) and foreigners represents a serious challenge: many *leitī*, particularly pageant contestants, speak minimal English, as poverty and marginality have barred them from opportunities to learn the language. A significant number have not traveled overseas, and those who have resided in industrial countries have not done so under privileged conditions.

By centralizing the English language and its associations, *leitī* position them-selves on the side of prestige and worldliness, and in opposition to the use of Tongan and its localized connotations. But their sociolinguistic behavior, both in and out of the pageant, adds further complexity. Indeed, despite the obvi-ous difficulties that *leitī* experience in speaking English during the pageant, many Tongans expect them to speak English more readily on a day-to-day basis than non-transgendered Tongan men, for a number of reasons. First, Tongans generally see *fakaleitī* as self-assured and brash creatures that know no shame (*ta'emā*).[9] While in actuality a significant percentage of *leitī* are self-effacing, the demeanor of other *leitī* underscores this stereotype. One illustration of this shamelessness is their very participation in a pageant that constitutes the prime locus of the formation and reinforcement of popular stereotypes of *fakaleitī*: contestants' behavior in the pageant can be moderately outrageous and is certainly viewed as exhibitionistic.

Second, stereotypes of *leitī* view them as oriented toward modernity, the West, transnationalism, and social change. Once again, the extent to which this stereotype reflects reality varies across individuals, but here as well it is certainly founded on undeniable (if partial) evidence. The uncompromisingly extra-local design of the pageant falls right in line with this expectation, both establishing and confirming the stereotypes held by audience members. Viewed in this light, the prominence of English in both public and private contexts is hardly surprising, since English is the language of extra-locality.

Finally, Tongans tend to view the use of English as having feminine undertones: as in many other societies in which a language of modernity competes with a code of traditionalism (e.g. Gal 1979), the former is associated with women's aspirations for upward mobility and emancipation from the strictures of traditionalism (compare Meyerhoff, this volume). When questioned on the matter, most Tongan men and women will state that women speak better English overall than men, and that this is due to the fact that girls study harder in school and that women are talkative "by nature." These familiar-sounding assertions bear witness to the fact that the gendering of language use is tacit and embodied in practice, rather than explicit and grounded in overt consciousness.

As a result of this gendering, men who speak "too much" English do so at the risk of compromising their masculinity in the eyes of society at large. This concerns *fakaleitī*, who willingly go to great lengths to dislocate themselves from their masculine attributes. Interestingly, it also concerns overseas-born Tongans: their awkwardness in performing Tongan maleness, including speaking Tongan as a preferred language, frequently brands them as *fakaleitī*-like, regardless of whether they present any identifiable sign of effeminacy in their comportment. The use of English thus has many associations in addition to extra-locality: it potentially indexes deficient Tonganness, deficient masculinity, femininity, and transgendered identity, traits which may or may not overlap but which are all readily equated to one another. Thus failure to perform Tonganness can easily become a sign of imperfect masculinity and vice versa, unless it is mollified by convincing mitigating factors, such as elite status or wealth.[10]

Patterns of language use in the Miss Galaxy pageant, as well as the overall non-local ambience to which they contribute, are not without irony. As discussed earlier, most contestants live in relative poverty. In tune with their under-privileged status, many *leitī* speak English poorly. Sustaining the level of extra-locality expected of them is therefore difficult for many contestants, who switch to Tongan once they have delivered simple memorized lines. But English still remains dominant in the pageant: it is the language that the emcee uses to address the audience and, when he addresses the contestants, he does so first in English and then provides a Tongan translation, usually *sotto voce*. These communicative practices maintain English in the foreground, at the expense of Tongan.[11]

The difficulty contestants have in maintaining English as their working language during the pageant places them in an awkward position. For example, in the interview event, contestants are given the choice of answering in English or Tongan, and most choose the latter. In 1997, one contestant chose English, and the audience initially reacted with a loud murmur of temporary admiration for her courage. However, it took little time for her to stumble, as she searched for an English word while waving her hand campily, while the audience, satisfied with the expected proof of the fraudulence of her claim to cosmopolitanism, began hooting and ridiculing, forcing her to abort her brave attempt:

Emcee: What would you say about being a hairstylist, or- being- a working- what-what does it mean, like, to be working at Joy's Hair Styles? ((*sotto voce, summarizes the question in Tongan*)) *Ko e hā e me'a 'oku ke fai 'i he* hair salon?

Masha: ((*takes cordless mike*)) Well thank you very much. ((*audience laughs, then shouts with admiration and encouragement*)) If you want your hair to be curled, ((*beckons with her hand*)) come over. ((*audience explodes in laughter and whooping, Masha laughs and then becomes serious and requests silence with the hand*)) Uh, I like it very much, and uh- I enjoy working there, with uhmm- ((*pauses, word-searches, waves her hand, audience explodes in laughter, drowning the remainder of the answer*)) blowers, ((*unable to finish, mouths*)) (thank you). ((*hands mike back and returns to her position*))
(1997: Sony: 4 0:02:45–0:03:55)

Photograph 2 Masha Entura searches for the English word she needs to answer her interview question.

Contestants thus are caught between a rock and a hard place: if they answer in English and make mistakes, they will be laughed at, and if they answer in Tongan, this very fact will be ridiculed as evidence that they are unable to carry through the artifice of extra-locality to its logical end. The ridicule that greets the choice of Tongan is congruent with many other aspects of mainstream Tongans' attitudes toward *fakaleitī*, both at the pageant and in day-to-day interactions. Mainstream Tongans indeed consider *fakaleitī* identity as essentially bogus: here are these men pretending to be women, and not just any women but cosmopolitan sophisticates, and yet they cannot even maintain their end of a simple conversation in English. At the pageant, it is not uncommon for drunken men or women to try to rip contestants' outfits and expose them as what they "really" are, namely persons with male physiologies. Nothing generates greater hilarity than contestants losing their bra in the middle of a performance. In day-to-day interactions between *fakaleitī* and mainstream Tongans, the latter often express mock annoyance at the "fraudulence" of *leitī* self-presentation and identity, while *leitī* argue back with "proofs" that they are "real women."

However, like all ideological linkages that disadvantage some and benefit others, the linkages I have described are not immune to contestation on the part of those whom they marginalize. This was powerfully illustrated by a minor humorous incident in the 1997 pageant, when one of the contestants, the quick-witted 'Āmini or Lady Amyland, sponsored by Joey's Unisex Hair Salon, turned the tables on the audience during the interview event (and, perhaps, on society at large, even if only for a fleeting moment). Before she has a chance to answer the emcee's question, Lady Amyland is heckled by a drunken *leitī* in the audience, who urges her to answer her interview question in English (*faka-Pālangi*). The heckling draws some laughter, since everyone knows that Lady Amyland's English is poor and that she would make a fool of herself if she tried. But 'Āmini's repartee wins the prize:

Emcee:	Miss Joey's Unisex Hair Salon! What do you have to say to promote Joey's Unisex Hair Salon? ((*lowers voice, translating into Tongan*)) *Ko e hā e me'a 'oku ke fai ke* promote *ai 'a e-* ((*rolls eyes, searches for Tongan word*)) *fakalakalaka ai 'a Joey's Unisex Hair Salon.*
'Ahi:	((*heckling from audience*)) *Faka-Pālangi, 'Āmini!*
Audience:	((*laughter*))
'Āmini:	Sorry excuse me, I'm a Tongan ( ) ((*rest of answer drowned by deafening laughter, vigorous applause, cat-calls*)) (1997: Sony: 4 0:05:42–0:06:26, see Photograph 3)

'Āmini answers the heckler by reaffirming her Tongan identity and therefore her duty and privilege to answer the question in Tongan, an unexpected move which the audience (and any Tongan viewer of the video recording) found extremely humorous, because the claim is embedded in a context in which

Photograph 3   Lady Amyland savors the effect of her quick-minded repartee to a heckler.

everything is done to foreground non-locality.[12] What Lady Amyland is doing here is part of a wider tacit project on the part of at least some contestants to take greater charge of the pageant and its effect on the audience. This project consists in stripping the audience (and society at large) of its privilege to ridicule contestants, and to take control of the boundary between humor and seriousness.

But the project goes further, and its meaning becomes clear when viewed in light of the previous analysis. Note that Lady Amyland asserts her claim to Tongan identity not in Tongan, but in English; the covert message is that one can assert one's Tonganness while controlling the tools with which one does so, and while using tools that are not part of the sanctioned repertoire. In addition, the preface of her repartee ("Sorry excuse me") is an inside joke which non-*leitī* audience members are unlikely to make sense of, a reference to another *leitī*'s awkward attempt, a few years earlier, to speak English to a prospective *Pālangi* date. The overall effect of Lady Amyland's repartee contests the power of dominant forces to dictate what counts as markers of locality and what does not; asserts that the claim to be part of the "galaxy" does not necessarily deny one's local identity; and proclaims that being a *leitī* does mean giving up one's place in Tongan society.[13]

7   Conclusion: The Linguistic Constructions of Tongan Transgenderism

This chapter has investigated the linguistic behavior and ideologies of *fakaleitī* and mainstream Tongans, and the relationship of these various behaviors and ideologies in the constructions of identities, stereotypes, and life trajectories. I argued that, in a society that remains essentially monolingual, the presence of English is strongly felt, being associated with contexts where cosmopolitanism, modernity, and capitalism are foregrounded, elements of increasing importance to the very nature of Tongan society. Among the subgroups of Tongan society who are enthusiastic users of English, *fakaleitī* figure prominently, even though most do not have access to the kind of resources which might justify, in the eyes of greater Tongan society, the implicit claim to prestige status that the choice of English entails: wealth, status in the traditional hierarchy, cosmopolitanism, and grammatical fluency in English.

Fakaleitī code-switch for complex and diverse reasons, and in this respect they do not differ from code-switchers in all other societies of the world. However, one of the most salient, although largely unarticulated, motivations for code-switching that this chapter has explored is the fact that the use of English represents for many *fakaleitī* a symbolic escape hatch out of social marginality (compare Meyerhoff, this volume, on women on Malo, Vanuatu). The claims embedded in their use of English and their code-switching serve as an idiom of resistance against the symbolic and material oppression that they experience as both transgendered persons and poor Tongans. However, this strategy is not without risk. Like all resistant action, these claims can be turned around and used against them to further marginalize them. *Leitī*'s language choices place them at risk of being perceived by non-transgendered Tongans as alienating themselves from a local context that offers both unpleasant but also potentially rewarding symbols and resources for everyone. Being generally poor, *leitī* are not in a good position to define for the rest of society what counts as "local," and the perception that they are alienating themselves from a pre-defined localness over which they have little control is potentially disadvantageous.

This chapter has attempted to explore the intersection of gender, modernity, and locality by focusing on the differences and conflicts in the subjectivities of members of one society. Reading dominant characterizations of modernity from sociology and cultural studies (e.g. Featherstone, Lash, and Robertson 1995; Jameson and Miyoshi 1998), we are led to expect that Tongans would experience tokens of modernity and globalization, for example, in a kind of Durkheimian (solidarity-enhancing) unison. What I have shown here is that they not only differ from one another in the way they experience these tokens and in what they do with them, but they also actively challenge each other's experiences of these tokens. Furthermore, they enlist these experiences to argue over the meaning of seemingly highly localized categories and dynamics, including gender.

In this chapter, in line with a substantial body of recent research, I have explored the potentially heterogeneous nature of gender as a social category, and have sought to unravel this heterogeneity in terms of the varied positions that members of the "same" gender can take *vis-à-vis* modernity and localness. I have also sought to distinguish between different meanings of modernity, from material to ideational manifestations of it. Finally, I have investigated the complex interplay of modernity with locality. The chapter has explored the role of language in creating and indexing these social and cultural dynamics. The discourse- and ethnography-based analysis I have developed here illustrates the complex role that categories other than gender play in defining gender. It also shows that the meaning and valuation of such categories as gender, modernity, and localness are objects of conflict and contradiction, both across subgroups of society and across contexts and interests.

ACKNOWLEDGMENTS

I conducted fieldwork in 1994, 1995, 1997, and 1999–2000, grounding myself on a general understanding of Tongan society acquired during residence in a Tongan village in 1978–80. I thank many Tongan informants and friends for their help and devotion, and Janet Holmes and Miriam Meyerhoff for useful comments on an earlier version of this chapter. Financial support for fieldwork from the following sources is gratefully acknowledged: Marsden Fund of the Royal Society of New Zealand, Wenner Gren Foundation for Anthropological Research, Yale University Social Science Faculty Research Fund, and Victoria University of Wellington Faculty of Humanities and Social Sciences Research Fund. Portions of this chapter are reprinted from Besnier (2002) by permission of the American Anthropological Association, which is gratefully acknowledged.

NOTES

1 The fact that, in Tonga as in many other parts of the Pacific, English is the language of choice when one is drunk lends further support to this analysis (compare Harvey 1991 on the role of Spanish in Quechua drunken conversation).

2 Tongan has a notable system of honorifics ("speech levels"), centered principally on the lexicon: certain words are used solely when addressing or speaking of members of the nobility or the royal family other than the sovereign, and others when addressing or speaking of the sovereign or God. These register variations are the subject of ideological elaboration, but in practice they concern a very restricted range of linguistic structures and their use is very flexible (Philips 1991). They are of no significant relevance to the materials presented here.

3 One interviewee, who belongs to a small Charismatic Christian sect, explicitly linked her "liberated" stance to the fact that she had accepted Jesus into her heart, which enables her to ignore tradition-based gossip and shaming. Because they reject the (often oppressive) structuring of mainstream Christian denominations, Charismatic Christians place themselves on the margin of a society where church-mediated and church-directed exchange is so determinative of social life. This is also true, to a lesser extent, of Mormons (Gordon 1990) and other people who have somehow extricated themselves from the duties of reciprocity and exchange, often at a cost to their social standing.

4 There is a substantial and ever-growing corpus of borrowings from English in the contemporary Tongan lexicon, many of which have been phonologically nativized (Schütz 1970). Some words were borrowed early in the history of contact (e.g. *taimi* "time", *siasi* "church"), and have lost all connotations of foreignness. More recent borrowings, while highly integrated in everyday linguistic usage, continue to subtly index the connotations of English as a medium of communication, as evidenced, for example, by cases where both a borrowing and a word of Polynesian origin have roughly the same meaning (e.g. *kiti* and *leka* "kid"). The borrowing of "*leitī*" probably dates back to the early decades of the twentieth century (Futa Helu, personal communication).

5 In the orthography in general use for Tongan, an apostrophe represents a glottal stop, a macron superscripted to a vowel represents gemination, and an acute accent above a word-final vowel indicates that stress shifts from the penultimate to the accented vowel to denote the definiteness and specificity of the noun phrase ending with the word thus marked.

6 Don Kulick extends his criticism to analyses that focus primarily on talk produced in other "on-stage" circumstances, for example, for media dissemination, or during performances of various kinds. The point is well taken, and falls in line with a long tradition in linguistic anthropology of emphasizing the importance of seeking an understanding of social dynamics by focusing on day-to-day interaction. However, one should also not forget that "public" discourse may also act as an important medium through which identities are created and negotiated, representations constructed and challenged.

7 Some of the information provided is fake or unrealistic, while other details are designed to be humorous. For example, contestants regularly claim "high-status" feminine occupations such as "nurse" and "public relations" (*sic*) to add glamor to their profile, as well as "future plans" to be "computer operator," "flying attendant" (*sic*), and "to be a good wife." The same practice of emulating international beauty contests is found in the pageants that transgendered persons stage in Jolo, Southern Philippines (Johnson 1997) and in urban South Africa (Reid 1999), both of which exhibit fascinating similarities to the Tongan material.

8 In the following discussion, I have not attempted to hide the identity of those concerned since my analysis is based on a public event. Extracts are

identified by year of recording and video reference number.

9 A Tongan businessman told me that he had employed a *fakaleitī* to sell his products door-to-door precisely because *fakaleitī* worry little about shame, in addition to being gregarious and talkative. These traits are thus not necessarily seen as negative assets.

10 Many of the symbolic associations I describe here of course echo patterns found in many other societies. One is reminded of Willis's (1977) celebrated analysis of working-class masculinity among adolescents in English schools, Bourdieu's (1985) analysis of social class and "refinement" in France, particularly as it relates to gender, and Ortner's (1991) study of social class and gender in New Jersey, among many other relevant examples.

11 English, as with other tokens of modernity and cosmopolitanism, also occupies a prominent role in many other public events in Tonga, including the Miss Heilala beauty pageant for "real" women.

However, in other events, these tokens are commonly on a par with Tongan and tokens of "Tonganness." In the Miss Heilala pageant, for example, the contestants' ability to perform tokens of Tonganness, including their linguistic skills, are scrutinized very closely. This scrutiny frequently places overseas-born contestants at a disadvantage, as discussed in Teilhet-Fisk (1996) and Besnier (2002).

12 The humor already began with the heckle itself, which is uttered in Tongan, despite the fact it urges the contestant to speak English, and which refers to the contestant by his everyday name, rather than her transgendered name.

13 I do not wish to imply that Lady Amyland's act of resistance was the result of a carefully engineered strategy on her part. For one thing, she was probably drunk, as many contestants are. However, we know from Scott (1985, 1990) that everyday acts of resistance need not be the outcome of calculated designs.

REFERENCES

Appadurai, Arjun 1996: *Modernity at Large: Cultural Dimensions of Globalization*. Minneapolis: University of Minnesota Press.

Besnier, Niko 1994: Polynesian gender liminality through time and space. In Gilbert Herdt (ed.) *Third Sex, Third Gender: Beyond Sexual Dimorphism in Culture and History*. New York: Zone, pp. 285–328, 554–66.

Besnier, Niko 1997: Sluts and superwomen: The politics of gender liminality in urban Tonga. *Ethnos* 62: 5–31.

Besnier, Niko 2002: Transgenderism, locality, and the Miss Galaxy beauty pageant in Tonga. *American Ethnologist* 29: 534–67.

Bourdieu, Pierre 1985: *Distinction: A Social Critique of the Judgement of Taste*. Translated by Richard Nice. Cambridge, MA: Harvard University Press.

Campbell, I. C. 1992: *Island Kingdom: Tonga Ancient and Modern*.

Christchurch: Canterbury University Press.

Comaroff, Jean and Comaroff, John 1993: Introduction. In Jean Comaroff and John Comaroff (eds) *Modernity and its Malcontents: Ritual and Power in Postcolonial Africa*. Chicago: University of Chicago Press, pp. xi–xxxvii.

Daniel, E. Valentine 1996: *Charred Lullabies: Chapters in an Ethnography of Violence*. Princeton Studies in Culture/Power/History. Princeton, NJ: Princeton University Press.

di Leonardo, Micaela 1991: Introduction: Gender, culture, and political economy: Feminist anthropology in historical perspective. In Micaela di Leonardo (ed.) *Gender at the Crossroads of Knowledge: Feminist Anthropology in the Postmodern Era*. Berkeley, CA: University of California Press, pp. 1–48.

Featherstone, Mike, Lash, Scott, and Robertson, Roland (eds) 1995: *Global Modernities*. London: Sage.

Gal, Susan 1979: *Language Shift: Social Determinants of Linguistic Change in Bilingual Austria*. New York: Academic Press.

Gaudio, Rudolph P. 1997: Not talking straight in Hausa. In Anna Livia and Kira Hall (eds) *Queerly Phrased: Language, Gender, and Sexuality*. New York: Oxford University Press, pp. 416–29.

Gordon, Tamar 1990: Inventing the Mormon Tongan family. In John Barker (ed.) *Christianity in Oceania: Ethnographic Perspectives*. Association for Social Anthropology in Oceania Monographs, 12. Lanham, MD: University Press of America, pp. 197–219.

Gupta, Akhil and Ferguson, James (eds) 1997: *Anthropological Locations: Boundaries and Grounds of a Field Science*. Berkeley, CA: University of California Press.

Hall, Kira and O'Donovan, Veronica 1996: Shifting gender positions among Hindi-speaking Hijras. In Victoria Bergvall, Janet M. Bing, and Alice F. Freed (eds) *Rethinking Language and Gender Research: Theory and Practice*. New York: Longman, pp. 228–66.

Harvey, Penelope 1991: Drunken speech and the construction of meaning: Bilingual competence in the Southern Peruvian Andes. *Language in Society* 20: 1–36.

Jameson, Fredric and Miyoshi, Masao (eds) 1998: *The Culture of Globalization*. Durham, NC: Duke University Press.

Johnson, Mark 1997: *Beauty and Power: Transgendering and Cultural Transformation in the Southern Philippines*. Oxford: Berg.

Kulick, Don 1999: Transgender and language: A review of the literature and suggestions for the future. *GLQ* 5: 605–22.

Lovell, Nadia (ed.) 1998: *Locality and Belonging*. European Association of Social Anthropologists Series. London: Routledge.

Malkki, Liisa 1995: *Purity and Exile: Violence, Memory, and National Cosmology among Hutu Refugees in Tanzania*. Chicago: University of Chicago Press.

Marcus, George E. 1995: Ethnography in/of the world system: The emergence of multi-sited ethnography. *Annual Review of Anthropology* 24: 95–117.

Morton, Helen 1996: *Becoming Tongan: An Ethnography of Childhood*. Honolulu: University of Hawaii Press.

Morton, Helen 1998: Creating their own culture: Diasporic Tongans. *The Contemporary Pacific* 10: 1–30.

Ogawa, Naoko and Shibamoto Smith, Janet 1997: The gendering of the gay male sex class in Japan: A case study based on *Rasen No Sobyô*. In Anna Livia and Kira Hall (eds) *Queerly Phrased: Language, Gender, and Sexuality*. New York: Oxford University Press, pp. 402–15.

Ortner, Sherry B. 1991: Reading America: Preliminary notes on class and culture. In Richard G. Fox (ed.) *Recapturing Anthropology: Writing in the Present*. Santa Fe, NM: School of American Research Press, pp. 163–89.

Philips, Susan U. 1991: Tongan speech levels: Practice and talk about practice in the cultural construction of social hierarchy. In Robert Blust (ed.) *Currents in Pacific Linguistics: Papers on Austronesian Languages in Honour of George Grace*. Canberra: Pacific Linguistics C–117, pp. 369–82.

Philips, Susan U. 2000: Constructing a Tongan nation-state through language ideology in the courtroom. In Paul V. Kroskrity (ed.) *Regimes of Language: Ideologies, Polities, and Identities*. School of American Research advanced seminar series. Santa Fe, NM: School of American Research Press, pp. 229–57.

Reid, Graeme 1999: Above the Skyline: Integrating African, Christian and Gay or Lesbian Identities in a South African Church Community. MA thesis, Department of Anthropology, University of the Witswatersrand.

Schütz, Albert J. 1970: Phonological patterning of English loan words in Tongan. In S. A. Wurm and D. C. Laycock (eds) *Pacific Linguistic Studies in Honour of Arthur Capell*. Canberra: Pacific Linguistics C–13, pp. 409–28.

Scott, James C. 1985: *Weapons of the Weak: Everyday Forms of Peasant Resistance*. New Haven, CT: Yale University Press.

Scott, James C. 1990: *Domination and the Art of Resistance: Hidden Transcripts*. New Haven, CT: Yale University Press.

Small, Cathy A. 1997: *Voyages: From Tongan Village to American Suburbs*. Ithaca, NY: Cornell University Press.

Spencer, Jonathan 1996: Modernism, modernity and modernization. In Alan Barnard and Jonathan Spencer (eds) *Encyclopedia of Social and Cultural Anthropology*. London: Routledge, pp. 376–9.

Stroud, Christopher 1992: The problem of intention and meaning in code-switching. *Text* 12: 127–55.

Teilhet-Fisk, Jehanne 1996: The Miss Heilala beauty pageant: Where beauty is more than skin deep. In Colleen B. Cohen, Richard Wilk, and Beverly Stoeltje (eds) *Beauty Queens on the Global Stage: Gender, Contests, and Power*. London: Routledge, pp. 185–202.

Willis, Paul 1977: *Learning to Labour: How Working Class Kids Get Working Class Jobs*. Westmead, England: Saxon House.

13   Claiming a Place: Gender, Knowledge, and Authority as Emergent Properties

MIRIAM MEYERHOFF

1   Introduction

This chapter examines aspects of language use and gender ideologies in Vanuatu (located in the southwest Pacific). It also discusses local ideologies about authority and knowledge, two other important social attributes, and shows how all three are linked. It adds a historical dimension to their analysis which stresses the longitudinal dimension to the ways gender is interpreted and enacted today.[1]

Three themes will be developed and subsequently drawn together. First, I will discuss evidence which suggests that in Vanuatu, gender *emerges* through relationships with people, perhaps in an even more fundamental sense than it emerges in the Western societies that are used more frequently as the basis for theorizing gender and language. I will adopt Marilyn Strathern's (1988) analysis of gender in Melanesia. She argues that in Melanesia as a whole, gender is understood as a trope of relationships with others, rather than as an opposition of different kinds (as it generally is in Western thought).

Second, I will take the position that relationships not only are negotiated in the here and now, but also carry historical baggage. Variationist sociolinguistics has shown us that synchronic variation often offers valuable insights into changes that have taken place in the past. This chapter builds on that tradition and links the historical record of how women and men have been talked about, to the way gender and sex roles are talked about now. I will try to show how historical factors influence synchronic manifestations of the emergence of gender. In particular, I will consider the significance that colonial, mission era, and current Western ideologies about gender have for the ways in which gender is talked about and which patterns of talk indirectly index (Ochs 1992) gender in Vanuatu today.

Third, I will show that gender is not the only social quality which is emergent in Vanuatu. Knowledge and authority also emerge through relationships, but in relationships with the indigenous concept *ples* 'place'. For this, I will make use of Bob Rubinstein's ethnographic discussion of how knowledge, identity, and language are linked together on Malo. We will see that relationships with *ples* are highly gendered on Malo. As a result of this, claiming knowledge or authority is likewise gendered. I will suggest that this underlies the importance that linguistic strategies which express empathy play in the speech of women. Toward this end, I will adopt a distinction between empathy and sympathy that highlights the relative degree to which a person claims or suggests shared *experience of* something, and not just shared *feelings about* it.

I start with an anecdote that set me rethinking my overly simplistic assumptions about ideologies of gender in the community where I lived in northern Vanuatu. Some people from the coastal villages on western Malo, an island in the north of Vanuatu, had gone "on top" to one of the villages on the hill in order to attend a double wedding. I was visiting friends there after several years away, and they invited me to come along too. At the end of the day, Leipakoa,[2] the woman I was staying with, sent me down the hill in the company of her younger, 12-year-old daughter before all of the ceremonies were finished so we would get home before dark. As Elise and I set off we were joined by another child, Vira, from Elise's class at school, and the three of us raced the setting sun down the hill carrying bags of food from the wedding and the family's gardens. When we made it to the flat land by the coast again, Elise's friend turned off in another direction to go home and she and I walked alone together. She turned to me and said (in the local creole, Bislama), "Vira used to be a girl, but now he's a boy." I wasn't sure if I had heard her correctly, so I said, "What?" She repeated, "Vira used to be a girl, but now he's a boy." I was still unsure whether that was really what she had said, so I asked her to explain what it meant. She tried to oblige but (unlike me) she obviously found the comment itself perfectly transparent. What was peculiar to her was the need to explain it. He used to be a girl, and he used to be with the girls, but now he is a boy so he isn't with the girls so much any more.

In the following days, I reported this conversation to a number of adults (women and men). All of them knew who Elise was referring to and they all essentially gave me paraphrases of Elise's explanation: Vira had done things with the girls and in girls' fashion before, but not so much now. I was told, with good humor (but I also thought some amusement at my curiosity), that there just are some boys who do things girl-fashion, some into adulthood.

What's going on here? One could look at this story with Western eyes and apply various Western labels to a boy like Vira. Or we might be tempted to think that Vira belongs to a transgendered category like the ones found in many parts of Oceania, especially Polynesia. But in Vanuatu there is no lexically codified transgendered category of men like the *fakaleitī* in Tonga (Besnier, this volume) or the *māhū* in Hawaii.[3] I explained to some of my adult friends that part of my confusion about how to interpret Elise's comments was because I know Malo is famous for its hermaphrodite pigs, and there is a specific lexical item for them. I wondered if it was possible that Vira was likewise intersexed.

They laughed this off, but they also failed to present an alternative term for a person who is culturally inter-gendered, as it were.

Instead, I think that there is another way to look at the significance of how Vira was talked about and how people talked to me about him during all of these exchanges, and this ties gender (in this case, what it is to be a boy or girl) more closely to vernacular, Ni-Vanuatu[4] ideologies about gender. As with other chapters in this section of the Handbook, this provides us with a different cultural and linguistic context in which to evaluate and better understand the basis on which linguistic forms come to be seen as gendered behaviors.

2   Elaboration of Emergent Gender

In this section, I outline in more detail Strathern's (1988) arguments about the emergence of gender through personal relationships in Melanesia. I draw a distinction between thinking of gender as emergent and gender as being fluid, showing that gender may be tied quite closely to sex. Crucially, though, this is a superficial association between gender and sex, and following Strathern, it can be seen to be an artefact of what the most important relationships are in the culture.

Strathern's position is that gender is an emergent attribute in much of Melanesia, and that it emerges through an individual's same-sex and cross-sex interactions. Melanesian orthodoxy, she argues, "requires that gender differences must be made apparent, drawn out of what men and women do" (1988: 184). She contrasts the Melanesian perspective with Western social constructionist analyses of gender. She argues that, at the time of her writing, social constructionism continued to be characterized by an underlying essentialism, that is, the "Western orthodoxy that gender relations consist in the "social or cultural construction" of what already has differentiated form through the biological sexing of individuals" (1988: 184). Arguably, this has since changed. A useful aspect of Strathern's theoretical framework is that it highlights the fact that there are at least two ways of viewing social categories such as gender. They may be viewed as end results, that is, we can focus on the way they are at any given point in time, or they may be viewed as a synchronic process (Niko Besnier, personal communication). Strathern argues that ideologies about gender in Melanesia fall into the latter camp, and more recent constructionist and performative developments in the analysis of identity in Western literature have similarly shifted the focus from results to ideologies of process.[5]

This does not mean that at all times gender is more fluid and contestable in the region of Vanuatu where I worked than it is in, for instance, the New Zealand and United States cultures I have most first-hand familiarity with. Nor does it mean that the emergent categories are themselves any more or less fluid than elsewhere. On the contrary, once gendered bases for interaction begin to crystallize there are extremely strong normative pressures on people to continue to engage in those practices that serve as clear social markers of gender boundaries. Though many customary practices which enforce physical separation of the sexes are falling into abeyance on Malo (such as proscriptions on women standing in front of their classificatory brothers (i.e. men treated as, and called, brothers), or wearing red in front of them, or using the same door of the house), there continues to be fairly rigid differentiation of the sexes in public spaces. So, when traveling between Malo and Santo, women and men generally sat in different places on the truck or boat (men, especially young men, often stood in the transports holding onto the roof of the cab, and they often sat on or in the covered prow of the boat).

Or, to give another example, the family I was living with would set off from their home as a mixed-sex group, but by the time we reached the main road, men (including all but the very littlest boys) and women (and girls and the very littlest boys) would start to gravitate to different sides of the road. As we walked along the road and met other people going in the same direction, the group boundaries would become even more marked, so that by the time we reached our destination, men's and women's groups would often be walking too far away from each other to have a conversation across them. At the social event, women, girls, and babies would sit in one area, while men and boys would take up seats in another. If there were Western-style seats or a convenient log to sit on, these always went to men, while the women's group would sit on mats, usually in the shelter of a house. In public gatherings, whether it be customary events such as a wedding, or more contemporary events such as a school fundraiser, the principal public roles as speakers or comperes go to men.[6]

Superficially, then, it could seem that gender roles in Vanuatu are even more closely tied to biological sex than they are in New Zealand or the United States, but following Strathern's analysis of gender this should rather be seen as an artefact of the way relationships are generally defined. That is, gender emerges as a function of interactions in the culturally most important relationships, and these are very often direct indexes of sex, for example, sister, uncle, or mother. What the anecdote about Vira reminds us is a point that has become almost axiomatic in language and gender research since the 1990s, namely that gender is one of many identities that is constructed in the day-to-day practices of individuals interacting with (or avoiding) other individuals.

Strathern's position may seem very similar to social constructionist approaches to gender, or even (with its emphasis on the emergence of identity through practices that define relationships) to the more specific construct, the community of practice. It can be differentiated from both of these, though. Perhaps the clearest point of departure from a social constructionist view of gender is Strathern's claim that in Melanesian thought, the child is seen as ungendered, or androgynous; this is a direct consequence of the fact that maleness or femaleness emerges only through interactions with others (see also note 5). Becoming a woman happens in interactions with men, but also in interactions with other women and through participation in same-sex activities.

Strathern's analysis of gender in Melanesia is also distinct from the highly subjective and agentive approach to theorizing gender that underlies communities of practice. This is because there are long-standing regional associations in Melanesia between specific interpersonal relationships and the role a person plays in formalized social exchanges of things of value. Here is one example of what I mean by this: the formalized exchanges bound up in a marriage help to consolidate the importance of certain relationships and individuals' roles in terms of those relationships. A woman marrying into a new family is seen as bringing with her items of great value, namely her future children, so this is reciprocated by an exchange of valuable material goods from her husband's classificatory brothers to her family. These are the kinds of relationships that Strathern is referring to. Gender emerges through father–daughter, wife–husband, sister–brother interactions and exchanges. So the relationships that are most important for the emergence of gender are characterized by a good deal of conventionalized behavior. In this respect, the picture Strathern paints differs from the community of practice, which in language and gender studies to date has stressed the agentiveness of the participants.

Given the orientation to gender in this social context, then, the anecdote about Vira does not so much illustrate that he was a gendered curiosity, bending or re-constructing his male identity, but rather it can be seen as an example illustrating how, as children, people have a good deal of latitude in determining how fast and which gender emerges through interactions with others. Vira's relationships as a younger child were with girls as a peer, therefore the gender emerging through such relationships could reasonably be described by Elise as "a girl." Social pressures that stress interactions and exchanges within the normative, social relationships that are conventionally linked to sex may mean that, by adulthood, most people will identify with the gender roles conventionally associated with one sex, but this will be the outcome of a lengthy engagement in same-sex and cross-sex activities or practices.

3   Knowledge and Authority as Emergent Properties: The Importance of *Ples*

Rubinstein's (1978, 1981) work on the social and linguistic construction of identity on Malo had a significant impact on Strathern's analysis of gender. This can be seen principally in Rubinstein's description of knowledge and authority which he characterizes as emergent qualities, too.

Rubinstein's doctoral thesis (1978) deals in detail with the processes by which people on Malo "place" themselves and construct an identity as being of or belonging to a particular place.[7] Since placing oneself on Malo first and foremost involves establishing natal associations with land, this means that the process of placing self is a highly gendered notion to begin with. "[M]en stay on the land, women leave it" (Rubinstein 1978: 287), or in the words of a woman I was talking to in 1994, *ol gel oli nating* 'girls are nothing' – at least partly because they leave the land they were born on.

Bolton (1999) discusses the relationship between gender and *ples* 'place' in the wider context of Vanuatu, where women (as a group) are often described with metaphors that suggest the ease with which they can relocate from their home. Bolton notes that when a woman marries she becomes associated with her husband's natal *ples* and no longer with that of her brothers or father. This contrasts markedly with the situation for men, who always are associated with the *ples* of their fathers (even among those who have relocated to the towns). This was technically true on Malo, but in the village community I lived in I also found that the category of *woman nara aelan* "woman from another island" was highly salient. Hence, there, a woman retains a vestige of her own *ples*, yet gives birth to children who are clearly identified as of her husband's *ples*. One could say, therefore, that *ples* for men is a constant, while *ples* for women is not. (Besnier, this volume, also discusses linguistic consequences arising from problems associated with finding a "place".) To the extent that she remains *woman nara aelan* and also becomes so integral a part of her new community that she creates (through birth) *man ples*, I would want to say that *ples* for women is both partible and subject to re-creation.

But according to Rubinstein, *ples* is more than a property defining in-group membership. Rubinstein (1981: 142) observes that traditionally on Malo information or knowledge acquires authority in two ways: one is personalized, that is to say, "connected with a powerful individual and with his success"; the other is more objective, that is, it is seen to have "an external reality in a unified and thoroughly unquestioned social system" such as traditional *kastom* ('custom(ary)') knowledge. Either of these may be established through a claim to *ples*. A person may have authority to know or pass on information because it is information that is tied to that person's *kastom* family associations, particularly their family's special (*tapu*) places. However, a person may also establish authority to voice some knowledge by grounding it in detailed information about where they were and what they were doing when they learnt it, again linking the knowledge overtly to some specific *ples*. Having authority and knowledge in turn affords the possessor a degree of social power. Rubinstein notes that progressive changes to the meaning of *kastom* in the community on Malo (see also Bolton, 2003) has given rise to a situation where knowledge increasingly derives its authority from a personalized base, rather than the unquestioned social system. This shift means that authority and knowledge is becoming a little less stable, in the sense that it becomes appropriate to speak of lots of individual knowledges (1981: 148–9).

In this way we can see that Rubinstein's explanation of the dynamics of knowledge and authority on Malo stands as a counterpoint to Strathern's explanation of the dynamics of gender. Where Strathern argues that gender emerges through participation in same- and cross-sex relationships, Rubinstein argues that knowledge and authority emerge through the speaker's relationships with specific places. Both gender and authority, then, are properties that are open to negotiation and emerge as a consequence of tensions between what had customarily been the norm in a community and the changes wrought by contact with other communities and/or contact with a supralocal culture of modernity (see also Besnier, Leap, Philips, this volume).

4   The Need for Special Linguistic Strategies for Claiming *Ples*

Clearly, though, if (natal) *ples* is stable and constant for men, while for women *ples* is partible, this creates rather different opportunities for placing oneself, establishing authority, and exercising power. I would argue that the whole business of placing oneself is a task that is more nuanced for a woman on Malo than it is for a man. A man can assert authority by invoking his family lineage and information about important landmarks or stories associated with a piece of land which place him as rightfully belonging there, while a woman once married and relocated cannot do this by such direct means. The task of placing herself (and hence asserting authority) socially must be addressed more indirectly. As the next two examples show, linguistic strategies are an important resource.

First, I begin with the story of Undu, because I think it illustrates well the differences in how women and men place themselves linguistically. I heard the story of Undu twice, from two different men.[8] The younger man explicitly established his ownership of the story and the information he was passing on to the listeners by explaining his family relationship to Undu (he would use the kinship term *tawean* for Undu[9]), thereby invoking personal authority in Rubinstein's terms. However, a more interesting telling of the tale occurred the first time I heard the story of Undu. This was from an older man, as some of his extended family sat around in conversation after dinner one night. Undu's name came up and a visiting teenager, Bretian, identified him as someone who had died:

Bretian:	*Be hem i ded, afta i lus no?*
Visi:	*No.*
Miriam:	*No, hem i stap.*
Papa:	*No hem i stap. Oli daeva finis, oli kam . . .*
Lolan:	*Hemia nao stret stori.*
Papa:	*A, hem i stap long kenu. Wan fren blong hem i go antap long bus. Afta i kambak nao, i no gat . . .*

Bretian:	But he died and he went missing, didn't he?
Visi:	No.
Miriam:	No, he's still around.
Papa:	No, he's still around. They had gone diving, and they came . . .
Lolan:	Here it is, the real story.
Papa:	Ah, he was in his canoe. One of his friends went into the bush. Then when he came back, he was gone . . .

Among the corrections to Bretian, the family's father says, "No, he's still around" and begins the story. At this point, his daughter-in-law, Lolan, interjects "Here it is, the real story," before Papa proceeds with only the slightest pause ("Ah, he was in his canoe . . ."). Papa's knowledge of Undu's story and his ability to have it accepted as an authoritative account is partly due to personal factors (everyone present knows Papa is related to Undu, also his age and standing within the community imbue his telling with authority), but the account also derives its authority from the external acceptance throughout the community of the supernatural cause of Undu's disappearance (Undu's violation of *kastom*).

However, I am particularly interested in Lolan's small interjection. This can be interpreted as accomplishing two things. At the most obvious level, she is signposting and helping to establish Papa's authority in this matter (and by extension, I would argue, his knowledge and authority in other similar domains of information). In this, her behavior is similar to the role Ochs and Taylor (1995) show mothers playing in the White middle-class family dinners that they recorded. Ochs and Taylor characterized these activities as helping to construct a "father knows best" dynamic in the family. But this is not all.

4.1 Supportiveness and the speaker's own authority

What Lolan is doing here also seems to me to fit in with a larger pattern of women using language to help place their social selves on Malo. As a woman, and especially as a woman who has married in from an island a long way away (as opposed to an island which has historical ties to Malo), Lolan needs to find indirect means by which to place her self. She is a school teacher and is active in the local church, so she has some authority vested in what Rubinstein calls the externally "unified . . . social system." But within the family her identities as teacher and church-goer are de-accentuated, and therefore I would argue that the authority associated with these roles is less directly indexed in her interactions within the family.[10] I interpret her overt tagging of Papa's story as an attempt to place her self as a member of the family. That is, she is establishing a share in or a claim to the authority associated with knowing stories that are part of that family's history and their more literal sense of place. Papa's story requires no imprimatur of authority from anyone else, and certainly not that of a younger woman who has married into his family, so it seems reasonable to suppose that at least part of the work that this small interjection is doing is to place Lolan in the family while using the frame of supporting someone else's conversational turn.

A second, similar example occurred in another family's after-dinner conversation. Talk turned to religion and Mesek began to reminisce about a trip he had made to a Buddhist temple in Japan. His wife, Leipakoa, provided supporting comments and interpretive paraphrases while Mesek explained the layout of the temple and the custom that visitors try to wriggle through a hole in a stone pillar ("for luck," says Leipakoa). Leipakoa has clearly heard the story often before and must be nearly as familiar with the details as Mesek himself is, but after a short digression about whether Buddhists believe in heaven or reincarnation, Leipakoa says to Mesek, "*Afta yu go?* (And then did you go through it?)"; Mesek says, "*Ye, mi mi go* (Yeah, I went through)" and gives some more orientation to the story. Leipakoa then asks, "*Be i naf blong hed blong yu i go insaed?* (But was there enough room for your head to go in?)" and in reply Mesek launches into the real drama of the story, telling me how he got stuck halfway through.

There are a number of things that Leipakoa may be doing in eliciting the story so carefully from Mesek. She might be wanting to keep a happy after-dinner conversation running as long as possible for her own enjoyment. She might be putting off a decision on who will do the dishes. She might be showing me how well-traveled members of her family are (not just visiting linguists go to exotic places). However, like Lolan with the story of Undu, I would suggest that one of the things Leipakoa is doing is using a supportive conversational mode (in this case, characterized by elicitations) to indirectly display knowledge that belongs to someone else. The experience was her husband's and takes its authority from the fact that Mesek can situate the experience in specific places and times, thus the authority of the story is most directly indexical to him. But Leipakoa can indirectly access that authority by acting as Mesek's muse, calling forth the story as it has been told before.

One might feel that this is placing undue emphasis on the act of speaking and the act of eliciting speech, but in presenting this analysis I again follow an emphasis on utterance that Rubinstein documents. People on Malo can reify words to an extreme. They explained to Rubinstein that words can be traded for other valuables such as pigs (1981: 152), so they are, in *kastom* thought, objective units. In other words, the indexicality between telling a tale and having social authority is similar to the relationship that exists between possessing and killing pigs and being wealthy.

What we seem to see here is a synchronic pattern in which women use a wide range of linguistic strategies in order to position themselves socially. While I have gone to effort to differentiate the Melanesian conceptualization of gender from others, I do not want to exoticize the situation overly. The end result has parallels in other cultures. Some of the sociolinguistic literature has claimed that women's sociolinguistic repertoire makes active use of a greater range of styles than men's (see Goodwin, this volume; Eckert 2000: 11, 19). In Rubinstein's terms, this might be glossed as indicating that a woman is making use of significantly different resources with which she can place her social self. Much as Eckert (2000) concluded about the high school girls she worked with, it appears that language is an important vehicle used by Malo women to place themselves, and that linguistic practices are especially important as a way of enabling a gendered self to emerge and be sustained.

5 Empathy and Gender

But I want to go further still. I want to characterize Lolan's and Leipakoa's strategies as expressions of empathy and I want to explore the importance of empathy in the expression of gender. In everyday parlance, "empathy" and "sympathy" are frequently used interchangeably; however, it is useful to differentiate them on the basis of the kind of subjective experience each involves. Wispé (1986: 316) distinguishes empathy from sympathy in the following way: empathy involves the speaker's experience of subjective qualities *in* the object of their empathy, whereas sympathy involves the speaker's experience of subjective qualities *about* it. Elsewhere, I have found it helpful to observe this distinction as a basis for understanding the distribution of the phrase "[I'm] sorry" that I recorded in Vanuatu (Meyerhoff 2000). Thus, empathy is fundamentally about claiming shared subjective experience, while sympathy involves a claim of shared orientation to or evaluation of an experience.

By making this distinction, Lolan and Leipakoa's strategies can be drawn into the fold of other expressions of empathy which seem to be more fundamentally grounded in concern for others. In other work, I have discussed the use and functions of linguistic variables that occur in spoken Bislama, specifically, the use of inclusive pronouns and the use of apology routines in everyday speech. Here, I will use them to explore the role of expressions of empathy in women's speech more broadly. This will enable us to see how empathy fits into the larger picture of knowledge, authority, and power, specifically, how these properties are claimed or indirectly indexed by linguistic means.

5.1 Empathy at linguistic work: Use of inclusive pronouns

Bislama is a typical Austronesian language in making a distinction in the first person plural between referents that include the addressee and referents that exclude the addressee. The Bislama forms are *yumi* (from English 'you [and] me') and *mifala* (from English 'me fellow[s]') respectively. I have found it useful to distinguish between a literal (truth-conditional) form of co-reference and what I have called a metaphorical form of co-reference (Meyerhoff 1998).[11] Thus, when a speaker says *"Bae yumi go nao? (Shall we go now?)"* and the addressee is one of the people who will leave, I would say this is a literal use of the inclusive pronoun. However, we also find in Bislama (and in several other languages that make this distinction) instances of *yumi* being used where the addressee is not, or could not have been, one of the people undertaking the event described. For instance, my landlord had been telling me about his former job in the regional health board, and he summed up his discussion saying, *"Be ol risej we yumi mekem . . .* (But the research that we [inclusive] conducted . . .)" when clearly it was not the case that I had participated in any of said research.

I argued (Meyerhoff 1998) that this metaphorical use of the inclusive indexes a perceived, salient, shared in-group membership. I show that I was addressed with this non-literal use of the inclusive pronoun most frequently by other women, and men only occasionally used the metaphorical inclusive with me. I suggested that this distribution of the variable reflected the generally high social salience of the intergroup boundary between the sexes. The apparent exceptions with male speakers occurred when one could point to evidence that some other in-group identity that we shared had become more salient in the conversation.

5.2 Empathy at linguistic work: Saying "sorry"

My discussion of the linguistic routine associated with apologies, "*Sore* ([I'm] sorry)," likewise focused on non-canonical uses of the form (Meyerhoff 1999, 2000). I examined a distributional difference in the use of *sore* to express empathetic concern rather than to express contrition for some social transgression. Although both men and women used it to apologize for a transgression, I only observed women using the form to express concern. So while a man (or woman) might say "*Mi sore tumas blong talem olsem long yu* . . . (I'm very sorry to say this to you)," I only noted women using *sore* to empathize with their interlocutor or the subject of discussion, for example:

Lisa: *Afta bebi i stap, ledaon gud*
Adelin: *Awe, sore!*

Lisa: And the baby stayed there [by itself] lying quietly
Adelin: Oh no!

5.3 General functionality of empathy

If we observe the distinction between empathy and sympathy outlined above, then both *sore* and the use of the inclusive pronoun when the addressee was not a literal co-participant or co-experiencer of an event can be seen as expressions of empathy. Both claim shared experience in subjective qualities, though interestingly, the two reverse the polarity of the term. When using *sore*, a speaker claims that she shares the subjective experience of her addressee; when she uses *yumi* she claims that the addressee shared her experience.

In my analysis of empathetic apologies (Meyerhoff 2000), I argued that the claim of shared knowledge inherent to an empathetic apology is extremely important for its distribution. Because a statement of empathy implies shared knowledge, and because knowledge (in my own culture, too) confers covert power or authority on the bearer, I suggested that the distribution of an empathetic strategy like *sore* was a way in which the users could index not only their role as caregivers and nurturers (which is part of macro-level ideologies about gender), but could also imply personal authority at the micro-level where authority is not a quality directly associated with them in general ideologies about gender.

I believe this insight holds more generally. The discourse strategies I have shown Malo women using to frame or elicit stories from others provides a similar opportunity to indirectly associate themselves with knowledge, in those cases *ples*-specific knowledge that directly indexes the authority of the male speakers. As with an empathetic apology, these strategies manage to do this while ostensibly maintaining a posture of supportiveness and care.

Up to this point, this chapter has been concerned with providing details of the synchronic situation with respect to language and gender in Vanuatu. I have drawn parallels between the emergent quality of gender and the emergent quality of authority. Insofar as the latter also has a gendered dimension, I have made the case that the two are more than ontological parallels, they are in fact related. I have made a case for the apparent functionality of linguistic expressions of empathy in the context of Ni-Vanuatu beliefs about gender, knowledge, and authority, and the role of *ples* in Ni-Vanuatu *kastom*.

In the next section, I introduce historical data on the way gender has been perceived and more specifically, the way women have been represented since the colonial and missionary period in Vanuatu. The reason for doing this is so that we can consider the historical baggage that this (like every other) ideological system carries. Just as in the study of sound change, we consider synchronic variation to be a reflex of ongoing and historical processes, I try to draw some links between the synchronic and the diachronic conceptualization of gender identity in Vanuatu, and will discuss aspects of the tension between them, especially the tensions that may emerge for women.

6   A Diachronic Perspective on Gender in Vanuatu

We often spend considerable energy providing an account of the synchronic social and linguistic context of the variation observed in a speech community, but patterns of discourse (like the ones outlined here) do not emerge from a diachronic vacuum. Although research in language and gender is increasingly concerned with providing an accurate picture of the way in which gender is both reflected and constructed through verbal interactions and in discourses about gender, we sometimes fail to place the construction of gender in its full social and historical context (some exceptions to this are Inoue 1994; Cameron 1995; Romaine 1996; Pauwels 1998). In the Pacific, this may be because we do not have access to a detailed or stable record of the social context going back earlier than European contact. In order to consider the longitudinal context of the patterns of language and gender that we see in Vanuatu today, we are limited to records since the eighteenth century. In the remainder of this chapter, I turn to this historical record and consider what it reveals about gender ideologies in Vanuatu when they are seen longitudinally. I then explore the extent to which these facts inform an analysis of the current situation.

6.1   Early contact and representations

Contact between the local, Ni-Vanuatu people and Europeans first occurred in the seventeenth century when various European explorers passed through the area. Longer-term contact was only established in the nineteenth century when traders and whalers set up stations in Vanuatu.[12] Shortly thereafter came the first missionaries, Marist, Presbyterian, and Anglican. In what follows, I consider how the Europeans perceived the sexes and how they tried to understand the gendering of social space and social routines in Vanuatu. I will focus mainly on their perceptions of women.

Forster (1996 [1778]: 164), traveling on Cook's second voyage, describes Ni-Vanuatu women in terms that were already shaping the broader European stereotypes of the Pacific. The Pacific societies were believed to reveal various stages in human development. Forster found Ni-Vanuatu women "deformed," they were generally "ill-favored, nay some are very ugly" (1996: 181). The most womanly aspects of their bodies are cartooned as odious, their breasts "flaccid and pendulous" (1996: 181). He noted that their social role seemed to be that of "pack-horses . . . for their indolent husbands," doing "all the most laborious drudgery in the plantations" (1996: 164). In marked contrast to this were his perception of Tahitian women. In Tahitian society women were "tall and beautiful" (1996: 179), "Venus of Medicis" (1996: 154) (needless to say, their breasts were "well proportioned" and "extremely feminine"). Forster clearly saw these differences in the women's appearance and their lifestyle as indicating Tahitian culture to have reached superior heights to that in Vanuatu (1996: 195). Jolly (1992a) points out that this means women played a particularly important role in shaping the social, political, and aesthetic evaluations early Anglo-Europeans made of Ni-Vanuatu.

The one positive thing Forster had to say about the socially subordinate position of women in Vanuatu was that he felt that this had obliged them to develop much keener intellects than the men around them, and also to better develop empathetic skills than men had (1996: 259).[13] So apparently empathy (though it is unclear whether Forster would have meant it in the very specific sense that Wispé and I use it) or concern for others has been an overtly displayed quality for some time.

These skills appear to have been less evident to European colonists, and during the colonial era the nature of discourses about gender change tack. Jolly (1993) points out that this should be seen in terms of the gendered dimension of colonialism itself. Until recently, discourses of a colonial heritage tended to off-set such "masculine" traits of colonization as hierarchy, authority, and

control, against the tempering "feminine" qualities of sympathetic understanding, egalitarian relations, and flexibility (Jolly 1993: 109).

Jolly's work is interesting because she not only documents how colonial
women were the subjects of a larger (re)construction of a middle-class domestic aesthetic in the European mind, but she also shows how colonial women
collaborated in actively constructing these new roles and models of femininity.
She compares the writings of a missionary, Charlotte Geddie, and a colonist/
adventurer, Beatrice Grimshaw, and demonstrates a pervasive maternalism at
work in the early period of extended European/Ni-Vanuatu contact.

Geddie's writings, for instance, exhibit a tension between two stances: her
perception of racial difference between herself and Ni-Vanuatu women, and
an in-group identity based on being of the same sex. Geddie resolves this by
recasting her relationship with Ni-Vanuatu women as not being between a
colonizer and the colonized. Instead, by invariably referring to the Ni-Vanuatu
converts as the "girls," the relationship is likened to a mother guiding and
training her daughters in the arts and bearing appropriate to a middle-class
woman. Mission women, all "aching hearts and cushioning bosoms" (Jolly
1993: 113), saw their role as rescuing Ni-Vanuatu women from a state of servitude in which they were perceived to exist at the time.

Similarly, Grimshaw's writings show a deep ambivalence about her relationship with Ni-Vanuatu women. Although Grimshaw writes in overtly racist
terms (which is not true of Geddie's writing), like Geddie, Grimshaw casts
herself as someone able to bring beauty and femininity to the betterment of
Ni-Vanuatu women's lives.

Geddie clearly operates within a masculinist ideology of colonialism, but
Jolly points out (1993: 115) that she and Grimshaw effectively construct a
relationship with local women that combines idealized masculine features,
such as control of other and a control of an aesthetic and economic hierarchy,
with aspects of an idealized femininity, such as an inherent sympathy with
and for the women who are the objects of their attention. This dissonance was
hardly the only one created by the situation, since the women missionaries'
own lives in the colonies and women's lives in Europe at the time were far
from being perfect models of the gendered ideals that so clearly colored
Geddie's and Grimshaw's interactions with local women (Jolly 1991: 31).[14]
However, one thing that the missionary families did provide was a fairly
consistent model of a world in which a dichotomous and natural gender division was assumed, and moreover one in which the most salient division of
labors was, again, in the idealized dichotomy between the public and the
domestic (Jolly 1991: 46) (a point I will return to shortly).

6.2 Twentieth-century colonial representations

As colonial contact took firmer hold in the area, the profile of the colonists
became more diverse. Numbers of younger men arrived looking for economic

profit, and they also actively engaged with the cultures they encountered, attempting to impose their own conceptions of gender (and race) relations on the general and particular situations they found themselves in. Illuminating data on this is to be found in a lengthy record of correspondence between an Englishman identified as Asterisk and a close friend back in England at the start of the twentieth century (Lynch 1923). Asterisk's letters reveal a deep ambivalence about Ni-Vanuatu women. When referring to his partner (and soon to be mother of his child) he could write positively and even chide himself for his racism, as in "[she] is much cleaner than a good proportion of the white women I have 'met.' And yet six months ago I was lampooning her to you as a savage beast." Nonetheless, in the next sentence he goes on, "But do you think I could tolerate her in civilization? Not for a week" (Lynch 1923: 166–7). Even as he appears to grow fonder of the woman he dubs "Topsy" in his letters ("I miss her horribly now when she goes away"; Lynch 1923: 172), he continues to regularly call her a "savage" or "childish."

The whole process of "going native" for Europeans in the Pacific tended to be, and still very often is, a process that is both highly gendered and highly sexualized. To really "go native" often entailed acquiring local sexual partners, with an increase in prestige all round (Manderson and Jolly 1997 has much discussion related to this). Given the demographics of the White population in the Pacific and social constraints on women (both in the colonial period, and to a lesser extent today), this means that "going native" was very much more a male activity than a female activity. The increase in prestige that this affords has suggestive parallels with some of the issues I have already raised and shows that the relationship between gender, practice, knowledge, and authority is germane to more than just Ni-Vanuatu society. By acquiring a specialized form of local knowledge, a European man increases his ability to speak with authority about what remains the unknowable to his confrères back home. For a Ni-Vanuatu woman, the relationship provides not only access to money and Western accessories, but potentially also a half-White child. If a woman's *ples* is partible partly by virtue of her ability to give birth to children belonging to some place other than her own natal *ples*, then this dynamic of the colonial social system introduces a further complication to traditional Ni-Vanuatu ideologies. What it means is that *ples* is not only tied up with ideologies about gender, but also with ideologies of race.

The dichotomy between male and female, and the sexualization or the infantilization of one half of that dichotomy, seem to be tropes of Europeans' own view of women as "damned whores or God's police" (Summers 1994) – that is, of their own preoccupations with and assumptions about gender – rather than an accurate representation of what was found. Webb (1995) makes it clear how pervasive this phenomenon was in the Pacific at the time. Photographs of Pacific themes were often posed or retouched in the studio to suit expectations about the subject matter "at home," posing women, for example, either in cozy family shots with their children or in poses suggesting sexual availability.

The point of this extended discussion of some of the sociohistorical dynamics of gender in Vanuatu is to make the case that when we consider how gender and language interact today we need to take into account that we are dealing with a tension between multiple ideologies, some indigenous, some external, and all of which carry some historical baggage. *Kastom* ways of knowing (including customary ways of knowing what constitutes a gendered person) play off against a Western, essentialized gender dichotomy that is explicitly identified with modern social values. *Kastom* ways of knowing also play off against competition for control in the public sphere, and yet as I have shown, the idealization of a public–private contrast itself arose from Western ideals about the family and the sexes (see also McElhinny 1997 on this supposed distinction). This means that it is all very well to evaluate discourse patterns against traditional Melanesian ideologies of gender, as I have attempted to do in the earlier parts of this chapter, but we also have to evaluate independent social forces. These introduce an element of change in the culture and in ideologies of power which intersect with the simultaneous reification of tradition.

Reflexes of the colonial idealization of gender roles and family roles continue to influence the way gender is talked about in Vanuatu today. These ideals did not come alone. A number of other concepts became salient in Melanesia following colonization and missionization, and some of these are entangled with gender ideologies in particularly salient ways. The complex and sometimes contradictory contrasts between modernity and tradition, and Christianity and *kastom*, that also emerged following European contact in Vanuatu intersect with an idealized opposition between manliness and womanliness in ways that sometimes shed further light on the way in which gender is tied up with the emergence of social authority or power. There is much to say on this (and much of it is expressed more thoughtfully in Bolton (2003) than I can here), so my discussion will be somewhat superficial. The purposes of these brief comments, though, is to bring up-to-date the discussion of the impact of intercultural contact on the negotiation of and emergence of gender as a social category.

The gendered dimensions of the contrast between *skul* ('school', which refers to parochial education and church learning in general, as well as secular schools) on the one hand, and *kastom* and tradition on the other, are especially rich. Rhetoric about *skul* and *kastom* often takes on a Manichaean quality in Vanuatu discourse (Tabani 1999). In practice, the opposition between the two is by no means so neat; as Jolly (1992b) points out, *kastom* is a polysemous word. It can refer to specific practices (in which case it stands in opposition to Christianity) but it can also refer to an entire way of life, in which case it stands in opposition to the values of other cultures and groups (e.g. Western, European culture). Some of the attitudes toward customary ways of life that appeared in Geddie's writings have, however, become thoroughly integrated into Vanuatu social and political thought. It is now axiomatic in many quarters that the time before conversion, when Ni-Vanuatu lived according to *kastom* and *kastom* law, was a bad time, a time of darkness, and one of the aspects of social life that most needed reorganizing was the role of women and men in the family.

As we saw, the relationship (and division of labor) between the sexes was an important criterion for defining a distinct post-Christian culture. The post-Christian ideal was a nuclear household with the father at the public head of the family, and a mother responsible for domestic work.[15] However, despite mission rhetoric about the wretched lives of Vanuatu women pre-contact, the Western models of family life and the gender roles imposed with evangelism increased the workload of most women (see Philips, this volume). They generated new expectations about domesticity, mothering, and support of one's spouse, all of which were to be played out in more individualistic or private domains than had existed before (Jolly 1993; Ralston 1992).

This move to identify women's work with the domestic sphere was accompanied by a move to exclude them from the public. Thus, where aspects of *kastom* nevertheless have continued to be an important basis for the organization of social life in Vanuatu, the European ideologies about gender roles contribute to a destabilization of traditions or *kastom* that do not reflect the naturalized hierarchy of men and women. For example, matrilineal land rights and clan descent were the norm in various parts of Melanesia including parts of northern Vanuatu (Clark 1985) before contact.[16] However, the importance of maternal descent lines for defining your *ples* in these regions continues to be weakened even today, and this (internal) destabilization of *kastom* may be justified in part by referring to biblical teaching (Jolly 1996). The late Grace Mera Molisa, poet, politician, and advocate of women's rights in Vanuatu, spoke forcefully about her feelings of being progressively robbed and disenfranchised by the weakening of the traditional social importance of women in the customarily matrilineal region from which she comes.

The situation of urban young people reveals further aspects of the tension between *kastom* and Western culture that are gendered. These tensions highlight the other meaning of *kastom*, namely the way it stands for indigenous, Ni-Vanuatu values and culture in contrast with external cultures. In an outstanding piece of ethnography, the Vanuatu Young People's Project (VYPP) shows how many urban young people distrust some of the colonial institutions of power and authority, such as the police, which for them are simply organs of oppression and harassment (Vanuatu Young People's Project n.d. [1998?]). For them, *kastom* is a necessary and desirable alternative to such institutions, and they speak of *kastom* practices as offering a viable code of conduct as they navigate the challenges of modernity in the capital city, Port Vila.

Yet it is clear that there is no simple return to an idealized (and equally essentialized) *kastom* past. There may be some attractions to *kastom* knowledge and *kastom* authority, but these have to be mediated through their experience of late modernity (Leap, this volume). For example, young women may have mixed feelings about *kastom*; it may offer value for some aspects of their social life, but conversely it may threaten others. As noted above, the notion of *kastom* itself now reflects a synthetic, postcolonial set of values and may be interpreted as a codification of male power over women. As the VYPP observes, *kastom* may be interpreted as an expectation that a woman will stay with an abusive husband (or agree to an arranged marriage). Some of the young women interviewed in *Kilim Taem* understandably resist its control over this aspect of their lives.

However, they may not speak out very loudly against *kastom*, because such young women find themselves in a delicate philosophical and political situation. Not only is it possible that they will be seen as inconsistent (arguing for a strengthening of *kastom* in some domains of their lives and rebelling against it in others), but voicing a resistance to *kastom* may provide a justification for their further marginalization and silencing. Because adherence to *kastom* can be seen as an expression of Ni-Vanuatu identity (versus Western identities), women speaking up for women's and children's rights in families may be perceived as aligned too much with external value systems (such as Western feminism). This can in turn be transformed into a rationale for further excluding them from the processes and debates of nation-building.

In some senses, the vexed status of *kastom* for young people in Port Vila matches the complications that their lives introduce to their claim on a *ples*. Although many people in Vila continue to live in neighborhoods that have affiliations to a particular island, this is by no means always true. The road (both metaphorical and literal) back to their island may be hard to navigate (and this may be particularly true for young women; Eriksen 2000). Thus, again, we see how *ples* and gender may be tied together. Customary relationships to land and people are destabilized by the same sorts of social change, and the qualities that emerge from relationships with places and people are in turn further problematized.

6.3   *The place of Bislama in claiming* ples

Finally, I return to a linguistic matter. In this section of the chapter, I consider the role that the national creole, Bislama, plays for some people in the emergence of gender in Vanuatu today.

Many people (Ni-Vanuatu and external researchers) have observed that in the last decades of the twentieth century, there was an appreciable increase in the numbers of women using Bislama as the main medium of communication. It was unclear, however, how much of a direct effect (if any) this was having on the development of the language. Indirectly, it was clear that the increased use of Bislama as the basis for communication in the home was deepening the pool of first-language speakers of Bislama. Since this phenomenon was assumed to be more prevalent in towns than in villages, it was possible that distinct varieties of Bislama might be taking shape (one used in towns and one used in villages). This was the background to my research in Vanuatu in the first place.

On arriving in Vanuatu, however, I found that use of Bislama in the home was more widespread in the village community on Malo than I had been led to believe it might be. Formerly, it had been expected that when a woman married out of the area in which her first language was spoken, she would learn the language of her new home, and this language would be the back-drop to her children's home life. On Malo, I met a number of women whose experiences still followed this pattern, but I also met a number of women who spoke only (or principally) Bislama to their children. Here I will explore some possible motivations and the possible significance of this linguistic choice for the latter group of women.

First, they can be contrasted with the women who learnt the local vernacular, Tamambo. Two such women were older (with grown children and grandchil-dren) and had moved from central Vanuatu to Malo after meeting their hus-bands while working in Vila, and two were younger women (with school-age children). The younger women who regularly used Tamambo at home and who were trying hard to learn it both came from islands closer to Malo (one from west Ambae; one from south Santo), specifically linguistic regions where their first language shares a relatively large proportion of core vocabulary with Tamambo. Both women noted that this paved the way for them and made their task of learning Tamambo comparatively easy.

On the other hand, the women who used Bislama in their homes were all younger (their children were still at school; the oldest had a son finishing secondary school). They came from a wide range of home islands: some in central and southern Vanuatu; some from northern Vanuatu (like Malo). By comparing the two groups, it is clear that neither the age of the speaker nor the degree of linguistic relatedness between a woman's first language and her husband's can account for all the differences observed.

The second thing to consider, then, is the wider function and significance of Bislama in Vanuatu. Bislama is the only national language of Vanuatu (English and French are co-official languages). Its spread and use in the latter half of the twentieth century is tightly intertwined with the nationalist movement that led ultimately to independence. Historically, too, Bislama rings with moral and social connotations. It was originally the language of the migrant, internation-alized labor force that left Vanuatu in the late eighteenth and early nineteenth centuries to work on plantations in Australia, Fiji, and elsewhere. For this reason, it was mainly, but not exclusively, a language of men, and for some time it remained a language learnt by men and associated with male activities, crystallizing in a less variable form with the participation of increasing numbers of people in the paid workforce and by its use on Radio Vanuatu (Bolton 2000). In short, Bislama has for most of its history been more or less strongly associated with movement and the fashioning of supralocal identity. These are the features indexed by the language; it is only to the extent that men in the past had freer access to movement and more frequent opportunities to associ-ate themselves with supralocal interests that the language was in any sense a "men's" language.

One of the factors contributing to the increased use of Bislama by women in their homes on Malo is, I believe, the ongoing association between Bislama and movement and national identity. This is by no means the only factor contributing to its use, but other interpersonal factors are beyond the scope of this discussion. A woman who chooses to use Bislama with her children can in some ways be seen as pragmatically exploiting her outsider status, and foregrounding a claim to be a woman, not of her husband's very local *ples*, but of a *ples* that defines Vanuatu as a nation.

In sum, the associations between Bislama and movement and the choice by some *woman nara aelan* to use Bislama bring us back to my earlier point. They shed further light on women's task of having to (re)create a *ples* for themselves on marriage and the challenge of claiming authority. Bislama provides a linguistic constant for them that is perhaps analogous to the constant of *ples* that men have staying in their home village.

7   Conclusion

One of the main goals of this chapter has been to explore the ties between the way gender is understood and voiced in its historical and synchronic contexts. For gender, one could substitute any other social category, since what I have tried to demonstrate is a broader principle, namely that the synchronic indexing of a category such as gender in talk disguises aspects of how that category has been talked about over time.

I have suggested that when looking at language and gender in Vanuatu, the use of empathy is best seen in this light. Empathy can be a covert linguistic action allowing the speaker to indirectly establish some control over knowledge and stake some claim to *ples*, but the significance of both these concepts and the veiled way in which women often tap into them derive from historical notions of gender, not just current ones. What I have also tried to show is that both internal and external historical forces are part of the picture. This is particularly stark in Vanuatu, given its history of colonial contact, but must surely be equally true in any context.

Which leads me to my final point. This section of the Handbook has presented a series of local case-studies. However, I hope that in both its methodology and its unification of themes, this chapter has a more general relevance, beyond a description of language and gender in Vanuatu. Clearly, it would be extraordinary indeed to find that only in Vanuatu is there such a nuanced relationship between gender, language, social history, and the current social climate. Indeed, a number of the chapters in this volume attest to that. I suspect, too, that even the quintessentially Ni-Vanuatu concept of *ples* (and how it relates to the establishment of knowledge and authority) is of practical use for the analysis of gender elsewhere, and indeed Besnier (this volume) explores how contestations of and problems with defining place contribute to the dynamics of gender and multilingualism in Tonga. Naturally, claims to authority and knowledge and the way these attributes feed ideologies of gender and the details of the power structures associated with them will differ from place to place. As we have seen, they have looked very different even at different periods in Vanuatu. But what may look more similar are the patterns relating power, place, authority, and gender through language.

NOTES

1　I am grateful to Niko Besnier, Lissant Bolton, Atiqa Hachimi, Janet Holmes, Dorothy Jauncey, and the Advanced Sociolinguistics class in the MSc for Applied Linguistics at the University of Edinburgh for comments on and input to earlier drafts. My thanks also to the Wenner-Gren Foundation for funding my 1994–5 trip in the field (grant #5742), and to the people of Vanuatu, especially my ever-generous hosts on Malo for encouraging my curiosity and taking the time to teach me.

2　As always, I use pseudonyms for the people I worked with in Vanuatu.

3　*Fakaleitī*, as Besnier explains, literally means "in the manner of a lady"; *māhū* appears to be a reflex of a proto-Oceanic word meaning "gentle" (Robert Blust, personal communication). Hachimi and Besnier point out to me that I may be placing excessive weight on the presence or absence of a specific lexical item in writing off the category of transgendered individuals from Malo society. I take their point, but I do think that where a specific lexical item, such as *māhū*, does exist, we can assume a qualitative difference in the way the community thinks about such individuals compared to communities where there is no such lexicalization.

4　*Ni-Vanuatu* is the adjective form of *Vanuatu*.

5　However, my reading of (even) Butler, whose 1990 work is fundamental to the analysis of identity as a series of performative acts, takes the biological sexing of individuals as a basis in her discussion of the psychological processes and social acts contributing to identity formation.

6　Women would occasionally make an announcement in the public meeting after church. These were less formal and more spontaneous occasions, yet here too in general women remained at the edges or outside the church hall, while men took up places under the roof and on the benches.

7　For the record, Rubinstein does not characterize the sexes in the same way Strathern does. He describes them as being "complementary" and unequal in the social domain (1978: 286), but the hierarchy of male-over-female breaks down in the cosmic domain.

8　Undu went out diving and gathering shellfish with some friends and disappeared mysteriously while they weren't looking. He had been heard to speak disrespectfully of a stone at the beach that had *kastom* power and so it was presumed he had been carried off by devils. He has been seen since then, but no-one can get close enough to talk to him.

9   *Tawean* is a kinship term that on Malo can pick out the (natal or classificatory) brother of the speaker's wife. It can also designate other relationships (discussed in Rubinstein 1978); in this case it indexes a relationship between men only, the speaker's great-grandfather.

10   Naturally there are contexts in which a woman (even *woman nara aelan*) has objective authority. When Lolan is at school, and especially for the two years she was principal at her school, the challenges of discursively constructing authority differ. An interesting case-study would consist in following someone like Lolan and examining coherent threads in how they manage their shifting authority.

11   I have no particular theory of metaphor in mind when I call it this, but rather intend it to stand for a generalized non-literal use of the pronoun.

12   Known then as the New Hebrides.

13   "[T]he constant acts of indelicacy, oppression, and inhumanity [against women]. . . , and the more delicate frame of their bodies, together with the finer and more irritable texture of their nerves, have contributed more towards the improvement and perfection of their intellectual faculties, than of those of the male . . . because their nerves are finer and more irritable; this makes them more inclined to imitation, and more quick in observing the properties and relations of things; their memory is more faithful in retaining them; and their faculties

thereby become more capable of comparing them, and of abstracting general ideas from their perceptions. . . . Used implicitly to submit to the will of their males, they have been early taught to suppress the flights of passion; cooler reflexion, gentleness, and every method for obtaining the approbation, and for winning the good-will of others have taken their place, . . . all this may perhaps prepare [the race] for the first dawnings of civilization" (1996: 259). Again, notice the crucial role women's roles and behaviors play in defining the progress of civilization.

14   Forster seems to have missed the dissonance between his attitudes to what he saw in Melanesia and the reality of his own culture. Though he was a fairly self-aware observer, he appears to have been blind to the parallels between the servitude of Ni-Vanuatu women and the lives of most women and men in Europe. Arguably, at that time the entire European lower class worked like "pack-horses" in a state of "laborious drudgery."

15   This kind of transformation occurred widely in the region. Dureau (1998) discusses a similar process by which Christianity transformed family relationships on Simbo (Solomon Islands), changing a woman's most salient relationship from that of someone's "sister" to someone's "wife."

16   Allen (1981) suggests that the male secret societies found in most of Vanuatu developed historically as a response to dominant matrilineal systems.

REFERENCES

Allen, Michael 1981: Rethinking old problems: Matriliny, secret societies and political evolution. In Michael R. Allen (ed.) *Vanuatu: Politics, Economics and Ritual in Island Melanesia*. Sydney: Academic Press, pp. 9–34.

Bolton, Lissant 1999: Women, place and practice in Vanuatu: A view from Ambae. *Oceania* 70: 43–55.

Bolton, Lissant 2000: Radio and the redefinition of *kastom* in Vanuatu. In David L. Hanlon and Geoffrey M. White (eds) *Voyaging through the Contemporary Pacific*. Lanham, MD: Rowman & Littlefield, pp. 377–402.

Bolton, Lissant 2003: *Unfolding the Moon: Women,* Kastom *and Textiles in Vanuatu*. Honolulu: University of Hawaii Press.

Butler, Judith 1990: *Gender Trouble: Feminism and the Subversion of Identity*. New York/London: Routledge.

Cameron, Deborah 1995: *Verbal Hygiene*. London and New York: Routledge.

Clark, Ross 1985: Languages of north and central Vanuatu: Groups, chains, clusters and waves. In Andrew K. Pawley and Lois Carrington (eds) *Austronesian Linguistics at the 15th Pacific Science Congress*. Canberra: The Australian National University, pp. 199–236.

Dureau, Christine 1998: From sisters to wives: Changing contexts of maternity on Simbo, Western Solomon Islands. In Kalpana Ram and Margaret Jolly (eds) *Maternities and Modernities: Colonial and Postcolonial Experiences in Asia and the Pacific*. Oxford: Oxford University Press, pp. 239–74.

Eckert, Penelope 2000: *Linguistic Variation as Social Practice*. Oxford: Blackwell.

Eriksen, Annelin 2000: Ambrym women on the move: Effects of female migration and wage labors. Paper presented at the workshop Walking About: Travel, Migration, and Movement in Vanuatu – a Cross-disciplinary Discussion. Center for Cross-Cultural Research, Australian National University, Canberra, October 2000.

Forster, Johann Reinhold 1996 [1778]: *Observations Made During a Voyage Round the World*. Honolulu: University of Hawaii Press.

Inoue, Minako 1994: Gender and linguistic modernization: Historicizing Japanese women's language. In Mary Bucholtz, Anita C. Liang, Laurel A. Sutton, and Caitlin Hines (eds) *Cultural Performances: Proceedings of the Third Berkeley Women and Language Conference*. Berkeley, CA: Berkeley Women and Language Group, University of California, pp. 322–33.

Jauncey, Dorothy 1997: A Grammar of Tamambo. Unpublished PhD dissertation, Australian National University.

Jolly, Margaret 1991: "To save the girls for better and brighter lives": Presbyterian missions and women in the south of Vanuatu: 1848–1870. *The Journal of Pacific History* 26: 27–48.

Jolly, Margaret 1992a: "Ill-natured comparisons": Racism and relativism in European representations of ni-Vanuatu from Cook's second voyage. *History and Anthropology* 5: 331–64.

Jolly, Margaret 1992b: Custom and the way of the land: Past and present in Vanuatu and Fiji. *Oceania* 62(4): 330–54.

Jolly, Margaret 1993: Colonizing women: The maternal body and empire. In Sneja Gunew and Anna Yeatman (eds) *Feminism and the Politics of Difference*. St Leonard's, NSW: Allen and Unwin, pp. 103–27.

Jolly, Margaret 1996: Woman ikat raet long human raet o no?: Women's rights, human rights and domestic violence in Vanuatu. *Feminist Review* 52: 169–90.

Lynch, Bohun (ed.) 1923: *Isles of Illusion: Letters from the South Seas*. Boston: Small, Maynard & Co.

Manderson, Lenore and Jolly, Margaret (eds) 1997: *Sites of Desire: Economies of Pleasure: Sexualities in Asia and the Pacific*. Chicago and London: University of Chicago Press.

McElhinny, Bonnie 1997: Ideologies of public and private language in sociolinguistics. In Ruth Wodak (ed.) *Gender and Discourse*. London: Sage, pp. 106–39.

Meyerhoff, Miriam 1998: Accommodating your data: The use and misuse of accommodation theory in sociolinguistics. *Language and Communication* 18: 205–25.

Meyerhoff, Miriam 1999: *Sorry* in the Pacific: Defining communities, defining practices. *Language in Society* 28(2): 225–38.

Meyerhoff, Miriam 2000: How apologies get to be gendered work. In Janet Holmes (ed.) *Gendered Speech in Social Context*. Wellington: Victoria University Press, pp. 52–62.

Ochs, Elinor 1992: Indexing gender. In Alessandro Duranti and Charles Goodwin (eds) *Rethinking Context: Language as an Interactive Phenomenon*. Cambridge: Cambridge University Press, pp. 335–58.

Ochs, Elinor and Taylor, Carolyn 1995: The "father knows best" dynamic in dinnertime narratives. In Kira Hall and Mary Bucholtz (eds) *Gender Articulated: Language and the Socially Constructed Self*. New York and London: Routledge, pp. 97–120.

Pauwels, Anne 1998: *Women Changing Language*. London and New York: Longman.

Ralston, Caroline 1992: The study of women in the Pacific. *The Contemporary Pacific* 4(1): 162–75.

Romaine, Suzanne 1996: Why women are supposed to talk like ladies: The glamour of grammar. In Natasha Warner, Jocelyn Ahlers, Leela Bilmes, Monica Oliver, Suzanne Wertheim, and Melinda Chen (eds) *Gender and Belief Systems: Proceedings of the Fourth Berkeley Women and Language Conference*. Berkeley, CA: Berkeley Women and Language Group, University of California, pp. 633–44.

Rubinstein, Robert L. 1978: Placing the Self on Malo: An Account of the Culture of Malo Island, New Hebrides. Unpublished PhD dissertation, Bryn Mawr College, Pennsylvania.

Rubinstein, Robert L. 1981: Knowledge and political process on Malo. In Michael R. Allen (ed.) *Vanuatu: Politics, Economics and Ritual in Island Melanesia*. Sydney: Academic Press, pp. 135–72.

Strathern, Marilyn 1988: *The Gender of the Gift: Problems with Women and Problems with Society in Melanesia*. Berkeley, CA: University of California Press.

Summers, Anne 1994: *Damned Whores and God's Police: The Colonization of Women in Australia*. Ringwood, Victoria and New York: Penguin.

Tabani, Marc Kurt 1999: *Kastom* et traditionalisme: Quelles inventions pour quelles traditions à Tanna (Vanuatu)? *Journal de la Société des Océanistes* 109: 121–31.

Vanuatu Young People's Project (no date [1998?]) *Kilim Taem (Killing Time)*. AusAID and UNICEF.

Webb, Virginia-Lee 1995: Manipulated images: European photographs of Pacific peoples. In Elazar Barkan and Ronald Bush (eds) *Prehistories of the Future: The Primitivist Project and the Culture of Modernism.* Stanford, CA: Stanford University Press, pp. 175–201.

Wispé, Lauren 1986: The distinction between sympathy and empathy: To call forth a concept a word is needed. *Journal of Personality and Social Psychology* 50(2): 314–21.

14 Constructing and Managing Male Exclusivity in Talk-in-interaction

JACK SIDNELL

> *One keeps forgetting to go right down to the foundations. One doesn't put the question marks deep enough down.*
>
> Ludwig Wittgenstein, *Culture and Value* (1980: 62)

1 Introduction

This chapter addresses the issues involved, for both members and analysts, in the production and recognition of exclusively male contexts and attends to the organization of talk within so-established contexts.[1] In this respect it differs in outlook and mode of argumentation from much, if not most, work in the field of interactional sociolinguistics where the facts of the "context" (including the relevance of the participants' gender) are often treated as pre-established. The concern of much work in interactional sociolinguistics is to discover correlations between some feature of the "context" and the talk seen to occur "within" it.[2] It is argued here, in contrast, that members' production and recognition of a social setting, including the visibility of the participants' gender, is a topic worthy of sustained empirical investigation. Rather than taking the social setting or context as a backdrop against which the phenomena of real analytic interest occur (e.g. talk), it is suggested that practices of talk-in-interaction are implicated in the very recognizability of the determinate features of those settings.

The discussion is divided into three sections: the first (section 2 below) examines theoretical issues at the nexus of conversation analysis and gender and language studies. The second (section 3) provides an analysis of the way context or social situations are constructed through talk-in-interaction as exclusively male. The third (section 4) looks at two practices of speaking which weave gender into the seen-but-unnoticed backdrop of everyday life. Taken together, sections 3 and 4 present an extended case-study of a male domain: the rural Guyanese rumshop.

2   The Visibility of Gender in Talk: Some Initial Considerations

The characterization of a setting as "male-only" or "exclusively female" is not simply a description to be judged as to its accuracy but also a formulation of that setting. Such a characterization formulates the setting in so far as it extracts one feature of the context and proposes its relevance to the organization of the activities embedded therein.[3] To see that this is the case one need only note that the same setting might just as accurately be described as "adult-only," "exclusively human," "conversations involving people more than four feet tall," "rumshop talk," "kitchen talk," "conversations between vegetarians," or what have you, ad infinitum.[4] So such a description as "male-only" presupposes the relevance of gender to the organization of any setting so formulated.

A first question raised then, at least from the perspective adopted in this discussion, is whether it can be shown that there is any warrant for describing a particular setting in this way.[5] Once it is recognized that descriptions of this kind ("male-only," "men's talk" etc.) are in fact formulations, it becomes necessary to specify the grounds on which any particular formulation is selected. If such grounding is not made a requirement, the analyst is free to formulate the context in any way that suits his or her present purposes, the intellectual context of the time, the particular prejudices and analytical interests of that researcher, and so on. The alternative route, and the possibility which is at least explored in this chapter, is that such formulations be grounded in the observable and publicly displayed orientations of the participants themselves. Such a goal is not at all straightforward and it is complicated by the overwhelming presumed "obviousness" of gender – an obviousness apparent in both analysts' and members' attitudes to the phenomenon. To summarize, it is here being proposed that a formulation such as "male-only" (a basic feature of sex-differences research) contains within it a members' analysis which requires explication and cannot be simply imported as a resource of sociological analysis. An ethnomethodological respecification takes precisely this members' work, implicated in the recognizability of gendered persons and settings, as a focus of analytic inquiry.[6]

2.1 Producing and recognizing gender: The case of interactional sociolinguistics and sex-differences research

It is plainly the case that much sociolinguistic research presupposes the analytic relevance of gender.[7] Within such an approach, the fact that the participants are observably men or women is taken as warrant for formulating them, in the analysis, in such terms.[8] The problem as noted in several places with respect to gender is that, for instance, the fact that some speaker is a woman is not sufficient grounds for analyzing her talk as "women's talk" since "she is, by the same token, a Californian, Jewish, a mediator, a former weaver, [. . .] and many others" (Schegloff 1997: 165). From a conversation analytic perspective, as Kitzinger (2000: 170) notes, there are problems inherent in much research which reports sex differences in talk "because it imposes the analysts' selective adoption of members' categories ('male', 'female', 'heterosexual', lesbian' and so on) on the data, without troubling to show that the participants themselves are orienting to doing gender or sexuality in the talk."

These same considerations apply to research which focuses on the assumed gender of the context rather than the gender of individual speakers. Sex-differences research investigating differences between talk in all-male versus all-female groups takes these designations as self-evident ("obvious") and as a starting point of empirical analysis. In many cases the purported relevance of gender to these contexts is built directly into the methods of data collection as women (or men) are instructed to make recordings that fit the description. This demands of subjects that they do an analysis of the setting in which the recordings are made and, presumably, encourages them to police or, at least, to regulate it in ways that will produce a data set that can be seen to fit the specifications of the researcher's instructions. How subjects do this is rarely, if ever, discussed. What will they do, for instance, if a male child enters the room (calls in from another room, calls on the telephone, etc.)? Will this count, for members or analyst, as a disruption of the all-female context of interaction? Data derived from such procedures is, for these reasons, problematically designated "spontaneously occurring" (Coates 1997: 108). With respect to data collection, Cameron (1997: 47) reports: "In 1990, a 21-year-old student in a language and gender class I was teaching at a college in the southern USA tape-recorded a sequence of casual conversation among five men; himself and four friends. This young man [. . .] had decided to investigate whether the informal talk of male friends would bear out generalizations about 'men's talk' that are often encountered in discussions of gender differences." Researchers do not discuss the ways in which, given the mandate to record male or female conversations, settings were constructed and managed to assure that this was accomplished. Moreover, the researchers do not acknowledge the possibility that, given a mandate to find women's or men's talk, the people collecting the data might already be predisposed to producing features of talk-in-interaction consistent (or otherwise) with its stereotypic understanding.[9]

Such research is then predicated on certain managed, produced, accomplished features of social settings. The problem with research to date lies in the fact that the production of such underlying features is not adequately explicated in the analysis (they are rather taken as essential features of those settings). However, members routinely go about providing for the recognizability of some setting as "exclusively male" or "exclusively female." What we want to uncover are the everyday methods which underlie the production and recognition of such exclusivity. Once we have shown that members have oriented to the exclusive character of a particular setting, and moreover methodically went about producing that exclusivity as a recognizable feature of that setting, we will be in a better position to analyze the talk contained within it as "men's talk," etc.

2.2   Respecifying gender: Exemplary studies and outstanding issues

When we look at the management of gender exclusivity in particular contexted case-studies, it is clear that the "all-male" or "all-female" character of an interactive setting is not something that simply happens – rather, it is an accountable and contingent accomplishment requiring several different kinds of interactional work. In the first place work is devoted to creating the conditions under which a setting might be seen as involving some kind of gender exclusivity. Minimally, this involves some policing of the participants, on gender grounds. Second, once those conditions are met, work is involved in providing for the recognizability of gender as an organizing feature of that setting. That is to say that even once the gender exclusivity is provided for it is still up to the participants to ensure that that feature can be seen as constitutive of *that* setting.

This interactional work is seen perhaps most clearly in interaction between children where gender is often deployed as a basic organizing feature of a wide range of activities (see Farris 2000; Goodwin 1990, 1998; Thorne 1990). In a discussion of cross-sex jump-rope, Goodwin (1998: 181) includes the following example:

> ((*The girls have practiced several minutes*))
> Malcolm: All the girls have to go bye bye.
> Girls: ((*Girls start to move to another area*))
> Malcolm: Okay. Now the boys get to practice.
> Ron: This is our home field.

In this example the children collaboratively organize the setting in ways that provide for the recognizability of its gender exclusivity: the boy, Malcolm, by issuing instructions which formulate the setting as involving gender exclusivity, and the girls by complying with such instructions in ways that show their shared orientation to perceived gender as a relevant feature of the emergent social setting. By building a categorization based on gender into the sequential organization of the talk, the participants endow it with procedural conse-quentiality. Jointly recognized gender categories are taken as the basis of further action and thus made an organizing feature of the social world.

Things are, however, rarely made explicit in this way, particularly, it seems, in adult interactions. In his well-known discussion of these issues, Schegloff (1997: 182) provides an example in which a rule of etiquette, "ladies first," is reformulated, "ladies last," so as to produce an ironic account of an in-progress course of action (not passing the butter despite multiple requests to do so). Schegloff goes on to note that although the example he isolates for analysis involves explicit mention of a gender-relevant category (here "ladies"), orien-tation to the category need not be invoked in this way. Other researchers have examined the multitude of ways in which participants' orientation to gender as a relevant feature of the social setting is displayed in particular interactional contexts (Schegloff mentions Garfinkel 1967, Ochs 1992, West and Zimmerman 1987, among others). A particularly clear case is presented by Limon in his discussion of barbecues among "periodically unemployed working-class men" in Mexican-American south Texas. He describes one activity as follows:

> Simon takes Jaime's hand as if to shake it but instead yanks it down and holds it firmly over his own genital area even as he responds to Jaime's "¿Como estas?" with a loud "¡Pos, chínga ahora me siento a toda madre, gracias!" (Well, fuck, now I feel just great, thank you!) There is more laughter which only intensifies when "Midnight" in turn actually grabs and begins to squeeze "el Mickey's" genitals. With his one free hand, for the other is holding a taco, el Mickey tries to pull on Jaime's arm unsuccessfully. Finally in an effort to slip out of Jaime's grip, he collapses to the ground cursing and trying to laugh at the same time and loses his taco in the process. (Limon 1989: 473)

According to Limon's description, such occasions are organized in large part around a kind of speech play of which the above excerpt is typical. This is often, as in the example given here, accompanied by and embedded in forms of mutual physical engagement which involve one man either actually or virtually handling another's genitals. Such activities then display the relevance of gender by virtue of the central and organizing role played by perceived "male insignia" (penis and testes).[10] The fact that this is relevantly character-ized as "men's talk" for the participants is thus recoverable from an analysis of the organization of the activities themselves.

Again such examples present somewhat extreme cases where the role of gender in the organization of activity is readily apparent. As such, while these examples are useful in showing the clear orientation of participants to a cat-egory, they are not representative of the way gender, as Hopper and LeBaron (1998) put it, "creeps in to" everyday affairs. Work such as that of Garfinkel's on Agnes in fact makes the case for the near omnirelevance of gender (see also West and Zimmerman 1987). A vast array of actions and behaviors may be inspected for what they say about the gender of the speaker, the recipient, the referent. Garfinkel (1967) goes so far as to suggest that for Agnes, who at the time he interviewed her was a pre-operative male-to-female transsexual, there was "no time out" and that

> the work and socially structured occasions of sexual passing were obstinately unyielding to (her) attempts to routinize the grounds of daily activities. This obstinacy points to the omnirelevance of sexual statuses to affairs of daily life as an invariant but unnoticed background in the texture of relevances that comprise the changing actual scenes of everyday life.   (1967: 118)

As Heritage (1984a: 182) notes, one general conclusion that can be reached from Garfinkel's study is that "the reproduced differentiation of culturally specific 'males' and 'females' is [. . .] the outcome of a mass of indiscernible, yet familiar, socially organized practices" (see also Ochs 1992). As such, the social scientist is set with the work of describing the ways in which members of a society methodically go about producing their gender as a recognizable "social fact." In this respect Agnes's accomplishment was to

> treat the "natural facts of life" of socially organized, socially managed sexuality as a managed production [. . .] so as unavoidably in concert with others to be making these facts of life visible and reportable – accountable – for all practical purposes.   (Garfinkel 1967: 180)

This managed production was implemented in a vast array of self-evident practices of dress, make-up, and grooming which formed, for Agnes, the groundwork for being taken as female. The managed production of sexual status secondly involved adopting appropriate modes of recognizable "feminine comportment" – sitting, walking, talking. These behaviors were "minutely accountable" and yet Agnes was largely successful in her attempt to adopt them (Heritage 1984a: 183). But the managed production of female sexual status, even after Agnes had mastered such fundamental aspects of appropriately gendered comportment, remained a persistent source of trouble. This residue of trouble was in part, it seems, a result of the fact that gender or sexual status made up a significant dimension of the seen but unnoticed backdrop of everyday, ordinary, mundane activity – a backdrop whose familiarity and banality made it almost impossible to reconstruct or imitate. Agnes was well aware of this deeper source of trouble and repeatedly emphasized in sessions with Garfinkel the problems caused by her lack of a girl's biography. Garfinkel writes:

> Another common set of occasions arose when she was engaged in friendly conversation without having biographical and group affiliation data to swap off with her conversational partner. As Agnes said, "Can you imagine all the blank

years I have to fill in? Sixteen or seventeen years of my life that I have to make up for. I have to be careful of the things that I say, just natural things that could slip out . . . I just never say anything at all about my past that in any way would make a person ask what my past life was like. I say general things. I don't say anything that could be misconstrued.

"Going along with" her interlocutor's assumptions about her gender thus in some ways proved more difficult than creating the reasonable grounds for those assumptions.[11] This issue is addressed in the final section of the present chapter. Picking up on the problem of biography from Garfinkel's discussion of Agnes, the analysis turns to look at the way in which men in a Guyanese rumshop publicly ratify one another's "boyhood" recollections and by that weave gender into the seen-but-unnoticed fabric of context. At the same time they actively exclude women (and children) from the situated activities of the rumshop and thus provide for the recognizability of the talk as "men's talk."[12]

The remainder of this chapter addresses these issues through an extended case-study. It begins with some ethnographic considerations concerning the construction of these exclusively-male contexts before moving to look in detail at the delivery and receipt of biographical talk as a way of investigating the seen but unnoticed character of gender. A concluding section returns to discuss some of the theoretical issues raised by the analysis and makes some recommendations for further research.

3   Producing and Recognizing Gender in a Guyanese Rumshop

The Guyanese rumshop is typically a one- or two-room structure often built onto the front of a house and facing the road.[13] There are several varieties of rum but one that is consumed on a daily basis (the so-called "white ball"). This is often acquired by advancing to a counter and requesting either a half or a full bottle. This is then taken back to the table with water, ice, and pop. The bottle of rum is passed around and each participant mixes his own drink – for most this consists of a shot of rum, about the same amount of water, ice, and a dash of coke. Each man drinks down his drink more or less at the same time but there is no strict timing adhered to. Rather, the bottle circulates the table in a coordinated fashion, and its travel provides for an inspection of each participant's glass to see if the drink has been consumed. It is, then, the orderly passage of the bottle which institutes an evenly distributed pattern of drinking.

Some fair amount of talk in the rumshop more or less obviously topicalizes and organizes the activities of drinking but most of the conversation is concerned with other matters. So while not completely unconnected, there are two relatively independent orders of activity underway at any given moment in the rumshop: on the one hand – drinking, and on the other, *gyafing*, the local term for ordinary conversation. It is important, for purposes of the present analysis, to recognize that the social organization and orderliness of drinking is accomplished, in part, through practices of talk-in-interaction but also that these practices are produced as independent of the main line of conversational activity simultaneously taking place. Both activities play an important role in organizing features of the setting including its visibly constructed social structure.

The activities of drinking and *gyafing* take place within a framework of social norms which specify a relationship between rumshop and gender. There is, in this respect, an often invoked rule which can be variously formulated but whose underlying sense amounts to something like, "no respectable woman goes into a rumshop," or put with a positive valence, "a woman in a rumshop is a prostitute." The power of invokable rules such as this does not depend on their definiteness and specificity in relating prescribed actions to well-defined contexts. Rather, it is the vague and unbounded character of such rules which permits searches of "indefinite scope and detail so as to see and evaluate whatever details of conduct" occur within their purview (Heritage 1984a: 207; see also Wieder 1974). From this perspective norms do not determine action, rather they provide for its intelligibility.

Norms, in this sense, may be treated as publicly available frameworks for the analysis and production of conduct (after Garfinkel 1967). In the specific case under examination, rules such as "a respectable woman never enters a rumshop" "provide for the intelligibility of perceivedly normal conduct and for the visibility of conduct which deviates from this" (Heritage 1987: 240). Norms, then, function in multiple ways. In the first place, norms are a resource drawn on in the production of normatively compliant conduct. In this respect we may note that women often call their husbands home from the rumshop. When they do this they come to the road outside the shop and yell in to the man closest the door and thus visibly avoid entering the shop. Women also often, for a variety of reasons, have reason to buy rum. On such occasions they routinely send a young male member of the extended household to purchase it for them. Thus, women display an orientation to the rule "a respectable woman never enters a rumshop" in building normatively compliant conduct.

An orientation to the rule is also visible in conduct which might be seen as deviant. It is to this set of cases that we now turn our attention. My goal is to show, in the examination of a particular example, the way in which male spaces, male domains, exclusively male contexts of conversation are actively constructed, sustained, and made visible through practices of talk-in-interaction.

On many occasions, women are, in fact, present within the space of the rumshop. These women (along with children and other men who are co-resident or simply passing through) are routinely engaged in the ongoing construction of simultaneous activities including those involved in the day-to-day maintenance of a household. The rule and the perceived respectability of the women involved are preserved, in such cases, through various secondary accounting practices. In particular, members work to maintain the sense in which women in such situations, while physically present, can be seen to be excluded from the framework of ongoing, exclusively male, activity. So, for example, if a woman works in the rumshop, serving rum over the counter or perhaps cooking fried fish a short distance away, she is routinely disattended by the men except in the course of those activities where she must be engaged – for example, in order to request the rum, to pay for it, etc. This produced disattention then operates to preserve the recognizability of the setting as an exclusively male domain.

When on occasion men do address their talk to co-present women in the rumshop, both the design of the talk and the manner in which it is fitted to the sequential context once again work to preserve the for-all-practical-purposes male exclusivity of the setting. Consider in this respect the following example, one of the few cases I have of talk directed to a woman in the rumshop. Two relatively independent courses of action are being pursued in the talk represented by the transcript. On the one hand, Ralph and John are here challenging Jaio to substantiate a claim he has made (lines 9–11, 18, 21, 29–31), which as they seem to understand it, contains the questionable assertion that Jaio knew a now deceased resident of the village.[14] When Jaio does not answer their questions in a way that they find satisfactory (line 16) they proceed to mock him (through imitation, lines 17, 26–27; see also Sidnell 2000 and below). We are interested at present in the quite distinct line of action implemented in Jaj's talk which emerges more or less simultaneous to the one just described. Jaj has found that there is no ice at the table and attempts to procure some through Sam's wife, Baby, who happens to be within earshot at the time.

(1) Rumshop[15]

1	Jaio:	yu na sopoos to bii moor	You're not supposed to be more
2		dan foor yiir fo mii.=	than four years older than me.
3	Ralph:	=di man na laik fu hiir	The man doesn't like to hear
4		s-laang taim stoorii.	old time story.
→ 5	Jaj:	ee. Sam waif. kom.	Hey. Sam's wife. Come.
6	Ralph:	nobadii na arguu hia	Nobody's arguing here
7		fu fait.	to start a fight
8	Jaj:	kom.	Come.
9	Ralph:	yuu noo, mis mana?	Do you know who Miss Manners is?
10		aks a-aks am	Ask, a-ask him.
11		if i noo mis mana	If he knows Miss Manners.
12	John:	( ) boloo shit op batii	Bolo shit his pants
13	??:	hhhh	hhhh
14	John:	di – aa jos di oda dee.	the – aa just the other day
15	Jaj:	( ) rait?	( ) right?
16	Jaio:	Mis mana darsii moma or=	Miss Manners is Darcy's mother or
17	John:	=ya darsii muma.	Yeah, Darcy's mother
18	Ralph:	eh he we shi bin liv den?	Ah-ha Where did she live then?

19	Jaj:	EE.	HEY
20	John:	miz: bee:bii:[a darsii muma	Miss Baby is Darcy's mother
21	Ralph:	[we shi bin liv?	Where did she live?
22	Jaio:	oo mi-am-tchh-	Oh my-uhm-tchh
23		[nat am beebii muma	not -uhm- Baby's mother
24	Ramish:	[pot a ais de	Put the ice there
25	Jaj:	huu ga chroo wid mii.	Who will drink with me?
26	John:	miz beebi muma	Miss Baby's mother
27		da-a-a mis mana	that is Miss Manners
28	Ramish:	[pot som ( )	Put some
29	Ralph:	[eh-he.	ah-ha
30		we shi bin <u>liv</u>?	Where did she live?
31		[°da mi wan fu noo.°]	That's what I want to know
32	John:	[<u>we</u> [<u>shi bin liv</u>.]	Where did she live?
33	Jaj:	[°som moor ais°]	Some more ice
34	Ralph:	[ii noo piiopl]	He knows people
35	John:	[weer shi woz] living?	Where was she living?
36	Jaj:	kaal fo wan bool ais.	Call for a bowl of ice
37	Ralph:	<u>hee</u>(hhh)?	Huh?

There are several ways in which the design of Jaj's talk here displays an orientation to the gender-exclusive character of the setting and its constituent activities. We may begin by noting that the turn in question is a directive and stands at the boundary between the activities taking place at the table and those in the immediate surround. Jaj's participation in the exclusively male group at the table is a witnessable feature of the emergent setting. At the same time his talk in line 5 is specifically designed to establish contact with the ongoing framework of activity in which Baby is engaged. The rumshop activities are organized by reference to a normative mutual exclusivity of men's and women's activities. We may ask then how Jaj's talk can be seen as preserving that feature of the setting.

The turn at line 5 is made up of three components, each engaged in a particular kind of interactional work (see figure 14.1). The first component is clearly a summons – an action which requests a display of availability from a recipient. A summons is an action that can be done either as the first pair part of its own summons–answer (pre-)sequence or as a component of a turn which

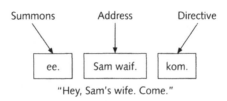

"Hey, Sam's wife. Come."

Figure 14.1 Components of Jaj's turn (line 5)

is engaged in other interactional work (the summons usually occurs in turn-initial position). As Schegloff (1995: 53) notes:

> some utterance forms which serve as common pre-expansion first pair parts can also be deployed instead as initial parts of the first pair part turn of a base adjacency pair. [. . .] An important issue is involved here, . . . , and that is the possible trade-offs between turn-organization and sequence organization in getting various interactional jobs done. . . . [s]ome jobs can either have a sequence dedicated to them or can be done as part of a turn's construction.

In his discussion of summons–answer sequences, Schegloff (1968) notes that a summons is fundamentally prefatory in so far as it projects further talk. Participants' orientation to this feature of the summons is observable in deferrals such as "wait a minute," "not now," and the like which convey a recipient's unavailability for the talk which they take to be projected in the summons. In the summons–answer sequences Schegloff studied, the summons serves as a request for a display of availability and willingness to talk. In the canonical sequence (e.g. T1 = Name, T2 = "What?"), the recipient is provided with a place to display that availability, a place to show a willingness to go along with what is being proposed.

In this example, however, Jaj does not build the summons as the first pair part of a pre-sequence and as such does not provide a place for an answer to it; rather he immediately launches into the next two components of his turn. This is significant in several ways. First, it suggests that the interaction the summons projects is likely to be cursory and not open-ended. Second, by launching directly into the rest of the turn, Jaj subordinates the request for a public display of recipiency, conveyed by the summons, to the directive which follows. This is an intervention into an order of relevances such that it reformulates what Baby can take to be proposed as a proper next action on her part.[16] Third, and perhaps most important, the summons without the provision of an answer proposes that Baby *should* be available, that is, it does not question her availability, but demands it.

The second component of this turn, "Sam waif," is likewise revealing. Rather than address this woman by her name, which he knows well, Jaj uses an address term that makes visible her relationship to one of the owners of the shop, who is also a participant in the conversation underway.[17] The address term does not treat the woman as an individual in her own right but rather as an individual associated with one of the men with whom Jaj is drinking. In formulating her in this way, Jaj displays a link between the recipient for his talk and a legitimate participant in the rumshop activities (Sam). Finally, the directive component of the turn ("kom") displays, to some extent at least, the warrant for talking to a woman in this context. It is not to engage in conversation but rather to have some task accomplished – a task which requires her to move into close proximity. The preferred response for a directive such as "kom" is non-vocal. As such, it is possible for Baby to properly respond to Jaj's talk without becoming publicly engaged in the ongoing course of the activities taking place at the table.

So Jaj has designed his talk here to preserve the observable gender exclusivity of the activity.[18] While summonses in other contexts call for a vocal response and project further talk, Jaj builds in additional turn components so as to provide for a non-vocal response from the recipient. Jaj's later talk is further suggestive in that, when his directive (reissued in line 8) is left unanswered, he soon abandons this course of action. After a second and again unsuccessful attempt to summon Baby (line 19), Jaj re-engages the course of action underway at the table (line 25). In line 33 Jaj publicly notices a need for ice and then somewhat ambiguously directs Ramish to "call for a bowl of ice" (line 36).[19] In this way he avoids further interaction with the woman and furthermore avoids topicalizing her in his own talk. Jaj's talk to the co-present woman should be contrasted with his talk in, for instance, line 25. While his talk to Baby is specifically designed to provide for only minimal further interaction, that directed to the co-present men invites collaborative activity (e.g. toasting, drinking).

While analysis in the preceding has focused on the design of Jaj's talk, one could argue that Baby is actively engaged in preserving the exclusively male character of the setting also. Baby and others are engaged in the construction and organization of a set of activities of which these recordings provide only brief glimpses. Our records thus do not provide an adequate basis for an analysis of what is going on in this respect. However, it is possible to see that, for whatever reason, Baby fails to hear, or perhaps more to the point, she fails to publicly acknowledge the talk directed to her. As I noted earlier, women often visibly avoid entering the rumshop. In this and other ways, then, women work to preserve the exclusivity of the setting just as men do.

It is the managed and produced non-engagement of co-present women in the two intertwined activities of drinking and talking which provides for and sustains the perceived male exclusivity of the setting. That is to say, even when women can be said to be co-present given some definition of the here-now, that co-presence is not disruptive of the seen-at-a-glance exclusively male character of the setting as long as the women remain non-participants in the two focal activities of drinking and conversing. I have attempted here to show that this peripheralization-exclusion does not simply happen but is rather a situated accomplishment. It is the product of concerted interactional work. Approaches which gloss actions such as we examined above as "directives" and correlate their frequency of occurrence with pre-determined gender categories and other presumed-to-be-already-established features of the setting run the risk of obscuring that interactional work. Sex-differences research in sociolinguistics generally excludes from consideration, by methodological fiat (that is, by building the exclusivity into the methodological basis of the study), the members' production and recognition of the gender exclusivity of particular settings.

So far we have discussed the way in which participants provide for, and sustain, the perceived gender exclusivity of the setting – the way they provide for its recognizability as a male domain. What has not been addressed is the way gender is systematically and persistently woven into the seen-but-unnoticed backdrop of the life-world. It will be recalled that, in her discussions with Garfinkel, Agnes frequently remarked upon the trouble caused by her lack of a female biography – she was left without "biographical and group affiliation data to swap off with her conversational partner" (Garfinkel 1967: 148). The next section of this chapter takes up this issue in relation to the activities of the rumshop.

4   Swapping-off Biographical Talk: Two Practices of Talk-in-interaction

As a way of getting at the methods by which participants weave gender into the settings of everyday life, some specification will now be given of the language game in which conversationalists swap-off biographical and group affiliation data: what might this consist in and how is it accomplished? The phenomenon that Garfinkel points to with this phrase might be taken to include a wide array of practices of talk-in-interaction. Here we will examine only two modes of "swapping-off": anticipatory sentence completion and second stories, as discussed in the lectures of Harvey Sacks (1995). The datum for the discussion will be a single story and its immediately surrounding talk. At the heart of the exchange is a story told by John primarily to Raja who, along with several other members of their "crew," were taking a drink in the rumshop.

Briefly, the story as it emerges in John's telling involves two central characters, himself and somebody these people refer to as Buddy['s] Daddy (hereafter BD).[20] The larger segment of talk from which this fragment is extracted involves a series of stories in which BD is portrayed as a menacing antagonist (on stories in a series see Jefferson 1978; Ryave 1978). Each man, it seems, has a story to tell about BD. The fragment here begins with Ramish suggesting that, on occasion, someone got the better of BD (and his brothers).[21] John follows this up with a story that illustrates this. The story John tells involves BD getting his comeuppance because of his own predictable behavior. The young John – these events took place many years earlier – knows that if he is walking with a stick, BD will want it and insist that John give it to him. John prepares for this eventuality by putting one end of the stick in a latrine before he encounters BD. As predicted, BD grabs the stick, takes it away from John, and in the process the contents of the latrine are transferred to his hand.

Although the roles of storyteller and story-recipient are relatively consistent across the course of the telling, a number of participants contribute in one way or another to the talk represented in the transcript. In particular, a reading of the transcript will reveal a significant element of byplay (see Goffman 1980;

Goodwin 1997). Not all aspects of the byplay and storytelling will be discussed here; however, they are provided for the sake of completeness.

John starts the story with a clear preface, "One time there now," before moving into what turns out to be important background material for the development of his story. For the purposes of the present analysis, the talk represented as lines 10–16 is of particular importance. At about line 27 (not included in the transcript) Jaj and Ramish begin what becomes a byplay sequence that constitutes an impediment to John's successful telling of the story. Jaio's role in the storytelling is incidental.

Despite the distraction of the story's grotesque content, we can see that it is in fact built quite artfully and with some subtlety despite a number of attempts to derail it. In particular, the byplay – surrounding the botanical knowledge implied by the use of a name, *chichilelee* – presents a significant potential obstacle to the telling of the story. This section is more or less confined to lines 25–73 (although Jaj persists till the end of the telling). After John's story reaches recognizable completion there follows a series of "second stories" which constitute a second focal point for analysis here (lines 140 and following).

(2) John's BD story (simplified)

1	Ramish:	Yaro prapa biit dem man,	Yaro really beat them
2		(tuu)~	(too)
3	Jaj:	aal de fokin (leta) bodii.	All of those brothers
4	Raja:	Wodiialii?	Wodiialii?
5	Ramish:	tchh-bodi dadii.	tchh- Buddy's father
6	Jaj:	oo-ya	Oh yeah
7	John:	[wan taim deer nou,	Now, one time
8	Raja:	[ya-a-a-a-a-	Yaaaaa
9	John:	ya-ii a bad bai.(.)	Yes, he was a bad man
10		i a wikid kaal.(.)	He'd call you with wicked intention
11		an yu ge wan lil pis stik	and you have a little stick
12		an soo,(.)	or something
13		kom bai.(.)	"come boy"
14	Sam:	gi mi di fo:king [stik hi.	"give me the fucking stick here"
15	Jaj:	[foking	"fucking
16		stik hi.	stick here"
. . .			
25	John:	[yu noo	Do you know what
26		chichilelee?	*chichilelee* is?
. . .			
29	Raja:	if yu tel mi bak wan neks	If you tell me another
30		- odinrii nemor it.	ordinary name for it
31	John:	beebii shuu.	"Baby's shoes"
32		dee doz kaal am man.	they call it, man.
33	Ramish:	chichilelee a wan	*Chichilelee* is a
34		griin staak ting man	green stalk thing man
35		(wid a bal)	(with a ball)
36	John:	yu noo chichilelee?	Do you know what *chichilelee* is?

37	Sam:	yea. mi na mos	Yeah, How could I not?
38		min nof=	There was a lot
39	Jaio:	=a da eria de.	in that area there
40	Raja:	oo.	Oh.
41		wan=wan wiid ya taak bou?	Is it a weed you are talking about?
42	??:	ai.	Yes
43	John:	n[o::.	No
44	Raja:	[oo-oo-aaa	Oh-oh-ahhh
...			
46	John:	wat rilii hapm,	What really happened
47	Ralph:	wan griin ting bai.=	It's a thing with green leaves
...			
49	John:	flowa plant rait	a flower plant right
50		bot ii-ii ting	but it's
51	Raja:	mmmm	mhhh
52	John:	wel i doz bos wan la:ng	Well it produces a long
53		(.) ting.	thing.
...			
74	John:	=nou wen mi -mi kot wan	Now, when I-I cut one
75	Ralph:	i kyaan see	He can't say it.
76	Jaj:	ah?	What?
77	John:	wan aftanuun, (.)	One afternoon
78		mi see [am gona laarn yu]	I said I'm goin to teach you
79	Ralph:	[( )]	
80	John:	a sens.	a lesson.
81	Jaj:	flowa plant	Flower plant.
82	Raja:	da yu tel yuself?	You told yourself that?
83	John:	yes.	Yes.
...			
91	Sam:	=[chichilelee de.	That's *chichilelee* there
92	John:	=[yu na sii abi lachrin?	you never saw our latrine?
93		abi lachrin don ool.	The latrine was already old.
...			
95	Jaj:	le mi [shoo yu	Let me show you
96	John:	[mi pul out wan bood	I pulled out a board
97	Jaj:	if yu wan noo	If you want to know
98		[wa neem chichilelee	what *chichilelee* is
99	John:	[mi jos mek so rait dong	I just went like this right down
...			
103	John:	yu wok wid a	You work with
104		( ) an yu push am in a	and you push it in the
105		a lachrin pit [soo	latrine like this.
106	Jaj:	[le mi sho yu	Let me show you.
107	John:	fol a shit.	It was full of shit.
...			
111	John:	wel mi gu out a rood di-	Well I went out on the road the-
112		obou sevn aklak	about seven o'clock.
113		siks torty – sevn=	six-thirty, seven
...			

115	John:	abi de out-	We were out-
116		abi liv rait hi.=	We use to live right here
117	Jaj:	=mi oz chrim am.	I used to trim them
118	Raja:	ya mi noo de aiyu bin liv	Yes I know that you lived there.
119	John:	ee yu bai.	"Hey you boy"
. . .			
121	John:	<u>bring da s</u>tik le mi sii bai.	"Bring that stick let me see, boy."
. . .			
124	John:	mi se (.) <u>ma:</u>n	I said, "Man,
125		na tek wee mi stik man.	don't take away my stick man."
126		mi se hee.	I said, "hey."
127		yu sii bai taim mi see hee	You see by the time I said "hey."
128		ii mek [soo an ii hool am.	he went like this, and he held it.
129	Jaj:	[( )	
130	John:	an ii jos mek soo	and he just went like this.
131		shit de in ii han.	There was the shit in his hand.
132	Jaj:	(chichilelee)	*chichilelee*
133	John:	oo skont man.	Oh skont man.
134		shit de in ii han.	The shit was in his hand.
135		na tek wee hool	Don't take away
136		nada foking bodii stik.	any-fucking-body else's stick.
137		(.)	
138		wa woz ii [op tu todee	What was he up to today.
139	Jaj:	[(hooz)	
140	Sam:	hee	Hey.
141		wan taim Diizil biit	One time Diesel beat
142		am bad do~	him bad though.
143	Ramish:	ii a plee foking bad man.	He used to pretend he was real bad
144	Sam:	Diizil biit bodii dadii	Diesel beat up Buddy's father
145		skont. rait a front	right in front
146		-in front a Mazjibit	-in front of Mazjibit
147		le mi tel yu,	Let me tell you,
148		tek out ii <u>shuuz.</u>	he took out his shoes
149		an ii biit ii skont	and he beat his skont
150	Ralph:	ii tek out ii shuuz	He took out his shoes
151		an biit mongkii tuu	and beat Monkey too
152		jost in fron de	Just in front there.
153	Raja:	dem teelii na don	Those Tally's are forever
154		gu an biit wid foking shuuz.	beating people with shoes.

John initially attempts to start the story with "Now, one time." Such a preface projects some immediate recounting of the specifics of an encounter. However, John abandons this projected course of action and in line 11 rather re-initiates the story by establishing a scene. There are several features of this turn that are worth remark. Note first that in lines 9 and 10 John has begun to sketch out the character of Buddy Daddy. His talk represented as line 11 is meant to be heard as following up on the specifics of this characterization (displayed by the use of *and*-prefacing). Whereas John's talk in line 7 had projected the telling of a specific encounter, here his talk is designed to convey something generic, not limited to a specific occasion; quite the contrary, this is a situation that John takes it others might recognize. This is conveyed in part through John's use of *you*. The pronoun selected invites the recipient to position themselves in this scene. This is an invitation that both Sam and Jaj appear to recognize and accept as displayed in their anticipatory completions (14, 15). As Sacks noted, anticipatory completion allows a recipient to display not only that they are listening (and understanding) the talk in progress but also that they can project its course. Here, the completion is in part invited by John's selection of *you*. For the purpose of the present analysis what we want to notice is that the scene, in which the participants are invited to imagine themselves, is a gendered one. This is true in some general way because boys in rural Guyana are more likely to wander around playing with sticks than girls (who, charged with a significant portion of the domestic labor of a household, are expected to stay close to home). But it is also true in the much more specific sense that the reported speech which John, Sam, and Jaj collaboratively voice is explicitly addressed to a boy. John's "kom bai" locates these events within a typical male child's biography. As such, when Sam and Jaj complete the talk, one of the things they are doing is displaying their access to (or at least familiarity with) a typical boy's biography. In the participants' silent acceptance of the voicing that Sam and Jaj offer they ratify that access. This is then perhaps one way in which gender is woven into the taken-for-granted, seen-but-unnoticed backdrop of everyday life.

The "swapping-off" here is done with some considerable degree of subtlety and before we leave the example it is worth noting at least one of the resources which John, Sam, and Jaj draw on in building this turn collaboratively. Sacks (1978: 257) mentions, in one of his lectures, a discussion of Gogol by Nabokov where Nabokov makes the point that "[b]efore Gogol, if when the curtain rises, there's a gun on the mantelpiece, you can be sure the gun will go off before the end of the play." That is, features of the constructed setting routinely turn out to matter, and participants can and do inspect settings, fully expecting that this will be the case. Something like this appears to be happening in the fragment under examination. John's mention of the stick is surely not coincidental. Rather, Sam uses that reference to anticipate what John is getting at (line 14) before John says it.

It has been suggested that some of the swapping-off that Garfinkel remarked upon could be accomplished within the course of a single collaboratively built turn. A phenomenon which is probably closer to what Garfinkel originally had in mind involves the telling of what Sacks called second stories. In several places in his lectures Sacks notes that, upon completion of a story in conversation, a response from the recipient is due. In responding in the appropriate place with an appropriate turn the recipient not only displays their monitoring of the story's progress (i.e. that it has reached completion) but also its sense, the reason it was told in the first place. Compare in this respect the way in which laughter, expressions of sympathy, displays of surprise or disbelief, each convey a distinct sense on the part of the recipient as to why the story was told – what its upshot is. One of the things that recipients routinely do upon completion of a story is tell another story, not just any story but one that conveys their hearing of the first. These second stories, according to Sacks, offer recipients a way of showing their detailed understanding of a first story and also their particular sense of the import of its telling at this juncture in the conversation.

Upon completion of John's story, we find Sam launching his own, responsive second story with the words "Hey, one time Diesel beat him bad, though." In this turn, Sam establishes a contrast between his projected story and the one that has just been told by John, through the use of "though." At the same time Sam ties his story to the one that precedes it through the use of anaphora (*am* "him"). Sam proceeds to tell a story in which Buddy Daddy received a public beating. Rather than dwell on the details of the telling of this second story and the further story-like response which Ralph offers upon its completion, I want to briefly note the way in which such second stories provide opportunities for swapping-off personal biography.

In some significant respects, John's story is built around his own involvement in the events he narrates. Here, then, his own personal biography is worked into the organization of the story. Now it may appear that Sam's story does not involve personal biography in the same way. After all the characters are now Buddy Daddy and Diesel. However, although Sam does not explicitly make himself a character in his story, he implicates himself as a witness (see Sidnell 2000). Sam's citing of a place where the events took place and the manner in which they were done (beat him bad, take out his shoes) index his seeing of those events, his position as a witness to them. In this sense Sam's story involves the swapping-off of biographical knowledge with John. Sam has heard in John's talk both particular details (i.e. the characters and what happened to them) as well as a more general theme (someone "getting the better" of this particular character) and uses those features to build a responsive story – one that displays his own understanding of John's story and his access to, in some sense, similar experiences and similar understandings of those experiences. With respect to the latter, I have argued elsewhere (Sidnell 2000) that a recurrent aspect of these stories is that, in them, the tellers are positioned as relatively impotent boys in contrast to the adult characters. Although John manages to get the better of an adult in his story he does this through trickery. Both Sam and John position themselves in the telling of their stories as children looking up through the age-stratified ranks of their community.

What Sam, John, and Jaj achieve here with apparent ease, this swapping-off of appropriately gendered personal biography, became for Agnes a major stumbling block in her attempt to construct herself as a recognizable woman. The case of Agnes then points to the way in which, in trading personal biography, members are weaving gender into the taken-for-granted scenes of everyday life. Here we have examined two practices of talk-in-interaction through which this swapping is accomplished: anticipatory completion and second stories. It should be noted that while in the specific case examined here these resources are put to this interactional task, they are not in any way specific to that task. This then points to the contingent nature of the connection between particular practices of speaking and socially recognized gender. In other words, practices of speaking are not necessarily linked to gender in any straightforward way. Rather, gender emerges as a recognizable feature of social settings (and social structure) within situated activities (such as story-telling, etc.). These activities have, as constituent features, particular, generic, practices of speaking which nevertheless themselves remain completely am-bivalent with respect to the gender of the speaker. Coates (1997) suggests that anticipatory completion is more characteristic of women's talk than of men's. However, the phenomenon was first noted in Sacks' discussion of the Group Therapy Sessions, and in particular a fragment involving three teenage boys.[22] In fact, there appears to be no one-to-one correlation between such practices of speaking and the perceived gender of the participants; rather, the point is that such practices are deployed in courses of action which provide for the production and recognition of gender.

5 Conclusion

In this chapter I have pointed to one way in which, by wedding the close analysis of talk-in-interaction with ethnography, it is possible to examine the manner in which the settings of everyday life, and the relevance to them of the participants' gender, are constructed and managed through practices of talk-in-interaction. It has been suggested that the recognizable gender exclusivity of particular settings is the product of members' interactional work. Such work was exemplified in an analysis of a particular male domain – the rural Guyanese rumshop. Even when women are present within the space of the shop, mem-bers work to preserve the for-all-practical-purposes male exclusivity of the setting. An attempt has also been made to describe some features of the talk which takes place in the rural Guyanese rumshop. Following up on observa-tions contained in Garfinkel's discussion of Agnes, it has been suggested that gender is woven into the seen-but-unnoticed settings of everyday life in part through practices of "swapping-off." An attempt to specify what such a lan-guage game might consist in led to an examination of two particular practices of talk-in-interaction, anticipatory completion and the telling of second stories. Taken together the analyses suggest that the rumshop, as an exclusively male domain and a place where "men's talk" occurs, is not simply a physical space but rather a social setting which is the product of concerted and collaborative interactional work by both men and women.

APPENDIX

For the sake of simplicity, readability, and consistency I have used the phonemic transcription system most commonly used by scholars of Guyanese Creole. Most of the characters are equivalent to IPA symbols; exceptions which occur in the transcripts are listed below:

sh [ʃ] voiceless alveopalatal fricative
ch [ʧ] voiceless alveopalatal affricate
y [j] palatal approximant/semi-vowel
ii [i] high, tense, front unrounded
i [ɪ] lower-high, lax, front unrounded
ee [e] mid, tense, front unrounded
e [ɛ] lower-mid, lax, front unrounded
a [a] low/open, short, central unrounded
aa [a:] low/open, long, central unrounded
ai [aɪ] falling diphthong
o [ə] short, central unrounded, unstressed, or [ʌ] short, back unrounded, frequently
      (but not always) stressed
ou [ʌʊ] falling diphthong
oo [o] long, mid, back rounded
u [ʊ] lax, lower-high, back rounded
uu [u] tense, high, back rounded

Other transcription conventions are adapted from Sacks, Schegloff, and Jefferson (1974):

[ ] Square parentheses mark the onset and resolution of overlap.
°soft° Superscripted zeros indicate that the talk contained within them was produced with decreased amplitude.
noo:: Colons indicate lengthening of the preceding vowel sound.
noo Underlining used to indicate emphasis.
( ) Single parentheses used to indicate a transcriber's best guess.
(( )) Double parentheses used to mark additional glosses.
? Question mark indicates rising intonation.
. Period indicates falling intonation.
(0.2) Numbers in single parentheses indicate a pause in tenths of seconds.
= Equals sign indicates that there is no interval between adjacent utterances, the second being latched immediately to the first (without overlapping it).

ACKNOWLEDGMENTS

Funding for the research reported in this chapter was provided by the Social Sciences and Humanities Research Council of Canada, the Wenner-Gren Foundation for Anthropological Research, the Ontario Graduate Scholarship Program, and the University of Toronto Alumni Association. During the early stages of writing I had several discussions with Chuck and Candy Goodwin. I'd like to acknowledge their help in stimulating the line of thinking advanced in this chapter (although they are in no way responsible for what I have done here). Both Janet Holmes and Miriam Meyerhoff gave extensive and very helpful comments on an early version of this chapter. For comments on still earlier versions I'd like to thank Allison Greene and Craig Tower as well as members of the Northwestern Discourse and Social Analysis group. This work was also made possible by the loving support of Allison Greene, Sula Sidnell-Greene, and Ginger Sidnell-Greene. Finally, thanks go to the Indo-Guyanese people who generously opened up their homes and lives to me between 1994 and 1996. The author alone is responsible for any remaining inadequacies.

NOTES

1 The term "member" is used to refer to a non-specific member of the society under investigation.

2 For discussion of the various ways in which "context" has been conceptualized in sociolinguistics and linguistic anthropology see Goodwin and Duranti 1992.

3 "Formulate" is a technical term in conversation analytic literature: for discussion, see Schegloff 1972, 2000. The term is used with a somewhat different nuance, but essentially the same meaning, by Garfinkel and Sacks 1970. See also note 16.

4 The incompleteness of all descriptions is often discussed under the heading of the "etcetera principle" (see Sacks 1963).

5 And of course there is a question as to what counts as evidence here – that is where one might look for the warrant. Conversation analysts tend to focus that investigation on the talk but the anthropologist might be predisposed to looking elsewhere.

6 In his lecture of February 16, 1967, Sacks remarked: "Is it possibly the case that, first, the phenomenon of a 'setting' needs to be recognized as also a Members' phenomenon, and not, for example, one of those things which, as social scientists, we construct and manage? And if so, then we have got to find out what

kind of thing it is that they're doing with it – what kind of thing this is" (Sacks 1995, vol. 1: 516).

7 This in and of itself should not be taken as a critique. Research in this area, with the relevance of gender presupposed, has clearly been the source of significant insight.

8 There is an underlying tension here in so far as many researchers advance anti-essentialist, theoretical conceptions of gender (suggesting that gender emerges through practices of talk) but at the same time employ the very same categories in their analysis. The theoretical notion of "performance," offered as an anti-essentialist antidote, is problematic in so far as it presupposes some "real" set of actors who inhabit the roles of the dramatis personae. Furthermore, the notion of performance fails to account for the fact that, in the first place, performances are necessarily embedded in socially organized activities, and second, performances admit of any number of interpretations – the problem of recognition, understanding, recipiency, is radically undertheorized. Dramatists have long been aware of these issues. Stoppard (1967: Act II, p. 62) for instance, writes: "audiences know

what to expect, and that is all they are prepared to believe in."

9   Some research has been conducted in settings organized by members rather than analysts, e.g. fraternities (for instance Kiesling 1997). Such an approach points to the possibilities of a productive dialogue between interactional sociolinguistics and ethnography.

10   West and Zimmerman (1987) use this term "insignia" to convey the relatively permanent yet socially constructed significance accorded to the genitalia in determining sex-category membership. A reliance on such a perceived once-and-for-all criterion for determining such matters is made explicit in many legal rulings: for instance, "[. . .] the law should adopt in the first place, the first three of the doctors' criteria, i.e. the chromosomal, gonadal and genital tests, and if all three are congruent, determine the sex for the purpose of marriage accordingly, and ignore any operative intervention. The real difficulties, of course, will occur if these three criteria are not congruent. This question does not arise in the present case and I must not anticipate, but it would seem to me to follow from what I have said that the *greater weight should probably be given to the genital criteria than to the other two*" (emphasis added: Mr Justice Ormrod as excerpted in Douglas 1973: 115–17).

11   Agnes reported that she was able to defuse potential problems by suggesting that she didn't like to talk about herself.

12   The issues tackled in this chapter raise certain difficulties given the framework within which the arguments are developed. The seen-but-unnoticed character of gender poses some serious problems for a conversation analytic perspective which places a premium (even a constraint) on grounding analytic claims in members' displayed orientations – that is, their "noticings." Such problems have surfaced in a number of previous accounts. Thus, for instance, Hopper and LeBaron (1998) begin by noting the omnirelevance of gender (citing Garfinkel) and develop an analysis in which gender is said to "creep into talk" through noticings which have describable antecedents ("peripheral gendered activity") and consequences (extensions of explicit gender topic talk) in the talk. However, while the analysis they present is useful in many respects, it skirts the main, problematic issues raised in much of the work on language and gender. In that body of scholarship, the focus is generally not on the gender of the things talked about (those features of the topic which can be perceived as "gendered") but rather the gender of the participants who produce that talk and, in the process, produce and recognize their own recognizably gendered selves. So while Hopper and LeBaron mention and to some extent attend to the well-known argument of Ochs (1992) regarding the "indirect indexing" of gender, they do not substantively address the issues to which that paper and the bulk of the language and gender literature is directed. Kitzinger, recognizing such problems, writes (2000: 171–2):

> From my own perspective, it would be unbearably limiting to use CA if it meant that I could only describe as "sexist" or "heterosexist" or "racist" those

forms of talk to which actors orient as such. Indeed, it is precisely the fact that sexist, heterosexist and racist assumptions are routinely incorporated into everyday conversations without anyone noticing or responding to them that way which is of interest to me. [. . .] These questions can be addressed without violating the precepts of CA – as evidenced by Sacks' analysis of a telephone conversation between two white women, Estelle and Jeanelle, neither of whom orients in any way to the white privilege and class privilege, yet Sacks draws our attention to precisely these features.

In her own substantive discussion of "coming out" in conversation, Kitzinger develops a not unrelated analysis of the way in which such actions are accomplished as visibly "not news," as completely ordinary, and as seen-but-unnoticed. This is achieved through members' methodic deployment of turn-taking practices. Kitzinger notes (p. 185). "Information about the speaker's sexuality is often deeply embedded within turn constructional units in ways that would render as interruptive any acknowledgement or assessment of this information from a co-conversationalist." That is to say that "coming out" is an action that seems to get routinely "buried" within a turn-at-talk so as to insulate it from modes of receipt that would mark it as "news" or as an "announcement" (e.g. "oh": see Heritage 1984a, 1984b).

13 This way of stating things accords particular rumshops a transcendental existence above and beyond members' production

and recognition of such spaces as rumshops. Such an account cannot in fact adequately deal with the phenomenon under study. The same space can be seen as, and oriented to as, a wake house, a shop front, a family home, etc. This is to say that it is the activity of men drinking in the space that affords it the status of a rumshop for members. This is particularly the case given that, because most rumshops sell liquor without a license, there are times when proprietors and patrons collectively work to obscure the seeing of this space as a "rumshop" – i.e. by quickly hiding the glasses, rum, and money.

14 All names have been changed to protect the anonymity of the participants.

15 The example is taken from a corpus of over 85 hours of recordings made during fieldwork in a rural Indo-Guyanese village between 1994 and 1996. Transcription conventions are given in the Appendix.

16 The first pair part of an adjacency pair is related to a second pair part by a relation of conditional relevance: a question establishes a next position for an answer, and talk in this position is routinely inspected to see how it might be seen as doing answering (see Heritage 1984a; Schegloff 1968). Here Jaj has intervened into the relations of conditional relevance by talking in the position that might otherwise have been occupied by the response to the summons. Another feature of conversational organization then comes into play – where two actions are done in a single turn at talk, recipients routinely respond to the second action first (see Sacks 1987).

17 We may speak of formulating persons here just as we spoke of formulating settings or contexts earlier. What is particularly clear in a consideration of place (Schegloff 1972) or person formulation is the way a referent remains constant while, to borrow from Frege, the "mode of presentation" differs (see Frege 1960 [1892]).

18 As Miriam Meyerhoff (personal communication) points out, the form of the directive also serves a boundary-marking function – marking this talk as somehow "external" to the "official" rumshop activities. In this respect note that Jaj's talk hails and beckons someone who is, by virtue of the talk, recognizably outside the immediate interactive environment occupied by the men.

19 Jaj's selection of Ramish may be prompted by the fact that they have together, just prior to this talk, distributed the few remaining pieces of ice.

20 The relevance of this formulation – "Buddy Daddy" – is discussed in Sidnell 2000.

21 Raja's "Wodiialii?" (line 4) is offered as candidate hearing of an earlier mention of "Buddy Daddy" and serves as a next turn repair initiator to which Ramish responds with the correction "tchh-Buddy Daddy."

22 The transcript reads as follows (Sacks 1995, vol. 1: 136):

Joe: (*cough*) We were in an automobile discussion,
Henry: Discussing the psychological motives for
Mel: Drag racing on the streets.

REFERENCES

Cameron, Deborah 1997: Performing gender identity: Young men's talk and the construction of heterosexual masculinity. In Sally Johnson and Ulrike Hanna Meinhof (eds) *Language and Masculinity*. Oxford: Blackwell, pp. 47–64.

Coates, Jennifer 1997: One-at-a-time: The organization of men's talk. In Sally Johnson and Ulrike Hanna Meinhof (eds) *Language and Masculinity*. Oxford: Blackwell, pp. 107–29.

Douglas, Mary (ed.) 1973: *Rules and Meanings: The Anthropology of Everyday Knowledge*. Harmondsworth: Penguin.

Farris, Catherine 2000: Cross-sex peer conflict and the discursive production of gender in a Chinese preschool in Taiwan. *Journal of Pragmatics* 32: 539–68.

Frege, Gottlob [1892] 1960: On sense and reference. In P. Geach and M. Black (eds) *Translations from the Philosophical Writings of Gottlob Frege*. Oxford: Blackwell, pp. 77–102.

Garfinkel, Harold, 1967: *Studies in Ethnomethodology*. Englewood Cliffs, NJ: Prentice-Hall.

Garfinkel, Harold and Sacks, Harvey 1970: On formal structures of practical actions. In John C. McKinney and Edward A. Tiryakian (eds) *Theoretical Sociology: Perspectives and Developments*. New York: Appleton-Century-Crofts, Educational Division, pp. 338–66.

Goffman, Erving 1980: Footing. In *Forms of Talk*. Pennsylvania: University of Pennsylvania Press.

Goodwin, Charles and Duranti, Alessandro 1992: Rethinking context: An introduction. In Alessandro Duranti and Charles Goodwin (eds) *Rethinking Context: Language as an Interactive Phenomenon*. Cambridge: Cambridge University Press, pp. 1–42.

Goodwin, Marjorie Harness 1990: *He-Said-She-Said: Talk as Social Organization among Black Children*. Bloomington: Indiana University Press.

Goodwin, Marjorie Harness 1997: Byplay: Negotiating evaluation in storytelling. In Gregory Guy, C. Feagin, Deborah Schiffrin and John Baugh (eds) *Towards a Social Science of Language: Papers in Honor of William Labov*. Vol. 2: *Social Interaction and Discourse Structures*. Amsterdam: John Benjamins, pp. 175–86.

Goodwin, Marjorie Harness 1998: Gender and language in cross-sex jump rope: The relevance of longitudinal studies. In Suzanne Wertheim, Ashlee C. Bailey, and Monica Carston-Oliver (eds) *Engendering Communication: Proceedings of the Fifth Berkeley Women and Language Conference*. Berkeley, CA: Berkeley Women and Language Group, University of California, pp. 175–86.

Heritage, John 1984a: *Garfinkel and Ethnomethodology*. Cambridge: Polity Press.

Heritage, John 1984b: A change-of-state token and aspects of its sequential placement. In J. Maxwell Atkinson and John C. Heritage (eds) *Structures of Social Action: Studies in Conversation Analysis*. Cambridge: Cambridge University Press, pp. 299–345.

Heritage, John 1987: Ethnomethodology. In Anthony Giddens and Jonathan Turner (eds) *Social Theory Today*. Cambridge: Polity Press, pp. 224–72.

Hopper, Robert and LeBaron, Curtis 1998: How gender creeps into talk. *Research on Language and Social Interaction* 31(1): 59–74.

Jefferson, Gail 1978: Sequential aspects of storytelling in conversation. In Jim Schenkein (ed.) *Studies in the Organization of Conversational Interaction*. New York: Academic Press, pp. 219–48.

Kiesling, Scott 1997: Power and the language of men. In Sally Johnson and Ulrike Hanna Meinhof (eds) *Language and Masculinity*. Oxford: Blackwell, pp. 65–85.

Kitzinger, Celia 2000: Doing feminist conversation analysis. *Feminism and Psychology*. 10(2): 163–93.

Limon, José 1989: Carne, carnales, and the carnivalesque: Bakhtinian batos, disorder, and narrative discourses. *American Ethnologist* 16(3): 471–86.

Ochs, Elinor 1992: Indexing gender. In Alessandro Duranti and Charles Goodwin (eds) *Rethinking Context: Language as an Interactive Phenomenon*. Cambridge: Cambridge University Press, pp. 335–58.

Ryave, Alan L. 1978: On the achievement of a series of stories. In Jim Schenkein (ed.) *Studies in the Organization of Conversational Interaction*. New York: Academic Press, pp. 113–32.

Sacks, Harvey 1963: Sociological description. *Berkeley Journal of Sociology* 8: 1–16.

Sacks, Harvey 1978: Some technical considerations of a dirty joke. In Jim Schenkein (ed.) *Studies in the Organization of Conversational Interaction*. New York: Academic Press, pp. 249–69.

Sacks, Harvey 1987: On the preferences for agreement and contiguity in sequences in conversation. In Graham Button and John R. E. Lee (eds) *Talk and Social Organisation*. Clevedon, England: Multilingual Matters, pp. 54–69.

Sacks, Harvey 1995: *Lectures on Conversation*, edited by Gail Jefferson. Oxford: Blackwell.

Sacks, Harvey, Schegloff, Emanuel A., and Jefferson, Gail 1974: A simplest systematics for the organization of turn-taking for conversation. *Language* 50(4): 696–735.

Schegloff, Emanuel A. 1968: Sequencing in conversational openings. *American Anthropologist*. 70: 1075–95.

Schegloff, Emanuel A. 1972: Notes on a conversational practice: Formulating place. In David N. Sudnow (ed.) *Studies in Social Interaction*. New York: Free Press, pp. 75–119.

Schegloff, Emanuel A. 1995: Sequence Organization. Unpublished MS, University of California, Los Angeles.

Schegloff, Emanuel A. 1997: Whose text? Whose context? *Discourse & Society* 8(2): 165–88.

Schegloff, Emanuel A. 2000: On granularity. *Annual Review of Sociology* 26: 715–20.

Sidnell, Jack, 2000: Primus inter pares: Story-telling and male peer groups in an Indo-Guyanese rumshop. *American Ethnologist* 27(1): 72–99.

Stoppard, Tom 1967: *Rosencrantz and Guildenstern are Dead*. London: Faber.

Thorne, Barrie 1990: Children and gender: Constructions of difference. In Deborah Rhode (ed.) *Theoretical Perspectives on Sexual Difference*. New Haven, CT: Yale University Press, pp. 100–13.

West, Candace and Zimmerman, Don H. 1987: Doing gender. *Gender and Society* 1: 125–51.

Wieder, Lawrence D. 1974: *Language and Social Reality: The Case of Telling the Convict Code*. The Hague: Mouton.

Wittgenstein, Ludwig 1980: *Culture and Value*. Edited by G. H. von Wright, translated by Peter Winch. Chicago: University of Chicago Press.

15 Exceptional Speakers: Contested and Problematized Gender Identities

KIRA HALL

1 Introduction

The field of language and gender has witnessed several pivotal shifts in its interpretation of normative and non-normative gender identity. This review aims to expose these shifts in an examination of the ways in which scholars have supported theoretical claims about the interplay of language, gender, and society by referencing the speech patterns of "the linguistic deviant" – the speaker who fails to follow normative expectations of how men and women should speak. What immediately becomes apparent in an overview of the literature is that linguistic deviance takes as many forms as the field has theories. In foundational discussions of language and gender in the early 1900s (e.g. Jespersen 1922) the linguistic deviant is the "woman" herself, whose speaking patterns are peculiarly divergent from more normative (in this era of scholarship, male) ways of speaking. In early feminist work by those arguing for what has been termed a *dominance model* of language and gender (e.g. Lakoff 1975), which theorizes women's divergent speech patterns as a byproduct of male dominance, the linguistic deviant is multiplied in some texts to include all speakers who are in some way disenfranchised from institutionalized male power – women, hippies, homosexuals, and even academic men. When the field shifted in the 1980s to a *difference* or *two-cultures model* of language and gender (e.g. Maltz and Borker 1982), which works on the assumption that children are socialized into divergent interactional patterns within single-sex playgroups, the linguistic deviant resurfaced as tomboy and sissy, whose preference for other-sex playmates was discussed, oddly enough, as proving the more normative, two-cultures rule. This latter use of the linguistic deviant could be said to parallel early discussions of non-Indo-European "women's languages" and "men's languages" in the first half of the twentieth century (e.g. Chamberlain 1912; Sapir 1915, 1929; Furfey 1944; Haas 1944; Flannery 1946), where the effeminate man, and occasionally the "feminist" or "young" woman, appear in the footnotes as strange and deviant exceptions to an otherwise unshakable linguistic dichotomy.

But footnote deviance does not end with effeminates and feminists. Because the overwhelming majority of our field's theories have been based not just on the speech patterns of heterosexuals (see McElhinny, this volume), but also on those of White middle-class English speakers, the deviant "ethnic" is also a common character, particularly in discussions that seek to make universal claims about how women and men speak (see Trechter, this volume). Most notable in this respect are studies supporting a two-cultures model of language and gender, where women whose speech styles do not conform to those identified for the unmarked middle-class White woman become problematic for the theory. Here, the "African American female" surfaces as our most marked footnote deviant, whose supposedly more direct speaking style wins her regular and honorable mention. When scholars began to diversify the canon by studying the speech patterns of men and women in a variety of communities, societies, and cultures, a new theory of language and gender was born that has as its focus organizations of language and gender in particular *communities of practice* (Eckert and McConnell-Ginet 1992). It is only when the field shifts to this perspective that we begin to see the purported linguistic deviant on her or his own terms, as a member of a community whose speaking styles are influenced by more localized norms of language and gender (see Besnier, this volume; Leap, this volume). Because what is "normative" becomes potentially infinite within this theoretical paradigm, the research canon becomes diversified as well, enabling not only more sophisticated research on language, gender, and ethnicity, but also the development of a field that has the sexual and gender deviance of previous generations at its center: *queer linguistics*.

This chapter, then, serves as what we might call an "underbelly" review of major works in language and gender research. It is not my intention to criticize earlier studies for their exclusions of certain communities of speakers; such an undertaking would be an unfair and pointless enterprise, particularly as all theories are limited by the intellect of the time in which they were developed. In contrast, I offer this review as an exposition of the historical shifts governing our field's understanding of normativity on the one hand and deviance on the other. What I illustrate here is that the concept of non-normative gender identity, while addressed in the gender and language literature in a peripheral manner until quite recently, is nevertheless foundational to the major theoretical perspectives that have developed within the field of language and gender.

2   Footnote Effeminates and Feminists

The field's first exceptional speakers surface in a flurry of anthropological discussions on sex-based "languages" that appeared at the turn of the twentieth century. Early anthropologists and ethnographers, in their explorations of non-European languages and cultures, developed the twin concepts of "women's language" and "men's language" as a means of explaining the morphological and phonological differences they observed between the speech of women and men. It is appropriate to begin our discussion here, not only because the work of these anthropologists ushered in a long trajectory of intertextual discussion regarding the social origins of gendered ways of speaking, but also because their representations of non-Indo-European languages initiated a dichotomous understanding of normative linguistic behavior that remains surprisingly influential in the field today.

What many of these texts have in common is what I identify here as "footnote deviance" – the casual and cursory mention of speakers who, simply put, do not play by the linguistic rules. Because so many of these scholars were, in pre-Whorfian mode, discussing the divergent patterns of speaking for women and men in these societies as reflecting and reinforcing a social configuration of gender unknown to more "civilized" European cultures, the unyielding nature of the dichotomy between women's speech and men's speech was repetitively emphasized, so much so that scholars regularly spoke of these gender-influenced varieties as "separate languages" (see, for instance, Richard Lasch's 1907 discussion of "Frauensprache"). What results is the kind of representation aptly identified by Sara Trechter (1999) as linguistic exoticism, where non-European languages, and the cultures carried through them, are portrayed as having rigidly defined gender roles, even to the point of restricting the way people talk on the basis of sex. The early portraits of languages like English are hardly parallel, for even when divergent patterns of speaking for women and men are acknowledged, as in Otto Jespersen's (1922) early piece on "The Woman," they are discussed more as a matter of individual choice, if not taste. And so we arrive at the long-standing distinction in the literature between "sex-exclusive languages" on the one hand and "sex-preferential languages" on the other, with the first designation giving the impression of rigidity and coercion and the second of fluidity and choice. In Trechter's own words, the exoticizing logic goes something like this:

> People who have gendered linguistic forms are radically different from European Americans; they are the people who actively restrict the speech of others in their rigid societies, whereas we have the choice to prefer certain linguistic variables over others in our free, modern society.   (1999: 104)

It may come as some surprise, then, that linguistic deviance is at all discussed in the early literature on so-called sex-exclusive languages. Yet even as scholars are presenting the "women's languages" and "men's languages" of various non-European cultures as rigidly dichotomized and mutually exclusive, they also make mention of the speakers who buck the system. The most popular of these deviants is the effeminate man, the cross-talker whose non-conformity to a sex-exclusive language model makes him not just a linguistic anomaly, but a social weirdo, an outcast. The fact that he is labeled as "effeminate" or "womanly" by the rest of society for using women's language is then held up as evidence for the extreme and unforgiving nature of the model. An early example of this approach comes to us from Alexander Chamberlain (1912) who, in a two-page review that appeared in *American Anthropologist* entitled "Women's Languages," discusses how male Caraya speakers interpret women's language as "'very bad' and make jests about it" (1912: 580). After pointing out that one of the chief differences in the speech of the two sexes is that women insert consonants (most commonly *k* or *h*) between vowels, Chamberlain offers the following aside:

> Dr. Krause confirms this, and cites the jest of the Caraya Indian Pedro, who said one day that Dr. Krause's companion, Francisco Adam, "was a woman," because he pronounced the Brazilian word *jacuba* (a kind of drink), not *šăúbă*, as a man would have done, but *šăkúbă* after the fashion of the women. (Chamberlain 1912: 580)

The anecdote works to affirm the "separateness" of the two varieties, since a male speaker who crosses the linguistic divide will not just be seen as womanly or effeminate, he will actually *be* a woman. It is noteworthy that this statement occurs only after Chamberlain has reviewed a number of different theories regarding the origin and significance of women's languages, in which he rejects an early argument by the explorer Bréton, that such languages might have occurred as a result of the tribal stealing of foreign women, in favor of later socio-economic explanations developed by Sapper (1897) and Lasch (1907). For Chamberlain, the severity of the sex-divide illustrated by this anecdote affirms the severity of the sex-based division of occupation and labor "among primitive peoples" (1912: 579). The resulting portrait of women's and men's language use is rigidly dichotomous, so much so that a speaker's use of the "other" variety changes his sex altogether in the public perception.

A more modern example of this same approach is found thirty years later in Paul Furfey's (1944) review entitled "Men's and Women's Language," which includes the following footnote as a quick aside: "Particularly interesting was Dr. Herzfield's observation that a man using a woman's expression would be considered effeminate" (1944: 223n). As the author offers no further explanation in the footnotes as to why this observation is "particularly interesting," the import of the comment is clear only when read alongside the larger argument developed within the text. Throughout the review, Furfey repeatedly suggests that the sex-based linguistic differences evident in many non-European languages point to a "consciousness of men and women as different categories of human beings" – one that is, in his own words, "bound up with a masculine assertion of superiority" (1944: 222). The implication, of course, is that the same sort of hierarchical consciousness does not exist in European cultures, a point Furfey alludes to early on in his stated goals for writing the article: "The present paper will discuss divergencies in the language usages of men and women, a phenomenon which is barely discernible in the familiar languages of Europe, but which is not at all uncommon among primitive peoples" (1944: 218). In fact, Furfey compares the gender stratification evident in these so-named "primitive" cultures with the class stratification of European cultures, arguing that their use of women's and men's languages parallels the use of standard and non-standard dialects in English. Whereas language in English is used "as an aid to upper-class control," says Furfey, language in these more primitive groups "serves as a tool of sex dominance." Furfey's review, then, by avoiding any in-depth discussion of gender in European languages, works to exoticize the oppressive nature of gender in non-European cultures. And the most exotic proof of this oppression is the linguistic effeminate, whose use of women's speech situates him on the social hierarchy as squarely female. Since it is through men's language that masculine superiority is asserted, a man who uses women's language is necessarily emasculated to a position of powerlessness.

The significance of this emasculation potential is also articulated in Regina Flannery's (1946) article on "Men's and Women's Speech in Gros Ventre," albeit for a rather different reason. We find a slight shift of tone in this article, as Flannery appears to move away from previous representations of sex-based speaking styles as distinct "languages" with her use of the term "speech differences" (a theoretical positioning reflected in the article's title). But in keeping with previous research, Flannery nevertheless emphasizes the mutually exclusive nature of these gendered styles, making bold statements such as "there are numerous interjections which may be used only by men and others equally numerous which may be used only by women" (1946: 133). Two pages later, however, we find out that there are indeed exceptions to what is presented here as an unyielding rule when we learn, somewhat abruptly, of the place of the "mannish" woman and "effeminate" man in language shift:

> One such woman said that the expressions used by women are "more modest" and that if a woman used men's words she would be considered mannish, and likewise a man who used women's words would be considered effeminate. A much older woman said that if a member of either sex "talked like the other" he or she was considered bisexual. This she illustrated by telling of the mortification suffered by the parents of a boy who persisted in acting like a girl in every way. The boy's mother was so sensitive that "she never went about and she just bowed her head in shame when her son was heard talking like a woman." (Flannery 1946: 135)

Flannery's use of the terms "mortification" and "shame" toward the end of this brief passage is telling, in that she wants to underscore the dichotomous nature of these linguistic varieties by exposing the social damage caused by their misuse. We later learn that it is this very mortification and shame that is accelerating language loss in the more general population. Because children are afraid that they will be "laughed at" by older generations for being bisexual if they make a linguistic mistake of this nature – knowing, as they do, "the connotations in the minds of older generations" (1946: 135) – they choose to avoid using Gros Ventre altogether by speaking only English. Flannery's argument, then, is a historical one, and our footnote effeminate wins the dubious distinction of promoting language shift.

It is perhaps not incidental that Flannery discusses English as "freeing" the younger generations of Gros Ventre speakers from the rigidity of linguistic gender in their mother tongue. The kind of evolutionary logic reflected in her discussion of language shift is evident in the vast majority of these early descriptions of men's and women's languages, which regularly contrast the "archaic" and "primitive" nature of sex-exclusive language systems with the modernity carried by sex-preferential systems such as English. A case in point is Otto Jespersen's (1922) early discussion entitled "The Woman," in which he outlined the many different kinds of sex differentiation evident in the world's languages. An important fact that has gone unnoticed about Jespersen's article – now infamous in language and gender studies for its representation of "the woman" as the linguistic Other – is the evolutionary logic betrayed by its organization.

This is apparent in the way in which he contrasts the types of linguistic differences that exist in "primitive tribes" with those of "civilized peoples." The extreme phonetic differences existing in non-European languages give way to "very few traces of sex dialects in our Aryan languages" (1922: 206) followed by only "a few differences in pronunciation between the two sexes" (1922: 209) in contemporary English. The vocabulary and word-choice differences evident for the sexes in English, in contrast to the phonetic differences evident for the sexes in non-European languages, hold a more advanced position on the evolutionary linguistic continuum. This representation hinges on Jespersen's sociological explanations for phonetic divergence, with primitive tribes and early civilized peoples sharing a sex-based division of labor that resulted in different phonological systems for men and women. Modern-day languages like English do not have distinctive grammars for the two sexes since the age-old division of labor has, in Jespersen's understanding, only "lingering effects" (1922: 219) in the twentieth century.

This teleological logic is also betrayed by the kinds of exceptional speakers Jespersen chooses for three of his four "time periods" in language and gender relations. We move from the young Carib-speaking man who is not "allowed" to pronounce the war-words of men's language until passing certain tests of bravery and patriotism, to the sixteenth-century French-speaking effeminate who imitates women in his reduction of the trilled *r*, to the modern-day English-speaking feminist who imitates the slang of men. The gendered rigidity evident in the non-European languages mentioned at the beginning of the article gives way to a certain fluency in the European languages discussed later, with the crucial turning point being sixteenth-century France. It is at this juncture, suggests Jespersen, that the sex-based division of labor, with its rigid linguistic reflexes, is replaced by a sex-based public–private dichotomy – a sociological shift that leads not to separate languages, but to slight differences in pronunciation in men's and women's speech (Jespersen 1922: 208–9).

Significantly, Jesperen cites Erasmus's note that female impersonators are the sole exception to what would otherwise be a "woman's" phonetic rule; this marks a transitional moment between the sex-exclusive systems of primitive times and the less rigid gender distinctions of modern-day English (see Freed, this volume, on the rigidity of gender distinctions in general). In the subsequent paragraph, Jespersen makes this transition overtly clear when he concludes:

> In present-day English there are said to be a few differences in pronunciation between the two sexes [. . .], but even if such observations were multiplied – as probably they might easily be by an attentive observer – they would be only more or less isolated instances, without any deeper significance, and on the whole we must say that from the phonetic point of view there is scarcely any difference between the speech of men and that of women: the two sexes speak for all intents and purposes the same language.   (1922: 209)

Jespersen's exceptional speakers, then, enter the text in order to illuminate how our present-day linguistic and cultural situation differs from that of the less civilized world that precedes us. The height of this linguistic evolution is captured by the educated feminist of the final time period. Her use of the "new and fresh expressions" of men, precipitated by "the rise of the feminist movement" (1922: 212), points to an equality between the sexes that was heretofore non-existent. The divergent uses of vocabulary and syntax that Jespersen subsequently identifies are then theorized not as sociological, but as cognitive, psychological, and personal.

3   The Woman

Given the care with which many of these early anthropologists describe both "men's language" and "women's language" as normative aspects of a particular linguistic and cultural system, Jespersen's more concentrated focus on "the woman" marks an important theoretical shift in the literature. Jespersen ushered in a new understanding of linguistic deviance, with English-speaking women and their speech peculiarities usurping the cross-talking effeminates of non-European cultures. In contrast to some of the more balanced discussions of language and gender that preceded him, Jespersen – in his more concentrated gaze on "the woman" and her conversational patterns – portrays men's speech as normative and women's as deviant. This is a new form of linguistic exoticism, one that has "women's speech" in modern-day English as its target instead of the women's and men's languages of non-European cultures. The scholars who followed Jespersen, also observing differences between women's conversational patterns and the more socially accepted or dominant patterns of men, tended to represent women's speech as abnormal, as the marked case, as norm-breaking. In this segment of our field's early history, then, the most contested and problematized gender identity becomes "the woman" herself.

This trend intersects with the anthropological tradition in important ways. Even though a surprising number of anthropologically oriented scholars had argued, for various non-European languages, that women's forms were sometimes more archaic than men's forms – among them Albert Gatchet (1884) for Hitchiti, Paul Ehrenreich (1894) and Fritz Krause (1911) for Caraya, Waldemar Bogoras (1922) for Chukchee, Mary Haas (1944) for Koasati, and Edward Sapir (1929) for Yana – the academic prose tends to position women's forms as nevertheless derivational. Gatchet, for instance, spends some time discussing the existence of an "ancient female dialect" in Hitchiti, still spoken by women and elders in the community. But even though he claims that this dialect was formerly the language of men as well as women, he goes on to give a grammar only of the newer "common form (or male language)," avoiding any further discussion of the dialect. Although the women's variety is older and apparently basic, Gatchet's prose positions it as both "uncommon" and marked. We see a comparable positioning in Edward Sapir's (1929) discussion of "Male and Female Forms of Speech in Yana," a text that aims to make a claim about the "linguistic psychology" of women and men. In the beginning of the article, Sapir is careful to argue for two different directions of derivation in Yana, with male forms fundamental in some cases and female forms fundamental in others. Yet in his conclusion, when theorizing why these sex forms might have come to exist in the first place, he ignores the latter of these directions altogether and discusses women's forms as purely reductive and derivational (a decision that seems to rest on an earlier observation that the male form in both cases "is longer than the female form"): "Possibly the reduced female forms constitute a conventionalized symbolism of the less considered or ceremonious status of women in the community. Men, in dealing with men, speak fully and deliberately; where women are concerned, one prefers a clipped style of utterance!" (1929: 212). There is no way for women to win in these early texts: when their language forms are discussed as fundamental or older, they are theorized as conservative and archaic before their more innovative and youthful male counterparts; when their language forms are discussed as derived or newer, they are theorized as psychologically deviant or otherwise abnormal.

But Sapir deserves credit for at least considering derivational processes, unlike many of his contemporaries who unreflectingly assumed men's speech to be basic. Typifying this approach is the work of Chatterji (1921), who equates the Bengali language with men's speech and discusses the speech of women, children, and the uneducated classes as derivational (he describes all three groups, for instance, as pronouncing the Bengali initial *l* as *n*). As Ann Bodine (1975) argues in her insightful review of this literature, Chatterji's description, without historical or internal evidence to the contrary, could just as appropriately be rendered in the opposite direction, particularly since women, children, and the uneducated classes make up the overwhelming majority of the

Bengali-speaking population. The simple fact that so many of the early articles on sex differentiation in language carry the title "Women's Speech" or "Women's Language" points to an understanding of male speech as *the* language and women's speech as a kind of oddity (see Bodine).

In fact, the term *peculiar* becomes the most common descriptor for women's speech in the literature of this period. Jespersen (1922) himself is a big fan of this buzzword, using it to describe women's divergent uses of vocabulary (e.g. "The use of *common* in the sense of "vulgar" is distinctly a feminine peculiarity"), as well as to theorize women's divergent uses of syntax ("These sentences are the linguistic symptoms of a peculiarity of feminine psychology"). His prose parallels that of Bogoras (1922) in his article on Chukchee published during the same year, who also discusses certain facets of women's pronunciation as sounding "quite peculiar":

> Women generally substitute š for č and r, particularly after weak vowels. They also substitute šš for rk and čh. The sounds č and r are quite frequent, so that the speech of women, with its ever-recurring š, sounds quite peculiar, and is not easily understood by an inexperienced ear. (Bogoras 1922: 665)

Bogoras's discussion is an especially clear case of the male linguistic gaze that characterizes much of this literature, with the author assuming a male readership that would identify with male uses of the language as opposed to female ones (certainly these phonetic forms do not sound so peculiar to the women who use them). The same gaze is evident in Sapir's (1915) article on "Abnormal Types of Speech in Nootka," published just seven years earlier, where he describes the "peculiar forms of speech" used by and for a variety of social deviants, among them fat people, abnormally small people, hunchbacks, lames, left-handed people, cowards, and circumcised males. Sapir's attempt to render these kinds of distinctions "less glaringly bizarre" by paralleling them to the sex distinctions found in non-European languages such as Eskimo is a noble undertaking. But it forces a parallel between women and other "deviants" that paves the way for subsequent representations of women as the peculiar linguistic Other.

4   Hippies, Historians, and Homos

We find reflexes of this early trend even in the ethnographically informed discussions of women's and men's speech patterns that surfaced with the rise of speech act theory in the 1960s and 1970s. Elinor Keenan (Ochs)'s ([1974] 1996) oft-cited study of Malagasy-speakers in Madagascar, entitled "Norm-Makers, Norm-Breakers: Uses of Speech by Men and Women in a Malagasy Community," is a case in point. Keenan (Ochs) spends the first three-quarters of her article outlining the linguistic repertoire of "the people of

Namoizamanga" (1996: 100), describing in great detail their varied discursive strategies for avoiding direct affront. It is only in the last few pages of the article that we come to realize that women are not included in this description because of their preference for a more direct and confrontational speaking style. Although Keenan (Ochs) presents Malagasy-speaking men as "norm-makers" and Malagasy-speaking women as "norm-breakers," the women of her study are certainly adhering to "a norm" just as much as the men are: their expected participation in more direct forms of information-finding, bargaining, and child-scolding speaks to the strength and persistence of that very norm. But since it is a norm deemed inferior by the more dominant male-speaking population, Keenan (Ochs) chooses to portray the speech of these Madagascar women as deviant, or even (as the title of her article might imply) subversive. The representation of women as a problematized gender identity, then, becomes central to feminists working within the *dominance model* of language and gender, which focuses on how women's speech patterns are trivialized, or otherwise marginalized, in male-dominant societies. Norms in such studies are viewed as singular, and women become the non-normative exception.

But the women of these texts rarely stand as the lone exception to an oppressive discursive regime. As with Sapir's (1915) work on deviant speech in Nootka, early researchers frequently discussed the speech patterns of women with reference to other marginalized identities in order to emphasize their abnormality, or as in the case of Robin Lakoff (1975), to highlight their disenfranchisement from the powers that be. Lakoff's text *Language and Woman's Place* is worth spending some time on here, not only because it is generally considered the prototype of dominance models of language and gender, but also because it established a new way of conceptualizing the relationship between gender, language, and marginality. Most scholars have read Lakoff's work as being exclusively concerned with women's patterns of speaking, ignoring her rather extensive discussions of a variety of other identities presented as problematic, among them the effeminate homosexual, the anti-capitalist hippie, and the asocial male professor. Because Lakoff is interested in the socializing forces that produce an asymmetry in the way women and men speak, she tests her theoretical argument with reference to the speakers who are in some way tangential to this socialization. For Lakoff, women have much in common with homosexuals, hippies, and academics: specifically, all of these identities share a marginality determined by their exclusion from institutionalized male power.

Central to Lakoff's explanation for this shared marginality is the gendered division of labor, and more specifically, the divergent ways of speaking brought about by this division. This concern prompted her to devote several pages of her discussion to Lionel Tiger's *Men in Groups*. Tiger's book, published in 1969, develops a classic anthropological argument about how gender works, attributing divergent behaviors in women and men to an evolutionary division of labor along the lines of biological sex. Like many physical anthropologists of this era, Tiger supports the explanatory power of a "man-the-hunter" model of human evolution, which holds that the evolution of male-dominant human societies was initiated by cooperative male hunting, a sex-based behavior observed in primates and supposed to have existed in primitive human communities. For Tiger, this evolutionary argument is key to an understanding of the concept for which he is most well known: male bonding in human societies. While primitive females stayed behind with their young and made decisions primarily in an individual capacity, the males were forced by the circumstances of labor to develop a group mentality. Because the hunt would be successful only if the hunters found ways to cooperate with one another, primitive males, unlike their female counterparts, began to develop interactive techniques to enhance group enjoyment and minimize personal friction. These interactive techniques, according to Tiger, find their modern-day realization in human male-bonding rituals.

Scores of articles written by feminist anthropologists subsequently challenged the man-the-hunter model of human evolution, including Nancy Tanner and Adrienne Zihlman's (1976; see also Zihlman 1978) female-focused model of human evolution often referred to as the "woman-the-gatherer" challenge (see di Leonardo 1991), a perspective that presumably allows for the possibility of some kind of group mentality for women as well. But Lakoff did not have the benefit of these critiques, writing as she was in the early 1970s, and she embraces Tiger's evolutionary discussion of male bonding as one way of explaining women's and men's differential orientations to politeness. Women, excluded from a male workplace built on "present-day reflexes of male bonding" (1975: 77), tend to orient themselves to politeness forms that discourage bonding, gravitating toward the first two rules of Lakoff's politeness paradigm: Formality (keep aloof) and Deference (give options). Men, on the other hand, as a result of their socialization within workplace situations that require them to develop techniques of working together as a group, are more likely to embrace Lakoff's third rule of politeness: Camaraderie. The latter rule would be essential in, for example, a male-dominated corporate workplace, as group members must develop interactive measures to gloss over emotional reactions and disagreements that might hinder progress toward a common goal. These are measures women have generally not needed to develop, Lakoff suggests, since they have historically been excluded from these group-oriented work environments.

Lakoff's remark that women's use of terms like *divine* is "not a mark of feelings of inferiority but rather a mere badge of class" (1975: 52) is telling in this respect, as she situates women within a powerless "female class" that exists outside of the institutionalized power structure and employs a non-work-related vocabulary deemed irrelevant by this very power structure. Her use of the term *female class*, incidentally, is quite consistent with radical feminist discussions of the time that identified women as a *fourth world* (e.g. Burris 1973) or *separate caste* (e.g. Dunbar 1970). Barbara Burris, for instance, in her "Fourth World Manifesto," argued that women around the world form a caste colonized and denigrated by male imperialism. But while for Burris "the long suppressed and ridiculed female principle" is "a female culture of emotion," for Lakoff the ridiculed principle is a female culture of talk. Certainly Lakoff's emphasis on the discriminating effects of the dichotomization of public and domestic spheres is prominent in the work of many feminist theorists of the time, not the least of which include Sherry Ortner's (1974) and Michelle Rosaldo's (1974) socially based arguments for the universal subordination of women in the early 1970s. "Woman's place," to borrow from the title of Lakoff's book, is a place excluded from the public sphere of men's work, and the language patterns that have developed as a result of this exclusion are devalued as "women's language."

The notion of a masculine workplace, then, is fundamental to Lakoff's theoretical explanation for men's and women's differential use of linguistic phenomena. This explains why academic males, hippies, and homosexuals occupy the margins of Lakoff's text as problematized gender identities. Like women, these groups are in some way excluded from a social history of male bonding in the labor force, and as with women, this exclusion leads to language patterns dissociated from what Lakoff terms "real-world power." The following excerpts from Lakoff's text – concerned with hippies, academic men, and homosexuals, respectively – underscore the fact that her text is not so much about gender as it is about power:

Hippies
I think it is significant that this word ["groovy"] was introduced by the hippies, and, when used seriously rather than sarcastically, used principally by people who have accepted the hippies' values. Principal among these is the denial of the Protestant work ethic: to a hippie, something can be worth thinking about even if it isn't influential in the power structure, or moneymaking. Hippies are separated from the activities of the real world just as women are – though in the former case it is due to a decision on their parts, while this is not uncontroversially true in the case of women. (Lakoff 1975: 13)

Academic men
Another group that has, ostensibly at least, taken itself out of the search for power and money is that of academic men. They are frequently viewed by other groups as analogous in some ways to women . . . what they do doesn't really count in the real world . . . The suburban home finds its counterpart in the ivory tower: one is supposedly shielded from harsh realities in both. Therefore it is not too surprising that many academic men . . . often use "women's language." (Lakoff 1975: 14)

Homosexuals
It is of interest, by the way, to note that men's language is increasingly being used by women, but women's language is not being adopted by men, apart from those who reject the American masculine image [for example, homosexuals]. This is analogous to the fact that men's jobs are being sought by women, but few men are rushing to become housewives or secretaries. The language of the favored group, the group that holds the power, along with its nonlinguistic behavior, is generally adopted by the other group, not vice versa. (Lakoff 1975: 10)

For Lakoff, male hippies, male academics, and male homosexuals are all in some sense gender deviants – identities who have forsaken a capitalistic power structure built on masculine ideals for pursuits considered trivial in the "real world." This would explain, suggests Lakoff, why the language patterns of hippie, academic, or homosexual so often appear to resemble that of the American middle-class housewife. That these disenfranchised groups are likely to use some of the same specialized lexical items as American middle-class women, she argues, points to a more general conclusion: "These words aren't, basically, 'feminine'; rather they signal 'uninvolved' or 'out of power'" (1975: 14). While certain patterns of speech may be considered feminine because women are, in her own terms, the "'uninvolved' 'out of power' group *par excellence*," Lakoff is careful to note that any group in society may use patterns associated with "women's language" (an observation that best explains her consistent use of scare quotes around the term). For Lakoff, then, it is the feminine-sounding male, marginal to the world of institutionalized masculinity, who ultimately enables her to formulate the crux of her argument: "The decisive factor is less purely gender than power in the real world" (1975: 57).

Yet in spite of their centrality to Lakoff's theory, these marginal figures are frequently, if not entirely, overlooked in subsequent discussions of her work. The majority of her critics, swept up in an imperative to test her argument empirically, interpreted Lakoffian "women's language" to be only about women, developing study upon study to determine whether or not female speakers actually use "women's language" more than their male interlocutors. What is amusing, in retrospect, is that a great number of these studies analyze the speech patterns of the very academics that Lakoff identifies as linguistically divergent. Betty Lou Dubois and Isabel Crouch (1975), for instance, in an adversarial critique often cited as "disproving" Lakoff's hypothesis (see, for example, Cameron 1985: 44), offer as empirical data an analysis of the "conversational give-and-take" in a question-and-answer period at an academic conference. Besides the fact that the authors of this article give us no information on how many women are actually participating in the discussion analyzed, the empirical finding that "33 tag questions were spoken by men, *none* by women" (1975: 293) is hardly relevant to Lakoff's overall theoretical argument, particularly in the context of an article that makes no mention of the Lakoffian buzzword *power*.[1] Perhaps this oversight is also behind Crosby and Nyquist's (1977) seeming portrayal of themselves as original authors of the claim that both men and women may use "women's language." Quoting Lakoff out of context as asserting that women's language is "language restricted in use to women" (1977: 315, fn. 3), they choose to rename Lakoff's "women's language" as *the female register* so as to allow for men's use of these variables as well. While the authors do recognize that Lakoff's central argument has to do with power, they reinterpret her discussion of power as being more about job status than about access to male work environments (or institutionalized masculinity), opposing her claim with the finding that there is no difference in the speech of high-status (male) police officers and low-status (male) police clerks.

Misreadings like these point to a more general critique regarding the unsophisticated manner in which such concepts as "power" and "status" have been theorized and evaluated in quantitatively oriented language and gender research. But Crosby and Nyquist's mission to distinguish the female register from the female speaker is nevertheless admirable, and it is this distinction, also voiced by O'Barr and Atkins (1980) in their focus on the use and perception of "powerful" and "powerless" language in the speech of trial witnesses, that in many ways enabled the development of *queer linguistics* – a field that explicitly questions the assumption that gendered ways of talking are indexically derived from the sex of the speaker.

5 Sissies and Tomboys

The 1980s ushered in an alternative flavor of language and gender research, marked in part by Daniel Maltz and Ruth Borker's (1982) proposal of a new framework for examining differences in the language use of American women and men. Their approach, sometimes identified as a *two-cultures* or *difference model* of language and gender, holds that American women and men come from two different sociolinguistic subcultures, in which they learn different rules for interacting with one another and interpreting conversational contributions. In a gender-oriented extension of John Gumperz's (1982) cultural approach to inter-ethnic communication, Maltz and Borker based their argument on a variety of studies on childhood playgroups that find that boys and girls orientate to their own sex as preschoolers and develop divergent interaction patterns. The singular norm of studies in the dominance approach becomes dual again, with male and female speakers traveling on different (and frequently oppositional) tracks of normativity. What is interesting about Maltz and Borker's platform for this review is a short aside in their concluding notes, where they give us the "tomboy," together with "lesbians and gay men," as one of "a number of specific problems that appear to be highly promising for future research" (1982: 94). Why these marginal identities might be problematic for a two-cultures approach to language and gender (or "potential research problems," in the words of Maltz and Borker) is fairly clear. Because the argument is based on the assumption that boys and girls are socialized into interaction differently in their single-sex playgroups, what happens to the theory when we find children who appear to shun this very socialization? Do they, for instance, grow up to be lesbians and gay men who share conversational patterns with the other sex? The sissy and the tomboy, then, as apparent exceptions to a socialization rule presented as having few if any defectors, become oddly important to a two-cultures perspective.

The most overtly theorized discussion of sissies and tomboys appears in Eleanor Maccoby's (1998) *The Two Sexes: Growing Up Apart, Coming Together,* a comprehensive review of previous research that supports a two-cultures approach to the subject of gender. Maccoby is interested in how biological, social, and cognitive forces come together to constitute what she calls gender's "explanatory web," creating divergent patterns of behavior for the two sexes that begin in the womb, materialize in early childhood, remain through adulthood, and are ultimately transferred to the next generation. In contrast to much of the two-cultures research that has as a main goal a description of "what boys do" as opposed to "what girls do" (offering linguistic evidence, for instance, to support the claim that boys' interaction is more "hierarchical" while girls' is more "collaborative"), Maccoby seeks to determine *why* these interactional differences arise in the first place. As her focus is on gender conformity in same-sex childhood playgroups, not dissension, tomboys and sissies appear in the text not so much as trouble-shooters for a two-cultures approach (or as identities whose interaction is interesting in their own right), but as exceptions that prove the more normative rule. And because this normative rule is produced biologically as well as socially for Maccoby, our tomboy and sissy come to play an interesting role in her theorizing of each of these influences.

Maccoby's primary sociological argument for why divergent patterns of interaction exist between the two sexes has to do with the "greater strength" (1998: 41) of boys' playgroups as opposed to girls'. The forces binding groups of boys together, she argues, are much stronger than those binding girls together, leading to a much more exclusionary kind of play in which peer group acceptance becomes the overriding concern. Boys therefore have a much greater need for recognition from other boys, and this drives them to engage in the status-oriented discursive behaviors identified by many linguists for all-boys' groups. What better way to prove the strength of boys' groups than to reference the sissy, whose inappropriate participation in these male rituals wins him rejection from his peers? The sissy not only evidences the strength of male socialization, says Maccoby, since we find boys accusing other boys of sissy behavior from preschool on if their activities are deemed too girl-like, he also highlights the restrictive nature of that socialization. The fact that girls do not enact sanctions against tomboy behavior in the same way that boys enact sanctions against sissy behavior illustrates that boys' groups are more cohesive, more conforming, more gender-exclusionary: "Clearly, an essential element in becoming masculine is becoming not-feminine, while girls can be feminine without having to prove that they are not masculine" (1998: 52). It is worth noting that Maccoby's use of the tomboy is diametrically opposed to Lakoff's (1975), who points to the "little girl [who] talks rough like a boy" as evidence for the strength of female socialization. For Lakoff, the fact that the tomboy is "ostracized, scolded, or made fun of" by parents and friends is suggestive of how society "keeps her in line, in her place" (1975: 5). In fact, this scenario functions as one half of the Batesonian double-bind that Lakoff employs as central to her overall argument:

If she refuses to talk like a lady, she is ridiculed and subjected to criticism as unfeminine; if she does learn, she is ridiculed as unable to think clearly, unable to take part in a serious discussion: in some sense, as less than fully human. (1975: 6)

The disparity between Lakoff's and Maccoby's sociological analysis of the tomboy could be a result of the twenty-year time differential between the two texts. Barrie Thorne (1993), in her ethnographic study of gender in American elementary schools, suggests that attitudes toward tomboys had probably changed over the two decades, with more and more girls entering team sports, schools loosening their dress codes, and parents putting less pressure on girls to be "ladylike." But to say that boys' groups are more cohesive because the label "sissy" operates as an insult whereas "tomboy" does not, as Maccoby does, ignores the import of age on peer acceptance of gender deviance. Certainly, Penelope Eckert's (1996, 2002) research on adolescent girls' management of the "heterosexual marketplace" suggests that it would be quite difficult, if not socially detrimental, for a girl to continue her tomboy leanings into the teen years. The differences of perspective voiced here undoubtedly have much to do with the fact that there is very little ethnographic, much less linguistic, research on so-called "deviant" gender identities in either childhood or adolescence. The tomboy's unwritten nature, then, makes her ripe for all sorts of scholarly pickings. In fact, Thorne discusses tomboys and sissies as part of a larger critique of the very two-cultures approach espoused by scholars like Maccoby, arguing that the variation we find within genders is greater than the variation we find between boys and girls taken as groups. For Thorne, the tomboy is just one aspect of a "complicated continuum of crossing" (1993: 112) – a continuum that is, in her opinion, obscured by research that operates on the assumption of gender as separation and difference. Thorne's chapter entitled "Crossing the Gender Divide," in which she provides contextualized examples of when and why children participate in the group activities of the other gender, serves as a demonstration of how research on gender can proceed in a non-dichotomous fashion: "An emphasis on social context shifts analysis from fixing abstract and binary differences to examining the social relations in which multiple differences are constructed and given meaning" (1993: 109).

But what most distinguishes Maccoby's tomboy from other social science toms is that hers begins in the womb. Maccoby argues that gendered behavior in childhood is a function of biology as well as socialization, so it is not surprising that we find extended discussions of prenatal deviants. We learn, for instance, about the male play patterns of girls who were exposed to excess amounts of adrenal androgen while in the womb (identified in the scientific literature as AGS females), as well as the rough-and-tumble play of female rhesus monkeys whose mothers had been injected with testosterone when pregnant. Maccoby is careful to avoid drawing links between this scientific research and sociological discussions of actual tomboys, but here again we see deviance embraced as evidence for normativity. The argument goes something like this. "Normal" boys and girls, as a result of prenatal hormonal priming, have different rates of maturation when it comes to particular kinds of behavior. Girls appear to self-regulate their behavior much earlier than boys do, having earlier success at potty-training, for example, and showing faster progress in language development. A boy's lack of self-control earns him more hierarchical, disciplinary commands from his parents as well as more rough-and-tumble play; a girl's more advanced language capacity invites more relational and nurturant talk about feelings. These same children eventually come to self-select playmates who behave as they do. The resulting single-sex playgroups begin to accentuate the behaviors encouraged earlier by parents, until definitively divergent patterns of interaction emerge for the two groups. The AGS girl stands on the sidelines of this discussion, stepping in at critical junctures as evidence for the biological component of Maccoby's explanatory web. The fact that AGS girls prefer male play partners and high levels of rough-and-tumble play gives Maccoby the evidence she needs to argue for biology's role in the construction of dichotomous gendered behaviors. And it is the biological aspect of Maccoby's argument, of course, that is particularly powerful, as it enables her to make a universal claim about how gender operates. Our bio-tom, then, in her conjoined biological and social deviance, provides evidence not only for a two-cultures gender normativity, but also for its cross-cultural persistence.

One last remark is called for here regarding the way in which Maccoby suggests that the phenomenon of early same-sex attraction might have an additional evolutionary purpose. Referring to the research of anthropologist Arthur Wolf (1995), she remarks that sex segregation in children's playgroups might occur so as to prevent incest and minimize the risks of inbreeding. Wolf conducted a study of boys and girls in southern China who, because they had been affianced by their parents at an early age, lived together in the same household for several years in preparation for marriage. He found that such children come to lack sexual interest in each other when they reach adolescence, offering as evidence the fact that their subsequent marriages have exceptionally low rates of fertility. Maccoby's interest in Wolf's research again has to do with the biological aspect of the explanatory web, as his findings provide yet another biologically oriented reason for why same-sex segregation might occur: "Children's spontaneous avoidance of cross-sex others who are not kin serves the biological function of keeping these others within the pool of potential mates" (Maccoby 1998: 94). Now this claim is problematic for all sorts of reasons, but what I want to focus on is the way in which this observation forces a connection between gender identity and sexual orientation. If tomboys and sissies spend much of their childhood with "the other sex" instead of their own, do they then, as Wolf's theory implies, grow up to lack sexual interest in the opposite sex? Is this where lesbians and gay men come from? Certainly, Maltz and Borker's (1982) juxtaposition of "tomboys" and "lesbians and gay men" as potential problems in their early research platform implies some connection between early deviant gender identities and the sexual orientation of adults. Indeed, the conflation of gender and sexual identity appears through much of the language and gender literature (McElhinny, this volume), where, until quite recently, the conversational practices of lesbians and gay men are discussed not as indexing community membership, but as instancing gender deviance (see also Kulick, this volume).

A telling example of this conflation surfaces in Burrell and Fitzpatrick (1989), where we find the heterosexualization of a conversational excerpt that takes place between two gay men in Deborah Tannen's (1986) *That's Not What I Meant!: How Conversational Style Makes or Breaks Relationships*. In her bestseller, which includes a chapter on the cross-cultural nature of male–female communication, Tannen gives us one of the field's first gay couples in the form of Mike and Ken, whom she describes, refreshingly, as "two people who lived together and loved each other" (1986: 126). The excerpt at issue regards a fight over salad dressing, where, according to Tannen, each partner misunderstands the conversational frame used by the other. But while Tannen discusses this exchange in gender-free terms in order to demonstrate the kinds of misunderstandings that can occur in close relationships (she is specifically interested, for instance, in demonstrating Gregory Bateson's notion of *complementary schismogenesis*), in Burrell and Fitzpatrick virtually the same exchange is reinterpreted entirely along gendered lines; Mike and Ken even surface as "Bob" and "Joanne." The two excerpts – Tannen's followed by Burrell and Fitzpatrick's – are reproduced below:

From Tannen (1986: 119)

Mike: What kind of salad dressing should I make?
Ken: Oil and vinegar, what else?
Mike: What do you mean, "what else?"
Ken: Well, I always make oil and vinegar, but if you want, we could try something else.
Mike: Does that mean you don't like it when I make other dressings?
Ken: No, I like it. Go ahead. Make something else.
Mike: Not if you want oil and vinegar.
Ken: I don't. Make a yogurt dressing.
(Mike makes a yogurt dressing, tastes it, and makes a face.)
Ken: Isn't it good?
Mike: I don't know how to make a yogurt dressing.
Ken: Well, if you don't like it, throw it out.
Mike: Never mind.
Ken: What never mind? It's just a little yogurt.
Mike: You're making a big deal about nothing.
Ken: *You* are!

From Burrell and Fitzpatrick (1989: 176–7)

Bob: What kind of salad dressing should I make?
Joanne: Vinaigrette, what else?
Bob: What do you mean, "what else?"
Joanne: Well, I always make vinaigrette, but if you want make something else.

Bob: Does that mean, you don't like it when I make other dressings?
Joanne: No, I like it. Go ahead. Make something else.
Bob: Not if you want vinagrette.
Joanne: I don't. Make a yogurt dressing.
(Bob makes a yogurt dressing, tastes it, and makes a face.)
Joanne: Isn't it good?
Bob: I don't know how to make a yogurt dressing.
Joanne: Well, if you don't like it, throw it out.
Bob: Never mind.
Joanne: What never mind? It's just a little yogurt.
Bob: You're making a big deal about nothing.
Joanne: You are!

What interests me with respect to the Burrell and Fitzpatrick version is how the authors reformulate the excerpt as a conversation between "the independent spouse" Bob and the "traditional wife" Joanne. "Throughout this admittedly trivial interaction," the authors explain, "the independent spouse, Bob, saw his wife as becoming increasingly more demanding, whereas the traditional wife Joanne, perceived her husband as becoming more hypersensitive and temperamental" (1989: 177). That an excerpt between two gay men is so easily recast into a heterosexual discussion of "The Psychological Reality of Marital Conflict" betrays a much larger theoretical problem in the language and gender literature of the 1970s and 1980s: namely, the persistent assumption that sexual identity is really about gender. How Tannen's gay men wound up as heterosexuals in Burrell and Fitzpatrick's book is not entirely clear,[2] but their transformation offers an illuminating example of how sexual identity is often disregarded, or ignored altogether, within a two-cultures model of language and gender.

When gays and lesbians do receive mention in the model, they tend not to be subjects of study in their own right, but tangential characters who provide extreme evidence for a dichotomous view of gendered behavior. Tannen (1990), for instance, in her subsequent bestseller *You Just Don't Understand*, refers to Philip Blumstein and Pepper Schwartz's (1984) popular finding that "lesbians have sex less often than gay men and heterosexual couples" as support for her argument that men tend to be initiators and women respondents: "But among lesbians, they found, often neither feels comfortable taking the role of initiator, because neither wants to be perceived as making demands" (Tannen 1990: 147–8). This discussion surfaces at the end of a chapter subtitled "Lecturing and Listening," in which Tannen explores the unequal roles played by men and women in conversation. Here, lesbians come to serve as a test-case for Tannen's theory, providing an archetypal female–female example of the behaviors she identifies as enabling the conversational inequality. Tannen reads the lesbian hesitancy to initiate sex as a gendered trait, and offers it as evidence for a more general theory regarding women's discomfort with self-assertion. Lesbians, then, as same-sex partners, are discussed as a kind of "grown-up" version of the childhood all-girl playgroups so instrumental to two-cultures theorizing.

Tannen's occasional comparisons of lesbians with gay men, as in a later chapter in the book when she contrasts lesbian and gay understandings of the relationship between money and independence (1990: 292), are intended not as discussions of sexual identity, but as paradigmatic examples of difference between women and men more generally.

6　Queers and the Rest of Us

What is exceptional about Tannen's lesbians and gay men, however, is precisely that they are not exceptional; that is, their interactive behaviors are viewed not as deviant, but as entirely in line with the interactive behaviors of heterosexual women and men. While we may fault her work for failing to consider the potential influences of sexual identity on conversational exchange, as Greg Jacobs (1996) does in a review of the literature for *American Speech*, her refusal to portray lesbians and gay men as peculiarly deviant, in the manner of former generations of researchers, is better understood as progressive for the linguistic scholarship of the time. Her work might even be said to reflect a transitional point in the academic treatment of sexual identity, when identities previously viewed as deviant or non-normative began to be brought into the mainstream of scholarly discussion. I want to argue here that three theoretical moves in the language and gender research of the early to mid-1990s precipitated this transition: first, the introduction of the notion of *communities of practice* (Eckert and McConnell-Ginet 1992); second, the more sophisticated development of *ideological* approaches to the study of language and gender (e.g. Gal 1991; Bucholtz and Hall 1995; Bucholtz, Liang, and Sutton 1999); and finally, the birth of *queer linguistics* (Livia and Hall 1997), a field that activates, albeit critically, the philosophical notion of performativity. All of these moves were formulated within, and influenced by, larger theoretical moves in the academy. Most notable in this respect is multicultural feminism, which encouraged the intellectual embracement of heretofore understudied identities in a postmodern drive to diversify the academic canon. The linguistic reflexes of this drive, accordingly, share a focus on more localized organizations of language, gender, and sexuality. The two-norm approach of the previous generation gave way to a paradigm that reframes the normative as ideologically produced within specific practice-based communities. Norms of feminine and masculine speech, then, although always constrained and influenced by dominant ideologies of language and gender, become potentially infinite in local articulation, particularly as gendered ideologies are produced only in interaction with localized understandings of race, class, sexuality, and age.

The concept of gender performativity, as developed within queer linguistics and more generally in sociolinguistics, is closely allied with ideological and practice-based approaches to the study of language and gender, although this fact has been little discussed in the literature. As Anna Livia and I argue in our introduction to *Queerly Phrased* (Livia and Hall 1997), the concept is much needed in the field as a way out of the circular research paradigm encouraged by the theoretical tenets of social constructionism. The feminist distinction between *sex* and *gender*, with the first term being used for the biological and the second for the social, was a politically necessary one, as it threw a decisive wrench in essentialist arguments that limited social agency to biological predisposition. But this distinction also had a compromising effect on ethnographic research, leading language and gender scholars, for example, to seek out the sociolinguistic reflexes of a prediscursive biological sex. Working from the assumption that the social maps onto the biological (a perspective criticized by feminist Linda Nicholson (1994) as a "coat-rack model" of sex and gender),[3] researchers pre-identified their subjects as "male" and "female" and then isolated the conversational strategies that distinguished these groupings from one another. Sexual identity, as a subjective designation not easily related to biology, remains invisible within this paradigm.

But the performativity of gender, as formulated by Judith Butler (1990, 1993) via a Derridean reworking of J. L. Austin's (1962) notion of the "performative utterance," disallows sociolinguistic approaches to identity that view the way we talk as directly indexing a prediscursive self. To a post-structuralist like Butler, there is no prediscursive identity, as even our understanding of biological sex is produced through cultural understandings of social gender. This kind of thinking puts much more weight on the speech event itself, requiring us to examine how speakers manage ideologies of feminine and masculine speech in the ongoing production of gendered selves. It also gives us a non-essentialist understanding of personhood, as what becomes important is not how speakers affirm or resist a pre-given biological designation, but how they activate various identity positions within particular conversations and localized contexts. Rusty Barrett's (1999) work on the "polyphonous identity" displays of African American drag queens in a Texas gay bar is an exemplary model of how such research might proceed, as he illustrates the ways in which speakers make use of linguistic variables with indexical associations to a variety of social categories.

Yet Butler's theory also has its limits for ethnographic sociolinguistic research. Most pressing in this regard is the restricted agency awarded the subject in a post-structuralist focus on discursive determinism (see Livia and Hall 1997), together with the undertheorization of the local in a philosophical text concerned with universal explanations for how gender works. Here is where the field would do well to remember how Austin's performative was taken up by linguistic anthropologists such as Dell Hymes, Charles Briggs, and Richard Bauman in the early ethnography of speaking. While Butler focuses almost exclusively on the rigid regulatory frames that make femininity and masculinity intelligible (in Austinian terms, the "conventional procedures" that make a performative utterance felicitous), these authors focus also on the emergent properties of specific speech events. Their perspective, as I have argued elsewhere (Hall 1999), is an ethnographic extension of the "dual-direction-of-fit" that Elizabeth Anscombe (1957) and then John Searle (1979) identify for Austin's classic performative. While the words of a performative do in some sense "fit" the world, conforming to the conventions that govern their success, they also constitute it, so that by their very utterance the world is also made to fit the words.

When we recognize this duality as existing within ritualized performance (as Tambiah 1979 does in a direct application of Austin's felicity conditions to ritual in the late 1970s), or more relevantly within conversational exchange, then we are compelled to examine the creative qualities of the speech event alongside the constraining ones. Hymes's (1975) repeated call to "understand structure as emergent in action" is critical here, as he and other scholars of performance, most notably Bauman and Briggs (cf. 1990), led us away from the analysis of ritual as mere reiteration. What moves into focus with their work is not Derridean iterability but "the total speech act," as they uncover not just the cultural conventions that make performance, ritual, and even everyday conversation felicitous, but also the creative aspects that govern any speech event. Butler's limitation of creativity to resignification – as, for instance, when a drag queen performs the "wrong" gender and thereby exposes the constructed nature of gender perceived as natural – is impoverished in ethnographic terms, since it reduces drag queen performance to an appropriation of a dominant ideology of femininity. This is, indeed, the assumption behind Butler's argument that drag is a kind of "double mimesis," that is, men acting like women acting like women. But as Barrett so cogently demonstrates in his linguistic research, drag queens are not acting like *women*, they are acting like *drag queens*. Their interwoven appropriations of African American Vernacular English, the "Standard" English phonology associated with *White-woman style*, and lexical items indexical of gay male speech suggest that gender identity is a multivocal phenomenon that depends on interaction with other social identities for its articulation. Because drag queen identity is always localized and produced through a variety of conflicting cultural scripts (race, class, sexuality, and gender among them), it would be ethnographically reductive to discuss their performances purely as a subversion of a non-localizable "femininity."

This brings me to the crux of an argument about how Butler's theory of gender performativity must be reworked, or at least acquire new focus, in the sociolinguistic study of language, gender, and sexuality. The only way identities previously regarded as non-normative can be brought into the mainstream of scholarship is if we localize what constitutes "felicitous" and "infelicitous" performances of gender and sexual identity within the language ideologies circulating in specific communities of practice. To discuss drag queen performance as the infelicitous enactment of dominant conventions of gender, as Butler does in her focus on drag as subversion, assumes a kind of singularity to drag queen identity, one that becomes interesting only in its potential to denaturalize heterosexual normativity. Queer linguistics, in contrast, invites us to discuss the conversational practices of all sexual identities – whether marginal or central to organizations of heterosexual kinship – as potentially felicitous on a more localized level. While much of the early research in the field has focused on the language practices of understudied sexual identities (just as much of the early research in language and gender focused on the language practices of women), its boundaries also embrace the findings of such scholars as Penelope Eckert (1996, 2002), whose ethnographic work on "the heterosexual marketplace" illustrates how heterosexual identity structures the adolescent social order in an American elementary school. Like queer theory, queer linguistics is necessarily concerned with how heterosexual normativity is produced, perpetuated, and resisted, but it seeks to localize these productions within specific communities of practice.

Recently, the field of queer linguistics, and indeed the entire study of language and identity, has come under fire from Don Kulick, who argues that the language practices of, for instance, gays and lesbians must be "unique to gays and lesbians" (2000: 259) if they are to be of interest to sociolinguists. But Kulick's criterion of "distinct and describable linguistic features and patterns" (Harvey and Shalom 1997: 3; cited by Kulick 2000: 276) puts him out of step with most recent work on language and identity. Indeed, in his article for the *Annual Review of Anthropology*, Kulick takes difference to be the necessary starting point for scholarship on language and sexuality, arguing that because linguistic differences across sexual identities have not been satisfactorily demonstrated, the entire field is therefore not viable. Now this is an odd claim given Kulick's (1999) strong praise for research on "transgender and language" in a previous review for the *GLQ*. We are left to assume that what makes transgender speech "distinctive" and thereby worthy of attention for Kulick, as opposed to the speech of gays and lesbians, is the mismatch between the original biological sex of the speaker and the social gender he or she produces. This recalls the problematic associated with the coat-rack theory of sex and gender, except that what comes into focus is not the men and women who affirm their biology, but the men and women who betray it. Certainly, there is nothing structurally "unique" about the feminine self-reference employed by the transgendered Hindi-speaking *hijras* of my own research (Hall and O'Donovan 1996, cited by Kulick 1999: 613; Hall 1997), as Hindi-speaking women make regular use of these linguistic forms on a daily basis.

Kulick's insistence on difference, then, not only requires linguistic deviance as a prerequisite for sociolinguistic research, it also recalls the much criticized difference model of language and gender (see Bucholtz and Hall 2002 for a fuller discussion). This approach, as noted earlier, has been extensively problematized for its tendency to emphasize cross-gender variation at the expense of potentially more significant intragender variation and cross-gender similarity. The practice-based and ideological models of language and gender that developed in response to these critiques, such as queer linguistics, seek not to describe how women's language use differs from men's, or how homosexuals' language use differs from heterosexuals', but to document the diverse range of women's and men's linguistic repertoires as developed within particular contexts. In these models, gender is seen as materializing only in interaction with other sociological discourses, including historical, national, ethnic, racial, age-related, and sexual ones. This, I would argue, is the direction that research on language and sexual identity must continue to take if the exceptional speakers of previous generations are to move squarely out of the footnotes.

ACKNOWLEDGMENTS

I would like to express my thanks to editors Miriam Meyerhoff and Janet Holmes for several careful readings of this chapter, and to Mary Bucholtz and Donna Goldstein for their continued support and insightful suggestions.

NOTES

1 Nora Newcombe and Diane B. Arnkoff (1979) are among the few scholars who noticed the oddity of scholars disputing Lakoff's claims with empirical research on the speech patterns of academics. In a criticism of Dubois and Crouch's (1975) findings, they assert: "Furthermore, an academic population may have distinctive speech styles. Lakoff (1975, 1977) has discussed at some length her belief that academic men are exceptions to her rules and use a speech style generally identified as 'female.' Many of the same reservations can be expressed about another study reporting no sex differences in the use of tag questions (Baumann 1976)."

2 Deborah Tannen (1996) discussed this "heterosexualization" in a plenary lecture at the fourth annual meeting of the Lavender Languages and Linguistics Conference in Washington, DC. I am grateful to her for allowing me to discuss this here, although for rather different reasons. According to Tannen, Burrell and Fitzpatrick have explained that they were unaware that the excerpt had originally appeared elsewhere, stating that one of their students had shared the data with them in class as self-collected.

3 See Bonnie McElhinny (2002) for a thorough and engaging discussion of divergent feminist approaches to the relationship between sex and gender.

REFERENCES

Anscombe, G. Elizabeth M. 1957: *Intention*. Oxford: Basil Blackwell.

Austin, John L. 1962: *How to Do Things with Words*. Cambridge, MA: Harvard University Press.

Barrett, Rusty 1999: Indexing polyphonous identity in the speech of African American drag queens. In Mary Bucholtz, Anita C. Liang, and Laurel A. Sutton (eds) *Reinventing*

Identities: The Gendered Self in Discourse. New York: Oxford University Press, pp. 313–31.

Bauman, Richard and Briggs, Charles L. 1990: Poetics and performance as critical perspectives on language and social life. *Annual Review of Anthropology* 19: 59–88.

Baumann, M. 1976: Two features of "women's speech." In Betty Lou Dubois and Isabel Crouch (eds) *The Sociology of the Languages of American Women.* San Antonio, TX: Trinity University.

Blumstein, Philip and Schwartz, Pepper 1984: *American Couples: Money, Work, Sex.* New York: William Morrow.

Bodine, Anne 1975: Sex differentiation in language. In Barrie Thorne and Nancy Henley (eds) *Language and Sex: Difference and Dominance.* Rowley, MA: Newbury House, pp. 130–51.

Bogoras, Waldemar 1922: Chukchee. In Franz Boas (ed.) *Handbook of American Indian Languages* 2. Bureau of American Ethnology Bulletin 40. Washington, DC: Smithsonian Institution, pp. 631–903, esp. 665–6.

Bucholtz, Mary and Hall, Kira 1995: Twenty years after *Language and Woman's Place.* In Kira Hall and Mary Bucholtz (eds) *Gender Articulated: Language and the Socially Constructed Self.* New York: Routledge, pp. 1–22.

Bucholtz, Mary and Hall, Kira 2002: Tactics of Subjectivity. Paper presented at the Ninth Annual Meeting of Lavender Languages and Linguistics, American University, Washington, DC, February.

Bucholtz, Mary, Liang, Anita C., and Sutton, Laurel A. (eds) 1999: *Reinventing Identities: The Gendered Self in Discourse.* New York: Oxford University Press.

Burrell, N. and Fitzpatrick, Mary Anne 1989: The psychological reality of marital conflict. In Dudley D. Cahn (ed.) *Intimates in Conflict: A Communication Perspective.* Hillsdale, NJ: Erlbaum, pp. 167–86.

Burris, Barbara 1973: Fourth world manifesto. In Anne Koedt, Ellen Levine, and Anita Rapone (eds) *Radical Feminism.* New York: Quadrangle Books, pp. 322–57.

Butler, Judith 1990: *Gender Trouble: Feminism and the Subversion of Identity.* New York: Routledge.

Butler, Judith 1993: *Bodies That Matter: On the Discursive Limits of "Sex."* New York: Routledge.

Cameron, Deborah 1985: *Feminism and Linguistic Theory,* 2nd edn. New York: St Martin's Press.

Chamberlain, Alexander F. 1912: Women's languages. *American Anthropologist* 14: 579–81.

Chatterji, Suniti Kumar 1921: Bengali phonetics. *Bulletin of the School of Oriental Studies* 2(1): 1–25.

Crosby, F. and Nyquist, L. 1977: The female register: An empirical study of Lakoff's hypotheses. *Language in Society* 6: 313–22.

di Leonardo, Micaela 1991: Introduction: Gender, culture, and political economy: Feminist anthropology in historical perspective. In Micaela di Leonardo (ed.) *Gender at the Crossroads of Knowledge: Feminist Anthropology in the Modern Era.* Berkeley, CA: University of California Press, pp. 1–48.

Dubois, Betty Lou and Crouch, Isabel 1975: The question of tag questions in women's speech: They don't really use more of them, do they? *Language in Society* 4: 289–94.

Dunbar, Roxanne 1970: Female liberation as the basis for social revolution. In Robin Morgan (ed.) *Sisterhood is Powerful.* New York: Random House, pp. 477–92.

Eckert, Penelope 1996: Vowels and nail polish: The emergence of linguistic style in the preadolescent linguistic marketplace. In Natasha Warner, Jocelyn Ahlers, Leela Bilmes, Monica Oliver, Suzanne Wertheim and Melinda Chen (eds) *Gender and Belief Systems*. Berkeley, CA: Berkeley Women and Language Group, University of California, pp. 183–90.

Eckert, Penelope 2002: Demystifying sexuality and desire. In Kathryn Campbell-Kibler, Robert J. Podesva, Sarah J. Roberts, and Andrew Wong (eds) *Language and Sexuality: Contesting Meaning in Theory and Practice*. Stanford, CA: CSLI Publications, pp. 99–110.

Eckert, Penelope and McConnell-Ginet, Sally 1992: Think practically and look locally: Language and gender as community-based practice. *Annual Review of Anthropology* 21: 461–90.

Ehrenreich, Paul 1894: Materialien zur Sprachenkunde Brasiliens. *Zeitschrift für Ethnologie* 26: 20–4.

Flannery, Regina 1946: Men's and women's speech in Gros Ventre. *International Journal of American Linguistics* 12: 133–5.

Furfey, Paul Hanly 1944: Men's and women's language. *American Catholic Sociological Review* 5: 218–23.

Gal, Susan 1991: Between speech and silence: The problematics of research on language and gender. In Micaela di Leonardo (ed.) *Gender at the Crossroads of Knowledge: Feminist Anthropology in the Modern Era*. Berkeley, CA: University of California Press, pp. 175–203.

Gatchet, Albert S. 1884: *Hitchiti. A Migration Legend of the Creek Indians*. Philadelphia: Brinton, pp. 79–81.

Gumperz, John J. (ed.) 1982: *Language and Social Identity*. Cambridge: Cambridge University Press.

Haas, Mary R. 1944: Men's and women's speech in Koasati. *Language* 20:

142–9. Reprinted in Dell Hymes (ed.) 1964: *Language in Culture and Society*. New York: Harper and Row, pp. 228–33.

Hall, Kira 1997: "Go suck your husband's sugarcane": Hijras and the use of sexual insult. In Anna Livia and Kira Hall (eds) *Queerly Phrased: Language, Gender, and Sexuality*. New York: Oxford University Press, pp. 430–60.

Hall, Kira 1999: Performativity. *Journal of Linguistic Anthropology* 9(1–2): 184–7.

Hall, Kira and O'Donovan, Veronica 1996: Shifting gender positions among Hindi-speaking Hijras. In Victoria Bergvall, Janet Bing, and Alice Freed (eds) *Rethinking Language and Gender Research: Theory and Practice*. London: Longman, pp. 228–66.

Hymes, Dell 1975: Breakthrough into performance. In Dan Ben-Amos and Kenneth S. Goldstein (eds) *Folklore: Performance and Communication*. The Hague and Paris: Mouton, pp. 11–74.

Jacobs, Greg 1996: Lesbian and gay male language use: A critical review of the literature. *American Speech* 71(1): 49–71.

Jespersen, Otto 1922: The woman. In *Language: Its Nature, Development, and Origin*. London: Allen and Unwin. Reprinted in Deborah Cameron, (ed.) 1990: *The Feminist Critique of Language: A Reader*. New York: Routledge, pp. 201–20.

Keenan (Ochs), Elinor [1974] 1996: Norm-makers, norm-breakers: Uses of speech by men and women in a Malagasy community. Reprinted in Donald Brenneis and Ronald K. S. Macaulay (eds) *The Matrix of Language: Contemporary Linguistic Anthropology*. pp. 99–115

Krause, Fritz 1911: *In den Wildnissen Brasiliens: Bericht und Ergebnisse der*

Leipziger Araguaya-Expedition 1908. Leipzig: R. Doigtländers Verlag, pp. 60, 343–4, 416–57.

Kulick, Don 1999: Transgender and language: A review of the literature and suggestions for the future. *GLQ* 5(4): 605–22.

Kulick, Don 2000: Gay and lesbian language. *Annual Review of Anthropology 2000* 29: 243–85.

Lakoff, Robin 1975: *Language and Woman's Place.* New York: Harper Colophon Books.

Lakoff, Robin 1977: Language and sexual identity. *Semiotica* 19: 119–30.

Lasch, Richard 1907: Über Sondersprachen und ihre Entstehung. *Mitteilungen der Anthropologischen Gesellschaft in Wien* 37.

Livia, Anna and Hall, Kira 1997: "It's a girl!" Bringing performativity back to linguistics. In Anna Livia and Kira Hall (eds) *Queerly Phrased: Language, Gender, and Sexuality.* New York: Oxford University Press, pp. 1–18.

Maccoby, Eleanor E. 1998: *The Two Sexes: Growing Up Apart, Coming Together.* Cambridge, MA: Harvard University Press.

Maltz, Daniel N. and Borker, Ruth A. 1982: A cultural approach to male–female miscommunication. In John J. Gumperz (ed.) *Language and Social Identity.* Cambridge: Cambridge University Press, pp. 196–216.

McElhinny, Bonnie 2002: Language, sexuality, and political economy. In Kathryn Campbell-Kibler, Robert J. Podesva, Sarah J. Roberts, and Andrew Wong (eds) *Language and Sexuality: Contesting Meaning in Theory and Practice.* Stanford, CA: CSLI Publications, pp. 111–34.

Newcombe, Nora and Arnkoff, Diane B. 1979: Effects of speech style and sex of speaker in persona perception. *Journal of Personality and Social Psychology* 37: 1293–1303.

Nicholson, Linda 1994: Interpreting gender. *Signs* 20(1): 79–105.

O'Barr, William M. and Atkins, Bowman K. 1980: "Women's language" or "powerless language"? In Sally McConnell-Ginet, Ruth Borker, and Nelly Furman (eds) *Women and Language in Literature and Society.* New York: Praeger, pp. 93–109.

Ortner, Sherry 1974: Is female to male as nature is to culture? In Michelle Rosaldo and Louise Lamphere (eds) *Woman, Culture, and Society.* Stanford, CA: Stanford University Press, pp. 67–87.

Rosaldo, Michelle Z. 1974: Woman, culture, and society: A theoretical overview. In Michelle Rosaldo and Louise Lamphere (eds) *Woman, Culture, and Society.* Stanford, CA: Stanford University Press, pp. 17–42.

Sapir, Edward 1915: Abnormal types of speech in Nootka. Reprinted in David Mandelbaum (ed.) 1949: *Selected Writings of Edward Sapir.* Berkeley, CA: University of California Press, pp. 179–96.

Sapir, Edward 1929: Male and female forms of speech in Yana. Reprinted in David Mandelbaum (ed.) 1949: *Selected Writings of Edward Sapir.* Berkeley, CA: University of California Press, pp. 206–12.

Sapper, Carl 1897: Mittelamericanische Caraiben. *Internationales Archiv für Ethnographie* 10: 53–60.

Searle, John R. 1979: A taxonomy of illocutionary acts. In *Expression and Meaning: Studies in the Theory of Speech Acts.* Cambridge: Cambridge University Press, pp. 1–29.

Tambiah, Stanley J. (1979): A performative approach to ritual. *Proceedings of the British Academy* 65. Oxford: Oxford University Press.

Tannen, Deborah 1986: *That's Not What I Meant! How Conversational Style Makes or Breaks Relationships.* New York: Ballantine.

Tannen, Deborah 1990: *You Just Don't Understand: Women and Men in Conversation*. New York: Ballantine.

Tannen, Deborah 1996: Gay Men's English – A Look Back. Paper presented at the Fourth Conference on Lavender Languages and Linguistics, American University, September.

Tanner, Nancy and Zihlman, Adrienne 1976: Women in evolution, Part One: Innovation and selection in human origins. *Signs* 1(3): 585–608.

Thorne, Barrie 1993: *Gender Play: Girls and Boys in School*. New Brunswick, NJ: Rutgers University Press.

Tiger, Lionel 1969: *Men in Groups*. London: Thomas Nelson & Sons, and New York: Random House.

Trechter, Sara 1999: Contextualizing the exotic few. In Mary Bucholtz, Anita C. Liang, and Laurel A. Sutton (eds) *Reinventing Identities: The Gendered Self in Discourse*. New York: Oxford University Press, pp. 101–22.

Wolf, Arthur 1995: *Sexual Attraction and Childhood Association: A Chinese Brief for Edward Westermarck*. Stanford, CA: Stanford University Press.

Zihlman, Adrienne 1978: Women in evolution, Part Two: Subsistence and social organization among early hominids. *Signs* 4(1): 4–20.

16 Language and Gender in Adolescence

PENELOPE ECKERT

1 Introduction

Adolescence is a critical site for the study of language and gender. First, it is a life-stage at which a tremendous amount of identity work is being done, and gender is perhaps more salient in this work than at any other life-stage. Adolescents are moving away from identities based in the family to identities based in a newly organized and newly heterosocial peer social order, and this heterosociability both makes gender more salient, and changes its constitution. Second, adolescents are the major institutionalized population within industrial, and perhaps particularly within US, culture, and this institutionalization intensifies identity work, giving rise to an unusual amount of symbolic activity – much of it linguistic. Finally, institutionalization also subjects adolescents to particular kinds of monitoring and policing, much of which is gendered, and much of which focuses on language.

2 Adolescence as Ideology

In introducing my discussion of gender and adolescent language, and of adult activity around this use, I would like to emphasize that adolescence, like gender, is an ideological construct. The joint consideration of gender and adolescence provides a double opportunity to discuss the problems of power, homogenization, reification, and essentialism in the study of language and social groups. Just as gender does not unfold naturally from biology, neither do life-stages such as childhood, adolescence, adulthood, or old age. Biology imposes some constraints, and culture takes off from there. Adolescence is an outgrowth of industrialization – of the shift to institutionalized preparation for work, and the need to keep the young out of the workforce. While there are physiological changes that coincide to some extent with the entrance into adolescence, to attribute "adolescent behavior" to "raging hormones" is to ignore the obvious: that above all, adolescence is an age- and generation-based location in the political economy.

What is commonly ignored is the fact that adolescents are not simply left to develop into adults, but are put into institutions that isolate them from adults. This situation produces a social hothouse, in which a social order emerges that solidifies the gender hierarchy as well as class, racial, and ethnic hierarchies. Adolescence slows time for the age group as, rather than focusing on getting to adulthood, adolescents enter into a kind of time warp – or a cultural sink – in which adolescence is not something to pass through, but something to achieve. And in the process, people become not more adult, but more adolescent, as the ultimate adolescent is the oldest: the high school senior. "Adolescent culture," in other words, is very much the product of the place given to adolescents in our society. If we want to consider gender in adolescence (and beyond), then, we need to consider how our adolescent institutions constrain the construction of gender (see, for example, Connell et al. 1982; Thorne, 1993).

If adolescents and women share a naturalizing discourse, they also share stigma and trivialization of their activities and concerns. Discourses of gender, and of race and class, are built on discourses of age – discourses of responsibility, maturity, control, emotionality, intellectual capacity, and rationality. The ultimate legitimate person in the social order, the White upper-middle-class male,[1] is slated to be unemotional, rational, focused on "business," and endowed with global and objective knowledge. Women and adolescents, on the other hand, are viewed as emotional, changeable, irrational, trivial, and unobjective. Adults can always get a sigh, a groan, or a laugh of commiseration just by announcing that they have adolescent offspring. People joke with those of us who work with adolescents about our bravery and forbearance. At a campus celebration of books published by Stanford faculty in 2000, I was even awarded a tongue-in-cheek prize for "work above and beyond the call of duty" for the ethnographic research involved in my book on adolescent linguistic and social practice (Eckert 2000). Colleagues have actually sat me in front of their adolescent children and asked me to "do my thing" with them – as if I were an animal psychologist and their children were problematic cats.

The purpose of this introductory diatribe has been to emphasize that life-stage and gender are intertwining constructions, and the examination of one calls for the examination of the other. Adolescence is a particularly rich life-stage for the study of the interplay between the construction of language and the construction of social identity because while it is eminently transitional, it is also highly reified and experienced as static (by many as painfully so). In the following discussion, I will step back a bit from adolescence to include the transition into adolescence. For it is in this transition that one can see the extent to which adolescence is not simply an abstract stage, but the dynamic accomplishment of an age cohort.

3 School as Site for the Construction of Adolescence

As the official transition from childhood to adulthood, adolescence is the time when the age cohort moves from their parents' and families' social sphere to one that they construct for themselves – one that is transitional from the social order of their childhood to the social order of their adulthood. Because adolescence is defined by secondary education, this takes place primarily in reference to schools. Even for those who are not in school, or who don't spend much time there, the very fact of their relation to the school is central to their place in society as *dropouts* or *truants*. And within the school, those who choose to minimize their institutional participation are labeled *anti-social*. In other words, participation in the secondary school institution defines legitimate adolescence. In the USA, the role of the high school in defining adolescence is particularly intense because, more than elsewhere, the high school in the USA is a total institution (Goffman 1961), not only providing academic and vocational instruction, but organizing the age group's civic, social, artistic, and athletic activities as well.

The dominant adult view of adolescence is of an "unfinished" population – a population in which judgment has not quite caught up with desire. This attribution constructs the age group as not yet responsible but harmless, their antics relatively predictable. And it defines adolescents as a special leisure class – without family and financial responsibilities, living out of danger and with comfortable adult caretakers, and content to participate in the school institution until it's "time" to join the adult world. Those people in their teens who for whatever reason do not fit this description are cast as anti-adolescents. For them, adolescence and adulthood are blurred, both in day-to-day experience and in treatment by the institutions of society – schools, social services, the courts. Any focus on adolescence as a life-stage locates struggle between adolescents and adults, erasing the ways in which adult-built institutions have set up a struggle among adolescents – a struggle that will endure into the cohort's own adulthood.

3.1 Accomplishing heterosociability

The adolescent social order is sufficiently reified in Western society that it begins consciously to take shape well before adolescence. Beginning in elementary school, there is a gradual appropriation of power and authority from adults into the age cohort, the development of an integrated social order, and the reorganization of normative relations within the cohort from asexual to heterosexual. By the time the cohort moves into secondary school, it has accomplished the social changes that move it into a heterosexual and hierarchical social order. And as the official locus of adolescence, the US high school brings an institutionalization of traditional gender arrangements, heterosexuality, and romance. The female supportive role is formalized in the pairing of such activities as girls' cheerleading and boys' varsity athletics, and in the feminization of organizational activities such as holding bake sales, organizing dances, and so on. Girls tend to do the majority of the behind-the-scenes work for school activities, while boys predominate in top managerial roles (class president, student body president, etc.). And the heterosexual couple is institutionalized in the king and queen of the high school homecoming and prom, and the yearbook's choice of "cutest couple." Heterosexuality and romance are also publicly constructed in high school through formal activities such as dances, in the relation between dating and social status, and in the careful following of the antics of the "famous couples" of each graduating class.

Achieving adolescence is a goal for younger children – not just individually but as a cohort – and the business of social change within the cohort and the business of individual change are closely and consciously intertwined. The move to adolescence is not an individual experience – it is an age cohort's *prise de conscience*. The following discussion is based on my own ethnographic work, in which I followed a diverse age cohort in Northern California from fifth grade (10–11 years) into eighth grade (13–14 years) – from elementary school into junior high. During this time the cohort moved from late childhood into early adolescence. The initial stages of this process involve a transcendence of the teacher-dominated classroom, developing a social order that spans the age cohort, moving toward age-group autonomy. This transcendence is accomplished through the emergence of a heterosexual market (Thorne 1993), dominated by a *crowd* – a socially heterosexual community of practice that comes to dominate attention and space, and comes to be known as the "popular crowd." In the crowd, heterosexual pairing takes place as a group endeavor, providing support and encouragement for individuals as they experiment, on behalf of the rest of the cohort, with unfamiliar and face-threatening practices. As the visible locus of emerging social heterosexuality, the crowd dominates attention through its fast-paced new heterosexual activity, as couples form and break up at a dizzying rate. The rapid negotiation of alliances creates a market, constructing desirability and worth in heterosexual terms. Within this enterprise arises a new gender differentiation and division of labor. Boys come to dominate certain arenas of recognized accomplishment – most notably sports and overt competition of many kinds. They begin to accomplish masculinity – to expand themselves physically, developing sports moves and postures that maximize the appearance of contained volume and strength, and engaging in aggressive, competitive talk about "masculine" subjects. And as girls become marginalized in these activities, they establish and dominate new spheres of activity and accomplishment. They engage with the technology of beauty and personality, experimenting with cosmetics, clothing, hairstyles, and the development of cute or clever personalities. And more important, they engage in *social engineering*. The entire heterosexual enterprise at this point is about alignments within the cohort rather than about individual boy–girl relationships. The pairs are brokered by members of the crowd, and the individual couples generally do not spend time together except in a few cases for very brief ritual appearances. And it is the girls who do the brokering. Girls control the heterosexual market – they decide who will go with whom, they arrange meetings and alliances, and they negotiate desirability.

As part of their role as brokers in the market, girls take up new forms of verbal activity. On the fifth grade playground, boys come to dominate the large games that take up the central area – to become *athletes* rather than *boys playing*. And girls, one by one and group by group, move away from some of their old playground activities, and take to standing, sitting, or walking around the periphery, watching the boys, heckling them, or talking intensely together. The practice of walking around has in itself symbolic significance. Moving away from the crowd and walking around slowly, intensely engaged in conversation, draws attention to those who do it. It stands in stark contrast to the fast movements of their peers, with play, with the larger groups engaged in games, and with the louder tone of children's talk and shouting. This walking, furthermore, is a visible occasion on which girls engage in intense negotiation of heterosexual pairings and realignment of friendships. This talk activity is a skill that girls consciously develop. In Eckert (1996), I recount how two girls, Trudy and Katya, gave up playground games for "talking" in February of fifth grade. Trudy had acquired a boyfriend, and as part of a move into prominence on the heterosexual market, she and Katya quite deliberately and self-consciously sat visibly aside and "just talked." It was not the desire to talk that brought them to sit aside on these occasions; rather, it was the cachet of sitting aside that brought them to talk. In fact, at first they sat awkwardly, not knowing what kind of conversation to engage in.

One might be inclined to attribute girls' engagement in negotiating relationships as evidence of the kind of connection orientation that is commonly attributed to girls and women (Belenky et al. 1986; Gilligan et al. 1990). If this is so, then *connection* has a different meaning than is commonly assumed. The focus on connection in the literature portrays girls as benign and positive in their relationships, in spite of the fact that any observer of adolescents during this period knows that girls can get quite mean and their friendships volatile, while boys' relationships tend to remain on a fairly even keel. A major activity among girls during this period is the development of cliques, ganging up on each other, shunning individuals, changing friends – a development of social toughness comparable to boys' development of physical or athletic toughness. Marjorie Harness Goodwin has chronicled this kind of activity in a variety of venues, and what is particularly striking about her findings is the elaborateness of girls' verbal activity in the accomplishment of exclusivity and the termination of relationships. The drawn-out nature of *he-said-she-said*, as girls police and sanction each other's behavior (Goodwin 1990), and the cleverness of girls' insults as they shun undesirables (Goodwin 2000),[2] all show an engagement in mean articulateness. It may be that a certain amount of this nastiness comes from the feeling of subordination and exclusion in the new gender order, but the fact is that girls are not sugar and spice.

This emerging social order brings with it – indeed depends on – an increase in peer-based social control and negotiation. Much of the linguistic activity observed as "adolescent" is part of the means of construction and maintenance of the social order. Certain kinds of speech acts gain particular prominence in the search for social control, and in the monitoring, particularly, of individuals' and groups' conformity to new gender norms. With the new heterosexual social order comes an intensification of pressure on boys to be aggressively masculine and heterosexual. Teasing is one of the more important and obvious verbal forms of social control that is certainly common in childhood, but continues in later elementary school and junior high school in highly focused encounters (Eder 1991). Much of this pressure comes from other boys, but Eder et al. (1995) found in their research in a junior high school that girls participate in sexual and homophobic verbal teasing and aggression as well. The use of labels such as *fag* to refer to any male who does not match up to masculine norms, or of *gay* to refer more generally to someone who also does not match up to norms, brings together the heterosexual and the masculine imperatives. And the gender asymmetry of terms like *slut* and *stud* create gender-asymmetrical categorizations based on sexual behavior – or in fact, at this stage, on behavior only remotely related to, but nonetheless linked to, sexuality. The meaning of *slut* in early adolescence, and even to some extent in adolescence, is closer to the meaning of *hussy* – a female who oversteps general bounds of propriety, whether a girl who dates too many boys, or who is loud, or who does what she pleases.

Just as "talking" emerges with the heterosexual market, so does another speech activity often taken as indicative of females' connection orientation. Perhaps the most interesting verbal means by which girls monitor progress in the accomplishment of new feminine norms of behavior and adornment is the use of compliments. As the heterosexual market takes off, one can see girls learning to do compliments, and indeed complimenting becomes a heightened verbal activity. As in the adult population (Holmes 1995), compliments are overwhelmingly addressed to females, and focus on appearance. Like the pairing of couples on the heterosexual market, complimenting is intense and almost compulsive among girls engaged in the market. And like trade on the market, it serves to establish norms of behavior and appearance. Girls accomplish this work through both sincere and sarcastic complimenting. Sincere compliments to players in the market add value to the receiver as evidence of her quality, and to the giver as evidence of her possession and exercise of cultural knowledge. The practice of offering obviously false compliments to stigmatized girls is a major means of pointing out infractions of the new norms, but more important, of establishing and enforcing social hierarchies and boundaries. As with the more direct forms of social engineering, this use of compliments might lead us to reconsider the source of behaviors commonly viewed as reflecting girls' greater "connection" orientation.

Gender differences begin to appear in data on phonological and grammatical variation at around the time that the adolescent social order begins to emerge in elementary school. Several authors have found boys leading girls in the use of non-standard variants at about the age of 10 (Biondi 1975; Macaulay 1977; Romaine 1984). Macaulay shows gender differences setting in between the earlier age in his sample (10 years old) and the later age (14 years old). It is certainly a general pattern that at least where clear non-standardisms (particularly grammatical) are concerned, from early adolescence on, males in general use more of them than females. The use of vernacular language – language that is sanctioned by adults, particularly teachers – is one means to establish one's independence, one's toughness, and one's right to "make the rules." And closely related to the use of vernacular language, for many, is the use of expletives and sexual references (deKlerk 1997; Eder et al. 1995; Kiesling 1997). Inasmuch as this is an important goal for boys as they try to achieve hegemonic masculinity, one might expect them to make greater use of vernacular variants. This attitudinal gender difference is what Trudgill invokes in his discussion of *covert prestige* (Trudgill 1972). And this may well explain the pattern that John Fischer found in his study of elementary school children (Fischer 1958), as boys reduced more occurrences of -*ing* than girls, and "typical" boys reduced more than "model" boys. Cheshire's study (Cheshire 1982) of an adolescent social network as defined by the use of a playground in Reading showed correlations between linguistic variables and participation in "vernacular" culture, which Cheshire defined primarily in terms of "toughness" (carrying weapons, criminal activity, skill at fighting, swearing) – which, in turn, was strongly related to gender. In her work with adolescents in Sydney, Edina Eisikovits (Eisikovits 1987) found boys increasing their use of vernacular variables in their interviews with her, apparently as a show of defiance in the face of an authority figure. But we need to be careful not to automatically equate the search for autonomy and toughness with male gender, however much societal norms may lean in this direction. For however compelling this view of gender may be, it breaks down in part when we take a closer look at general patterns, as becomes particularly clear in the data on adolescent speakers.

3.2 Constructing adolescent social categories

The arrival in secondary school marks the official beginning of adolescence, and with heterosociability firmly in place in the cohort, there is increased attention to other forms of diversity. In most places, primary schools feed into larger secondary schools, where there is often greater class, racial, and ethnic diversity – and sufficient numbers to form crowds based in these categories. Thrown together in a close environment for the better part of the week, students engage in identity politics, vying for space, visibility, social resources, legitimation. Space is exploited in such a way that the school layout becomes a highly charged social map, providing a variety of stages from which people can mount cultural performances. The semiotic activity that constitutes social categories within and beyond the school permeates just about every aspect of people's day-to-day practice. Styles emerge laden with social significance, mapping out the ideological terrain of the age cohort within an adult-defined environment. Differences in class, race, religion, and ethnicity, and positioning in relation to adult institutions (not only the school but government, police, courts, the media), to adult control, and to adolescence itself, create a highly charged atmosphere for the creation of distinction (Irvine 2001). These categories, in turn, are saturated with gender in a complex variety of ways. Categories may be constructed around different gender practices, for example, with more or less gender segregation, more or less gender hierarchy, more or less consensuality – and these within different kinds of activities. The degree of hostility and/or segregation of categories may differ among males and among females, as may the need to exercise difference. It is the magnitude of this complexity that can make generalizations about gender problematic.

Labeling is an important means of producing and maintaining social distinctions. The simple existence of a term for a social type creates a category, allowing it to enter into everyday discourse. At the same time, the potential for labeling can serve as a strong means of social control. Labels arise in real use, and in relation to real people in real situations (Bucholtz 2001; Eckert and McConnell-Ginet 1995). We make social meaning by labeling as we chat. It is in speech activities such as making observations and judgments about people, pointing people out to others, describing absent people, that we endow labels with meaning. And in thus endowing labels with meaning, we create categorizations. In this way, the day-to-day use and re-use of labels brings about the continual ebb and flow of meaning and social change. This goes for the use of *fag, gay, slut,* and *stud* mentioned above, as well as for the huge range of category names that constitute an important part of the lexicon in any high school. In every school, a proliferation of labels maps out the local social terrain, the margins of respectability, and the terms of evaluation (T. Labov 1992). These labels connect to those in other schools, but always with either small differences in meaning or with strikingly different inventories – depending on the nature of the local social order. And these terms are used differentially by gender. Eckert and McConnell-Ginet (1995) have noted that the hegemonic categories (such as *jock* and *burnout*) tend to be primarily defined in terms of males, and female participants in these categories need to work harder to emphasize their category status. (Striking evidence of the hegemonically male status of these categories appeared in one writer's claim that my first book about jocks and burnouts (Eckert 1989) was only about boys.) On the other hand, certain categories may be specifically male or female (such as *nerd* or *ditz*), while others may be used differently when referring to males and females. At any rate, the practice of labeling is a powerful means of co-constructing gender and other social categorizations, and of controlling social meaning within the community.

The volatility of these labels attests to – indeed is an agent of – social change. Mary Bucholtz's account of a group of girls (Bucholtz 1996) claiming status as *nerds* – a status normally reserved for males – is a striking example of the process of change through the contestation of categories, the regendering of categories, and the reclaiming of epithets. While nerds in schools have been generally stigmatized, their increased power and visibility in the high tech industry – and the increasing visibility of technological expertise in school itself – feeds back into an increasingly self-proclaimed status in high school. These girls, in appropriating an aggressively intellectual and independent style, are making a claim about their ability not only to be smart but, like boys, to "make the rules." In laying claim to nerd status, these girls are constructing a particular style that includes not only being smart, but being independently smart, beyond the control of teachers. They lay this claim by constructing an entire style of speech that includes specialized names, lexicon, and phonological variables signaling articulateness (e.g. the hyper-articulation of stops). Thus as labels serve to produce and reproduce categories in discourse, speech style joins with other aspects of style (e.g. dress and other adornment, substance use, musical taste, territory, activities, movement) to make claims about one's own relation to those labels. Norma Mendoza-Denton's study of Mexican American girls in Northern California (Mendoza-Denton 1994, 1996) shows how gang girls use a wide range of semiotic means, from language choice and variation to make-up and dress, to lay claim to gang identity and practice that has been traditionally reserved for males. Specific features of this style (e.g. the span of black eyeliner) are iconic of toughness, simultaneously signaling ethnic identity to non-Latinos, claiming access to the male prerogative of toughness, and setting themselves off from tamer girls.

General ideology would have it that many adolescent labels and the styles that go with them are trivial, manifesting as they do "purely adolescent" concerns. Adolescent styles are viewed as ever-changing, but trivialized as stylistic activity for its own sake, and limited to adolescence. These styles and the concerns they represent are expected to have no lasting effect on language or society since individuals are expected to drop them as they move into adulthood. This attitude toward stylistic activity is more general, and part of the construction of hegemony by which style is an add-on for people who are not sufficient in their "natural state." The business suit and the man who wears it are "style-less" – and this stylelessness goes with seriousness of purpose, the important work of the world. Women in high heels and make-up, teeny-boppers, goths, and hip-hoppers, on the other hand, are frivolous: their stylistic activity a bid to be noticed or to rebel, and their activities just noise in the world. The opposition between the real and the styled is repeated across society in many ways. Most crucial to this discussion is the recursiveness of this opposition (Gal and Irvine 1995), as it not only separates adolescents from other age groups – and particularly adults – it also separates delegitimated adolescents from the legitimated.

In his study of White middle-class Parisian adolescents, Stephen Albert (Albert 2000) noted how they distinguish themselves from adolescents who are "into" youth styles (*à fond dedans*). For these teenagers, knowledge of youth styles – of dress, of music, etc. – is crucial to being cosmopolitan, but so also is a lack of engagement in conscious stylistic activity, and an avoidance of specific youth styles. In this way, they lay claim to naturalness by claiming to choose what they like, what's comfortable, and, presumably, what's objectively good. Being *à fond dedans* ("into") styles, for them, signals a lack of the self-control and perspective that come with maturity – and with class. Unmarked, they are *hors style* – needing no explanation, packaging, or self-presentation.

At the same time, the situated appropriation of elements of these styles allows "mainstream" adolescents to lay temporary claim to bits of meaning. The use of Latino and African American Vernacular English (AAVE) features by White Anglo teenagers in the USA signals coolness, toughness, attitude. And while these acts of identity may indicate admiration, the admiration is for a specific set of attributes, and as such, as argued by people such as Mary Bucholtz, Cecilia Cutler, and Jane Hill (Bucholtz 1999; Cutler 1999; Hill 1993), preserves the racial hierarchy. Based on her work in Rio Di Janeiro, Jennifer Roth-Gordon (Roth-Gordon 2001) argues that middle-class Brazilian adolescents engage in just enough slang use to establish their connection to youth culture. But the youth culture that they're connected to is a kind of imagined community in which youth are aligned in their up-to-dateness in opposition to their out-of-date parents. Originating in the tough poor favelas, urban slang represents youthful autonomy, but it is also linked to crime, race, and poverty. In their selective use of favela slang, middle-class adolescents assert that they are the upcoming generation, but signal restraint. And their ability to dispassionately appropriate favela youth resources constitutes, in their and their parents' view, legitimate adolescence, and an anticipation of legitimate adulthood. In other words, they construct their age group as aligned with their parents' class position. The favela youth, on the other hand, engage in slang "for real," and are expected to carry their slang into adulthood – an adulthood that will not differ significantly from youth.

4   Adolescents as Leaders in Linguistic Change

I don't think that I need to argue that stylistic innovations of adolescence do carry over into adult language. This should be self-evident. But the social work that brings into opposition the marked and the unmarked, the vernacular and the standard, the delegitimized and the legitimized, is an important source of change throughout the linguistic system. There is every reason to believe that linguistic change is propelled – or accelerated – by social upheaval. Historical linguists have noted that languages tend to change more rapidly during historical periods of unrest, and we have seen major linguistic developments at specific times of social change (Clermont and Cedergren 1979; Zhang 2001). One might consider that very similar dynamics are at work during the adolescent life-stage. The cohort is undergoing rapid social change, with changing alliances, and ever-emerging new forms of identity. It is in, and by virtue of, this process that adolescents act as major agents of linguistic change. Early arguments (Halle 1962) that linguistic change is the result of reinterpretation at the moment of acquisition have been challenged by the fact that it is adolescents, not children, who lead in linguistic change. And this is not a purely linguistic phenomenon, but goes hand in hand with the fact that adolescents are also engaged in social change.

By virtue of their transitional place in the life-course, adolescents are in a particularly strong position to respond to change in the conditions of life, and in so doing bring about lasting social change. It is particularly apparent with immigrant groups that adolescents are society's transition teams, reinterpreting the world, resolving the old with the new, substrate with superstrate, culture with culture, local with transnational. Chantal Tetrault (2000) describes the multilingual punning of French adolescents of North African descent. In *hachek*, a competitive word duel played by two participants, rhyming play between Arabic and French allows these teenagers to play with cultural meaning as they construct a new cultural space, or as she puts it, "creating cultural crossroads from which to speak." Norma Mendoza-Denton's examination (Mendoza-Denton, forthcoming) of the raising of [I] and the fortition of [θ] in the speech of Latino adolescents shows the importation of Spanish phonology into English, transforming English into a language that can construct Latino identities. Particularly, the heightened use of this particular phonological feature in a highlighted discourse use of *and everything* relates it directly to the US life of these adolescents. Teenagers in immigrant communities are simultaneously mediating cultures, and they can do it not simply because they are some transitional generation, but precisely because of their life-stage. As youth, they are expected to mess with meaning. By virtue of their location in time and social and cultural space, they have special knowledge, and in working with this knowledge – in making new meanings – they are constructing authenticity of a new kind. They are not just resolving ethnicity, gender, class, and race for today, but constructing permanent meanings that they will carry into adulthood, to be worked on by the next generation.

Work in phonological and grammatical variation has shown adolescents interrupting what might otherwise be smooth age grading, leading all other age groups – younger and older – in sound change and in the use of vernacular forms. Adolescents are producing linguistic patterns that are no longer reflecting their family of origin, but that reflect their own search for a place in the peer social order. Walt Wolfram's data (1969) on African American English in Detroit and Ronald Macaulay's data (1977) from Glasgow show better correlations of language use with parents' socio-economic class for pre-adolescents than for adolescents. My own Detroit suburban study (Eckert 2000), which included only adolescents, saw parents' socio-economic class give way as a significant correlate with variation in favor of the age-specific social categories that mediate social class for the adolescent age group. Potentially more striking evidence of the role of adolescent social practice on language change is Sarah Roberts' (2000, forthcoming) powerful argument, on the basis of historical Hawaiian data, that creolization in the case of Hawaiian Creole was effected not by children learning pidgin as their first language, but by older children and adolescents in peer-based communities of practice as they mutually constructed local-based identities.

I mentioned earlier that general gender differences begin to emerge at about the same time as the heterosexual market. The more detailed data on variation in adolescence shows gender as a crucial aspect of the development of phonological distinctions among emerging social categories. In Ronald Macaulay's data, for example (Macaulay 1977), the relation between boys' and girls' speech interacts strikingly with class. The middle-class boys use fairly consistently more vernacular variants than the middle-class girls; but the difference decreases as one moves through the lower middle class and upper working class, and disappears or reverses in the lower working class. In the lower working class, girls take a significant lead over boys in the use of vernacular variants of two variables, boys take a significant lead over girls in one variable, and there is no difference in the remaining two. It is worth noting, too, that the only consistent class stratification pattern across all five variables is among the 15-year-old girls, suggesting that this population is the most sensitive to the use of language to construct whatever social differences are embedded in class.

William Labov has found this crossover pattern among adults as well (Labov 1991), and it is repeated dramatically in my own data on Detroit suburban speech (Eckert 2000). In my ethnographic study of a Detroit suburban high school, the use of sound changes moving out from the urban area distinguishes the two main opposed social categories that constitute the working and the middle class for the age group. It is important to reiterate that these social categories are based not on parents' socio-economic class, but on the speakers' own class trajectory, which is based only partially on parents' class. The *burnouts*, constituting a school-based working-class culture, reject the school as the locus of their social lives, and orient themselves to the local and urban area. The *jocks*, on the other hand, participate in the school on the institution's terms, locating their social as well as their academic lives in the school, isolating themselves to a great extent from the local area and avoiding the urban area. The opposition between these two dominant categories is manifested in a burnout lead in the use of urban sound changes, and of the vernacular feature of negative concord. However, it is the girls' use that shows the greatest difference: the jock girls are the most standard speakers, and the burnout girls are the most vernacular, with the jock and burnout boys falling between them. It is important to point out that not all burnout girls use vernacular variants more than all burnout boys. Particularly, the most vernacular speakers in the school – dramatically leading all other speakers – are a group of girls known to be the "wildest" burnouts. These girls' extreme speech style is an integral part of their proud construction of themselves in opposition to all of their classmates, male and female, whom they view as tame. (As one of them put it, the other burnouts in the school are really jocks.) If there is a consistent gender pattern in all these data, then, it is the girls' greater overall use of linguistic variability across social categories.

5 Policing Adolescent Language

An important part of the verbal culture of adolescence is produced not by the adolescents but by the media they engage with. It is continually observed that adolescence provides a crucial market for consumer goods and services, and that the media are poised to exploit that market. The media that target adolescents do not stop there, but target pre-adolescent audiences with adolescent-oriented consumerism. Thus the pre-adolescent market is prepared in advance, and hurried along, through the marketing of adolescence itself. An examination of magazines aimed at adolescents shows an overwhelming gender ideology, with magazines aimed at boys focusing on activities (skateboarding, sports) and magazines aimed at girls focusing on romance and the production of the self.[3] The encouragement of a preoccupation with the self as object is an important means for building a market (Chanda 1991), and it is well known that the media target adolescents with sexually oriented consumerism, and target girls in particular with the technology of physical and spiritual perfection. These magazines do not simply put forth ideas, they set up a gendered discourse for adolescents to participate in, engaging them in imagined communities that are formed to a great extent by linguistic practice. Mary Talbot (1992) examines the discourse of a British teen magazine, *Jackie*, and shows how the writers engage girls in a "synthetic sisterhood." Through the use of such things as emotive punctuation, first- and second-person pronouns, response-demanding utterances, and through setting up shared presuppositions, the writers engage the reader in imaginary dialogue – all the while constraining the reader's part in the dialogue. Many of these magazines, as well, introduce the readers to the writing and editorial staff, showing photographs and portraying their speech as cool, perky, and "teenage," and inviting them into friendship. In the process, the young adult writers recycle a form of discourse that they view as adolescent. In this way, the readers are engaged in an adolescent discourse invented by adults.

Adolescent language is also directly policed – in school, in after-school programs, even colleges. The recent fervor about "Mallspeak" in the USA is a particularly dramatic illustration of the convergence of the stigmatization of the language of adolescents and females. In 1999, Smith and Mount Holyoke Colleges (private universities in Massachusetts) made a big media splash by introducing programs in speaking across the curriculum. Aimed at training students to be articulate public speakers, a reasonable goal in itself, this initiative was unfortunately couched in a discourse of verbal hygiene (Cameron 1995), locating the problem not in the need to learn an academic register, but in the need to eradicate "Mallspeak." In an article in *The Seattle Times*, Elizabeth Mehren characterized Mallspeak thus:

> A product of both the urban street scene and the consumer cathedrals of the San Fernando Valley in Los Angeles, Mallspeak is the speech form that gave forth the dreaded phrase "gag me with a spoon" and made "like" the first word to be a verb, adjective, adverb and conjunction – all at once. "Minimalist", "repetitive", "imprecise", and "inarticulate" are some of the words Smith College President Ruth Simmons uses to describe Mallspeak, adding, "It drives me crazy." (Mehren 1999)

Smith College English professor Patricia Skarda was quoted in the *New Jersey Star Ledger* (August 29, 1999) as offering the following "Mallspeak lexicon": "'Like' is an approximation – an unwillingness to say one thing. 'You know' begs for agreement, as if the speaker is terribly unsure of him or herself. 'I mean' indicates that the student does not, in fact, know what he or she means."

Despite Skarda's acknowledgment that males as well as females use these forms, the very fact that this way of speaking is referred to as "Mallspeak" points to gender – to the girls who hang out in shopping malls. The actual object of attention in the famous college courses designed to eradicate Mallspeak is more general inarticulateness, and the new efforts at "speaking across the curriculum" are aimed at developing argumentation skills. Professor Skarda's examples – *like, you know, I mean*, are certainly not specific to women or girls (nor does she claim them to be). Yet they are folded into a female style and related to what is commonly thought of as a trivial female activity. (I will not, here, go into the untriviality of hanging out in malls – among the few safe spaces where girls can "go public.")

This construct of inarticulate female/adolescent language is popular in the media. In recent years, considerable attention has been paid to the use of *like* as a discourse marker, and to the use of rising intonation on declaratives (dubbed "uptalk"). Both are attributed to adolescents, and particularly to adolescent girls. And both are interpreted as hedges, and taken to signal the adolescents' lack of concern with precision, or unwillingness to take responsibility for their statements. And when they are discussed specifically with respect to girls, they are taken to indicate insecurity, and an unwillingness to state a forceful opinion. There is some evidence that young people, and females, make greater use of both of these than older and male people. What is problematic is the situated nature of the evidence and the interpretation of this use.

Suzanne Romaine and Deborah Lange (1991) note that in an informally gathered corpus of quotative uses of *like*, the vast majority were used by women and girls. They do not claim, however, that girls are more likely to use *like* more as a quotative, but that they actually use more of the kind of constructed dialogue that calls for the use of *like*. My own data on the more general use of *like* as a discourse marker (which includes, but does not separate out, the quotative use) in Belten High shows no gender difference across the population. However, gender does interact with social category in this use of *like*. The most frequent users of the discourse marker *like* are the jock girls, and the most infrequent are the burnout boys, while the differences among the jock boys, the burnout boys and the burnout girls are statistically insignificant. But there are also boys who use *like* far more than average – the in-between boys (i.e. boys who affiliate with neither category). Since the sample of in-betweens in this study is quite heterogeneous, it is difficult to speculate about the significance of this finding. But it suffices to observe that there is no simple relation between gender and the discourse marker use of *like*.

Women and adolescents also appear to lead in the use of rising intonation on declaratives. In Australia, this feature is used most frequently by working-class speakers, teenagers, and women, and in description and narrative (Guy et al. 1986). Cynthia McLemore, in a study of sorority speech, found that this intonational contour is part of "sorority" style, and that within the sorority it carries authority. However, a *Darwin Magazine* article (August 2001) says:

> A speech pattern called uptalk – ending sentences with an upward inflection that makes it seem like you're asking a question – is inhibiting success in many people, especially women. So says Diane DiResta, author of *Knockout Presentations: How to Deliver Your Message with Power, Punch and Pizzazz* (Chandler House Press, 1998).

While this intonation pattern, like the discourse marker *like*, is widely accepted as signaling hesitation and/or insecurity, it deserves the kind of pragmatic treatment that Deborah Cameron and her colleagues have given to tags (Cameron et al. 1988). A class project observed 300 people ordering drinks at a Stanford University juice stand during parents' weekend. As part of the ordering process, the female undergraduate server asked the customer to give his or her name. The demographic group that overwhelmingly used rising intonation the most in stating their names were middle-aged men. How many analysts would be ready to label this as an expression of insecurity?

Marginalized, delegitimized youth are singled out for their own kind of verbal hygiene. Cathryn Houghton (1992) chronicles the practice of group therapy in an institutional setting, which aims at socializing a group made up largely of poor Latina adolescents into "productive and independently functioning adults" (p. 282). Key to this socialization is the imposition of a discourse style that constructs the speaker as autonomous (i.e. referring to the self rather than the group). It is worth noting that the kind of group-oriented language that is being problematized in this therapy group is precisely the kind of language that is commonly celebrated in discussions of "women's language." While I am not endorsing the view of women's language as particularly collaborative, I do note that it is apparently all right for some women and girls to conform to the maternalistic construction of female speech, but not for others.

6   Conclusion

My purpose in this chapter has been twofold: to consider the interactions among language, gender, and other aspects of identity in adolescence, and to consider the status of adolescence as a site for the study of language and social identity. It should be clear by now that I believe that age-related ideology is inseparable from gender ideology, as well as from ideologies of class, race, and ethnicity. The study of language and gender, therefore, needs to move into the study of the life span, and the gendering of life-stages.

As the move into and through adolescence is a particularly important crossroads for gender, it is one place to look to examine some of our most deeply engrained beliefs about gender. Work on girls moving toward adolescence, for example, clearly calls into question any view that girls' language use reflects any more of a "connection" orientation than boys' (e.g. Cameron 1997). A focus on other life-stages may well provide a new way of looking at other aspects of gender. Consider, for example, the view of women as nurturant. This, I would argue, is one of those essentialist ideals built on something that is in fact specific to a particular life-stage. Nurturing is an activity, which can become a long-term quality for those who identify with nurturing activity in a long-term way. Just as competitiveness is required of any athlete and studiousness is required of any scholar, nurturing is required of any caretaker of small children, including mothers. And being an athlete, a scholar, or a caretaker of small children can be temporary phases in one's life. I would argue that there is nothing particularly nurturant about girls. Children who have strong attachments to young pets may feel nurturant toward them, and girls may be more encouraged than boys to nurture their pets. But this nurturance does not carry into other relationships. But gender norms constrain many women to develop a nurturing persona as they seek to qualify as potential (wives and) mothers, and while gender norms may also lead women to maintain this persona after it has served its purpose, many older women are impatient and eager to move away from nurturing activity. Serious thought about life-stages, therefore, may be an important aspect of the study of gender, and of its manifestations in language. This exploration of language and gender in adolescence should, I hope, encourage people to explore language and gender in young adulthood, in old age, and in any other stages that may or may not have names, that emerge as relevant in people's lives.

NOTES

1 I have argued elsewhere (Eckert 1997: 151–67) that the study of language and age (or anything else and age) has been dominated by the middle-aged bias of those who do most of the research, and those who "manage" the age groups other than their own. Indeed, one might argue that the study of the life-stage of middle age could be analogous to the study of Whiteness.

2 It was particularly striking, when, during the discussion period after this talk of Goodwin's, an elementary school teacher in the audience expressed excitement that someone

was finally paying attention to the kind of nastiness that was, in his experience, rampant among girls, and not mentioned in the literature on language and gender.

3 I subscribed to a set of boys' magazines and a set of girls' magazines under two different names for several years. The two names found their ways onto quite different sets of mailing lists. My girls' magazine name received invitations to enter beauty contests, while my boys' magazine name received offers of credit cards.

REFERENCES

Albert, Steve J. 2000: The Language of Authenticity: French Adolescents Talk about Personality, Style, and the Individual. Paper presented at the Annual Meeting of the American Anthropological Association, San Francisco.

Belenky, Mary F., Clinchy, B. M., Goldberger, N. R., and Tarule, J. M. 1986: *Women's Ways of Knowing*. New York: Basic Books.

Biondi, L. 1975: *The Italian-American Child: His Sociolinguistic Acculturation*. Washington, DC: Georgetown University Press.

Bucholtz, Mary 1996: Geek the girl: Language, femininity and female nerds. In Natasha Warner, Jocelyn Ahlers, Leela Bilmes, Monica Oliver, Suzanne Wertheim, and Melinda Chen (eds) *Gender and Belief Systems*. Berkeley, CA:

Berkeley Women and Language Group, University of California, pp. 119–31.

Bucholtz, Mary 1999: You da man: Narrating the racial other in the production of white masculinity. *Journal of Sociolinguistics* 3: 443–60.

Bucholtz, Mary 2001: Word up: Social meanings of slang in California youth culture. Language and culture symposium 8. http://www.language-culture.org/colloquia/symposia/bucholtz-mary/

Cameron, Deborah 1995: *Verbal Hygiene*. London and New York: Routledge.

Cameron, Deborah 1997: Performing gender identity: Young men's talk and the construction of heterosexual masculinity. In Sally Johnson and Ulrike Hanna Meinhof (eds) *Language and Masculinity*. Oxford: Blackwell, pp. 47–64.

Cameron, Deborah, McAlinden, F., and O'Leary, K. 1988: Lakoff in context: The social and linguistic function of tag questions. In Jennifer Coates and Deborah Cameron (eds) *Women in Their Speech Communities: New Perspectives on Language and Sex*. London and New York: Longman, pp. 74–93.

Chanda, P. S. 1991. Birthing terrible beauties: Feminisms and "women's magazines." *Economic and Political Weekly*: WS 67–70.

Cheshire, Jenny 1982: *Variation in an English Dialect*. Cambridge: Cambridge University Press.

Clermont, Jacques and Cedergren, Henrietta 1979: Les "R" de ma mère sont perdus dans l'air. In Pierrette Thibault (ed.) *Le français parlé: Etudes sociolinguistiques*. Edmonton, Alberta: Linguistic Research, pp. 13–28.

Connell, Robert W., Ashenden, D. J., Kessler, S., and Dowsett, G. W. 1982: *Making the Difference: Schools, Families and Social Division*. Sydney: George Allen and Unwin.

Cutler, Cecilia A. 1999: Yorkville crossing: White teens, hip hop and African American English. *Journal of Sociolinguistics* 3: 428–41.

deKlerk, Vivian 1997: The role of expletives in the construction of masculinity. In Sally Johnson and Ulrike Hanna Meinhof (eds) *Language and Masculinity*. Oxford: Blackwell, pp. 144–58.

Eckert, Penelope 1989: *Jocks and Burnouts: Social Categories and Identity in the High School*. New York: Teachers College Press.

Eckert, Penelope 1996: Vowels and nailpolish: The emergence of linguistic style in the preadolescent heterosexual marketplace. In Natasha Warner, Jocelyn Ahlers, Leela Bilmes, Monica Oliver, Suzanne Wertheim, and Melinda

Chen (eds) *Gender and Belief Systems*. Berkeley, CA: Berkeley Women and Language Group, University of California, pp. 183–90.

Eckert, Penelope 1997: Age as a sociolinguistic variable. In Florian Coulmas (ed.) *Handbook of Sociolinguistics*. Oxford: Blackwell, pp. 151–67.

Eckert, Penelope 2000: *Linguistic Variation as Social Practice*. Oxford: Blackwell.

Eckert, Penelope and McConnell-Ginet, Sally 1995: Constructing meaning, constructing selves: Snapshots of language, gender and class from Belten High. In Kira Hall and Mary Bucholtz (eds) *Gender Articulated: Language and the Socially Constructed Self*. London: Routledge, pp. 469–507.

Eder, Donna 1991: The role of teasing in adolescent peer group culture. In S. Cahill (ed.) *Social Studies of Child Development*. Greenwich, CT: JAI Press, pp. 181–97.

Eder, Donna, Evans, Catherine Colleen, and Parker, Stephen 1995: *School Talk: Gender and Adolescent Culture*. New Brunswick, NJ: Rutgers University Press.

Eisikovits, Edina 1987: Sex differences in inter- and intra-group interaction among adolescents. In Anne Pauwels (ed.) *Women and Language in Australian and New Zealand Society*. Sydney: Australian Professional Publications, pp. 45–58.

Fischer, John L. 1958: Social influences on the choice of a linguistic variant. *Word* 14: 47–56.

Gal, Susan and Irvine, Judith T. 1995: The boundaries of languages and disciplines: How ideologies construct difference. *Social Research* 62: 967–1001.

Gilligan, Carol, Lyons, Nona P., and Hanmer, Trudy J. (eds) 1990: *Making*

Connections: The Relational Worlds of Adolescent Girls at Emma Willard School. Cambridge, MA: Harvard University Press.

Goffman, Erving 1961: *Asylums: Essays on the Social Situation of Mental Patients and Other Inmates*. New York: Anchor.

Goodwin, Marjorie Harness 1990: *He-Said-She-Said: Talk as Social Organization among Black Children*. Bloomington: Indiana University Press.

Goodwin, Marjorie Harness 2000: Constituting the Moral Order in Girls' Social Organization: Language Practices in the Construction of Social Exclusion. Paper presented at IGALA 2 (Conference of the International Gender and Language Association). Stanford, California.

Guy, Gregory, Horvath, Barbara, Vonwiller, Julia, Daisley, Elaine, and Rogers, Inge 1986: An intonational change in progress in Australian English. *Language in Society* 15: 23–52.

Halle, Morris 1962: Phonology in a generative grammar. *Word* 18: 54–72.

Hill, Jane H. 1993: Hasta la vista, baby: Anglo Spanish in the American Southwest. *Critique of Anthropology* 13: 145–76.

Holmes, Janet 1995: *Women, Men and Politeness*. London and New York: Longman.

Houghton, Cathryn 1992: "Talking it out" or talking it in: An ethnography of power and language in psychotherapeutic practice. In Kira Hall, Mary Bucholtz, and Birch Moonwomon (eds) *Locating Power: Proceedings of the Second Berkeley Women and Language Conference*. Berkeley, CA: Berkeley Women and Language Group, University of California, pp. 272–85.

Irvine, Judith 2001: "Style" as distinctiveness: The culture and ideology of linguistic differentiation. In Penelope Eckert and John Rickford (eds) *Stylistic Variation in Language*. Cambridge: Cambridge University Press, pp. 21–43.

Kiesling, Scott 1997: Power and the language of men. In Sally Johnson and Ulrike Hanna Meinhof (eds) *Language and Masculinity*. Oxford: Blackwell, pp. 65–85.

Labov, Theresa 1992: Social and language boundaries among adolescents. *American Speech* 67: 339–66.

Labov, William 1991: The intersection of sex and social class in the course of linguistic change. *Language Variation and Change* 2: 205–51.

Macaulay, Ronald K. S. 1977: *Language, Social Class and Education: A Glasgow Study*. Edinburgh: University of Edinburgh Press.

Mehren, Elizabeth 1999: Schools attack "Mallspeak," stress import of diction. *The Seattle Times*, March 25.

Mendoza-Denton, Norma 1994: Language attitudes and gang affiliation among California Latina girls. In Mary Bucholtz, Anita C. Liang, Laurel A. Sutton, and Caitlin Hines (eds) *Cultural Performances: Proceedings of the Third Berkeley Women and Language Conference*. Berkeley, CA: Berkeley Women and Language Group, University of California, pp. 478–86.

Mendoza-Denton, Norma 1996: "Muy Macha": Gender and ideology in gang girls' discourse about makeup. *Ethnos* 6(91–2): 47–63.

Mendoza-Denton, Norma forthcoming: *Homegirls: Symbolic Practices in the Making of Latina Youth Styles*. Cambridge, MA and New York: Blackwell.

Roberts, Sarah 2000: Nativization and the genesis of Hawaiian Creole. In John H. McWhorter (ed.) *Language Change and Language Contact in Pidgins and Creoles*. Amsterdam: John Benjamins, pp. 257–300.

Roberts, Sarah forthcoming: *The Genesis of Hawai'i Creole English in the Early 20th Century: Social and Linguistic Factors of Language Change*. Department of Linguistics, Stanford University.

Romaine, Suzanne 1984: *The Language of Children and Adolescents*. Oxford: Blackwell.

Romaine, Suzanne and Lange, Deborah 1991: The use of *like* as a marker of reported speech and thought: A case of grammaticalization in progress. *American Speech* 66: 227–79.

Roth-Gordon, Jennifer 2001: Slang and the Struggle Over Meaning: Race, Language, and Power in Brazil. PhD dissertation, Department of Cultural and Social Anthropology, Stanford University.

Talbot, Mary 1992: A synthetic sisterhood: False friends in a teenage magazine. In Kira Hall, Mary Bucholtz, and Birch Moonwomon (eds) *Locating Power: Proceedings of the Second Berkeley Women and Language Conference*. Berkeley, CA: Berkeley Women and Language Group, University of California, pp. 573–80.

Tetrault, Chantal 2000: Adolescents' multilingual punning and identity play in a French *cité*. Paper presented at the Annual Meeting of the American Anthropological Association, San Francisco.

Thorne, Barrie 1993: *Gender Play*. New Brunswick, NJ: Rutgers University Press.

Trudgill, Peter 1972: Sex, covert prestige and linguistic change in the urban British English of Norwich. *Language in Society* 1: 179–95.

Wolfram, Walt 1969: *A Sociolinguistic Description of Detroit Negro Speech*. Washington, DC: Center for Applied Linguistics.

Zhang, Qing 2001: Changing Economics, Changing Markets: A Sociolinguistic Study of Chinese Yuppies. PhD dissertation, Department of Linguistics, Stanford University.

17 Language and Gendered Modernity

WILLIAM L. LEAP

To a self who participates in the construction of known discourses, the problem is not to fragment surroundings or to emerge from silence into speech, but to piece together what is daily fragmented by the Other...

Stewart (1990: 55)

1 Introduction

This chapter[1] explores how relationships between language and gender reflect and respond to the content and contexts of modernity – that is, the "modes of social life or organization which emerged in Europe from about the seventeenth century onward and which subsequently became more or less worldwide in their influence" (Giddens 1991: 1). Under Giddens' argument, modernity is not a label for a time period, so much as a reference to the complex changes in political economy which enabled the emergence of North Atlantic capitalism, the predatory expansion of capitalist economies into South Atlantic (Africa, Latin America), Asian, and other Pacific domains, and the construction of regimes of economic and political control linking home countries to colonial outposts worldwide. Recently, these regimes of control have assumed new forms, as colonial rule gave way to post-colonial configurations of independence and nation-building, and as colonial powers, like former colonies, struggle to position themselves and their citizenry within the palimpsest of empire.

These struggles for position are reflected in disputes over borders and boundaries, in disagreements over the meanings and messages of history, in tensions between local communities, in "ethnic" divisions and broader political allegiances, as well as in the seemingly unending conditions of displacement and diaspora. They are also reflected in the uncertainties of outcome which have become characteristic of modernity as a whole, and have had profound effects on the formation of *late modern* experience. Gender has also been profoundly affected by these uncertainties and discontents, and the same is true for the linguistic practices and products through which gendered meanings and practices – as well as the *understandings* of those meanings and practices – are constructed, negotiated, and contested in everyday life. Certainly, language has always been a useful resource for expressing and contesting claims to gendered subjectivity. But the fragmented, seemingly decentralized conditions of (late) modernity has made language an especially valuable resource in that regard– even if, at the same time, modernity imposes its own demands on gender-related grammar, discourse, and text-making.

This chapter examines several examples of speakers using linguistic practices and products to claim a late modern, gendered subjectivity: a personal advertisement in a South African lesbian/gay newspaper, a poem by (self-identified) gay Irish poet Cathal Ó Searcaigh, and a portion of the life-story narrative of a Filipino *bakla*. The textual formats differ in each example, and so do the social and historical conditions underlying each of the sites of text-making. Even so, a close analysis of the language of text-making in each case shows how speakers use the textual moment to assert gendered position in these settings, and how speakers construct those assertions *in relation to* site-specific struggles over race/ethnicity, class position, sexual diversity, cultural allegiance, national identity, and other features shaping and fragmenting everyday life within the late modern period.

There are provocative parallels to be drawn between the linguistic practices attested in these texts and the performative claims to gendered subjectivity (Butler 1990: 25, passim) which emerge from text-making in such complex and contested settings. And one of the goals of this chapter is to examine these parallels and to trace their connections to the *flexible strategies of accumulation* (Harvey 1989: esp. pp. 147ff) which have come to be so closely associated with economic and social practices of late modernity.

2 Assumptions: "Text" Makes "Gendered Modernity" Accessible

Genders are cultural constructions, and not determined entirely or primarily by bodily form or biological function. Accordingly, studies of gendered experience frequently use *text* as an entry point for such inquiry, because gender is negotiated and contested through the production and circulation of life stories, personal anecdotes, gossip and other narratives, legal statements, ritual oratory, words of advice and practical caution, jokes, songs, and other forms of expressive language, as well as through word borrowings, modifications to existing vocabulary, and new word formations.[2]

I refer here to these linguistic materials as *texts*, to underscore the idea that these linguistic practices, and the messages about gender expressed through them, take place within specific economic contexts and social and historic "moments." And because *text* is *situated language use*, texts always contain formal marking which identifies their location within the larger setting and their connections to other textual materials within the same economic, social, and historical setting.

Moreover, texts also express meanings which are relevant to the situation of text-making. Accordingly, Halliday (1978: 108–9) reminds us that "text is choice, . . . selected from the total set of operations that constitute what can be meant" within the given setting. Accordingly, analysis of text needs to take into account the evidence of *choice-making* and the other indications of *intentionality of message* which the text contains.

Choice and intentionality are properties of speaker-performance, but not exclusively so. As Mary Bucholtz observes, " '[t]exts,' or stretches of discourse, take on meaning only in interaction and [. . .] as consumers of cultural 'texts,' audiences are active participants in this process of meaning making" (1999: 349, citing McIlvenny 1996). So it is helpful to think of texts as the product of speaker/audience *co-construction*, to think of textual meanings as something *interpellated* through the mutual engagement of speakers and audience within the social moment. Such site-specific engagement does not divorce text pro-duction or textual meanings from the workings of broader social and historical process. Speakers and audience are located within opportunity structures and relations of power, and the outcomes of text production are always shaped accordingly (Fairclough 1989: 4). Equally important here are the connections between textual meanings and broader frames of reference in terms of which those meanings claim authority. Birch Moonwomon (1995: 45) explains the characteristics of "lesbian text" in these terms:

> In verbal interactions communicants assume shared knowledge of many kinds. Some of the knowledge that is taken to be common is the stuff of societal dis-courses, which are often discourses of conflict. Lesbian text evidences assump-tions of shared knowledge of various societal discourses and participation in them. Importantly, text also evidences assumptions of common stances, lesbian perspectives within the societal discourses, which are not points but territories within [the] societal discourses invoked in interaction.

Noting how text production is closely tied to political economy, and how interpolations of meanings are shaped by local and broader discursive domains, we understand why "telling sexual stories" and sharing other narratives of intimate life have become widely attested forms of linguistic performance within late modernity (Plummer 1995: 6, 16), and why text-making so often provides occasions for negotiating and contesting late modern gendered subjectivities. The identities which are displayed and confirmed through story-telling and conversation may be reflections of personal desire. But the textual details which

give "voice" to those identities position those voices within systems of reference and meaning which are socially, not just personally, constructed. (See
again, Hennessy's statement in note 2.) And by doing so, as the following
examples will show, texts make gendered claims accessible, if not entirely
acceptable, to other participants in the speech event and to the broader audience beyond it.

3   Looking Beyond the Dorp: Language Choices and Gendered Meanings in a South African Gay Personal Advertisement

Late modernity in Southern Africa has been closely entwined with systems of
racial/class-based inequalities which derive both from colonial administration
and from attempts to stabilize White rule during the initial years of post-
colonial independence. These regimes of state power have engaged in various
ways female- and male-based, same-sex oriented, desires, practices, and identities. The lesbian/gay visibility in the "new" South Africa (including the
freedom from discrimination on the basis of sexual orientation outlined in
the new South African constitution) is the latest reflection of this engagement.
Gay-oriented bars and clubs advertise openly in the popular press. The sexual
preferences of politicians and other national figures are regularly discussed on
television programs and in other public forums. Gay pride events and other
celebrations of vibrant lesbian/gay cultures are regular events in major urban
centers such as Johannesburg, Cape Town, and Durban, and same-sex business
districts and residential neighborhoods have emerged in these cities, as well.

   In the small towns (*die dorp*) in the countryside, at a distance from urban
areas (and much of the South African terrain falls within this category), homosexual presence is not always so visible, and is often submerged beneath
references to "confirmed bachelor" and "the dutiful, stay-at-home daughter."
Finding a partner for anything more than casual sex (or even for that) can be
difficult in those settings, especially when local sex/gender ideologies remain
firmly anchored within Afrikaner-based, Calvinist value systems.

   Example (1) is one of several "personal ads" included in the back pages of
the August, 1997 issue of *The Exit*, South Africa's monthly gay and lesbian
newspaper, and speaks directly to these concerns. The writer self-identifies as
a G(ay),W(hite) M(an) in his late 30s and uses Calvinist-inspired, Afrikaner
notions of purity, wholesomeness, and honesty to frame his self-description as
well as to specify the type of man with whom he hopes to make contact. At the
same time, the presentation of these remarks is decidedly trans-global. In fact,
the organization of the text resembles that widely attested in sexually oriented
personal advertising in North Atlantic and other print media, both "straight"
as well as gay: an eye-catching title, relevant facts about the writer, a brief

description of the desired respondent, listing of any characteristics which the writer will find undesirable in a respondent, additional stipulations, and the necessary contact information.

(1)   *Huislik en Opreg*
      GWM, laat 30s, eerlik, opreg, liefdevol, sin vir humor, eensaam, huislik, manlik maar geen hunk. Gesoek: 'n opregte eelike saggaarde standvestige ordentlike GWM vir vriendskap moontlik verhounding later. Jou bate jou persoonlikheid nie "looks" nie. Geen drienkers, drugs of queens. English guys welcome. ALA. [reply number]

In this case, the information presented in each of these categories (with English translation) is as follows:[3]

1   *Title*: Huislik en Opreg
2   *About the writer*: GWM, laat 30s, eerlik, opreg, liefdevol, sin vir humor, eensaam, huislik, manlik maar geen hunk.
3   *About the intended respondent*: Gesoek: 'n opregte eelike saggaarde stand-vestige ordentlike GWM vir vriendskap moontlik verhounding later. Jou bate jou persoonlikheid nie "looks" nie.
4   *Undesirable traits*: Geen drienkers, drugs of queens.
5   *Additional stipulations:* English guys welcome. ALA.
6   *Contact information*: [the reply number, to which any response should be directed]

1   *Title*: Homebody and wholesome
2   *About the writer*: Gay White man, late 30s, honest, wholesome, loving, sense of humor, lonely, homebody, "masculine"/straight-acting, but not a "hunk."
3   *About the intended respondent*: What I am looking for: an upright, honest, soft-natured, reliable cleancut GWM for friendship, possibly relationship later. Your strong point will be your personality, not your "looks."
4   *Undesirable traits*: No heavy drinkers, drugs, or queens.
5   *Additional stipulations*: English guys welcome. A(ll) L(etters) A(nswered).
6   *Contact information*.

On first reading, and consistent with the text's repeated references to Calvinist values, the primary language of this statement would appear to be Afrikaans. Yet note how much of the textual message is expressed through English rather than Afrikaans vocabulary: *GWM, humor, hunk, later, "looks", drugs, queens, English guys welcome, ALA.*[4] Importantly, the late modern Afrikaans vocabulary contains words and phrases corresponding to each of these English lexical references, and using those words and phrases would have positioned the advertisement (and its message) even more securely within an Afrikaans-centered cultural framework. The choice of English, rather than Afrikaans, in these instances becomes especially significant in those instances, and researchers as well as potential respondents need to read the usage accordingly.

For example, when telling us that he does not want replies from heavy drinkers, drug users, or flamboyant, effeminate men, the writer uses Afrikaans *drienkers* but English *drugs* and *queens*. Alcohol consumption aside, party drugs (and addiction to them) are not traditional features of Afrikaner culture, and religious tracts published by the Dutch Reform Church often use references to the ever-pervasive drug culture as markers for the external (i.e. British/American/North Atlantic-based) influences now competing for the hearts and minds of the Afrikaner faithful. The writer's use of English *drugs*, rather than Afrikaans *dwelmmidel* (or Afrikaans *dwelmslaaf*, "drug addict") is consistent with this broader, English/outsider versus Afrikaans/insider dichotomy.

The writer's choice of English *queens* in this statement requires discussion. In South African English usage (but see note 5, below), much as is the case in North Atlantic settings and elsewhere, *queens* refers to publicly flamboyant, highly effeminate gay men, and is a term used by heterosexual persons as well as by gay-identified men and by lesbians. But South African everyday discourse also includes another term for flamboyant, effeminate men: *moffie*. This term derives from a particular component of South African sexual history, as Chetty (1994: 127) explains: "'Moffie,' coined in the coloured communities of the western Cape, has become the South African equivalent of 'queer,' 'faggot,' or 'flikker,' with extremely derisive connotations." Today, *moffie* is part of the sexual vocabularies maintained by speakers of English, Afrikaans, Xhosa, and other Southern African languages. And while "derisive connotations" may still be invoked by this term, *moffie* does not always command negative reference in its late modern usage. Gay/male-identified men, regardless of language background, use *moffie* to underscore feelings of intimacy or mutual affection during conversations with other gay friends. And even when Afrikaans-speaking heterosexuals use *moffie* to mark male effeminacy, they are not necessarily equating effeminacy and male-centered, same-sex desire. *Moffie* may identify a married man with children, a school teacher, or even a local minister, if any of these individuals appears to fall short of a more aggressive, masculine ideal. Similarly, and paralleling one meaning of English *bachelor*, *moffie* may also identify a man who remains unmarried, lives at home, and takes care of elderly parents or other relatives – regardless of his sexual orientation or style of expressive masculinity (Hambidge 1995).

Queens and *moffie* are in some ways quite similar, but *moffie* commands a broader and more complex range of meanings than does *queens*, while *queens* identifies a more limited domain of visible, flamboyant, and decidedly sexualized identities. This is the category of persons being excluded when the writer says *geen . . . queens*, "no . . . queens." Yet excluding *queens* from the pool of desirable respondents affirms the writer's willingness to receive replies from men whose sexual personae, while not flamboyantly effeminate, are also not aggressively masculine, either. Note the word-choice in the next statement in the advertisement: *English guys welcome*. Ordinary guys – who, in South African linguistic usage could be *moffies* but are not *queens*, and might be speakers of Afrikaans and/or English – are the men whom the writer hopes to contact through this advertisement, and he has constructed the text which reaches across linguistic and cultural traditions, accordingly.[5]

Far from being an arbitrary or random component of text design, the interplay of Afrikaans and English usages in this text here contributes directly and richly to the writer's presentation of his intended message and to his outreach to his intended audience. In contrast, framing the statement entirely in Afrikaans would have limited the writer's chances of making contact with English-speaking respondents, since a sizeable number of speakers of English in South Africa are not sufficiently familiar with Afrikaans to be able to read a text written in that language.[6] Moreover, enduring associations between Afrikaans and the everyday administration of apartheid rule could even discourage first-language fluent Afrikaans speakers from responding to an advertisement framed entirely in that language, since such an assertion of language loyalty could overlap with loyalty to other, less desirable social stances.[7]

Finally, framing the text entirely in Afrikaans would also delete usages like *GWM* and *ALA*, codings which indicate the writer's familiarity with the international language of male-centered personal advertising, and imply a familiarity with other, broadly circulating domains of male-centered sexuality. While the ample use of Calvinist references suggests that the writer is not trying to present himself or to position his (homo)sexuality in cosmopolitan terms, these codings and other features of English usage (particularly, the possibility of a US-based English usage, in the sense of note 4) confirm the writer's willingness to explore sexual possibilities beyond the boundaries and restrictions of the home village.

4 Getting Back to Sources: Language, Gender, and Rural Tradition in the Poetry of Cathal Ó Searcaigh

Sexual diversity is also prominent in the everyday discourses of Irish late modernity. And while laws criminalizing homosexual practices have been rescinded in the Republic of Ireland, conservative voices still charge that homosexual persons undermine the obligations of responsible sexual citizenship. To build support for lesbian/gay rights in this setting, same-sex desire has to claim a secure place within the broader frameworks of national identity and national unity. References to Irish cultural tradition provide useful resources to this end, and so does the emergence of a "gay Gaelic" as a language appropriate for public and private (homo)sexual discursive practice.

Cathal Ó Searcaigh, "the first openly gay poet writing in the Irish language" (Kennedy, forthcoming: 2), draws heavily on both of these resources in his poetic explorations of male homoerotic experience. As Kennedy explains, the content of his poems is not always explicitly "gay," and very few of the poems actually address the connections between sexual identity and national identity directly. However, because "Ó Searcaigh [is] the first Irish-language poet to claim the political importance of identifying himself as a gay man, this self-identification . . . provides a clear context for reading his love poetry as homoerotic" (Kennedy, forthcoming: 2, footnote 3).

Much of the imagery in Ó Searcaigh's poetry lends itself quite effectively to homoerotic and other gay-centered readings; this is especially the case for his depictions of life in the Irish countryside, as I explain below. But homoerotic/ gay-centered messages are not presented in isolation in these texts, and these themes always have to be read in terms of broader social tensions which define late modern experience within the Irish setting.

For example, in *An Tobar* /"The Well," Ó Searcaigh contrasts the *Uisce beo bioguil, fioruisce gle* /"lively, lively water, pellucid spring-water" which can be drawn from the family well, with the *uisce lom gan loinnir* /"mawkish [water] without sparkle" which comes from the kitchen faucet.[8] This imagery fore-grounds the traditional resources of the Irish countryside, and highlights their vulnerability under the pressures of modernization. Read more generally, the imagery reminds the reader that, whenever modernity takes hold, "a mechan-ical world of convenience, forgetful of sensual pleasure and stimulation" will eventually replace the more traditional "purer, more organic connection[s] with nature" (Kennedy, forthcoming: 5).

In other settings, the "mechanical . . . , forgetful . . ." world of modernity is not always so disruptive. Indeed, the countryside's "pure . . . organic connec-tion to nature," valuable as it is in many ways, did not support Ó Searcaigh's earliest efforts to come to terms with male-centered, sexual desires. To find suitable opportunities to that end, he moved away from rural Donegal, and eventually took up residence in London. The anonymity of urban life (he explains in other texts) helped him move easily within the city's many homo-sexual venues. But urban anonymity left other desires unfulfilled. After several years in self-imposed cultural exile, and as his interests in poetry took priority over continuing a career in television broadcasting, he returned to Donegal to pursue his writing within its more familiar terrain.

Ó Searcaigh did not renounce his urban-based homosexual identity when he returned to Donegal, but he did have to think carefully about appropriate ways to claim that identity within rural Irish settings, and reflections on that task are deeply entwined throughout *An Tobar's* depictions of modernity. An unnamed narrator, whose remarks suggest that he speaks for the poet within the text, provides some of this commentary. A second voice is also attested in this poem: *Sean Bhrid*/Old Brigit. Her name and title identify her as a grandmother-like figure, a matriarch, a wise woman, and a village elder. She also carries the name of an important Irish Catholic saint, as well as the name often given to the local busybody in jokes and other stereotypic depictions of rural Irish life. Like the narrator, she brings a variety of intertextual perspect-ives into the discussion, but unlike the narrator, whose point of view is shaped by urban and rural differences, Sean Bhrid views rural Irish life primarily from within.

An Tobar begins with Sean Bhrid's reminder that regional improvements have made obsolete Donegal's ancient family wells, but, at the same time, indoor plumbing has made water from the now-abandoned family wells all the more valuable. And, consistent with her status as matriarch and village elder, she speaks here not only for herself, but on behalf of the larger local constituency.

This discussion continues into the poem's middle stanzas, as Ó Searcaigh remembers how well water provided much needed refreshment during the summer heat. Sean Bhrid is silent during these remarks, realizing perhaps that the poet is now developing the argument she set out to propose. All that remains is to bring the argument to conclusion, and Sean Bhrid does so by offering the following words of advice in the poem's final stanza:

(2)
Aimsigh do thobar fein, a chroi
Oir ta am an anais romhainn amach;
Caithfear pilleadh aris ar na foinsi.

Seek out your own well, my dear,
for the age of want is near;
There will have to be a going back to sources.

Read in terms of the poem's discussion of modernity, these remarks propose a rejection of modern-day conveniences and a return to the traditional practices of the Irish countryside. This position is consistent with Sean Bhrid's opening commentary, and also follows from her many intertextual connections with rural Irish culture. But Sean Bhrid's suggestions take on a more subversive reading when read against Ó Searcaigh's male-centered sexuality. A second person singular reference in the imperative verb – *Aimsigh do thobar fein*/ "seek out *your own* well" – urges the poet to look beyond the expectations of rural Ireland's family-centered, community-based sexuality, and to define his sexual subjectivity in terms of *his* own understanding of what is an appropriate "source."

Linguistic details are significant to the poem's presentation of messages in other ways. Remember that in example (1), the writer framed his personal advertisement by combining materials from the resources of two locally available languages (Afrikaans and English). But while two languages (Gaelic and English) are also available in the rural Irish setting, Ó Searcaigh does not attempt to combine them in *An Tobar* (or in any of his writings). Instead, he crafts two versions of the poem, one in Gaelic, the other in English. There are no English loan-words in the Gaelic text, and no evidence of English "interference" structuring Gaelic vocabulary and syntax. Similarly, there are no Gaelic loan-words in the English text and (by my reading) no evidence of Gaelic interference structuring the English vocabulary and syntax. And while the two texts are published together, they are presented as separate texts, each within its own column on the page, and each under its own title.

Because Ó Searcaigh writes poetry in Gaelic, and has earned praise for his creative use of that language in written form, it is tempting to view the Gaelic text of *An Tobar* as the "poem," and the English text as the "translation." Doing so positions Ó Searcaigh's Gaelic poetry (as well as his writing of poems in Gaelic) as an example of the *aris ar na foinsi/* "getting back to sources" proposed by Sean Bhrid in the final stanza of *An Tobar*. Moreover, since Gaelic is the language of the countryside and, more generally, Gaelic provides a performative marker for allegiance to Irish tradition, there are additional reasons to consider the Gaelic text as the primary site of message-making in this setting.

At the same time, the particulars of (sexual) subjectivity which the poet will be claiming through his *aris ar na foinsi* are deeply embedded in the modernist condition.[9] And given its associations with urban experience, its close ties to the workings of British colonial rule, its international status, and its enduring connections to structures of power and opportunity, English – not Gaelic – is the language of modernity within the rural Irish setting. Because of these linkages to modern experience, there is nothing remarkable about Ó Searcaigh, or any Irish writer, trying to explore same-sex desires by writing poetry in English. But even when working within an English language format, Ó Searcaigh makes clear that he wants to see discussions of (homo)sexuality move beyond English-centered linguistic domains. Remember that the sources highlighted in Sean Bhrid's final remark are Irish tradition/Gaelic in basis, and "getting back to [those] sources" requires a willingness to "seek out" (in Sean Bhrid's terms) what are unavoidably new and unfamiliar forms of linguistic as well as social practice.

Such explorations were very much a part of Ó Searcaigh's earlier efforts to claim his own sexual subjectivity. Exploration was a motive prompting him to leave home and, eventually, settle in (English-speaking!) London. And in other texts, he describes evenings when he walked the London streets and explored its homosexual haunts, searching for a sex partner who also could speak a few words of Gaelic. Now that he has returned to Donegal, finding speakers of Gaelic is no longer a difficult task, but with same-sex identities and desires not given broad public expression in rural Ireland, "seeking out" a Gaelic-speaking sex partner is still a matter of uncertainty, though now for entirely different linguistic reasons.

Breaking down linguistic boundaries, and (in a fashion similar to example (1)) incorporating (sexualized) English into (traditional) Gaelic text construction, will not solve the problem here. As Sean Bhrid observed above, when indoor plumbing brings well water into the house, the water loses its sparkle. More appropriate is the creation of an entirely new, entirely Gaelic-based language of same-sex desire, whose references are not bound to modernist assumptions about sexuality and whose formal details are not dependent on modernist forms of sexual representation. The all-Gaelic text of *An Tobar* needs to be read as movement toward this goal. The absence of explicit references to male sexuality, and of other markers which signify "gay poetry" to an English audience and are highly visible in the English version of the poem, makes good sense under this reading. These absences are not expressions of coded or closeted gay meanings, nor do they suggest any reluctance to talk about (homo)sexual issues in public text-making. Rather, these absences reflect Ó Searcaigh's attempts to construct an alternative presentation of sexual meaning – in Gaelic and in English, a presentation which affirms Gaelic understandings of same-sex desire in terms of Gaelic linguistic and cultural practices.

5   Growing Muscles and Going in Drag: Language and Gender in Transnational Relocation

Unlike the situation in rural Ireland, some forms of same-sex identities and desires do receive rich public expression in Filipino contexts. One of the more visible forms of same-sex identity is *bakla*, male-bodied Filipino persons who use cross-dressing, effeminate behavior, particular forms of linguistic reference,[10] and related practices to express a male-centered gendered subjectivity in female-centered terms (Manalansan 1994: 61). At an earlier time, the *bakla* sense of the feminine may have been constructed entirely according to indigenous models and practices. Today, meanings of *bakla* incorporate North Atlantic, mainland pan-Asian, as well as Philippine-based gendered imaginaries. And while public expressions of *bakla* "identity" continue to affirm the subject's ties to Filipino culture and tradition, *bakla* also incorporates expressions of local place for those living outside of the homeland. (For more discussion of these issues, see Besnier, this volume.)

Understandably, there are tensions and conflicts between traditional and diasporic readings of *bakla* subjectivity, and how individual *bakla* address these issues is always a primary theme in their life-story narratives. Example (3) is an excerpt from one such narrative. Tony, the speaker in this text, was born just outside of Manila and is now (mid-1990s) a resident of New York City. He is talking with Filipino anthropologist Martin Manalansan about his decision to leave Manila and move to the USA, and about his reactions to the new forms of gendered opportunity which voluntary relocation provided him.[11]

> (3)
> 1   Noong nasa Manila ako,
> 2   kunyari pa akong pa-min ang drama ko
> 3   although alam ng lahat na bading talaga ang truth.
> 4   Pag-step ng aking satin shoes dito sa New York,
> 5   o biglang nagiba ang pagrarampa ko.
> 6   May I try ko ang pagmu-mu and also nag-gym ako.
> 7   Ang sabi ng ibang Pinay na bading na parang lukresiya ako.

8   Bakit daw ako nagpapmuscles and then nagmumujer ako.
9   Alam mo, pag wala ka sa pakikialam ng pamilya at kaibagan mo sa Pilipinas,
10   kahit ano puwede.

Manalansan translates Tony's statements as follows:

1   When I was still in Manila,
2   I was still putting on the macho drama
3   although I knew that all the badings[12] knew the truth.
4   When my satin shoes hit New York,
5   I suddenly changed the way I walked the ramp.
6   I tried going in drag and going to the gym.
7   Many Filipinos told me that I was crazy.
8   Why, they asked, was I growing muscles and going in drag?
9   You know, when you live far away from your parents and friends in the Philippines,
10   anything is possible.   (Manalansan 1998: 141)

Central to the organization of this text and to the gendered messages it conveys are the contrasts in location – Manila (lines 1–3) versus New York City (lines 4–8), and the differing styles of gendered performance which unfold at each site: *pa-min ang drama ko/* "macho drama" in Manila, versus *ang pagmu-mu* ("drag") and *nag-gym ako* ("going to the gym") in New York City. These close associations between location and style of gendered performance are reflected in the language choices evidenced throughout this multilingual text. For example, Tony uses Tagalog words to identify features of *bakla* experience which are closely associated with *bakla* life in the homeland, and may also be relevant to *bakla* experience elsewhere. In some cases, these "Tagalog" words may have been borrowed from Spanish or English sources, but have become fully incorporated in Tagalog grammar and lexicon, and now they conform to Tagalog rules of pronunciation and word structure: e.g. *pa-min* ("macho," English *man*, line 2), *pagmu-mu*, *nagmumujer*[13] ("drag," Spanish *mujer*, lines 6 and 8), *pamilya* (Spanish "familia," line 9), or *lukresiya* (English "crazy," line 7).[14]

Other English words appear in Tony's remarks without any Tagalog modification of their linguistic form. Some of these English words simply provide support to text structure: *although* (line 3), *and also* (line 6), *and then* (line 8). More generally (and I discuss a small group of exceptions, below), English words identify meanings which are not uniquely *bakla* in basis, but are still relevant to *bakla* experience in the diasporic setting: *step* (line 4), *satin shoes* (line 4), *ramp* (line 5), *gym* (line 6), *muscles* (line 8), and of course *New York* (line 4).

While Tagalog versus English word choices are found throughout this text, their presence makes especially important contributions to textual meaning in several of its sentences. In line 6, word choices draw attention to the broader contrasts in homeland versus diasporic gendered performance structuring Tony's efforts to construct *his own* version of *bakla* subjectivity:

(line 6) *May I try ko ang pagmu-mu and also nag-gym.*
  "I tried going in drag[Tagalog] and going to the gym[English]."

In line 8, word choices suggest that Tony's friends react to his efforts to claim *bakla* subjectivity in terms of similar contrasts:

(line 8) *Bakit daw ako nagpapmuscles and then nagmumujer ako*
  "Why, they asked, was I growing muscles[English] and going in drag[Tagalog]?"

In a small number of cases (*truth, drama, may I ____ verb*) English words signal a third type of gendered/locational reference: meanings which are fundamental to *bakla* experience, whatever the site of gendered performance. *Truth* has the same meaning here as in everyday English conversation. *Drama* in this usage refers to particular details shaping a person's life experience, a reference similar to "that's the role he is playing/he is meant to play." *Drama* may also be used to specify the individual who serves as role-model for a specific moment of gendered performance, as Manalansan explains:

> When someone wants to ask about the drag persona of another bakla for the night, the question could be framed this way: *Ano ang drama niuya ngayon?* [What is his drama today?] The answer could be, *Tina Turner ang drama niya.* [Tina Turner is his/her drama.] (Manalansan 1995: 257)

May I ____ verb commands a somewhat more complex reference: this construction introduces sentences which describe forms of action attempted by the speaker, but not necessarily brought to completion. The presence of *May I try* in line 6,

May I try ko ang pagmu-mu and also nag-gym ako.
"I tried going in drag and going to the gym."

underscores the experimental nature of his attempts to reconstruct *bakla* subjectivity, and sets the stage for the skeptical reaction of his friends as reported in the following two lines.[15]

The list of English terms which apply to *bakla* experience, broadly defined, does not include English-language names for the *bakla* subject: instead, and the other textual movement between Tagalog and English word choices notwithstanding, Tony refers to *bakla* by using the Filipino/swardspeak term *bakla* throughout this text, never by using *gay, homosexual,* or *queer.* English words do not appear in lines 9–10, where Tony weighs the costs of displacement against the benefits of diasporic residence:

Alam mo, pag wala ka sa pakikialam ng pamilya at kaibagan mo sa Pilipinas, kahit ano puwede.
"You know, when you live far away from your parents and friends in the Philippines, anything is possible."

The all-Tagalog wording in this statement reiterates the position which Tony voiced at an earlier point in the text (see again, line 6): leaving home has not led him to reject his Filipino-based *bakla* "identity" so much as given him opportunities and incentives to redesign the female-centered references already associated with *bakla* tradition. And by constructing lines 9–10 entirely in Tagalog,[16] Tony confirms that "traditional" understandings of *bakla* can be meaningful to his gendered performance in the diasporic setting, just as he has shown elsewhere in the text how diasporic understandings of *bakla* can inform efforts to claim male, same-sex identities and practices within contexts back home.

6   Discussion: Gender, Modernity, and Flexible Language

Tony is one of many *bakla* who regularly combine linguistic materials from Tagalog, English, and Spanish when responding to questions during structured interviews and when talking with friends in less formal speech settings. In fact, text-making across linguistic boundaries is one of the defining characteristics of *swardspeak*, the language closely associated with *bakla* experience worldwide. As Manalansan explains, while all gay "argots" (as he calls them) provide gay men with

> linguistic strategies that enable gay men to negotiate and express their unique experience and views, . . . *swardspeak* reflects the historical, cultural, and politico-economic processes   of a mobile group of multiply-minoritized men from a former American colony in the Third World. [It is] in fact a "syncretic" dynamic that "critically appropriates elements from the master codes of the dominant culture and 'creolizes' them, disarticulating signs and rearticulating their symbolic meaning."   (Manalansan 1995: 250, quoting Mercer 1988: 57)

Manalansan continues,

> The argot is a fast changing one. The movement of people between the Philippines and America provides a way by which innovations in both areas provide the grist for exchange and revitalization. . . . While many of the phrases and words presented [in his 1995 essay – WL] will actually be out of date by the time [that essay] is published, the fundamental mechanisms and dynamics of the argot remain strongly continuous.   (Manalansan 1995: 252)

Among other points, this description of swardspeak suggests that the social and political experiences shaping *bakla*-related gendered modernity are mirrored in the language pluralism, and carefully mediated movement between language traditions, which are characteristic of swardspeak text-making. Importantly, and as explained in previous sections of this chapter, similar parallels between experiences of gendered modernity and the textual descriptions of those experiences can be found outside of the Filipino context. For instance, the gay personal advertisement in example (1) drew richly on Afrikaans understandings of male-centered desire and on Afrikaans linguistic conventions which regularly express them. But the language of the advertisement also incorporated understandings of male-centered desire which circulate outside of South African linguistic, cultural, and gendered domains, and against which Afrikaans (homo)sexual discourse is now being redefined.[17] And similarly, in example (2), the social and sexual meanings which Ó Searcaigh explored through his pairing of linguistically distinct texts spoke directly to his moving away from English-speaking urban domains and the English-dominant (homo)sexual opportunities available there, and his return to a sexual subjectivity framed entirely within Gaelic-centered traditions.

This convergence of language pluralism and gendered experience attested in these texts is neither accidental nor arbitrary. Other studies of social groups especially hard hit by the disruptions of late modernity have identified text-making practices which use contrasts in language tradition to mark tensions between local versus regional, ethnic versus national, and personal versus more corporate allegiances which shape the details of everyday experience within the late modern setting.[18] Most of those discussions use claims about *code-switching* to describe the dynamics of language pluralism attested in the text-making. Carol Myers-Scotton observes, however, that in some instances of code-switching, the individual movement from one language option to another "does not necessarily have a special indexicality; rather it is the *overall pattern* which carries the communicative intention" (1993: 117, my emphasis). Under this arrangement, Myers-Scotton continues, "code switching itself becomes the unmarked choice" – that is, an expected, anticipated, an unremarkable component of text-related language pluralism.

David Harvey's discussion of *flexible accumulation* (1989: 147 ff) helps us understand why, particularly in the moments of gendered text-making of interest to this chapter, an "overall pattern" of code-switching, not particular movements from one language to the next, would become the unmarked (linguistic) practice in such settings.[19] The tensions between nationalism, citizenship, and sexual subjectivity which are so evident in those speech settings, and addressed in such detail in the texts constructed there, are central to the late modern experience worldwide, and are closely associated with the workings of political economy which underlies those experiences, what Lash and Urray (1988) have described as a *disorganized capitalism*. Under an already unstable, unpredictable, and disorganized modernity, Harvey argues, investors, managers, and workers so often become engaged in projects which bring together – generate an *accumulation* of – opportunities, resources, valued statuses, and symbols of "success" which would otherwise not be available or accessible to them. Importantly, the sources of opportunity, resources, status, and symbols are not limited to the immediate home terrain, but are widely cast across local and regional domains, and beyond, and the resulting accumulations are always open to further modification, elaboration, and change. In other words, and adding more meaning to Harvey's initial phrasing, the accumulation of opportunities, resources, statuses, and symbols does not adhere to some predetermined inventory, but is always fluid and flexible.

Aiwa Ong's (1999) discussion of cultural logic underlying the Chinese resettlement throughout the Asian-Pacific rim shows how Harvey's claims about the economic dimensions of flexible accumulation extend into efforts to maintain cultural identity in the context of displacement and diaspora. Note the multiple sites of social action, and the strategic (re)construction of cultural and social ties in response to them, which Ong identifies in the following remarks:

> Chinese traders in transnational settings have been viewed mainly as skillful handlers of money, but rarely have they been seen as agents actively shaping their self-identity in a cross-cultural context. . . . What is often missing in accounts of diasporan experiences is an account of diasporan subjects as active manipulators of cultural symbols [. . .].

She continues:

> Hong Kong emigrants seek the kinds of symbolic capital that have international recognition and value, not only in the country of origin but also in the country of destination and especially in the transnational spaces where the itineraries of traveling businessmen [*sic*] and professionals intersect with those of local residents. As a result, . . . multiple geographies were and continued to be engaged by ethnic Chinese whose earlier diaspora are continually evolving into a network of family ties, kinship, commerce, sentiments, and values spread throughout regions of dispersal and settlement.   (Ong 1999: 12)

The relationships between language, cultural practices, and political economy which Ong identifies in these remarks – and specifically the *flexible accumulation* of linguistic and other symbolic resources, on which these relationships are based – are not limited to the transnational experiences of affluent, Asian/ Pacific diasporic Chinese. Similar accumulations of expressive resources from diverse language and cultural traditions can be found throughout late modernity, including sites of gendered modernity of the sort examined in this chapter. Importantly, these accumulations of language traditions and linguistic practices through which speakers and their audiences engage in gendered identities and practices at these sites resemble the "flexibility with respect to labour processes, labour markets, products and patterns of consumption" (Harvey 1989: 147) which structures (and in some ways, may also restrict) accumulation within the economic domain.

To foreground these connections between text-making and political economy, and to underscore the parallels between linguistic practices and the *flexible accumulation* of other forms of valued resources in late modernity, I propose describing the "overall pattern" of language use in such settings as occurrences of *flexible language*. Doing so draws attention to how code-switching, language pluralism, and other "familiar" linguistic practices actually claim new significance within contexts of late modern, gendered text-making and within the economic and social "moments" within which those texts are situated. Flexible language reminds us that, when staring in the face of a disorganized capitalism and confronted by the other unstable and unpredictable meanings of gender which now circulate widely throughout the late modern social order, having access to a diverse range of linguistic and other symbolic resources becomes valuable. In fact, having access to such a flexible linguistic/symbolic inventory becomes *all the more* valuable, if, as Ken Plummer has claimed (see discussion in section 2 above), text-making provides the primary means for making sense out of local uncertainties of gendered late modernity and for claiming one's own place within it.

If speakers find that *flexible language* provides an effective format for describing gendered experiences in late modernity and for making sense out of its local disorganization, speakers are telling us that *gender itself* is fragmented, decentralized, constantly subjected to negotiation and change within contexts of late modernity, and that gendered identities are accessible to late modern subjects only in flexible, accumulative terms. This understanding of gender is consistent with recent efforts to theorize gender in performative rather than prediscursive terms. Particularly important here is the argument (Butler 1990: 15, 25) that gendered meanings do not exist prior to the social moment, but emerge from forms of social practice, some of which are heavily gendered, others of which are not necessarily gender-specific or even intended to be.

Text-making in flexible terms – that is, where the production and interpretation of text is not confined to the structures and references from a single linguistic tradition, but draws on a broad accumulation of linguistic and other symbolic resources – seems especially suited to the demands of these performative tasks. As discussion in this chapter has shown, flexible language provides speakers with linguistic options which address the concerns of the gendered moment, but which can easily be adjusted or reconstituted once the concerns or the text-making task begin to change.

But while text-making in flexible terms is directly linked to broader conditions of late modern experience, flexible language is also a product of that experience, and has to be studied accordingly. For example, since economic accumulations unfold unevenly across boundaries of race, sexuality, class, and nationality, the same should be true for linguistic accumulations and for the gendered identities constructed in terms of those accumulations. In the examples reviewed here, efforts to give voice to gender have benefited from literacy, mobility, and other privileged forms of textual practice. In instances where speakers do not have access to such privileged practices, accumulations of linguistic resources and meanings of gender which follow from them will be constructed quite differently. In that sense, it would be worthwhile to move beyond the textual similarities attested in these examples, and to examine the economic and social implications expressed through the *different* styles of language choices and code-mixing which each example displays.

NOTES

1   My thanks to Denis Provencher, Miriam Meyerhoff, and Janet Holmes for the helpful critiques they gave to each of the earlier versions of this text. And my thanks to Wolfram Hartmann, Kieran Kennedy, and Martin Manalansan for supporting the development of the South African, Gaelic, and Filipino examples, respectively.

2   I am not suggesting here that the text-based negotiations/contestations of gender take place only within the domains of text-making, and thereby, independently of material conditions lying outside of the text. As Rosemary Hennessy (2000: 19) explains, the material requirements that allow human life to continue depend on social relations that encompass *more* than language, consciousness, identity, discourse – although they do depend on them too. It is this "more" that constitutes the material "outside" of language – the human relations through which needs are met – but which is only made meaningful through language.

3   My thanks to Wolfram Hartmann, Columbia University and University of Namibia, for his assistance with the preparation of this English translation.

4   The spelling of *humor*, and the presence of such references as *hunk* and "*looks*", suggest that the author is drawing specifically on a US-based English usage in this regard.

5   Miriam Meyerhoff reminds me that *queens* could function as an Afrikaans term (e.g. borrowed from English) in this usage, and not be the result of a mid-phrase code-switching. If so, *geen . . . queens* makes even clearer the writer's lack

of interest in effeminate men, while *English guys welcome* shows that, Afrikaans usage notwithstanding, he is still willing to receive replies from non-effeminate English speakers.

6   When I have discussed the "readability" issue with English-speaking South African gay-identified men, they have consistently reported that they skip over personal ads written in Afrikaans, assuming from the writer's linguistic usage that he only wants replies from other Afrikaner men.

7   Each issue of *The Exit* contains two or three personal advertisements written entirely in Afrikaans and oriented exclusively in terms of Afrikaner interests. Other associations notwithstanding, the wording of these texts always makes clear that the writers are from rural areas of Southern Africa and are hoping to meet same-sex-identified Afrikaner men from similar locales. Occasionally, the personal advertisements will also include statements written in Zulu, though usually these texts also include enough vocabulary from English and other Western language sources to make the text accessible to a wider audience. In other words, Zulu-language personal ads are in no sense written exclusively for a Zulu readership.

8   Unfortunately, copyright restrictions make it impossible to reprint the entire poem, but the text is available in Ó Searcaigh (1993).

9   By linking homosexuality to modernity here, I am not proposing that same-sex desires and practices were absent from Irish tradition. However, just as modernity

reshaped other segments of social experience, modernity prompted the formation of same-sex-based subjectivities not possible at earlier points in time. And, following arguments outlined in D'Emilio (1983), Sedgwick (1990), and Katz (1995), modernist forms of same-sex desires had profound effects on other segments of modern social experience, and the resulting articulation of a homosexual/ heterosexual binary greatly influenced popular *understandings* of modernity itself.

10 The language associated with *bakla* experience is called *swardspeak* (Manalansan 1995); see discussion in the following section of this chapter.

11 My analysis of this passage builds on Manalansan's several studies of *bakla* (1994, 1995, 1998), and has benefited from his many helpful suggestions. I reformatted the passage and added line numbering to facilitate discussion of the textual detail.

12 *Bading* is one of many terms for *bakla* identity commonly used in Tagalog and in swardspeak conversations.

13 Note the reduplicated first syllable – *mu* – of the base in both words. Marking the plural of animate nouns by duplicating the first syllable of the base is a widely attested Tagalog morphemic process. The two versions of this word, each with its own phonetic and morphemic forms, may suggest borrowings from Spanish at two different points in time or under two different sets of linguistic and social circumstances. Compare, for example, Trager's (1939) explanation for the different forms of Spanish loan-words found in the language of Taos pueblo, New Mexico.

14 Manalansan notes (personal communication) that *lukresiya* may be a combination of Spanish *loca* and English *crazy*. (The deletion of the final vowel in the first word segment is widely attested in Tagalog word compounding.) Perhaps more consistent with the foregrounding of assertive feminine presence in this passage, Manalansan also suggests that *lukresiya* may be a Tagalog/ swardspeak rendering of the first name of the notorious Italian noblewoman, Lucrezia Borga. The contrasts in reference resemble the several intertextual meanings surrounding the name *Sean Bhrid* in example (2). Miriam Meyerhoff (personal communication) reminds me that, in all such instances, the multiple readings intensify the stylistic force of the term's textual reference.

15 Manalansan (1995) speculates that the phrase derives from the English language-based children's game, *Mother, May I*. Miriam Meyerhoff (personal communication) suggests that this usage may be an English-based reflection of the Tagalog, sentence-level modality marking. It is likely that both explanations apply with equal force here.

16 *Pamilya*, while a Spanish loan-word, is part of Tagalog vocabulary.

17 I have in mind here both the writer's use of *GWM*, *ALA*, and other linguistic codings, as well as his framing of male same-sex(uality) with a North Atlantic derived identity category, *gay*, rather than in terms of *moffie* or some other Afrikaans-based marker of sex/ gender subjectivity.

18 For example, Susan Gal (1987) connects the dynamics of language loyalty and language shift on the part of certain linguistic minority

groups within the European periphery to the speakers' associations between language choices available to them, and the relative status imposed on them by the surrounding society. Jane Hill (1995) shows how Don Gabriel shifts between Mexicano and Spanish when telling the story of his son's death, so that he can mark the differences in "community-centered" versus "personal profit-oriented" orientations and underscore other contrastive ideological stances as the narrative unfolds. Kathryn Woolard (1989) explains the shifting between Catalan and Castilian Spanish in everyday Catalunyan conversations as a symbolic marker of the Catalan speaker's unique location – historically, politically, culturally, and linguistically – within the Spanish nation-state. And Suzanne Romaine (1994) argues that the introduction of English expressions into Tok Pisin (the "English based pidgin/creole" widely spoken throughout Papua New Guinea) is leading to the rapid depidginization of Tok Pisin and, ultimately, the demise of this linguistic tradition, at least within PNG's urban areas. The reluctance of some Tok Pisin speakers to switch between Tok Pisin and English in vernacular conversations, and even to acquire English, is understandable under these circumstances, just as the emerging stratification of Tok Pisin speakers along the lines of English, rather than Tok Pisin fluencies, is now unavoidable.

19   Myers-Scotton's explanation for the occurrence of unmarked code-switching (1993: 119ff) focuses almost entirely on characteristics of the speakers' linguistic background and their face-to-face interaction. Larger issues of political economy are not attested in her analysis. My use of flexible accumulation in the following paragraphs is not intended to dispute Myers-Scotton's analysis, but only to situate that analysis within a broader frame of reference.

REFERENCES

Bucholtz, Mary 1999: Purchasing power: The gender and class imaginary on the shopping channel. In Mary Bucholtz, Anita C. Liang, and Laurel A. Sutton (eds) *Reinventing Identities*. New York: Oxford University Press, pp. 348–68.

Butler, Judith 1990: *Gender Trouble*. New York: Routledge.

Chetty, Dhiannaraj 1994: A drag at Madame Costello's: Cape moffie life and the popular press in the 1950s and 1960s. In Mark Gevisser and Edwin Cameron (eds) *Defiant Desire*. Johannesburg: Ravan Press, pp. 115–27.

D'Emilio, John 1983: Capitalism and gay identity. In Ann Snitnow, Christine Stansell, and Sharon Thompson (eds) *Powers of Desire*. New York: Monthly Review Press, pp. 100–15.

Fairclough, Norman 1989: *Language and Power*. London: Longmans.

Gal, Susan 1987: Code switching and consciousness in the European periphery. *American Ethnologist* 14: 637–53.

Giddens, Anthony 1991: *Modernity and Self-Identity*. Stanford, CA: Stanford University Press.

Halliday, Michael A. K. 1978: Language as social semiotic. In *Language as Social Semiotic*. London: Edward Arnold, pp. 108–24.

Hambidge, Joan 1995: *Die Gawe Moffie op die Dorp* – An analysis of Afrikaans literature's obsession with Gays. Paper presented at the First Colloquium on Gay and Lesbian Studies in Southern Africa, University of Cape Town, October 19–21, 1995.

Harvey, David 1989: *The Condition of Postmodernity*. Oxford: Blackwell.

Hennessy, Rosemary 2000: *Profit and Pleasure: Sexual Identities in Late Capitalism*. New York: Routledge.

Hill, Jane H. 1995: The voices of Don Gabriel: Responsibility and self in a modern Mexicano narrative. In Dennis Tedlock and Bruce Mannheim (eds) *The Dialogic Emergence of Culture*. Urbana: University of Illinois Press, pp. 97–147.

Katz, Jonathan Ned 1995: *The Invention of Heterosexuality*. New York: Dutton.

Kennedy, Kieran forthcoming: Cathal O'Searcaigh: Local gael or global gay? In William Leap (ed.) *Gay Language without Gay English? Globalization, Sexual Citizenship, and the "New" Languages of Same-Sex Desire*.

Lash, Scott and Urray, John 1988: *The End of Organized Capitalism*. Oxford: Oxford University Press.

McIlvenny, Paul 1996: Heckling and Hyde Park: Verbal audience participation in popular discourse. *Language in Society* 25: 27–60.

Manalansan, Martin 1994: Searching for community: Gay Filipino men in New York City. In *Dimensions of Desire. Ameriasia Journal*, Special Issue, 20: 59–74.

Manalansan, Martin 1995: "Performing" the Filipino gay experience in America: Linguistic strategies in a transnational context. In William L. Leap (ed.) *Beyond the Lavender Lexicon*. Newark, NJ: Gordon and Breach, pp. 249–66.

Manalansan, Martin 1998: Remapping Frontiers: The Lives of Filipino Gay Men in New York. Doctoral dissertation, Department of Anthropology, University of Rochester.

Mercer, Kobina 1988: Diasporic cultures and the dialogic imagination. In Mbye B. Cham and Claire Andrade-Watkins (eds) *Blackframes: Critical Perspectives on Black Independent Cinema*. Cambridge, MA: MIT Press, pp. 50–61.

Moonwomon, Birch 1995: Lesbian discourse, lesbian knowledge. In William L. Leap (ed.) *Beyond the Lavender Lexicon*. Newark, NJ: Gordon and Breach, pp. 45–64.

Myers-Scotton, Carole 1993: *Social Motivations for Codeswitching: Evidence from Africa*. Oxford: Clarendon Press.

Ong, Aiwa 1999: *Flexible Citizenship: The Cultural Logics of Transnationality*. Durham, NC: Duke University Press.

Ó Searcaigh, Cathal 1993: *Homecoming: An Bealach 'na Bhaile/Selected Poems: Rogha Danta*. Indreabhan, Conamura: Clo Iar-Chonnachta.

Plummer, Ken 1995: *Telling Sexual Stories*. London: Routledge.

Romaine, Suzanne 1994: Language standardization and linguistic fragmentation in Tok Pisin. In Marcyliena Morgan (ed.) *Language and the Social Construction of Identity in Creole Situations*. Los Angeles:

Center for African American Studies, University of California at Los Angeles, pp. 19–42.

Sedgwick, Eve 1990: *The Epistemology of the Closet*. Berkeley, CA: University of California Press.

Stewart, Katherine Claire 1990: Backtalking the wilderness. In Faye Ginsburg and Anna H. Tsing (eds) *Uncertain Terms: Negotiating Gender in American Culture*. Boston: Beacon Press, pp. 43–57.

Trager, George L. 1939: Spanish and English loanwords in Taos. *International Journal of American Linguistics* 10: 144–58.

Woolard, Kathryn A. 1989: *Double Talk: Bilingualism and the Politics of Ethnicity in Catalonia*. Stanford, CA: Stanford University Press.

18 A Marked Man: The Contexts of Gender and Ethnicity

SARA TRECHTER

1 Introduction

As many chapters in this volume illustrate, the field of language and gender has expanded significantly in recent years to consider the relevance of ethnicity, sexual preference, and to a lesser extent class, to the construction of spoken and signed gendered identities (Hall and Bucholtz 1995; Livia and Hall 1997a; Bucholtz et al. 1999). In not-so-distant-past studies, the ethnic background of research participants was without question assumed because it was "unmarked" – White – and conclusions about gender and language based on research participants from this single ethnic background were often generalized to reflect on women and men as a whole. Because of ground-breaking work critiquing the lack of ethnic voices in relation to matrix languages and dialects and a growing body of work in languages outside the Euro-American context, this situation has begun to change (see this volume and this chapter for citations).

Nevertheless, if one glances at the titles of work in gender and language, it is still common for studies considering ethnicity and gender to prominently feature the non-matrix language name or a non-White ethnic label in their title ("Good Guys and 'Bad' Girls: Identity Construction by Latina and Latino Student Writers"; "No Woman No Cry: Claiming African American Women's Place"). Ethnicity is foregrounded most often when it is non-White. Imagine changing some titles that just specify "women" to what they truly consider – White women, such as "White Women's Identities at Work." The field of gender and language still treats ethnicity as "marked" through the construction of oppositional pairs that oppose non-White to White, dialect to standard, non-English gender to English, non-matrix language speakers to matrix within a society. Thus, we might suppose that any contribution on gender and ethnicity will discuss research on each of the marked members of these oppositions and how they have added to a more highly diversified field of data, much as research in gender variation has taken us beyond essentialist definitions of "male" and "female."

These two aspects of language and gender research have not developed apace. Researchers have complicated the notion of binary gender by pointing out its interactional and contextually constructed nature (see Bergvall, Bing, and Freed 1996; Eckert and McConnell-Ginet 1992), interconnectedness and ideological associations with sexual preference (Livia and Hall 1997b), and its indexical rather than isomorphic nature (Ochs 1992). Except for some recent exceptions, there has not been an extensive engagement with redefining linguistic ethnicity in the field of language and gender. This may partially be because there is still a great deal of work to be done toward making the field of language and gender more attentive to issues of ethnicity and to the diverse voices of gender before the constructional nature of ethnicity can be dealt with in detail. A recent, important contribution to gender and ethnicity research is one that examines how gender is constructed intra-ethnically and interactionally within an in-group (Morgan 1999). A focus on interactional sequences in single-sex or cross-sex interactions emphasizes both the strategies for gendering that are available and interactive differences between men and women (Goodwin, this volume; 1999). Yet in such ethnic studies, there is some risk in assuming the gender (or ethnic) identity of participants as obvious or given as we look to their interactional strategies in constructing such identities (Urciuoli 1995; Kulick 2000). In effect, the available data on gender, language, and ethnicity has moved at a slower rate than our attempts to theorize it has. In practice, the mutually constructive properties of gendered/ethnic identity are complex and difficult to balance within any one study, especially when constrained by markedness relations with society's matrix language. As a focus, this chapter balances the importance of studies that demonstrate the role of ethnicity in the construction of linguistically gendered identities with those that emphasize the ways ethnicity itself gets gendered in both practice and ideology.

A great deal of gender and ethnicity research has addressed past stereo-typing and attempted to create a more accurate and complete picture of ethni-cally gendered language in groups that have been neglected in the mainstream of gender and language research. The first section of this chapter considers how such work has changed the field of our inquiry. Without the continuation of these efforts, gender and language research will continue with a rather skewed focus, where the unmarked focus will be women who just happen to be Anglo and middle-class. In so far as sociolinguistic research is in constant danger of losing the complexity of either gender or ethnicity when demon-strating the relevance of one to a specific interactional context, the second focus of this chapter examines recent work that addresses two central ques-tions: (1) how do gender and ethnicity mutually construct each other in nego-tiated discourse, and (2) how do some features of gender or ethnicity become iconic – ideologically part of a community as easily recognizable and inter-pretable features that are then taken as natural? Finally, a central assumption of this chapter is that even when gender and language research does not address ethnicity (i.e. it is assumed), the ethnicity of both the researched and the researcher should become highly marked. In fact, it probably is already quite salient in the interpretation of those readers whose ethnicity is most often deemed worth commenting on in an academic context. Thus, the conclusion of this chapter is a proposal, re-emphasizing the gender and language researcher's responsibilities toward changing the field of research rather than merely plowing in new directions. Geneva Smitherman remarked explicitly on this obligation when advocating the use of African American English Vernacular in public and even corporate contexts:

> So many of us who came in in the 60s on the struggles of Black people ... got these degrees. We joined the mainstream. We should have been changing the course of that stream because the stream is polluted.   (*Oprah Winfrey Show*, 1987)

Rather than assuming that the work we do merely describes the lamentable nature of fields and streams, as researchers we both effect and reflect that nature, and therefore have obligations to advocate and empower others in our work (Cameron et al. 1992). To the extent that gender and ethnicity research reflects and promulgates dominant social norms, activist researchers should, without inordinate reflexiveness or self-indulgence, attempt to direct such reflections productively. Language and gender research has not just studied "women's language," but has emphasized a political agenda that encourages the redefinition of men's language as "marked" (see Black and Coward 1981). The conclusion of this chapter therefore argues for similar work in the field of gender and ethnicity. Drawing on feminist perspectives as well as work by hooks (1992), Dyer (1997), and Ignatiev and Garvey (1996), I examine and propose strategies to make a man, a White man, as marked as any of the rest of us.

2   Revealing Ethnic Gender

The evolution of the field of language and gender has a great deal in common with language, gender, and ethnicity in that critical approaches in both have responded to the refusal to "see" the complexity or sometimes even the presence of the Other. Cameron (1985), for instance, critiques the work of Labov (1972b) in New York and Trudgill (1974) as predefining a core social world as male-dominated. Because women's socio-economic status in these studies was partially determined by their father's or husband's occupations, their linguistic gender could also only be viewed within a power dynamic where male behaviors were defined as core and females' as deviant. Likewise, in viewing the social world in terms of sex, rather than in terms of interaction, community contact, and gendered social action, nuanced behaviors that were outside of the centrally defined prototype were lost (Eckert 1989). In a similar vein, Foster (1995) and Morgan (1999) call for a renewal in the field of African American Vernacular English (AAVE) that recognizes the voices and interactions of women as central and the work of African American women scholars in this field as valid. Morgan proposes that sociolinguistic work that types competitive genres in AAVE such as "playing the dozens" as particular to juvenile, male, culture obscures the gender complexity of the field and ignores women's voices and genres. She cites Labov's (1972a) work as also excluding other "deviant" genders such as boys who were considered "lame" because of their sexual preference or non-stereotypical behaviors. By giving examples of women's "reading," a genre used by both African American male and female speakers, Morgan demonstrates that the inclusion of women's voices in the analysis of AAVE leads to a more explanatory and socially grounded account. Like the dozens, reading is a public performance, where (often) women denounce the actions and attitudes of the hearer to her/his face in what is often an extended monologue. Both types of performance test the ability of the addressee to save face and be publicly cool. Along with Goodwin's (1990, 1999) analysis of AAVE-speaking girls' and boys' games and "he-said-she-said" interactions in Philadelphia, these analyses stress the importance of maintaining public face, confronting what others may have said behind one's back, and preserving a public cool. Without the additions of the interactional resources and analysis of how these are taken up by women, or with an analysis of these genres as only competitive boy talk, the complex connections between these genres and historical oppression of African Americans as well as construction of community values would be lost. The addition of women's voices to the study of ethnicity is vital.

Likewise, Galindo and Gonzales (1999: 4) argue that hitherto there has been no far-reaching insider account of Chicana language in the research on gender and ethnicity, and though outsider accounts are important, they cannot recount the "lived experience" of women who live with the crossing of borders, an excellent metaphor for both gender and ethnicity (see Anzaldúa 1987). There are two ways that this border-crossing becomes particularly relevant for the study of gender and ethnicity. First, women in ethnic communities are sometimes the mediators between traditional culture and language, preserving older forms, and the matrix language culture. Gonzales (1999) focuses on women in New Mexico who must cross between the borders of the local community of Córdoba and the larger Chicano- and English-speaking community, and are therefore cultural and linguistic innovators, maintaining their Spanish through strong local networks, but switching code to accommodate to outsiders. The role of ethnic women as "cultural brokers" in such situations is arguably related to their economic role in the community. For instance, Hill (1987) connects the fact that older Mexicano-speaking women were not as likely to speak Spanish but to maintain their Mexicano with their employment patterns. Where men were more likely to leave for a time to work in a Spanish-speaking urban center, women's cottage industry production affected their language choices. Even though women's ways of speaking were often devalued by the community at large, they were also envied by some young men who had shifted to Spanish. Conversely, young Gullah women from the Sea Islands of the Eastern US coast were more likely to speak a dialect nearer to Standard English because of their service work in the mainland industry (Nichols 1983). Finally, Medicine (1987) argues that Lakhota-speaking women maintain the language through their role as socializers of children, but are cultural brokers because of their bilingual skills (see also Goldstein 1995 on gender and bilingualism).

Ethnic women's borderland linguistic fluency does not just apply to mediating between languages; it also concerns gender borders. Much of the work on Latinas and Chicanas in the gender and language literature has purposefully sought to debunk gender stereotypes of Latinas as submissive followers (Orellana 1999). Galindo (1999), in particular, argues that Chicanas are often stereotyped from within their culture and by outsiders who regard Chicanas as pure, chaste, and conservative speakers. Slang vocabularies such as *pachuco* or *caló* in this tradition are associated with big-city male gang members, the lower classes, or prison inmates. Galindo offers examples of Texas women who choose to use such "rough" vocabulary and pronunciation to defy gender stereotypes and traditional gender expectations for Chicanas. Likewise, Zentella (1998: 641) examines an ideology constructing a distinction between "the Spanish/poor/non-white female identity . . . subordinate to an English/rich/ white male identity," and the conflict between this ideology and the Madonna ideology which equates Spanish with country and motherhood. To the extent that Puertorriqueñas are responsible for passing on their *mother* language, while ensuring their own advancement and their children's success in English-speaking schools in America, they are in a double bind. Zentella maintains that they are switching to English at phenomenal rates.

Such work demonstrates the need for more studies that explore the linguistic behavior and choices of ethnic women, especially in how they view their linguistic choices as constructing a powerful, gendered, ethnic voice for themselves despite expectations from the matrix culture and gender expectations within their own community (see Mendoza-Denton 1999a for a summary). Inasmuch as heritage language and ideologies equating heritage language with ethnic membership are connected to women's available linguistic choices, studies which demonstrate women's place in the maintenance and evolution of heritage language, and how this gendered expectation comes into being, are vital to understanding how ethnicity, linguistic gendered ethnicity, is constructed within a predefined community.

3 Conflicting Styles

Although such representations allude to the multiple pressures of borderland gender, they do so primarily at the level of an overarching community ideology. They also demonstrate, however, that the ideologies of gender and ethnicity and the accompanying interactional behavior are not straightforward or necessarily standardized within such a "community." Drawing more heavily on the methodologies of Conversation Analysis and ethnography, Goodwin (this volume; 1999) consequently sees identities and, in particular, moral development as continually emerging from interactional contexts such as complex games rather than as static, predefined positions from which language emerges. Although the girls in her studies are both "markedly" ethnic – primarily Mexican and Central American children in Los Angeles, who speak Spanish – and gendered, her work primarily demonstrates how different aspects of identity emerge in situations of play and conflict. Ethnicities and genders are consequently performative acts brought into being within particular contexts, rather than contained in traditional binaries of male/not male and White/non-White. In such a complex field of performance, it is not simple to pinpoint exactly how gender and ethnicity are mutually constructed or even that a particular linguistic behavior is necessarily "ethnic." The values of particular linguistic behaviors are multiple: in performance and uptake, they transform throughout an interchange. Goodwin consequently (1999: 402) notes: "Much more work is required to sort out the effects of ethnicity, age and social class on norms of speaking." Nevertheless, by paying close attention to performative data, the linguistic detail of how "community" membership is regulated emerges in the face of different personal styles.

Mendoza-Denton (1999b) provides further nuances to our understanding of Latina intra-group ethnicity. It is complicated by both class and urban versus rural associations, and the fact that linguistic actions contain multiple meanings. In high school girl intra-group conversations about class and ethnic affiliations, the stances that participants take do not always involve neat correlations of discourse markers with conversational effect; the same discourse marker may show oppositional co-construction or a collaborative denial (see Modan 1994 for similar strategies among ethnic Jewish women). By utilizing conversations in which the teenagers argue about and explore their allegiance to different identities, Mendoza-Denton is able to compare the girls' stances concerning their own ethnic affiliations, while exploring the concomitant linguistic behaviors that serve to include or exclude. The girls' ideological profession of affiliation or allegiance to the Mexican Rural Class is not matched by their Mexican Urban Middle Class interactional style, and a speaker with Mexican Rural Class style has difficulty gaining and maintaining the floor.

That participants within any given community of practice will not always have similar styles, especially as they cross back and forth between borders displaying multiple allegiances, is central to the study of how ethnicity and gender are mutually constructed. As people use different voices to perform multiple identities, they may both invoke and challenge the prototypical categories associated with those identities. Hall (1995) and Barrett (1999) investigate such switching between voices as people utilize their performance for linguistic and material capital. The sex workers in Hall (1995) invent and "call on" the voices of ethnic (White Southern, Latino/a, African American) gender stereotypes, often catering to their clients' desires. African American Texas drag queens engage in abrupt shifts into and out of White women's "speech"

(Barrett 1999); this is middle-class, and "refined," exhibiting many of the stereo-typic vocabulary and pronunciation characteristics for women's speech, such as empty adjectives like "adorable" or "marvelous," hypercorrect pronuncia-tion, and "dynamic" intonation (cf. Lakoff 1975). In crossing such borders, the drag queens inadvertently make the connections between stereotypic gender and ethnicity more explicit. To be really "woman-like," the drag queens invoke a voice that is "White." As people create different identities in such overt performances, the question remains whether the voices that such performers use are their "real" identities – those which form a stable sense of self (see also Weatherall and Gallois, this volume). Of course, such a question could be asked for any performance – if participants are bringing different voices to bear, then to what extent does the performance necessarily construct gender and ethnic identity? If identity is interactionally constructed, for instance in children's games (Goodwin, this volume) or the workplace (Holmes and Stubbe, this volume), then the validity of heritage ethnic categorizations such as African American, Latino/a, White, Panjabi, is questionable.

This latter question has been addressed in some detail by Walters (1996) as well as Anzaldúa (1991: 250), who defend identity categories against a perceived onslaught of performative umbrella analyses of identity. In effect, they argue that the practice of focusing on "performance" or interactional construction of identity prematurely effaces social categorization and a politically motivated conception of community. With the erasure of ethnicity, the non-White voice is assimilated into White, and the lesbian, female voice is subsumed into a queer, unmarked, therefore male, perspective. The very social categorization that enables discrimination may ultimately be the political rallying point for the formation of a community of practice to resist historically rooted domin-ance. To the extent that performative analyses deal with individuals' use of multiple voices, gender and ethnicity researchers are in a double bind. The work summarized above both emphasizes the need to address a lack of ethnic (usually considered to be non-White) women's voices in gender and language research, but also seeks to reveal the complexity of voices within an estab-lished category. Those researchers who have focused on the interactional construction of identity apparently also feel obligated to address the lack of diversity in the gender and language tradition by categorizing participants first by gender and ethnic background. Work that addresses a lack of women's or ethnic voices in the gender and language literature assumes a priori both the gendered and ethnic identity of its subject by asking the question, "How do women and girls who identify as X speak or sign?" And if identity is not defined a priori through a common social construct such as Chicana, African American, Jew, or White, it may be through a particular kind of linguistic performance: those who speak Spanish, those who signify, and so on. This kind of definition is tautological: linguists simultaneously try to define the practices of a linguistic community while maintaining that the community as an entity is defined by its practice (Urciuoli 1995; Trechter 2000; Kulick 2000).

An approach which focuses on the emergent identity of participant(s) in a community of practice need not be in conflict with one that recognizes historically enforced social categories as sites of resistance and identity formation, nor should we be forced to abandon any study of linguistic communities or the social aspects of semiosis because participants in interactions draw on multiple voices. The relationship between gender and ethnicity *should* emphasize different definitions of linguistic communities as they come into prominence, especially considering the specific political goals of the researched and researcher: a community of *practice* (Eckert and McConnell-Ginet 1992), an *imagined* community (Anderson 1991; Queen 1997), one of *contact* "that placed at its center the operation of language *across* lines of social differentiation . . . that focused on modes and zones of contact between dominant and dominated groups" (Pratt 1987: 60; Barrett 1997), or even a *speech* community, defined by "participation in a set of shared norms . . . observed in overt types of evaluative behavior" (Labov 1972b: 120–1). Recognizing that ethnic, community, and gender identities are fluid social constructs in practice, which index and draw on semiotic resources while simultaneously creatively constructing new resources through contextual interaction, is difficult to capture. Yet both historically grounded and performative meanings of community as well as linguistic judgments about such constructions explain why gender and ethnicity are neither static nor singular. Different definitions of "community" (identity-based, interaction-based, community-based) are also highlighted as they emerge from interaction.

4   Use and Construction of Models

Given an available repertoire and some notion of what choices of expression are associated with a particular projection of identity in a given context, a speaker can project multiple gender and ethnic affiliations. Myers-Scotton (1998) proposes a Markedness Model in which participants in speech events perform as rational actors who have in mind specific sets of rights and obligations (RO), and which therefore provides a heuristic for how participants might choose possible moves within an interaction. For a specific interaction type, a speaker would often be aware of the language, dialect, or genre (linguistic features) that index an unmarked RO set. A speaker usually chooses an unmarked move, but may sometimes opt to build a new interactional norm by choosing a marked feature. For instance, the African American drag queen performances may shift from indexing stereotypic White woman speech to that of an African American man for shock humor in a performance as a marked shift (Barrett 1998).

Rampton (1991, 1995) examines how switches between unmarked norms for speech events operate in inter-ethnic language crossing among urban youth. He primarily focuses on the ideology behind the unmarked uses of SAE (Stylized

Asian English) – used to disrespect; Caribbean Creole – used to demonstrate urban vitality and dissent; and Panjabi – associated with local networks. In particular, agonistic Panjabi words were especially prevalent in inter-ethnic interactions among younger boys and were highly associated with the activity of tag games. Panjabi was thus an unmarked choice for agonistic boys' play. As the boys grew older, however, Panjabi use decreased in inter-ethnic interactions, and White girls were not often recorded using Panjabi words unless they were discussing *bhangra* (a popular music extending beyond the local interaction networks) or had Panjabi boyfriends. Additionally, Rampton argues that the crossing among urban, ethnic linguistic varieties dissociates one variety from a natural marker of ethnicity so that ethnicity is interactionally negotiated. He does not discuss crossing as a possible marker for gender – White girls were not recorded speaking Panjabi, even though they do claim to use some Panjabi words.

Such work that traces inter-ethnic crossing demonstrates more than how speakers make choices about which variety to use for an appropriate context. It demonstrates the performative change or historical development of an ethnic variety as a preferential gender variety for the playful expression of conflict or teasing, as well as its association with age-related and historically sedimented genres. The political and social resistance associated with Caribbean Creole or African American dialects, Rampton theorizes, springs from political and social resistance movements of the 1960s and therefore is more likely to be adapted to function in the cool urban youth culture as a less local language of dissent. Thus, for gender (see discussions of Barrett and Hall in section 3 above) or ethnic "crossing" to be possible, interactional participants draw on, as well as create, gendered and ethnic interactional norms. Gender crossing is consequently ethnic, as in White women's speech being the most "female," and ethnic crossing is apparently gendered, as researchers associate it primarily with male behaviors (Bucholtz 1999; Hewitt 1986; Kiesling 2001).

Because the interactional obviously draws on and creates new historical linguistic norms, how such notions become naturalized or "denaturalized" (as in the case of Rampton's new ethnicities) becomes of primary importance, especially if our desire is to disrupt and resist such processes. Obviously, such work calling attention to the socially constructive nature of ethnicity and gender is not new to the social sciences and can be traced from Boas in the early twentieth century to Butler (1993). However, Irvine and Gal (2000) and Irvine (2001) theorize how *linguistic* differentiation gets constructed as a typical semiotic process in culture. They identify three semiotic processes through which people create ideologies of *linguistic* difference: *iconization, fractal recursivity,* and *erasure. Iconization* is a process by which linguistic features that normally index stances, genres, or dialect become so strongly associated with a social group that they are thought to be inherent or essential characteristics of that group (for a discussion of indexicality see Kiesling, this volume). Even those group members who do not frequently use the linguistic features in question are associated with them by default. Through *fractal recursivity* the linguistic relationship between form and social meaning that is salient from one level of interaction or context is projected into new areas or levels of discourse as speakers draw on salient resources to create shifting "identities" or communities. In other words, form(s) including pronunciation, word choice, phrases, dialect, or even a particular language associated iconically with one group may be utilized by both in- and out-group members, sometimes projecting new meanings. Such projection can have the effect, however, of further stabilizing the iconic connection between linguistic form and social group identity through repetition and expansion of the form into multiple contexts, despite some potential of destabilizing the original iconic form.[1] Finally, the ideological process of *erasure* effectually removes some groups and social behaviors from vision and sight. They become subsumed under the totalizing and dominant ideology. In effect, they become *unmarked* (see Bucholtz 2001; Trechter and Bucholtz 2001 for further discussion). Erasure may be perpetuated on a number of different levels both as it occurs within the interactional norms of a community and as that community is viewed by outsiders. Together these ideological processes serve to equate social identity with linguistic form.

Multiple-level erasure has often occurred in accounts of the phonological or morphological gender indicators in several Native American languages. Lakhota, a Siouan language, currently spoken by about 12,000 people in the northern middle-west of the United States, has often been characterized by academic researchers and native speakers alike as possessing a series of sentence-final particles which indicate illocutionary force and gender of the speaker. These are usually reported by native speakers through the citation of one or two iconic forms: men say *lo* and women say *le*; men say *yo*, and women say *ye*. To some extent it is difficult to tell how much native speakers have been influenced by academic researchers in creating such a neat complementary distribution of forms in their claims about Lakhota. They typically volunteer the iconic sayings above, but the others are most likely from elicitation in the context of textual interpretation or production. In some sense, through further representation the academic community has taken this iconization and potentially the erasure of women's voices to new levels (see Trechter 2000 for a detailed discussion). Table 18.1 represents data from Rood and Taylor (1997) and from what native speakers have told me about their language.[2]

Table 18.1 Lakhota clitics, by gender and speech act

Illocutionary/affective force	Man	Woman
Formal question	hũwo	hũwe (obsolete)
Imperative	yo	ye$_a$
Opinion/emphasis	lo	le (archaic), ye$_a$
Emphatic statement		kʃto
Entreaty	ye$_e$	na
Surprise/opinion	wã	mã

I have found that by examining a variety of Lakhota speech acts, genres, and conversations that, of course, in interaction this neat table of "separate but equal" behavior for men and women breaks down. This is because men and women engage in different discourse genres which index their gender, use some of the same particles pretty regularly, and because some forms are dying out (Trechter 2000). Women tend to use *kʃto* more often, and men use *wã* more often than women. However, there are three forms that are used almost exclusively by men (*lo*, *yo*, and *hũwo*) and two that are used exclusively by women (*na*, *mã*). By "exclusive" use here, I mean that to use the forms that are exclusive is to give a clearly gendered flavor to one's voice. Thus, men using the exclusively women's particles are considered to be acting in a womanly manner or maternally, and women who use the men's particles are "tomboys." The particles *lo* and *yo* have in fact become highly salient to speakers, and it is only in conjunction with these that the "women's" forms are defined as appropriate to women's use at all. It is considered "natural" or an essential quality for men to use *lo* and *yo* (*hũwo* as a rhetorical question indicator is a bit more rare), and though some speakers acknowledge that some boys in situations of limited linguistic access have difficulty nowadays picking up the male forms, others have told me that boys do this naturally without correction. In this sense, certain of the gender deictics in Lakhota that point to the gender of the speaker have gone beyond indexical relationships and become *iconic*.

Iconization of these forms, as Irvine and Gal (2000) assert, seems to have come from their repeated association with certain speech events. As these markers became an increasingly salient part of their speech the participants in these events were considered to "naturally" speak in a certain way. In fact, in a vast collection of multi-genred text collected by native speaker and linguist Ella Deloria in the 1920s and 1930s and in the conversational data in my own fieldwork, *lo* "m. assertion" as a gender and assertion particle is considerably higher in frequency than any other gender particle. It occurred thousands of times. Its supposed female counterpart, *le* "f. assertion," was very rare, and it is now obsolescent, and *kʃto* "emphatic," often associated with women and especially the genre of gossip, was used only forty times. The largest concentration of men using male assertion particles is found in the conversations of men speaking publicly.

In a speech transcribed by Ella Deloria in the 1930s (example (1)), a group of men who do not know each other well are jokingly and agonistically talking about political speeches. There are nine uses of *lo* in a text that is only eleven lines long. I reproduce the text in full because it illustrates the good humor but polite distancing evoked with the use of *lo*, its association with public speaking, and assertion of opinion in public. There is a tendency for the men to end their turn with an assertion particle after they make their point. The interactions between B and C (an insistent and slightly critical participant) contain more masculine assertions as the two men negotiate the perceived proper length of a good political speech and whether the old guard have been thrust aside or have given up their power willingly. Potentially, every sentence could end with *lo*, but there is an especial increase of use in line 9 as the younger man (speaker B) reflects personally and gives his opinion on larger public concerns of the Lakhota people. When speaker C authoritatively continues this reflection combining personal and public matters, he also ends his opinions with *lo*.[3]

(1): *Comments around the inauguration*

1   A: hũhũ hi! Tʰakoȝa, ʃicaya ukoyakix'āpe **ló**!!
2   B: Tókʰel hé?
3   A: óx, le pcelyéla ũkóyakaksāu kī he wakʰé kī. Tuwá wóyute wāȝí otʰá cʰą̄ke cʰa cʰį̄ʃká ogná iyáta iyéyī ną̄ yawáʃteʃte yatʰī nā iyókʰpiyexcī napcī nā akʰé ocápa yũkʰā cʰī̄ʃká-inũpa kī akʰé wóyute-waʃte ũ hé etāhā ogná él aúpi nā kákʰel ihá icáxtake kī hécʰegna kícigluzāu kī iyécʰel ũkókyakix'āpe **ló**!
4   B: Hā, éyaʃ tʰũkaʃila, cʰī waná líla tʰéhā-yākʰapi cʰāke hécʰamū?. Tʰiyókʰatī nā oyāk-ʃice éyaʃ líla wóglakau kī ótapi ecʰíyatāhā oʃílya? Niyéʃ wanáx'ũ yāke kī tʰawát'elcʰicʰiyapiʃni nā hécʰamū we **ló**!
5   A: Hũhí, niʃnálaʃ onáx'ũ-awaʃtecʰilake ũ. ímnayexcī iyáyīkte séce ũ!
6   B: Wā, tʰũkaʃila, tkʰáʃ henála slolwáya cʰa epʰé séca **wā**!
7   A: ox, tuwá akʰákʃá!
8   C: Kʰola, kahāskeyala s'e iyáyeʃni, ehāni. Takúku mahétuya ilúkcā nā yuhá ináyaȝī-iteke ʃā owehāhāpi ecé ecʰánu nā ílotake **ló**.
9   B: Hā, Wā, itéʃniyā oíyokʃice? Táku éyaʃ iyúha oíhāke yukʰā keyápi k'ū wicákʰape **ló**. Lé āpétu kī Lakʰóta wicʰaxca wakícʰūza-ūpi k'ū wicʰákicigluzapi nā kʰoʃkálaka wicʰák'upi yũkʰā kítāla s'e iyōmayake **ló**. Heū eháʃ áwicakʰeya-iwayīkte kī omáyatʰake **ló**.
10   C: Tó, éyaʃ cʰī hécʰetu? Waná Lakʰólwichox'ā-tʰanila k'ū hécʰeyá-inaȝī s'elél. éyaʃ hākéyela ecʰél ehé **ló**, tʰakoȝa, hé wicʰákicigluzapi ehé k'ū hé hécʰetuʃni?. Iyecʰīka xeyáp ináȝīpe **ló**.
11   B: Hā, hāk'u. icʰe?

1   A: Well, of all things! Grandson, that was no way to treat us **m**!
2   B: What do you mean by that?
3   A: What you did to us was exactly like what happens to a man who has taken a spoonful of the best tasting food, and chewed it with ecstasy, and then swallowed it most agreeably, and again opened his mouth for more; but this time, the second spoonful of the same fine food is brought to his lips, and the instant it touches his lips, it is immediately withdrawn, leaving him wanting more **m**.
4   B: Yes, perhaps, grandfather, but you know the audience had already been sitting there quite a while. The room was warm, and the seats uncomfortable, but there were so many speakers which made it bad. It was only out of consideration for you listeners that I did as I did **m**.
5   A: Oh, and you are the only one I really like to hear, too. I thought you would talk so satisfyingly!
6   B: But grandfather, there's just a chance that that was all I knew to say **m.surprise**!
7   A: Impossible!
8   C: My friend, why didn't you speak a little longer? It was obvious you had various worthwhile ideas which you had thought up and kept in mind, but all you did was "wise-crack" and then you sat down **m**.

9   B: Yes, I guess so; but really, don't you know, it was a sorrowful occasion. They
          are right who say that everything must end sometime **m**. On this day, the
          leadership of the Dakota has been taken away from the old men and given
          over to the young, and it affected my spirit, the very least bit **m**. On that
          account, I couldn't talk really seriously. It stuck in my throat **m**.
10   C: Of course, well, you are right. It seems that the old Dakota ways are really
          and truly at an end. But grandchild, you got only part of it right **m**. To say the
          leadership was wrested from the old men is not to put it accurately. Of their
          own accord, the old men have stepped aside **m**.
11   B: Yes, really; isn't it so? (Deloria 1937?: 212–20)

Authoritative male opinions often contain the use of *lo* even when not in
cases of overt public opinion-making, but I would argue that the frequency of
lo in these contexts makes this particular genre a prototype for its use. Women
who must make speeches and offer opinions in public contexts tell me they do
use *lo*, but that this in no way means that they are gay (a common interpretation). They know that the iconic use would mean that they would be expected
to act like men (have desire for women) because they are using the male particle,
but they are merely using the particle in its authoritative context (Trechter 2000).
They do so in professions that may have formerly been male-dominated.

Fractal recursivity occurs when this gender indicator is used in other contexts.
Even though *lo* suggests an authoritative stance, when males are not acting
particularly authoritatively, they may feel constrained to use it as the pressures
of iconization and recursivity act as semiotic forces. Deloria (*ca.* 1937: 306)
notes such an instance as a man (example (2)) speaks to her of his experiences
in *Wokiksikuye K'eya* 'Some Memories.'

> When the ending *lo* is used simply as a closing to a statement by a man who isn't
> trying to be authoritative, he sometimes "swallows" it instead of accenting it for
> emphasis. This informant does so constantly, except where he is quoting.

Unlike the speakers in example (1), this particular man was relating stories
about himself where he was truly frightened but kept his calm, or where he
appeared weak or silly to himself and others, but ultimately proved his strength
of character. In the introduction and conclusion to his story, his use of *lo*
reflects a narrative frame of a differently-authoritative self as it is "swallowed."

> (2):   *Introduction to "Some Memories"*
>   Oglálata tʰoká wahí k'ūhā wóixa wãʒígʒi awákʰipʰa k'éyaʃ iyúhaxcī wóixaʃni.?
>   Woyuʃ'iyaye nakū slolwáye **lo**. Yūkʰā wãʒi lecʰetū.
>   "When I first came among the Oglala, laughable experiences were mine but not
>   everything was funny. I also knew fear **m**. And one such time was as follows."
>   (Deloria *ca.* 1937: 306)

> (3):   *Conclusion to "Some Memories"*
>   maya-apʰaʒeʒe ekawĩgapi kĩ lecʰel wicʰūt'etaha wakpapte **lo**.
>   "I had just come through, escaping death just as one might turn about just at
>   the very rim of a cliff **m**."   (ibid.: 309)

This man's constrained use of *lo* in his introduction to his stories and in the conclusion in example (3) illustrates that he is under some pressure to display masculinity. Not all men do this. Because men are now constrained to use *lo* in a variety of discourse contexts, even when not speaking authoritatively or publicly, iconization and recursion for this form is rampant. Although the original meanings of authority and public opinion are still apparent through a thorough examination of discourse contexts, it has become an indicator of maleness rather than only one of stance, affect, or discourse context.

Erasure in the context of gendered discourse particles in Lakhota should by now be obvious. *Le*, the phonologically similar and iconically female assertive counterpart of *lo*, has become obsolescent. *Le* as a form was associated both with opinion and also with maternal care-giving. Although I have heard males use the form in a care-giving context (see Trechter, forthcoming, for a detailed analysis), it has not been refracted in numerous contexts. The form *kʃto* "emphatic" which is currently becoming the iconic counterpart of *lo* (see Rood and Taylor 1997) also does not seem to be a good candidate for broad recursive spread because it is often associated with the genre of gossip. It is perhaps the negative associations of some forms that marks them for a type of erasure even in cultures where the balance between men's and women's cultural activities and rights and semiotic resources is highly emphasized ("men say *x*; women say *y*").

5 Conclusion

Such a model of linguistic and semiotic differentiation is important to the treatment of language, gender, and ethnicity for three reasons: (1) it demonstrates how through iconization we establish categories of ethnic and gendered linguistic forms; (2) it demonstrates how and why gender are often mutual constructions as people draw on different voices for self and other representation; and (3) why certain populations, behaviors, genders, and ethnicities are continually effaced despite attempts to call attention to their presence. The academic study of language and gender is also a type of cultural community. As we examine the construction of linguistic differentiation, however, we as a community of practice are potentially susceptible to the same constructive ideological processes we are examining: iconization, recursivity, and erasure. Interestingly, the process of erasure has permeated not just the folk conceptualizations of language, gender, and ethnicity, but in reviewing this chapter, it is apparent that such erasure continues to be an unconscious process in current gender and ethnicity research. Recognizing previous erasure among academics of ethnic women's voices and styles – even those which are iconic within ethnic communities, Morgan, Galindo and Gonzales, and others make them more audible in gender and ethnic research. Goodwin and Mendoza-Denton draw our attention to hitherto unobserved competitiveness and stylistic differences in intra-group interactions among girls of different ethnicities, focusing on actual interaction, whereas Anzaldúa notes the possible erasure of ethnicity if performative theory is overly emphasized. Though much current work attends to current iconization of ethnic and gender language and subsequent recursivity through double-voiced uses (Barrett 1999; Hall 1995), there is still some danger of promulgating the practice of erasure at the academic, research level. In examining the process of recursivity and the liminal language or border crossings among urban and White youth, and the consequent creation of "new ethnicities" (Rampton 1995) or the appropriation of ethnic language in fraternities (Kiesling 2001), Morgan's critique of Labov's (1972a) work on ethnic vernacular springs to mind. The appropriation by trendy youth of ethnic varieties appears largely to be male practice. The question is whether ethnic appropriation by Whites is a male-gendered practice, or whether by unconsciously focusing attention primarily on boys and young men's appropriations, through repetition, the presence and practice of girls and women are erased.

In a variety of ways, language and gender researchers have sought to examine the connections between interactional work and the formation of ideology about gender and ethnicity while working to include greater diversity of gender and ethnic voices. Yet the complex semiotic processes associated with erasure cannot be addressed by only emphasizing alternative practices and voices that hitherto have been ignored. In the tradition of gender and language, Black and Coward (1981) early on encouraged a turning of the tables. Rather than only focusing on "women's language" to counteract men's historical hegemony and resulting erasure of women's voices, an important step to upsetting the hegemonic balance was men's recognition of themselves as also living within gendered subjectivities (see Johnson and Meinhof 1997). Similar challenges have been put forth by researchers in ethnic studies and the growing field of Whiteness studies (hooks 1992; Dyer 1997; Ignatiev and Garvey 1996), going so far as to claim that the objective of Whiteness studies is ultimately to eradicate such an ethnic category, partially through the realization of its hegemonic and destructive nature.

Although it may seem that there are already many studies done on gender and language about White folk, few of these engage with the topic by considering participants' *Whiteness* to be ethnic or this ethnicity to be part of their linguistic gender construction, leaving it unconsidered as an unmarked norm. A shift toward recognizing or marking White ethnicity in gender and language studies is not only important for complicating our view of ethnicity in the political realm; it is also a responsible research move. For in much of the research interactions described in this chapter, in the local network of interactions, Whiteness is not always the unmarked norm, though it may be taken up in that way by our academic community. For instance, Hartigan (1999), Modan (2001), and Trechter (2001) argue that in many locales – Detroit, Washington, DC, Pine Ridge Indian reservation, respectively – "whiteness" is clearly marked. Hillbillies living in predominantly African American neighborhoods in Detroit, for example, are ethnically marked in their local network because of their Whiteness, and also in the larger American context because of their obviously deviant non-middle-class White ethnicity. Bucholtz (2001: 96) argues that nerd speech, by being a hyperstandard White variety (non-appropriative of de-racialized African American English), "undermines the racial project of white-ness as a normative and unmarked construct." In effect, focusing the lens of gender and ethnicity in one direction only leads us to miss how the ideological and interactional processes of linguistic differentiation, erasure, and discrimi-nation operate.

Because sociolinguistic variables of gender and ethnicity are not consistently regarded in the same light within a community, "authentic" indicators, though salient, do not always become iconic representations for a community. For instance, Besnier (this volume) discusses how the most salient marker of iden-tity for the *fakaleitī* in Tonga is not always their linguistic orientation toward English and modernization, but their vocal pitch and ways of speaking. More-over, gender and ethnicity are often constructed in terms of each other, enabling erasure along the axis of either. For instance, "authentic" male ethnic language may be quite different from women's, but both are not always treated as equally ethnic by researchers or within a community. Schilling-Estes (1998) notes that speakers of Ocracoke English considered the most authentic ethnic speech (though she does not refer to it in racial terms) to be located in the speech of White men who have historical connections to traditional maritime occupations and who "play poker".[4] These men had exaggeratedly raised /ay/ and did not actually possess another typical feature of Ocracoke Island speech (fronted /aw/) to the degree of many other speakers, yet they were most often mentioned as "real" examples of the dialect by people on the island. She concludes that women and gay Ocracokan men who use fronted /aw/ and a less exaggerated pronunciation of /ay/ also have a strong sense of Ocracoke (ethnic) identity. Nevertheless, *erasure* takes place along a gendered axis within this community, because the speech of the poker players is held up as authentic and because the other common pronunciation feature is not analyzed as an identification marker. Ethnicity becomes *de facto* male as it is indexed by a poker-playing, maritime community of practice. Another com-mon kind of erasure takes place at the level of language and gender research. As the focus in Schilling-Este's study is the gendering of language and how community membership is linguistically and ideologically realized through gender, the construction of presumably White ethnicity is largely obscured.

The linguistic study of gender and ethnicity may have come a long way since the early 1970s, especially as notions of gender and ethnicity have been firmly rooted in social interaction and ideological promulgation, and more work on a greater diversity of voices is slowly being published. The workings of cultures (or models of them) are, however, not absolutes. One objective in reflecting on the processes of linguistic differentiation in culture is to destab-ilize the process and to effectively counteract the hegemonic force of erasure. Increased attention to how such erasure is accomplished at different levels of construction, both folk and in the academy, is now possible. However, there is still a great deal of work to be done in providing adequate data from a variety of languages, dialects, and ethnic perspectives. This chapter is a call to step up the work in both of these areas.

NOTES

I would like to thank the editors of this volume for their excellent comments, patience, and support, and Mary Bucholtz for her encouragement as well as thought-provoking discussions with me concerning markedness and Whiteness.

1   This "double effect" of recursivity has been one of the recurrent criticisms of drag queen speech that draws on stereotypic features of women's language: that it fails to destabilize the connection between the stereotype of women's speech and women, and in some interpretations actually reinforces it.

2   Ye_a and ye_e are pronounced the same, but trigger and undergo different morphophonemic processes. They are homophonous but definitely different morphemes (see Trechter, forthcoming).

3   For reasons of length, I omit the interlinear gloss of the original and only provide a running translation with the relevant gender particles highlighted and translated with *m.* (male assertion), *m.surprise*, etc. Lakhota transcription is in the International Phonetic Alphabet, with /c/ indicating an alveopalatal affricate.

4   One cannot be sure that these men are White in Schilling-Estes (1998). It is common practice not to mention race when research participants are White or easily subsumed into that category.

REFERENCES

Anderson, Benedict 1991: *Imagined Communities: Reflections on the Origin and Spread of Nationalism.* London: Verso.

Anzaldúa, Gloria 1987: *Borderlands/La Frontera: The New Mestiza.* San Francisco: Aunt Lute Books.

Anzaldúa, Gloria 1991: To(o) queer the writer – Loca, excritora y chicana. In Betsy Warland (ed.) *Writings by Dykes, Queers, and Lesbians.* Vancouver: Press Gang Publishers, pp. 249–63.

Barrett, Rusty 1997: The "homo-genius" speech community. In Anna Livia and Kira Hall (eds) *Queerly Phrased: Language, Gender, and Sexuality.* New York: Oxford University Press, pp. 181–201.

Barrett, Rusty 1998: Markedness and styleswitching in performances by African American drag queens. In Carol Myers-Scotton (ed.) *Codes and Consequences: Choosing Linguistic Varieties.* New York: Oxford University Press, pp. 139–61.

Barrett, Rusty 1999: Indexing polyphonous identity in the speech of African American drag queens. In Mary Bucholtz, Anita C. Liang, and Laurel A. Sutton (eds) *Reinventing Identities: The Gendered Self in Discourse*. New York: Oxford University Press, pp. 313–31.

Bergvall, Victoria, Bing, Janet, and Freed, Alice (eds) 1996: *Rethinking Language and Gender Research*. New York: Longman.

Black, Maria and Coward, Rosalind 1981: Linguistic, social and sexual relations: A review of Dale Spender's *Man Made Language*. Reprinted in Deborah Cameron (ed.) *The Feminist Critique of Language*. London: Routledge, pp. 111–33.

Bucholtz, Mary 1999: You da man: Narrating the racial other in the production of white masculinity. *Journal of Sociolinguistics* 3(4): 443–60.

Bucholtz, Mary 2001: The whiteness of nerds: Superstandard English and racial markedness. *Journal of Linguistic Anthropology* 11(1): 84–100.

Bucholtz, Mary, Liang, Anita C., and Sutton, Laurel A. (eds) 1999: *Reinventing Identities: The Gendered Self in Discourse*. New York: Oxford University Press.

Butler, Judith 1993: *Bodies That Matter: On the Discursive Limits of "Sex."* New York: Routledge.

Cameron, Deborah 1985: *Feminism and Linguistic Theory*. London: Macmillan.

Cameron, Deborah, Frazer, Elizabeth, Harvey, Penelope, Rampton, Ben, and Richardson, Kay (eds) 1992: *Researching Language: Issues of Power and Method*. London: Routledge.

Deloria, Ella 1937?: Dakota Ethnographic and Conversational Texts. MS 30 (x8a.7). Philadelphia: American Philosophical Society.

Deloria, Ella *ca*. 1937: Dakota Autobiographies. Bosas Collection, MS 30 (x8a.6). Philadelphia: American Philosophical Society.

Dyer, Richard 1997: *White*. New York: Routledge.

Eckert, Penelope 1989: The whole woman: Sex and gender differences in variation. *Language Variation and Change* 1: 245–67.

Eckert, Penelope and McConnell-Ginet, Sally 1992: Think practically and look locally: Language and gender as community-based practice. *Annual Review of Anthropology* 21: 461–90.

Foster, Michèle 1995: Are you with me?: Power and solidarity in the discourse of African American women. In Kira Hall and Mary Bucholtz (eds) *Gender Articulated: Language and the Socially Constructed Self*. New York: Routledge, pp. 329–50.

Galindo, Letticia 1999: Caló and taboo language use among Chicanas: A description of linguistic appropriation and innovation. In Letticia Galindo and María Dolores Gonzales (eds) *Speaking Chicana: Voice, Power and Identity*. Tucson: University of Arizona Press, pp. 175–93.

Galindo, D. Letticia and Gonzalez, María Dolores (eds) 1999: *Speaking Chicana: Voice, Power and Identity*. Tucson: University of Arizona Press.

Gaudio, Rudi 2001: White men do it too: Racialized (homo)sexualities in postcolonial Hausaland. *Journal of Linguistic Anthropology* 11(1): 36–51.

Goldstein, Tara 1995: "Nobody is talking bad": Creating community and claiming power on the production lines. In Kira Hall and Mary Bucholtz (eds) *Gender Articulated: Language and the Socially Constructed Self*. New York: Routledge, pp. 375–400.

Gonzales, María Dolores 1999: Crossing social and cultural borders: The road to language hybridity. In Letticia Galindo and María Dolores Gonzales (eds) *Speaking Chicana: Voice, Power and Identity.* Tucson: University of Arizona Press, pp. 13–38.

Goodwin, Marjorie Harness 1990: *He-Said-She-Said: Talk as Social Organization among Black Children.* Bloomington: Indiana University Press.

Goodwin, Marjorie Harness 1999: Constructing opposition within girls' games. In Mary Bucholtz, Anita C. Liang, and Laurel A. Sutton (eds) *Reinventing Identities: The Gendered Self in Discourse.* New York: Oxford University Press, pp. 388–409.

Hall, Kira 1995: Lip service on the fantasy lines. In Kira Hall and Mary Bucholtz (eds) *Gender Articulated: Language and the Socially Constructed Self.* New York: Routledge, pp. 183–216.

Hall, Kira and Bucholtz, Mary 1995: *Gender Articulated: Language and the Socially Constructed Self.* New York: Routledge.

Hartigan, John 1999: *Racial Situations: Class Predicaments of Whiteness in Detroit.* Princeton, NJ: Princeton University Press.

Hewitt, Roger 1986: *White Talk Black Talk.* Cambridge: Cambridge University Press.

Hill, Jane 1987: Women's speech in modern Mexicano. In Susan Philips, Susan Steele, and Christine Tanz (eds) *Language, Gender and Sex in Comparative Perspective.* Cambridge: Cambridge University Press, pp. 121–60.

hooks, bell 1992: *Black Looks: Race and Representation.* Boston: South End Press.

Ignatiev, Noel and Garvey, John (eds) 1996: *Race Traitor.* New York: Routledge.

Irvine, Judith 2001: "Style" as distinctiveness: The culture and ideology of linguistic differentiation. In Penelope Eckert and John R. Rickford (eds) *Stylistic Variation in Language.* Cambridge: Cambridge University Press, pp. 21–43.

Irvine, Judith and Gal, Susan 2000: Language ideology and linguistic differentiation. In Paul Kroskrity (ed.) *Regimes of Language: Ideologies, Polities, and Identities.* Santa Fe, NM: School of American Research Press, pp. 35–84.

Johnson, Sally and Meinhof, Ulrike Hanna (eds) 1997: *Language and Masculinity.* Oxford: Blackwell.

Kiesling, Scott 2001: Stances of whiteness and hegemony in fraternity men's discourse. *Journal of Linguistic Anthropology* 11(1): 101–15.

Kulick, Don 2000: Gay and lesbian language. *Annual Review of Anthropology* 29: 243–85.

Labov, William 1972a: *Language in the Inner City: Studies in the Black English Vernacular.* Philadelphia: University of Pennsylvania Press.

Labov, William 1972b: *Sociolinguistic Patterns.* Philadelphia: University of Pennsylvania Press.

Lakoff, Robin 1975: *Language and Woman's Place.* New York: Harper & Row.

Livia, Anna and Hall, Kira (eds) 1997a: *Queerly Phrased: Language, Gender, and Sexuality.* New York: Oxford University Press.

Livia, Anna and Hall, Kira 1997b: "It's a girl!": Bringing performativity back to linguistics. In Anna Livia and Kira Hall (eds) *Queerly Phrased: Language, Gender, and Sexuality.* New York: Oxford University Press, pp. 3–18.

Medicine, Beatrice 1987: The role of American Indian women in cultural continuity and transition. In Joyce Penfield (ed.) *Women and Language in*

Transition. New York: State University of New York Press, pp. 159–65.

Mendoza-Denton, Norma 1999a: Sociolinguistics and linguistic anthropology of US Latinos. *Annual Review of Anthropology* 28: 375–95.

Mendoza-Denton, Norma 1999b: Turn initial *no*: Collaborative opposition among Latina adolescents. In Mary Bucholtz, Anita C. Liang, and Laurel A. Sutton (eds) *Reinventing Identities: The Gendered Self in Discourse*. New York: Oxford University Press, pp. 273–92.

Meyerhoff, Miriam 1996: Dealing with gender identity as a sociolinguistic variable. In Victoria Bergvall, Janet Bing, and Alice Freed (eds) *Rethinking Language and Gender Research*. New York: Longman, pp. 202–27.

Modan, Gabriella 1994: Pulling apart is coming together: The use and meaning of opposition in the discourse of Jewish American women. In Mary Bucholtz, Anita C. Liang, Laurel Sutton, and Caitlin Hines (eds) *Cultural Performances: Proceedings of the Third Berkeley Women and Language Conference*. Berkeley, CA: Berkeley Women and Language Group, University of California, pp. 501–8.

Modan, Gabriella 2001: White, whole wheat, rye: Jews and ethnic construction in Washington, D.C. *Journal of Linguistic Anthropology* 11(1): 116–30.

Morgan, Marcyliena 1999: No woman no cry: Claiming African American women's place. In Mary Bucholtz, Anita C. Liang, and Laurel A. Sutton (eds) *Reinventing Identities: The Gendered Self in Discourse*. New York: Oxford University Press, pp. 27–45.

Myers-Scotton, Carol 1998: A theoretical introduction to the markedness model. In Carol Myers-Scotton (ed.) *Codes and Consequences: Choosing Linguistic Varieties*. New York: Oxford, University Press, pp. 18–39.

Nichols, Patricia 1983: Linguistic options and choices for Black women in the rural South. In Barrie Thorne, Cheris Kramarae, and Nancy Henley (eds) *Language, Gender and Society*. Rowley, MA: Newbury House, pp. 54–68.

Ochs, Elinor 1992: Indexing gender. In Alessandro Duranti and Charles Goodwin (eds) *Rethinking Context: Language as an Interactive Phenomenon*. Cambridge: Cambridge University Press, pp. 335–58.

Orellana, Marjorie Faulstich 1999: Good guys and bad girls: Identity construction by Latina and Latino student writers. In Mary Bucholtz, Anita C. Liang, and Laurel Sutton (eds) *Reinventing Identities: The Gendered Self in Discourse*. New York: Oxford University Press, pp. 64–82.

Pratt, Mary Louise 1987: Linguistic utopias. In Nigel Fabb, Derek Attridge, Alan Durant, and Colin MacCabe (eds) *The Linguistics of Writing: Arguments between Language and Literature*. Manchester: Manchester University Press, pp. 48–66.

Queen, Robin 1997: I don't speak spritch: Locating lesbian language. In Anna Livia and Kira Hall (eds) *Queerly Phrased: Language, Gender, and Sexuality*. New York: Oxford University Press, pp. 233–56.

Rampton, Ben 1991: Interracial Panjabi in a British adolescent peer group. *Language in Society* 20(3): 391–422.

Rampton, Ben 1995: *Crossing: Language and Identity among Adolescents*. London: Longman.

Rood, David and Taylor, Alan 1997: A Lakhota sketch. In William Sturtevant and Ives Goddard (eds)

Handbook of North American Indians, vol. 17. Washington, DC: Smithsonian Institution, pp. 440–82.

Schilling-Estes, Natalie 1998: Reshaping economies, reshaping identities: Gender-based patterns of language variation in Ocracoke English. In Suzanne Wertheim, Ashlee C. Bailey, and Monica Corston-Oliver (eds) *Engendering Communication: Proceedings of the Fifth Berkeley Women and Language Conference.* Berkeley, CA: Berkeley Women and Language Group, University of California, pp. 509–20.

Trechter, Sara 1999: Contextualizing the exotic few: Gender oppositions in Lakhota. In Mary Bucholtz, Anita C. Liang, and Laurel A. Sutton (eds) *Reinventing Identities: The Gendered Self in Discourse.* New York: Oxford University Press, pp. 101–22.

Trechter, Sara 2000: Review of *Queerly Phrased*. *Language* 76(2): 444–6.

Trechter, Sara 2001: White between the lines: Ethnic positioning in Lakhota discourse. *Journal of Linguistic Anthropology* 11(1): 22–35.

Trechter, Sara forthcoming: *Gendered Voices in Lakhota.* New York: Oxford University Press.

Trechter, Sara and Bucholtz, Mary 2001: White noise: Bringing language into whiteness studies. *Journal of Linguistic Anthropology* 11(1): 3–21.

Trudgill, Peter 1974: *The Social Differentiation of English in Norwich.* Cambridge: Cambridge University Press.

Urciuoli, Bonnie 1995: Language and borders. *Annual Review of Anthropology* 23: 55–82.

Walters, Suzanna 1996: From here to queer: Radical feminism, postmodernism, and the lesbian menace. *Signs* 21: 831–69.

Zentella, Ana Celia 1998: Spanish Madonnas: U.S. Latinas and language loyalty. In Suzanne Wertheim, Ashlee Bailey, and Monica Corston-Oliver (eds) *Engendering Communication: Proceedings from the Fifth Berkeley Women and Language Conference.* Berkeley, CA: Berkeley Women and Language Group, University of California, pp. 637–52.

Part IV
Stereotypes and Norms

19 Gender and Language Ideologies

DEBORAH CAMERON

1 Introduction

Language ideologies have emerged in recent years as a distinct focus for research and debate among sociolinguists and linguistic anthropologists (see e.g. Schieffelin, Woolard, and Kroskrity 1998). The term "language ideologies" is generally used in this literature to refer to sets of *representations* through which language is imbued with cultural meaning for a certain community. In these representations of language, certain themes recur: examples include where and how language originated, why languages differ from one another and what that means, how children learn to speak, and how language should properly be used. Accounts of these matters may be more or less widely diffused. Some myths of linguistic origin, for example, are localized to a single small community; others, such as the biblical account in the Book of Genesis of Adam naming God's creatures, have been much more widely disseminated. A more recent example of a "diffused" ideology of language is the representation of ancestral vernacular languages as privileged carriers of the identity or spirit of a people. Originating in the thought of German-speaking philosophers and historically associated with the political ideology of nationalism, this language ideology has spread and persisted: it remains salient in the post-colonial and post-Cold War debates of the present day.

It is worth commenting briefly on the definition of language ideologies in terms of *representations* of language rather than, say, *beliefs* or *attitudes* relating to it. The term "ideology" is often used in ordinary discourse to denote beliefs or belief systems (e.g. "communism," "feminism," "racism"), and it is especially likely to be used in connection with belief systems which the speaker takes to be misguided and/or partisan. Explicitly or implicitly, "ideology" is opposed to "truth" (or sometimes more specifically to "science," as a mode of thinking which makes particularly strong claims to truth). One reason why academic commentators prefer not to equate "language ideology" with "beliefs about language" is precisely to avoid this common-sense identification of ideology with false or objectionable beliefs. The linguist's axiom "all languages are equal" will probably be regarded by readers of this book as both scientifically "true" and socially "progressive" – which is to say, neither false nor objectionable – but it is nevertheless also "ideological." It is part of a "liberal" ideology which has deeply influenced the social and human sciences since the mid-twentieth century. This example also shows why "language ideologies" cannot be equated simply with folklinguistic stereotypes (see Talbot, this volume).

In addition, such terms as "attitude" and "belief" denote, or are commonly assumed to denote, *mental* constructs which essentially "belong" to individuals. Ideologies, by contrast, are *social* constructs: they are ways of understanding the world that emerge from interaction with particular (public) representations of it. The study of language ideologies, then, involves examining the texts and practices in which languages are represented – not only spoken and written but also spoken and written *about*. It is from these representations that language users learn how linguistic phenomena are conventionally understood in their culture. That need not imply, however, that they internalize a particular understanding as a set of fixed beliefs: representation is also a means for *contesting* current understandings of language and creating new alternatives.

Challenging established ideologies of language has been among the aims of many social and political movements, including feminism. Nineteenth- and twentieth-century feminist writings on language took up the subject of what I have been calling "language ideologies" long before that term was used in its present scholarly sense. It was a salient issue for feminists because of the salience of gender itself in many (pre- and non-feminist) representations of language. Ideas about how women and men use language, and how they ought ideally to use it, have been a recurring theme in discourse about language produced by many societies in many historical periods. Women in particular have also been prime targets for the kind of ideological discourse I have elsewhere labelled "verbal hygiene" (Cameron 1995), which sets out actively to intervene in language use with the aim of making it conform to some idealized representation.

These observations suggest a number of questions which need to be considered in an essay about gender and language ideologies. How has the relationship between language and gender been represented in different times and places, and what purposes have been served by representing it in particular ways? Has political (feminist) intervention succeeded in changing the repertoire of representations? How and to what extent do ideological representations of the language/gender relationship inform everyday linguistic and social practice among real women and men?

Before I examine these questions in more detail, though, it is relevant to consider the more general question of what ideological work is done by representations of language. In an earlier discussion (Cameron 1995), I argued that many such representations belong to a "double discourse" in which language is simultaneously both itself and a symbolic substitute for something else.

Pronouncements on the "proper" uses of language at one level express the desire to control and impose order on *language*, but at another level they express desires for order and control in other spheres. Putting language to rights becomes a surrogate for putting the world to rights. One familiar example of this is the persistent equation of grammatical "correctness" with law-abiding behavior, and of failure to follow prescriptive grammatical rules with lawlessness or amorality.

Recent writers on language ideologies have also called attention to their symbolic dimension, the sense in which they are always concerned with more than just the linguistic issues they purport to be about. Kathryn Woolard (1998: 4) quotes Raymond Williams: "a representation of language is always a representation of human beings in the world," while Susan Gal (1995: 171) reminds us that ideas about what is desirable in language are always "systematically related to other areas of cultural discourse such as the nature of persons, of power, and of a desirable moral order." These insights are highly relevant to any analysis of representations which focus on the relation of language to gender. In many cases it is not difficult to argue that the underlying subject of these representations is gender itself: one purpose of making statements about men's or women's language is to instruct the hearer or reader in what counts as gender-appropriate behavior. To take a now notorious example, Otto Jespersen's assertion that ". . . women exercise a great and universal influence on linguistic development through their instinctive shrinking from coarse and vulgar expressions and their preference for refined and (in certain spheres) veiled and indirect expressions" (1922: 246) is readily understood as an expression of what were at the time mainstream societal views on proper femininity.

Yet the idea of the "double discourse" suggests that language does not only stand in for other things when it is represented, it also remains "itself." It might be observed, for instance, that Jespersen's assertion about women's linguistic refinement is not only a representation of gender, it is also part of a discourse on the supposed nature of language. If you read the whole chapter in which Jespersen expounds on the subject of "The Woman," it becomes clear that he is adopting a view of languages as ideally balanced between "masculine" and "feminine" elements. The natural inclinations of men are needed to give a language "variety and vigour," while those of women are needed to keep it within the bounds of propriety that civilized society requires. As well as telling us something about historical understandings of gender, this tells us something about historical understandings of language.

2 Representing Language and Gender: Uniformity and Diversity

Jespersen's chapter "The Woman" provides us with a prototypical example, from early twentieth-century Europe, of what is probably the most general, most culturally widespread, and most historically persistent of all language ideologies pertaining to gender: that there are clear-cut, stable differences in the way language is used by women and by men. In many versions of this ideology the differences are seen as natural, and in most they are seen as desirable. Beyond that, however, representations of gendered linguistic behavior are extremely variable historically and culturally. From the most accessible popular texts on the subject (e.g. Lakoff 1975; Spender 1980; Tannen 1990) it would be easy to get the impression that women have always and everywhere been measured against a similar linguistic ideal, constituted by such qualities as reticence, modesty, deference, politeness, empathy, supportiveness, and cooperation. On inspection, however, the picture is more complicated.

Joel Sherzer (1987) has suggested one useful overarching generalization: that in any community the normal linguistic behavior of women and men will be represented in ways congruent with the community's more general representation of the essential natures of the two groups. If women are said to be "naturally" modest, for example, their speech will be represented as expressing that modesty – community members may explain that "women don't like to speak in public," for instance. In observed reality, there may be little evidence for this generalization, or the evidence may be contradictory. Or it may be that women do indeed behave "modestly," precisely because the representation of women as modest has the force of a norm, which is enforced in various ways (e.g. denying women the opportunity to practice speaking in public, or sanctioning individual women who are insufficiently reticent). Women themselves may actively try to conform to prevailing ideals of feminine behavior, though the effort and calculation this often demands makes clear that the behavior in question is not simply "natural."

As Sherzer also points out, while the assumption that women's language proceeds from women's nature is culturally very widespread, there is considerable cross-cultural variation in precisely what "women's nature," and therefore women's language, is taken to consist of. Jespersen thought women more "refined" than men, and claimed that this was reflected in women's instinctive avoidance of coarse, vulgar, and abusive language. In the Papua New Guinea village of Gapun, however, a distinctive genre of speech called a *kros* in Tok Pisin, which is a tirade of obscene verbal abuse delivered in monologue, is represented by villagers as a primarily female genre (Kulick 1993). Women in this community are not regarded as more reticent, delicate, or verbally cooperative than men. Among the Malagasy of Madagascar, a highly valued traditional style of speech known as *kabary*, which is characterized by a high degree of indirectness, is associated with men, on the grounds that women are by nature direct speakers (Keenan 1974). Among Western anglophones, by contrast, the opposite belief prevails: men are supposed to be more direct speakers than women.

It is also the case that cultural representations of gendered speech may change over time. The ideal most frequently criticized by feminists – that of the modest, deferential, and publicly silent woman – is sometimes presented as if it had prevailed throughout recorded history, but in some times and places, the ideal woman speaker was represented very differently. In a discussion of the "conduct books" which instructed readers in proper behavior from the medieval period onward, Ann Rosalind Jones (1987) observes that texts of this genre addressed to upper-class women in the royal courts of Renaissance Europe were very far from exhorting women to be silent and deferential. On the contrary, the court lady was expected to hold her own in verbal duels and witty exchanges which took place in public and in mixed company. The "silent woman" ideal with which we are now more familiar emerged, Jones argues, with the rise to prominence of the European bourgeoisie. Especially where they espoused puritan religious beliefs, the bourgeois class had different notions of the proper relationship between women and men. Conduct literature written for a bourgeois readership emphasized the subordination of wives to husbands, and the confinement of women to the domestic sphere. The specifically linguistic corollary of this can be seen in the following extract from a 1614 conduct book entitled *A Godly Forme of Household Gouernmente* (quoted in Armstrong and Tennenhouse 1987: 8). The respective linguistic duties of men and women in a household are graphically laid out in two columns:

Husband	*Wife*
Deal with many men	Talk with few
Be "entertaining"	Be solitary and withdrawn
Be skillfull in talk	Boast of silence

Jones also points out that bourgeois conduct literature was often intended as an implicit or explicit critique of the "decadent" aristocracy. The license of aristocratic women to speak freely in public was represented in bourgeois texts as a sign of the immorality of the upper classes. Discourse on the ideal of the silent woman, then, was not just part of an ideology of gender, but also played a part in an ideological conflict between social classes. In this particular conflict, the bourgeoisie were the eventual victors. Over time, Jones observes, gender norms which were once specifically bourgeois would be adopted by the upper class as well, becoming an ideal to which women in general were exhorted to aspire. In later eras, the withdrawn and reticent middle-class woman would be favorably contrasted not with the articulate but immoral aristocrat, but with the vulgar and undisciplined working-class woman. Even today, in British English at least, a loose and vulgar female tongue is still sometimes figured in the person of the "fishwife," though few people have ever encountered a real member of that traditional occupational category.

The examples just given remind us that there is *intra-* as well as intercultural variation in the representation of language and gender. From outside a culture this variation may not be salient or even visible, but inside, the representation of differences *between* women, or between men, does ideological work. The "fishwife," for example, represents a supposedly general (not just gendered) characteristic of low-status speakers – their lack of refinement compared to higher-status speakers. The effect of the interaction of class and gender representations is to define low-status women as "unfeminine." Or, we could consider the commonplace representation (which is not confined to a single culture[1]) of Asian speakers – of both sexes – as more reticent and polite than Western speakers. The interaction between ethnic and gendered representations in this case leads to the stereotypical perception of Asian women as "superfeminine." Though this stereotype can be exploited for its positive value (in parts of the sex industry, for instance, and by the Asian airlines who use the subservience of their female cabin crew as a selling point), it can also prompt more negative evaluations of Asian women as *excessively* feminine. The work done by representations like these is to establish a norm of desirable feminine behavior which is identified with a particular *kind* of femininity – in the cases I have used as examples here, the norm is White, Western, and middle-class. Of course, the norm is not necessarily an accurate description of the way White middle-class women in a given community really behave: rather, it is a representation incorporating the characteristics ideologically ascribed to them as female members of a favored social group. But the way "other" women are represented foregrounds the idea that they are *different* from the norm – just as women-in-general are typically represented as different from the "human" norm, that is, from men.

Ideologies of language and gender, then, are specific to their time and place: they vary across cultures and historical periods, and they are inflected by representations of other social characteristics such as class and ethnicity. What is constant is the insistence that in any identifiable social group, women and men are *different*. Gender differences are frequently represented as complementarities, that is, whatever men's language is, women's language is not. But as the examples in the above discussion illustrate, there may be great variation in the actual substance of claims about how men and women speakers differ from or complement one another.

Whatever their substance, though, these representations of gender and language are part of a society's apparatus for maintaining gender distinctions in general – they help to naturalize the notion of the sexes as "opposite," with differing aptitudes and social responsibilities (see Talbot, this volume). In many cases they also help to naturalize gender *hierarchies*. Jespersen may praise the "refinement" he attributes to women speakers, but this quality is readily invoked to exclude women from certain spheres of activity on the grounds they are too refined to cope with the linguistic demands of, say, military service. Among the Malagasy and in Gapun, the qualities attributed to men's speech are also ones the society accords particular respect to. In these communities too, we find women being excluded or marginalized from certain important public forums, in part because it is supposed they cannot master the appropriate public language.

Here it may be as well to remind ourselves that ideological representations do not, in and of themselves, accomplish the exclusion, marginalization, or subordination of women. Their particular role in those processes is to make the relationship of women and men in a given society appear natural and legitimate rather than merely arbitrary and unjust. Conversely, attacks on particular representations (such as feminist criticisms of the idea that women are "naturally" silent/modest/delicate) do not in and of themselves produce changes in the position of a subordinate group. Rather, they help to undermine the legitimacy of the present order, the sense that the way things are is desirable, natural, and immutable. If enough people can be induced to doubt that the status quo is natural or legitimate, a climate is created in which demands for change are much harder for their opponents to resist.

Feminist demands for change have often included demands that restrictions on women's linguistic behavior be removed, and those demands have often been supported by criticism of the ideological representations which justified the restrictions. The 1848 Seneca Falls Convention, a landmark event in nineteenth-century American feminism, demanded for instance that women be accepted as speakers at mixed public gatherings such as political meetings, attacking the argument that public speaking was incompatible with respectable femininity. Christian religious women have challenged the idea that women cannot be effective preachers (an argument often deployed by opponents of women's ordination to the priesthood). These challenges have been successful: while for a variety of reasons it remains true that discourse in many public forums is dominated by men, the argument that women should not be permitted to speak publicly because it is indecent, or because they are incompetent to do so, have been fairly decisively discredited. When these arguments are heard today, they are widely perceived as eccentric and reactionary; and when instances from the past are cited (such as the solemn debate within the BBC during the 1970s on whether a woman television newsreader would so inflame male viewers' passions as to render them incapable of concentrating on current events) they are received with incredulity. In the matter of women's public speech, at least, mainstream ideologies of language and gender have changed dramatically in recent decades.

In the very last decade of the twentieth century, another shift in representations of language and gender began to become apparent. In the following sections I will examine this shift, exploring what it might tell us about changing concepts of both gender and language.

3 Shifting Ideological Landscapes: The Fall and Rise of "Women's Language"

Much of the feminist criticism produced on the subject of language ideologies since the mid-1970s has addressed itself in particular to the idea, implied if not stated in most mainstream representations of "women's language," that women are linguistically *inferior* to men. The tradition of commentary that

1970s feminists inherited portrayed women's language by and large as a deviation from the (implicitly masculine) norm, and this deviance tended to be evaluated in negative terms. Despite Jespersen's overt championing of male/ female complementarity, it is difficult not to read his account of male/female differences as sexist – not merely stereotypical but biased in favor of men's alleged vigor, creativity, and more complex sentence structure. Early feminist commentators, most notably Robin Lakoff (1975), also made use of what would now be labeled a "deficit model," according to which women's characteristic way of speaking was, indeed, a factor making women unsuitable candidates for positions of public authority and responsibility. Feminists, however, differed from prefeminists like Jespersen in pointing out that women were not "naturally" weak and deferential speakers: rather they were socialized into "feminine" ways of behaving, in a sexist society which systematically strove to keep women in their (subordinate) place. Nevertheless, the solution proposed by many feminists was for women to adopt alternative and "better" ways of speaking. This was the idea behind, for example, "assertiveness training" for women (Cameron 1995; Crawford 1995; Gervasio and Crawford 1989). The late twentieth-century equivalents of conduct literature (self-help books, radio and TV talkshows, and articles in women's magazines, for example) often advised women in a more piecemeal manner on how to be taken more seriously by deliberately eschewing such "women's language" features as high pitch, "swoopy" intonation, expansive body language, allowing oneself to be interrupted, phrasing commands in the form of questions, adding question tags to statements, and producing declaratives with rising intonation. As I have argued elsewhere (Cameron 1995), a good deal of this advice implicitly boils down to "talk [more] like a man" – or more exactly, perhaps, since we are dealing here with representations rather than empirical realities, "try to approximate the popular linguistic stereotype of a man."

This kind of guidance still circulates, but the climate in which it now exists is no longer one in which it is generally assumed that women are "deficient" as language users. On the contrary, more and more mainstream discourse on language and gender stresses the opposite proposition – that women are actually *superior* to men. The problem of the unassertive or insecure woman speaker may not have disappeared entirely, but it is increasingly being eclipsed by anxiety about a quite different phenomenon, namely the problem of the inarticulate, linguistically unskilled man. In the new deficit model, it is men who are represented as deficient, and women whose ways of speaking are frequently recommended as a model for them to emulate. To illustrate this point, I will reproduce a number of texts in which the proposition "women are superior language users" is explicitly or implicitly asserted.

Example (1) comes from an advertisement, part of an extended multimedia advertising campaign run by British Telecom (the UK's largest provider of telephone services) in the late 1990s. The idea that men should emulate women's styles of speaking was central to this campaign, a primary goal of which (according to a spokesperson for the advertising agency) was to encourage men to make more extended telephone calls, after market research had found significant differences in men's and women's attitudes to talking on the phone. Here I reproduce part of the text of a print advertisement, which provides a particularly striking example of the strategy BT's advertisers adopted (in fact it is the first part of a text whose second part is quoted by Talbot, this volume; see also Talbot 2000). It should be acknowledged, by the way, that this strategy includes some degree of irony: it is not clear that the claims made about gender difference (e.g. "men make phone calls standing up") are meant to be taken at face value. However, even if these claims are made entirely in jest (which is not clear either), the joke depends on readers' familiarity with the more "serious" discourse they allude to. Serious or not, then, this text affirms certain generalizations about language and gender as "common knowledge."

> (1): *British Telecom advertisement*
> *(Radio Times* magazine, December 1994)
> Men and women communicate differently. Have you noticed? Women like to sit down to make phone calls. They know that getting in touch is much more important than what you actually say. Men adopt another position. They stand up. Their body language says this message will be short, sharp and to the point. "Meet you down the pub, all right?" That's a man's call. Women can't understand why men are so abrupt. Why can't they share the simple joys of talking as other men have? "Conversation is one of the greatest pleasures of life. But it wants leisure." W. Somerset Maugham. Or, as another writer said, "The conversation of women is like the straw around china. Without it, everything would be broken."

Example (2) comes from an interview conducted by two sociologists with the manager of a call center in the northeast of England. Call centers are workplaces where employees sell products and/or provide customer services by telephone: they are a rapidly growing sector of the "new" hi-tech service economy. In this extract from the interview transcript, the manager is explaining why the call center operators he recruits are predominantly women, even though his center is in an area of high unemployment where any job attracts numerous applicants of both sexes.

> (2): *Interview with a call center manager*
> (Tyler and Taylor 1997: 10)
> . . . We are looking for people who can chat to people, interact, build rapport. What we find is that women can do this more, they're definitely more natural when they do it anyway. It doesn't sound as forced, perhaps they're used to doing it all the time anyway . . . women are naturally good at that sort of thing. I think they have a higher tolerance level than men . . . I suppose we do, yes, if we're honest about it, select women sometimes because they are women rather than because of anything they've particularly shown at the interview.

Example (3) comes from an advice booklet with the subtitle *How To Get More Out of Life Through Better Conversations* (BT 1997). Like example (1), this was produced on behalf of British Telecom, but for a different purpose. It was part of a community service project undertaken by BT under the heading "TalkWorks," which involved producing and distributing learning materials on the theme of "better communication." This particular text was written by an external consultant, with the assistance of a qualified psychologist and counsellor. It was available at no charge to any UK household requesting it (i.e. not just customers of BT), and more than two million copies were distributed in the 18 months following its appearance.

> (3): *Advice booklet*
>   (British Telecom 1997: 17–18)
>   Just as we can only get to know about another person's "real self" through
>   their words, we can only become familiar with our own real self by commun-
>   icating openly and fully with other people. Conversation, it turns out, is the
>   best way we have of exploring the full range and diversity of our own thoughts,
>   memories and emotions . . . talking candidly about ourselves not only helps
>   other people get to know us, it also helps us to get to know ourselves and
>   be more genuine. . . . Some people actively struggle to avoid becoming known
>   by other people. We now know that this struggle can lead to a form of stress
>   which is capable of producing a whole set of physical and emotional
>   problems . . . As a rule, women are more comfortable with talking about their
>   real selves than men. Women also live longer than men. This may not be a
>   coincidence.

Example (4) comes from a document entitled *Boys and English*, produced by a British government agency, the Office for Standards in Education, in 1993. The function of Ofsted is to assess and monitor the standards achieved by schools in England and Wales; it also issues guidance to schools on improving standards. This text is addressing a subject that has featured prominently in discussions of education in Britain since the late 1990s, namely the academic "under-achievement" of boys relative to girls. It summarizes recent research findings and offers guidance on how boys could be helped to do better in English, a subject where the gender gap in achievement is particularly striking.

> (4): *Ofsted Report on Boys and English*
>   (1993: 16, emphasis in original)
>   [Boys] were more likely [than girls] to interrupt one another, to argue openly
>   and to voice opinions strongly. They were also less likely to listen carefully to
>   and build upon one another's contributions . . . *It is particularly important for
>   boys to develop a clearer understanding of the importance of sympathetic listening as a
>   central feature of successful group and class discussion.*

These texts show how pervasive a particular representation of language and gender has become in recent years, at least in the UK where all four examples were produced. The texts are drawn from different genres, including both "popular" ones like advertising and advice literature, and "expert" ones like the Ofsted report. They represent language and gender differences in a range of contexts: personal relationships (examples (1) and (3)), work (example (2)) and education (example (4)). But what they say about language and gender is essentially similar: each one represents the verbal behavior of men as in some way problematic, and contrasts it unfavorably with the behavior of women in the same situation. In all four texts the "problem" is defined explicitly or implicitly as a lack of skill in using language for the purpose of creating and maintaining rapport with other people. Males in these texts do not spend sufficient time interacting with friends and relatives, do not share their feelings and problems openly, cannot chat to customers in a "natural" manner, and are unable to listen "sympathetically" in group discussions designed to promote learning. These deficiencies are represented as having serious consequences for men, including educational underachievement (example (4)), unemployment (example (2)), personal unhappiness and even premature death (example (3)).

The consistent focus on men's communicational shortcomings in these texts (and many others which I do not have space to reproduce) marks a real shift in public discourse on men, women, and language. For most of the 1970s and 1980s, representations of language and gender – both popular and expert – focused either on women's alleged shortcomings as language users (e.g. their lack of skill in public speaking and performance genres such as comedy or political debate) or else, where discussion was informed by feminist ideas, on the relationship between women's speech styles and their subordinate position in society. Even those feminists who valued women's language positively were apt to represent it as an obstacle to women's advancement because of the widespread prejudice it inspired. Today, by contrast, women are regularly represented as model language users: their verbal skills are seen, moreover, as central to what is portrayed as the fulfillment of that old prophecy, "the future is female." Compared to their male peers, today's women and girls are said to be doing better in education, gaining employment more easily, living happier as well as longer lives – and it is suggested that they owe this good fortune at least partly to their linguistic accomplishments.

What accounts for this shift, and how should it be interpreted? A number of possibilities suggest themselves. One might be that the new representations reflect real gains made by feminism since the 1970s. The value of women's ways of doing things has been recognized, and women are finally getting the (material and symbolic) rewards they deserved all along. Another possibility is that on the contrary, all this discourse about women's superiority is intended to distract attention from factual evidence suggesting that in material reality, women are still "the second sex." It is evident, for instance, that women's superior educational qualifications have not translated into higher-status and better-paid jobs: one Australian study found that boys leaving school with low levels of literacy were soon out-earning not only girls with similar qualifications, but also girls who had left school with high or very high levels of literacy

(Gilbert 1998). There is still a significant gender gap in earnings, and women remain more likely than men to end their lives in poverty.

In the following section, however, I will argue that the shift toward a language ideology of female superiority and male deficit is neither a simple case of successful feminist intervention in a tradition of sexist representations, nor straightforwardly part of a "backlash" discourse in which feminism has "gone too far," leaving men as the new victims of sexist oppression. I would agree that these are both elements in the new discourse of female verbal superiority. But that discourse, in my view, is more fundamentally a product of changing ideals concerning language itself – what it is for, and what constitutes skill in using it. In contemporary Western societies, recent social changes have given new value to linguistic genres and styles that were and are symbolically associated with femininity. It is this development, more than any radical change in gender relations as such, that underlies the new discourse of female verbal superiority.

4   "Communication": The Language Ideology of Late Modernity?

In the foregoing section I have referred to the "female verbal superiority" discourse as instantiating a *change* in the way gendered language is represented. Yet readers might well ask themselves how much has really changed. The idea that women are better than men at sharing their feelings or listening sympathetically to others is hardly novel: on the contrary, it is a hoary old stereotype. Complaints about men's taciturnity, insensitivity, and lack of emotional openness are not new either. And the idea that women are more inclined to use talk as a means for maintaining close relationships, and are more skilled at doing so than men, was emphasized in a number of spectacularly successful self-help and advice texts published in the early 1990s, notably Deborah Tannen's *You Just Don't Understand* (1990) and John Gray's *Men are from Mars, Women are from Venus* (1992). However, neither Tannen nor Gray overtly argued for the superiority of women. Rather, both took the line that the sexes are "different but equal" and need to understand and accept one another's differences in order to avoid misunderstandings. Nevertheless, their texts seem to have been read by many people as implicitly suggesting that women are superior and that men would do well to emulate them. Subsequent works of advice literature (example (3), for instance) have drawn that conclusion more explicitly. What has changed, then, is not the dominant stereotypes of men's and women's linguistic behavior, but the value judgments made on that behavior. And the obvious question is, why?

To put briefly what I have argued at greater length elsewhere (Cameron 2000), the conditions obtaining in late modern societies have given rise to a new linguistic ideal: the skilled interpersonal communicator who excels in such verbal activities as cooperative problem-solving, rapport-building, emotional self-reflexivity and self-disclosure, "active" listening, and the expression of empathy. If we ask what it is about contemporary life that brings this ideal to the fore, two important considerations immediately suggest themselves. One is the changing nature of work in the global economy, especially in post-industrial societies where most work is no longer about manufacturing objects, but rather involves selling services. Service sector workers are required to engage intensively in interaction with other people. And this interaction is not purely instrumental in nature, but foregrounds the interpersonal functions of language. A good server does not just provide efficient service, s/he creates rapport with customers, making them feel that they are individually valued and cared for, and that their needs are more important than the server's own. It is a role that has elements of both nurturance and low status or powerlessness – qualities which also figure in many familiar representations of "women's language." Hence the assertion by the call center manager quoted in example (2) above that women are more "naturally" suited than men to customer service work.

The other relevant consideration is the changing nature of *personal* life in late modern societies, some key features of which are described by the sociologist Anthony Giddens (1991). Late modern subjects, Giddens asserts, live in a more complex, mobile, rapidly changing, and individualistically oriented society than their ancestors did, and their sense of identity depends on being able to order the various fragments of their life-experience into a coherent, ongoing autobiographical narrative. This requires a high degree of self-reflexivity, the ability and willingness to reflect on one's experience. As Giddens puts it, the self in late modern society becomes a "reflexive project," something subjects must think about and work on rather than simply taking for granted. Another thing late modern subjects have to work at is the creation of intimate relationships with others. The individualism and mobility of contemporary societies weaken social networks, making it more difficult to become close to others while at the same time raising our expectations of the few people to whom we *are* close (modern marriages, for instance, are no longer economic and social alliances between extended families, but are ideally supposed to be unions between "soul mates" who will meet one another's needs for friendship as well as sex, romance, and domesticity). Under these conditions, intimacy has to be created and sustained through mutual self-disclosure, the open and honest sharing of experiences and feelings. The reflexively constructed self cannot remain a private creation, then, but must be *communicated* continuously to significant others. In that context it becomes easier to understand why such skills as emotional expressiveness and empathetic listening are so idealized in many present-day representations of language.

In a study of what the term "communication" meant to mainstream Americans, Katriel and Phillipson (1981) found that their informants differentiated it from mere "talk" or "chat." "Communication" for them meant honest, serious, problem-solving talk within significant relationships, where it functioned as a means for overcoming the otherwise invincible isolation of the individual. They also represented "communication" as a kind of "work," worthwhile but also difficult and requiring continuous effort. As Katriel and Phillipson note (1981: 304), from the perspective on the world which their informants adopted, communication is "both vitally important and highly problematic. If people are unique, the kind of mutual disclosure and acknowledgement entailed in communication provide a necessary bridge from self to others. But if people are unique, they also lack the mutuality necessary for achieving interpersonal meaning and co-ordination." This problem can only be overcome by working hard to develop the skills "communication" demands.

It is because "communication" has come to be conceived in this way, as a means to greater self-knowledge and more satisfying intimate relationships (or in the service economy, more convincingly *simulated* intimate relationships), that contemporary advice literature on speech is so different from the advice literature of the past.[2] Victorian authorities, or the denizens of eighteenth-century salons who wrote treatises on the art of conversation, would scarcely recognize British Telecom's late twentieth-century account of what constitutes "better conversation." Nor would the authors of early modern conduct books like the one quoted earlier in this chapter. The advice writers of the past emphasized qualities such as wit, taste, propriety, politeness, and modesty. Invariably, for example, they dwelt on the vulgarity of talking about oneself and recommended that "delicate" topics be avoided in polite company. Today's authorities are equally insistent that talking about oneself (self-disclosure or "sharing") is a crucial skill for communicators to master, and that personal problems of every kind can and should be addressed by talking about them. In the past, advice writers about conversation were usually literary and cultural luminaries, or else high-ranking members of polite society who took it upon themselves to share their knowledge of that milieu with others who aspired to join. By contrast, today's authorities are psychologists and therapists – their expertise is in the area of human behavior and relationships, and many of the linguistic strategies they recommend (e.g. "being assertive," "sharing your feelings," "listening without judging") originated as rules specifically for various kinds of therapeutic discourse.

In the last few paragraphs I have been discussing what I take to be a pervasive and powerful ideology of language in late modern societies, the ideology of "communication" as a set of skills which are needed to sustain both personal identity and interpersonal relationships. One effect of the rise of this "communication" ideology has been to alter prevailing definitions of linguistic "skill," so that the interpersonal skills of, for instance, self-disclosure and empathetic listening are foregrounded while traditionally admired skills of a more forensic or rhetorical kind – such as the ability to engage in formal debate or public oratory – recede into the background.[3] The shift could also be analyzed as a foregrounding of "private" linguistic genres relative to "public" ones, illustrating a phenomenon discussed by a number of analysts of language and social change (notably Fairclough 1992), namely the growing "informalization" or "conversationalization" of Western public discourse. Service encounters, for instance, increasingly simulate personal conversations between acquainted parties;

addresses by politicians and even monarchs, influenced strongly by the demands of the television medium for which most of them are now primarily designed, are less "oratorical" and more "personal" (Montgomery 1999); institutional written documents such as job specifications and health education materials adopt a more informal and direct mode of address than they did in the past.

What does all this have to do with *gender*, and more specifically with the recent tendency to represent women as linguistically superior to men? My answer would be that the representation of women as model language users is a logical consequence of defining "skill" in communication as primarily skill in using language to maintain good interpersonal relationships, and of emphasizing traditionally "private" speech genres (e.g. conversations about personal feelings and problems) rather than "public" ones. The management of feelings and of personal relationships are culturally coded as female domains, and have been throughout the modern era in the West. Nancy Armstrong and Leonard Tennenhouse, discussing early modern conduct books, point out that this literature helped to establish a division of the social world into "public and private, economic and domestic, labor and leisure, according to a principle of gender that placed the household and sexual relations under *female* authority" (Armstrong and Tennenhouse 1987: 12, my emphasis).

In late modern societies, however, the public/private boundary is increasingly blurred. Ways of speaking traditionally associated with the private sphere (e.g. emotionally expressive ones) are now equally favored in public contexts and economic transactions (e.g. service encounters), while the conduct of domestic, sexual, and other intimate relations is no longer just a matter for private contemplation, but a major preoccupation of the popular media. By the gendered logic that has prevailed in the West for several centuries, these changes are bound to be perceived as *feminizing* the values and the language of public discourse, and consequently as advantaging women while simultaneously marginalizing men.

What kind of ideological work is done by the representations of language and gender I have been examining in this discussion? To begin with, they do the usual work of affirming the existence of fundamental differences between women and men. The differences are represented variously as biologically based (e.g. Skuse et al. 1997, a widely publicized study suggesting that there is a gene on the X chromosome controlling certain social and verbal skills), as "facts of life" which are "natural" in some unspecified way (cf. the comments of the call center manager in example (2) above), as socially constructed but too "deep" to be amenable to change (this is Deborah Tannen's (1990) position), or as constructed and alterable with effort (probably the commonest position, exemplified by examples (1), (3), and (4) above). In all cases, however, one effect of the representations is to reproduce the proposition that gender difference or complementarity is part of the normal order of things.

In discussions of globalization and the new economy, representations of female verbal superiority and male deficit do particular ideological work. As example (2) demonstrates, common-sense ideas about women as "naturally" skilled communicators help to naturalize the way women are channeled into low-paid and low-status service occupations – as if the issue were all about women's aptitude for the work and not at all about their greater willingness (born of historical necessity rather than choice) to accept the low pay, insecurity, and casualization which were endemic to "women's work" in the past and are now becoming the lot of many more workers. Example (2) also shows that ideas about "natural" gender difference can license discrimination in the workplace: the call center manager admits that he sometimes hires women "because they are women rather than because of anything they've particularly shown at the interview." Here representation (what women are said to be "good at") takes precedence over reality (how the woman in front of you actually performs).

A corollary of employers selecting women for certain occupations "because they are women" is, presumably, *not* selecting men because they are men. Another kind of ideological work done by current representations of language and gender is, in fact, to scapegoat men (or more exactly, certain groups of them, especially young working-class men) for misfortunes not of their making. Economic globalization has particularly affected the life-chances of non-elite male workers in Western societies by exporting the jobs they would once have expected to do to parts of the world where labor is cheaper, thus leaving many Western working-class men chronically un- or under-employed. A good deal of discourse on boys' educational underachievement arises from anxiety about this development (for a feminist critique, see Epstein et al. 1998; Mahony 1998). Some of this discourse blames young men for being unable or unwilling to develop the communication skills that would make them employable in new conditions. It is implied, and sometimes said, that if boys and young men made more effort to improve their communication skills, they would not be unemployed, poor, socially marginalized, and disaffected – though arguably it is a naive oversimplification of the economic realities to suggest that young men by their own efforts could avoid the inevitable systemic problems associated with the transition to a post-industrial order. Men's alleged poor verbal and social skills are also sometimes invoked in a "pathologizing" way, to explain the involvement of lower-class males in disruptive classroom behavior, violence, and criminal activity. Some commentators propose remedial instruction in communication and "emotional literacy" skills as a solution (e.g. Goleman 1995; Phillips 1998). Others suggest that anti-social males may be suffering from various clinical syndromes which could be controlled by medication (see Mariani 1995). Once again, this approach obscures the impact on certain men of systemic factors, particularly economic deprivation and inequality.

I will close this discussion by pointing out, however, that the "communication ideology" with which new representations of gendered language are strongly linked does ideological work of a broader kind – it is not concerned only or even primarily with gender, but is engaged in constructing a new model of the "good *person*." It presents, for the contemplation of women and men alike, a new ideal which, symbolically speaking, has both masculine and feminine elements: the enterprising, self-aware, interpersonally skilled individual who will flourish rather than flounder in the demanding conditions of twenty-first-century life. Despite the emphasis currently given to the "feminine" qualities of the good communicator, the individuals who most closely approximate the new ideal in the real world are often men: men who combine the traditionally "masculine" qualities of authority, enterprise, and leadership with a command of the more "feminine" language of emotional expressiveness and rapport. Outstanding examples of this type include the former US president Bill Clinton and the British Prime Minister Tony Blair. That both are male only underlines the point that valuing "feminine" characteristics need not threaten the dominant position of men in a society. On the contrary, a man who has some of these characteristics – always provided he remains clearly a man – will often be particularly applauded for his "sensitivity," whereas the same qualities in a woman attract no special approbation, since after all, they are "only natural" (which is to say, they are normative) for women. At the same time, women receive less credit for adopting characteristics that are admired when displayed by men, such as competitiveness, decisiveness, and strength of will. Nobody ever said approvingly of Margaret Thatcher that she was "in touch with her masculine side."

5   Representations and Realities

The comments just made bring us back to one of the questions posed in the introduction to this chapter: what is the relationship between language ideologies, the representations of language that circulate within a culture, and the actual linguistic behavior of that culture's members? Overall there is something rather contradictory about feminist discussions of this question. On one hand feminists have been at pains to stress the gulf that exists between representations and reality. Many empirical studies have been undertaken in an effort to disprove common gender stereotypes, such as that women don't swear and men don't gossip. The claim here is that actual gendered behavior is typically remote from cultural representations of it. On the other hand, sexist representations are sometimes criticized as pernicious, precisely because it is supposed that regular exposure to them may cause people to take them as models for their own behavior. Here, there is an implicit claim that representations *do* affect behavior. Ideological statements such as "women's language lacks forcefulness" can become self-fulfilling prophecies; that is why it is important to challenge them so vigorously. In which case, it might well be asked why so many common stereotypes find little support in empirical studies of naturally occurring language use.

   In my view, the way out of this contradiction is to bear in mind that human beings do not "behave," they *act*. They are not just passive imitators of whatever they see and hear around them: they must actively produce their own ways of behaving – albeit not always in a fully conscious and deliberate way and never, as Marx said in another context, "under conditions of their own choosing." Since human beings are social beings, their identities and practices are produced from social (which is to say, collective rather than purely individual) resources. And the representations that circulate in a culture are among those collective resources. They do not determine our behavior in the way the laws of physics determine the behavior of matter, but neither are they entirely irrelevant to it. Occasionally we may learn ways of acting from them directly (as when people claim they learned to kiss or to smoke from scenes in movies), but more usually we integrate them into the broader understandings of the world on which we base our own actions.

That this process is both active and selective is illustrated by reception studies carried out with readers of self-help books (e.g. Lichterman 1992; Simonds 1992). No genre could be more overtly didactic than self-help, and one might suppose that no group of readers would be more susceptible to the ideological norms embedded in representations than self-help readers. Yet both the researchers cited above found that their informants claimed not to read self-help books for the advice they offered – indeed they often could not remember, when questioned, what a recently enjoyed text had recommended readers to do. Rather, the informants said they read self-help for the pleasure of "recognizing" themselves. They said that the texts helped them to understand themselves better, and that far from being inspired by this to change themselves, they usually felt "reassured" that their own ways of acting were normal, even if they were also problematic.

What these readers described doing with self-help texts can be readily linked to what Anthony Giddens calls "the reflexive project of the self," the process whereby people ongoingly construct autobiographical narratives in an effort to understand themselves in relation to the world. It could be argued that representations are particularly powerful in shaping this kind of understanding, precisely because they are *not* accurate reproductions of the complexity of lived experience. Compared to an actual life, for example, a life *story* is simpler, more condensed, and far more orderly. It is private and personal experience ordered by public generic (in this case, narrative) conventions, and as such it provides the reader with a template s/he can use to order and reflect on his/her own experience.

If representations are resources for the work of producing identities and actions, then the interesting question about them becomes less "what does this representation say about language and gender – is it accurate or misleading, sexist or anti-sexist?" than "what do people *do* with this representation of language and gender?" – always bearing in mind, of course, that different people may do different things with it. It is by investigating what people do with representations *in* reality that we will discover the relationship *between* representations and reality.

Language and gender scholars are not excluded from the category of "people who do things with representations of language and gender." Just as those representations are resources for the production of gender in everyday life, so they are also resources for the production of theoretical understandings of gender. A simple illustration is the way empirical research on language and gender has often begun from folklinguistic stereotypes (e.g. "women talk incessantly"). Researchers may be motivated by a wish to explode the stereotype, but still the stereotype has set the agenda – and the researcher cannot avoid recirculating it, even if she presents it critically. Of course, popular representations do not always set research agendas, but there is no escaping the influence of prior "expert" representations: it is a strict rule of academic discourse that one *must* refer to (and so recirculate) the discourse of one's predecessors in the same field of inquiry. Nor is this necessarily an undesirable limitation. Even if one *could* think without reference to prior understandings of the phenomenon one is trying to think about, the resulting ideas would be difficult or impossible for others to integrate into their own understandings of the world, and therefore useless as a contribution to public discourse. (This is a particularly salient point for feminists who view their scholarship as a contribution to a movement for social *change*.)

It is impossible to "transcend" ideology, but it is not impossible for language and gender scholars to be *reflexive* about the cultural resources that have shaped their own understandings, as well as the understandings of the people whose language use they study. This, too, is an argument for the serious study of language ideologies. Cultural representations of language and gender are part of our inheritance, as social beings and also as linguists. Arguably, the better we understand them – where they "come from" and how they work – the more control we will have over what we do with them.

NOTES

1   This is an "orientalist" representation, i.e. it portrays Asia from a Western standpoint, but I hesitate to call it simply "Western" because the idea of Asian speakers as more polite and reticent is often found in Asian *self-representations* too. On the appropriation and internalization of others' stereotypes by members of the group they stereotype, see Talbot, this volume.

2   On the history of advice literature about conversation, see Burke 1993; Zeldin 1998.

3   In a sample of recent "communication skills" texts and training materials I examined, most of which were produced for professional rather than personal self-improvement purposes, there was virtually no reference – in some texts, none at all – to any speech event that necessitated addressing an audience or using formal generic conventions. Even such routine responsibilities as chairing a business meeting often went unmentioned. By contrast, a sample of comparable materials from the 1930s and 1950s placed emphasis on such rhetorical performances as "making a presentation" or "proposing a toast." (See further Cameron 2000.)

REFERENCES

Armstrong, Nancy and Tennenhouse, Leonard (eds) 1987: *The Ideology of Conduct: Essays on Literature and the History of Sexuality*. New York: Methuen.

BT 1997: *TalkWorks: How To Get More Out of Life Through Better Conversations*. London: British Telecommunications plc.

Burke, Peter 1993: *The Art of Conversation*. Ithaca, NY: Cornell University Press.

Cameron, Deborah 1995: *Verbal Hygiene*. London and New York: Routledge.

Cameron, Deborah 2000: *Good To Talk? Living and Working in a Communication Culture*. London and Thousand Oaks, CA: Sage.

Crawford, Mary 1995: *Talking Gender*. London: Sage.

Dunbar, Robin 1996: *Grooming, Gossip and the Evolution of Language*. London: Faber & Faber.

Epstein, Debbie, Elwood, Jannette, Hey, Valerie, and Maw, Janet (eds) 1998: *Failing Boys: Issues in Gender and Achievement*. Buckingham: Open University Press.

Fairclough, Norman 1992: *Discourse and Social Change*. Cambridge: Polity.

Gal, Susan 1995: Language, gender and power: An anthropological review. In Kira Hall and Mary Bucholtz (eds) *Gender Articulated: Language and the Socially Constructed Self*. London: Routledge, pp. 169–82.

Gervasio, Amy and Crawford, Mary 1989: Social evaluations of assertiveness: A critique and speech act reformulation. *Psychology of Women Quarterly* 13: 1–25.

Giddens, Anthony 1991: *Modernity and Self-Identity: Self and Society in the Late Modern Age*. Cambridge: Polity.

Gilbert, Pam 1998: Gender and schooling in new times: The challenge of boys and literacy. *Australian Educational Researcher* 25(1): 15–36.

Goleman, Daniel 1995: *Emotional Intelligence*. New York: Bantam Books.

Gray, John 1992: *Men are from Mars, Women are from Venus*. New York: HarperCollins.

Jespersen, Otto 1922: *Language: Its Nature, Development and Origin*. London: Allen and Unwin.

Jones, Ann Rosalind 1987: Nets and bridles: Early modern conduct books and sixteenth century women's lyrics. In Nancy Armstrong and Leonard Tennenhouse (eds) *The Ideology of Conduct: Essays on Literature and the History of Sexuality*. New York: Methuen, pp. 39–72.

Katriel, Tamar and Phillipson, Gerry 1981: "What we need is communication": "Communication" as a cultural term in some American speech. *Communication Monographs* 48: 301–17.

Keenan, Elinor Ochs 1974: Norm-makers, norm-breakers: Uses of speech by men and women in a Malagasy community. In Richard Bauman and Joel Sherzer (eds) *Explorations in the Ethnography of Speaking*. Cambridge: Cambridge University Press, pp. 125–43.

Kulick, Don 1993: Speaking as a woman: Structure and gender in domestic arguments in a New Guinea village. *Cultural Anthropology* 8(4): 510–41.

Lakoff, Robin 1975: *Language and Woman's Place*. New York: Harper & Row.

Lichterman, Philip 1992: Self help reading as a thin culture. *Media, Culture & Society* 14: 421–47.

Mahony, Pat 1998: Girls will be girls and boys will be first. In Debbie Epstein, Jannette Elwood, Valerie Hey, and Janet Maw (eds) *Failing Boys: Issues in Gender and Achievement*. Buckingham: Open University Press, pp. 37–55.

Mariani, Philomena 1995: Law-and-order science. In Maurice Berger, Brian Wallis, and Simon Watson (eds) *Constructing Masculinity*. New York: Routledge, pp. 135–56.

Montgomery, Martin 1999: Speaking sincerely: Public reactions to the death of Diana. *Language and Literature* 8(1): 5–33.

Office for Standards in Education (Ofsted) 1993: *Boys and English*. London: Ofsted.

Phillips, Angela 1998: *Communication: A Key Skill for Education*. London: BT Forum.

Schieffelin, Bambi, Woolard, Kathryn, and Kroskrity, Paul (eds) 1998: *Language Ideologies: Practice and Theory*. New York and Oxford: Oxford University Press.

Sherzer, Joel 1987: A diversity of voices: Men's and women's speech in ethnographic perspective. In Susan Philips, Susan Steele, and Christine Tanz (eds) *Language, Gender and Sex in Comparative Perspective*. New York: Cambridge University Press, pp. 95–120.

Simonds, Wendy 1992: *Women and Self-Help Culture: Reading Between the Lines*. New Brunswick, NJ: Rutgers University Press.

Skuse, D. H., James, R. S., Bishop, D. V. M., et al. 1997: Evidence from Turner's syndrome of an imprinted X-linked locus affecting cognitive function. *Nature* 387(6634): 705–8.

Spender, Dale 1980: *Man Made Language*. London: Routledge and Kegan Paul.

Talbot, Mary 2000: "It's good to talk?" The undermining of feminism in a British Telecom advertisement. *Journal of Sociolinguistics* 4: 108–19.

Tannen, Deborah 1990: *You Just Don't Understand*. New York: William Morrow.

Tyler, Melissa and Taylor, Steve 1997: "Come Fly With Us": Emotional Labour and the Commodification of Sexual Difference in the Airline Industry. Paper presented to the Annual International Labour Process Conference, Edinburgh.

Woolard, Kathryn 1998: Language ideologies as a field of inquiry. In Bambi Schieffelin, Kathryn Woolard, and Paul Kroskrity (eds) *Language Ideologies: Practice and Theory*. New York and London: Oxford University Press, pp. 3–47.

Zeldin, Theodore 1998: *Conversation: How Talk Can Change Your Life*. London: Harvill Press.

20 Gender Stereotypes: Reproduction and Challenge

MARY TALBOT

> *Oh*
> *Bossy Women Gossip*
> *Girlish Women giggle*
> *Women natter, women nag*
> *Women niggle-niggle-niggle*
> *Men Talk*
> (From Liz Lochhead, *Dreaming Frankenstein*)

1 Introduction

For an individual to be assigned to the category of male or female has far-reaching consequences. Gender is often thought of in terms of bipolar categories, sometimes even as mutually exclusive opposites – as in "the opposite sex." People are perceived through a "lens" of gender polarization (Bem 1993) and assigned to apparently natural categories accordingly. On the basis of this gender assignment, naturalized norms and expectations about verbal behavior are imposed upon people. There is a strong tendency for gender stereotyping to set in. Stereotyping involves a reductive tendency: to "stereotype someone is to interpret their behaviour, personality and so on in terms of a set of common-sense attributions which are applied to whole groups (e.g. 'Italians are excitable'; 'Black people are good at sport')" (Cameron 1988: 8). Like caricatures, they focus obsessively on certain characteristics, real or imagined, and exaggerate them.

Early work in the field that we now know as language and gender was highly speculative and certainly did not reflect on the category of gender itself. Instead, it simply accepted and used the commonsensical categories of female and male. As a consequence, it tended to reproduce sexist stereotypes. Indeed, early pre-feminist scholarship was profoundly androcentric. In 1922, Otto Jespersen wrote on *Language: Its Nature, Development and Origin* including a single chapter on "The Woman." He presents various alleged characteristics of women as speakers, including softspokenness, irrational topic shift, and, not least, volubility and vacuity; in other words, talking a lot but making no sense. The "evidence" (other than his own opinion) that he refers to for his claim about women's voluble vacuity consists of proverbs, witticisms, and the views of authors and fictional characters:

> The volubility of women has been the subject of innumerable jests; it has given rise to popular proverbs in many countries; as well as to Aurora Leigh's resigned "A woman's function plainly is – to talk" and Oscar Wilde's sneer, "Women are a decorative sex. They never have anything to say, but they say it charmingly". A woman's thought is no sooner formed than uttered. Says Rosalind, "Do you not know I am a woman! When I think, I must speak" (*As You Like It*, III. 2. 264). (Jespersen 1922: 250)

The stereotype of the empty-headed chatterer represented in this passage is still very much with us. As Deborah Cameron observes, "Jespersen is caught between his fantasies (soft-spoken, retiring child-women) and his prejudices (loquacious but illogical bird-brains) to produce a sexist stereotype which is still recognizable sixty years on" (1985: 33). Several years later this is still true. Other variations or inflections on this caricature are, of course, the gossip and the nagging wife or scold. A notable feature of stereotypes of women as language users is how negative they are. Women are, as Graddol and Swann put it, "consistently portrayed as chatterboxes, endless gossips or strident nags patiently endured or kept in check by strong and silent men" (1989: 2). The English language has a remarkable variety of words for vocal, particularly verbally aggressive, women. Here are some of them: *scold, gossip, nag, termagant, virago, harpy, harridan, dragon, battleaxe, (castrating) bitch, fishwife, magpie, jay, parrot,* and *poll.* They are all highly pejorative, though some of them have fortunately fallen out of use.

Stereotypical representations of women as language users are never far away. Women's verbal excess is treated as a legitimate source of laughter in television situation comedies, newspaper cartoons, and so on. In situation comedy centered on female characters, the comedy very often rests on their speech spiralling into excess, because it is either abusive or simply relentless and never-ending (Macdonald 1995: 56). In a typical episode of the BBC's comedy *Birds of a Feather*, as Myra Macdonald notes, "Tracey's attempts to improve Sharon's table manners and housekeeping skills are met with the charge: 'you're turning into a right nag, you are, Trace', while Sharon's humour at Tracey's expense leads Tracey to dub her sister a 'sarkie cow' (BBC1, 11 October 1990)" (Macdonald 1995: 56). In other words, their verbal behavior was frequently represented as either "nagging" or "bitching." In sitcoms centered on male characters (here Macdonald cites the BBC's *Steptoe and Son* and ITV's *Home to*

Roost), their slanging matches and other verbal confrontations, while capable of being every bit as vituperative and excessive, are not perceived in terms of nagging and bitching. As far as sitcom writers are concerned, then, it seems that vituperation among men is neither nagging nor bitching, and is not gendered.

Sexist stereotypes are not always articulated for humorous ends. The horror writer James Herbert draws in women's empty chatter as part of his scene-setting in the novel *The Survivor*. After an account of bizarre and grisly deaths in the locality following a plane crash, we are informed that:

> The women met in shops and in the High Street, infecting each other with their own personal fear; the men discussed the peculiar happenings at their desks or work benches, many scornful of the suggestion that some evil was afoot in the town, but admittedly perplexed by the sequence of events.   (Herbert 1976: 110)

The men discuss the situation intelligently and in public. They respond to suggestions; they admit to being perplexed by the bizarre events that have taken place, or are scornful of supernatural explanations put forward to account for them. The women, on the other hand, are just making trouble: they respond emotionally, "infecting" one another with "their own personal fear." Their talk is trivial, personal, and lacks content. (The occupational stereotyping is also notable: women shop, while men work.)

This chapter begins with some preliminary theoretical observations about the phenomenon of stereotyping in general, and its function. I then briefly overview shifts in the use of the category of gender by language and gender practitioners, from early unreflective use to more recent recognition that gender is a problematic category which is susceptible to stereotyping. I then consider recent fruitful applications of the concept of stereotyping itself. Particular attention is given to the argument that a stereotypical "women's language" operates as a powerful hegemonic construct of preferred feminine behavior, for which I draw upon some coverage of recent explorations of it as a resource for constructing cross-gendered and sexualized personas. The chapter also considers how gender stereotypes are contested in a range of contexts, and concludes with attention to the resilience of the gossip. (See Besnier, this volume; Sidnell, this volume.)

2   Stereotyping

As a representational practice, stereotyping involves simplification, reduction, and naturalization. Some theorists are careful to distinguish it from the more general process of *social typing* (e.g. Dyer 1977; Hall 1997). In order to make sense of the world – and the events, objects, and people in it – we need to impose schemes of classification. We *type* people according to the complexes of classificatory schemes in our culture, in terms of the social positions they inhabit, their group membership, personality traits, and so on. Our understanding of who a particular person is is built up from the accumulation of such classificatory detail. Stereotyping, by contrast, reduces and simplifies. Both social typing and stereotyping are practices in the maintenance of the social and symbolic order; both involve a strategy of "splitting," whereby the normal and acceptable are separated from the abnormal and unacceptable, resulting in the exclusion of the latter. Stereotyping differs from more general social typing in its rigidity; it "reduces, essentializes, naturalizes and fixes 'difference' . . . facilitates the 'binding' or bonding together of all of Us who are 'normal' into one 'imagined community'; and it sends into symbolic exile all of Them" (Hall 1997: 258).

Power is clearly a key consideration here. Stereotypes tend to be directed at subordinate groups (e.g. ethnic minorities, women) and they play an important part in hegemonic struggle. As Richard Dyer explains:

> The establishment of normalcy (i.e. what is accepted as "normal") through social- and stereo-types is one aspect of the habit of ruling groups . . . to attempt to fashion the whole of society according to their own world view, value system, sensibility and ideology. So right is this world view for the ruling groups that they make it appear (as it does appear to them) as "natural" and "inevitable" – and for everyone – and, in so far as they succeed, they establish their hegemony. (Dyer 1977: 30)

Hegemony involves control by consent, rather than by force. The representational practice of stereotyping plays a central role in it, by endlessly reiterating what amount to caricatures of subordinate groups.

Stereotypes are (re)produced in a wide range of practices of representation, including scholarship, literature, television situation comedy, and both "high" and "low" art (including particularly newspaper cartoons). What I have presented above is a cultural studies perspective; the stereotypes that Dyer and Hall investigated were predominantly pictorial representations of gay and Black people respectively. Hall elaborates on the ambivalence of stereotyping and the possible co-existence of conflicting – "good" and "bad" – stereotypes of Black men: "blacks are both 'childlike' *and* 'oversexed', just as black youth are 'Sambo simpletons' and/or 'wily, dangerous savages'; and older men both 'barbarians' and/or 'noble savages' – Uncle Toms" (Hall 1997: 263).

Returning to the pre-feminist linguistics that I referred to in my opening section, Jespersen's single chapter on "The Woman" clearly marks out the boundaries of Us and Them (another chapter in the same section of the book deals with "The Foreigner"). My quotation from the chapter on "The Woman" provides an example of a "bad" stereotype of women as speakers. Cameron's comment about Jespersen being caught between "his fantasies (soft-spoken, retiring child-women) and his prejudices (loquacious but illogical bird-brains)" hints at just how closely the good and the bad may co-exist.

Stereotyping as a representational practice is at the center of the notion of folklinguistics. Folklinguistics is a term linguists sometimes use to refer to (generally) non-linguists' beliefs about language; for example, the belief about women's verbal incontinence that has been the staple of misogynist newspaper cartoons for decades, if not centuries. Indeed, folklinguistics is the basis of Cameron's glossary entry for "stereotype" in her reader: "in linguistics, a folklinguistic characterization of some group's speech" (1985: 189–90).

Within the field of language and gender, the term "stereotype" is often used to refer to prescriptions or unstated expectations of behavior, rather than specifically to representational practices. A study of a mixed group of American engineering students provides a good example of this usage. Victoria Bergvall (1996) conducted a study of verbal interaction among a group of students studying in the traditionally masculine area of engineering. The academic domain of engineering is still highly androcentric and, simultaneously, traditional expectations about gender behavior and identity prevail. This places women who want to become engineers in a predicament. Conflicting demands are made upon them. On the one hand, if they want to take part in heterosexual social and sexual relationships, they need to behave in stereotypically "feminine" ways: presenting their own views tentatively, displaying supportiveness of men, and generally exhibiting cooperative behavior. On the other hand, if they are to succeed in their studies, they have to behave in ways perceived as "masculine": asserting themselves and their views, thereby putting themselves in competition with other students. Bergvall's study shows these women striving and contriving to comply with both sets of expectations, with some degree of success:

> In the course of examining the linguistic actions of these engineering students, it becomes clear that the women display speech behaviours that transcend easy boundaries: they are assertive, forceful, facilitative, apologetic and hesitant by turns. It appears at times to be a double-bind, no-win situation: when the women are assertive, they are resisted by their peers; when they are facilitative, their work may be taken for granted and not acknowledged. These interactions suggest that these women are subject to the forces of traditional stereotypes, even though, in interviews, they assert that the classroom is gender-neutral territory with equal opportunities for women and men.   (Bergvall 1996: 192)

Gender stereotypes are closely linked with and support gender ideologies. If we view them as ideological prescriptions for behavior, then actual individuals have to respond to the stereotypical roles expected of them.

Gender stereotypes linked to gender ideology reproduce naturalized gender differences. In doing so, they function to sustain hegemonic male dominance and female subordination. A study of British adolescents' experience and expectations of talk in the classroom provides a second example. Michelle Stanworth (1983) found that boys were encouraged by teachers to be assertive in classroom interaction and that the girls admired most those boys who demonstrated most ability to do so. Girls demonstrating the same abilities, however, were not admired at all. On the contrary, vocal girls had scorn heaped on them by other girls. In evaluating their behavior differently, one could say that the non-vocal girls colluded in their own oppression, since they supported the view that it is only right that boys should dominate, and deplorable that girls should try to make themselves heard in the same way. In this way, hegemonic male dominance and female subordination are sustained.

To draw out what the gender stereotypes are, one could say that the American engineering students *should be* apologetic, hesitant, and supportive; the British schoolgirls *should be* silent and subordinate. These are ideological prescriptions or norms of behavior that weigh heavily on them: they are under the pressure, if you like, of "good" stereotypes, highly reductive and simplifying ones. The representational "bad" stereotypes of the verbal incontinent and the scold can be seen as punitive responses or "correctives" to the "problem" of women trying to control, dominate or, at worst, even contribute to talk. It has been suggested (e.g. Spender 1985) that women are perceived as too talkative because how much they talk is measured not against how much men talk, but against an ideal of female silence. Ideally women should be saying nothing at all. The "good" stereotypes, then, present how to behave, and the "bad" how not to. In his investigation of the stereotyping of Black people, Hall remarks on the way the double-sided nature of representation and stereotyping traps men in a no-win situation. Referring to the work of Staples (1982) and Mercer and Julien (1994), he observes the following:

> black men sometimes respond to . . . infantilization by adopting a sort of caricature-in-reverse of the hyper-masculinity and super-sexuality with which they had been stereotyped. Treated as "childish", some blacks in reaction adopted a "macho", aggressive-masculine style. But this only served to confirm the fantasy amongst whites of the ungovernable and excessive sexual nature . . . Thus, "victims" can be trapped by the stereotype, unconsciously confirming it by the very terms in which they try to oppose it and resist it.   (Hall 1997: 263)

Similarly, sexist stereotypes lie in wait for women and girls who dare to transgress. Of course, in the research referred to above, one can only speculate about the actual use of stereotypes by the people involved, but we do know that they are available as a resource for teenage girls to pillory fellow schoolgirls and for male engineering students to ridicule and ostracize their female counterparts.

3 Reproduction of Gender Stereotypes in Feminist Linguistics

I want to turn now from practitioners' productive use of the notion of stereotype to their unintentional reproduction (see also Romaine, this volume;

Kiesling, this volume). I began with an example of a "bad" stereotype in early pre-feminist work on gender and language: Jespersen on the alleged volubility of women. With the benefit of hindsight, it is clear that early feminist scholarship tended to reproduce some of the androcentrism of pre-feminist work, and hence some of the stereotypes. In *Language and Woman's Place*, the first exploration of language and the socialization of women as subordinates, Robin Lakoff (1975) presented women as disadvantaged language users. This early, introspective work speculated that women used, or were expected to use, language which presented them as uncertain, weak, and empty-headed. Its androcentrism lay principally in the fact that she accounted for women's language (henceforth WL) in terms of its deficiencies – its deviation when measured against a norm, which was assumed to be male – and thereby, curiously for feminist scholarship, marked out the boundaries of Us and Them with women on the outside. Lakoff certainly did not set out to reproduce sexist stereotypes; indeed she was a robust challenger of sexism (and apparently a force to be reckoned with among her colleagues in the Linguistics department at Berkeley in the 1970s). However, some of her speculations about how women's alleged deficiency manifested itself are equally curious echoes of Jespersen; for example, her attention to indirectness, use of euphemism, avoidance of swearing, and so-called "empty" or meaningless lexical choices echoes Jespersen's earlier speculations. Lakoff's claim that WL is weak and uncertain was probably heavily influenced by stereotypical expectations. For example, she claims that, when women use tag questions, they indicate hesitancy inappropriately, though she concedes that she has no "precise statistical evidence" (1975: 16) for this claim (actually she has no *evidence* at all, precise or otherwise, other than her own introspection). It seems that when she reflected on men and women using tag questions, she "interpreted" them according to the sex of the person producing them: seeing tentativeness in women's use of the linguistic feature, but not in men's use of exactly the same. As Janet Holmes has observed, one person's feeble hedging is another's perspicacious qualification (Holmes 1984: 169). In other words, it may be that what was perceived as an inadequacy in women, in men was seen otherwise. In fact, in Lakoff's early ideas about WL, she shifts between interest in women's *actual* behavior and interest in restrictive *cultural expectations* about appropriate behavior for women; in other words, stereotypes. I will return to this point later.

It is possible to identify three frameworks or "models" shaping early feminist research into language and gender: "deficit," "dominance," and "difference." This is a considerable oversimplification, but convenient here. The early "deficit" framework was briefly considered above. Later researchers were careful not to approach their subject in terms of male norm and female deficiency. In the "dominance" framework, language patterns are interpreted as manifestations of a patriarchal social order. In this view, asymmetries in the language use of women and men are enactments of male privilege. The "difference" framework rests on assumptions about distinct male and female sub-cultures into which boys and girls are said to be socialized. The argument goes that, by the time they reach adulthood, men and women have acquired distinct male and female interactional styles. The idea that women and men have distinct styles has proved popular, but it is problematic. While there is extensive research to support such a view, including research on politeness (e.g. Brown 1980, 1993; Holmes 1995) and on physical alignment and eye contact in conversations (e.g. Tannen 1990), it needs extensive contextual grounding, as ethnographic studies of women in specific speech communities emphasize (e.g. Eckert and McConnell-Ginet 1992). "Women" and "men" are not homogeneous groups. Overall, there is support for the view that women in many speech communities and settings tend to be less competitive conversationalists than men, but there is a tendency to overgeneralize and disregard contextual differences. This is basically a problem of allowing gender to override other considerations. A prominent feature of work within the difference framework is its positive reassessment of forms of talk that women are supposed to engage in, such as gossip. As Cameron has remarked, the two frameworks can be seen as distinct "moments" in feminist linguistics: "dominance was the moment of feminist outrage, of bearing witness to oppression in all aspects of women's lives, while difference was the moment of feminist celebration, reclaiming and revaluing women's distinctive cultural traditions" (1996: 41).

Difference-and-dominance have often been used together. Over two decades of language and gender research has been overwhelmingly preoccupied with gender *differences*. This has sometimes been inflected with a view of those differences embodying, at the level of individual interaction, male dominance over women in the wider social order. Both dominance and difference approaches rest on a dichotomous conception of gender; neither problematizes the category of gender itself.

The reification of gender *as* difference in this enormous body of research has inevitably led, again, to the reproduction of gender stereotypes. Gender is reified as difference when the agenda is set solely in terms of identifying male and female differences. It has "fixed" difference. As Barrie Thorne remarks, such "static and exaggerated dualisms" can only lead to a "conceptual dead end" (1993: 91). Various critics (e.g. Cameron 1992; Talbot 1998) have pointed out that the male and female interactional styles, as described, would equip them perfectly for traditional roles. After all, the nurturant, supportive verbal behavior characteristic of the female interactional style is just what is needed to be a good mother. Binary oppositions like these are supposed to characterize women's and men's different styles of talk:

Sympathy	Problem-solving
Rapport	Report
Listening	Lecturing
Private	Public
Connection	Status
Supportive	Oppositional
Intimacy	Independence

The left-hand column reminds us that women are nurturers. It could be a celebration of maternal qualities; indeed, it could be used to support a traditional idealization of the mother and womanhood in general. The right-hand column could be used in defense of male power and privilege.

The views of feminist linguists have had their influence on other areas, sometimes leading to further reproduction of stereotypes about women's language use. The familiar features of WL are often listed in introductory texts of the kind students appreciate for their uncomplicated clarity. The reductiveness of such books is made worse by their lack of scholarly referencing; this seems a high price to pay for student-friendliness. In the 1980s, Cameron argued that non-academic feminist workshops and discussion groups had developed a feminist folklinguistics which might have come "straight from the pages of Jespersen" (Cameron 1985: 34). She characterizes feminist folklinguistic beliefs about women's language use as follows:

1   Disfluency (because women find it hard to communicate in a male language).
2   Unfinished sentences.
3   Speech not ordered according to the norms of logic.
4   Statements couched as questions (approval seeking).
5   Speaking less than men in mixed groups.
6   Using co-operative strategies in conversation, whereas men use competitive strategies. (1985: 35)

It seems clear that the alleged male and female styles are highly stereotypical. Interestingly, one group of experimental researchers reports on having inadvertently elicited features of an allegedly "feminine" interactional style from a group of both women and men (Freed 1996). By asking them to engage in collaborative activities viewed as female, they unintentionally set up a "feminine" experimental space where everyone "did" woman talk. They conclude that the task engaged in was all-important in the language choices made; and the task was stereotypically feminine. Others have cautioned against the unreflective use of gender stereotypes, as preconceptions limiting a researcher's perception of their data (e.g. Cameron 1997: 25). As Cameron has incisively observed, *"gender is a problem, not a solution.* 'Men do this, women do that' is not only overgeneralized and stereotypical, it fails utterly to address the question of where 'men' and 'women' come from" (1995: 42).

4   WL: A Stereotype in Operation

More recently, questions such as these – where the categories of men and women come from – are starting to be addressed by feminist linguists. In a recent volume of research, for example, many of the contributors directly or indirectly interrogate categories such as masculine, feminine, heterosexual,

White, and middle-class (Bucholtz, Liang, and Sutton 1999). It is notable that all are conscious of theoretical shortcomings in earlier work by feminist linguists. Running through the volume is a careful avoidance of bipolar categories of gender, and the comparative approach that goes with them. Indeed, a striking feature of the book is its repeated rejection of gender identity as a static category altogether. Interestingly, Lakoff's early speculative work on WL has recently been revisited and reinterpreted in terms of stereotypes in operation. For example, Rusty Barrett returns to Lakoff's speculations about a stereotypical "women's language" in a study of African American drag queens' performances of an "uptown white woman" style (Barrett 1999). He points out that WL is a hegemonic notion of gendered speech that, he argues, is used by African American drag queens in the cultivation of an exaggerated "feminine" persona which is ultimately neither gendered nor ethnic, but *classed* (Barrett 1999: 321). Barrett's study illuminates the insight that WL is a potent ideological construct (Bucholtz and Hall 1995; Cameron 1997; Gal 1995).

Other research referring back to the early notion of WL is a study of fantasy-line operators offering telephone sex services (Hall 1995). Hall found that in order to "sell to a male market, women's pre-recorded messages and live conversational exchange must cater to hegemonic male perceptions of the ideal woman" (Hall 1995: 190). In catering for their customers' expectations, telephone sex workers pander to sexist and racist assumptions by vocalizing the stereotypes they assume their customers and "dial-a-porn" clients want to hear ("dial-a-porn" is the colloquial term used for pre-recorded messages containing erotic fantasies). In interviewing phone-sex operators about their occupation, Hall did not specify her intention to focus on language use until the end of the interview. Nevertheless, the interviewees were very much aware of the linguistic nature of their job. This is hardly surprising, since their livelihoods depended on their verbal ability; the sexual personas they performed over the telephone are entirely verbal. So it is not really a surprise that some of them volunteered a good deal of linguistic detail about what made their voices marketable commodities; for instance, they described their selection of what they regarded as "feminine" words (including precise color terms), high pitch, whispering, and a wide-ranging "feminine, lilting" pattern of intonation. One operator reported describing the appearance of her fantasy persona using "words that are very feminine":

> I always wear peach, or apricot, or black lace- or charcoal-colored lace, not just black. I'll talk about how my hair feels, how curly it is. Yeah, I probably use more feminine words. Sometimes they'll ask me, "What do you call it [female genitalia]?" And I'll say, well my favorite is *the snuggery* . . . And then they crack up, because it's such a feminine, funny word.   (Hall 1995: 199–200)

In reflecting on her language use, one interviewee makes a link between WL and sexual submissiveness, describing her customers' perception of it as indicating a sexually submissive position (Hall 1995: 206). Another of the phone-sex operators Hall interviewed was a Mexican American bisexual man who posed as a woman for his male callers. Like the drag queens in Barrett's study, this sex worker performs a Euro-American woman over the telephone for the benefit of his clients. In projecting this WL stereotype, he is not so much cross-dressing as "cross-expressing" (Hall 1995: 202). For these sex workers, WL is a lucrative commodity in the phone-sex marketplace.

WL, then, operates as a powerful hegemonic construct of preferred feminine speech patterns. As a symbolic resource, it is not only available to women. Its first description – Lakoff's *Language and Woman's Place* – is used by cross-dressers as an instructional text, whether directly or indirectly. For example, it is referred to in a booklet entitled *Speaking as a Woman: A Guide for Those Who Desire to Communicate in a More Feminine Manner* (Liang 1989) catering for men who want to "pass" as women. This booklet contains simple descriptions of such WL features as "feminine" lexis, high pitch, and wide-ranging intonation patterns, along with advice on how to achieve them. Deborah Tannen's popularizing books are put to similar use. It is perhaps ironic that research founded on a dichotomous view of gendered verbal behavior is being used by male-to-female cross-dressers to subvert the binary division of male and female. While the obsession with difference and the unreflective reproduction of bipolar categories are now seen as a conceptual dead-end and pose problems for feminist linguists in the academic world, it seems they have helped to develop a rich symbolic resource for "gender-benders." As academic feminists are beginning to theorize the fluidity of gender identities, non-academics are appropriating earlier feminist research to help them engage in the practice of making their own gender identities more fluid. Not all appropriations can be viewed so positively.

5   Challenging Sexist Stereotypes

WL, then, is a hegemonic construct of preferred feminine speech patterns that is a resource for the construction of cross-gendered and sexualized personas. Cross-dressers, drag artists, and phone-sex workers have appropriated it for their own purposes. Gays' exploitation of the stereotypes enshrined in WL no doubt impacts on the stereotypes themselves in some way, possibly subversively. Livia and Hall remark on the knock-on effect that drag has on all other gender performances: "Drag, in its deliberate misappropriation of gender attributes, serves to queer not only the gender performance of the speaker but, by implication, all the other terms in the gender paradigm, according none the innocence of the natural or the merely descriptive" (1997: 12). But the queering of stereotypes does not eliminate them. What it does begin to do is undermine the naturalization of gender categories and destabilize the link between them and particular attributes and patterns of behavior. WL is clearly not only the province of women.

For sex workers on the fantasy lines, WL is lucrative; it is an asset enabling access to economic power and relative social freedom. Several of Hall's interviewees commented on their freedom from the sorts of constraint that employment in corporate America imposes. But this freedom they enjoy comes at the cost of perpetuating sexist stereotypes in the phone-sex marketplace. The situation is an interesting one for feminist linguists: a powerless speech style is a source of economic power for both women and men. As Hall observes, "this high-tech mode of linguistic exchange complicates traditional notions of power in language, because the women working within the industry consciously produce a language stereotypically associated with women's powerlessness in order to gain economic power and social flexibility" (1995: 183). Hall refers to a training manual produced by a phone-sex company that explicitly recommends striving to be "the ideal woman" (as though this were unproblematic) before going on to try "bimbo, nymphomaniac, mistress, slave, transvestite, lesbian, foreigner, or virgin." The phone-sex workers themselves argue that they cannot afford the luxury of quibbling over representations, though they identify themselves with feminism; they are, understandably, more concerned about improving working conditions and securing health-care benefits. But, be this as it may, they are actively involved in the perpetuation of reductive, ultimately denigrating representations of women and in the naturalization of potentially abusive kinds of relationship between women and men (it seems appropriate here to recall the link made between WL and a submissive sexual position in the context of "phone sex").

So, while such appropriations of stereotypes are interesting, they are not in themselves overt contestations of the reductive sexist assumptions embodied in them. This is not to say that stereotypes go uncontested, however. On the contrary, struggles in and over language and representation are taking place all the time and in different modes. Whenever we complain about sexist practices, such as the use of reductive stereotypes about women's language use, we are contesting them. Elsewhere I have suggested shouting at the television as a bottom line in thinking about resistance and contestation – not a bit effective in bringing about change, but better than nothing and a good way of letting off steam (Talbot 1998: 219). A more public, and hence perhaps rather more influential, mode of contestation by an individual might be writing letters of complaint, or indeed graffiti on the wall. Collective forms of contestation include stickering activities and related guerrilla-like practices. A stickering campaign on the London Underground was particularly effective. The Underground was once notorious for the sexist advertising images flanking the escalators in stations; strategically placed stickers announcing that "this poster degrades women" eventually had the desired effect of their removal.

In the academic domain, research countering the stereotype of the verbal incontinent has provided vast amounts of quantitative evidence that men talk more than women, in public places at least. Feminist research has produced extensive evidence of public talk being dominated by men (it must be noted, however, that some of this research has tended to treat women and men as if they were homogeneous groups, and none of it problematizes gender itself). It has shown schoolboys dominating classrooms, with the encouragement of their teachers, men doing most of the talking in university seminars and academic conferences, men dominating management meetings, and so on. However, mere empirical evidence such as this is unlikely to undermine the deeply held belief that women talk more than men, a belief entrenched in the gossip stereotype. It is unlikely that such research has reduced the number of newspaper cartoons using women's verbal incontinence as the butt of their humor. It certainly did not deter the *Daily Telegraph* from producing the headline: "It's official: women really do talk more than men" (February 24, 1997) for some science coverage (a report of some neurological research indicating that, in a sample of eleven women and ten men, the women had proportionately larger language areas). The fact that there was no mention of amount of talk at all in the report itself did not appear to matter. Headlines, like advertising slogans, are about gaining the reader's attention, not striving for accuracy. For the sub-editor writing the headline, the opportunity to resurrect the attention-grabbing gossip stereotype was presumably irresistible.

Direct interventions are another way of challenging sexist practices such as the use of reductive stereotypes about women's language use. Some guidelines produced by the National Union of Journalists (NUJ) in Britain take issue with stereotypical representations of women and men in the press:

> There is no reason why girls and women should be generally characterized as emotional, sentimental, dependent, vulnerable, passive, alluring, mysterious, fickle, weak, inferior, neurotic, gentle, muddled, vain, intuitive . . . Nor is there any reason why boys and men should be assumed to be dominant, strong, aggressive, sensible, superior, randy, decisive, courageous, ambitious, unemotional, logical, independent, ruthless.   (1982: 6)

In the late 1980s, it was suggested that, as the profession employs increasing numbers of women, their presence would disturb "the 'men-only' vacuum" in the newsroom and bring about change (Searle 1988: 257). However, scrutiny of contemporary tabloid newspapers in Britain suggests that the guidelines have not been very influential at all. The NUJ's ethics council, which provides a channel for the views of the general public, has done very little with complaints about sexism (though it has fared less badly in dealing with press misrepresentation of gays, lesbians, disabled people, and ethnic minorities). Anti-sexist guidelines tend to be perceived as a form of censorship by men working in journalism. Codes of conduct are difficult to impose by union members because to implement them they would have to tackle their own immediate superior, the newspaper editor.

The trouble is that traditional sexist stereotypes are so resilient and so well entrenched that they may be contested repeatedly without undermining their commonsensical status. Even a chorus of dissenting voices is unlikely to dislodge them. Moreover, as I have argued elsewhere with specific regard to the gossip stereotype, it is possible for them to be contested and reasserted in the same text (Talbot 2000). I return to this point in the next section.

6 The Resilience of the Gossip

Of late we have borne witness to the apparent undermining and reversal of the perception of women as deficient language users; now it is *men* who are deficient (see Cameron, this volume). New gender stereotypes about language use seem to be emerging, just as essentializing and reductive as the older ones, but placing men and women rather differently. In her recent studies of "communication skills" discourse, Cameron has identified a discourse about men's communicative deficiencies which has evolved from popularized notions of distinct male and female interactional styles (Cameron 1998, 2000).

This relatively new view of women as expert communicators has been taken up with enthusiasm by "management gurus" and advertisers. I will go through one example of each. Allan and Barbara Pease, owners of an Australian management training empire, draw on it in a best-selling book aimed at a general audience, *Why Men Don't Listen and Women Can't Read Maps*. The back cover offers the following motley list of "revelations" about the behavioral characteristics of women and men:

Why men really can't do more than one thing at a time
Why women make such a mess of parallel parking
Why men should never lie to women
Why women talk so much and men so little
Why men love erotic images and women aren't impressed
Why women prefer to simply talk it through
Why men offer solutions, but hate advice
Why women despair about men's silences
Why men want sex and women need love

Cruder by far than Tannen's popularizing work on gender differences, this book claims to be based on (and indeed gives references to) scientific sex differences research. Notwithstanding its claims to scientific founding, what it actually espouses is an extreme, and very crude, form of biological essentialism. As one might expect, it completely disregards any research findings that might interfere with its simple, endlessly repeated claims: such as that women, among other things, talk more than men. The result is a volume unselfconsciously reproducing a raft of weary clichés and tired jokes, rigged up with an illusion of "scientificity." For example, their chapter on "Talking and Listening" contains a section headed "Women Talk, Men Feel Nagged." It opens as follows:

The building of relationships through talk is a priority in the brain-wiring of women. A woman can effortlessly speak an average of 6,000–8,000 words a day. She uses an additional 2,000–3,000 vocal sounds to communicate, as well as 8,000–10,000 body language signals. This gives her a daily average of more than 20,000 communication "words" to relate her message. That explains just why the British Medical Association recently reported that women are four times more likely to suffer with jaw problems.

> "Once I didn't talk to my wife for six months," said the comedian. "I didn't want to interrupt."

Contrast a woman's daily "chatter" to that of a man. He utters just 2,000–4,000 words and 1,000–2,000 vocal sounds, and makes a mere 2,000–3,000 body language signals. His daily average adds up to around 7,000 communication "words" – just over a third the output of a woman.   (Pease and Pease 1999: 89–90)

The stereotype of the over-talkative woman is given factual status, with the help of some spurious figures and a reference to the British Medical Association. A shaded box between the two paragraphs reinforces the point with an old familiar joke. While communication skills discourse may appear to undermine traditional stereotypes of women as language users, it seems that such stereotypes are readily resurrected and may be with us for some time yet. In 2000 Allan Pease addressed a personnel conference at Harrogate in England; the event was covered in *The Times* in an article referring to his most recent publication – the article was headed "Women rule as a natter of fact." Stereotypes, it would appear, rule ok.

An advertisement in a British Telecom (the UK's main provider of phone services) campaign in the 1990s criticized men for making women feel guilty about running up phone bills. "Why can't men be more like women?" we were asked, this being the slogan in a banner across the advertisement (another part of the text of this advertisement is discussed in Cameron, this volume). The slogan was a reversal of the talk-song "Why can't a woman be more like a man?" from the musical *My Fair Lady*. The appeal of this banner headline lies in its ironic reversal of the familiar folklinguistic negative assessment of women's talk. In this recent reversal, women are held up as model communicators. As Cameron has pointed out, its use in an advertising campaign shows the extent to which a proposition such as "women are better at talking" has moved from expert discourse into popular common-sense; advertisers, after all, must make their appeals to the familiar and recognizable (Cameron 1998).

The advertisement, and indeed the whole campaign, draws a sharp contrast between men's instrumental use of the telephone with women's interpersonal, and specifically phatic, use of it. Drawing on the familiar distinction between men's report-talk and women's rapport-talk, the campaign drew fathers' attention to their wives' superior ability in keeping in contact with their daughters at university. This was a stark contrast with British Telecom's preceding advertising campaign which, while promoting the value of the phone for keeping families in touch with one another, worked with the gossip stereotype (this earlier advertising campaign featured the actor Maureen Lipman as a mother endlessly phoning her family in Australia). However, the very advertisement that ironically reversed *My Fair Lady*'s talk-song and held women up as model communicators was curiously ambivalent about the value of phatic talk. The same text contains some aphorisms on the theme of conversation; oddly chosen ones, since they are not particularly positive about phatic talk at all. One anonymous aphorism, for example, compares women's conversation to "the straw around china. Without it everything would be broken." The simile of empty packaging material is hardly complimentary. Elsewhere in the advertising copy, the subject of domestic budgeting (comparing unlike things in terms of their relative cost) reduces women's talk to a commodity. The text of the advertising copy concludes with the implications that women's gossip is acceptable both because it is cheap and because licensing it is a way of avoiding domestic disputes:

> This difference between the sexes becomes rather more than academic when the phone bill hits the mat.
> Some men have a way of making women feel guilty about it.
> Would it help, gentlemen, if you knew the true costs?
> That a half hour chat at local cheap rate costs less than half a pint, for example?
> Or that a five minute local call at daytime rate costs about the price of a small bar of chocolate?
> Not so much when you think about it.
> Particularly compared with the cost of not talking at all.

In her investigation of other British Telecom material, Cameron has remarked on the continued presence of the gossipy woman, not to mention the nagging wife and hen-pecked husband, despite all the overt claims about the superiority of women as communicators (2000: 174). It seems that the evolving stereotypes involving female fluency and male inarticulacy slide back into their older versions very readily indeed.

7   Conclusion

So, in recent years we have seen an apparent turnabout in the perception of women's verbal abilities. Women are no longer the deficient communicators, but the superior ones. But this view is predicated on a "differences" framework which, as I have indicated above, is highly problematic. It tends to shore up gender stereotypes rather than undermine them. It is a view that is shot through with problems (dealt with in detail in Cameron 2000), and anyway even as it is presented it is undermined. To be rather more positive, it may be that widespread perception of communication skills as feminine will have lasting impact on one of the "good stereotypes" considered earlier: it seems that, sometimes at least, women's talk is no longer being judged against an ideal of female silence. What is less sure, however, is that holding aloft the nurturant, supportive verbal behavior supposedly characteristic of the female interactional style as superior "communication" actually does anything to disturb hegemonic male dominance and female subordination.

REFERENCES

Barrett, Rusty 1999: Indexing polyphonous identity in the speech of African American drag queens. In Mary Bucholtz, Anita C. Liang, and Laurel A. Sutton (eds) *Reinventing Identities: The Gendered Self in Discourse.* New York and Oxford: Oxford University Press, pp. 313–31.

Bem, Sandra Lipsitz 1993: *The Lenses of Gender: Transforming the Debate on Sexual Inequality.* New Haven, CT: Yale University Press.

Bergvall, Victoria 1996: Constructing and enacting gender through discourse: Negotiating multiple roles as female engineering students. In Victoria Bergvall, Janet Bing, and Alice Freed (eds) *Rethinking Language and Gender Research: Theory and Practice.* London: Longman, pp. 173–201.

Brown, Penelope 1980: How and why women are more polite: Some evidence from a Mayan community. In Sally McConnell-Ginet, Ruth Borker, and Nelly Furman (eds) *Women and Language in Literature and Society.* New York: Praeger, pp. 111–36.

Brown, Penelope 1993: Gender, politeness and confrontation in Tenejapa. In Deborah Tannen (ed.) *Gender and Conversational Interaction.* Oxford: Oxford University Press, pp. 144–62.

Bucholtz, Mary and Hall, Kira 1995: Introduction: Twenty years after *Language and Woman's Place.* In Kira Hall and Mary Bucholtz (eds) *Gender Articulated: Language and the Socially Constructed Self.* London and New York: Routledge, pp. 1–22.

Bucholtz, Mary, Liang, Anita C., and Sutton, Laurel A. (eds) 1999: *Reinventing Identities: The Gendered Self in Discourse.* New York and Oxford: Oxford University Press.

Cameron, Deborah 1985: *Feminism and Linguistic Theory.* Basingstoke: Macmillan.

Cameron, Deborah 1988: Introduction. In Jennifer Coates and Deborah Cameron (eds) *Women in Their Speech Communities.* London: Longman, pp. 3–12.

Cameron, Deborah 1992: Review of Tannen 1991. *Feminism and Psychology* 2–3: 465–89.

Cameron, Deborah 1995: Rethinking language and gender studies: Some issues for the 90s. In Sara Mills (ed.) *Language and Gender: Interdisciplinary Perspectives.* London: Longman, pp. 31–44.

Cameron, Deborah 1996: The language–gender interface: Challenging co-optation. In Victoria Bergvall, Janet Bing, and Alice Freed (eds) *Rethinking Language And Gender Research: Theory and Practice.* London: Longman, pp. 31–53.

Cameron, Deborah 1997: Theoretical debates in feminist linguistics. In

Ruth Wodak (ed.) *Discourse and Gender*. London: Sage, pp. 21–36.

Cameron, Deborah 1998: "Communication skills" as a gendered discourse. In Suzanne Wertheim, Ashlee C. Bailey and Monica Corston-Oliver (eds) *Engendering Communication: Proceedings of the Fifth Berkeley Women and Language Conference*. Berkeley, CA: Berkeley Women and Language Group, University of California, pp. 105–16.

Cameron, Deborah 2000: *Good to Talk? Living and Working in a Communication Culture*. London: Sage.

Dyer, Richard 1977: *Gays and Film*. London: British Film Institute.

Eckert, Penelope and McConnell-Ginet, Sally 1992: Think practically and look locally: Language and gender as community-based practice. *Annual Review of Anthropology* 21: 461–90.

Freed, Alice 1996: Language and gender research in an experimental setting. In Victoria Bergvall, Janet Bing, and Alice Freed (eds) *Rethinking Language and Gender Research: Theory and Practice*. London: Longman, pp. 54–76.

Gal, Susan 1995: Language, gender and power: An anthropological review. In Kira Hall and Mary Bucholtz (eds) *Gender Articulated: Language and the Socially Constructed Self*. London and New York: Routledge, pp. 169–82.

Graddol, David and Swann, Joan 1989: *Gender Voices*. Oxford: Blackwell.

Hall, Kira 1995: Lip service on the fantasy lines. In Kira Hall and Mary Bucholtz (eds) *Gender Articulated: Language and the Socially Constructed Self*. London and New York: Routledge, pp. 183–216.

Hall, Stuart 1997: The spectacle of the "Other". In Stuart Hall (ed.) *Representation: Cultural Representations and Signifying Practices*. London: Sage, pp. 223–90.

Herbert, James 1976: *Lair*. London: New English Library.

Holmes, Janet 1984: "Women's language": A functional approach. *General Linguistics* 24(3): 149–78.

Holmes, Janet 1995: *Women, Men and Politeness*. London: Longman.

Jespersen, Otto 1922: *Language: Its Nature, Development and Origin*. London: Allen and Unwin.

Lakoff, Robin 1975: *Language and Woman's Place*. New York: Harper and Row.

Liang, Alison 1989: *Speaking as a Woman: A Guide for Those Who Desire to Communicate in a More Feminine Manner*. King of Prussia, PA: Creative Design Services.

Livia, Anna and Hall, Kira (eds) 1997: *Queerly Phrased: Language, Gender, and Sexuality*. Oxford: Oxford University Press.

Lochhead, Liz 1986: *Dreaming Frankenstein*. London: Polygon.

Macdonald, Myra 1995: *Representing Women: Myths of Femininity in the Popular Media*. London: Edward Arnold.

Mercer, Kobena and Julien, Isaac 1994: Black masculinity and the politics of race. In Kobena Mercer (ed.) *Welcome to the Jungle*. London: Routledge, pp. 131–70.

NUJ 1982: *Non-sexist Code of Practice for Publishing*. London: National Union of Journalists.

Pease, Allan and Pease, Barbara 1999: *Why Men Don't Listen and Women Can't Read Maps*. New South Wales: Pease Training International.

Searle, Denise 1988: The National Union of Journalists' attitude to controlling media sexism. In Gail Chester and Julienne Dickey (eds) *Feminism and Censorship*. Bridport, Dorset: Prism, pp. 253–60.

Spender, Dale 1985: *Man Made Language*, 2nd edn. London: Routledge and Kegan Paul.

Stanworth, Michelle 1983: *Gender and Schooling: A Study of Sexual Divisions in the Classroom*. London: Hutchinson.

Staples, Robert 1982: *Black Masculinity: The Black Man's Role in American Society*. San Francisco, CA: Black Scholar Press.

Talbot, Mary M. 1998: *Language and Gender: An Introduction*. Cambridge: Polity.

Talbot, Mary M. 2000: "It's good to talk"?: The undermining of feminism in a British Telecom advertisement. *Journal of Sociolinguistics* 4: 108–19.

Tannen, Deborah 1990: Gender differences in conversational coherence: Physical alignment and topical cohesion. In Bruce Dorval (ed.) *Conversational Organization and its Development*. Norwood, NJ: Ablex, pp. 167–206.

Thorne, Barrie 1993: *Gender Play*. Milton Keynes: Open University Press.

21 Gender and Identity: Representation and Social Action

ANN WEATHERALL AND CINDY GALLOIS

1 Gender Identity: A Pervasive Social Categorization

Gender identity has long been understood as one's social identification as a boy or a girl, a man or a woman. For the vast majority of people, a clear gender classification is given at (or with ultrasound technology, well before) birth. Thereafter, all social interactions are influenced by gender assignment (see, for example, Condry and Condry 1976). Identification with a gender group is considered by many developmental psychologists as a fundamental social categorization in the life of a child (Yelland 1998). Indeed, there is general agreement among psychologists that gender is the single most important social category in people's lives (Bem 1993). Despite this agreement there is little consensus about how best to conceptualize gender identity and its relationship to language. In this chapter, we discuss two major psychological approaches to gender and language. The first takes a social-cognitive perspective, where gender identity is considered to be the internalization of social norms about gender that predispose individuals to act, talk, and think largely in accordance with them. The second perspective comes from discursive psychology, where the emphasis is on language rather than cognition as the prime site for understanding social conduct.

The social-cognitive perspective generally assumes that behavior, including language and communication, is mainly driven by and is a reflection of underlying cognitive characteristics and processes. For example, a study showing differential treatment by teachers in response to the same behavior displayed by either boys or girls was interpreted as demonstrating that teachers' gender preconceptions influenced their responses to children (Fagot et al. 1985). Such preconceptions are thought to derive from a proclivity of the human cognitive system to categorize information, in order to make sense of the huge amount of sensory information with which people are confronted in daily life. Cognitive shortcuts tend to assimilate items into culturally available categories (cf. Tajfel 1981). Thus, social beliefs about gender function as a guide in the perception of others and in interactions with them. In addition, a psychological need for a positive personal and social identity may, in some situations, influence the kinds of judgments made about other people, depending on whether they belong to the same or a different gender category to you.

The social-cognitive perspective involves an assumption that gender identity develops as a relatively stable, pre-discursive trait, which resides in individuals and which is more or less salient, depending on its relevance to a particular social context. For this perspective, although identity both drives and reflects the language around it, cognition is conceptually prior to its expression in language and communication. In contrast, the discursive psychology perspective considers gender to be the accomplishment and product of social interaction. Discursive psychology emphasizes the study of language over minds as the best way for understanding the significance of social categories in human conduct. In this approach, social categories are also verbal categories whose use provides insights into the structure and organization of social life. For example, generalizations about gender may be used to support differential treatment of women and men, and the specific characteristics of individual women or men may be mobilized in arguments to contradict the validity of gender generalizations (Billig et al. 1988).

The development of discursive psychology has been influenced by ethnomethodological approaches to the study of social life. This influence is particularly relevant to the topic of gender identity and language, because one of the earliest non-essentialist approaches to gender in psychology developed from ethnomethodology. This approach considers how the taken-for-grantedness and ordinariness of belonging to one and only one of two gender groups is achieved in everyday life (Kessler and McKenna 1978). Garfinkel's (1967) study of a transsexual, Agnes, provided compelling evidence that gender identity is more than a reflection of biology or an internalization of social norms. Agnes, unlike most people, had to consciously work at achieving and securing her gender identity status. Thus, she made "observable *that* and *how* normal sexuality is accomplished" (Garfinkel 1967: 80). Garfinkel noted that among Agnes's "passing" devices were the use of pitch control, a lisp, and stereotypical features of women's speech such as euphemism.

The differing theoretical assumptions of the discursive and social-cognitive approaches about the nature of gender identity and its relationship to language have profoundly influenced the research agendas of psychologists studying gender and language. Sections 2 and 3 describe the kinds of questions asked about gender and language, and the insights achieved, from each approach. Section 4 highlights similarities and differences between them. Finally we consider what the two psychological approaches can contribute to and take from other gender and language research traditions.

2 Language and Social Cognition: Representations of Gender in Language and Interaction

A fundamental assumption made by psychologists taking a social-cognitive approach to gender identity is that language is both a medium for expressing gender identity and a reflection of it. The idea that language holds a represent-ation of social identity motivated much early social-cognitive research on gender. An early question was: if speech is a reflection of gender identity, then to what extent can a speaker's gender identity be accurately assessed by listen-ers? A related concern has been with how much real gender differences in speech, and how much beliefs about gender differences, influence evaluations of speakers. In research since the early 1970s, definitive answers to these ques-tions have not been found. From a social-cognitive perspective, a possible explanation for the lack of resolution has been that the salience of gender identity in speech and communication fluctuates as a function of the specific conversational context. Social identity theory and communication accommod-ation theory, discussed later in this section, offer two key frameworks for explicating the subtleties of context for the expression of gender identity in language and speech.

Giles, Smith, Ford, Condor, and Thakerar (1980) were among the first to report a high degree of consistency in ratings of speakers on masculinity and femininity. This finding prompted speculation about the degree of correspondence between people's self-reported gender identity and others' perceptions of them as masculine or feminine. Smith (1985) tested whether speech-based attributions of masculinity and femininity bore any resemblance to speakers' self-assessed masculinity and femininity. In this study, speakers' gender identities were measured by their degree of endorsement of sex-role stereotypes as characterizing themselves. The results showed a high level of correspondence between listeners' perceptions of the speakers' gender iden-tity and speakers' self-ratings of masculinity and femininity. In an additional experimental twist, Smith examined whether listeners' gender identities would affect their ratings. The results suggested that the stronger the gender identity of the listeners, the more likely they were to polarize the differences between female and male speakers, and to exaggerate the similarities among same-gender speakers.

The idea that factors other than the gender identity of the speaker may influence the perception and evaluation of speech has continued as an import-ant theme in social-cognitive research on gender and language. A variable that has received considerable attention is gender stereotypes about speech. Early work established a high degree of consensus about the speech traits associated with women and men (Kramer 1978). Aries (1996) confirmed that there is broad agreement in Anglo-American culture on beliefs about how men and women talk, and that stereotypes about gender and language have changed little since the 1970s (see also Mulac et al. 1998).

Cutler and Scott (1990) investigated the influence of speaker gender (i.e. gendered speech stereotypes) on listeners' judgments of speaker verbosity. They recorded two-person dialogues taken from plays, where each person contributed equal amounts of speech to the conversation. The gender of the speaker taking each role in the conversation was systematically varied. In this work, the general social categories of "women" and "men" were being used as a proxy for gender identity. When the dialogues were between a man and a woman, the woman was judged to be talking more than her conversational partner. When members of the same gender performed the dialogues, however, each speaker was judged as contributing to the conversation equally. Thus, gender as a social category appeared to trigger psychological processes that resulted in a halo effect, where a gendered speech style was somewhat in the ear of the beholder.

Given that speakers' gender identity and gender stereotypes about speech influence how other speakers are perceived and evaluated, an obvious question is how much we evaluate women's and men's speech based on actual differences in language style, as opposed to stereotyped beliefs about the way men and women talk. A supposition here, of course, is that there are real and stable gender differences in speech (e.g. Mulac et al. 1998). Lawrence, Stucky, and Hopper (1990) tested what they called the sex-stereotype and the sex-dialect hypotheses. The sex-stereotype hypothesis asserts that speaker gender alone triggers differential evaluative responses in listeners. In contrast, the sex-dialect hypothesis is that different evaluations of men and women are due to real differences in their speech patterns. The conversations used in the study were based on short segments of a previously recorded naturally occurring conversation between a woman and a man. The conversational segments were transcribed and re-recorded. In one condition, actors of the same gender as the original speaker reproduced the language and paralanguage. In the other condition, each actor took the other gender role.

The sex-dialect hypothesis would predict that listeners' ratings would be influenced by the original speaker gender, whereas the stereotype hypothesis would predict that listeners would be influenced by the gender of the actor. The results of the study did not straightforwardly support either hypothesis. Rather, listeners were influenced by both original and attributed speaker gender. In addition, the influence varied depending on the particular conversational segment. Lawrence et al. concluded that the impact on listeners of speech style and stereotypes may be fluctuating and transitory, and that there was a need for descriptive research on how speakers produce and orient to social identities such as age, gender, and social class in interactions. Other possible explanations are, among others, that stereotypes may differ in strength and that stereotypes may have different functions.

2.1   Gender and social identity theory

One of the most influential contemporary theories to consider the importance of social identities and their impact on language use and interaction is social identity theory (SIT: Tajfel 1981). According to SIT, people's sense of who they are comprises aspects deriving both from them as individuals and from their membership of social groups (see Augoustinos and Walker 1995 for a comprehensive overview of this theory). SIT emphasizes that the ways people think and behave depend strongly on the social groups they belong to, particularly in contexts where group membership is salient for some reason. Characteristics of group behavior associated with social identity include stereotyping and in-group favoritism. An important aspect of the theory is that it recognizes that different social groups vary in terms of the power and status that they have in society, a recognition that is essential to a comprehensive understanding of women and men as social groups.

SIT is based on the assumption that people are generally motivated to view themselves in a favorable way. Achieving a positive self-concept requires making social comparisons in order to evaluate the opinions and abilities of people who share or do not share a social group membership. If a group to which a person belongs has a low social status, the person may try to overcome any sense of inferiority stemming from that group membership through a number of identity maintenance mechanisms. One possible strategy, social mobility, is to leave the low-status group and join the higher-status group (i.e. to "pass"): this is an individual strategy. Where passing is not possible and group membership is stable (as is generally the case with gender), other strategies may be employed to achieve more positive self-esteem. These include social creativity, or finding new dimensions of comparison where one's own group comes out better (e.g. using nurturance or people-centeredness as a key dimension, rather than leadership), and social competition, or entering into social or political conflict to gain more status for the group (e.g. joining the feminist movement).

Social identity theory was conceived to explain the ways that oppressed groups challenge their social disadvantage, but the methodology originally developed to test it involved experiments on the behavioral patterns of reward allocation by individuals assigned randomly to minimally different groups (Tajfel 1970). Much of the research on SIT has diverged from the original purpose and is more relevant to contexts of social rivalry (such as opposing sports teams) than to social inequality. Nevertheless, the theory was soon applied as a framework for understanding the influence of important social group memberships (e.g. ethnicity, religious affiliation) on cognition and behavior. For example, Williams and Giles (1978) argued that this theory could be used to demonstrate that the diverse actions and perspectives of women in a feminist era, far from being trivial and irrational, were coherent strategies for promoting social change. The identity maintenance strategies they described frequently involved language.

Williams and Giles (1978) suggested that prior to the women's liberation movement of the 1960s–1970s, women had largely accepted their secondary status in society. Thus, before the second wave of feminism, many women achieved a positive social identity by individual means. For example, individual women could achieve a positive self-concept by comparing themselves with other women on dimensions such as performance of domestic duties, or by comparing the social status of their husbands to other women with husbands of lower social standing. The feminism of the 1960s and 1970s led to a raised consciousness of the illegitimacy of women's secondary social status, however, and the American Civil Rights movement meant that the possibility of social change was salient. Williams and Giles argued that it was precisely under such social conditions that SIT would predict a mobilization of women in a political movement. They interpreted attempts to gain equality with men in employment, legal, and political contexts as consistent with the social mobility strategy outlined in SIT (cf. Augoustinos and Walker 1995).

More recently, feminist psychologists have criticized social identity theory for treating women as a single, coherent social group. The limitations of SIT for understanding the multifaceted nature of womanhood in contemporary society have been well documented (see Skevington and Baker 1989). Despite these problems, however, this theory has been useful for interpreting aspects of women and language use. For example, Coates (1986) used SIT in a discussion of the impact of feminism on women's language. Coates suggested that, in terms of language, a social mobility strategy was a widespread identity maintenance tactic used by women to enhance their social identity. The linguistic evidence she cited of women trying to be like men included the use of deeper voices, increased swearing, adoption of falling rather than rising intonation patterns, and increasing use of non-standard accents. Women also redefined the language characteristics of women positively, for example by emphasizing the relative merits of cooperative as opposed to competitive strategies in conversation. There have also been moves, particularly in feminist academic circles, to redefine positively features of women's language such as gossip.

2.2   Communication accommodation theory

The psychological concept of social identity in general, and gender identity in particular, appears in a different guise in another influential theory called communication accommodation theory (CAT: Giles, Coupland, and Coupland, 1991; see also Gallois and Giles 1998). CAT and its precursor, speech accommodation theory (SAT), have been widely used as frameworks for understanding social identity, language variation, and their consequences during intergroup interactions.

If a fundamental psychological process is the categorization of people into different groups, then speech is likely to be a key basis for social categorization and a consequential marker of social identities. In considering the processes influencing language use in any interaction, speech accommodation theory (see Giles and Powesland 1975; Giles and Smith 1979) applied four social psychological theories to language use. First, influenced by similarity-attraction theory, SAT proposed that speech convergence (adjusting the way we speak to be more like the person we are speaking to) is used to indicate that we like or want to be liked by the interlocutor or to identify with the interlocutor's group. For example, a young man wanting to signal his liking of a young woman may reduce his use of swearing and taboo language (i.e. converge to what he believes is her more polite speech). A corollary of this pattern is that we may judge the speech of a person we like to be more similar to our own speech than that of a person we do not like or who is a member of a group we disparage.

Similarity-attraction theory emphasizes the benefits of speech convergence: an increase in attraction or approval. Such convergence also has costs; for example, the young man using more polite speech, while he shows his identification with his love, may be losing language markers identifying him as masculine. Social exchange theory predicts that convergent speech acts occur only when the advantages of the exchange outweigh the disadvantages. Carli (1990) highlighted the potential dilemmas for women in using a particular language style. Carli found that women who used a more tentative speech style were more persuasive when talking to a man than when talking to a woman. People with more tentative speech styles were rated by both women and men as less competent, however. These results indicate that the cost of using assertive language for women may be not being influential, particularly to men, but the benefit of using such language is that they are perceived as more competent.

Third, causal attribution theory suggests that the way speech shifts are evaluated depends on the motives and intentions that are attributed to them. For example, if the young man in the example above reduces his swearing only when the young woman's mother is around, the young woman may be less likely to attribute that change to the young man's attraction to her (even though his intention may actually be to signal his attraction).

The final theoretical influence on SAT was social identity theory. Giles and Smith (1979) argued that in situations where group membership is salient, speech divergence (shifting language style to make it more dissimilar to the interlocutor's) reflects a group identity maintenance process; that is, a strategy to mark oneself as distinct from another social group. For example, a woman wanting to emphasize her femininity may exaggerate the features associated with women's language in a mixed-sex interaction.

The paragraphs above show that SAT is a well-developed example of the social-cognitive approach. As such, this theory was, at its conception, distinct from sociolinguistic approaches to language variation. At the time, Giles and Powesland (1975) argued that the latter constructed people as (in their words) "sociolinguistic automata," whose social identifications were expressed by particular features of language in deterministic ways. In contrast, SAT proposed that motivation, in context, to identify with or show liking for another person (or the reverse) is what determines the use of language markers, rather than a stable trait of group identity. Indeed, they argued that Labov's (1966) findings of style change might best be explained as a motivation to converge with the interviewer, rather than an indication of social group or social identity *per se*.

From the beginning, research using SAT found complexities that the theory was not well equipped to handle. For example, Thakerar, Giles, and Cheshire (1982) found that nurses converged to stereotypes of a higher-status group's speech style, rather than to the actual speech characteristics of members of that group. In a similar vein, Bilous and Krauss (1988) found that men and women in friendly interactions (where a motivation to converge could be expected) converged to each other's style on some variables (even crossing over in some cases), but diverged on others; this appeared to involve behavioral divergence driven by convergent motivation. Complexities like these led to the transformation of SAT into communication accommodation theory (CAT: see Giles et al. 1991).

CAT, compared to SAT, has significantly broadened and extended the variables seen to influence sociolinguistic choices and responses to them. The theory now links the larger sociohistorical context to the orientations and goals of individual speakers, who use a large array of strategies (including convergence/divergence, management of the discourse, emotional and relational expression, role-related language, and face-maintenance, among others) to direct their communication. Accordingly, listeners respond, attribute, and evaluate the interaction, and make judgments about future interactions. Identity, along with intergroup and interpersonal orientation, are negotiated during the course of interactions, in a continual interplay between communication and social-psychological variables. Thus, CAT is less clearly a social-cognitive approach, and shows some similarity to the discursive approach described below. Nevertheless, for CAT, identity and motivation are still conceptually prior to language and communication.

To date, few studies have invoked the full complexity of CAT in the area of gender and language. Instead, research has often continued to rely on stereotypes about gender differences in speech. For example, Hannah and Murachver (1999) operationalized a (feminine) facilitative speech style as the higher use of minimal responses, fewer interruptions, and not looking away during an interaction. They then looked for divergence or convergence to the facilitative or non-facilitative style across two conversations in same- and mixed-sex dyads. Their results showed no compelling patterns of change related to gender identity, perhaps because the salience of gender identity was marked in a way other than what they measured (e.g. intonation, phonology).

One exception to this trend is research by Boggs and Giles (1999), who studied patterns of accommodation and non-accommodation in workplaces where women were coming into previously male-dominated jobs. They argued that communication breakdown in such workplaces reflects socio-structural factors built into the organization that normalize male domination of the jobs and encourage miscommunication when women take the jobs. Using CAT along with closely related theory, they modeled a non-accommodation cycle, beginning with threats to the men's identity, progressing through non-accommodation by men as a consequence, and leading to tit-for-tat responses by women. They concluded that this cycle reflects and maintains the organizational structure, and that in particular it undermines attempts at affirmative action. In their view, the usual construction of communication breakdown between men and women in these workplaces as interpersonal (and therefore the "fault" of either the men or the women involved), or at best as arising from cultural differences in men's and women's language, is unhelpful. Instead, they advocate considering these situations in terms of the language that reflects the social structure.

Social identity theory (SIT) and communication accommodation theory (CAT) have been influential in interpreting language behaviors that seem to be motivated by the desire to achieve a positive social identity as a woman or a man. For example, SIT has been used to explain the use of lower pitch by women in politics, feminist challenges to sexist language, and the promotion of a co-operative communication style in business. SIT and CAT provide a framework for understanding why communication style changes during the course of an interaction, depending on the relative salience of interpersonal and intergroup dimensions. Indeed, the work of Boggs and Giles (1999) and that of other recent researchers (see Gallois and Giles 1998) shows how CAT gives priority to both communication and social-cognitive factors, and it represents a significant move in the direction of constructionist theory. Both SIT and CAT, however, are open to the charge that they treat "women" (and "men") as a homogeneous group, when in fact there are few or perhaps no experiences that all women (or men) share. Discursive psychology aims to avoid this problem by avoiding essentialist and realist assumptions about identity altogether.

3 Discursive Psychology: Gender as Action in Talk

A discursive psychological (DP) perspective to identity rejects the essentialist assumptions of social cognition, where gender identity is expressed through language. This approach treats identity as primarily a verbal categorization that occurs in the process of interaction *in order to do things*. Thus, identity is not viewed in essentialist terms as something that people *are*. Rather, identity is something that people *do* during the business of everyday interaction. Furthermore, the kinds of identifications or categorizations that are resources for social action are available, and have their nature defined, through systems of meaning which have cultural and ideological histories (Wetherell and Edley

1998). In discursive psychology the emphasis is on talk, not cognition, as the most important site for studying identity (e.g. see Edwards 1997).

There are different styles of discourse analysis within DP. At a general level, however, discursive psychological approaches have been more or less influenced by conversation analysis, ethnomethodology, post-structuralism, and speech act theory. For example, Foucault's ideas about subjectivity being the product of discursive practices or epistemic regimes have influenced the theoretical stance of DP on identity. According to this approach, a sense of self emerges not from an inner core but out of a complex of historical, cultural, and political processes and practices. Individuals are located in and opt for a variety of different positions, depending on the social, historical, political, and economic aspects of their situations. The influence of ethnomethodology and conversation analysis is evident in discursive studies where the focus is on the everyday linguistic practices that function to organize and structure interaction and social action.

Following Potter and Wetherell (1987) the concepts of action, construction, and variation are often used as analytic tools in discursive psychology. In this work, an important focus is what is being achieved (i.e. social action or function) in an interaction. Often, an analysis concentrates on the management of an *issue* or *dilemma*, for example presenting something as factual (e.g. sex differences) when there is a personal stake involved (e.g. a need to justify discriminatory practices). The term *ideological dilemma* has been coined to refer to the contradictory beliefs and ideas that constitute our common-sense understanding of the world (Billig et al. 1988). For example, when referring to many people working together on a talk we may say "many hands make light work" or "too many cooks spoil the broth." This reflects an underlying dilemma, whose resolution depends on what we are doing with the idea – recruiting or discouraging volunteers.

A further characteristic of Potter and Wetherell's (1987) discourse analytic approach is that it aims to identify the linguistic and rhetorical resources used by a speaker to construct behavior or social action as reasonable and rational. The identification of broader patterns of language use, sometimes referred to as *interpretative repertoires, practical ideologies*, or *discourses*, is often an aim of the research. These patterns involve the "often contradictory and fragmentary notions, norms and models which guide conduct and allow for its justification and rationalisation" (Wetherell, Stiven, and Potter 1987: 60). The use of the term "ideology" in ideological dilemmas and practical ideologies suggests the critical nature of many discursive studies. Ideology refers to the systems of beliefs or thoughts that contribute to the maintenance of asymmetrical power relations and social inequalities between groups. For example, the belief that women are "naturally" more nurturing than men contributes to women having to shoulder the major burden for child-care and elder-care.

An early example of a discourse-analytic study in psychology that utilized the concepts of interpretative repertoires and practical ideologies was Wetherell et al.'s (1987) investigation into the accounts that university students gave of employment opportunities for women. The interpretative repertoires that emerged from the analysis were called "individualism" and "practical consideration" talk. These two repertoires functioned in the students' accounts to naturalize and justify sexual inequality in employment. On the one hand, students argued, using an individualism interpretative repertoire, that it was up to individuals to show they had the knowledge, experience, and skills worthy of employment. On the other hand, the participants noted that there were practical considerations (e.g. lack of adequate child-care) making the employment of women a problem (also see Gough 1998). Wetherell et al. suggested that the repertoires of individualism and practical considerations allowed speakers to endorse the concept of equal opportunity, thus presenting themselves as liberal and open-minded. At the same time, however, they also denied the possibility that bias against women in employment existed. The simultaneous endorsement of equity and denial of bias constructs a discursive context that discourages actions that would encourage women into employment.

3.1 Gender differences as interactional resource

The issue of gender differences in speech has been a key theme in gender and language research (Cameron 1998). Instead of trying to establish what the "real" differences are, a discursive approach examines how ideas of gender are used for argumentative purposes. Billig et al. (1988) noted that there is a fundamental dilemma associated with discussions about men and women. The dilemma is associated with the contradictory common-sense ideas that all human beings are essentially "the same" and also that all individuals are essentially "different." The availability of these contradictory notions means that making generalizations about people can always be countered by particular exceptions. An important point is that generalizations and particularizations have a moral status. There are tensions between beliefs and values of human equality and those of human variety. As a result, the extent of similarity or difference between people is always an ideological dilemma. Billig et al. illustrated the articulation of the dilemma of gender versus individual difference in student discussions about the statement "there are some jobs men can do better than women." Discussions of this question followed what Billig et al. referred to as a "generalization–particularization chain," with each categorical statement about women or men sparking a reference to individual differences or exceptions.

The "fact" of being a man or a woman and what that means, at least in discussions about gender, is not fixed but a process of stabilizing and destabilizing notions that generalize about gender and that highlight the uniqueness of individual women and men. The contradictory purposes to which gender can be put were noted by Ehrlich (1999), when a tribunal member's identity as a woman was used to justify claims that she was both biased and not biased. Similarly, Marshall and Wetherell (1989) found variability and inconsistency in how gender identity was used in discussion of men's and women's suitability as lawyers. The similarity between women and men was used to support the argument that both make good lawyers, but the differences between them were also used to argue that both women and men make good lawyers. Of course, the notion of gender differences was also used when claims were made that men were more suited to careers as lawyers than women.

Gill's (1993) study of how radio station personnel explained the lack of female disc jockeys (DJs) also shows how the notion of gender differences becomes implicated in the discursive patterning of sexism. The first and most prevalent explanation given by the radio station workers was that women just did not apply for jobs when vacancies were advertised. A typical reason given for women's non-application was that women are not interested in doing that kind of work. Gill suggested that a function of this kind of explanation is that it deflects possible charges of sexism away from the radio station. Women's non-application is a compelling explanation for the lack of female DJs. However, a characteristic of discourse analytic studies is not to endorse the "truth" of any one explanation, but rather to identify the different accounts given (sometimes by the same person) and to consider any inherent contradictions. The contradictions are key to the analytic approach because they highlight the discursive nature of the problem, reveal the ideological dimensions of common-sense ideas, and suggest why social problems (such as gender segregation in the labor market) are so resistant to change.

A contradiction in the accounts collected by Gill (1993) was highlighted by the second type of explanation given for the lack of female DJs. This reason (and sometimes both explanations were used within the same interview) focused on audiences' alleged negative reactions to female presenters and their preference for men's voices. The interesting thing to note here is the inherent inconsistency between the two explanations, of women's non-application and of audiences' preference for men. In the light of the latter explanation, the lack of women in broadcasting looks less like the result of non-application and more like a deliberate policy not to employ women because of audience preference for men's voices. Despite the inconsistency, a common feature is that both explanations deflect the attribution of blame away from the radio station (Gill 1993). These two seemingly common-sense explanations function discursively to excuse the radio station from any responsibility to increase the number of women DJs.

The third type of explanation given invoked the notion of gender differences. Women supposedly lacked the qualities and skills necessary to be radio presenters. In this case, Gill (1993) paid close attention to the exact nature of the skills that the men interviewed listed as being necessary for the job. Interestingly, the interviewees tended to avoid being explicit about the skills required, but when they were, the skills mentioned (e.g. being dextrous and having a personality) did not seem to fit more readily with masculine than feminine stereotypes. Thus, the *notion* rather than the reality of difference was sufficient to justify sexual inequality. A final type of explanation in the broad-casters' explanations revolved around the supposed unsuitability of women's voices. As might be expected, women's voices were not described in positive terms; rather, adjectives like "shrill" or "grating" were used.

A further interesting aspect of Gill's (1993) analysis was the identification of a "Catch–22" situation with the way women's voices were described. On the one hand, if women sounded grating and shrill they turned listeners off, justi-fying not employing women as presenters. On the other hand, the duskiness and sexiness of some women's voices could switch audiences on, thus justify-ing limiting female DJs to unpopular night shifts. Every description of women's voices supported discriminating against them in broadcasting jobs. Further-more, despite the contradictions and inconsistencies among the four types of explanations, they formed a compelling set of discourses that could be used to undermine accusations of sexism and weaken the justification for affirmative action campaigns. Thus, the sexual inequality evident in broad-casting may be seen, in part, as an effect of the discourses about the lack of female DJs.

3.2 Identity work in talk

The discourse analytic studies discussed so far have approached gender as a social category that is produced and reproduced through interpretative reper-toires, or common-sense meaning systems. The systems of meaning are ideo-logical because they are implicated in maintaining the gendered structure of society. A different thread of discursive psychology focuses less on broad patterns of meaning and more on the production of social identities as verbal categories mobilized during interaction in order to do things. Both types are constructionist in so far as gender is viewed as a discursive and/or interactional product. In contrast, a cognitive approach generally construes gender in more essentialist terms as an internal characteristic of individuals that sometimes causes, or at least influences, behavior.

The influence of conversation analysis (CA), with its focus on the joint ac-complishment of social action, is important to this second thread of discursive psychology, as is the CA perspective of context. Historically, gender and lan-guage research has treated the sex of participants as one of the features of the interactional context that may influence language use (see Aries 1996); thus, whether a conversation is held in a mixed-sex group or a same-sex group is an important influence on language use. The CA perspective on context is markedly different. Context is not seen as a combination of independent variables that define the nature of the interaction in advance; rather, context is viewed as being constituted by the interaction itself.

The conversation analytic approach to context and its influence on discur-sive psychology is evident in Antaki and Widdicombe's (1998) approach to the study of identity. According to this perspective, the important question is:

> ... not therefore whether someone can be described in a particular way, but to show *that* and *how* this identity is made relevant or ascribed to self or others ... If there is one defining principle displayed in this kind of analytic approach, it is the ethnomethodological one that identity is to be treated as a resource for the participant rather than the analyst.   (Widdicombe 1998: 191)

Many gender and language studies assume that participants have an internalized gender identity and that people's speech is somehow causally related to that identity. Speakers' identities as "men" or "women" are often invoked in analyses to explain speech, without any evidence that these identities are salient to the participants. This practice has been criticized by conversation analysts as an act of intellectual hegemony, where the researcher's concerns about what is relevant to the participants is imposed onto the analysis (Schegloff 1997). One way of avoiding the imposition of a researcher's concerns is to take the approach that Widdicombe (1998) alludes to above. Taking a more conversation analytic approach means not treating identities as a kind of demographic or psychological fact whose relevance to behavior can simply be assumed. Instead of asking about the strength of gender identity or the kind of contexts where that identity is salient, the focus is on whether, when, and how identities are used. Thus, the existence and relevance of any feature of the interactions is introduced into an analysis only when the participants have demonstrated their orientation to that feature as relevant.

Edwards (1998) is one of the rare examples of discursive psychology's conversation analytic approach being applied to the study of gender identity (but also see Stokoe 1998, 2000). The data for the study were transcripts of family counselling sessions. The analysis focuses on one session with a couple, Connie and Jimmy. Early in the first session, the counsellor asked a series of questions in order to "make some sense" of the couple's "rich and complicated lives" (Edwards 1998: 20–1). Those inquiries offered up various kinds of identity categories (e.g. age, marital status, parenthood) that presumably had some relevance to understanding Connie and Jimmy's relationship problems. One of the more general theoretical points made by Edwards was that it is possible to speculate on how the details requested by the counsellor can be used to make sense of the couple's lives. Following a CA approach, however, the task is to examine what, if anything, the participants in the sessions *do* when they invoke these social categorizations in their talk.

In his analysis Edwards (1998) focused on the terms "girl" and "woman" to investigate the rhetorical subtleties of gender as it was mobilized as a relevant category in the counselling session. Edwards was interested in how these words, with their different connotations of age, marital status, and potential sexual availability, were applied to highlight the relevant aspect of the person being referred to. One instance was when the topic of their relationship difficulties arose: the issue was how Jimmy had left Connie with the children. Connie attributed Jimmy's walking out to an extra-marital relationship, whereas Jimmy blamed his leaving on various aspects of Connie's social activities.

During the discussion of Jimmy's walking out, Edwards (1998) noted that the terms "girl" and "woman" were used variably for the same referent. For example, Connie referred to the other person in the extra-marital affair as "this girl," which seemed to downgrade her status as someone worth bothering about. In contrast, Jimmy denied leaving Connie for another "woman" and reformulated what Connie referred to as "an affair" as a "fling" with a "girl." Edwards argued that Jimmy's use of the term "girl" functioned to downgrade the status of the relationship and helped to counter Connie's claim that it was a serious and long-term threat to their relationship.

Edwards (1998) found a similar kind of rhetorical variation in the use of gender identity terms in descriptions of Connie's social activities. Jimmy's objection to Connie's going out was her flirtatiousness. However, Connie claimed she wanted the freedom to go out with her "friends" for a "girls' night out." Edwards argued that the categories of "friends" and "girls" worked together to define going out as unthreatening and harmless. Jimmy maintained his objection to the way Connie behaved "out with company." A bit later Connie reformulated the relevant identities of her friends from "girls" to "married women." This reformulation attended to Jimmy's complaint about her going out as being an opportunity for unfaithfulness.

In this brief description, we have only been able to give a flavour of Edwards's (1998) analysis, but his substantive point is important. Identity categories such as "girls," "married women," and "the other woman" are not used merely because that is what the people being referred to *are*, or even because that is how those people *think* of themselves. Instead, the categories of girls and women are used to attend to the local, rhetorically important business of the interaction at hand.

3.3   Gender relevance

A definitive aspect of the conversation analytic thread in discursive psychology is an insistence on focusing on features that are demonstrably relevant to the participants in the interaction. Thus, analysts avoid seeking the influence of predetermined categories on interactions (such as "gender" or "sexist language"), but instead only analyze what the speakers or members explicitly orient to as relevant. The feminist psychologist Elizabeth Stokoe (1998) suggested that the analytic approach of CA may provide a way of escaping the historical tendency of research in the gender and language field to perpetuate and endorse stereotyped beliefs about the ways women and men speak. A conversation analytic approach to gender, following the CA view of context, supports a grounded, empirical approach for documenting the theoretical notion of "doing gender." Thus, CA provides a method of analysis that is consistent with the social constructionist perspective currently advocated by many gender and language researchers (e.g. Bergvall, Bing, and Freed 1996; Crawford 1995).

Influenced by a CA approach, Stokoe (1998) restricted her analysis of gender and language to those moments during an interaction when gender as a topic was raised in interactions. The data she examined were recordings of groups of young adults discussing the future, employment, and family orientations. She found that participants' orientations to gender tended to be occasioned when the topics of employment and family were discussed. Thus, utterances where women and men were contrasted followed people's orientation to gender and recognition of gender as a societal division. Statements about the nature of women and men often occasioned extended discussions of gender. In these discussions gender stereotypes were invoked to support or contest arguments. Stokoe (1998) noted that sequential structures of conversations about gender included generalization–particularization chains (see Billig et al. 1988) and assessment–agreement/disagreement adjacency pairs.

Stokoe (1998) used discussions about child-care facilities to illustrate the kinds of interactional sequences that organized talk about gender. In such discussions it was commonly assumed that the facilities were largely for the benefit of women. This assumption of a "generic mother" invoked extended discussion about gender. Other participants called attention to (i.e. "noticed") the implicit assumption of women as caregivers. Stokoe found that these noticings occasioned extended discussions about the relative roles of women and men in child-care. Furthermore, disclaimers of the kind "I'm not sexist but . . ." or "I'm not chauvinistic but . . ." were used to occasion a non-sexist identity for a speaker precisely at the moment when he or she was invoking sex stereotypes (e.g. associating wives with washing and ironing). Stokoe's analysis is an initial step toward understanding the kinds of norms and structures that organize talk about gender maintain the gendered status quo.

The extent to which it is justifiable or even desirable to invoke gender as an analytic category when it is not transparently relevant to participants engaging in an interaction has been a matter of heated debate (see Billig 1999; Schegloff 1997; Weatherall 2000; Wetherell 1998). Arguing against using a conversation analytic mentality, Wetherell suggested that for a complete rather than just a technical analysis of texts it is necessary to consider the "argumentative texture of social life" upon which everyday sense-making practice depends. Compelling evidence that gender constitutes part of the "argumentative texture" for meaning-making is found in Cameron's (1998) analysis of the vignette "Is there any ketchup, Vera?" In this example, Vera understands that her husband is not inquiring as to the presence of ketchup in the house, but is requesting that she fetch it for him. The relevance of gender here is marked not by "gender noticing" but through a consideration of the pragmatics of the exchange (i.e. a similar request from a daughter may have received a different response). Arguably, gender is "omni-relevant" to all social interaction. However, an ongoing challenge for feminist gender and language researchers is to analyze its significance for language and talk without endorsing the gender binaries and sex stereotypes that we are seeking to challenge.

4 Parallels and Disjunctures in Approaches to Gender Identities in Language

Discursive psychology developed in part as a reaction against an overly cognitive focus in psychology, where individual mental processes were emphasized as primary in human behavior and everyday talk as a central activity of social life was largely ignored. Social-cognitive approaches tend to be interested in language only in so far as it provides a way of understanding cognitive structures and mental processes. In contrast, discursive psychology takes language, in its own right, as the object of study, examining how talk and social interaction construct the social world and make things happen. DP also endorsed established critiques of psychology's conventional research practices and its dominant epistemological assumptions of realism and positivism (see Potter and Wetherell 1987; Edwards 1997). Thus, it is quite common for DP to be set up in opposition to approaches that have a more cognitive and experimental flavor. A fundamental difference between the two approaches that cannot be ignored is that social cognition conceptualizes gender identity as existing prior to language in the minds of individuals, whereas discursive psychology views gender identity as indexical and occasioned, discursively constituted in the ongoing business of interaction.

Despite the considerable differences, we would like to suggest some similarities between the two approaches, and to highlight what each contributes to the strengths and limitations of feminist work on gender identity and its relationship to language. When compared to studies of gender and language from other fields, both social-cognitive and discursive psychological approaches put more emphasis on the relation between language and larger social variables, constructed either as pre-existing intergroup relations (SIT), verbal categories occasioned in talk (DP), or a combination of the two (CAT). Both approaches, thus, aim to link language and communication in interaction to larger issues about gender.

In addition, a theme common to social-cognitive and discursive psychology is that of variability. For the former, language variation in accent, speech rate, lexis, and the like may indicate the influence of social identity on the interaction. DP has focused less on variation in paralanguage and non-verbal behavior and more on how common-sense beliefs and verbal categories are used to conduct the business of the interaction. Historically, social psychologists have endeavored to introduce psychological explanations of patterns of linguistic variation reported in sociolinguistic surveys, arguing that concepts such as motivations, identities, and intentions were required to increase explanatory power (Giles 1979). Twenty years later, Holmes and Meyerhoff (1999) noted that SIT and CAT were regularly used in the interpretation of linguistic variation. In contrast, there is little evidence that the theoretical ideas and analytic concepts from discursive psychology are being mobilized in sociolinguistic work on gender (but see Ehrlich 1999), though there is considerable scope to do so.

There are some strong similarities in the conceptualization of gender identity in the two approaches we have described, especially when CAT is considered. Both approaches allow for variation in the salience and relevance of gender identity. CAT proposes that in contexts where particular social identities are relevant, predictable changes in communication strategies and behavior should be evident. For DP the relevance of gender identities to interaction is also variable. In styles of DP that are more heavily influenced by conversation analysis, psychological concepts such as identities (e.g. gender identity) are only relevant to an analysis when the participants explicitly attend to them.

A relatively recent development in sociolinguistics has been a "community of practice" approach to gender and language (see McConnell-Ginet, this volume). The two psychological approaches described in this chapter can gain from and also contribute to this perspective, where shared social practices are viewed as mediating the relationship between social identity and language variation (see Eckert 2000; McConnell-Ginet, this volume). The community of practice approach also acknowledges that the relationship between gender identity and language is dynamic and situated in the ebb and flow of social interactions. What differentiates discursive psychology in particular from both social-cognitive psychology and the community of practice approach is its reluctance to invoke (gender) identity as relevant to interaction, unless that relevance is interactionally displayed.

Treating identity as a concern of participants avoids the difficulties of specifying exactly what gender identity is (e.g. a pattern of responses to sex-stereotypical traits or to an assigned gender category), as well as the problems associated with the ontological status of gender categories (deciding in advance the defining characteristics of a woman or a man). Furthermore, it avoids reproducing gender stereotypes by assuming, for example, that when women talk about "female" things and men talk about "male" things, the participants are "doing" gender. Thus, an important advantage of DP is that it avoids making the assumption that identity always guides behavior. Instead, the relevance of gender identity is grounded in the interaction itself, rather than relying on the researcher's assumptions. In recent years, CAT has moved in this direction by invoking the notion that identities are continually negotiated in interaction (e.g. Boggs and Giles 1999; Gallois and Giles 1998). The cost of this move is a loss of parsimony, as is also the case for DP, but the gain in explanatory power makes this cost bearable.

What advantages does a community of practice framework bring to the social psychology of gender and language? Supporting a social constructionist perspective, the community of practice framework has moved attention away from a simple notion of gender differences in speech to an investigation of the role of linguistic variation in constructing social identities. Linguistic practices are understood to form part of a more general pool of resources for constructing identity. Some versions of DP have tended to focus on labeling practices or verbal categories to study identities in talk. The study of linguistic variation within a community of practice framework shows that verbal categories (e.g. lexical items such as "girl," "woman," and so on) are not the only linguistic resources available for doing identity work; variation in phonology, prosody, and so forth (and by extension, non-verbal behavior) may also be used to make identities relevant to an interaction. A challenge for discursive psychologists and some other social psychologists of language is to broaden the range of linguistic resources they consider in studies of identity in talk and social interaction.

Furthermore, the community of practice framework encourages researchers to focus attention on the local linguistic accomplishment of identity, and to focus on how gendered social identities are accomplished through the activities and practices of specific speech communities. The advantage of attending to the local and practical accomplishment of identity is that it avoids treating gender as a monolithic category and making universal claims about gender.

What focusing on the particular misses, however, is the power of broader meaning systems to shape local practices. An important element of discursive psychology and of CAT is that issues of similarities and differences among and between women and men do not simply emerge out of local practice but also have an ideological dimension. Gender identities are not just social categories to which people belong, but are also verbal categories that can be invoked in order to do things that are consequential for social action. The link between larger social issues and local practices, *as they are engaged in and responded to by individual men and women in interaction*, will remain the focus of psychological research on gender and language into the future.

REFERENCES

Antaki, Charles and Widdicombe, Sue 1998: Identity as an achievement and as a tool. In Charles Antaki and Sue Widdicombe (eds) *Identities in Talk*. London: Sage, pp. 1–14.

Aries, Elizabeth 1996: *Men and Women in Interaction: Reconsidering the Differences*. New York: Oxford University Press.

Augoustinos, Martha and Walker, Iain 1995: *Social Cognition: An Integrated Introduction*. London: Sage.

Bem, Sandra L. 1993: *The Lenses of Gender: Transforming the Debate on Sexual Inequality*. New Haven, CT: Yale University Press.

Bergvall, Victoria L., Bing, Janet M., and Freed, Alice F. (eds) 1996: *Rethinking Language and Gender Research: Theory and Practice*. London: Longman.

Billig, Michael 1999: Whose terms? Whose ordinariness? Rhetoric and ideology in conversation analysis. *Discourse & Society* 10: 543–58.

Billig, Michael, Condor, Susan, Edwards, Derek, Gane, Mike, Middleton, Derek, and Radley, Alan (eds) 1988: *Ideological Dilemmas: A Social Psychology of Everyday Thinking*. London: Sage.

Bilous, F. R. and Krauss, Robert M. 1988: Dominance and accommodation in the conversational behaviors of same- and mixed-gender dyads. *Language and Communication* 8: 183–94.

Boggs, Cathy and Giles, Howard 1999: "The canary in the coalmine": The nonaccommodation cycle in the gendered workplace. *International Journal of Applied Linguistics* 9: 223–46.

Cameron, Deborah 1998: "Is there any ketchup, Vera?": Gender, power and pragmatics. *Discourse and Society* 9: 437–55.

Carli, L. 1990: Gender, language and influence. *Journal of Personality and Social Psychology* 59: 941–51.

Coates, Jennifer 1986: *Women, Men and Language*. London: Longman.

Condry, John C. and Condry, Sandra M. 1976: Sex differences: A study in the eye of the beholder. *Child Development* 56: 225–33.

Crawford, Mary 1995: *Talking Difference: On Gender and Language*. London: Sage.

Cutler, Anne and Scott, Donia R. 1990: Speaker sex and perceived apportionment of talk. *Applied Psycholinguistics* 11: 253–72.

Eckert, Penelope 2000: *Linguistic Variation and Social Practice*. Malden, MA: Blackwell.

Edwards, Derek 1997: *Discourse and Cognition*. London: Sage.

Edwards, Derek 1998: The relevant thing about her: Social identity categories in use. In Charles Antaki and Sue Widdicombe (eds) *Identities in Talk*. London: Sage, pp. 15–33.

Ehrlich, Susan 1999: Communities of practice, gender and representation of sexual assault. *Language in Society* 28: 239–56.

Fagot, Beverly I., Hagen, Richard, Leinbach, Mary D., and Kronsberg, Sandra 1985: Differential reactions to assertive and communicative acts of toddler boys and girls. *Child Development* 56: 1499–505.

Gallois, Cindy and Giles, Howard 1998: Accommodating mutual influence in intergroup encounters. In M. T. Palmer and G. A. Barnett (eds) *Mutual Influence in Interpersonal Communication: Theory and Research in Cognition, Affect, and Behavior*. New York: Ablex, pp. 130–62.

Garfinkel, Harold 1967: *Studies in Ethnomethodology*. Cambridge, MA: Polity.

Giles, Howard 1979: Sociolinguistics and social psychology: An introductory essay. In Howard Giles and Robert St Clair (eds) *Language and Social Psychology*. Oxford: Blackwell, pp. 1–20.

Giles, Howard, Coupland, Nikolas, and Coupland, Justine 1991: Accommodation theory: Communication, context, and consequence. In Howard Giles, Justine Coupland, and Nikolas Coupland (eds) *Contexts of Accommodation*. Cambridge: Cambridge University Press, pp. 1–68.

Giles, Howard and Powesland, Peter F. 1975: *Speech Style and Social Evaluation*. London: Academic Press.

Giles, Howard and Smith, Phillip M. 1979: Accommodation theory: Optimal levels of convergence. In Howard Giles and Robert St Clair (eds) *Language and Social Psychology*. Oxford: Blackwell, pp. 45–65.

Giles, Howard, Smith, Peter, Ford, Barry, Condor, Susan, and Thakerar, Jitendra 1980: Speech style and the fluctuating salience of sex. *Language Sciences* 2: 260–82.

Gill, Ros 1993: Justifying injustice: Broadcasters' accounts of inequality in radio. In Erica Burman and Ian Parker (eds) *Discourse Analytic*

Research: Repertoires and Readings of Texts in Action. London: Routledge, pp. 75–93.

Gough, Brendon 1998: Men and the discursive reproduction of sexism: Repertoires of difference and equality. *Feminism and Psychology* 8: 25–49.

Hannah, Annette and Murachver, Tamar 1999: Gender and conversational style as predictors of conversational behaviour. *Journal of Language and Social Psychology* 18: 153–95.

Holmes, Janet and Meyerhoff, Miriam 1999: The community of practice: Theories and methodologies in language and gender research. *Language in Society* 28: 173–83.

Kessler, Suzanne J. and McKenna, Wendy 1978: *Gender: An Ethnomethodological Approach.* New York: Wiley.

Kramer, Cheris 1978: Male and female perceptions of male and female speech. *Language and Speech* 20: 151–61.

Labov, William 1966: *The Social Stratification of English in New York City.* Washington, DC: Center for Applied Linguistics.

Lawrence, Samuel G., Stucky, Nathan P., and Hopper, Robert 1990: The effects of sex dialects and sex stereotypes on speech evaluations. *Journal of Language and Social Psychology* 9: 209–24.

Marshall, Harriette and Wetherell, Margaret 1989: Talking about career identities: A discourse analysis perspective. In Sue Skevington and Deborah Baker (eds) *The Social Identity of Women.* London: Sage, pp. 106–29.

Mulac, Anthony, Erlandson, Karen T., Farrar, W. Jeffrey, Hallett, Jennifer S., Molloy, Jennifer L., and Prescott, Margaret E. 1998: "Uh-huh. What's that all about?" Differing interpretations of conversational backchannels and questions as sources of miscommunication across gender boundaries. *Communication Research* 25: 641–68.

Potter, Jonathon and Wetherell, Margaret 1987: *Discourse and Social Psychology: Beyond Attitudes and Behaviour.* London: Sage.

Schegloff, Emanuel A. 1997: Whose text? Whose context? *Discourse & Society* 8: 165–87.

Skevington, Sue and Baker, Deborah (eds) 1989: *The Social Identity of Women.* London: Sage.

Smith, Phillip M. 1985: *Language, the Sexes and Society.* Malden, MA and Oxford: Blackwell.

Stokoe, Elizabeth 1998: Talking about gender: The conversational construction of gender categories in academic discourse. *Discourse & Society* 8: 217–40.

Stokoe, Elizabeth 2000: Toward a conversation analytic approach to gender and discourse. *Feminism and Psychology* 10: 552–63.

Tajfel, Henri 1970: Experiments in intergroup discrimination. *Scientific American* 223: 96–102.

Tajfel, Henri 1981: *Human Groups and Social Categories.* Cambridge: Cambridge University Press.

Thakerar, Jitendra N., Giles, Howard, and Cheshire, Jenny 1982: Psychological and linguistic parameters of speech accommodation theory. In Colin Fraser and Klaus R. Scherer (eds) *Advances in the Social Psychology of Language.* Cambridge: Cambridge University Press, pp. 205–55.

Weatherall, Ann 2000: Gender relevance in talk-in-interaction and discourse. *Discourse & Society* 11: 290–2.

Wetherell, Margaret 1998: Positioning and interpretative repertoires: Conversation analysis and post-structuralism in dialogue. *Discourse & Society* 9: 387–412.

Wetherell, Margaret and Edley, Nigel 1998: Gender practices: Steps in the analysis of men and masculinities. In Karen Henwood, Christine Griffin, and Ann Phoenix (eds) *Standpoints and Differences: Essays in the Practice of Feminist Psychology.* London: Sage, pp. 156–73.

Wetherell, Margaret, Stiven, Hilda, and Potter, Jonathon 1987: Unequal egalitarianism: A preliminary study of discourse and employment opportunities. *British Journal of Social Psychology* 26: 59–71.

Widdicombe, Sue 1998: Identity as an analyst's and a participant's resource. In Charles Antaki and Sue Widdicombe (eds) *Identities in Talk.* London: Sage, pp. 191–206.

Williams, Jennifer and Giles, Howard 1978: The changing status of women in society: An intergroup perspective. In Henri Tajfel (ed.) *Differentiation Between Social Groups.* London: Academic Press, pp. 431–46.

Yelland, Nicola (ed.) 1998: *Gender in Early Childhood.* London: Routledge.

22 Prestige, Cultural Models, and Other Ways of Talking About Underlying Norms and Gender

SCOTT FABIUS KIESLING

1 Introduction

In this chapter I will focus on how speaker norms have been conceived in language and gender studies, and attempt to arrive at a synthesis which suggests how a speaker's knowledge about language and social context contributes to the patterning of language by gender. I will focus both on what we can "objectively" describe about a society, as well as how speakers "subjectively" conceive of society, and then how these conceptions might have consequences for behavior (language use in particular). In addition, I want to explore the connection between what gender meanings arise in a particular interaction and wider societal meanings.

2 What Are Norms?

2.1 Norms and sociolinguistic meaning

The first important distinction that needs to be made is between norms about the social identity of a speaker (*social group norms*) and norms about the social meaning of a linguistic item (*social action norms*). These two have often been conflated in correlational studies of variationist sociolinguistics, such that a given variant will be claimed to "mean" membership in the group that uses it the most. While this is sometimes the case, the picture is usually more complex. For example, we might propose that a low-pitched voice is indicative of (i.e. means) masculinity. But we can show that the same kind of voice has connotations of authority, even for women. We are thus more accurate in describing the relationship between masculinity and voice pitch by saying there is an (arbitrary) linguistic norm that connects authority and pitch, and a further social norm that connects masculinity and authority (see Connell 1995; Kiesling 2001a). (Whether or not the meaning of low pitch came from its association with men is not important here, just that there is a linguistic feature connecting a social group norm with a linguistic norm.) The connection between authority and masculinity is a social group norm, while the connection between low pitch and authority is a social action norm.

Ochs (1992) has characterized the connection between linguistic forms and social identity as *indirect indexicality*, because there are one or more social actions (a stance, speech act, or speech activity) that come between a linguistic feature and the group that uses it the most, rather than a *direct indexicality* between the group and the linguistic feature. The distinction I am making names the two parts of indirect indexicality, which include both social action norms and social group norms. Social action norms are those norms that describe the indexing of stances, acts, and activities by linguistic forms, while social group norms are those that describe the connection between stances, acts, and activities and the social identities of speakers. This distinction is similar to, but slightly different from, that between *social significance* and *social meaning*, originally made by Lavendera (1982) and discussed by Milroy (1992) and Holmes (1996). Social significance is meaning that comes from the statistical connection between a group and a linguistic feature, so it is a *direct index*. But social meaning is meaning that derives, at least in part, from the function of the linguistic feature. If I claim that low pitch directly indexes "male," then that is social significance. If I claim that tag questions index tentativeness, then that is social meaning. The difference between these terms and what I am suggesting is that I want to say that all variables have social meaning but not necessarily social significance. The social meaning of a linguistic item is ontologically primary, while its social significance derives ultimately as a kind of short circuit between social meaning and social action.

We thus have three interrelated norms: social group norms, social action norms, and social significance norms. While I believe social action norms are ontologically primary, the connection between each type of norm is functionally bidirectional, and in fact a linguistic form can be used to indirectly index a stance by first indexing a social group. For example, a White American speaker might use a feature of African American English to index a stance stereotypically associated with African Americans (as shown in Kiesling 2001a). This bidirectional, web-like view of these norms is illustrated more fully below.

In interactional discourse gender studies, such as summarized in Tannen (1990), the distinction between social group norms and social action norms has in fact been the point: that different linguistic features carry different social meanings for men and women (and other groups). Thus, Maltz and Borker (1982) suggest that questions play different roles in conversations for men and women. Further, if groups share social action norms, they still may value norms differently. Goodwin (1980), for instance, shows how boys and girls use different forms of directives to accomplish their goals and organize their groups. Of course, the distinction between social group and social action norms (as we will see with all types of norms) is not necessarily kept separate by speakers, but interact and influence one another. I will explore these interactions below.

Another more common way of describing norms is as *descriptive* or *prescriptive*. Descriptive norms are those that simply describe a group, usually through some statistic like the average, such as "the average height of men." Prescriptive norms are those values that people are expected to adhere to (or at least strive for), such as "Men should be tall." Both kinds of norms have played a part in language and gender research; often, they are difficult to tease apart, as prescriptive norms often affect descriptive norms. Moreover, both social group norms and indexical norms each have a prescriptive and a descriptive flavor. In general, studies try to find out what the descriptive norm is (see especially Romaine, this volume), and then use prescriptive norms to help explain those norms, although in practice the two often get confused. Indeed, prescriptive norms, such as "Women should be more polite" (see Lakoff 1975), often turn out to be descriptively accurate: "Women are more (positively) polite" (see Holmes 1995). The interaction between the two, however, can be quite complex, with each kind of norm influencing the other. For example, men are, on average, taller than women in most societies, but this has led to a complete gender dichotomy whereby all men are expected to be taller than women. This prescriptive norm makes life difficult for short men and tall women, and one rarely sees couples in the USA and perhaps throughout Western society in which the man is shorter than the woman. Below I will revisit this notion when I discuss the connection between social power and masculinity.

The height example shows how prescriptive norms affect descriptive norms: a descriptively average difference has been turned into a prescriptively categorical difference, such that men and women are prescriptively completely separate categories and differ categorically on many traits. "Men should not be like women and women should not be like men." In turn, we find a much more categorical pattern in couple's relative heights than would appear by chance.

I want to make a further distinction among norms that characterize a society, norms that characterize institutions, and norms that characterize speech events. As I see it, we need to distinguish among at least these three interacting levels when thinking about language and gender: (1) the wider society, consisting of large census group categories; (2) institutions such as corporations, clubs, families, universities, etc.; and (3) specific speech events with their individual speakers. At each level there are norms of each type, and they interact. On the societal level we have patterns such as those described by Romaine (this volume) on variation and Talbot (this volume) on stereotypes. At the institutional level, we have patterns described in Part V of this volume, and by McConnell-Ginet (this volume) on community of practice. Finally, each speech event will develop both types of norm as the event unfolds, and as a type of speech event recurs, prescriptive norms for those events will develop, as seen in Bucholtz (this volume, on discourse analysis). Speakers have knowledge of all these levels of norms, and of course each individual has a way of approaching these norms (among these approaches are resistance, compliance, and active promotion).

How might this knowledge be characterized, and how do different "levels" of norms interact? In order to explore this question further, I want to rely on an extended example, based on my own research with fraternity men. I will briefly look at how norms have been used in language and gender through this example, and then explore how they might be combined to arrive at an understanding of the relationships among the various underlying norms that speakers use when making choices about how to say something, and making meaning out of the choices of other speakers.

2.2   *The fraternity study: Background and data*

I spent a little more than a year in 1993–4 with a fraternity at a university in Northern Virginia, in the suburbs of Washington, DC. A fraternity of this kind is an all-male social group. It is essentially an institutionalized friendship network which also does volunteer work to help the university and the surrounding community. I chose this site because there had been very little work until then specifically focusing on men's gender identity; most work had focused on explaining why women did not act the way men were assumed to behave. Also, there was increasing evidence that we could learn much about language and gender by focusing on the differences within genders as well as among or between them (see Eckert 1989).

I investigated both variation and discourse strategies in the fraternity, and possible connections between these kinds of linguistic features. I specifically looked at style shifting by individual men: how did they speak differently in varying situations? For variation (see Kiesling 1998), I focused on how they used the (ing) variable when socializing, in interviews with me, and in fraternity meetings. I found that, while most men used a high percentage of the alveolar N variant in socializing situations, in the meeting and interview situations there were some men who continued to use the high N, while most of the men used a lower N (see figure 22.1). In discourse (see Kiesling 1997, 2001a), I explored what discourse features and strategies men used to create authority (power and hierarchy), and, most importantly, what *kind* of power and authority the men construct based on their position in the fraternity and the speech event. In all of these investigations, I have explained the patterns I find based on a number of underlying norms the men have about gender and society, usually as described in their own words. Below I will introduce some of these terms in the context of the fraternity research.

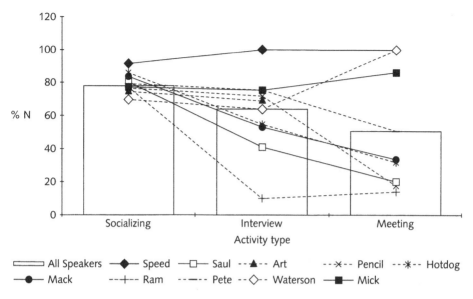

Figure 22.1 Cross-tabulation of speaker and activity type for progressive verb forms only (from Kiesling 1998: 84)

2.3 *Prestige*

What explanatory norms have been proposed for patterns of variation in census categories? The first kind of norm, proposed by Labov (1966), is in terms of prestige. Prestige in variation studies has always been assumed to be some shared value (norm) of a single speech community, but in fact it is something that has at its root the identification of certain linguistic forms with upper-class speakers. The assumption has been (and this has often been corroborated in experiments) that the speech of such speakers is the more desirable kind of speech for everyone in a speech community.

In the fraternity example, G is what is usually called the prestigious variant, and men use it less than women, following a recurrent pattern in variation studies for stable variables of this kind (see Romaine, this volume). So why do men use more N, if there is more prestige in G (especially if one assumes they would want to display greater societal power)? Labov left the door open to other kinds of prestige as well. Trudgill (1972) pursued this notion and found that in fact men in Norwich, England, valued the vernacular variant, even though they didn't come right out and say it. Following Labov, he called this "covert prestige." So one type of underlying evaluative norm that has been used is the notion of prestige, and the corresponding notion of covert prestige.

2.4   *Power, solidarity, and politeness*

Now let's have a look at the most important norms that have been used in interactional sociolinguistics: power, solidarity, and the related notion of politeness. These kinds of norms, while cultural, describe norms for different speech activities and speech acts. In this view, speakers orient themselves (because of their culture, gender, and so on, and the specific nature of the speech activity or act) more toward relationships of power (hierarchy or rank) or relationships of solidarity (social distance). Power and solidarity have been investigated most closely on the discourse level, but the claim is that cultures and subcultures have different orientations to these values. In language and gender, for example, it has been claimed that men concern themselves more with relationships of power, while women are more concerned with relationships of solidarity. A good example of this is Goodwin's (1980) study, in which she found that the boys tended to use directives that emphasized and created hierarchy, while the girls used directives which emphasized solidarity and inclusiveness.

Brown and Levinson's (1987) politeness theory is related: they make a distinction between negative politeness (minimizing interference with an addressee's freedom of action) and positive politeness (focusing on the similarity between speakers' wants). However, their theory is more focused on individual speech acts and speakers, and less on conversational goals and cultural expectation. But it is close enough to include it in this set of norms, and it has been used profitably to explain gender differences in language use, most notably by Holmes (1995). However, positive and negative politeness strategies are often tied to meanings of solidarity and power, such that positive politeness is tied to solidarity (because of its focus on connections) and negative politeness to power (because of its focus on freedom and independence, which a powerful person has more of than a non-powerful person). These connections are essentially a conflation of distance with inequality and closeness with equality. But Brown and Levinson clearly intend these three concepts (power, positive politeness, and negative politeness) to be kept separate. As Tannen (1993b) points out, hierarchy and distance are separable, and are often bound together differently depending on the culture. This view suggests that another type of norm for describing gender differences is how hierarchy relationships are bound with distance relationships.

These norms could help us explain the differences in the men's use of (ing) in the fraternity, but only in the most general terms. Moreover, the pattern in the fraternity raises problems for the generalization that men focus on power. We could say that the men are more focused on solidarity in the socializing situation, and more on power in the interview and meeting situations. We could extend this generalization to suggest that the men who use more N in the interview and meeting situations are focusing more on solidarity than the others. But this explanation cannot be more specific while relying only on general notions of power and solidarity. In addition, since these are all men, why aren't they all more focused on power all the time, even in the socializing situation? I will return to these questions below.

2.5   *Immediate speech event norms*

Before I move to a synthesis, I want to briefly touch on what we might call the local effects of norms. We can exemplify this if we consider one of the principles of accommodation theory, which holds that under situations of positive affect, speakers try to adjust their speech so it more closely matches the patterns of their interlocutor(s). Speech accommodation theorists have identified a number of motivations for accommodating behavior, as summarized in Weatherall and Gallois (this volume) and Giles, Coupland, and Coupland (1991). It is these *motivations*, rather than the accommodating behavior, that I would classify as true norms, and hence accommodation can be said to be a local norm *effect*.

A related notion used to explain the patterning of linguistic variation is network analysis, as pioneered by Milroy (1980) and used recently by Eckert (2000). As with accommodation, social networks work in concert with specific norms to produce linguistic patterns. Denser and more multiplex networks tend to amplify the importance of norms with more immediate and local meaning for speakers in those networks, while less dense and multiplex networks tend to allow for a wider range of norms to influence speech behavior. However, the network analysis points to the need for a subtle understanding of and differentiation among the different kinds and levels of norms that may impact the speech of a given person in a given speech event.

3   Norms and Identity: Toward a Synthesis

Accommodation patterns highlight a very important aspect of sociolinguistic research: that all patterns arise from decisions people make in interaction, when they are talking to someone and thinking about "who they are" with respect to that person or people. So in explaining these patterns, we must ask what kinds of (sub)conscious knowledge speakers draw on to achieve these stances. Most of the above norms have been claimed at one time or another to be The Primary Motivation for sociolinguistic patterns, including and especially those about language and gender. But in fact people can multi-task, and even apprehend multiple levels of meaning, as indirect speech acts show us (see also Silverstein 1976). Here I want to propose a way of characterizing the knowledge people rely on during the process outlined above.

Following Ochs (1992), I propose that people's primary way of organizing interaction (including language) is through stances. This focus does not mean that knowledge relating to larger "census" categories does not come into play, just that this knowledge is invoked in the service of creating stances and performing certain acts situated in particular activities. With respect to the fraternity data above, then, I claim that the men who use a high level of N in the meeting do so because they want to construct a certain kind of stance in that meeting, specifically one of practicality and hard work. However, N does not directly index this stance, but relies on a web of indexicality associated with the wider linguistic style that N is a part of. Another way of thinking about stance is in terms of personal style (Eckert 2000), where a single linguistic feature is part of a wider personal style of a speaker, or even category of speakers. In this view, a linguistic feature does not, in speaker's real-time processing, do the work of creating an identity. Rather, the correlations that linguists find between gender and a particular linguistic feature are simply a heuristic indication of similar personal styles. As the California Style Collective (1993) explains, each style is unique, made up of a bricolage of linguistic (and other) behaviors that index various sociological and cultural meanings. Stances are local instantiations of a personal style, performed in a particular speech event. It is the nature of these various sociological and cultural meanings to which I now turn.

3.1   (Ing) and the web of norms in the fraternity

In order to make this discussion more concrete, let us return to the fraternity. Given the explanation above, N should indicate (but not necessarily fully index) a certain general personal style, which can be discerned through an examination of the specific personal styles of those who use it. We should be able to show that it helps create specific stances in interaction. In this regard, the three men who use high amounts of N in the meeting are worth focusing on, because they provide a contrastive category with the other, "control" category. We should thus be able to analyze the stances and styles of these three men and identify how they are specifically different in this regard. This analysis will yield a better understanding of the kinds of specific indexicality being used when these men use N and the others use G (the velar variant).

I will focus on the following speech, given by Brian Waterson, a first-year member of the fraternity. In this speech he is running for the office of vice-president. It is unusual for someone in his position in the fraternity (new) to run for such an office (and even more unusual to succeed, which he does not). In fact, this is the only time in my corpus when he speaks in a meeting, and this passage is thus responsible for Waterson's categorical (4/4) use of N in the meetings.

Waterson's Speech
1   Hotdog: Could we have Brian Waterson
2   (7.3)   ((*Waterson walks in, goes to the front of the room*))

3	Waterson:	Um (1.1) I'm not gonna f:- um put a load of shit in you guys whatever.
4		Um (0.7) You guys know I'm a **fuckin'** hard worker.
5		I work my ass off for everything.
6		I don't miss anything
7		I'm always I'm always there,
8		I'll do anything for you guy:s,
9		and if you nominate me for this position
10		I'll put a hundred percent ef-effort towards it,
11		I mean I have **nothin'** else to do 'cept **fuckin'** school work.
12		and the fraternity.
13		and uh and uh like uh like you guys said um this:
14		we need a change because we're **goin'** down?
15		A:nd I know I don't have a lot of experience?
16		In like position-wise?
17		But when this fraternity first started (0.5)
18		back in uh April of of nineteen eighty-nine,
19		um the guys that were elected for positions then didn't have too much (0.9) uh: experience in positions either.
20		So just keep that in mind when you vote.
21		Thank you boys.
22		Remember I'm the I'm the ice ma:n. ((*final two words said in an emphasized whisper as he walks out of the room*))

(Numbers in parentheses represent silence in seconds; text in double parentheses are comments; colons represent lengthening of the preceding sound; a dash represents an incomplete morpheme. The four coded (ing) tokens are in bold; *anything* and *everything* are not bold because a secondary stress on the *-ing* morpheme in trisyllabic words makes them categorically G, similar to monomorphemic *thing*; see Houston 1985.)

Since Waterson cannot perform an "electable identity" based on his experience in the fraternity, or on past offices he has held, he must construct some other kind of electable identity suitable for the authority of this office. He does this by presenting a "hard-working" stance, where hard-working means giving time to the fraternity to perform often mundane and tedious chores requiring stamina and consistency. His use of N helps create this stance, through its social significance indexing of the working class, which in turn indexes stances (through social group norms) of tough physicality. Below I explore this connection more fully.

3.2 Linguistic norms, linguistic ideology, metapragmatics: Standard versus non-standard

I have already characterized N as non-standard and G as standard. So we might say that Waterson is simply a non-standard speaker and leave it at that.

But the non-standard is sometimes equated with a covertly prestigious form, a term which suggests that a speaker will gain something in their use of it. So we should ask what specifically Waterson gets by using N – how it builds his status. The answer is that it helps build his *ability*-oriented authority rather than a *structurally* oriented authority. Speakers who use more G tend to identify themselves with the established age hierarchy of the fraternity, which Waterson is trying to circumvent since he is low down on that hierarchy. He is relying on his audience's linguistic ideology to help create his stance: G is indexed to an establishment hierarchy, while N is indexed to an anti-establishment hierarchy. I have shown elsewhere (Kiesling 1998) that the other men who use a high N create similar stances through similar indexings. So here we find that the linguistic feature N actually indexes an entire ideology, but crucially, it is still used in interaction as a resource to create a stance. This indexing is the kind of indexing referred to by Silverstein (1993, 1996; see also Morford 1997) as a second-order indexical, because it relies on speakers' knowledge of the social distribution and evaluation of linguistic forms.

This perspective suggests a picture of indexicality in which both direct and indirect indexicality are at work, but one in which the stance of the speaker is still central. In this case, the speaker is relying on a social significance relationship between a social group and a linguistic feature, and then using that value to help create a stance through a social group norm. This kind of indexing is found in other studies of language and gender, but only when there is existing metalinguistic and metapragmatic knowledge in a community such that the linguistic feature itself has some social value. This is more typically the situation for instances of bilingualism (and of course diglossia), as well as many cases of stable sociolinguistic variation (such as the (ing) case) and changes from above the level of consciousness (Labov 1972).

3.3   Cultural models/figured worlds: Rocky and the lawyer

Another way of making the concept of (covert) prestige more powerful is to explore the kinds of cultural models or figured worlds that Waterson may index, in a similar way as he indexes a linguistic ideology (see Holland and Quinn 1987; D'Andrade and Strauss 1992; Holland et al. 1998 for discussions of these terms). Here I want to suggest that he is doing more than indexing a shared social hierarchy – rather, he is indexing a shared narrative: cognitive schemas known as cultural models (and the related and more recent term, figured worlds). An example of such a model is Holland and Skinner's (1987) study of how college students talk about gender types, particularly derogatory terms. They show that the women they interviewed categorize men based on their conformity to a shared prototypical narrative of how intimate relationships proceed. Other ways of organizing their data did not work for Holland and Skinner (1987: 104): "Without knowledge of the [cultural model] scenarios, we would have been at a loss to explain why respondents thought some terms for gender types could be used as insults whereas others could not."

We can apply this "scenario" approach to the fraternity case, by appealing to cultural models of masculinity. We can identify one cultural model for men that follows a trajectory of technical, intellectual, and eventually structural attainment and expertise. We might call this model the corporate lawyer model, as such people are structurally powerful, have established hierarchies and ideologies in their interest, and as a prototype are assumed to come from families that already have societal structural power. Opposing this model is what I call the Rocky model, after the movie character who wins a world boxing title through hard work, physical power, determination, and stamina, and who also comes from a working-class background. Waterson's N use helps bring this underdog scenario to mind (or something like it; I'm not claiming this is the specific scenario), and helps Waterson create an electable identity of the underdog who works hard and in the end does a good job.

Cultural models have been shown by cognitive anthropologists to provide the most rich and reliable descriptions of cultural norms: knowledge, shared by people in a culture, which gives rise to patterns of behavior. I have been concerned in this chapter with what knowledge speakers use to make decisions about what language forms to use, and how they "subjectively" understand their decisions. Cultural models are a powerful resource in this endeavor, and I want to encourage researchers to use the concept more widely than has been the case, as well as the methods of cognitive anthropologists (see D'Andrade 1995; Bernard 1994), in order to come to a richer understanding of the gender patterns we find in talk, and the speaker knowledge that leads to these patterns (and how talk helps to build this knowledge).

Eckert (2000), while not using the cultural model concept in her discussion, seems to make a similar point. She explores the local, "subjective," meanings associated with different variables in vowel shift in Detroit. In her ethnographic variation analysis of a suburban high school, she shows that the variables have meanings such as "urban" versus "suburban," and are understood in terms of rich cultural models of the social landscape. These cultural models help Eckert explain with precision the kinds of social forces and meanings at work in the variation patterns in the school, particularly those relating to gender. Rather than discussing the variables in terms of prestige (or power or solidarity or politeness), Eckert shows, for example, that girls are evaluated against a particular narrative which includes sexuality, urbanness, and school engagement. In addition, girls' orientations to that narrative are displayed through behavioral symbols, including linguistic variables. Boys play a different role in this model, one focusing more on athletics and "toughness," so that we find that differences among boys are better explained by relating them to this role in the model, and that gender differences can be ascribed to their qualitatively different roles in the cultural model. (Other studies that use a cultural-model-like perspective are Bucholtz 1999; Gal 1978; Kendall 1999; Mendoza-Denton 1997; Meyerhoff 1999; Morford 1997.)

Cultural models thus give the researcher an important explanatory tool which does not exclude traditional explanatory terms such as prestige, power, and solidarity, but rather renders these terms more specific to the speakers being investigated, and thus more thickly explanatory. Researchers must use ethnographic methods to discover what models exist, then determine how different speakers relate themselves and others to these models (whether they follow them or deviate from them in some way). Then these relationships to models can be correlated with various linguistic features such as sociolinguistic variables or discourse strategies to find the motivations for the speakers' choices.

3.4   Institutional norms: Experience and hard work hierarchies

On the institutional level, we find yet more specific realizations of cultural models, so that norms in the institution to some extent mirror those of society as a whole. This "fractal recursivity" (Irvine and Gal 2000: 38) can be found in the hierarchies the men construct within the fraternity. These can be seen as institutional cultural models, in that they construct normative paths and categories of members through their stories. They are similar to the institutional categories identified by Eckert in her study of the school in two ways. First, they reproduce with local meaning "objective" categories found by social scientists looking at the larger society (e.g. socio-economic class). Second, they represent not just abstract categories, but entire life (institutional) trajectories and styles of behavior.

In the fraternity, I found multiple interacting hierarchies in play. The most obvious was the age hierarchy, with probationary members (pledges) at the bottom, and senior members and alumni at the top. This hierarchy in many respects paralleled the formal offices of the fraternity such as president and treasurer, in that older members tended to hold the higher offices. As I have suggested, however, there isn't a perfect correlation between the two hierarchies, in that members are evaluated for an office based on experience, past "hard work," and intellectual or leadership abilities specific to performing a certain office. These competing evaluative hierarchies can be seen as competing cultural models of how a member moves up both the age and office hierarchies. In the first model, one comes in to the fraternity ready-made with certain abilities, and "naturally" moves up as one gets older. In the second model, one comes to the fraternity as a *tabula rasa*, and one learns the ropes and proves oneself to other members through hard work. (These themes are elaborated in Kiesling 1997.) In the meeting, a speaker's orientation to these kinds of hierarchies helps explain why some used N more than others. The three speakers who did so are all oriented more to the hard work model than the experience model, whereas the G users focused more on the experience (and natural ability) model. These models help us connect the wider, global indexings to the narrower, local social indexings, and account for institutional variants of dominant patterns of gender behavior.

3.5   Speech activity norms and indexing: Markedness and contrast

Speech activities also have norms: norms for the kind of language expected, the kind of stances expected, and generic structure. These norms have been called *frames* in the discourse analysis literature (see Tannen 1993a). In general, speakers use such norms to help them make sense of meaning in a speech activity (for instance, whether someone is following or flouting Gricean conversational maxims), and many misunderstandings have been shown to be based on a mismatch of frames (Tannen and Wallat 1982). However, the norms can be broken, or, viewed another way, more marked linguistic forms can be used. In this case, the marked form in fact may index another speech activity. For example, note that in the style-shifting picture for the fraternity presented in figure 22.1, the Socializing speech activity (which is broadly conceived, from hanging out in dorm rooms to conversations in bars) has a high N use by all speakers (Waterson actually has the lowest N use in Socializing, but the individual differences here are not statistically significant). So in the Socializing speech activity, the use of N is unmarked in the sense that its use is the "rule" for the speech activity. We might suggest that a similar rule holds for the Meeting speech activity, although in this case the G variant is unmarked. The high N users in the meeting are therefore using a marked form to index the Socializing speech activity within the Meeting speech activity (i.e. momentarily reframing the speech activity).

This reframing is thus done in order to help the men create a stance similar to that typically created in the Socializing activity. What is it from the Socializing activity that these men would want to bring into the Meeting activity? We can see this in Waterson's speech, more so in the second half, when he begins to try to take a stance of *casual* hard work (line 11): *I mean I have nothin' else to do 'cept fuckin' school work.* He also seems to be relying on his less formal (hierarchical) relationship with the men, as evidenced by his reminder of his fraternity nickname (*I'm the Iceman*) and by addressing the men with the term *boys*. In this case, using aspects of a speech activity in which stances of casual confidence and non-hierarchical relationships prevail (as in the Socializing activity type) helps to create such a stance. (This activity type is of course a creation of the analyst, but it need not be the emically veridical activity type to allow the argument to go through. One focus of future research might be to what extent speakers do rely on such speech activity norms for creating stances.)

This approach is not always successful. In the discussion following the speeches for the vice-president office, Pete, the current vice-president, broke frame and began boasting in a way more typical of Socializing situations. The other members shouted him down until he focused his topic on the issue at hand (see Kiesling 2001b).

This indexing of other speech activities is related to gender patterns in a somewhat subtle, but important, way. First, we are likely to find a different style-shifting pattern for women in similar situations in terms of overall percentages, and, more importantly, we are also unlikely to find any high N users in the meeting. I make this prediction because there really is no high-status parallel to the Rocky cultural model for women, so women would be less likely to appeal to hard work through this variable. In essence, I'm suggesting that women would not create the kind of stance that Waterson creates in a similar situation, which means they would not index the Socializing situation. Moreover, stances in the corresponding female Socializing activity type are likely to be different, especially for this population. What's important to notice is the centrality of stance and its relation to gender performance: an activity type has an unmarked stance which can be created in another activity type by using a linguistic feature associated with the "embedded" speech activity. And again, we can find a parallel in these frames to the more global cultural models discussed above: Socializing is related to the Rocky cultural model, to less concern for formal hierarchy, and to non-establishment linguistic ideologies.

3.6   The interaction of different cultural models: The web of indexicality

I do not want to say that any one of these kinds of norms is necessarily primary in indexicality; in fact, I want to argue that they create a web of underlying norms that it would be unwise to try to pull apart. Far from being a Gordian knot, these norms have intricately related relationships which reinforce and inform one another. Of course one level may come to the fore depending on other aspects of context, such as the topic. We can observe some structure in these indexical webs in the fractal recursivity noted at various points above. A speaker's stance does emerge as the central construct, however, since it is mostly on this level that speakers will experience language and interaction, especially when we are dealing with probabilistic features such as (ing). That is, as Silverstein (1985) points out, even if speakers evaluate N and G differently when asked, they don't consciously keep track of their and others' percentages. Rather, they take a stance to their interlocutors, and it is in the service of this stance-taking that other levels of social organization and indexicality come into play. I want to be clear here that I am not claiming that stance (or footing or framing) is the "prime indexicality" (in fact I would say there is no such thing); I do claim that speakers' experience of social meaning is primarily stance-focused. Stance is primary interactionally but not indexically.

How does all this relate to the notions of prescriptive/descriptive norms, prestige, networks, power, solidarity, and accommodation, summarized above? It suggests a way of connecting these generalizing concepts to the ways that speakers actually experience interaction. By focusing on stances and different kinds of schemata (cultural models and frames), we have a way of accounting for the way speakers "subjectively" feel interaction to happen. We can then connect these subjective explanations with the "objective" terms discussed above. Cultural models also give us a more specific way of formulating concepts such as norm, prestige, power, solidarity, accommodation, and peer pressure.

An identity, and Eckert's personal style, can therefore be seen as a repertoire of stances in particular speech events, and an orientation to one or more dominant cultural models, whether that be following the model or indexing some kind of deviation from it. Furthermore, things like masculinity and femininity can be seen as cultural generalizations of these stance bundles, so that masculinity as a social trait becomes recognized through confrontational, hierarchical, or "tough" stances, for example.

Where do norms come from and how are they reproduced, especially if they are not conscious? This is accomplished through interactions, and by repeated use of the kinds of indexings explored above. Thus, a performance of indexicality reinforces that indexical relationship, much the way the use of a particular neural pathway in the brain strengthens the connection between neurons. Sidnell (this volume) illustrates other interactional processes in which gender norms, especially the rules for speech activities, can be reinforced through interaction. However, interlocutors must share a particular cultural model or schema with the speaker for these social meanings to be successfully created. It is through this sense-making that indexicality occurs, and thus the reinscription of these underlying norms. These webs of indexicality are perhaps another way of thinking about the ideological Discourse as discussed by Foucault (1980, 1982) and used by Critical Discourse Analysts in their work (see Wodak, this volume).

3.7 Norms and perception

I want to mention one other relationship of underlying norms to language, and that is how these norms form a context which predisposes our perception of them. Very little work has been performed in this area, but it is potentially very important for an understanding of language and gender. It seems that our knowledge of a speaker's identity changes how we perceive his or her speech at a very low level. This means that we could actually perceive what is physically the "same thing" (word, sentence, pitch, vowel formants) as different depending on gender. These perceptual "inconsistencies" go beyond simply normalizing for differences in voice quality. Strand (2000) is the starkest example of such work. She showed that when speakers were shown stereotypically feminine faces which spoke in a stereotypically feminine way, phonetic processing was significantly faster than when a male face was matched with a female voice. This shows that speakers rely on schemata of prototypical speakers at an extremely early stage in language processing, and that the distinction between prescriptive and descriptive norms is even more difficult and entangled than previously thought, as prescriptive norms may in fact distort how we perceive descriptive norms at a very basic level. Social information and norms are thus not something that is added on to language after we have "decoded" the denotational meaning of an utterance, but rather a central and basic part of our knowledge of language.

4 Conclusion

In this chapter, I have tried to survey and synthesize a rather wide array of views on how underlying norms are used by speakers to create social meaning, especially gender meanings, and how hearers use these norms to interpret the meanings (in the broadest sense) of utterances. I have tried to square the "objective" norms described by linguists, anthropologists, and psychologists with the "subjective" experience of speakers. In that vein, I've argued that a speaker's stance is their primary concern, and that linguistic features index social meanings in the service of the speaker, creating or performing a certain stance. Schemata in the form of cultural models have figured prominently in this discussion, and I hope that researchers continue to widen their use of these constructs in the future. Using such constructs requires more effort on the part of researchers, since one needs to triangulate an in-depth linguistic analysis with a number of different kinds of social analyses. However, I believe that by using these underlying norms and concepts, we can arrive at a more faithful picture of the relationship of language to gender identity.

REFERENCES

Bernard, H. Russell 1994: *Research Methods in Anthropology*. Thousand Oaks, CA: Sage.

Brown, Penelope and Levinson, Stephen 1987: *Politeness: Some Universals in Language Use*. Cambridge: Cambridge University Press.

Bucholtz, Mary 1999: You da man: Narrating the racial other in the production of white masculinity. *Journal of Sociolinguistics* 3: 443–60.

California Style Collective (Jennifer Arnold, Renee Blake, Penelope Eckert, Catherine Hicks, Melissa Iwai, Norma Mendoza-Denton, Julie Solomon, and Tom Veatch) 1993: Variation and Personal/Group Style. Paper presented at NWAVE-XXII, University of Ottawa, Canada.

Connell, Robert 1995: *Masculinities*. Berkeley, CA: University of California Press.

D'Andrade, Roy G. 1995: *The Development of Cognitive Anthropology*. Cambridge: Cambridge University Press.

D'Andrade, Roy G. and Strauss, Claudia 1992: *Human Motives and Cultural Models*. Cambridge: Cambridge University Press.

Eckert, Penelope 1989: The whole woman: Sex and gender differences in variation. *Language Variation and Change* 1: 245–67.

Eckert, Penelope 2000: *Linguistic Variation as Social Practice.* Oxford: Blackwell.

Foucault, Michel 1980: *Power/Knowledge: Selected Interviews and Other Writings 1972–1977.* New York: Pantheon.

Foucault, Michel 1982: The subject and power. *Critical Inquiry* 8: 777–95.

Gal, Susan 1978: Peasant men can't get wives: Language change and sex roles in a bilingual community. *Language in Society* 7: 1–16.

Giles, Howard, Coupland, Nikolas, and Coupland, Justine 1991: Accommodation theory: Communication, context, and consequence. In Howard Giles, Nikolas Coupland, and Justine Coupland (eds) *Contexts of Accommodation.* Cambridge: Cambridge University Press, pp. 1–68.

Goodwin, Marjorie Harness 1980: Directive–response speech sequences in girls' and boys' task activities. In Sally McConnell-Ginet, Ruth Borker, and Nelly Furman (eds) *Women and Language in Literature and Society.* New York: Praeger, pp. 157–73.

Holland, Dorothy, Lachicotte, William, Skinner, Debra, and Cain, Carole 1998: *Identity and Agency in Cultural Worlds.* Cambridge, MA: Harvard University Press.

Holland, Dorothy and Quinn, Naomi (eds) 1987: *Cultural Models in Language and Thought.* Cambridge: Cambridge University Press.

Holland, Dorothy and Skinner, Debra 1987: Prestige and intimacy: The cultural models behind Americans' talk about gender types. In Dorothy Holland and Naomi Quinn (eds) *Cultural Models in Language and*
Thought. Cambridge: Cambridge University Press, pp. 78–111.

Holmes, Janet 1995: *Women, Men, and Politeness.* London: Longman.

Holmes, Janet 1996: Women's role in language change: A place for quantification. In Natasha Warner, Jocelyn Ahlers, Leela Bilmes, Monica Oliver, Suzanne Wertheim, and Melinda Chen (eds) *Gender and Belief Systems: Proceedings of the Fourth Berkeley Women and Language Conference, April 19–21, 1996.* Berkeley, CA: Berkeley Women and Language Group, University of California, pp. 313–30.

Houston, Ann 1985: Continuity and Change in English Morphology: The Variable (ING). PhD dissertation, University of Pennsylvania, Department of Linguistics.

Irvine, Judith and Gal, Susan 2000: Language ideology and linguistic differentiation. In Paul Kroskrity (ed.) *Regimes of Language: Ideologies, Polities, and Identities.* Santa Fe, NM: School of American Research Press, pp. 35–83.

Kendall, Shari 1999: The Interpenetration of (Gendered) Spheres: An Interactional Sociolinguistic Analysis of a Mother at Work and at Home. PhD dissertation, Georgetown University.

Kiesling, Scott F. 1997: Power and the language of men. In Sally Johnson and Ulrike Hanna Meinhof (eds) *Language and Masculinity.* Oxford: Blackwell, pp. 65–85.

Kiesling, Scott F. 1998: Variation and men's identity in a fraternity. *Journal of Sociolinguistics* 2: 69–100.

Kiesling, Scott F. 2001a: Stances of whiteness and hegemony in fraternity men's discourse. *Journal of Linguistic Anthropology* 11(1): 101–15.

Kiesling, Scott F. 2001b: "Now I gotta watch what I say": Shifting constructions of masculinity in discourse. *Journal of Linguistic Anthropology* 11(2): 250–73.

Labov, William 1966: *The Social Stratification of English in New York City*. Washington, DC: Center for Applied Linguistics.

Labov, William 1972: *Sociolinguistic Patterns*. Philadelphia: University of Pennsylvania Press.

Lakoff, Robin 1975: *Language and Woman's Place*. New York: Harper and Row.

Lavendera, Beatrice 1982: Le principe de réinterpretation dans la théorie de la variation. In Norbert Dittmar and Brigitte Schlieben-Lange (eds) *Die Soziolinguistik in Romanischsprächigen Landern*. Tübingen: Narr.

Maltz, Daniel N. and Borker, Ruth A. 1982: A cultural approach to male–female miscommunication. In John J. Gumperz (ed.) *Language and Social Identity*. Cambridge: Cambridge University Press, pp. 196–216.

Mendoza-Denton, Norma 1997: Chicana/Mexicana identity and linguistic variation: An ethnographic and sociolinguistic study of gang affiliation in an urban high school. PhD dissertation, Stanford University.

Meyerhoff, Miriam 1999: *Sorry* in the Pacific: Defining communities, defining practices. *Language in Society* 28: 225–38.

Milroy, Lesley 1980: *Language and Social Networks*. Oxford: Blackwell.

Milroy, Lesley 1992: New perspectives in the analysis of sex differentiation in language. In Kingsley Bolton and Helen Kwok (eds) *Sociolinguistics Today: International Perspectives*. London: Routledge, pp. 163–79.

Morford, Janet 1997: Social indexicality in French pronominal address. *Journal of Linguistic Anthropology* 7: 3–37.

Ochs, Elinor 1992: Indexing gender. In Alessandro Duranti and Charles Goodwin (eds) *Rethinking Context: Language as an Interactive Phenomenon*. Cambridge: Cambridge University Press, pp. 335–58.

Silverstein, Michael 1976: Shifters, linguistic categories, and cultural description. In Keith H. Basso and Henry A. Selby (eds) *Meaning in Anthropology*. Albuquerque, NM: University of New Mexico Press, pp. 11–55.

Silverstein, Michael 1985: Language and the culture of gender: At the intersection of structure, usage, and ideology. In Elizabeth Mertz and Richard J. Parmentier (eds) *Semiotic Mediation: Sociocultural and Psychological Perspectives*. Orlando, FL: Academic Press, pp. 219–59.

Silverstein, Michael 1993: Metapragmatic discourse and metapragmatic function. In John A. Lucy (ed.) *Reflexive Language: Reported Speech and Metapragmatics*. Cambridge: Cambridge University Press, pp. 33–58.

Silverstein, Michael 1996: Indexical order and the dialectics of sociolinguistic life. In Risako Ide, Rebecca Parker, and Yukako Sunaoshi (eds) *SALSA III: Proceedings of the Third Annual Symposium about Language and Society – Austin*. Austin, TX: University of Texas Department of Linguistics, pp. 266–95.

Strand, Elizabeth 2000: Gender stereotype effects in speech processing. PhD dissertation, Ohio State University, Department of Linguistics.

Tannen, Deborah 1990: *You Just Don't Understand: Women and Men in Conversation*. New York: William Morrow.

Tannen, Deborah (ed.) 1993a: *Framing in Discourse*. New York: Oxford University Press.

Tannen, Deborah 1993b: The relativity of linguistic strategies: Rethinking power and solidarity in gender and dominance. In Deborah Tannen (ed.) *Gender and Conversational Interaction*. New York: Oxford University Press, pp. 165–88.

Tannen, Deborah and Wallat, Cynthia 1982: A sociolinguistic analysis of multiple demands on the pediatrician in doctor/mother/ child interaction. In Robert J. Di Pietro (ed.) *Linguistics and the Professions*. Norwood, NJ: Ablex, pp. 39–50.

Trudgill, Peter 1972: Sex, covert prestige and linguistic change in the urban British English of Norwich. *Language in Society* 1: 179–95.

23 Communicating Gendered Professional Identity: Competence, Cooperation, and Conflict in the Workplace

CAJA THIMM, SABINE C. KOCH,
AND SABINE SCHEY

1 Introduction

Job profiles and work organization are changing rapidly. Driven by new technology and Internet-based communication, the concept of the "virtual company" influences professions, such as tele-work and on-line project management, worldwide. Presumed changes in the working world not only concentrate on technology-based communication but also raise hopes for more female participation in the workforce. To date, however, sex segregation has been one of the "backbones of social stratification and inequality" (Achatz, Allmendinger, and Hinz 2000: 2).

Explanations for sex segregation are various. Apart from the classical "barriers" theories based on social inequality (Luzzo and Hutcheson 1996), there are theories about the cultural dimensions of gendered organizations and employment gratification (Hultin and Szulkin 1999), and concepts which focus more on the political system and its influence on equal opportunity in different countries (von Wahl 1999). Success and failure in professional careers is often perceived as a result of multidimensional influences. Many women experience the effects of sex segregation: they are confronted, for example, with gender stereotypes, gendered expectations, and their related behavioral manifestations. Contrary to expectations, these have changed surprisingly little over recent years (Jacobs 1995; Eckes 1997). In a large international study on the "typical man/woman," Williams and Best (1986) found scarcely any changes compared to a study by Broverman et al. (1972), undertaken almost twenty years earlier.

In this chapter we explore the hypothesis that gendered attitudes and expectations toward women and men influence not only gender roles and self-perception, but also *communication styles at work*. We begin by asking how women and men judge the function of verbal interaction in terms of career and professional life in general, and how they perceive themselves in situations of conflict, competence, and cooperation. Earlier research suggests that experiencing negative communication at work can cause frustration and may lead to reduced self-esteem. Our empirical work builds on this research, examining the influence of interpersonal relations and communication styles at work on women's professional development.

2 Gendered Organizations and Gender Stereotypes

Researchers such as Kanter (1977) and Acker (1991) characterize organizations as engaged in *gendered processes*, in which both gender and sex are regulated through a gender-neutral, asexual discourse. While Acker holds the position that gender differences are not emphasized sufficiently, Reskin (1993) regards gender differences as overemphasized, at least in some organizational contexts. We believe that verbal communication at work influences the professional performance of men and women in gender-specific ways, and that the communication of *social categories* plays an important part in the construction of gendered professional worlds. Social categories – such as age or gender – are related to social values and attitudes which underlie social stereotypes. These influence identity processes, beliefs of self-efficacy, and, consequently, professional success. How, and to what effect, social stereotypes are communicated has been an issue in socio-psychological research for many years (Eckes 1997), and has also become an important issue for sociolinguistics (Talbot 1998; this volume).

In line with Robert Merton's theory of the "self-fulfilling-prophecy" (1948), a theory which was supported by Rosenthal and Jacobson's (1968) findings regarding a teacher-expectancy effect, a number of studies have shown that the way people treat each other is largely determined by their expectations. The explanation for these effects seems to be quite simple; as Snyder (1981) states, how others present themselves to us is largely a product of how we first treat them.

Expectations are influenced by personal and social experiences, stereotypes, and general attitudes (Blanck 1993). Like other kinds of expectations, gendered expectations are subject to situational variation. In addition to individual characteristics such as gender, age, ethnicity, personality traits, attitudes, group membership, and so on, situational factors such as relative status, power, and position in a hierarchy may also contribute to the formation of expectations. Deaux and LaFrance regard gender stereotypes as "the most fundamental aspect of the gender belief system, both in terms of their durability over time and their pervasive influence on the other aspects of the system" (1998: 793).

One important way to convey those stereotypes is through language, particularly in face-to-face situations.

3   Social Categorization, Stereotypes, and Language

Linguistic research on "women's language" has been a very productive component of gender research more broadly. The earliest language and gender research (e.g. Lakoff 1975; Kramer 1975) identified ways in which women's and men's patterns of verbal interaction reflected male dominance in society as a whole (see overview in Talbot 1998; Crawford 1995). In mixed-gender conversations, women were typically interrupted more often, for instance; they needed to devote greater effort than men to get attention for their topics; and in general, women conversationalists did not receive the same degree of verbal support as their male interlocutors (Fishman 1978). A good deal of subsequent research confirmed these patterns of male dominance in verbal interaction with females (e.g. Tannen 1995; Woods 1988; Watts 1995). It is worth noting, however, that this approach tends to present women as inactive and helpless "objects" of male power. But it is equally possible to conceive of women as taking a more active role: they are also actively constructing their identity, their social environment, and their interpersonal relationships. In other words, we can conceptualize gendered communication in terms of mutuality, as a *mutual construction of gender*. This does not imply, however, that we can neglect the force of societal influences, such as gender-related stereotypes. On the contrary, there are many studies which have shown that knowing the sex of an individual can influence judgments on mental and physical health, on personality traits, achievements, emotional experience, mathematical competence, or power (for an overview of sex stereotypes and performance, see Ussher 1992).

Consequently, it is necessary to consider the role of gender stereotypes in the development of attitudes to communication when examining workplace communication and interpersonal verbal interaction. In contrast to those who claim that gender is salient in all communication situations, we begin from the hypothesis that gender differences will be salient in some, but not necessarily in all situations. We adopt the interactive model of "gender-related behavior" outlined by Deaux and Major (1987) and Deaux and LaFrance (1998). The authors assume that gender has an impact only in those situations where specific factors, such as the type of task or conversational topic, are associated with stereotypical images of women and men, and that these must be activated by certain cues. Gender salience and gender-related behavior are thus conceptualized as a function of the actor, the target, and – foremost – the situation. This interactive model relates to the concept of "doing gender" (Braun and Pasero 1997; West and Zimmerman 1987), concentrating on the *processes* through which the construction of gender and (stereo)typing takes place.

4   Gendered Communication

Since the early 1990s, researchers have investigated the relationship between gender and communication variables from a number of perspectives, such as language use (e.g. Tannen 1995; Woods 1988), competence and competence expectations (Foschi 1992), interpersonal distance (Lott 1995), leadership behavior and leadership perception (Butler and Geis 1990), and many more. Talk at work has received attention from feminists worldwide, reflecting the growing importance of professional communication for women in different countries (Fine, Johnson, Ryan, and Luftiyya 1987; Woods 1988; Holmes 1992; Rossi and Todd-Mancillas 1987; Tannen 1995; Thimm and Ehmer 1997; Thimm 1998). Communication at work has been accepted as an integral part of the study of the "gendered organization" (Kanter 1977).

The importance of *speech style* in work-related interactions has been investigated in several studies. Steffen and Eagly (1985), for example, found that high-status persons were assumed to use a more direct and less polite style, and were also thought more likely to gain compliance by using this style. Lower-status individuals were more concerned with face-saving, and also perceived the style of their partner's talk as more direct and less polite. Softening and politeness strategies were directly related to status: the higher the status, the more direct and less polite the style of talk was perceived to be (cf. also Holmes 1995).

In this context, we outline two particularly relevant approaches (for more detail see Thimm 1995): first, the "sex-dialect hypothesis" (also called "genderlect" or "female register" hypothesis) and, second, the "sex-stereotype hypothesis." The "genderlect" hypothesis assumes that the judgment of communication of women and men is based on actual language performance differences. Typical female language is characterized, it is suggested, by such features as tag questions, softeners, or hedges (Crosby and Nyquist 1977). In contrast, the sex-stereotype hypothesis does not assume that actual language differences are a necessary precondition for differential judgments, but rather proposes that judgments are determined by *stereotypical* expectations. Support for the sex-stereotype hypothesis can be found in Burgoon, Birk, and Hall (1991), who analyzed the category "verbal intensity" in doctor–patient communication. The authors showed that greater expression of intensity by male speakers (indicated, for example, by the use of intensifiers such as "very," "especially," by directives, and by verbs of judgment) was perceived as an effective tool for reaching interactive goals, whereas women were judged as more effective when using a less intensive and more neutral style of talk.

It seems, then, that men are allowed to use an explicitly powerful style, but similar behavior by women does not elicit the same kind of approval, a case of "double standard" for men and women (Foschi 1992). Carli (1990) provides further support for this proposition. She showed that women used more "tentative" language (hedges, softeners, tag questions) and were successful in achieving their communicative goals using this strategy when talking to men, but not when talking to women. In contrast, the use of the tentative style by men was not judged as less successful. These results can be interpreted as a higher tolerance of variety in men's communication styles than women's, reflecting more stereotyped expectations of women's speech style. This interpretation is further illuminated by research which showed that, regardless of gender, certain verbal cues accounted for more successful talk (Erickson, Lind, Johnson, and O'Barr 1978). The authors read out two types of texts from a defendant in a simulated jury setting. One version was formulated as "powerful," the other as "powerless." The powerless version was characterized by a low speech rate, less talk, more pauses as a sign of "non-dynamic delivery," fewer interruptions and attempts to interrupt, more softeners, tag questions, intensifiers, deictic phrases, and more politeness markers. Individuals who employed powerless talk were judged as less competent and less convincing, without gender being disclosed. When asked for associations with the sex of the speakers, *women* were associated with *powerless style* whereas the typical male style was described as more powerful.

This study, as well as others (see overview in Mulac, Incontro, and James 1985), demonstrates how strongly language attitudes and judgments of discourse rely on stereotype-based categorizations of how men and women ought to behave. The results suggest that stereotypical expectations restrict women's interactional behavior more than men's. Whereas men are allowed a wide variety of styles, women very often are not.

5   Gendered Workplace Communication: Empirical Research

There is still relatively little research on the relationship between communication and gender, even in the organizational communication area, based on spoken discourse in natural workplace settings (cf. Poro 1999). In exploring this area, it is important at the initial stage to discover more about the communication expectations and experiences of professional women and men, and their beliefs about what constitutes effective communication.

The empirical research we have undertaken attempts to address this requirement, as well as some of the related research questions and issues mentioned above:

1   Research Study 1: Communication experiences and expectations of men and women in different work settings. This study examines the expectations held by women and men concerning the role and function of verbal communication in relation to workplace success and job satisfaction.
2   Research Study 2: Verbal strategies at work: gender differences in communication situations involving conflict and status asymmetries. This study focuses on the actual verbal strategies used by women and men in particular kinds of workplace interaction.[1]

Both studies were carried out at the University of Heidelberg (Germany), and the participants were native speakers of German. The text excerpts below are translated from German in order to illustrate the kinds of verbal output produced by the participants.

5.1   Gendered expectations and professional communication experience

In the first study two female interviewers conducted two-hour interviews with 13 men and 13 women. The interview comprised a structured questionnaire and a less structured component involving open questions. The interview guidelines included questions on the following topics:

*   Associations regarding communication in general
*   Personal experiences concerning communication in different settings
*   Communication at work
*   Team communication
*   Experience and expectations of successful communication
*   Communication and gender

Subjects' age ranged from 26 to 52 years (mean = 38). The participants came from a variety of professional backgrounds, such as kindergarten teacher, journalist, computer consultant, and management assistant. The interviews were transcribed and the analysis focused on the following six research hypotheses. The women were expected to report:

*   (1): more orientation and differentiation toward persons and situations versus contents and objects;
*   (2): more socio-emotional orientation versus task orientation in terms of communication goals;
*   (3): a more cooperative versus competitive style;

- (4): more consensus orientation versus influence orientation in conflict situations;
- (5): more emphasis on social competence versus professional competence in their professional self-image.

It was also expected that women as well as men would concede that

- (6): women (versus men) receive more sex discrimination, i.e. are more often named as a group (where men are seen as the "default" gender).

Table 23.1 indicates the results of the analysis of responses to the interview questions relating to these six hypotheses. Results suggest differences as well as similarities in the judgment of communicative behavior by men and women. The women from our sample reported that they perceived themselves as more relationship-oriented in their communicative goals, more cooperative in their communicative style, and more consensus-oriented in their conflict behavior. Looking at the total frequency of utterances relating to selected hypotheses in table 23.1, it can be seen that men provided an equal number of relationship-oriented and task-oriented statements, whereas women's responses indicated a more relationship-oriented focus. The female participants also emphasized their use of a cooperative style; there is a highly significant difference between men and women in relation to the category "cooperative versus competitive style" ($p < 0.005$). Other categories indicate similarities between men and women: e.g. "person orientation" versus "object orientation" and definition of "professional competence" as the main part of their professional self-image.

Table 23.1   Results of content analysis on selected hypotheses (frequency = number of utterances; * = significant p-values)

Content	Frequency		Chi^2	p
	Women	Men		
1 Focus: person-oriented vs. content/object-oriented	95 / 45	104 / 57	0.36	0.551
2 Goals: relationship-oriented vs. task-oriented	101 / 47	62 / 62	9.35	0.002*
3 Style: cooperative vs. competitive	96 / 8	90 / 24	7.75	0.005*
4 Conflict style: consensus- vs. influence-oriented	45 / 11	22 / 18	7.12	0.007*
5 Self-image: social vs. professional competence	21 / 22	16 / 23	0.50	0.477
6 Women receive more sex discrimination	36 / 26	49 / 13	6.32	0.012*

Figure 23.1 Female conflict strategies at work (n of persons = 12, n of utterances = 35)

Interestingly, both groups showed a preference in the category "professional competence" versus "social competence." The most important characteristic for positive professional identity was "competence": to be accepted and treated as a professionally competent individual ranked high in both groups. On the other hand, career orientation as part of "professional competence" was mentioned only by men. Another interesting result relates to the category "sex discrimination": significantly more men reported that they saw women as being the target of sex discrimination, whereas a large number of women did not report feeling that they experienced discrimination of this kind. Apparently women are still more easily convinced of personal failure than of overall gender-related disadvantages!

Since we found the most striking differences concerning communication styles in the context of *conflict management*, we were particularly interested in examining how men and women reported dealing with conflict situations. Figure 23.1 presents the results of the analysis of female participants' answers concerning conflict communication.

The most obvious difference concerning conflict management strategies relates to avoidance of confrontation: 35 per cent of utterances by women on how they handled conflicts could be attributed to that category: "I tend to avoid confrontation"; "I am just a terribly peace-loving person," are examples of utterances relating to this issue. For men, on the other hand, avoiding conflicts was not a preferred strategy: they rather reported a tendency toward problem-solving and aggressive demands for compliance in dealing with conflict at work (figure 23.2).

Another striking difference is the self-perception regarding aggressive types of behavior: 32 per cent of the men's utterances referred to aggressive behavior as a potential strategy for dealing with conflict. Some examples: "I start yelling";

Figure 23.2   Male conflict strategies at work (n of persons = 12, n of utterances = 34)

"I can get real loud"; "I can put pressure on people"; "I can get angry and shout at someone."

In general we concluded that participants displayed a high degree of consciousness of the fact that the workplace constitutes a gendered world. Communication in the workplace is still guided by familiar sociocultural stereotypes of men's and women's roles, some expressed very bluntly by the participants, as in the following comment by a male participant: "women should stay in the kitchen, and the fact that we now have a female boss is sad but true."

Men and women in the sample regarded men as more assertive, direct, analytical, logical, aggressive, and verbose, with a higher need for self-presentation, and less flexibility than women. Women were regarded as being friendlier, more cooperative, empathic, holistic, less assertive, more indirectly aggressive, and with higher communicative competence than men. These results obviously coincide with stereotypical gender perspectives on behavior: women described themselves as non-confrontational in situations of conflict; men on the contrary saw themselves as aggressive and goal-oriented. Furthermore, we found evidence for gender-related judgments of work performance: according to our participants, women had to do better at their jobs, but at the same time be more humble and less demanding in order to be equally accepted in the workplace. In everybody's descriptions men appeared as the "default" gender in successful or leading positions; formulations referring to women subcategorized them as, for example, "a successful woman" or "the woman in leading position." In this respect, then, our participants conformed to the concept of double standards in their expectations of success for women and men (cf. Foschi 1992; Heilman and Guzzo 1978).

In one category, however, the professional self-image of men and women at work was surprisingly similar. For both genders the most important aspect of their professional self-image was being regarded as a *competent professional*. Perhaps this can be seen as a reflection of the ongoing German debate on quotas for some professions, such as university professors or higher managerial positions, where women currently hold less than 10 per cent of these positions. Women want to be accepted as qualified and competent, so that they can feel equal to their male counterparts.

5.2   Gendered language use

Investigating the speech variables identified within the framework of the sex-dialect approach (see above), we examined not only the verbal strategies used by women and men in the recorded interviews, but also their verbal behavior in carefully designed role-plays. The focus of the analysis was on the style of self-presentation by male and female participants. A number of linguistic features were chosen for analysis:

- Hedges: e.g. *somewhat, somehow*
- Intensifiers: e.g. *really, very, totally, truly, clearly, extremely*
- Softeners: e.g. *maybe, probably, generally speaking, well*
- Vagueness: e.g. *could be, may, might, maybe, I think*
- Emotiva: statements which express personal involvement, e.g. *I feel like, I like, I hate*
- Use of technical terms: lexical features of business-related or office talk

All of the interviews were coded accordingly in the process of transcription. Linguistic variables were counted automatically as part of our computer-based transcription program (Neubauer, Hub, and Thimm 1994).

The results indicated that women and men differed only slightly in their linguistic self-presentation. We found some small, non-significant differences in language use by women and men on the coded parameters, especially in relation to the use of intensifiers by women. An interesting difference was found, however, in the use of technical terms, a category we described as "lexical features of business-related talk." We identified a ratio of 12 terms used by men to 50 terms used by women, providing a significant difference of $p < 0.04$. Even though the results of quantitative analyses based on counting isolated categories should be interpreted with care, this finding is suggestive in relation to the issue of impression management: the female participants seemed more inclined to demonstrate professional competence by their choice of vocabulary. Whether this is a general property of their professional style or just an accommodation to the task, to the interview situation, or to the respective interviewer, is open to interpretation.

5.3   Strategic interaction in the workplace

The second study focused on the issue of how gender and power influence strategic verbal interaction in workplace situations. This study used two different types of role-play situations in order to compare the influence of partner information and task in relation to choice of verbal strategies. One situation can be described as potentially face-threatening, the other one as a routine task in everyday office communication. The potentially face-threatening situation is characterized by the relation between the task and the authority of the speakers. Where the authority of the speaker in a professional situation is given (as in a superior–subordinate relation), but the subordinate is not likely to comply or might even resist, we label this a "reactance prone situation" (RPS). Situations where speakers feel free to ask for something and do not expect resistance are labeled a "standard situation" (SS). To compare the effects of task, status, situation, and gender we conducted role-plays of both situational types. As a task we chose a pair of routine activities: typing up a letter and preparing coffee for the superior. The following instructions were given to the participants:

Standard situation (SS)
"You are participating in a role-play study between the head of a department of a company and her/his secretary. Please imagine you are the boss of a department in a large company, and you have your own secretary. When you are seated at your desk in a minute, call in your secretary to take a letter. Dictate her a circular letter addressing all members of staff. Point out that you want everyone to lock up their offices after work. Think up an appropriate text for this letter. When you have finished dictating, you also want your secretary to make some coffee. This is one of her duties as a secretary. *You know she will be willing to make coffee.*"

Reactance prone situation (RPS)
The instructions the participants were given were the same as above, with one modification:
"*You know that she does not like making coffee and might be unwilling to do so.*"

Altogether 109 individuals participated, all of them graduate students of the department of business administration at the University of Mannheim; 109 role-play texts were collected, 48 produced by female, 61 by male speakers. In the RPS, 26 women and 34 men took part, whereas in the SS there were 22 women and 27 men, all between 21 and 27 years of age. The part of the secretary was played by a confederate of the research team.

The communicative situation of this role-play is distinguished by the expectation of the speaker in one case that the target person (the secretary) likes making coffee and is willing to do so (standard situation), while in the other case she dislikes this task although it is one of her duties (reactance prone situation). In both situations (SS and RPS), the legitimacy of the speaker to pose the request is high, while the willingness of the partner to comply is high in one situation (SS), but low in the other (RPS).

As we were particularly looking for conflict management strategies, the reactance prone situation seemed more likely to confront the participants with potential conflict and was therefore our main focus. Since the confederate "secretary" was asked to minimize her verbal input, the texts cannot be classi-fied as strictly "dialogues." However, since the participants were not informed about her status as a confederate, but rather assumed that she was also a role-play participant, we began from the hypothesis that partner orientation was a manifest property in our data.

5.4   *Typology of strategic interaction*

Strategic interaction can be regarded as central to reactance prone situa-tions. If we expect resistance or unwillingness from our interaction partners, we prepare ourselves and plan our own actions in more detail. Strategy is defined as a *sequence of speech patterns serving the purpose of reaching the interactional goals of the speaker in a situation of actual or perceived reactance.* We distinguish *type of strategy* from *strategic moves*, which serve to carry out the strategy in the context of the verbal interaction. The strategy itself is named in accordance with the goal aimed for. The exact speech patterns, that is, the strategic moves, are analyzed in relation to the strategy (Thimm 1990).

To analyze strategic interaction in the context of gendered communication at work the strategies described in table 23.2, and their concomitant strategic moves, were taken as the base line. We shall focus on those outcomes which yielded significant results in terms of gender differences.

Table 23.2   Typology of strategies and strategic moves

Goals	Strategies	Strategic moves
Avoiding a conflict, preventing a conflict, securing one's position	Face-saving strategy	Delegation, changing the topic, vagueness, mentioning external sources, softeners
Maintaining a relationship, securing the interaction	Relationship-securing strategy	Personal address, confirming, reassuring, idiomatic phrasing, metacommunication
Getting a person to cooperate	Cooperation strategy	Complimenting, praising, asking further questions, offering compensation, cooperative informing, positive assessment, self-disclosure
Establishing or confirming power over others	Power strategy	Orders, threats, mentioning status or hierarchy, demonstrating competence, direct requests

5.5 Face-saving strategy

As the possibility of reactance includes the risk of loss of authority for the superior, we assumed that participants would try to minimize this risk by employing face-saving strategic moves. Besides the features shown in table 23.2, a number of other linguistic categories were used to test for this strategy, including the analysis of the *syntactic form of the request*. Methodologically this comprised two steps. First, the requests for making coffee were evaluated with respect to degree of directness (direct request, question, or command, as illustrated below). Second, the whole text was analyzed for *syntactic complexity*. Depending on the context, syntactic complexity can be regarded as a partial face-saving strategy in that it demonstrates verbal competence (and thereby attends to the speaker's face needs), or it may introduce an element of vagueness by expressing the propositional content in a complex and difficult to process construction.

Both men and women used significantly more softeners in the RPS than in the SS. Analysis for gender differences yielded a clear, but unexpected, result: male participants used significantly more softeners than female. So contrary to other research, this so-called female feature functioned in these role-plays as a male strategy. Hedging on the part of the male speakers was thus employed with strategic considerations, particularly with face-saving implications. As this result contradicted other findings on powerless talk, a separate analysis for each variable in the category of "softeners" was carried out, aiming at a more detailed differentiation between various types of softeners. On the basis of German research on feminist linguistics concerning gendered language usage (Gottburgsen 2000), the following features were analyzed:

- *somehow, somewhere*
- conditional phrases (e.g. *could you, would you*)
- hedges
- politeness phrases (e.g. *please, be so kind, if you'd be so kind*)
- softening particles (e.g. *just, maybe*)
- diminutives (e.g. *little*)

Regardless of the gender of the participants, a particularly high number of softeners were found in the introductory phase of the request where the ground for positive cooperation was being laid. However, the analysis also indicated that the women handled the RPS role-play situation differently from men: the male participants employed significantly more softeners, conditional forms, and explicitly polite talk features than the women. As mentioned above, we interpret the findings in the light of strategic interaction. If a situation is seen as face-threatening with respect to personal goals and statuses, men seem entirely capable of employing features of the "powerless" talk typically associated with women's genderlect.

Another face-saving strategic move, which is used frequently, is *delegation of responsibility by referring to external authorities*. In the role-play texts, a delegation of responsibility was realized by referring to external authorities (*my boss; I've been instructed to*) or by referring to external force (*due to safety regulations; due to some complaints*). Men and women differed from one another in a highly significant way, independently of the role-play conditions, with women using many more delegating moves. Moreover, the male participants did not differentiate between the conditions, whereas female participants used forms of delegation or justification more often in the reactance prone situations. Some examples of gendered usage are:

- female participant: *this is an office regulation; I was told to . . .*
- male participant: *in the last meeting of managerial directors, we decided that . . . ; I've been told by my superior . . .*

Those males who used delegating moves, often employed a more personal and less general reference to authority, and sometimes even managed to emphasize their status as a boss, as can be seen in the first example from a male speaker above.

5.6   *Relationship-securing strategy*

Since the role-plays provided little or no possibility to engage in a conversation, there were only a few typical elements of the relationship-securing strategy to be found. One of these was *personal address*. A significant gender difference between the direct form of address with *Mrs. X* (*Frau Maier*) and *Miss X* (*Fräulein Maier*) was found. In German the second form of address (*Fräulein*) is hardly ever used for older women, and has a pejorative connotation. The male participants in the RPS addressed their "secretary" more often with a personal name than the participants in the SS did. Since no specific names had been given in the instruction, participants could choose freely (the proper name Maier, one of the most frequent German family names, was chosen by 36 participants). Another important category includes the personal pronoun *we*. By using this pronoun, participants tried to refer explicitly to a mutual perspective and demonstrate cooperation:

- *We will have to come up with something for that* (male speaker)
- *Ok, we can leave it at that for now* (female speaker)
- *All right, let's have a nice cup of coffee, don't you think so? Now that we've finished work* (female speaker)

Another relevant category for the analysis of asymmetrical communication is the use of *metacommunication*. Those phrases which communicate awareness of the underlying conflict and formulate the directive using explicit metacommunication can also be analyzed with respect to the relationship-securing strategy. We defined metacommunication as mentioning the task (*I have a request for you*), and as mentioning the potential conflict (*I know you don't like to do that*).

Comparing conditions, results yielded a highly significant difference, with more metacommunicative utterances in the reactance prone situation. This suggests the important contribution made by metacommunicative interaction in work settings in general, since both male and female participants often used this strategic move. The more precise analysis, however, showed that women did not differentiate as much between SS and RPS as the men did.

When looking at the content of metacommunicative messages, possible resistance plays an important role. Male participants used the following phrases:

- *Well, ahm, I know you don't like doing this, but would you please make some coffee for me*
- *Ok, hm, and then I have a little request. Could you maybe make some coffee for me? I know this is not one of your favorite occupations, but that would be very nice of you.*

Whereas this type of direct, upfront addressing of the secretary was used frequently by male speakers, it was found in only three instances with female speakers, for example:

- *Ahm, Mrs. Mueller, could you make some coffee for me nonetheless anyway?*
- *Ahm, I'd like some coffee, would you be willing to make some coffee for me, you can make some for yourself, too.*

Just like the men's, the women's messages included reference to the underlying conflict, but they also often offered compensation. Offering compensation, such as promising personal activities in the future, sometimes takes on a ritual character, especially in institutional talk. The following excerpt shows that some of the female participants even went out of their way to offer compensation:

- *Ahm, Mrs. Maier, would you please make some coffee for me; I know that you don't really like doing that, but tomorrow I'll do it again myself, ok?*

This formulation takes on the character of an apology for the demand. If we see the task of coffee-making as part of a symbol of status asymmetry this seems to be a very "un-bossy" thing to offer!

5.7   *Cooperation strategy*

Cooperative management depends to a great extent on the way a superior shares information with his/her subordinates. Our first study indicated that women perceived themselves as very cooperative and less aggressive than men. The second study was designed to compare male and female degrees of cooperativeness when asking someone to undertake a task which they might be unwilling to do. A request such as this could involve a degree of face-threat or risk to one's own authority; this seemed an appropriate situation to test whether women would actually behave in the way they perceived themselves.

The participants in the role-play dealt with the problem presented by the task in different ways. Sometimes the explanations the participants gave to their secretary concerning the circular letter were lengthy and detailed. These explanatory introductions were counted as a move of *cooperative inform-ing*. When looking at gender differences, we found that male participants typically formulated this informational part in more detail than the women. One example:

- *Good morning Mrs. Maier. Please come in and have a seat, please. I'd like you to take dictation. This is to be a circular letter to our colleagues, which includes some important information . . .*

The speech act of informing someone about something is usually performed by a person in a higher position and has to be seen in the context of the hierarchical structure of the relationship. Analyzing the cooperative informing moves, it became obvious that the male participants regarded this type of communication with their secretary as an important aspect of their role. They took time to explain the circumstances of the task in nearly every role-play of the RPS.

The *positive assessment of the work* of the secretary is another strategic move in the cooperative strategy. Both men and women seemed concerned about this issue, but differed in the positive assessment with respect to some details. Women thanked their secretary much more often after they finished taking notes for the letter (*Ok, that's about it, thank you*). Men tended to comment more generally on the secretary's skills or qualifications (*I know you can do this, just finish it up as usual*).

One move that differed between women and men in the context of strategic cooperation was *self-disclosure moves*, that is, the voluntary passing on of rather intimate information by the participants. Self-disclosure is recognized as an important and well-researched phenomenon in interpersonal interaction (e.g. Pearce and Sharp 1973). The role-plays provided examples of personal messages used in the RPS to reduce the level of face-threat in the situation. Indicators of such self-disclosure phrases were personal pronouns such as *we* which suggest mutuality, speech acts such as asking further questions, indicating implicit support for the secretary, or requesting advice from her (*And now? Sincerely? Can we leave it that way?*). The most obvious way to formulate self-disclosures are phrases such as: *I'm so overworked*, or personal requests to the secretary such as: *Now that we've finished our work we can have a nice cup of coffee, don't you think so?*

The data showed highly significant differences in self-disclosure between male and female participants. The differences were qualitative as well as quantitative in nature and became obvious within the structure of arguments. If female participants employed self-disclosure it often took on the character of an excuse:

- *And then I want to ask you a big favor: I've just too much to do and feel really burdened, could you please make some coffee for me?*
- *Then I would like to ask you to make some coffee for me, I have such a headache. Thank you.*

For some male participants, on the other hand, self-disclosure was employed to demonstrate importance:

- *Well, so much for this, and now for the other thing, ahm, I would ask you to, by way of exception, I do know that you don't like to do it, but today I still have so much work to do, so today I have to stay in late, and I want to ask you to make some coffee for me.*

Here the women mention stress and headaches, while the male speaker underlines the necessity of working overtime. Describing yourself as *burdened* does not refer to competence, but rather conveys the impression of not being able to cope. And having a headache comes across as a classical stereotype of female incapability.

5.8   Power strategy

Many interactional situations in the workplace are heavily influenced by differences of position in the hierarchy and status differences. Not surprisingly, linguistic features also strongly reflect the influence of status and hierarchy.

One indicator of dominance in interactions and of powerful talk is the type of speech act used. On the assumption that syntactic phrasing and speech act type indicate different power strategies, the texts were analyzed for different types of request formulations: direct request, indirect requests, and commands. Orders or commands included utterances such as: *And then make some coffee for me*; indirect requests involved sentences such as: *Coffee would be nice now, wouldn't it?* Other ways of asking for coffee were coded as direct requests: *All right, and now you could make some coffee for me, please.* The results of analyzing all the available texts in this way are recorded in table 23.3.

In the potentially face-threatening situation (RPS), women used significantly more indirect requests than any other strategy, and they completely avoided orders or commands. Indirect requests are generally regarded as one means of expressing politeness (Holmes 1995). Men, on the other hand, showed a greater preference than women for direct requests in both conditions. Looking at this

Table 23.3 Types and frequency of requests

	Women (n = 48)		Men (n = 61)	
	SS (22)	RPS (26)	SS (27)	RPS (34)
Direct requests	6	11	9	18
Indirect requests	13	21	19	18
Orders/commands	3	0	4	2
Total	22	32	32	38

result from the perspective of powerful talk, it appears that gender stereotypes are being confirmed: men are more direct in phrasing their requests, and some even employ canonical power-oriented strategies such as commands, whereas women are typically more polite and less direct.

Acting the "boss" is realized even more explicitly in some texts. One of the most striking and explicit features is the use of the title or position of the speaker, a strategy used only by male speakers. When finishing up the dictation they often added a title or a position, referring to themselves as *the head of the department, the management* or *sincerely – Your board of directors*. These titles refer to official positions and therefore emphasize their superior position.

Another category which yielded highly significant differences between men and women was the type of technical language used, that is, business-related talk or "office talk." Office talk is characterized by lexical features, particularly nouns, and by certain phrases used in business settings (e.g. *mail it out; distribute the copies; xerox the letter*, etc.) and by specific routines. The category "office talk" not only reflects a higher identification with the job (or rather the role-play situation), it is also very much part of powerful talk at work. Using the right "code" signals competence. This code consists mainly of the technical terminology relevant to the situation. Male participants used such terminology significantly more frequently than the female participants did.

6 Summary and Conclusions

The results from the studies described in this chapter suggest that similarities and differences in gendered communication in the workplace should be considered from a range of perspectives. First, it is clear that for both men and women verbal communication plays an important role in interpersonal interaction at work. Second, our interview study showed that, for both men and women, conveying professional competence was the most important goal for their work-related self-image. Furthermore, men and women in the interview study claimed to use different cooperative and conflict strategies at work, a self-assessment whose accuracy was confirmed by the role-play study.

Third, the data from the role-play study suggested that, overall, male participants used a wider variety of communicative strategies than women. Male participants used features of a "powerless style" and related strategies in order to pursue their interactional goals more frequently than female participants did. Female participants, on the other hand, did not rely as much on verbal references to status or personal position; their approach tended to be brief and highly structured. Our data showed that elements of the "female register" or "powerless register" are equally accessible to men and women and must be regarded as highly context-dependent. The strategic use of elements of powerless talk may in some circumstances be an advantage to all interlocutors. However, professional men and women are frequently measured by different standards (Foschi 1992); hence women are often sanctioned into less flexible ways of behaving, while a greater range of acceptable behaviors is available to men (Carli 1990).

In line with the view that gender differences are salient only in some situations, as suggested by the "gender-in-context model" (Deaux and Major 1987; Deaux and LaFrance 1998), one needs to identify precisely those contexts where gender has an impact. Factors such as task or conversational topic are often associated with sex-stereotypical images, and these may be activated by particular cues, as in the different role-play situations devised for our second study, especially where the female secretary was asked to prepare coffee. In many cases it is the small details, the tone of voice or the wording, which makes gender and verbal gender differences salient. Notwithstanding that there are social and political barriers and disadvantages for women which have to be taken into account, we believe it to be of decisive importance to look at *female activities* from the perspective of the mutual construction of reality. This suggests a gender-construction perspective – which we believe is a perspective of change and chance, adequately taking into account the complexity of gendered interaction.

NOTE

1   Both of these studies were supported by grants from the German Science Foundation (DFG), Bonn.

REFERENCES

Achatz, Juliane, Allmendinger, Jutta, and Hinz, Thomas 2000: Sex Segregations in Organisations: A Comparison of Germany and the U.S. Paper presented in the Session "Occupational and Job Segregation at the Workforce", ASA, Washington.

Acker, Joan 1991: Hierarchies, jobs, bodies: A theory of gendered organizations. In Judith Lorber and Susan A. Farell (eds) *The Social Construction of Gender*. Newbury Park, CA: Sage, pp. 162–79.

Blanck, Peter D. (ed.) 1993: *Interpersonal Expectations: Theory, Research and Applications*. Cambridge: Cambridge University Press.

Braun, Friederike and Pasero, Ursula 1997: *Kommunikation von Geschlecht – Communication of Gender*. Kiel: Centaurus.

Broverman, Inge, Vogel, Susan, Broverman, Donald, Clarkson, Frank, and Rosenkrantz, Paul 1972: Sex role stereotypes: A current appraisal. *Journal of Social Issues* 28(2): 59–78.

Burgoon, Michael, Birk, Thomas, and Hall, Judith 1991: Compliance gaining and satisfaction with physician–patient communication: An expectancy theory interpretation of gender difference. *Human Communication Research* 18: 177–208.

Butler, Doré and Geis, Florence L. 1990: Nonverbal affect responses to male and female leaders: Implications for leadership evaluations. *Journal of Personality and Social Psychology* 58(1): 48–59.

Carli, Linda L. 1990: Gender, language, and influence. *Journal of Personality and Social Psychology* 59(5): 941–51.

Crawford, Mary 1995: *Talking Difference: On Gender and Language*. London: Sage.

Crosby, Fave and Nyquist, Linda 1977: The female register: An empirical study of Lakoff's hypotheses. *Language in Society* 6: 313–22.

Deaux, Kay and LaFrance, Marianne 1998: Gender. In Daniel Gilbert, Susan Fiske, and Gardener Lindzey (eds) *The Handbook of Social Psychology*, vol. 1. Boston: McGraw-Hill, pp. 788–827.

Deaux, Kay and Major, Brenda 1987: Putting gender into context: An interactive model of gender-related behavior. *Psychological Review* 94(3): 369–89.

Eckes, Thomas 1997: Talking about gender: A sociopsychological perspective on language and gender stereotyping. In: Friederike Braun and Ursula Pasero (eds) *Kommunikation von Geschlecht – Communication of Gender*. Kiel: Centaurus, pp. 30–53.

Erickson, Bonnie, Lind, Allan E., Johnson, Bruce, and O'Barr, William M. 1978: Speech styles and impression formation in a court room setting: The effects of "powerful" and "powerless" speech. *Journal of Experimental Social Psychology* 14: 266–79.

Fine, Marlene G., Johnson, Fern J., Ryan, M. Sallyanne, and Lytfiyya, M. Nawal 1987: Ethical issues in defining and evaluating women's communication in the workplace. In Lea P. Stewart and Stella Ting-Toomey (eds) *Communication, Gender and Sex Roles in Diverse Interaction Contexts*. Norwood, NJ: Ablex, pp. 105–18.

Fishman, Pamela M. 1978: Interaction: The work women do. *Social Problems* 25(4): 397–406.

Foschi, Martha 1992: Gender and double standards for competence. In Cecilia Ridgeway (ed.) *Gender, Interaction, and Equality*. New York: Springer, pp. 181–207.

Gottburgsen, Angelika 2000: *Stereotype Muster des sprachlichen "doing gender."* Opladen: Westdeutscher.

Heilman, Madeline E. and Guzzo, Richard A. 1978: The perceived cause of work success as a mediator of sex discrimination in organizations. *Organizational Behavior and Human Performance* 21: 346–57.

Holmes, Janet 1992: Women's talk in public contexts. *Discourse & Society* 3(2): 131–50.

Holmes, Janet 1995: *Women, Men and Politeness*. London: Longman.

Hultin, M. and Szulkin, R. 1999: Wages and unequal access to organizational power: An empirical test of gender discrimination. *Administrative Science Quarterly* 44: 453–72.

Jacobs, Jerry A. 1995: *Gender Inequality at Work*. Newbury Park, CA: Sage.

Kanter, R. Moss 1977: *Men and Women of the Corporation*. New York: Basic Books.

Kramer, Cheris 1975: Women's speech: Separate but unequal? In Barrie Thorne and Nancy Henley (eds) *Language and Sex: Difference and Dominance*. Rowley, MA: Newbury House, pp. 43–56.

Lakoff, Robin T. 1975: *Language and Woman's Place*. New York: Harper and Row.

Lott, Bernice 1995: Distancing from women: Interpersonal sexist discrimination. In Bernice Lott and Diane Baluso (eds) *The Social Psychology of Interpersonal Discrimination*. New York: Guilford Press, pp. 12–49.

Luzzo, Darrell A. and Garrison Hutcheson, Kathy 1996: Causal attributions and sex differences associated with perceptions of occupational barriers. *Journal of Counseling and Development* 11(12): 124–30.

Merton, Robert K. 1948: The self-fulfilling prophecy. *Antioch Review* 8: 193–210.

Mulac, Anthony, Incontro, Carol R., and James, Margaret R. 1985: Comparison of the gender-linked language effect and sex role stereotypes. *Journal of Personality and Social Psychology* 49(4): 1098–109.

Neubauer, Marion, Hub, Ingrid, and Thimm, Caja 1994: Transkribieren mit LATEX: Transkriptionsregeln, Eingabeverfahren und Auswertungsmöglichkeiten. Arbeiten aus dem Sonderforschungsbereich 245 Sprache und Situation, 76.

Pearce, William and Sharp, Stephen 1973: Self-disclosing communication. *Journal of Communication* 23: 409–25.

Poro, Susanne 1999: *Beziehungsrelevanz in der beruflichen Kommunikation*. New York and Frankfurt: Lang.

Reskin, Barbara 1993: Sex segregation in the workplace. *Annual Review of Sociology* 19: 241–70.

Rosenthal, Robert and Jacobson, L. 1968: *Pygmalion in the Classroom*. New York: Holt, Rinehart & Winston.

Rossi, Ana M. and Todd-Mancillas, William R. 1987: Male/female differences in managing conflicts. In Lea P. Stewart and Stella Ting-Toomey (eds) *Communication, Gender and Sex Roles in Diverse Interaction Contexts*. Norwood, NJ: Ablex, pp. 96–104.

Snyder, Marc 1981: On the self-perpetuating nature of social stereotypes. In David L. Hamilton (ed.) *Cognitive Processes in*

Stereotyping and Intergroup Behavior.
Hillsdale, NJ: Lawrence Erlbaum,
pp. 183–212.

Steffen, Valerie J. and Eagly, Alice H.
1985: Implicit theories about
influence of style: The effects of
status and sex. *Personality and Social
Psychology Bulletin* 11(2): 191–205.

Talbot, Mary M. 1998: *Language and
Gender: An Introduction.* Cambridge:
Polity.

Tannen, Deborah 1995: *Job Talk. Wie
Frauen und Männer am Arbeitsplatz
miteinander Reden.* Hamburg: Kabel.

Thimm, Caja 1990: *Dominanz und Sprache.
Strategisches Handeln im Alltag.*
Wiesbaden: Deutscher
Universitätsverlag.

Thimm, Caja 1995:
Durchsetzungsstrategien von
Frauen und Männern: Sprachliche
Unterschiede oder stereotype
Erwartungen? In Christa M.
Heilmann (ed.) *Frauensprechen–
Männersprechen.
Geschlechtsspezifisches Sprechverhalten.*
Munich and Basel: Reinhard,
pp. 120–9.

Thimm, Caja 1998: Frauen, Sprache,
Beruf. Sprachliches Handeln am
Arbeitsplatz. In Giesela Schoenthal
(ed.) *Feministische Linguistik –
Linguistische Geschlechterforschung.
Ergebnisse, Konsequenzen,
Perspektiven.* Hildesheim: Georg
Olms, pp. 323–46.

Thimm, Caja and Ehmer, Heidi 1997:
Strategic interaction at the
workplace. How men and women

deal with power differences. In
Friederike Braun and Ursula Pasero
(eds) *Kommunikation von Geschlecht –
Communication of Gender.* Kiel:
Centaurus, pp. 303–19.

Ussher, Jane M. 1992: Sex differences in
performance: Fact, fiction or fantasy.
In Andrew P. Smith and Dylan M.
Jones (eds) *Handbook of Human
Performance*, vol. 3. London:
Academic Press, pp. 63–94.

Wahl, Annette von 1999:
*Gleichstellungsregime. Berufliche
Gleichstellung von Frauen in den USA
und der Bundesrepublik Deutschland.*
Opladen: Leske & Buderich.

Watts, Richard 1995: Male vs. female
discourse strategies: Tabling
conversational topics. In G. Brünner
and Gabriele Graeffen (eds) *Texte
und Diskurse. Methoden und
Forschungsergebnisse der funktionalen
Pragmatik.* Opladen: Westdeutscher,
pp. 218–38.

West, Candace and Zimmerman,
Don H. 1987: Doing gender.
Gender and Society 1(2): 125–51.

Williams, John E. and Best, Deborah L.
1986: Sex stereotypes and intergroup
relations. In S. Worchel and W. G.
Austin (eds) *Psychology of Intergroup
Relations.* Chicago: Nelson-Hall.

Woods, Nicola 1988: Talking shop: Sex
and status as determinants of floor
apportionment in a work setting.
In Jennifer Coates and Deborah
Cameron (eds) *Women in Their
Speech Communities.* London:
Longman, pp. 141–57.

24 Linguistic Sexism and Feminist Linguistic Activism

ANNE PAUWELS

1 Women and Men as Language Users and Regulators

The popular portrayal of women and men as language users has stressed their fundamental differences. A quick perusal of some writings about male and female speakers across languages (e.g. Baron 1986) leaves no doubt that men are perceived not only as powerful speakers but especially as authoritative language users. Women, on the other hand, are often seen as garrulous, frivolous, and illiterate language users. These popular stereotypes gained in stature when they were endorsed by or validated in the "academic" and "scientific" literature of the day (for an overview see e.g. Baron 1986; Kramarae 1981). This "scientific" validation in turn led to the desire for the codification and regulation of women's speech, and of women as speakers. Cameron (1995; this volume) as well as other scholars of language and gender have documented the many rules, codes, and guides that were developed to codify and control women's language behavior over the past centuries. Essentially this action cemented men's status as norm-makers, language regulators, and language planners. Men signaled their authority in language through their roles in the dictionary-making process, in the writing of normative grammars, in the establishment of language academies and other normative language institutions, and through their involvement in language planning activities. The history of women as language regulators is very different. As stated above, women were subjected to linguistic regulation much more than men. However, women were given some authority in language regulation as norm enforcers: both as mothers and as school teachers (especially in elementary education) women were to ensure that children learned to use language according to the prescribed norms.

It was the linguistic activism associated with the women's movement starting in the 1970s that posed the first major female challenge to male dominance in language regulation and planning. Women of all walks of life started to expose the biased portrayal of the sexes in language use and demonstrated that this portrayal was particularly discriminatory and damaging to women. Furthermore, their activities targeted the uncovering of the gendered nature of many linguistic rules and norms. For example, Bodine's (1975) paper on "Androcentrism in prescriptive grammar" showed that sex-indefinite *he* gained its dominant status as generic pronoun as a result of male regulation. Baron's (1986) comprehensive analysis of grammar in relation to gender similarly exposes androcentric practices. Another powerful expression of language regulation is the dictionary. Scholars such as Kramarae (1992), Pusch (1984), and Yaguello (1978) revealed sexism in lexicographic practices, especially in older versions of dictionaries of English, German, and French: the works of the "best" male authors were a major source for dictionary definitions of words. Female authors or women-oriented publications (especially women's magazines) were seldom included in the source material. These exposures of bias cast women in the role of critical commentators on "men's rules." Some women reacted to the bias by becoming *norm-breakers* who subverted established norms and rules: examples include the use of *she* as sex-indefinite pronoun, and in German, the introduction of the word *Herrlein* (literally, little man) for a single man to match the existing *Fräulein* (literally, little woman – Miss).

Perhaps most threatening to men's role as norm-makers were the attempts women made at becoming norm-makers themselves through the formulation of proposals and guidelines for non-sexist language use. Developing women's own norms and implementing them across a speech community is clearly the strongest challenge, if not threat, to male authority in language regulation. This assumption is borne out by the often vehement reactions expressed by (male-dominated) language academies and other linguistic authorities against analyses of linguistic sexism and against proposals for non-sexist language use (for details see e.g. Blaubergs 1980; Hellinger 1990; Pauwels 1998). In many negative reactions to the guidelines the author tries to discard a proposed change by questioning the linguistic expertise of the feminist language planner or linguistic activist. In other words, he or she expresses the belief that the female language planner does not have the knowledge or the expertise to propose new language norms.

In the following sections I will examine the language (planning) activities which were triggered by the newly gained female consciousness associated with women's movements across the Western world during the 1970s and 1980s. I will also examine the extent to which their attempts at becoming *norm-makers* have been successful.

2   Feminist Linguistic Activism – Non-sexist Language Reform

2.1   *Feminist non-sexist language campaigns as an instance of language planning*

It is important to acknowledge that the debates, actions, and initiatives around the (non-) sexist language issue are a form of language planning. The marginalization of feminist perspectives on gender and communication in the 1970s and early 1980s had a particularly strong effect on the recognition of feminist linguistic activism as a genuine case of language planning, in this instance a form of *corpus planning* (see Kloss 1969). In fact, "mainstream" literature on language planning either ignored or denied the existence of feminist language planning until Cooper's (1989) work on language planning and social change which includes the American non-sexist language campaign as one of its case-studies.

It will become clear from the description and discussion below that feminist campaigns to eliminate sexist bias from language have all the trademarks of language reform. In my previous work (e.g. Pauwels 1993, 1998) I have analyzed feminist language reform using a sociolinguistic approach to language planning (e.g. Fasold 1984). The sociolinguistic approach emphasizes the fact that reforms are directed at achieving social change, especially of the kind that enables greater equality, equity, and access. Within this framework the language planning process is divided into four main stages. The *fact-finding* stage is concerned with documenting the problematic issues and concerns. The *planning* stage focuses on the viability of change as well as on developing proposals for change. In the *implementation* stage the methods and avenues for promoting and implementing the changes are assessed and the preferred proposals are implemented. In the *evaluation/feedback* stage language planners seek to assess to what extent the planning and implementation processes have been successful in terms of achieving the goal of the language planning exercise. This involves examining whether the changes are being adopted by the speech community and how they are being used.

2.2   *Documenting sexist language practices*

Exposing and documenting sexist practices in language use and communication has been, and continues to be, a grassroots-based activity by feminists with an interest in language and the linguistic representation of the sexes. There is no denying that feminist activists in the USA were the trailblazers in both exposing sexist bias and proposing changes. Amongst a (linguistic) academic readership the works of Lakoff (1975) and Spender (1980) and the collection of essays in Nilsen et al. (1977) became the main reference points for elaborate descriptions of linguistic sexism as it affected the English language. Other speech communities in which feminists took an early and active interest in exposing sexist linguistic practices included Norway (Blakar 1977), France (Yaguello 1978), Germany (e.g. Troemel-Ploetz 1978; Guentherodt 1979; Guentherodt et al. 1980; Hellinger and Schräpel 1983) as well as Spain (e.g. Garcia 1977). More recently the documentation of gender bias has spread to languages such as Chinese, Icelandic, Lithuanian, Italian, Japanese, Polish, and Thai (see Hellinger and Bussman 2001; Pauwels 1998).

Feminist explorations into the representation of women and men revealed commonalities across speech communities as well as across languages. A striking feature across many languages and speech communities is the *asymmetrical treatment* of women and men, of male/masculine and female/feminine concepts and principles. The practice of considering the man/the male as the prototype for human representation reduces the woman/female to the status of the "subsumed," the "invisible," or the "marked" one: women are invisible in language when they are subsumed in generic expressions using masculine forms. Generic reference in many languages occurs via the use of forms which are identical with the representation of maleness (e.g. *he* as generic and masculine pronoun, generic nouns coinciding with nouns referring to males). When women are made visible in language, they are "marked": their linguistic construction is often as a derivative of man/male through various grammatical (morphological) processes.

This asymmetry also affects the lexical make-up of many languages. The structure of the lexicon often reflects the "male as norm" principle through the phenomenon of lexical gaps, that is, the absence of words to denote women in a variety of roles, professions, and occupations (e.g. Baron 1986; Hellinger 1990; Sabatini 1985; Yaguello 1978). The bias against women in the matter of lexical gaps is particularly poignant when we consider the reverse, namely, the absence of male-specific nouns to denote men adopting roles or entering professions seen to be female-dominant. The male lexical gaps tend to be filled rather quickly, even to the extent that the new male form becomes the dominant one from which a new female form is derived. An example of this practice is found in German where the word *Hebamme* (midwife) is making way for the new word *Entbindungspfleger* (literally "birthing assistant") as a result of men taking up the role of midwife. Meanwhile a female midwife has been coined *Entbindungspflegerin*, a form derived from *Entbindungspfleger*.

The semantic asymmetry that characterizes the portrayal of women and men in language is of particular concern to feminist activists, as it is an expression of women's and men's perceived values and status in society. The core of this semantic asymmetry is that woman is a sexual being dependent on man, whereas man is simply defined as a human being whose existence does not need reference to woman. Schulz (1975) highlights the practice of semantic derogation which constantly reinforces the "generic man" and "sexual woman" portrayal. Schulz (1975: 64) finds that "a perfectly innocent term designating a girl or a woman may begin with neutral or positive connotations, but that gradually it acquires negative implications, at first only slightly disparaging, but after a period of time becoming abusive and ending as a sexual slur." This practice has also been observed and examined for French (e.g. Sautermeister 1985), German (e.g. Kochskämper 1991), and Japanese (e.g. Cherry 1987).

Linguistic *stereotyping* of the sexes was also seen as problematic, especially for women as it reinforced women's subordinate status. Stereotyped language was particularly damaging to women in the context of the mass media and educational materials. It is therefore not surprising that both these spheres of language use were subjected to thorough examinations of sexism (see e.g. Nilsen et al. 1977).

Community reaction to these feminist analyses was predominantly negative: the existence of linguistic sexism was vigorously denied. Reasons for its denial varied according to the status and linguistic expertise of the commentator. Whereas non-experts rejected the claim on (folk) etymological assumptions, or because of an unquestioned acceptance of the wisdom of existing language authorities, linguistic experts refuted the claims by arguing that feminist analyses of the language system are fundamentally flawed as they rest on erroneous understandings of language and gender, particularly of grammatical gender. For example, the reaction of the Department of Linguistics at Harvard University to suggestions from students at the Divinity School to ban *Man, man,* and generic *he* as they are sexist, and the reaction by the German linguist Hartwig Kalverkämper (1979) to a similar observation for the German language by fellow linguist Senta Troemel-Ploetz (1978), stated that feminist analysts held a mistaken view about the relationship between grammatical gender and sex. These denials were in turn scrutinized and refuted by feminist linguistic commentators who exposed historical practices of grammatical gender reassignment (e.g. Baron 1986; Cameron 1985) or who presented evidence from experimental work on people's perceptions of gender and sex in language (e.g. Mackay 1980; Pauwels 1998).

2.3   Changing language: How?

Most feminist language activists were and are proponents of language change as a measure for achieving a more balanced representation of women and men in language. Taking linguistic action to improve the plight of women was seen as an integral part of women's liberation. Furthermore, many language activists subscribe to an interactionist view of language and reality which has its origins in a weaker version of the Sapir–Whorf hypothesis: language shapes and reflects social reality.

Despite this consensus on the need for linguistic action there is considerable diversity in the activists' and planners' views on how to change sexist practices in language. Their views on strategies for achieving change are shaped by many factors, including their own motivation for change, their understanding and view of language, and the nature and type of the language to be changed. Planners whose motivation to change is driven by a belief that language change lags behind social change will adopt different strategies from those activists whose main concern is to expose patriarchal bias in language. Whereas the former may consider linguistic amendments as a satisfactory strategy to achieve the linguistic reflection of social change, the latter activists would not be satisfied with mere amendments. Proposals for change are also shaped by one's understanding of the language system, of how meaning is created, and of how linguistic change occurs. For example, a linguist's suggestions for change may be heavily influenced by his or her training – training in recognizing the distinctive structural elements and properties of language such as phonemes, morphemes, and grammatical categories, and in recognizing how these elements contribute to creating meaning. Reformers without such training may focus their efforts for change mainly at the lexical level as this level is often considered the only one susceptible to change. The nature and type of language also influences proposals for change: languages that have grammatical gender pose different challenges from those that do not.

Among this multitude of opinions and views on the question of change, three main motivations for change can be discerned: (1) a desire to expose the sexist nature of the current language system; (2) a desire to create a language which can express reality from a woman's perspective; or (3) a desire to amend the present language system to achieve a symmetrical and equitable representation of women and men.

Causing *linguistic disruption* is a strategy favored by those wishing to expose the sexist nature of the present language system. Its advocates claim that this strategy helps people to become aware of the many subtle and not so subtle ways in which the woman and the female are discriminated against in language. This disruption is achieved through various forms of linguistic creativity including breaking morphological rules, as in *herstory* (based on *history*), or grammatical conventions, such as the generic use of the pronoun *she*; using alternative spellings, as in *wimmin, LeserInnen* (female readers); or inverting gender stereotypes, as in "Mr X, whose thick auburn hair was immaculately coiffed, cut a stunning figure when he took his seat in Parliament for the first time since his election." The revaluation and the reclaiming of words for women whose meaning had become trivialized or derogatory over time (e.g. *woman, girl, spinster*) is another form of linguistic disruption, as is the creation of new words (e.g. *male chauvinism, pornoglossia*) to highlight women's subordination and men's domination.

More radical proposals have come from those activists who do not believe that the present language system is capable of expressing a woman's point of view. They call for the creation of a new woman-centered language. Examples range from the experimental language used by Gert Brantenberg (1977) in her (Norwegian) novel *The Daughters of Egalia*, the creation of the Láádan language by the science fiction writer and linguist Suzette Haden Elgin "for the specific purpose of expressing the perceptions of women" (Elgin 1988: 1), to the experiments in "writing the body" – *écriture féminine* – emerging from the postmodern feminist theories and approaches associated with Hélène Cixous and Luce Irigaray. To date these experiments in women-centered languages and discourses have remained largely the domain of creative writers.

More familiar to the general speech community are feminist attempts at achieving linguistic equality of the sexes by proposing amendments to existing forms, rules, and uses of language (sometimes labeled *form replacement* strategy). *Gender-neutralization* and *gender-specification* are the main mechanisms to achieve this. Whereas gender-neutralization aims to do away with, "neutralize," or minimize the linguistic expression of gender and/or gender-marking in relation to human referents, the gender-specification (also called *feminization*) strategy promotes the opposite: the *explicit* and *symmetrical* marking of gender in human referents. An illustration of gender-neutralization is the elimination in English of female occupational nouns with suffixes such as *-ess, -ette, -trix* (e.g. *actress, usherette, aviatrix*). An example of gender-specification in English is the use of *he or she* to replace the generic use of *he*. The application of both mechanisms has been confined mainly to word level as there was a belief that changes at word level could have a positive effect on eliminating sexism at discourse level.

Given the prominence of the linguistic equality approach and the form replacement strategy it is worthwhile examining which factors influence the feminist language planners in opting for gender-neutralization or gender-specification.

2.4 Choosing non-sexist alternatives

Social and linguistic factors play a role in the selection of the strategies. Social factors revolve around questions of social effectiveness: the chosen strategy should achieve linguistic equality of the sexes by both *effecting* and *reflecting* social change relating to women and men in society. This is particularly relevant with regard to occupational nomenclature. Linguistic factors focus on the issue of *linguistic viability* as well as on matters of *language typology*. Proposed changes need to take account of the typological features and the structural properties of a language; for example, languages which mark gender through morphological processes may have different options from those that don't. Linguistic viability is also linked to linguistic prescriptivism: proposed alternatives which are seen to violate deeply ingrained prescriptive rules or norms could obstruct or slow down the process of adoption in the community.

Most non-sexist language proposals generated for a range of languages contain explicit or implicit evidence that these social and linguistic factors have played a role in the choice of the principal strategy (gender-neutralization or gender-specification). However, feminist activists and language planners proposing changes for the same language may differ in the priority they assign to arguments of social effectiveness and of linguistic viability, or how they interpret these concepts. This has led to debates about the preferred principal strategy. The Dutch and German feminist language debates are examples of the tensions about the choice of the main strategy for language change. Dutch and German are typologically closely related languages with a grammatical gender system. Languages with a grammatical gender system classify nouns into gender categories on the basis of morphological or phonological features (see Corbett 1991). Whilst many have claimed that a grammatical gender system which classifies nouns in the masculine, feminine, or neuter categories is a purely linguistic invention, and is not linked to the extralinguistic category of biological sex, Corbett (1991: 34) acknowledges that "there is no purely morphological system" and that such systems "always have a semantic core." This is particularly obvious in the gender assignment of human (agent) nouns, with most nouns referring to women being feminine, and those referring to male persons being masculine.

In the case of Dutch the grammatical gender system operates with a three-gender system: masculine, feminine, neuter. However, Dutch does not mark the distinction between masculine and feminine nouns in relation to a range of qualifiers and gender agreement markers, including definite articles, demonstrative pronouns, and attributive adjectives. For example, both masculine and feminine nouns attract the same definite article: *de*. This gender system is labeled *common gender*. In the case of human agent nouns grammatical gender largely coincides with biological sex. Dutch still has a large number of female human agent nouns (especially occupational nouns) which have been formed by means of a suffixation process involving suffixes such as *-a*, *-euse*, *-in*, *-e*, *-ster*. German also operates with a three-gender system: masculine, feminine, and neuter, but unlike Dutch is not of the common gender type. The grammatical gender assignment of human agent nouns similarly displays substantial overlap with biological sex. Although German also has a range of feminine suffixes including *-euse*, *-ess/eß*, *-ette*, the most frequently used one is *-in*. Furthermore, this suffix is still very productive in the formation of feminine occupational and other human agent nouns, for example *Pilotin* (female pilot), *Polizistin* (female police officer).

In the Dutch debates proponents of the gender-neutralization strategy are in favor of phasing out the use of feminine forms of occupational nouns and of not using them in the creation of new female nouns. They promote the use of a single form to denote a male, female, or generic human referent. Their choice for this new gender-neutral form is almost invariably the existing masculine/ generic form, e.g. *de advokaat* (the lawyer). They consider this strategy socially effective as it detracts attention from the categories of sex and gender which in their view ultimately benefits women. De Caluwe (1996: 40) claims that "it is even questionable whether women would be served by the practice of mentioning gender in each and every case. As long as women are not represented equally strongly among all occupations/professions at all levels . . . the feminine forms threaten to be seen as marginalized or even stigmatized forms" (my translation). The advocates of gender-neutralization also see this strategy as linguistically more viable for the following reasons: gender-neutralization is more in tune with current structural developments in the Dutch language, which is becoming more analytic and is moving away from the use of gender-marking suffixes (Brouwer 1991). Choosing gender-neutralization also reduces speaker insecurity with regard to the formation of new feminine forms: as Dutch has many feminine suffixes language users often face the sometimes difficult decision which suffix to use: "Is the female derivation of *arts/dokter* (physician/medical doctor) arts*e* or arts*in*/dokter*es* or dokter*in*?" (Brouwer 1991: 76). Furthermore, gender-neutralization supporters claim that there is a definite trend away from the use of feminine occupational nouns among language users.

For the advocates of the gender-specification/feminization strategy (e.g. Van Alphen 1983; Niedzwiecki 1995), making women visible in all occupations and professions through systematic use of feminine occupational forms is seen to achieve social effectiveness. In response to claims from the gender-neutralization camp that feminine suffixes have connotations of triviality, the feminization supporters respond that it is better to be named and to be visible in language, even if there are some connotations of triviality: Niedzwiecki (1995) believes that the latter will abate and eventually disappear when there is consistent and full use of feminine forms in all contexts. They are confident that this strategy is linguistically viable and do not believe that continued feminization is at odds with trends in the Dutch language. They rely on a study by Adriaens (1981) which recorded an increase in the number of feminized occupational nouns. However, judging by current trends in language use and by existing policy documents the gender-neutralization strategy is the one most likely to be adopted and implemented in Dutch-speaking communities (e.g. Pauwels 1997a).

In the German context the same social arguments are used by advocates of either strategy. The feminization supporters opine that their strategy is the more socially effective because it not only makes women visible and reveals that women are increasingly found in a variety of occupations and professions, but it also ensures that all occupations and professions are seen as accessible to men *and* women. Those opting for gender-neutralization in German claim that gender equality in language is best served by minimizing gender reference, especially in generic contexts. The linguistic proposals emerging from either side do include more radical suggestions than those found in the Dutch context. For example, the radical feminist linguist Luise Pusch (1990) proposes total or radical feminization by means of reversing the current practice of attributing generic status to the masculine form. In her proposal the feminine form becomes the appropriate (unmarked) form. Well aware of the radical nature of this proposal, Pusch defends it as an important transitional strategy to rectify the many centuries of androcentrism in language. She asserts, somewhat provocatively, that this strategy is socially effective as it gives men the chance to experience personally what it means to be subsumed under a feminine form and it gives women the opportunity to experience the feeling of being named explicitly in generic contexts. She also defends the linguistic viability of her proposal by claiming that it is simple and does not involve the creation of any new forms.

A less radical version of the feminization strategy involves the explicit and consistent use of the feminine forms in gender-specific as well as generic contexts. In generic contexts preference goes to the use of gender-paired formulations (often labelled *gender splitting*) such as *der/die Lehrer/in* (the male/female teacher) or *der Lehrer und die Lehrerin* or the graphemically innovative *der/die LehrerIn*. This proposal is seen as a linguistically viable option since the German language system is suited for continued formation of feminine occupational and human agent nouns through gender suffixation. Unlike Dutch, German has a dominant feminine suffix which continues to be productive: the -*in* suffix. There is minimal speaker uncertainty in creating new feminine forms as speakers are not faced with making a selection from a wide variety of options. Concerns about the semantic ambiguity of -*in* are downplayed, as the meaning "wife of a male incumbent of an occupation" rather than "female incumbent of" is disappearing fast.

Whilst some gender-neutralization supporters follow the same path as their Dutch counterparts and accord the current (masculine) generic form the status of gender-neutral form, others make much more radical proposals. In response to a request from the Institute of German Language regarding eliminating gender bias from occupational nomenclature, Pusch (1984) proposed to change gender assignment in human agent nouns (mainly occupational nouns). This would entail the elimination of all feminine forms derived by suffixation and a gender reassignment for the noun in generic contexts. The neuter gender is to be used for generic reference, leading to the following pattern: **das** *Professor* for generic reference, **die** *Professor* (instead of *die Professorin*) for female-specific reference, and **der** *Professor* for male-specific reference. Pusch argues that the use of the neuter gender in generic contexts is socially the most effective in conveying gender-neutrality. However, she is aware that a drastic overhaul of part of the German gender system may make this proposal less linguistically viable than others. Judging on policy initiatives in Germany, Austria, and German-speaking Switzerland it is the feminization strategy which is promoted more heavily.

Similar debates and discussions about the most effective and desirable strategies have occurred in relation to the French and Spanish languages, where regional linguistic differences (e.g. Canada versus France) have also affected discussion (see Pauwels 1998). In the case of English there has been little if any debate about gender-neutralization being the principal strategy in promoting linguistic equality. Discussions have been more about selecting alternative forms within the gender-neutralization strategy: for example, should the word *chairman* be replaced by an existing, semantically related noun, such as *president*, *chair*, or should a new form be created, for example, *chairperson*? Replacing generic *he* by pronouns such as singular *they*, by a new pronoun, or by generic *she*, *it*, or *one* is another example of this (e.g. Bodine 1975; Mackay 1980; Baron 1986; Henley 1987).

2.5   *Implementing changes – guidelines for non-sexist language use*

A crucial component in language planning is the implementation of the proposed changes. Language planners need to identify pathways and mechanisms to implement their proposals so that these can reach and spread through the speech community. In many forms of corpus planning (e.g. orthographic reform) implementation is top-down with language academies and other authoritative language bodies leading, and educational authorities facilitating the implementation process. However, in the case of feminist language planning these language authorities were and are often strongly opposed and resistant to the proposed changes. Being principally a grassroots-driven phenomenon, feminist language planning had limited (if any) access to, and cooperation from, the main channels for the implementation of language change. These include the education system, the media, legislative measures, and linguistic authorities. Instead their main mechanisms for spreading change were, and remain, promotion through personal use, the use of role models, and pressure on key agencies to adopt guidelines for non-sexist language use.

The promotion of linguistic disruption and of a newly created woman-centered language was primarily achieved through personal language patterns, often in speech but mainly in writing. Prominent feminist activists who practiced forms of linguistic disruption became role models for and of feminist linguistic change. Mary Daly's (1978) linguistic practices in *Gyn/ecology: The Metaethics of Radical Feminism* are a typical illustration of this. Feminist publications – both academic and general – became vehicles for spreading feminist linguistic practices throughout the feminist community. For example, in its early publication days the German feminist magazine *Emma* played an important role in familiarizing German feminists with, and promoting, feminist language change. The magazine practiced gender splitting, used the new indefinite pronoun *frau* (instead of *man*, meaning "one"), and created many new compounds with *-frau* (-woman) to make women more visible in language. The creative work of feminist novelists and poets such as Monique Wittig, Audre Lorde, Adrienne Rich, Gert Brantenberg, Verena Stefan, and others who experiment with new forms of language use is a further illustration of this.

Exerting pressure on key agencies in language spread became a prominent mechanism for the promotion of change emanating from the linguistic equality approach. Feminist individuals and women's action groups not only developed guidelines and policies on non-sexist language use but also acted to convince professional organizations and key agencies to adopt the policies. These language-oriented actions were often part of general initiatives by women's groups to eliminate gender-biased practices from society. Early targets for feminist linguistic activism were publishers of educational material, the print media, education, and legislative writing. These agencies were targeted because of their key role in shaping the representation of women and men and because of their potential to facilitate and spread change through a community. Feminist language activists also used the introduction of Sex Discrimination, Equal (Employment) Opportunity and Human Rights Acts, and other legislative measures to demand linguistic changes. A case in point is the need to amend professional and occupational nomenclature to comply with Equal Employment Opportunity (EEO) Acts. Terminology commissions, education ministries, employment councils, language academies, and other public agencies charged with making amendments to official (occupational) nomenclature and terminology called upon feminist language planners to assist them in this task. This in turn triggered requests for non-sexist language guidelines and policies to be developed for other public and private agencies covered under EEO and anti-discrimination legislation. To date non-sexist language policies are in place in most public sector and in many large private sector organizations in English-language countries. They are also increasingly found in European countries and in supranational organizations such as UNESCO (see Pauwels 1998; Hellinger and Bussman 2001).

2.6 Assessing feminist language planning

The success of feminist language activism needs to be judged ultimately against the goals it set out to achieve. These include raising awareness of the gender bias in language and getting the speech community to adopt the proposed changes in a manner that promotes gender equality. The relatively recent nature of feminist language planning activities (from the mid-1970s at the earliest) and the scant number of investigations (Fasold 1987; Fasold et al. 1990) to date which have charted non-sexist language changes make a comprehensive assessment of success or failure as yet impossible. Nevertheless some comments can be made with regard to evidence of a greater community awareness of gender bias in language. Furthermore, the findings of recent and current research projects (admittedly small-scale) can shed some light on the adoption patterns of some non-sexist proposed changes in the community.

2.7 Increased awareness of gender bias

There is no doubt that in English-language communities and in some other speech communities (mainly European) the awareness of gender bias in language has been raised markedly as a result of feminist linguistic activism. Although many people still disagree with the claim that there is a gender bias in language, or refuse to adopt non-sexist language changes, they have nevertheless been made aware of the problematic nature of language in this respect. A growing number of people display metalinguistic behavior which points toward a greater awareness of sexist language. This includes apologizing for the use of generic *he* – some authors now feel compelled to justify the use of generic *he* in textbooks, or for using -*man* compounds in a generic context. Others self-correct generic *he* constructions or comment about title use and gender stereotypes. Whilst many such comments continue to be made in a deprecatory manner they nevertheless show awareness of the problem. The community's awareness is also evident in surveys on issues such as gender stereotyping, masculine generic *he* use, linguistic asymmetries in occupational nouns, and terms of address and naming practices (for an overview, see Pauwels 1998). For example, in 1986, 13 per cent of 250 female respondents were not familiar with *Ms* as an alternative title for women; by 1996 this had decreased to 4 per cent of 300 women (Pauwels 2001a). It is not possible at this stage to discern whether this awareness has been raised more through contact with linguistic disruption strategies or through language guidelines striving for linguistic equality.

2.8   *Adopting feminist language change*

Investigating the adoption of feminist language change is a much more complex issue. It involves exploring which types of feminist language change are being adopted: change resulting from linguistic disruption strategies, women-centered language developments, or form replacement proposals. It also requires investigating the process by which these changes spread through a speech community. Does change spread from public forms of written discourse to public speech? Which sector of the community leads the change and how does it spread from this group to other groups in the community? Furthermore, there is the fundamental question of whether the adoption and spread of non-sexist language through a community occurs in such a way that it promotes gender equality and eliminates the bias against women in language.

To date many of these questions have not yet been addressed and present an opportunity for further research, especially in communities which have witnessed feminist linguistic activism for a number of years. To my knowledge there have not yet been any systematic investigations into community adoption of changes linked to the strategies of linguistic disruption or women-centered language developments. In fact the linguistic disruption strategy was not intended to be adopted by the community at large; rather, it was used by linguistic activists to raise the community's awareness, sometimes in a more provocative manner. There is certainly evidence that some feminist publications in English, German, Dutch, French, and Spanish continue to use linguistic disruption as a way of keeping readers aware of gender bias in language. Developing women-centered languages has remained a preoccupation of poets and creative writers.

The adoption of proposals emerging from the linguistic equality approach and involving form replacements has received more attention. To date most such explorations have focused on the adoption and spread of non-sexist alternatives for generically used nouns and pronouns and on symmetrical naming practices or title use. The reduction or avoidance of gender-stereotyped language has also been examined. Although these investigations are relatively small-scale and mainly involve English, they nevertheless allow an insight into the issue of the adoption and spread of feminist language planning.

2.9 Non-sexist generic nouns and pronouns in writing

The studies by Cooper (1984), Markovitz (1984), Ehrlich and King (1994), and Pauwels (1997b, 2000), among others, concern the adoption of non-sexist generic nouns and pronouns in English. All report a decrease in use of masculine generic nouns and pronouns in favor of non-sexist alternatives both in forms of written discourse and in public speech. Cooper's (1984) corpus of 500,000 words taken from American newspapers and magazines covering the period 1971 to 1979 noted a dramatic decline in the use of masculine generic nouns (including -*man* compounds) and some decline in the use of generic *he*. Markovitz (1984) and Ehrlich and King's (1994) work focuses on university documents and reveals that the use of non-sexist alternatives for masculine generic nouns and generic *he* had increased markedly. Pauwels' (1997b) survey of non-sexist generic nouns and pronouns in 2,000 job advertisements in Australian newspapers found a very high degree of use of such forms. Only 5.4 per cent of all generic nouns (i.e. 128 different occupational and human agent nouns) used in the advertisements could be considered sex-exclusive terms: there were a few instances of -*man* compounds and of -*ess* words. With the exception of *chairman* and *handyman*, all -*man* compounds occurred less than their gender-inclusive counterparts. There were many instances of -*man* compounds having been replaced by -*person* compounds such as *chairperson*, *draftsperson*, *foreperson*, *groundsperson*, *handyperson*, even *waitperson*. The investigation also showed that the (already) few female-exclusive terms had been abandoned in favor of gender-neutral ones. For example, there were no *air hostesses*, only *flight attendants*; no *salesgirls*, *saleswomen*, or *salesladies*, only *salesperson(s)* or *salespeople*. The study also revealed zero use of generic *he*. In job advertisements generic *he* was replaced mainly by the practice of repeating the generic noun, although there were some instances of *He/She*.

In more recent work I have started to investigate the use of non-sexist alternatives to masculine generic nouns and pronouns in public, non-scripted speech (Pauwels 2000, 2001b). A comparison of (non-scripted) speech derived from radio programs and parliamentary debates recorded in Australia between the 1960s and 1970s and in the 1990s showed a steep decline in the use of generic *he* from the pre-feminist reform period (i.e. between the 1960s and 1970s) to the post-feminist reform period (in the 1990s). In the pre-reform period approximately 95 per cent of all generic pronouns were generic *he*. Singular *they* recorded less than 1 (0.4) per cent, and *he or she* only 2.25 per cent. The post-reform period revealed a significant turnaround for singular *they*, which had

Table 24.1   Generic pronoun use by academics and teachers

Pronouns	Number (2,189)	%
Singular *they*	763	34.85
He or she	1,105	50.47
Generic *he*	258	11.78
Generic *she*	60	2.74
It	3	0.13

become the most frequently used generic pronoun recording a 75 per cent usage rate. Generic *he* had dropped from 95 to 18 per cent, whereas *he or she* had increased only slightly to 4.5 per cent. The users of these pronouns were mainly educated speakers including health professionals, journalists, lawyers, judges, members of the clergy, academics, teachers, and athletes. Changes in the patterns of generic noun use could not be investigated as there were very few examples of morphologically marked masculine generic nouns in the pre- and post-reform database.

Another recent study (Pauwels 2000) explored generic pronoun use by Australian academics and educators when they were lecturing or giving papers at conferences, or in workshops or symposia. This study revealed that generic *he* has become the exception rather than the norm in generic pronoun use, as can be gleaned from table 24.1.

These investigations also reveal some difference in the choice of pronoun which is most likely linked either to type of speaker, or to type of speech genre, or both. Educators and academics display a greater use of *he or she* than other educated speakers, whose preference is for the gender-neutral alternative singular *they*. The observed difference may also reflect the type of speech genre: the first study (Pauwels 2001b) consisted mainly of parliamentary debates and one-on-one interviews on radio programs, whereas the second study (Pauwels 2000) focused on lectures in university or other educational settings.

The academic pronoun study (Pauwels 2000) also provided an opportunity to investigate which type of speaker leads the adoption of non-sexist pronouns. The study comprised 165 women and 187 men, which facilitated the examination of gender patterns as presented in table 24.2. Seven different patterns emerged from the data: (1) prevalent use of generic *he* by an individual, (2) prevalent use of generic *she*, (3) prevalent use of *he or she*, (4) prevalent use of singular *they*, (5) variable use of *he or she* and singular *they*, (6) variable use of generic *he* and singular *they*, (7) variable use of *he* and *he or she*. There were a small number of speakers (9 women and 10 men) whose pronoun use did not reveal any discernible patterns. Although both women and men use non-sexist alternatives more than generic *he*, it is women, not surprisingly, who lead the adoption. Their combined use of non-sexist alternatives (i.e. patterns 3, 4, 5) is 82.34 per cent whereas that of men is 62.02 per cent. Another indicator

Table 24.2 Women's and men's use of generic pronouns

Pronouns used	Women (n = 165) (%)	Men (n = 187) (%)	Total use (%)
Generic *he*	0.6	10.16	5.68
Generic *she*	3.63	1.6	2.55
He or she	44.24	29.41	36.36
Singular *they*	17.5	16.57	17.04
He or she/singular *they*	20.6	16.04	18.18
He/singular *they*	4.24	8.5	6.53
He/*he or she*	3.63	12.29	8.23
No discernible pronoun pattern	5.45	5.34	5.39

of women leading this change is the almost complete absence of generic *he* among female speakers, whereas men still record 10.16 per cent use of this form.

2.10 Naming practices and titles

Another prominent aspect of feminist linguistic reform concerned naming practices and terms of address for women (e.g. Kramer 1975; Stannard 1977; Spender 1980; Cherry 1987). Symmetrical use of titles and terms of address for women and the elimination of derogatory and discriminatory naming practices were the goals of feminist linguistic activism. There is some evidence of change in this arena of language use as well: an increasing number of women adopt naming practices which assert their linguistic independence from men. Women are more likely to keep their pre-marital name after marriage; there is a growing tendency for the mother's surname to be chosen as the family surname upon the birth of children; naming practices which render women invisible (e.g. Mrs John Man) are starting to disappear.

Investigations to date have focused on the introduction and spread of the new title *Ms* as a term of address for women, replacing *Miss* and *Mrs* (for a discussion of the viability of *Ms* as a new title for women, see Pauwels 1998). Evidence from English-language countries (especially the USA, Canada, and Australia) shows that women are increasingly adopting the new title, with estimates for the USA ranging between 30 and 45 per cent (Atkinson 1987; Pauwels 1987). For Australia I examined the use of *Ms* among women in 1986 and again in 1996 (Pauwels 1987, 2001a). In 1986 approximately 20 per cent of 250 women used *Ms*. This percentage had almost doubled by 1996: 37 per cent. The 1996 study also collected socio-demographic information on the *Ms* users, revealing that women with a tertiary education and between the ages of 25 and 65 (i.e. the working population) lead the adoption of *Ms*. Education was the most significant factor in determining title use. Age was also significant but because of the large age groupings it was not possible to pinpoint the most significant age group for *Ms* use. Correlations between marital status and title use showed that *Ms* is being adopted first by those who fall "outside" the traditional categories of "married" and "single/unmarried," but *Ms* use is increasingly found among the latter groups. Although these studies reveal an increase in the use of *Ms* there is not yet strong evidence that *Ms* is in fact replacing the titles *Mrs* or *Miss*. At this stage *Ms* has been added as a new option besides *Mrs* and *Miss* with the latter titles unlikely to become obsolescent in the near future. As to men's use of *Ms* to address women, preliminary evidence from Australia suggests that few attempts are made by men to use *Ms*, even where a woman's preference for this form is known.

3   Are the Changes Effective?

Investigating the effectiveness of the changes is the most important form of evaluation of the success or failure of (social) linguistic reform. Non-sexist language reform can be considered truly successful if there is not only evidence of the adoption of non-sexist alternatives but also evidence that these alternatives are being used in a manner promoting linguistic equality of the sexes. The investigation of the social effectiveness of non-sexist language reform is still in its infancy. The basis for most comments on the effectiveness of this reform is anecdotal evidence. For example, there is some evidence that the newly created *-person* compounds are not used generically but simply replace *-woman* compounds (Ehrlich and King 1994; Pauwels 2001a). Another observation is that some feminist linguistic creations are not used in their intended manner, leading to a depoliticization of these innovations: Ehrlich and King (1994: 65) comment that "while feminist linguistic innovations (such as *feminism, sexism, sexual harassment*, and *date rape*) pervade our culture, it is not clear that their use is consistent with their intended, feminist-influenced, meanings." To what extent the current usage patterns of *Ms* are an indication of potential failure is less clear cut: it is certainly true that the feminist intention of *Ms* being a replacement for *Miss* and *Mrs* has not yet been achieved and may not be achieved for a long time. In fact at the moment it is being used as an additional option to the existing titles of *Mrs* and *Miss*, leading to even greater asymmetry than before. However, my research into the use of *Ms* does show that women who use *Ms* do so with its intended meaning. The effectiveness of non-sexist alternatives to generic *he*, especially *he or she* and singular *they*, has also received mixed feedback: studies into the mental imagery associated with masculine generic nouns and pronouns had shown that the use of more gender-inclusive or gender-neutral forms reduced the maleness of the mental imagery (e.g. Moulton et al. 1978; Hamilton 1988; Wilson and Ng 1988). Khosroshahi's (1989) study, however, revealed no real difference in the mental imagery associated with masculine generic and gender-inclusive or gender-neutral generic forms, except in the case of women who had reformed their language. She concludes that the adoption of gender-inclusive/gender-neutral forms will only be effective if there is a personal awareness of the discriminatory nature of the other forms and there is a personal commitment to change. This view concurs with Cameron's (1985: 90) comment that "in the mouths of sexists, language can always be sexist." However, I do not believe that this observation is cause for a pessimistic assessment of the effectiveness of non-sexist language reform: there is evidence that feminist linguistic activism has raised the community's awareness of gender bias in language. There is also proof that those who adopt the changes do so because they are aware of the bias and have a personal commitment to change. Of course, ultimately meanings are not fixed and will change over time and according to context. This applies as much to feminist meanings as to any other meanings.

4   Concluding Remarks

In this chapter I have discussed feminist linguistic activism as a genuine form of language reform, showing women in the new roles of critical linguistic commentators, norm-breakers, and norm-makers. Even if the ultimate goals of feminist language reform may not be achieved these linguistic initiatives and actions, many of which have been undertaken at the grassroots level, have made a major contribution to exposing the ideologization of linguistic meanings to the speech community at large and to challenging the hegemony of the meanings promoted and authorized by the dominant group or culture, in this case men.

REFERENCES

Adriaens, Geert 1981: Vrouwelijke beroepsnamen in het Nederlands [Female occupational titles in Dutch]. Unpublished thesis, University of Leuven.

Atkinson, Donna L. 1987: Names and titles: Maiden name retention and the use of Ms. *Women and Language* 10: 37.

Baron, Dennis 1986: *Grammar and Gender.* New Haven, CT and London: Yale University Press.

Blakar, Rolv M. 1977: *Språk er makt* [Language and power]. Oslo: Pax.

Blaubergs, Maija 1980: An analysis of classic arguments against changing sexist language. *Women's Studies International Quarterly* 2(3): 135–47.

Bodine, Ann 1975: Androcentrism in prescriptive grammar: Singular "they", sex-indefinite "he", and "he or she". *Language in Society* 4: 129–46.

Brantenberg, Gert 1977: *Egalias døttre* [Daughters of Egalia]. Oslo: Novus.

Brouwer, Dédé 1991: Feminist language policy in Dutch: Equality rather than difference. *Working Papers on Language, Gender and Sexism* 1(2): 73–82.

Cameron, Deborah 1985: *Feminism and Linguistic Theory*. London: Macmillan.

Cameron, Deborah 1995: *Verbal Hygiene*. London: Routledge.

Cherry, K. 1987: *Womansword: What Japanese Words Say about Women*. Tokyo: Kodansha International.

Cooper, Robert L. 1984: The avoidance of androcentric generics. *International Journal of the Sociology of Language* 50: 5–20.

Cooper, Robert L. 1989: *Language Planning and Social Change*. Cambridge: Cambridge University Press.

Corbett, Greville 1991: *Gender*. Cambridge: Cambridge University Press.

Daly, Mary 1978: *Gyn/ecology: The Metaethics of Radical Feminism*. Boston: Beacon Press.

De Caluwe, Johan 1996: Systematische vervrouwelijking van functiebenamingen? [Systematic feminization of occupational titles?] In *Taal en beeldvorming over vrouwen en mannen*. Zoetermeer: Ministerie van Onderwijs, Cultuur en Wetenschappen, pp. 39–41.

Ehrlich, Susan and King, Ruth 1994: Feminist meanings and the (de)politicization of the lexicon. *Language in Society* 23: 59–76.

Elgin, Suzette Haden 1988: *A First Dictionary and Grammar of Láádden*. Madison, WI: Society for the Furtherance and Study of Fantasy and Science Fiction.

Fasold, Ralph 1984: *The Sociolinguistics of Society*. Oxford: Blackwell.

Fasold, Ralph 1987: Language policy and change: Sexist language in the periodical news media. In Peter Lowenberg (ed.) *Language Spread and Language Policy*. Washington, DC: Georgetown University Press, pp. 187–206.

Fasold, Ralph, Yamada, Haru, Robinson, David, and Barish, Steven 1990: The language planning effect of newspaper editorial policy: Gender differences in *The Washington Post*. *Language in Society* 19: 521–39.

Garcia, Meseguer A. 1977: *Lenguaje y discriminación sexual* [Language and sex discrimination]. Madrid: Editorial Cuadernos para el Diálogo, S.A. Edicusa.

Guentherodt, Ingrid 1979: Berufsbezeichnungen für Frauen. Problematik der deutschen Sprache im Vergleich mit Beispielen aus dem Englischen und Französischen. [Occupational nouns for women. Problems for German in comparison with examples from English and French]. *Osnabrücker Beiträge zur Sprachtheorie*, Beiheft 3: 120–32.

Guentherodt, Ingrid, Hellinger, Marlis, Pusch, Luise, and Troemel-Ploetz, Senta 1980: Richtlinien zur Vermeidung sexistischen Sprachgebrauchs [Guidelines for the elimination of sexist language use]. *Linguistische Berichte* 69: 15–21.

Hamilton, Mykol C. 1988: Using masculine generics: Does generic "he" increase male bias in the user's imagery? *Sex Roles* 19: 785–99.

Hellinger, Marlis 1990: *Kontrastive Feministische Linguistik* [Contrastive feminist linguistics]. Ismaning: Hueber.

Hellinger, Marlis and Schräpel, Beate 1983: Über die sprachliche Gleichbehandlung von Frauen und Männern [About linguistic equality of women and men]. *Jahrbuch für Internationale Germanistik* 15: 40–69.

Hellinger, Marlis and Bussmann, Hadumod (eds) 2001: *Gender Across Languages: The Linguistic Representation of Women and Men*. Amsterdam: John Benjamins.

Henley, Nancy 1987: The new species that seeks a new language: On sexism in language and language change. In Joyce Penfield (ed.)

Women and Language in Transition. Albany: State University of New York Press, pp. 3–27.

Kalverkämper, Hartwig 1979: Die Frauen und die Sprache [Women and language]. *Linguistische Berichte* 62: 55–71.

Khosroshahi, Fatemeh 1989: Penguins don't care, but women do: A social identity analysis of a Whorfian problem. *Language in Society* 18: 505–25.

Kloss, Heinz 1969: *Research Possibilities on Group Bilingualism: A Report.* Quebec: International Center for Research on Bilingualism.

Kochskämper, Birgit 1991: Language history as a history of male language policy: The history of German *Mensch, Frau, Mann, Mädchen, Junge, Dirne* . . . and their Indo-European cognates. *Working Papers on Language, Gender and Sexism* 1(2): 5–17.

Kramarae, Cheris 1981: *Women and Men Speaking.* Rowley, MA: Newbury House.

Kramarae, Cheris 1992: Punctuating the dictionary. *International Journal of the Sociology of Language* 94: 135–54.

Kramer, Cheris 1975: Sex-related differences in address systems. *Anthropological Linguistics* 17: 198–210.

Lakoff, Robin 1975: *Language and Woman's Place.* New York: Harper and Row.

Mackay, Donald G. 1980: Psychology, prescriptive grammar and the pronoun problem. *American Psychologist* 35: 444–9.

Markovitz, Judith 1984: The impact of the sexist language controversy and regulation on language in university documents. *Psychology of Women Quarterly* 8(4): 337–47.

Moulton, Janice, Robinson, George M., and Elias, Cherin 1978: Sex bias in language use: neutral pronouns that

aren't. *American Psychologist* 33: 1032–6.

Niedzwiecki, Patricia 1995: *Handleiding voor de taalvervrouwelijking. Deel 1* [Guidance for the feminization of language]. Brussels: Kabinet van Onderwijs en Ambtenarenzaken.

Nilsen, Aileen P., Bosmajian, Haig, Gershuny, H. Lee, and Stanley, Julia P. (eds) 1977: *Sexism and Language.* Urbana, IL: National Council of Teachers of English.

Pauwels, Anne 1987: Language in transition: A study of the title "Ms" in contemporary Australian society. In Anne Pauwels (ed.) *Women and Language in Australian and New Zealand Society.* Sydney: Australian Professional Publications, pp. 129–54.

Pauwels, Anne 1993: Language planning, language reform and the sexes in Australia. *Australian Review of Applied Linguistics* (Series S) 10: 13–34.

Pauwels, Anne 1997a: Non-sexist language policy debate in the Dutch speech community. In Friederike Braun and Ursula Pasero (eds) *Kommunikation von Geschlecht – Communication of Gender.* Kiel: Centaurus, pp. 261–79.

Pauwels, Anne 1997b: Of handymen and waitpersons: A linguistic evaluation of job classifieds. *Australian Journal of Communication* 24(1): 58–69.

Pauwels, Anne 1998: *Women Changing Language.* London: Longman.

Pauwels, Anne 2000: Women Changing Language. Feminist Language Change in Progress. Paper presented at the First International Gender and Language Association Conference, Stanford University, May 2000.

Pauwels, Anne 2001a: Spreading the feminist word? A sociolinguistic study of feminist language change in Australian English: The case of the new courtesy title "Ms". In Marlis Hellinger and Hadumod

Bussmann (eds) *Gender Across Languages: The Linguistic Representation of Women and Men*. Amsterdam: John Benjamins, pp. 137–52.

Pauwels, Anne 2001b: Non sexist language reform and generic pronouns in Australian English. *English World Wide* 22: 105–19.

Pusch, Luise 1984: *Das Deutsche als Männersprache* [German as a men's language]. Frankfurt/Main: Suhrkamp.

Pusch, Luise 1990: *Alle Menschen werden Schwestern* [All men will become sisters]. Frankfurt/Main: Suhrkamp.

Sabatini, Alma 1985: Occupational nouns in Italian: Changing the sexist usage. In Marlis Hellinger (ed.) *Sprachwandel und feministische Sprachpolitik: Internationale Perspektiven* [Language change and feminist language policy: International perspectives]. Opladen: Westdeutscher, pp. 64–75.

Sautermeister, Christine 1985: La femme devant la langue [The woman before language]. In *Frauenthemen im Fremdsprachenunterricht* [Women's topics in foreign language teaching. Working papers]. *Arbeitsberichte 3*. Hamburg: University of Hamburg, Zentrales Fremdspracheninstitut, pp. 63–97.

Schulz, Muriel 1975: The semantic derogation of women. In Barrie Thorne and Nancy Henley (eds) *Language and Sex: Dominance and Difference*. Rowley, MA: Newbury House, pp. 64–73.

Spender, Dale 1980: *Man Made Language*. London: Routledge and Kegan Paul.

Stannard, Una 1977: *Mrs Man*. San Francisco: Germainbooks.

Troemel-Ploetz, Senta 1978: Linguistik und Frauensprache [Linguistics and women's language]. *Linguistische Berichte* 57: 49–68.

Van Alphen, Ingrid 1983: Een vrouw een vrouw, een woord een woord. Over gelijke behandeling van vrouwen en mannen en de konsekwenties voor beroepsbenamingen in het Nederlands [A woman, a woman, a word, a word. About equal treatment of women and men and the consequences for occupational nouns in Dutch]. *Tijdschrift voor Vrouwenstudies* 14(4): 307–15.

Wilson, Elizabeth and Ng, Sik H. 1988: Sex bias in visuals evoked by generics: A New Zealand study. *Sex Roles* 18: 159–68.

Yaguello, Marina 1978: *Les Mots et les femmes* [Words and women]. Paris: Payot.

Part V
Institutional Discourse

25 "Feminine" Workplaces: Stereotype and Reality

JANET HOLMES AND MARIA STUBBE

1 Introduction

The notion of the "gendered" workplace arose repeatedly during our research on workplace discourse in New Zealand.[1] Both those participating in the research and members of the wider New Zealand community were very willing to identify some workplaces as particularly "feminine" and others as very "masculine," though they were not always so articulate about what exactly they meant by such descriptions. This chapter explores the notion of the gendered workplace, and examines, in particular, how such notions develop, as well as how they unravel when subjected to more detailed analysis of actual workplace interaction.

Gender appears to be a particularly salient dimension of social interaction in New Zealand. Indeed, New Zealand has been described as a "gendered culture," a culture in which "the structures of masculinity and femininity are central to the formation of society as a whole," a culture in which "the intimate and structural expressions of social life are divided according to gender" (James and Saville-Smith 1989: 6–7). Gender, it has been suggested, is the motif and preoccupation of New Zealand society, as class is in Britain. And perhaps gender appears particularly salient in New Zealand because social class categorization is generally weaker than in Britain. Rags to riches stories of people (usually men) who have succeeded in making their fortunes in business and have joined the commercial elite are endemic in New Zealand newspapers. New Zealanders firmly believe that social mobility is easier in New Zealand than in Britain, especially for men.

The recent rise to prominence of a raft of successful career women suggests, however, that New Zealand social patterns are changing. In the year 2000 in New Zealand, as almost every newspaper and magazine noted, women held the positions of Prime Minister, Leader of the Opposition, Chief Justice, Attorney-General, and Governor-General, as well as the top position in Telecom, and the position of Chief Executive in a number of Ministries and influential government organizations. Nevertheless, the rapidity of this change, its potentially ephemeral nature, and the specific characteristics of the women who have made it to the top (most had no brothers, none had an older brother, and many have no children), all support the view that New Zealand may be a particularly interesting focus for exploring the notion of the "gendered" workplace.

2 "Feminine" and "Masculine" Workplaces

What exactly do people mean when they refer to a "feminine" or "masculine" workplace? While non-linguistic characteristics such as the gender composition of the workforce, the nature of the organization's work, and how often people socialize in and out of work are undoubtedly components of the picture, it is also clear that specific kinds of communication pattern are equally important. In fact, many distinguishing features of what are widely considered male versus female styles of interaction have been identified since the early 1970s (e.g. see Aries 1996; Coates 1996; Crawford 1995; Holmes 1995; Romaine 1999; Talbot 1998; Tannen 1993; Wodak 1997). In addition to scholarly research in this area, there are also many "self-help" texts identifying typical, and often stereotypical, components of gendered communicative styles both at work and at home (e.g. Elgin 1993; Gray 1992; Rearden 1995; Tannen 1990, 1994b). Table 25.1 provides a summary of some of the most widely cited features of "feminine" and "masculine" interactional styles.

The inevitable simplification involved in such a list, and the resulting dichotomizing of male and female style, is clearly misleading, and popular approaches which focus only on contrasts such as these have been severely criticized, especially when they suggest that such differences are unavoidable, culturally conditioned, or even innate (see, for example, Cameron 1992; Crawford 1995; Freed 1992; Meyerhoff 1991; Troemel-Ploetz 1991). A list such

Table 25.1 Widely cited features of "feminine" and "masculine" interactional style

Feminine	Masculine
indirect	direct
conciliatory	confrontational
facilitative	competitive
collaborative	autonomous
minor contribution (in public)	dominates (public) talking time
supportive feedback	aggressive interruptions
person/process-oriented	task/outcome-oriented
affectively oriented	referentially oriented

as this takes no account of the many sources of diversity and variation (such as age, class, ethnicity, sexual orientation, and so on) which are relevant when comparing styles of interaction. It largely ignores stylistic variation arising from contextual factors, including the social and discourse context of an interaction, and the participants' goals. And there is no consideration of how such differences develop: fundamental underlying issues such as the social distribution of power and influence are inevitably factored out.

Nevertheless, such a list captures quite well the components people typically have in mind when they refer to "masculine" and "feminine" workplaces (see also Talbot, this volume). And, while obviously crude and simplistic, the list summarizes many of the distinguishing features of male and female styles of interaction which emerged from the first raft of language and gender research, much of which was well conceived and carefully executed. As Cameron (1996) points out, the findings of this research have proved remarkably robust (see also McElhinny, this volume).

Research on interaction at work, in particular, has generally confirmed these patterns. In interviews, team discussions, in classrooms, and in department meetings, patterns of domination of talking time, aggressive interruption, and competitive and confrontational discourse have been found to characterize men's rather than women's discourse, and it is certainly true that such features are habitually labeled "masculine" rather than "feminine" (see Tannen 1994a; Swann 1992; Stanworth 1983; Nelson 1998; West 1984). Men have been found to interrupt more than women in similar employment positions (e.g. Case 1988; West 1984; Woods 1988), to take more and/or longer turns (e.g. Eakins and Eakins 1976; Edelsky 1981; Holmes 1992; James and Drakich 1993), and to adopt an aggressive rather than a facilitative personal style in many workplace interactions (e.g. Ainsworth-Vaughn 1992; Case 1991; Tannen 1994b; Holmes 2000a). Moreover, the "masculine" style tends to be more highly valued, largely due to the fact that men have dominated most workplaces until relatively recently, occupying nearly all the influential and powerful positions. Hence, as Kendall and Tannen point out, "styles of interaction more common among men have become the workplace norm" (1997: 85).

It is perhaps worth emphasizing at this point that we are not talking about places that are literally "women's" workplaces and "men's" workplaces, but rather about cultural dimensions and perceptions, which are a matter of degree. Some men can and do interact at times and in ways that contribute to the perception of a workplace as more "feminine," just as the behavior of some women reinforces the view of their workplaces as particularly "masculine." Moreover, different workplaces can be characterized as more or less "feminine" and more or less "masculine" in different respects. So, in a particular workplace, meeting structures may conform to a more "masculine" style, while the way small talk is distributed may fit a more "feminine" stereotype. Moreover, individuals may behave in stereotypically "masculine" or "feminine" ways even at different points within the same interaction. The notion of the gendered workplace is thus a considerable simplification with potentially misleading implications. This point will be elaborated more fully in the final section of the chapter.

3   "Masculine" and "Feminine" Styles of Interaction in New Zealand Workplaces

What evidence is there of female and male patterns of interaction in the New Zealand workplaces we have studied, and how do these patterns relate to the notion of the "gendered" workplace? In exploring this point we first focus on some broad patterns identified in three different aspects of workplace interaction, namely features of the structure of talk in meetings, the distribution of humor in meetings, and the distribution of small talk at work.

The data we draw on was collected by the Wellington Language in the Workplace (LWP) Project (Holmes 2000b). The Project was designed to analyze features of effective interpersonal communication in a variety of New Zealand workplaces and used a methodology which allowed workplace interactions to be recorded as unobtrusively as possible (Stubbe 1998a). The LWP Project currently has a corpus of over 1,500 workplace interactions to use as the basis for analysis.

It is both impossible and unilluminating to examine workplace talk in a functional vacuum. People participate in a wide range of types of workplace talk, from one-to-one meetings, through small group discussions, to large-scale formal meetings, as well as variable amounts of social talk around the edges of task-oriented talk, and at ratified social breaks. Any analysis of gendered styles of interaction, and the related issue of what people mean when they talk of a "feminine" or "masculine" workplace, must therefore compare reasonably similar activities, with reasonably similar objectives. We first consider, then, aspects of formal meetings, a type of interaction which dominated the timetable of many participants in the workplaces studied.

3.1   Meeting talk

A number of features of meeting talk tend to be associated with one gender rather than the other. It is widely believed, for instance, that meetings with a majority of female participants are more likely to digress from the agenda than meetings with predominantly male participants. There is no evidence to support such broad generalizations in the data from our workplace meetings. The style of a meeting or, more often, a particular section of a meeting, typically reflected its function rather than the gender of its participants. Meetings with an explicit agenda, a strict time limit, and a number of issues requiring a decision tended to be predominantly linear in structure, following the agenda from item to item, with only minor and brief digressions. More exploratory meetings, or sections of meetings, where participants were brainstorming a problem, or discussing options for future action, were typically more spiral in structure, pursuing a range of different ideas for a short period, and returning to elaborate some at a later point. Movement through the agenda was less straightforward in these cases. The complexity of such patterns is illustrated in the qualitative analyses below (see also Marra, forthcoming; Stubbe, forthcoming a).

Another prototypically gendered aspect of meetings, mentioned above, is the amount of talk engaged in by meeting participants. The general consensus among researchers who have analyzed talk in formal meetings is that men typically contribute a good deal more talk than women in such contexts (see James and Drakich 1993; Holmes 1995). Indeed, even within more "feminine" workplaces, such as educational institutions, formal contexts have proved to be male-dominated with respect to the distribution of talk (e.g. Eakins and Eakins 1976; Stanworth 1983). One might expect, then, that at least in the more formal meetings in our corpus, men would dominate the talking time. The reality, however, proved rather more complex.

We analyzed the distribution of talk in a set of formal meetings from four different but comparable workplaces, two of which were publicly perceived as relatively "feminine" (though only one was actually dominated by women workers), and two as more "masculine" workplaces (where both were in fact numerically dominated by males). The results suggested that organizational role and status, rather than gender, were the most influential factors in determining who contributed most talk. The meetings were selected to be reasonably similar in function; they were reporting meetings of teams or groups who met regularly. In every meeting the person chairing the meeting talked most (Holmes 2000a). Even in "masculine" workplaces, when women managers or project leaders chaired the meetings they dominated the talking time. And the proportion of the total talking time taken by female chairs and male chairs was remarkably similar (ranging from 37 to 53 per cent with no significant variation along gender lines). Factors such as organizational responsibility and role predominated in accounting for who contributed most talk in workplace meetings, regardless of the "gender" of the workplace. Patterns such as these suggest that stereotypes of gendered workplaces may need updating. The same is true of claims about women's sense of humor.

3.2 Humor in the workplace

Popular stereotypes portray women as humorless creatures, rarely cracking jokes and slow to respond to the humor of others (Crawford 1995). Similar claims have been made about women at work; researchers suggest that "women may have a lower propensity to use humor as a part of their professional repertoire" (Cox, Read, and Van Auken 1990: 293; see also Walker 1981; McCauslan and Kleiner 1992). The implication is that stereotypically "feminine" workplaces are serious work contexts where humor rarely intrudes into discussion. Like many stereotypes, this one seems to have developed with minimal observation of the actual patterns of use of humor by women and men at work. Again, the reality turns out to be different.

We examined the distribution of humor in 22 meetings from our workplace corpus: the dataset comprised 16 mixed-gender meetings, three from a stereotypically "feminine" workplace with only women participants, and three from a stereotypically "masculine" workplace with just male participants. The resulting analysis of 396 instances of humor provided ample evidence to challenge the stereotypes (Holmes, Marra, and Burns, forthcoming).[2] Overall, the women produced more humor than the men in these meetings. So, for example, the average ratio for women was 25 instances per 100 minutes compared to the men's ratio of 14 instances per 100 minutes. This pattern held both for the relative contributions of women and men in the mixed-gender meetings, and on the basis of a comparison of the six single-gender meetings. Moreover, not only did women produce more humor overall than men in these meetings, the very presence of women tended to be associated with higher levels of humor: as the proportion of female participants in a meeting increased, so did the amount of humor. There is no support here for the picture of the serious businesswoman who lacks a sense of humor, nor for the suggestion that a "feminine" workplace is a humorless setting.

It is worth noting that the stereotype of the humorless businesswoman is to some extent inconsistent with the widely accepted view that "feminine" workplaces are warm, friendly places where a high value is placed on solidarity and collegiality. One possible explanation for this apparent contradiction is that women become more serious, and less inclined to encourage or contribute to humor, as they ascend the organizational ladder; in other words, it is women in roles of responsibility, especially in "masculine" workplaces, who lack a sense of humor. Exploring this hypothesis, we examined the influence of the chair, typically the section manager, on the amount of humor in meetings (Holmes, Marra, and Burns, forthcoming). While all the chairs in our database responded positively to humor, some of them were more active than others in initiating humor. The analysis indicated that in both mixed-gender and single-gender groups, female chairs contributed a higher proportion of humor than their male counterparts, providing no support for the suggestion that women lose their sense of humor as they gain seniority. Where there was a gender difference, it was in the relative amounts of different *types* of humor engaged in by women and men. In general, women were more likely than men in these meetings to initiate extended humor sequences, a collaborative activity which tended to generate good feeling and positive collegial attitudes.

In a number of ways, then, women played a proactive positive role in contributing to the humor in meetings. These analyses of workplace humor provide convincing evidence that "feminine" workplaces do not lack humor, and that women's contributions to workplace humor are typically frequent and collegial in orientation. We turn now to the third component in this overview of trends in workplace communication, namely a consideration of the relation between stereotype and reality in the distribution of small talk at work.

3.3 Small talk at work

While humor is stereotypically, and inaccurately, associated predominantly with "masculine" workplaces, small talk is stereotypically associated with "feminine" workplaces. In "feminine" workplaces, the stereotype suggests, small talk is copious and obligatory. In fact, of course, small talk and social talk occurred in all the workplaces we studied. People used small talk at the boundaries of interaction, at the beginning and end of the day, at the start and end of meetings, and sometimes at points within meetings (Holmes 2000c).

It is not possible to rigorously compare the amount of small talk used in different workplaces given the fact that our recordings were collected from volunteers who, despite our request to include all their workplace talk, sometimes edited out talk they regarded as unimportant, irrelevant, and non-serious. Three pieces of evidence, however, are worth considering in assessing the accuracy of the stereotype. First, the data analyzed in the papers in Coupland (2000), a collection devoted to small talk, but without gender as an explicit focus, is overwhelmingly dominated by women. Female participants contribute by far the most, and sometimes all, of the small talk analyzed in these papers. Second, of the papers which specifically examine small talk in the workplace, the majority select domains which are most commonly associated with women (hairdresser, supermarket checkout, travel agent, call center, women's health care), and the remainder provide examples and extracts featuring many more female than male protagonists. While the first point suggests that women engage in small talk more often than men, the second indicates that caution is necessary in interpreting such research. Just as some researchers appear to have looked for data in places which can be designated as stereotypically "feminine" workplaces, others may have been predisposed to identify women's contributions as prototypical exemplars of small talk.

The third piece of evidence comes from our analysis of the gender distribution of small talk in meetings from a range of the white-collar workplaces researched. In all workplaces, whether "masculine" or "feminine," the beginning of a meeting was an obligatory site for small talk, especially when participants had not met before that day. Its absence was perceived as "marked." Small talk was also usual while waiting for participants at larger meetings. However, in the most "masculine" white-collar organization with whom we worked, the small talk at the beginning of meetings was noticeably briefer, and the small talk topics less personal than in all other workplaces. The meetings got under way relatively quickly, and social talk digressions were few and brief. Conversely, in the most "feminine" workplace where we recorded, small talk at the beginning of meetings was more extended, and often very personal, indicating that the participants regularly maintained their relationships through such talk (Holmes 2000c). Social talk often "leaked" into meetings in this workplace, though an apparent social digression frequently turned out to have relevance for the organization's business in the longer term (a point elaborated below). Certainly, it appeared that there was greater tolerance for small talk in the more "feminine" white-collar workplaces researched.

This relatively neat pattern, however, was challenged by two sets of data, one from a factory, the second from meetings in one particular private, commercial organization. In the factory, small talk was frequent throughout the day, and was typically very personal in its content. In the private, commercial organization, which was in some respects a stereotypically "masculine" workplace, small talk, social banter, and witty repartee based on knowledge of their colleagues' recent social activities was the norm at the beginning of meetings. Interestingly, both workplaces had a dynamic female manager, with a strong personality and very good sense of humor, though there were other social factors at work too. Distributional and frequency data provide only part of the story.

As more women move into senior positions and take on managerial responsibility, our analyses suggest that they may influence the traditional stereotypes of gendered workplaces. On the one hand, they may influence the amount of social talk and humor which is considered acceptable in meetings and other workplace settings. On the other, they may adopt patterns of talk and interaction which have previously been considered stereotypically "masculine." This trend was also apparent in other dimensions of our analysis. Women managers were demonstrably skilled at getting their message across, at giving authoritative directives, at managing meetings, and providing leadership (see Holmes, Stubbe, and Vine 1999; Holmes 2000a). But the analyses which provided this evidence also indicated the complexity of the way effective women managers operate in the modern workplace. These analyses benefit from an approach which examines the detailed "practice" of talk at work, within a community of practice framework. We turn now to a more detailed qualitative analysis of the way individual women "do gender" in two contrastingly gendered workplaces.

4   A Community of Practice Approach to Analyzing the "Gendered" Workplace

The term "community of practice" was introduced to language and gender research by Eckert and McConnell-Ginet (1992; see also Wenger 1998; Eckert and McConnell-Ginet 1999; Holmes and Meyerhoff 1999; and McConnell-Ginet's and Eckert's chapters in this volume). A community of practice (henceforth, CofP) is

> an aggregate of people who come together around mutual engagement in an endeavour. Ways of doing things, ways of talking, beliefs, values, power relations – in short, practices – emerge in the course of this mutual endeavour.   (1992: 95)

The CofP approach focuses on what members do – the practice or activities which indicate that they belong to the group, and also the extent to which they belong. It also takes account of the attitudes, beliefs, values, and social relations which underlie their practice. Hence, the CofP model encourages a focus on "not gender differences but the difference gender makes" (Cameron 1992: 13). It is therefore useful in examining the issue of what people mean when they talk about a "feminine" or "masculine" workplace or workplace culture.

Wenger (1998: 73) identifies three criterial features of a CofP: (1) mutual engagement, (2) a joint negotiated enterprise, and (3) a shared repertoire of negotiable resources accumulated over time. The linguistic manifestations of a shared repertoire provide a basis for comparison between workplaces, and suggest some of the ways in which a distinctive workplace "culture" is constructed through interaction. Indeed, Wenger (1998: 125–6) identifies a number of more specific "constitutive characteristics" of a CofP, some of which lend themselves to the analysis of patterns of interaction and, more specifically, patterns of discourse (for further discussion, see Holmes and Meyerhoff 1999; Holmes and Marra, forthcoming). In our analyses to date, as indicated in the first section of the chapter, we have focused particularly on contrasting *styles* of workplace interaction, with attention to a number of Wenger's characteristics, including shared ways of engaging in doing things together, and discursive ways of sustaining relationships and displaying group membership, such as social talk, small talk, and the use of humor. In the next section, we explore how some of these aspects of workplace interaction are manifested in complex and detailed practice at the micro-level, and how gender is "produced and reproduced in differential forms of participation in particular CoPs" (Eckert and McConnell-Ginet 1995: 491).

5   The Gendered Workplace in Practice

As noted above, people often have quite definite views about whether the culture of their own or other workplaces is based on "feminine" values in the sense that it is hospitable to women, or whether it is more traditionally "masculine" and male-dominated. Perceptions are influenced by stereotypes relating to the nature of the work carried out, the gender composition of the workforce, and individuals' personal experiences, as much as by the actual practices found there. Nevertheless, such informal assessments tend to be remarkably consistent, and have generally been in accord with our own judgments, based on ethnographic data, of where the different workplaces included in our study might fit on a continuum from "feminine" to "masculine" organizational culture. We therefore considered it would be interesting to take these subjective comparisons as a starting point for exploring in more detail how particular discourse practices relate to gender in actual interactions.

We compare the interaction styles of teams in two sharply contrasting New Zealand workplaces. The first is a stereotypically "feminine" workplace, an office in a white-collar "knowledge industry" government organization, while the second, a factory, can be characterized as having a more "masculine" organizational culture. We briefly describe the distinguishing characteristics of each workplace as a gendered community of practice, before looking more closely at examples of how gender is constructed through discourse in each setting. These analyses draw on typical excerpts from the interactions of a competent female manager and her team, focusing on the aspects of discourse introduced above: strategies for managing meetings, and the functions of humor and social talk at work. The excerpts selected are designed to illustrate the richly textured underpinning of aspects of the gender stereotypes, as well as the way other aspects of these stereotypes unravel when put under the microscope.

6   Doing Gender in a "Feminine" Workplace

The office workplace represents the stereotypically feminine end of the gender continuum. It is a relatively small organization with a predominantly female staff whose main task is to monitor and advise on economic and social issues in New Zealand from the perspective of equality for women. When we tested our ethnographic data against the three criterial features for a CofP of mutual engagement, joint enterprise, and shared repertoire, it was clear that the "feminine" cap fitted this workplace well in broad terms at the time the data was collected.

First, members of the organization, and in particular members of the work units within it, engaged with one another many times a day in a variety of ways. They spoke face-to-face in formal meetings and informal problem-solving sessions, engaged in informal work-related and social chat in their workspaces, at breaks, and in passing; they communicated by telephone or e-mail on occasion, and they regularly read and commented on one another's written output (e.g. letters, reports, etc.). There were organized opportunities for socializing at work with colleagues and with external contacts, with some individuals also choosing to mix socially outside of work. In short, the communication patterns in this workplace could be characterized as "high involvement" and heavily context-embedded, with a strong emphasis on face-to-face interpersonal talk, all features consistent with the feminine end of the style continuum.

Second, there was a very clear sense of joint enterprise both in the organization as a whole and within individual teams, which went beyond simply doing the tasks at hand to encompass the pursuit of certain ideals relating specifically to gender issues. For instance, its staff included women who had joined the organization largely because they felt a particular commitment to furthering the aspirations of women. The organization is also perceived by outsiders as promoting a feminist agenda, something which its staff are sensitive to, as illustrated in this brief excerpt (transcription conventions are provided at the end of the chapter):

(1)

> *Context: Two female workers informally discussing a forthcoming publication*
>
> there was a meeting to discuss the titles when I was away. . . . I suppose my concept of what we want to convey is not something that . . . we sort of don't want to sound like it's an agenda we're trying to push because we're feminists right. . . . I'm trying to think who we're targeting I just think the word agenda goes puts them right off

In terms of workplace culture this shared philosophy was reflected in an overt emphasis on practicing the principles of employment equity, and on creating a professional environment that was comfortable for women to work in. It also influenced the kinds of communicative practices shared by the workers in this office – the third criterial feature of a CofP.

There is ample evidence, both from our analysis of actual interactions and observations reported by our informants, that these shared practices were typified by many of the features stereotypically associated with a feminine style. For example, participants in the study explicitly noted to us that although there was a recognized workplace hierarchy, this tended to be downplayed in most contexts, with managers adopting a relatively egalitarian and consensus-seeking approach in their interactions with their teams. Participants' understandings of their particular roles within the work unit or project team, and their unit's collective role within the larger institution or organization, were typically negotiated in this workplace, rather than being laid down from above. Our informants also commented that interactions were relatively informal in tone, and that the boundaries between people's personal and work lives were fuzzier than at other workplaces they had experience of, where maintaining such boundaries was often seen as an important aspect of "being a professional." They felt there was an acceptance, even an expectation, that people could and would talk about aspects of their personal lives with their colleagues in the course of the working day, and they explicitly attributed this to its being a workplace which operated with a distinctively feminine culture.

These patterns are realized in the data through a variety of specific discourse practices which interact in complex ways. Managers would often negotiate directives and decisions at some length, or embed them in collaborative problem-solving, rather than issuing direct instructions. For instance, the chair of a meeting would take specific steps to ensure that participants had genuinely reached consensus before moving on to the next issue or agenda item. This was particularly noticeable when someone had expressed a contrary view, or a reservation, at an earlier stage in the discussion. In such cases, the chair would quite explicitly seek the views of the formerly dissenting participant on the decision which was being considered.

At a more extended level of analysis, meetings often did not follow a strictly linear pattern of topical organization and decision-making. Digressions and topic shifts back and forth were common, and our analysis also revealed many examples of the seamless integration of personal or affectively oriented talk and collaborative humor sequences with business talk. For instance, sequences of jointly constructed humorous talk and amusing anecdotes were commonly interleaved with the business at hand during formal meetings and other discussions. Although strictly speaking "off-topic," such digressions were usually related in some way to the issue being discussed, and performed important discourse management and affective functions. The overall effect is one of high-energy, good-humored, friendly interaction, with many of the features of "all-together-now" talk identified by Coates (1988, 1996) in describing the talk of women friends. To illustrate some of these points, we next analyze in some detail a meeting typical of many recorded at this workplace.

6.1   The Flying Filers

The data excerpts below come from a fairly lengthy regular team meeting which provided an especially rich illustration of the above points, while also allowing us to explore the extent to which the picture it paints of this office as a "feminine" workplace is complicated by other discursive features. The team is discussing the allocation of responsibilities in relation to a range of tasks over the next period of time. These intersect with problems relating to loss of personnel and the fact that the departmental filing has got severely behind. A number of possible solutions are discussed, some involving the reassignment of duties. One solution, first proposed at a relatively early point in the meeting, is to bring in external filers, "the flying filing squad." A senior team member, Zoe, is clearly not happy with this suggestion, and throughout the discussion she raises objections whenever it re-emerges, as it regularly does. Leila, the manager, uses a number of strategies to defuse and resolve this tension.

Example (2) illustrates how Leila encourages the participation of all those present in the decision-making process right from the start. In introducing the issue, she acknowledges that it may prove insoluble:

(2)
Leila: I mean we may not be able to find a solution but that I mean you're the people
         who are in the best situation for knowing that # what's your feeling?

When the suggestion of bringing in outsiders to deal with the filing backlog is first mooted, Zoe comes in immediately:

(3)
Zoe: mm/but\ okay but hang on what are our other options here um we've also got
         Hannah
Leila: /mm\
         yeah

Leila responds positively, saying *that's a good suggestion*, and she allows Zoe to express at some length the reasons for her reservations. The discussion then develops into a collaborative consideration of the staffing problems raised by Zoe's alternative solution. Leila explicitly seeks agreement, and checks that all are happy with the final resolution of each problem.

However, despite the collaborative tone overall, at various points during this discussion, Leila does invoke her managerial status rather more explicitly. In example (4), she refers to her expectations about the need for further staff, and by her repetitive use of *I*-statements she makes it clear that, while she is happy to consult, this type of planning nevertheless falls within her prerogative as manager:

(4)

Leila:	I think we have the solution here I think the good news is that I'll- I probably don't have to think about recruiting someone else
Zoe:	oh right
Leila:	I mean /I-\ that's that's the first bit of good news that I guess I see that that's =
Zoe:	/yeah\
Leila:	= what it looks that's what it feels for me # am I being overly optimistic
Hannah:	I'm not clear what you're planning for nominations
Leila:	well I'm not planning anything yet

Leila also regularly uses various strategies which explicitly control the way in which the interaction develops. In example (5), for instance, she summarizes and ratifies the decisions reached so far:

(5)

Leila:	. . . so I think what we need though we need extra help with information requests # Emma has that immediately # effectively we have a nominations vacancy I would prefer if we could solve our nominations problem in-house probably

At another point, she initiates an abrupt topic shift after several minutes of off-topic talk to get the discussion back on track.

At the same time, throughout this sequence Leila pays a great deal of attention to the positive face needs of her colleagues, and to Zoe's in particular, often using humor to maintain the solidarity of the group, thus helping to avert the possibility of the disagreement turning into unresolved conflict. In example (6), Leila points out that she and Zoe have been working together on this issue, and pays her a humorous compliment on her ability to "mother" new staff, which raises a laugh from the group as a whole:

(6)

Leila:	Zoe Zoe and I'd been talking I mean one we're gonna need Zoe um anyway to do handing over with the other librarians when they come /on\ board and I think that =
Karen:	/yeah\

Leila: = they're probably going to feel a need for a little bit of mothering and I think
            Zoe will be good at that and the /other thing she's been\ really good with
            Kerry I've =
Karen: /[laughs]\
Leila: = watched her [laughs] I've seen her doing it = /
Emma: /=mother librarian
Leila: she'll be sort of the great aunt librarian /[laughs]\
All: /[laughter]\

Soon after this, they return to the issue of the filing, and Leila reintroduces the
suggestion of the flying filing squad with a humorous anecdote describing
how she saw their van and attempted to get the phone number from the side
of the van while driving along:

(7)
Leila: . . . and I was trying to sort of /edge round and I was [laughs]:\ stretching
            this way =
All: /[laughter]\
Leila: = in the /car: [laughs] I was a wee\ bit like ( ) [laughs] you must have been =
Emma: /( ) thought you were a maniac\
Leila: = away the day that I told this that I'd found these funny people and er Zoe
            tracked them down
All: [laughter]

While this could be seen as an unnecessary digression, it in fact serves a
number of useful purposes, by fostering good collegial relationships and
reframing the proposed solution in a non-threatening way. Notice particularly
the way in which Emma contributes to the humor, and how Leila closes her
short narrative with *I'd found these funny people and Zoe tracked them down*, thus
subtly pointing out that she and Zoe are a team, and also implying that Zoe
must have been open to the idea at that time.

   Gradually a solution to a number of the staffing problems identified begins
to emerge. At this point there is a good deal of collaborative humor, reflecting
relief that a solution is in sight:

(8)
[laughter throughout this section]
Leila: Emma you are part of the solution in that I think that ( )
Emma: I only want to be part of the problem
XX: really
Leila: [laughs] [in fun growly tone]: don't you dare be part of the problem I'll keep
            on giving you vitamin c bananas [laughs] chocolate fish [laughs] I gave I gave
            um I you know everyone had chocolate fish last week but Emma had more
            chocolate fish than anybody the only thing was she had holes in her teeth
            /[laughs]\ she couldn't =
Emma: /I couldn't eat them\
Leila: = eat them /[laughs]\

Emma: /I've been putting\off going to the dentist for /six months now and\ I've =
Leila: /[drawls]: oh no:\
Emma: = got a hole in /my tooth\ [laughs] anyway
Leila: /oh yuck\

The way Leila shares information about the holes in Emma's teeth and jokingly threatens to feed her with various goodies simultaneously reinforces the supportive team culture, and constructs Leila in a nurturing role somewhat akin to that of a mother with a child – benevolent but nonetheless an authority figure.

Zoe continues to raise objections (e.g. *it seems to me um a bit silly to bring in the flying filers if all they're gonna do is file for us when we can get Robyn to do it*), and it takes over half an hour for her to come to terms with Leila's proposed solution. But finally it is clear that she is reconciled to it (see Holmes 2000a). Leila's strategies of clearly stating and restating the contentious issues, requesting Zoe to make explicit her reservations, and overtly seeking her agreement before proceeding have resulted in a satisfactory ending. The final resolution of all the staffing issues leaves the team feeling very positive, as indicated by a good deal of collaborative and mutually supportive humor at the end of the meeting. Leila's use of humor at this point lightens the tone, and reasserts the solidarity of the group after a meeting in which she has needed at times to be assertive and overtly managerial. In example (9), Leila first jokingly threatens two people who are about to move from the library to another section with the fact that they will have to work harder, and then pretends that her own skills are limited to making coffee:

(9)
Leila: you have to work hard you two /no I mean round there [laughs]\
All: /[laughter]\
Emma: as opposed to the library
Leila: [laughs] absolutely
All: /[laughter]\
XX: /there's a benefit\ I- the coffee's constant round there
Emma: [laughs] this is a constant
Leila: the coffee is con- yeah I can make coffee /it's one thing I know I can do
            [laughs] =
Emma: /lot of very strong black coffee
            good\
Leila: = 'cause it's one thing I feel confident about in my cool competency # making
            [laughs] coffee: [laughs] it's one thing I really got a good performance on
            [laughs]
All: [laughter]

We have dealt with this example in some detail to illustrate some of the discursive practices typical of this workplace. There is a marked orientation toward collaborative styles and processes of interaction, together with a high level of attention to the interpersonal dimension. While Leila is clearly in charge, she usually chooses less direct, more linguistically polite strategies to achieve her goals in a consensual way. Such patterns are of course consistent with both the "feminine" stereotype and the research evidence on preferred "feminine" styles of interaction, especially in same-sex groups (cf. Coates 1996). However, as illustrated above, even in such a workplace, managers do still exert their authority overtly and directly in certain situations, colleagues openly disagree with one another and compete to push their own point of view, and it was clearly regarded by participants in the interaction as unremarkable for them to do so. Just because a workplace has a predominantly "feminine" culture, this does not mean individuals will always use "feminine" discourse strategies, nor does it rule out the use of stereotypically more "masculine" strategies where these are appropriate and necessary.

7   Doing Gender in a "Masculine" Workplace

It is often claimed that females who attain high-status positions in traditional male-dominated workplaces succeed by adopting a "masculine" style of management and communication. Our data provided an opportunity to test this claim by comparing the discursive practices identified in the "feminine" workplace described above with those of female managers in a number of stereotypically "masculine" workplaces. Not unexpectedly, operating in a mixed-gender environment and a more masculine workplace culture does indeed appear to influence the discursive practices of women managers. However, while it is certainly apparent from their discourse strategies that women in these workplaces are interacting in a differently gendered CofP from the more "feminine" one described above, it is not the case that they shift wholesale to a "masculine" style; and nor do they all use exactly the same mix of strategies. Rather, just as in the meeting analyzed above, these women skillfully blend a range of communication strategies from right across the masculine–feminine continuum in a way that is appropriate to the norms of their workgroup, and to the specific situation at any given time.

We first briefly describe the CofP characteristics of a particular work team in a stereotypically "masculine" workplace, and then illustrate in more detail the different ways in which gender is constructed through the discursive practices found in this setting. The "masculine" workplace selected for this discussion provides a maximal contrast with the "feminine" workplace already described. It is a multicultural factory with a majority of male staff engaged in skilled trade and semi-skilled manual work, in what is traditionally a male occupational area. Because gender differences are often more apparent in male working-class and trade contexts (e.g. Weigel and Weigel 1985; Bernsten 1998), we might predict a greater tendency in such an environment for a woman manager to adopt discourse and management strategies from the "masculine" end of the continuum in order to develop and maintain her credibility with her male subordinates. However, although our data confirms this hypothesis to an extent, the actual picture is more complex.

7.1   *The Power Rangers*

As elsewhere in the factory, men form a majority in the close-knit production team, pseudonymed the Power Rangers, which was the focus of our study. Their level of mutual engagement on a day-to-day basis is not uniformly high, as the packers and manufacturers work in two adjacent but separate areas on different floors of the factory, and there are long intervals where individual team members may not need to communicate with one another. Moreover, talk is not the main currency of work as in the office workplace described above – rather, talk is regarded as a means to a practical end. Nevertheless, the team enjoys sustained and multiplex mutual relationships. They have daily briefing sessions, individuals have regular contact with one another in the course of their 12-hour shifts, they see one another at "smoko" (tea/coffee breaks), and there is regular social contact between many team members outside work hours. Moreover, because many of the team members have worked together for a relatively long time, and have developed a strong sense of group identity, they are a very cohesive group. There is a real sense of joint enterprise in this team, which is highly motivated both in terms of completing the immediate tasks during a shift, as well as meeting longer-term goals such as continuing to out-perform other production teams, and meeting quality and safety targets. Teamwork is highly and explicitly valued, something which is further reinforced by the Polynesian cultural background of a majority of the team, which tends to privilege the group over individuals.

One of the more noticeable ways in which these characteristics are reflected in discourse is in a strong orientation to team morale, and a very distinctive sparky communicative style. The team uses many markers of solidarity in their interactions, and there is a lot of in-group talk and gossip. The Power Rangers also have a well-deserved reputation at the factory for uninhibited swearing, and constantly joking around and "having each other on" which sits alongside their status as the top-performing team. At the time of the study, their particular blend of verbal humor, jocular abuse, and practical jokes contributed to a unique team culture, and generally helped to create positive relationships within the team (see also Stubbe 2000; Stubbe, forthcoming b; Holmes and Marra, forthcoming). These kinds of playful yet highly competitive and "in your face" strategies for building solidarity are well documented as common characteristics of all-male groups (e.g. Kuiper 1991; Kiesling 2001).

Example (10) provides a typical illustration of how members embed the team culture in the course of routine task-oriented interactions. Ginette, the manager, is participating in a longstanding team ritual when using the intercom, by the mock-serious use of ham radio conventions like *copy kiwi* and *stand by* to initiate the interaction with Russell. Her use of the nickname *kiwi* and the familiar and friendly term of address *bro* when addressing Russell, and his use in return of *bro*, are also characteristic of the way this team interacts.[3]

(10)
Context: Ginette the team leader talks to Russell in manufacturing via the intercom

Ginette: copy kiwi copy kiwi
Russell: what's up
Ginette: stand by and I'll give you the figures bro
Russell: yep go
Ginette: for the line 1 acma rainbow flight we need 24 tonnes 24
Russell: yo bro
Ginette: . . . then we are on orange wave orange wave # for the line 1

As mentioned above, the amount and style of humor used by members of this team is one of its defining characteristics. Example (11) is a classic example of the sort of no-holds-barred contestive humor that is commonplace between members of the Power Rangers:

(11)
Context: Two male production workers talking during a lull in their work

Peter: oh man I'm starving I am starving . . . I might go and join the war remind me
         of the old days the army and the front row . . .
David: you'd be the first one to get shot
Peter: why /what makes\ you say that
David: /you're so\   you're so big
Peter: brother [warningly]
David: it's very rare that a bullet will miss you
         [laughter]
Peter: yes /(that's not on)\
David: /look at the\ size of your stomach
Peter: that's NOT on (3)
David: actually they'll close their eyes and sh- fire a shot
         [laughter]
Peter: [drawls]: oh: I see
David: they got no problem missing that

Although this example happens to involve two men, Ginette the manager, like the other female team members, actively participates in such joking, and in fact she often deliberately initiates it as a way of countering boredom and maintaining morale amongst the team. A classic example occurred on April Fools' Day when she tricked several team members into ringing the zoo to ask for "Mr Lion," much to the mirth of their colleagues.

Ginette's routine use of such high solidarity discourse strategies when she interacts with members of her team clearly serves to minimize the difference in status between them. What is less clear is whether this is best explained as a "feminine" tendency on the part of Ginette to emphasize social connection ahead of her individual status as team leader (cf. Tannen 1990), something which also happens to be a typical feature of Polynesian culture (Metge 1995), or as an attempt by her to accommodate to the "masculine" mateship culture of the factory. In this instance, the same discourse strategies can in fact be interpreted in a number of different ways, and as they are all mutually re-inforcing, the inherent ambiguity does not much matter, and may in fact be useful to Ginette in trying to balance the different aspects of her identity as a Polynesian woman who leads a predominantly male production team (cf. Stubbe 1998b).

At the same time, as example (12) illustrates, she routinely adopts a stereotypically very "unfeminine" direct, no-punches-pulled style when it comes to giving instructions or meting out criticism (see also Stubbe 1999). Notice the explicit directives, and also the appeal to individuals not to let the rest of the team down:

(12)
Context: Some team members have not been filling out packing codes correctly

Ginette: check the case . . . make sure you check them properly 'cause like I said it's just one person's stupid mistake makes the whole lot of us look like eggs +++ check them properly

There is then a bit of horseplay from team members, one of whom says he didn't have a pen. Ginette responds:

Ginette: no pen you come out here and get one

These are very direct imperative forms, expressed forcefully with an explicit *you* in the final instance. At the end of this long harangue, which has been spiked sporadically with humor, she says:

Ginette: please fill them out properly fuck youse

The comic mix of imperative form and forceful expletive, alongside the for-mally polite *please*, and the friendly colloquial pronoun *youse*, an in-group solidarity signal, elicits appreciative laughter from the team. Ginette thus ends the instructions on a less serious note, while nevertheless getting her message over very explicitly.

Her direct style in this context works well, not just because it accommodates to masculine discourse practices, but also because she has developed a strong, positive relationship with her team: they trust her and are confident that she will look after their interests when dealing with higher management, for instance. They also know that later in the day she will be just as ready to join in with a joke or a tease as anyone else in the team, and that she does not abuse her position of authority.

When dealing with team members on a one-to-one basis or in training sessions, Ginette's style is often quite different. She is sensitive to their particular problems, and takes care to preserve their face. In example (13) she follows up on a team member who has still not understood the correct procedure for entering the packing codes onto a stock form, despite the very explicit briefing earlier in the day.

(13)

Context: Ginette is explaining the correct way of entering the packing codes to Sam

Ginette: what do we have on here
Sam: four five six seven
Ginette: why have you put four five six seven
Sam: 'cause I was taking it off that one but gonna take it off that one
Ginette: you don't take it off that one
Sam: no er well yeah I did I know I was my- that was my mistake
Ginette: yeah
Sam: yeah
Ginette: no the way you did it this morning is good that's what we're supposed to
           do (9) see how important important the checks a- are you know if you do
           them properly
Sam: well I yeah I'm usually pretty good on on that sort of thing now so-
Ginette: yeah
Sam: if you go by the book you can't go wrong
Ginette: that's right just remember that when you're doing the check list you put
           down what YOU find not what it should be so you're checking against what
           it should be   if it don't match then there's something wrong

In such situations Ginette acts more as a coach or mentor, following up on what the team member is doing, leading them through the solution to a problem, and patiently waiting and encouraging them to work out things for themselves rather than simply demonstrating or instructing.

It could be argued that much (though certainly not all) of the time, Ginette constructs her leadership role as akin to that of a mother, although this is never expressed quite as explicitly as it is in the office setting (examples (6) and (8) above). This is reflected in the way Ginette talks to the team – by turns bossy, giving direct instructions, and supportive and nurturing – as well as the way she very consciously looks after their practical and emotional needs. Indeed, she explicitly promotes the model of the team as a family that sticks together, a view which appears to be shared by the rest of the team as shown by the affectionate nicknames Camp Leader and Camp Mother, used to refer to her and another female team member who was co-team leader at one time.[4]

These brief analyses of interaction in the factory team highlight the complexity of the notion of a "feminine" or "masculine" workplace. On just about any measure, a factory can be characterized as a particularly "masculine" workplace, yet the patterns identified do not coincide neatly with the discursive practices typically associated with masculine styles of interaction. In this setting the high premium placed on solidarity and team cohesion means that social talk, usually associated with the feminine end of the spectrum, is frequent and very personal; and while there is a good deal of the contestive humor associated with male groups, there is a similar proportion of collaborative and supportive humor (Holmes and Marra, forthcoming). Ginette clearly accommodates to many typically male discursive practices, but she blends these with features associated with more "feminine" styles of interaction. Because of the unique interplay between gender and many other variables such as culture, class, educational background, gender composition, and the different kinds of work involved, the way in which Ginette enacts her gender identity, and balances this with her professional role in the context of a "masculine" organizational culture, is quite different from the way Leila achieves this in the context of a much more "feminine" organization. However, neither manager restricts herself to narrowly defined "feminine" or "masculine" discursive practices in order to do so. Rather, both draw creatively on a wide range of discursive resources to perform their roles as effective managers in these differently gendered workplace contexts.

To sum up, then, given its salience in New Zealand society, it is inevitable that the social category of gender will be used to guide people's behavior at work. Stereotypes provide simplifications which reduce the complexity of ongoing decisions about how to act, talk, dress, and so on, and how to respond to the actions, talk, and dress of others (but see Cameron, this volume; Talbot, this volume, for further discussion). For those involved, describing a given workplace as more or less "masculine" or "feminine" serves as a useful shorthand to describe the discourse practices and cultures in relative terms. In this section, however, using detailed analyses of interactions in New Zealand workplaces, we have demonstrated that the reality is rather more complex and difficult to interpret than such polarized terminology implies. First, there is no one-to-one correspondence between gender and the use of a given linguistic or discourse feature in any specific context. And second, gender is only one of a number of relevant social and contextual variables affecting the way an interaction unfolds. The dangers of over-reliance on stereotypes are quite apparent. To mention only the most obvious, simplistic notions of "appropriate" styles of interaction based on gender stereotypes inevitably underestimate the impressive management skills of practitioners such as Ginette and Leila, skills which were especially evident in their sensitive responsiveness to the complexities of the very varied contexts in which they were negotiating meaning.

8 Conclusion

This chapter has explored discourse features which have been widely used to characterize the organizational culture of different workplaces as being relatively more "feminine" or "masculine." The first section summarized patterns observed in a large set of data recorded in a range of New Zealand workplaces. Analyses of the structure and distribution of talk in the workplaces in our data suggest that factors other than gender determine the patterns of talk in meetings: the function of the meeting and the relative status of participants are among the most obvious of these. Our analysis of the distribution of humor in workplace meetings directly contradicts the stereotype which suggests that humor is more characteristic of "masculine" workplaces. It was apparent that women typically contributed more humor than men in the meetings analyzed, and the women chairs, in particular, encouraged workplace humor. While patterns of small talk in most workplaces appear to support the stereotype that "feminine" workplaces are more tolerant of off-task social talk, there are exceptions in the form of apparently "masculine" workplaces where, at least in some contexts, small talk is frequent and social talk is encouraged.

The second section of the chapter challenged the stereotypical assumptions underlying the notion of a gendered workplace by focusing on the discursive practices of two particular women managers. Like their male counterparts, they convey their instructions clearly and directly, and skillfully control meetings making use of a variety of strategies: they typically dominate the talking time, control the opening and closing stages of meetings, keep the discussion on track, summarize progress, and check that consensus has been reached. But they also use a wide variety of more subtle strategies to keep control of the discourse, with choice of strategy influenced by specific context. Directness, it appears, is generally appropriate in meetings when giving instructions to subordinates about routine tasks within their area of responsibility. However, these women tend to use a much less confrontational and more ameliorative style when dealing with problems on a one-to-one basis, when the task is more complicated, or when criticism of an individual is implied. In such cases, mitigation and indirectness are more often evident, even where this might appear to be a less immediately efficient style. Similarly, women managers typically use humor and social talk strategically to construct solidarity and cement good relationships in the workplace, as well as to control the behavior of others in an acceptable and collegial manner.

Gender is such a salient dimension that interaction is typically viewed through "gendered" spectacles much of the time. Consequently, people tend to overlook data which does not fit gender stereotypes. But, as we have illustrated, the reality is that much of what goes on at work does *not* fit the gender stereotype. The data produced by the New Zealand women managers in our study suggests that they typically make use of a wide verbal repertoire style (Smith-Hefner 1988; Chambers 1992; Case 1995), integrating features typically associated both with masculine and with feminine speech styles in earlier research.

It is here that the CofP approach provides an especially useful framework for exploring workplace norms and teasing out distinctive aspects of workplace culture in relation to gender. It also provides a basis for examining the ways in which individual women and men construct their gender identities and balance these with their professional roles within the parameters established as acceptable by the group with which they work. Each workplace team over time constructs a unique set of discursive practices from the resources available to them, compatible with other aspects of the way they work together. These shared practices, and the ways in which individuals conform to or challenge the group's norms, contribute to the construction of differently gendered communities of practice in each workplace.

So, finally, how would we characterize the contribution of the sociolinguist in the analysis of the concept of the "gendered" workplace? It can be argued that it is at least threefold. First, we can check, and challenge if appropriate, the content of the broad generalizations which constitute the inevitable stereotypes that develop in a community. Second, we can provide detailed evidence to unravel and complexify the stereotypes themselves, moving a stereotype in the direction of a more accurate "social type" perhaps (see Hall 1997; Talbot, this volume). Third, we can contribute to the development of analytical approaches which avoid reifying social categories that distort perceptions of what people are achieving through discourse, and which capture more satisfactorily the complexities of meaning negotiated through discourse in workplace interaction.

TRANSCRIPTION CONVENTIONS

All names are pseudonyms.

XX	Unidentified speaker
YES	Capitals indicate emphatic stress
[laughs]	Paralinguistic features in square brackets
+	Pause of up to one second
(3)	Pause of 3 seconds
..../......\\... ..../.......\\...	Simultaneous speech
(hello)	Transcriber's best guess at an unclear utterance
?	Rising or question intonation
-	Incomplete or cut-off utterance
#	Signals end of "sentence" where it is ambiguous on paper
=	Utterance continues on speaker's next line
...	Section of transcript omitted
(. . .)	Indecipherable speech
:	Indicates the scope of the paralinguistic feature it accompanies

NOTES

1 We would like to thank Meredith
   Marra and Miriam Meyerhoff for
   valuable comments on a draft of this
   chapter. We also thank all those who
   allowed their workplace interactions
   to be recorded, and other members
   of the Language in the Workplace
   Project team who assisted with
   collecting, transcribing, and analyzing
   the data, especially Bernadette Vine,
   Meredith Marra, Megan Ingle, and
   Louise Burns. The research was
   supported by a grant from the New
   Zealand Foundation for Research
   Science and Technology.
2 Humorous utterances were defined as
   utterances identified by the analyst,
   on the basis of paralinguistic,

prosodic, and discoursal clues,
as intended by the speaker(s) to
be amusing and perceived to be
amusing by at least some
participants (Holmes 2000d: 164).
3 Although *bro* is an abbreviation
   of *brother*, and therefore more
   commonly used as a solidarity
   marker between males, it is not
   unusual for it to be used in
   addressing women who are members
   of the in-group, particularly in
   Polynesian contexts.
4 These nicknames are drawn from
   an act in the repertoire of a popular
   New Zealand comedy duo, the Topp
   Twins, who portray two bossy female
   youth group leaders.

REFERENCES

Ainsworth-Vaughn, Nancy 1992: Topic
   transitions in physician–patient
   interviews: Power, gender and
   discourse change. *Language in
   Society* 21(3): 409–26.
Aries, Elizabeth 1996: *Men and Women
   in Interaction: Reconsidering the
   Differences.* Oxford: Oxford
   University Press.
Bernsten, Janice 1998: Marked versus
   unmarked choices on the auto
   factory floor. In Carol Myers-Scotton
   (ed.) *Codes and Consequences:
   Choosing Linguistic Varieties.*
   Oxford: Oxford University Press,
   pp. 178–91.
Cameron, Deborah 1992: "Not gender
   differences but the difference gender
   makes": Explanation in research
   on sex and language. *International
   Journal of the Sociology of Language*
   94: 13–26.

Cameron, Deborah 1996: The language–
   gender interface: Challenging co-
   optation. In Victoria L. Bergvall,
   Janet M. Bing, and Alice F. Freed
   (eds) *Rethinking Language and
   Gender Research: Theory and Practice.*
   New York: Longman, pp. 31–53.
Case, Susan Schick 1988: Cultural
   differences, not deficiencies: An
   analysis of managerial women's
   language. In Suzanna Rose and
   Laurie Larwood (eds) *Women's
   Careers: Pathways and Pitfalls.* New
   York: Praeger, pp. 41–63.
Case, Susan Schick 1991: Wide verbal
   repertoire speech: Gender, language
   and managerial influence. *Women's
   Studies International Forum* 16(3):
   271–90.
Case, Susan Schick 1995: Gender,
   language and the professions:
   recognition of wide-verbal-repertoire

speech. *Studies in the Linguistic Sciences* 25(2): 149–92.

Chambers, J. K. 1992: Linguistic correlates of gender and sex. *English World-Wide* 13(2): 173–218.

Coates, Jennifer 1988: Gossip revisited: Language in all-female groups. In Jennifer Coates and Deborah Cameron (eds) *Women in Their Speech Communities*. London: Longman, pp. 94–121.

Coates, Jennifer 1996: *Women Talk*. Oxford: Blackwell.

Coupland, Justine (ed.) 2000: *Small Talk*. London: Longman.

Cox, Joe A., Read, Raymond A., and Van Auken, Philip M. 1990: Male–female differences in communicating job-related humor: An exploratory study. *Humor* 3(3): 287–95.

Crawford, Mary 1995: *Talking Difference: On Gender and Language*. London and Thousand Oaks, CA: Sage.

Eakins, Barbara Westbrook and Eakins, R. Gene 1976: Verbal turn-taking and exchanges in faculty dialogue. In Betty Lou Dubois and Isabel Crouch (eds) *The Sociology of the Languages of American Women*. San Antonio, TX: Trinity University Press, pp. 53–62.

Eckert, Penelope and McConnell-Ginet, Sally 1992: Communities of practice: Where language, gender and power all live. In Kira Hall, Mary Bucholtz, and Birch Moonwomon (eds) *Locating Power: Proceedings of the Second Berkeley Women and Language Conference*. Berkeley, CA: Berkeley Women and Language Group, University of California, pp. 89–99.

Eckert, Penelope and McConnell-Ginet, Sally 1995: Constructing meaning, constructing selves: Snapshots of language, gender, and class from Belten High. In Kira Hall and Mary Bucholtz (eds) *Gender Articulated: Language and the Socially Constructed Self*. London: Routledge, pp. 469–507.

Eckert, Penelope and McConnell-Ginet, Sally 1999: New generalizations and explanation in language and gender research. *Language in Society*, Special Issue: *Communities of Practice in Language and Gender Research* 28(2): 185–201.

Edelsky, Carole 1981: Who's got the floor? *Language in Society* 10: 383–421.

Elgin, Suzette H. 1993: *Genderspeak, Men, Women and the Gentle Art of Self Defense*. New York: Wiley.

Freed, Alice 1992: We understand perfectly: A critique of Tannen's view of cross-sex communication. In Kira Hall, Mary Bucholtz, and Birch Moonwomon (eds) *Locating Power: Proceedings of the Second Berkeley Women and Language Conference*. Berkeley, CA: Berkeley Women and Language Group, University of California, pp. 144–52.

Gray, John 1992: *Men are from Mars, Women are from Venus*. New York: HarperCollins.

Hall, Stuart 1997: The spectacle of the "Other". In Stuart Hall (ed.) *Representation: Cultural Representations and Signifying Practices*. London: Sage, pp. 223–90.

Holmes, Janet 1992: Women's talk in public contexts. *Discourse & Society* 3(2): 131–50.

Holmes, Janet 1995: *Women, Men and Politeness*. London: Longman.

Holmes, Janet 2000a: Women at work: Analysing women's talk in New Zealand workplaces. *Australian Review of Applied Linguistics (ARAL)* 22(2): 1–17.

Holmes, Janet 2000b: Victoria University of Wellington's Language in the Workplace Project: An overview. *Language in the Workplace Occasional Papers* 1. http://www.vuw.ac.nz/lals/wlp/resources/op1.htm

Holmes, Janet 2000c: Doing collegiality and keeping control at work: Small talk in government departments. In Justine Coupland (ed.) *Small Talk*. London: Longman, pp. 32–61.

Holmes, Janet 2000d: Politeness, power and provocation: How humor functions in the workplace. *Discourse Studies* 2(2): 159–85.

Holmes, Janet and Marra, Meredith forthcoming: Having a laugh at work: How humor contributes to workplace culture.

Holmes, Janet, Marra, Meredith, and Burns, Louise forthcoming: *Women's Humor in the Workplace: A Quantitative Analysis*. (To appear in *Language in the Workplace Occasional Papers*.)

Holmes, Janet and Meyerhoff, Miriam 1999: The community of practice: Theories and methodologies in language and gender research. *Language in Society* 28(2): 173–83.

Holmes, Janet, Stubbe, Maria, and Vine, Bernadette 1999: Constructing professional identity: "Doing power" in policy units. In Srikant Sarangi and Celia Roberts (eds) *Talk, Work and Institutional Order: Discourse in Medical, Mediation and Management Settings*. Berlin and New York: Mouton de Gruyter, pp. 351–85.

James, Bev and Saville-Smith, Kay 1989: *Gender, Culture and Power*. Auckland: Oxford University Press.

James, Deborah and Drakich, Janice 1993: Understanding gender differences in amount of talk. In Deborah Tannen (ed.) *Gender and Conversational Interaction*. Oxford: Oxford University Press, pp. 281–312.

Kendall, Shari and Tannen, Deborah 1997: Gender and language in the workplace. In Ruth Wodak (ed.) *Gender and Discourse*. London: Sage, pp. 81–105.

Kiesling, Scott 2001: "Now I gotta watch what I say": Shifting constructions of masculinity in discourse. *Journal of Linguistic Anthropology* 11(2): 250–73.

Kuiper, Koenraad 1991: Sporting formulae in New Zealand English: Two models of male solidarity. In Jenny Cheshire (ed.) *English Around the World*. Cambridge: Cambridge University Press, pp. 200–9.

McCauslan, Jenny A. and Kleiner, Brian H. 1992: Women and organizational leadership. *Equal Opportunities International* 11(6): 12–15.

Marra, Meredith forthcoming: Decisions in New Zealand Business Meetings. PhD thesis, Victoria University of Wellington, New Zealand.

Metge, Joan 1995: *New Growth from Old: The Whaanau in the Modern World*. Wellington: Victoria University Press.

Meyerhoff, Miriam 1991: Review of Tannen 1990. *Australian Journal of Linguistics* 11: 236–41.

Nelson, Marie Wilson 1998: Women's ways: Interactive patterns in predominantly female research teams. In Jennifer Coates (ed.) *Language and Gender: A Reader*. Oxford: Blackwell, pp. 354–72.

Rearden, Kathleen Kelley 1995: *They Don't Get It Do They*. Boston: Little, Brown.

Romaine, Suzanne 1999: *Communicating Gender*. Mahwah, NJ: Lawrence Erlbaum.

Smith-Hefner, Nancy J. 1988: Women and politeness: The Javanese example. *Language in Society* 17(4): 535–54.

Stanworth, Michelle 1983: *Gender and Schooling*. London: Hutchinson.

Stubbe, Maria 1998a: Researching language in the workplace: A participatory model. In *Proceedings of the Australian Linguistics Society Conference*, Brisbane, University of Queensland, July 1998. http://www.cltr.uq.edu.au/als98

Stubbe, Maria 1998b: Striking a balance: Language, gender and professional identity. In Suzanne Wertheim, Ashlee C. Bailee, and Monica Corston-Oliver (eds) *Engendering Communication: Proceedings of the Fifth Berkeley Women and Language Conference*. Berkeley, CA: Berkeley Women and Language Group, University of California, pp. 545–56.

Stubbe, Maria 1999: Just Joking and Playing Silly Buggers: Humor and Teambuilding on a Factory Production Line. Paper presented at NZ Linguistics Society Conference, Massey, 24–26 November 1999.

Stubbe, Maria 2000: "Just do it . . . !": Discourse strategies for "getting the message across" in a factory production team. In *Proceedings of the Australian Linguistics Society Conference*, University of Western Australia, September 1999. http://www.arts.uwa.edu.au/LingWWW/als99/

Stubbe, Maria forthcoming a: "I've got a little problem!" The discourse organization of task-oriented discussions in professional workplaces. (To appear in *Language in the Workplace Occasional Papers*).

Stubbe, Maria forthcoming b: Miscommunication and Problematic Discourse in the Workplace. PhD thesis, Victoria University of Wellington, New Zealand.

Swann, Joan 1992: *Girls, Boys and Language*. Oxford and New York: Blackwell.

Talbot, Mary M. 1998: *Language and Gender: An Introduction*. Oxford: Polity.

Tannen, Deborah 1990: *You Just Don't Understand: Women and Men in Conversation*. New York: William Morrow.

Tannen, Deborah (ed.) 1993: *Gender and Conversational Interaction*. Oxford: Oxford University Press.

Tannen, Deborah 1994a: *Gender and Discourse*. Oxford: Oxford University Press.

Tannen, Deborah 1994b: *Talking from 9 to 5: Women and Men in the Workplace*. London: Virago Press.

Troemel-Ploetz, Senta 1991: Review essay: Selling the apolitical. *Discourse & Society* 2(4): 489–502.

Walker, Nancy A. 1981: Do feminists ever laugh? Women's humor and women's rights. *International Journal of Women's Studies* 4(1): 1–9.

Weigel, M. Margaret and Weigel, Ronald M. 1985: Directive use in a migrant agricultural community: A test of Ervin-Tripp's hypothesis. *Language in Society* 14: 63–79.

Wenger, Etienne 1998: *Communities of Practice: Learning, Meaning, and Identity*. Cambridge and New York: Cambridge University Press.

West, Candace 1984: When the doctor is a lady: Power, status and gender in physician–patient dialogues. *Symbolic Interaction* 7(1): 87–106.

Wodak, Ruth (ed.) 1997: *Gender and Discourse*. London: Sage.

Woods, Nicola 1988: Talking shop: Sex and status as determinants of floor apportionment in a work setting. In Jennifer Coates and Deborah Cameron (eds) *Women in Their Speech Communities*. London: Longman, pp. 141–57.

26 Creating Gendered Demeanors of Authority at Work and at Home

SHARI KENDALL

1 Introduction

The movement of women into managerial and professional positions in the workplace is one of the most significant organizational changes in the past century (Burke and Davidson 1994). As women entered professions tradition-ally occupied by men, studies addressed the question of whether women and men in comparable positions linguistically constitute those positions in similar ways. The women in these studies were more likely to use "polite" language and/or less likely to use linguistic strategies that would make their authority more visible (Ainsworth-Vaughn 1998; Case 1995; Fisher 1993; Preisler 1986; Tannen 1994a; West 1990). At the same time, research on language and gender in the family addressed the question of whether mothers and fathers speak with their children in similar ways. In these studies, the mothers tended to take up less powerful roles (Ochs and Taylor 1995) or use more "polite" language than fathers (Bellinger and Gleason 1982; Gleason and Greif 1987; Snow et al. 1990). However, despite a shared focus on power and the linguistic construction of gender, studies of gender and language in the workplace and the family have proceeded independently. This chapter uses a framing approach to compare one woman's linguistic creation of authority as a parent with her ten-year-old daughter at home and as a manager with her two female subordinates at work.

This woman, whom I call Elaine, creates disparate, gendered demeanors of authority at home and at work through her face-related practices as she performs directives to influence and control her daughter and subordinates. During dinnertime at home, Elaine creates a demeanor of explicit authority characterized by values of parental care-giving and "civilized" behavior. Her directives vary linguistically based on the discursive positions she takes up within the frames she creates and maintains during dinnertime, and they reflect the dinner-related and socialization functions of mealtime. In the workplace, Elaine creates a benevolent demeanor of authority by linguistically maintaining the faces of her subordinates when asking them to perform tasks in five short encounters and in a longer review in which she provides one subordinate with feedback on her work. Her controlling actions vary linguistically based on the functions they perform within these encounters and reflect the teaching component of the review. Ironically, when Elaine directs the actions of her subordinates, she draws on mitigating strategies that evoke the qualities associated with sociocultural conceptions of "mother"; however, she does not use these strategies to the same extent to "do" her identity as a mother.

After introducing research relevant to the linguistic creation of gender and authority in the workplace and the family, I explain how individuals linguistically create gendered identities through face-related practices, and how this construction is linked with authority. The model is based on Goffman's (1967) notions of face, deference, and demeanor; Tannen's (1994b) advances in framing theory (Bateson 1972; Goffman 1974); and Davies and Harré's (1990) positioning theory. I then present the analysis of Elaine's directives to her daughter and subordinates; and, finally, I compare Elaine's directives at home and at work to ascertain whether she draws on language strategies she uses as a mother when she is speaking as a manager.

The analysis demonstrates that a framing approach can contribute a more complex understanding of the role directives play in the linguistic construction of social identities and relations. A framing approach relates the linguistic forms and meanings of utterances to the speaker's frame of the activity (as realized through talk) because the pragmatic, interactional, and social meanings of any utterance are dependent upon the frame in which they occur – that is, what the speaker is *doing* when he or she produces an utterance (Tannen 1994b). In addition, although studies find that women use face-saving strategies in both the workplace and the home, no study has examined one or more woman's actual language practices in both domains. Therefore, important differences in how women use face-saving strategies, and the extent to which they use these strategies, have not been investigated. Finally, although extensive research, including Brown and Levinson's (1987) thorough analysis of linguistic politeness phenomena, has explored the linguistic dimensions of deference, these discussions have not integrated the related concept of demeanor, even though Goffman (1967: 77) introduces deference and demeanor as "two basic elements" of the expressive component of language – that component through which individuals convey face-related meanings. As I have shown elsewhere (Kendall 1993, 1999), re-incorporating demeanor into the analysis of deference reveals that women in positions of authority in the workplace use a face-saving style both as a strategy for accomplishing work and for linguistically enhancing their identities. The analysis in this chapter provides further evidence that women use a face-related style to agentively enact – and, in fact, enhance – their authority by demonstrating that one woman creates different demeanors of authority in her roles as mother and manager.

2   Language, Gender, and Authority at Work and at Home

Studies of gender and language in the workplace suggest that some women in positions of authority use a face-saving style with their subordinates and equal-ranking colleagues in some situations in which men do not. For example, the female managers in Tannen's (1994a) study of language in several large corporations gave directives and feedback to their subordinates in ways that saved face for the subordinates. One manager used directives phrased as suggestions to get her subordinate to make changes on a document (e.g. *You might put in parentheses*) (p. 81). In contrast, a male manager gave directives and feedback in ways that reinforced status differences (e.g. *Oh, that's too dry. You have to make it snappier!*) (p. 53). West (1990) observes a similar pattern in her analysis of medical encounters: male doctors tended to aggravate directives to their patients, whereas female doctors tended to mitigate their commands. In problem-solving situations in the industrial community, Preisler (1986) finds that the managers who contributed most actively when accomplishing a task with subordinates also used more linguistic "tentativeness features," and these managers were usually women.

Studies that address parental authority in the family find that mothers take up less powerful roles and use more face-saving strategies and politeness phenomena. In their study of narrative roles at dinnertime, Ochs and Taylor (1995) discover that the mothers tended to introduce narratives, taking up the powerful role of narrative introducer, the person who controls who and what will be the focus of attention. However, fathers took up the even more powerful narrative role of problematizer or family judge, the "primary audience, judge, and critic of family members' actions, conditions, thoughts, and feelings." Both patterns contribute to a traditional arrangement of "Father knows best," which, Ochs and Taylor observe, is a configuration of power that is generally thought to be extinct in middle-class families. In a classic study of directives, Bellinger and Gleason (1982) demonstrate that the fathers in three families at home gave more directives and were more likely than the mothers to phrase directives as imperatives (*Turn the bolt with the wrench*), rather than questions (*Could you turn the bolt with the wrench?*) or statements (*The wheel is going to fall off*). Gleason and Greif (1983: 148–9) conclude, regarding this study, that fathers' "more direct, controlling, and relatively impolite" language acts as a "bridge to the outside world" because it is more cognitively and linguistically challenging than mothers' language to children. Aronsson and Thorell's (1999) analysis of children's controlling actions in role-plays of family conflict scenarios suggests that these children perceive mothers as being more likely to give reasons for their directives. The children enacted the father as "the man of ultimate action" and the mother as "compromiser and negotiator – the one who provides reasons, justifications and other mitigating accounts" (p. 43). Snow et al. (1990:

294) demonstrate that the mothers in twenty-four families were more likely to use the politeness forms *please, thank,* and *excuse*. Finally, Greif and Gleason (1980) discovered that, although both mothers and fathers prompted girls and boys to say *thank you* for a gift and *good-bye* to the researchers, the parents modeled gendered behavior themselves because the mothers were more likely than the fathers to address these forms to the researchers.

Although no studies have compared women's talk at work and at home, a few have posited a relationship between women's talk in the two domains. In two studies of women's speech in the workplace, the researchers suggest that women may draw upon language associated with mothers to enact their authority at work. In her analysis of directives given by female detectives to subordinates on a Japanese drama series, Smith (1992: 78) observes that the detectives used a "Motherese Strategy" that is not typically found in the public sphere, but is commonly used by mothers to children. These forms invoke both the authority of the mother and the solidarity between mother and child. Similarly, Wodak (1995: 45) concludes that the leadership styles of three head-mistresses (the Austrian equivalent of the principal in US schools) share a linguistic "pattern of maternity," in which they pursue their agendas through what she calls a "we discourse" that "establishes and maintains the boundaries of intimacy." Two studies of talk at home differ in their assessment of the relative power of mothers' language to children, but assume the powerlessness of women's speech, or images of women's speech, in the public domain. Based on her comparison of American and Samoan mothers' communicative practices, Ochs (1992: 337) traces powerless images of women in US society to powerless images of mothering which, she suggests, are based on the relatively accommodating language middle-class American mothers use with their children. In contrast, Cook-Gumperz (1995: 401) demonstrates that two three-year-old girls constituted mothers as speaking with power in a make-believe game of "mummies and babies" by "controlling the resources and destiny of others." As a result of her analysis, she poses the question: why do children experience the mother's role as "all-powerful," but later assume a "publicly demonstrated powerlessness" as adult women?

In summary, research pertaining to the linguistic creation of gender and authority in the workplace and the family suggests that mothers tend to take up less powerful roles than fathers at home and use a more face-saving style in both domains. The framing analysis of a woman's directives in this chapter reveals that this woman does use face-saving strategies in both domains; however, the frequency and form of these strategies differ in significant ways.

3   Creating Gendered Demeanors of Authority

A framing approach conceptualizes the creation of gendered identities as a component of the creation of identities in general and, consequently, reveals how this construction is mediated by other social parameters, roles, and identities – as scholars have recently advocated (Bucholtz 1999; Cameron 1997; Eckert and McConnell-Ginet 1992). Women and men do not generally choose linguistic options for the purpose of creating masculine or feminine identities; instead, they draw upon gendered linguistic strategies to perform pragmatic and interactional functions of language and, thus, constitute roles in a gendered way. It is the manner in which people constitute their identities when acting within a social role that is linked with gender – that is, being a "good mother," being a "good manager" (Kendall 1999). This conceptualization of language and gender is captured by Goffman's (1967: 83) conception of *demeanor*: the individual's expression of "certain desirable or undesirable qualities." Individuals interactionally construct the self through both demeanor and *deference*: the "appreciation an individual shows of another to that other." Whereas expressions of deference tend to "point to the place the individual has achieved in the hierarchy of this society," expressions of demeanor tend to point to "qualities which any social position gives its incumbents a chance to display during interaction" (pp. 82–3). Thus, demeanor is expressed through the manner in which the individual "handles" his or her social positions. Furthermore, an individual expresses deference to create and sustain the other's self, but deference is also a "means by which [the individual] expresses the fact that he [or she] is a well or badly demeaned individual" (p. 81). In other words, people display certain qualities through actions that convey demeanor, and an important component of these qualities is the manner in which they extend deference to others – that is, their face-related practices.

From this perspective, women in positions of institutional authority who linguistically downplay status differences when enacting their authority are not reluctant to exercise authority, nor are they expressing powerlessness; instead, they are exercising and constituting their authority by speaking in ways that accomplish work-related goals while maintaining the faces of their interlocutors. A number of studies provide evidence that higher-ranking individuals' use of deference with lower-ranking individuals may actually enhance their demeanor. For example, Reynolds (1985: 35) ascertains, in her examination of Japanese sentence-final particles, that higher-status individuals' use of deference may be "interpreted as a virtue of the superior" and may help the speaker "gain the inferior's genuine respect." Pearson (1988: 87) discovered, in her investigation of directives, disagreements, and suggestions in church meetings, that the minister, the highest-status individual present, used the most strategies of both power and politeness: the minister's "intentional underplaying of status and/or power, may actually enhance his prestige and power because he is not abusing the privileges of his role." Similarly, Smith-Hefner (1988: 548) concludes in her study of "basic" and "polite" language styles in Javanese society that men may "create a favorable image" by using the polite speech style that is typically used by lower-status individuals to confer respect or humble the self *vis-à-vis* a respected other. Similarly, women who use a face-saving style with their subordinates and their children may enhance their identities, albeit in a gendered way.

4 Participants and Procedure

The analysis presented in this chapter is part of a larger research study which explores the relations among work, family, gender, and talk of one woman at work and at home (Kendall 1999). The mother in this family, Elaine, volunteered to participate in the study in response to a request for volunteers that was sent over e-mail in her workplace, a large government institution in the Washington, DC area. She and her husband, Mark, work outside the home full-time. Elaine supervises two employees, Janice and Lauren; and Mark owns and operates a small roofing business. At the time of recording, Elaine and Mark were in their mid-forties and their daughter, Beth, was ten years old. The family is White and middle-class. Elaine tape-recorded naturally occurring talk herself by carrying a tape-recorder with her for a week at work and at home.

The analysis of talk is based on all the directives, excluding offers and requests for information, that Elaine addresses to Beth during dinnertime at home (71 directives) and to her subordinates at work (33 directives). Directives were classified for syntactic form (imperative, statement, question); directness (direct, indirect, off-record); and types of mitigation/aggravation (e.g. point-of-view shifts, expressions of need/obligation, lexical minimizers). Based on these classifications and the analysis of each directive in context, seven directive categories were identified, representing the primary face-related strategies Elaine uses in these encounters. These strategies range along a continuum from most face-saving to most face-threatening (see figure 26.1).

First, conventionally polite requests are questions constituted by modals and subject–auxiliary inversion (*Would you double check that for me*) (Brown and Levinson 1987). They may also include rising intonation, formulaic expressions (*please*), tag-type questions (*Would that be okay*), and prerequests (*Could you do me a favor*).

Second, directives framed as joint activity are constituted by suggestions, which are statements mitigated by modals such as *might* and *can* (*And then you can bring the plate over to Daddy*), hedges (*maybe*), and/or subjectivizers such as *think* (*I think that probably both of these should come out*) (Goodwin 1990; Tannen 1994a). In general, suggestions frame the requested action as optional, and thus convey that the participants are jointly engaged in the activity. Directives may also be framed as joint activity by the inclusion of reasons that lead the addressee "to see the reasonableness" of the directive and thus convey that the

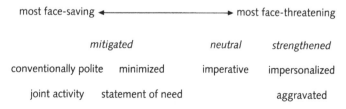

Figure 26.1   Face continuum

participants are "cooperatively involved in the relevant activity" (Brown and Levinson 1987: 125, 128).

Third, minimized imperatives are mitigated by the lexical items *just*, *little*, and *real quick* (*Just draft up a little memo to him*). They generally save the face of the other through non-imposition.

Fourth, *statements of need/obligation*, which attribute the source of the directive to exigencies of the situation, are constituted by expressions of *need* (*I need cheese grated*) and modals of obligation such as *should*, *have to*, and *supposed to* (*Beth, you're gonna have to uh heat your tortilla up*). Minimized imperatives and statements of need are mitigated, but not to the extent of requests and suggestions.

Fifth, *unmitigated imperatives* are neither mitigated nor aggravated (*Wash your hands*). They are neutral in terms of face (Blum-Kulka 1997).

Sixth, *impersonalized directives* frame the need for the directive as external to the speaker and addressee by framing the directive as a *general rule* through assertions of what the addressee will or will not do, or through avoidance of "I" and "you" by inclusive points of view (*we*, *let's*), agent deletion, general *you*, existentials, and passives (*Hey, let's not use that language. It would be "droppings," thank you*).

Finally, *aggravated directives* are constituted by any of the forms above, but are aggravated by linguistic structures or prosodic elements that increase the force of the directive (*Hey! Excuse me, let's not use that language!*) (Aronsson and Thorell 1999; Culpeper 1996; Goodwin 1990).

In the following sections, I describe Elaine's directives at home and at work, in turn. For each domain, I first describe the discursive structure of the encounter and then present the directive analysis. The first step is necessary because a framing approach requires contextual analysis of directives in order to assess their interactional and social meanings. In the dinnertime encounters, I identify the frames that Elaine creates and maintains and the positions that she takes up within these frames. A *frame* (Bateson 1972; Goffman 1974) is a set of expectations about a situated speech activity, including the participants' speaking rights and responsibilities. Davies and Harré's (1990: 46) conceptualization of *position* provides a way to refer to a participant's discursive roles within a frame: positions incorporate "a conceptual repertoire and a location for persons within the structure of rights for those that use that repertoire." In the work encounters, I identify the functions Elaine performs through her directives and the patterned sequence in which these functions occur.

5   Face-related Practices at Home

5.1   *Discursive structure: Frames and positions at dinnertime*

During the dinnertime encounters, Elaine produces the following directives: 10 polite, four joint activity, 14 minimized imperatives, four statements of necessity/obligation, 23 unmitigated imperatives, six impersonalized, and 10 aggravated. She expends linguistic effort to maintain her daughter's face in 46 per cent (n = 32), she does not use mitigating or aggravating strategies in 32 per cent (n = 23), and she strengthens 22 per cent (n = 16). The mitigating strategies she uses at dinnertime vary based on the frames she creates and maintains and the positions she takes up within these frames. There are five higher-level frames that account for "what is going on" at dinnertime: in a dinner frame, family members prepare, serve, and eat dinner; in a conversational frame, they engage in social talk; in a managerial frame, they plan and carry out activities that will occur after dinner; in a care-giving frame, parents attend to children's needs at dinnertime; and, in a socialization frame, parents monitor and correct children's behavior. Each of these frames makes discursive positions available to family members. For example, the care-giving frame makes the position of Care-giver available to parents and Care-receiver available to children. The parental positions in the other frames are Head Chef, Conversationalist, Manager, and Civilizer.

In addition, each higher-level frame and its associated framing position are linguistically realized through several lower-level frames. Like the higher-level frames, these frames are constituted, in part, by the positions that the frames make available to the participants. As Head Chef in the dinner frame, Elaine serves food (Host) and directs the preparation of food (Chef). As Care-giver in the care-giving frame, Elaine assists Beth (Assistant), teaches her dinnertime skills (Teacher), and monitors Beth's dinnertime needs (Caretaker). As Civilizer in a socialization frame, Elaine monitors Beth's dinnertime etiquette (Etiquette Enforcer), behavior (Behavior Monitor), and appearance (Appearance Monitor), and she makes sure that Beth performs dinnertime rituals (Ritual Enforcer). As Manager, Elaine plans future activities (Planner) and gets Beth ready to go (Social Secretary). The analysis excludes the Host, because Elaine addresses directives to Beth and Mark collectively; the Assistant, which is constituted by commissives rather than directives; and the conversational frame, which is constituted by requests for information rather than action. The remaining frames, principal positions, and positions appear in figure 26.2.

Frame	Dinner	Care-giving	Managerial	Socialization
Principal positions	Head Chef	Care-giver	Manager	Civilizer
Positions	Chef (Host)	Caretaker Teacher (Assistant)	Planner Social Secretary	Ritual Enforcer Appearance Monitor Behavior Monitor Etiquette Enforcer

Figure 26.2 Frames and positions at dinnertime

5.2   *Directives at dinnertime*

The first lower-level position Elaine takes up in the dinner frame is the Chef: directing the preparation of dinner. Elaine performs ten directives in this position: three conventionally polite requests, two suggestions conveying joint activity, one minimized imperative, and four unmitigated imperatives. Although this position is split evenly between directives with and without face-saving strategies (requests and suggestions versus imperatives), the sequential and functional distributions of these directive categories reveal the greater salience of the mitigated forms: Elaine uses conventionally polite requests and suggestions to identify tasks for Beth to perform, and she uses imperatives to give Beth instructions for accomplishing these tasks. In example (1), Elaine uses conventional politeness to ask Beth to bring her something (dots indicate pauses of one second per dot):

(1)
Elaine: Can you get that for me please . . .
          Just about have all this coming together.

Elaine phrases the directive as a conventionally polite request by using a modal and question inversion, *can you*, and the politeness form, *please*. Using conventional politeness conveys that Beth is worthy of having her face maintained, even though she is performing tasks that, in actuality, may not be voluntary.

In (2), Elaine uses a suggestion to identify a task for Beth to perform and then uses imperatives to provide her with specific instructions (dashes indicate aborted utterances):

(2)
Elaine: Um . you could spoon in that –
          Uh . shake this up.
          Don't get it on the recorder.
          Just spoon in that, and stir it around.

Elaine frames the initial directive as a suggestion by telling Beth that she *could* perform the action, conveying that Beth's actions are voluntary and, thus, framing Beth's actions as joint activity.

Elaine takes up the framing position of the Care-giver in a care-giving frame when she attends to Beth's needs at dinnertime. The first position in this frame is the Caretaker, in which she directs Beth to perform, for herself, the kinds of actions a parent would perform for a younger child. In (3), Elaine first takes up the position of the Host (a position constituted by offers in the form of questions) by offering Beth some food, but she then reframes the offer as a directive, shifting from Host to Caretaker:

(3)
Elaine: You want some milk? water?
  → You need to have some fluids.
Beth: Yeah, I'm getting some milk.
Elaine: Go ahead and get some.

Elaine frames the directive as being for Beth's own good by referring to Beth's *need* for fluids as the basis of the command. Likewise, other directives in this position are ultimately for Beth's benefit. Therefore, since these actions do not represent a significant face threat, it is not surprising that unmitigated imperatives predominate in this position: six unmitigated, one minimized imperative, and two statements of Beth's needs.

Elaine takes up the position of the Teacher in the care-giving frame when she teaches Beth to do specific tasks to help prepare dinner, to serve herself, or to help clean up. This position is characterized by imperatives accompanied by praise: four unmitigated, four minimized, and one suggestion. In (4), Elaine instructs Beth as she prepares her burrito (square brackets enclose simultaneous talk; angle brackets enclose the manner in which an utterance is spoken):

(4)
Elaine: Okay, just kind of flip it over.
  Keep it compact . . .
  That's it. [Roll, roll.]
Beth: [Shoot.   ]
Elaine: Okay, tuck that under . . .
  <*increasing emphasis*> You got it. You've got it. You've got it!
  You did it yourself!
  Great!

This teaching method tends to take longer than it would if Elaine did the task herself, but she is teaching Beth dinnertime skills.

In the socialization frame, Elaine takes up the framing position of the Civilizer when she gives Beth explicit injunctions to behave and speak in appropriate ways. Although this frame involves teaching, the focus is on appropriate behavior at the dinner table rather than eating and cooking skills. The first two positions in this frame are characterized by conventional politeness. Elaine takes up the first position, the Ritual Enforcer, three times when she asks or reminds Beth to perform formal rituals at dinnertime. In (5), she uses a conventionally polite request to ask Beth to say the blessing:

(5)
Elaine: Do you want to say the blessing real quick?
Beth: Okay.
. . .
Elaine: After you finish chewing that carrot? <*chuckles*>

In this position, Elaine uses two conventionally polite requests and one imperative mitigated by *please* (to remind her to ask to be excused before leaving the table).

Elaine takes up the position of Appearance Monitor when she tells Beth to attend to her appearance at the dinner table. In (6), Elaine asks Beth to clean some hair off her face:

(6)
Elaine: → You have hair on your face. Will you clean it off for me?
          I'm talking about one side, on your cheek,
          → see just brush it off, right there, that far side by me.

Elaine uses a conventionally polite form to tell Beth to remove the hair. She then uses a minimized imperative (*just brush it off*) when Beth does not comply. In this position, Elaine uses one conventionally polite directive, two minimized imperatives, and one unmitigated imperative.

Elaine takes up the third position in the socialization frame, the Behavior Monitor, when she tells Beth to perform an action or to cease one that is not directly tied to dinnertime etiquette. The majority of directives in this position are aggravated: eight aggravated directives and two unmitigated imperatives. In (7), Elaine asks Beth to help clean up, using a conventionally polite request. When Beth does not comply, Elaine reprimands her (empty parentheses indicate unintelligible speech):

(7)
Elaine: Can you help clear up both ( ).
Beth: I cleaned up my plate!
          <singing> ( ).
Elaine: → How about helping us, thank you!

Although the directive is phrased as a suggestion, it is aggravated by emphatic intonation and the otherwise polite *thank you*. Snow et al. (1990: 296) find similar cases in which the use of "politeness forms often actually reinforced the parental position of power by expressing exasperation or impatience."

Elaine takes up the final position in the socialization frame, the Etiquette Enforcer, when she monitors and teaches Beth appropriate language at dinnertime. This position is characterized by impersonalization: six impersonalized directives and one aggravated. In (8), Elaine uses impersonalizing strategies to reprimand Beth for inappropriate language. What Beth says is not intelligible on the tape-recording, but Elaine's response clearly indicates that she finds it offensive:

(8)
Beth: ( )
Elaine: ((*apparently gives Beth a disapproving look*))
Beth: What.

Elaine: → That's not something we hear at the table, please. Thank you.
((*to Mark*)) Dad, will you give her a little dish?

Elaine uses impersonalizing strategies to frame the directive as a general rule: the statement form and inclusive pronoun *we* cast the directive as being applicable to everyone, not to Beth alone. In this way, she phrases the directive as though she is "merely drawing attention to the existence of a rule" (Brown and Levinson 1987: 207). The impersonalizing strategies strengthen the force of the directives by endowing them with an existence outside Elaine's control.

In the final frame, managerial, Elaine takes up the framing position of the Manager when she plans Beth's social life and makes sure that Beth gets where she needs to go. In the first position, the Planner, Elaine identifies actions that Beth must perform in the near future. This position is characterized by strategies that appeal to Beth's voluntary compliance: four conventionally polite requests, a suggestion, and two statements of need/obligation. In the latter case, she frames the required action as obligatory, but provides reasons as well, conveying the desire for Beth not only to perform an action, but to perform it willingly. In (9), she tells Beth that she has to go to bed early so that she can get up early:

(9)
Elaine: You have to go to bed . earlier . so . because you're getting up and going to work with me tomorrow so . 'cause I have to leave earlier.

Elaine frames the required action (going to bed early) as being obligatory through a statement of necessity (*you have to*), but she appeals to Beth for cooperative involvement as well.

The second position in the managerial frame is the Social Secretary. This position is not a dinnertime position *per se*, but occurs after dinner when the family is still chatting in the kitchen. For example, on the first night, Beth has her horse-riding lesson later that evening so she has to get ready to go as soon as she finishes eating. In (10), Elaine shifts from the conversational frame, in which they are discussing how long a drive would be on a future vacation, to the managerial frame by telling Beth to get ready:

(10)
Elaine: I don't think it's very far.
Mark: ( )
Elaine: It couldn't be any further than when we drove to Ohio.
Mark: No, about six hours.
Beth: Excuse me!
Elaine: → Okay, go ahead and get your vitamin, and go up and brush your teeth, 'cause you're gonna . probably have to leave about . quarter after or so.
Beth: The only weird thing is, remember when I rode O'Connor?

Although Elaine tells Beth to get ready, Beth introduces a new topic, which they discuss for several minutes before Elaine repeats her directive. The Social Secretary position is characterized by rapid lists of short imperatives: six unmitigated, five minimized, and one aggravated (when Beth does not comply with a previous directive).

5.3   Summary: Directives at dinnertime

Table 26.1 summarizes the face-related strategies Elaine uses in her directives to Beth at dinnertime. Elaine's directives vary linguistically based on the discursive positions she takes up, and they reflect the dinner-related and socialization functions of mealtime. The majority of her directives at dinnertime are unmitigated imperatives (32 per cent, n = 23). Together, unmitigated imperatives and minimized imperatives constitute more than half of her directives (52 per cent, n = 37). Imperatives reflect the dinner-related function of mealtime: she uses them in the dinner and care-giving frames to give Beth instructions for preparing dinner (Chef), to teach her dinnertime skills (Teacher), and to perform dinner-related actions (Caretaker). The directive categories that Elaine uses the most frequently, following imperatives, are aggravated (14 per cent, n = 10), conventionally polite (14 per cent, n = 10), and impersonalized (8 per cent, n = 6). These strategies reflect the socialization function of mealtime. Elaine gives aggravated and impersonalized directives for Beth to behave in socially appropriate ways (Monitor, Etiquette Enforcer); and she uses conventional politeness when asking Beth to do something she might ask of another adult: helping to prepare dinner (Chef), requesting that she say the blessing (Ritual Enforcer), and arranging future activities with her (Planner). Based on these patterns, Elaine creates a demeanor of explicit authority characterized by values of parental care-giving and "civilized" behavior.

Table 26.1   Face-related strategies at home

	n	%
Polite	10	14
Joint activity	4	6
Necessity/obligation	4	6
Minimized imperative	14	20
Imperative	23	32
Impersonalized	6	8
Aggravated	10	14
Total	71	100

6 Face-related Practices at Work

6.1 Directives at work: Five short encounters

The analysis of workplace interaction is based on all Elaine's tape-recorded work encounters with her subordinates: five brief encounters (11 directives) and one longer encounter in which she provides Lauren with feedback on a contract (22 directives). I discuss directives in these two contexts in turn. In the five brief encounters, Elaine produces the following directives: two polite, seven joint activity, one minimized imperative, and one unmitigated imperative. She expends linguistic effort to maintain her subordinates' faces in 91 per cent (n = 10), and she does not use any strengthening strategies. In the previous section, I suggest that Elaine uses conventionally polite directives when asking Beth to perform actions she would ask of an adult and, thus, models the appropriate use of overtly polite language. In her directives to her subordinates, Elaine displays the behavior she models for her daughter at home. She uses conventionally polite requests when she contacts her subordinates to "request" that they do something for her. In (11), Elaine calls Lauren on the telephone and asks her to come to her office:

(11)
Elaine: Lauren, I just talked to Tim Brown,
and he said interest is not allowable so . um
→ Do you want to come in here real quick, are you busy.

The directive is conventionally polite based on the modal (*want to*) and inversion. She also minimizes the requested action (*come in here*) through the use of *real quick*; and she adds a tag question that further conveys her wish not to impose (*are you busy*).

In general, Elaine positions her subordinates as equals engaged in joint activity by phrasing her directives as suggestions, conveying that the subordinates can decide whether to perform the action or not. These linguistic forms influence the interactional positionings of the participants by casting the subordinates – at least interactionally – as status equals. In (12), Elaine and Janice discuss some issues in Elaine's office; then, as Janice is leaving, Elaine tells her to ask a visitor they are expecting about a site visit:

(12)
Janice: There are no other proposals coming in?
Elaine: → Right, and then let's ask her too . bout the site visit too.
Janice: Okay.
Elaine: So that doesn't slip our minds, so that she's thinking –
Janice: <*louder*> Yeah.

Elaine tells Janice to ask the visitor about the site visit by using the inclusive pronoun *let's*, even though Janice will perform the action alone. However, her point-of-view shift maintains Janice's face by creating "common ground" (Brown and Levinson 1987: 119). She reinforces the cooperative component by using inclusive *our* in the reason she provides, *so that doesn't slip our minds*. Finally, Elaine's lexical choice, *slip*, maintains Janice's face by minimizing the importance of the required action.

6.2   *Directives at work: Reviewing a subordinate's work*

Elaine produces 22 directives during the half-hour meeting with her subordinate, Lauren: two polite, eight joint activity, two necessity/obligation, five minimized imperatives, and five imperatives. She expends linguistic effort to maintain Lauren's face in 77 per cent (n = 17); the remaining 23 per cent are neutral (n = 5). However, although she frames directives as joint activity in only 36 per cent of the directives in the review (n = 8), an analysis of the discourse structure of the activity reveals the salience of this directive type within the activity and, thus, to the identities and relations Elaine creates. Elaine frames the review as a learning experience for her subordinate by identifying problems, identifying how Lauren can correct the problems, and providing reasons and explanations. As a result, the review is constituted by a series of ten sequences. In each sequence, Elaine first identifies the problematic area by referring to the contract they are reviewing; she then gives an *identifying directive* that identifies how Lauren can correct the problem. Following this initial directive, Elaine gives directives that perform four other functions: she *explains* how to correct errors addressed by identifying directives; she *instructs* her with specifics about how to accomplish a previous directive; she *responds* to Lauren's questions not previously discussed by Elaine; and she *summarizes* previous directives. In addition to patterns of directive functions, the ten sequences are discursively delineated by the discourse markers *okay, then,* or *and then*. Elaine gives one identifying directive for each of the ten sequences, but one is repeated, bringing the total to eleven. She produces four explaining, two instructing, two responding, and three summarizing directives.

The five directive functions in the review vary, first, in terms of mitigation type (presence or absence of reasons) and the syntactic forms in which these reasons occur. All fifteen of the identifying and explanatory directives have reasons. Eleven of these have internal reasons in the syntactic form "reason *so* directive" or "directive *because* reason." The remaining four have external reasons. In contrast, the instructing, responding, and summarizing directives do not have reasons. The summarizing directives are differentiated by discourse markers within the syntactic form "*yeah* or *so* directive." Second, the five directive functions are distinguished by face-related strategies. The responding, instructing, and summarizing directives are imperatives (the two responding are unmitigated and the two instructing are minimized). In contrast, the majority of identifying directives are suggestions (45 per cent, n = 5). Together, suggestions and requests constitute 67 per cent (n = 7) of the eleven identifying directives. Of the remaining, two are imperatives and two are statements of need. The following analysis of two directive sequences illustrates the structure of the review and how the linguistic forms of the directives reflect (and constitute) this structure.

Elaine begins the review by noting that Lauren made some positive revisions to the first draft of the contract. She then introduces the first problem that remains in the second draft (double parentheses enclose lexical changes to protect anonymity):

(13)
Elaine: Okay . um all this stuff that you've . picked up was fine.
          Let me get the ((client's)) contract.
          Under the travel clause –
          Remember when we had that . definition of domestic travel .
Lauren: Mhm.
Elaine: They didn't put that in.

The problem Elaine points out is that the contract does not have the correct *definition of domestic travel*. Elaine's identification of the problem is potentially face-threatening because Lauren should have discovered the discrepancy. Elaine maintains Lauren's face by emphasizing joint activity: she evokes shared knowledge by reminding Lauren of the definition (*remember when*) and by using inclusive *we*. These strategies contrast with possible unmitigated criticism, such as "You didn't make sure the contract included the definition I gave you." Elaine also saves Lauren's face by attributing the error to the client alone, *They didn't put that in*, rather than criticizing Lauren for not identifying and correcting the error herself.

After pointing out the problem, Elaine gives an identifying directive in (14) to identify how Lauren can correct it (double question marks indicate continuative high-rise intonation):

(14)
Elaine: → You might want to mention that to them, and see what they say about it.
Lauren: Okay, [will you]–
Elaine: [I'm sure] it's probably like a universal definition?? but–

Elaine maintains Lauren's face by downplaying the importance of the error. She phrases the directive as a suggestion through the use of *might want*, which makes the action seem optional; and she uses the word *mention*, which downplays the importance of the error by downplaying the corrective action. She further maintains Lauren's face by acknowledging that it was common sense to use this definition: *I'm sure it's probably like a universal definition??*

In (15), Lauren explains her reasoning for not checking or changing the definition. However, Elaine reiterates the necessary action by issuing a second directive to explain why Lauren must talk to the client (*her* in the example):

(15)
Lauren: You know what I thought, else, they might be doing?
Elaine: Hm?
Lauren: You know is . negotiating ahead of time . money. ( )
Elaine: Yeah, which is fine.
          → That's just what we had talked about before so ask her about that.
Lauren: Okay.
Elaine: Okay.

Elaine maintains Lauren's face in this explanatory directive by appealing to joint activity through inclusive *we* and providing a reason in the form "reason *so* directive": (*That's just what we had talked about before*) *so* (*ask her about that*).

Elaine begins the second directive sequence in (16) by using the discourse marker *okay*, and then pointing out the problem in the contract:

(16)
Elaine: Okay, now see all this stuff?? the sharing of ((samples))??
Lauren: Mhm.
Elaine: and all this stuff right here??
          is not in their . contract.
          So I'm not sure where this . came from .
Lauren: Well–

When Elaine points out the information that is not in the contract, Lauren begins to explain (*Well–*), but Elaine does not let her take the floor at this point. Instead, in (17), she attempts to give the initial directive that will identify how Lauren can correct the error:

(17)
Elaine: Excuse me, so I think we need to check with–
Lauren: Remember they want . them . to interact?? . . with each other??

Although Elaine is not able to complete her directive because Lauren again begins to explain, it is clear that the directive displays the face-related strategies Elaine typically uses for identifying directives: she frames the directive with *I think*, which makes the specified action seem optional because it is phrased as Elaine's opinion, and she gives a reason in the form "reason *so* directive": (*I'm not sure where this . came from*) *so* (*I think we need to check with–*). She also conveys joint activity by using *we* when it is actually Lauren who will be checking.

Elaine's second attempt to give the identifying directive in this sequence, in (18), is less mitigated than her attempt in (17) above. She omits the subjectivizer

I think and eliminates the point-of-view shift by stating that *you need* instead of *we need*, putting on-record the fact that it is Lauren who must perform the action:

(18)
Elaine: Right.
  → But . what you'll need to do–
  this is where I said . for these . two things??–

Although Elaine uses *you* instead of *we*, she mitigates this directive through the use of *need*, mitigating the required action by presenting it as being obligatory for external reasons, not because Elaine requires it. However, again, Elaine does not finish the directive. This time, she backs up to provide further information.

Lauren asks a question and, at this point, Elaine abandons the unfinished directive to respond. Example (19) illustrates a typical response sequence in which Elaine responds with an unmitigated imperative and then gives instructions with a minimized imperative:

(19)
Lauren: Oh, that should be in the work statement, right?
Elaine: No, that's fine.
  → Ask um . Kent.
Lauren: Okay.
Elaine: Isn't he the ((person responsible)) now?
Lauren: uh huh.
Elaine: → Just draft up a little memo to him .
  asking him to look over this . draft subcontract agreement
  and see if you [have any .]
Lauren: [Okay.]
Elaine: questions

In the first directive, Elaine answers Lauren by telling her that she needs to ask Kent and, in the second directive, she tells her how to ask him. In the latter, she uses a non-imposing imperative in which she minimizes the action Lauren must perform with *just* (*just draft*) and the required product with *little* (*a little memo*).

6.3 Summary: Directives at work

Table 26.2 summarizes the face-related strategies Elaine uses in her directives to her subordinates at work. Elaine's directives to her subordinates vary linguistically based on the functions they perform within these encounters and the teaching component of the review. Elaine positions her subordinates as equals engaged in joint activity in 46 per cent of her directives (n = 15). She

Table 26.2   Face-related strategies at work

	n	%
Polite	4	12
Joint activity	15	46
Necessity/obligation	2	6
Minimized imperative	6	18
Imperative	6	18
Impersonalized	0	0
Aggravated	0	0
Total	33	100

uses this strategy in the review to identify solutions to problems and to give further explanations, and she uses them to direct her subordinates on a regular basis. She uses minimized imperatives and unmitigated imperatives much less frequently, both at 18 per cent (n = 6). In the review, she uses minimized imperatives to give instructions and to summarize previous directives, and she uses unmitigated imperatives to respond to questions. In the shorter encounters, she uses imperatives to close encounters.

Through these strategies, Elaine creates a benevolent demeanor of authority, a gendered mode of enacting authority that is recognized and appreciated by her subordinates. In an interview with Lauren, I asked her to describe an ideal "group leader," which is the position that Elaine holds. She responded to the question by referring to Elaine:

(20)
Lauren: Honestly. . . . I–I mean I would say Elaine would be.

When asked why, Lauren referred to the manner in which Elaine gives her feedback on her work, which is the speech event examined in this section:

(21)
Lauren: She's a–um, she's–she always gives you–
            she'll give constructive criticism.
            She'll never say "well, this was just terrible," and mark everything up.
            She'll explain to you, "Well the–you know, what you did was fine"
            you know,
            "but let me send you a–a sample of," you know,
            "the way I've done it in the past and next time you can use that."

In her portrayal of Elaine, Lauren uses many of the mitigating strategies Elaine actually uses in the review. She uses an aggravated lexical item to illustrate how Elaine does not give feedback: *She'll never say "well, this was just terrible."* When Lauren provides an example of how Elaine does give feedback, she casts Elaine as beginning with reassurance, *what you did was fine*; emphasizes Elaine's teaching approach, *She'll explain to you*; and gives a directive phrased as a suggestion: *"but let me send you a–a sample of,"* you know, *"the way I've done it in the past and next time you can use that."* Lauren phrases the directive (in Elaine's voice) as being an opinion, *the way I've done it*, and as being optional by saying *and next time you can use that* – as though the end of the sentence were: *if you want to.*

7 Speaking as Mother and Manager

There are two possible ways to address the question of whether Elaine draws on strategies she uses as a mother when speaking as a manager: first, whether Elaine uses similar language structures and mitigating strategies, and/or creates similar demeanors of authority when speaking as mother and manager; and, second, when she speaks as a manager, whether she uses linguistic options and strategies that evoke the qualities associated with sociocultural conceptions of "mother." The latter claim would predict that some women in positions of authority may speak in ways associated with mothers whether or not they have children themselves. The answer to the first question is both yes and no. Elaine does draw from a limited repertoire of linguistic structures when speaking as mother and manager: for example, she uses the same minimizers in both domains (*just, little, kind of,* and *real quick*). In addition, she uses a limited repertoire of mitigating strategies in both domains as well: conventional politeness, joint activity, expressions of need/obligation, minimizers, and impersonalizing strategies. However, overall, she does not construct similar demeanors of authority in these positions.

The primary difference between the demeanors of authority Elaine creates when speaking with her daughter and her subordinates is the extent to which she makes this authority manifest. Table 26.3 shows the percentages of mitigation types in both domains, using the face continuum that was introduced in figure 26.1.

Table 26.3 Face continuum: home and work

	Home		Work	
	n	**%**	**n**	**%**
Mitigated	14	20	19	58
Minimally mitigated	18	26	8	24
Neutral	23	32	6	18
Strengthened	16	22	0	0
Total	71	100	33	100

Elaine uses face-related strategies at all points on the continuum when speaking with her daughter: mitigated (20 per cent), minimally mitigated (26 per cent), neutral (32 per cent), and strengthened (22 per cent). In contrast, in the workplace, she gives directives only on the mitigated end of the scale, and the most frequent are the most mitigated: mitigated (58 per cent), minimally mitigated (24 per cent), neutral (18 per cent), and none strengthened. Through her face-related practices, Elaine creates a demeanor of explicit authority at home by using directive forms that make her authority more visible, whereas she creates a benevolent demeanor of authority at work by using directive forms that interactionally downplay status differences. Through the use of these strategies, she creates a frame in which she and her subordinates are jointly engaged in the activity as contributors who (on the surface) both decide what needs to be done. In this way, she expends linguistic effort to save the faces of her subordinates when performing a task which, in its very nature, positions her as an authority: telling her subordinates what to do. However, the asymmetrical frame of the encounter is the key to her construction of authority: if she draws authority from her institutional status, this status itself frames the encounter, making it possible for her to make her contributions consistent with face rather than framing them in ways that explicitly recreate her status.

The answer to the second question is yes: Elaine does use linguistic options and strategies that evoke the qualities associated with sociocultural conceptions of "mother" when speaking as a manager. However, ironically, she does not use these strategies to the same extent to "do" her identity as a mother. In her description of the leadership styles of the three headmistresses, Wodak (1995: 45, 54) suggests that women in positions of authority may draw on a "we discourse" that "establishes and maintains the boundaries of intimacy." Her examples include strategies through which participants convey joint activity. It is these very strategies that most differentiate Elaine's directives at work and at home. Whereas the highest percentage of her directives at work appeal to joint activity (46 per cent, n = 15 of 33), very few of her directives at home are framed in this way (6 per cent, n = 4 of 71). By using this strategy in the workplace, Elaine uses a style that reflects sociocultural conceptions of a nurturing mother.

In conclusion, Elaine constitutes her parental and managerial authority through the frames she creates and maintains, the positions she takes up within these frames, the discursive functions she performs within these positions, and the linguistic forms she chooses to constitute these discursive structures. The face-related strategies Elaine uses when directing the actions of her daughter and subordinates reflect the discursive structures of the encounters, but they reflect socially relevant choices as well. Elaine chooses, to a certain extent, the frames she will create and maintain. At work, she chooses to frame the review as a learning experience for her subordinate, rather than, for example, giving her a list of items to correct. At home, she chooses to maintain certain of the frames at dinnertime; for example, although a socialization frame (enforcing appropriate language and dinnertime rituals) is common, it is not essential and, therefore, represents a choice. The frames she chooses make certain positions available to the participants, and these positions reflect and constitute the participants' identities and social relations. By choosing to frame the review as a learning experience, she takes up the position of a Teacher. In the dinner encounters, she takes up multiple positions in relation to her daughter: Head Chef, Caregiver, Conversationalist, Manager, and Civilizer. Finally, although the frames and positions Elaine creates and maintains entail certain pragmatic functions, she chooses the mitigating strategies and other linguistic forms to perform these functions within particular sequences (e.g. the suggestion–instruction sequence in the Chef position). Therefore, although Elaine's face-related practices reflect the discursive structure of these encounters, each level of interaction represents a choice as well and, thus, is a potential vehicle for the linguistic creation of gendered identities.

As previous research suggests, Elaine, like some other women in positions of authority, linguistically downplays her institutional authority through face-related practices. In contrast, although studies of mother–child interaction demonstrate that mothers use face-related strategies when giving directives to their children, the comparison of Elaine's directives at home and at work reveals that she does not use face-related strategies to the same extent in these domains. Through her face-related practices, Elaine constructs demeanors of authority differentiated by the extent to which she makes her authority manifest when speaking as a mother and a manager.

REFERENCES

Ainsworth-Vaughn, Nancy 1998: *Claiming Power in Doctor–Patient Talk*. Oxford: Oxford University Press.

Aronsson, Karin and Thorell, Mia 1999: Family politics in children's play directives. *Journal of Pragmatics* 31: 25–47.

Bateson, Gregory 1972: *Steps to an Ecology of Mind*. New York: Ballantine.

Bellinger, David C. and Gleason, Jean Berko 1982: Sex differences in parental directives to young children. *Sex Roles* 8: 1123–39.

Blum-Kulka, Shoshana 1997: *Dinner Talk: Cultural Patterns of Sociability and Socialization in Family Discourse*. Mahwah, NJ: Lawrence Erlbaum.

Brown, Penelope and Levinson, Stephen 1987: *Politeness: Some Universals in Language Usage*. Cambridge: Cambridge University Press.

Bucholtz, Mary 1999: Bad examples: Transgression and progress in language and gender studies. In Mary Bucholtz, Anita C. Liang, and Laurel A. Sutton (eds) *Reinventing Identities: The Gendered Self in Discourse*. New York: Oxford University Press, pp. 3–24.

Burke, Ronald J. and Davidson, Marilyn J. 1994: Women in management: Current research issues. In Ronald J. Burke and Marilyn J. Davidson (eds) *Women in Management: Current Research Issues*. London: Paul Chapman Publishing, pp. 1–8.

Cameron, Deborah 1997: Performing gender identity: Young men's talk and the construction of heterosexual masculinity. In Sally Johnson and Ulrike Hanna Meinhof (eds) *Language and Masculinity*. Oxford: Blackwell, pp. 47–64.

Case, Susan Schick 1995: Gender, language and the professions: Recognition of wide-verbal-repertoire speech. *Studies in the Linguistic Sciences* 25: 149–92.

Cook-Gumperz, Jenny 1995: Reproducing the discourse of mothering: How gendered talk makes gendered lives. In Kira Hall and Mary Bucholtz (eds) *Gender Articulated: Language and the Socially Constructed Self*. New York and London: Routledge, pp. 401–19.

Culpeper, Jonathan 1996: Towards an anatomy of impoliteness. *Journal of Pragmatics* 25: 349–68.

Davies, Bronwyn and Harré, Rom 1990: Positioning: Conversation and the production of selves. *Journal for the Theory of Social Behavior* 20: 43–63.

Eckert, Penelope and McConnell-Ginet, Sally 1992: Think practically and look locally: Language and gender as community-based practice. *Annual Review of Anthropology* 21: 461–90.

Fisher, Sue 1993: Gender, power, resistance: Is care the remedy? In Sue Fisher and Kathy Davis (eds) *Negotiating at the Margins: The Gendered Discourse of Power and Resistance*. New Brunswick, NJ: Rutgers University Press, pp. 87–121.

Gleason, Jean Berko and Greif, Esther Blank 1983: Men's speech to young children. In Barrie Thorne, Cheris Kramarae, and Nancy Henley (eds) *Language, Gender and Society*. Rowley, MA: Newbury House, pp. 140–50.

Gleason, Jean Berko and Greif, Esther Blank 1987: Sex differences in parent–child interaction. In Susan U. Philips, Susan Steele, and Christine Tanz (eds) *Language, Gender, and Sex in Comparative Perspective*. Cambridge: Cambridge University Press, pp. 189–99.

Goffman, Erving 1967: *Interaction Ritual: Essays on Face-to-face Behavior*. New York: Pantheon.

Goffman, Erving 1974: *Frame Analysis: An Essay on the Organization of Experience*. Boston, MA: Northeastern University Press.

Goodwin, Marjorie Harness 1990: *He-Said-She-Said: Talk as Social Organization among Black Children*. Bloomington, IN: Indiana University Press.

Greif, Esther B. and Gleason, Jean Berko 1980: Hi, thanks, and goodbye: More routine information. *Language in Society* 9: 159–66.

Kendall, Shari 1993: Constructing Competence: Gender and Mitigation at a Radio Network. Paper presented at the Annual Meeting of the American Association for Applied Linguistics, Baltimore.

Kendall, Shari 1999: The Interpenetration of (Gendered) Spheres: An Interactional Sociolinguistic Analysis of a Mother at Work and at Home. Unpublished dissertation, Georgetown University.

Kendall, Shari under review: The balancing act at home: Framing gendered identities at dinnertime. Unpublished MS.

Ochs, Elinor 1992: Indexing gender. In Alessandro Duranti and Charles Goodwin (eds) *Rethinking Context: Language as an Interactive Phenomenon*. Cambridge: Cambridge University Press, pp. 335–58.

Ochs, Elinor and Taylor, Carolyn 1995: The "father knows best" dynamic in dinnertime narratives. In Kira Hall and Mary Bucholtz (eds) *Gender Articulated: Language and the Socially Constructed Self*. New York and London: Routledge, pp. 97–120.

Pearson, Bethyl 1988: Power and politeness in conversation: Encoding of face-threatening acts at church business meetings. *Anthropological Linguistics* 30: 68–93.

Preisler, Bent 1986: *Linguistic Sex Roles in Conversation: Social Variation in the Expression of Tentativeness in English*. Berlin: Mouton de Gruyter.

Reynolds, Katsue Akiba 1985: Female speakers of Japanese. *Feminist Issues* 5: 13–46.

Smith, Janet S. 1992: Women in charge: Politeness and directives in the speech of Japanese women. *Language in Society* 21: 59–82.

Smith-Hefner, Nancy J. 1988: Women and politeness: The Javanese example. *Language in Society* 17: 535–54.

Snow, Catherine E., Perlmann, Rivka Y., Gleason, Jean Berko, and Hooshyar, Nahid 1990: Developmental perspectives on politeness: Sources of children's knowledge. *Journal of Pragmatics* 14: 289–305.

Tannen, Deborah 1994a: *Talking from 9 to 5: Women and Men in the Workplace: Language, Sex and Power*. New York: Avon Books.

Tannen, Deborah 1994b: The sex-class linked framing of talk at work. In Deborah Tannen (ed.) *Gender and Discourse*. New York: Oxford University Press, pp. 95–221.

West, Candace 1990: Not just "doctor's orders": Directive-response sequences in patients' visits to women and men physicians. *Discourse & Society* 1: 85–113.

Wodak, Ruth 1995: Power, discourse, and styles of female leadership in school committee meetings. In David Corson (ed.) *Discourse and Power in Educational Organizations*. Cresskill, NJ: Hampton, pp. 31–54.

27 Schooled Language: Language and Gender in Educational Settings

JOAN SWANN

1 Introduction

In referring to "schooled language," I have in mind the spoken and written language that, in various guises, pervades schools and classrooms: the language through which teaching and learning, school and classroom organization, and "discipline" take place; the language that is taught and assessed as part of the formal curriculum; but also the language that escapes adult intervention – that hangs around playgrounds, corridors, the fringes of lessons. Through their participation in diverse educational language events, girls and boys develop certain ways of using language; they also become certain kinds of students, and, more generally, certain kinds of people. Insofar as gender is "done" in educational settings it is done, to a large extent, through language. And insofar as language is gendered in educational settings, this will affect girls' and boys' development as "schooled subjects," their experiences of education, and what they get out of it.

Research carried out in educational settings may (like research in other contexts) contribute to theoretical debate about language and gender. But it is also bound up with distinctly practical concerns, which raise equally important issues for researchers. In this chapter I want to examine three "shifts" that have taken place in recent years, that are relevant to the conduct of research in education and that are, to differing degrees, relevant to research carried out in other contexts. These are shifts in conceptions of "language" and "gender"; in educational policy and practice; and in contexts of communication – principally, the increasing importance of electronic communication. Educational research has become "unsettled" in several respects, and the points I identify below pose certain dilemmas for researchers.

2 Shifting Conceptions of "Language" and "Gender"

A great deal of research on language, gender, and education has been concerned to document differences and inequalities in girls' and boys' language behavior. Girls and boys were observed to have different speaking styles, they made different reading choices, they wrote in different ways and about different topics. But boys' speaking styles allowed them to dominate classroom interaction, so that girls had limited opportunities to contribute; books and other resources used in schools contained many more male than female characters and examples; male characters in stories were more active and had less restricted roles than female characters; information books often neglected women's and girls' experiences and contributions to society; even in literacy, an area associated with high achievement amongst girls, there were arguments that girls' success in school did not help them – and in certain respects hindered them – in doing well outside school, and particularly in gaining high-status careers. "Equal opportunities" initiatives, designed to counteract such imbalances and inequalities, have included encouraging girls to contribute more in class discussions, encouraging more collaborative talk between students, introducing books/resources containing less stereotyped images, and broadening the range of reading and writing carried out by girls and boys. (For a review of these developments, see Swann 1992.)

The picture of difference and (consequent) inequality that I have sketched out above comes from research carried out, in the main, since the 1970s. It is, therefore, an "established" set of research findings that has had an impact on policy and practice in Britain and several other countries. It is, however, challenged by a shift in conceptions of language and gender that has both theoretical and practical implications. I'm referring here to what might be termed the postmodern shift that has affected language and gender research in general, not just in educational settings: a development that may be represented as running from relative fixity to relative fluidity in terms of how "language" and "gender" are conceived and how the two are seen to inter-relate. Recent research on language and gender has tended to focus on diversity (prioritizing differences amongst women/girls and amongst men/boys rather than seeing gender as a "binary" distinction); on context and performativity (seeing gender as something that is "done" in context rather than as a social attribute, and also seeing language as inherently context-dependent); and on uncertainty and ambiguity (in terms of the meanings of what language users say and do). Several collections covering aspects of language and gender both address and exemplify such preoccupations (e.g. Bergvall, Bing, and Freed 1996; Bucholtz, Liang, and Sutton 1999; Hall and Bucholtz 1995; Johnson and Meinhof 1997; Wodak 1997).

To illustrate the implications of this shift I shall look at three papers that, in various ways, challenge a distinction that has often been made in research on spoken language, between "cooperative" speaking styles (associated with female speakers) and "competitive" speaking styles (associated with male speakers). I have chosen the cooperative/competitive distinction because it is educationally relevant. It has been associated, for instance, with "male dominance" in classroom settings, with female students having less opportunity to participate in class discussion, and with certain inequalities in assessment practices (see e.g. Cheshire and Jenkins 1991; Jenkins and Cheshire 1990; Holmes 1994; and various studies discussed in Swann 1992). There has also been some debate over whether changes to classroom talk to render this more collaborative may be considered a process of "feminization" (see discussion of this in Swann and Graddol 1995). Any challenges to the cooperative/competitive distinction, therefore, have practical as well as theoretical significance.

Roger Hewitt (1997) argues that "cooperation" has functioned more as a moral or political term than as an analytical one, and that insufficient attention has been paid to the different ways in which cooperation may be done, or the different forms this may take. Hewitt distinguishes between "declarative" (individually oriented) and "coordinative" (collectivity oriented) dimensions in talk. Cooperation, he suggests, may be done by asserting the coordinative dimension (emphasizing interconnectedness) or by denying the declarative dimension (downplaying self-interest).[1] Hewitt also notes that the declarative and coordinative dimensions may be carried out simultaneously in an utterance – a smile, or intonation, could be doing the coordinative work while the words have a declarative function. Furthermore, surface forms of expressions may not relate directly to these dimensions – a style that appears highly competitive, for instance, may allow speakers to cooperate effectively on a certain task. This last point of Hewitt's relates to an established distinction between language forms and functions. Cooperation and competition are best regarded as functional categories: something achieved in an interaction. They may be differently realized – cooperation may be realized through a range of linguistic forms, including some that do not immediately "look" cooperative. Hewitt goes rather further than this, however, claiming that a form may simultaneously function as competitive and collaborative.

Hewitt illustrates this framework with an example of a game known as "boxing out and taxing," played by boys in a South London secondary school. The game is played within groups – players have to opt in (and may subsequently opt out). Within the groups, players try to catch one another unawares and box (i.e. knock) something out of another player's hand. They may then claim the object or, more usually, an amount of money due after a few days. Players who don't pay up in time may be "taxed" – that is, charged interest on their debt. In practice, players who have been boxed out try to cancel the debt by boxing out the person to whom they owe money, or another player. A lot of talk takes place around this game – for example, standard performatives, such as calling "box-out" to indicate that a player has knocked something out of another's hand, and that this counts as a box-out within the game; arguments about box-outs; and appeals to bystanders/other group members to resolve disputes. The game is highly competitive: Hewitt notes that it displays "ferocious levels of competitive individualism" (1997: 40). Nevertheless, Hewitt claims that some cooperation is evident, for example in the simultaneous assertion and denial of the declarative dimension (by using some degree of mitigation, or even in the use of an insult – "you tight arse" – which claims the right to insult but also familiarity).

Hewitt's framework, at least as described in the paper I have referred to, is still rather sketchy, but the main point of relevance here is that Hewitt is attempting to complexify notions of competition and cooperation, drawing attention to some degree of ambiguity in the ways these may be worked out interactionally, and to the difficulty of drawing a categorical distinction between them.

Similarly, Amy Sheldon's concern (1997) is to problematize straightforward conceptions of gendered language use. Sheldon takes issue with a dichotomous model of gender (in which female groups and female conversations are characterized as cooperative and egalitarian, and male groups/conversations as competitive and hierarchical). She argues that girls will do competitive and oppositional talk, but how this is done will vary across cultures and contexts. In relation to her own work with US Midwestern preschool children, she draws a distinction between two types of conflict style: "double-voice discourse" and "single-voice discourse." In double-voice discourse, "the 'voice' of mitigation and social sensitivity is bound up with the 'voice' of self-interest and egocentricity"; in single-voice discourse, "[i]nteractants have the single orientation of pursuing their own self-interest without orienting to the perspective of the partner or tempering their self-interest with mitigation" (1997: 231). Double-voice discourse seems to be consistent with Hewitt's suggestion that, in his terms, declarative and coordinative dimensions may exist simultaneously in interactions. Sheldon suggests that such discourse will be found in solidarity-based groups where harmony and collaboration are important.

Sheldon found that both girls and boys in her study engaged in conflict talk; both girls and boys used double-voice discourse in managing this, but girls used double-voice discourse more frequently, sometimes engaging in highly elaborate negotiations. Like Hewitt, then, Sheldon seeks to question any straightforward distinction between notions such as cooperation and competition in talk. She is also concerned to complexify gender, seeing this as performative ("I will discuss how gender can be 'done' in children's discourse": 1997: 225) and as differentiated. Although she actually finds a fairly clear gender difference in children's interactional strategies – a difference illustrated in transcripts and that she can also express in numerical terms – she tends to downplay this difference, emphasizing the importance of culture, context, and children's social goals. In contrast to earlier research (and to an earlier paper drawing on similar data: Sheldon 1990) she is concerned with "reframing" conceptions of gender and moving away from a "dichotomous" distinction between speakers.

Some of my own work has addressed the notion of cooperation, in this case focusing on different readings of the same spoken texts. One example of this is a (re-)analysis of a discussion between two students, a girl and a boy, who were working together on a writing task they had been set by their teacher. They had to produce a jointly authored story and key this into a computer. The discussion had been video-recorded and previously analyzed by researchers working on a project on Spoken Language and New Technology (SLANT), carried out in the southeast of England.[2] The original analysis was concerned not with gender issues but with collaborative talk and learning. The researchers suggested that the girl was more "spontaneous," and tended to take the lead in the interaction. The boy, on the other hand, was more reserved and unwilling to assert himself (Scrimshaw and Perkins 1997). Two female members of the SLANT team, on seeing the video, disputed this interpretation, arguing that the boy took a dominant role in the interaction, exercising more control over the process of writing, whereas the girl was more cooperative and supportive, seeking agreement from the boy for any suggestions she made. These team members also related their interpretation to gender, seeing the interaction as a classic example of "male dominance." In analyzing the interaction, I tried to identify what features might have given rise to two apparently conflicting interpretations, and whether a "dominance" reading of the interaction was compatible with other readings (Swann 1997).

The girl speaker did seem to encourage the boy to contribute (using questions or phrases that required completion) and she also sought the boy's agreement for her own suggestions (again, using questions and question intonation). The boy did not give this kind of verbal support, nor did he seek any agreement for his suggestions. This strategy favored the boy to the extent that more of his suggestions found their way into the piece of writing produced by the students. This might be consistent with a reading of the interaction that saw the girl as having a more cooperative speaking style that also led to her "giving away power," and that saw the boy as "dominant." However, the two students also expressed different views on how they should be working, or perhaps how they wished to work. The girl was insistent that they had to agree, whereas the boy never mentioned this, and occasionally seemed slightly exasperated by the girl's insistence. In this context there seemed to be an ambiguity in the girl's use of question forms or intonation to solicit agreement: these could be read as supportive/cooperative, but also as part of an overall strategy to impose her own definition on the working relationship, with which she expected the boy to comply – that this had to be a relationship based on mutual agreement. It was difficult, then, to give a definitive reading of the text: the text seemed to be open enough to allow the co-existence of alternative – and to some extent competing – interpretations.

In combination, these studies problematize the notion of language, or more specifically linguistic meaning. In all cases, what it means to be cooperative or competitive is questioned. Rather than being distinct, these categories overlap and shade into one another. Utterances are seen as, at least, multifunctional, but also as uncertain, ambiguous, and context-dependent. Sheldon's study, in particular, also problematizes the notion of gender, seen in her desire to "reframe" research and break away from a dichotomous model – her insistence on gender as performative and bound up with culture and context. In terms of Sheldon's interpretation of her data, this gives rise to a shift in emphasis. I suggested above that she found gender differences but played these down, whereas earlier research, with similar data, might have played them up. But the model of gender that she espouses would actually go rather further: a differentiated, contextualized, and performative model of gender has more substantial implications for empirical research, calling into question any generalized claims about gender, and about educational inequality. Sally Johnson discusses similar issues in relation to internally differentiated models of masculinity (Johnson 1997: 19–20; the Connell referred to is Bob Connell's work on gender and power; see also Connell (1995) on masculinities):

> Work within pro-feminist approaches to masculinity has explored men in terms of "multiple subjectivities," and this has led writers to abandon the idea of "masculinity" in the singular, in preference for the pluralized "masculinities". The concept of "male power" is then dislodged by the notion of "hegemonic" or "hierarchical" masculinities, perhaps best characterized as those forms of masculinity able to marginalize and dominate not only women, but also other men, on the grounds of, say, class, race and/or sexuality   (Connell, 1987).

According to this view of masculinities, where gender identities and power relations are seen as highly contextualized practices, it becomes rather more difficult to make clear and generalizable statements about how men are or what they do.

Within education, Alison Jones has addressed similar problems and possibilities of working with a more fragmented notion of "girl" or "girlhood":

> the language of discourse and subjectivity offers ways of talking about complexities and contradictions in understanding girls' schooling. However, there are problems. A focus on women's/girls' multiple and fragmented experience calls into question any straightforward – and compelling – notion of power, and it also challenges the use of the term "girls" in educational research.   (Jones 1993: 157)

Jones distinguishes different forms of femininity – for instance, when, in New Zealand, it is appropriate to talk about "girls" and when about "Maori girls." Johnson, similarly, distinguishes forms of masculinity differentiated by class, race, and sexuality. But these categories still seem rather too fixed. If "girl" is "multiple" and "fragmented" so, presumably, is "Maori girl." Within an interaction, seen as a contextualized practice, several aspects of identity would come into play, not all of them as obvious as gender, class, and race, and not all of them as readily specifiable by a researcher.

There are several implications here for empirical research. For instance, how do researchers assess whether a speaker is "doing gender," or any other aspect of identity? What aspects of identity are relevant at any point in an interaction? How do these relate to any one of a number of other things speakers may be doing as they talk? More contextualized models of language and meaning have similar implications: how do researchers establish the meaning of an utterance? Is one interpretation as good as any other? Given the importance of context, what should count as relevant context, and what sort of warrants or decision procedures do researchers need to draw on to make inferences about this?

I have discussed this issue elsewhere, focusing on the range of warrants evident in research on language and gender – from quantitative/variationist work to highly localized, qualitative studies (see Swann 2002). The point I want to make here is that it is necessary to have some way of relating observations to gender, but that highly contextualized studies are not always best placed to do this. Amy Sheldon's study could be interpreted in terms of gender (though she played this down). In this case, Sheldon was able to draw a direct comparison (expressible in numerical terms) between the speech of girls and boys. My own study, however, focused on a single interaction between two students who differed in several respects, including the fact that one was female and the other male. Each of the students had their own perceptions of the task they were engaged in and their own interactional purposes. The study did not – and could not – demonstrate that the students were "doing gender." The perception of two observers that the interaction was a classic example of "male dominance" is framed by, and reliant on, earlier research, carried out in other contexts. Similarly, Roger Hewitt's study is set against a generalization about male speakers' competitive styles derived from other research. It is of interest because it challenges notions of cooperation/competition, but attributing the boys' speaking styles to gender (or to masculinity, or certain forms of masculinity) would be problematical (Hewitt does not directly make this claim, but the paper is included in an edited collection on language and masculinity).

I have suggested (Swann 2002) that despite the current emphasis on context and performativity, language and gender researchers do not actually dispense with gender as an a priori explanatory category – and probably they cannot. The perception that someone is "doing gender" (or masculinity, or girlhood, or Maori girlhood) seems necessarily to depend upon an observer's prior assumptions about at least the potential salience of gender/masculinity/femininity. The danger is that researchers may make such assumptions without an appropriate warrant to support them. The issue of how local, contextualized observations may plausibly be related back to gender is something that requires further debate. Methodologically, I would favor a form of "pragmatic eclecticism": an appeal to a wider range of warrants and associated research methods drawn on as and when to target specific questions and issues; and a more explicit acknowledgment of the possibilities and limitations of all methodological choices. This would include the currently less fashionable enterprise of making direct, even quantifiable comparisons across groups and contexts so that we can more clearly establish commonalities and differences between these; and the use of quantitative (e.g. corpus-based) approaches to complement an analysis of more contextualized examples (cf. Holmes 1996).

Although I have used research carried out in educational settings as the basis for discussion in this section, the points I have made are also relevant to research carried out in other contexts. Challenges to gendered patterns of "competitive" and "cooperative" talk, however, have more direct educational relevance. For instance, while not identical, the characteristics that have been attributed to feminine "cooperative" styles are consistent with the kind of "collaborative" talk that has been advocated as an aid to learning in educational settings. As I mentioned earlier, there has been some debate over whether educationally collaborative talk may be considered a process of "feminization" – and, if so, what the implications would be for female and male learners. The terms of any such debate are clearly thrown into question by research that challenges the nature of cooperation/competition as well as the notion of "gendered talk" more generally. The working out of such issues requires a hospitable research climate – more hospitable, I think, than currently obtains within education. I shall look further below at the articulation between contemporary research on language and gender and educational policy contexts.

3   Shifting Research Contexts: Educational Policy and Practice

In this section I want to document a shift in education as a context for research and enquiry that has led some feminists to question the nature of the research that it is possible to carry out. Although I think the points I make will have more general relevance, I shall focus mainly on developments that cover England and Wales, which is the educational context with which I am most familiar. Writing about research and educational policy developments in England and Wales, Miriam David, Gaby Weiner, and Madeleine Arnot (2000) refer to the constraints of operating in a "cold climate" – one in which feminist interests and insights have been marginalized. The climatic change is a gradual one that has taken place from the late 1980s, through the 1990s, and up to the present. It is almost a parallel, then, to the shift in conceptions of language and gender that I referred to above, and I suppose may be regarded as the other side of the coin. Certainly I want to argue that there has been a widening gap between language and gender as a research area and the design of educational policy.

I mentioned earlier that concerns about "male dominance" of talk gave rise to a number of "equal opportunities" initiatives designed to rectify perceived imbalances in classroom interaction. In this respect, there was some degree of overlap in the interests of researchers and at least some educational policy-makers. Language issues formed part of several equal opportunities initiatives developed during the 1980s – often at local (school and local education author-ity) levels but also with the support of national institutions such as HMI (Her Majesty's Inspectorate).[3] Since the late 1980s (with, for instance, the advent of the Education Reform Act in 1988) control of several aspects of education has become more centralized. Developments such as the introduction of a national curriculum have been associated with the marginalization of gender issues, or equal opportunities initiatives in language, as in other aspects of school and classroom life. Within the English curriculum, for instance, initial proposals drawn up by the English working group chaired by Brian Cox (the "Cox Report," DES/WO 1989) contained a chapter on equal opportunities which discussed educational implications of gender differences in language use, and was clearly informed by research in this area. Subsequent non-statutory guid-ance for English reduced this to a few passing references (e.g. NCC 1989); and there was no mention at all of gender, or equal opportunities, in the later streamlined version of the curriculum (DFE/WO 1995).

Since the early 1990s, there has been an increasing swell of concern about the position of boys in education, and specifically about boys' "underachieve-ment." This has become an issue in several countries – Epstein, Elwood, Hey, and Maw claim it has acquired the status of a "globalized moral panic" (1998: 3) – though it is likely to be articulated differently in different policy contexts. Within England and Wales, David et al. (2000) suggest that concern about "underachievement" dates from around 1994, and they relate it to increasing government (and media) interest in comparing examination performance across schools. Boys' "underachievement" refers to their performance relative to girls in national examinations and other forms of testing. Examinations such as the General Certificate of Secondary Education (GCSE) reveal increasing levels of performance amongst both girls and boys, but with girls, overall, increasing their levels of performance relative to boys.[4] This disguises a number of im-portant factors – for instance, where pupils choose subjects, their choices are still often gender-stereotyped; there are substantial differences in educational performance between boys, and between girls; and performance in school may not be consistent with post-school achievements: the "glass ceiling" in employ-ment is still in evidence. (For a discussion of factors that may contribute to gender differences in educational performance, see Murphy and Elwood 1998.)

The discourse of "underachievement," however, seems to allow little scope for such qualifications. To give a brief illustration that came up at the time of writing: the A Level examination results that were released in 2000 showed an overall increase in pass rates, but whereas girls increased their performance in the higher (A and B) grades, boys' performance declined very slightly (by 0.2 per cent).[5] This was greeted by the headline "Boys in crisis" in the tabloid *Mirror* newspaper, and by "Boys left scrambling for places after A-level slump" in *The Times* (in both cases, August 17: 1). As an illustration of the "crisis," the *Mirror* ran a feature on triplets (two girls and a boy) who had just received their results. The girls had each achieved four A grades; the "underachieving" boy, two As and two Bs. Several educationists were called upon to provide explanations – ranging from a "laddish culture" that was hostile to academic achievement, to boys' and girls' different learning styles, differences in maturity, and the effects of "girl-friendly" schooling brought about by earlier equal opportunities initiatives. *The Times* ran a rather more cautious appraisal by Alan Smithers, Director of the Centre for Education and Employment Research at Liverpool University, which discussed the relationship between subject choice and grading (subjects chosen by girls tend to give higher grades), the nature of the examination, and girls' improved job opportunities. Within a few days of the release of the results, David Blunkett, Secretary of State for Education and Employment, had outlined "a package of measures to narrow the gender gap in educational achievement." These included asking all local education authorities to provide a detailed evaluation of programs they had been asked to set up two years previously to tackle boys' underachievement; getting more male teachers into the classroom ("changing the status of the teaching profession by offering higher salaries and career opportunities"); changing primary school reading lists to "make books more stimulating and engaging for boys"; promoting the importance of literacy to boys; using role models such as professional footballers in after-school study centers at Premiership and Nationwide football clubs; setting up a "Gender and Achievement" web site to provide advice to schools; commissioning research; organizing regional conferences for schools and education authorities to hear the views of experts; and introducing various measures, including a large advertising campaign, to encourage young people to stay on in education. Mr. Blunkett acknowledged that the problem was an international one, but commented: "I am determined that our boys should not miss out" (Department for Education and Employment, August 20, 2000).[6] One might ask where such massive government intervention was when "our girls" were identified as "missing out" during the 1970s and 1980s.

The discourse of "underachievement" is of interest in its own right, but I am referring to it here because it represents a challenge to feminist interests in gender issues, including feminist interests in language and gender. It signals a potential reversal of the kinds of equal opportunities initiatives I mentioned earlier, that were carried out particularly during the 1980s. In reading the literature on underachievement, there is a sense that girls have had their day – it's now the boys' turn. In a report of a survey of equality projects in schools and local education authorities (LEAs), Arnot, Millen, and Maton comment:

> the most significant finding was the current primacy of "improving boys' achievement" projects. Out of 96 named school or LEA projects, 40 were targeted on boys only, 35 projects focused on both sexes, although often boys' underachievement was mentioned as a particular issue to be tackled, and only three projects were specifically targeted at girls. (Arnot et al. 1998: 18)

Specific concerns have often been raised (as in the DfEE press release above) about boys' language use and about their learning of language and literacy. Several publications have been designed to address boys' "underachievement" in English (e.g. Frater 1997; Ofsted 1993; Qualifications and Curriculum Authority (QCA) 1998; School Curriculum and Assessment Authority (SCAA) – undated, but around 1997). I shall look briefly at one example, the Qualifications and Curriculum Authority's *Can Do Better*. *Can Do Better* illustrates, I think, the potential marginalization of girls' interests and the incompatibility with contemporary research on gender that has characterized many policy statements on underachievement.

Can Do Better discusses boys' performance in different aspects of English (speaking and listening, reading and writing); how the implementation of the English curriculum may affect boys' learning; how teachers can investigate boys' achievements in their own schools; and various forms of positive action to help boys. The booklet explicitly prioritizes boys' interests over girls':

> There are still major issues to be addressed relating to girls' achievements and aspirations, and these must not be forgotten. However, more recently public attention has shifted to boys and their relative underachievement up to and including GCSE across wide areas of the curriculum. In some subjects, including English and English literature, the difference in achievements is particularly pronounced. (QCA 1998: 9)

The sop to girls' interests here is a common strategy. For instance, Terry Reynolds, an inspector of English in a London borough, sees "underachievement" as a moral panic and is also cynical about a move to reduce the coursework element in GCSE examinations: "I'm sure I'm not alone in believing that the decision to limit coursework [. . .] was at least in part prompted by a desire to give the boys a better chance in competing against the girls" (1995: 15). Despite this apparent skepticism, Reynolds advocates teaching strategies to deal with "underachievement" that he claims will be more appealing to boys, and relegates girls' interests to parentheses or an afterthought.

Can Do Better attributes boys' "underachievement" to several factors, such as an anti-academic "male culture," but also to certain features of the English curriculum: English is seen as a girls' subject, for instance; English is sedentary, whereas boys prefer more active participation; and boys have limited tolerance of ambiguity: they need more well-defined tasks. English teaching, therefore, needs to appeal to boys' interests as well as extending them. The booklet's characterization of boys' speaking styles is consistent with earlier evidence from language and gender research. Boys are "generally more competitive in discussion," for instance, and "enjoy the verbal cut and thrust of debate" (pp. 12, 16). However, within the discourse of underachievement this is now reframed. Boys' speaking styles mean that they will learn less well from others, and the "cut and thrust" is not always relevant to the task in hand. Attention is thus shifted from girls (whose learning may be inhibited by boys' speaking styles) to boys (whose styles may inhibit their own learning).

Similar points emerge in relation to reading and writing. *Can Do Better* comments on boys' preference for non-fiction, and for action and fantasy. Suggestions for strategies to improve boys' literacy include selecting resources that they would find more appealing. In one case study:

> Reluctant boys showed greater interest when pupils worked collaboratively in groups on structured tasks related to short stories which had been selected to appeal to boys in particular. There was no reduction in interest from girls. (1998: 35)

This suggests a willful return to a situation documented in feminist research studies since the 1970s and 1980s, in which girls' interests could be systematically marginalized on the grounds that disaffected girls made less trouble (see, for instance, Swann 1992). Sue Adler comments also that appealing to boys' interests does little to challenge these:

> Our library fiction stock now consciously caters for reluctant young male readers, trying to entice them with stories featuring sport and computers, and seeking out books with cool covers. The pedagogy of the National Literacy Strategy, which makes reading seem active and breaks activities into short periods of time, may well suit boys. I do not, however, see anything in the courses and lists promoting boys' fictional reading that confronts the resistance to read anything that could be construed as "girls' books". Rather, the spin on reading is that it can be a "laddish" activity.   (Adler 2000: 211)

Can Do Better comments on the predominance of narrative in writing tasks set for students. The claim is that this may leave students ill-equipped to cope with later writing demands, such as the need to write to inform and persuade in work contexts. Because boys are more inclined toward non-fiction, a lack of attention to this may disadvantage them more. Boys may also be disadvantaged because teachers value writing that is neatly presented and without spelling errors. Teachers may "undervalue structure and action in boys' stories and appear to give greater emphasis to handwriting and spelling" (p. 20). More evidence is needed to support assumptions such as the link between boys' "non-fiction" writing preferences and workplace persuasive writing. But the main point of interest is that very similar assumptions underpinned a claim twelve years earlier that such educational practices disadvantaged girls – that girls' very success in English limited their success in other subject areas (because they were not given practice in a wider range of genres) and did not prepare them for high-status careers. In a paper that was influential at the time, Janet White argued:

> The English Department which operates with a punctilious view of "good" writing (a matter of prescriptive correctness) and enshrines only a few types of writing as the "best" (fictional narrative, varieties of "creative" description) is ultimately doing as great a disservice to its predominantly female students as are the overtly "unfriendly" male-dominated subject areas.   (White 1986: 570)

I have singled out this study because White is also credited as a member of the working party that, in a very different context, contributed to *Can Do Better*. This raises issues about the way feminists operate, and are able to operate in the current educational climate – I shall return to these below.

Can Do Better demonstrates how a concern with "underachievement" represents a shift in focus – toward boys, and away from girls; and how this may involve a certain amount of reframing: activities that were once taken as evidence of girls' educational disadvantage may be re-interpreted as disadvantaging boys. There is a fear amongst feminists that this may lead to a diversion of energy, resources, and general consideration toward boys, and to a consequent marginalization of girls' interests.

Put this way, the issues seem rather polarized, and bound up with fixed and static notions of both language and gender. It is significant that I have related discussion and examples in the booklet back to earlier (1970s and 1980s) feminist research and initiatives. The booklet itself presents a uniform picture of boys/masculinity: there is no consideration of different types of boys or girls; nothing on other social factors such as race or class; nothing on context; no attempt to problematize masculinity – or, for that matter, underachievement; and no concession to uncertainty in the meaning of language or language practices. If the booklet may be critiqued in this way then so, of course, may any feminist concerns (my own included). If the meaning of language practices is relatively open and subject to (re)negotiation, then why should change to these (whatever the motivation) necessarily disadvantage "girls"? Faced with the heavy binarism of the underachievement debate, however, I do not think "every girl for herself" is an appropriate response. If boys are positioned as "boys," who underachieve in relation to "girls" and who require certain "boy-friendly" strategies to help them, there seems to be every reason for concern about the position of girls.

It is possible to engage on different terms with issues of "underachievement." More critical, and more sophisticated responses are found, as might be expected, in academic texts (see e.g. the papers in Epstein, Elwood, Hey, and Maw 1998, and in Epstein, Maw, Elwood, and Hey 1998). They may also be found in "official" publications in certain policy contexts. Nola Alloway and Pam Gilbert tackled the issue of boys' underachievement in a package of materials entitled *Boys and Literacy*, published by the Australian Curriculum Corporation. *Boys and Literacy* was produced in a climate in many ways similar to that which inspired *Can Do Better* – as a response to widespread concerns about boys' participation and performance in English and language arts (Alloway and Gilbert 1997a: viii).

While the publication takes such concerns seriously, and focuses on practical suggestions to help teachers tackle boys' performance in literacy, it also adopts a relatively complex model of masculinity. Alloway and Gilbert discuss "the ways that boys take themselves up as masculine subjects," and emphasize differences between boys and between girls:

[Looking at the interaction between race, class, geographical location and gender] allows for more complex readings of which groups of boys and girls are at risk of under-achieving in school-based literacy, and which groups are most privileged. [. . .] An exploration of the performance and achievement of boys in school literacy learning needs to take this intragroup difference seriously. (1997a: 5)

The complex relationships between class, ethnicity and masculinity [. . .] may mean that privileged groups of boys are more likely to be encouraged to accept some forms of school regulation in anticipation of career and professional rewards in the post-schooling period. (1997a: 8)

Alloway and Gilbert also acknowledge the dangers of a "competing victim syndrome" (1997a: 12), in which a focus on boys means a reallocation of resources, time, and energy away from girls. They argue that what it means to be literate is under constant renegotiation (e.g. in relation to technological change) and they emphasize the need for critical literacy, which would (amongst other things) engage with the social construction of masculinity. The materials address the issue of boys' achievement in literacy:

- by questioning school literacy practices
- by making visible the tensions associated with being positioned as literate within school culture and being identifiably male within boys' culture
- by developing strategies for contesting these tensions with boys.
 [. . .] a critical approach to gender and literacy will give boys the skills to critique and to challenge their own practices. (1997a: 13)

Teaching units (Alloway and Gilbert 1997b) include activities to "deconstruct" video and print texts, to explore tensions between dominant masculinities and school literacy practices, and to explore alternative masculinities.

At issue here is the extent to which this relatively complex and critical approach to gender and literacy is compatible with participation in an initiative to tackle boys' "underachievement." The focus of such initiatives is necessarily on boys, even if masculinities are pluralized and held up to question. I am not sure whether researchers can avoid a binary position if they enter the "underachievement" arena (i.e. if they are complicit in any way with this rather than critiquing from the outside). I shall return below to alternative positions that may be taken up by educational researchers.

4 Shifting Contexts for Communication

Alloway and Gilbert's critical approach to literacy suggests that literacy is in a constant state of flux. The point would apply to language practices in general, which constantly change with the advent of new contexts, communication technologies, and communicative purposes. Such changing practices would affect not only how girls and boys communicate but also, necessarily, how they do gender.

Electronic communication has given rise to a range of diverse texts and practices. These have sometimes been said to undermine traditional notions of authorship, readership, and text, and to open up opportunities, as well as posing severe challenges for the English curriculum and for education more generally (e.g. Spender 1995; Tweddle 1995). There has been continuing speculation about the extent to which electronic communication might permit, or encourage, new forms of interpersonal relations. Sherry Turkle (1995) looked at the practices adopted by US higher education students, who, at any one time, might engage in different communication activities via different windows on their computer screen. Students could, for instance, travel between several MUDs whilst also engaging in a "real life" activity (e.g. work or study).[7] The MUD characters could be gendered in a variety of ways or their gender could be uncertain. Turkle comments that many users felt they were taking on different identities as they interacted in each window. Furthermore, the distinction between the virtual world of the MUDs and real life sometimes blurred: one student cited by Turkle claimed "RL [real life] is just one more window, and it's not usually my best one" (1995: 13). Mindy McAdams, similarly, speculated on the possibility/desirability of hiding or changing one's gender on-line (McAdams 1996).

According to this view, electronic communication would seem to be an archetypally postmodern medium, allowing contributors a certain flexibility in how they present themselves to others, and in the terms on which they interact with others, and giving rise to a kind of "identity-hopping" that would be difficult to match in face-to-face communication. Feminists have also suggested that electronic communication may have specific advantages for girls/women. Dale Spender draws a favorable comparison between certain uses of computer-mediated communication (CMC) and the kinds of talk traditionally associated with female speakers, such as "gossip" or chat:

> Women will be drawn in through an emphasis on the communication potential of the computer. Once women see that it is dead easy to natter on the net – to reach people all around the world, to consult bulletin boards, to "meet" in cafes and houses and art galleries without leaving home – there will be no stopping them.
>
> The only obstacle that they will have to contend with is the men who are already there: the men who have written the rules of the road.   (Spender 1995: 192)

In the second part of this quotation, however, Spender is hinting at some of the problems electronic communication may pose for women and girls. Some empirical studies (Herring 1993, this volume; Herring, Johnson, and DiBenedetto 1995; Wylie 1995) have suggested that men's interactional dominance on the Net may be similar to their dominance in face-to-face interactions.

Within education, there is also well-documented evidence of girls' low take-up of computing, and of boys' dominance of computing resources where these are meant to be available to all in the classroom (e.g. Beynon 1993; Culley 1988; Hoyles and Sutherland 1989). As familiarity with computing has become more essential, considerable concern has been expressed about girls' educational disadvantage in this area. Spender draws an analogy with print, suggesting that new communication practices may reinforce traditional inequalities:

> After five hundred years, women were just beginning to look as though they were drawing even with the men. They have reached the stage in countries like Australia where, for the first time, more women than men have been gaining higher education qualifications. But this success has been achieved in an education system still based on print, where the skills needed to succeed have been reading, writing and memory – all things that women are good at.
>
> And just when it looks as though equity is about to be realized – the rules of the game are changed. The society (and soon, the education system) switches to the electronic medium. And "everyone" knows that girls are not as good as boys – with machines!   (1995: 185)

An important and unresolved issue, then, relates to the extent to which CMC offers alternative positions for girls/women and boys/men; and the extent to which it simply returns us to traditional polarized notions of gender difference and disadvantage.

In *Can Do Better* the Qualifications and Curriculum Authority suggested that boys' knowledge of and interest in computing was not always fully used in the English classroom. More recently, Nicholas McGuinn (2000) has suggested that information technology may be a way of motivating boys, and so raising their achievements. Boys' interests in IT may encourage them to read and write more widely; and writing may seem less daunting to boys because "accuracy" is downplayed – texts are often more spontaneous than carefully crafted. The possibilities that exist for relative anonymity and for collaborative writing (relieving the pressure on individual authors) may also be helpful. It is interesting that McGuinn uses Lorraine Culley's (1988) work as support for his suggestion that greater use of IT may benefit boys. Culley, as I mentioned above, demonstrated that boys dominated computing resources – which has, not surprisingly, given rise to concern about girls. McGuinn is, like the QCA in *Can Do Better*, reframing earlier educational research, although in a slightly different way: in this case, boys' dominance of resources is taken as an indicator of their potential advantage in the area of computing (as it was in earlier feminist studies), but the interest of girls is totally neglected.

5   Conclusion

In this chapter I have pointed to certain changes that have taken place within language and gender as a research area and within education as an important context for research. I have suggested that the current emphasis on "language" and "gender" as differentiated and contextualized practices, while a useful corrective to earlier relatively "static" models, makes it harder for empirical researchers to relate instances of language use plausibly to gender, or femininity/ies, or masculinity/ies. I have given my own view that, having usefully problematized "language" and "gender," it is time to begin some reconstruction work. I have also pointed to problems and possibilities afforded by the increasing importance attached to electronic communication – this suggests, at least, that researchers need to take on board a wider range of texts and practices. In both cases, these are matters for continuing debate – they affect the conduct of research and have implications for the development of language and gender as a research field.

I have also, however, pointed to a widening gap between language and gender as a research field and the educational policy context in which some language and gender researchers may wish to operate. Whereas earlier approaches to language and gender seemed able to articulate fairly readily with the practices and policy-making of the day, more recent approaches sit uneasily alongside current educational debate and policy-making. Research that takes on board complex and highly contextualized models of language and gender will be wary of over-ready generalizations about boys' "underachievement." On the other hand, in the current educational climate, with its emphasis on the speedy identification of problems such as "underachievement" and the provision of immediate and straightforward solutions, some research interests will appear, at least, rather esoteric.

Faced with a difficult research climate there are a number of strategies that researchers may adopt. Academic researchers have sometimes been able to maintain a critical stance – I referred above to the papers in Epstein, Elwood, Hey, and Maw (1998) and Epstein, Maw, Elwood, and Hey (1998), many of which sought to challenge the notion of boys' "underachievement." Such challenges are academically relevant – that is, they contribute to academic debate within education. But they are unlikely to have an early impact on educational policy or practice in Britain. Alloway and Gilbert's work on boys and literacy is an attempt to engage more directly with educational policy and practice, but on the researchers' own terms (which involves, in this case, reformulating the "underachievement" debate). The effectiveness of such an approach depends on a policy context that is, at least to some extent, open to critical debate. I have also suggested that it may be difficult to engage with policy on boys' "underachievement" without, in effect, bolstering a binary position in relation to gender. In some contexts, educationists may have little choice but to play along with educational policy that they may find uncongenial, perhaps in the hope that they may take the edge off certain developments (in relation to "underachievement," maybe keeping girls' interests within the margins of policy-making).[8] Feminists and others concerned about gender issues have always had to make choices about how to represent themselves and their work to others – this seems to be a matter of particular importance within contemporary educational research.

NOTES

1 This bears more than a passing resemblance to Brown and Levinson's (1987) politeness system, and to the notions of positive and negative politeness. Hewitt claims that his own categories are more inclusive than Brown and Levinson's, and they do not involve the concept of "face."

2 Spoken Language and New Technology (SLANT) was an ESRC-funded project directed by John Elliott, University of East Anglia, and Neil Mercer, Open University.

3 Language-related initiatives are reviewed in Swann (1992); David et al. (2000) and Myers (2000) provide more general reflections on equal opportunities initiatives during this period.

4 The GCSE (General Certificate of Secondary Education) is an examination taken mainly by students at the age of 16 or over.

5 The A Level (General Certificate of Education, Advanced Level) examination is taken mainly by students between the ages of 17 and 19. A Levels are widely used as entrance qualifications for higher education.

6 Department for Education and Employment "News," at http://www.dfee.gov.uk/news/ (August 20, 2000).

7 MUDs are Multi-User Dungeons, or sometimes Multi-User Domains: multi-user computer games in which participants play characters who meet and interact with one another.

8 I have taken the expression "playing along" from Gemma Moss (1989). Moss discusses a number of strategies that girls may make in response to sexism – there are some parallels between this and responses feminist and other researchers may make to an inhospitable research climate.

REFERENCES

Adler, Sue 2000: When Ms Muffett fought back: A view of work on children's books since the 1970s. In Kate Myers (ed.) *Whatever Happened to Equal Opportunities in Schools? Gender Equality Initiatives in Education.* Buckingham: Open University Press, pp. 201–13.

Alloway, Nola and Gilbert, Pam 1997a: *Boys and Literacy: Professional Development Units.* Carlton, Victoria: Curriculum Corporation.

Alloway, Nola and Gilbert, Pam 1997b: *Boys and Literacy: Teaching Units.* Carlton, Victoria: Curriculum Corporation.

Arnot, Madeleine, Millen, Diane, and Maton, Kath 1998: *Current Innovative Practice in Schools in the United Kingdom: Network Strategy Research Study on Education as a Policy Issue of Gender Equality.* Final Report, November, University of Cambridge.

Bergvall, Victoria L., Bing, Janet M., and Freed, Alice (eds) 1996: *Rethinking Language and Gender Research.* London: Longman.

Beynon, John 1993: Computers, dominant boys and invisible girls: Or, "Hannah, it's not a toaster, it's a computer!" In John Beynon and

Hughie Mackay (eds) *Computers into Classrooms: More Questions than Answers*. London: Falmer, pp. 160–89.

Brown, Penelope and Levinson, Stephen 1987: *Politeness: Some Universals in Language Usage*. Cambridge: Cambridge University Press.

Bucholtz, Mary, Liang, Anita C., and Sutton, Laurel A. (eds) 1999: *Reinventing Identities: The Gendered Self in Discourse*. New York: Oxford University Press.

Cheshire, Jenny and Jenkins, Nancy 1991: Gender issues in the GCSE oral English examination, Part II. *Language and Education* 5(1): 19–40.

Connell, Robert W. 1987: *Gender and Power: Society, the Person and Sexual Politics*. Cambridge: Polity.

Connell, Robert W. 1995: *Masculinities*. Cambridge: Polity.

Culley, Lorraine 1988: Girls, boys and computers. *Educational Studies* 13: 3–8.

David, Miriam, Weiner, Gaby, and Arnot, Madeleine 2000: Gender equality and schooling, education policy-making and feminist research in England and Wales in the 1990s. In Jane Salisbury and Sheila Riddell (eds) *Gender, Policy and Educational Change: Shifting Agendas in the UK and Europe*. London and New York: Routledge, pp. 19–36.

Department of Education and Science and the Welsh Office (DES/WO) 1989: *English for Ages 5–16: Proposals of the Secretary of State for Education and Science and the Secretary of State for Wales* (the Cox Report). London: Department of Education and Science and the Welsh Office.

Department for Education and the Welsh Office (DFE/WO) 1995: *English in the National Curriculum*. London: HMSO.

Epstein, Debbie, Elwood, Jannette, Hey, Valerie, and Maw, Janet (eds) 1998: *Failing Boys? Issues in Gender and Achievement*. Buckingham: Open University Press.

Epstein, Debbie, Maw, Janet, Elwood, Jannette, and Hey, Valerie (eds) 1998: *International Journal of Inclusive Education*: Special Issue, *Boys' "Underachievement"*, 2(2).

Frater, Graham (1997) *Improving Boys' Literacy Skills*. London: Basic Skills Agency.

Hall, Kira and Bucholtz, Mary (eds) 1995: *Gender Articulated: Language and the Socially Constructed Self*. New York and London: Routledge.

Herring, Susan 1993: Gender and democracy in computer-mediated communication. *Electronic Journal of Communication* 3. (Reprinted in Rob Kling (ed.) 1996: *Computerization and Controversy*, 2nd edn. New York: Academic Press, pp. 476–89.)

Herring, Susan, Johnson, Deborah A., and DiBenedetto, Tamra 1995: "This discussion is going too far!" Male resistance to female participation on the Internet. In Kira Hall and Mary Bucholtz (eds) *Gender Articulated: Language and the Socially Constructed Self*. New York and London: Routledge, pp. 67–96.

Hewitt, Roger 1997: "Boxing out" and "taxing". In Sally Johnson and Ulrike Hanna Meinhof (eds) *Language and Masculinity*. Oxford: Blackwell, pp. 27–46.

Holmes, Janet 1994: Improving the lot of female language learners. In Jane Sunderland (ed.) *Exploring Gender: Questions and Implications for English Language Education*. London: Prentice-Hall, pp. 156–62.

Holmes, Janet 1996: Women's role in language change: A place for quantification. In Natasha Warner, Jocelyn Ahlers, Leela Bilmes, Monica Oliver, Suzanne Wertheim, and Melinda Chen (eds) *Gender and Belief Systems: Proceedings of the Fourth*

Berkeley Women and Language Conference, April 19–21, 1996. Berkeley, CA: Berkeley Women and Language Group, University of California, pp. 313–30.

Hoyles, Celia and Sutherland, Rosamund 1989: *Logo Mathematics in the Classroom.* London: Routledge.

Jenkins, Nancy and Cheshire, Jenny 1990: Gender issues in the GCSE oral English examination, Part I. *Language and Education* 4(4): 261–92.

Johnson, Sally 1997: Theorizing language and masculinity. In Sally Johnson and Ulrike Hanna Meinhof (eds) *Language and Masculinity.* Oxford: Blackwell, pp. 8–26.

Johnson, Sally and Meinhof, Ulrike Hanna (eds) 1997: *Language and Masculinity.* Oxford: Blackwell.

Jones, Alison 1993: Becoming a "Girl": Post-structuralist suggestions for educational research. *Gender and Education* 5: 157–66.

McAdams, Mindy 1996: Gender without bodies. *CMC Magazine,* http://www.december.com/cmc/1996/mar/mcadams.html

McGuinn, Nicholas 2000: Electronic communication and under-achieving boys: Some issues. *English and Education* 34(1): 50–7.

Moss, Gemma 1989: *Un/Popular Fictions.* London: Virago.

Murphy, Patricia and Elwood, Jannette 1998: Gendered learning outside and inside school: Influences on assessment. In Debbie Epstein, Jannette Elwood, Valerie Hey, and Janet Maw (eds) *Failing Boys? Issues in Gender and Achievement.* Buckingham: Open University Press, pp. 162–81.

Myers, Kate (ed.) 2000: *Whatever Happened to Equal Opportunities in Schools? Gender Equality Initiatives in Education.* Buckingham: Open University Press.

National Curriculum Council (NCC) 1989: *English Key Stage 1: Non-statutory Guidance.* York: NCC.

Office for Standards in Education (Ofsted) 1993: *Boys and English.* London: Ofsted.

Qualifications and Curriculum Authority (QCA) 1998: *Can Do Better: Raising Boys' Achievements in English.* London: QCA.

Reynolds, Terry 1995: Boys and English. *The English and Media Magazine* 33 (Autumn): 15–18.

School Curriculum and Assessment Authority (SCAA) (undated): *Boys and English.* London: SCAA.

Scrimshaw, Peter and Perkins, Gary 1997: Tinkertown: Working together. In Rupert Wegerif and Peter Scrimshaw (eds) *Computers and Talk in the Primary Classroom.* Clevedon: Multilingual Matters, pp. 113–32.

Sheldon, Amy 1990: Pickle fights: Gendered talk in preschool disputes. *Discourse Processes* 13(1): 5–31. (Reprinted in Deborah Tannen (ed.) 1993: *Gender and Conversational Interaction.* Oxford: Oxford University Press, pp. 83–109.)

Sheldon, Amy 1997: Talking power: Girls, gender enculturation and discourse. In Ruth Wodak (ed.) *Gender and Discourse.* London: Sage, pp. 225–44.

Spender, Dale 1995: *Nattering on the Net: Women, Power and Cyberspace.* North Melbourne: Spinifex Press.

Swann, Joan 1992: *Girls, Boys and Language.* Oxford: Blackwell.

Swann, Joan 1997: Tinkertown: Reading and rereading children's talk around the computer. In Rupert Wegerif and Peter Scrimshaw (eds) *Computers and Talk in the Primary Classroom.* Clevedon: Multilingual Matters, pp. 133–50.

Swann, Joan 2002: Yes, but is it gender? In Jane Sunderland and Lia Litosseliti (eds) *Discourse Analysis and Gender Identities*. Amsterdam: John Benjamins.

Swann, Joan and Graddol, David 1995: Feminizing classroom talk? In Sara Mills (ed.) *Language and Gender: Interdisciplinary Perspectives*. London: Longman, pp. 135–48.

Turkle, Sherry 1995: *Life on the Screen: Identity in the Age of the Internet*. New York: Simon and Schuster.

Tweddle, Sally 1995: A curriculum for the future: A curriculum built for change. *English in Education* 29(2): 3–11.

White, Janet 1986: The writing on the wall: Beginning or end of a girl's career? *Women's Studies International Forum* 9: 561–74.

Wodak, Ruth (ed.) 1997: *Gender and Discourse*. London: Sage.

Wylie, Margie 1995: No place for women. *Digital Media* 4 (January): 3–6.

28 Coercing Gender: Language in Sexual Assault Adjudication Processes

SUSAN EHRLICH

1 Introduction

This chapter investigates the linguistic representation and (re)production of gender ideologies in institutional discourse. More specifically, it examines the language of sexual assault adjudication processes as a way of gaining greater insight into how dominant ideologies of sexual violence against women are reproduced, sustained, and (potentially) contested in these kinds of institutional settings. While concerted lobbying by feminists in the 1970s, 1980s, and 1990s has resulted in sweeping statutory reform to sexual assault legislation in Canada and the United States, the adjudication of sexual assault cases continues to be informed by culturally powerful interpretive frameworks that legitimate male violence and reproduce gendered inequalities. That is, whether or not androcentric definitions and understandings of rape or sexual harassment are actually encoded in law, the interpretation and characterization of events in such cases are "overwhelmingly directed toward interrogating and discrediting the woman's character on behalf of maintaining a considerable range of sexual prerogatives for men" (Crenshaw 1992: 409). Given the often large discrepancy that exists between "law as legislation" and "law as practice" (Smart 1986), following Conley and O'Barr (1998), this paper locates the law's failure to live up to its statutory ideals in the details of everyday legal practices. And, because "the details of everyday legal practices consist almost entirely of language" (Conley and O'Barr 1998: 3), linguistic analysis, of the type exemplified here, can be revealing of the cultural mythologies that inhabit such practices (e.g. a trial) and have a determining effect on legal outcomes.

Central to an investigation of language as it is embodied within institutional settings is both an understanding of the relationship between linguistic practices and speakers' social identities and an exploration of the institutional and cultural backdrop against which speakers adopt such practices. In this chapter I bring together what have traditionally been two separate (but related) strands of research within feminist language studies: (1) the study of language use: how individuals draw upon linguistic resources to produce themselves as gendered, and (2) the study of linguistic representations: how culturally dominant notions of gender are encoded (and potentially contested) in linguistic representations. While distinguishing between these two kinds of research has served as an organizing principle for much work in the field of language and gender, Cameron (1998: 963) problematizes the distinction, as I do, suggesting that "in many cases it is neither possible nor useful to keep these aspects apart":

> When a researcher studies women and men speaking she is looking, as it were, at the linguistic construction of gender in its first- and second-person forms (the construction of "I" and "you"); when she turns to the representation of gender in, say advertisements or literary texts she is looking at the same thing in the third person   ("she" and "he").

Put in Cameron's terms, this chapter explores the way that the linguistic representation of gender "in the third person" shapes the enactment of gender "in the first person." Encoded in third-person forms, talk by lawyers and adjudicators *about* the accused, the complainants, and violence against women more generally represents male sexual aggression in particular ways: specifically, "his" sexual prerogatives are privileged and protected at the expense of "her" sexual autonomy. Such representations transmit androcentric values and attitudes; yet, they also have a strongly constitutive function: they shape and structure witnesses' *own* accounts of the events and concomitantly the way that gender is enacted in the first person. Put another way, my approach elucidates how the "talk" of participants, specifically witnesses, is filtered through cultural and institutional ideologies which themselves are manifest in talk.

2   Institutional Coerciveness

Debates over the nature of gender identity and its social construction, originating in feminist work of the 1990s, have in recent years informed research in sociolinguistics generally and feminist linguistics more specifically. In particular, conceptions of gender as categorical, fixed, and static have increasingly been abandoned in favor of more constructivist and dynamic ones. Cameron (1990: 86), for example, makes the point (paraphrasing Harold Garfinkel) that "social actors are not sociolinguistic 'dopes'," mindlessly and passively producing linguistic forms that are definitively determined by social class membership, ethnicity, or gender. Rather, more recent formulations of the relationship between language and gender, following Butler (1990), emphasize the performative aspect of gender: linguistic practices, among other kinds of practices, continually bring into being individuals' social identities. Under this account, language is one important means by which gender – an ongoing social process

– is enacted or constituted; gender is something individuals *do* – in part through linguistic choices – as opposed to something individuals *are* or *have* (West and Zimmerman 1987). Cameron's (1995: 15–16) comments are illustrative:

> Whereas sociolinguistics would say that the way I use language reflects or marks my identity as a particular kind of social subject – I talk like a white middle-class woman because I am (already) a white middle-class woman – the critical account suggests language is one of the things that *constitutes* my identity as a particular kind of subject. Sociolinguistics says that how you act depends on who you are; critical theory says that who you are (and are taken to be) depends on how you act. [emphasis in original]

Here Cameron argues for an understanding of gender that reverses the relationship between linguistic practices and social identities traditionally posited within the quantitative sociolinguistics or variationist paradigm.

While the theorizing of gender as "performative" has succeeded in problematizing mechanistic and essentialist notions of gender that underlie much variationist work in sociolinguistics, for some feminist linguists (e.g. Wodak 1997) Butler's formulation ignores the power relations that impregnate most situations in which gender is "performed" and in so doing affords subjects unbounded agency. For Cameron (1997), Butler's (1990) discussion of performativity does, arguably, acknowledge these power relations, that is, by alluding to the "rigid regulatory frame" within which gendered identities are produced. Yet, as Cameron (1997: 31) also points out, often philosophical treatments of this "frame" remain very abstract: "for social researchers interested in applying the performativity thesis to concrete instances of behavior, the specifics of this 'frame' and its operation in a particular context will be far more significant considerations than they seem to be in many philosophical discussions." The routine enactment of gender is often, perhaps always, subject to what Cameron calls the "institutional coerciveness" of social situations; in other words, dominant gender ideologies often mold and/or inhibit the kinds of gendered identities that women (and men) produce.

Addressing the tensions between local and more universal accounts of language and gender, Bergvall (1999) emphasizes the need to analyze dominant gender ideologies that pre-exist and structure local (linguistic) enactments of gender. That is, while more local and contextual accounts of language and gender (e.g. Eckert and McConnell-Ginet 1992a, 1992b, 1999) move us away from overarching and excessive generalizations about women, men, and "gendered" talk, Bergvall (1999: 282) suggests that we also consider the force of socially ascribed gender norms – "the assumptions and expectations of (often binary) ascribed social roles against which any performance of gender is constructed, accommodated to, or resisted." Likewise, Woolard and Schieffelin (1994: 72) argue that we must connect the "microculture of communicative action" to what they call "macrosocial constraints on language and behavior." Certainly, the examination of language and gender within institutions elucidates some of the macro-constraints that pre-exist local performances of gender. Indeed, Gal (1991) suggests that because women and men interact primarily in institutions such as workplaces, families, schools, and political forums, the investigation of language and gender in informal conversations, outside of these institutions, has severe limitations. It "creates the illusion that gendered talk is mainly a personal characteristic" (p. 185), whereas, as much feminist research has revealed, gender is also a structuring principle of institutions.

Sexual assault adjudication processes are a rich and fertile site for the investigation of gendered ideologies that pre-exist and "coerce" many performances of gender. Embedded within legal structures, as feminist legal theorists (e.g. MacKinnon 1987, 1989; Bartlett and Kennedy 1991; Lacey 1998) have argued, are androcentric and sexist assumptions that typically masquerade as "objective" truths. The crime of rape, in particular, has received attention from feminists critical of the law, because in Smart's (1989: 50) words, "the legal treatment of rape epitomizes the core of the problem of law for feminism." Not only are dominant notions about male and female sexuality and violence against women implicated in legal statutes and judicial decisions surrounding sexual assault, I argue they also penetrate the discursive arena of the trial. Moreover, the material force with which the law legitimates a certain vision of the social order, through, for example, fines, imprisonment, or execution, means that the discursive imposition of ideologies in legal settings will have a particular potency. Hence, by locating my analysis of gendered linguistic practices in the context of sexual assault adjudication processes, I propose to explore the "institutional coerciveness" of these particular institutional settings or, put differently, the way that these settings shape and constrain performances of gender.

While acknowledging the dynamic and performative nature of gendered identities, I demonstrate in what follows how particular institutions make available or thwart certain definitions of femininity and masculinity, thereby homogenizing what in other contexts might be realized as variable and heterogeneous performances of femininity or masculinity. That is, outside of these institutional settings, when unaffected by the discursive and ideological constraints that permeate these contexts (e.g. when participating in other kinds of communities of practice), the male defendant and female complainants might recount their narratives quite differently. Concomitantly, the nature of their gendered (linguistic) identities, because they are mediated by the particular social practices and activities within which participants are engaged, might also be quite different outside of these institutions. While, as Eckert and McConnell-Ginet (1992a, 1992b, 1999) suggest, gendered identities, and social identities more generally, arise out of individuals' participation in a diverse set of communities of practice, institutional forces may constrain such identities, belying the complexity of their formation. And, to the extent that certain gendered identities are inhibited or facilitated by the sexual assault hearings analyzed here, this kind of institutional discourse provides a window onto the "rigid regulatory frame" (Butler 1990) within which gender is often enacted.

Previous scholarship on the language of institutional settings has investigated the *interactional* (i.e. inter-sentential) mechanisms by which certain ideological or interpretive "frames" dominate institutional interactions, while others are suppressed (Philips 1992). Todd (1989) and Fisher (1991), for example, document how doctors' medical and technical concerns prevail in interactions with patients, even when patients articulate their problems in social and/or biographical terms. In her comparison of a doctor–patient interaction and a nurse-practioner–patient interaction, Fisher (1991: 162) isolates aspects of interactional structure related to such discursive control. The doctor, much more than the nurse-practitioner, asked questions that "both allow a very limited exchange of information and leave the way open for his [the doctor's] own assumptions to structure subsequent exchanges." By contrast, the nurse-practitioner used open-ended, probing questions which maximized the patient's own "voice" and interpretation of medical problems. In Fisher's (1991: 162) terms, in these kinds of interactions "both the questions and the silences – the questions not asked – do ideological work." Not only was Fisher's doctor–patient interaction structured by the doctor's assumptions (due to questions that allowed a limited exchange of information), but implicit in these assumptions were views about the centrality of the nuclear family to this mother's sense of well-being or ill-health. According to Fisher, the doctor's questions functioned to reinscribe the hegemonic discourse that "justif[ies] the traditional nuclear family which has at its center a *mother*" (Fisher 1991: 162, emphasis in original).

In this chapter I too consider the "ideological work" performed by questions in institutional settings. While others have documented the way that judges' decisions in sexual assault cases can be informed by rape mythologies (Coates 1997; Coates et al. 1994), this chapter focuses on discriminatory views of violence against women as they (re)circulate within adjudication processes themselves. Indeed, embedded within the questions asked of complainants, rape mythologies become much more insidious, I argue, because of the structuring potential of language. Not only do questions, with their implicit and explicit propositions, frame and structure the complainants' "talk" about their experiences of sexual assault, they also produce the complainants as particular kinds of subjects – as subjects who are "passive" in their responses to sexual aggression, as opposed to strategic and active. Fairclough's (1995: 39) comments on his use of the term "subject" within institutional contexts are relevant here: "the term 'subject' is used . . . because it has the double sense of agent ('the subjects of history') and affected ('the Queen's subjects'); this captures the concept of *subject as qualified to act through being constrained – 'subjected' – to an institutional frame*" (emphasis mine). In the terms of this investigation, one manifestation of Fairclough's "institutional frame" are the questions asked of complainants; that is, the questions' presuppositions embody ideological perspectives which have consequences for the way in which the complainants are "qualified to act" linguistically.

3   Data

The data analyzed here come from two sources. They were transcribed from audiotaped recordings of a York University (Toronto, Canada) disciplinary tribunal dealing with sexual harassment; in addition they come from transcripts of a Canadian criminal trial in which the same defendant was charged with two counts of sexual assault. Both adjudication processes dealt with the same events – two alleged instances of acquaintance rape with two different women. The complainants were casual acquaintances prior to the alleged instances of sexual assault. They met coincidentally a short time after the incidents, discovered each other's experience with the accused, and together launched complaints against him in the context of York University and later in the context of the Canadian criminal justice system. Within the context of York University, the accused was alleged to have violated York University's Standards of Student Conduct, specifically the provisions of its sexual harassment policy. Within the context of the criminal justice system, the accused was charged on two separate counts of sexual assault on two separate complainants.

The accused and the complainants were all White, undergraduate students at York University. (Pseudonyms are used throughout this chapter to refer to the accused and the two complainants.) Each of the women, on two separate nights three days apart, had been socializing with the defendant and had invited him to her dormitory room on the university campus. The first complainant, Connie, was a casual acquaintance of the accused. On the night of the alleged assault, Connie met the accused, Matt, for dinner at approximately 10:30 in the evening. After an enjoyable dinner, according to the complainant's testimony, Connie invited Matt back to her room in university residence. At that point, he briefly massaged her and they then engaged in some consensual kissing. From that point on, Connie reported in her testimony that she objected to his further sexual advances; in spite of her objections, Matt allegedly persisted in unwanted sexual aggression. His acts of unwanted sexual aggression, according to Connie's testimony, included: removing her clothes, putting his fingers inside her vagina, putting his penis between her legs and rubbing it against her, and pushing her face onto his lap so that she was forced to perform fellatio on him until orgasm. In both the university tribunal and the criminal trial, these facts were not at issue. What was at issue was whether or not the sexual acts were consensual.

The second case involved the complainant Marg. Matt and Marg had met for the first time the night before the alleged sexual assault. On the night of the assault, Marg was socializing with her friend, Melinda, at a downtown Toronto club. Marg's car was towed away during the time Marg and Melinda were at the club and, as a result, they sought help from Matt and his friend, Bob (also Melinda's boyfriend). Given the lateness of the hour (3:00 or 4:00 in the morning), it was decided that the four would spend the night in Marg's university residence room and that Matt would help Marg retrieve her car the next morning. After deciding that the men would massage the women, and vice versa, Marg agreed that Matt could sleep in her bed, but warned him on a number of occasions that if he crossed the line "he was dead." That is, in this case, the complainant did not admit to any consensual sexual activity as the first complainant did. Once in bed, according to the complainant's testimony, Matt initiated a number of unwanted sexual advances: he began to go under her clothes and touched her breasts and vagina. On a number of occasions, as a result of the unwanted sexual aggression, Marg asked Melinda, who was in the other bed with Bob, to join her in the washroom. In spite of Marg's attempts to solicit help from Melinda, and by association, Bob, Matt continued to initiate unwanted acts of aggression, according to Marg's testimony. These included: putting his foot between her legs and inserting his toe in her vagina, unbuttoning her shirt, sucking on her breasts and putting his fingers in her vagina. As in the first case, in both the tribunal and the criminal trial, the occurrence of these particular sexual acts was not at issue; what was at issue was whether or not they were consensual.

3.1 The York University disciplinary tribunal

York University disciplinary tribunals are university trials that operate outside of the provincial or federal legal system. Members of the university community can be tried for various kinds of misconduct, including unauthorized entry or access, theft or destruction of property, assault or threat of assault and harassment, and discrimination that contravenes the provincial Human Rights Code or the Canadian Charter of Rights and Freedoms. Each case is heard by three tribunal members who are drawn from a larger pool consisting of university faculty members and students. The tribunal members decide upon the guilt or innocence of defendants and on penalties. Penalties range from public admonition to expulsion from the university. Normally, these tribunals are open to the public and are audiotaped. The tribunal members hearing this particular case consisted of a man who was a faculty member in the Law Faculty (the tribunal's chair), a woman who was a faculty member in the Faculty of Arts, and a woman graduate student in the Faculty of Arts. The case against the accused was presented by the university's legal counsel. The accused was at times represented by a family friend, at times by his mother, and at times represented himself.

While not technically a criminal court of law, the York University disciplinary tribunals function like one to the extent that each side, the prosecution and the defense, presents its version of the events at issue to the members of the disciplinary tribunal. In the case described here, the complainants, the accused, and their witnesses testified under questioning by their own representatives and by the tribunal members. All participants were also cross-examined by representatives from the other side. Thus, unlike jury trials, the "talk" of this disciplinary tribunal was not designed for an overhearing, *non-speaking* audience – the jury (Atkinson and Drew 1979), but rather for members of the disciplinary tribunal who themselves had the right to ask questions of the accused, complainants, and witnesses. The testimonies of witnesses seemed to follow no strict order in this particular tribunal. For example, both complainants testified under questioning from the university lawyer, the tribunal members, and the accused's representative(s) at the beginning of the hearing and then again at the end of the hearing.

As stated previously, within the context of the university tribunal the accused was alleged to have violated York University's Standards of Student Conduct, specifically the provisions of its sexual harassment policy. According to the regulations of York University, *sexual harassment* is defined as "the unwanted attention of a sexually oriented nature made by a person who knows or ought reasonably to know that such attention is unwanted." In determining whether the accused had violated the standards of student conduct deemed appropriate by the university, I am assuming that the university tribunal members were employing the standard of proof that other administrative tribunals in Canada (i.e. the normal standard in civil law) employ – that of "balance of probabilities." That is, according to a "balance of probabilities," the tribunal members were to decide which of the parties was to be believed more.

3.2   *The criminal trial*

The accused was charged by the same plaintiffs under the Criminal Code of Canada on two counts of sexual assault. In this particular criminal trial, a judge determined the guilt or innocence of the accused and the accused's sentence. The complainants were witnesses for the province (i.e. the state), which is represented by a Crown attorney; the accused was represented by a defense lawyer. In the criminal trial, then, it was the prosecuting and defense lawyers who asked questions of the defendant, the complainants, and witnesses in direct and cross-examination. Unlike the university tribunal, testimony and question-asking in criminal trials follow a prescribed order: the Crown first presents its case whereby its witnesses provide testimony under questioning (from the Crown) in direct examination and (from the defense lawyer) in cross-examination; the defense then presents its case whereby its witnesses provide testimony under questioning (from the defense lawyer) in direct examination and (from the Crown) in cross-examination. All criminal trials are conducted according to three foundational principles: (1) the accused is presumed innocent until proven guilty; (2) the Crown must prove "beyond a reasonable doubt" that the accused committed the offense; and (3) the accused has the right to silence. In this particular case, the accused testified. Moreover, both the Crown and the defense agreed that the sexual acts in question had occurred. Thus, the onus was on the Crown to prove "beyond a reasonable doubt" that the complainants had not consented to the sexual acts in question.

4 Ideological Frame: The Utmost Resistance Standard

Until the 1950s and 1960s in the United States, the statutory requirement of utmost resistance was a necessary criterion for the crime of rape (Estrich 1987); that is, if a woman did not resist a man's sexual advances to the utmost, then rape did not occur. Estrich (1986: 1122) comments: "in effect, the 'utmost resistance' rule required both that the woman resist to the 'utmost' and that such resistance must not have abated during the struggle." Because women were thought to fabricate accusations of rape, strict – and unique – rules of proof, of which resistance requirements were a part, were imposed upon rape cases in the nineteenth century (Schulhofer 1998). About resistance requirements in particular, Schulhofer (1998: 19) says the following: "to make sure that women complaining of rape had really been unwilling, courts required them to show physical resistance, usually expressed as 'earnest resistance' or even resistance 'to the utmost'." Within the Canadian context, Busby (1999: 275) argues, like Schulhofer (1998), that "special evidence rules" have been applied to sexual violence cases, focusing far more attention on the complainant's behavior than is possible in other kinds of criminal cases. While resistance requirements, in particular, have not been encoded in statutes in Canada, they have often been operative in the adjudication of sexual violence cases. Backhouse (1991: 103) argues that a very high standard of resistance was set in the Ontario case of *R. v. Fick* in 1866 when the trial judge in this case stipulated that in order for rape to occur "the woman [must have] been quite overcome by force or terror, she resisting as much as she could, and resisting so as to make the prisoner see and know that she really was resisting to the utmost" (cited in Backhouse 1991: 103). In the 1970s, Clark and Lewis (1977) investigated the characteristics of Toronto-area rape cases leading to perpetrator arrest and prosecution in 1970, and determined that a victim's testimony of lack of consent was deemed credible only when she resisted her attacker to the utmost of her capabilities. Thus, whether or not strict rules of proof or "special evidence rules" are actually encoded in law, the adjudication of sexual assault cases can still require such strict rules of proof in order to convict the accused. Indeed, in the remainder of this chapter I argue that the "utmost resistance standard" is the primary ideological frame through which the events in question and, in particular, the complainants' actions are understood and evaluated. This (re)framing functions to characterize the women as not "resisting to the utmost" and ultimately (re)constructs the events as consensual sex.

5 Analysis

What follows is an analysis of various propositions that emerged in question–answer sequences between cross-examining questioners, including the so-called neutral tribunal members, and complainants. Taken together, I argue that these propositions "frame" the way the events come to be understood: they function as an ideological filter through which the complainants' acts of resistance are characterized as "inaction" and the events generally are (re)constructed as consensual sex. (These examples and analyses are taken from a much larger study investigating the language of sexual assault adjudication processes. See Ehrlich (2001) for a fuller treatment of this topic.)

5.1   The complainants as "autonomous individuals"

The so-called options and choices available to the complainants in the context of escalating sexual violence was a theme evident in many of the questions asked of them. Consider example (1) where Matt's cross-examining representative, TM, in the university tribunal questions Connie.

(1)   *Tribunal*
TM: So I guess my my question to you is uh <u>you had a choice</u> at this point even though you say in your your oral testimony that you *didn't* have a choice. <u>Everybody has a choice</u> . . . and your choice was that you could have asked him to leave. So I'm wondering why you didn't ask him to leave? <u>We all have free will</u>. Let me rephrase the question or put another question to you then in the absence of an answer of that one. Why did you let uh what you say happened happen?
CD: ((*crying*)) I didn't let it happen.
TM: But <u>you had certain options</u>. You could have left the room. By your admission there was a time when he was asleep. You could have called through a very thin wall. Uh:: you actually left the room to go to the washroom. Uh <u>you had a number of options here and you chose not to take any of them</u>.

More often in the form of declaratives than interrogatives, as the underlined excerpts in (1) show, TM focuses on the *options* and *choices* Connie ostensibly had. Moreover, he makes assertions about the free will and choices that we all enjoy. One is reminded here of the classic liberal subject – the rational, autonomous, and freely choosing individual. Yet, as socialist feminists, among others, have argued, such a view denies the socially structured inequalities among individuals that shape and restrict so-called options. In an analogous way, TM's talk about options, choice, and freedom fails to acknowledge the power dynamics that can shape and restrict women's behavior in the context of potential sexual violence.

In keeping with this view of the complainants as unconstrained by socially structured inequalities, many of the question–answer sequences involving complainants (and cross-examiners or tribunal members) identified the seemingly numerous and unlimited options that they did not pursue. Example (2), from a tribunal member's questioning of Marg, displays a delineation of options not pursued by the complainant: GK lists (i.e. asserts) a series of actions that Marg did not perform – *You never make an attempt to put him on the floor . . . to close the door behind him or . . . to lock the door* – and then asks whether they were offensive to her. GK's use of *only* in *You only have to cross the room* is indicative of her own view of such actions: Marg could have *easily* performed them.

(2)   *Tribunal*
GK: What I'm trying to say and I I realize what I'm saying is not going. . . . You never make an attempt to put him on the floor, or when he leaves the room to close the door behind him, or you know you have several occasions to to lock the door. You only have to cross the room. Or to move him to the floor, but these things are offensive to you?
MB: I was afraid. No one can understand that except for the people that were there. I was extremely afraid of being hurt. Uhm: as for signals, they were being ignored. I tried I mean maybe they weren't being ignored I don't know why he didn't listen to them. I shouldn't say they were being ignored but he wasn't listening. And I kept telling him, I kept telling him, I was afraid to ask him to sleep on the floor. It crossed my mind but I didn't want to get hurt. I didn't want to get into a big fight. I just wanted to go to sleep and forget about the whole entire night.

Examples (3) and (4), from the criminal trial, show the cross-examiner suggesting that "seeking help" was a reasonable option for Connie.

(3)   *Trial*
Q: And I take it part of your involvement then on the evening of January 27th and having Mr. A. come back to your residence that you felt that you were in this comfort zone because you were going to a place that you were, very familiar; correct?
CD: It was my home, yes.
Q: <u>And you knew you had a way out if there was any difficulty</u>?
CD: I didn't really take into account any difficulty. I never expected there to be any.
Q: I appreciate that. <u>Nonetheless, you knew that there were other people around who knew you and obviously would come to your assistance, I take it, if you had some problems</u>, or do you know? Maybe you can't answer that.
CD: No, I can't answer that. I can't answer that. I was inviting him to my home, not my home that I share with other people, not, you know, a communal area. I was taking him to my home and I really didn't take into account anybody else around, anybody that I lived near. It was like inviting somebody to your home.
Q: Fair enough. And I take it from what you told us in your evidence this morning that it never ever crossed your mind when this whole situation reached the point where you couldn't handle it, or were no longer in control, to <u>merely</u> go outside your door to summons someone?
CD: No.

(4)   *Trial*
Q: What I am suggesting to you, ma'am, is that as a result of that situation with someone other than Mr. A., you knew what to do in the sense that if you were in a compromising position or you were being, I won't use the word harass, but being pressured by someone you knew what to do, didn't you?

CD: No, I didn't. Somebody had suggested that, I mean, I could get this man who wasn't a student not be be permitted on campus and that's what I did.

Q: What – but I am suggesting that you knew that there was someone or a source or a facility within the university that might be able to assist you if you were involved in a difficult situation, isn't that correct, because you went to the student security already about this other person?

CD: Yeah, okay. If you are asking if I knew about the existence of student security, yes, I did.

The underlined sentences in examples (3) and (4) are "controlling" questions in Woodbury's (1984) sense. That is, in producing such questions the defense attorney is signaling his (ostensible) belief in the truth of their propositions and his expectation that the propositions will be confirmed by the addressee. Moreover, these questions all contain the factive predicate *know*, a predicate that presupposes the truth of its complement. More specifically, what is taken for granted and assumed in the cross-examiner's remarks is the "fact" that help was readily available on the university campus for those in trouble; what is "declared" – in the form of controlling questions – is Connie's awareness of these sources of help. The juxtaposition of these propositions has the effect of implicitly undermining Connie's claim that she was sexually assaulted. That is, if it is established in the discourse that help was available and that Connie was aware of its availability, then her "failure" to seek assistance casts doubt on her credibility. The final question of example (3) further undermines the charges of sexual assault – It *never ever crossed your mind . . . to merely go outside your door to summons someone?* – insofar as the word *merely* characterizes the seeking of help as unproblematic and effortless. Examples (5) and (6), both from the criminal trial, show the judge and the cross-examining lawyer asking Connie and Marg, respectively, why they didn't utter other words in their various attempts to resist Matt's sexual aggression. Connie reports saying "Look, I don't want to sleep with you" at a certain point that night and Marg recounts one of several incidents when she attempts to elicit Bob's help, saying "Bob where do you get these persistent friends," yet these expressions of resistance are problematized by the questioners. Both of the underlined questions in (5) and (6) are negative *wh*-questions. First, then, they presuppose the fact that the complainant has not uttered the words suggested by the questioner: "Don't undue [sic] my bra" and "Why don't you knock it off" in (5) and "Bob, he was doing it again, please help me" in (6). More significantly, however, negative questions signal a speaker's surprise at or conflict with the presupposed proposition contained therein (Lyons 1977; Woodbury 1984). Hence, when the judge and the cross-examining lawyer produce utterances of the form "Why didn't you say X?" they are subtly communicating their surprise at/opposition to the complainants' failure to produce the suggested utterances. Indeed, Lyons (1977: 766) argues that negative questions are "commonly . . . associated, in utterance, with a prosodic or paralinguistic modulation indicative of *impatience* or *annoyance*" (emphasis mine). Of added import is the fact that in example (5), it is the judge – the ostensibly neutral adjudicator – who is expressing his impatience or annoyance with the complainant's "inaction."

(5)   *Trial*
Q: And in fact just raising another issue that I would like you to help us with if you can, this business of you realizing when the line was getting blurred when you said "Look, I don't want to sleep with you," or words to that effect, yes, you remember that?
CD: Yes.
Q: Well, when you said that, what did that mean or what did you want that to mean, not to have intercourse with him?
CD: Yeah, I mean, ultimately, that's what it meant. It also, I mean –
The Court: You didn't want to sleep with him but why not, "Don't undue [sic] my bra" and "Why don't you knock it off"?
CD: Actually, "I don't want" – "I don't want to sleep with you" is very cryptic, and certainly as he got his hands under my shirt, as he took off my shirt, as he undid my bra, as he opened my belt and my pants and pulled them down and I said, "Please don't, please stop. Don't do that. I don't want you to do that, please don't," that's pretty direct as well.

(6)   *Trial*
MB: . . . And then we got back into bed and Matt immediately started again and then I said to Bob, "Bob where do you get these persistent friends?"
Q: Why did you even say that? You wanted to get Bob's attention?
MB: I assumed that Bob talked to Matt in the hallway and told him to knock it off.
Q: You assumed?
MB: He was talking to him and came back in and said everything was all right.
Q: Bob said that?
MB: Yes.
Q: But when you made that comment, you wanted someone to know, you wanted Bob to know that this was a signal that Matt was doing it again?
MB: Yes.
Q: A mixed signal, ma'am, I suggest?
MB: To whom?
Q: What would you have meant by, "Where do you get these persistent friends?"
MB: Meaning Bob he's doing it again, please help me.
Q: Why didn't you say, "Bob, he was doing it again, please help me?"
MB: Because I was afraid Matt would get mad.
Q: You weren't so afraid because you told Bob, "Where do you get these persistent friends?" Did you think Matt would be pleased with that comment because it was so general?
MB: I didn't think about it but I thought that was my way of letting Bob know what was going on.

In examples (7) and (8) the option of "asking Matt to leave" is explored by the questioners. The underlined sentence in (7) contains the matrix clause *it's quite obvious that*, which presupposes the truth of its embedded clause. Thus, what is taken for granted by the defense lawyer is that it never occurred to Connie that she might tell Matt to leave. The underlined sentence in (8) displays the same presuppositions as the underlined sentence in (7) in addition to possessing other pragmatic properties. As a negative *wh*-question, not only does it presuppose the truth of its proposition – "You did not ask him to leave," it also expresses the speaker's surprise at or conflict with this proposition. The preceding negative question in (8), *did you not have a choice?*, has a similar effect: the cross-examining questioner expresses his surprise at Connie's failure to pursue options that would seem to be "freely chosen."

(7)   *Trial*
Q: I am not trying to be critical here. We weren't there, you were, but when you talk about I think instinct, ma'am, the muscle memory was there when Matt had already offered to leave once, and I take it <u>it's quite obvious that it never crossed your mind at that point to tell him to leave</u> and in fact he never did?
CD: No, the context was certainly different. Before I could even think of him leaving I wanted him to stop. I mean, that came first.

(8)   *Tribunal*
TM: My question to you is although you say you have no choice . . . uh did you not have a choice? You could have asked him to leave at this point. <u>Why did you not ask him to leave?</u>
CD: Because . . . I wanted to explain to him why I wanted him to stop. I wanted him to understand I didn't want him to be angry. I didn't want him to be offended, I wanted him to understand.

In response to many questions about options not pursued, both complainants would sometimes make reference to the fact that they were physically incapable of carrying out the suggested actions. In (9) below, for example, Connie explains that she was *underneath* Matt at a certain point in time and cites her immobility as the reason she did not leave, did not pick up a phone, etc.: *I mean, before I could be in a position to pick up a phone to, to leave, I had to be in a position to move and I wasn't.* In spite of her assertions throughout example (9) (this example continues immediately after example (7)) that she was underneath Matt, that she couldn't move, that she couldn't get her arms free, the cross-examiner continues to ask Connie about her acts (or lack thereof) of physical resistance: whether she tried to push him off (*Did you try to push him off?*) and whether she sat up to express her resistance verbally (*Did you ever sit up at the point that he was trying to remove your pants and say, "What's going on here? Look at the two of us, how far we have gone here"?*). Such questions are reminiscent of Schulhofer's (1998: 20) description of a 1947 Nebraska Supreme Court decision, which applied the utmost resistance standard to a woman's charge of rape: "only if a woman resisted physically and 'to the utmost' could a man be expected to realize that his actions were against her will."

(9) *Trial*

Q: And all of this happened fairly quickly. Again, I realise it's ridiculous to suggest that you are looking at a watch, but I take it that we've got this ongoing behaviour, that it's so physical that you are in no position to leave or do anything?

CD: That's right. I mean, before I could be in a position to pick up a phone to, to leave, I had to be in a position to move and I wasn't. So before thinking of I have to pick up the phone and I have to walk out the door, I had to think of how am I going to get out from underneath this man.

Q: Right. <u>Did you try to push him off?</u>

CD: Yes, I did.

Q: You weren't able to?

CD: No, I wasn't.

Q: Is that because you weren't able to get your arms free or because he was on top of you?

CD: I couldn't get my arms free and I couldn't push him off.

Q: At one point you were naked?

CD: Yes.

Q: At what point was that?

CD: I can't even pinpoint a specific time.

Q: Well, your shirt came off first as a result of the fondling of the breasts, right?

CD: Yes.

Q: And Mr. A. started to undue [*sic*] your belt and try to take your pants and try to take them down to which you responded "don't" and all of that other stuff?

CD: Yes.

Q: And yet he was still able to do that with your other pants?

CD: Yes.

Q: And were your arms still in the same position above your head and crossed over and being held by one hand?

CD: Yes. I am not sure at what point exactly he let go of them.

Q: But I take it, whatever he did, if he let go of your hands they went to another part of your body that rendered you incapable of getting out from under?

CD: Yes.

Q: Ma'am, <u>did you ever sit up at the point that he was trying to remove your pants and say, "What's going on here? Look at the two of us, how far we have gone here", nothing like that.</u>

CD: Everytime I tried to sit up, I got pushed back down.

Example (10), from the tribunal, also shows the cross-examining questioner posing questions to the complainant, Marg, about physical acts of resistance. (This question–answer sequence concerns Marg's responses to Matt's attempts to put his toe in her vagina.) A negative *wh*-question, the first underlined sentence, presupposes the proposition "Marg didn't get up" and, in addition, signals the speaker's surprise at/conflict with such a proposition. Moreover, the word *just* in *Why didn't you just get up?* expresses the speaker's belief that such an action could have been performed easily and unproblematically by Marg. Further on in the example, we see that the questioner asks two more questions about Marg "getting up": a negative tag question – *you did not get up. Is that correct?* – and a negative prosodic yes–no question – *And you still did not get up?* Both continue to express the cross-examiner's (ostensible) surprise at her "lack of action"; furthermore, the word *still* suggests that the act of getting up was long overdue. Despite the fact that several of Marg's responses point to a physical act of resistance she did perform – pushing Matt's toe away – this act was clearly not "vehement" enough to satisfy the cross-examiner's standard of resistance. (Equals signs represent "latched" or immediately continuing speech; square brackets signal overlapping speech.)

(10) *Tribunal*
TM: It's after that point that you're sitting on a windowsill and now comes a rather bizarre incident according to you.
MB: Yeah.
TM: Uh:: he attempts to stick his toe =
MB: = Right =
TM: = in your vagina?
MB: Yes.
TM: Uh::: . . . now you were very upset the previous night when a total stranger whom you picked up in a bar took your hand and put it on his . . . uh crotch. Uh::m . . . yet you don't deny that you continue to sit there at the windowsill while this is going on.
MB: I didn't sit there and let him do that. I was sitting in the fetal position, he kept trying to put his toe there and I kept pushing it away.
TM: <u>Why didn't you just get up?</u>
MB: *I didn't know what to do. You don't understand. The whole entire time. I didn't know what to do. I was not thinking clearly. Where would I have gone?*
TM: You've now had a whole night's experience with this young man according to you =
MB: = And I [still didn't know what to do.]
TM: [And you're still prepared] to uh to to tell this panel that you are sitting there allowing this kind of bizarre [behaviour to go on?]
MB: [No I wasn't allowing it.] I kept pushing his foot away and telling him that I did not want to go to his house.
TM: <u>But I come back to the fact you did not get up. Is that correct?</u> When he first began to do this?
MB: No I pushed his foot away.
TM: And then he continued to do it?
MB: Right.
TM: <u>And you still did not get up?</u>
MB: I:: don't think so.

Repeatedly posing questions that presupposed and (pseudo)asserted the complainants' access to unlimited, freely chosen options, I am suggesting that the defense and the supposedly neutral tribunal members transformed the complainants' strategic responses to sexual aggression into ineffective acts of resistance. Consider example (6) above. This example displays one kind of strategic response adopted by the complainants to Matt's sexual aggression. When Matt begins his sexual aggression once again, Marg attempts to attract

Bob's attention. Rather than saying "Bob, he is doing it again, please help me," as the defense lawyer suggests, however, Marg employs a somewhat more indirect formulation: "Bob where do you get these persistent friends?" Asked by the defense lawyer why she uses what he characterizes as a mixed signal, Marg responds that she was afraid Matt would get mad. That is, what drives the complainants' actions in a situation of escalating sexual violence is not the free will of an autonomous individual, but rather the strong emotions of fear, shock, and confusion engendered by Matt's sexual aggression. Viewed within an alternative contextualizing framework, where the structural and systemic inequalities of male/female sexual relations are acknowledged and foregrounded, Marg's utterance could be construed as a strategic response to her fear of Matt's escalating violence. Yet, within the context of example (6), where Marg's options are represented as unlimited and her fear of Matt discounted, the utterance "Bob where do you get these persistent friends?" is (re)constructed as "passive" and "lacking in appropriate resistance."

5.2 The transformative work of questions

In keeping with Fisher's (1991) claim that questions perform ideological work, I have attempted to demonstrate the way that propositions presupposed and (pseudo)asserted in questions formed a powerful ideological frame through which the events under investigation in this trial and tribunal were understood. Specifically, the ideological frame of utmost resistance functioned as a discursive constraint, restricting the complainants' "talk" about their experiences and transforming their strategic agency into ineffectual agency. Example (11), from the testimony of the complainants' witness Melinda in cross-examination, is illustrative of the women's self-characterizations as they respond to (i.e. are subjected to) the barrage of questions delineating the numerous and unlimited options available to them.

(11) *Trial*
Q: Guess I am just asking you did you have it in your mind that your room at some point might be a place that you can go, particularly when you started to get into trouble with Mr. A.?
MK: That didn't even enter my mind.
Q: Why didn't it enter your mind?
MK: Because as things were happening they were happening so fast and I didn't have a lot of time to think about what to do, what to do. Everything clouded over on me.
Q: Right. I know it did, but what about from 4:30 in the morning until ten or 11 in the morning, it still didn't cross your mind?
MK: No.
Q: You know your roommate was there because you said "I am home", or words to that effect?
MK: Yes.

((*a few intervening questions*))

Q: It never crossed your mind to go back and speak to Wayne again since that was his job?

MK: No.

Q: Did it ever cross your mind?

((*a few intervening questions*))

Q: You didn't think that he might be a safe person to help you out of your dilemma?

MK: I wasn't thinking. I wasn't thinking clearly and I didn't know what to do.

Q: Is it because of your exhaustion you don't know what to do now? You sure seemed to know what to do when the car was towed and the fact that you wanted to get back up to see Bob and that suggests a presence of mind you have?

MK: I have never been put in a situation like that and, as I said, things were happening quickly and I was at a loss of what to do. I have never been put in that position. I am not experienced with that. I just didn't even think about it.

Implicitly claiming that Melinda has "failed" to seek help for Marg, the defense attorney asks a number of questions about possible sources of help. Melinda is questioned about whether she thought of her residence room as a safe refuge and whether she enlisted the help of her roommate or the residence adviser, Wayne. Faced with repeated questions about her "failure" to pursue such options, Melinda responds by referring to her inability to think clearly under the circumstances. Indeed, this is one "stroke" in the portrayal of what I'm calling ineffectual agency – a portrayal produced in the "talk" of the complainants and their witness in the process of being "subjected . . . to an institutional frame" (Fairclough 1995: 39). Contributing to the realization of this depiction are a variety of grammatical forms (illustrated in example (11)), used by the complainants and their witness, that emphasize their inability to *act* in ways that effectively express their resistance to Matt's sexual aggression. That is, when questioned about the "numerous" and unlimited "options" that they were "free" to pursue, the complainants and their witness did not generally respond by casting themselves in the roles of agents and actors, that is, as individuals who "purposefully initiate[d] or cause[d] actions" (Capps and Ochs 1995: 67). Rather, when they did represent themselves as initiators or causers of actions (i.e. as agents or actors) their causal role was severely diminished; otherwise, they represented themselves as experiencers of cognitive or emotional states or as patients – entities that were acted upon. Specifically, the complainants and their witness (1) referred to themselves as agents or actors of negated actions, that is, actions that were *not* performed; (2) referred to themselves as agents or actors of unsuccessful actions; (3) referred to themselves as agents or actors of actions, the force of which was diminished by adverbial or adjectival phrases; (4) referred to themselves as experiencers of negated cognitive states; (5) referred to themselves as experiencers of fear; and (6) referred to themselves as patients, that is, entities that were *acted upon*. Specific examples follow.

5.2.1   Negated actions

In examples (12)–(14), the underlined sentences display the complainants and/or the witness as the agents or actors of grammatically negated acts. Generally, then, all of the underlined predicates designate actions that were not caused or initiated by the referents of their subjects.

(12)   I just sat there, and I didn't – <u>I didn't do anything. I didn't say anything</u>. (CD, Trial)

(13)   <u>I didn't fight and I didn't scream. I didn't say anything</u>. (MB, Trial)

(14)   And everything was happening so fast, <u>I didn't even think about knocking on the neighbour's door or anything</u>. (MK, Tribunal)

5.2.2   Unsuccessful actions

In a similar way, the underlined sentences in examples (15)–(17) all represent the complainants as agents or actors of actions that were *not* performed. In these examples, however, the acts are represented as "attempted" but "unsuccessful," given the presence of the main verb *try*.

(15)   Well, <u>I tried to</u> [talk to Bob about Matt's aggression]. The incident in the bathroom when I asked Bob to go talk to Marg . . . was the only thing I could think of . . . to get someone to tell Matt to stop it. (MK, Tribunal)

(16)   I was afraid. No one can understand that except for the people that were there. I was extremely afraid of being hurt. Uhm: as for signals, they were being ignored. <u>I tried</u> [to give signals of non-consent] I mean maybe they weren't being ignored I don't know why he didn't listen to them. (MB, Tribunal)

(17)   <u>I kept trying to move away and push my head back up</u> but he had my hair and every time – <u>every time I tried to</u>, he just pushed me back down. (CD, Trial)

5.2.3   Actions with limited force

Whereas examples (12)–(17) represent actions *not* caused or achieved by the complainants and/or their witness, examples (18)–(20) do depict the women as agents or actors of actions. The underlined sentences in (18)–(20), however, contain adverbial or adjectival phrases that diminish the force or effectiveness of these actions. The adverbial *just* modifies the events represented in (18)–(19), signifying that the actions were minimal or limited in some way. Likewise, in (20) CD's use of the phrase *the best I could come up with* suggests that there were *better* ways of resisting Matt.

(18) Q: Right. So what, so you did what?
     MB: So <u>I just sat there</u> and desperately hoped he would leave. (MB, Trial)

(19) Q: And you didn't encourage that and said, [*sic*] "Thanks for coming fel-
          lows, see you around," anything to jolly him out?
     MB: I was afraid and <u>I just sat there staring</u> I was so afraid. (MB, Trial)

(20) Q: So you didn't sort of then say, okay try plan "B." You didn't say, "Matt,
          I want you to leave." That would have been clear as a bell.
     CD: I didn't really have a well thought out plan "A" and plan "B." I was
          running on I think instinct and is <u>the best I could come up with was
          "Don't, stop, no, please don't."</u> (CD, Trial)

5.2.4   *Experiencers of negated cognitive states*

As with many of Melinda's utterances in example (11), examples (21)–(24) show
the complainants as experiencers of negated cognitive states. First, then, the
women are not representing themselves as purposefully or willfully initiating
actions. Second, they are not representing themselves as experiencers of *positive*
cognitive states, that is, as having ideas and/or knowledge about possible
actions. On the contrary, the underlined sentences in (21)–(24) depict the complainants as unable to act purposefully or willfully because they lack knowledge or are unable to think clearly.

(21) Because I was in shock and everything started coming in on me and <u>I didn't
     know what to do</u>. I was tired and <u>I wasn't sure what to do</u>. (MB, Trial)

(22) All I wanted was to take – someone to take control of the situation and help
     me because <u>I wasn't thinking of what to do for myself</u>. (MB, Trial)

(23) He seemed very angry and I realized I had lost control of the situation and
     <u>didn't really know what to do about it</u> and <u>couldn't really think straight</u> at
     this point other than wanting him to stop. (CD, Trial)

(24) <u>I didn't know what to do</u>. I just felt overwhelmed, I was so tired. I felt so
     helpless. <u>I didn't know what to do</u>. (CD, Trial)

5.2.5   *Experiencers of fear*

By far, the most frequent response to questions concerning the complainants'
and their witness's "failure" to pursue the numerous options presented to them
was that they had been motivated by fear. I provide the following question–
answer sequence as a representative example:

(25) *Trial*
Q: And you didn't encourage that and said, [*sic*] "Thanks for coming fellows, see you around," anything to jolly him out?
MB: <u>I was afraid and I just sat there staring I was so afraid</u>.
Q: You were afraid that Mr. A. was saying to Bob, "Let's go out of here, let's leave"?
MB: No. <u>I was afraid because he was mad</u> because I didn't want to do anything with him so he was mad with me, <u>so I was afraid that he was going to physically hurt me</u> because I didn't want to do anything with him.

5.2.6 *Patients or entities acted upon*

Using grammatical constructions that even further diminish their agency, the complainants and their witness at times represented themselves as entities that were *acted upon*. That is, not only did they not portray themselves as initiators of events, they represented events or psychological states as controlling *them*. Connie's utterance in (26) is an explicit statement about her increasing sense that she was not in control:

(26) From that point that I realized that it had gotten out of control. (CD, Trial)

Examples (27) and (28) represent this same complainant as an experiencer of unrealized cognitive states (e.g. knowing how to react, being logical and coherent). Indeed, Connie is both patient and experiencer in these two examples; the events are represented as happening *to her* too quickly to allow for careful reflection.

(27) I mean actions were happening too fast for me to know how to react to them, for me to know what to do, and be logic and coherent about what the next move would be. (CD, Trial)
(28) Everything was happening too quickly for me to react to it. (CD, Trial)

The idea that the women's thoughts were not within their control has a more explicit grammatical realization in examples (29)–(31). Their minds are depicted in the grammatical role of *patient* – as entities that were subjected to certain thoughts and not others.

(29) Q: Guess I am just asking you did you have it in your mind that your room at some point might be a place that you can go, particularly when you started to get into trouble with Mr. A.?
      MK: <u>That didn't even enter my mind</u>. (MK, Trial)

(30) Q: Why didn't you say "Look, you can't do this to me," whatever. "I've got a class in the morning," why did that come to your mind? . . . Were you still worried about his feelings?
      CD: No. I don't know why <u>that's the first thing that came to my mind</u>. (CD, Trial)

(31)   <u>It never even crossed my mind of anything sexual happening</u>. (MB, Tribunal)

Examples (32)–(34) also show the women as acted upon, either by the force of emotions or by the overwhelming strength of the events. That the underlined portions of examples (32)–(34) all have verbs of motion further reinforces this representation: the women are controlled by potent and *active* forces.

(32)   I was like . . . I was so confused and <u>so so many emotions running through me</u> that I didn't know what to do that I just rolled over. (MB, Tribunal)

(33)   Because I was in shock and <u>everything started coming in on me</u> and I didn't know what to do. I was tired and I wasn't sure what to do. (MB, Trial)

(34)   Because as things were happening they were happening so fast and I didn't have a lot of time to think about what to do, what to do. <u>Everything clouded over on me</u>. (MK, Trial)

Overwhelmed by uncontrollable forces, Marg, in examples (35) and (36), expresses a desire for help, again casting herself in the semantic role of patient. As she so eloquently articulates her plight, someone has to act upon her (i.e. help her) because she no longer can think (or act) for herself.

(35)   I was waiting for or hoping <u>somebody would help me</u> and say, "Let's leave." (MB, Trial)

(36)   All I wanted was to take – <u>someone to take control of the situation and help me</u> because I wasn't thinking of what to do for myself. (MB, Trial)

The cumulative effect of the grammatical forms delineated in this section can be seen in the question–answer sequence of example (11). Responding repeatedly to questions about help she did *not* seek, Melinda is produced, not as a purposeful initiator of actions that would solicit help, but as an entity acted upon by paralyzing emotions (e.g. *Everything clouded over on me*) or as an experiencer of cognitive states that yielded no action (e.g. *I wasn't thinking clearly; I just didn't even think about it*). Set against a landscape peopled by autonomous subjects whose "choices" are unencumbered by socially structured inequities, this portrait of Melinda renders her purposeful acts (i.e. her agency) as weak, unsuccessful, or non-existent. Returning to Fairclough's notion of the "institutional subject," we can view the complainants and their witness as subjects "acting through" discursive (and material) constraints, producing themselves as ineffectual agents. They are "entered" involuntarily into this subject position (Hirsch and Lazarus-Black 1994) by questions that accomplish ideological work – questions that not only represent their actions as passive and ineffectual but also "produce" them as such.

6 Conclusion

In a discussion of representations of violence against women in the mainstream media, Chancer (1997: 227) cites Stuart Hall (Hall et al. 1978) on the difficulty of alternative "voices" emerging within such contexts: "what debate there is tends to take place almost exclusively *within the terms of reference* of the controllers . . . and this tends to repress any play between dominant and alternative definitions" (emphasis in original). I have argued similarly that the "debate" evident within these adjudication processes tended to be "framed" almost exclusively by a culturally dominant ideological perspective that presupposed the complainants' behavior to be lacking in appropriate resistance – this lack of resistance being equivalent to consent. Yet, the *interactional* (i.e. question–answer) quality of these adjudication processes (i.e. they are literally dialogic) had consequences for the particular potency with which alternative perspectives were submerged in these contexts. While Chancer (1997: 227), following Hall et al. (1978), argues that "viewpoints which challenge dominant perspectives seldom shine in the spotlight of contemporary mass culture,"[1] my data show that linguistically encoded dominant ideologies acted as a constraint on the complainants' *own* linguistic practices. That is, not only did the dominant perspectives obscure and/or render invisible the complainants' acts of strategic agency (i.e. did not allow them to "shine"), they also *produced* them as subjects who had not acted strategically. Questions, as we have seen, can mold or exert control over the forms of answers. And, in response to innumerable questions whose presuppositions and (pseudo)assertions embodied the utmost resistance standard, the complainants cast themselves as agents who were ineffectual: their performances of strategic acts within "the external reality" were transformed into performances of ineffectual acts of resistance within the linguistic representations of "the courtroom reality." (This distinction is made by Hale and Gibbons 1999.) And, without effectual and appropriate resistance, the dominant discourse (re)framed the sexual activity as consensual.

 The kinds of "coerced" identities that I have claimed the complainants and their witness produced in these institutional settings, in large part due to the institutionally sanctioned strict role integrity of questioner and respondent, are subject to interpretation and reception along gendered dimensions. The complainants' representation and production of themselves as "ineffectual agents" is intelligible insofar as it reinforces and perpetuates stereotypical images of women as weak and passive. Particularly pervasive in the area of male/female sexual relations are stereotypes of "active and aggressive masculinity and passive and victimised femininity" (Lacey 1998: 100), images confirmed by the representations (self- and other-generated) of the complainants. Significant about the identities constituted in these contexts is the degree of institutional *coerciveness* involved: the complainants and their witness were "called into" their subject positions involuntarily by a dominant discourse that constrained their possibilities for representing their strategic agency. Indeed, the discursive constraints imposed upon the complainants within the adjudication processes mirrored the highly restrictive circumstances surrounding the sexual assaults. Just as the complainants and their witness had few opportunities to challenge the prevailing narrative of the court, so they had few possibilities for action within the context of Matt's intimidating and frightening demeanor and his escalating sexual and physical violence.

NOTE

1   I thank Sue Levesque for directing my attention to this particular formulation of Chancer's.

REFERENCES

Atkinson, J. Maxwell and Drew, Paul 1979: *Order in Court*. Atlantic Highlands: Humanities Press.

Backhouse, Constance 1991: *Petticoats and Prejudice: Women and Law in Nineteenth-Century Canada*. Toronto: Osgoode Hall Society of Law.

Bartlett, Katharine and Kennedy, Rosanne 1991: Introduction. In Katharine Bartlett and Rosanne Kennedy (eds) *Feminist Legal Theory: Readings in Law and Gender*. Boulder, CO: Westview Press, pp. 1–11.

Bergvall, Victoria 1999: Toward a comprehensive theory of language and gender. *Language in Society* 28: 273–93.

Busby, Karen 1999: "Not a victim until a conviction is entered": Sexual violence prosecutions and legal "truth". In Elizabeth Comack (ed.) *Locating Law: Race/Class/Gender Connections*. Halifax, Nova Scotia: Fernwood Publishing, pp. 260–88.

Butler, Judith 1990: *Gender Trouble: Feminism and the Subversion of Identity*. London: Routledge.

Cameron, Deborah 1990: Demythologizing sociolinguistics. In J. Joseph and T. Taylor (eds) *Ideologies of Language*. London: Routledge, pp. 79–93.

Cameron, Deborah 1995: *Verbal Hygiene*. London: Routledge.

Cameron, Deborah 1997: Theoretical debates in feminist linguistics: Questions of sex and gender. In Ruth Wodak (ed.) *Gender and Discourse*. London: Sage, pp. 21–36.

Cameron, Deborah 1998: Gender, language, and discourse: A review essay. *Signs: Journal of Women in Culture and Society* 23: 945–73.

Capps, Lisa and Ochs, Elinor 1995: *Constructing Panic: The Discourse of Agoraphobia*. Cambridge, MA: Harvard University Press.

Chancer, Lisa 1997: The seens and unseens of popular cultural representations. In Martha Fineman and Martha McCluskey (eds) *Feminism, Media and the Law*. Oxford: Oxford University Press, pp. 227–34.

Clark, Lorenne and Lewis, Debra 1977: *Rape: The Price of Coercive Sexuality*. Toronto: Women's Press.

Coates, Linda 1997: Causal attributions in sexual assault trial judgments. *Journal of Language and Social Psychology* 16: 278–96.

Coates, Linda, Bavelas, Janet, and Gibson, J. 1994: Anomalous language in sexual assault trial judgements. *Discourse & Society* 5: 189–206.

Conley, John M. and O'Barr, William M. 1998: *Just Words: Law, Language and Power*. Chicago: University of Chicago Press.

Crenshaw, Kimberle 1992: Whose story is it anyway? Feminist and antiracist appropriations of Anita Hill. In T. Morrison (ed.) *Race-ing Justice, En-gendering Power*. New York: Pantheon Books, pp. 402–40.

Eckert, Penelope and McConnell-Ginet, Sally 1992a: Think practically and look locally: Language and gender as community-based practice. *Annual Review of Anthropology* 21: 461–90.

Eckert, Penelope and McConnell-Ginet, Sally 1992b: Communities of practice: Where language, gender, and power all live. In Kira Hall, Mary Bucholtz, and Birch Moonwomon (eds) *Locating Power: Proceedings of the Second Berkeley Women and Language Conference*. Berkeley, CA: Women and Language Group, University of California, pp. 88–99.

Eckert, Penelope and McConnell-Ginet, Sally 1999: New generalizations and explanations in language and gender research. *Language in Society* 28: 185–201.

Ehrlich, Susan 2001: *Representing Rape: Language and Sexual Consent*. London: Routledge.

Estrich, Susan 1986: Real rape. *Yale Law Journal* 1087, 1122.

Estrich, Susan 1987: *Real Rape*. Cambridge, MA: Harvard University Press.

Fairclough, Norman 1995: *Critical Discourse Analysis: The Critical Study of Language*. London: Longman.

Fisher, Sue 1991: A discourse of the social: Medical talk/power talk/oppositional talk. *Discourse and Society* 2: 157–82.

Gal, Susan 1991: Between speech and silence: The problematics of research on language and gender. In Micaela di Leonardo (ed.) *Gender at the Crossroads of Knowledge*. Berkeley, CA: University of California Press, pp. 175–203.

Hale, Sandra and Gibbons, John 1999: Varying realities: Patterned changes in the interpreter's representation of courtroom and external realities. *Applied Linguistics* 20: 203–20.

Hall, Stuart, Critcher, C., Jefferson, T., Clarke, J., and Roberts, B. 1978: *Policing the Crisis: Mugging, the State, and Law and Order*. New York: Holmes and Meier.

Hirsch, Susan and Lazarus-Black, Minnie 1994: Performance and paradox: Exploring law's role in hegemony and resistance. In Minnie Lazarus-Black and Susan Hirsch (eds) *Contested States: Law, Hegemony and Resistance*. London: Routledge, pp. 1–31.

Lacey, Nicola 1998: *Unspeakable Subjects: Feminist Essays in Legal and Social Theory*. Oxford: Hart Publishing.

Lyons, John 1977: *Semantics*. Cambridge: Cambridge University Press.

MacKinnon, Catharine 1987: *Feminism Unmodified*. Cambridge, MA: Harvard University Press.

MacKinnon, Catharine 1989: *Toward a Feminist Theory of the State*. Cambridge, MA: Harvard University Press.

Philips, Susan 1992: A Marx-influenced approach to ideology and language: Comments. *Pragmatics* 2: 377–85.

Schulhofer, Steven 1998: *Unwanted Sex: The Culture of Intimidation and the Failure of Law*. Cambridge, MA: Harvard University Press.

Smart, Carol 1986: Feminism and the law: Some problems of analysis and strategy. *International Journal of the Sociology of Law* 14: 109–23.

Smart, Carol 1989: *Feminism and the Power of Law*. London: Routledge.

Todd, Alexandra 1989: *Intimate Adversaries: Cultural Conflicts between Doctors and Women Patients*. Philadelphia: University of Pennsylvania Press.

West, Candace and Zimmerman, Don 1987: Doing gender. *Gender and Society* 1: 25–51.

Wodak, Ruth 1997: Introduction: Some important issues in the research of gender and discourse. In Ruth Wodak (ed.) *Gender and Discourse*. London: Sage, pp. 1–20.

Woodbury, Hannah 1984: The strategic use of questions in court. *Semiotica* 48: 197–228.

Woolard, Kathryn A. and Schieffelin, Bambi 1994: Language ideology. *Annual Review of Anthropology* 23: 55–82.

29 Multiple Identities: The Roles of Female Parliamentarians in the EU Parliament

RUTH WODAK

1 Introduction: Gender, Identity, and the Workplace

At the beginning of the twenty-first century, equal rights and equality of treatment are anchored in laws of equal opportunity in many Western countries (cf. Kargl, Wetschanow, Wodak, and Perle 1997). Attitudes, values, stereotypes, and role-images, however, are still severely encumbered by patriarchal traditions, and inequalities of treatment in professional and public life can be found everywhere (cf. Tannen 1995; Kendall and Tannen 1997; Kotthoff and Wodak 1997; de Francisco 1997; Martin-Rojo 2000; Gherardi 1995). Political life and the political world, in particular, are dominated by men (cf. Mazey 2000: 334). Despite the attempt to introduce the concept of "gender" into many areas of politics, including the EU (European Union), those who lead and dominate are still White men, and the agenda is still clearly determined by traditional values. For example, only one of twelve EU satellite committees, the EUMC (European Monitoring Center against Racism, Xenophobia and Anti-Semitism), is led by a woman. The legal norms on "gender anti-discrimination guidelines" are still at a developmental stage (cf. Eglström 2000), and experiences in the USA of "affirmative action" are clearly ambivalent in their value (cf. Appelt and Jarosch 2000).

This unequal treatment of men and women in our society is manifest – apart from women's lower payment for the same work and their much-quoted additional burden – in language and linguistic behavior. For human beings develop language on the basis of reality: in other words, dependent on the particular social conditions in which they live. Language, therefore, reflects social structures in its own structure, and at the same time reacts on human beings in the form of world-views and ideologies, thereby legitimizing the economic imbalance (Fairclough and Wodak 1997; Wodak 2001b, forthcoming). Social power is reinforced; the powerful everywhere are mostly elites, and these consist, for the most part, of White men. The same behavior is judged differently in men and women: we hear of "careerist women" but of "dynamic men." And in Women's Studies many stereotypes have also taken root, as in the "deficit hypothesis" (Lakoff 1975): this suggests that women lack something which men possess, and that where men are forceful, women are perceived as uncertain and hesitant. Dichotomizations did and still do partially dominate the academic debate (Wodak 2001c; Cameron 1997; Tannen 1997, 1989): men are accordingly seen as evil, dominant, and dedicated to competition, whereas women are good, subordinate, and cooperative (but see Sheldon 1997); in fact they come from "different cultures" (but see Cameron 1997). I believe that several levels are being combined here which – as the sample analyses below will demonstrate – interact with each other: the levels of self-definition, stereotypes, and the history of genders, the levels of power, hierarchy, and organization, and finally the level of observable real behavior.

Equal rights for women and men and equal treatment in professional and public contexts have long been sought by prominent women and women's organizations (Saurer, forthcoming). Yet when we look at this more precisely we have to say that women still have to justify their existence in the public domain, and often have to compete with conservative stereotypes, whereas men are spared this kind of legitimization pressure. They are simply, and more easily, accepted. In recent years, however, it has become clear that so-called feminine behavior is being revalued; trainers in organizational sociology are now attaching increasing value to cooperative and consumer-friendly behavior that is believed to increase both pleasure and efficiency in work. Some mixing of feminine and maternal stereotypes is taking place; powerful women are being forced into maternal roles and confronted with precisely these kinds of positive and negative transferences (Wodak 1996). The "mama" is undoubtedly powerful, but at the same time protective and understanding. Research among women leaders has shown that "gender" and organizational *habitus* (Bourdieu 1993, 1994) and rules overlap. Often an organization makes a greater impact in its norms and values than socially conditioned gender behavior (Diem-Wille 1996; Martin-Rojo 2000).

Unfortunately these almost banal truths have not always entered general awareness. In particular, consequences are so far rarely visible, such as similar career-paths for men and women, and similar degrees of acceptance in the various public domains (Diem-Wille 1996; Martin-Rojo 2000; Wodak 1997). In this connection gender cannot be separated from other identities: combinations of different identities and roles are always appearing, and so it is more sensible to look at holistic behavior and interactions than to try to identify the variables of gender in isolation.

This chapter is therefore concerned with "multiple identities" in elite women, in female members of the EU parliament (cf. Wodak et al. 1999; Wodak 2001a).

This public domain is particularly complex, and is determined by intercultural, ideological, ethnic, national, and gender conflicts (Muntigl, Weiss, and Wodak 2000). I ask how women can or do establish themselves in such a complex setting and what strategies they employ to present and promote themselves and to guarantee that they are taken seriously (Straehle 1998; Wodak 2001a).

First I will deal with the concept of fragmented and multiple identities; then a number of examples from authentic interviews with female EU parliamentarians will help to illustrate our claims and their resulting tendencies against the background of comprehensive statistical data. My principal hypothesis is that elite women must succeed in coming to terms with conflict-ridden role requirements and in developing their own individual images in order to be accepted in the political arena. For they will only have a chance of being taken seriously as exotic "flowers" or "birds of paradise" – not in competition with their male colleagues but outside of such competition. Then they will not be a threat but simply different, perhaps even admirable, but certainly acceptable. (The complete analysis may be found elsewhere; similarly, an explanation of the full methodology, and its location within the discourse-historical approach in the context of Critical Discourse Analysis, could not be undertaken here for reasons of space: cf. Muntigl, Weiss, and Wodak 2000; Wodak 2000a; Wodak and Meyer 2001; Reisigl and Wodak 2001.)

2 Sociopolitical Background: The European Parliament and the European Community

Since its beginnings in the 1950s, the shape of what is now known as the European Union (EU) has been constantly evolving. The original six members have grown to fifteen, the number of official languages to eleven, and the economic, legal, and political ties have expanded and deepened. With former Eastern Bloc countries preparing for membership in the coming decades, the EC's development and expansion will continue. At its core, this largely political and economic process also concerns identity constructions. No longer merely a geographical conglomeration of individual and, in the past, frequently belligerent nation-states, the web of ties connecting the member states of the EC seems to be evolving toward something beyond the sum of its parts. But what does this something look like? How is the European Union defined? Can we already speak of a European[1] identity or identities? What does it mean to be a member of the EU? How are national, organizational,[2] and individual identities invoked and oriented to in the discourses of EU organizations and those who represent them? And coming back to the main focus of this chapter, how are gender identities displayed and enacted in the midst of this complexity?

This chapter takes a sociolinguistic and discourse analytical critical perspective – one that shares the viewpoint that the EU, its organizations, and representatives are largely constructed (and construct themselves) discursively – in order to investigate these sorts of question. This is done on the basis of interviews, conducted in Brussels during a period of intensive fieldwork, with delegates to the European Parliament (EP), civil servants in the European Commission, and representatives from COREPER (Committee of Permanent Representatives) and its working groups, the secretariat of the Council of Ministers. In this chapter, I will have to dispense with any comparison of EU organizations and will focus only on the EP. The analyses presented here form part of a larger multidisciplinary study[3] that examines the communicative processes shaping the discourses on unemployment that take place in the multinational, multilingual, and multicultural organizations of the EU in multiple genres (see Muntigl, Weiss, and Wodak 2000). More specifically, then, this chapter looks at expressions of identity in the context of interviews that focused (1) on unemployment in the EU in general, (2) on the preparation of and follow-up to a meeting in Luxembourg in November 1997, and (3) on the roles of what are viewed as the EU's primary organizational bodies – the European Parliament, European Commission, and Council of Ministers (including COREPER) – and individuals working within them.

In this chapter, I will focus on the multiple identities of female MEPs and the construction of gender roles in such a complex domain as the multilingual, multi-ideological, and multinational setting of the EP.

3 Perspectives on Concepts of "Identity"

Sociolinguistic and discourse analytical studies of relevance to the analysis of identity in this chapter fall roughly into three groups: those using ethnomethodological/conversation analytic approaches to charting identity, such as Antaki and Widdicombe (1998), Widdicombe (1998), and Zimmerman (1998); studies conducted at the Department of Applied Linguistics in Vienna using a discourse-sociolinguistic/-historical approach, in particular Wodak et al. (1999); and those drawing on concepts such as footing, framing, and positioning, such as Goffman (1981), Tannen and Wallat (1993), and Davies and Harré (1990), or focusing on pronouns or person deictics, such as Wilson (1990) and Wortham (1996). My theoretical understanding of the notion of identity is most influenced by the first two groups of studies, and they are therefore highlighted in this short summary.

According to the ethnomethodological/conversation analytic perspective, identity is not something static that people *are* or *have* (as is the case in much social science research where social categories assigned a priori are often seen as predictive of certain types of behavior), but as something that they can orient to and use as a resource in the course of interaction. As Widdicombe (1998: 191) puts it: "The important analytic question is not therefore whether someone can be described in a particular way, but to show that and how this identity is made relevant or ascribed to self or others." In other words, although a person may be potentially classifiable by gender, ethnicity, class, or age, or as a doctor, mother, sister, and so on, these particular identities are not automatically relevant in every interaction she or he engages in. A person may invoke any number of aspects of identity depending on the contingencies of a particular conversation, or one may be positioned by one's interlocutors in a particular way (e.g. as someone in need of sympathy or help). The main point is that rather than using identities as "demographic facts, whose relevance to a stretch of interaction can simply be assumed" (Widdicombe 1998: 194–5), the analyst should "focus on whether, when and how identities are used . . . [C]oncern is with the occasioned relevance of identities here and now, and how they are consequential for this particular interaction and the local projects of speakers" (Widdicombe 1998: 195). To sum up, identities are locally occasioned, interactively constructed, and are resources "used in talk" (Antaki and Widdicombe 1998: 1).

With respect to the individuals interviewed for this study, it is important to note that while I have introduced them above as delegates to the European Parliament, civil servants in the European Commission, and representatives from COREPER and the working groups that serve the Council of Ministers, these labels represent exogenous identities, that is, identities that these individuals can be interpreted as "wearing" by virtue of their positions within particular institutions of the EU. In the light of the theoretical introduction here, it is important to stress that these classifications may or may not ultimately be relevant for these individuals in their discursive behavior in an interview situation, even if the interviewer has selected them specifically because of the expertise associated with their professional titles. Thus, for example, in one interview a Member of the European Parliament (MEP) may speak with any range of identities (or "voices" in the sense of Bakhtin 1981): as an MEP speaking as he/she might to a journalist, as one woman to another, as a Finn or Spaniard or Belgian, as a member of a particular committee or political group, and so on. Precisely which identity(ies) is (are) relevant at a given moment will depend on any number of factors obtaining for the particular discourse in which the interlocutors are engaged.

Zimmerman (1998: 90ff) makes a useful distinction between three types of identity found in talk: discourse (e.g. speaker, listener, narrator), situated (e.g. shopkeeper, customer), and transportable (e.g. African American, European, female). In this chapter, I am particularly interested in transportable identities, those that

> travel with individuals across situations and are potentially relevant in and for any situation and in and for any spate of interaction. They are latent identities that "tag along" with individuals as they move through their daily routines . . . they are identities that are usually visible, i.e. assignable or claimable on the basis of physical or culturally based insignia which furnish the intersubjective basis for categorization . . . it is important to distinguish between the registering of *visible* indicators of identity and *oriented-to* identity which pertains to the capacity in

> which an individual should *act* in a particular situation. Thus, a participant may
> be *aware* of the fact that a co-interactant is classifiable as a young person or a male
> without orienting to those identities as being relevant to the instant interaction.
> (Zimmerman 1998: 90–1)

In a sense, then, I am interested in the degree to which these potential, transportable identities, for example Parliamentarian, Commission official, Greek, female, are actually *oriented to* in the interview data.

A word of caution is called for here: to some, labeling identities as "transportable" may seem incongruous with my claim that identities are not fixed and "out there" but are changeable and constructed in talk. Perhaps therefore it is useful to think of these potential transportable identities in terms of groups of characteristics, much like semantic fields. While a whole range of characteristics may make up our individual definitions of, say, "bird" (or in our case, Parliamentarian, Commission official, etc.), the context in which "bird" is used will ultimately determine whether what we are invoking is more like a hummingbird or an ostrich. In other words, if the transportable identity of "politician" or "female" or "Commissioner" is oriented to in conversation, even if we have, at some level, certain expectations (i.e. the characteristics constituting the semantic fields) of what "politician" or "female" or "Commissioner" mean, the specifics of any one of these identities are not predetermined and inevitable, but drawn in the contingencies of real-time talk. Moreover, I claim that gender – while constructed in the specific interaction in a specific way – is always out there. In contrast to Butler (1990), I believe that ultimately we are always perceived as women or men, in every interaction; this is validated by very banal facts such as the different payment of men and women for the same jobs. In such basic and fundamental social domains, human beings are reduced to their biological gender. On the other hand, I would like to emphasize that we all have a whole range of possibilities of enacting our gender roles, and that in many other situations gender is certainly not the basic issue. But as a result of long years of gender research and my own experience, I have come to see that gender classification seems – consciously or subconsciously – to direct the interaction and behavior of many people (see also Wodak in press) in very many contexts.

Among the transportable identities we could imagine as potentially relevant for the individuals interviewed is that of nationality, or even *supra*-nationality, a particular *European*-ness. In a recent study on Austrian national identity, Wodak et al. (1999) offer a discursively based definition of nation as well as a viable framework for its study. In this research, Wodak et al. draw on Benedict Anderson's (1988) characterization of nations as "imagined communities," noting that

> If a nation is an imagined community and at the same time a mental construct,
> an imaginary complex of ideas containing at least the defining elements of collect-
> ive unity and equality, of boundaries and autonomy, then this image is real to
> the extent that one is convinced of it, one believes in it and identifies with it

emotionally. The question of how this imaginary community reaches the minds of those who are convinced of it is easy to answer: it is constructed and conveyed in discourse, predominantly in narratives of national culture. National identity is thus the product of discourse.   (1999: 44–5)

Based on the concept of "national identities," it is important to provide a working definition of "gender identities" and "multiple identities," which will be primarily drawn from premises of Pierre Bourdieu (1990), Paul Ricoeur (1992), Denis Martin (1995), Stuart Hall (1996a, 1996b), Michael Billig (1989), and the gender research of Peggy Watson (2000) and Jo Shaw (2000). Within the framework of Critical Discourse Analysis, in particular the discourse-historical approach, multiple identities are analyzed, while comparing discursive strategies of difference with strategies of sameness and describing a number of context-determined "narratives of gender and professional identities."

Though a very detailed account of the theoretical assumptions developed in our study (Wodak et al. 1999; Wodak 1997) would leave no space to examine the data which gave them their warrants (Toulmin 1964), it is nonetheless important to review three of these which are of particular relevance. The first is that we must understand Anderson's notion of "imagined community" (1988) as meaning that national identities are discursively produced and reproduced. Discourse, in turn, must be viewed as social practice.

Our second assumption draws on Pierre Bourdieu's notion of "habitus" (1993, 1994). National, gender, professional, or other identities have their own distinctive habitus which Bourdieu defines as a complex of common but diverse notions or schemata of perception, of related emotional dispositions and attitudes, as well as of diverse behavioral dispositions and conventions – practices, all of which are internalized through socialization. In our case the schemata in question refer to the idea of "*homo/femina europeus/a*," a European person, a common culture, history, present, and future, as well as to a type of "transnational corpus" or territory, but also to stereotypical notions of other nations, groups of "the others" and their culture, history, and so on. Second, in the specific context of gender identities and their construction, habitus refers to gender habitus (see Kotthoff and Wodak 1997). The emotional dispositions and attitudes refer to those manifested toward the specific "in-group" on the one hand and the respective "out-groups" on the other (be they different nations, genders, or political parties). Behavioral dispositions and practices include both dispositions toward solidarity with one's own group as well as the readiness to exclude the "others" from this constructed collective.

Thus, the discursive construction of gender/professional/national identities is always also a discursive construction of difference. Seyla Benhabib (1996: 3ff) states: "Since every search for identity includes differentiating oneself from what one is not, identity politics is always and necessarily a politics of the creation of difference. One is a Bosnian Serb to the degree to which one is not a Bosnian Moslem or a Croat." "What is shocking about these developments," she argues, "is not the inevitable dialectic of identity and difference that they display but rather the atavistic belief that identities can be maintained and secured

only by eliminating difference and otherness. The negotiation of identity/
difference [. . .] is the political problem facing democracies on a global scale."

A further premise – and this is our third central assumption – is that there is
essentially no such thing as one national/gender/professional identity, but
rather that different identities are discursively constructed according to context,
that is according to the audience to which they are addressed, the setting of
the discursive act, the topic being discussed, and so on. I would like to emphasize here that identities constructed in this way are dynamic, vulnerable, fragmented, and ambivalent. We assume that there are certain systematic relations
(of transfer and contradiction) between the models of identity offered by the
political elite or the media (the system) and "everyday discourse" (life-world)
(Habermas 1998). The fragmentations oppose existing dichotomies of the
"private" and "public" which has been very well argued by McElhinny (1997).

I would like to turn now to the relationship between identity and discursive
construction: if we regard gender identities purely as discursive constructs
which are made up of specifically constructed narratives of identity, the
question remains why somebody will reproduce a specific given discursive
construction. Martin (1995: 13) offers a convincing answer:

> To put it in a nutshell, the identity narrative channels political emotions so that
> they can fuel efforts to modify a balance of power; it transforms the perceptions
> of the past and of the present; it changes the organization of human groups and
> creates new ones; it alters cultures by emphasizing certain traits and skewing
> their meanings and logic. The identity narrative brings forth a new interpretation
> of the world in order to modify it.

However, we assume that we are dealing not only with representations and
discourses of gender/national/political/professional identities but also with
social practices – how people enact their identities. This leads us back to Bourdieu's concept of habitus, which I elaborated earlier (see also Scollon 2000).

With regard to examining discursive data for instances of or orientations to national as well as gender identities, we have used the discourse-
sociolinguistic/-historical approach which emphasizes three dimensions of
analysis: contents, strategies, and means and forms of realization (see Reisigl
and Wodak 2001 for the discourse model and argumentation strategies). Most
importantly, I will be concerned with "narratives of identity" of female MEPs
and their discursive strategies of establishing "sameness" and "difference" (in
Paul Ricoeur's sense, 1992).

4   Survey Data

The European Union has decided to propose a strategy of "gender mainstreaming" (European Commission final report 96/67; see www.europa.int/
comm/employment_social/equ_opp/gms_en.html) (cf. Pollack and Hafner-

Burton 2000; Commission of the European Communities reports, 1995, 1996; Council of Europe report 1998; Nelen 1997). "Gender mainstreaming" can be defined as follows: "Action to promote equality requires an ambitious approach and represents the recognition of male and female identities and the willingness to establish a balanced distribution of responsibilities between men and women." Moreover, the Commission report states

> The promotion of equality must not be confused with the simple objective of balancing statistics: it is a question of promoting long-lasting changes of parental roles, family structures, institutional practices, organizational work and time, their personal development and independence, but also of men and the whole society, in which it can encourage progress and establishment of democracy and pluralism.

Reading through all these proposals makes it obvious that we are dealing with very interesting suggestions, but the proposals stay on an abstract level (Braithwaite 2000). Employment policies are still to a considerable extent the responsibility of each member state (subsidiarity; Muntigl, Weiss, and Wodak 2000; Wagner 2000). Thus, the implementation of certain aspects is left to the member states, with their varying policies, traditions, and cultures (see Kargl, Wetschanow, and Wodak 1998). In the European organizations themselves, gender mainstreaming has led to higher participation of women, but not on the highest levels, as some recent statistics illustrate (see discussions in Rossilli 2000).

In the European commission, there are a total of 16,279 employees at all levels of hierarchy: 7,739 are women, 8,540 men. This means that women constitute 47.5 per cent of the sample. Looking more closely reveals that only 5.9 per cent are women at the highest level of the hierarchy (51 total: 3 women, 48 men). Such a distribution presents us with a picture that we know all too well: women advance only to a certain point in their careers. (Statistics from March 1, 2000.)

If we now look at the European Parliament (without having statistics available for the political parties), there is a total of 27 per cent of women from the total number of MEPs (169 women). Interestingly, they are distributed very differently along the fifteen member states: 34 from Germany and 27 from France are the highest numbers, but Finland and Luxembourg have the highest percentages according to their total number of MEPs (50 per cent). Sweden has 45 per cent, Denmark 44 per cent. These numbers illustrate the specific stance of the Scandinavian countries, which we find reproduced in the interview sequences below. Italy, Portugal, and Greece have the lowest number of female MEPs (11, 12, and 16 per cent respectively). (Statistics from July 28, 1999.) (See table 29.1.)

Although we would certainly need more data and more context information, these results already point to the large gap between North and South, to the different cultural traditions of the Mediterranean countries and the Scandinavian

Table 29.1 Women in the European Parliament

	Belgium	Denmark	Germany	Greece	Spain	France	Ireland	Italy	Luxembourg	Netherlands	Austria	Portugal	Finland	Sweden	UK	Total
1994–1999[a]	8	7	34	4	21	27	3	10	3	10	7	3	8	9	15	169
Percentage of women	32	44	34	16	33	31	20	11	50	32	33	12	50	45	17	27
1999–2004[b]	7	6	36	4	22	35	5	10	0	11	8	5	7	9	21	186
Percentage of women	28	38	36	16	34	40	33	11	0	35	38	20	44	45	24	30
Change in percentage of women	–13	–14	6	0	5	30	67	0	–100	10	14	67	–13	0	40	10

a The numbers on Sweden, Austria, and Finland relate to the first European election (Sweden, 1995; Austria/Finland, 1996).
b Status: July 28, 1999.

countries where gender roles are defined in significantly different ways. The Southern countries are still very male-oriented (except for the famous role of the "mama"), whereas the Scandinavian countries have a long tradition in gender equality. Austria, Germany, The Netherlands, and Belgium are all situated in the middle range (around 30 per cent), whereas the UK and Ireland fall toward the bottom of the scale (17 and 20 per cent respectively).

Of course, these numbers tell us nothing about the quality of the attendance of these MEPs, of their initiatives and their positioning. In addition, we do not know if certain political parties (such as the Greens) favor women in contrast to more rightwing parties. And lastly, these numbers do not illustrate any success of the gender mainstreaming strategies mentioned above. Very different qualitative research, in the EU organizations and in the member states, is needed to provide some answers to the question of possible and promoted changes in gender structures.

4.1   The interviews

The data for this analysis consist of 28 interviews, with fourteen Members of the European Parliament, all members of the Committee on Employment and Social Affairs; ten Commission officials, among them eight from DGV (one of 24 directorates-general, DGV the administrative service responsible for employment policy), and one each from DGXV (financial institutions/company law) and the Commissioner in charge of employment and social issues; and four Austrian delegates to the Council of Ministers, one to COREPER II (ambassador-level, permanent representative), one to COREPER I (deputy level), one a bureaucrat of high standing in the employment directorate, and one a member of the Council's working group responsible for issues of employment and social affairs.

It is important to note that I make no claims of having representative samples of individuals from the EP, European Commission, and Council. All persons participating in the study were self-selected to the extent that they responded to our written and/or telephone requests for an interview. Moreover, of the MEPs who participated, ten were from three, largely left-oriented, political groups: the European Socialists, the European United Left, and the Greens. Only four MEPs came from what would be considered as representing more conservative groups (e.g. the European People's Party). In addition to the fact that we were able to interview only four individuals from the Council, all of those interviewed were Austrian and thus we can make no comparison with members from other countries. Finally, with regard to language, only those interviews conducted in English or German are analyzed here, these languages being either the first or second language of both the interviewers and most of the interviewees. All interviews were audio-recorded and later transcribed. In sum, then, we are working with a body of data that is suitable for in-depth qualitative, but not statistical, analysis.

The interviews focused on four general topic areas, which means that although certain topic-related questions were generally included in all interviews (e.g. "What do you feel are the reasons for the rise in unemployment in recent years?"), interviews were sufficiently loosely structured for interviewees to have considerable freedom in developing the topics and steering the conversation as they wished. The main topic groups in the interview protocol, each with several subcategories of possible questions, were:

1   unemployment, including reasons for and possible solutions to it, and perspectives on current employment-related policy-making, especially the Luxembourg Employment Summit of November 1997;
2   the role of the EU organization in which the interviewee works, including relationships with other EU bodies, the interviewee's own role within the organization, and his or her "access points," or contact with "ordinary" EU citizens;
3   day-to-day working life, including multicultural issues and the development of documents such as reports, opinions, etc.; and
4   the interviewee's personal history, such as career development, and definition of "being European." In this chapter, I focus on the construction of gender identities by women throughout the whole interview.

5   Methods of Analysis

Essentially, I am looking for when and how certain identities are constructed, achieved, and oriented to. In the data analyzed here, narratives (or personal examples and anecdotes that may or may not follow the "canonical" narrative form, i.e. consisting of abstract, orientation, complicating actions, evaluation, and coda as described by Labov 1972, Labov and Waletzky 1967) are particularly fruitful sites for the analysis of the discursive construction of multiple and gender identities in interaction. As noted by Schiffrin (e.g. 1996, 1997), Linde (1993), Mumby (1993), Ochs (1997), Benke and Wodak (2000, forthcoming), and others, narrative is among other things "a tool for instantiating social and personal identities" (Ochs 1997: 202). Schiffrin argues that

> narratives can provide . . . a *sociolinguistic self-portrait*: a linguistic lens through which to discover people's own views of themselves (as situated within both an ongoing interaction and a larger social structure) and their experiences. Since the situations that speakers create through narratives – the transformations of experience enabled by the story world – are also open to evaluation in the interactional world, these self-portraits can create an interactional arena in which the speaker's view of self and world can be reinforced or challenged. (Schiffrin 1997: 42, emphasis in original)

What Schiffrin highlights in particular is the dynamic aspect of identity construction in interaction, especially in narratives. Most relevant for the analysis here, however, is simply that narratives can reveal "footings" in Goffman's sense that in turn reveal orientations to particular constructions of self. Moreover, the strategies of self-presentation and the topoi[4] used in defining one's own identities will be focused on in the analysis of some examples. The questions I seek to address as a result of the analyses are the following: what kinds of identities do the individuals in these interviews – whose exogenous positions potentially mark them as representatives of the European Union, of particular organizations within the EU's political structure, of particular units (e.g. committees, working groups) within those organizations, of particular nationalities or political persuasions – orient to and use in their talk? Do gendered or other identities come into play? Most importantly, though, I am interested in whether the MEPs, men and women, present themselves differently and in what way professional women characterize their experiences and their careers.

6 Some Results of the Analysis

In contrast to the European Commission officials, who tended to speak of themselves in terms of "we" referring to "the Commission" and equated this with the European Union or the European level, the MEPs oriented to numerous identities, both professional and personal. Among the professional identity types frequently oriented to are those such as (specific) EP political group member, EP committee member, rapporteur (elected to summarize a debate before motions are voted on), national party member, representative from a particular member state, and so on; very often, however, relatively more personal aspects of identity emerged as well, from that of social worker, family man or woman, grandmother, to more abstract presentations of personal or moral positions such as tolerant, or active, or diplomatic, or pragmatic. Many of these presentations of self manifest themselves in brief personal anecdotes or longer narratives.

As discussed previously, narratives are particularly revealing indices of identity because they offer a sort of "window" on to how individuals evaluate their past experience and position themselves in their world. Example (1) is a narrative in which MEP2 talks about her first experience as a rapporteur.

(1)[5]
1   when I – entered the parliament – *Orientation (lines 1–3)*
2   on my first report it was about Leonardo
3   I don't know if you know:
4   ((*smiles*)) well – I said "I'm going to speak to the commissioner"
5   and – I –/ I knew – he only speaks very bad French
6   and my eh my French was very bad as well.

```
 7  so I said "I want to have interpretation"
 8  So – I went to the commissioner          Complicating Actions (lines 4–14)
 9  with a very good int/ int/ interpreter
10  and I/ I/ I/ I talked more than an hour with him.
11  because we talked the same about it
12  and at the end he said –
13  "well: I have here the advice of my: civil servants but I – agree with you:
14  and this and this and this all goes through. – "
15  so you have to be: – eh: –
16  I don't know h/ how do we call it in English in/ I
17  in the Netherlands we say (brutaal)
18  so you have to: ((laughs)) be polite          Evaluation (lines 16–20)
19  but you have to – you:/ you mustn't be/
20  you mustn't sit behind your –/ your desk. –
21  because that doesn't help. ((laughs))
22  but then/then then you have the worse system
23  that I tried several times          Coda (22–31)
24  then you have the Council. –
25  a:nd – it's very difficult eh:
26  to negotiate with the Council is my: –/ eh is my experience:
27  it's possible to do: –
28  bu:t – – now they have their own strategy:
29  and their own – reasons:
30  eh: and they don't like the power of the parliament
31  so: the:/ the/ that's –/ that's the most difficult part.
```

In example (1), which has been marked for basic narrative structure according to Labov (1972) and Labov and Waletzky's (1967) model, we see that MEP2's story is objectively about having a successful meeting with a Commissioner while acting as rapporteur on a report about Leonardo.[6] In lines 4–14, the complicating actions, she shows how she went to the Commissioner with an interpreter, and because she and the Commissioner had the same understanding of the issues involved ("because we talked the same about it"), he was willing to support her, despite contrary advice by his "civil servants" on the matters involved. The main point of the story, or evaluation, from MEP2's perspective, is to show that as an MEP, to get things done, you must be active and assertive, "not sit behind your desk." While MEP2 might have felt hindered by her (and the Commissioner's) limited language skills in French, she found help through an interpreter and argued her points before the Commissioner – with success. Thus, in this narrative, MEP2 positions herself as an MEP who is proactive and who will do what it takes, including arguing directly with Commissioners, to see that her voice is heard. She also orients to being a rapporteur (line 2), which carries some responsibility in a committee, and to being from the Netherlands (line 17), although this last identity is evoked only to characterize her style of work (*brutaal* in Dutch, or "assertive").

At the same time that she presents herself as a proactive MEP who has served as rapporteur on more than one occasion, she paints a picture of both the Commission and the Council in a way that is consistent with what many other MEPs and EC officials in these data observe about the respective organizations. Here we see a benevolent Commissioner who is willing to listen to an individual MEP and to make decisions according to reason and his own conviction, even if that means occasionally going against the advice of his directorate-general or perhaps cabinet ("well, I have here the advice of my civil servants but I agree with you and this and this and this all goes through"). In the coda of the story we see that MEP2 compares the accessibility and cooperativeness of the Commissioner to the difficulty and uncooperativeness of the Council ("it's very difficult to negotiate with the Council . . . they have their own strategy and their own reasons"). Thus, MEP2's narrative also constructs a world in which the Parliament and Commission can work together as partners, whereas the Parliament and Council remain at odds. The gender identity constructed here, through an account of her activities and a description of her meeting with a powerful person, is that of a woman who knows what she wants and how to proceed (*"brutaal* but polite"). Women who tend to be successful have to be active, to fight for their opinions and not "sit behind their desk." Thus, a very active role is portrayed which might be in conflict with traditional gender roles, a role where women are viewed as dominant, threatening, and maybe even irritating if fighting for a cause.

In example (2), taken from the part of the interview with MEP10 that focused on the reasons for unemployment, we see how national and party identities may be oriented to as a context for understanding a particular interpretation of a political, economic, and social issue, in this case unemployment.

(2)
1   it/ it's quite <u>simple</u>. – why we have this – <u>high</u> – unemployment rate no
2   and it's because we are changing soti/ <u>society</u>
3   I mean we had a – highly in/ industrial society and now we are <u>changing</u>
4   so. – so: eh – this is completely <u>new</u> for us
5   and –/ and then we are <u>trying</u> – to <u>amend that</u>
6   and to try to – eh: help that up
7   with –/ with – kind of <u>old</u> –/ old <u>structures</u>: and – <u>old</u> – <u>answers</u>. –
8   eh: and – we don't want to <u>face</u> that we really <u>have</u> to –
9   adjust a <u>lot</u> of – <u>thinking</u>
10 I mean that/ that's –/ what it is <u>about</u>. – and –/ and –
11 we have to – <u>reconsider</u> –
12 eh what is <u>full</u> employment and what is
13 what is eh: –/ to have a eh/ eh – a <u>work</u> for <u>salary</u>: –
14 and a lot of that so/ sort of things. –
15 because I don't think that – we will <u>ever</u> –
16 ever <u>have</u> what called –
17 usually *in Sweden/* fo/ <u>full employment</u> ((*laughs*))/
18 and –/ and –/ and <u>my</u> solution to that and/ and
19 *the* <u>*Green group*</u> is of course that
20 for the <u>first</u> you have to <u>see</u>: –
21 *we* have a/ had a –/ eh have another – eh eh another eh: – <u>approach</u>

22   and another – <u>view</u>: of – full employment. –
23   just to say that a – <u>okay</u>. – this is – nineteen ninety. – <u>seven</u>
24   and h –/ we had so many f/ people in –/ unemployed.
25   so the <u>first</u> thing we should <u>do</u>: – is of course to <u>reduce</u>: – the <u>working time</u>. –
26   because – eh forty hours:
27   a week *as we are working in <u>Sweden</u>* now
28   it was not – eh institution of <u>god</u>. –
29   it/ it was – decided of with/ us ((*laughs*))/
30   the/ the time when we –/ when we <u>needed</u> a lot of people to <u>work</u>
31   so – re–/ reduction of working time of course
32   and <u>also</u> – to change the attitudes in society against
33   the people that <u>have</u> work and <u>don't</u> have work
34   . . .
35   <u>and</u> eh: –/ and <u>then</u> also of course we have to – <u>support</u> and/
36   and say that <u>flexibility</u> in that sense
37   you could work the hour that you <u>like</u>
38   and you could have a half-time <u>jo:b</u> and so on
39   and have a small company in size
40   so all these <u>taxations</u>
41   and all – the regulations
42   has to be: – sh –/ <u>changed</u>
43   and <u>altered also</u>. – to make this <u>possible</u>
44   eh: – and of course – the <u>taxation</u> or the/ the: –
45   you don't say taxation you say – eh: –
46   the tax on <u>labor</u> –/ on <u>labor</u>. –
47   <u>it's</u> it's quite <u>high</u>
48   I s:uppose it's – eh: – all the same in the European Union
49   but *in <u>Sweden</u>* – eh which I/ know most of course ((*laughs*))/
50   in the North West
51   there eh –/ there we have – <u>really high</u>
52   percentage of tax <u>on</u> – labor. –
53   and that should be <u>s:witched</u> and <u>changed</u>
54   of course so you put it on – *as I'm a Green* –
55   *eh MEP* – on energy:
56   and non resourceable –
57   eh: eh:m – ninedren/ non
58   <u>renewable resources</u> and energy and so on
59   so – <u>this</u>: should be <u>switched</u> of course

In example (2), MEP10 orients both her nationality (Swedish) and her political affiliation (Green). Although it is not clear why she points out her nationality in lines 17 and 27, in lines 19–26, where she has included herself as belonging to the Green group, she appears to use this identity as a resource (in the sense of Antaki and Widdicombe 1998) or context (Zimmerman 1998) for understanding the measures she advocates for addressing unemployment: reinterpreting the traditional understanding of "full employment" and reducing the standard number of hours worked per week. In line 49 she again orients to her national identity, even to a more local identity (northwest Sweden), as a type of frame for her claims about high labor taxes. She is from northwest Sweden, where labor taxes are quite high, so she can speak as an authority on this issue. Finally, in this excerpt, she resumes her orientation to her political affiliation. She favors a switch in taxation from labor to energy and non-renewable resources, a position fully consistent with her identity as an MEP from the European Greens. Thus, in this example, we see how national and political identities can be invoked as a resource or context for understanding a particular perspective or presenting a frame of expertise. This female MEP defines herself mostly with the help of other identities (political, local, professional); the organizational identities seem to dominate gender issues (see Wodak 1997 for different types of female leaders and the overlap of gender roles and images with organizational pressures; see also Kendall and Tannen 1997; Alvesson and Billing 1997). She displays her expertise, primarily, and does not overtly reflect on her gender role. Of course, this interview displays only a single context; we do not know how this MEP perceives the organization on other occasions.

At this juncture, it is worth observing that among all the MEPs interviewed, it tended to be Swedes and Finns, as well as MEPs from either the European Greens or the United European Left (many of whose members are from Green parties in their home countries), who mentioned their nationality and/or party affiliation at several points throughout an interview. In other words, while almost all MEPs make reference to their party affiliation or nationality in the course of the interview (long before the "Do you consider yourself to be European" question), the Swedes and Finns, and/or Greens, appeared to draw on this resource more than others (see Wodak 2001b, forthcoming). The one EC official who invoked his national identity before being asked the "European" question also belonged to the Scandinavian group (a Finn). Although the analysis of more data (with more representative distribution of nationalities and political affiliations) would be necessary to confirm these tendencies, one might conjecture that Swedes and Finns, who have a long history of political association (e.g. in the Nordic Council and the European Free Trade Association, EFTA), and whose countries were two of the last three to join the EU in 1995, may tend to identify more strongly with each other as Scandinavians and less so as "Europeans" in the strictly EU sense.[7] One EC official (not a Scandinavian) illustrates this in an anecdote:

(3)
1   I was at a conference in Stockholm recently and I said
2   Someone was asking me, a Scanda/
3   It had to be a Scandinaviena because
4   And I said I lived in Brussels
5   And they said, "well you know, well are you Irish or something"
6   And I said, "well, I'm also a European"
7   And they looked at me and said
8   "that doesn't mean anything.
9   What does that mean?

10 I mean, you're a European commission official, that's why"
11 "I'm European you know, I live on the continent
12 and you all live –
13 not the continent as distinct from the British Isles
14 but I mean continent, the territory of Europe
15 and that for me has meaning
16 I mean it has influenced my history, thinking and economics
17 And will continue to do so"
18 I mean this girl was absolutely shocked
19 "you are the first person who ever said that to me", she said.
20 "I never never thought of it that way."
21 She said, "I know many people – "
22 It was, I know now
23 She was from Finland
24 And she said "I don't think anyone in Finland will think of themselves as European."
25 So that's very interesting.

This kind of observation is also relayed by the Scandinavians themselves. Almost all Swedes and Finns interviewed made comments to the effect of a "Scandinavian way of thinking" or noted the fact that (especially in Sweden) only a very slim majority of popular votes led to joining the EU, as in this excerpt:

(4)
1 I know that *we* are a very stubborn country.
2 Most of the people ah: are now: ah well.
3 A ha./ mo/ most of the people –
4 At least when was it fifty-one point four percent or something like that
5 Voted in the referendum for entering the European Union
6 But today *we* – almost never meet anyone who did –
7 I don't know what they did
8 Yeah because everybody said – do/ they said "no: I voted no:" and
9 Ye said "well I really do I re – I really do regret" ((*laughs*))
10 Aha:. – so it (happened) ((*laughs*)) okay:
11 So I mean it's make/ it doesn't make the whole ah – /
12 The whole billing – easier. (MEP3)

This anecdote reports a reluctance of many Swedes to associate themselves with the EU, which is not unlike the fact that it was largely Scandinavian MEPs (who were also Greens) who qualified their self-definitions of "being European" as *not* being restricted to just the EU. These examples illustrate our claims of the perception and construction of "multiple identities" on the one hand, and of the overriding of "gender" through national affiliation in the European context of the EP on the other hand.

While I have focused on the evidence suggesting that Swedes and Finns may identify strongly as a group, a similar pattern is suggested for the Greens.

In the interview data, it is predominantly Greens who repeatedly identify their political affiliation in explicit terms (e.g. "I am a Green"; "I'm left"). Perhaps both "Scandinavians" and "Greens" see themselves as slightly on the periphery of mainstream EU politics and orient to this difference in talk to provide part of the frame for understanding particular points of view or interpretations of economic and social issues. Thus, these narratives evoke many strategies of "difference" and of the construction of distinctive groups. They also allow insight into the dynamics of this European organization, of the fragmentation that many MEPs experience, and of the loyalty conflicts between national, cultural, supranational, political, and gender identities.

Let us return, however, to the idea of the greater relative variety of identities oriented to by MEPs when compared to EC officials (see Wodak, forthcoming for details). The profession of an MEP, because of the enormous complexity of the domain, allows for individuality to be seen and heard. Moreover, it seems to allow for women to enact an active gender role, to succeed in being heard and listened to, and to succeed in implementing certain political goals.

MEP3, for example, oriented to a particularly wide range of identities (left, woman, Swedish, mother, political outsider, and so on) during her interview. Most striking is the way in which she repeatedly positions herself as being an "atypical MEP," thus using very distinct strategies of difference. Here we see one such occasion.

(5)
1   I figure here the most common – eh civil – job. – for an MEP
2   is eh to be a lawyer.
3   me myself *I'm far from that*
4   the job I had doesn't even <u>exist</u> outside *Scandinavia.*
5   so: – it's a sort of a social teacher – so
6   so I'm/ I'm very in/ an:/ a very special bird in this a:
7   IF mhm mhm so now you don't feel like you – fit into sort of a <u>typical</u> MEP eh
8   ME *no. no: no: I'm not. I'm left I'm a woman I'm Swedish* and I'm also
9   everything –/ everything's wrong. ((*laughs*))

In example (5), MEP3 contrasts herself with what she considers to be a typical profile for an MEP (lawyer by profession), emphasizing the degree to which she feels different ("I'm far from that . . . I'm a very special bird . . . everything's wrong"). She also points out many of the identities that she associates with, and that she perceives as marking her as different from the norm set by traditional, conservative, patriarchal Europeans (social teacher, left, female, Swedish). This sequence is a very good illustration of a successful woman who has managed to come to terms with all her differences, which have served to marginalize her, and to emphasize them. She "turns the tables," and strategically redefines the traditionally negative connotations into positive attributes. "She is a very special bird," and this way of self-presentation allows for her success. Conflicting ideological problems and dilemmas (Billig 1989) seem to be solved through self-irony, self-reflection, and assertiveness.

At other points in the same interview, MEP3 emphasizes that not only is she an atypical MEP, she is not a typical politician either. This is illustrated in example (6):

(6)
1   I mean I know that – even on/ on a: national level
2   I mean there are very many politicians all sorts in all parties –
3   that <u>prefer</u> to/ to meet the/ the – eh/ the citizens through – media.
4   eh –/ so *I know that I'm not that sort.*
5   so I prefer to meet the people. –
6   it/ it could be hard but it's more interesting. .
7   and that's the way I̱ learn at the same time – a lot.
8   . . . and a (xx) of –/ I met so very many politicians – during my – living 45 years
9   ((*laughs*)) so: – and it's the –/
10 I mean do you really – when you've seen them in action
11 when you were a child or
12 all through the years – you say oh – how disgusting and –
13 what behavior they've done and instead I –/
14 *for sure I will not be that sort of person that I always despised!*
15 that means that if you go to a meeting
16 you just don't go there. –
17 and you just don't talk for forty-five minutes
18 telling everybody how the situation really is
19 and then you leave <u>off</u>. –
20 mostly with the plane first a limo and then a plane and
21 that's – not a boring life

Just before this excerpt begins, MEP3 and the interviewer have been talking about the kind of contacts MEPs have with their constituencies. In this context, MEP3 contrasts her own behavior with that of what she considers to be typical of (male) politicians. In lines 1–3 she casts the typical politician as preferring to meet with citizens indirectly, through the media. Alternatively, this typical politician "drops in" on his constituency only briefly, in a condescending, patronizing ("telling everybody how the situation really is"), and elitist ("then you leave off – mostly with the plane, first a limo and then a plane") manner. In lines 10–14 she elaborates on her point of view and emotional reaction to this sort of politician, emphasizing that her opinion of what is "typical" has been supported by observations over many years and that this to her is "disgusting." Thus, through irony, and overt criticism, she marks her difference from other (male) MEPs and constructs the negative out-group. All these strategies serve to construct her own identity. Moreover, in contrast to the other female MEPs presented above (both the active MEP as well as the expert), she does not align with a group, does not use an inclusive "we," and does not seem to belong to any one group. She constructs herself as belonging to numerous "deviant" groups (deviant from a normative perspective), thus emphasizing her uniqueness and her difference from others (much in line with "*idem*" and *"ipse"* as described by Ricoeur 1992). In both lines 4 and 14, she explicitly dissociates herself from being "that sort of person." In other words, although by virtue of being an MEP she is technically a "politician," she is not of the sort one might imagine. What is implied is the "typical dominant male politician," who is not really interested in political content nor in the citizens and their needs, but mostly in persuasive rhetoric and sampling votes. Throughout the interview, she emphasizes her difference and uniqueness, according to our theory of the discursive construction of identity (Wodak et al. 1999).

This interview is one of five interviews with female MEPs which all use similar discursive strategies for constructing their gender and political identities. Of course one cannot generalize from such a small sample. I assume, however, that there may well be a more general tendency visible here which corresponds to my own experiences of working for thirty years in male academia and to numerous accounts in many studies throughout the professions (Saurer, forthcoming).

Although I have already suggested elsewhere that the types of identity oriented to by the EC officials dovetail nicely with the Commission's being described as carrying the "European conscience" (Cini 1996), that is, as promoting specifically European interests, I have still not made it entirely explicit why we might find the degree of variation in identities oriented to by female and male MEPs. In some ways, this multiplicity of orientations appears to be functional for the way in which the EP operates. Corbett et al. (1995, especially pp. 44–63) nicely describe the pressures under which MEPs work, and the directions in which they can be torn: although many EC officials undoubtedly also travel extensively, for the most part they are based in Brussels. MEPs deal with extreme time and location pressures tied to the EP's four-week cycle of activities (e.g. meetings and sessions in Brussels, one-week plenary sessions in Strasbourg, regular travel to the home country, visits to other countries as part of being members of inter-parliamentary delegations, etc.). At the same time, MEPs are involved with their political groups (both in the Parliament and possibly at home), sit on several committees, are called on to speak as experts at conferences and other public events, and act as hosts to visiting groups from their own or other countries. In short, there is no simple description for the "job" of being an MEP. Corbett et al. (1995: 63) suggest that in order to cope, an MEP must ultimately make choices and prioritize:

> the priorities of individual members are very different, as are their profiles within the European Parliament. Some become known as men or women of the House, and are constantly present in the plenary. Others are more effective within committee, or in their Group or their national party delegation, others concentrate more on their national or regional political image. Some members remain generalists, whereas others become specialists, and are always allocated reports or opinions within a particular policy area. Some even develop functional rather than policy specialities . . . Some only pay short visits to Brussels or Strasbourg, whereas others are always present, and have even bought accommodation there.

Depending on how individual MEPs organize their priorities, we may find very different kinds of identity relevant for MEPs across the board, and for an individual MEP. Thus the variability that we find in the interviews with MEPs as to the types of "we" and "I" identities they orient to seems to be functional, reflecting to a large extent the peculiarities of the European Parliament itself. However, I have emphasized the specific strategies used by female MEPs, which mark their uniqueness and their different attitudes to politics and ideologies in general.

Basically, we have found three "types" or "habitus" of female gender role constructions, which seem to provide success in "doing politics": "assertive activist," "expert," and "positive difference (special bird)" (or combinations of these). These habitus and their related social practices are very different from other roles of successful women or female leaders as described in studies of female principals in schools (Wodak 1997) or in big businesses (Kendall and Tannen 1997). This first pilot study does not allow us to make strong generalizations; however, it is necessary to contrast the different types of organizations and professions with each other in order to explain these differences. Schools in the Austrian system in the above-mentioned study are extremely rigid organizations which allow for very little flexibility and are organized in a very hierarchical way; thus, possible gender constructions, moreover in a setting with children, evoke variations of mother roles and of carers (Wodak and Schulz 1986). In businesses, other dynamics are at stake, as described also by the general tendencies of marketization and consumerism. In such organizations, serving the client becomes more and more important; and many previously "female" attributes are regarded highly as promoting flexibility and endorsing a comfortable, thus more efficient, work environment (Fairclough 1992). The EP, as described above, through its complexity is much more open and less organized, and thus more flexible. This allows for a wider range of identity constructions: the self-definitions are not monitored as closely as in other organizations. More research into these organizational aspects will provide more detailed answers.

In conclusion, therefore, a caveat is in order. The analyses presented here are not intended to be interpreted as *the* way that the European Parliament or female MEPs *are*. In addition to being inaccurate, such a conclusion vitiates the premise underlying this chapter namely that identities are dynamic in talk, and that potential, transportable identities may or may not be invoked in a given interaction. Instead, this chapter has set out to provide a plausible interpretation for some of the similarities and differences in *orientations to* and *uses of identities* by those women in the EP who participated in the interview component of our study, including their understandings of *European*-ness, if, indeed, they felt it could be defined. Moreover, I have used these interviews to respond to some of the questions we posed in the beginning: when can women succeed, when are they allowed to succeed? And how are multiple identities coped with? How are they enacted? It will be of interest in the future to see if women will have to remain "special birds," if women like to be special birds, if women are made into special birds, or if there are other alternatives which women would like and which could arise. Or we could, perhaps, ask ourselves which special bird we would like to be . . .

TRANSCRIPTION CONVENTIONS

:	A colon indicates an extension of the sound it follows. Longer extensions are shown by more colons.
–	A dash stands for an abrupt cut-off.
word	Emphasized syllables, words, or phrases are underlined.
(xx)	Words in single parentheses were difficult to understand and could not be transcribed with complete certainty.
((*smiles*))	Double parentheses contain descriptions of non- and paralinguistic utterances by the speakers.
h	"h" without a period stands for audible exhalations.

NOTES

1 I use "Europe(an)" (unless noted otherwise) in the sense of "Europe consisting of the EU." As pointed out by several Members of the European Parliament (MEPs) who were interviewed for this chapter, what is geographically "Europe" extends considerably beyond the EU's current borders. Nevertheless, since the focus of this chapter is European identity-building in the European Union, I will use "Europe(an)" in the more restrictive sense.

2 In this chapter as in other work (e.g. Straehle et al. 1999; Weiss and Wodak 1999, 2000; Wodak and Weiss 2001; Muntigl, Weiss, and Wodak 2000) written at the Research Centre Discourse, Politics, Identity (see note 3 for description of Centre), a distinction is made between organization and institution that follows Rehberg (1994: 56). While "institution" is defined as the "social

regulations" in which the principles, rules, and claims to validity (*Geltungsansprüche*) of a specific social order are expressed, organizations are the social formations that embody institutions. Thus, in this chapter I refer to the European Parliament, the Council of Ministers, and the European Commission as EU organizations rather than institutions.

3 The Discourses of Unemployment in Organizations of the European Union is one of the projects undertaken at the Research Centre Discourse, Politics, Identity at the University of Vienna (Austria) with the support of the Wittgenstein Prize for Elite Researchers (1996) awarded to Ruth Wodak. Research Centre projects build on numerous previous studies on organizational discourse and identity under the direction of Professor Wodak at the Department of Applied Linguistics at the University of Vienna. See

www.oeaw.ac.at/wittgenstein for
more information on the Centre.

4   Within argumentation theory, "topoi"
    or "loci" can be described as parts of
    argumentation which belong to the
    obligatory, either explicit or inferable,
    premises. They are the content-
    related warrants or "conclusion
    rules" which connect the argument or
    arguments with the conclusion, the
    claim. As such, they justify the
    transition from the argument or
    arguments to the conclusion
    (Kienpointner 1992: 194).

5   Transcription conventions are given
    at the end of the chapter.

6   One of three EU youth- and education-
    related programs – Socrates, Leonardo,
    and Youth for Europe – established
    in 1995. Leonardo provides financial
    support for professional development
    and job training.

7   Individuals interviewed from Austria,
    the third of the most recent states to
    join the EU, did not seem to mention
    their nationality as often or in as
    explicit ways as the Swedes and
    Finns.

REFERENCES

Alvesson, Mats and Billing, Yvonne
    (eds) 1997: *Understanding Gender
    and Organizations*. London: Sage.

Anderson, Benedict 1988: *Die Erfindung
    der Nation: Zur Karriere eines
    folgenreichen Konzepts*. Frankfurt
    am Main and New York: Campus.
    (Original English publication:
    Anderson, Benedict 1983: *Imagined
    Communities: Reflections on the Origin
    and Spread of Nationalism*. London:
    Polity.)

Antaki, Charles and Widdicombe,
    Sue (eds) 1998: *Identities in Talk*.
    London: Sage.

Appelt, Erna and Jarosch, Monika (eds)
    2000: *Combating Racial Discrimination:
    Affirmative Action as a Model for
    Europe*. Oxford and New York: Berg.

Bakhtin, Mikhail 1981: *The Dialogic
    Imagination*. Austin: University
    of Texas Press.

Benhabib, Seyla 1996: The democratic
    movement and the problem of
    difference. In Seyla Benhabib
    (ed.) *Democracy and Difference:
    Contesting the Boundaries of the
    Political*. Princeton, NJ: Princeton
    University Press, pp. 3–18.

Benke, Gertraud and Wodak, Ruth
    2000: Stories about the past. Paper
    delivered at the IPRA Conference,
    Budapest, 2000.

Benke, Gertraud and Wodak, Ruth
    forthcoming: Memories of the
    Wehrmacht: The discursive
    construction of generational
    memories. In D. Nelson and
    M. Dedaic (eds) *War with Words*.
    The Hague: de Gruyter.

Billig, Michael 1989: *Ideological
    Dilemmas*. London: Sage.

Bourdieu, Pierre 1990: *Was heißt
    sprechen?* Vienna: Braumüller.

Bourdieu, Pierre 1993: *Soziologische Fragen*.
    Frankfurt am Main: Suhrkamp.

Bourdieu, Pierre 1994: *Zur Soziologie der
    symbolischen Formen*. Frankfurt am
    Main: Suhrkamp.

Braithwaite, Mary 2000: Mainstreaming
    Gender in the European Structural
    Funds. Paper prepared for the
    Mainstreaming Gender in European
    Public Policy Workshop, University
    of Wisconsin-Madison, October
    14–15, 2000.

Butler, Judith 1990: *Gender Trouble*. New
    York: Routledge.

Cameron, Deborah 1997: Theoretical debates in feminist linguistics: Questions of sex and gender. In Ruth Wodak (ed.) *Gender and Discourse.* London: Sage, pp. 21–36.

Cini, Michelle 1996: *The European Commission: Leadership, Organisation and Culture in the EU Administration.* Manchester and New York: Manchester University Press.

Corbett, Richard, Jacobs, Francis, and Shackleton, Michael 1995: *The European Parliament*, 3rd edn. London: Cartermill.

Davies, Bronwyn and Harré, Rom 1990: Positioning: Conversation and the production of selves. *Journal for the Theory of Social Behavior* 20(1): 43–63.

De Francisco, Victoria 1997: Gender, power and practice: Or, putting your money (and your research) where your mouth is. In Ruth Wodak (ed.) *Gender and Discourse.* London: Sage, pp. 37–56.

Diem-Wille, Gertraud 1996: *Karrierefrauen und Karrieremänner.* Opladen: Westdeutscher.

Elgström, Sven 2000: Norm negotiations. The construction of new norms regarding gender and development in EU foreign aid policy. In Sonia Mazey (ed.) *Women, Power and Public Policy in Europe.* Special Issue, *Journal of European Public Policy* 7(3): 457–76.

Fairclough, Norman 1992: *Discourse and Social Change.* London: Polity.

Fairclough, Norman and Wodak, Ruth 1997: Critical discourse analysis. In Teun A. van Dijk (ed.) *Introduction to Discourse Analysis*, vol. 2. London: Sage, pp. 258–84.

Gherardi, Silvia 1995: *Gender, Symbolism and Organizational Cultures.* London: Sage.

Goffman, Erving 1981: *Forms of Talk.* Philadelphia: University of Pennsylvania Press.

Habermas, Jürgen 1998: *Die postnationale Konstellation. Politische Essays.* Frankfurt am Main: Suhrkamp.

Hall, Stuart 1996a: The question of cultural identity. In Stuart Hall, D. Held, D. Hubert, and K. Thompson (eds) *Modernity: An Introduction to Modern Societies.* Cambridge, MA. and Oxford: Blackwell, pp. 595–643.

Hall, Stuart 1996b: Introduction: Who needs "identity"? In Stuart Hall and Paul du Gay (eds) *Questions of Cultural Identity.* London: Sage, pp. 1–17.

Kargl, Maria, Wetschanow, Karin, and Wodak, Ruth 1998: Sprache und Geschlecht. In Johanna Dohnal (ed.) *Eine andere Festschrift. Reihe Dokumentation*, Band 17. Vienna: Milena Verlag.

Kargl, Maria, Wetschanow, Karin, Wodak, Ruth, and Perle, Nela. 1997: *Kreatives Formulieren: Anleitungen zu geschlechtergerechtem Sprachgebrauch.* Vienna: Schriftenreihe des Bundesministeriums für Frauenangelegenheiten und Verbraucherschutz.

Kendall, Shari and Tannen, Deborah 1997: Gender and language in the workplace. In Ruth Wodak (ed.) *Gender and Discourse.* London: Sage, pp. 81–105.

Kienpointner, Manfred 1992: *Alltagslogik. Struktur und Funktion von Argumentationsmustern.* Stuttgart-Bad Cannstatt: Frommann-Holzboog.

Kotthoff, Helga and Wodak, Ruth (eds) 1997: *Communicating Gender in Context.* Amsterdam: John Benjamins.

Labov, William 1972: *Language in the Inner City.* Philadelphia: University of Pennsylvania Press.

Labov, William and Waletzky, Joshua 1967: Narrative analysis: Oral versions of personal experience. In J. Helm (ed.) *Essays on the Verbal and Visual Art.* Seattle: University of Washington Press, pp. 12–44.

Lakoff, Robin 1975: *Language and Woman's Place.* New York: Harper and Row.

Linde, Charlotte 1993: *Life Stories: The Creation of Coherence.* New York: Oxford University Press.

Martin, Denis-Constant 1995: The choices of identity. *Social Identities* 1(1): 5–20.

Martin-Rojo, Luisa 2000: Narratives at Work: When Women Take on the Role of Managers. Paper delivered at the Workshop on Theory and Interdisciplinarity in CDA, July 6–7, 2000, Department of Linguistics, University of Vienna.

Mazey, Sonia 2000: Introduction: Integrating gender-intellectual and "real world" mainstreaming. In Sonia Mazey (ed.) *Women, Power and Public Policy in Europe.* Special Issue, *Journal of European Public Policy* 7(3): 333–45.

McElhinny, Bonnie 1997: Ideologies of public and private language in sociolinguistics. In Ruth Wodak (ed.) *Gender and Discourse.* London: Sage, pp. 106–39.

Mumby, Denis (ed.) 1993: *Narrative and Social Control: Critical Perspectives.* Newbury Park, CA: Sage.

Muntigl, Peter, Weiss, Gilbert, and Wodak, Ruth 2000: *European Union Discourses on Un/employment. An Interdisciplinary Approach to Employment Policy-making and Organizational Change.* Amsterdam: John Benjamins.

Nelen, Sorah 1997: Three Challenges for the Future of the European Union's Gender Policy Examined: The Intergovernmental Conference, Kalanke, and Mainstreaming. PhD Thesis, College of Europe, Bruges.

Ochs, Elinor 1997: Narrative. In Teun A. van Dijk (ed.) *Introduction to Discourse Analysis,* vol. 1: *Discourse*

as Structure and Process. London: Sage, pp. 185–207.

Pollack, Mark and Hafner-Burton, E. 2000: Mainstreaming gender in the European Union. Unpublished MS.

Rehberg, Karl-Siegbert 1994: Institutionen als symbolische Ordnungen. Leitfragen und Grundkategorien zur Theorie und Analyse institutioneller Mechanismen. In G. Göhler (ed.) *Die Eigenart der Institutionen: Zum Profil politischer Institutionentheorie.* Baden-Baden: Nomos, pp. 47–84.

Reisigl, Martin and Wodak, Ruth 2001: Discourse and discrimination. In Martin Reisigl and Ruth Wodak (eds) *Rhetorics of Racism and Antisemitism.* London and New York: Routledge.

Ricoeur, Paul 1992: *Oneself as Another.* Chicago: University of Chicago Press.

Rossilli, Mariagrazia (ed.) 2000: *Gender Policies in the European Union.* New York: Peter Lang.

Saurer, Edith forthcoming: *Liebe und Arbeit: Geschlechterbeziehungen in Europa (19. und 20. Jahrhundert).*

Schiffrin, Deborah 1996: Narrative as self-portrait: Sociolinguistic constructions of identity. *Language and Society* 25: 167–203.

Schiffrin, Deborah 1997: The transformation of experience, identity, and context. In Gregory Guy, C. Feagin, Deborah Schiffrin, and John Baugh (eds) *Towards a Social Science of Language: Papers in Honor of William Labov,* vol 2: *Social Interaction and Discourse Structures.* Amsterdam and Philadelphia: John Benjamins, pp. 41–55.

Scollon, Ron 2000: *Mediated Discourse: The Nexus of Practice.* London: Routledge.

Shaw, Jo 2000: Importing gender: The challenge of feminism and the analysis of the EU legal order. In

Sonia Mazey (ed.) *Women, Power and Public Policy in Europe*. Special Issue, *Journal of European Public Policy* 7(3): 6–31.

Sheldon, Amy 1997: Talking power: Girls, gender enculturation and discourse. In Ruth Wodak (ed.) *Gender and Discourse*. London: Sage, pp. 225–44.

Straehle, Carolyn 1998: "We are not Americans and not Japanese, we are Europeans." Looking Inside the European Union. Unpublished MS, Academy of Sciences, Research Centre Discourse, Politics, Identity, Vienna.

Straehle, Carolyn, Weiss, Gilbert, Wodak, Ruth, Muntigl, Peter, and Sedlak, Maria 1999: Struggle as metaphor in EU discourses on unemployment. In Ruth Wodak and R. Iedema (eds) *Organizational Discourse*. Special Issue, *Discourse & Society*, 10(1): 67–99.

Tannen, Deborah 1989: *Talking Voices: Repetition, Dialogue, and Imagery in Conversational Discourse*. Cambridge: Cambridge University Press.

Tannen, Deborah 1995: *Talking from 9 to 5*. New York: Random House.

Tannen, Deborah 1997: *The Argument Culture*. New York: Random House.

Tannen, Deborah and Wallat, Cynthia 1993: Interactive frames and knowledge schemas in interaction: Examples from a medical examination/interview. In Deborah Tannen (ed.) *Framing in Discourse*. New York: Oxford University Press, pp. 57–76.

Toulmin, Stephen 1964: *The Uses of Argument*. Cambridge: Cambridge University Press.

Wagner, Ina 2000: Frauen in innovativen Betrieben. Project Proposal to the DFG, Vienna, Technical University.

Watson, Peggy 2000: Politics, policy and identity: EU eastern enlargement and East–West differences. In Sonia Mazey (ed.) *Women, Power and Public Policy in Europe*. Special Issue, *Journal of European Public Policy* 7(3): 369–85.

Weiss, Gilbert and Wodak, Ruth 1999: Organisation and Communication. On the Relevance of Niklas Luhman's Systems Theory for a Discourse-Hermeneutic Approach to Organizations. Working paper, Academy of Sciences, Research Centre Discourse, Politics, Identity, Vienna.

Weiss, Gilbert and Wodak, Ruth 2000: Debating Europe: Globalisation rhetoric and European Union employment policies. In I. Bellier and T. M. Wilson (eds) *An Anthropology of the European Union*. New York: Berg, pp. 75–92.

Widdicombe, Sue 1998: Identity as an analysts' and a participants' resource. In Charles Antaki and Sue Widdicombe (eds) *Identities in Talk*. London: Sage, pp. 191–206.

Wilson, John 1990: *Politically Speaking: The Pragmatic Analysis of Political Language*. Oxford: Blackwell.

Wodak, Ruth 1996: *Disorders of Discourse*. London: Longman.

Wodak, Ruth 1997: Introduction: Some important issues in the research of gender and discourse. In Ruth Wodak (ed.) *Gender and Discourse*. London: Sage, pp. 1–20.

Wodak, Ruth 2000a: Recontextualization and the transformation of meaning: A critical discourse analysis of decision making in EU meetings about employment policies. In S. Sarangi and M. Coulthard (eds) *Discourse and Social Life*. Harlow: Pearson Education, pp. 185–206.

Wodak, Ruth 2000b: "La sociolingüística necesita una teoria social"? Nuevas perspectivas en el analisis critico del discurso. *Discurso y Sociedad* 2(3): 123–47.

Wodak, Ruth 2001a: What CDA is about – a summary of its history, important concepts and its developments. In Ruth Wodak and Michael Meyer (eds) *Methods of Critical Discourse Analysis.* London: Sage, pp. 1–14.

Wodak, Ruth 2001b: Politikwissenschaft und Diskursanalyse: Diskurs in/der Politik. In Andrei S. Markovits and Sieglinde K. Rosenberger (eds) *Demokratie. Modus und Telos.* Beiträge für Anton Pelinka. Vienna: Böhlau, pp. 75–99.

Wodak, Ruth 2001c: Diskurs, Politik, Identität. In Oswald Panagl, Hans Goebl, and Emil Brix (eds) *Der Mensch und seine Sprache(n).* Vienna: Böhlau, pp. 133–55.

Wodak, Ruth in press: Gender and language (cultural concern essay). In *International Encyclopedia of the Social and Behavioral Sciences.* Oxford: Elsevier Science.

Wodak, Ruth forthcoming: Multinational organisations: Europe in the search of new identities. *Conference Proceedings.* City University of Hong Kong Press.

Wodak, Ruth, de Cillia, Rudolf, Reisigl, Martin, and Liebhart, Karin 1999: *The Discursive Construction of National Identity.* Edinburgh: Edinburgh University Press.

Wodak, Ruth and Meyer, Michael (eds) 2001: *Methods of Critical Discourse Analysis.* London: Sage.

Wodak, Ruth and Schulz, Muriel 1986: *The Language of Love and Guilt: Mother–Daughter Relationships from a Cross-cultural Perspective.* Amsterdam: John Benjamins.

Wodak, Ruth and Weiss, Gilbert 2001: "We are different than the Americans and the Japanese?" A critical discourse analysis of decision-making in European Union meetings about employment policies. In Edda Weigand and Marcelo Dascal (eds) *Negotiation and Power in Dialogic Interaction.* Amsterdam: John Benjamins.

Wortham, Stanton 1996: Mapping participant deictics: A technique for discovering speakers' footing. *Journal of Pragmatics* 25: 331–48.

Zimmerman, Don H. 1998: Identity, context and interaction. In Charles Antaki and Sue Widdicombe (eds) *Identities in Talk.* London: Sage, pp. 87–106.

Epilogue: Reflections on Language and Gender Research

ALICE F. FREED

1 Introduction

In the second half of the twentieth century, social science researchers, among them linguists, directed what might easily be considered an excessive amount of attention to the discussion of *differences* between the sexes, including sex differences in language. Starting in the 1960s, sociolinguists, working as urban dialectologists, began providing detailed descriptions of characteristics that were said to distinguish women's and men's speech (Wolfram 1969; Trudgill 1972; Labov 1972). In 1973, Robin Lakoff's now classic article, "Language and Woman's Place" (Lakoff 1973), changed the research landscape and launched a new era of work on "women and language." Lakoff's work did not change the emphasis on difference, however, and women's and men's speech continued to be compared and contrasted. With some notable exceptions (e.g. Gal 1978; Nichols 1983), it has only been since the early 1990s that researchers have seriously rethought the validity of taking sex and gender *difference* as a starting point for research on the interaction of language, sex, and gender. It has only been in recent years that sociolinguists have finally begun examining and reporting the significant heterogeneity within women's linguistic practices and within men's, and have begun noticing the similarity of the language of many women and many men. Perhaps even more importantly, since the early 1990s, researchers have increasingly understood the need to examine the complexity and the fluidity of the concept of gender. Despite the changes that have taken place in the scholarly field of language and gender and the innovative approaches that have emerged in the years since 1990 (see, for example, Eckert and McConnell-Ginet 1992, 1995; Hall and Bucholtz 1995; Bergvall, Bing, and Freed 1996; Livia and Hall 1997; and Bucholtz, Liang, and Sutton, 1999), there are still relatively few widely available published discussions which criticize the approach that takes female–male difference as both a starting point and as an explanation for linguistic behavior.

In this final chapter of the *Handbook of Language and Gender*, I would like to outline what we have now learned from language and gender research, drawing in part from the chapters in this collection and in part from other research published since 1973. Many (but not all) of the chapters in this volume reflect the shift that has taken place in the field of language and gender. This shift, as Janet Holmes and Miriam Meyerhoff explain in the Introduction, is best described as a movement away from "essentialist and dichotomous conceptions of gender to a differentiated, contextualized, and performative model which questions generalized claims about gender" (Introduction, p. 7). Despite this change, popular accounts of male and female language remain unchanged; institutional discourse and the invocation in institutional settings of stereotypes about women and men remain strong. Many of the authors in this volume address this phenomenon as they focus on the culturally constructed ideological underpinnings that help secure the belief in a sharp dichotomy between men and women.

In what follows, I will provide evidence that indicates that neither trade, academic, nor scholarly publications adequately represent the research findings of this area of sociolinguistics. I will illustrate that despite limited corroboration that significant language distinctions even exist between women and men, a considerable amount of print media continues to characterize women's and men's language as different. This will lead me to the principal theme of this chapter, namely an examination of why public perceptions of the way women and men talk do not match the language patterns that researchers have identified through careful investigation. I will examine the basis for the pervasive fascination with and emphasis on sex and gender difference, and I will investigate the tenaciousness of the public portrayal of women and men as speaking in ways that are distinctly different from one another regardless of how each is depicted. I will propose three reasons or possible causes for this persistent and most curious phenomenon.

First of all, it occurs to me that those of us doing language and gender research are partially responsible for the mismatch between research findings and public discussions of language and gender. We have not sufficiently concerned ourselves, and I include myself in this criticism, with public attitudes about language, sex, and gender. We commonly dismiss popular views about language as uninformed and continue talking to and writing only for one another. Second, we have not always adequately guarded against perpetuating, albeit unintentionally, a fair number of sex and gender stereotypes by overgeneralizing our own research results as well as the findings of others. Deborah Cameron, Janet Holmes and Maria Stubbe, Bonnie McElhinny, Mary Talbot, and Sara Trechter make similar points in their chapters in this volume. Mary Talbot goes so far as to suggest that the mere act of listing features of speech traditionally, but incorrectly, assumed to be associated with women or men serves to perpetuate the belief in these very language characteristics. Deborah Cameron makes a similar point in her chapter on gender and language ideologies (this volume, p. 463). Finally and most importantly, it is my contention that at least in the West, we are witnessing a reaction to (perhaps a backlash against) the process of gender destabilization whereby the supposed certainty of two sexes and two genders, and the concomitant certainty of the naturalness of heterosexuality, is gradually being eroded.

2 Research Findings: Language and Gender from 1973 to the Present

From 1973 to the end of the twentieth century, language and gender research was dominated by three major themes which theorized both the impressions and the presumed realities of female and male speech. Because these frameworks have been exhaustively described, evaluated, and critiqued elsewhere in the language and gender literature (see Crawford 1995; Freed 1995; Cameron 1998), and are reviewed in a number of the chapters of this volume (e.g. Bucholtz, Cameron, Romaine, Sidnell, and Talbot), I will sketch them only briefly. The earliest modern theory about "women's language," most often associated with Robin Lakoff (1973), is commonly referred to as the *deficit theory*. It described women's language as ineffective in comparison to men's and explained women's manner of speaking as being a reflection of women's insecurity and powerless place in society. By contrast, the *dominance theory* of language and gender, presented first by Barrie Thorne and Nancy Henley in 1975 (see also Fishman 1983), focused on issues of patriarchy – that is, male power and dominance. Researchers characterized the social and political arrangement between the sexes as one in which women were viewed and treated as unequal to men because the norms of society had literally been established by men. The division of labor between women and men was seen to include a division of language practices, one belonging to the powerful and the other belonging to women. Language differences were identified as part of a structure of unequal access and influence. Finally, the *difference theory*, represented by the writings of Daniel Maltz and Ruth Borker (1982) and Deborah Tannen (1990, 1994), hypothesized that women and men used specific and distinct verbal strategies and communicative styles which were developed in same-sex childhood peer groups. Researchers who adhered to this framework believed that by focusing on language difference instead of power difference (or male dominance), the antagonistic comparison between women and men could be avoided and the positive values of each language style could be celebrated. Feminist linguists who objected to the difference framework (Troemel-Ploetz 1991; Freed 1992; Uchida 1992) argued that the particular sets of verbal strategies associated with women and men emerged not in a vacuum but were an integral part of the power arrangements between men and women in societies around the world.

As has been argued by numerous researchers in recent years, all three of these approaches are limited and flawed. (For useful discussions see Henley and Kramarae 1991; Eckert and McConnell-Ginet 1992, 1995.) Each of the frameworks concentrates on the verbal characteristics of women, or as Sally Johnson (1997) observes, each of the approaches is "characterized by almost exclusive *problematization of women*" (Johnson, 1997: 10), and each makes use "of a concept of gender based on *binary opposition*. The tacit hypothesis of many studies seems to be that men and women are essentially different and that this difference will be reflected in their contrasting use of language" (1997: 11). The shortcomings of this essentialist view are rigorously argued in many chapters of this volume and the analyses provided explain how women and men have been continually naturalized into separate categories by a variety of deeply embedded social, historic, and linguistic ideologies. (For further discussion, see, among others, the chapters in this volume by Deborah Cameron, Penelope Eckert, Bonnie McElhinny, Miriam Meyerhoff, and Susan Philips.)

Not only did considerable debate develop about how to conceptualize the nature of language and gender research but, as Penelope Eckert and Suzanne Romaine each describe in their chapters of the Handbook, a substantial body of criticism arose of the entire quantitative sociolinguistics paradigm, a paradigm that attempted to correlate linguistic behavior with sex (or gender), race, and social class, as straightforward categories of social scientific investigation. We have now established with sizeable amounts of data the diversity of speech patterns and the mosaic of language practices within the category called "male" and within the one designated as "female." As magnificently portrayed in many of the chapters in this book, the over-reaching conclusion to be drawn about language practices among girls, boys, women, and men is the presence of elaborate variability. Janet Holmes and Maria Stubbe (this volume) remind us that when studied closely, gendered linguistic practices that have been over-generalized "unravel" and become more complex. Marjorie Goodwin's data (this volume) confirm that "the notion that girls are fundamentally interested in cooperative, face-saving interaction" is called into question by "transcripts of naturally occurring behavior in disputes" in cross-cultural comparisons (this volume, p. 243). Penelope Eckert concludes that "if there is a consistent gender pattern in all these data, then, it is the girls' greater overall use of linguistic variability across social categories" (this volume, p. 393). We can cite large numbers of examples in which men and boys talk the way "women" are expected to sound; similarly, we have determined that girls' and women's speech often fails to conform to the speech patterns that had been assumed. And yet, despite the extensive body of data that have been amassed, analyzed, interpreted, and published, the general impression that the lay public and the academic community (at least in North America) seem to have about the way women and men speak remains fairly unaltered. (See James and Clarke 1993; James and Drakich 1993; and James 1996 for reviews of conflicting findings regarding three language features that have repeatedly been described as characteristic of women's speech.)

3 Disputing "Female" and "Male" as Binary Categories

Disagreement with and opposition to studies that frame social scientific research around binary dichotomous categories (whether considering difference between the sexes, among socio-economic classes, between public and private activities, or racial and ethnic groups) is gaining ground in all the social sciences and is well represented in this volume. (For additional discussion, see Bem 1993; Crawford 1995; Bing and Bergvall 1996; Gibbon 1999.) The fundamental problem with describing human beings in terms of difference is that the concept invariably leads to a ranking or privileging of one group over another. Establishing one group as "different" from another situates one of the two groups as the standard or norm by which the second is judged; the second group can then be characterized as deviant, deficient, or just slightly on the margin. In the case of sex or gender, the masculine norm has defined activities in the arts, in education, in publishing, in government, in sports, in the health industry, in work, play, and sexual practice. Accordingly, women are measured and their nature determined based on how they differ from men.

Discussions that emphasize difference also lead to a reification of the notion of human social difference, thereby creating a sense that these distinctions are natural, static, and immutable. Catherine MacKinnon (1984) provides a useful illustration of this principle when she cautions that if women and men are theorized to be different, then the notion of different but equal under the law in the United States is an impossible goal. As she explains it, in the realm of the law, equality is a prize awarded to likes:

> According to the approach to sex equality that has dominated politics, law, and social perception, equality is an equivalence, not a distinction, and sex is a distinction. The legal mandate of equal treatment ... becomes a matter of treating likes alike and unlikes unlike; and the sexes are defined as such by their natural unlikeness. Put another way, gender is socially constructed as difference epistemologically, ... a built-in tension exists between this concept of equality, which presupposes sameness, and this concept of sex, which presupposes difference. (MacKinnon 1984: 32–3)

Similar themes have long surfaced in feminist scholarship. Cynthia Fuchs Epstein in her book *Deceptive Distinctions: Sex, Gender and the Social Order* (1988) explains:

> Analyses of research on modes of communication, like research on other behavioral and attitudinal differences between the sexes, indicate that what "everyone knows" to be true may turn out not to be true at all. Differences tend to be superficial, and they are often linked to power differentials – associated with female and male status but not necessarily paired with them – and they are situation-specific.

> But beyond these findings, the research shows that many widely assumed differ-
> ences turn out to be mere stereotypes; that there are more similarities in men's
> and women's behavior than is commonly believed. Whether humans need to
> create differences between the sexes actively or symbolically . . . or whether the
> creation and maintenance of distinction are a self-conscious activity of the pow-
> erful whose interests are served by them or whether differences once created by
> intent or accident become perpetuated through a process of institutionalization,
> it seems clear that most gender differences are socially created and therefore may
> be socially altered.   (1988: 231)

As expressed repeatedly in the chapters of this volume, feminist researchers
writing on this topic consider that it is the popular and prevailing understanding of *gender* as the social and behavioral manifestation of *sex* that lies at the
heart of the issue we are dealing with. That *language* is the vehicle for conveying expectations about gendered behavior further complicates matters because
this deeply entrenched view of gender is recursively articulated and becomes
naturalized and normalized through countless everyday language activities
and linguistic practices. As William Leap explains (this volume), texts, that is,
various forms of linguistic production, are a primary site of gender construction.
He writes:

> Genders are cultural constructions, and not determined entirely or primarily by
> bodily form or biological function. Accordingly, studies of gendered experi-
> ence frequently use *text* as an entry point for such inquiry, because gender is
> negotiated and contested through the production and circulation of life stories,
> personal anecdotes, gossip and other narratives, legal statements, ritual oratory,
> words of advice and practical caution, jokes, songs, and other forms of expressive
> language, as well as through word borrowings, modifications to existing vocabu-
> lary, and new word formations.   (p. 402)

The simple acts of referring to, describing, and addressing one another, the
topics so well captured in Sally McConnell-Ginet's chapter on social labeling,
all create notions of gender as seemingly fixed and stable. Proverbs and folktales,
as Robin Lakoff points out (this volume), as well as the multitude of ways that
language represents us, the "linguistic sexism" that Anne Pauwels studies
(this volume), all conspire to create a sense of fixed reality. We are constantly
reminded, however, that reality is indeed in the eyes of the beholder.

This is a good place to digress with a terminological concern. A key element
of my discussion is that we need to break down various destructive dichotomies in order to learn more about the legitimate character and interworkings
of language, sex, and gender. I am contesting the widely held view that humans
can be naturally and categorically classified into two neat groups called either
"women" and "men" or "females" and "males." Yet in the process of criticizing
the use of these dichotomies, I am invoking several dichotomies of my own and
I want to acknowledge straight away my awareness of this inconsistency. In
this chapter, I am focusing on the dichotomy between perceived or believed as
distinct from actual or empirical accounts of language use. I am simultaneously

assuming the existence of an essentialist versus a constructed theory of sex and gender. Furthermore, I am continuing to use the words *female* and *male* and *woman* and *man* (see Rosenblum and Travis 1996) while arguing against the immutable nature of the very categories that these terms are said to name. This predicament is forced upon me by the nature of the language available to us for the purposes of a discussion such as this. (See Bing and Bergvall 1996.) So as we contemplate the public perceptions of language use that are distinct from established linguistic evidence, we need to recognize the ways that our own use of language infiltrates and partly shapes what we are able to say.

4 The Language Data

Three decades into the study of language, sex, and gender, we still find a remarkable discrepancy between public perceptions of how women and men speak (and how they are expected to speak) and the actual character of the language that people use. The persistence of this contradiction underscores the vitality of well-entrenched stereotypes about sex and gender and the weight and influence of societal efforts to maintain the impression of difference between women and men.

Sociolinguists, linguistic anthropologists, and other scholars have now analyzed vast quantities of naturally occurring speech samples from a wide range of contexts. These data demonstrate in vivid detail that the amount of talk, the structure of narratives, the use of questions, the availability of cooperative and competitive speech styles, the employment of prestige speech forms, the use of intimate friendly talk, the occurrence of various phonological and prosodic patterns sometimes representative of linguistic change, the occurrence of vernacular speech forms, lexical choices, the use of silence, interruption, aggravated forms of address, and forms of politeness – these do not correlate in any consistent pattern with either sex or gender. Researchers have substantiated again and again that speakers use language in creative and divergent ways depending on a wide range of factors including (but not limited to) setting and context, type of activity engaged in, group, social, and personal identity, topic of conversation, channel of communication, community of practice, audience, language repertoires of various sorts, economic and symbolic resources, political purpose, symbolic and actual resistance to various forms of oppression, relative rank, and nature of relationship to addressee. Despite our knowledge base, the stereotypes, the ideas that we might call folklinguistic beliefs, remain strong. As Mary Talbot reminds us (this volume), "Stereotyping as a representational practice is at the center of the notion of folklinguistics" (p. 472).

Consider just a fraction of the research findings for English: we have an analysis of the speech of United States senators speaking at the confirmation hearings for the nomination of Clarence Thomas to be a Justice of the United

States Supreme Court (Mendoza-Denton 1995); a study of Latina teenagers engaged in and resisting therapeutic discourse in California (Cathryn Houghton 1995); details about middle-aged African American women telling stories in their homes in Chicago (Marcyliena Morgan 1991); an ethnography of groups of European American high school students talking among themselves in Detroit, some identified with mainstream culture and others rebelling against it (Penelope Eckert 1989a, 1989b). We have a description of female and male telephone sex-workers (Kira Hall 1995), of female and male police officers at work (Bonnie McElhinny 1995), of White middle-class adolescents verbally engaged at the dinner table (Alice Greenwood 1996), of college students talking about friendship as part of an experiment (Alice Freed and Alice Greenwood 1996); of members of a Canadian university tribunal examining cases of sexual assault (Susan Ehrlich and Ruth King 1996; Susan Ehrlich 1998). There are investigations of male students speaking in American college fraternity houses (Scott Kiesling 1997), of an African American teacher working with her students in a classroom (Michele Foster 1995), of college-aged men gossiping (Sally Johnson and Frank Finlay 1997), of lesbians telling their coming-out stories (Kathleen Wood 1999), of White middle-class American women telling their pregnancy stories (Freed 1996), of people interacting over the Internet (Susan Herring et al. 1995), of school-aged children playing jump-rope (Marjorie H. Goodwin 1999), of middle-class British women talking to close personal friends (Jennifer Coates 1996), of doctors and patients interacting (Candace West 1990), of people talking in the workplace (Shari Kendall and Deborah Tannen 1997), gay speech (William Leap 1995), lesbian language, heterosexual communication, political and legal discourse, conversation at university faculty meetings, testimony before grand juries and special prosecutors, telephone exchanges, old speakers, young speakers, speakers with a variety of kinds of aphasia and dementia. From a wide array of published accounts we have learned that our language use is vital, ever-changing, flexible and creative, sometimes stilted, other times polite, occasionally rude and vulgar, alternately filled with slang or with literary forms, useful for political, social, and personal affirmation, rebellion, resistance, confrontation, conformity, argumentation, love-making, and friendship.

From this we have definitively substantiated significant degrees of linguistic variation in the speech of women; we have clear evidence that men's language does not constitute a single style or form. Yet despite the enormity of our research results, the public representation of the way women and men speak is almost identical to the characterization provided thirty years ago. These deeply entrenched gender-specific linguistic stereotypes apparently serve critical social purposes; they appear to maintain not only a status quo that advantages men over women and heterosexuals over homosexuals and lesbians, but one that helps establish and maintain rules of feminine and masculine behavior even if these generalizations fail to reflect social or linguistic reality.

5   Sources of Evidence about Public Views of Language Difference

We may ask what evidence exists that our research has not had an impact on public perceptions, or at least public discourse about women's and men's language. I will provide two types of data to support my claim: (1) an informal and anecdotal review of twenty-five years of students' comments on the topic, and (2) an analysis of several on-line library databases of print media sources.

When I have queried my own American university students about how women and men talk, they have always quickly and easily provided predictable responses. Although I no longer ask the question, they still volunteer the same information – just less directly. My students say that women curse less than men and that little girls are explicitly taught not to curse at all. Students report that men use obscenities quite freely, though in theory, not around women because boys are admonished from cursing in the presence of their mothers or sisters. I learn each year from a new crop of students that women are less direct in their speech, though students find it hard to describe what it means to be verbally indirect. Women are consistently portrayed as more polite, friendlier in their use of language, and are said to use better grammar than men. Men make more sexual comments, my students report. Men use blunter language. Women are more hesitant in their speech than men. Women ask more questions than men. Men won't ask for directions when they are lost. Some of these verbal myths have even passed into American popular culture and turn up on Internet lists of "100 reasons why it is good to be a man" (or a woman, as the case might be). These are all well-known examples of linguistic practices stereotypically associated with women and men.

When I ask my students if they believe what they are saying, they quickly, unhesitatingly, reply that they are merely reporting stereotypes. Then the personal stories emerge. The students, one by one, describe a friend or relative who talks like a woman – even though he is a man. They talk about how their own language was corrected by parents or teachers when they were children but how they pay little attention to these instructions now that they are adults – except maybe during a job interview or perhaps, they admit, in class. The students I interact with never fail to give me specific examples that are in direct contradiction to the very list of characteristics that they have helped compile.

If the students realize that the speech characteristics that they are cataloguing are not real, why do they supply almost identical lists, year after year? Is it the question itself about male/female verbal differences that prompts their reply? Why don't they resist the question? The list of linguistic features is on the tips of their tongues and the thoughts about the assumed nature of women's speech and men's speech are very much part of their cultural knowledge. Just as much part of their knowledge, however, is the reality that each of them speaks in different ways at various times and that they are able to alter their language, change their projected image, shape their identity, and affect their interactions with others through the language they use. Where do our students', or at least my students', impressions originate? How do their ideas, let us agree to call them folklinguistic beliefs, evolve? What creates and maintains their beliefs? What mechanism is at work that perpetuates these sex- and gender-related stereotypes?

In order to answer some of these questions, I decided to investigate the degree of coverage given to the topic of sex and gender difference in the English-language press. Following the lines of Deborah Cameron's suggestion that the popular press is obsessed with differences between women and men (1995: 202), I decided to search a variety of databases for evidence that academics and the public at large are being exposed to an avalanche of information (or propaganda) about sex differences – including material on language and sex difference.

6   On-line Databases of Popular, Educational, and Academic Print Media

I searched a variety of large on-line databases that indexed four different kinds of published material; these comprised widely circulated magazines and journals, major English-language newspapers, educational publications, and academic (i.e. scholarly) journals. The results of this database search quickly confirmed my suspicions. Despite the innovative and ground-breaking writing done on language and gender since the 1990s, work that has criticized using female–male difference as a starting point, I did not find discussions reflecting this fact in popular, news, or academic publications. In such widely circulated popular publications as *USA Today, Parade Magazine, Newsweek Magazine*, or the *New York Times*, there was little that suggested that the boundary between the sexes was becoming fuzzy or that the edges of the two-gender system were softening. Instead readers were repeatedly exposed to articles that conformed to existing assumptions and common perceptions about sex and gender. A great deal of excitement was generated by reports about negligible and obscure scientific findings related to sex differences in the brain; a significant amount of discussion connected academic findings of gender differences to their possible application for educators, therapists, industry managers, government in-service training centers, parents, etc. Not surprisingly, the traditional view of the relationship between the sexes was the one conveyed in the popular press. It is not difficult to conclude that the treatment of this topic by the mass media constitutes a very effective mechanism for reinforcing and maintaining the impression of sex and gender difference as a normal aspect of human existence.

I began with the on-line version of the *Reader's Guide to Periodic Literature* where a total of 306 popular magazines and journals are indexed. (Some of these have been added since this database was created in 1983, while other magazines have ceased publication in the intervening years.) Using the key-words "sex differences" (the words "gender differences" were not among the searchable terms in this database), and checking for a period of ten years, January 1990 through December 1999, I found no fewer than 280 articles that dealt with sex (or "gender") differences in one form or another. It was evident from scanning the titles that some of these articles dealt with topics from the social sciences and some were from the so-called hard sciences; a few treated topics related to species other than our own, such as one entitled "How cardinals tell her songs from his," which appeared in *Science News* in August 1998. Most of the articles, however, were what we would expect: "Listening in on girl-talk," *Newsweek*, November 1998; "Sex talk (male–female language differences)," *Esquire*, January 1997; "Why men lose weight faster than women," *Jet*, July 1996; "What I got when I acted like a guy," *Redbook*, April 1995; "All I want for Christmas . . . (differences in boys' and girls' letters to Santa)," *Good Housekeeping*, December 1995; "The difference between macho sex and true intimacy," *Ebony*, July 1995; "How to give orders like a man," *The New York Times Magazine*, August 1994; "What women do better," *Redbook*, August 1993; "Sex differences in the brain," *Scientific American*, September 1992; "Why women live longer than men and what men can do about it," *Ebony*, February 1991; "It's all in your head: Gender and pain," *Esquire*, April 1990.

For the magazines indexed by the *Reader's Guide to Periodic Literature*, the peak coverage of the topic "differences between the sexes" was in 1994 when 44 articles appeared; there were 32 in 1993, and 39 in 1995. (This pattern was roughly duplicated in my other searches.) For the period considered, the number of articles ranged from a low of 20 (1990) to a high of 44 (1994). Because I was unable to determine the exact number of magazines scanned per year, thus leaving open the possibility that the higher and lower numbers reflected the fluctuation in the total number of scanned magazines, I compared the number of articles found for "sex differences" with the number for "race differences." Searching for "race differences" in place of "sex differences" for the same ten-year period, January 1990 through December 1999, I found only 63 articles (as compared to 280).

I decided to explore a bit further, noting that this was a relatively small number of articles given the hundreds of magazines that were involved in the search. I wondered whether I would find different sorts of number in databases for newspapers, educational, or academic publications. Using the on-line data-base *Lexis-Nexis*, I examined the number of articles that appeared under the category "General News" based on keyword searches for "sex differences," "gender differences," "racial differences," and "ethnic differences." (The choice of "race difference" versus "racial difference" was again determined by the available keywords in the particular database being used.) The category "General News" is described as "U.S. & international newspapers, magazines, newsletters & journals." Under this rubric are "Major Newspapers," described in the on-line *Lexis-Nexis* site as consisting of US newspapers which "must be listed in the top 50 circulation in Editor & Publisher Year Book. Newspapers published outside the United States must be in the English language and listed as a national newspaper in Benn's World Media Directory or one of the top 5 per cent in circulation for the country."

The results of this second search were slightly different from those of the *Reader's Guide to Periodic Literature*. While there was an increase in the number of references for five-year periods under both sex differences and gender differences, comparable increases showed up also for racial differences. Again a search was done for the ten-year period from January 1990 through December 1999. For this particular database, the keywords "gender differences" and "racial differences" turned up more sources than either "sex differences" or "ethnic differences." "Gender differences" produced a total of 319 articles; "sex differences" revealed 117. Surprisingly – a result not duplicated in any other search – under "racial differences" a similar total, 314 references, was found; for "ethnic differences" 213 articles were cited.

Also using *Lexis-Nexis* but this time for the category "Magazines and Journals," the pattern was as found in the *Reader's Guide to Periodic Literature*. (As before, the keywords "gender differences" and "racial differences" turned up more sources than either "sex differences" or "ethnic differences.") Thus, searching with the keywords "gender differences," from January 1990 through December 1999, I found 59 articles. For the same time-period for the same database, using "racial differences" from January 1990 through December 1999, 24 articles appeared.

The exercise was repeated with two more databases: (1) ERIC, the US Department of Education's Educational Resource Information Center database, which contains citations and abstracts from over 980 educational and education-related journals and the full text of more than 2,200 digests; and (2) EBSCO's "Academic Search Premier," a privately operated database which provides full text for 3,288 scholarly publications covering academic areas of study including social sciences, humanities, education, computer sciences, engineering, language and linguistics, arts and literature, medical sciences, and ethnic studies.

For ERIC, the keywords "sex differences" and "racial differences" turned up more sources than either "gender differences" or "ethnic differences." Thus, searching with the keywords "sex differences" from January 1990 through December 1999, a stunning 9,233 articles were found. For the same time-period with the same database, using "racial differences" from January 1990 through December 1999, only 2,214 articles were cited.

EBSCO's "Academic Search Premier" revealed the same pattern. Again using the keywords "sex differences" and "racial differences," the following numbers appeared: with the keywords "sex differences," there were 4,309 articles from January 1990 through December 1999. For this same time-period with the same database, using "racial differences," 481 articles appeared.

The results of all these searches are summarized in table 1.

Table 1 Keyword searches, January 1990 to December 1999 (number of articles)

Reader's Guide to Periodic Literature	
"Sex differences"	280
"Race differences"	63
Lexis-Nexis "General News"	
"Gender differences"	319
"Sex differences"	117
"Racial differences"	314
"Ethnic differences"	213
Lexis-Nexis "Magazines and Journals"	
"Gender differences"	59
"Racial differences" .	24
ERIC	
"Sex differences"	9,233
"Racial differences"	2,214
EBSCO Academic Search Premier	
"Sex differences"	4,309
"Racial differences"	481

These searches were undertaken in an attempt to document the degree of interest in, or at least the degree of coverage given to, the topic of male and female difference (including language difference) in popular, educational, and scholarly publications. These numbers bear out and verify the impression that many of us have, that "sex difference" and "gender difference" are extremely fashionable topics, topics that we, the reading public, come across with tremendous regularity in both professional and personal contexts. The numbers substantiate the existence of a bedrock ideological foundation that feeds the interest and belief in the two-gender system. Not coincidentally, a discussion of the existence of such powerful ideologies is a common thread in the chapters of this Handbook. While the topics and approaches of the chapters vary considerably, we find this theme, perhaps more than any other theme. A consideration of the ideological underpinnings which provide the cultural foundation for public views of gender, combined with an analysis of the degree to which public discourse provides a forum for the expression of these views permeates the volume. Deborah Cameron's chapter focuses specifically on gender and language ideologies, but in addition, no less than half of the other articles herein discuss the phenomenon of ideology and its role in constructing and naturalizing such diverse but everyday notions as: adolescence (Eckert), authority (Meyerhoff), sex- and gender-related roles and practices (Philips), sociolinguistic research (McElhinny), judicial processes (Ehrlich), the place of ethnicity in language and gender research (Trechter), advertising (Cameron), management training (Talbot), and labeling/naming (McConnell-Ginet). A detailed analysis of how ideologies shape and help perpetuate the belief that women and men are different (regardless of how each is represented) is also addressed in the chapters by Besnier, Lakoff, Swann, and Wodak.

7   What the Database Numbers Reveal

In the remainder of this chapter I would like to explore what the numbers from these databases contribute to our understanding of the continued discrepancy between public views of language and gender and our own empirical observations about language. That an ideological basis for this trend exists is now transparent; that such deeply rooted and nearly invisible ideologies mold our belief systems and infiltrate our public and private institutions is not surprising. What remains mysterious, however, is why the strength of our research findings has not enabled us to make inroads into changing, or at least adjusting, the public discourse on language and the sexes. I will suggest three reasons for what appears to be remarkable stability in discussions of the two-gender and two-sex system.

First of all, considering the extensive research findings generated by years of studying language and gender, it seems that we, as feminist linguists, have done a fairly dismal job of conveying to the public what we have learned about language and the sexes. Why, we might ask, are professional linguists so little able to make headway in showing the public, even though they seem to already know this, that language is much more diverse than represented by stereotypes? Why have we failed to influence people outside the small group doing related research? It is my impression that language and gender researchers, including myself, have tended to dismiss (as nonsense and therefore as unimportant) the public's ideas about how women and men talk. We express our dismay but, in general, we have simply not made this a research priority. (In a related commentary, Joan Swann (this volume) addresses the "alarming" gap that is developing between educational policy and language and gender research. Also see Susan Herring's discussion (this volume) about gender equality and the Internet.) The continued mismatch between what sociolinguists working in this field know and what the public and other self-appointed language experts express about language and gender is, therefore, in part due to the fact that we as a field have not chosen to address this inconsistency. In my view, the contrast between speakers' actual language use and others' perceptions of and expectations about language use should be more rigorously taken into account in our work. There are certainly many practical obstacles to our accomplishing this – such considerations as limited research time, tenuring and publishing pressures within the academy, issues of funding, the preferences shown by major media outlets, to say nothing of researchers' personal intellectual priorities. Nonetheless, our failure to communicate to the public our acquired knowledge about language and gender is a critical component of the perpetuation of gendered stereotypes and is thus part of the very problem that needs to be addressed.

A second reason that an incongruity persists between perceptions and actual speech practices seems to stem from a continued emphasis on sex and gender difference within the academic community itself. The perils of the difference paradigm are quite real due to its capacity for creating stereotypes and over-generalizations. For this reason, it is disappointing that many researchers are themselves slow to give up this approach. Barbara Johnstone (1996), in her book *The Linguistic Individual*, reminds us of the dangers of generalizing about the speech behavior of any individual based on that person's group identity. She says:

> No student of variation in discourse structure or style would expect any individual to be a perfect match for the generalized description of regions, classes, genders and so on generated by research; . . . Aware as we may be of the fact that we are generalizing away from particular cases, and as well as we may understand what we gain and lose by doing this, there is still some danger in it. The danger is that idealized descriptions sometimes come to be used as explanatory devices. From discovering that, in some respects, an individual's style matches expectations generated in other studies of groups to which the individual belongs, it is a short and easy step to supposing that group identifications account for the individual's behavior. (1996: 86)

Simple observations about similarities in the speaking styles of superficially related groups of people fail to explain the mechanism whereby individual speakers make the choices that they make. Linguists themselves need to be more cautious about the generalizations that they draw from their own work and from that of others. Editors compiling anthologies and scholars writing textbooks need to be more aware of the traditional nature of the choices they make with regard to the content of their books; their decisions help shape the opinions of the next generation of students and scholars.

Deborah Cameron makes similar points in her chapter in this volume. She notes that while "Researchers may be motivated by a wish to explode the stereotype [about language and gender] . . . the stereotype has set the agenda" (p. 465); and while conceding that it is difficult to think about language and gender "without reference to prior understandings of the phenomenon" she urges language and gender scholars "to be *reflexive* about the cultural resources that have shaped their own understandings, as well as the understandings of the people whose language use they study" (p. 465).

Altogether, the evidence is compelling that the world around us is convinced that women and men are essentially different and that the way we speak is a perfect indicator of just how different we are. Our students say so, our colleagues in other fields say so, the articles, newspapers, and books that we read say so. And yet we have compiled substantial evidence that neither biological nor linguistic data support these assumptions. We know that reports of small brain differences between women and men have minimal (if any) effect on either how we conduct ourselves in our social lives or how we function as thinking individuals. We understand that the linguistic choices that speakers make, those which set their language off from the language practices of others, are often manifestations of speaker-determined agency and indices of speaker identity. *Language as used* regularly reflects speaker-driven decisions about how we, as speakers, want to present ourselves and how we want others to view us. *Language as perceived* is another matter entirely and it is precisely these stereotyped perceptions of language use that are cause for concern. We may conclude that the sheer volume of published reports about sex differences provides energetic sustenance for the continuing misperceptions of how we speak and the enduring disparity between this view and the data that document how we actually use language. But, there must be more.

8   The Breakdown of the Two-gender System

There is a third reason that I would like to suggest for the trend of emphasizing, over-reporting, and even exaggerating evidence of sex and gender difference: it appears that some cracks in the towering edifice of the two-sex, two-gender system are beginning to show. I suspect that discomfort or concerns about the weakening of distinctions between the sexes has aroused public resistance to acknowledging variability in gendered behavior. I have the impression, as Deborah Cameron (1995) also suggests, that it is the fear of gender instability that is galvanizing the insistence on difference. "It is striking," she reminds us, "that popular discourse on gender, though seemingly prompted by the increasing complexity and fuzziness of gender boundaries, continues to be organized around a simple binary opposition" (1995: 202). Perhaps the urgency of attention being conferred to male and female difference is due to the public's gradual realization that things are falling apart. Perhaps, when a sufficiently large number of men and women deviate from the stereotyped expectations that society has had for them, change actually begins to take hold. Perhaps, as Cameron (1997) suggests, the insistence on gendered behavior is part of the mechanism not only for constructing but for attempting to maintain traditional gendered distinctions.

The real threat to the two-gender system may be that people are increasingly aware that women and men are able to recreate themselves (that is, create different selves) in part through language. People are experiencing first-hand the constructed nature of gender and grasping the degree to which gender is "performed" and variable. Changes and variations in speech behavior thus become symbolic (or even represent concrete evidence) that things are not the way they used to be, or perhaps, that things never were as they had been represented. Indeed, several chapters in this collection make specific reference to social and linguistic changes that are occurring. Sally McConnell-Ginet provides examples of address term usage that "seem to indicate something about ongoing changes in the gender order" (p. 81). Robin Lakoff, while examining a number of public events covered by the press, remarks that "change is coming" and that the clock cannot be turned back. Niko Besnier and Kira Hall provide detailed examples of innovative language practices employed by people in transgendered communities; Anna Livia examines how authors create alternative gender identities for their characters. If there is a threat to the central ideology on which White Western heterosexual male-based norms and power rest, then perhaps public efforts to affirm the "naturalness" of gendered patterns of behavior need to be redoubled.

Overall, the American landscape is gradually changing and evidence is abundant that conceptualizations and public displays of sexuality and gendered behavior are in flux. In recent years in the United States, we have had many surprising images. We looked upon Bob Dole, a White man in his early seventies, former Majority Leader of the United States Senate and once Republican Presidential candidate, as he appeared in advertisements for the drug Viagra which combats "erectile dysfunction," while at the same time his wife was setting up an exploratory committee to consider launching a campaign to become the first female president of the United States. On American day-time television, we watch talk-show host Jerry Springer interview young adults as they reveal their sexual infidelities that invariably turn out to be with same-sex partners, always to the apparently staged bewilderment of their current heterosexual lovers. We read *Newsweek* magazine's cover-story about the increasing popularity of bisexuality on and off college campuses (July 17, 1995) and *The New York Times Sunday Magazine* featured story on the persistence of polygamy (May 1999). We notice that *The New York Times* Sunday "Styles" section describes an increasingly large number of traditional wedding ceremonies while it also reports that in the United States, hair color, hairstyle, and hair lengths for men and women vary widely, and body piercing, tattoos, and jewelry cover more and more parts of young American male and female bodies. We learn from newspaper accounts that women in their fifties and sixties are having babies as younger men and older women pair off. We witness female sports stars taking center stage at high schools across the United States and Canada.

Transsexuals, cross-dressers, and transgendered individuals are not as rare as they used to be. In the remarkable 1999 movie *Boys Don't Cry*, screen actress Hilary Swank dramatizes the true story of Brandon Teena, a young woman who takes on a male identity in the rural town of Falls City, Nebraska. What is most noteworthy about this film is that the fairly conservative Academy Awards Association bestowed on Swank the coveted Academy Award for Best Actress for her unglamorous role as a female–male cross-dresser/transgendered individual. It is hard to imagine that this could have happened twenty years earlier. It is not yet a new world. Sexual violence against women has not declined. Pay differentials between women and men are still in evidence. White men still dominate most major institutions in the West and, in countries around the world, women are veiled, raped, or often under the equivalent of house arrest in their own homes. The two-sex, two-gender system is still enforced but the edges are blurring and the signs of discomfort are on the rise.

In 1992 Robin Lakoff (1992, 1995), gave a fascinating account of five highly publicized events, each involving a different American woman, events which Lakoff believes served to change the nature of women's public voices. (Her essay in this volume develops a similar theme.) In this earlier work Lakoff discusses the significance of the actions, escapades, and misfortunes surrounding the lives of Anita Hill (who accused US Supreme Court Justice nominee Clarence Thomas of sexual harassment), first lady Hillary Clinton, Lorena Bobbitt (who was brought to trial for cutting off her husband's penis while he slept), Olympic figure skaters Tonya Harding and Nancy Kerrigan, and Nicole Brown Simpson, murdered ex-wife of football star O. J. Simpson. According to Lakoff, as a result of what transpired in these women's lives, women began to appropriate what Lakoff called "interpretive control" or the "making of meaning" (1995: 29) for the first time in history. These events, Lakoff claims, "increased women's interpretive control over public discourse, [that is] their ability to determine the meaning of events in which they were involved" (1995: 30). She observes:

> the existence of all of these cases and the extraordinary interest focused on all of them say several things. They show the culture at a nodal moment, when it may go forward or back but can never really revert to the pre-[Anita] Hill situation. Male discourse control has been wrested from the realm of presupposition and "normality," allowing it to be seen as only one possible choice and to be commented upon as an aberration. . . . The passions generated by all these events make perfect sense seen in this light: we are enmeshed in the most serious cultural revolution of all time, and the stakes are very high.   (1995: 43)

I would like to place Lakoff's comments in the context of the present discussion, and have the reader observe with me what amounts to a continuation and intensification of the trends that Lakoff noted at that time. The cast of public female luminaries has changed in dramatic detail in the United States in the intervening years and the various circumstances involving women have been quite remarkable. Think for a moment about some of the women who were prominent in the news at the end of the twentieth century in the United States, that is at the beginning of the new millennium. First Lady and now Senator from New York, Hillary Rodham Clinton; former Attorney General Janet Reno; Former Secretary of State Madeleine Albright; former Governor of the State of New Jersey and now Presidential Cabinet member and head of the Environment Protection Agency, Christine Todd Whitman; Paula Jones, Monica Lewinsky, and Linda Tripp, three prominent figures in scandals associated with former President Bill Clinton; television actress Ellen Degeneres, television talk-show host Oprah Winfrey; NBC's "Today Show" Host, Katie Curac; and pop-singer Madonna. This list could certainly be expanded. What we are dealing with here is not simply, as was the case with the five events analyzed by Lakoff, specific identifiable incidents in which women played important roles. Instead the women I have named have been associated with a diversity of circumstances and situations, each of which is symbolically identified with particular trends involving women. These women have been simultaneously mistreated and adored by the mass media and the American public. Several of them have suffered breathtaking humiliation and denunciation. Many have undergone "make-overs" while their appearance, marital status, sexual habits, personal tragedies, and moral character has been dissected. As Lakoff said of the women she discussed: "The list . . . may seem tendentious because it mixes the holy with the profane, or at least the serious with the trivial. . . . What unites them is the media frenzy every one of them has occasioned" (1995: 31) I would add, that what unites the women I have mentioned is the firmness of their images and places in the American social and political scene.

9   Conclusion

I do not pretend for one moment that the popular press has turned soft on women or that women are now portrayed more positively and less stereotypically than a decade ago. But what I do think is different is the nature of the activities that women are routinely engaged in, the stories that their lives represent, and the public's reactions to events that even ten years ago would have seemed unthinkable. Women are not being silenced in the same fashion as was true just ten years ago; each of the women mentioned above has been heard and each has managed to effect some change in her own self-definition and in public images of women. The details of what women are saying and doing, their activities, speech, and behavior, are sufficiently different from the stereotypes that we have been handed in the past that there is undeniable evidence that things are changing; despite enormous efforts to hold the line, social patterns are not settling back down into familiar configurations. There is persistent confirmation that long-established notions of sex-determined and gender-determined differences are being destabilized. And while these changes are occurring, while these unprecedented events are unfolding, the popular press, television programs, the self-help industry, books on popular psychology, relentlessly inform us that women and men are different. We are told that we shop differently, that we vote differently, that we think differently, that we process information differently, and that we speak differently. Some of the time, it is true, some women and some men do some things differently from some particular subset of other men and women. But we know with certainty that this is not simply based on sex. What we may well be witnessing in the press's obsession with sex difference is a new tactic to counter the changing tides. Instead of simply ridiculing women, as the press has done in the past, we may wonder if what we are observing is not a deliberate or perhaps unwitting intensification of the volume of the rhetoric of difference. The insistence on the authenticity and naturalness of sex and gender difference may be part of an ideological struggle to maintain the boundaries, to secure the borders, and to hold firm the belief in women and men as essentially different creatures. We will be watching as a new age dawns and as language and other social practices continue to reveal the real texture and complexity of people's everyday lives.

REFERENCES

Bem, Sandra L. 1993: *The Lenses of Gender: Transforming the Debate on Sexual Inequality*. New Haven, CT: Yale University Press.

Bergvall, Victoria, Bing, Janet, and Freed, Alice F. (eds) 1996: *Rethinking Language and Gender Research: Theory and Practice*. [Real Language Series.] London: Longman.

Bing, Janet and Bergvall, Victoria 1996: The question of questions: Beyond binary thinking. In Victoria Bergvall, Janet Bing, and Alice F. Freed (eds) *Rethinking Language and Gender Research: Theory and Practice*. London: Longman, pp. 1–30.

Bucholtz, Mary, Liang, Anita C., and Sutton, Laurel A. (eds) 1999: *Reinventing Identities: The Gendered Self in Discourse*. New York: Oxford University Press.

Cameron, Deborah 1995: *Verbal Hygiene*. London: Routledge.

Cameron, Deborah 1997: Performing gender identity: Young men's talk and the construction of heterosexual masculinity. In Sally Johnson and Ulrike Hanna Meinhof (eds) *Language and Masculinity*. Oxford: Blackwell, pp. 47–64.

Cameron, Deborah 1998: Gender, language and discourse: A review. *Signs: Journal of Women, Culture and Society* 23(4): 945–60.

Coates, Jennifer 1996: *Women Talk*. Oxford: Blackwell.

Crawford, Mary 1995: *Talking Difference: On Gender and Language*. London: Sage.

Eckert, Penelope 1989a: *Jocks and Burnouts: Social Categories and Identity in the High School*. New York: Teachers College Press.

Eckert, Penelope 1989b: The whole woman: Sex and gender differences in variation. *Language Variation and Change* 1: 245–67.

Eckert, Penelope and McConnell-Ginet, Sally 1992: Think practically and look locally: Language and gender as community-based practice. *Annual Review of Anthropology* 21: 461–90.

Eckert, Penelope and McConnell-Ginet, Sally 1995: Constructing meaning, constructing selves: Snapshots of language, gender and class from Belten High. In Kira Hall and Mary Bucholtz (eds) *Gender Articulated: Language and the Socially Constructed Self*. New York: Routledge, pp. 469–507.

Ehrlich, Susan 1998: The discursive reconstruction of sexual consent. *Discourse Society* 9(2): 149–71.

Ehrlich, Susan and King, Ruth 1996: Consensual sex or sexual harassment: Negotiating meaning. In Victoria Bergvall, Janet Bing, and Alice F. Freed (eds) *Rethinking Language and Gender Research: Theory and Practice*. London: Longman, pp. 153–72.

Epstein, Cynthia Fuchs 1988: *Deceptive Distinctions: Sex, Gender and the Social Order*. New Haven, CT: Yale University Press and New York: Russell Sage Foundation.

Fishman, Pamela 1983: Interaction: The work women do. In Barrie Thorne, Cheris Kramarae and Nancy Henley (eds) *Language, Gender and Society*. Rowley, MA.: Newbury House, pp. 89–101.

Foster, Michele 1995: "Are you with me?" Power and solidarity in the discourse of African American women. In Kira Hall and Mary Bucholtz (eds) *Gender Articulated: Language and the Socially Constructed Self*. New York: Routledge, pp. 329–50.

Freed, Alice F. 1992: We understand perfectly: A critique of Tannen's view of cross-sex conversation. In Kira Hall, Mary Bucholtz, and Birch Moonwomon (eds) *Locating Power: Proceedings of the Second Berkeley Women and Language Conference*, vol. 1. Berkeley, CA: Berkeley Women and Language Group, University of California, pp. 144–52.

Freed, Alice F. 1995: Applied linguistics: Language and gender. In William Grabe (ed.) *An Overview of Applied Linguistics: Annual Review of Applied Linguistics*, vol. XV. Cambridge: Cambridge University Press, pp. 1–20.

Freed, Alice F. 1996: The language of pregnancy: Women and medical experience. In Natasha Warner, Jocelyn Ahlers, Leela Bilmes, Monica Oliver, Suzanne Wertheim, and Melinda Chen (eds) *Gender and Belief Systems: Proceedings of the 1996 Berkeley Women and Language Conference*. Berkeley, CA: Berkeley Women and Language Group, University of California, pp. 237–45.

Freed, Alice F. and Greenwood, Alice 1996: Women, men and type of talk: What makes the difference. *Language in Society* 25(1): 1–26.

Gal, Susan 1978: Peasant men can't get wives: Language change and sex roles in a bilingual community. *Language in Society* 7: 1–17.

Gibbon, Margaret 1999: *Feminist Perspectives on Language*. London and New York: Longman.

Goodwin, Marjorie Harness 1999: Constructing opposition within girls' games. In Mary Bucholtz, Anita C. Liang, and Laurel A. Sutton (eds) *Reinventing Identities: The Gendered Self in Discourse*. New York: Oxford University Press, pp. 388–409.

Greenwood, Alice 1996: Floor management and power strategies in adolescent conversation. In Victoria Bergvall, Janet Bing, and Alice F. Freed (eds) *Rethinking Language and Gender Research: Theory and Practice*. London: Longman, pp. 77–97.

Hall, Kira 1995: Lip service on the fantasy line. In Kira Hall and Mary Bucholtz (eds) *Gender Articulated: Language and the Socially Constructed Self*. New York: Routledge, pp. 183–216.

Hall, Kira and Bucholtz, Mary (eds) 1995: *Gender Articulated: Language and the Socially Constructed Self*. New York: Routledge.

Henley, Nancy and Kramarae, Cheris 1991: Gender, power and miscommunication. In Nikolas Coupland, Howard Giles, and John M. Wiemann (eds) *Miscommunication and Problematic Talk*. Newbury Park, CA: Sage, pp. 18–43.

Herring, Susan, Johnson, Deborah A., and DiBenedetto, Tamra 1995: "This discussion is going too far!" Male resistance to female participation on the Internet. In Kira Hall and Mary Bucholtz (eds) *Gender Articulated: Language and the Socially Constructed Self*. New York: Routledge, pp. 67–96.

Houghton, Cathryn 1995: Managing the body of labor: The treatment of reproduction and sexuality in a therapeutic institution. In Kira Hall and Mary Bucholtz (eds) *Gender Articulated: Language and the Socially Constructed Self.* New York: Routledge, pp. 121–41.

James, Deborah 1996: When and why do women use more prestige speech forms than men? A critical review. In Victoria Bergvall, Janet Bing, and Alice F. Freed (eds) *Rethinking Language and Gender Research: Theory and Practice.* London: Longman, pp. 98–125.

James, Deborah and Clarke, Sandra 1993: Women, men and interruptions: A critical review. In Deborah Tannen (ed.) *Gender and Conversational Interaction.* Oxford: Oxford University Press, pp. 231–80.

James, Deborah and Drakich, Janice 1993: Understanding gender differences in amount of talk: A critical review of research. In Deborah Tannen (ed.) *Gender and Conversational Interaction.* Oxford: Oxford University Press, pp. 281–312.

Johnson, Sally 1997: Theorizing language and masculinity: A feminist perspective. In Sally Johnson and Ulrike Hanna Meinhof (eds) *Language and Masculinity.* Oxford: Blackwell, pp. 8–26.

Johnson, Sally and Finlay, Frank 1997: Do men gossip: An analysis of football talk on television. In Sally Johnson and Ulrike Hanna Meinhof (eds) *Language and Masculinity.* Oxford: Blackwell, pp. 130–43.

Johnson, Sally and Meinhof, Ulrike Hanna (eds) 1997: *Language and Masculinity.* Oxford: Blackwell.

Johnstone, Barbara 1996: *The Linguistic Individual: Self-expression in Language and Linguistics.* New York: Oxford University Press.

Kendall, Shari and Tannen, Deborah 1997: Gender and language in the workplace. In Ruth Wodak (ed.) *Gender and Discourse.* London: Sage, pp. 81–105.

Kiesling, Scott F. 1997: Power and the language of men. In Sally Johnson and Ulrike Hanna Meinhof (eds) *Language and Masculinity.* Oxford: Blackwell, pp. 65–85.

Labov, William 1972: *Sociolinguistic Patterns.* Philadelphia: University of Pennsylvania Press.

Lakoff, Robin 1973: Language and woman's place. *Language in Society* 2: 45–80.

Lakoff, Robin 1992: The silencing of women. In Kira Hall, Mary Bucholtz, and Birch Moonwomon (eds) *Locating Power: Proceedings of the Second Berkeley Women and Language Conference,* vol. 1. Berkeley, CA: Berkeley Women and Language Group, University of California, pp. 344–55.

Lakoff, Robin 1995: Cries and whispers: The shattering of the silence. In Kira Hall and Mary Bucholtz (eds) *Gender Articulated: Language and the Socially Constructed Self.* New York: Routledge, pp. 25–50.

Leap, William (ed.) 1995: *Beyond the Lavender Lexicon: Authenticity, Imagination and Appropriation in Lesbian and Gay Languages.* New York: Gordon and Breach.

Livia, Anna and Hall, Kira (eds) 1997: *Queerly Phrased: Language, Gender, and Sexuality.* New York: Oxford University Press.

MacKinnon, Catherine A. 1984: Difference and dominance: On sex discrimination. In *Feminism Unmodified: Discourses on Life and Law.* Cambridge, MA: Harvard University Press, pp. 32–45.

Maltz, Daniel N. and Borker, Ruth A. 1982: A cultural approach to male–female miscommunication. In John J.

Gumperz (ed.) *Language and Social Identity*. Cambridge: Cambridge University Press, pp. 196–216.

McElhinny, Bonnie 1995: Challenging hegemonic masculinities: Female and male police officers handling domestic violence. In Kira Hall and Mary Bucholtz (eds) *Gender Articulated: Language and the Socially Constructed Self*. New York: Routledge, pp. 215–43.

Mendoza-Denton, Norma 1995: Pregnant pauses: Silence and authority in the Anita Hill-Clarence Thomas hearings. In Kira Hall and Mary Bucholtz (eds) *Gender Articulated: Language and the Socially Constructed Self*. New York: Routledge, pp. 51–66.

Morgan, Marcyliena 1991: Indirectness and interpretation in African American women's discourse. *Pragmatics* 1: 421–52.

Nichols, Patricia 1983: Linguistic options and choices for Black women in the rural south. In Barrie Thorne, Cheris Kramarae, and Nancy Henley (eds) *Language, Gender, and Society*. Rowley, MA: Newbury House, pp. 54–68.

Rosenblum, Karen and Travis, Toni-Michelle 1996: Constructing categories of difference: Framework essay. In Karen Rosenblum and Toni-Michelle Travis (eds) *Meaning of Difference*. New York: McGraw-Hill, pp. 1–34.

Tannen, Deborah 1990: *You Just Don't Understand: Women and Men in Conversation*. New York: William Morrow.

Tannen, Deborah 1994: *Gender and Discourse*. New York: Oxford University Press.

Tannen, Deborah 1998: Listening-in on girl talk. *Newsweek*, November 1998.

Thorne, Barrie and Henley, Nancy (eds) 1975: *Language and Sex: Difference and Dominance*. Rowley, MA: Newbury House.

Troemel-Ploetz, Senta 1991: Review essay: Selling the apolitical. *Discourse & Society* 2(4): 489–502.

Trudgill, Peter 1972: Sex, covert prestige, and linguistic change in the urban British English of Norwich. *Language in Society* 1: 179–95.

Uchida, A. 1992: When "difference" is "dominance": A critique of the "anti-power-based" cultural approach to sex differences. *Language in Society* 21(4): 547–68.

West, Candace 1990: Not just "doctors' orders": Directive–response sequences in patients' visits to women and men physicians. *Discourse & Society* 1: 85–113.

Wolfram, Walt 1969: *A Sociolinguistic Description of Detroit Negro Speech*. Washington, DC: Center for Applied Linguistics.

Wood, Kathleen 1999: Coherent identities amid heterosexist ideologies: Deaf and hearing lesbian coming-out stories. In Mary Bucholtz, Anita C. Liang, and Laurel A. Sutton (eds) *Reinventing Identities: The Gendered Self in Discourse*. New York: Oxford University Press, pp. 46–63.

Index

AAVE *see* African American Vernacular
  English
abortion, in United States 265
abstract individualism 27–8, 30, 35
  defined 28
Abu-Lughod, Lila, *Veiled Sentiments*
  262
academic discourse,
  analysis of women and power 4, 163,
    165–9, 713
  expert representations 465
  men's 364
academic print media, on-line databases
  708–12
academies, language 550
accent,
  and identity 114
  power in social transformation 104–5
Acker, Joan 529
activism, feminist linguistic 14–16, 22,
  550–70
activity, gender as an 29–32, 51, 495–502
activity theory, Soviet 29, 31
address,
  as attention-getting 77
  epithets in 82–3
address forms 77–87, 337–8, 715
  abusive to women 83–4
  children's 241
  endearments 85
  English typology 77–8
  familial 86–7
  Ms 565–6

non-sexist 562, 565–6
  and reference 72–7
relationship-securing strategies 541–2
relationships in 337–8
respectful 86
tag with labels 73
adjudication processes, sexual assault
  645–70
Adler, Patricia 237, 243
Adler, Peter 237, 243
Adler, Sue 635
adolescence, as ideology 381–2, 711
adolescent language, policing 393–6
adolescents,
  identities 5, 9, 368, 375, 706
  language and gender 381–400
  as leaders in linguistic change 390–3
  talk in the classroom 472–3
Adriaens, Geert 558
advertising,
  gay personal 5–6, 402, 404–7
  gender assumptions in 56, 57
  gender and power in 14, 215
  and ideology 711
  men as deficient communicators
    454–5, 482–3
  on-line 215
  sexist 479
  use of generic forms 563
advice literature 458–9, 460
  see also conduct books; self-help
    books
affirmative action, US 671

African American Vernacular English,
and Standard English 47, 374
White US teenagers' use of 390, 510
and women's voices 425–6
African Americans,
boys' and girls' play and social
organization 29, 231, 232–3, 237,
238–9, 242
church terms of address 78–9
drag queens' linguistic strategies 26,
373, 428–9, 430, 477
female terms of address 84–5
women's discourse 47, 354, 706
"Africanism" 133
Afrikaans 2, 415
and English 405–7
age,
deference to and intimacy 81
and gender segregation 232
ideology related to gender ideology
381–400
and ostracism from girls' groups
242–3
agency 27, 30, 36
and discourse analysis 45, 54, 58, 60
in language choice 31–2, 62, 713–14
and power 63
aggression,
in children's negotiations 229–30,
236, 237, 243
defined 230
direct physical 230
direct verbal 230, 242, 469
indirect 230, 242
male 256, 536, 575
in on-line male communication 206,
207, 209, 211–12
self-perception at work 535–6
"Agnes" 51, 332–3, 339, 344–5, 488
agoraphobia study, Los Angeles 131–2
Albert, Stephen 390
Albright, Madeleine 173, 716
Alloway, Nola, *Boys and Literacy* 636–7,
640
ambiguity 154–6, 625
American Anthropologist 356
American English 101
American Speech 372
Americans, East European Jewish 180

anaphora 146
Anderson, Benedict 72, 676–7
androcentrism 469, 472, 474, 551, 558
in definitions of sexual assault 645–6,
648
androgen, adrenal 368–9
Angier, Natalie 93
anonymity, of on-line communication
202–3, 205, 206–9, 213
Anscombe, Elizabeth 374
Antaki, Charles 499–500, 674–5
anthropology 1, 44, 120, 279
commodity logic 28–9
culture and personality school 243
feminist 21, 253–4, 261, 363
gender ideologies and power in 5
and metadiscourse 59
sex-based languages notion 354–5
see also cognitive anthropology;
cultural anthropology; linguistic
anthropology; physical
anthropology; psychological
anthropology
anticipatory sentence completion 339,
343, 345
Anzaldúa, Gloria 426, 429, 437
apologies, empathy and 311, 312
Appadurai, Arjun 279
applied linguistics 2
Arabic, and French 391
Ardener, Shirley 2, 261
argument of verb 73
argumentation, gender differences in
497–9, 502
Aries, Elizabeth 489–90, 499
Armstrong, Nancy 451, 461
Arnot, Madeleine 631, 633
Aronsson, Karin 602
Arpanet 203–4
arts, discourse analysis of women and
power 4, 163–4, 169–72
Aryan languages 358
Asian cultural gender stereotypes 452
assertiveness training 454, 493
assessment–agreement/disagreement
adjacency pairs 502
"Asterisk" 316
Atkins, Bowman K. 104, 366
Atkinson, J. Maxwell 238

attitudes, public   700–18
audience, as active participants in
    meaning making   403
Augostinos, Martha   491, 492
Austin, J. L.   122–3, 373–4
Australia   395, 563, 564, 565
  boys' literacy levels   457
  preschool children   232, 235
Austria, Oberwart   103, 114–15
authenticity, and place   277–443
author,
  gender assumptions and
    representations   56, 62, 142, 715
  intentions   170
authority,
  at work   600–23
  creating gendered demeanors of
    603–4
  in the domestic sphere   256, 600–23
  as emergent   306–8
  and face-saving strategies   540–1
  female at work   7, 583–8, 594, 602,
    619–21
  gender, knowledge and   302–26
  ideology   14, 711
  linguistic and social norms   510
  male in language regulation   550
  parental and managerial   7, 600–23
  and place in Vanuatu   5, 306–8
  supportiveness and   309–10
autobiography, transsexual   56, 62, 94,
    154

babies, gender labeling   90–1
Backhouse, Constance   653
"bad" language, use of   163
Bailey, Ashlee C.   2
Baker, Carolyn   235
Bakhtin, Mikhail   675
bakla, Filipino   402, 411–14
Barbin, Herculine   62, 94, 156
Barnes, Melanie K.   236, 243
Baron, Dennis   551
Barrett, Rusty   26, 373, 374, 428, 430,
    477
Barthes, Roland   120, 136
Bateson, Gregory   188, 370
Bauman, Richard   373, 374
Bavelas, Janet Beavin   180

Belfast, standard and non-standard use
    by women   113–14 (table 4.3)
belief systems   2, 396
  ideologies and   712–14
  politics and   161, 168
  production and reproduction of   57–8
Bellinger, David C.   602
Bengali   360–1
Benhabib, Seyla   677–8
Benke, Gertraud   682
Berentzen, Sigurd   234, 235, 237
Bergman, Ingmar, *Scenes from a Marriage*
    147
Bergvall, Victoria L.   2, 472, 647
Berlant, Lauren   134
Bernsten, Jan   75
Bersianik, Louky   155
Besnier, Niko   x, 5, 12, 26, 115, 279–301,
    307, 321, 354, 411, 438, 470, 715
Best, Deborah L.   528–9
Best, Raphaela   235
Bilik, Naran   75
bilingualism   2, 518
Billig, Michael   130–1, 132, 496, 497, 677,
    689
Bilmes, Jack   238
Bilous, F. R.   494
binary opposition, gender as   23, 33,
    475–6, 636, 640, 702, 703–5, 714
Bing, Janet M.   2
biographical talk   333, 339–45
biography, lack of   332–3, 339
biology   23, 24, 255, 256, 368–9, 381, 461
Birk, Thomas   531–2
bisexuality   715
Bislama   2, 303
  and claiming *ples*   319–21
  pronominal choice   89, 311–13
  sore   12, 312
Bjorkqvist, Kaj   230
Black, Maria   437
Black men, stereotypes of   26, 471, 473
Blair, Kristine   213, 214
Blair, Tony   463
Blum, Susan D.   78
Blum-Kulka, Shoshana, *Dinner Talk*   180,
    184
Blumstein, Philip   371
Blunkett, David   633

Boas, Franz 431
Bobbitt, Lorena 716
Bodine, Ann 360–1
  "Androcentrism in prescriptive
    grammar" 551
body,
  decoration 715
  male representation of the 264
  and women's writing 147–8, 556
Boggs, Cathy 494–5
Bogoras, Waldemar 360, 361
Bolton, Lissant 307, 317, 320
Borker, Ruth 49, 161, 231, 366, 369–70,
  510–11, 701
Bortoni-Ricardo, Stella M. 114
boundaries,
  breaking down linguistic 410–11, 414
  disputes over political 401–2
  normative 304–5
  policing of gender 26
Bourdieu, Pierre 27, 672, 677
bourgeoisie, European 451
boys,
  academic underachievement 456, 462,
    632–7, 640
  "boxing out and taxing" 626–7
  language use 634–6
  and literacy 634–7, 640
Boys Don't Cry 715
boys' groups, constructing gender
  identity in 234–8, 367–8, 511
Bradford, Barbara Taylor 144
brain, sex differences in the 708, 713–14
brainstorming 577
Brantenberg, Gert, *The Daughters of Egalia*
  555, 560
Brazil,
  rural migrants to urban areas 114
  travestis 26
  youth culture 390
Briggs, Charles 59–60, 61, 62, 262, 373,
  374
British Telecom,
  advertisements 454–5, 482–3
  *How to Get More Out of Life Through
    Better Conversations* 456
Brookner, Anita, *Hotel du Lac* 144
Brossard, Nicole, *L'Amer* 155
Broverman, Inge 529

Brown, Janelle 217, 219
Brown, Penelope 161, 514, 601
Brown, Roger 4, 79–80, 181
Bucholtz, Mary x, 2, 3, 10, 12, 30,
  43–68, 372, 375, 388, 389, 390, 403,
  432, 438, 512
Bull, Tove 115–16
Burgoon, Michael 531–2
burnouts, and *jocks* 238, 388, 392–3, 395
Burrell, N. 370–1
Burris, Barbara, "Fourth World
  Manifesto" 363–4
Burton, Pauline 2
Busby, Karen 653
Bush, George W. 172, 173
Bussmann, Hadumod 2
Butler, Judith 24, 27–8, 31–2, 90, 121,
  123, 128, 130–1, 373, 374, 402, 417,
  431, 646–7, 676
  Gender Trouble 126–7, 148–9
  on Larsen 133

CA *see* Conversation Analysis
Cahill, Spencer 92
Cairns, Beverly D. 242
Cairns, Robert B. 242
California,
  age cohort ethnographic study 384
  children's language 232, 234, 236–7,
    243
California Style Collective 516
call centers 455–6, 459, 462
caló 427
Calvinism 405, 407
Cameron, Deborah x, 2, 6, 10, 13, 14,
  25, 31, 57, 59, 133–4, 329, 365, 394,
  395, 425, 447–67, 469, 472, 475, 482,
  497, 502, 550, 567, 575, 646, 647,
  700–1, 708, 711, 713, 714
Can Do Better (Qualifications and
  Curriculum Authority) 634–6, 639
Canada 645–70
  Charter of Rights and Freedoms 651
canonical texts 21
capitalism 296
  disorganized 415–17
  ideologies of 36
  and liberalism 28
Capps, Lisa 131–2

Caraya 356, 360
Cardiff, glottalization 110
Carib 358
Caribbean Creole 431
Carlassare, Elizabeth 215–16
Carli, L. 493, 532
CAT *see* Communication
    Accommodation Theory
categories,
  of analysis 22, 24–5, 30, 502
  bipolar gender 468, 476–7, 703–5
  gender-based cognitive 15, 123
  iconization and 431–5, 436
  identity and performance 429
  of kinds of people 69–71, 244
  labels for 69–71
  multiple and fragmented 629
  naturalizing 478–9, 702, 705
  prescriptive 511
  role of other than gender 297
  use of identity 500–1
  see also social categories
category, gender as a 8–10, 22, 630
Caudwell, Sarah 91, 149, 151
causal attribution theory 493
CDA *see* Critical Discourse Analysis
censorship, and the Internet 209
Chamberlain, Alexander, "Women's
    Languages" 356
Chamberlain, Lori 155
Chambers, J. K. 99, 103–4
Chancer, Lisa 667
Channell, Joanna 135
Chatterji, Suniti Kumar 360–1
Chawaf, Chantal 147
Cherny, Lynn 210, 211
Cheshire, Jenny 2, 387, 494
Chetty, Dhiannaraj 406
Chicanas 426–7
child-care 502
children,
  bilingual Spanish/English 232, 240
  conflict talk 238–41, 627
  effect on use of standard language
    115–16
  emergence of gender through
    interaction 305–6, 706
  gender as an organizing feature in
    play 330–1

identifying sex by tape-recordings of
    speech 110
  in role-plays of family conflict 602
  sissies and tomboys 366–8
  socialization and inter-ethnic
    communication 366
children's negotiations 4–5, 229–51
  framing in 236
  relevance of ethnicity, class, and
    gender 229–51
  sequential organization 4–5, 12, 230
Chinese 553
  children's gendered language 233
  terms of address 75, 78
Chinese culture,
  diaspora and cultural identity 416
  power in 181, 182, 183
  sex segregation in playgroups 369
Christian religious identities 252
Christianity,
  ideology of family 317, 318
  and women preachers 453
Chukchee 360, 361
Cini, Michelle 691
citationality (Butler) 31
Cixous, Hélène 147, 148, 556
Clancy, Patricia M. 131
Clark, Lorenne 653
Clarke, Sandra 163, 168
classification 470–1
Clément, Catherine 148
Clinton, Bill 173, 463, 716
Clinton, Hillary Rodham 164, 172,
    173–6, 716
clique formation 243
closeness 181–2, 187–90
CMC *see* computer-mediated
    communication
co-construction, of meaning 403
co-reference, truth-conditional and
    metaphorical 311–12
Coates, Jennifer 2, 345, 492, 584, 706
code-switching 415
  and language contact 48
  multiple identities and 428–9
  Stylized Asian English 430
  Tongan–English 5, 286–96
coerciveness, institutional 646–9
CofP *see* communities of practice

cognitive anthropology 519
cognitive approach 13, 488
  see also social cognitive approach
cognitive schema *see* cultural models
cohesive devices 146, 148
colonialism,
  gendered 283, 314–15, 401
  and naming practices 75
  representations in Vanuatu 315–19
Comaroff, Jean 280
Comaroff, John 286
commercialization, World Wide Web
  214–16, 219
commodity-based societies, gender in
  28, 30
common ground, strategy of creating
  614
communication,
  development of skills 460–3, 481–3, 484
  gendered 2, 531–45
  as the language ideology of late
    modernity 458–63
  or talk as work 459–60
  see also computer-mediated
    communication; electronic
    communication
Communication Accommodation Theory
  (CAT) 6, 13, 489, 492–5, 503–5
communication styles,
  in the classroom 626–31
  influence on women's professional
    development 6, 495, 529
communicative action, and macrosocial
  constraints 647–8
communities of practice 2, 11, 354, 372,
  504–5
  analysis of the gendered workplace
    7, 267, 580–1, 594–5
  constitutive characteristics 581
  defined 29–30, 71, 580
  gender and ethnicity 429–36
  and heterosexual ideology 375
  institutional forces and 648
  and language variation 71–2
  local and global connections 30, 71–2
  memberships in different 30
  norms and 512
  and social constructionism 305–6
  and terms of address 81–3

community,
  different definitions of 430
  ideology and borderlands 427–8
  and political organization in the
    Internet 216–17
"complementary schismogenesis" 188,
  370
compliments 386
computer conferencing 205–6
computer-mediated communication
  205–12
  asynchronous 206–9
  discourse style and gender
    identification 206–9, 210–12, 218
  and educational opportunities 7,
    638–9, 640
  future projections 219–21
  gender and power in 4, 11, 202–28
  synchronous 210–12
  text-based as gender-irrelevant 202
  see also electronic communication;
    on-line communication
Condor, Susan 489
conduct books 451, 454
conflict management 535–6 (figs 23.1,
  23.2), 538–9
conflict talk, children's 238–41, 627
Conley, John 161, 645
connection,
  girl talk and 385–6, 396
  power and 181 (fig. 8.1)
  and power in the family 180–7, 194–9
Connell, Bob 629
consciousness,
  different male and female 261
  fragmented 143–4
  social origins of 29
consciousness raising 56, 255, 561–2
context,
  in children's negotiations 232–4
  in discursive psychology 494–5,
    497–501
  problematization of 62–3
  relevant 630
  and talk in interactional
    sociolinguistics 9, 327–8
  talk varies across 11, 29
contextualization cues 5
  culturally specific 49

convergence, speech   493–4
conversation,
    competence model   147
    dinner-table   180, 184–7
    floor-holding in   162
    the modern art of   458–63
    self-revelation as a gender-specific
        ritual   187–90
    sequential organization of   51, 244
    supportive mode   309–10
    topic control   162, 165
    turn-taking in   51, 52, 162–3, 575
    unequal roles by men and women
        371–2
Conversation Analysis   12, 51–4, 63, 327,
    428, 674–5
    and desire   130–1, 135
    in discursive psychology   496, 499–502
    feminist   53, 169
    mixing of levels   166
    relevance of gender in   33–5
    Schegloff's treatment of gender in   4,
        10, 33–5, 51–2, 163, 165–9, 329
    transition relevance place (TRP)   168–9
conversational strategies,
    and inequalities   165–6
    male and female   373
    of men and women in literature
        146–7
Cook-Gumperz, Jenny   232, 234, 603
Cooper, Robert L.   552, 563
cooperation strategy   542–4
    cooperative informing   543
cooperative–competitive speaking styles,
    in the classroom   626–31
Coplan, David B.   262–3
Corbett, Greville   557, 691
COREPER *see* European Union,
    Committee of Permanent
    Representatives
corpus planning   552, 560
Corsaro, William A.   232, 235, 239–40
Corston-Oliver, Monica   2
cosmopolitanism   283, 286, 296
Coupland, Justine   492–3, 515, 579
Coupland, Nikolas   492–3, 515
couples, dual-career with children
    179–201
Coward, Rosalind   437

Cox, Brian, *The Cox Report*   632
Crapanzano, Vincent   62
creativity   5, 492, 555, 705, 706
    language as a resource for   11, 94,
        112, 430
    as resignification   374
criminal trial, acquaintance rape   650–1,
    652, 653–66
Critical Discourse Analysis   13, 52, 54,
    57–8, 166, 168, 523
    feminist   55, 56
    liberatory   55–6, 63
    study of elite women   673–4, 677
critical linguistics   55
critical literacy   637
critical theory   55
    and sociolinguistics   647
Crosby, F.   365–6
cross-cultural differences,
    in children's negotiations   231, 233–4
    in communicative norms   49–50
cross-cultural patterns, of language use
    258–9, 702
cross-cultural tensions in contact   315–22
cross-dressing   715
    and use of women's language   477–8
Crouch, Isabel   365
crowd   384
Culley, Lorraine   639
cultural anthropology   254
cultural models   509–27
    Rocky and the lawyer   518–20
cultural studies   1, 471
culture,
    in the borderlands   30
    discourse as   46–50
    and ethnography   36
    and gender   24
    and nature   255–6
    and place   279–80
culture and personality school   243
Curac, Katie   716
Curtis, Pavel   212
Cutler, Anne   490
Cutler, Cecilia   390
cyberspace   206

Daly, Mary, *Gyn/ecology: The Metaethics of
    Radical Feminism*   560

Danby, Susan 235
Danet, Brenda 210, 212
data collection 705–6
  unelicited data 46, 54, 329–30
data elicitation 46
databases, on-line 708–12
David, Miriam 631, 632
Davies, Bronwyn 601, 606, 674
Davis, Madeleine 265
De Caluwe, Johan 557
de Certeau, Michel 27
Deaux, Kay 530–1
Deaver, Michael 174–5
declaratives, rising intonation 395
decoding 523–4
deconstructive feminism 24–5
deep structures 119
deference 601, 604
deficit model, of women's and
    men's language 454–5, 474, 672,
    701
definitional rights, within academic
    disciplines 165–9
Degeneres, Ellen 716
deindustrialization 112
Delarue-Mardrus, Lucie, *L'Ange et les
    Pervers* 155–6
Deleuze, Gilles 127–9
Deloria, Ella 433–5
demeanor 601, 604
Derrida, Jacques 122–3, 130, 374
descriptive approach 2, 511, 524
desire 4, 119–41
  and courtly love 128
  defining 124–9
  fear and 131–2
  gustatory 132
  kinds of 124
  in language 130–7
  and language socialization 130,
    131–2, 137
  and sexual difference 23, 126
determinism,
  discursive 373
  technological 203, 220
Detroit, Belten High studies 238, 391–2,
    392–3, 395, 519, 706
developmental psychology 229–30
  and gender assignment 487

deviance,
  from gender norms 25, 353–9
  as identification 690–1
  and normativity 353–80
dialect geography 99
dialectology 99
dialects, sociolinguistic studies of urban
    100–2, 699
dialogue, constructed 146–7
Dibbell, Julian 211
dictionaries 550, 551
difference,
  but equality 458
  discursive construction of 677–8
  and dominance 475
  economy of 123
  evidence of public views of language
    707–18
  and similarity 497, 703–4
difference perspective 161, 474, 475,
    483–4, 701
  in research 699–701
differences, between women 451–2
diglossia 518
directives,
  aggravated 606
  at dinnertime 600, 602, 605, 608–12
  at work 602, 613–19
  impersonalized 606
  use by children 233, 511, 514
  use in male exclusive contexts 337–8
directness 540, 591, 594, 605
  female 47, 59, 115, 257, 361–2, 450, 452
disc jockeys, lack of female 498–9
discourse,
  as culture 46–50
  defining 44–5
  dominant institutional 645–67
  "double" 448–9
  Foucauldian 45, 58, 496
  and gender 43–68
  as history 58–62
  natural histories of 61–2
  power of gender ideologies in 252–76
  as social practice 677
  as society 50–1
  as text 54–8
  see also performativity;
    recontextualization

Discourse & Society   163
discourse analysis,
    in discursive psychology   496–7
    and the family   179–201
    feminist   43
    ideological diversity and   265–6,
        272
    issues in   63
    in language and gender studies   3,
        43–68
    multiple approaches   64
    norms as frames   521
    quantitative and qualitative   12–13,
        43–4
    sociolinguistic-historical approach
        674–5, 677
    women and power   4
    see also Critical Discourse Analysis
discursive psychology   6, 11, 51, 53,
    119–20, 487, 488, 503–5
    and Conversation Analysis   12, 496
    and desire   130–1
    gender as action in talk   495–502
    issues or dilemmas in   496
discussione   238
dispreferred response   53
disputes, gender and ethnicity in
    children's   238–41
distance,
    agentless passives and   168
    and closeness   181–2
    and inequality   514
    pronominal marking of   79–80
diversity, and uniformity   449–53
division of labor,
    gender   23, 256, 315, 318, 356, 358,
        362, 384, 701
    into paid and unpaid work   32
doctor–patient communication   531–2,
    602, 649, 706
Dole, Bob   715
domestic violence   260, 270
dominance,
    and difference   475
    in husband–wife relations   269
    in sister–brother relations   269
    see also male dominance
dominance theory   161, 353, 362, 474,
    475, 701

dorp   404
Dowd, Maureen   164, 173
drag queens,
    identity and linguistic strategies   26,
        373, 374, 477, 478
    pronoun choice   93–4, 153–4
    transnational location   411–14
Drant, Thomas   155
Drew, Paul   238
Dubois, Betty Lou   365
Duffy, Maureen, *Love Child*   149, 150–1
Duranti, Alessandro   36
Dutch   2
    feminist language debates   557–9
dyads,
    conversational   162, 176
    gender   36, 265, 268
Dyer, Richard   425, 471
Dyson, Ketaki Kushari   2

Eagly, Alice H.   531
earnings, gender gap   458
EBSCO, "Academic Search Premier"
    710, 711
Eckert, Penelope   x, 5, 9, 11–12, 13, 15,
    29–30, 52, 70, 71, 116, 238, 267, 310,
    354, 368, 372, 375, 381–400, 425, 504,
    512, 515, 516, 519, 520, 580, 648, 702,
    706
écriture féminine   147–8, 556
Eder, Donna   232, 237, 239, 242, 386
Edinburgh   110–11
Edley, Nigel   495–6
education,
    access to   109
    boys' underachievement   456, 457,
        462, 632–7, 640
    and electronic communication
        638–9
    gender and power in   14
    level and use of standard language
        115
    policy and practice   2, 631–7, 712
    stereotyped materials   554
    Universal Education Act (1872)
        105
    as a woman's issue in politics   172
educational print media, on-line
    databases   708–12

educational research, feminist 7
educational settings, language and
    gender 624–44
Edwards, Carolyn Pope 231
Edwards, Derek 500–1
Edwards, John 110
effeminates, footnote and feminists
    354–9
Ehrenreich, Paul 360
Ehrlich, Susan xi, 7, 12, 13, 53, 146,
    497–8, 504, 563, 566, 645–70, 706
Eisikovits, Edina 387
electronic communication, education and
    638–9, 640
Elgin, Suzette Haden 555–6
Eliot, T. S. 143
elite women, fragmented and multiple
    identities 7, 671–98
Ellem, Elizabeth Wood 272
ellipsis, literary use of 151
Ellis, Sarah 105
Elwood, Jannette 632, 640
emotion,
    expression of 163, 259
    female culture of 363–4
    as indexed in discourse 59–60
emotion talk 236
emotional literacy skills 462–3
empathy 148, 151, 459
    compared with sympathy 303, 311
    functionality of 312–13, 321
    and gender 311–13
employment 14, 496–7, 502
    EU gender mainstreaming 678–9
    female and male unemployment
        112–13
    "glass ceiling" 632
    gratification 528
engineering 472
England and Wales, educational
    practices 631–40
English 2, 110
    address forms typology 77–8
    and Afrikaans 405–7
    school curriculum 634–6, 638–9
    sexism in 553, 559
    of Shakespeare 148
    and Tongan 283–4
entextualization 61, 62

Epstein, Cynthia Fuchs, *Deceptive
    Distinctions: Sex, Gender and the Social
    Order* 703–4
Epstein, Debbie 632, 640
Equal Employment Opportunity (EEO)
    Acts 561
equal opportunities initiatives 625,
    631–2, 671, 679
equality,
    closeness and 514
    and hierarchy 181–2, 514
    law and likes 703
    of men in liberal capitalism 28
    and on-line communication 217–19
    and variety 497
erasure 431, 432, 436, 437–9
ERIC *see* United States, Department of
    Education, Educational Resource
    Information Center (ERIC) database
Ervin-Tripp, Susan 183, 185, 236–7
Eskilstuna studies of gender
    differentiation 106–10 (table 4.2),
    112, 113
Eskimo 361
essentialism 9–10, 15, 30, 259, 265, 304,
    396, 481–2, 700, 702, 705
Estrich, Susan 173, 653
ethnicities, "new" 437
ethnicity,
    in children's negotiations 232–4,
        238–41
    gender and 26, 423–43
    and ideology 711
    interactional negotiation of 430–1
    marking of White 437–8
ethnography 12, 36, 280, 297, 318, 428,
    475
    activities analysis 31, 231
    of children's negotiation 4–5, 230,
        234–8
    limitations of interviews 288–9
    and talk-in-interaction 327–45
ethnography of communication 46–8,
    63, 373
ethnomethodology 34, 50–1, 130–1, 328,
    488, 496, 500, 674–5
EUMC *see* European Union Monitoring
    Center Against Racism, Xenophobia
    and Anti-Semitism

euphemism 488
European Union 673–4
  Committee of Permanent
    Representatives (COREPER) 674
  Council of Ministers 674
  gender mainstreaming strategy
    678–81
European Union (EU) Parliament 673–4
  roles of female members 7, 671–98
  women in 679–81 (table 29.1)
European Union Monitoring Center
    Against Racism, Xenophobia and
    Anti-Semitism (EUMC) 671
"Europeanness" 676–7, 692–3
everyday interaction 331–45
evolution, "man-the-hunter" model
    362–3
exchange-societies, marriage 306, 307
exclusion,
  in girls' groups 230, 242–3
  patterns of 31, 32, 161–5
  of women from public sphere 318,
    362–5, 452
  of women in male-only settings
    327–52
exoticism, linguistic 355–7, 359
expectations,
  cultural and ideological 35, 468, 474
  double standards 532, 536
  gendered stereotypical 529–30, 531–2,
    533–7 (table 23.1)
  and perceptions of gender 676, 704,
    712–18
expressive power, denial of 162

face 601
  continuum 605–6 (fig. 26.1; table 26.3)
face-related practices,
  at home 600, 604, 605, 606–12
    (table 26.1), 621
  at work 601, 613–19 (table 26.2)
face-saving strategies 7, 243, 531, 540–1,
    601, 602
factory talk 580, 582, 588–95
Fairclough, Norman 57, 58, 403, 460,
    649, 666
fakaleitī (or *fakafefine*) 5, 280–1, 296, 303,
    438
Faludi, Susan 112–13

familiarity, and respect 183
family,
  address forms within 86–7
  break-up of structure 115
  Christian ideology of 317, 318
  counselling 500–1
  dinnertime face-related practices 602,
    606–12
  gendered authority in the 600–23
  power and connection in arguments
    194–9
  power–connection grid 180–4
    (figs 8.2, 8.3)
family interaction, gender and 4, 32,
    179–201
family therapy, control maneuvers 180
Fanua, Tupou Posesi 270
Farr, Marcia 241
Farris, Catherine 233–4
"father-knows-best" dynamic 184–7,
    309, 602, 606–12
Faupula, Manu 270, 272
fear, socialization of 131–2
Feld, Steve 262
female empowerment, and the Internet
    202–28
female register hypothesis *see* sex-dialect
    hypothesis
femaleness, linked with childishness
    92–3
femininity,
  cultural ideals of 451–2
  different forms of 629
  historically and socially constructed
    112, 116
  idealized colonial 315
  and moral order 449
  self-assessed 489
  subversion by drag queens 374
feminism,
  American 453
  backlash 457–8
  and Conversation Analysis 53
  and discourse analysis 3, 259
  and language ideologies 448
  marginalization of 631–7
  multicultural 372–6
  rape and the law 648
  second wave 492

sex and gender in Western 22
social activism 14–16
see also radical feminism; socialist
feminism; standpoint feminism
feminist linguistics 21, 475, 701
activism 14–16, 22, 550–70
methods of analysis 165
performative aspects of gender 646–7
reproduction of gender stereotypes in
473–6
feminists, and footnote effeminates
354–9
feminization,
classroom 626, 631
of politics 164
of professions 220
of public discourse 461–3
strategy 556, 558
Ferguson, Charles 259
fiction,
characters without gender 149–50,
157
male and female characters in 143–7
Filipino, *bakla* 402, 411–14
Fine, Gary Alan 238
Finlay, Frank 706
Finnish children 230
Fischer, John 387
Fisher, Sue 649, 661
Fishman, Pamela 162
Fitzpatrick, Mary Anne 370–1
Flannery, Regina, "Men's and Women's
Speech in Gros Ventre" 357–8
flexible language, gender and modernity
27, 414–17
flexible strategies of accumulation 402,
415–16
focalization 143–4, 148
folklinguistic stereotypes 448, 465, 472,
482, 705–6, 707–8
folklinguistics, feminist 476
folktales 162, 704
footing 674, 683
Ford, Barry 489
foreclosures 130–1
form replacement strategy 556, 562–3
format tying 239–40, 243
formulaic expressions 605
Forster, Johann Reinhold 314

Foster, Michèle 425, 706
Foucault, Michel 45, 58, 129, 130, 156,
496, 523
Fox, Jennifer, "An American Love Story"
188–9
fractal recursivity 431–2, 435–6, 437,
520, 522
frames,
defined 606
of expertise 687
ideological regulatory 647, 648–9,
653, 661–6
institutional 645–70
norms as 521, 523
framing 265, 601, 674
at dinnertime 606–7
during children's disputes 236, 242
framing approach 12–13, 132, 135–6,
600–3
France 553
Frankfurt School *see* critical theory
fraternities 437, 512–13, 520–1, 706
web of norms 516–18
Freed, Alice F. xi, 2, 8, 10, 359, 699–721
French 2, 79, 110, 358, 554, 559
and Arabic 391
gender agreement 89, 94, 149
of Molière 148
passé simple and *passé composé* 150
pronoun use 152–3
use of gender marking to subvert 56
Freud, Sigmund 119, 122, 124–7, 128,
134
Friedrich, Paul 80
friendship, women's 187–90, 706
Frith, Hannah 53
Fromkin, Victoria 119
Furfey, Paul, "Men's and Women's
Language" 356–7

Gaelic, Irish, and English 407–11
Gaelic, Scottish 2
Gal, Susan 32, 103, 114–15, 261, 292,
372, 389, 431, 433, 449, 648
Galford, Ellen, *Moll Cutpurse* 144
Galindo, D. Letticia 426, 427, 436
Gallois, Cindy xi, 6, 10, 11, 12, 13, 52,
429, 487–508, 492, 515
Gapun, Papua New Guinea 450, 452

Garfinkel, Harold   50–1, 331–3, 339, 343, 344–5, 488
Garréta, Anne, *Sphinx*   149–50
Garvey, John   425
Gatchet, Albert   360
Gaudio, Rudolf P.   25
gay argots   414
gay vocabulary   120–1
gays and lesbians   371–2
   personal ads   404–7
   studies of language   121, 375, 706
   tomboys and   369–70
   in USA   25
   use of women's language   478
   see also homosexuals; lesbians
Gayspeak   134
Geddie, Charlotte   315, 317
Geertz, Hildred   183
gender,
   as action in talk   495–502
   as activity and relation   27–32
   breakdown of the two-gender system   714–17
   characterization of a setting by   327–52
   coercing   645–70
   common   557
   and discourse   43–68
   "doing"   501–2, 531, 582–95, 624
   emergent   304–6
   and empathy   311–13
   ethnic   423–43
   and family interaction   179–201
   fluidity of concept   3, 478, 699–718
   institutional definitions   32–3
   knowledge and authority   302–26
   and language ideologies   447–67
   in literary texts   142–58
   morphological and cultural   142, 154–6
   mutual construction of   530–1
   and power in on-line communication   202–28
   and power in the workplace   537–9
   as relation   27–30
   relationship to sex and sexuality   22–7
   relevance   501–2, 504
   relevance in children's negotiations   229–51

   relevance and salience in different settings   22, 31, 33–6
   and self-reference   88–90
   sex and language   103–5
   shifting conceptions of   625–31
   as a social category   9–11, 22, 71–2, 297, 304–5
   as a topic of conversation   502
   and translation   61, 154–6
   and underlying norms   509–27
   see also linguistic gender
gender assignment,
   developmental psychology and   487
   see also sex attribution
gender concord, literary use of   148–54
gender crossing,
   continuum   368–9
   ethnic   431, 437
gender differences,
   as complementarities   452
   evidence of public views of language   707–18
   exaggeration of   23
   in ideology   261–3
   as interactional resource   497–9
   in language use and regulation   550–1
   or male dominance   49
   naturalized   472–3
   Separate Worlds Hypothesis   230, 231–4, 243, 672
   in various institutional settings   32
   see also sex differences
gender exclusivity, case-studies and issues   330–3
gender identity,
   constructing in boys' and girls' groups   234–8
   creation of   603–4
   in late modernity   5–6, 59–60
   negotiation in the family via power–connection   179–201
   normative and non-normative   353–80
   practice-based methods of analysis   3–4
   problematization of   5, 353–80
   representation and social action   487–508
   social categorization   487–8
   as a social construct   11–14

gender liminality, Polynesia 26
gender practices,
    social labeling and 69–97
    USA 715–17
gender segregation,
    barriers theories 528
    challenging universality of 231–2
    in early childhood 262
    explanations for 528–9
gender splitting 559, 560
gender-neutralization 556, 557–8,
    559
gender-specification 556, 558
gender-switching, in on-line
    communication 210–12, 638
gendering 90–4, 267, 292
genderlect *see* sex-dialect hypothesis
generalization–particularization chain
    497–8, 502
generalizations 494, 514, 595, 706,
    713
generations, gender ideologies of women
    in different 265
genre,
    discourse 265–6
    and gender patterns 259
    and social identity 266
    see also speech genre
German 2, 79, 80, 533, 541, 553, 554
    shift from Hungarian to 103, 115
Germany 553
    feminist language debates 557–9
Giddens, Anthony 27, 401, 459, 464
gift-based societies, gender in 28
Gilbert, Pam, *Boys and Literacy* 636–7,
    640
Giles, Howard 489, 491–2, 492–5, 503,
    515
Gill, Ros 498–9
Gilligan, Carol 231, 261
Gilman, Albert 4, 79–80
girls,
    AGS 368–9
    cooperative and supportive talk
    628
    as cultural brokers 234
    "double-voice discourse" 235, 236,
    627
    fragmented notion of girlhood 629

gang semiotics 389
    language development 369
    marginalization of educational
        interests 634–7
    as *nerds* 389, 438
    social engineering 384–5
    variability across social categories
        702
girls' groups,
    constructing gender identity within
        234–8, 367–8, 511
    political processes and forms of
        exclusion 230, 242–3
Glasgow 391
    glottalization 98
Gleason, Jean Berko 602, 603
globalization, and representations of
    females 461–3
glottalization 98, 110
Godard, Barbara 155
Godly Forme of Household Governmente, A
    451
Goffman, Erving 12–13, 92–3, 240, 383,
    601, 604, 674, 683
Gonzalez, María Dolores 426, 436
Goodwin, Marjorie Harness xi, 4–5, 12,
    29, 30, 31, 35, 47, 52, 229–51, 310,
    330–1, 385, 426, 428, 436, 511, 702,
    706
Gordon, Elizabeth 110
Gore, Al 172, 173
gossiping 47, 60, 469, 475, 480, 481–3,
    492, 638
Graddol, David 205, 469
graffiti, sexual 120, 479
grammars 550, 551
grammatical approach 13, 557–9
grammatical cohesion 146
Gramsci, Antonio 268
Gray, John, *Men are from Mars, Women
    are from Venus* 458
Greenwood, Alice 706
Greif, Esther Blank 602, 603
Grimshaw, Beatrice 315
Gros Ventre 357–8
Grossman, Wendy M. 210
Grosz, Elizabeth 126
group affiliation, biographical talk in
    339–45

group attitudes, homophobic   70
group membership, and social identity
    theory   491–2
Guattari, Félix   127–9
Gullah Creole   110, 426–7
Gumperz, John   48–9, 366
Guo, Jiansheng   233
Guyana, rumshop as male-only   5, 12,
    333–45
Guyanese Creole   2, 335–6, 340–2

Haas, Mary   360
habitus (Bourdieu)   672, 677–8, 692
Hall, Judith   531–2
Hall, Kira   xi, 2, 5, 25, 31–2, 93–4, 122,
    136, 353–80, 428, 471, 473, 477–8,
    479, 706, 715
Hall, Stuart   667, 677
Halliday, Michael A. K.   403
halo effect   490
Hannah, Annette   494
Harden, Blaine   175
Harding, Susan   231, 256
Harding, Tonya   716
Harlem, teenagers in   114
Harré, Rom   601, 606, 674
Harris, Katherine   174
Hartigan, John   437
Hartley, Sue   110
Harvey, David   402, 415–16
Hawaii, *mahu*   303
Hawaiian Creole   392
He-Said-She-Said   29, 47, 232–3, 385–6,
    426
hedging   53, 241, 394–5, 474, 531, 537,
    605
hegemony,
    in definitions of sexuality   25–6,
        471
    of ideologized meanings   567
    in US gender ideology   32–3
Heidelberg, University of   533
Hellinger, Marlis   2
Hemingway, Ernest   146
Henley, Nancy   161, 231, 701
Henwood, Karen L.   190
Herbert, James, *The Survivor*   470
Heritage, John   332
hermaphrodites   154, 155–6

Herring, Susan   xi, 4, 9, 11, 14, 202–28,
    706, 712
heterosexuality,
    cathexis   126
    identity structures US adolescent social
        order   375
    naturalizing narratives of compulsory
        149
    as normative   23, 354, 706
    performance of   133–4
    and romance in high school   384
    study of gender in context of   22, 23
heterosociability, in adolescence   381,
    383–7
Hewitt, Roger   626–7, 630
Hey, Valerie   632, 640
Heywood, John   135–6
hierarchies, multiple   520–1
hierarchy,
    and equality   181–2
    and gender ideologies   452
hijras, in India   25, 93–4, 375
Hill, Anita, and Clarence Thomas *see*
        Hill-Thomas case
Hill, Jane   390, 426
Hill-Thomas case of sexual harassment
        161, 164, 169, 171, 265, 716
Hindi   93–4, 375
Hines, Caitlin   2
Hinton, Leanne   82, 84, 86–7
hippies, historians, and homos   361–6
Hirsch, Susan F.   262, 265
historians, hippies, and homos   361–6
historical linguistics   390–1
history,
    feminist challenge to assumptions   21,
        32
    turning points for women and for men
        3, 21
Hitchiti   360
Holland, Dorothy   518–19
Holmes, Janet   xii, 1–17, 110, 111, 386,
        474, 503, 510, 511, 514, 573–99, 700,
        702
    Language in Society   71
home,
    face-related practices at   606–12
    family interaction   179–201
    and work   267

homosexuality 120–2
  cathexis 126–7
  in Irish poetry 407–11
homosexuals,
  and heterosexual language use 372–6
  hippies and historians 361–6
  language use 6, 401–22
  see also gays and lesbians
hooks, bell 425
Hooks, Patricia 175
Hopper, Robert 331–2, 490
Horace 155
hormones, prenatal priming 368–9
Houghton, Cathryn 395, 706
Hughes, Linda A. 236
human relations 2
human resources 2
Human Rights Act 561, 651
humanist feminism 27–8
humor,
  boundaries of 295
  in the workplace 7, 577–9, 593, 594
Hungarian, shift to German 103, 115
Hymes, Dell 46, 373, 374
hypercorrection 21, 102

Icelandic 553
iconicity, of gender or ethnicity 424,
  432
iconization 431–5, 436
Ide, Sachiko 77, 88
identities,
  "coerced" 7, 645–67
  contested and problematized gender
    353–80
  discursively constructed 675, 677–8
  exogenous 675
  multiple 7, 428–9, 671–98
  parental 190–9
  situated 675
  transportable 675–6
identity,
  ambiguous 154–6
  aspects relevant to conversational
    analysis 34–5
  conflation of gender and sexual
    369–70
  European 673–4
  fractured and pronoun use 93–4

large-group 165
  maintenance mechanisms 491–2, 493
  and norms 515–24
  perspectives on concepts of 674–8
  "polyphonous" 373
  sexual 120–1
  see also gender identity; national
    identity; social identity
identity formation,
  in adolescence 381–400
  children's storytelling and
    disagreements 237, 238–9
identity politics 387–8
identity work, in talk 499–501
ideological approaches 372, 431–6, 505,
  699–718
ideological dilemma 496, 497
ideologies,
  about language 59, 116
  and belief systems 712–14
  changes in communication 6
  dominant, and Western inequality 12,
    36, 715
  heritage language and 426–7
  in legal settings 648–68
  and linguistic strategies 55–8
  mediation of intimacy 134–5
  multiple about women 316–17
  practical 496–7
  as social constructs 448
  texts and 55
ideologies, gender,
  in anthropology 5, 255–60
  in conversation analysis 53
  cross-cultural comparison 9
  diversity in 260–6
  and gender stereotypes 472–3
  hegemony in USA 32–3
  institutional discourse 7, 266–72,
    645–70, 700
  intra-societal diversity 263–6
  multiple 268–72
  in on-line databases 708–12
  political roots of interest in 254–5
  political and social relevance 14
  power in discourse 252–76
  supported by gender stereotypes 6
  of women in different generations
    265

ideology,
  adolescence as 381–2
  family 180
  gender differences in 261–3
  language and power 13
  liberal 448
  linguistic 517–18
  production and reproduction of 57–8
  role in concept construction 711–12
  role of representations of language 6
  use of term 254, 447–8, 496–7
  Western 182
  see also language ideologies
idiolects 100
Ignatiev, Noel 425
imagined community 72, 390, 393, 430, 471, 676–7
immanence 128
imperatives,
  minimized 606
  unmitigated 606, 613
  use by children in play 233
indexical model, of gender and social identity 35–6, 286, 424
indexicality 431
  of gender identity 503
  indirect and direct 510, 518
indexing, and speech activity norms 521–2
India,
  hijras 25, 93–4, 375
  language contact and code-switching 48
  widow-burning 265
individualism 497
  American 33
  competitive 627
  and expectations of relationships 459
  see also abstract individualism
individuals, gender as property of 27–8, 33
Industrial Revolution 105, 381
inequalities,
  between groups 496–7
  conversational strategies and 165–6
  educational 7
  gender 22, 107–8, 279
  and gender segregation 528

in girls' and boys' language behavior 625–31
and the law on sexual assault 645–70
new technologies and 639
systematic 32–3, 36, 462
information technology 639
innovations, spread of 103
innuendo 120
Inoue, Miyako 26, 60, 62
instigating 47, 242
Institute of German Language 559
institutional contexts, for gender ideologies in discourse 266–72, 645–70
institutional discourse 571–721, 700
  dominant ideologies in 7, 645–70
institutions,
  coerciveness 646–9
  and critical discourse analysis 57
  gender as a structuring principle of 648
  main American 163
  mediation of intimacy 134–5
  norms 511, 520–1
  and system of social relations 31, 268
insults 82–3, 93–4, 385
  sexual 554
  see also ritual, insults
intention,
  authorial 170
  fallacy of 123
intentionality of message 493
  choice-making in text and 403, 407, 415
inter-ethnic communication, children's socialization and 366
interaction,
  dynamic aspects of 11, 429, 504–5, 530–1, 554
  gender differences as resource 497–9
  of gender and language 9, 35–6
  institutional influences 649, 667
  inter-ethnic 49
  rather than possession 28–32
  see also strategic interaction
interactional sociolinguistics 2, 48–50, 63, 514
  analyst's role 63
  context and talk 327–8
  and sex differences research 329–30

interactional style,
features of "feminine" and
"masculine" 574 (table 25.1)
"feminine" and "masculine" in New
Zealand workplaces 576–80
feminine of men and women 476
interests, and gender categories 24–5,
280
intergroup theory 71
interior monologue 143
Internet 204, 706
access 203–5
and censorship 209
community and political organization
216–17
control of resources 218, 220–1
as democratic 202, 209, 712
female entrepreneurs 215–16
female users 203, 204
gender and power 4, 11, 202–28,
638–9
and privacy 209
Internet Relay Chat (IRC) 210–12
Internet Service Providers (ISPs) 204
interpellation 403
interpretation, politics of 164, 171
interpretative repertoires 496–7
interruptions,
as cooperative overlap 168
studies 34–5, 51, 52, 162–3, 165, 168,
530, 575
intertextuality 61
interviews,
amount of talk in single-sex and
mixed-sex 111
with female MEPs 681–2
limitations of ethnographic 264,
288–9
playback 54
intimacy,
boundaries of 603
communication in 458, 459–60
gender interaction 49–50, 187–90
male communicative strategies in
50
power and solidarity 180–1
pronominal use 89
public mediation of 130, 134–6
women's control of 80, 162

intonation,
in children's disputes 240–1
feminine 477
rising 605
Ireland *see* Belfast; Gaelic; Irish
Irigaray, Luce 153, 556
Irish, rural gay poetry 402, 407–11
Irvine, Judith T. 388, 389, 431, 433
Islam, access to masculine power 25
Israelis, dinner conversation 180
Italian 553
Italian children's negotiations 235, 238,
239–40
iterability 122–4, 130, 136, 374

Jacklin, Carol Nagy 230
Jacobs, Greg 372
Jacobson, L. 529
James, Deborah 69, 70, 163, 168
James, Henry 76, 146
Portrait of a Lady 143–4
Japan 280
communicative style of children 131
drama series 603
power in 181, 182, 183
preschool children 231, 233
resistance to femininity norms 26
women's views on roles 265
Japanese 553, 554
deference in 604
pronoun use 86, 88, 89
Japanese women's language (JWL) 26,
60, 62
Javanese culture 181, 183, 604
Jefferson, Gail 186
Jeffords, James 70
Jespersen, Otto,
*Language: Its Nature, Development and
Origin* 469, 474
"The Woman" 355, 358–61, 449–50,
452, 469, 471
jocks, and *burnouts* 238, 388, 392–3, 395
Johnson, Sally 2, 629, 702, 706
Johnston, Alexandra 200
Johnstone, Barbara, *The Linguistic
Individual* 713
Jolly, Margaret 314–15, 317
Jones, Alison 629
Jones, Ann Rosalind 451

Jones, Paula 716
journalism, sexism in 480
Joyce, James 143
judicial processes, ideology and 645–70, 711
Jugaku, A. 88
Julien, Isaac 473
justifying 53

kabary see Malagasy
Kalverkämper, Hartwig 554
Kanemura, Hasumi 86
Kant, Immanuel 125
Kanter, R. Moss 529
Katriel, Tamar 459–60
Kaukiainen, Ari 230
kava ceremony 271
Keenan, Elinor (Ochs) 47, 115, 450
    "Norm-makers, Norm-breakers:
        Uses of Speech by Men and Women
        in a Malagasy Community" 256–7,
        361–2
    see also Ochs, Elinor
Keesing, Roger 261
Kendall, Shari xii, 7, 12, 13, 111, 200,
    575, 600–23, 706
Kennard, Hicks 82, 89–90
Kennedy, Elizabeth 265
Kennedy, Kieran 407–8
Kerrigan, Nancy 716
Key, Mary Ritchie 179
Khatru 145
Khosroshahi, Fatemeh 566–7
Kibby, Marge 214
Kiesling, Scott Fabius xii, 6, 13, 431,
    437, 474, 509–27, 706
kin-based societies, and male power
    256, 257
King, Ruth 563, 566, 706
kinship terms, English 91–2, 287
Kitzinger, Celia 53, 329
knowledge,
    as emergent 306–8
    gender and authority 302–26
    personalized in traditional societies
        307
    shared 312–13, 403–4
knowledge industry, white-collar 582–8
knowledge–power discourse 45

Koasati 360
Koch, Sabine C. xii, 6, 11, 528–49
Kotthoff, Helga 2, 238
Kramarae, Cheris 551
Krause, Fritz 360
Krauss, Robert M. 494
kros (Tok Pisin) 450
Kulick, Don xii, 4, 12, 26, 59–60,
    119–41, 259, 288, 370, 375, 450
Kuna Indians, Panama 47, 258–9
Kurath, Hans 99
Kyratzis, Amy 233, 236–7

labeling,
    gay by heterosexual men 25–6,
        134
    as social control 388
    social and gender 69–97, 504–5, 704,
        712
labels,
    adolescent boys' 386
    categorizing 69–71
    "empty" 72–7
    gendering 90–4
    insulting 69
    predicative 69–71
    rejection of 71
    uses by men and women 83
labor,
    ownership of 28
    see also division of labor
Labov, Theresa 388
Labov, William 98, 99, 103, 111, 114,
    392, 425, 426, 437, 494, 513, 684
Lacan, Jacques 125–6, 128, 129
LaFrance, Marianne 530–1
Lagerspetz, Kirsti M. J. 230
Lakhota 2, 427, 432–6
    clitics by gender and speech act 432
    (table 18.1)
Lakoff, Robin Tolmach xii, 4, 10, 35, 47,
    104, 111, 146–7, 161–78, 179, 255,
    353, 367–8, 429, 454, 474, 477, 511,
    552, 701, 704, 715, 716
    Language and Woman's Place 362–5,
        478, 699
laments 59–60, 260, 262
Lange, Deborah 394–5
Langford, Wendy 135

language,
  beliefs about 472, 712–18
  data 705–6
  and desire 119–41
  and the law 645–70
  power and ideology 13
  as a resource for creativity 11, 94, 112, 430
  sex and gender 103–5
  and sexuality 119, 120–4
  shifting conceptions of 625–31
  and social cognition 489–95
  and society 1, 112–16
  structurally limited indeterminacy 36
  structuring potential of 649, 671–2
language change,
  feminist activism and 554–6, 562–7
  "from above" or "from below" 103, 109
  role of adolescents in 390–3
  and sociolinguistic patterns 102–3
language choice,
  agency in 31–2, 62, 713–14
  gender and 116, 401–22, 426–7
language contact,
  and code-switching 48
  in Vanuatu 317–22
language games, biographical swapping off 339–45
language and gender,
  in adolescence 381–400
  authority at work and at home 600–23
  canonical texts 2
  deficit model 454, 474, 701
  difference/two cultures model 353–4, 366–8, 371, 375, 474, 701
  discourse analysis in studies 43–68
  dominance model 353, 362, 474, 701
  in educational settings 624–44
  global patterns 15
  history of the study 19–158
  ideological approaches 372, 375
  interdisciplinary studies 43–4
  representing 449–53
  reproduction of sexist stereotypes 468–9
  role in negotiations of relations 159–276

themes and issues 8–10
theory and methodologies 8, 10–14, 503–5, 630–1, 646
use of models 430–6
variation in 98–118
White middle-class male models 231, 243, 354, 382
see also research
language ideologies 32, 59–61, 255, 447–67
  use of term 447
language planning 550, 551
  feminist non-sexist language campaigns 552–67
language shift 115–16
  evolutionary logic 358
language socialization 131, 137
language typology 556
language use,
  cross-cultural patterns 258–9
  and gender identity 285–8
  gendered 537, 627
  non-sexist guidelines 551, 560–1
  perceived versus actual 704–18
language variation, and communities of practice 71–2
Larsen, Nella, *Passing* 133
Larson, Karen 111
Lasch, Richard 355, 356
Lash, Scott 415
Latina women's talk 241, 243, 427, 428, 706
Latino 390, 391
Lave, Jean 71
Lavendera, Beatrice 510
law,
  equality and likes 703
  on sexual assault and inequalities 645–70
Lawrence, D. H. 143
Lawrence, Samuel G. 490
Le Guin, Ursula, *The Left Hand of Darkness* 151
Leap, William L. xii–xiii, 5–6, 12, 115, 318, 354, 401–22, 704, 706
Leaper, Campbell 231
learning, framing approach 13
LeBaron, Curtis 331–2
Leclerc, Annie 147

Lee Jung Bin   173
Leeds-Hurwitz, Wendy   80–1
Lefanu, Sarah   145
leitī   280, 281
   and English   285–8
   public construction of identity   288–95
Leontyev, Aleksei N.   29, 31
lesbians   120–1, 369–70, 371–2, 706
   text   403
   see also gays and lesbians
Lesotho   263
Lever, Janet Rae   231
Levinson, Stephen   161, 514, 601
Lewinsky, Monica   174, 716
Lewis, Debra   653
lexical cohesion   146
lexicography, sexism in   551
lexicon, male as norm   553
Lexis-Nexis   709–10, 711
Liang, Anita C.   2, 372
   Speaking as a Woman   478
liberal political philosophy   28, 261, 448
libertarianism   209, 219
libido   125
life-stages, gendering of   381–2, 396
Limon, José   264, 331
Lind, E. Allen   161
Linde, Charlotte   682
linguistic anthropology   3, 46, 229–30,
      254, 705
   theorizing gender in   21–42
linguistic disruption strategies   555, 560,
      562
linguistic gender,
   literary uses of   142, 148–51, 157
   use to subvert   55–6
linguistic strategies,
   as control and connection maneuvers
      200
   different in same context   31
   of exclusion   32
   female sociolinguistic repertoire
      49–50, 309–10
   of gay men   411–14
   gender agency and flexibility in   26–7,
      424
   ideologies and   55–8
   in literature   148–54
   subversive   56–8, 149

   in the workplace   537
   see also conversational strategies
Lipman, Maureen   483
listening, empathetic   459, 460–1
literacy, boys and   634–7, 640
literacy practices   61
literary criticism,
   expansion into cultural criticism   55
   feminist   55–6
   language and desire   120
   stylistics in   54–5, 144
literary styles,
   feminist   144
   male and female conventions   4, 56,
      142–8, 156
literary theory   119
literature,
   "Africanism" in American   133
   female writers   21, 147–8, 556
   linguistic approaches to gender in   91,
      142–58
   linguistic gender in   55–6
Lithuanian   553
Livia, Anna   xiii, 4, 12, 13, 31–2, 55–6,
      62, 91, 94, 122, 142–58, 372–3, 478,
      715
   Pronoun Envy   149
local education authorities, equality
      projects   633
locality   9, 279–80, 296–7, 373
Lochhead, Liz   468
Lorde, Audre   560
Los Angeles, agoraphobia study   131–2
loss   127
Lott, Trent   175
love songs   269–70, 271
Lowry, Malcolm, *Under the Volcano*   144
Lubiano, Wahneema   265
Luker, Kristin   265
lullabies   260
Lyons, John   656

ma   283, 284
McAdams, Mindy   638
Macaulay, Ronald K. S.   387, 391, 392
Macaulay, Thomas   105
Maccoby, Eleanor   230, 231
   *The Two Sexes: Growing Up Apart,
      Coming Together*   366–9

McConnell-Ginet, Sally xiii, 3–4, 11–12, 15, 29–30, 52, 69–97, 267, 354, 372, 388, 504, 512, 580, 648, 704, 714–15
Macdonald, Myra 469
McElhinny, Bonnie xiii, 3, 12, 21–42, 86, 104, 267, 268, 317, 354, 370, 575, 678, 700, 706
McGuinn, Nicholas 639
MacKinnon, Catherine 703
McLemore, Cynthia 395
Madagascar *see* Malagasy
Madonna 716
magazines, adolescent 393
Major, Brenda 530–1
Malagasy, women's direct speech style 47, 59, 115, 257, 361–2, 450, 452
male bonding 363, 589
male dominance 254, 262, 272, 472–3, 530, 575
  in the classroom 626–31
  or gender differences 49
  ideological resistance to 262–3, 429
  on the Internet 638–9
  of public talk 258–9
male exclusivity 5, 12, 333–45
  in talk-in-interaction 327–52
"Mallspeak" 393–4
Malo 303, 305, 306, 307, 308, 310, 320
Maltz, Daniel 49, 161, 231, 366, 369–70, 510–11, 701
Mamet, David, *Oleanna* 4, 164, 169–72
management training 711–12
manager, female authority as a 7, 583–8, 594, 602, 619–21
Manalansan, Martin 411–12, 414
Mandarin 233
Mani, Lata 265
Marcus, George E. 280
marginality,
  escape by linguistic means 284–95, 296
  gender, language and 362–5
markedness,
  and contrast 521–2
  of female grammatical forms 553
  of gender and ethnicity 423–43
  Myers-Scotton's Markedness Model 430
Markovitz, Judith 563

Marks, Shula, *Not Either an Experimental Doll* 263
Markus, M. Lynne 203
marriage,
  exchange-societies 306, 307
  as patriarchal 50
  women's names after 74–5, 81, 565
Marshall, Harriette 498
Martin, Denis 677, 678
Martin, Emily, *The Woman in the Body* 264
Marx, Karl 254, 464
  "Sixth Thesis on Feuerbach" 29
Marxism 25, 27, 30, 55, 57, 58, 254, 262
  psychology 29
  social theory 31
Mary, Queen of Scots, letters written to 109
masculinity 2
  association of technology with 204
  construction in boys' groups 234–5
  cultural models of 519–20
  historically and socially constructed 112–13, 116
  institutionalized 364–5
  internally differentiated models 629
  literary style 4, 144
  self-assessed 489
  Tonganness and 292
mass culture 55
mass media,
  adolescents and 393
  discursive control by 57
  infiltration of the Internet by 214–16
  male interests 215, 219
  stereotyped language in the 554, 708
  treatment of women 717
  use of language 165
Mathews, Holly 268
  on "La Llorona" 264
Maton, Kath 633
matrilineal land rights 318
Maw, Janet 632, 640
Maynard, Douglas W. 239–40
meaning,
  co-construction of 403
  ideologization of linguistic 567

meaning (*cont'd*)
implied 49
more than intention 122–3
norms and sociolinguistic 509–12
situational 31, 35–6
struggles for control of 164
systems of 495–6, 499, 505
media *see* mass media
medical books 264
medical procedures,
hegemonic discourse in 649
sexual norms and 24–5
see also doctor–patient communication
Medicine, Beatrice 427
meeting talk 7, 575, 576–7, 584–8, 594
Mehren, Elizabeth 394
melancholia 127
Melanesia,
gender analysis 302, 304, 318
metaphors of interaction 28–9
men,
communication deficits 6, 454–7, 462, 481–3
constructing themselves as heterosexual 25–6
dominance of White 715
gender identity work 512–13
ideal modern types 463
recognition as gendered subjectivities 437
Mendoza-Denton, Norma 161, 389, 391, 427, 428, 436, 706
men's language 329–30, 331, 333, 353–4, 355
as normative 359–61
quantitative evidence 479–80
redefinition as marked 425
Mercer, Kobena 473
Merton, Robert 529
metacommunication 541–2
metadiscourse 59
metalinguistic behavior 561–2
metaphors,
for gender 27
of interaction rather than possession 28–9
metapragmatics 517–18
Mexican folktale, "La Llorona" 264
Meyer, Paul R. 206

Meyerhoff, Miriam xiii, 1–17, 89, 292, 296, 302–26, 503, 700
Language in Society 71
middle class, language use 104–5
military, gendering of the 267
Millar, Frank E. 180
Millen, Diane 633
Mills, Sara 56, 144
Milroy, James 110
Milroy, Lesley 110, 113–14, 510, 515
miscommunication 49, 166–7
missionaries,
and naming practices 75
in Vanuatu 314, 315, 317
Mitchell-Kernan, Claudia 47
mitigating strategies 601, 602–3, 605, 627
Modan, Gabriella 437
modern societies, gendered language compared with traditional 259
modernism 143
modernity,
alternative 280
association of English language use with 286, 292–5, 296
definition 401
gender identities in late 5–6, 59–60
language and gendered 401–22
language ideology of late 458–63
languages as symbols of 110, 410
meanings of 280, 297
Molisa, Grace Mera 318
Moonwomon, Birch 2, 403
Moore, Dinty 146
moral order, and symbolic aspects of language 449
Morgan, Marcyliena 242, 425–6, 436, 437, 706
Morrison, Toni 133
mother,
generic assumption 502, 672
idealization of 476
as language regulator 550
leadership style 592, 603, 619–21
narrative roles 602, 606–12
power and connection 183–4
as problematizee 185
role in middle-class family 309, 619–21

"Motherese strategy" 603
multicultural societies, language use in
    48–50, 415
Mumby, Denis 682
Murachver, Tamar 494
Myers-Scotton, Carol 415, 430

Nakamura, Keiko 233
name-calling 76–7
names,
    children's changing use of 87
    in cyberspace 206–7, 210
    gendered 81
    masculine and feminine pairs 74
    occupational 556, 561, 562
    "official" changes 74–5
    on tombstones 76
    see also nicknames; surnames
naming,
    forms identical to pronouns 76
    kinship relations and 75
    non-sexist 565–6
    practices 75, 712
narrative analysis 119
narratives,
    autobiographical and reflexivity 459,
        464–5
    characters and narrators in 143–4,
        151
    coming out 121
    gay 6, 135–6
    girls' disputes 242
    naturalizing of compulsory
        heterosexuality 149
    power and connection in family
        184–7
    professional identity 677–93
    roles at dinnertime 602, 606–12
    sexual stories 403–4, 411–14
    as sociolinguistic self-portraits 682–3
narrator, omniscient 143–4
nation-state representations, Tongan
    268–72
national identity 686–7
    and the imagined community 72,
        676–7
    and language choices 319–21
    and sexual identity 408–11, 415–16
National Union of Journalists (NUJ) 480

nationalism, and language ideologies
    447
nationality, and identities 676–7
natural histories, of discourse 61–2, 63
nature, and culture 255–6, 408
need/obligation, statements of 606
negotiating relations, role of language
    and gender in 159–276
Nepal, Tamang 75
Netherlands 102, 115
network analysis 113–14, 515
New York City, postvocalic /r/ 98, 99,
    102, 111
New York Times 164, 173
New Zealand,
    "feminine" and "masculine"
        interactional workplace styles 267,
        576–80
    as a gendered culture 573–4
    Maori girls 629
New Zealand English 110
Newsweek 173
Newton, Esther 93
Ni-Vanuatu 304, 313, 319
Nichols, Patricia 110
Nicholson, Linda 373
nicknames 75, 84
Niedzwiecki, Patricia 558
Nigeria, *'yan daudu* 25
Nilsen, Aileen P. 553
non-Indo-European languages 353–4,
    355
non-sexist language campaigns 552–67
non-verbal behavior 503
non-Western cultures, language varieties
    109, 115
Nootka 361, 362
Nordberg, Bengt 102, 106–9, 109–10,
    113
NORM (non-mobile older rural male)
    99
normativity,
    and deviance 353–80
    heterosexual 375
    as ideologically produced 372
norms,
    in adolescence 386, 473
    application of masculine to women
        35, 362, 703

norms (*cont'd*)
   defining   509–15
   as descriptive or prescriptive   511, 524
   and expectations   35, 468
   of gender categories   24–5, 31
   gender and linguistic strategies   149
   and identity   515–24
   institutional   520–1
   internalization of social   487
   linguistic   517–18
   and perception   523–4
   representation of women as modest
      450
   as social framework   334–5
   socially ascribed gender   647–8
   and sociolinguistic meaning   509–12
   and stereotypes   13, 15, 445–570
   underlying   509–27
   workplace male   575–6
Norway,
   language contact and code-switching
      48
   preschool children   231, 234
   Sami-speaking women and use of
      Norwegian   115–16
   sexist language practices   553
   women's speech   111
Norwegian   110, 115–16
Norwich,
   class, style, and sex differentiation in
      -*ing* forms   101 (table 4.1), 102, 104,
      513
   initial /h/   98
nouns, non-sexist generic in writing
   563–5
Nuku'alofa, Tonga   281–3
nurses   494, 649
Nyquist, L.   365–6

Ó Searcaigh, Cathal, poetry   402, 407–11,
   415
O'Barr, William M.   104, 161, 366, 645
Oberwart, Austria   103, 114–15
Ochs, Elinor   4, 13, 35–6, 59, 131–2,
   184–7, 302, 309, 510, 515–16, 602,
   603, 682
   see also Keenan
O'Connor, Mary Catherine   183, 185
Ocracoke English   438

O'Donovan, Veronica   93–4, 375
Office for Standards in Education
   (Ofsted), *Boys and English*   456
office talk   582–8
Ogawa, Naoko   86, 88
Oleanna (Mamet)   4, 164, 169–72
on-line communication,
   anonymity of   202–3, 205, 206–9, 213
   discussion forums   216–17
   gender and power in   202–28, 638
   interpersonal   220–1
on-line databases   708–12
Ong, Aiwa   416
opinion formation   165
oppositional sequences, children's
   229–30, 239–41
organizational culture, continuum from
   feminine to masculine   581–95
organizational sociology   672
organizations,
   gendered   528–31
   structure and gender interaction in the
      workplace   495
origin,
   myths of linguistic   447
   place of   279–80
Ortner, Sherry   30, 33, 258, 260, 364
   "Is Female to Male as Nature is to
      Culture?"   255–6
Osterman, Karin   230
Other,
   desire of the   124, 126
   objectification of the foreign   280
   woman as the linguistic   358–61
"outliers", gender   25

pachuco   427
Panama, Kuna Indians   47, 258–9
Panjabi   431
Papua New Guinea   59, 450
paralanguage   503
parapraxes   119
parents,
   authority   7, 184–7, 606–12
   gender-specific roles   190–4
   identities   190–9
parody   149
passing   491
passives, agentless   168

patriarchy   115, 219, 254–5, 262, 474, 671, 701
Pauwels, Anne   xiii, 6, 13, 550–70, 704
Pearson, Bethyl   604
Pease, Allan and Barbara, *Why Men Don't Listen and Women Can't Read Maps*   481–2
peer interaction, children's   229–51
Peltonen, Tarja   230
perception,
    and expectations   712–18
    gender, identity and   677
    and norms   523–4
performance, gender as   11, 402, 417, 428–9, 629, 646–7, 700, 714–15
performative utterance   373–4
performativity   31, 119, 121, 122–3, 127, 128, 148–9
    in education   625
    and erasure   437
    and ethnography   373
    in queer linguistics   372–6
personhood model   27–8, 30, 373–4, 462–3
Philadelphia Quaker school   236
Philips, Susan U.   xiii–xiv, 5, 9, 12, 13, 14, 252–76, 282, 318
Phillipson, Gerry   459–60
philology   120
philosophy, language and desire   120
physical anthropology   24
Piercy, Marge, *Woman on the Edge of Time*   151–2
place,
    and authenticity   277–443
    and culture   279–80
    see also ples
play,
    children's fantasy   236–7
    gender-segregated patterns   49
    peer negotiation during   229–51
    as socialization   231
    "with-then-apart"   232, 234
ples   303
    Bislama in claiming   319–21
    knowledge and authority   5, 306–8
    linguistic strategies for claiming   308–10
Plummer, Ken   417

poetry,
    Bedouin women's   262
    homosexual language use   5–6, 402, 407–11, 415
point of view *see* focalization
police officers,
    deference in forms of address   86
    sexual identity and   24, 26, 32, 267, 706
Polish   553
politeness   4, 104, 229, 475, 601, 603
    Lakoff's paradigm   363
    negative and positive   514
    in on-line communication   207–8
    power and solidarity   514–15
    pragmatics of   238
    socialization of   131
    strategies at work   531, 544–5, 600, 613
political correctness   164, 169, 171
political discourse, extending definition of   176
political economy,
    age- and generation-based location in   382
    text-making and   415–16
political parties, and female MEPs   681, 687–9
politics,
    academic   165–9
    defined   161
    discourse analysis of women and power   4, 161–78
    feminization of   164
    use of lower pitch by women   495
    women and   4, 172–6, 671–98
polygamy   715
Polynesians   26, 281–2, 591
popular culture   55, 707–8
popular print media   708–12
pornography   135
    on the Web   213–14, 216, 218
positioning theory   601, 606–7, 674
positivism   503
possession   28–9
postfeminism   217
postmodernism   12, 372, 625, 638
post-structuralism   12, 24–7, 36, 45, 53, 57, 62, 373, 496

Potter, Jonathon 496
Pound, Ezra 143
power,
    and address options 77–87
    and belief systems 57–8
    colonial ideologies and 316–17
    and connection 181 (fig. 8.1)
    and connection in the family 180–7,
        194–9
    defined 182
    establishment of normalcy and 471
    and gender 364–6
    and gender in on-line communication
        202–28
    and gender in the workplace 537–9
    and knowledge 36, 45, 129
    language and ideology 13
    male over women 260, 364–5, 629
    in sexual violence 654–61
    social of White men 672
    solidarity and politeness 514–15
    and women's language 104–5
    see also women and power
power games 161–5, 169
power strategy 544–5
powerlessness,
    images of mothering 603
    women's language 104, 357, 363, 366,
        479, 532, 540, 546
Powesland, Peter F. 493–4
practice-based approaches 27–32
pragmatic homonymy 147
pragmatic identity 147
pragmatic synonymy 147
preference hierarchies 119
Preisler, Bent 602
preschool children, gender segregation
    231–2, 233
prescriptivism,
    linguistic 59, 449, 550–1, 556
    normative 511
prestige 509–27
    covert 6, 104, 387, 513, 518
    English in Tonga as language of 283,
        296
    overt 6, 104, 387
prestige varieties, roles of men and
    women and functions of 101,
    109–11

print media 4, 165
    on-line databases 708–12
private property, and liberalism 28
pro-drop languages 88
professional communication experience,
    and gendered expectations 533–7
professional competence 535, 536–7,
    545–6
professional identity 1, 528–49
progressive aspect 146
progressive school children, ethnicity
    232, 233
prohibition 134–5
pronouns,
    boys' use of 235
    choice and sex attribution 90–4
    cross-expressing gender 93–4, 153–4
    familiar and formal second-person
        forms 79–80
    first-person reference 88–9
    inclusive for empathy 311–12
    Japanese 86, 88, 89
    literary use of ellipsis and 151–2
    neologisms in fiction 152, 153, 157
    non-sexist generic in writing 563–5
        (tables 24.1, 24.2)
    referring 73–4, 674
    self-reference 88–90
    usage by gays 121
    use of third person to shape first-
        person enactment 646
pronunciation, sex differences in 358–9,
    361
propaganda 163
proper names, referring 73–4
protest, women's 259, 262
Proust, Marcel 145
proverbs 162, 469, 704
psychoanalysis,
    desire and 4, 119–20, 121, 124–5,
        127–8
    Lacanian 125–6, 128, 129
psychological anthropology 231
psychological approaches 360–1, 487
psychology,
    feminist 492
    gender segregation and 231, 243
    Marxist 29
    and therapeutic discourse 460

see also discursive psychology; social
  psychology; Soviet psychology
public discourse,
  feminization 461–3
  informalization of 460–3
  quality of 163
  women's interpretive control 716–17
public sphere,
  different kinds of 268
  female representation in the 453
  male authority in 256
  sex differentiation 305
public–private divide 256–8, 358, 364,
  461–3, 678
publication, feminist 560–2
publishing, on-line 215–16
Pusch, Luise 551, 558, 559

Qing Zhang 72
quantitative sociolinguistics 4, 631, 702
queer, use of term 70
queer language 122, 478
queer linguistics 354, 366, 372–6
queer theory 149
questions,
  "controlling" 656
  ideological work in institutional
    settings 649, 661–6, 667
  negative 656–7, 659–60
  role in conversations for men and
    women 510–11
  role in sexual assault tribunals 653–66
  transformative work of 661–6
quotability 123
quotation 61

racism 259
radical feminism 50
Rampton, Ben 430–1, 437
rape 124, 260
  criminal trial on acquaintance rape
    650–1, 652, 653–66
  criterion in USA for 653
  in cyberspace 211
  date rape 53
  definitions and understandings of
    645, 648
  mythologies 26, 649
rationality, and equality of men 28

Raymond, Alan and Susan 190
Reader's Guide to Periodic Literature
  709–10, 711
reading, AAVE 426
realism 503
recontextualization 61
recursivity *see* fractal recursivity
reference,
  and address 72–7
  control of terms of 667
  generic 553, 557–9, 563–5
  second-person 77
  voices within systems of 403–4
  see also names; pronouns; self-reference
referential models, of language and
  social identity 35
referring expressions, grammatical roles
  72–3
reflexivity 459–65, 713
reframing 132, 180, 521–2, 627, 636
refugees 280
register,
  for desire 120
  female *see* sex-dialect hypothesis
Reid, Elizabeth M. 211–12
Reiter, Rayna, "Men and Women in the
  South of France: Public and Private
  Domains" 256, 257
relabeling 71
relationship-securing strategy 541–2
Renaissance, court lady 451
Reno, Janet 173, 716
repertoires, interpretative 496–7
reported speech, use in literature 146
representations,
  cultural changes over time 450–1
  of gender in language and interaction
    489–95
  gender on the World Wide Web
    212–17
  of language, ideological role 6, 59–61,
    646
  of language and gender 447, 449–53
  of men and women in literature
    146–7
  as resources for identity production
    464–5
  and social action in gender and
    identity 487–508

representations (*cont'd*)
    stereotypes and practices of   463–5,
        471–2
    of women in the speech community
        553
repressions   120, 130–1, 133–4, 137
requests,
    formulations   544–5, 613
    and pre-requests   605
    types and frequency of   545 (table 23.3)
research   630, 699–721
    aspects of identity relevant to   630
    current   1–17
    empirical gaps   21
    findings from 1973 to the present
        701–2
    methods of analysis   682–3
    participants' orientation to gender
        331
    persistence of stereotypes in   8, 162,
        700–1, 705–6
    quantitative and qualitative   9, 12–13,
        15
    relevance and use of   1–2, 9–10
    salience of gender   630
resignification   374
resistance,
    ethnic   431
    ideological to domination   262–3, 266,
        429–30
    linguistic to use of English   283, 296
Reskin, Barbara   529
respect, and familiarity   183
response cry   240
Reynolds, Katsue Akiba   88, 604
Reynolds, Terry   634
rhetorical patterns   13
Rich, Adrienne   560
Richardson, Dorothy,
    Revolving Lights   142–3
    The Tunnel   143
Ricoeur, Paul   677, 678, 691
ritual,
    insults   47, 233, 237–8, 238–9
    as performative utterance   374
    "telling your day"   184–7
    wailing   59–60, 61, 259
Roberts, Sarah   392
Rodino, Michelle   211

Rogers, L. Edna   180
role-plays   537–9, 546
roles,
    elite female constructions   682–93
    family   184–7, 604–12
    gender-specific of parents   190–4
    identity and conversational   34–5
    ideology and   264, 711
    of men and women and the functions
        of prestige varieties   109–11
    sexual   126
    of women in political discourse   164,
        176
    women's reproductive   256
Romaine, Suzanne   xiv, 4, 11, 98–118,
        394–5, 473, 511, 513, 702
romantic partners   32
Rood, David   432, 436
Rosaldo, Michelle   256, 257, 364
Rosenberg, Jarrett   183, 185
Rosenthal, Robert   529
Roth-Gordon, Jennifer   390
RP (received pronunciation)   114
Rubin, Gayle   146
Rubinstein, Bob   303, 306, 307, 310
Russian   80

Sacks, Harvey   12, 339, 343, 345
Sahlins, Marshall   27
salience, conversational of gender   10,
        504, 531
Sālote, Queen of Tonga   270, 272
sameness   703
sanctions, gender-based   24–5
Sanford, Stephanie   242
Sapir, Edward   360, 361, 362, 554
Sapir–Whorf hypothesis   554
Sapper, Carl   356
SAT *see* speech accommodation theory
Schegloff, Emanuel   4, 10, 33–5, 51–2,
        53, 77, 163, 329, 331, 337, 500
    and Billig   130–1
    "Whose Text? Whose Context?"
        165–9
Schey, Sabine   xiv, 6, 11, 528–49
Schieffelin, Bambi   647
Schiffrin, Deborah   34, 682–3
Schilling-Estes, Natalie   438
Schofield, Janet Ward   232

"schooled language" 624
schools,
    boys' and girls' subject choices
      632–3
    language and gender in 624–44
    "second curriculum" of gender
      difference 235
    as sites for the construction of
      adolescence 383–90
Schulhofer, Steven 653, 658
Schultz, Muriel 553–4
Schwartz, Pepper 371
science fiction 56, 145, 151–2, 157
Scotland 109, 110–11
Scots vernacular 110–11
Scott, Donia R. 490
scripted texts, performance of 61
scripts 260
Searle, John 374
second language education 2
self, as reflexive project 459–65
self-disclosure 459–60, 543–4
    gender-specific conversational ritual
      187–90
self-fulfilling prophecies, stereotypes as
      463, 529–30
self-help books 464, 574
self-knowledge 460–4
self-presentation, at work 537–9, 672,
      682–93
self-reference, and gender 88–90
Selfe, Cynthia L. 206
selves, gendered 373–4
semantic derogation 553–4
semiotic model, of gender and ethnic
      linguistic differentiation 423–43
semiotic practices,
    desire and 123–4
    girls' gangs 389
    ideology creation and 431–2, 437
    social aspects 430
Sen, Amartya 107
Seneca Falls Convention (1848) 453
sentence, the "female" 142–3, 144,
      145
Separate Worlds Hypothesis 230,
      231–4, 243
setting, characterization by gender
      327–52

sex,
    and grammatical gender 554
    language and gender 103–5, 704
sex attribution,
    in literature 91
    pronominal choice and 90–4
    to babies 90–1
    see also gender assignment
sex differences,
    and desire 126
    in language, identifying and reifying
      10
    psychological studies 230
    research and interactional
      sociolinguistics 329–30
    stereotypes and expectations 162
    style and social class 100–2
    versus class differences 105–9
    see also gender differences
sex discrimination, workplace 462, 671
Sex Discrimination Act 561
sex and gender,
    "coat-rack" model 23, 373, 375
    definitions 22–7
sex-dialect hypothesis 365–6, 490, 531
sex-exclusive languages 355, 358
sex-preferential languages 355, 358
sex-stereotype hypothesis 490, 531–2
sexism 56, 259, 474, 554
    challenging stereotypes 468–9,
      478–81
    discursive patterning of 498–9, 648
    in lexicography 551
    linguistic and feminist activism
      550–70, 704
sexist language 2, 6, 13, 495
    choosing non-sexist alternatives
      556–9
    documenting practices 552–4
sexual assault,
    feminist campaigns to change
      legislation 645
    issue of consensuality 650–66
    use of language in adjudication
      proceedings 645–70, 706
sexual harassment 161, 171, 212, 645
    defined 652
sexual violence 7, 645–70, 715
    options and choices discourse 654

sexuality,
  language and   119, 120–4
  procreative   23, 26
  transgendered   284–5
sexualization,
  of native women by colonists   316
  and objectification of women in
    politics   4, 173–6
  of women on the Web   213–14, 218
Shantz, Carolyn Uhlinger   229
Shaw, George Bernard, *Pygmalion*
    104–5, 482
Shaw, Jo   677
Sheldon, Alice   145
Sheldon, Amy   235, 236, 627, 629, 630
Sherzer, Joel   47, 258–9, 262, 450
Shibamoto Smith, Janet   86, 88
Shona address practices   75
Shuman, Amy   242
Sidnell, Jack   xiv, 5, 10, 12, 327–52, 470,
    523
Siegal, Meryl   26
signature   122
Signature Event Context   122–3
signification   122–3, 125–6
signifying, conversational   47
Silberstein, Sandra   265
silence, of ideal woman   451, 473
silences,
    structure interaction   130, 133–4,
      137
    women's   261–3
Silverberg, Robert   145
Silverstein, Michael   59, 515, 518, 522
similarity-attraction theory   493
Simmonds, Felly Nkweto   74–5
Simon, Sherry   154
Simpson, Nicole Brown   716
Sinhala   182
sissies, and tomboys   366–72
sister–brother relations, Tongan   268,
    269, 270, 272
SIT *see* social identity theory
situated language use   45, 504, 530–1,
    538–9
    text as   403
situational meaning   31, 35–6
Skarda, Patricia   394
Skinner, Debra   518–19

slips of the tongue *see* parapraxes
small talk, at work   7, 575, 579–80,
    594
Smart, Carol   648
Smith, Janet S.   603
Smith, Phillip M.   489, 493
Smith-Hefner, Nancy J.   604
Smitherman, Geneva   425
Smithers, Alan   633
Smitherson, Janet   10
Snow, Catherine E.   602–3
Snyder, Marc   529
social action, and representation in
    gender and identity   487–508
social action norms   509–10
social capital   105
social categories,
    adolescent   386, 387–90
    gender identity as   487–8
    and language behavior   9, 304
    as sites of resistance   429–30
    stereotypes and language   530–1
    as verbal categories   488, 499, 505
    in work organizations   529–30
social change   12, 391, 465, 491–2
    feminist linguistic activism and
      552–67
social class,
    and adolescents' use of vernacular
      392
    in children's negotiations   232, 233–4,
      243
    differences, versus sex differences
      105–9
    gender and   25, 26, 112–16
    and ideologies of gender   451
    patriarchal concept of   115
    and social networks   114
    style and sex   100–2
    US displacement of idea   33
social cognitive approach   6, 11, 487–8,
    489–95, 503
social comparison   491–2
social constructionism   2, 11–14, 15, 24,
    304, 495, 501, 705
    and communities of practice   305–6,
      504–5
    and ethnic identity   431–2
    and performativity   373

social dialect literature 11
social engineering, by girls 384–5
social group norms 509–10
social identity,
  emergence and negotiation of 6, 13,
    31–2
  genre and 266
  how language constructs 21
  indexical model 35–6, 286, 424
  and linguistic form 432
  referential models 35
  variation approach 34–5
social identity theory (SIT), gender and
    489, 491–2, 493, 495, 503
social meaning, and social significance
    510
social mobility 491–2
social networks 71, 113–16, 515
  and social class 114
social order,
  and computer-mediated
    communication 202–3
  law and ideologies 648
  and normative gender categories 25
social organization,
  conversation analysis and 51–4
  functional model 23, 24
  and gender ideologies 266–72
social psychology 1, 13, 51, 52, 503
  theories of language use 493–4
social realism 143
social science research 14, 699, 703
social significance norms, and social
    meaning 510
social theory,
  Marxist 31
  structural-determinist 27
  unitarian approach 34–5
social typing, compared with
    stereotyping 470–1
socialist feminism 654
socialization,
  and biology 368–9
  of children in the family 180
  framing approach 12, 474–5
  into gender 25, 219, 243, 353
  and use of standard and non-standard
    varieties 113–14
  see also language socialization

sociobiological approach 23
sociocultural conceptions, of gendered
    roles 15, 32, 268–72
sociolinguistic patterns, and language
    change 102–3
sociolinguistics 1, 12–13
  city studies 99
  and critical theory 647
  difference perspective 699
  and discursive psychology 503–4
  and feminist language reform 552–67
  gender and ethnicity 424–5
  gender performativity in 372–3
  masculine bias 111
  norms and meaning 509–12
  research and ideology 36, 711
  theorizing gender in 21–42
  use of gender category in 22
  see also interactional sociolinguistics;
    quantitative sociolinguistics;
    variationist sociolinguistics
sociology 1, 32, 44, 243
softeners 531, 537, 540
solidarity,
  and address options 77–87
  power and 180–1
  power and politeness 514–15
South Africa 263
  gay personal advertisement 402,
    404–7
  women in Muslim courts 262, 265
South African English 405–7
Soviet psychology 27, 29, 31
Spain, sexist language practices 553
Spanish 559
  and English 232, 391, 426–7
speaker intention 122
speaking across the curriculum 393–4
speaking, ways of 46–7, 490
  girls' and boys' 231–4
  male and female 353–9, 475
  as mother and manager 619–21
  transgendered 285–8
speech accommodation theory (SAT)
    492, 493–4
  motivations 515
speech act theory 361–2, 496
  and institutional constraints 31–2
  total speech act 374

speech community 71, 505
  definitions 21, 430
  regularities 100
  representation of women in the 553
speech convergence 493–4
speech event norms 511, 515
  and indexing 521–2
speech genre, the concept of 259, 260, 262, 564
speech styles,
  direct and indirect and gender 47, 257
  work-related interactions 531–2
Spender, Dale 162, 552, 638–9
spirit possession 259
splitting, stereotyping and 471
Spoken Language and New Technology (SLANT) 628
sports talk 133–4
Springer, Jerry 715
stances 515–16, 522–3, 524
standard languages, and vernacular languages 21, 113–14
standard speech,
  versus non-standard 517–18
  and women 101, 103–9, 374
standpoint feminism 261–2
Stannard, Una 76
Stanworth, Michelle 472–3
Staples, Robert 473
state formation, and male power 256, 257
state–civil institutions 268, 271
status,
  forms of address 80–7
  linguistic means for women to achieve 104–5
  and politeness strategies at work 531
Stefan, Verena 560
Steffen, Valerie J. 531
Steiner, George 154–5
stereotypes,
  about on-line communication styles 208–9
  challenging sexist 478–81, 486–7
  ethnicity and gender 424–5
  maternal 672
  and norms 13, 15, 445–570

persistence of 8, 162, 700–1, 705–6
as self-fulfilling prophecies 463, 529–30
set the agenda in research 713–14
social categorization and language 529, 530–1
of Tongan *leitī* 284–5
of women in sexual assault cases 645–67
stereotypes, gender,
  about speech 29, 329–30, 489–90, 523–4, 550, 707–8
  and gender ideologies 6, 472–3
  and gendered organizations 529–30
  reproduction and challenge 468–86
  in research 15
  role of 530–1
  use by telephone sex workers 136
stereotyping 468, 470–3
Stewart, Katherine Claire 401
Stokoe, Elizabeth H. 10, 53, 501–2
storytelling,
  children's 237
  initiating conflict through 47
  men's talk 339–45
  second stories 339, 343–4
Strand, Elizabeth 523
strategic interaction,
  reactance prone situations 538–9
  typology 539 (table 23.2)
  in the workplace 537–45
strategy, defined 539
Strathern, Marilyn 28, 302, 304, 305–6, 307
stratification, gender or class 357
Streeck, Jürgen 232, 233
structural-functionalism 27
structuralism, French 27, 255–6
Stubbe, Maria xiv, 7, 12, 13, 14, 573–99, 700, 702
Stucky, Nathan P. 490
students,
  accounts of employment opportunities for women 496–7
  comments on language difference 707–8
style,
  ethnic gender and 427–30
  gender differences in 490

modern compared with traditional
  societies 259
shifting by men 512–13, 521–3
social class and sex 100–2
uniqueness of 516
see also communication styles;
  interactional style; literary styles
stylelessness 389–90
stylistics 5, 54, 55–6
  analysis 143–7, 148–54
  feminist 55–6
  in literary criticism 54–5, 144
Stylized Asian English (SAE) 430–1
subcultures, sociolinguistic gender 366
subjectivity,
  gendered 402
  Lacanian registers of 125–6
subjectivizers 605
subjects,
  constructed as passive by language
    649, 664–6
  "institutional" 666
subordination 31, 254, 266, 272, 364,
  451, 472–3
subversion 149, 214, 478, 551
suggestions 605, 613
summons 77, 337
Sunderland, Jane 2
Sundgren, Eva 106–9, 113
surnames,
  use of bare 81–2
  woman adopts husband's 74–5, 81,
    565
Sutton, Laurel A. 2, 84, 372
Swank, Hilary 715
Swann, Joan xiv, 7, 205, 469, 624–44,
  712
swapping off, biographical talk 339–45
swardspeak, Filipino 413–14
Sweden 102, 103
  see also Eskilstuna
Sweet, Henry 104
symbolic capital 104, 116, 416, 449
Szymanski, Margaret 232, 234

taboos 134–5
tag games 431
tag questions 35, 111, 365, 395, 474, 531,
  605

Tagalog 2, 412–14
Tahiti 314
Taiwanese preschool children 233–4
Tajfel, Henri 491
Takayoshi, Pamela 213, 214
Talbot, Mary M. xiv–xv, 6, 13, 14, 57,
  393, 448, 452, 455, 468–86, 511, 575,
  700, 705
talk,
  at work 531–2
  or communication as work 459–60
  constructs different styles 11
  declarative and coordinative
    dimensions 626–7
  gender as action in 495–502
  gender differences in style 475–6
  identity work in 499–501
  phatic 483
  varies across context 29
  visibility of gender in 328–33
talk-in-interaction,
  biographical swapping-off 339–45
  case-studies 12, 231
  male exclusivity in 327–52
  Tongan–English 289–95
"TalkWorks" (BT) 456
Tamambo 320
Tamang, in Nepal 75
Tambiah, Stanley J. 374
Tannen, Deborah xv, 2, 4, 12, 34, 49, 79,
  146–7, 161, 168, 179–201, 461, 478,
  510, 514, 521, 575, 601, 602, 674, 701,
  706
  That's Not What I Meant! 370–2
  You Just Don't Understand 164, 371–2,
    458
Tanner, Nancy 363
Taylor, Alan 432, 436
Taylor, Carolyn 184–7, 309, 602
Taylor, Maureen 190–4
teachers,
  gender preconceptions 487–8, 529
  as language regulators 550
teamwork, male 589–93
teasing 386
technical language, use of 537, 545
technological determinism 203, 220
technology, association with masculinity
  204

Teena, Brandon   715
teknonyms   75
telephone sex workers   136, 428, 477–8, 479, 706
television, sitcoms   469–70
"telling your day"   184–7
temporal linking   146
Tennenhouse, Leonard   451, 461
tentativeness   602
testosterone   368–9
Tetrault, Charles   391
text,
   discourse becomes   61–2
   language choices in multilingual   412–14
   makes gendered modernity accessible   402–4
   as site of gender construction   704
   as situated language use   403
text analysis,
   feminist   56
   relevance of gender in   4, 142–58
text linguistics,
   discourse in   54–8
   feminist   57–8
textual cohesion   146, 148
Thai   553
Thakerar, Jitendra   489, 494
Thatcher, Margaret   463
Thelma and Louise   164, 171
therapeutic discourse   460
Thimm, Caja   xv, 6, 11, 13, 111, 528–49
Thomas, Clarence   705–6
   see also Hill-Thomas case
Thorell, Mia   602
Thorne, Barrie   33, 92, 161, 232, 234, 244, 368, 475, 701
Tiger, Lionel, *Men in Groups*   362–3
Tiptree Junior, James *see* Sheldon, Alice
Todd, Alexandra   649
Tok Pisin, *kros*   450
tomboys, and sissies   366–72
Tonga,
   fakaleitī (transgendered)   5, 280–1, 296, 303, 438
   gender roles and ideology   5, 252–4, 268–72, 322
   Miss Galaxy beauty contest   289–95
   society as a diaspora   281–2

Tongan, and English   2, 283–4
Tongans, overseas   281–2, 283
trade, and language contact   314–15
traditional societies,
   gendered language compared with modern   259
   personalized knowledge   307
traditionalism, and modernity   280, 292–5
transcription practices   61
transgender,
   language research   375, 715
   linguistic construction in Tonga   5, 279–301
   pronominal choice in   93–4
   in Vanuatu   303–4
transgression,
   of gender norms   25, 61–2, 136
   of taboos   134–5
translation   61, 154–6
   metaphors for   4, 154–5, 157
   of Tongan texts   252
translators   4, 142, 154–6, 157
transnationalism,
   drag queens   411–14
   and Tonganness   282
transsexuals   715
   autobiography   56, 62, 94, 154, 344–5, 488
   omnirelevance of gender   332–3
   pronominal choice   93–4, 154
travestis, Brazil   26
Trechter, Sara   xv, 6, 354, 355, 423–43, 700
tribunals   497–8
   sexual harassment   650–2, 653–66
Tripp, Linda   716
Troemel-Ploetz, Senta   554
"troubles talk"   186
Trudgill, Peter   2, 99, 101, 102, 104, 387, 425, 513
Turkle, Sherry   638
turn types,
   in talk   12, 239–41, 244
   utterance forms   337
tying techniques   239–40

unconscious   119, 122
underachievement, discourse of   456, 462, 632–7

Undue Attention Test   164–5
unemployment,
  EU discourse on   674, 682, 683–93
  male   112–13, 457, 462
UNESCO   561
uniformity, and diversity   449–53
United Kingdom (UK)   103, 115
  educational concerns about boys'
    academic underachievement   456
  "old boy network" of public schools
    114
United States (USA)   103, 115, 265, 565
  affirmative action   671
  attitudes to language and gender
    715–17
  Civil Rights movement   492
  criterion for rape   653
  Department of Education, Educational
    Resource Information Center (ERIC)
    database   710, 711
  Equal Rights Amendment   107
  hegemony in gender ideology   32–3
  high school as a total institution   383
  "Mallspeak"   393–4
  preschool children   232, 233, 235
  sexual assault legislation   645–70
  southeastern address forms   81, 86
  southeastern Gullah Creole   110
  southern terms of Black/White
    address   78–9
  treatment of gays and lesbians   25
  women voters   172–6
  women's role in social reform   257
universalist claims   259
unmarkedness   423, 432
"uptalk"   394–5
urban dialectology   100–2, 699
Urry, John   415

van Dijk, Teun   57
Vangelisti, Anita L.   236, 243
Vanuatu,
  Bislama in   2, 89, 303, 311–13
  colonial representations in 20th
    century   315–19
  diachronic perspective on gender in
    313–21
  early contact and representations   313,
    314–15

language use and gender ideologies
    302–26
  place and authority   5, 319–21
  story of Undu   308–9
Vanuatu Young People's Project (VYPP)
    318
Varenne, Herve, *Ambiguous Harmony*
    180
variation,
  adolescent phonological and
    grammatical   387, 391–2
  intragender   375
  in language and gender   98–118, 702,
    706
  quantitative and qualitative research
    98
  in social cognitive and discursive
    psychological approaches   503–5
  synchronic   102–3, 302
variationist sociolinguistics   4, 11, 12,
    98–118, 509–10
  criticisms and limitations   109–16
  findings   100–3
  research methods   99–100
Venezuela, Warao in   59–60, 61
ventriloquizing   199
verbal hygiene   394, 448
  see also prescriptivism, linguistic
verbal intensity   531–2, 537
verbosity, listeners' judgments of speaker
    gender   490
vernacular languages,
  ideology of ancestral   447
  and standard languages   21
  use by adolescents   387, 391–2
victims,
  of the stereotype   473
  women as   49–50
villages   257, 258, 268
violence, sexual norms and   24
Virago   146
virtual realities   213–14
vocabulary, sociocultural qualities and
    120–1
voices,
  Bakhtin's   675
  children's repertoire of   233–4
  double   437, 627
  emergence of alternative   667

voices (*cont'd*)
  single 627
  women's 265, 426, 498–9, 716–17
Vygotsky, Lev Semenovich 27, 29

Waletzky, Joshua 684
Walker, Iain 491, 492
Wallat, Cynthia 674
Walters, Suzanna 429
Warao, in Venezuela 59–60, 61, 262
Warner, Michael 134
Warner, Natasha 2
Waterson, Brian 516–17
Watson, Peggy 677
Watts, Richard, *Power in Family Discourse*
  180, 182
Weatherall, Ann xv, 6, 10, 11, 12, 13, 52,
  53, 163, 166, 429, 487–508, 515
Webb, Virginia-Lee 316
Weiner, Gaby 631
Wellington Language in the Workplace
  Project (LWP) 576
Wenger, Etienne 71, 581
Wertheim, Suzanne 2
West,
  cultural shift toward individual
    fulfillment 217
  and modernity 280
  multiple ideologies about women
    316–17
  reaction to gender destabilization
    701–18
West, Candace 34, 162, 602, 706
Wetherell, Margaret 53, 163, 166, 495–7,
  498, 502
Wetzel, Patricia J. 182
White, Janet 635
Whiteness, ethnic marking of 437–8
Whiteness studies 437
Whiting, Beatrice Blyth 231
Whitman, Christine Todd 716
Widdicombe, Sue 499–500, 674–5
Williams, Jennifer 491–2
Williams, John E. 528–9
Williams, Raymond 449
Wilson, John 674
Winfrey, Oprah 172, 175, 716
Winterson, Jeanette 149
  Written on the Body 151

Wispé, Lauren 311, 314
Wittgenstein, Ludwig 327
Wittig, Monique 560
  Le Corps lesbien 153
  Les Guérillères 152–3
  L'Opoponax 152
Wodak, Ruth xv, 2, 7, 13, 57, 111, 523,
  603, 671–98
Wolf, Arthur 369
Wolfram, Walt 391
woman-centered language 555–6, 560,
  562
women,
  complicity in reproducing traditional
    gender roles on-line 214, 219
  differences between 451–2
  ethnic as cultural brokers 426–7
  as a fourth world or separate caste
    363–4
  as intersections of various aspects of
    social identity 260
  Jespersen's portrayal 355, 358–61,
    449–50, 452, 469, 471
  and linguistic ideals 450–1
  as norm-breakers and norm-makers
    256–7, 361–2, 551, 567
  objectification and sexualization in
    politics 4, 173–6
  as objects of heterosexual desire and
    violence 56
  in politics 4, 172–6, 671–98
  problematization of 702
  public images of 716–17
  and standard speech 101, 103–9
  third world 259
  Tongan models for 269
  as voters 164, 172–6
women and language studies 699
women and power, discourse analysis
  4, 161–78
women's experiences 21, 311
  crossing of borders 426–7
women's language 329, 353–5, 396
  deficit model 454, 474, 701
  as deviant 359–61
  facilitative 494
  the fall and rise of 453–8
  feminist folklinguistic beliefs about
    476

impact of feminism on 492
as language of powerlessness 104,
 357, 363–4, 366, 479
as new ideal 458–63
positive images of 455–7, 481–3,
 492
and power 104–5
regulation by men 550
stereotypes of 6, 29, 353–4, 476–8,
 530–2
women's movement 105–6, 115, 148,
 254, 261, 359, 492
 and linguistic activism 550–1
women's professional development,
 influences on 6, 529
women's studies 120, 672
women's work 284–5, 462
women's writing 144, 147–8, 556
Wong, Andrew 72
Wood, Kathleen 706
Woodbury, Hannah 656
Woolard, Kathleen 449, 647
Woolf, Virginia 142–3, 146, 156
work,
 changing nature of 528
 face-related practices 613–19
 and home 267
 men's and women's 32
 operation of gender norms at 24–5
 small talk at 7, 579–80
workplace,
 Communication Accommodation
  Theory in the 494–5
 competence, cooperation, and conflict
  528–49
 doing gender in a "feminine" 582–8

"feminine" 573–99
gender and identity in the 671–3
gender and power in the 14, 267
the gendered 7, 26, 31, 573–4, 580–2,
 595
gendered communication in the
 532–45
humor in the 577–9
"masculine" 364, 574–6, 588–95
segregation 32
sex discrimination 462
strategic interaction 6, 49, 537–9
World Wide Web 212–17
 commercialization 214–16, 219
 graphical representation 213–14
 opportunities for women 202, 205,
  215–16, 217
 self-representation on the 213
 usage patterns 215, 218
Wortham, Stanton 674
written discourse 4, 12
 see also text
Wyld, H. C. 105

Xhosa 406

Yaguello, Marina 551
'*yan daudu*, Nigeria 25
Yana 360
Yanagisako, Sylvia 265
Yeliseyeva, Alla 188
youth culture, and slang use 390

Zentella, Ana Celia 427
Zihlman, Adrienne 363
Zimmerman, Don 34, 162, 674, 675–6

Lightning Source UK Ltd.
Milton Keynes UK
UKOW06f1509221214

243546UK00002B/6/P